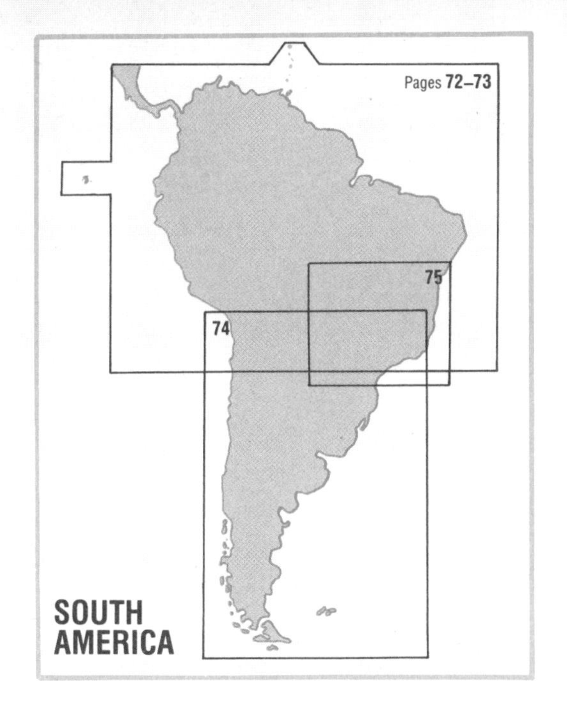

Pages **72–73**

75

74

SOUTH AMERICA

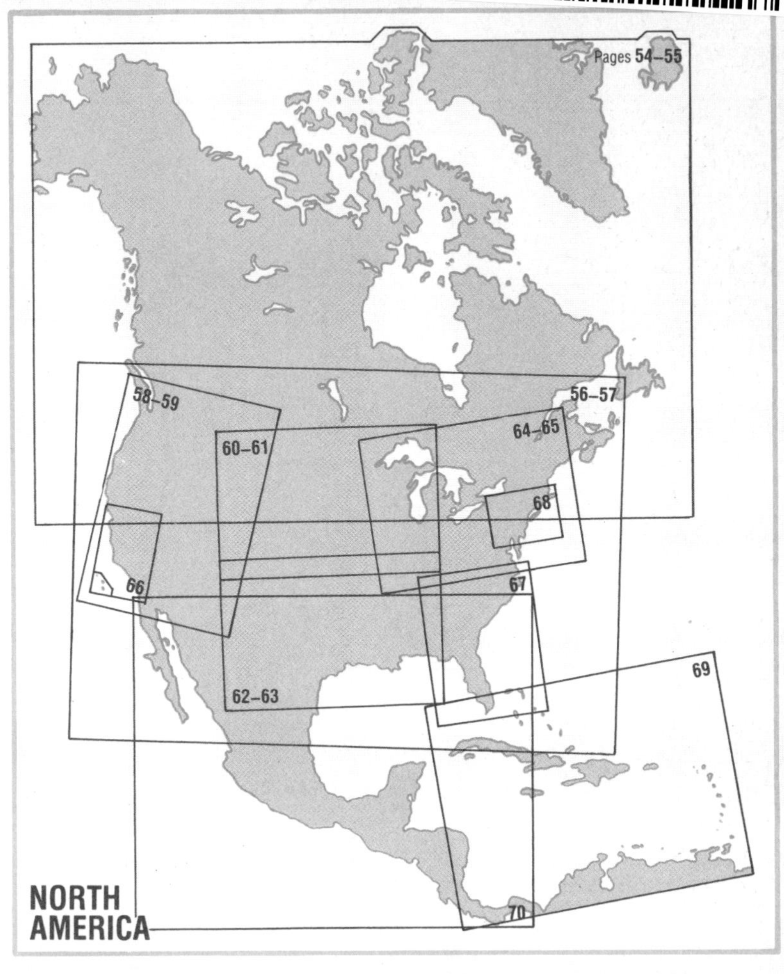

Pages **48–49**

50–51

47

AFRICA

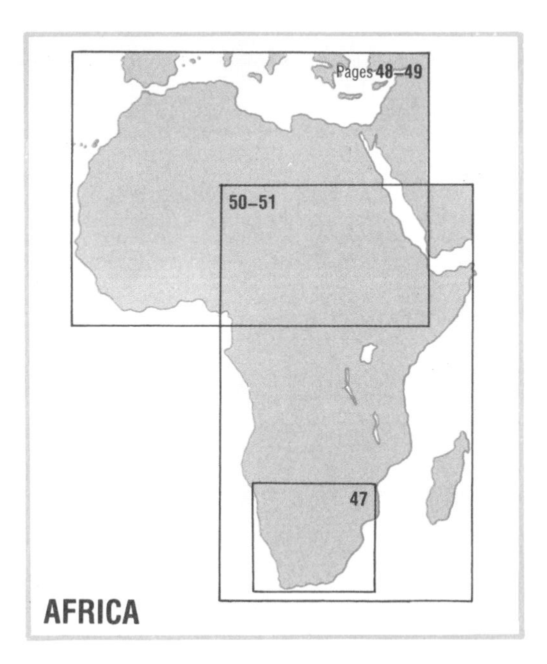

Pages **54–55**

58–59

56–57

60–61

64–65

68

66

67

69

62–63

70

NORTH AMERICA

GENERAL MAPS

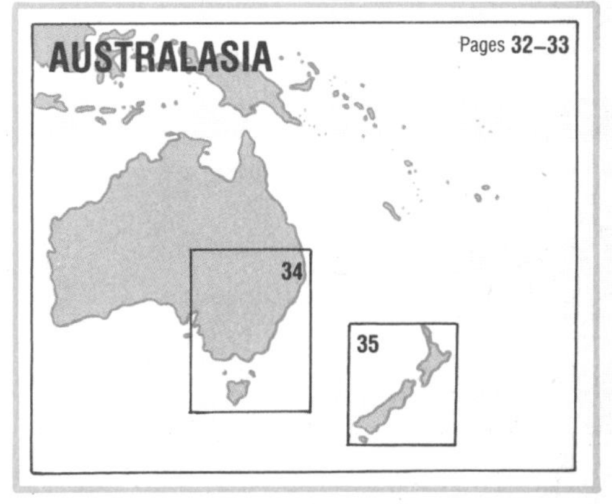

AUSTRALASIA

Pages **32–33**

34

35

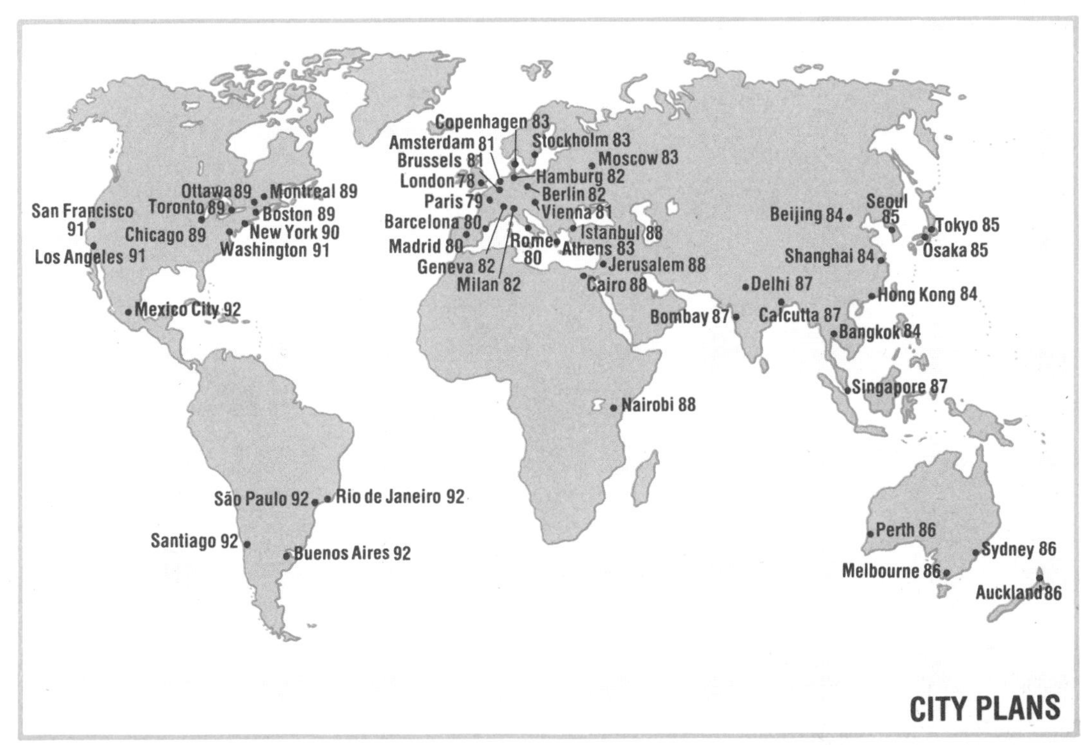

Copenhagen 83
Amsterdam 81   Stockholm 83
Brussels 81   Moscow 83
London 78   Hamburg 82
Paris 79   Berlin 82
Barcelona 80   Vienna 81
Madrid 80   Istanbul 88
Rome   Athens 83
80
Geneva 82   Jerusalem 88
Milan 82   Cairo 88

Ottawa 89   Montreal 89
San Francisco   Toronto 89   Boston 89
91   Chicago 89   New York 90
Los Angeles 91   Washington 91

Beijing 84   Seoul 85
  Tokyo 85
Shanghai 84   Osaka 85
Delhi 87   Hong Kong 84
Bombay 87   Calcutta 87
Bangkok 84

Mexico City 92

Nairobi 88

Singapore 87

São Paulo 92   Rio de Janeiro 92

Santiago 92   Buenos Aires 92

Perth 86   Sydney 86
Melbourne 86   Auckland 86

CITY PLANS

THE TIMES

ATLAS OF THE WORLD

FAMILY EDITION

TIMES BOOKS

Published in 1990 by
TIMES BOOKS,
16 Golden Square,
London W1R 4BN

First published 1988
Reprinted 1988
Reprinted with revisions 1989
Reprinted with revisions 1990

Copyright © Times Books and
Bartholomew 1990

Maps prepared by
Bartholomew, Edinburgh
the cartographic division of Collins
and Times Books, London
with the assistance of
Thames Cartographic Services, Maidenhead
Cosmographics, Watford

Index and statistical data prepared by
Geographical Research Associates,
Maidenhead

Geographical Dictionary prepared by
Professor B.W. Atkinson

Index processed and typeset by
Computaprint Data Services,
Haywards Heath

Physical Earth Maps
Duncan Mackay

Design
Ivan Dodd
Vivienne Hookings

Editorial Direction
Alison Ewington
Paul Middleton
H. A. G. Lewis, OBE
Barry Winkleman

Printed and bound in Italy by
Mondadori, Verona.

British Library Cataloguing in
Publication Data

The Times atlas of the world.
Family ed.
1. World : Atlases
912

ISBN 0-7230-0307-6

This new, family-edition, the third to bear the name *The Times Atlas of the World* is no less important for being the smallest and youngest. It is a reference work for use in the home, office or school, for those who travel the world and also those, like Francis Bacon, who journey only "in map and chart".

An index of no fewer than 30,000 entries, keyed to the main map plates, will aid those who, whilst familiar with the name of a place, are uncertain of just where it lies on the map.

It is by no means always easy to ascertain the correct title and status of a country as distinct from its everyday name used on maps. The list of states and territories gives in addition to name, title and status, the population and area, the national currency, the major religions and the national flag.

Maps, being an efficient way of storing and displaying information, are used to amplify the list of states and territories and the geographical comparisons of continents, oceans, lakes and islands. They form the basis of the section on earthquakes, volcanoes, economic minerals, vegetation, temperature, rainfall and population.

Maps are also, by nature, illustrative and a 14-page section shows the world's major physical features in the way they appear from space but with the names of the features added.

Amongst the statistical data contained in the Atlas is a listing of the major metropolitan areas with their populations. For the past several decades there has been, throughout the world, an accelerating flow of people from the land to towns and cities and especially the major cities, some of which now contain the bulk of the national population. Growth in air travel has turned those same cities into centres of tourism. Influx of population and the demands of tourism have enhanced the status of cities. Generous space has, therefore, been allocated to maps of major cities and their environs.

Geographical names in this Atlas are given in their anglicized (conventional) form where such a form is in current use. Other names are given in their national Roman alphabet or else converted into English by transliteration (letter-to-letter) or transcription (sound-to-sound). Because Roman alphabet letters, sometimes modified, are pronounced in a variety of ways, a brief guide to pronunciation has been included. The whole is supplemented by a dictionary of geographical terms.

In the names, in the portrayal of international boundaries and in the list of states and territories, the aim has been to show the situation as it pertains in the area at the time of going to press. This must not be taken as endorsement by the publishers of the status of the territories concerned. The aim throughout has been to show things as they are. In that way the Atlas will best serve the reader to whom, it is hoped, it will bring interest, benefit and continuing pleasure.

H.A.G. Lewis, OBE
Geographical Consultant to *The Times*

ABU DHABI
(see **UNITED ARAB EMIRATES**)

AFGHANISTAN

STATUS: Republic
AREA: 652,225 sq km (251,773 sq miles)
POPULATION: 15,510,000
ANNUAL NATURAL INCREASE: 2.4%
DENSITY: 23.8 per sq km
CAPITAL: Kabul
LANGUAGE: Pushtu, Dari (Persian dialect)
RELIGION: 90% Sunni and 9% Shiah Moslem.
Hindu, Sikh and Jewish minorities
CURRENCY: afghani (Af)
ORGANISATIONS: UN, Col. Plan

Afghanistan is a mountainous landlocked country in south-west Asia with a climate of extremes. In summer the lowland south-west reaches a temperature of over 40°C (104°F); in winter this may drop to −26°C (−15°F) in the northern mountains. Rainfall varies between 10 and 40cm (4–16in). The country is one of the poorest in the world with hardly 10% of the land suitable for agriculture. Main crops are wheat, fruit and vegetables. Sheep and goats are the main livestock. Mineral resources are rich but underdeveloped with natural gas, coal and iron ore deposits predominating. The main industrial area is centred on Kabul.

AJMAN
(see **UNITED ARAB EMIRATES**)

ÅLAND

STATUS: Self-governing Island Province of Finland
AREA: 1,505 sq km (581 sq miles)
POPULATION: 23,761

ABBREVIATIONS	
ANZUS	Australia, New Zealand, United States Security Treaty
ASEAN	Association of South East Asian Nations
CACM	Central American Common Market
CARICOM	Caribbean Community and Common Market
CEAO	West African Economic Community
Col. Plan	Colombo Plan
COMECON	Council for Mutual Economic Assistance
Comm	Commonwealth
Council of Eur	Council of Europe
ECOWAS	Economic Community of West African States
EEC	European Economic Community
EFTA	European Free Trade Association
NATO	North Atlantic Treaty Organisation
OAS	Organization of American States
OAU	Organization of African Unity
OECD	Organisation of Economic Co-operation and Development
OPEC	Organization of Petroleum Exporting Countries
UN	United Nations
WEU	Western European Union

ALBANIA

STATUS: People's Socialist Republic
AREA: 28,750 sq km (11,100 sq miles)
POPULATION: 3,140,000
ANNUAL NATURAL INCREASE: 2.0%
DENSITY: 109.2 per sq km
CAPITAL: Tirana (Tiranë)
LANGUAGE: Albanian (Gheg, Tosk)
RELIGION: mainly atheist. Moslem, Roman Catholic and Greek Orthodox minorities
CURRENCY: new lek
ORGANISATIONS: UN

Situated between Yugoslavia and Greece on the eastern seaboard of the Adriatic, Albania is politically and economically isolated from the rest of Europe. The climate is Mediterranean type with a high rainfall of more than 180cm (7in) in the mountains which cover most of the country. There are considerable mineral resources of chrome, copper, and iron ores; also oil and natural gas. Major exports are now metal products, textiles and grain. Albania became a people's republic in 1946, drifted away from Soviet influence towards China in the 1960's, but since the death of Mao Zedong in 1976 has slowly improved relations with western Europe.

ALEUTIAN ISLANDS

STATUS: Territory of USA
AREA: 17,665 sq km (6,820 sq miles)
POPULATION: 6,730

ALGERIA

STATUS: Democratic and Popular Republic
AREA: 2,381,745 sq km (919,355 sq miles)
POPULATION: 23,840,000
ANNUAL NATURAL INCREASE: 3.2%
DENSITY: 10 per sq km
CAPITAL: Algiers (El-Djezaïr)
LANGUAGE: Arabic, French, Berber
RELIGION: Moslem
CURRENCY: Algerian dinar (AD)
ORGANISATIONS: UN, Arab League, OAU, OPEC

Physically the country is divided between the coastal Atlas mountain ranges of the north and the Sahara desert to the south. Arable land occupies small areas of the northern valleys and coastal strip with wheat, barley and vines leading crops. Sheep, goats and cattle are the most important livestock. Although oil from the southern deserts dominates the economy it is now declining. Economic policy has concentrated on encouraging smaller manufacturing industries. Tourism is a growth industry and now earns important foreign exchange.

AMERICAN SAMOA
STATUS: Unincorporated Territory of USA
AREA: 197 sq km (76 sq miles)
POPULATION: 37,000
CAPITAL: Pago Pago

ANDORRA

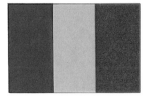

STATUS: Principality
AREA: 465 sq km (180 sq miles)
POPULATION: 51,400
ANNUAL NATURAL INCREASE: n.a.
DENSITY: 110.5 per sq km
CAPITAL: Andorra la Vella

LANGUAGE: Catalan, French, Spanish
RELIGION: mainly Roman Catholic
CURRENCY: French franc, Spanish peseta

Andorra is a tiny alpine state high in the Pyrenees between France and Spain. Agriculture and tourism are the main occupations. Tobacco and potatoes are the principal crops, sheep and cattle the main livestock. Important sources of revenue are the sale of hydro-electricity, stamps and duty-free goods.

ANGOLA

STATUS: People's Republic
AREA: 1,246,700 sq km (481,225 sq miles)

POPULATION: 9,287,000
ANNUAL NATURAL INCREASE: 2.5%
DENSITY: 7.5 per sq km
CAPITAL: Luanda
LANGUAGE: Portuguese, tribal dialects
RELIGION: mainly traditional beliefs. Large Roman Catholic and Protestant minorities
CURRENCY: kwanza (K)
ORGANISATIONS: UN, OAU

Independent from the Portuguese since 1975, Angola is a large country south of the equator in south-western Africa. Much of the interior is savannah plateaux with rainfall varying from 25cm (10in) in the north to 60cm (24in) in the south. Most of the population is engaged in agriculture producing cassava, maize and coffee, but Angola is very rich in minerals. Petroleum, diamonds, iron ore, copper and manganese are exported with petroleum accounting for at least 50% of earnings. The small amount of industry is concentrated around Luanda. Most consumer products and textiles are imported.

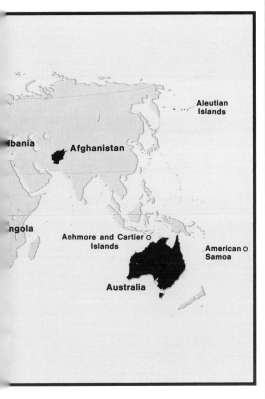

ANGUILLA

STATUS: UK Dependent Territory
AREA: 91 sq km (35 sq miles)
POPULATION: 6,700
CAPITAL: The Valley

ANTIGUA & BARBUDA

STATUS: Commonwealth Nation
AREA: 442 sq km (171 sq miles)
POPULATION: 76,296
ANNUAL NATURAL INCREASE: 1.0%

DENSITY: 172.6 per sq km
CAPITAL: St John's (on Antigua)
LANGUAGE: English
RELIGION: Anglican Christian majority
CURRENCY: East Caribbean dollar (EC$)
ORGANISATIONS: Comm., UN, CARICOM, OAS

The country consists of two main islands in the Leeward group in the West Indies. Tourism is the main activity but local agriculture is being encouraged to reduce food imports. The production of rum is the main manufacturing industry.

ARGENTINA

STATUS: Republic
AREA: 2,766,889 sq km (1,068,302 sq miles)
POPULATION: 31,960,000
ANNUAL NATURAL INCREASE: 1.6%
DENSITY: 11.6 per sq km
CAPITAL: Buenos Aires
LANGUAGE: Spanish
RELIGION: 90% Roman Catholic, 2% Protestant
CURRENCY: austral (A)
ORGANISATIONS: UN, OAS

The country stretches over 30 degrees of latitude from the thick sub-tropical forests of the north through the immense flat grass plains of the pampas to the cool desert plateaux of Patagonia in the south. The economy of Argentina was long dominated by the produce of the rich soils of the pampas, beef and grain. Agricultural products account for over 60% of export revenue with grain crops pre-dominating, although the late 1980's have seen a decline due to competition and falling world grain prices. Beef exports, the mainstay of the economy from 1850, decreased by over 50% between 1970 and 1983, again due to strong competition from Western Europe. Industry has also declined during the last decade. Shortage of raw materials and foreign aid debts have meant lower production, unemployment and a strong decline in home demand. The expansion of the oil and gas industry and the steady growth of coal, hydro-electricity and nuclear power, is providing a base for industrial expansion but internal inflation and foreign financial sanctions have not yet allowed this expansion.

ARUBA

STATUS: Self-governing Island of Netherlands Antilles
AREA: 193 sq km (75 sq miles)
POPULATION: 60,000
CAPITAL: Oranjestad

ASCENSION

STATUS: Island Dependency of St Helena
AREA: 88 sq km (34 sq miles)
POPULATION: 1,007
CAPITAL: Georgetown

ASHMORE AND CARTIER ISLANDS

STATUS: External Territory of Australia
AREA: 3 sq km (1.2 sq miles)
POPULATION: No permanent population

AUSTRALIA

STATUS: Commonwealth Nation
AREA: 7,682,300 sq km (2,965,370 sq miles)
POPULATION: 16,532,000
ANNUAL NATURAL INCREASE: 0.8%
DENSITY: 2.2 per sq km
CAPITAL: Canberra
LANGUAGE: English
RELIGION: 88% Christian. Aboriginal beliefs. Jewish minority
CURRENCY: Australian dollar ($A)
ORGANISATIONS: Comm, UN, ANZUS, Col. Plan, OECD

AUSTRALIAN CAPITAL TERRITORY (CANBERRA)

STATUS: Federal Territory
AREA: 2,432 sq km (939 sq miles)
POPULATION: 273,000
CAPITAL: Canberra

NEW SOUTH WALES

STATUS: State
AREA: 801,430 sq km (309,350 sq miles)
POPULATION: 5,699,000
CAPITAL: Sydney

NORTHERN TERRITORY

STATUS: Territory
AREA: 1,346,200 sq km (519,635 sq miles)
POPULATION: 156,000
CAPITAL: Darwin

QUEENSLAND

STATUS: State
AREA: 1,727,000 sq km (666,620 sq miles)
POPULATION: 2,743,000
CAPITAL: Brisbane

SOUTH AUSTRALIA

STATUS: State
AREA: 984,380 sq km (79,970 sq miles)
POPULATION: 1,408,000
CAPITAL: Adelaide

TASMANIA

STATUS: State
AREA: 68,330 sq km (26,375 sq miles)
POPULATION: 448,000
CAPITAL: Hobart

VICTORIA

STATUS: State
AREA: 227,600 sq km (87,855 sq miles)
POPULATION: 4,260,000
CAPITAL: Melbourne

WESTERN AUSTRALIA

STATUS: State
AREA: 2,525,500 sq km (974,845 sq miles)
POPULATION: 1,544,000
CAPITAL: Perth

Australia is both a continent and a country and is the sixth largest country in terms of area. The centre and the west, over 50% of the land area, are desert and scrub with less than 25cm (10in) of rain. Only in the subtropical north and the eastern highlands does rainfall exceed 100cm (39in) annually. Australia is rich in both agricultural and natural resources. Wool, wheat, meat, sugar and dairy products account for over 40% of export revenue despite the immense growth in mineral exploitation. The country has vast reserves of coal, oil, natural gas, nickel, iron ore, bauxite and uranium ores. Gold, silver, lead, zinc and copper ores are also exploited. In 1984 minerals accounted for about 38% of export revenue. Recent high deficits in balance of trade have been caused by fluctuations in world demand, competition from the E.E.C. and recent unfavourable climatic conditions affecting agricultural surpluses. Increasing trade with eastern Asia, and Japan in particular has opened up new areas of commerce to counteract the sharp decline in Europe as a market.

AUSTRALIAN ANTARCTIC TERRITORY

STATUS: Territory
AREA: 6,120,000 sq km (2,320,000 sq miles)
POPULATION: No permanent population

AUSTRIA

STATUS: Republic
AREA: 83,855 sq km (32,370 sq miles)
POPULATION: 7,605,000
ANNUAL NATURAL INCREASE: 0.0%
DENSITY: 90.7 per sq km
CAPITAL: Vienna (Wien)
LANGUAGE: German
RELIGION: 89% Roman Catholic, 6% Protestant
CURRENCY: Schilling (Sch)
ORGANISATIONS: UN, Council of Europe, EFTA, OECD

Austria is an alpine, land-locked country in central Europe. The mountainous Alps which cover 75% of the land consist of a series of east-west ranges enclosing lowland basins. The climate is continental with cold winters and warm summers. About 25% of the country, in the north and north-east, is lower foreland or flat land containing most of Austria's fertile farmland. Half is arable and the remainder is mainly for root or fodder crops. Manufacturing and heavy industry however, account for the majority of export revenue particularly pig-iron, steel, chemicals and vehicles. Over 70% of the country's power is hydroelectric. Tourism and forestry are also important to the economy.

AZORES

STATUS: Self-governing Island Region of Portugal

AREA: 2,335 sq km (901 sq miles)
POPULATION: 253,500
CAPITAL: Ponta Delgada

BAHAMAS

STATUS: State
AREA: 13,865 sq km (5,350 sq miles)
POPULATION: 245,000
ANNUAL NATURAL INCREASE: 1.9%
DENSITY: 17.7 per sq km
CAPITAL: Nassau (on New Providence)
LANGUAGE: English
RELIGION: mainly Anglican Christian, Baptist and Roman Catholic
CURRENCY: Bahamian dollar (B$)
ORGANISATIONS: Comm, UN, CARICOM, OAS

About 700 islands and over 2000 coral sand cays (reefs) constitute the sub-tropical Commonwealth of The Bahamas. The island group extends from the coast of Florida to Cuba and Haiti in the south. Only 29 islands are inhabited. Most of the 100cm (39in) of rainfall falls in the summer. The tourist industry is the main source of income and although fluctuating through recession, still employs over 70% of the working population. Recent economic plans have concentrated on reducing imports by developing fishing and domestic agriculture. Other important sources of income are ship registration (the world's third largest open-registry fleet), income generated by offshore finance and banking and export of rum, salt and cement.

BAHRAIN

STATUS: State
AREA: 661 sq km (225 sq miles)
POPULATION: 421,040
ANNUAL NATURAL INCREASE: 2.8%
DENSITY: 636.9 per sq km
CAPITAL: Al Manāmah (Manama)
LANGUAGE: Arabic, English
RELIGION: 60% Shiah and 40% Sunni Moslem. Christian minority
CURRENCY: Bahrain dinar (BD)
ORGANISATIONS: UN, Arab League

The sheikdom is a barren island in the Persian Gulf with less than 8cm (3in) rainfall. Summer temperatures average 32°C (89°F). Bahrain was the first country in the Arabian peninsula to strike oil, in 1932. In 1985, oil accounted for 65% of revenue, but a decline in value of the product and lower production is now causing the government to diversify the economy with expansion of light and heavy industry and chemical plants, and the subsequent encouragement of trade and foreign investment.

BALEARIC ISLANDS (BALEARES)

STATUS: Island Province of Spain
AREA: 5,015 sq km (1,935 sq miles)
POPULATION: 754,777
CAPITAL: Palma de Mallorca

BANGLADESH

STATUS: People's Republic
AREA: 144,000 sq km (55,585 sq miles)
POPULATION: 104,530,000
ANNUAL NATURAL INCREASE: 2.7%

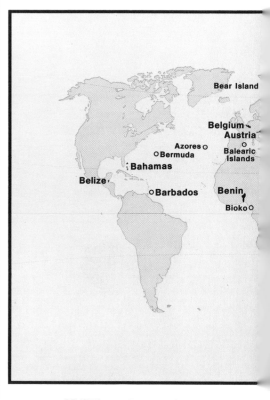

DENSITY: 725.9 per sq km
CAPITAL: Dhaka (Dacca)
LANGUAGE: Bengali (Bangla), Bihari, Hindi, English
RELIGION: 85% Moslem. Hindu, Buddhist and Christian minorities
CURRENCY: taka (tk)
ORGANISATIONS: Comm, UN, Col. Plan

Bangladesh is one of the world's poorest countries. Life expectancy averages only 48 years. Most of the territory of Bangladesh comprises the vast river systems of the Ganges and Brahmaputra which drain from the Himalayas into the Bay of Bengal, frequently changing course and flooding the flat delta plain. The climate is tropical, and agriculture is dependent on monsoon rainfall. When the monsoon fails there is drought. 82% of the population of Bangladesh are farmers, the main crops being rice and jute. There are no extensive mineral deposits, although large reserves of natural gas under the Bay of Bengal have not yet been exploited. The main export goods are jute, animal skins and tea.

BARBADOS

STATUS: State
AREA: 430 sq km (166 sq miles)
POPULATION: 253,881
ANNUAL NATURAL INCREASE: 0.9%
DENSITY: 590 per sq km
CAPITAL: Bridgetown
LANGUAGE: English
RELIGION: Anglican Christian majority.
Methodist and Roman Catholic minorities
CURRENCY: Barbados dollar (BDs$)
ORGANISATIONS: Comm, UN, CARICOM, OAS

The former British colony of Barbados in the Caribbean is the easternmost island of the

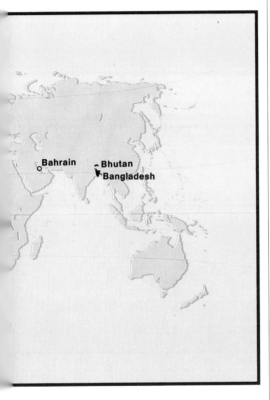

Antilles chain. The gently rolling landscape of the island is lush and fertile, the temperature ranging from 25°–28°C(77°–82°F) with 127–190cm(50–75in) rainfall per year. Sugar and its by-products, molasses and rum, form the mainstay of the economy. Tourism has become a growing industry in recent years.

BASUTOLAND
(see **LESOTHO**)

BEAR ISLAND (BJØRNØYA)
STATUS: Island of Svalbard, Norway
AREA: 176 sq km (68 sq miles)
·POPULATION: 14

BECHUANALAND
(see **BOTSWANA**)

BELGIUM

STATUS: Kingdom
AREA: 30,520 sq km (11,780 sq miles)
POPULATION: 9,920,000
ANNUAL NATURAL INCREASE: 0.1%
DENSITY: 325.1 per sq km
CAPITAL: Brussels (Bruxelles/Brussel)
LANGUAGE: French, Dutch, German
RELIGION: Roman Catholic majority. Protestant, Jewish minorities
CURRENCY: Belgian franc
ORGANISATIONS: UN, Council of Europe, EEC, NATO, OECD, WEU

Belgium is situated between the hills of Northern France and the North European plain. Over two thirds of the country comprises the Flanders plain, a flat plateau covered by fertile wind-blown loess which extends from the North Sea coast down to the forested mountains of the Ardennes in the south, which rise to a height of 692m(2270ft). The climate is mild and temperate, although the country's proximity to the Atlantic means that low pressure fronts bring changeable weather and frequent rainfall (72–120cm or 28–47in per annum). Over half the country is intensively farmed – cereals (mainly wheat), root crops, vegetables and flax are the main crops. Extensive pastureland ensures that Belgium is self-sufficient in meat and dairy products. Belgium lacks mineral resources, except for coal, but its metal and engineering industries account for nearly one third of its exports. The Flanders region is famous for its textiles. Most of Belgium's trade passes through the North sea port of Antwerp, and an efficient communications network links the port with the rest of Europe.

BELIZE

STATUS: State
AREA: 22,965 sq km (8,865 sq miles)
POPULATION: 176,000
ANNUAL NATURAL INCREASE: 2.5%
DENSITY: 7.7 per sq km
CAPITAL: Belmopan
LANGUAGE: English, Spanish, Maya
RELIGION: 60% Roman Catholic, 40% Protestant
CURRENCY: Belizean dollar (BZ$)
ORGANISATIONS: Comm, UN, CARICOM

Bordering the Caribbean Sea, sub-tropical Belize is dominated by its dense forest cover. Principal crops for export are sugar-cane, fruit, rice, maize and timber products. Since independence from Britain in 1973 the country has developed agriculture to lessen reliance on imported food products. Fish is a staple diet and also provides valuable foreign exchange.

BENIN

STATUS: People's Republic
AREA: 112,620 sq km (43,470 sq miles)
POPULATION: 4,440,000
ANNUAL NATURAL INCREASE: 3.0%
DENSITY: 39.4 per sq km
CAPITAL: Porto Novo
LANGUAGE: French, Fon, Adja
RELIGION: traditional beliefs majority, 15% Roman Catholic and 13% Moslem
CURRENCY: CFA franc
ORGANISATIONS: UN, CEAO, ECOWAS, OAU

Benin, formerly Dahomey, is a small strip of country descending from the wooded savannah hills of the north to the forested and cultivated lowlands fringing the Bight of Benin. The economy is dominated by agriculture with palm oil, cotton, coffee, groundnuts and copra as main exports. The developing off-shore oil industry has proven reserves of over 20 million barrels.

BERMUDA
STATUS: Self-governing UK Crown Colony
AREA: 54 sq km (21 sq miles)
POPULATION: 58,080
CAPITAL: Hamilton

BHUTAN

STATUS: Kingdom
AREA: 46,620 sq km (17,995 sq miles)
POPULATION: 1,447,000
ANNUAL NATURAL INCREASE: 2.0%
DENSITY: 31.1 per sq km
CAPITAL: Thimphu
LANGUAGE: Dzongkha, Nepali, English
RELIGION: Mahayana Buddhist. Hindu minority
CURRENCY: ngultrum, Indian rupee
ORGANISATIONS: UN, Col. Plan

The country spreads across the Himalayan foothills between China and India east of Nepal. Rainfall is high at over 300cm (118in) per year but temperatures vary between extreme cold of the northern ranges to a July average of 27°C (81°F) in the southern forests. Long isolated, the economy of Bhutan is dominated by agriculture and small local industries. All manufactured goods are imported.

BIOKO (FERNANDO PÓO)
STATUS: Island of Equatorial Guinea
AREA: 2,034 sq km (785 sq miles)
POPULATION: 57,190
CAPITAL: Malabo (Sta. Isabel)

BJØRNØYA

(see **BEAR ISLAND**)

BOLIVIA

STATUS: Republic
AREA: 1,098,575 sq km (424,050 sq miles)
POPULATION: 7,000,000
ANNUAL NATURAL INCREASE: 2.8%
DENSITY: 6 per sq km
CAPITAL: La Paz
LANGUAGE: Spanish, Quechua, Aymara
RELIGION: large Roman Catholic majority
CURRENCY: Boliviano
ORGANISATIONS: UN, OAS

With an average life expectancy of 51 years, Bolivia is one of the world's poorest nations. Landlocked and isolated, the country stretches from the eastern Andes across high cool plateaux before dropping to the dense forest of the Amazon basin and the grasslands of the south-east. Development of the economy relies on the growth of exploitation of mineral resources as subsistence agriculture occupies the majority of the population. Crude oil, natural gas, tin, zinc and iron ore are the main mineral deposits.

BONAIRE

STATUS: Self-governing Island of Netherlands Antilles
AREA: 288 sq km (111 sq miles)
POPULATION: 10,625
CAPITAL: Kralendijk

BONIN ISLANDS (OGASAWARA-SHOTO)

STATUS: Islands of Japan
AREA: 104 sq km (40 sq miles)
POPULATION: 200

BOTSWANA

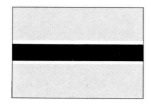

STATUS: Republic
AREA: 582,000 sq km (224,652 sq miles)
POPULATION: 1,211,816
ANNUAL NATURAL INCREASE: 3.3%
DENSITY: 2.1 per sq km
CAPITAL: Gaborone
LANGUAGE: Setswana, English
RELIGION: traditional beliefs majority. Christian minority

CURRENCY: pula (P)
ORGANISATIONS: Comm, UN, OAU

The arid high plateau of Botswana with its poor soils and low rainfall, supports little arable agriculture, but over 2.5 million cattle graze the dry grasslands. Diamonds, copper, nickel and gold are mined in the east and are the main mineral exports. The growth of light industries around the capital has stimulated trade with neighbouring countries.

BOUGAINVILLE ISLAND

STATUS: Part of Papua New Guinea
AREA: 10,620 sq km (4,100 sq miles)
POPULATION: 77,880

BRAZIL

STATUS: Federative Republic
AREA: 8,511,965 sq km (3,285,620 sq miles)
POPULATION: 144,428,000
ANNUAL NATURAL INCREASE: 2.3%
DENSITY: 16.9 per sq km
CAPITAL: Brasília
LANGUAGE: Portuguese
RELIGION: 90% Roman Catholic. Protestant minority
CURRENCY: Cruzado (CZ$)
ORGANISATIONS: UN, OAS

Brazil is not only the largest country in South America but also has the fastest growing economy. Brazil is now an industrial power but with development limited to the heavily populated urban areas of the eastern coastal lowlands. The Amazon basin tropical rain forest covers roughly one third of the country; savannah grasslands of the centre west give way to light forest – now much cleared – of the eastern Brazilian Highlands, and the cool southern plateau of the south. This varied landscape is dominated by three river systems of the Amazon, São Francisco and Paraguay/Paraná. Economic variety reflects the changing landscape. In agricultural production Brazil is one of the world's leading exporters with coffee, soya beans, sugar, bananas, cocoa, tobacco, rice and cattle major commodities. Mineral resources, except for iron ore, at the moment do not play a significant role in the economy, but recent economic policies have concentrated on developing the industrial base – road and rail communications, of light and heavy industry and expansion of energy resources, particularly hydro-electric power harnessed from the great river systems.

BRITISH INDIAN OCEAN TERRITORY

STATUS: British Dependency comprising the Chagos Archipelago
AREA: 52 sq km (20 sq miles)
POPULATION: No permanent population

BRUNEI

STATUS: Sultanate
AREA: 5,765 sq km (2,225 sq miles)
POPULATION: 241,000
ANNUAL NATURAL INCREASE: 2.6%
CAPITAL: Bandar Seri Begawan
DENSITY: 41.8 per sq km
LANGUAGE: Malay, English, Chinese
RELIGION: 65% Sunni Moslem. Buddhist and Christian minorities
CURRENCY: Brunei dollar (B$)
ORGANISATIONS: Comm, UN, ASEAN

The Sultanate of Brunei is situated on the north-west coast of Borneo. Its tropical climate is hot and humid with annual rainfall ranging from 250cm(98in) on the thin coastal strip to

500cm(197in) in the mountainous interior. Oil, both on-shore and off-shore is the mainstay of the Brunei economy. Other exports include natural gas, which is transported to Japan, rubber and timber. Apart from oil, most other industries are local.

BULGARIA

STATUS: People's Republic
AREA: 110,910 sq km (42,810 sq miles)
POPULATION: 8,973,600
ANNUAL NATURAL INCREASE: 0.2%
DENSITY: 80.9 per sq km

CAPITAL: Sofia (Sofiya)
LANGUAGE: Bulgarian
RELIGION: atheist, Eastern Orthodox and Moslem
CURRENCY: lev
ORGANISATIONS: UN, Warsaw Pact, COMECON

Most of the landscape consists of low alpine mountain ranges with broad fertile valleys. The climate is continental with hot summers and cold winters. Rainfall ranges between 45 and 120cm (18–47in) per year. Tobacco is the main export crop but rice, wine, fruit and vegetables are also important. Bulgaria has experienced significant industrial growth since the end of the Second World War and been transformed from an agricultural economy to one based on light and heavy engineering and manufacturing. Most of this industry is concentrated around Sofia. Nuclear power is expected to provide up to 60% of electricity by the end of the century. Copper, lead, zinc and coal mining have helped stimulate this transformation. Tourism is a developing industry.

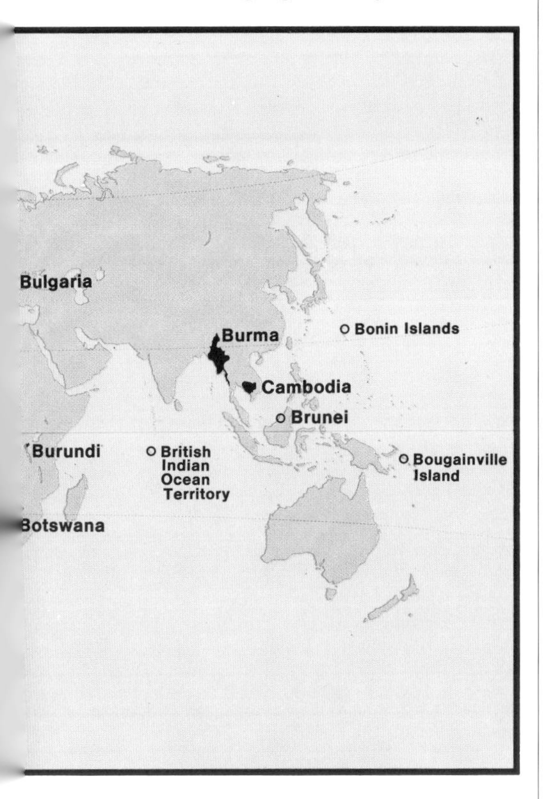

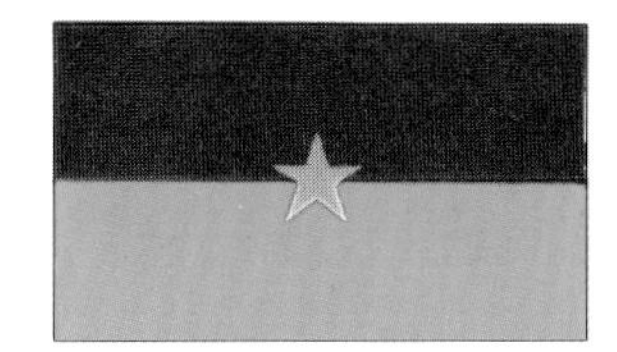

BURKINA

STATUS: People's Democratic Republic
AREA: 274,122 sq km (105,811 sq miles)
POPULATION: 8,530,000
ANNUAL NATURAL INCREASE: 2.6%
DENSITY: 31.1 sq km
CAPITAL: Ouagadougou
LANGUAGE: French, Moré (Mossi), Dyula
RELIGION: 60% animist, 30% Moslem, 10% Roman Catholic
CURRENCY: franc CFA
ORGANISATIONS: UN, CEAO, ECOWAS, OAU

Situated on the southern edge of the Sahara in West Africa, Burkina is a poor, landlocked republic with thin soils supporting savannah grasslands. Frequent droughts, particularly in the north, seriously affect exports of cattle and cotton and the economy which is mainly subsistence agriculture. There is virtually no industry.

BURMA

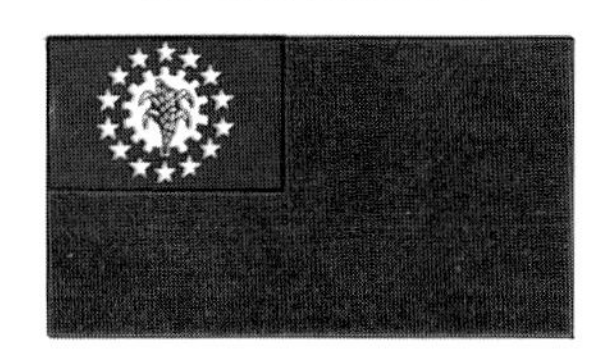

STATUS: Socialist Republic
AREA: 678,030 sq km (261,720 sq miles)
POPULATION: 39,840,000
ANNUAL NATURAL INCREASE: 2.0%
DENSITY: 58.8 per sq km
CAPITAL: Rangoon
LANGUAGE: Burmese
RELIGION: 85% Buddhist. Animist, Moslem, Hindu and Christian minorities
CURRENCY: kyat
ORGANISATIONS: UN, Col. Plan

Much of Burma is covered by tropical rain forest divided by the central valley of the Irrawaddy, the Sittang and the Salween rivers. The western highlands are an extension of the Himalayas; hills to the east and south are a continuation of the Yunnan Plateau of China. The Burmese economy is based on export of rice and forestry products. The irrigated central basin and the coastal region to the east of the Irrawaddy delta are the major rice-growing areas. Hardwoods, particularly teak, cover the highlands. There is potential for growth in areas of tin, copper, oil and natural gas exploitation, as there are significant deposits. The small amount of industry concentrates on food processing.

BURUNDI

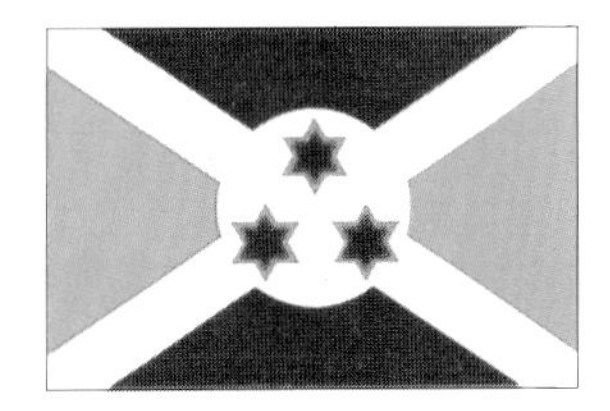

STATUS: Republic
AREA: 27,835 sq km (10,745 sq miles)
POPULATION: 5,130,000
ANNUAL NATURAL INCREASE: 3.0%
DENSITY: 184.3 sq km
CAPITAL: Bujumbura
LANGUAGE: French, Kirundi, Swahili
RELIGION: 60% Roman Catholic. Large minority Animist
CURRENCY: Burundi franc
ORGANISATIONS: UN, OAU

This central African republic is one of the world's poorest nations. Manufacturing industry is almost non-existent as the population barely produces enough food for itself. Burundi is close to the equator but because of its altitude temperatures range between 17° and 23°C (63° and 74°F). The poverty has two basic causes – repetitive droughts and slow recovery from tribal conflicts.

CAMBODIA

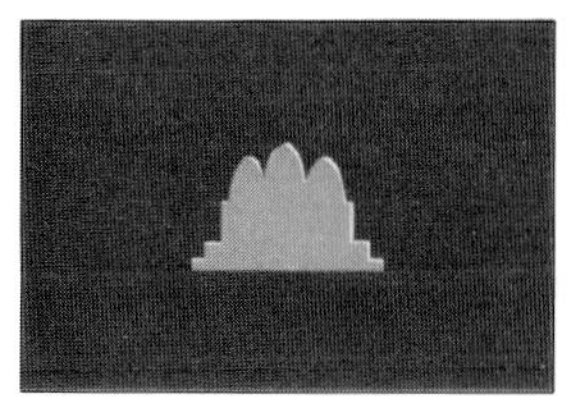

STATUS: People's Republic
AREA: 181,000 sq km (69,865 sq miles)
POPULATION: 7,870,000
ANNUAL NATURAL INCREASE: 2.3%
DENSITY: 43.5 per sq km
CAPITAL: Phnom Penh
LANGUAGE: Khmer
RELIGION: Buddhist majority. Roman Catholic and Moslem minorities
CURRENCY: riel
ORGANISATIONS: UN, Col. Plan

Cambodia is a potentially rich country in S.E. Asia whose economy has been damaged since the 1970's by the aftermath of the Vietnam War. The central plain of the river Mekong covers over 70% of the country and provides ideal conditions for rice production and harvesting of fish. Over 50% of Cambodia is covered by monsoon rain forest.

CAMEROON

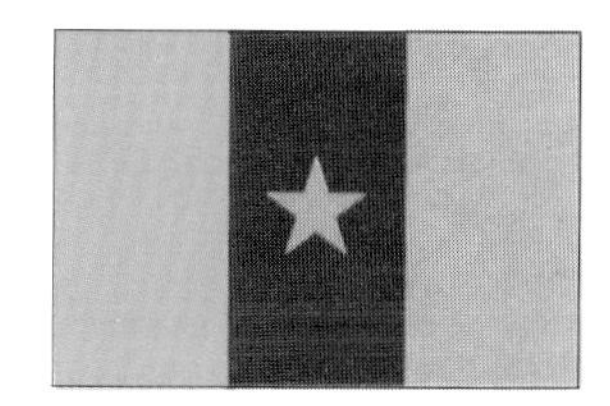

STATUS: Republic
AREA: 475,500 sq km (183,545 sq miles)
POPULATION: 11,082,000
ANNUAL NATURAL INCREASE: 2.7%
DENSITY: 23 per sq km
CAPITAL: Yaoundé
LANGUAGE: English, French
RELIGION: 40% Christian, 39% traditional beliefs, 21% Moslem
CURRENCY: CFA franc
ORGANISATIONS: UN, OAU

Cameroon is situated on the coast of West Africa just north of the equator. Coastal lowlands rise to densely forested plateaux. Rainfall varies from over 1000 to only 50cm per year. The majority of the population are farmers with agricultural products accounting for over 80% of export revenue. Coffee and cocoa are the main cash crops. Mineral resources are underdeveloped but Cameroon already is Africa's greatest producer of bauxite, aluminium ore. Oil exploitation is playing an increasing role in the economy.

CANADA

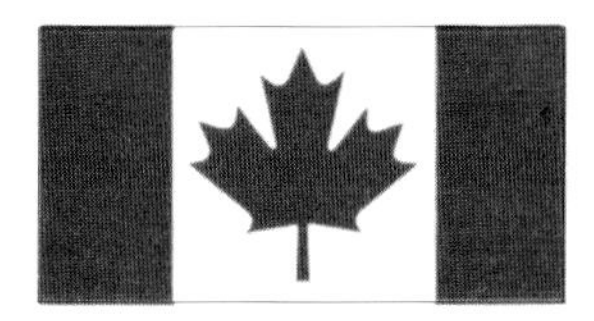

STATUS: Dominion
AREA: 9,922,385 sq km (3,830,840 sq miles)
POPULATION: 26,028,000

ANNUAL NATURAL INCREASE: 0.8%
DENSITY: 2.6 per sq km
CAPITAL: Ottawa
LANGUAGE: English, French
RELIGION: 46% Roman Catholic. Protestant and Jewish minority
CURRENCY: Canadian dollar (C$)
ORGANISATIONS: Comm, UN, Col. Plan, NATO, OECD

ALBERTA

STATUS: Province
AREA: 661,190 sq km (255,220 sq miles)
POPULATION: 2,414,000
CAPITAL: Edmonton

BRITISH COLUMBIA

STATUS: Province
AREA: 948,595 sq km (366,160 sq miles)
POPULATION: 3,009,000
CAPITAL: Victoria

MANITOBA

STATUS: Province
AREA: 650,090 sq km (250,935 sq miles)
POPULATION: 1,085,000
CAPITAL: Winnipeg

NEW BRUNSWICK

STATUS: Province
AREA: 73,435 sq km (28,345 sq miles)
POPULATION: 715,000
CAPITAL: Fredericton

NEWFOUNDLAND AND LABRADOR

STATUS: Province
AREA: 404,520 sq km (156,145 sq miles)
POPULATION: 569,000
CAPITAL: St. John's

NORTHWEST TERRITORIES

STATUS: Territory
AREA: 3,379,685 sq km (1,304,560 sq miles)
POPULATION: 52,000
CAPITAL: Yellowknife

NOVA SCOTIA

STATUS: Province
AREA: 55,490 sq km (21,420 sq miles)
POPULATION: 885,000
CAPITAL: Halifax

ONTARIO

STATUS: Province
AREA: 1,068,630 sq km (412,490 sq miles)
POPULATION: 9,484,000
CAPITAL: Toronto

PRINCE EDWARD ISLAND

STATUS: Province
AREA: 5,655 sq km (2,185 sq miles)
POPULATION: 129,000
CAPITAL: Charlottetown

QUEBEC

STATUS: Province
AREA: 1,540,680 sq km (594,705 sq miles)
POPULATION: 6,653,000
CAPITAL: Quebec

SASKATCHEWAN

STATUS: Province
AREA: 651,900 sq km (251,635 sq miles)
POPULATION: 1,007,000
CAPITAL: Regina

YUKON TERRITORY

STATUS: Territory
AREA: 482,515 sq km (186,250 sq miles)
POPULATION: 25,000
CAPITAL: Whitehorse

Canada is the world's second largest country stretching from the great barren islands of the Arctic north to the vast grasslands of the central south, and from the Rocky Mountain chain of the west to the farmlands of the Great Lakes in the east. This huge area experiences great climatic differences but basically a continental climate prevails with extremes of heat and cold particularly in the central plains. The Arctic tundra of the far north provides summer grazing for caribou. Further south coniferous forests grow on the thin soils of the ancient shield landscape and on the extensive foothills of the Rocky Mountains. In contrast, the rich soils of the central prairies support grasslands and grain crops. The Great Lakes area provides fish, fruit, maize, root crops and dairy products; the prairies produce over 20% of the world's wheat; and the grasslands of Alberta support a thriving beef industry. Most minerals are mined and exploited in Canada with oil and natural gas, iron ore, bauxite, nickel, zinc, copper, gold and silver the major exports. The country's vast rivers provide huge amounts of hydro-electric power but most industry is confined to the Great Lakes and St Lawrence margins. The principal manufactured goods for export are steel products, motor vehicles, and paper for newsprint. Despite economic success, Canada still remains one of the world's most under-exploited countries so vast are the potential mineral resources and areas of land for agricultural development.

CANARY ISLANDS

STATUS: Island Province of Spain
AREA: 7,275 sq km (2,810 sq miles)
POPULATION: 1,614,882
CAPITAL: Las Palmas (Gran Canaria) and Santa Cruz (Tenerife)

CAPE VERDE

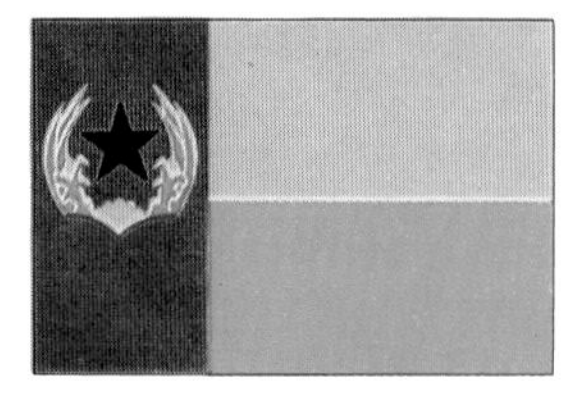

STATUS: Republic
AREA: 4,035 sq km (1,560 sq miles)
POPULATION: 359,000
ANNUAL NATURAL INCREASE: 2.4%
DENSITY: 88.9 per sq km
CAPITAL: Praia
LANGUAGE: Portuguese, Creole
RELIGION: 98% Roman Catholic
CURRENCY: Cape Verde escudo
ORGANISATIONS: UN, ECOWAS, OAU

Independent since 1975, the ten inhabited volcanic islands of the republic are situated in the Atlantic 500km (310 miles) west of Senegal. Rainfall is low but irrigation encourages growth of sugar-cane, coconuts, fruit and maize. Fishing accounts for about 70% of export revenue. All consumer goods are imported and trading links continue to be maintained with Portugal.

CAROLINE ISLANDS

(see **MICRONESIA, FEDERATED STATES OF, AND PALAU**)

CAYMAN ISLANDS

STATUS: UK Dependent Territory
AREA: 259 sq km (100 sq miles)
POPULATION: 23,700
CAPITAL: George Town

CELEBES (SULAWESI)

STATUS: Island Province of Indonesia
AREA: 229,110 sq km (88,435 sq miles)
POPULATION: 11,552,917

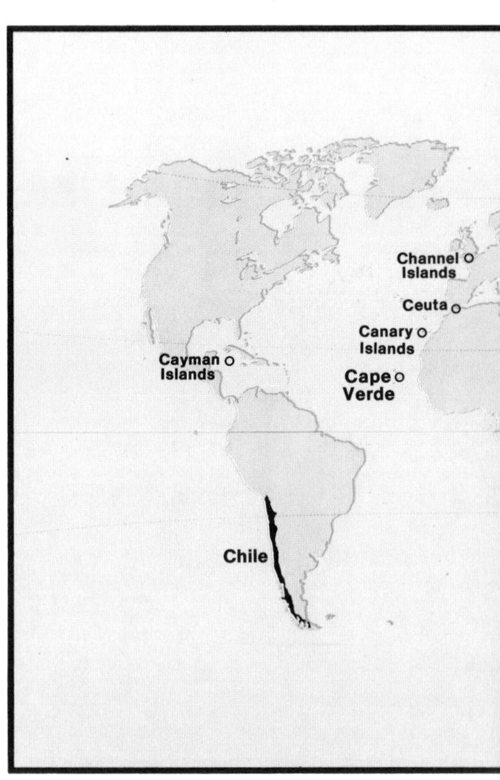

CENTRAL AFRICAN REPUBLIC

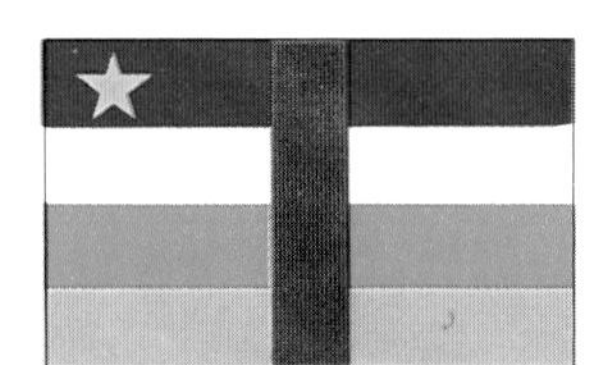

STATUS: Republic
AREA: 624,975 sq km (241,240 sq miles)
POPULATION: 2,860,000
ANNUAL NATURAL INCREASE: 2.8%
DENSITY: 4.6 per sq km
CAPITAL: Bangui
LANGUAGE: French, Sango
RELIGION: animist majority. 33% Christian. Moslem minority
CURRENCY: CFA franc
ORGANISATIONS: UN, OAU

The republic is landlocked and remote from both east and west Africa. The natural vegetation is tropical savannah on the rolling plateaux but despite 100cm (39in) or more rainfall per year, the economy is based on subsistence agriculture. A small amount of crops are exported – cotton, coffee, oil palm and cocoa. Diamonds and uranium ore are the major mineral exports. Hardwood forests in the south-west provide timber for export.

CEUTA

STATUS: Spanish External Territory
AREA: 19.5 sq km (7.5 sq miles)
POPULATION: 67,188

CEYLON
(see SRI LANKA)

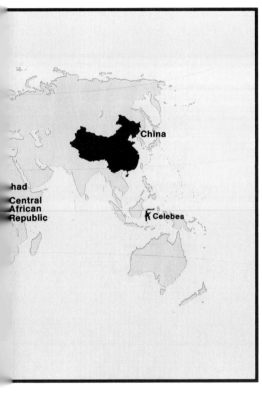

CHAD

STATUS: Republic
AREA: 1,284,000 sq km (495,625 sq miles)
POPULATION: 5,396,000
ANNUAL NATURAL INCREASE: 2.0%
DENSITY: 4 per sq km
CAPITAL: Ndjamena
LANGUAGE: French, Arabic, local languages
RELIGION: 50% Moslem, 45% animist, 5% Christian
CURRENCY: CFA franc
ORGANISATIONS: UN, OAU

Chad is a vast state of central Africa stretching deep into the Sahara. The economy is based on agriculture but only the south with

100cm (39in) of rainfall can support crops for export – cotton, rice and groundnuts. Severe droughts, increasing desertification and border disputes have severely restricted development. Life expectancy at birth is still only 43 years. Salt is mined around Lake Chad.

CHANNEL ISLANDS

STATUS: British Crown Dependency
AREA: 194 sq km (75 sq miles)
POPULATION: 138,668
CAPITAL: St Helier (Jersey), St Peter Port (Guernsey)

CHILE

STATUS: Republic
AREA: 751,625 sq km (290,125 sq miles)
POPULATION: 12,907,000
ANNUAL NATURAL INCREASE: 1.6%
DENSITY: 17.2 per sq km
CAPITAL: Santiago
LANGUAGE: Spanish
RELIGION: 85% Roman Catholic. Protestant minority
CURRENCY: Chilean peso
ORGANISATIONS: UN, OAS

Chile is a long thin country on the west coast of South America stretching throughout 38° degrees of latitude from the Atacama desert of the north to the ice deserts of Tierra del Fuego. Apart from a thin coastal strip of lowland, the country is dominated by the Andes mountains. The economy is based upon the abundance of mineral resources with copper (the world's largest reserve), iron ore, nitrates, coal, oil and gas all major exports. Most energy is provided by hydroelectric power. Light and heavy industries are based around Concepción and Santiago.

CHINA

STATUS: People's Republic
AREA: 9,597,000 sq km (3,704,440 sq miles)
POPULATION: 1,072,200,000
ANNUAL NATURAL INCREASE: 1.0%
DENSITY: 111.7 per sq km
CAPITAL: Beijing (Peking)
LANGUAGE: Mandarin Chinese, regional languages
RELIGION: Confucianist, Buddhist, Taoist. Small Christian and Moslem minority
CURRENCY: Renminbi or yuan
ORGANISATIONS: UN

ANHUI (ANHWEI)
STATUS: Province
AREA: 139,900 sq km (54,000 sq miles)
POPULATION: 52,170,000
CAPITAL: Hefei

BEIJING (PEKING)
STATUS: Municipality
AREA: 17,800 sq km (6,870 miles)
POPULATION: 9,750,000

FUJIAN (FUKIEN)
STATUS: Province
AREA: 123,000 sq km (47,515 sq miles)
POPULATION: 27,490,000
CAPITAL: Fuzhou

GANSU (KANSU)
STATUS: Province
AREA: 530,000 sq km (204,580 sq miles)
POPULATION: 20,710,000
CAPITAL: Lanzhou

GUANGDONG (KWANGTUNG)
STATUS: Province
AREA: 231,400 sq km (89,320 sq miles)
POPULATION: 63,460,000
CAPITAL: Guangzhou

GUANGXI-ZHUANG (KWANGSI-CHUANG)
STATUS: Autonomous Region
AREA: 220,400 sq km (85,075 sq miles)
POPULATION: 39,460,000
CAPITAL: Nanning

GUIZHOU (KWEICHOW)
STATUS: Province
AREA: 174,000 sq km (67,165 sq miles)
POPULATION: 30,080,000
CAPITAL: Guiyang

HEBEI (HOPEI)
STATUS: Province
AREA: 202,700 sq km (78,240 sq miles)
POPULATION: 56,170,000
CAPITAL: Shijiazhuang

HEILONGJIANG (HEILUNGKIANG)
STATUS: Province
AREA: 710,000 sq km (274,060 sq miles)
POPULATION: 33,320,000
CAPITAL: Harbin

HENAN (HONAN)
STATUS: Province
AREA: 167,000 sq km (64,460 sq miles)
POPULATION: 78,080,000
CAPITAL: Zhengzhou

HUBEI (HUPEH)
STATUS: Province
AREA: 187,500 sq km (72,375 sq miles)
POPULATION: 49,890,000
CAPITAL: Wuhan

HUNAN (HUNAN)
STATUS: Province
AREA: 210,500 sq km (81,255 sq miles)
POPULATION: 56,960,000
CAPITAL: Changsha

JIANGSU (KIANGSU)
STATUS: Province
AREA: 102,200 sq km (39,450 sq miles)
POPULATION: 62,700,000
CAPITAL: Nanjing

JIANGXI (KIANGSI)
STATUS: Province
AREA: 164,800 sq km (63,615 sq miles)
POPULATION: 35,090,000
CAPITAL: Nanchang

JILIN (KIRIN)
STATUS: Province
AREA: 290,000 sq km (111,940 sq miles)
POPULATION: 23,150,000
CAPITAL: Changchun

LIAONING (LIAONING)
STATUS: Province
AREA: 230,000 sq km (88,780 sq miles)
POPULATION: 37,260,000
CAPITAL: Shenyang

NEI MONGOL (INNER MONGOLIA)
STATUS: Autonomous Region
AREA: 450,000 sq km (173,700 sq miles)
POPULATION: 20,290,000
CAPITAL: Hohhot

NINGXIA HUI (NINGHSIA)
STATUS: Autonomous Region
AREA: 170,000 sq km (65,620 sq miles)
POPULATION: 4,240,000
CAPITAL: Yinchuan

QINGHAI (CHINGHAI)
STATUS: Province
AREA: 721,000 sq km (278,305 sq miles)
POPULATION: 4,120,000
CAPITAL: Xining

SHAANXI (SHENSI)
STATUS: Province
AREA: 195,800 sq km (75,580 sq miles)
POPULATION: 30,430,000
CAPITAL: Xian

SHANDONG (SHANTUNG)
STATUS: Province
AREA: 153,300 sq km (59,175 sq miles)
POPULATION: 77,760,000
CAPITAL: Jinan

SHANGHAI
STATUS: Municipality
AREA: 5,800 sq km (2,240 sq miles)
POPULATION: 12,320,000

SHANXI (SHANSI)
STATUS: Province
AREA: 157,100 sq km (60,640 sq miles)
POPULATION: 26,550,000
CAPITAL: Taiyuan

SICHUAN (SZECHWAN)
STATUS: Province
AREA: 569,000 sq km (219,635 sq miles)
POPULATION: 103,200,000
CAPITAL: Chengdu

TIANJIN (TIENTSIN)
STATUS: Municipality
AREA: 4,000 sq km (1,545 sq miles)
POPULATION: 8,190,000

YUNNAN (YUNNAN)
STATUS: Province
AREA: 436,200 sq km (168,375 sq miles)
POPULATION: 34,560,000
CAPITAL: Kunming

XINJIANG UYGUR (SINKIANG UIGHUR)
STATUS: Autonomous Region
AREA: 1,646,800 sq km (635,665 sq miles)
POPULATION: 13,840,000
CAPITAL: Urumqi

XIZANG (TIBET)
STATUS: Autonomous Region
AREA: 1,221,600 sq km (471,540 sq miles)
POPULATION: 2,030,000
CAPITAL: Lhasa

ZHEJIANG (CHEKIANG)
STATUS: Province
AREA: 101,800 sq km (39,295 sq miles)
POPULATION: 40,700,000
CAPITAL: Hangzhou

With population over one billion and vast mineral and agricultural resources China has made a tremendous effort during the late 1970's and 80's to erase the negative economic effects of the collectivisation policy implemented from 1955, and the cultural revolution of the late 1960's.

The land of China is one of the most diverse on Earth. The majority of the people live in the east where the economy is dictated by the great drainage basins of the Huang He and the Chang Jiang (Yangtze). Here, intensive irrigated agriculture produces one third of the world's rice as well as wheat, maize, sugar, soya beans and oil seeds. Pigs are reared and fish caught throughout China. The country is basically self-sufficient in cereals, livestock and fish.

Western and northern China are far less densely populated areas as cultivation is restricted to oases and sheltered valleys. In the south-west, the Tibetan plateau averages 4,900 m (16,000 ft) and supports scattered sheep herding. To the north are Sinkiang and the desert basins of Tarim and Dzungaria, and bordering Mongolia the vast dry Gobi desert. In the far north only in Manchuria does the rainfall allow extensive arable cultivation, mainly wheat, barley and maize.

The natural mineral resources of China are immense, varied and under-exploited. The Yunnan Plateau of the south-east is rich in tin, copper, and zinc; Manchuria possesses coal and iron ore; and oil is extracted from beneath the Yellow Sea. The main industrial centres are situated close to the natural resources and concentrate on the production of iron, steel, cement, light engineering and textile manufacturing. The economy is being built on this industrial base, with stable and adequate food production and increasing trade with the United States, Western Europe and Japan.

CHRISTMAS ISLAND
STATUS: External Territory of Australia
AREA: 135 sq km (52 sq miles)
POPULATION: 2,000

COCOS (KEELING) ISLANDS
STATUS: External Territory of Australia
AREA: 14 sq km (5 sq miles)
POPULATION: 616

COLOMBIA

STATUS: Republic
AREA: 1,138,915 sq km (439,620 sq miles)
POPULATION: 30,240,000
ANNUAL NATURAL INCREASE: 2.1%
DENSITY: 26.6 per sq km
CAPITAL: Bogotá
LANGUAGE: Spanish, Indian languages
RELIGION: 95% Roman Catholic. Small Protestant and Jewish minorities
CURRENCY: Colombian peso
ORGANISATIONS: UN, OAS

The landscape of Colombia falls into two distinct parts: the northern Andes and the

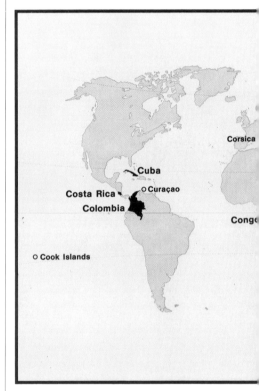

rain forests of the east.

Fertile river valleys in the Andean range produce tobacco, coffee, cotton, and rice.

Coffee has always been the major export crop, but manufacturing industry and mining of coal, iron ore, copper and precious stones are becoming more dominant in the economy. Immense illegal quantities of cocaine are exported.

COMOROS

STATUS: Federal Islamic Republic
AREA: 1,860 sq km (718 sq miles)
POPULATION: 422,500

ANNUAL NATURAL INCREASE: 3.1%
DENSITY: 227.2 per sq km
CAPITAL: Moroni
LANGUAGE: French, Arabic, Comoran
RELIGION: large Moslem majority. Christian
minority
CURRENCY: Comoros franc (CF)
ORGANISATIONS: UN, OAU

The Comoro Islands, comprising Moheli, Grand Comore, and Anjouan, are situated between Madagascar and the east African coast. In 1974, the island of Mayotte voted in referenda to remain a French dependency. A cool, dry season alternates with hot, humid monsoon weather between November and April, and annual rainfall ranges from 100–114cm(40–45in). Mangoes, coconuts and bananas are grown around the coastal lowlands. The island's economy is based on the export of coffee, vanilla, copra, sisal, cacao and cloves. Timber and timber products are important to local development. There is no manufacturing.

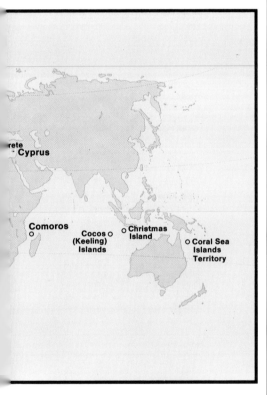

CONGO

STATUS: People's Republic
AREA: 342,000 sq km (132,010 sq miles)
POPULATION: 2,266,000
ANNUAL NATURAL INCREASE: 2.6%
DENSITY: 6.6 per sq km
CAPITAL: Brazzaville
LANGUAGE: French, Kongo, Teke, Sanga
RELIGION: 50% traditional beliefs, 30% Roman Catholic. Small Protestant and Moslem minority
CURRENCY: CFA franc
ORGANISATIONS: UN, OAU

The Congo, Africa's first Communist State still has strong economic ties with the west, especially France its former colonial ruler. Situated on the coast of West Africa it contains over two-thirds swamp and forest, with wooded savannah on the highlands of the Batéké plateau near the Gabon border. Its climate is hot and humid with average rainfall of 122–128cm(48–50in). Over 60% of the population are employed in subsistence farming, the main crops being plantains, maize and cassava, while coffee, groundnuts and cocoa are all exported. Timber and timber products accounts for 60% of all the Congo's exports. Its mineral resources are considerable including industrial diamonds, gold, lead, zinc and extensive coastal oilfields. Manufacturing industry is concentrated in the major towns and is primarily food processing and textiles.

COOK ISLANDS

STATUS: Self-governing Overseas Territory in free association with New Zealand
AREA: 233 sq km (90 sq miles)
POPULATION: 17,185
CAPITAL: Rarotonga

CORAL SEA ISLANDS TERRITORY

STATUS: External Territory of Australia
AREA: 22 sq km (8.5 sq miles)
POPULATION: No permanent population

CORSICA (CORSE)

STATUS: Island Region of France
AREA: 8,680 sq km (3,350 sq miles)
POPULATION: 248,700
CAPITAL: Ajaccio

COSTA RICA

STATUS: Republic
AREA: 50,900 sq km (19,650 sq miles)
POPULATION: 2,816,558
ANNUAL NATURAL INCREASE: 2.6%
DENSITY: 55.3 per sq km
CAPITAL: San José
LANGUAGE: Spanish
RELIGION: 95% Roman Catholic
CURRENCY: Costa Rican colón
ORGANISATIONS: UN, CACM, OAS

Costa Rica is a narrow country, situated between Nicaragua and Panama, with both a Pacific and a Caribbean coastline. The mountain chains that run the length of the country form the fertile uplands where coffee (one of the main crops and exports) and cattle flourish. Bananas are grown on the Pacific coast. Although gold, silver, iron ore and bauxite are mined, the principal industries are food processing and manufacture of textiles and chemicals, fertilizers and furniture.

CRETE (KRÍTI)

STATUS: Island Province of Greece
AREA: 8,330 sq km (3,215 sq miles)
POPULATION: 501,082
CAPITAL: Iráklion

CUBA

STATUS: Republic
AREA: 114,525 sq km (44,205 sq miles)
POPULATION: 10,487,000
ANNUAL NATURAL INCREASE: 1.1%
DENSITY: 91.6 per sq km
CAPITAL: Havana (Habana)
LANGUAGE: Spanish
RELIGION: Roman Catholic majority
CURRENCY: Cuban peso
ORGANISATIONS: UN, COMECON

Cuba, consisting of one large island and over fifteen hundred small ones, dominates the entrance to the Gulf of Mexico. It is a mixture of fertile plains, mountain ranges and gentle countryside with temperatures ranging from 22°–28°C(72°–82°F) and an average annual rainfall of 120cm(47in). Being the only Communist state in the Americas, most of Cuba's trade relations are with the USSR and Comecon countries. Sugar, tobacco and nickel are the main exports and the mining of manganese, chrome, copper and oil is expanding. Cuba has enough cattle and coffee for domestic use but many other food products are imported.

CURAÇAO

STATUS: Self-governing Island of Netherlands Antilles
AREA: 444 sq km (171 sq miles)
POPULATION: 153,736
CAPITAL: Willemstad

CYPRUS

STATUS: Republic
AREA: 9,250 sq km (3,570 sq miles)
POPULATION: 686,400
ANNUAL NATURAL INCREASE: 1.3%
DENSITY: 74.2 per sq km
CAPITAL: Nicosia
LANGUAGE: Greek, Turkish, English
RELIGION: Greek Orthodox majority. Moslem minority
CURRENCY: Cyprus pound (C£), Turkish Lira (TL)
ORGANISATIONS: Comm, UN, Council of Europe

Cyprus is a prosperous Mediterranean island. The summers are very hot (38°C, 100°F) and dry and the winters warm and wet. About two-thirds of the island is under cultivation and produces citrus fruit, potatoes, barley, wheat and olives. Sheep, goats and pigs are the principal livestock. The main exports are minerals (including copper and asbestos), fruit, wine and vegetables. Tourism is also an important source of foreign exchange, despite Turkish occupation of the north. Most industry consists of local manufacturing.

CZECHOSLOVAKIA

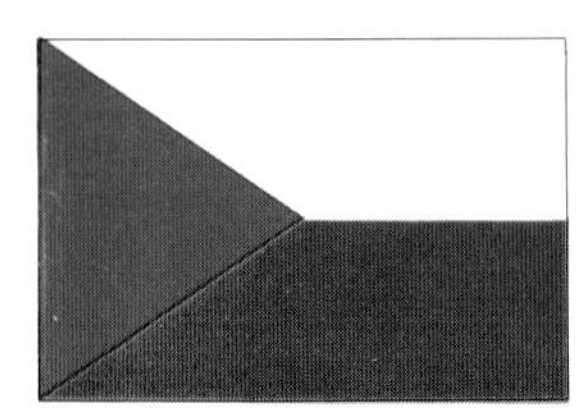

STATUS: Socialist Republic
AREA: 127,870 sq km (49,360 sq miles)
POPULATION: 15,620,000
ANNUAL NATURAL INCREASE: 0.3%
DENSITY: 122.2 per sq km
CAPITAL: Prague (Praha)
LANGUAGE: Czech, Slovak
RELIGION: 70% Roman Catholic,
15% Protestant
CURRENCY: koruna (Kcs)
ORGANISATIONS: UN, Warsaw Pact, COMECON

At the heart of central Europe, Czechoslovakia is fringed by forested uplands in the west and the Carpathians to the east. Winters are cold and wet, while summers are hot and humid with frequent thundery showers. Agriculture accounts for 65% of the land use and ranges from cereal crops, cattle and pig farming in the fertile lowlands, to the cultivation of oats, potatoes and rye and sheep farming in the less hospitable uplands. Czechoslovakia is rich in natural resources including coal, zinc, lead, mercury, iron ore, copper and tin. Timber and timber products are also important. These have been extensively exploited and Czechoslovakia's only industrial competitor in the Communist block is East Germany. Exports include machinery, industrial chemicals, coal, lignite, iron, steel and textiles.

DAHOMEY
(see **BENIN**)

DENMARK

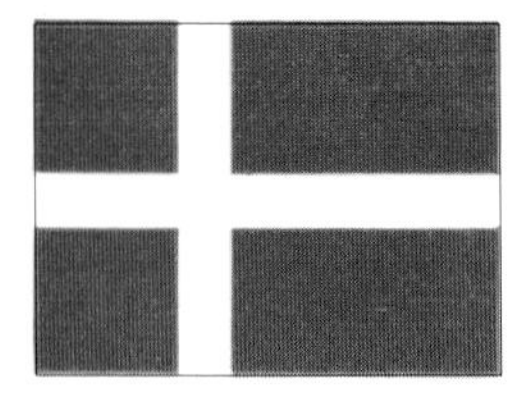

STATUS: Kingdom
AREA: 43,075 sq km (16,625 sq miles)
POPULATION: 5,129,254
ANNUAL NATURAL INCREASE: −0.1%
DENSITY: 119 per sq km
CAPITAL: Copenhagen (København)
LANGUAGE: Danish
RELIGION: 94% Lutheran. Small Protestant and Roman Catholic minority

CURRENCY: Danish krone
ORGANISATIONS: UN, Council of Europe, EEC, NATO, OECD

Denmark acts as a bridge between West Germany and Scandinavia. It consists of the Jutland Peninsula and over 400 islands. The low-lying landscape was scarred by retreating glaciers leaving distinctive 'moraines' (accumulations of earth and stones carried by glaciers). The climate is mild, especially in the North Sea area, with rainfall at all seasons. Exports are predominantly meat and dairy products – beef, butter, cheese, eggs, bacon and pork. Cereals, sugar beet and pototoes are also grown. An extensive fishing industry is centred on the shallow lagoons which have formed along the indented western coastline. Over 30% of the total workforce are involved in industry, and machinery and electrical products are amongst the most important.

DJIBOUTI

STATUS: Republic
AREA: 23,000 sq km (8,800 sq miles)
POPULATION: 484,000
ANNUAL NATURAL INCREASE: 2.5%
DENSITY: 21.0 per sq km
CAPITAL: Djibouti
LANGUAGE: French, Somali, Dankali, Arabic
RELIGION: mainly Moslem. Roman Catholic minority
CURRENCY: Djibouti franc
ORGANISATIONS: UN, Arab League, OAU

The former French colony of Djibouti, strategically situated at the mouth of the Red Sea, acts as a trade outlet for Ethiopia, as well as serving Red Sea shipping. Its climate is extremely hot and arid – average annual temperatures are 30°C(86°F) and the annual rainfall on the coast is as low as 38cm(15in), and there is consequently very little cultivation. Cattle, hides and skins are the main exports. The port of Djibouti is an important transit point for Red Sea trade.

DOMINICA

STATUS: Commonwealth Nation
AREA: 751 sq km (290 sq miles)
POPULATION: 80,000
ANNUAL NATURAL INCREASE: 1.7%
DENSITY: 106.5 per sq km
CAPITAL: Roseau
LANGUAGE: English, French patois
RELIGION: 80% Roman Catholic
CURRENCY: East Caribbean dollar (EC$)
ORGANISATIONS: Comm, UN, CARICOM, OAS

Dominica is located in the Windward Islands of the east Caribbean between Martinique and Guadeloupe. Tropical rain forest covers the island which obtains foreign revenue from sugar-cane, bananas, coconuts, soap, vegetables and citrus fruits. Main livestock are cattle, pigs and poultry. Tourism is the most rapidly expanding industry.

DOMINICAN REPUBLIC

STATUS: Republic
AREA: 48,440 sq km (18,700 sq miles)
POPULATION: 6,867,000

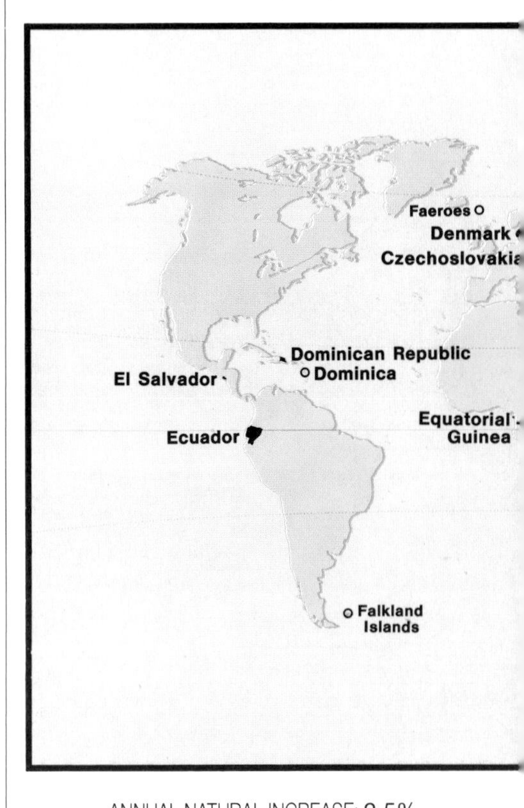

ANNUAL NATURAL INCREASE: 2.5%
DENSITY: 141.8 per sq km
CAPITAL: Santo Domingo
LANGUAGE: Spanish
RELIGION: 90% Roman Catholic. Small Protestant and Jewish minority
CURRENCY: Dominican Republic peso
ORGANISATIONS: UN, OAS

The Caribbean island of Hispaniola is divided between Haiti and the Dominican Republic. The landscape is dominated by a series of mountain ranges, thickly covered with rain forest, reaching up to 3000m(9840ft). To the south there is a coastal plain where the capital, Santo Domingo, lies. The annual rainfall exceeds 100cm(40in). Agriculture forms the backbone of the economy – sugar, coffee, cocoa and tobacco are the staple crops. Minerals include bauxite, nickel, gold and silver.

DUBAI
(see **UNITED ARAB EMIRATES**)

ECUADOR

STATUS: Republic
AREA: 461,475 sq km (178,130 sq miles)
POPULATION:10,200,000
ANNUAL NATURAL INCREASE: 2.8%
DENSITY: 22.1 per sq km
CAPITAL: Quito
LANGUAGE: Spanish, Quechua, other Indian languages
RELIGION: 90% Roman Catholic
CURRENCY: sucre
ORGANISATIONS: UN, OAS, OPEC

Ecuador falls into two distinctive geographical zones, the coastal lowlands which border the Pacific Ocean and, inland the Andean highlands. The highlands stretch about 400km(250

miles) north-south, and here limited quantities of maize, wheat and barley are cultivated. Ecuador's main agricultural exports–bananas, coffee and cocoa, are all grown on the fertile coastal lowlands. Large resources of crude oil have been found in the thickly forested lowlands on the eastern border. Ecuador is now South America's second largest oil producer after Venezuela.

EGYPT

STATUS: Arab Republic
AREA: 1,000,250 sq km (386,095 sq miles)
POPULATION: 51,900,000
ANNUAL NATURAL INCREASE: 2.6%
DENSITY: 51.9 per sq km
CAPITAL: Cairo (El Qâhira)
LANGUAGE: Arabic, Berber, Nubian, English, French
RELIGION: 80% Moslem (mainly Sunni), Coptic Christian minority
CURRENCY: Egyptian pound (£E)
ORGANISATIONS: UN, Arab League (suspended), OAU

The focal point of Egypt situated on the Mediterranean coast of north-east Africa is the fertile, irrigated Nile Valley, sandwiched between two deserts. Egypt is virtually dependent on the River Nile for water as average annual rainfall varies between only 20cm(8in) in the north and zero in the deserts. Cotton and Egyptian clover are the two most important crops with an increasing cultivation of cereals, fruits, rice, sugar-cane and vegetables. Buffaloes, cattle, sheep, goats and camels are the principal livestock. Tourism is an important source of revenue together with tolls from the Suez Canal. Major manufactures include cement, cotton goods, iron and steel, and processed foods. The main mineral deposits are phosphates, iron ore, salt, manganese and chrome.

EL SALVADOR

STATUS: Republic
AREA: 21,395 sq km (8,260 sq miles)
POPULATION: 5,110,000
ANNUAL NATURAL INCREASE: 2.4%
DENSITY: 238.8 per sq km
CAPITAL: San Salvador
LANGUAGE: Spanish
RELIGION: 80% Roman Catholic
CURRENCY: Salvadorean colón (C)
ORGANISATIONS: UN, CACM, OAS

Independent from Spain since 1821, El Salvador is a small, densely populated country on the Pacific coast of Central America. Temperatures range from 24 to 26°C(75–79°F) with an average, annual rainfall of 178cm(70in). Coffee and cotton are important exports and the country is the main producer of balsam. Industry has expanded considerably with the production of textiles, shoes, cosmetics, cement, processed foods, chemicals and furniture.

EQUATORIAL GUINEA

STATUS: Republic
AREA: 28,050 sq km (10,825 sq miles)
POPULATION: 420,000
ANNUAL NATURAL INCREASE: 2.3%
DENSITY:14.9 per sq km
CAPITAL: Malabo
LANGUAGE: Spanish, Fang, Bubi, other tribal languages
RELIGION: 96% Roman Catholic. 4% animist
CURRENCY: CFA franc
ORGANISATIONS: UN, OAU

Independent from Spain since 1968, Equatorial Guinea is made up of two separate provinces – mainland Mbini with hot, wet climate and dense rain forest but little economic development, and the volcanic island of Bioko. Agriculture is the principal source of revenue. Cocoa and coffee from the island plantations are the main exports with wood products, fish and processed foods manufactured near the coast in Mbini.

ETHIOPIA

STATUS: People's Democratic Republic
AREA: 1,023,050 sq km (394,895 sq miles)
POPULATION: 48,500,000
ANNUAL NATURAL INCREASE: 2.1%
DENSITY: 47.4 per sq km
CAPITAL: Adis Abeba (Addis Ababa)
LANGUAGE: Amharic, English, Arabic
RELIGION: Ethiopian Orthodox, Moslem and animist
CURRENCY: Birr
ORGANISATIONS: UN, OAU

Situated off the Red Sea coast, the landscape of Ethiopia consists of heavily dissected plateaux and plains of arid desert. Rainfall in these latter areas is minimal and unreliable. Drought and starvation are an ever-present problem. Farming, in the high rural areas, accounts for 90% of export revenue with coffee as the principal crop and main export together with fruit and vegetables, oil-seeds, hides and skins. Gold and salt are mined on a small scale. The most important industries are cotton textiles, cement, canned foods, construction materials and leather goods. These are concentrated around the capital, and Asmara in the north. Difficulty of communication has hindered development. In recent years the economy has been devastated by droughts and civil wars.

FAEROES (FØROYAR)
STATUS: Self-governing Island Territory of Denmark
AREA: 1,399 sq km (540 sq miles)
POPULATION: 47,000
CAPITAL: Tórshavn

FALKLAND ISLANDS (MALVINAS)
STATUS: UK Crown Colony
AREA: 12,175 sq km (4,700 sq miles)
POPULATION: 1,916
CAPITAL: Port Stanley

FIJI

STATUS: Republic
AREA: 18,330 sq km (7,075 sq miles)
POPULATION: 715,375
ANNUAL NATURAL INCREASE: 2.4%
DENSITY: 39 per sq km
CAPITAL: Suva
LANGUAGE: Fijian, English, Hindi
RELIGION: 51% Methodist Christian,
40% Hindu, 8% Moslem
CURRENCY: Fiji dollar ($F)
ORGANISATIONS: UN, Col. Plan

A country of some 320 tropical islands, of which over 100 are inhabited, in the south central Pacific Ocean. Fiji's economy is geared to production of sugar-cane, coconut oil, bananas and rice. Main industries are sugar processing, gold-mining, copra processing and fish canning. Important livestock are cattle, goats, pigs and poultry. Tourism is a major developing industry.

FINLAND

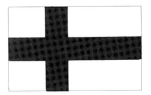

STATUS: Republic
AREA: 337,030 sq km (130,095 sq miles)
POPULATION: 4,955,000
ANNUAL NATURAL INCREASE: 0.4%
DENSITY: 14.7 per sq km
CAPITAL: Helsinki
LANGUAGE: Finnish, Swedish
RELIGION: 90% Evangelical Lutheran. Eastern
Orthodox minority
CURRENCY: markka (Finnmark)
ORGANISATIONS: UN, EFTA, OECD

Finland is a flat land of lakes and forests stretching from 60° to 70°N. The soils are thin and poor on the ice-scarred granite plateau, but ⅘ths of the country supports coniferous forest. Timber and timber products such as paper and dairy goods make up most of Finnish exports. Because of the harsh northern climate most of the population live in towns in the far south. Manufacturing industry has been developing rapidly in recent years.

FRANCE

STATUS: Republic
AREA: 543,965 sq km (209,970 sq miles)
POPULATION: 55,854,000

ANNUAL NATURAL INCREASE: 0.4%
DENSITY: 102.7 per sq km
CAPITAL: Paris
LANGUAGE: French
RELIGION: 90% Roman Catholic. Protestant,
Moslem and Jewish minorities
CURRENCY: French franc
ORGANISATIONS: UN, Council of Eur, EEC,
OECD, WEU

France encompasses a great variety of landscapes, a series of high plateaux, mountain ranges and lowland basins. The Pyrenees form the border with Spain in the south-west, and the Jura mountains form a border with Switzerland. The highest mountain range is the Alps, south of the Jura.

The highest plateau is the Massif Central which rises to 1886m(6188ft). The Vosges plateau borders the plain of Alsace, and the third major plateau, Armorica, occupies the Brittany peninsula.

The French climate is moderated by proximity to the Atlantic, and is generally mild. The south has a mediterranean climate with hot dry summers, the rest of the country has rain all year round. Much of the French countryside is agricultural. France is self-sufficient in cereals, dairy products, meat, fruit and vegetables, and a leading exporter of wheat, barley and sugarbeet. Wine is also a major export. France has reserves of coal, oil and natural gas, and is one of the world's leading producers of iron ore. It has large steel-making and chemical refining industries. Its vehicle, aeronautical and armaments industries are among the worlds most important. Leading light industries are fashion, perfumes and luxury goods. Most of its heavy industry is concentrated in the major industrial zone of the north-east. Tourism is a major source of revenue.

FRANZ JOSEF LAND

STATUS: Islands of USSR
AREA: 16,575 sq km (6,400 sq miles)
POPULATION: No reliable figure available

FRENCH GUIANA

STATUS: Overseas Department of France
AREA: 91,000 sq km (35,125 sq miles)
POPULATION: 90,500
CAPITAL: Cayenne

FRENCH POLYNESIA

STATUS: Overseas Territory of France
AREA: 3,940 sq km (1,520 sq miles)
POPULATION: 191,400
CAPITAL: Papeete

FRENCH SOUTHERN AND ANTARCTIC TERRITORIES

STATUS: Overseas Territory of France
AREA: 439,580 sq km (169,680 sq miles)
POPULATION: 180

FUJAIRAH

(see **UNITED ARAB EMIRATES**)

GABON

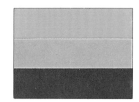

STATUS: Republic
AREA: 267,665 sq km (103,320 sq miles)
POPULATION: 1,226,000
ANNUAL NATURAL INCREASE: 1.6%
DENSITY: 4.6 per sq km
CAPITAL: Libreville
LANGUAGE: French, Bantu dialects, Fang
RELIGION: 60% Roman Catholic
CURRENCY: CFA franc
ORGANISATIONS: UN, OAU, OPEC

Gabon, which lies on the equator, consists of the Ogooúe river basin covered with tropical rain forest. It is hot and wet all year with average

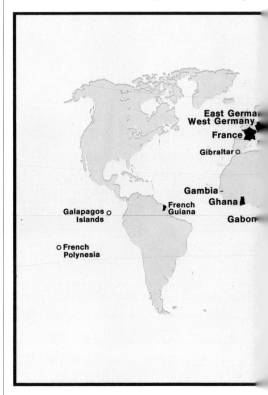

annual temperatures of 25°C(77°F). It is one of the most prosperous states in Africa with valuable timber and mineral resources.

GALAPAGOS ISLANDS

STATUS: Territory of Ecuador
AREA: 7,845 sq km (3,030 sq miles)
POPULATION: 7,954

GAMBIA, THE

STATUS: Republic
AREA: 10,690 sq km (4,125 sq miles)
POPULATION: 788,163

ANNUAL NATURAL INCREASE: 2.0%
DENSITY: 73.7 per sq km
CAPITAL: Banjul
LANGUAGE: English, Madinka, Fula, Wolof
RELIGION: 85% Moslem. Christian and animist minorities
CURRENCY: dalasi
ORGANISATIONS: Comm, UN, ECOWAS, OAU

The Gambia is the smallest country in Africa and, apart from its Atlantic coastline, is entirely surrounded by Senegal. It is 470km(292 miles) long, averages 24km(15 miles) wide and is divided by the Gambia river. The climate has two distinctive seasons. November to May is dry but July to October sees monsoon rainfall up to 130cm(51in). The temperatures average about 23°–27°C(73°–81°F) throughout the year. Groundnuts and subsidiary products are the mainstay of the economy but tourism is developing rapidly. The production of cotton, livestock, fish and rice is increasing to change the present economic reliance on a single crop – groundnuts.

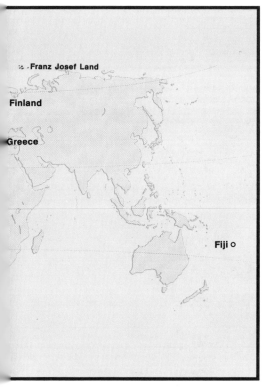

GERMANY, EAST

STATUS: Democratic Republic
AREA: 108,175 sq km (41,755 sq miles)
POPULATION: 16,666,000
ANNUAL NATURAL INCREASE: 0%
DENSITY: 154.1 per sq km
CAPITAL: Berlin (East)
LANGUAGE: German
RELIGION: atheist. 50% Evangelical Protestant, 8% Roman Catholic
CURRENCY: Mark of the GDR (DDR-M)
ORGANISATIONS: UN, COMECON, Warsaw Pact

East Germany is a leading European industrial nation and one of the most developed of the east European socialist bloc. Most of the northern part is flat or rolling hills covered with dark soils. Further south the Central Highlands rise towards the Erzgebirge (500–1000m or 1640–3280ft). The climate is central European with cold, wet winters and warm summers. The country trades predominantly with other Comecon members but is not rich in minerals although potash, copper and uranium are mined successfully and East Germany is the world's largest producer of lignite. Within the eastern bloc East Germany is also the leading supplier and producer of chemicals, synthetic fibres and plastics. There is also a thriving engineering industry and the manufacture of consumer goods is expanding. Although it is a largely urban-industrial economy, agriculture employs 10% of the workforce producing mainly cereal crops, potatoes and sugar-beet. Cattle, pigs, sheep and poultry are the main livestock.

GERMANY, WEST

STATUS: Federal Republic
AREA: 248,665 sq km (95,985 sq miles)
POPULATION: 61,320,000
ANNUAL NATURAL INCREASE: −0.2%
DENSITY: 246.6 per sq km
CAPITAL: Bonn
LANGUAGE: German
RELIGION: 50% Protestant, 50% Roman Catholic
CURRENCY: Deutsche Mark (DM)
ORGANISATIONS: UN, EEC, NATO

West Germany consists of three main areas – the Northern plain, the Central Uplands (the largest area) and the Bavarian Alps. It has extremely fertile farmland and although less than 10% of the population work in agriculture over 50% of the land is farmed. West Germany produces huge amounts of dairy products, pork, bacon, beef and ham. The main crops are barley, oats, wheat, rye, sugar-beet and potatoes. The iron, steel and chemical industries of the Ruhr are at the heart of the economy. West Germany is one of the world's leading producers of vehicles, machine tools, electrical and electronic goods and consumer products. Exploitation of the vast resources of coal, iron ore and lignite continues to be a priority. They also help Germany produce its vast electricity supply. The chemical industry relies on the country's great reserves of potash. The textile manufacturing industry is also important.

GHANA

STATUS: Republic
AREA: 238,305 sq km (91,985 sq miles)
POPULATION: 13,812,000
ANNUAL NATURAL INCREASE: 3.4%
DENSITY: 57.9 per sq km
CAPITAL: Accra
LANGUAGE: English, tribal languages
RELIGION: 42% Christian
CURRENCY: new cedi (C)
ORGANISATIONS: Comm, UN, ECOWAS, OAU

Ghana, the West African state once known as the Gold Coast, gained independence from Britain in 1957. The landscape varies from tropical rain forest to dry scrubland, with the annual rainfall ranging from over 200cm(79in) to less than 100cm(40in). The temperature averages 27°C(81°F) all year. Cocoa is the principal crop and chief export but although most Ghanaians farm, there is also a thriving industrial base around Tema,where local bauxite is smelted into aluminium, the largest artificial harbour in Africa. Other exports include gold and diamonds and principal imports are fuel and manufactured goods.

GIBRALTAR

STATUS: UK Crown Colony
AREA: 6.5 sq km (2.5 sq miles)
POPULATION: 30,000

GILBERT ISLANDS
(see **KIRIBATI**)

GREAT BRITAIN
(see **UNITED KINGDOM**)

GREECE

STATUS: Hellenic Republic
AREA: 131,985 sq km (50,945 sq miles)
POPULATION: 9,990,000
ANNUAL NATURAL INCREASE: 0.44%
DENSITY: 75.7 per sq km
CAPITAL: Athens (Athína)
LANGUAGE: Greek
RELIGION: 97% Greek Orthodox
CURRENCY: drachma
ORGANISATIONS: UN, Council of Eur, EEC, NATO, OECD

Mainland Greece and the many islands are dominated by mountains and sea. The climate is predominantly Mediterranean with hot, dry summers and mild winters. Poor irrigation and drainage mean that much of the agriculture is localised but the main crop, olives, is exported and agricultural output generally is increasing. The surrounding seas are important, providing two-thirds of Greece's fish and supporting an active merchant fleet. Athens is the manufacturing base and at least one-quarter of the population live there. Greece is a very popular tourist destination which helps the craft industries in textiles, metals and ceramics and other local products.

GREENLAND

STATUS: Self-governing Island Territory of Denmark
AREA: 2,175,600 sq km (839,780 sq miles)
POPULATION: 53,406
CAPITAL: Godthåb (Nuuk)

GRENADA

STATUS: Commonwealth Nation
AREA: 345 sq km (133 sq miles)
POPULATION: 98,000
ANNUAL NATURAL INCREASE: 1.8%
DENSITY: 284.1 per sq km
CAPITAL: St George's
LANGUAGE: English, French patois
RELIGION: Roman Catholic majority
CURRENCY: E. Caribbean dollar (EC$)
ORGANISATIONS: Comm, UN, CARICOM, OAS

The Caribbean island of Grenada is the southernmost of the Windward islands. It is mountainous and thickly forested with a settled warm climate, (average temperature of 27°C or 81°F), which ensures that its tourist industry continues to expand. Bananas are the main export, although the island is also famous for its spices, especially nutmeg and cloves. Cocoa is also exported.

GUADELOUPE

STATUS: Overseas Department of France
AREA: 1,780 sq km (687 sq miles)
POPULATION: 336,300
CAPITAL: Basse-Terre

GUAM

STATUS: Unincorporated Territory of USA
AREA: 450 sq km (174 sq miles)
POPULATION: 130,400
CAPITAL: Agaña

GUATEMALA

STATUS: Republic
AREA: 108,890 sq km (42,030 sq miles)
POPULATION: 8,990,000
ANNUAL NATURAL INCREASE: 3.1%
DENSITY: 82.6 per sq km
CAPITAL: Guatemala
LANGUAGE: Spanish, Indian languages
RELIGION: 75% Roman Catholic, 25% Protestant
CURRENCY: quetzal (Q)
ORGANISATIONS: UN, CACM, OAS

The central American country of Guatemala has both a Pacific and a Caribbean coastline. The mountainous interior, with peaks reaching up to 4000m (13,120ft), covers two-thirds of the country; in addition there are coastal lowlands and a thickly forested mainland to the north known as the Petén. Agricultural products form the bulk of Guatemala's exports, notably coffee, sugar-cane and bananas. Mineral resources including nickel, antimony, lead, silver and, in the north, crude oil, are only just beginning to be exploited.

GUINEA

STATUS: Republic
AREA: 245,855 sq km (94,900 sq miles)
POPULATION: 6,533,000
ANNUAL NATURAL INCREASE: 2.3%
DENSITY: 26.6 per sq km
CAPITAL: Conakry
LANGUAGE: French, Susu, Manika (Official languages: French and 8 others)
RELIGION: mainly Moslem, some animist, 1% Roman Catholic
CURRENCY: Guinea franc
ORGANISATIONS: UN, ECOWAS, OAU

Guinea, a former French colony is situated on the West African coast. Its drowned coastline, lined with mangrove swamps contrasts strongly with its interior highlands containing the headwaters of the Gambia, Niger and Senegal rivers. Agriculture occupies 80% of the workforce, the main exports being coffee, bananas, pineapple and palm products. Guinea has some of the largest resources of bauxite (aluminium ore) in the world as well as gold and diamonds. Both bauxite and aluminium are exported.

GUINEA-BISSAU

STATUS: Republic
AREA: 36,125 sq km (13,945 sq miles)
POPULATION: 932,000
ANNUAL NATURAL INCREASE: 1.9%
DENSITY: 25.8 per sq km
CAPITAL: Bissau
LANGUAGE: Portuguese, Crioulo, Guinean dialects
RELIGION: Animist and Moslem majorities. Roman Catholic minority
CURRENCY: Guinea-Bissau peso
ORGANISATIONS: UN, ECOWAS, OAU

Guinea-Bissau, on the West African coast was once a centre for the Portuguese slave trade. The coast is swampy and lined with mangroves, and the interior consists of a low-lying plain densely covered with rain forest. The coast is hot and humid with annual rainfall of 200–300cm (79–118in) a year, although the interior is cooler and drier. 80% of the country's exports comprise groundnuts, groundnut oil, palm kernels and palm oil. Fish, fish products and coconuts also make an important contribution to trade.

GUYANA

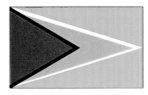

STATUS: Co-operative Republic
AREA: 214,970 sq km (82,980 sq miles)
POPULATION: 812,000
ANNUAL NATURAL INCREASE: 2.2%
DENSITY: 3.8 per sq km
CAPITAL: Georgetown
LANGUAGE: English, Hindu, Urdu, Amerindian dialects

RELIGION: mainly Christian, Moslem and Hindu
CURRENCY: Guyana dollar ($G)
ORGANISATIONS: Comm, UN, CARICOM

The ex-British colony of Guyana borders both Venezuela and Brazil. Its Atlantic coast, the most densely-populated area, is flat and marshy, while towards the interior the landscape gradually rises to the Guiana Highlands – a region densely covered in rain forest. Sugar, molasses and rum, once Guyana's main exports, are now being outstripped by bauxite.

HAITI

STATUS: Republic
AREA: 27,750 sq km (10,710 sq miles)
POPULATION: 5,523,000

ANNUAL NATURAL INCREASE: 2.3%
DENSITY: 199.1 per sq km
CAPITAL: Port-au-Prince
LANGUAGE: French, Creole
RELIGION: 80% Roman Catholic. Some Voodoo folk religion
CURRENCY: gourde
ORGANISATIONS: UN, OAS

Haiti occupies the western part of the island of Hispaniola in the Caribbean. It is the poorest country in Central America. The country is mountainous with three main ranges, the highest reaching 2680m(8793ft). Agriculture is restricted to the plains which divide the ranges. The climate is tropical. 85% of the workforce are farmers, and coffee is the main export. Light manufacturing industries are concentrated around the capital.

HAWAIIAN ISLANDS
(see UNITED STATES OF AMERICA)

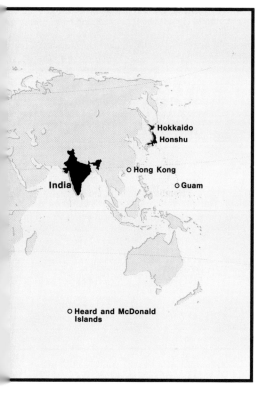

HEARD AND McDONALD ISLANDS

STATUS: External Territory of Australia
AREA: 412 sq km (159 sq miles)
POPULATION: No permanent population

HISPANIOLA

STATUS: Island of the West Indies comprising Haiti & Dominican Republic
AREA: 76,170 sq km (29,400 sq miles)
POPULATION: 12,154,000

HOKKAIDO

STATUS: Island of Japan
AREA: 78,460 sq km (30,285 sq miles)
POPULATION: 5,678,000

HONDURAS

STATUS: Republic
AREA: 112,085 sq km (43,265 sq miles)
POPULATION: 4,802,000
ANNUAL NATURAL INCREASE: 3.2%
DENSITY: 42.8 per sq km
CAPITAL: Tegucigalpa
LANGUAGE: Spanish, Indian dialects
RELIGION: large Roman Catholic majority
CURRENCY: lempira or peso
ORGANISATIONS: UN, CACM, OAS

The Central American republic of Honduras consists substantially of rugged mountains and high plateaux with, on the Caribbean coast, an area of hot and humid plains, densely covered with tropical vegetation. These low-lying plains are subject to high annual rainfall, an average of 250cm(98in), and it is in this region that bananas, accounting for half the nation's exports, are grown. Other crops include coffee, sugar, rice, maize, beans and tobacco. Exploitation of lead, iron, tin and oil may lead, however, to a change in the traditional agriculture-based economy. Most industries are concerned with processing local products.

HONG KONG
(INCLUDING KOWLOON & THE NEW TERRITORIES)

STATUS: UK Dependent Territory
AREA: 1,067 sq km (412 sq miles)
POPULATION: 5,680,000
CAPITAL: Victoria

HONSHU

STATUS: Main Island of Japan
AREA: 230,455 sq km (88,955 sq miles)
POPULATION: 97,283,000

HUNGARY

STATUS: Republic
AREA: 93,030 sq km (35,910 sq miles)
POPULATION: 10,584,000
ANNUAL NATURAL INCREASE: −0.2%
DENSITY: 113.8 per sq km
CAPITAL: Budapest
LANGUAGE: Hungarian
RELIGION: 60% Roman Catholic, 20% Hungarian Reformed Church, Lutheran and Orthodox minorities
CURRENCY: forint
ORGANISATIONS: UN, Warsaw Pact, COMECON

The undulating fertile plains of Hungary are bisected by the River Danube, and the country is surrounded by mountains – the northern highlands reach a height of 1000m(3280ft). In the centre of the country, Lake Balaton (600 sq km or 232 sq miles) is the largest lake in Europe. Winters in Hungary are severe, though in summer the enclosed plains can become very hot. Just over 50% of land is arable. Main crops are wheat and maize, and rice, sugar-beet and sunflowers are also grown. Bauxite is Hungary's only substantial mineral deposit. Engineering forms the basis of the economy and most of this industry is concentrated around the capital, Budapest, which is linked by road, rail and river to the rest of eastern Europe. Heavy industry specialises in the production of pig-iron, crude steel, cement and chemicals.

ICELAND

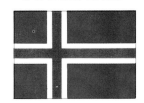

STATUS: Republic
AREA: 102,820 sq km (39,690 sq miles)
POPULATION: 247,357
ANNUAL NATURAL INCREASE: 1.0%
DENSITY: 2.4 per sq km
CAPITAL: Reykjavik
LANGUAGE: Icelandic
RELIGION: 93% Evangelical Lutheran
CURRENCY: Icelandic krona
ORGANISATIONS: UN, Council of Eur, EFTA, NATO, OECD

The northernmost island in Europe, Iceland is 850km(530 miles) away from Scotland, its nearest neighbour. The landscape is entirely volcanic – compacted volcanic ash has been eroded by the wind and there are substantial ice sheets and lava fields as well as many still active volcanoes, geysers and hot springs. The climate is cold, with average summer temperatures of 9°–10°C(48°–50°F), and vegetation is sparse. An average of 950,000 tonnes of fish are landed each year and 95% of Iceland's exports consist of fish and fish products.

INDIA

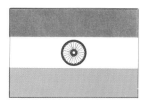

STATUS: Republic
AREA: 3,166,830 sq km (1,222,395 sq miles)
POPULATION: 824,000,000
ANNUAL NATURAL INCREASE: 2.3%
DENSITY: 260 per sq km
CAPITAL: New Delhi
LANGUAGE: Hindi, English, regional languages
RELIGION: 83% Hindu, 11% Moslem
CURRENCY: Indian rupee (R)
ORGANISATIONS: Comm, UN, Col. Plan

India has the world's second largest population. This vast country contains an extraordinary variety of landscapes, climates and resources.

The Himalaya in the north is the world's highest mountain range with many peaks reaching over 6000m(19,685ft). The Himalayan foothills are covered with lush vegetation, water is in abundant supply (rainfall in Assam reaches 1,070cm or 421in a year) and the climate is hot, making this region the centre for tea cultivation. To the south lies the vast expanse of the Indo-Gangetic plain, 2500km(1550 miles) east-west, divided by the Indus, Ganges and Brahmaputra rivers. This is one of the world's most fertile regions, although it is liable to flooding and failure of monsoon rainfall (June to September) can result in severe drought. In the pre-monsoon season the heat becomes intense – average temperatures in New Delhi reach 38°C(100°F). Rice, wheat, cotton, jute, tobacco and sugar are the main crops. To the south lies the Deccan plateau. India's natural resources are immense – timber, coal, iron ore and nickel, and oil has been discovered in the Indian Ocean. Nevertheless, 80% of the population live by subsistence farming. Main exports by value are precious stones, clothing, tea, iron ore, machinery and cotton.

INDONESIA

STATUS: Republic
AREA: 1,919,445 sq km (740,905 sq miles)
POPULATION: 174,950,000
ANNUAL NATURAL INCREASE: 2.1%
DENSITY: 91.2 per sq km
CAPITAL: Jakarta
LANGUAGE: Bahasa Indonesia
RELIGION: 78% Moslem, 11% Christian, 11% Hindu and Buddhist
CURRENCY: rupiah
ORGANISATIONS: UN, ASEAN, Col. Plan, OPEC

Indonesia is an arc of islands along the equator which includes Kalimantan (the central and southern part of Borneo), Sumatra, Irian Jaya (the western part of New Guinea), Sulawesi and Java. It is a Moslem nation and has the fifth largest population in the world. Most people live on Java, leaving parts of the other islands virtually uninhabited. The climate is tropical: hot, wet and subject to monsoons. Over three-quarters of the people live in villages and farm but the crops produced are hardly enough for the increasing population and the fishing industry needs developing. Timber and oil production are becoming very important as sources of foreign exchange and there are also rich mineral deposits, as yet not fully exploited.

IRAN

STATUS: Republic
AREA: 1,648,000 sq km (636,130 sq miles)
POPULATION: 53,920,000

ANNUAL NATURAL INCREASE: 2.9%
DENSITY: 32.7 per sq km
CAPITAL: Tehrān
LANGUAGE: Farsi, Kurdish, Arabic, Baluchi, Turkic
RELIGION: Shiite Moslem majority. Sunni Moslem and Armenian Christian minorities
CURRENCY: Iranian rial
ORGANISATIONS: UN, Col. Plan, OPEC

Iran is a large mountainous country situated between the Caspian Sea and the Persian Gulf. The climate is one of extremes with temperatures ranging from −20° to 55°C(−4° to 131°F) and rainfall varies from 200cm(79in) to almost zero. Agricultural conditions are poor except around the Caspian Sea and wheat is the main crop though fruit (especially dates) and nuts are grown and exported. The main livestock is sheep and goats. Iran is oil rich and the revenues have been used to improve communications and social conditions generally. War with neighbouring Iraq has restricted economic growth and particularly affected the Iranian oil industry in the Persian Gulf.

IRAQ

STATUS: Republic
AREA: 438,317 sq km (169,235 sq miles)
POPULATION: 17,064,000
ANNUAL NATURAL INCREASE: 3.3%
DENSITY: 38.9 per sq km
CAPITAL: Baghdad
LANGUAGE: Arabic Kurdish, Turkoman
RELIGION: 50% Shiite, 45% Sunni Moslem
CURRENCY: Iraqi dinar (ID)
ORGANISATIONS: UN, Arab League, OPEC

Iraq is mostly desert but because of the two great rivers, the Tigris and the Euphrates, there are pockets of fertile land. The two rivers join and become the Shatt al Arab which flows into the Persian Gulf. Iraq has a very short coastline making Basra, the principal port, very important. Oil is the major export and oil revenues enable agriculture to be improved and increased. Dates are the other main export. Light industry is situated around Baghdad, the capital, Basra and Kirkuk, the large oilfield. War with Iran has placed great strains on the economy with exports of oil, oil products and natural gas severely restricted.

IRELAND (EIRE)

STATUS: Republic
AREA: 68,895 sq km (26,595 sq miles)
POPULATION: 3,540,000
ANNUAL NATURAL INCREASE: 0.9%
DENSITY: 51.4 per sq km

CAPITAL: Dublin (Baile Atha Cliath)
LANGUAGE: Irish, English
RELIGION: 95% Roman Catholic, 5% Protestant
CURRENCY: punt or Irish pound (I£)
ORGANISATIONS: UN, Council of Eur, EEC, OECD

The Irish Republic forms 80% of the island of Ireland. It is a country where the cool, damp climate makes for rich pastureland, and livestock farming predominates. Meat and dairy produce is processed in the small market towns where there are also breweries and mills. Large-scale manufacturing is centred round Dublin, the capital and main port. Ireland also possesses reserves of oil and natural gas, peat and deposits of lead and zinc. Tourism is also important to the Irish economy.

IRIAN JAYA

STATUS: Province of Indonesia
AREA: 421,980 sq km (162,885 sq miles)
POPULATION: 1,268,600

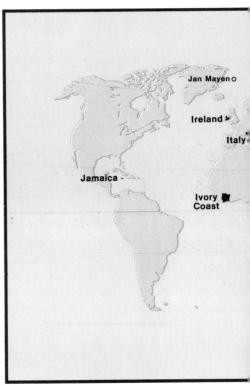

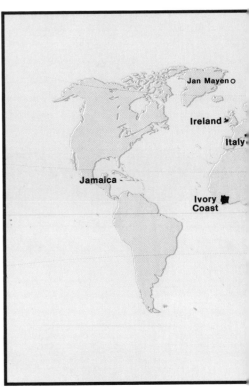

ISRAEL

STATUS: State
AREA: 20,770 sq km (8,015 sq miles)
POPULATION: 4,478,000
ANNUAL NATURAL INCREASE: 1.6%
DENSITY: 215.6 per sq km
CAPITAL: Jerusalem
LANGUAGE: Hebrew, Arabic
RELIGION: 85% Jewish, 13% Moslem
CURRENCY: new shekel
ORGANISATIONS: UN

This narrow country on the eastern Mediterranean littoral contains a varied landscape – a coastal plain bounded by foothills in the south and the Galilee Highlands in the north; a deep trough extending from the River Jordan to the Dead Sea, and the Negev, a desert region in the south extending to the Gulf of Aqaba. Economic development in Israel is the most advanced in the Middle East. Manufacturing, particularly diamond finishing and electronics, and mining are the most important industries although Israel also has a flourishing agricultural industry exporting fruit, flowers and vegetables to Western Europe.

ITALY

STATUS: Republic
AREA: 301,245 sq km (116,280 sq miles)

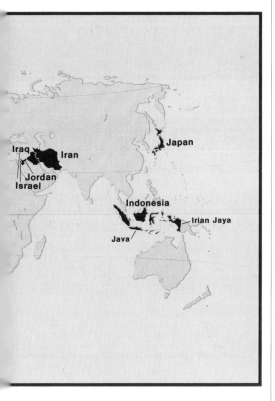

POPULATION: 57,440,000
ANNUAL NATURAL INCREASE: 0.1%
DENSITY: 190.7 per sq km
CAPITAL: Rome (Roma)
LANGUAGE: Italian, German
RELIGION: 90% Roman Catholic
CURRENCY: Italian lira
ORGANISATIONS: UN, Council of Eur, EEC, NATO, OECD, WEU

Over 75% of the landscape of Italy is hill or mountain, with the north dominated by the flat plain of the River Po rising to the high Alps. Climate varies from hot summers and mild winters in the south and lowland areas, to mild summers and cold winters in the Alps. Agriculture flourishes with cereals, vegetables, olives and vines the principal crops. Italy is the world's largest wine producer. Cheese is also an important commodity. In spite of the lack of mineral and power resources textiles, manufacturing industry: cars, machine tools, textile machinery and engineering, mainly in the north, are expanding rapidly and account for nearly 50%

of the work force. This is increasing the imbalance between the north and south where the average income is far less per head, and where investment is lacking.

IVORY COAST (CÔTE D'IVOIRE)

STATUS: Republic
AREA: 322,465 sq km (124,470 sq miles)
POPULATION: 11,630,000
ANNUAL NATURAL INCREASE: 3.0%
DENSITY: 36.1 per sq km
CAPITAL: Yamoussoukro
LANGUAGE: French, tribal languages
RELIGION: 65% traditional beliefs, 23% Moslem, 12% Roman Catholic
CURRENCY: CFA franc
ORGANISATIONS: UN, CEAO, ECOWAS, OAU

Independent from the French since 1960, the Ivory Coast is divided between the low plains of the south and the plateaux of the north. The climate is tropical with rainfall all year round in the south. Much of the population is engaged in agriculture producing rice, cassava, maize, sorghum, plantains and yams. Exports include coffee, timber and cocoa. The main industrial area and leading port is centred on Abidjan. Important industries are food-processing, textiles and timber products.

JAMAICA

STATUS: State
AREA: 11,425 sq km (4,410 sq miles)
POPULATION: 2,358,000
ANNUAL NATURAL INCREASE: 1.8%
DENSITY: 206.4 per sq km
CAPITAL: Kingston
LANGUAGE: English, local patois
RELIGION: Anglican Christian majority. Rastafarian minority
CURRENCY: Jamaican dollar (J$)
ORGANISATIONS: Comm, UN, CARICOM, OAS

Jamaica, part of the Greater Antilles chain of islands in the Caribbean is formed from the peaks of a submerged mountain range. The climate is tropical with an annual rainfall of over 500cm(197in) on the high ground. There is a plentiful supply of tropical fruits such as melons, bananas and guavas. Principal crops include sugar-cane, bananas and coffee. Jamaica is rich in bauxite which provides over half foreign-exchange earnings. Main manufacturing industries are food processing, textiles, cement and agricultural machinery.

JAN MAYEN
STATUS: Island Territory of Norway
AREA: 380 sq km (147 sq miles)
POPULATION: No permanent population

JAPAN

STATUS: Imperial monarchy
AREA: 369,700 sq km (142,705 sq miles)
POPULATION: 122,610,000
ANNUAL NATURAL INCREASE: 0.7%
DENSITY: 331.7 per sq km
CAPITAL: Tokyo
LANGUAGE: Japanese
RELIGION: Shintoist, Buddhist, Christian minority
CURRENCY: yen
ORGANISATIONS: UN, Col. Plan, OECD

Japan consists of the main islands of Hokkaido, Honshu, Shikoku and Kyushu which stretch over 1,600km(995 miles). The land is mountainous and heavily forested with small, fertile patches and a climate ranging from harsh to tropical. The archipelago is also subject to monsoons, earthquakes, typhoons and tidal waves. Very little of the available land is cultivable and although many of the farmers only work part-time Japan manages to produce enough rice for the growing population. Most food has to be imported but the Japanese also catch and eat a lot of fish. Japan is a leading economic power and most of the population are involved in industry. Because of the importance of trade, industry has grown up round the major ports especially Yokohama and Osaka and Tokyo, the capital. The principal exports are electronic, electrical and optical equipment. To produce these goods Japan relies heavily on imported fuel and raw materials and is developing the country's nuclear power resources to reduce this dependence. Production of coal, oil and natural gas is also being increased.

JAVA
STATUS: Island of Indonesia
AREA: 134,045 sq km (51,740 sq miles)
POPULATION: 99,852,812

JORDAN

STATUS: Kingdom
AREA: 90,650 sq km (35,000 sq miles)
POPULATION: 2,970,000
ANNUAL NATURAL INCREASE: 3.7%
DENSITY: 32.8 per sq km
CAPITAL: Amman

LANGUAGE: Arabic
RELIGION: 90% Sunni Moslem. Christian and Shiite Moslem minorities
CURRENCY: Jordanian dinar (JD)
ORGANISATIONS: UN, Arab League

Jordan is one of the few remaining kingdoms in the middle east. It is mostly desert, but has fertile pockets. Temperatures rise to 49°C(120°F) in the valleys but it is cooler and wetter in the east. Fruit and vegetables account for 20% of Jordan's exports and phosphate, the most valuable mineral, accounts for over 40% of export revenue. Amman is the manufacturing centre, processing bromide and potash from the Dead Sea. Other important industries are food processing and textiles.

KALIMANTAN

STATUS: Indonesian Province in Borneo
AREA: 550,205 sq km (212,380 sq miles)
POPULATION: 7,721,665

KAMPUCHEA

(see **CAMBODIA**)

KENYA

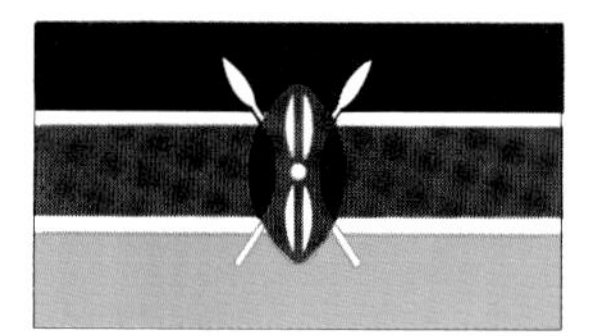

STATUS: Republic
AREA: 582,645 sq km (224,900 sq miles)
POPULATION: 22,800,000
ANNUAL NATURAL INCREASE: 4.2%
DENSITY: 39.1 per sq km
CAPITAL: Nairobi
LANGUAGE: Kiswahili, English, Kikuyu, Luo
RELIGION: traditional beliefs majority, 25% Christian, 6% Moslem
CURRENCY: Kenya shilling (KSh)
ORGANISATIONS: Comm, UN, OAU

Kenya lies on the equator but as most of the country is on a high plateau the temperatures range from 10° to 27°C (50° to 81°F). Rainfall varies from 76 to 250cm(30 to 98in) depending on altitude. Poor soil and a dry climate mean that little of the land is under cultivation but exports are nonetheless dominated by farm products – coffee, tea, sisal and meat. Nairobi and Mombasa are the manufacturing centres. The tourist industry is growing. Electricity is generated from both geothermal sources and hydro-electric power stations on the Tana river.

KERGUELEN ISLANDS

STATUS: Part of French Southern and Antarctic Territories
AREA: 7,215 sq km (2,785 sq miles)
POPULATION: 75

KHMER REPUBLIC

(see **CAMBODIA**)

KIRIBATI

STATUS: Republic
AREA: 717 sq km (277 sq miles)
POPULATION: 66,250
ANNUAL NATURAL INCREASE: 2.0%
DENSITY: 92.4 per sq km
CAPITAL: Bairiki (in Tarawa Atoll)
LANGUAGE: I-Kiribati, English
RELIGION: Christian majority
CURRENCY: Australian dollar ($A)
ORGANISATIONS: Comm

Kiribati consists of sixteen Gilbert Islands, eight Phoenix Islands, three Line Islands and Ocean Island. These four groups are spread over 5 million sq km(1,930,000 sq miles) in the central and west Pacific. The temperature is a constant 27° to 32°C (80° to 90°F). The islanders grow coconut, breadfruit, bananas and babai (a coarse vegetable). Copra is the only major export. Main imports are machinery and manufactured goods.

KOREA, NORTH

STATUS: Democratic People's Republic
AREA: 122,310 sq km (47,210 sq miles)
POPULATION: 21,890,000
ANNUAL NATURAL INCREASE: 2.3%
DENSITY: 178.9 per sq km
CAPITAL: Pyongyang
LANGUAGE: Korean
RELIGION: mainly Buddhist, Confucianist, Daoist and Chundo Kyo
CURRENCY: won

High, rugged mountains and deep valleys typify North Korea. Climate is extreme with severe winters and warm, sunny summers. Cultivation is limited to the river valley plains where rice, millet, maize and wheat are the principal crops. North Korea is rich in minerals including iron ore, coal and copper and industrial development has been expanding. Further potential exists in the exploitation of the plentiful resources of hydro-electricity. Main exports are metal ores and metal products.

KOREA, SOUTH

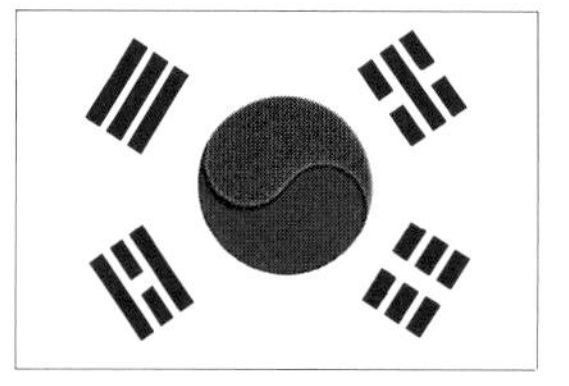

STATUS: Republic
AREA: 98,445 sq km (38,000 sq miles)
POPULATION: 41,970,000
ANNUAL NATURAL INCREASE: 1.6%

DENSITY: 426.3 per sq km
CAPITAL: Seoul (Sŏul)
LANGUAGE: Korean
RELIGION: 26% Mahayana Buddhism, 22% Christian. Confucianist minority
CURRENCY: won
ORGANISATIONS: Col. Plan

The terrain of South Korea is less rugged than the North and the climate is less extreme. Agriculture is still very primitive, with rice the principal crop. Tungsten, coal and iron ore are the main mineral deposits. The country is a major industrial nation with iron and steel, chemicals, machinery, shipbuilding, vehicles and electronics dominating. South Korea builds more ships than any other nation except Japan.

KURIL ISLANDS

STATUS: Islands of USSR
AREA: 15,540 sq km (6,000 sq miles)
POPULATION: No reliable figure available

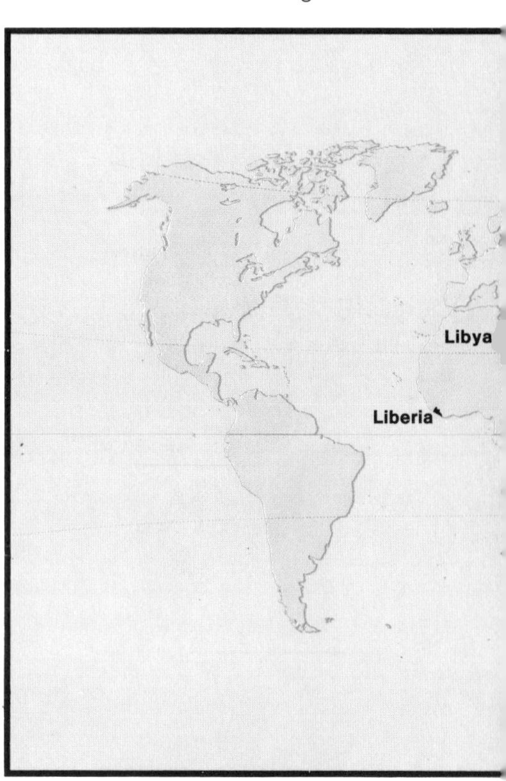

KUWAIT

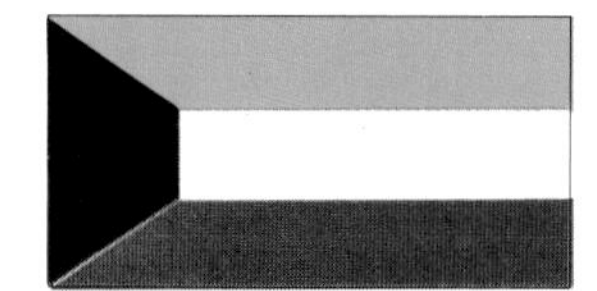

STATUS: State
AREA: 24,280 sq km (9,370 sq miles)
POPULATION: 1,958,000
ANNUAL NATURAL INCREASE: 3.2%
DENSITY: 80.6 per sq km
CAPITAL: Kuwait (Al Kuwayt)
LANGUAGE: Arabic, English
RELIGION: 95% Moslem, 5% Christian and Hindu
CURRENCY: Kuwaiti dinar (KD)
ORGANISATIONS: UN, Arab League, OPEC

Situated at the mouth of the Persian Gulf, Kuwait comprises low, undulating desert, with summer temperatures as high as 52°C(126°F). Annual rainfall fluctuates between 1 and

37cm(½–15in). Severe dust storms are a frequent occurrence in winter. Since the discovery of oil in 1946, Kuwait has been transformed into one of the world's wealthiest nations, exporting oil to Japan, France, the Netherlands and the UK. Apart from the sale of crude oil, Kuwait also refines and sells oil products. The natural gas fields have also been developed. Other industries include fishing (particularly shrimp), food processing, chemicals and building materials. However, it is the prolific public services which account for over 65% of the country's work force. In agriculture, the aim is to produce half the requirements of domestic vegetable consumption by expanding the irrigated area. Major crops are melons, dates and vegetables.

KYUSHU

STATUS: Island of Japan
AREA: 42,010 sq km (16,215 sq miles)
POPULATION: 13,295,000

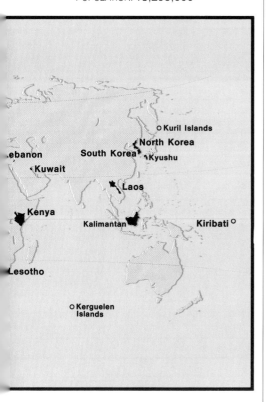

LAOS

STATUS: People's Democratic Republic
AREA: 236,725 sq km (91,375 sq miles)
POPULATION: 3,830,000
ANNUAL NATURAL INCREASE: 2.3%
DENSITY: 16.2 per sq km
CAPITAL: Vientiane (Viangchan)
LANGUAGE: Lao, French, tribal languages
RELIGION: Buddhist majority, Christian and animist minorities
CURRENCY: kip (K)
ORGANISATIONS: UN, Col. Plan

Laos is a poor, landlocked country in Indo-China. Temperatures range from 15°C (59°F) in

winter, to 32°C (90°F) before the rains, and 26°C (79°F) during the rainy season from May to October. Most of the sparse population are farmers growing small amounts of rice, maize, sweet potatoes and tobacco. The major exports are tin and teak, the latter floated down the Mekong river. Almost constant warfare since 1941 has hindered any possible industrial development. Main exports are timber products and coffee.

LEBANON

STATUS: Republic
AREA: 10,400 sq km (4,015 sq miles)
POPULATION: 2,762,000
ANNUAL NATURAL INCREASE: 2.1%
DENSITY: 265.6 per sq km
CAPITAL: Beirut (Beyrouth)
LANGUAGE: Arabic, French, English
RELIGION: 58% Shiite and Sunni Moslem, 42% Roman Catholic and Maronite Christian
CURRENCY: Lebanese pound (£L)
ORGANISATIONS: UN, Arab League

Physically, Lebanon can be divided into four main regions: a narrow coastal plain; a narrow, fertile, interior plateau; the west Lebanon and Anti-Lebanon mountains. The climate is of Mediterranean type with an annual rainfall ranging between 92cm (36in) on the coast and 230cm (91in) in the mountains. Trade and tourism have been severely affected by civil war since 1975. Agriculture accounts for nearly half the employed people. Cement, fertilisers, jewellery, sugar and tobacco products are all manufactured on a small scale.

LEEWARD ISLANDS
(see ANGUILLA, ANTIGUA, GUADELOUPE, MONTSERRAT & ST KITTS-NEVIS)

LESOTHO

STATUS: Kingdom
AREA: 30,345 sq km (11,715 sq miles)
POPULATION: 1,670,000
ANNUAL NATURAL INCREASE: 2.5%
DENSITY: 55.0 per sq km
CAPITAL: Maseru
LANGUAGE: Sesotho, English
RELIGION: 80% Christian
CURRENCY: loti
ORGANISATIONS: Comm, UN, OAU

Lesotho, formerly Basutoland, is completely encircled by South Africa. This small country is rugged and mountainous, and southern Africa's highest mountain, Thabana Ntlenyana

(3482m or 11,424ft) is to be found in the east Drakensberg. Because of the terrain, agriculture is limited to the lowlands and foothills and sorghum, wheat, barley, maize, oats and legumes are the main crops. Cattle, sheep and goats graze on the highlands.

LIBERIA

STATUS: Republic
AREA: 111,370 sq km (42,990 sq miles)
POPULATION: 2,436,000
ANNUAL NATURAL INCREASE: 3.1%
DENSITY: 21.9 per sq km
CAPITAL: Monrovia
LANGUAGE: English, tribal languages
RELIGION: Christian majority, 5% Moslem
CURRENCY: Liberian dollar (L$)
ORGANISATIONS: UN, ECOWAS, OAU

The West African republic of Liberia is the only nation in Africa never to have been ruled by a foreign power. The hot and humid coastal plain with its savannah vegetation and mangrove swamps rises gently towards the Guinea Highlands, and the interior is densely covered by tropical rain forest. Rubber, formerly Liberia's main export has now been supplemented by iron, discovered in the Bomi Hills. Liberia has the world's largest merchant fleet of over 2,500 ships due to its flag of convenience tax regime.

LIBYA

STATUS: Socialist People's Jamahiriyah
AREA: 1,759,180 sq km (679,180 sq miles)
POPULATION: 4,083,000
ANNUAL NATURAL INCREASE: 3.3%
DENSITY: 2.3 per sq km
CAPITAL: Tripoli (Tarabulus)
LANGUAGE: Arabic, Italian, English
RELIGION: Sunni Moslem
CURRENCY: Libyan dinar (LD)
ORGANISATIONS: UN, Arab League, OAU, OPEC

Libya is situated on the lowlands of North Africa which rise southwards from the Mediterranean Sea. 95% of its territory is hot and dry desert or semi-desert with average rainfall of less than 13cm(5in). The coastal plains, however, have a moister Mediterranean climate with rainfall of 20–61cm(8–24in), and this is the most densely populated region. In these areas, a wide range of crops are cultivated including grapes, groundnuts, oranges, wheat and barley. Dates are grown in the desert oases. Only 30 years ago Libya was classed as one of the world's poorest nations but the exploitation of oil has transformed Libya's economy and now accounts for over 95% of its exports. Most imported goods come from Italy.

LIECHTENSTEIN

STATUS: Principality
AREA: 160 sq km (62 sq miles)
POPULATION: 28,000
ANNUAL NATURAL INCREASE: 1.1%
DENSITY: 175.1 per sq km
CAPITAL: Vaduz
LANGUAGE: Alemannish, German
RELIGION: 87% Roman Catholic
CURRENCY: Franken (Swiss franc)
ORGANISATIONS: Council of Eur

Situated in the central Alps between Switzerland and Austria, Liechtenstein is one of the smallest states in Europe. Its territory is divided into two zones – the flood plains of the Rhine to the north and Alpine mountain ranges to the south where cattle are reared. Liechtenstein's other main sources of revenue comprise light industry chiefly the manufacture of precision instruments, also textile production, food products and tourism.

LUXEMBOURG

STATUS: Grand Duchy
AREA: 2,585 sq km (998 sq miles)
POPULATION: 377,000
ANNUAL NATURAL INCREASE: 0%
DENSITY: 146 per sq km
CAPITAL: Luxembourg
LANGUAGE: Letzeburgish, French, German
RELIGION: 95% Roman Catholic
CURRENCY: Luxembourg franc, Belgian franc
ORGANISATIONS: UN, Council of Eur, EEC, NATO, OECD, WEU

The Grand Duchy of Luxembourg is strategically situated between France, Belgium and Germany. In the north the Oesling region is an extention of the Ardennes which are cut through by thickly forested river valleys. The Gutland to the south is an area of rolling lush pastureland. The climate is mild and temperate with rainfall ranging from 70–100cm(28–40in) a year. Just over half the land is arable, mainly cereals, dairy produce and potatoes, and wine is produced in the Moselle Valley. Iron ore is found in the south and is the basis of the thriving steel industry. Other major industries are textiles, chemicals, metal goods and pharmaceutical products.

MACAU (MACAO)

STATUS: Overseas Territory of Portugal
AREA: 16 sq km (6 sq miles)
POPULATION: 444,000
CAPITAL: Macau

MADAGASCAR

STATUS: Democratic Republic
AREA: 594,180 sq km (229,345 sq miles)
POPULATION: 10,919,000
ANNUAL NATURAL INCREASE: 2.8%
DENSITY: 18.4 per sq km
CAPITAL: Antananarivo
LANGUAGE: Malagasy, French, English
RELIGION: 57% animist, 40% Christian, 3% Moslem
CURRENCY: Malagasy franc (FMG)
ORGANISATIONS: UN, OAU

Madagascar is the world's fourth largest island, situated 400km(250 miles) east of the Mozambique coast. The terrain consists largely of a high plateau reaching 1500m(4920ft), with steppe and savannah vegetation. The mountains of the Tsaratanana Massif to the north reach up to 2876m(9435ft). Much of the hot humid east coast is covered by tropical rain forest – here rainfall reaches 150–200cm(59–79in) per annum. Although farming is the occupation of about 85% of the population, only 3% of the land is cultivated. Coffee and rice are the main products. Forestry is rapidly gaining in importance.

MADEIRA

STATUS: Self-governing Island Region of Portugal
AREA: 796 sq km (307 sq miles)
POPULATION: 269,500
CAPITAL: Funchal

MALAWI

STATUS: Republic
AREA: 94,080 sq km (36,315 sq miles)
POPULATION: 7,755,000
ANNUAL NATURAL INCREASE: 3.2%
DENSITY: 82.4 per sq km
CAPITAL: Lilongwe
LANGUAGE: Chichewa, English
RELIGION: traditional beliefs majority, 10% Roman Catholic, 10% Protestant
CURRENCY: kwacha (K)
ORGANISATIONS: Comm, UN, OAU

Malawi, formerly Nyasaland, is located at the southern end of the East African Rift Valley. The area around Lake Malawi is hot and humid with swampy vegetation, gradually supplemented by highlands to the west and southeast, where conditions are cooler. Temperatures vary between 15° and 32°C(58° to 89°F). Average annual rainfall is 73–100cm(29–39in). Malawi has an intensely rural economy –

96% of the population work on the land. Maize is the main subsistence crop, and tea, tobacco, sugar and groundnuts are the main exports. Malawi has deposits of both coal and bauxite, but they are, as yet, largely unexploited. Manufacturing industry concentrates on consumer goods (mainly clothing) and building and construction material. All energy is produced by hydro-electric power stations.

MALAYSIA

STATUS: Federation
AREA: 332,965 sq km (128,525 sq miles)
POPULATION: 16,968,000
ANNUAL NATURAL INCREASE: 2.4%
DENSITY: 50.9 per sq km

CAPITAL: Kuala Lumpur
LANGUAGE: Bahasa Malaysia, English
RELIGION: 53% Moslem, 25% Buddhist, Hindu, Christian and animist, minorities
CURRENCY: ringgit/Malaysian dollar
ORGANISATIONS: Comm, UN, ASEAN, Col. Plan

PENINSULAR MALAYSIA

STATUS: States
AREA: 131,585 sq km (50,790 sq miles)
POPULATION: 14,005,000

SABAH

STATUS: State
AREA: 76,115 sq km (29,380 sq miles)
POPULATION: 1,342,631
CAPITAL: Kota Kinabalu

SARAWAK

STATUS: State
AREA: 124,965 sq km (48,235 sq miles)
POPULATION: 1,550,000
CAPITAL: Kuching

The federation of Malaysia consists of two separate parts; West Malaysia is located on the Malay Peninsula, while East Malaysia consists of Sabah and Sarawak on the island of Borneo 700km(435 miles) across the South China Sea. Despite this distance, both areas share a similar landscape, which is mountainous and covered with lush tropical rain forest. The climate is tropical, hot and humid all the year round, with annual average rainfall of 250cm(98in). Malaysia is the world's main tin producer, and also produces over 40% of the world's rubber, and is also a leading source of palm oil, bauxite and gold.

Chief exports by value are manufactured goods, rubber, crude oil, palm oil, timber and timber products and tin. Most industries are concerned with production and processing of local products – palm oil, furniture, food processing and petroleum products. Most of the population are engaged in agriculture for local needs but crops grown for export include pineapples, tobacco, cocoa and spices. Livestock is imported to the home economy with pigs, cattle, goats, buffaloes and sheep predominant.

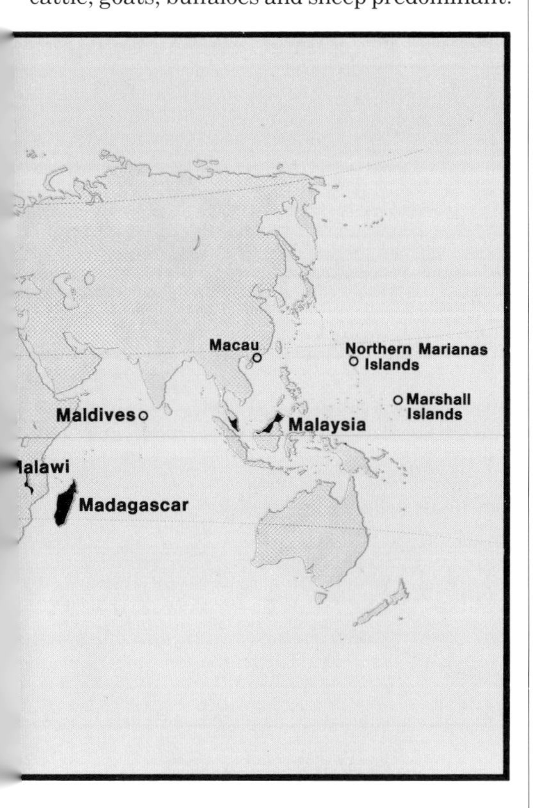

MALDIVES

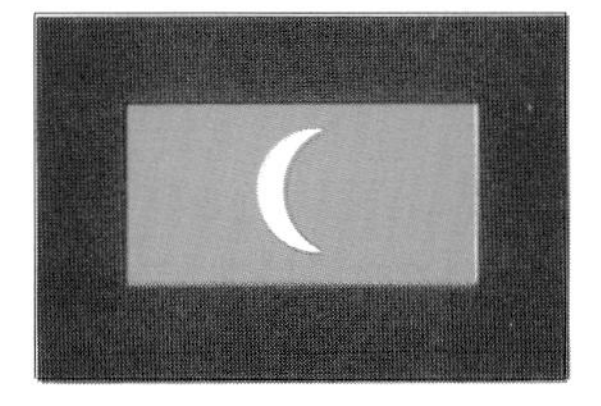

STATUS: Republic
AREA: 298 sq km (115 sq miles)
POPULATION: 200,000
ANNUAL NATURAL INCREASE: 3.1%
DENSITY: 671.1 per sq km
CAPITAL: Malé
LANGUAGE: Divehi
RELIGION: Sunni Moslem majority
CURRENCY: rufiyaa
ORGANISATIONS: Comm, UN, Col. Plan

The Maldive Islands are listed as one of the world's poorest nations. They consist of a series of coral atolls stretching 885km(550 miles)

across the Indian Ocean. Although there are 2000 islands, only about 215 are inhabited. The main island, Malé, is only 1½ miles long. Fishing is the main activity and fish and coconut fibre are both exported. Most staple foods have to be imported but coconuts, millet, cassava, yams and fruit are grown locally. Tourism is developing.

MALI

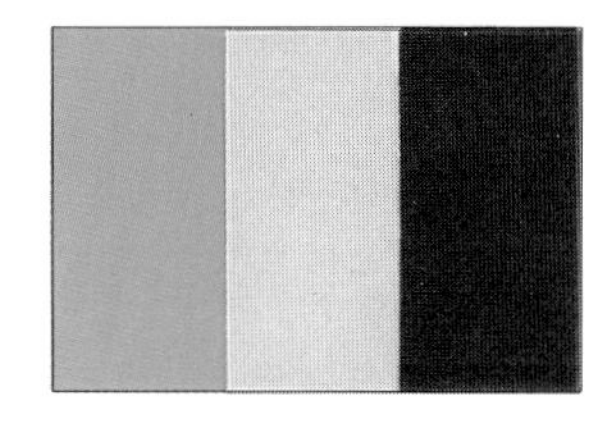

STATUS: Republic
AREA: 1,240,140 sq km (478,695 sq miles)
POPULATION: 7,784,400
ANNUAL NATURAL INCREASE: 2.8%
DENSITY: 6.3 per sq km
CAPITAL: Bamako
LANGUAGE: French, native languages
RELIGION: 65% Moslem, 30% traditional beliefs, 5% Christian
CURRENCY: CFA franc
ORGANISATIONS: UN, CEAO, ECOWAS, OAU

Mali is one of the world's most undeveloped countries. Over half the area is barren desert. South of Tombouctou the savannah covered plains support a wide variety of wildlife. Most of the population live in the Niger valley and grow cotton, oil seeds and groundnuts. Fishing is important. Mali has few mineral resources. Recent droughts have taken their toll of livestock and agriculture. Main exports are cotton and livestock. There is no industry.

MALTA

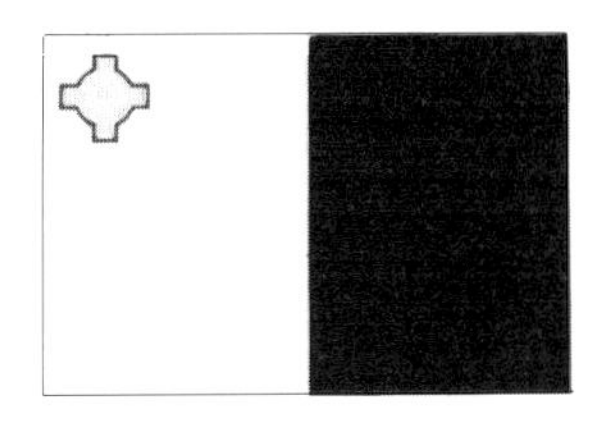

STATUS: Republic
AREA: 316 sq km (122 sq miles)
POPULATION: 345,636
ANNUAL NATURAL INCREASE: 0.8%
DENSITY: 1093.8 per sq km
CAPITAL: Valletta
LANGUAGE: Maltese, English, Italian
RELIGION: Great majority Roman Catholic
CURRENCY: Maltese lira (LM)
ORGANISATIONS: Comm, UN, Council of Eur

Malta lies about 96km(60 miles) south of Sicily, and consists of three islands; Malta, Gozo and Comino. Malta has a Mediterranean climate with mild winters, hot dry summers and an average rainfall of 51cm(20in). About 40% of the land is under cultivation with wheat, potatoes, tomatoes and vines the main crops. The large natural harbour at Valletta has made it a major transit port. Tourism is also an important source of revenue. Principal exports are machinery, beverages, tobacco, flowers, wine, leather goods and potatoes.

MAN, ISLE OF

STATUS: British Crown Dependency
AREA: 572 sq km (221 sq miles)
POPULATION: 67,000
CAPITAL: Douglas

MARIANA ISLANDS, NORTHERN

STATUS: Freely Associated State with USA
AREA: 471 sq km (182 sq miles)
POPULATION: 20,591

MARQUESAS ISLANDS
(see **FRENCH POLYNESIA**)

MARSHALL ISLANDS

STATUS: Freely Associated State with USA
AREA: 181 sq km (70 sq miles)
POPULATION: 40,609
CAPITAL: Majuro

MARTINIQUE

STATUS: Overseas Department of France
AREA: 1,079 sq km (417 sq miles)
POPULATION: 336,000
CAPITAL: Fort-de-France

MAURITANIA

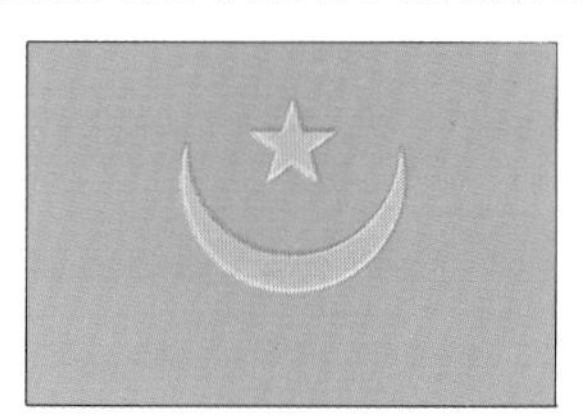

STATUS: Islamic Republic
AREA: 1,030,700 sq km (397,850 sq miles)
POPULATION: 1,894,000
ANNUAL NATURAL INCREASE: 2.9%
DENSITY: 1.8 per sq km
CAPITAL: Nouakchott
LANGUAGE: Arabic, French
RELIGION: Moslem
CURRENCY: ouguiya
ORGANISATIONS: UN, CEAO, ECOWAS, Arab League, OAU

Situated on the west coast of Africa, Mauritania consists of savannah, steppes and desert with high temperatures, low rainfall and frequent droughts. There is very little arable farming except in the Senegal river valley where millet and dates are grown. Most Mauritanians raise cattle, sheep, goats or camels. The country has only one railway which is used to transport the chief export, iron ore, from the mines to the coast at Nouadhibou. Severe drought during the last decade decimated the livestock population and forced many nomadic tribesmen into the towns. Coastal fishing contributes nearly 50% of foreign earnings. Exports are almost exclusively confined to iron ore, copper and fish products.

MAURITIUS

STATUS: State
AREA: 1,865 sq km (720 sq miles)
POPULATION: 1,056,867
ANNUAL NATURAL INCREASE: 1.5%
DENSITY: 566.7 per sq km
CAPITAL: Port Louis
LANGUAGE: English, French, Creole, Hindi, Bhojpuri
RELIGION: 51% Hindu, 31% Christian, 17% Moslem
CURRENCY: Mauritian rupee (R)
ORGANISATIONS: Comm, UN, OAU

Mauritius is a mountainous island in the Indian Ocean. It has a varied climate with temperatures ranging from 7° to 36°C(45° to 97°F) and annual rainfall of between 153 and 508cm(60 to 200in). Sugar-cane and its by-products are the mainstay of the economy and tourism is developing rapidly.

MAYOTTE

STATUS: French 'Territorial Collectivity', claimed by Comoros
AREA: 376 sq km (145 sq miles)
POPULATION: 77,300
CAPITAL: Dzaoudzi

MELILLA

STATUS: Spanish External Territory
AREA: 12.5 sq km (4.8 sq miles)
POPULATION: 57,167

MEXICO

STATUS: Federal Republic
AREA: 1,972,545 sq km (761,400 sq miles)
POPULATION: 82,734,454
ANNUAL NATURAL INCREASE: 2.6%
DENSITY: 41.9 per sq km
CAPITAL: Mexico City
LANGUAGE: Spanish
RELIGION: 96% Roman Catholic
CURRENCY: Mexican peso
ORGANISATIONS: UN, OAS

The landscape of Mexico consists of mountain ranges and dissected plateaux. As much of the land is above 500m(1640ft) temperature and rainfall are modified. The north is arid but the south is humid and tropical. Maize and beans are grown for local consumption. The population has outstripped food production and many Mexicans have moved to the cities. Minerals, especially silver, uranium and gold, are the main source of Mexico's wealth but the mines are mostly foreign-owned and Mexico aims to lessen this dependence on foreign investment as the country develops. Oil, natural gas and coal all have considerable reserves and are gradually becoming more important. Main exports are crude oil, and machinery.

MICRONESIA, FEDERATED STATES OF

STATUS: Freely Associated State with USA
AREA: 330 sq km (127 sq miles)
POPULATION: 86,094
CAPITAL: Kolonia

MOLUCCAS

STATUS: Island Group of Indonesia
AREA: 83,675 sq km (32,300 sq miles)
POPULATION: 1,411,006

MONACO

STATUS: Principality
AREA: 1.6 sq km (0.6 sq miles)
POPULATION: 27,000
ANNUAL NATURAL INCREASE: 1.4%
DENSITY: 16875 per sq km
CAPITAL: Monaco-ville
LANGUAGE: French, Monegasque, Italian, English
RELIGION: 90% Roman Catholic
CURRENCY: French franc

The tiny Principality is the world's smallest independent state after the Vatican City. It occupies a thin strip of the French Mediterranean coast near the Italian border and is backed by the Maritime Alps. It comprises the towns of Monaco, la Condamine, Fontvieille and Monte Carlo. Most revenue comes from tourism, casinos and light industry. Land has been reclaimed from the sea to extend the area available for commercial development.

MONGOLIA

STATUS: People's Republic
AREA: 1,565,000 sq km (604,090 sq miles)
POPULATION: 2,090,000
ANNUAL NATURAL INCREASE: 2.5%
DENSITY: 1.3 per sq km
CAPITAL: Ulaanbaatar (Ulan Bator)
LANGUAGE: Khalkha Mongolian
RELIGION: some Buddhist Lamaism
CURRENCY: togrog (tughrik)
ORGANISATIONS: UN, COMECON

Situated between China and the USSR, Mongolia has one of the lowest population densities in the world. Much of the country consists of a high undulating plateau (1500m or 4920ft) covered with grassland. To the north, mountain ranges reaching 4231m(13,881ft) bridge the border with the USSR, and to the south is the large expanse of the Gobi desert where rainfall averages only 10–13cm(4–5in) a year. The climate is very extreme with January temperatures falling to −34°C(−29°F). Mongolia is predominantly a farming economy, its main exports being cattle and horses, and wheat, barley, millet and oats are also grown. Its natural resources include some oil, coal, iron ore, gold, tin and copper.

MONTSERRAT

STATUS: UK Crown Colony
AREA: 106 sq km (41 sq miles)
POPULATION: 12,000
CAPITAL: Plymouth

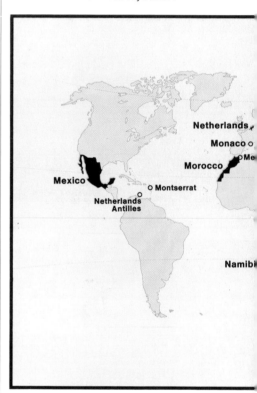

MOROCCO

STATUS: Kingdom
AREA: 710,895 sq km (274,414 sq miles)
POPULATION: 23,910,000
ANNUAL NATURAL INCREASE: 2.6%
DENSITY: 33.6 per sq km
CAPITAL: Rabat
LANGUAGE: Arabic, French, Spanish, Berber
RELIGION: Moslem majority, Christian and Jewish minorities
CURRENCY: Moroccan dirham (DH)
ORGANISATIONS: UN, Arab League

One third of Morocco, on the north-west coast of Africa, consists of the Atlas mountains reaching 4165m(13,665ft). Between the Atlas and the Atlantic coastal strip is an area of high plateau bordered on the south by the Sahara desert. The north has a Mediterranean climate and vegetation, and west-facing slopes of the Atlas have high annual rainfall and are thickly forested. Morocco has the world's largest phosphate deposits. The main crops are wheat and barley, and tourism is a major source of revenue.

MOZAMBIQUE

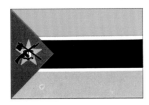

STATUS: People's Republic
AREA: 784,755 sq km (302,915 sq miles)

POPULATION: 14,907,000
ANNUAL NATURAL INCREASE: 2.5%
DENSITY: 18.9 per sq km
CAPITAL: Maputo
LANGUAGE: Portuguese, tribal languages
RELIGION: mainly traditional beliefs,
15% Christian, 15% Moslem
CURRENCY: metical
ORGANISATIONS: UN, OAU

The ex-Portuguese colony of Mozambique consists of a large coastal plain, rising towards the interior to the plateaux and mountain ranges which border Malawi, Zambia and Zimbabwe. The highlands in the north reach 2436m (7992ft). The climate is tropical on the coastal plain, although high altitudes make it cooler inland. Over 90% of the population are subsistence farmers cultivating coconuts, cashews, cotton, maize and rice. Mozambique also acts as an entrepôt, handling exports from South Africa, and landlocked Zambia and Malawi. Coal is the main mineral deposit and there are large reserves. Other underexploited minerals are iron ore, bauxite and gold.

NAMIBIA (S.W. AFRICA)

STATUS: UN Trust Territory
AREA: 824,295 sq km (318,180 sq miles)
POPULATION: 1,288,000
ANNUAL NATURAL INCREASE: 2.9%
DENSITY: 1.6 per sq km
CAPITAL: Windhoek
LANGUAGE: Afrikaans, German, English, regional languages
RELIGION: 90% Christian
CURRENCY: South African rand (R)

The south-west African country of Namibia is one of the driest in the world. The Namib desert on the coast has less than 5cm(2in) average rainfall a year, the Kalahari to the north-east 10–25cm(4–10in). The vegetation is sparse. Maize and sorghum are grown in the northern highlands and sheep are reared in the south. Namibia is, however, rich in mineral resources, with large deposits of diamonds, lead, tin and zinc, and the world's largest uranium mine.

NAURU

STATUS: Republic
AREA: 21 sq km (8 sq miles)
POPULATION: 8,000
ANNUAL NATURAL INCREASE: −0.3%
DENSITY: 381 per sq km
CAPITAL: Yaren
LANGUAGE: Nauruan, English
RELIGION: Nauruan Protestant majority
CURRENCY: Australian dollar ($A)
ORGANISATIONS: Comm (special member)

Nauru is one of the smallest republics in the world. Its great wealth is entirely derived from the phosphate deposits. The flat coastal lowlands encircled by coral reefs rise gently to the central plateau where the phosphate is mined. Most phosphate is exported to Australasia and Japan. Deposits may be exhausted by 1993.

NEPAL

STATUS: Kingdom
AREA: 141,415 sq km (54,585 sq miles)
POPULATION: 18,300,000
ANNUAL NATURAL INCREASE: 2.3%
DENSITY: 129.4 per sq km
CAPITAL: Kathmandu
LANGUAGE: Nepali, Maithir, Bhojpuri
RELIGION: 90% Hindu, 5% Buddhist, 3% Moslem
CURRENCY: Nepalese rupee (NR)
ORGANISATIONS: UN, Col. Plan

Nepal is a Himalayan kingdom sandwiched between China and India. The climate changes sharply with altitude from the southern Tarai plain to the northern Himalayas. Central Kathmandu varies between 2°C(35°F) and 30°C(86°F). Most rain falls between June and October and can reach 250cm(100in). Agriculture concentrates on rice, maize and cattle, buffaloes, sheep and goats. The small amount of industry processes local products.

NETHERLANDS

STATUS: Kingdom
AREA: 33,940 sq km (13,105 sq miles)
POPULATION: 14,714,948
ANNUAL NATURAL INCREASE: 0.4%
DENSITY: 433.6 per sq km
CAPITAL: Amsterdam (seat of Government: The Hague)
LANGUAGE: Dutch
RELIGION: 40% Roman Catholic, 30% Protestant. Jewish minority
CURRENCY: gulden (guilder) or florin
ORGANISATIONS: UN, Council of Eur, EEC, NATO, OECD, WEU

The Netherlands is situated at the western edge of the North European plain. The country is exceptionally low-lying, and about 25% of its territory has been reclaimed from the sea. The wide coastal belt consists of flat marshland, mud-flats, sand-dunes and dykes. Further inland, the flat alluvial plain is drained by the Rhine, Maas and Ijssel. A complex network of dykes and canals prevents the area from flooding. To the south and east the land rises. Flat and exposed to strong winds, the Netherlands has mild winters and cool summers.

The Dutch are leading world producers of dairy goods and also cultivate crops such as wheat, barley, oats and potatoes. Lacking mineral resources, much of the industry of the Netherlands is dependent on natural gas. Most manufacturing industry has developed around Rotterdam. Here are oil refineries, steel-works and chemical and food processing plants.

NETHERLANDS ANTILLES

STATUS: Self-governing part of Netherlands Realm
AREA: 800 sq km (308 sq miles)
POPULATION: 261,850
CAPITAL: Willemstad

NEW BRITAIN

STATUS: Island of Papua New Guinea
AREA: 36,500 sq km (14,090 sq miles)
POPULATION: 268,400

NEW CALEDONIA

STATUS: Overseas Territory of France
AREA: 19,105 sq km (7,375 sq miles)
POPULATION: 153,700
CAPITAL: Noumea

NEW GUINEA

STATUS: Island comprising Irian Jaya and part of Papua New Guinea
AREA: 808,510 sq km (312,085 sq miles)
POPULATION: 3,763,300

NEW HEBRIDES

(see **VANUATU**)

NEW ZEALAND

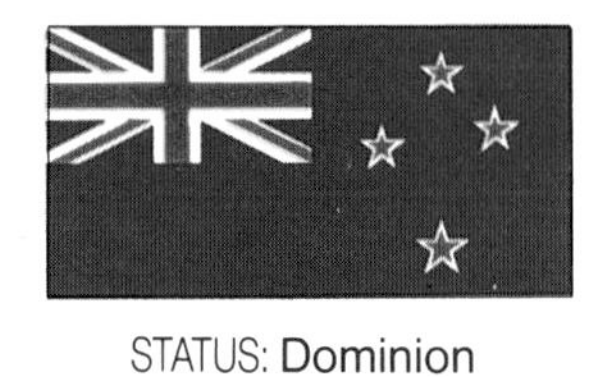

STATUS: Dominion
AREA: 265,150 sq km (102,350 sq miles)
POPULATION: 3,300,000
ANNUAL NATURAL INCREASE: 0.8%
DENSITY: 12.4 per sq km
CAPITAL: Wellington
LANGUAGE: English, Maori
RELIGION: 35% Anglican Christian, 22% Presbyterian, 16% Roman Catholic
CURRENCY: New Zealand dollar ($NZ)
ORGANISATIONS: Comm, UN, ANZUS, Col. Plan, OECD

The two main islands that make up New Zealand lie in the South Pacific Ocean. The Southern Alps run the length of South Island with a narrow coastal strip in the west and a broader plain to the east. Stewart Island lies beyond the Foreaux Strait to the south. North Island is less mountainous. Most of the country enjoys a temperate climate. Nearly 20% of the land is forested and 50% pasture. New Zealand is one of the world's leading exporters of beef, mutton and wool. Most exploited minerals are for industrial use – clay, iron sand, limestone, sand and coal. Manufacturing industries and tourism are of increasing importance. New trading links are developing with countries bordering the Pacific.

NICARAGUA

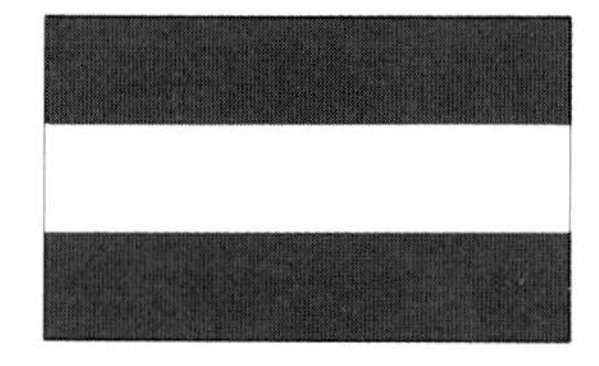

STATUS: Republic
AREA: 148,000 sq km (57,130 sq miles)
POPULATION: 3,620,000
ANNUAL NATURAL INCREASE: 3.4%
DENSITY: 24.5 per sq km
CAPITAL: Managua
LANGUAGE: Spanish
RELIGION: Roman Catholic
CURRENCY: cordoba (C$)
ORGANISATIONS: UN, CACM, OAS

Nicaragua is the largest of the Central American republics south of Mexico situated between the Caribbean and the Pacific. Active volcanic mountains parallel the western coast. The south is dominated by Lakes Managua and Nicaragua. Climate is tropical with rains May to October. Agriculture is the main occupation with cotton, coffee, sugar-cane and fruit the main exports. Gold, silver and copper are mined.

NIGER

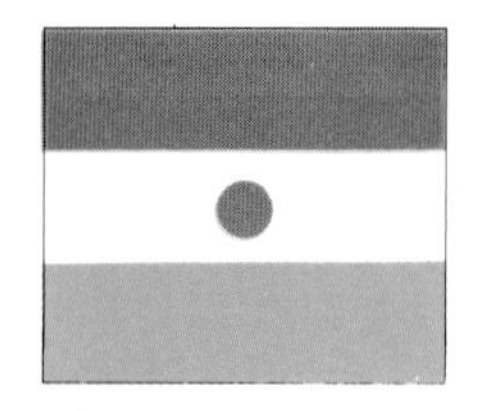

STATUS: Republic
AREA: 1,186,410 sq km (457,955 sq miles)
POPULATION: 7,249,596
ANNUAL NATURAL INCREASE: 2.8%
DENSITY: 6.1 per sq km
CAPITAL: Niamey
LANGUAGE: French. Hausa and other native languages
RELIGION: 85% Moslem, 15% traditional beliefs
CURRENCY: CFA franc
ORGANISATIONS: UN, CEAO, ECOWAS, OAU

Niger is a vast landlocked south Saharan republic with rainfall gradually decreasing from 56cm(22in) in the south to near zero in the north. Temperatures are above 35°C(95°F) for much of the year. Most of the population are farmers particularly cattle, sheep and goat herders. Recent droughts have affected both cereals and livestock. Large deposits of uranium ore and phosphates are being exploited. The economy depends largely on foreign aid.

NIGERIA

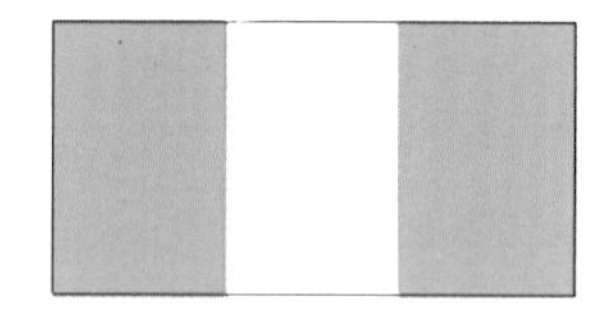

STATUS: Federal Republic
AREA: 923,850 sq km (356,605 sq miles)
POPULATION: 101,907,000
ANNUAL NATURAL INCREASE: 3.0%
DENSITY: 110.3 per sq km
CAPITAL: Lagos
LANGUAGE: English, Hausa, Yoruba, Ibo
RELIGION: Moslem majority, 30% Christian, animist minority
CURRENCY: naira (N)
ORGANISATIONS: Comm, UN, ECOWAS, OAU, OPEC

The most populous nation in Africa, Nigeria is bounded to the north by the Sahara and to the west, east and south-east by tropical rain forest. The southern half of the country is dominated by the Niger and its tributaries, the north by the interior plateaux. Temperature averages 32°C(90°F) with high humidity. From a basic agricultural economy, Nigeria is slowly being transformed by oil discoveries in the Niger delta which account for 95% of exports.

NIUE

STATUS: Self-governing Overseas Territory in free association with New Zealand
AREA: 259 sq km (100 sq miles)
POPULATION: 2,190
CAPITAL: Alofi

NORFOLK ISLAND

STATUS: External Territory of Australia
AREA: 36 sq km (14 sq miles)
POPULATION: 1,977
CAPITAL: Kingston

NORWAY

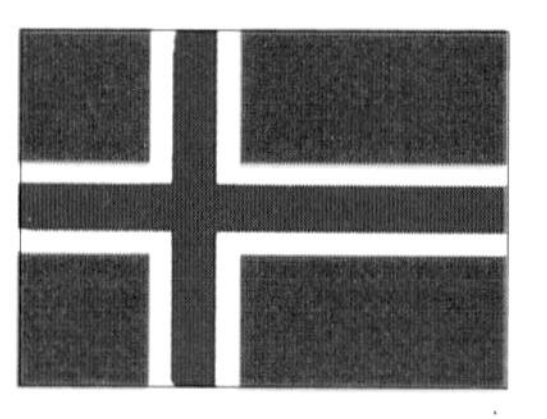

STATUS: Kingdom
AREA: 323,895 sq km (125,025 sq miles)
POPULATION: 4,198,300
ANNUAL NATURAL INCREASE: 0.2%
DENSITY: 12.9 per sq km
CAPITAL: Oslo

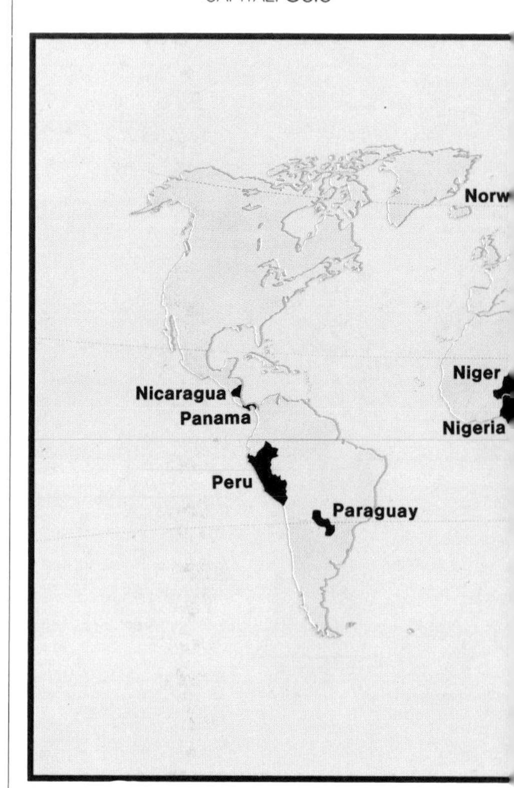

LANGUAGE: Norwegian (Bokmal and Nynorsk), Lappish
RELIGION: 92% Evangelical Lutheran Christian
CURRENCY: Norwegian krone
ORGANISATIONS: UN, Council of Eur, EFTA, NATO, OECD

Norway is a mountainous country stretching from 58° to 72°N. The climate on the indented western coast is modified by the Gulf Stream with high rainfall and relatively mild winters with temperatures averaging −3.9°C(25°F) in January and 17°C(63°F) in July. Rainfall may be as high as 196cm(79in). Most settlements are scattered along the fjords, the coast and around Oslo in the south. Norway is rich in natural resources. Coal, petroleum, natural gas predominate in exports but are supplemented by forestry products and fishing. By value, the most important exports are crude oil and natural gas, food manufacturing and machinery. The advanced production of hydro-electric power has helped develop industry, particularly chemicals, metal products and paper processing.

OMAN

STATUS: Sultanate
AREA: 271,950 sq km (104,970 sq miles)
POPULATION: 1,200,000
ANNUAL NATURAL INCREASE: 3.3%
DENSITY: 4.4 per sq km
CAPITAL: Muscat (Masqat)
LANGUAGE: Arabic, English
RELIGION: 75% Ibadi Moslem, 25% Sunni Moslem
CURRENCY: rial Omani (RO)
ORGANISATIONS: UN. Arab League

The Sultanate occupies the north-east coast of Arabia with a detached portion overlooking the

Straits of Hormuz. The desert landscape consists of a coastal plain and low hills rising to plateau in the interior. The two fertile areas are the Batimah in the north and Dhofar in the south. The main crop is dates. Oil provides over 95% of export revenue.

PAKISTAN

STATUS: Islamic Republic
AREA: 803,940 sq km (310,320 sq miles)
POPULATION: 105,409,000
ANNUAL NATURAL INCREASE: 2.8%
DENSITY: 131.1 per sq km

CAPITAL: Islamabad
LANGUAGE: Urdu, Punjabi, Sindhi, Pushtu
RELIGION: 90% Moslem
CURRENCY: Pakistani rupee (R)
ORGANISATIONS: Comm, UN, Col.Plan

The landscape and the economy of Pakistan are dominated by the river Indus and its tributaries which flow south flanked by the plateau of Baluchistan and the Sulaiman mountains to the west and the Thar desert to the east. The climate is dry and hot averaging 27°C(80°F). Rainfall reaches 90cm(36in) in the northern mountains. Over 50% of the population are engaged in agriculture which is confined to the irrigated areas near the great rivers. Main crops are wheat, cotton, maize, rice and sugarcane. There are many types of low-grade mineral deposits, such as coal and copper, but these are little developed. Main industries are food-processing and metals but these only contribute about 20% to the economy.

PALAU

STATUS: UN Trustee Territory
AREA: 497 sq km (192 sq miles)
POPULATION: 14,106
CAPITAL: Koror

PANAMA

STATUS: Republic
AREA: 78,515 sq km (30,305 sq miles)
POPULATION: 2,322,000
ANNUAL NATURAL INCREASE: 2.1%
DENSITY: 29.6 per sq km
CAPITAL: Panama
LANGUAGE: Spanish, English
RELIGION: large Roman Catholic majority
CURRENCY: balboa (B)
ORGANISATIONS: UN, OAS

Panama is situated at the narrowest part of Central America and has both Pacific and Caribbean coastlines. The climate is tropical with little variation throughout the year – average temperature 27°C(80°F). The rainy season is from April to December. Panama probably has the world's largest copper reserves but these are hardly developed. Most foreign revenue is earned from the Panama Canal, and export of petroleum products.

PAPUA NEW GUINEA

STATUS: Independent State
AREA: 462,840 sq km (178,655 sq miles)

POPULATION: 3,561,000
ANNUAL NATURAL INCREASE: 2.6%
DENSITY: 7.7 per sq km
CAPITAL: Port Moresby
LANGUAGE: Pidgin English, English, native languages
RELIGION: Pantheist, Christian minority
CURRENCY: kina (K)
ORGANISATIONS: Comm, UN, Col. Plan

Papua New Guinea (the eastern half of New Guinea and neighbouring islands) is a mountainous country. It has an equatorial climate with temperatures of 21° to 32°C(70° to 90°F) and annual rainfall of over 200cm(79in). Copper is the major mineral deposit with large reserves on Bougainville, one of the neighbouring islands. Sugar and beef-cattle are developing areas of production. Major exports are copra, timber, coffee, rubber and tea.

PARAGUAY

STATUS: Republic
AREA: 406,750 sq km (157,005 sq miles)
POPULATION: 4,010,000
ANNUAL NATURAL INCREASE: 2.8%
DENSITY: 9.9 per sq km
CAPITAL: Asunción
LANGUAGE: Spanish, Guarani
RELIGION: 90% Roman Catholic
CURRENCY: guarani (G)
ORGANISATIONS: UN, OAS

Paraguay is a landlocked country in South America with temperatures which average 15°C(59°F) all year. The country divides into lush, fertile plains and heavily forested plateau east of the River Paraguay and marshy scrubland (the Chaco) west of the river. Cassava, cotton, soyabeans and maize are the main crops but the rearing of livestock – cattle, horses, pigs and sheep – and food processing, dominate the export trade. The largest hydro-electric dam in the world is at Itaipú. This was constructed as a joint project with Brazil and will eventually have a capacity of 12.6 million kw.

PERU

STATUS: Republic
AREA: 1,285,215 sq km (496,095 sq miles)
POPULATION: 21,255,900
ANNUAL NATURAL INCREASE: 2.5%
DENSITY: 16.5 per sq km
CAPITAL: Lima
LANGUAGE: Spanish, Quechua
RELIGION: large Roman Catholic majority
CURRENCY: inti
ORGANISATIONS: UN, OAS

Peru divides into three geographical regions. The coastal region is very dry but fertile oases produce cotton, sugar, fruit and fodder crops. This is the most prosperous and heavily populated area which includes the industrial centres around Lima. In the ranges and plateaux of the Andes and the Amazon lowlands the soil is thin but the inhabitants depend on cultivation and grazing. Poor communications have hindered the development of Peru and there are great differences between rich and poor. Peru has rich mineral deposits of copper, lead, zinc and silver. There are oil reserves in the interior.

PHILIPPINES

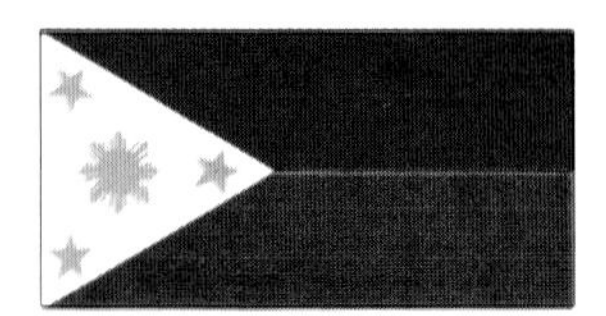

STATUS: Republic
AREA: 300,000 sq km (115,800 sq miles)
POPULATION: 58,721,307
ANNUAL NATURAL INCREASE: 2.5%
DENSITY: 195.7 per sq km
CAPITAL: Manila
LANGUAGE: Pilipino (Tagalog), English, Spanish, Cebuano
RELIGION: 90% Christian, 70% Moslem
CURRENCY: Philippine peso (P)
ORGANISATIONS: UN, ASEAN, Col. Plan

The Philippines consists of three main island groups, the Luzon and its neighbours, the Visayas and Mindanao, including the Sulus. The archipelago is subject to earthquakes and typhoons. It has a monsoon climate and over 40% of the country is covered by rain forest. Fishing is important but small farms dominate the economy, producing rice and copra for domestic consumption and other coconut and sugar products for export. Forestry is becoming an important industry but main exports are textiles, fruit and electronic products. Fishing is an important local industry.

PITCAIRN ISLAND

STATUS: UK Dependent Territory
AREA: 45 sq km (17.25 sq miles)
POPULATION: 59
CAPITAL: Adamstown

POLAND

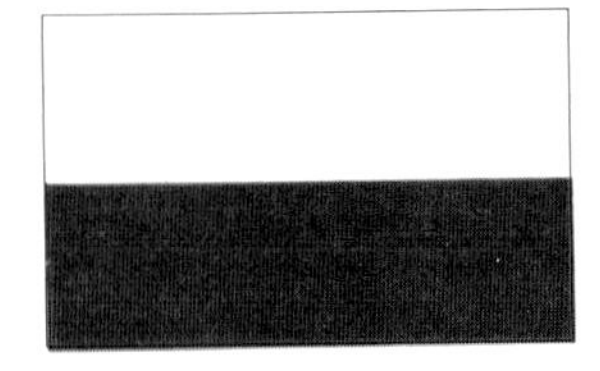

STATUS: Republic
AREA: 312,685 sq km (120,695 sq miles)
POPULATION: 37,811,000
ANNUAL NATURAL INCREASE: 0.9%
DENSITY: 120.9 per sq km
CAPITAL: Warsaw
LANGUAGE: Polish
RELIGION: 90% Roman Catholic
CURRENCY: zloty
ORGANISATIONS: UN, Warsaw Pact, COMECON

Poland occupies most of the southern coast of the Baltic Sea. Part of the North European Plain, the flat well-drained landscape rises gently towards the foothills of the Carpathians in the far south. The climate is continental with long severe winters. Average winter temperatures are below freezing point; rainfall averages between 52 and 73cm(21 and 29in). Both agriculture and natural resources play an important part in the economy and Poland is nearly self-sufficient in cereals sugar-beet and potatoes. There are large reserves of coal, copper, sulphur and natural gas. Major industries are ship-building in the north and production of metals and chemicals in the major mining centres in the south.

PORTUGAL

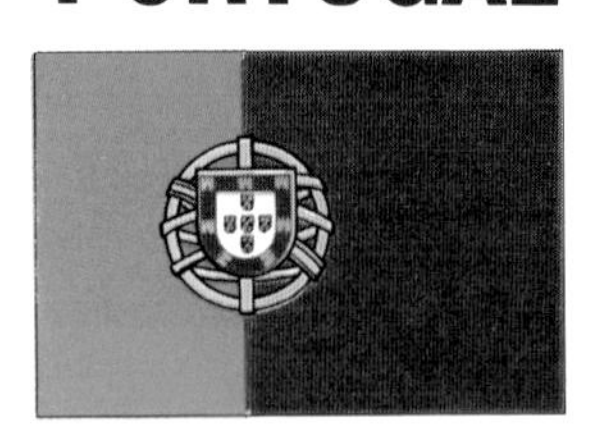

STATUS: Republic
AREA: 91,630 sq km (35,370 sq miles)
POPULATION: 10,410,000
ANNUAL NATURAL INCREASE: 0.5%
DENSITY: 113.6 per sq km
CAPITAL: Lisbon (Lisboa)
LANGUAGE: Portuguese
RELIGION: large Roman Catholic majority
CURRENCY: escudo
ORGANISATIONS: UN, Council of Eur, EEC, NATO, OECD

Portugal occupies the western, Atlantic coast of the Iberian Peninsula. The Mediterranean climate is modified by westerly winds and the Gulf Stream. This is reflected in the lusher mixed deciduous/coniferous forest in the northern mountains and the Mediterranean scrub in the far south. The rolling hills along the western coasts rise gently to the interior plateaux. A quarter of the population are farmers growing vines, olives, wheat, maize and beans, and rearing cattle and sheep. Minerals are coal, copper, kaolin and uranium. Over 9 million tourists visit the country each year.

PORTUGUESE GUINEA
(see GUINEA-BISSAU)

PUERTO RICO

STATUS: Self-governing commonwealth associated with USA
AREA: 8,960 sq km (3,460 sq miles)
POPULATION: 3,292,000
CAPITAL: San Juan

QATAR

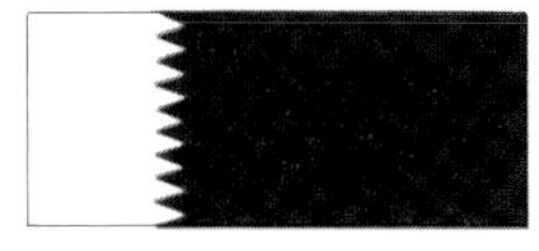

STATUS: State
AREA: 11,435 sq km (4,415 sq miles)
POPULATION: 371,863
ANNUAL NATURAL INCREASE: 2.9%
DENSITY: 32.5 per sq km
CAPITAL: Doha (Ad Dawhah)
LANGUAGE: Arabic, English
RELIGION: Moslem
CURRENCY: Qatar riyal (QR)
ORGANISATIONS: UN, Arab League, OPEC

The country occupies all of the Qatar peninsula which reaches north from the north-east Arabian coast into the Persian Gulf. The land is flat and dry desert; the climate is hot and humid. July temperatures average 37°C(98°F) and annual rainfall averages 62mm(2.5in). Irrigation schemes are expanding production of fruit and vegetables for home consumption. The main source of revenue is from the exploitation of oil and gas reserves. The N.W. Dome oilfield contains 15% of known world gas reserves.

RAS AL KHAIMAH
(see UNITED ARAB EMIRATES)

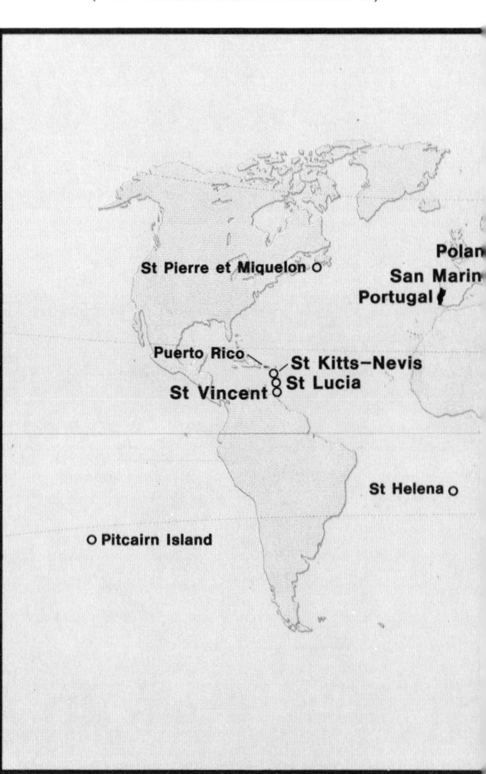

RÉUNION

STATUS: Overseas Department of France
AREA: 2,510 sq km (969 sq miles)
POPULATION: 574,800
CAPITAL: Saint-Denis

ROMANIA

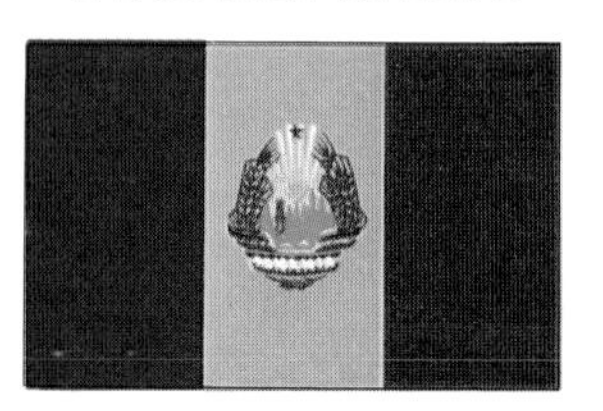

STATUS: Republic
AREA: 237,500 sq km (91,675 sq miles)
POPULATION: 23,050,000
ANNUAL NATURAL INCREASE: 0.4%
DENSITY: 97.1 per sq km
CAPITAL: Bucharest (Bucureşti)

LANGUAGE: Romanian, Magyar
RELIGION: 85% Romanian Orthodox
CURRENCY: leu
ORGANISATIONS: UN, Warsaw Pact, COMECON

The landscape of Romania is dominated by the great curve of the Carpathian mountains. Lowlands to the west, east and south contain rich agricultural land, especially north of Bucharest either side of the Danube. The climate is continental with variable rainfall, hot summers and cold winters. The economy, once mainly agricultural, is now based on mineral resources and the policy of industrialisation. Coal, oil and natural gas provide power; iron ore, manganese, lead, copper and uranium are mined.

ROSS DEPENDENCY

STATUS: Antarctic Territory Overseas of New Zealand
AREA: 425,000 sq km (164,050 sq miles)
POPULATION: No permanent population

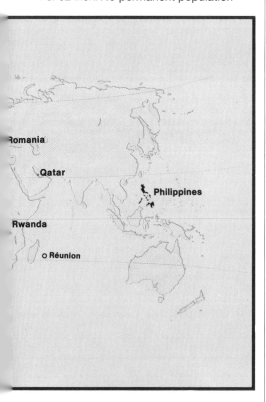

RWANDA

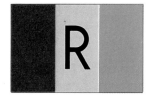

STATUS: Republic
AREA: 26,330 sq km (10,165 sq miles)
POPULATION: 6,710,000
ANNUAL NATURAL INCREASE: 3.8%
DENSITY: 254.8 per sq km
CAPITAL: Kigali
LANGUAGE: French, tribal languages, Kinyarwanda (Bantu)
RELIGION: 50% animist, 50% Roman Catholic
CURRENCY: Rwanda franc
ORGANISATIONS: UN, OAU

Small and isolated Rwanda supports a high density of population on the moist plateaux east of the Rift Valley. Agriculture is basically subsistence with coffee the major export. Few minerals have been discovered, and manufacturing is confined to food processing and construction materials.

SABAH

(see **MALAYSIA**)

ST HELENA

STATUS: UK Dependent Territory
AREA: 122 sq km (47 sq miles)
POPULATION: 5,564
CAPITAL: Jamestown

ST KITTS (ST CHRISTOPHER)- NEVIS

STATUS: Commonwealth Nation
AREA: 262 sq km (101 sq miles)
POPULATION: 48,000
ANNUAL NATURAL INCREASE: 1.8%
DENSITY: 183 per sq km
CAPITAL: Basseterre
LANGUAGE: English
RELIGION: Christian
CURRENCY: E. Caribbean dollar (EC$)
ORGANISATIONS: Comm, UN, CARICOM, OAS

St Kitts-Nevis, in the Leeward Islands, comprises two volcanic islands: St Christopher (St Kitts) and Nevis. The climate is tropical and humid with temperatures between 16°C and 33°C(61°F and 91°F) and an average annual rainfall of 140cm(55in). Main exports are sugar and molasses and cotton. Tourism is an important source of revenue.

ST LUCIA

STATUS: Commonwealth Nation
AREA: 616 sq km (238 sq miles)
POPULATION: 146,000
ANNUAL NATURAL INCREASE: 2.5%
DENSITY: 237.1 per sq km
CAPITAL: Castries
LANGUAGE: English, French patois
RELIGION: 80% Roman Catholic
CURRENCY: E. Caribbean dollar (EC$)
ORGANISATIONS: Comm, UN, CARICOM, OAS

Independent since 1979 this small tropical Caribbean island in the Lesser Antilles grows coconuts, cocoa, citrus fruit and bananas. Most of the population are small farmers. Main industries are food and drink processing and all consumer goods are imported. There are no commercial mineral deposits. Tourism is a rapidly developing industry.

ST PIERRE & MIQUELON

STATUS: Overseas Department of France
AREA: 241 sq km (93 sq miles)
POPULATION: 6,400
CAPITAL: St Pierre

ST VINCENT

STATUS: Commonwealth Nation
AREA: 389 sq km (150 sq miles)
POPULATION: 113,000
ANNUAL NATURAL INCREASE: 2.5%
DENSITY: 290.5 per sq km
CAPITAL: Kingstown
LANGUAGE: English
RELIGION: Christian
CURRENCY: E. Caribbean dollar (EC$)
ORGANISATIONS: Comm, UN, CARICOM, OAS

St Vincent in the Lesser Antilles comprises the main island and a chain of small islands called the Northern Grenadines. The climate is tropical. Most exports are foodstuffs: arrowroot, sweet potatoes, bananas, coconut products and yams. Some sugar-cane is grown for the production of rum and other drinks. Tourism is an expanding industry.

SAMOA

(see **AMERICAN SAMOA & WESTERN SAMOA**)

SAN MARINO

STATUS: Republic
AREA: 61 sq km (24 sq miles)
POPULATION: 22,746
ANNUAL NATURAL INCREASE: 1.2%
DENSITY: 372.9 per sq km
CAPITAL: San Marino
LANGUAGE: Italian
RELIGION: Roman Catholic
CURRENCY: Italian lira, San Marino lire

An independent state within Italy, San Marino straddles a limestone peak in the Apennines south of Rimini. The economy is centred around tourism and sale of postage stamps. Most of the population are farmers growing cereals, olives and vines and tending herds of sheep and goats. Wine and textiles are exported.

SÃO TOMÉ AND PRINCIPÉ

STATUS: Democratic Republic
AREA: 964 sq km (372 sq miles)
POPULATION: 115,600
ANNUAL NATURAL INCREASE: 2.9%
DENSITY: 119.9 per sq km
CAPITAL: São Tomé
LANGUAGE: Portuguese
RELIGION: Roman Catholic majority
CURRENCY: dobra (Db)
ORGANISATIONS: UN, OAU

Independent from Portugal since 1975, two large and several small islands make up this tiny state situated near the equator 200km(125 miles) off the west coast of Africa. The climate is tropical with temperatures averaging 25°C(77°F) and rainfall between 100 and 500cm (40 and 197in). Cocoa, coconuts and palm oil are the main crops grown on the rich volcanic soil. Other foods and consumer goods are imported.

SARAWAK

(see **MALAYSIA**)

SARDINIA (SARDEGNA)

STATUS: Island Region of Italy
AREA: 24,090 sq km (9,300 sq miles)
POPULATION: 1,651,218
CAPITAL: Cagliari

SAUDI ARABIA

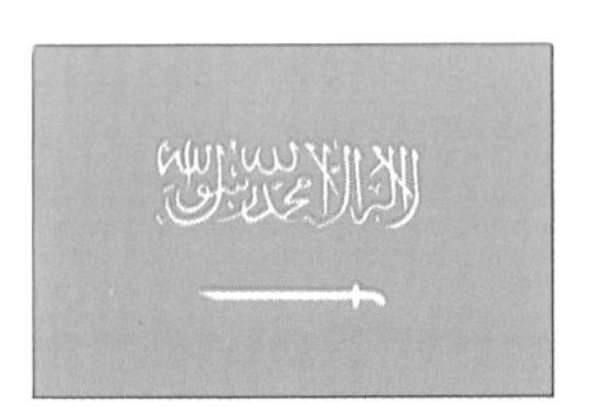

STATUS: Kingdom
AREA: 2,400,900 sq km (926,745 sq miles)
POPULATION: 11,520,000
ANNUAL NATURAL INCREASE: 3.0%
DENSITY: 4.8 per sq km
CAPITAL: Riyadh (Ar Riyad)
LANGUAGE: Arabic
RELIGION: Moslem (85% Sunni)
CURRENCY: riyal
ORGANISATIONS: UN, Arab League, OPEC

Saudi Arabia occupies the heart of the vast arid Arabian Peninsula. To the east, high mountains fringe the Red Sea but even here rainfall rarely exceeds 38cm(15in). Temperatures rise beyond 44°C(111°F) in the summer. The interior plateau slopes down gently eastwards to the Persian Gulf and supports little vegetation. Only in coastal strips and oases are cereals and date-palms grown. Oil is the most important resource and export commodity and economic development is dependent on its revenue. Irrigation schemes and land reclamation projects are attempting to raise food production.

SENEGAL

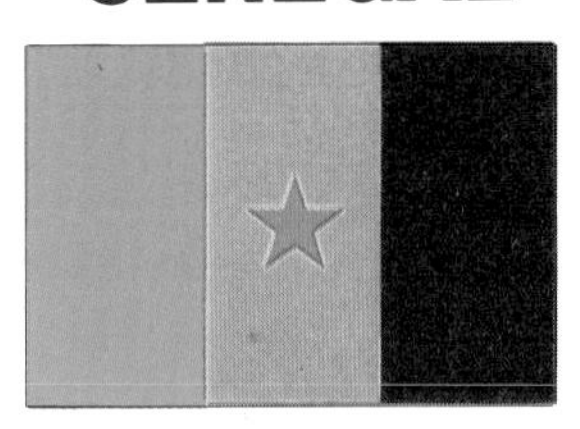

STATUS: Republic
AREA: 196,720 sq km (75,935 sq miles)
POPULATION: 6,982,000
ANNUAL NATURAL INCREASE: 2.9%
DENSITY: 35.5 per sq km
CAPITAL: Dakar
LANGUAGE: French, native languages
RELIGION: 90% Moslem, 5% Roman Catholic
CURRENCY: CFA franc
ORGANISATIONS: UN, CEAO, ECOWAS, OAU

Senegal on the coast of West Africa, is a flat, dry country cut through by the Gambia, Casamance and Senegal rivers. Rainfall rarely exceeds 58cm(23in) on the wetter coast. The interior savannah supports varied wildlife but little agriculture. Groundnuts, cotton and millet are the main crops, but frequent droughts have reduced their value as cash crops. Phosphate mining, ship-repairing and food processing are the major industries.

SEYCHELLES

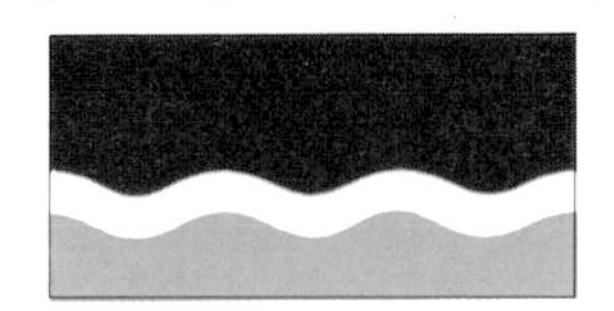

STATUS: Republic
AREA: 404 sq km (156 sq miles)
POPULATION: 67,000
ANNUAL NATURAL INCREASE: 1.9%
DENSITY: 165.8 per sq km
CAPITAL: Victoria
LANGUAGE: Creole
RELIGION: 90% Roman Catholic
CURRENCY: Seychelles rupee (SR)
ORGANISATIONS: Comm, UN, OAU

This archipelago in the Indian Ocean comprises some 86 granite or coral islands. Mahe, the largest covers 155sq km(60sq miles) rising steeply to over 900m(2953ft). The coral islands rise only a few metres above sea level. Temperatures are a constant 24°–29°C(75°–84°F), and rainfall is in the range 180–345cm(71–135in). Main exports are copra, coconuts and cinnamon. Fishing is also important to the economy. Tourism has expanded greatly since the opening of the international airport in 1978.

SHARJAH

(see **UNITED ARAB EMIRATES**)

SHIKOKU

STATUS: Island Prefecture of Japan
AREA: 18,755 sq km (7,240 sq miles)
POPULATION: 4,226,000

SIERRA LEONE

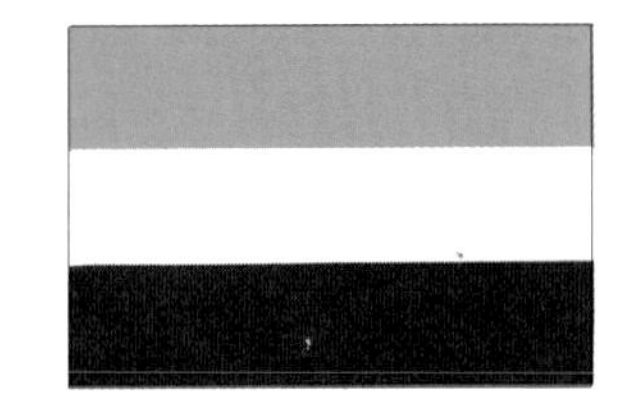

STATUS: Republic
AREA: 72,325 sq km (27,920 sq miles)
POPULATION: 3,875,000
ANNUAL NATURAL INCREASE: 1.8%
DENSITY: 53.6 per sq km
CAPITAL: Freetown
LANGUAGE: English, (also Krio Temne, Mende)
RELIGION: animist majority. Moslem and Christian minorities
CURRENCY: leone (Le)
ORGANISATIONS: Comm, UN, ECOWAS, OAU

A former British colony, the coastline of Sierra Leone is dominated by swamps broken only by

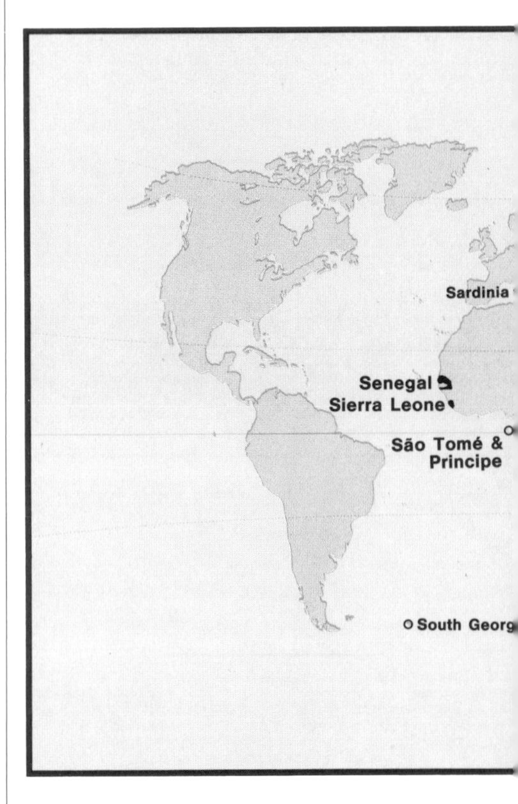

the mountainous peninsula south of Freetown. A wide coastal plain extends inland to the foothills of the interior plateaux and mountains. The land is not fertile due to the poor soils with most of the population farming at subsistence level. Mineral deposits include diamonds, iron ore and bauxite with manufacturing only developed around the capital. Oil-, rice- and timber-mills process these products for export.

SINGAPORE

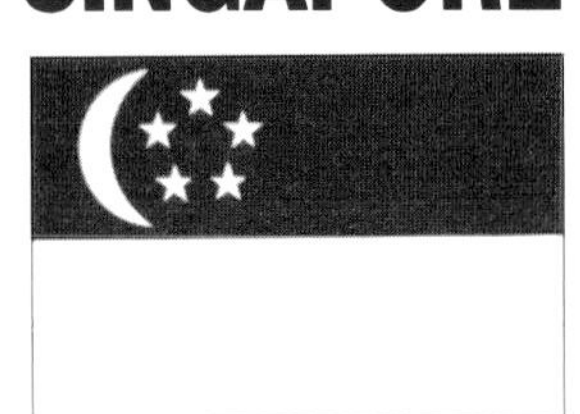

STATUS: Republic
AREA: 616 sq km (238 sq miles)
POPULATION: 2,647,000

ANNUAL NATURAL INCREASE: 1.1%
DENSITY: 4297.1 per sq km
CAPITAL: Singapore City
LANGUAGE: Malay, Chinese (Mandarin), Tamil, English
RELIGION: Daoist, Buddhist, Moslem, Christian, Hindu
CURRENCY: Singapore dollar (S$)
ORGANISATIONS: Comm, UN, ASEAN, Col. Plan

Founded by Sir Stamford Raffles, the state of Singapore has been transformed from an island of mangrove swamps into one the world's major entrepreneurial centres. The island, connected to Peninsular Malaysia by a man-made causeway, has a hot, humid climate with 224cm(96in) of rain per year. With few natural resources, Singapore depends on manufacturing precision goods and electronic products along with financial services.

SOCIETY ISLANDS
(see **FRENCH POLYNESIA**)

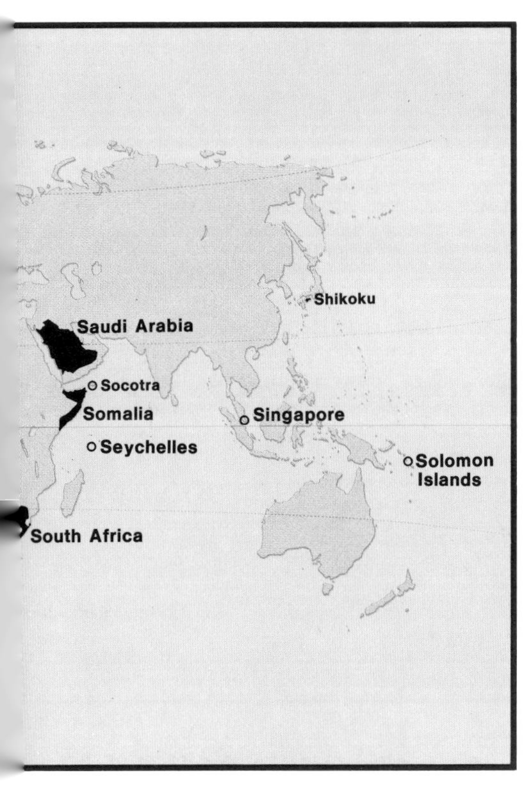

SOCOTRA
STATUS: Island of South Yemen
AREA: 3,625 sq km (1,400 sq miles)
POPULATION: No reliable figure available

SOLOMON ISLANDS

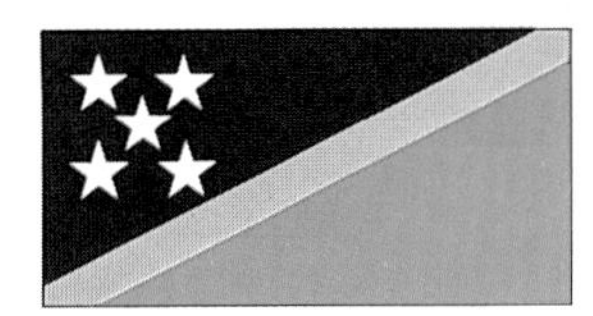

STATUS: Commonwealth Nation
AREA: 29,790 sq km (11,500 sq miles)
POPULATION: 299,000
ANNUAL NATURAL INCREASE: 3.7%
DENSITY: 10 per sq km
CAPITAL: Honiara
LANGUAGE: English, native languages
RELIGION: 95% Christian

CURRENCY: Solomon Islands dollar (SI$)
ORGANISATIONS: Comm, UN

Situated in the South Pacific Ocean the Solomon Islands consist of six main and many smaller islands. The mountainous large islands are covered by tropical rain forest reflecting the high temperatures and heavy rainfall. The main crops are coconuts, cocoa and rice with copra, timber and palm oil being the main exports. This former British protectorate became independent in 1978. There are reserves of bauxite, phosphate and gold.

SOMALIA

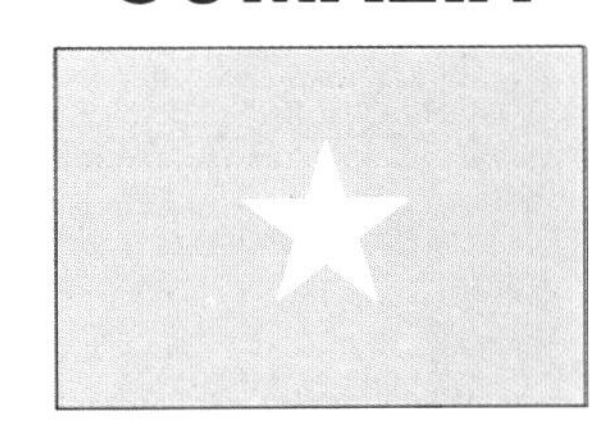

STATUS: Democratic Republic
AREA: 630,000 sq km (243,180 sq miles)
POPULATION: 6,220,000
ANNUAL NATURAL INCREASE: 2.5%
DENSITY: 9.9 per sq km
CAPITAL: Mogadishu (Muqdisho)
LANGUAGE: Somali, Arabic, English, Italian
RELIGION: Moslem. Roman Catholic minority
CURRENCY: Somali shilling (Som. Sh.)
ORGANISATIONS: UN, Arab League, OAU

Independent since 1960, Somalia, is a hot and arid country in north-east Africa. The semi-desert of the northern mountains contrasts with the plains of the south where the bush country is particularly rich in wildlife. Most of the population are nomadic, following herds of camels, sheep, goats and cattle. Little land is cultivated but cotton, maize, millet and sugar-cane are grown. Bananas are a major export. Iron ore, gypsum and uranium deposits are found but none are yet exploited.

SOUTH AFRICA

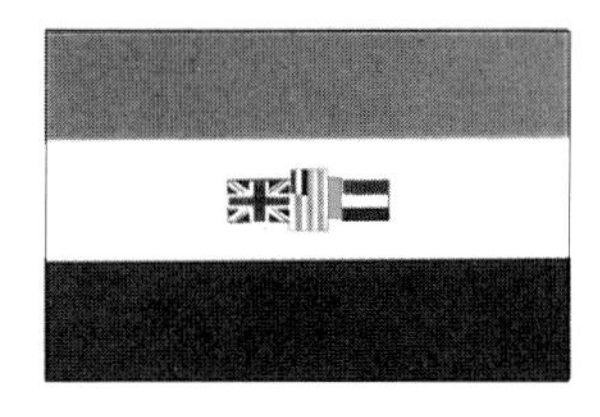

STATUS: Republic
AREA: 1,184,825 sq km (457,345 sq miles)
POPULATION: 29,600,000
ANNUAL NATURAL INCREASE: 2.3%
DENSITY: 24.9 per sq km
CAPITAL: Pretoria (administrative)
Cape Town (legislative)
LANGUAGE: Afrikaans, English, various African languages
RELIGION: mainly Christian. Hindu, Jewish and Moslem minorities
CURRENCY: rand (R)
ORGANISATIONS: UN

BANTU HOMELANDS
STATUS: Self-governing Territories of South Africa
AREA: 93,690 sq km (36,165 sq miles)
POPULATION: No reliable figure available

BOPHUTHATSWANA
STATUS: Self-governing Republic within South Africa
AREA: 40,000 sq km (15,440 sq miles)
POPULATION: 1,660,000

CAPE PROVINCE
STATUS: Province
AREA: 656,640 sq km (253,465 sq miles)
POPULATION: 4,901,251

CISKEI
STATUS: Self-governing Republic within South Africa
AREA: 4,000 sq km (1,545 sq miles)
POPULATION: 1,000,000

NATAL
STATUS: Province
AREA: 86,965 sq km (33,570 sq miles)
POPULATION: 2,145,018

ORANGE FREE STATE
STATUS: Province
AREA: 127,990 sq km (49,405 sq miles)
POPULATION: 1,863,327

TRANSKEI
STATUS: Self-governing Republic within South Africa
AREA: 43,190 sq km (16,670 sq miles)
POPULATION: 2,876,122

TRANSVAAL
STATUS: Province
AREA: 268,915 sq km (103,800 sq miles)
POPULATION: 7,532,179

VENDA
STATUS: Self-governing Republic within South Africa
AREA: 6,500 sq km (2,510 sq miles)
POPULATION: 459,986

The Republic of South Africa is the most highly developed country in Africa. Geographically, the interior consists of a plateau of over 900m(2955ft) drained by the Orange and Limpopo rivers. Surrounding the plateau is a pronounced escarpment below which the land descends by steps to the sea. Rainfall in most areas is less than 50cm(20in) becoming increasingly drier in the west. Agriculture is limited by poor soils but sheep and cattle are extensively grazed. Main crops are maize, wheat, sugar-cane, vegetables, cotton and vines. Wine is an important export commodity. South Africa abounds in minerals. Diamonds, gold, platinum, silver, uranium, copper, manganese and asbestos are mined and nearly 80% of the continent's coal reserves are in South Africa. Manufacturing and engineering is concentrated in southern Transvaal and around the ports. Most foreign revenue is earned through exports of minerals, metals, precious stones, textiles and chemicals and tobacco.

SOUTHERN & ANTARCTIC TERRITORIES
STATUS: Overseas Territory of France
AREA: 439,580 sq km (169,680 sq miles)
POPULATION: 180

SOUTH GEORGIA
STATUS: Dependency of Falkland Islands
AREA: 3,755 sq km (1,450 sq miles)
POPULATION: No permanent population

SOUTH SANDWICH ISLANDS

STATUS: Dependency of Falkland Islands
AREA: 337 sq km (130 sq miles)
POPULATION: No permanent population

SPAIN

STATUS: Kingdom
AREA: 504,880 sq km (194,885 sq miles)
POPULATION: 39,085,000
ANNUAL NATURAL INCREASE: 0.5%
DENSITY: 78 per sq km
CAPITAL: Madrid
LANGUAGE: Spanish, Catalan, Basque
RELIGION: Roman Catholic
CURRENCY: peseta
ORGANISATIONS: UN, Council of Eur, EEC, NATO, OECD

Once a great colonial power, Spain occupies most of the Iberian Peninsula. Mountain ranges fringe the meseta, a vast plateau averaging 600m(1970ft). Climate is affected regionally by latitude and proximity to the Atlantic Ocean and Mediterranean Sea. Much of the land is covered by Mediterranean scrub but wheat, barley, maize, grapes and olives are cultivated. Main cash crops are cotton, olives, tobacco and citrus fruit. Textile manufacturing in the north-east and steel, chemicals, consumer goods and vehicle manufacturing in the towns and cities has proved a magnet for great numbers of the rural population. Other major industries are cement, fishing and forestry. Main minerals are coal, iron ore, uranium and zinc. Tourism is of vital importance to the economy.

SPITSBERGEN

STATUS: Main Island of Svalbard
AREA: 39,045 sq km (15,070 sq miles)
POPULATION: 3,477

SRI LANKA

STATUS: Democratic Socialist Republic
AREA: 65,610 sq km (25,325 sq miles)
POPULATION: 16,600,000
ANNUAL NATURAL INCREASE: 2.0%
DENSITY: 253.0 per sq km
CAPITAL: Colombo
LANGUAGE: Sinhala, Tamil, English
RELIGION: 70% Buddhist, 15% Hindu. Roman Catholic and Moslem minorities
CURRENCY: Sri Lanka rupee (R)
ORGANISATIONS: Comm, UN, Col. Plan

Situated only 19km(12 miles) from mainland India, Sri Lanka (also called Ceylon) is an island of undulating coastal plain encircling the central highlands. The climate is divided accordingly between tropical on the coast and temperate in the hills. Annual rainfall averages only 100cm(39in) in the north and east while the south and west receive over 200cm(79in). Natural resources are limited but the rich agricultural land produces tea, rubber and coconuts. Gem-stones (sapphire, ruby, beryl, topaz), graphite and salt are mined. The main industries are food processing, textiles, chemicals and rubber. Tourism is a steadily growing area of foreign exchange earnings.

SUDAN

STATUS: Republic
AREA: 2,505,815 sq km (967,245 sq miles)
POPULATION: 25,560,000
ANNUAL NATURAL INCREASE: 2.9%
DENSITY: 10 per sq km
CAPITAL: Khartoum
LANGUAGE: Arabic, tribal languages
RELIGION: Moslem, animist and Christian
CURRENCY: Sudanese pound (£S)
ORGANISATIONS: UN, Arab League, OAU

Sudan, in the upper Nile basin, is Africa's largest country. The land is mostly flat and infertile with a hot, arid climate. The White and Blue Niles are invaluable, serving not only to irrigate cultivated land but also as a potential source of hydro-electric power. Subsistence farming accounts for 80% of the Sudan's total production. Major exports include cotton, groundnuts, sugar-cane and sesame seed. The principal activity is nomadic herding with over 20 million cattle and sheep and 14 million goats. Gum arabic is the only forest product exported.

SUMATRA (SUMATERA)

STATUS: Island of Indonesia
AREA: 524,100 sq km (202,305 sq miles)
POPULATION: 32,604,024

SURINAM

STATUS: Republic
AREA: 163,820 sq km (63,235 sq miles)
POPULATION: 415,000
ANNUAL NATURAL INCREASE: 2.0%
DENSITY: 2.5 per sq km
CAPITAL: Paramaribo
LANGUAGE: Dutch, English, Surinamese (Sranang Tongo), and others
RELIGION: 45% Christian, 28% Hindu, 20% Moslem
CURRENCY: Suriname guilder
ORGANISATIONS: UN, OAS

Independent from the Dutch since 1976, Surinam is a small state lying on the north-east coast in the tropics of South America. Physically, there are three main regions: a low-lying, marshy coastal strip; undulating savannah; densely forested highlands. Rice growing takes up 75% of all cultivated land. The introduction of cattle-raising for meat and dairy products is not yet complete. Bauxite accounts for 90% of Surinam's foreign earnings. Rice and timber products are also important. Timber resources are largely untapped.

SVALBARD

STATUS: Archipelago Territory of Norway
AREA: 62,000 sq km (23,930 sq miles)
POPULATION: 3,942

SWAZILAND

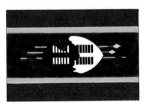

STATUS: Kingdom
AREA: 17,365 sq km (6,705 sq miles)
POPULATION: 740,000
ANNUAL NATURAL INCREASE: 3.0%
DENSITY: 42.6 per sq km
CAPITAL: Mbabane
LANGUAGE: English, SiSwati
RELIGION: 60% Christian, 40% traditional beliefs
CURRENCY: emalangeni (E) S. African rand
ORGANISATIONS: Comm, UN, OAU

Landlocked Swaziland in southern Africa, is a sub-tropical, savannah country. It is divided into four main regions: the High, Middle and Low Velds and the Lebombo Mountains. Rainfall is abundant promoting good pastureland for the many cattle and sheep. Major exports include sugar, meat, citrus fruits, textiles, wood products and asbestos.

SWEDEN

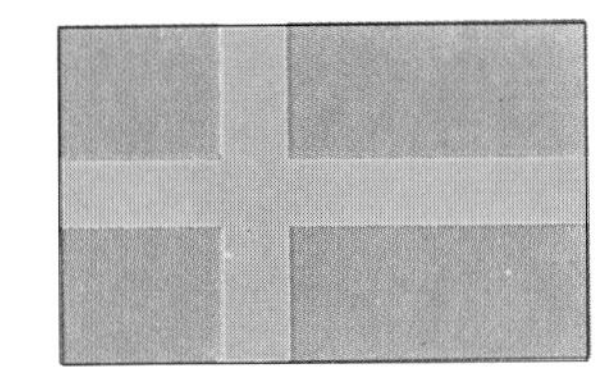

STATUS: Kingdom
AREA: 449,790 sq km (173,620 sq miles)
POPULATION: 8,469,000
ANNUAL NATURAL INCREASE: 0%
DENSITY: 18.8 per sq km
CAPITAL: Stockholm

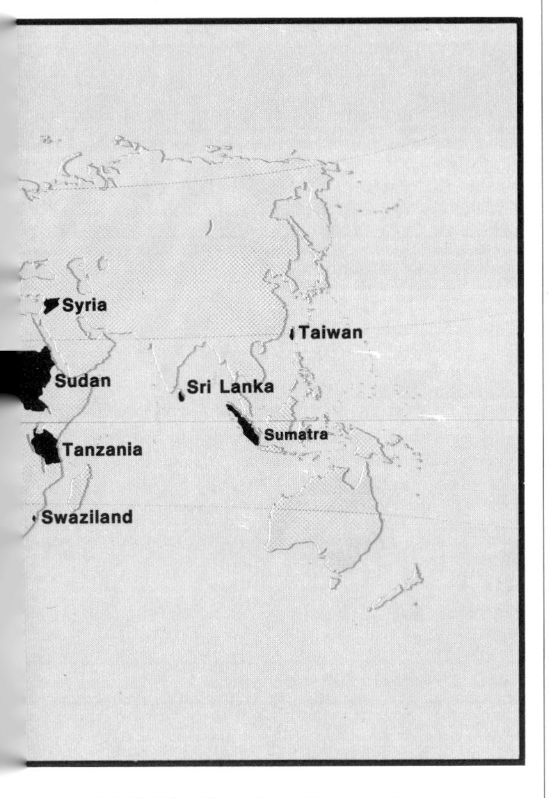

LANGUAGE: Swedish, Finnish, Lappish
RELIGION: 95% Evangelical Lutheran
CURRENCY: Swedish krona (kr)
ORGANISATIONS: UN, Council of Eur, EFTA, OECD

Glacial debris, glacier-eroded valleys and thick glacial clay are all dominant features of Sweden. Physically, Sweden comprises four main regions: Norrland the northern forested mountains; the Lake District of the centre south; the southern Uplands of Jönköping; and the extremely fertile Scania plain of the far south. Summers are short and hot with long, cold winters. Annual rainfall varies between 200cm(79in) in the west and south-west, to 50cm(20in) in the east and south-east.

Over half the land area is forested resulting in a thriving timber industry, but manufacturing industry, particularly cars and trucks, metal products and machine tools, is becoming increasingly dominant. Mineral resources are also rich and plentiful – iron-ore production alone exceeds 17 million tons a year. There are also deposits of copper, lead and zinc.

SWITZERLAND

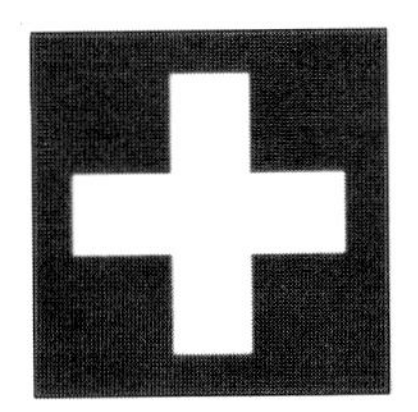

STATUS: Confederation
AREA: 41,285 sq km (15,935 sq miles)
POPULATION: 6,510,000
ANNUAL NATURAL INCREASE: 0.2%
DENSITY: 157.7 per sq km
CAPITAL: Bern (Berne)
LANGUAGE: German, French, Italian, Romansch
RELIGION: 44% Protestant, 48% Roman Catholic. Jewish minority
CURRENCY: Swiss franc
ORGANISATIONS: Council of Eur, EFTA, OECD

Switzerland is a mountainous, landlocked country in the Alps. Winters are very cold with heavy snowfall. Summers are mild with an average July temperature of 18–19°C(64°–66°F). Rainfall is normally restricted to the summer months. Agriculture is based mainly on dairy farming. Major crops include hay, wheat, barley and potatoes. Industry plays a major role in Switzerland's economy, centred on metal engineering, watchmaking, food processing, textiles and chemicals. Tourism is also an important source of income and employment. The financial services sector, especially banking, is also of great importance.

SYRIA

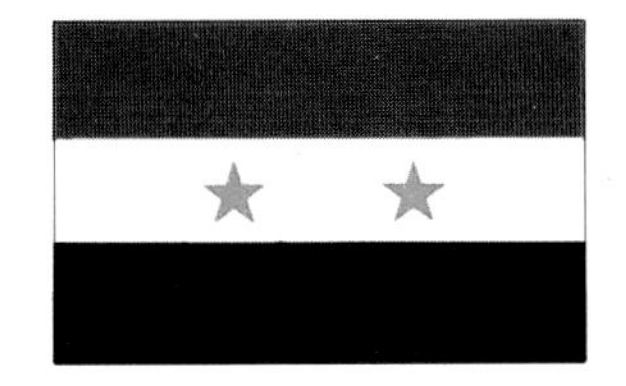

STATUS: Arab Republic
AREA: 185,680 sq km (71,675 sq miles)
POPULATION: 11,338,000
ANNUAL NATURAL INCREASE: 3.8%
DENSITY: 61.1 per sq km
CAPITAL: Damascus (Dimashq)
LANGUAGE: Arabic
RELIGION: 80% Sunni Moslem. Christian minority
CURRENCY: Syrian pound (£Syr)
ORGANISATIONS: UN, Arab League

Syria is situated at the heart of the Middle East bordered by Turkey, Iraq, Jordan, Israel and Lebanon. Its most fertile areas lie along the coastal strip, and in the depressions and plateaux of the north-east which are cut through by the rivers Orontes and Euphrates. In the south the Anti-Lebanon range is bordered to the east by the Syrian desert. While the coast has a Mediterranean climate, the interior becomes increasingly hot and arid – average summer temperatures in the desert reach 43°C(109°F). Rainfall varies between 22 and 40cm(9 and 16in). Cotton is Syria's main export crop, and wheat and barley are also grown. Cattle, sheep and goats are the main livestock. The country is rapidly becoming industrialised as oil, natural gas and phosphates are exploited. Salt and gypsum are mined.

TAHITI

STATUS: Main Island of French Polynesia
AREA: 1,042 sq km (402 sq miles)
POPULATION: 115,820

TAIWAN

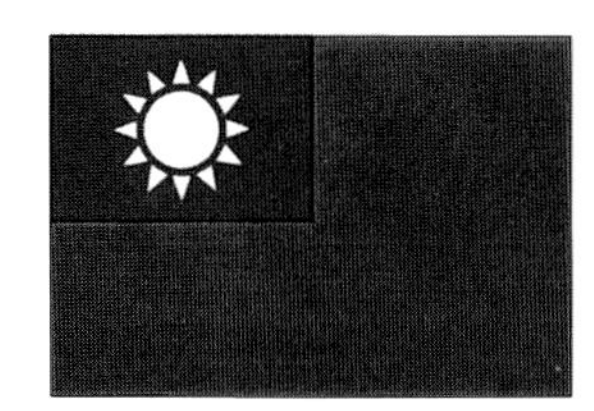

STATUS: Republic
AREA: 35,990 sq km (13,890 sq miles)
POPULATION: 19,700,000
ANNUAL NATURAL INCREASE: 1.5%
DENSITY: 547.4 per sq km
CAPITAL: Taipei
LANGUAGE: Mandarin Chinese
RELIGION: Buddhist majority. Moslem, Daoist and Christian minorities
CURRENCY: New Taiwan dollar (NT$)

Taiwan is situated off the coast of mainland China. Two-thirds of the island is mountainous, the highest point being 3,950m(12,959ft). Climate is tropical marine, with persistent cloudy conditions. The monsoon rains fall in June to August, annual average 260cm (102ins). Main crops are rice, tea, fruit, sugarcane and sweet potatoes. Highly industrialised, its principal exports are textiles, electrical and consumer goods. Natural resources are limestone, marble, asbestos, copper and sulphur.

TANZANIA

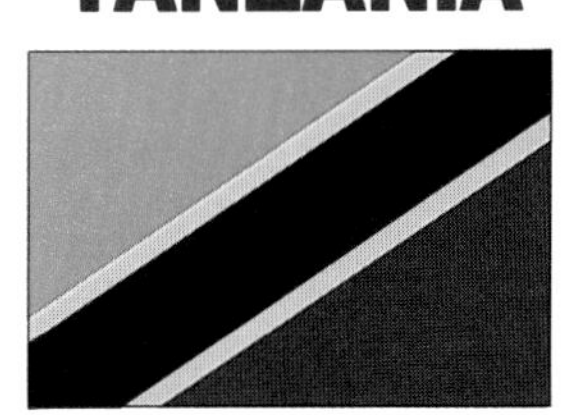

STATUS: United Republic
AREA: 939,760 sq km (362,750 sq miles)
POPULATION: 24,000,000
ANNUAL NATURAL INCREASE: 3.5%
DENSITY: 25.5 per sq km
CAPITAL: Dodoma
LANGUAGE: Kiswahili, English
RELIGION: Christian, Hindu, Moslem
CURRENCY: Tanzanian shilling
ORGANISATIONS: Comm, UN, OAU

Much of this East African country consists of high interior plateaux covered by scrub and grassland, bordered to the north by the volcanic Kilimanjaro region, to the east by Lake Tanganyika, and by highlands to the south. Despite its proximity to the equator, the altitude of much of Tanzania means that temperatures are reduced, and only on the narrow coastal plain is the climate truly tropical. Average temperatures vary between 19° and 28°C(67° and 82°F), and rainfall 57 to 106cm(23 to 43in). Subsistence farming is the main way of life, although coffee, cotton and sisal are exported. Industry is limited to textiles, food processing and tobacco.

THAILAND

STATUS: Kingdom
AREA: 514,000 sq km (198,405 sq miles)
POPULATION: 54,536,000
ANNUAL NATURAL INCREASE: 2.0%
DENSITY: 106.1 per sq km
CAPITAL: Bangkok (Krung Thep)
LANGUAGE: Thai
RELIGION: Buddhist, 4% Moslem
CURRENCY: baht
ORGANISATIONS: UN, ASEAN, Col. Plan

Thailand consists of a flat undulating central plain fringed by mountain ranges, and by a flat plain drained by the River Mekong. From May to October monsoon rains are heavy with an annual average rainfall of 150cm(59in). The climate is tropical with temperatures reaching 36°C(97°F). Over 50% of the country is covered by dense rain forest. Rice is the main export crop, although maize, beans, coconut and groundnuts are also grown. Thailand is one the world's largest producers of rubber and tin.

TIMOR

STATUS: Island of Indonesia
AREA: 33,915 sq km (13,090 sq miles)
POPULATION: 555,350

TOGO

STATUS: Republic
AREA: 56,785 sq km (21,920 sq miles)
POPULATION: 3,246,000
ANNUAL NATURAL INCREASE: 3.1%
DENSITY: 57.2 per sq km
CAPITAL: Lomé
LANGUAGE: French, Kabre, Ewe
RELIGION: 60% animist, 25% Christian, 7.5% Moslem
CURRENCY: CFA franc
ORGANISATIONS: UN, ECOWAS, OAU

This small African republic between Ghana and Benin has only 65km(40 miles) of coast. The interior consists of mountains and high infertile tableland. The climate is tropical with an average temperature of 27°C(81°F). Most of Togo's farmers grow maize, cassava, yams, groundnuts and plantains. Main exports are phosphates, cotton and coffee.

TOKELAU ISLANDS

STATUS: Overseas Territory of New Zealand
AREA: 10 sq km (4 sq miles)
POPULATION: 1,690

TONGA

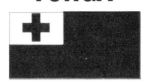

STATUS: Kingdom
AREA: 699 sq km (270 sq miles)
POPULATION: 95,200
ANNUAL NATURAL INCREASE: 0.9%
DENSITY: 136.2 per sq km
CAPITAL: Nuku'alofa
LANGUAGE: Tongan, English
RELIGION: Christian
CURRENCY: pa'anga ($T)
ORGANISATIONS: Comm

Tonga consists of an archipelago of 169 islands in the Pacific 180km(112 miles) north of New Zealand. There are seven groups of islands, but the most important are Tongatapu, Ha'apai and Vava'u. All the islands are covered with dense tropical vegetation, and temperatures range from 11° to 29°C(52° to 84°F). Main exports are coconut products and bananas.

TRINIDAD & TOBAGO

STATUS: Republic
AREA: 5,130 sq km (1,980 sq miles)
POPULATION: 1,243,000
ANNUAL NATURAL INCREASE: 1.8%
DENSITY: 242.3 per sq km
CAPITAL: Port of Spain
LANGUAGE: English
RELIGION: 60% Christian, 25% Hindu, 6% Moslem
CURRENCY: Trinidad & Tobago $ (TT$)
ORGANISATIONS: Comm, UN, CARICOM, OAS

These Caribbean islands lie only 11 and 30km(7 and 19 miles) respectively from the Venezuelan coast. Both islands have mountainous interiors – the central range of Trinidad reaches 940m(3084ft) – and are densely covered with tropical rain forest. Sugar was once the mainstay of the economy but oil is now the leading source of revenue.

TRISTAN DA CUNHA

STATUS: Dependency of St Helena
AREA: 98 sq km (38 sq miles)
POPULATION: 313

TUAMOTU-GAMBIER ARCHIPELAGO

(see **FRENCH POLYNESIA**)

TUBAI ISLANDS

(see **FRENCH POLYNESIA**)

TUNISIA

STATUS: Republic
AREA: 164,150 sq km (63,378 sq miles)
POPULATION: 7,810,000
ANNUAL NATURAL INCREASE: 2.7%
DENSITY: 47.6 per sq km
CAPITAL: Tunis
LANGUAGE: Arabic, French
RELIGION: Moslem
CURRENCY: Tunisian dinar (TD)
ORGANISATIONS: UN, Arab League, OAU

The flat central plains of Tunisia are fringed to the north-east and south-west by mountains and to the west by the sahel, a broad plain

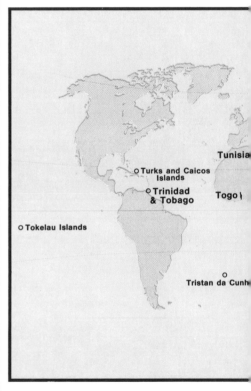

which leads to the Sahara. Average annual temperature ranges from 10° to 27°C(50° to 81°F) and while the coastal area has Mediterranean scrub, the interior is desert. Wheat, barley, olives and citrus fruit are the main crops and oil, natural gas and sugar refining are the main industries. Tourism is growing rapidly.

TURKEY

STATUS: Republic
AREA: 779,450 sq km (300,870 sq miles)
POPULATION: 52,420,000
ANNUAL NATURAL INCREASE: 2.5%
DENSITY: 67.3 per sq km

CAPITAL: Ankara
LANGUAGE: Turkish, Kurdish
RELIGION: Sunni Moslem. Christian minority
CURRENCY: Turkish Lira (TL)
ORGANISATIONS: UN, Council of Eur, NATO, OECD

Turkey has always occupied a strategically important position linking Europe and Asia. The central Anatolian plateau, is bordered to the north and south by mountain ranges which converge in the eastern Anatolian mountains crowned by Mt Ararat 5165m(16,945ft). The north, south and west coastlines are fringed by Mediterranean vegetation and have short, mild and wet winters and long, hot summers. The interior is arid with average rainfall less than 25cm(10in). The main crops are wheat and barley, but tobacco, olives, sugar-beet, tea and fruit are also grown, and sheep, goats and cattle are raised. Turkey is becoming increasingly industrialised and now leads the Middle East in the production of iron, steel, chrome, coal and lignite. Tourism is a rapidly growing industry.

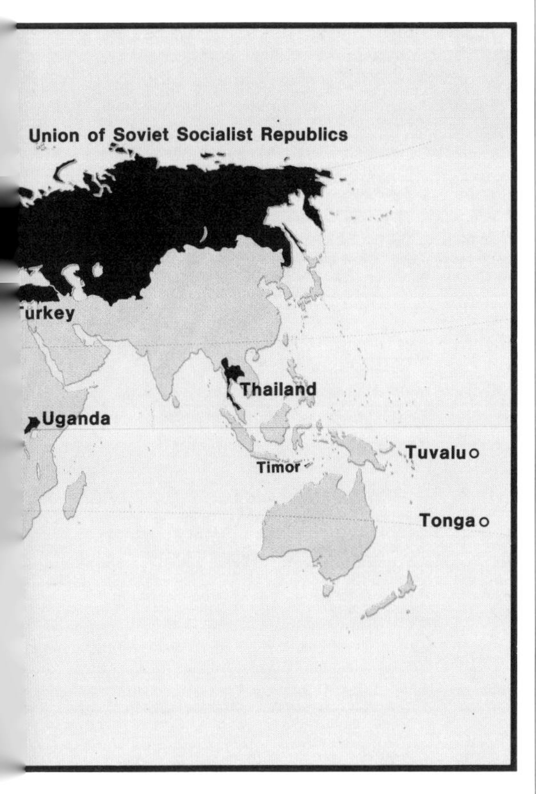

TURKS & CAICOS ISLANDS

STATUS: UK Dependent Territory
AREA: 430 sq km (166 sq miles)
POPULATION: 10,800
CAPITAL: Cockburn Town

TUVALU

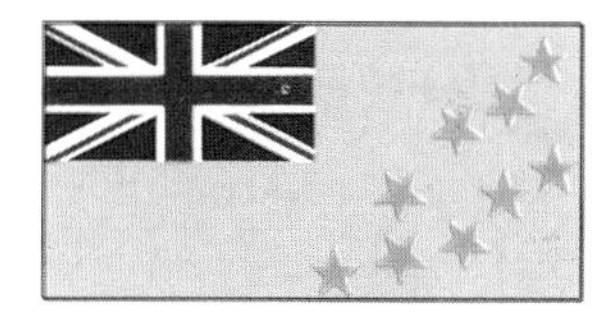

STATUS: State
AREA: 24.6 sq km (9.5 sq miles)
POPULATION: 8,000
ANNUAL NATURAL INCREASE: 1.5%
DENSITY: 325.2 per sq km
CAPITAL: Funafuti
LANGUAGE: Tuvaluan, English

RELIGION: 98% Protestant
CURRENCY: Australian and Tuvaluan $A
ORGANISATIONS: Comm (Special member)

Tuvalu consists of nine dispersed coral atolls 600–1200km(372–745 miles) north of Fiji in the Pacific Ocean. The climate is tropical; hot, with heavy annual rainfall (c300cm or 118in). Fish is the staple food but coconuts and bread-fruits are cultivated.

UGANDA

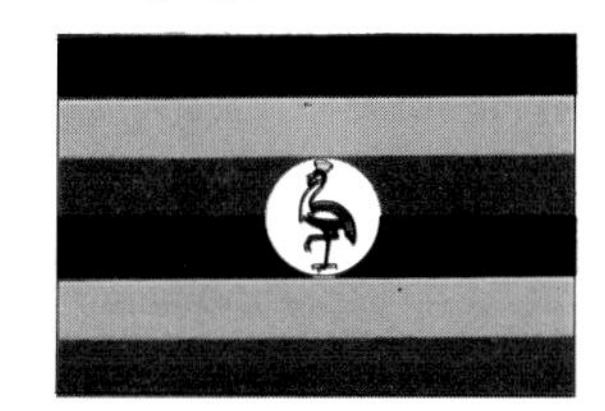

STATUS: Republic
AREA: 236,580 sq km (91,320 sq miles)
POPULATION: 15,500,000
ANNUAL NATURAL INCREASE: 3.4%
DENSITY: 65.5 per sq km
CAPITAL: Kampala
LANGUAGE: English, tribal languages
RELIGION: 60% Christian. Moslem minority
CURRENCY: Uganda shilling
ORGANISATIONS: Comm, UN, OAU

Uganda is bordered to the west by the African Rift valley and to the east by Kenya. The central high plateau is savannah, while the area around Lake Victoria has been cleared for cultivation. To the west are mountain ranges reaching 5110m(16,765ft). The climate is warm (21°–24°C or 70°–75°F), and rainfall ranges from 75–150cm(30–59in). The main export crop is coffee. Lake Victoria has great supplies of freshwater fish.

UMM AL QAIWAIN
(see UNITED ARAB EMIRATES)

UNION OF SOVIET SOCIALIST REPUBLICS (USSR)

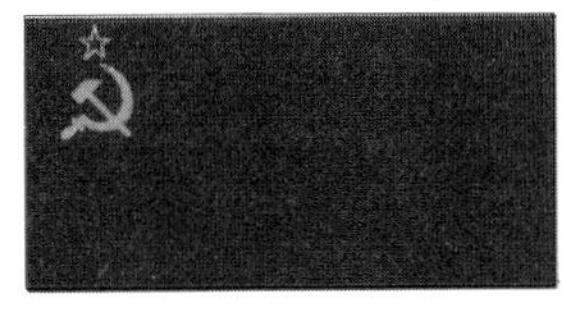

STATUS: Union of Soviet Socialist Republics
AREA: 22,400,000 sq km (8,646,400 sq miles)
POPULATION: 286,717,000
ANNUAL NATURAL INCREASE: 0.9%
DENSITY: 12.8 per sq km
CAPITAL: Moscow (Moskva)
LANGUAGE: Russian, regional languages
RELIGION: Russian Orthodox with Christian, Jewish and Moslem minorities
CURRENCY: rouble
ORGANISATIONS: UN, Warsaw Pact, COMECON

ARMENIA
STATUS: Union Republic
AREA: 30,000 sq km (11,580 sq miles)
POPULATION: 3,283,000
CAPITAL: Yerevan

AZERBAYDZHAN
STATUS: Union Republic
AREA: 87,000 sq km (33,580 sq miles)
POPULATION: 7,029,000
CAPITAL: Baku

BYELORUSSIA
STATUS: Union Republic
AREA: 208,000 sq km (80,290 sq miles)
POPULATION: 10,200,000
CAPITAL: Minsk

ESTONIA
STATUS: Union Republic
AREA: 45,100 sq km (17,410 sq miles)
POPULATION: 1,573,000
CAPITAL: Tallinn

GEORGIA
STATUS: Union Republic
AREA: 69,700 sq km (26,905 sq miles)
POPULATION: 5,449,000
CAPITAL: Tbilisi

KAZAKHSTAN
STATUS: Union Republic
AREA: 2,717,300 sq km (1,048,880 sq miles)
POPULATION: 16,538,000
CAPITAL: Alma-Ata

KIRGHIZIA
STATUS: Union Republic
AREA: 198,500 sq km (76,620 sq miles)
POPULATION: 4,291,000
CAPITAL: Frunze

LATVIA
STATUS: Union Republic
AREA: 63,700 sq km (24,590 sq miles)
POPULATION: 2,681,000
CAPITAL: Riga

LITHUANIA
STATUS: Union Republic
AREA: 65,200 sq km (25,165 sq miles)
POPULATION: 3,690,000
CAPITAL: Vilnius

MOLDAVIA
STATUS: Union Republic
AREA: 33,700 sq km (13,010 sq miles)
POPULATION: 4,341,000
CAPITAL: Kishinev

RUSSIAN SOVIET FEDERAL SOCIALIST REPUBLIC (RSFSR)
STATUS: Union Republic
AREA: 17,078,005 sq km (6,592,110 sq miles)
POPULATION: 147,386,000
CAPITAL: Moscow

TADZHIKISTAN
STATUS: Union Republic
AREA: 143,100 sq km (55,235 sq miles)
POPULATION: 5,112,000
CAPITAL: Dushanbe

TURKMENISTAN
STATUS: Union Republic
AREA: 488,100 sq km (188,405 sq miles)
POPULATION: 3,534,000
CAPITAL: Ashkhabad

UKRAINE
STATUS: Union Republic
AREA: 603,700 sq km (233,030 sq miles)
POPULATION: 51,704,000
CAPITAL: Kiev

UZBEKISTAN

STATUS: Union Republic
AREA: 447,400 sq km (172,695 sq miles)
POPULATION: 19,906,000
CAPITAL: Tashkent

The Union of Soviet Socialist Republics is the largest country in the world, covering one fifth of the earth's surface. After China and India, it has the worlds third largest population. From Moscow, in European Russia, to Vladivostok on the Sea of Japan is a journey of 9200km(5720 miles) which crosses eleven time zones.

The country encompasses a great diversity of different climates and environments ranging from the frozen wastes of eastern Siberia to the deserts of Central Asia. Nearly half of the USSR falls north of 60°, and large areas of its territory lie within the Arctic Circle.

European Russia, west of the Ural mountains, is an area of undulating lowlands cut through by broad rivers. To the south and west of this region lie the mountain ranges of the Caucasus, Carpathians and Crimean. East of the Urals lies the West Siberian plain, a vast tract of low-lying marshy land, drained by the great rivers Ob and Irtysh. This gradually rises towards the Central Siberian plateau which reaches a height of 1500m(4920ft), and lies between the Yenisey and Lena rivers. East of the River Lena the mountains reach a height of 3000m(9840ft). In the south of this region is Lake Baikal, at 1611m(5285ft), the world's deepest lake. South of the West Siberian plain is Soviet Central Asia.

The vegetation and climate of the USSR reflect this great diversity. Within the Arctic Circle there is a belt of tundra – sparse, scrubby vegetation. Here, reindeer herding is the only means of subsistence. South of the tundra lies the taiga belt, an area of thick coniferous forest which stretches from the Baltic to the Pacific. European Russia is an area of mixed and deciduous woodland while the steppe lands immediately to the east of the Urals are Russia's 'black soil' lands, the most fertile areas of the USSR. The climate of the USSR is one of extremes.

These conditions become more extreme towards the east; in Moscow, for example, annual snow cover is five months, on the east coast nine months. In the north-east January temperatures can fall to −60°C(−76°F). The central Siberian plateau is covered with permafrost – the ground is permanently frozen, and only the top soil thaws in the spring. Rainfall is erratic, particularly to the east of the Urals, where drought is common, and this can undermine the agricultural potential of the blacksoil belts. The steppes do, however, account for much of the 10% of Russian territory which is under cultivation. About 60% of this area is given over to cereals – wheat, barley, oats and rye – which are transported vast distances to supply the most far-flung regions of the USSR. In general fruit and vegetables are grown and consumed locally. In addition to cereals industrial crops are also grown in the steppe regions – sunflowers, sugar-beet, cotton, flax, hemp and potatoes.

The 12th Five Year Plan adopted in 1986, is dedicated to raising the living standards, implementing scientific and technical progress, greater economy in use of energy and natural resources and placing greater emphasis on energy, food programmes and development of consumer goods and services.

The Soviet economy is self-sufficient in energy requirements. Coal is in plentiful supply – the USSR has about 58% of the world's reserves – but is now being supplemented by oil and natural gas as the country's main source of energy. Over 80% of electricity is produced by fuel-burning power stations. The remainder is generated by hydro-electric schemes using the latent power of the great rivers of Siberia, in particular the rivers Yenisey, Angara and Kureyka. There are also at least four potential and one working tidal electric generation schemes in the White Sea. These could eventually provide electricity to the Moscow region and to the heavy industry of the southern Urals. Nuclear and nuclear thermal power stations also make an important contribution.

Recent discoveries of vast reserves of oil in the area of Saratov in West Siberia, supplement the supplies from the longer established Volga-Urals oilfields. A network of pipelines over 71,000km(44,120 miles) in length distributes oil to the industrial centres and to eastern European countries. The natural gas pipelines total over 124,000km(77,055 miles) and distribute to eastern Europe and Italy, West Germany and Austria. The USSR also has large reserves of iron ore and non-ferrous metals such as manganese, though it is not self-sufficient in copper, lead, zinc and tin. Uranium is mined in the Altai mountains.

Heavy industry is concentrated in the Urals around Sverdlovsk, Chelyabinsk and Magnitogorsk producing steel, turbines, piping, heavy machinery, chemicals and vehicles. Lighter, consumer industries are concentrated around Moscow with cotton and woollen textiles, leather goods, precision instruments, electric and electronic goods, and processed foods.

UNITED ARAB EMIRATES (UAE)

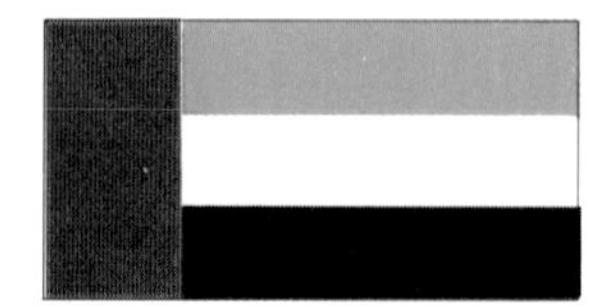

STATUS: United Arab Emirates
AREA: 75,150 sq km (29,010 sq miles)
POPULATION: 1,600,000
ANNUAL NATURAL INCREASE: 2.3%
DENSITY: 21.3 per sq km
CAPITAL: Abu Dhabi
LANGUAGE: Arabic, English
RELIGION: Sunni Moslem
CURRENCY: UAE dirham (Dh)
ORGANISATIONS: UN, Arab League, OPEC

ABU DHABI

STATUS: State
AREA: 64,750 sq km (24,995 sq miles)
POPULATION: 670,125

ÁJMĀN

STATUS: State
AREA: 260 sq km (100 sq miles)
POPULATION: 64,318

DUBAI

STATUS: State
AREA: 3,900 sq km (1,505 sq miles)
POPULATION: 419,104

FUJAIRAH

STATUS: State
AREA: 1,170 sq km (452 sq miles)
POPULATION: 54,425

RAS AL-KHAIMAH

STATUS: State
AREA: 1,690 sq km (652 sq miles)
POPULATION: 116,470

SHARJAH

STATUS: State
AREA: 2,600 sq km (1,005 sq miles)
POPULATION: 268,722

UMM AL QAIWAIN

STATUS: State
AREA: 780 sq km (300 sq miles)
POPULATION: 29,229

Seven emirates stretched along the south eastern shores of the Persian Gulf constitute this oil rich Arab state. Flat deserts cover most of the landscape rising to the Hajar mountains of the Musandam Peninsula. Summer temperatures reach 40°C(104°F)⁻ and winter rainfall 13cm(5in). Only the desert oases are fertile, producing fruit and vegetables. Trade is dominated by exports of oil and natural gas.

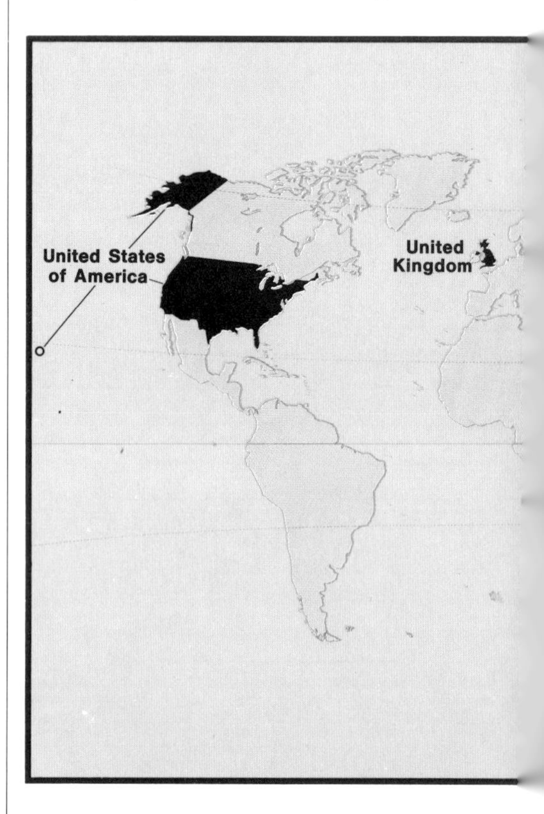

UNITED KINGDOM OF GREAT BRITAIN & NORTHERN IRELAND (UK)

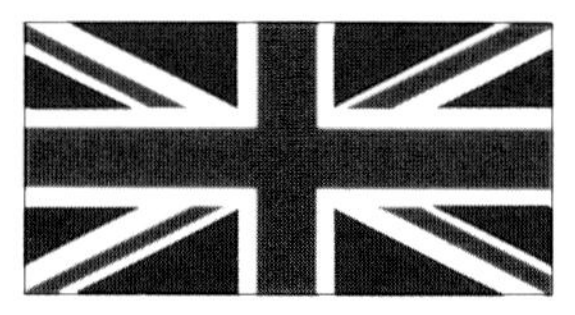

STATUS: Kingdom
AREA: 244,755 sq km (94,475 sq miles)
POPULATION: 57,065,000
ANNUAL NATURAL INCREASE: 0.2%
DENSITY: 233.2 per sq km
CAPITAL: London
LANGUAGE: English, Welsh, Gaelic
RELIGION: Protestant majority, Roman Catholic, Jewish, Moslem and Hindu minorities

CURRENCY: Pound Sterling (£)
ORGANISATIONS: Comm, UN, Col. Plan, Council of Eur, NATO, OECD, WEU

ENGLAND

STATUS: Constituent Country
AREA: 130,360 sq km (50,320 sq miles)
POPULATION: 47,536,300
CAPITAL: London

NORTHERN IRELAND

STATUS: Constituent Region
AREA: 14,150 sq km (5,460 sq miles)
POPULATION: 1,578,000
CAPITAL: Belfast

SCOTLAND

STATUS: Constituent Country
AREA: 78,750 sq km (30,400 sq miles)
POPULATION: 5,094,000
CAPITAL: Edinburgh

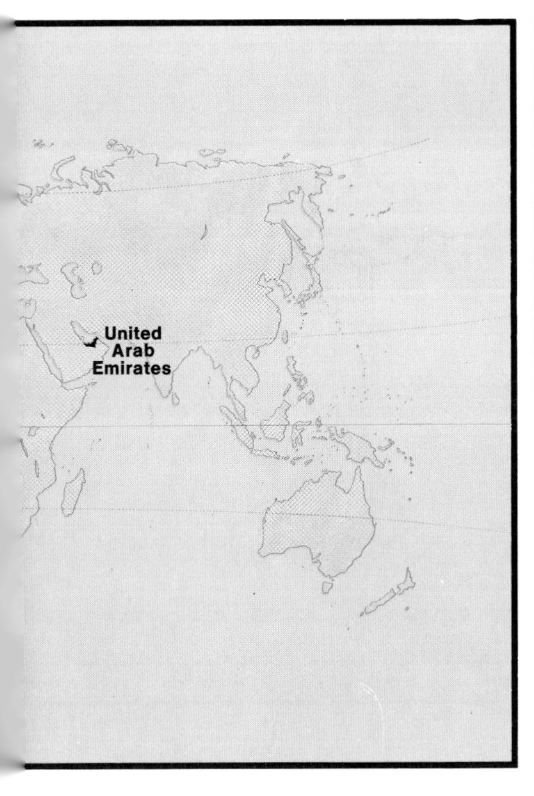

United Arab Emirates

WALES

STATUS: Principality
AREA: 20,760 sq km (8,015 sq miles)
POPULATION: 2,857,000
CAPITAL: Cardiff

The United Kingdom is part of the British Isles which are situated off the coast of north-west Europe separated from France by the English Channel and from Belgium, the Netherlands and Scandinavia by the North Sea. There are two main islands: the larger, Great Britain, comprises England, Scotland and Wales; the smaller, the island of Ireland separated from Britain by the Irish Sea, comprises Northern Ireland and the Irish Republic.

The Highland zone of Britain consists of ancient uplifted rocks which now form the mountainous-dissected and glaciated areas of Wales, the Lake District in the north-west, and the Southern Uplands and Grampians of Scotland which rise to the highest point in the UK to 1344m(4409ft) at Ben Nevis. The latter are divided by the wide Central Lowland rift valley. Central England is dominated by the Pen-nine mountain chain which stretches southwards from the Southern Uplands down the centre of England to the river Trent. The landscape of the south-west consists of the ancient uplifted granite domes of Dartmoor and Bodmin Moor.

Lowland Britain is a very contrasting landscape. Limestone and sandstone hills are separated by flat clay vales, east of a line joining the rivers Humber and Exe. Here is found both the richest agricultural land and the densest population.

The climate of the British Isles is mild, wet and variable. Summer temperatures average 13°–17°C(55°–63°F), and winter temperatures 5°–7°C(41°–45°F). Annual rainfall varies between 65 and 500cm(26 and 200in) with the highest in the central Lake District and the lowest on the coasts of East Anglia.

Although a tiny percentage of the nation's workforce are employed in agriculture, farm produce is important to both home and export markets. 78% of the total UK land area is farmland. The main cereal crops are wheat, barley and oats. Potatoes, sugar-beet and green vegetable crops are widespread.

About 20% of the land is permanent pasture for raising of dairy and beef stock; and 28% of the land, mainly hill and mountain areas, is used for rough grazing of sheep. Pigs and poultry are widespread in both England and lowland Britain. The best fruit-growing areas are the south-east, especially Kent, and East Anglia and the central Vale of Evesham for apples, pears and soft-fruit. Both forestry and fishing industries contribute to the economy.

The major mineral resources of the UK are coal, oil and natural gas. Most of coal output goes towards the generation of electricity but oil and natural gas from the North Sea, and to a lesser extent nuclear power, are divided between the needs of industry and the consumer. Iron ore, once mined in sufficient quantity to satisfy industry, is now imported to support the iron and steel manufacturing sector.

The UK produces a great range of industrial goods for home consumption and export. Heavy industry particularly the production of iron and steel is traditionally located close to fuel sources (coal) in South Wales, the North-East at Teesside and South Yorkshire. The majority of iron ore is imported. The main shipbuilding areas are Clydeside in western Scotland, Belfast in Northern Ireland and Tyneside in the North-East. Other heavy industrial goods, vehicles, engines and machinery are produced on Merseyside in Lancashire, Derby/Nottingham in the North Midlands, Birmingham in the West-Midlands, Cardiff in South Wales, Clydeside and Belfast.

General and consumer good manufacturing is located in all heavy industrial areas but the London area, West Midlands and Lancashire/Merseyside predominate. Main products are food and drinks, chemicals, light engineering products, cotton and woollen textiles, electrical and electronic goods.

The UK is a trading nation. The balance of trade has changed during the last 30 years because of stronger economic, military and political ties within Europe – the EEC and NATO – and consequently reduced trading links with former colonies particularly in Australasia. Major exports are cereals, meat, dairy products, beverages, tobacco products, textiles, metalliferous ores, petroleum and petroleum products, chemicals, pharmaceutical goods, plastics, leather goods, rubber, paper, iron and steel, other metal goods, engines and vehicles, machinery, electrical goods and transport equipment.

The UK has a highly developed transport network to move goods and services. Motorways, trunk roads and principal roads total over 50,000km(31,070 miles), the railway network covers 16,730km(10,395 miles). The inland waterway system, once a major freight carrier, totals only 563km(350 miles) but still carries over 4 million tonnes of goods annually.

UNITED STATES OF AMERICA (USA)

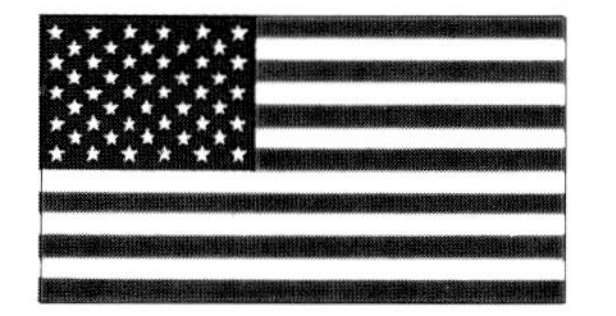

STATUS: Federal Republic
AREA: 9,363,130 sq km (3,614,170 sq miles)
POPULATION: 245,815,000
ANNUAL NATURAL INCREASE: 0.7%
DENSITY: 26.3 per sq km
CAPITAL: Washington, DC
LANGUAGE: English, Spanish
RELIGION: Christian majority. Jewish minority
CURRENCY: US dollar ($)
ORGANISATIONS: UN, ANZUS, Col. Plan, NATO, OECD, OAS

ALABAMA

STATUS: State
AREA: 131,485 sq km (50,755 sq miles)
POPULATION: 4,127,000
CAPITAL: Montgomery

ALASKA

STATUS: State
AREA: 1,478,450 sq km (570,680 sq miles)
POPULATION: 513,000
CAPITAL: Juneau

ARIZONA

STATUS: State
AREA: 293,985 sq km (113,480 sq miles)
POPULATION: 3,466,000
CAPITAL: Phoenix

ARKANSAS

STATUS: State
AREA: 134,880 sq km (52,065 sq miles)
POPULATION: 2,422,000
CAPITAL: Little Rock

CALIFORNIA

STATUS: State
AREA: 404,815 sq km (156,260 sq miles)
POPULATION: 28,168,000
CAPITAL: Sacramento

COLORADO

STATUS: State
AREA: 268,310 sq km (103,570 sq miles)
POPULATION: 3,290,000
CAPITAL: Denver

CONNECTICUT

STATUS: State
AREA: 12,620 sq km (4,870 sq miles)
POPULATION: 3,241,000
CAPITAL: Hartford

DELAWARE
STATUS: State
AREA: 5,005 sq km (1,930 sq miles)
POPULATION: 660,000
CAPITAL: Dover

DISTRICT OF COLUMBIA
STATUS: Federal District
AREA: 163 sq km (63 sq miles)
POPULATION: 620,000
CAPITAL: Washington

FLORIDA
STATUS: State
AREA: 140,255 sq km (54,140 sq miles)
POPULATION: 12,377,000
CAPITAL: Tallahassee

GEORGIA
STATUS: State
AREA: 150,365 sq km (58,040 sq miles)
POPULATION: 6,401,000
CAPITAL: Atlanta

HAWAII
STATUS: State
AREA: 16,640 sq km (6,425 sq miles)
POPULATION: 1,093,000
CAPITAL: Honolulu

IDAHO
STATUS: State
AREA: 213,455 sq km (82,390 sq miles)
POPULATION: 999,000
CAPITAL: Boise

ILLINOIS
STATUS: State
AREA: 144,120 sq km (55,630 sq miles)
POPULATION: 11,544,000
CAPITAL: Springfield

INDIANA
STATUS: State
AREA: 93,065 sq km (35,925 sq miles)
POPULATION: 5,575,000
CAPITAL: Indianapolis

IOWA
STATUS: State
AREA: 144,950 sq km (55,950 sq miles)
POPULATION: 2,834,000
CAPITAL: Des Moines

KANSAS
STATUS: State
AREA: 211,805 sq km (81,755 sq miles)
POPULATION: 2,487,000
CAPITAL: Topeka

KENTUCKY
STATUS: State
AREA: 102,740 sq km (39,660 sq miles)
POPULATION: 3,721,000
CAPITAL: Frankfort

LOUISIANA
STATUS: State
AREA: 115,310 sq km (44,510 sq miles)
POPULATION: 4,420,000
CAPITAL: Baton Rouge

MAINE
STATUS: State
AREA: 80,275 sq km (30,985 sq miles)
POPULATION: 1,206,000
CAPITAL: Augusta

MARYLAND
STATUS: State
AREA: 25,480 sq km (9,835 sq miles)
POPULATION: 4,644,000
CAPITAL: Annapolis

MASSACHUSETTS
STATUS: State
AREA: 20,265 sq km (7,820 sq miles)
POPULATION: 5,871,000
CAPITAL: Boston

MICHIGAN
STATUS: State
AREA: 147,510 sq km (56,940 sq miles)
POPULATION: 9,300,000
CAPITAL: Lansing

MINNESOTA
STATUS: State
AREA: 206,030 sq km (79,530 sq miles)
POPULATION: 4,306,000
CAPITAL: St Paul

MISSISSIPPI
STATUS: State
AREA: 122,335 sq km (47,220 sq miles)
POPULATION: 2,627,000
CAPITAL: Jackson

MISSOURI
STATUS: State
AREA: 178,565 sq km (68,925 sq miles)
POPULATION: 5,139,000
CAPITAL: Jefferson City

MONTANA
STATUS: State
AREA: 376,555 sq km (145,350 sq miles)
POPULATION: 809,000
CAPITAL: Helana

NEBRASKA
STATUS: State
AREA: 198,505 sq km (76,625 sq miles)
POPULATION: 1,601,000
CAPITAL: Lincoln

NEVADA
STATUS: State
AREA: 284,625 sq km (109,865 sq miles)
POPULATION: 1,060,000
CAPITAL: Carson City

NEW HAMPSHIRE
STATUS: State
AREA: 23,290 sq km (8,990 sq miles)
POPULATION: 1,097,000
CAPITAL: Concord

NEW JERSEY
STATUS: State
AREA: 19,340 sq km (7,465 sq miles)
POPULATION: 7,720,000
CAPITAL: Trenton

NEW MEXICO
STATUS: State
AREA: 314,255 sq km (121,300 sq miles)
POPULATION: 1,510,000
CAPITAL: Santa Fé

NEW YORK
STATUS: State
AREA: 122,705 sq km (47,365 sq miles)
POPULATION: 17,898,000
CAPITAL: Albany

NORTH CAROLINA
STATUS: State
AREA: 126,505 sq km (48,830 sq miles)
POPULATION: 6,526,000
CAPITAL: Raleigh

NORTH DAKOTA
STATUS: State
AREA: 179,485 sq km (69,280 sq miles)
POPULATION: 663,000
CAPITAL: Bismarck

OHIO
STATUS: State
AREA: 106,200 sq km (40,995 sq miles)
POPULATION: 10,872,000
CAPITAL: Columbus

OKLAHOMA
STATUS: State
AREA: 177,815 sq km (68,635 sq miles)
POPULATION: 3,263,000
CAPITAL: Oklahoma City

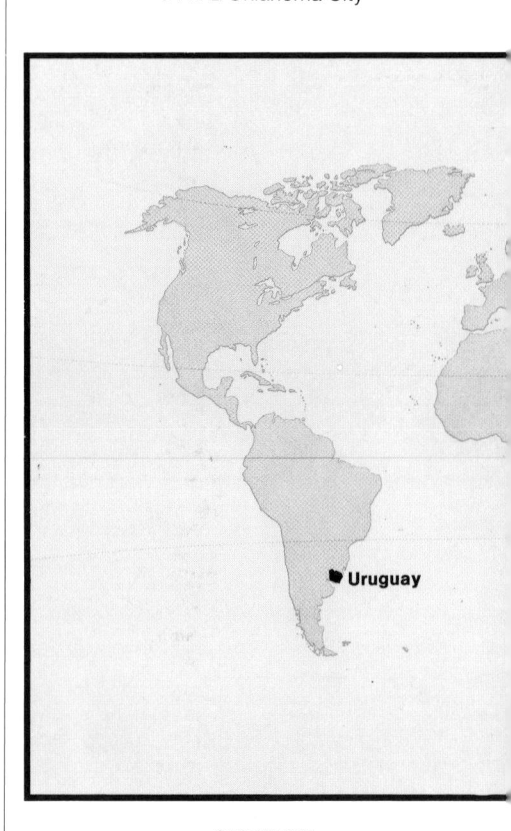

OREGON
STATUS: State
AREA: 249,115 sq km (96,160 sq miles)
POPULATION: 2,741,000
CAPITAL: Salem

PENNSYLVANIA
STATUS: State
AREA: 116,260 sq km (44,875 sq miles)
POPULATION: 12,027,000
CAPITAL: Harrisburg

RHODE ISLAND
STATUS: State
AREA: 2,730 sq km (1,055 sq miles)
POPULATION: 995,000
CAPITAL: Providence

SOUTH CAROLINA
STATUS: State
AREA: 78,225 sq km (30,195 sq miles)
POPULATION: 3,493,000
CAPITAL: Columbia

SOUTH DAKOTA
STATUS: State
AREA: 196,715 sq km (75,930 sq miles)
POPULATION: 715,000
CAPITAL: Pierre

TENNESSEE
STATUS: State
AREA: 106,590 sq km (41,145 sq miles)
POPULATION: 4,919,000
CAPITAL: Nashville

TEXAS
STATUS: State
AREA: 678,620 sq km (261,950 sq miles)
POPULATION: 16,780,000
CAPITAL: Austin

UTAH
STATUS: State
AREA: 212,570 sq km (82,050 sq miles)
POPULATION: 1,691,000
CAPITAL: Salt Lake City

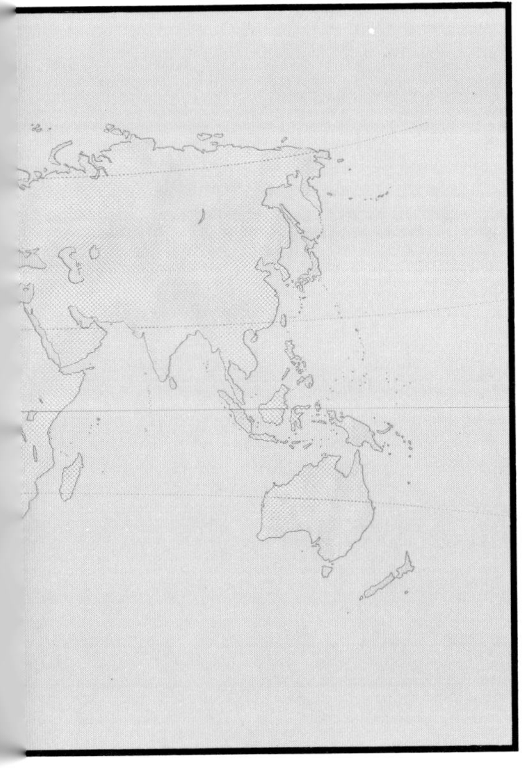

VERMONT
STATUS: State
AREA: 24,900 sq km (9,612 sq miles)
POPULATION: 556,000
CAPITAL: Montpelier

VIRGINIA
STATUS: State
AREA: 102,835 sq km (39,695 sq miles)
POPULATION: 5,996,000
CAPITAL: Richmond

WASHINGTON
STATUS: State
AREA: 172,265 sq km (66,495 sq miles)
POPULATION: 4,619,000
CAPITAL: Olympia

WEST VIRGINIA
STATUS: State
AREA: 62,470 sq km (24,115 sq miles)
POPULATION: 1,884,400
CAPITAL: Charleston

WISCONSIN
STATUS: State
AREA: 140,965 sq km (54,415 sq miles)
POPULATION: 4,858,000
CAPITAL: Madison

WYOMING
STATUS: State
AREA: 251,200 sq km (96,965 sq miles)
POPULATION: 471,000
CAPITAL: Cheyenne

The United States of America is the world's fourth largest country after USSR, Canada and China, with the world's fourth largest population. The 19th and 20th centuries have brought 42 million immigrants to its shores, and the population of the USA now has the highest living standard of any country in the world. The large land area covers a huge spectrum of different landscapes, environments and climates. The eastern coast of New England where the European settlers first landed, is rocky, mountainous and richly wooded. South of New England is the Atlantic coastal plain, rising to the west towards the Appalachian mountain system. Beyond the Appalachians lie the central lowlands, a large undulating plain cut through by the Mississippi and Ohio rivers. Further west lie the Great Plains crossed by the Missouri, Red and Arkansas rivers and rising gently towards the mighty Rockies a spine of mountains running south from Alaska. The highest point is Mt. Whitney in California, at 4418m(14,495ft). Beyond the Rockies lies the Great Valley of California and the Pacific coast.

Climatic variety within this vast region is enormous, ranging from the Arctic conditions of Alaska to the desert of the south-west – winter temperatures in Alaska plummet to −28°C(−19°F), whereas in Florida they maintain a steady 19°C(66°F). In California the weather varies little, being constantly mild with a range of only 9°C(16°F), whereas in the central lowlands winters are severe and the summers very hot. The centre of the continent is dry, but both the north-west Pacific and the New England Atlantic coast are humid with heavy rainfall. Many areas of the USA fall prey to exceptional, often disastrous, weather conditions: the north-eastern seaboard is susceptible to heavy blizzards, the southern lowlands are vulnerable to spring thaw flooding and the Mississippi valley is prone to tornadoes.

The natural vegetation of the USA reflects it's climatic diversity. The north-west coast is rich in coniferous forest, especially Douglas fir, while its Appalachian mountain region is well endowed with hardwoods, notably maple and oak. In the arid south-west, vegetation is limited to desert scrub whereas the Gulf and South Atlantic coast are fringed with swampy wetlands. The central lowlands are endowed with rich black-earth soils (the agricultural heartland), gradually supplanted – towards the Rockies, by tall-grass prairie. The north-eastern states of Illinois, Iowa, Indiana and Nebraska form the so-called corn belt, whereas further west wheat supplements corn as the main crop. Spring wheat is grown in the northern states of North and South Dakota and Minnesota. The north-eastern corner of the USA is predominantly dairy country, and the states of the deep south are famous for their cotton, though cotton cultivation is declining. Rice is grown in Texas, California and Louisiana, and fruit and vegetables in Florida, Texas and California.

The USA consumes 30% of all the world's energy resources but is well endowed with energy reserves. There are substantial coal resources in Pennsylvania, the Appalachian region, the Dakotas and Wyoming, and oil and natural gas regions in Texas, Louisiana, Alaska, and off-shore, in the Gulf of Mexico. The vast resources of America's great rivers have been harnessed extensively for hydro-electric power. In the west, mineral deposits include copper, lead, zinc and silver, and there is iron ore around Lake Superior. Most specialist industrial minerals are imported. Diamonds, tin, chromite, nickel, asbestos, platinum, manganese, mercury, tungsten, cobalt, antimony and cadmium are not found in sufficient quantities for home demand. Main non-metallic minerals extracted within the USA are cement, clays, gypsum, lime, phosphate, salt, sand, gravel and sulphur.

About one fifth of the land area of the USA is covered by commercially usable coniferous and deciduous forest. Exploitation and re-planting are closely controlled. Atlantic and Pacific fishing, particularly around Alaska, is mainly carried out within the 200 mile fishery zone.

America's first industrialised area lies to the south of the Great Lakes, and has gradually extended south and west to form one of the largest industrial zones in the world. Chicago is the main steel-producing town, while Pennsylvania and Pittsburgh are famous for their steel and chemical industries. Manufacturing industries are more predominant towards the east of this zone.

Most of the fastest growing industrial areas are along the west coast. These stretch from Seattle and Portland in the north to San Francisco, Oakland and San Jose in central California and to Los Angeles, Anaheim, Santa Ana and San Diego in the south. The main industries are vehicle manufacture, armaments, machinery, electrical goods, electronics, textiles and clothing and entertainment.

UPPER VOLTA
(see **BURKINA**)

URUGUAY

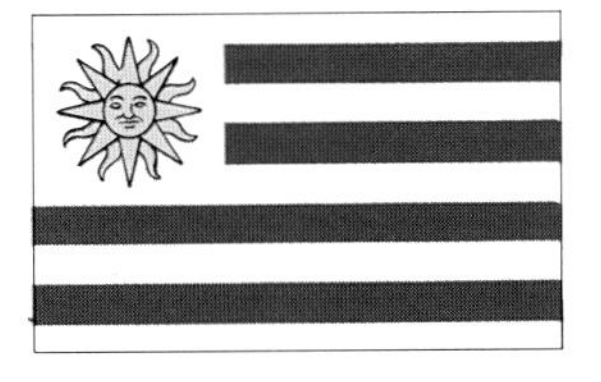

STATUS: Republic
AREA: 186,925 sq km (72,155 sq miles)
POPULATION: 3,080,000
ANNUAL NATURAL INCREASE: 0.9%
DENSITY: 16.5 per sq km
CAPITAL: Montevideo
LANGUAGE: Spanish
RELIGION: Roman Catholic
CURRENCY: Uruguayan new peso (N$)
ORGANISATIONS: UN, OAS

Situated on the coast of South America, Uruguay consists of a narrow coastal plain with rolling hills inland. Maximum elevation is around 200m(656ft). The temperate climate and adequate rainfall provide good agricultural potential but most of the land is given over to the grazing of sheep and cattle. The entire economy relies on the production of meat and wool. Most industry is devoted to food processing. 89% of the land area is farmed.

VANUATU

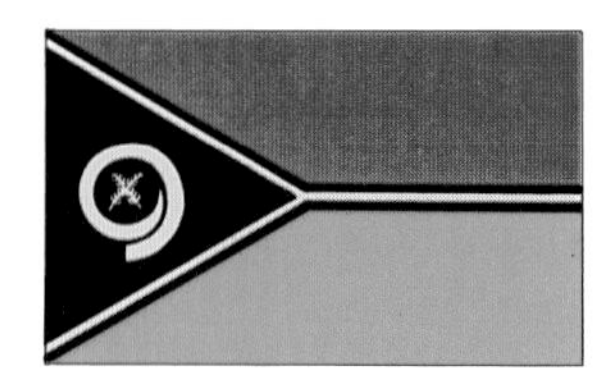

STATUS: Republic
AREA: 14,765 sq km (5,700 sq miles)
POPULATION: 149,400
ANNUAL NATURAL INCREASE: 3.6%
DENSITY: 10 per sq km
CAPITAL: Port Vila
LANGUAGE: Bislama, English, French, many Melanesian languages
RELIGION: Christian
CURRENCY: Vatu
ORGANISATIONS: Comm, UN

Vanuatu is a chain of densely forested, mountainous, volcanic islands in the South Pacific. Climate is tropical and cyclonic. Copra, cocoa and coffee are grown mainly for export. Fish, pigs and sheep are important for home consumption as well as yam, taro, manioc and bananas. Manganese is the only mineral.

VATICAN CITY

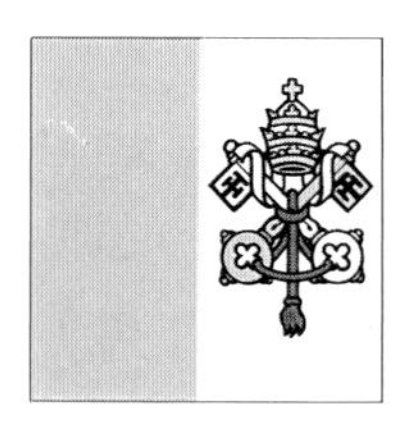

STATUS: Ecclesiastical State
AREA: 0.44 sq km (0.17 sq miles)
POPULATION: 766
DENSITY: Not applicable
LANGUAGE: Italian, Latin
RELIGION: Roman Catholic
CURRENCY: Italian lira, Papal coins

The headquarters of the Roman Catholic church, the Vatican in Rome is the world's smallest independent state. The papal residence since the 5th century AD, it is the destination for pilgrims and tourists from all over the world. Most income is derived from voluntary contributions and interest on investments. The only industries are those connected with the Church.

VENEZUELA

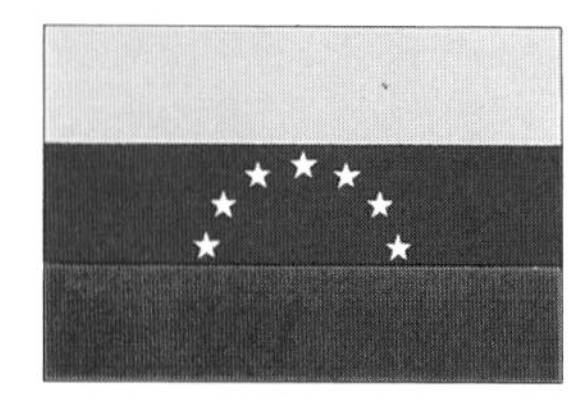

STATUS: Republic
AREA: 912,045 sq km (352,050 sq miles)
POPULATION: 18,770,000
ANNUAL NATURAL INCREASE: 2.7%
DENSITY: 20.6 per sq km
CAPITAL: Caracas
LANGUAGE: Spanish
RELIGION: Roman Catholic
CURRENCY: bolívar (B)
ORGANISATIONS: UN, OAS, OPEC

Venezuela, one of the richest countries of Latin America is divided into four topographic regions: the continuation of the Andes in the west; the humid lowlands around Lake Maracaibo in the north; the savannah-covered central plains (llanos) and the extension of the Guiana Highlands covering almost half the country. The climate varies between tropical in the south to warm temperate along the northern coasts. The economy is built around oil production in the Maracaibo region. Bauxite and iron ore are also important. The majority of employment is provided by industrial and manufacturing developments.

VIETNAM

STATUS: Socialist Republic
AREA: 329,566 sq km (127,246 sq miles)
POPULATION: 61,400,000
ANNUAL NATURAL INCREASE: 2.5%
DENSITY: 186.3 per sq km
CAPITAL: Hanoi
LANGUAGE: Vietnamese, French, Chinese
RELIGION: Buddhist
CURRENCY: dong
ORGANISATIONS: UN, COMECON

A long narrow country in South-East Asia, Vietnam has a mountainous backbone and two extensive river deltas: the Song Hong (Red River) in the north and the Mekong in the south. Monsoons bring 150cm(59in) of rain every year and rice is grown extensively throughout the north. Vietnam possesses a wide range of minerals including coal, lignite, anthracite, iron ore and tin. Industry is expanding rapidly, but decades of warfare and internal strife have impeded development.

VIRGIN ISLANDS (UK)

STATUS: UK Dependent Territory
AREA: 153 sq km (59 sq miles)
POPULATION: 13,000
CAPITAL: Road Town

VIRGIN ISLANDS (USA)

STATUS: External Territory of USA
AREA: 345 sq km (133 sq miles)
POPULATION: 106,000
CAPITAL: Charlotte Amalie

WALLIS & FUTUNA ISLANDS

STATUS: Self-governing Overseas Territory of France
AREA: 274 sq km (106 sq miles)
POPULATION: 15,400
CAPITAL: Mata-Utu

WESTERN SAMOA

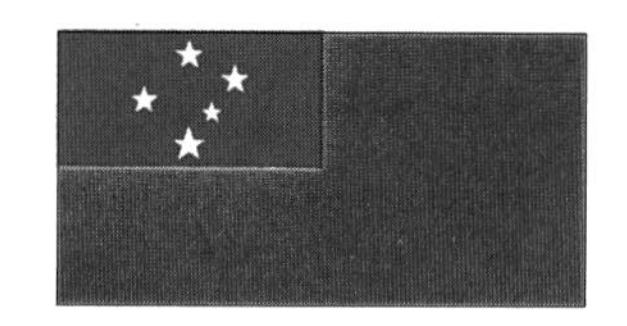

STATUS: Independent state
AREA: 2,840 sq km (1,095 sq miles)
POPULATION: 165,000
ANNUAL NATURAL INCREASE: 3.0%
DENSITY: 58.1 per sq km
CAPITAL: Apia
LANGUAGE: English, Samoan
RELIGION: local beliefs
CURRENCY: talà dollar ($WS)
ORGANISATIONS: Comm, UN

Nine volcanic tropical islands constitute this south Pacific state, of which only four are populated – Savaii, Upolu, Manono and Apolima. Annual rainfall is often 250cm(100in) per year. Temperatures average 26°C(79°F) for

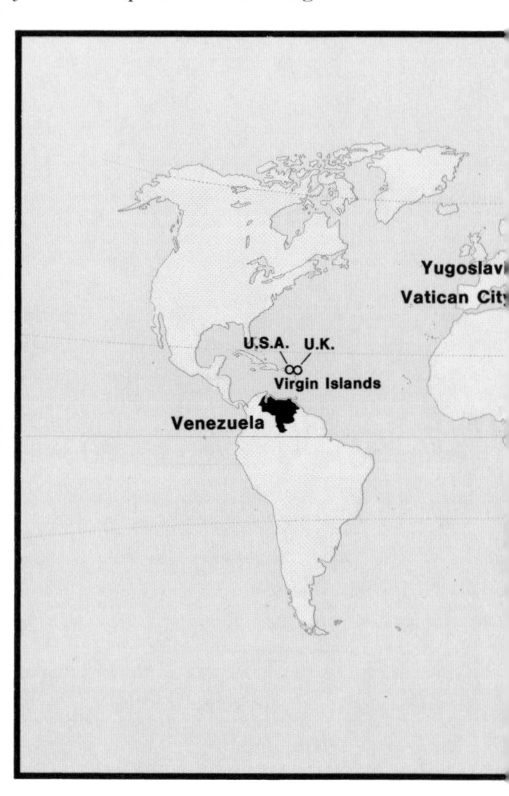

most months. Main exports are copra, timber, taro, cocoa and fruit. The only industries are food processing and timber products. Main imports are food products, consumer goods, machinery and animals.

WEST IRIAN
(see IRIAN JAYA)

WINDWARD ISLANDS
(see DOMINICA, GRENADA, MARTINIQUE, ST LUCIA & ST VINCENT)

WRANGEL ISLAND (VRANGELYA OSTROV)

STATUS: Island Territory of USSR
AREA: 7,250 sq km (2,800 sq miles)
POPULATION: No permanent population

YEMEN

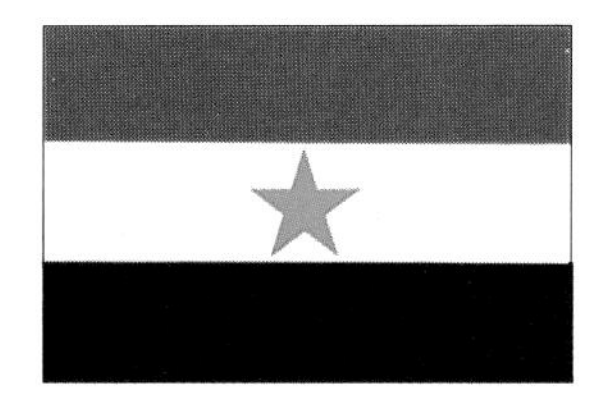

STATUS: Arab Republic
AREA: 189,850 sq km (73,280 sq miles)
POPULATION: 8,595,000
ANNUAL NATURAL INCREASE: 3.0%
DENSITY: 45.3 per sq km
CAPITAL: San'a
LANGUAGE: Arabic
RELIGION: Sunni and Shiite Moslem
CURRENCY: Yemeni riyal
ORGANISATIONS: UN, Arab League

Situated in the extreme south-west corner of the Arabian Peninsula, the Yemen Arab Republic is mountainous and relatively wet.

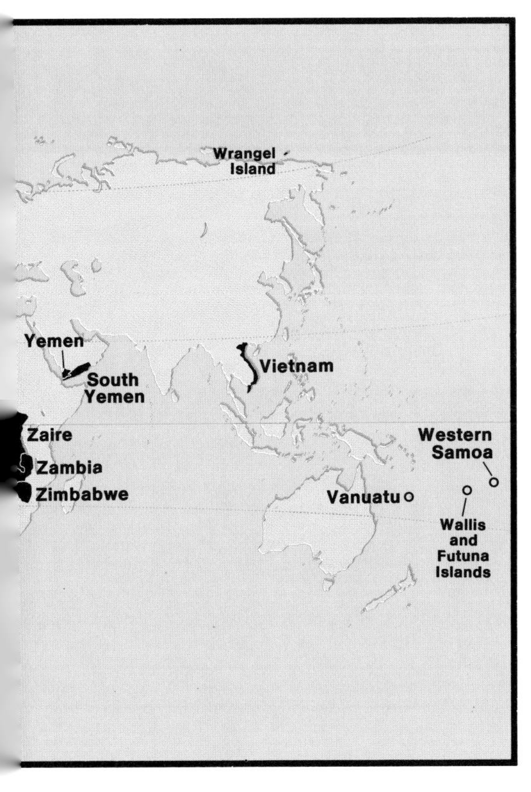

Temperatures vary between 14° and 22°C(57° and 70°F). Rainfall reaches 89cm(35in) inland and this helps to irrigate the cereals, cotton, coffee, fruits and vegetables which are mainly grown above 1500m(4920ft). Most of the population are farmers and herders of sheep and cattle. The main industries are textiles, cement and salt mining.

YEMEN, SOUTH

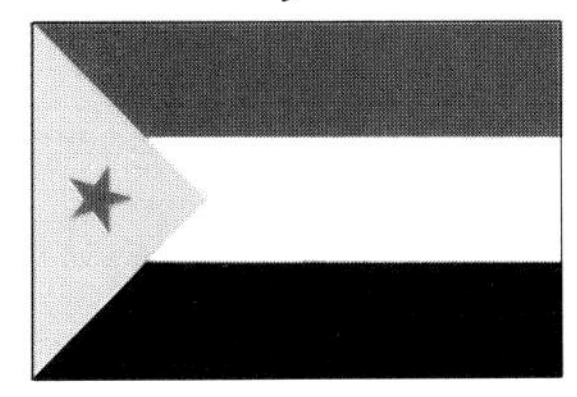

STATUS: People's Democratic Republic
AREA: 287,680 sq km (111,045 sq miles)
POPULATION: 2,345,266
ANNUAL NATURAL INCREASE: 3.0%
DENSITY: 8 per sq km
CAPITAL: Aden
LANGUAGE: Arabic
RELIGION: Sunni Moslem
CURRENCY: Yemeni dinar (YD)
ORGANISATIONS: UN, Arab League

This desert country stretches for 1100km(685 miles) along the south-east coast of Arabia from the mouth of the Red Sea to Oman. The narrow coastal plain fringes the wide irrigated Hadhramaut valley in which are grown sorghum, millet, wheat and barley. Main livestock are sheep, goats, cattle and poultry. Rainfall rarely exceeds 46mm(2in). Altitude of the inland desert restricts summer average temperature to 32°C(90°F). The country's major exports are cotton and fish.

YUGOSLAVIA

STATUS: Socialist Federal Republic
AREA: 255,805 sq km (98,740 sq miles)
POPULATION: 23,657,000
ANNUAL NATURAL INCREASE: 0.7%
DENSITY: 92.5 per sq km
CAPITAL: Belgrade (Beograd)
LANGUAGE: Serbo-Croat, Albanian, Macedonian, Slovene
RELIGION: 40% Orthodox Christian, 30% Roman Catholic
CURRENCY: dinar
ORGANISATIONS: UN

Yugoslavia is a federal union of very diverse republics. The long mountainous coastline, popular with tourists, enjoys a typical Mediterranean climate. The interior limestone 'karst' region has more extreme temperatures. The most productive areas, both agriculturally and industrially, are in the north and east. Cereals, root crops, cotton and fruit are grown. Mineral resources include iron ore, chrome, manganese, copper and lead.

ZAIRE

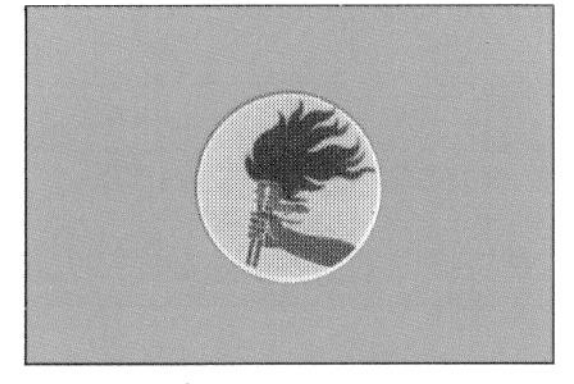

STATUS: Republic
AREA: 2,345,410 sq km (905,330 sq miles)
POPULATION: 32,564,000
ANNUAL NATURAL INCREASE: 2.8%
DENSITY: 13.9 per sq km
CAPITAL: Kinshasa
LANGUAGE: French, Kiswahili, Tshiluba, Kikongo, Lingala
RELIGION: traditional beliefs, 48% Roman Catholic, 13% Protestant
CURRENCY: zaïre
ORGANISATIONS: UN, OAU

Zaire, formerly the Belgian Congo, is Africa's second largest country and is dominated by the drainage basin of the Zaire river. The climate is very variable but basically equatorial with high temperatures and high rainfall. Soils are poor with the majority of the population engaged in shifting agriculture. Cassava, cocoa, coffee, cotton, millet, rubber and sugar-cane are grown. 60% of exports are minerals – copper, cobalt, diamonds, gold, manganese, uranium and zinc, with copper being the most important with 40% of total foreign exchange earnings. Zaire has abundant wildlife with tourism becoming increasingly important.

ZAMBIA

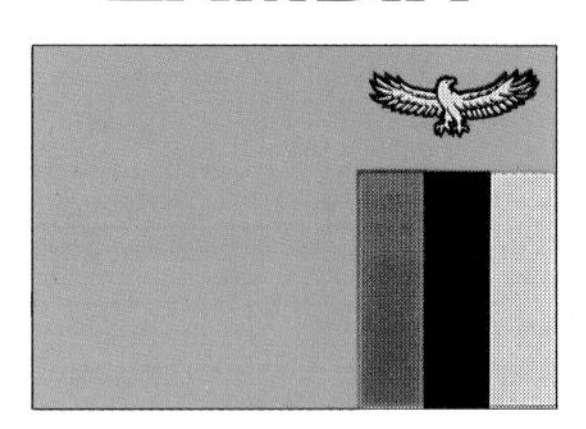

STATUS: Republic
AREA: 752,615 sq km (290,510 sq miles)
POPULATION: 7,531,000
ANNUAL NATURAL INCREASE: 3.3%
DENSITY: 10 per sq km
CAPITAL: Lusaka
LANGUAGE: English, African languages
RELIGION: 70% Christian, animist minority
CURRENCY: Kwacha (K)
ORGANISATIONS: Comm, UN, OAU

Mineral-rich Zambia consists mainly of high rolling plateaus. Altitude moderates the potentially tropical climate so that the summer temperature averages only 13°–27°C(55°–81°F). The north receives over 125cm(49in) of rain per annum, the south, less. Most of the country is grassland with some forest in the north. Farming is mainly at subsistence level. Copper, lead, zinc, cobalt and tobacco are the main exports. Wildlife is diverse and abundant and contributes to expanding tourism.

ZIMBABWE

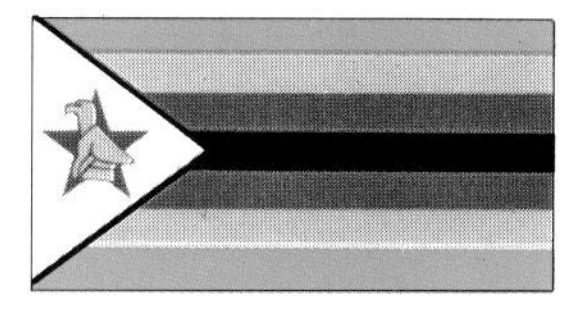

STATUS: Republic
AREA: 390,310 sq km (150,660 sq miles)
POPULATION: 8,870,000
ANNUAL NATURAL INCREASE: 3.5%
DENSITY: 22.7 per sq km
CAPITAL: Harare
LANGUAGE: English, Chishona, Sindebele
RELIGION: traditional beliefs, 20% Christian
CURRENCY: Zimbabwe dollar (Z$)
ORGANISATIONS: Comm, UN, OAU

Landlocked Zimbabwe consists of rolling plateaux (the high veld) 1,200–1,500m(3940–4920ft) and the low veld (the valleys of the Zambezi and Limpopo rivers). Altitude moderates the tropical climate of the high veld to temperate with low humidity. Mineral deposits include chrome, nickel, platinum and coal with gold and asbestos especially important. Tobacco, maize, tea and sugar-cane are grown. Manufacturing industry is slowly developing and now provides a wide range of consumer products.

North and Central America
25 349 000
9 785 000

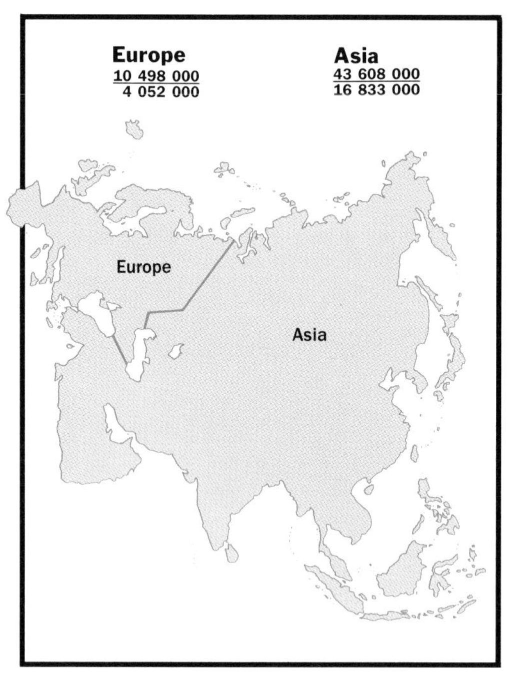

CONTINENTS

land area ▢ = 1 000 000 sq kms / 386 000 sq miles

Europe
10 498 000
4 052 000

Asia
43 608 000
16 833 000

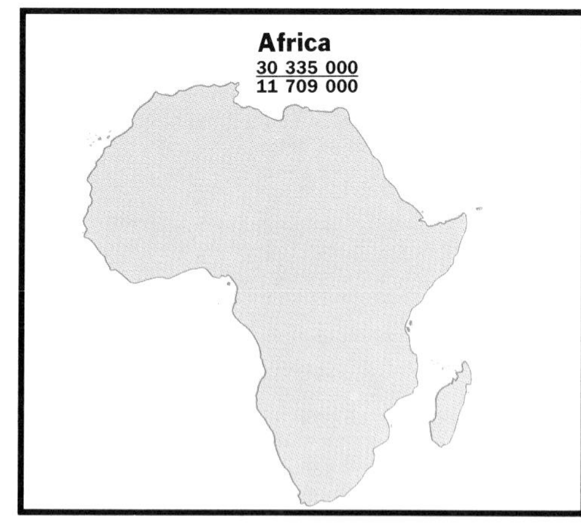

Europe

Asia

Africa
30 335 000
11 709 000

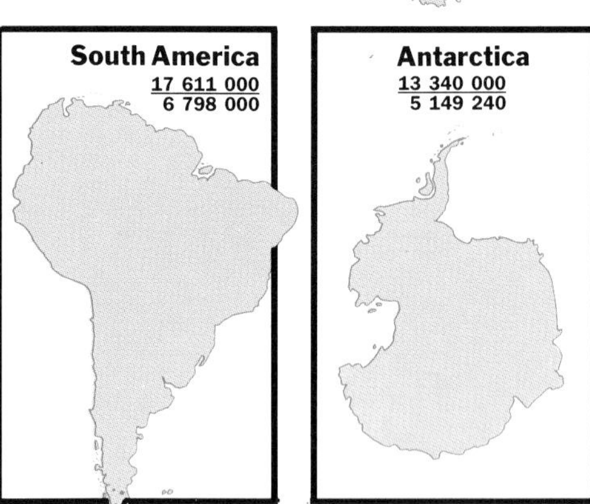

South America
17 611 000
6 798 000

Antarctica
13 340 000
5 149 240

Australasia
8 923 000
3 444 278

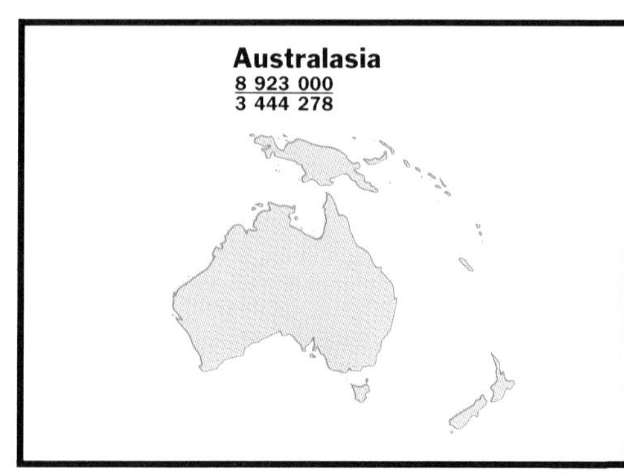

METROPOLITAN AREAS

Population	Metropolitan Area	Country
	ASIA	
2,548,057	Ahmadabad	India
2,251,533	Ankara	Turkey
2,517,080	Anshan	China
3,844,608	Baghdād	Iraq
2,921,751	Bangalore	India
5,670,692	Bangkok	Thailand
9,470,000	Beijing (Peking)	China
702,000	Beirut	Lebanon
8,243,405	Bombay	India
9,194,018	Calcutta	India
5,705,230	Changchun	China
2,459,920	Changsha	China
1,143,000	Cheyabinsk	USSR
4,025,180	Chengdu	China
6,511,130	Chongqing	China
3,430,312	Dhaka	Bangladesh
4,619,060	Dalian	China
2,500,000	Damascus	Syria
5,729,283	Delhi	India
2,045,150	Fushun	China
5,669,640	Guangzhou (Canton)	China
5,234,150	Hangzhou	China
2,878,000	Hanoi	Vietnam
2,670,000	Harbin	China
5,613,400	Hong Kong	UK colony
2,545,836	Hyderabad	India
7,347,800	Jakarta	Indonesia
482,700	Jerusalem	Israel
3,974,260	Jilin	China
3,375,830	Jinan	China
2,000,000	Kābul	Afghanistan
5,180,562	Karachi	Pakistan
937,875	Kuala Lumpur	Malaysia
2,952,689	Lahore	Pakistan
2,339,750	Lanzhou	China
4,289,347	Madras	India
6,720,050	Manila – Quezon City	Philippines
2,099,564	Nagoya	Japan
2,471,070	Nanchang	China
3,682,270	Nanjing	China
1,436,000	Novosibirsk	USSR
8,594,000	Osaka-Kobe	Japan
3,516,768	Pusan	South Korea
2,639,448	Pyôngyang	North Korea
4,204,840	Qingdao	China
2,458,712	Rangoon	Burma
4,000,000	Saigon (Ho Chi Minh)	Vietnam
9,645,824	Seoul	South Korea
12,050,000	Shanghai	China
5,054,640	Shenyang	China
2,647,100	Singapore	Singapore
2,223,600	Surabaya	Indonesia
2,030,649	Taegu	South Korea
7,990,000	Tianjin	China
2,640,000	Taipei	Taiwan
2,176,880	Taiyuan	China
2,073,000	Tashkent	USSR
6,042,584	Tehrān	Iran
11,680,282	Tokyo	Japan
4,273,080	Wuhan	China
2,911,580	Xian	China
2,300,000	Zibo	China
	EUROPE	
1,030,743	Amsterdam	Netherlands
3,027,331	Athens	Greece
1,703,744	Barcelona	Spain
1,407,073	Belgrade	Yugoslavia
3,236,009	Berlin	East and West Germany
2,311,000	Birmingham	UK
970,346	Brussels	Belgium
2,272,526	Bucharest	Romania
3,962,000	Budapest	Hungary
1,343,916	Copenhagen	Denmark
920,956	Dublin	Rep. of Ireland
2,745,700	Essen – Dortmund	West Germany
384,507	Geneva	Switzerland
1,593,600	Hamburg	West Germany
5,494,916	Istanbul	Turkey
2,587,000	Kiev	USSR
5,020,000	Leningrad	USSR
1,611,887	Lisbon	Portugal
9,021,683	London	UK
3,100,507	Madrid	Spain
2,577,700	Manchester	UK
1,589,000	Minsk	USSR
8,967,000	Moscow	USSR
1,115,000	Odessa	USSR
453,730	Oslo	Norway
8,510,000	Paris	France
1,200,266	Prague	Czechoslovakia
2,817,227	Rome	Italy
1,128,859	Sofia	Bulgaria
1,617,038	Stockholm	Sweden
1,531,000	Vienna	Austria
999,000	Volgograd	USSR
1,671,400	Warsaw	Poland
1,119,000	Yerevan	USSR
1,174,512	Zagreb	Yugoslavia
	AFRICA	
2,000,000	Abidjan	Côte d'Ivoire
1,464,901	Addis Ababa	Ethiopia
4,000,000	Alexandria	Egypt
2,600,000	Algiers	Algeria
13,300,000	Cairo	Egypt
1,911,521	Cape Town	South Africa
2,904,000	Casablanca	Morocco
1,096,000	Dar-es-Salaam	Tanzania
1,609,408	Johannesburg	South Africa
1,343,651	Khartoum	Sudan

2,653,558	Kinshasa	Zaire
4,200,000	Lagos	Nigeria
1,288,700	Nairobi	Kenya
	NORTH & CENTRAL AMERICA	
2,657,000	Atlanta	USA
2,303,000	Baltimore	USA
2,842,000	Boston	USA
6,199,000	Chicago	USA
3,725,000	Dallas – Fort Worth	USA
4,362,000	Detroit	USA
3,044,000	Guadalajara	Mexico
2,025,700	Havana	Cuba
3,228,000	Houston	USA
13,471,000	Los Angeles	USA
18,748,000	Mexico City	Mexico
2,954,000	Miami – Fort Lauderdale	USA
2,336,000	Minneapolis – St Paul	USA
2,335,000	Monterrey	Mexico
2,921,357	Montreal	Canada
18,054,000	New York	USA
819,263	Ottawa	Canada
4,866,000	Philadelphia	USA
1,960,000	Phoenix	USA
2,105,000	Pittsburg	USA
603,267	Quebec	Canada
1,336,000	Sacramento	USA
2,286,000	San Diego	USA
3,558,000	San Francisco – Oakland	USA
1,816,300	San Juan	Puerto Rico
1,550,739	Santo Domingo	Dominican Republic
2,458,000	St Louis	USA
3,427,168	Toronto	Canada
1,380,729	Vancouver	Canada
3,646,000	Washington DC	USA
600,700	Winnipeg	Canada
	SOUTH AMERICA	
3,475,541	Belo Horizonte	Brazil
4,486,000	Bogotá	Colombia
1,683,700	Brasília	Brazil
12,600,000	Buenos Aires	Argentina
3,247,698	Caracas	Venezuela
4,605,043	Lima	Peru
2,200,000	Medellín	Colombia
1,309,100	Montevideo	Uruguay
2,886,101	Pôrto Alegre	Brazil
1,093,278	Quito	Ecuador
2,912,016	Recife	Brazil
10,980,015	Rio de Janeiro	Brazil
2,329,604	Salvador	Brazil
4,858,342	Santiago	Chile
16,710,013	São Paulo	Brazil
	AUSTRALASIA	
842,000	Auckland	New Zealand
297,000	Canberra	Australia
3,001,000	Melbourne	Australia
3,594,000	Sydney	Australia
325,200	Wellington	New Zealand

MOUNTAIN HEIGHTS

metres feet

metres	feet		
8,848	29,028	**Everest (Qomolangma Feng)**	*China–Nepal*
8,611	28,250	**K2 (Qogir Feng) (Godwin Austen)**	*India–China*
8,598	28,170	**Kangchenjunga**	*India–Nepal*
8,481	27,824	**Makalu**	*China–Nepal*
8,167	26,795	**Dhaulagiri**	*Nepal*
8,156	26,758	**Manaslu**	*Nepal*
8,153	26,749	**Cho Oyu**	*China–Nepal*
8,125	26,657	**Nanga Parbat**	*India*
8,091	26,545	**Annapurna**	*Nepal*
8,088	26,470	**Gasherbrum**	*India–China*
8,027	26,335	**Xixabangma Feng (Gosainthan)**	*China*
7,885	25,869	**Distaghil Sar**	*India, Kashmir*
7,820	25,656	**Masherbrum**	*India*
7,816	25,643	**Nanda Devi**	*India*
7,788	25,550	**Rakaposhi**	*India*
7,756	25,446	**Kamet**	*China–India*
7,756	25,447	**Namjagbarwa Feng**	*China*
7,728	25,355	**Gurla Mandhata**	*China*
7,723	25,338	**Muztag**	*China*
7,719	25,325	**Kongur**	*China*
7,690	25,230	**Tirich Mir**	*Pakistan*
7,546	24,757	**Muztagata**	*China*
7,514	24,652	**Gongga Shan (Minya Konka)**	*China*
7,495	24,590	**Pik Kommunizma**	*USSR*
7,439	24,406	**Pik Pobedy (Tomur Feng)**	*USSR–China*
7,313	23,993	**Chomo Lhari**	*Bhutan–Tibet*
7,134	23,406	**Pik Lenina**	*USSR*
6,960	22,834	**Aconcagua**	*Argentina*
6,908	22,664	**Ojos del Salado**	*Argentina–Chile*
6,872	22,546	**Bonete**	*Argentina*
6,800	22,310	**Tupungato**	*Argentina–Chile*
6,770	22,211	**Mercedario**	*Argentina*
6,768	22,205	**Huascarán**	*Peru*
6,723	22,057	**Llullaillaco**	*Argentina–Chile*
6,714	22,027	**Kangrinboqê Feng (Kailas)**	*China, Tibet*
6,634	21,765	**Yerupaja**	*Peru*
6,542	21,463	**Sajama**	*Bolivia*
6,485	21,276	**Illampu**	*Bolivia*
6,425	21,079	**Coropuna**	*Peru*
6,402	21,004	**Illimani**	*Bolivia*
6,310	20,702	**Chimborazo**	*Ecuador*
6,194	20,320	**McKinley**	*USA*
5,951	19,524	**Logan**	*Canada*
5,896	19,344	**Cotopaxi**	*Ecuador*
5,895	19,340	**Kilimanjaro**	*Tanzania*
5,775	18,947	**Santa Marta (Cristobal Colon)**	*Colombia*
5,775	18,947	**Bolivar**	*Colombia*
5,671	18,605	**Damávand**	*Iran*
5,642	18,510	**El'brus**	*USSR*
5,610	18,405	**Citlatépetl (Orizaba)**	*Mexico*
5,489	18,008	**Mt St. Elias**	*Canada*
5,227	17,149	**Mt Lucania**	*Canada*
5,200	17,058	**Kirinyaga (Kenya)**	*Kenya*
5,140	16,860	**Vinson Massif**	*Antarctica*
5,123	16,808	**Büyük Aǧri (Ararat)**	*Turkey*
5,110	16,763	**Stanley (Margherita)**	*Uganda–Zaire*
5,030	16,503	**Jaya (Carstensz)**	*Indonesia*
5,005	16,421	**Mt Bona**	*USA*
4,996	16,391	**Mt Blackburn**	*Canada*
4,949	16,237	**Sanford**	*USA*
4,807	15,770	**Mont Blanc**	*France–Italy*
4,750	15,584	**Klyuchevskaya Sopka**	*USSR*
4,634	15,203	**Monte Rosa (Dufour)**	*Italy–Switzerland*
4,620	15,157	**Ras Dashen**	*Ethiopia*
4,565	14,979	**Meru**	*Tanzania*
4,545	14,910	**Dom (Mischabel)**	*Switzerland*
4,528	14,855	**Kirkpatrick**	*Antarctica*
4,508	14,790	**Wilhelm**	*Papua, New Guinea*
4,507	14,786	**Karisimbi**	*Rwanda–Zaire*
4,478	14,691	**Matterhorn**	*Italy–Switzerland*
4,418	14,495	**Whitney**	*USA*
4,398	14,431	**Elbert**	*USA*
4,392	14,410	**Rainier**	*USA*
4,351	14,275	**Markham**	*Antarctica*
4,321	14,178	**Elgon**	*Kenya–Uganda*
4,307	14,131	**Batu**	*Ethiopia*
4,205	13,796	**Mauna Kea**	*USA, Hawaii*
4,169	13,677	**Mauna Loa**	*USA, Hawaii*
4,165	13,664	**Toubkal**	*Morocco*
4,095	13,435	**Caméroun**	*Cameroon*
4,094	13,431	**Kinabalu**	*Malaysia*
3,794	12,447	**Erebus**	*Antarctica*
3,776	12,388	**Fuji**	*Japan*
3,764	12,349	**Cook**	*New Zealand*
3,718	12,198	**Teide**	*Canary Is*
3,482	11,424	**Thabana Ntlenyana**	*Lesotho*
3,482	11,424	**Mulhacén**	*Spain*
3,415	11,204	**Emi Koussi**	*Chad*
3,323	10,902	**Etna**	*Italy, Sicily*
2,743	9,000	**Mt Balbi**	*Bougainville, Papua, New Guinea*
2,655	8,708	**Gerlachovsky stit (Tatra)**	*Czechoslovakia*
2,230	7,316	**Kosciusko**	*Australia*

ISLANDS

land area □ = 10 000 sq kms / 3 860 sq miles

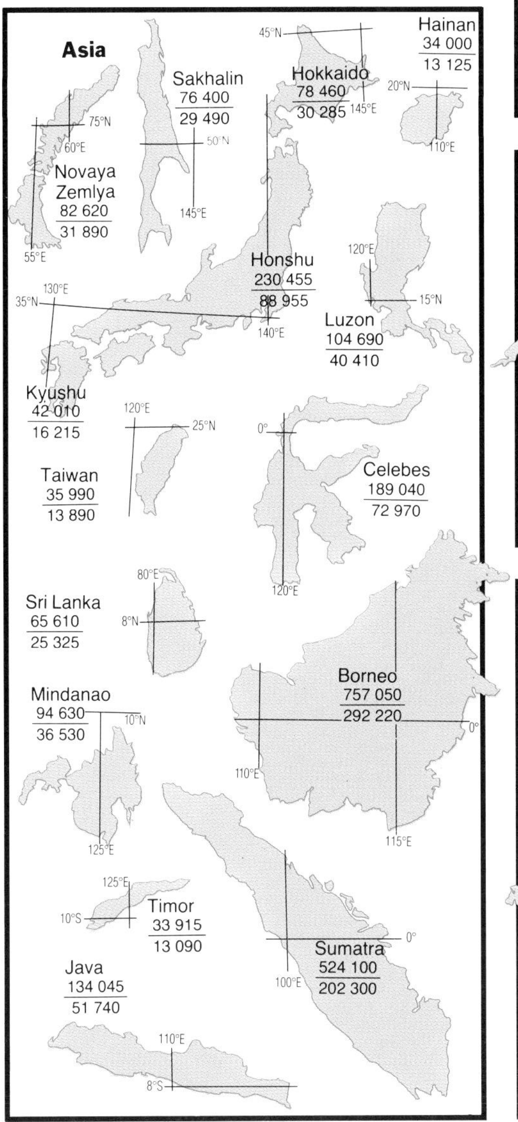

Asia

Sakhalin 76 400 / 29 490
Hokkaido 78 460 / 30 285
Hainan 34 000 / 13 125
Novaya Zemlya 82 620 / 31 890
Honshu 230 455 / 88 955
Luzon 104 690 / 40 410
Kyushu 42 010 / 16 215
Taiwan 35 990 / 13 890
Celebes 189 040 / 72 970
Sri Lanka 65 610 / 25 325
Borneo 757 050 / 292 220
Mindanao 94 630 / 36 530
Timor 33 915 / 13 090
Java 134 045 / 51 740
Sumatra 524 100 / 202 300

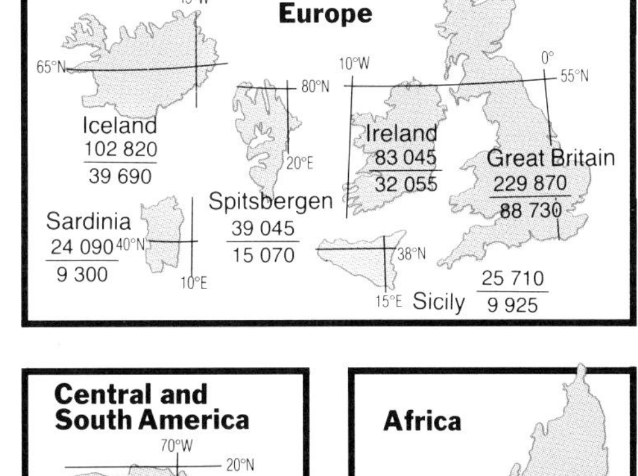

Europe

Iceland 102 820 / 39 690
Ireland 83 045 / 32 055
Great Britain 229 870 / 88 730
Sardinia 24 090 / 9 300
Spitsbergen 39 045 / 15 070
Sicily 25 710 / 9 925

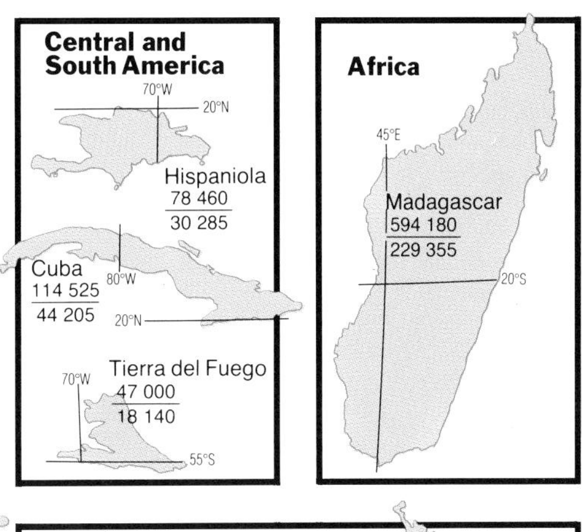

Central and South America

Hispaniola 78 460 / 30 285
Cuba 114 525 / 44 205
Tierra del Fuego 47 000 / 18 140

Africa

Madagascar 594 180 / 229 355

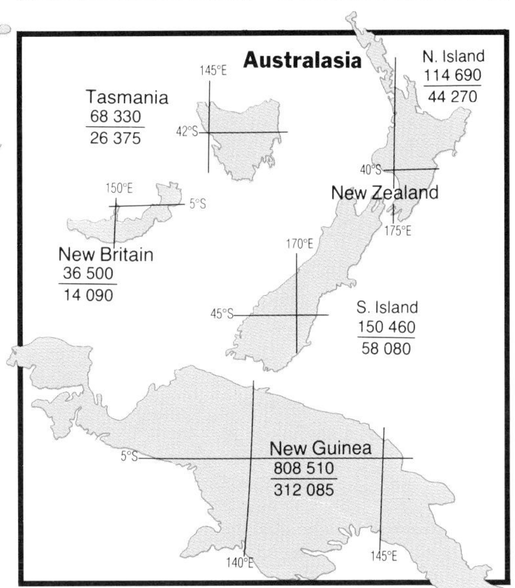

Australasia

Tasmania 68 330 / 26 375
N. Island 114 690 / 44 270
New Zealand
New Britain 36 500 / 14 090
S. Island 150 460 / 58 080
New Guinea 808 510 / 312 085

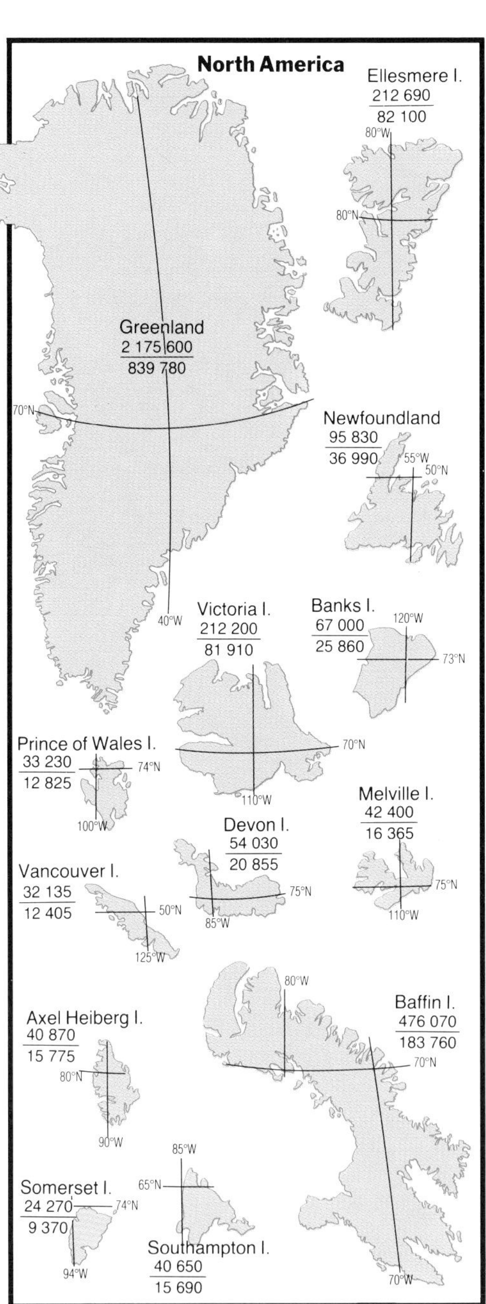

North America

Ellesmere I. 212 690 / 82 100
Greenland 2 175 600 / 839 780
Newfoundland 95 830 / 36 990
Victoria I. 212 200 / 81 910
Banks I. 67 000 / 25 860
Prince of Wales I. 33 230 / 12 825
Devon I. 54 030 / 20 855
Melville I. 42 400 / 16 365
Vancouver I. 32 135 / 12 405
Axel Heiberg I. 40 870 / 15 775
Baffin I. 476 070 / 183 760
Somerset I. 24 270 / 9 370
Southampton I. 40 650 / 15 690

OCEANS AND SEAS

water area ☐ = $\dfrac{1\ 000\ 000\quad \text{sq km}}{386\ 000\quad \text{sq miles}}$

OCEAN FACTS AND FIGURES

The area of the Earth covered by sea is estimated to be 361,740,000 sq km (139,670,000 sq miles), or 70.92% of the total surface. The mean depth is estimated to be 3554 m (11,660 ft), and the volume of the oceans to be 1,285,600,000 cu. km (308,400,000 cu. miles).

INDIAN OCEAN

Mainly confined to the southern hemisphere, and at its greatest breadth (Tasmania to Cape Agulhas) 9600 km. Average depth is 4000 m; greatest depth is the Amirante Trench (9000 m).

ATLANTIC OCEAN

Commonly divided into North Atlantic (36,000,000 sq km) and South Atlantic (26,000,000 sq km). The greatest breadth in the North is 7200 km (Morocco to Florida) and in the South 9600 km (Guinea to Brazil). Average depth is 3600 m; the greatest depths are the Puerto Rico Trench 9220 m, S. Sandwich Trench 8264 m, and Romansh Trench 7728 m.

PACIFIC OCEAN

Covers nearly 40% of the world's total sea area, and is the largest of the oceans. The greatest breadth (E/W) is 16,000 km and the greatest length (N/S) 11,000 km. Average depth is 4200 m; also the deepest ocean. Generally the west is deeper than the east and the north deeper than the south. Greatest depths occur near island groups and include Mindanao Trench 11,524 m, Mariana Trench 11,022 m, Tonga Trench 10,882 m, Kuril-Kamchatka Trench 10,542 m, Philippine Trench 10,497 m, and Kermadec Trench 10,047 m.

Comparisons (where applicable)	greatest distance N/S (km)	greatest distance E/W (km)	maximum depth (m)
Indian Ocean	—	9600	9000
Atlantic Ocean	—	9600	9220
Pacific Ocean	11,000	16,000	11,524
Arctic Ocean	—	—	5450
Mediterranean Sea	960	3700	4846
S. China Sea	2100	1750	5514
Bering Sea	1800	2100	5121
Caribbean Sea	1600	2000	7100
Gulf of Mexico	1200	1700	4377
Sea of Okhotsk	2200	1400	3475
E. China Sea	1100	750	2999
Yellow Sea	800	1000	91
Hudson Bay	1250	1050	259
Sea of Japan	1500	1100	3743
North Sea	1200	550	661
Red Sea	1932	360	2246
Black Sea	600	1100	2245
Baltic Sea	1500	650	460

EARTH'S SURFACE WATERS

Total volume	c.1400 million cu. km
Oceans and seas	1370 million cu. km
Ice	24 million cu. km
Interstitial water (in rocks and sediments)	4 million cu. km
Lakes and rivers	230 thousand cu. km
Atmosphere (vapour)	c.140 thousand cu. km

to convert metric to imperial measurements:
1 m = 3.281 feet
1 km = 0.621 miles
1 sq km = 0.386 sq miles

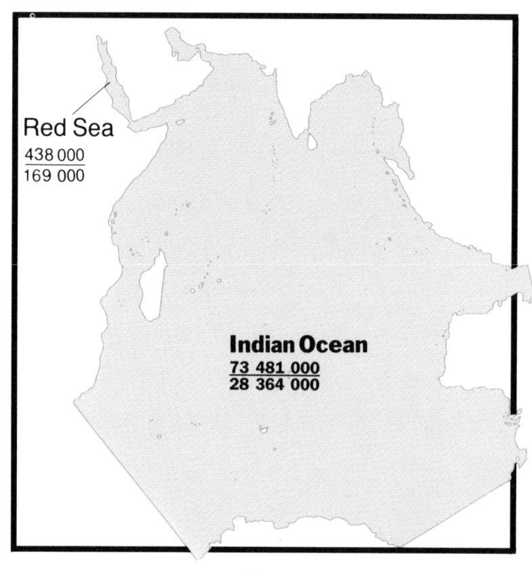

Red Sea
438 000
169 000

Indian Ocean
73 481 000
28 364 000

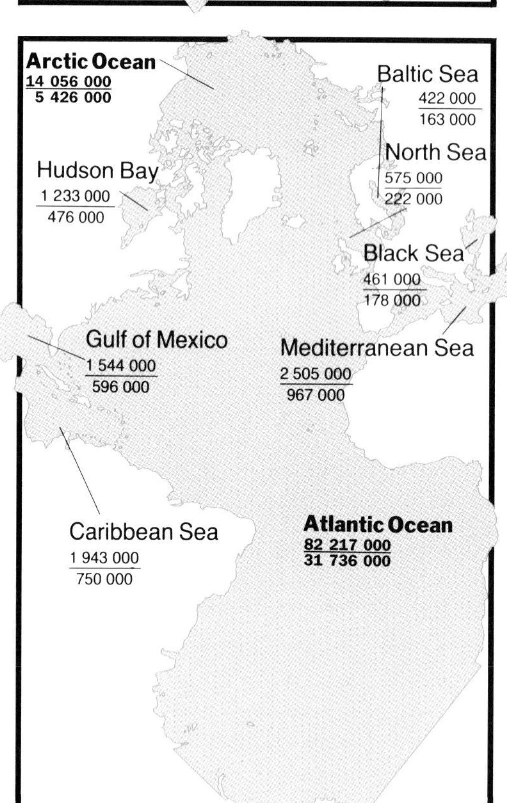

Arctic Ocean
14 056 000
5 426 000

Baltic Sea
422 000
163 000

Hudson Bay
1 233 000
476 000

North Sea
575 000
222 000

Black Sea
461 000
178 000

Gulf of Mexico
1 544 000
596 000

Mediterranean Sea
2 505 000
967 000

Caribbean Sea
1 943 000
750 000

Atlantic Ocean
82 217 000
31 736 000

FEATURES OF THE OCEAN BASIN

The majority of land drainage occurs in the Atlantic, yet this is the most saline ocean due to interchange of waters with its marginal seas. The continental margins (21% of ocean floors) are the most important economic areas.

	PACIFIC	ATLANTIC	INDIAN	WORLD
AVERAGE OCEAN DEPTH (metres)				
3000				
3500				
4000				
OCEAN AREA (million sq km)	180	107	74	361
LAND AREA DRAINED (million sq km)	19	69	13	101
AREA AS PERCENTAGE OF TOTAL				
Continental margin	15.8	27.9	14.8	20.6
Ridges, rises and fracture zones	38.4	33.3	35.6	35.8
Deep ocean floor	42.9	38.1	49.3	41.9
Island arcs and trenches	2.9	0.7	0.3	1.7

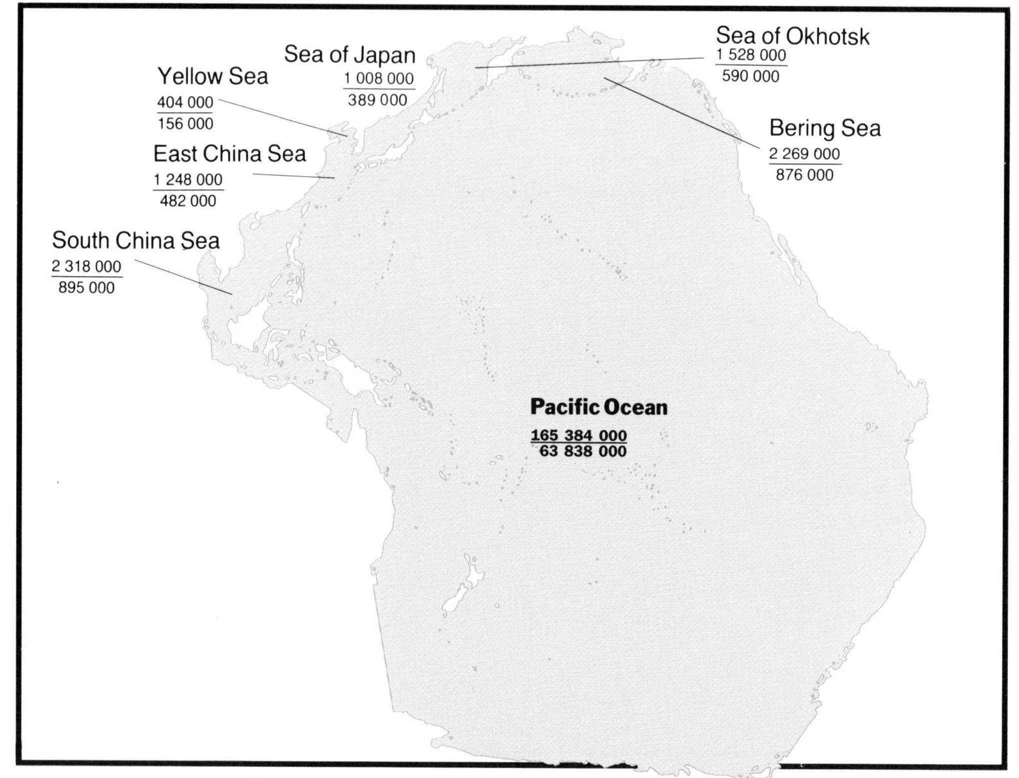

Sea of Japan
1 008 000
389 000

Sea of Okhotsk
1 528 000
590 000

Yellow Sea
404 000
156 000

Bering Sea
2 269 000
876 000

East China Sea
1 248 000
482 000

South China Sea
2 318 000
895 000

Pacific Ocean
165 384 000
63 838 000

RIVER LENGTHS

km	miles	
6,695	4,160	**Nile** *Africa*
6,515	4,050	**Amazon** *South America*
6,380	3,965	**Chang Jiang (Yangtze)** *Asia*
6,019	3,740	**Mississippi-Missouri** *North America*
5,570	3,460	**Ob'-Irtysh** *Asia*
5,550	3,450	**Yenisey-Angara** *Asia*
5,464	3,395	**Huang He (Yellow River)** *Asia*
4,667	2,900	**Zaire (Congo)** *Africa*
4,500	2,800	**Paraná** *South America*
4,440	2,775	**Irtysh** *Asia*
4,425	2,750	**Mekong** *Asia*
4,416	2,744	**Amur** *Asia*
4,400	1,730	**Lena** *Asia*
4,250	2,640	**Mackenzie** *North America*
4,090	2,556	**Yenisey** *Asia*
4,030	2,505	**Niger** *Africa*
3,969	2,466	**Missouri** *North America*
3,779	2,348	**Mississippi** *North America*
3,750	2,330	**Murray-Darling** *Australasia*
3,688	2,290	**Volga** *Europe*
3,218	2,011	**Purus** *South America*
3,200	1,990	**Madeira** *South America*
3,185	1,980	**Yukon** *North America*
3,180	1,975	**Indus** *Asia*
3,078	1,913	**Syrdar'ya** *Asia*
3,060	1,901	**Salween** *Asia*
3,058	1,900	**St Lawrence** *North America*
2,900	1,800	**São Francisco** *South America*
2,870	1,785	**Rio Grande** *North America*
2,850	1,770	**Danube** *Europe*
2,840	1,765	**Brahmaputra** *Asia*
2,815	1,750	**Euphrates** *Asia*
2,750	1,710	**Pará-Tocantins** *South America*
2,750	1,718	**Tarim** *Asia*
2,650	1,650	**Zambezi** *Africa*
2,620	1,630	**Amudar'ya** *Asia*
2,620	1,630	**Araguaia** *South America*
2,600	1,615	**Paraguay** *South America*
2,570	1,600	**Nelson-Saskatchewan** *North America*

km	miles	
2,534	1,575	**Ural** *Asia*
2,513	1,562	**Kolyma** *Asia*
2,510	1,560	**Ganges (Ganga)** *Asia*
2,500	1,555	**Orinoco** *South America*
2,490	1,550	**Shabeelle** *Africa*
2,490	1,550	**Pilcomayo** *South America*
2,348	1,459	**Arkansas** *North America*
2,333	1,450	**Colorado** *North America*
2,285	1,420	**Dnepr** *Europe*
2,250	1,400	**Columbia** *North America*
2,150	1,335	**Irrawaddy** *Asia*
2,129	1,323	**Xi Jiang (Pearl)** *Asia*
2,032	1,270	**Kama** *Europe*
2,000	1,240	**Negro** *South America*
1,923	1,195	**Peace** *North America*
1,899	1,186	**Tigris** *Asia*
1,870	1,162	**Don** *Europe*
1,860	1,155	**Orange** *Africa*
1,809	1,124	**Pechora** *Europe*
1,800	1,125	**Okavango** *Africa*
1,609	1,000	**Marañón** *South America*
1,609	1,005	**Uruguay** *South America*
1,600	1,000	**Volta** *Africa*
1,600	1,000	**Limpopo** *Africa*
1,550	963	**Magdalena** *South America*
1,515	946	**Kura** *Asia*
1,480	925	**Oka** *Europe*
1,445	903	**Godavari** *Asia*
1,430	893	**Senegal** *Africa*
1,480	925	**Belaya** *Europe*
1,410	876	**Dnestr** *Europe*
1,400	875	**Chari** *Africa*
1,368	850	**Fraser** *North America*
1,320	820	**Rhine** *Europe*
1,314	821	**Vyatka** *Europe*
1,183	735	**Donets** *Europe*
1,159	720	**Elbe** *Europe*
1,151	719	**Kizilirmak** *Asia*

km	miles	
1,130	706	**Desna** *Europe*
1,094	680	**Gambia** *Africa*
1,080	675	**Yellowstone** *North America*
1,049	652	**Tennessee** *North America*
1,024	640	**Zelenga** *Asia*
1,020	637	**Duena** *Europe*
1,014	630	**Wisła (Vistula)** *Europe*
1,012	629	**Loire** *Europe*
1,006	625	**Tejo (Tagus)** *Europe*
977	607	**Tisza** *Europe*
925	575	**Meuse (Maas)** *Europe*
909	565	**Oder** *Europe*
761	473	**Seine** *Europe*
354	220	**Severn** *Europe*
346	215	**Thames** *Europe*
300	186	**Trent** *Europe*

DRAINAGE BASINS

sq km	sq miles	
7,050,000	2,721,000	**Amazon** *South America*
3,700,000	1,428,000	**Congo** *Africa*
3,250,000	1,255,000	**Mississippi-Missouri** *North America*
3,100,000	1,197,000	**Paraná** *South America*
2,700,000	1,042,000	**Yenisey** *Asia*
2,430,000	938,000	**Ob'** *Asia*
2,420,000	934,000	**Lena** *Asia*
1,900,000	733,400	**Nile** *Africa*
1,840,000	710,000	**Amur** *Asia*
1,765,000	681,000	**Mackenzie** *North America*
1,730,000	668,000	**Ganges-Brahmaputra** *Asia*
1,380,000	533,000	**Volga** *Europe*
1,330,000	513,000	**Zambezi** *Africa*
1,200,000	463,000	**Niger** *Africa*
1,175,000	454,000	**Chang Jiang** *Asia*
1,020,000	394,000	**Orange** *Africa*
980,000	378,000	**Huang He** *Asia*
960,000	371,000	**Indus** *Asia*
945,000	365,000	**Orinoco** *South America*
910,000	351,000	**Murray-Darling** *Australasia*
855,000	330,000	**Yukon** *North America*
815,000	315,000	**Danube** *Europe*
810,000	313,000	**Mekong** *Asia*
225,000	86,900	**Rhine** *Europe*

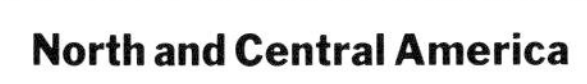

North and Central America

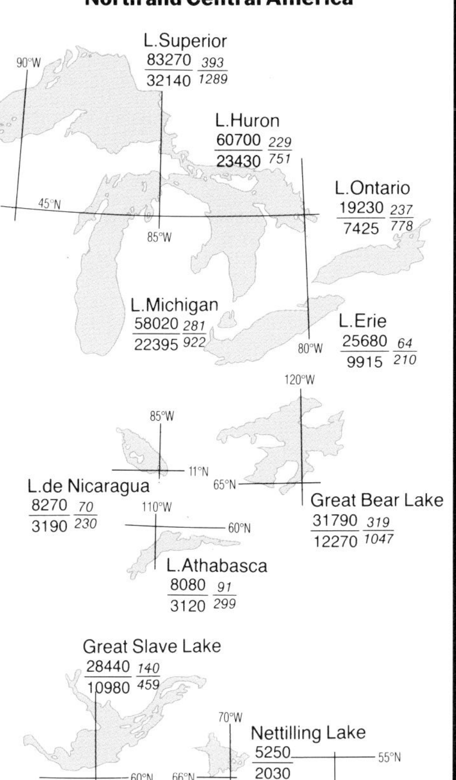

L.Superior 83270 *393* / 32140 *1289*
L.Huron 60700 *229* / 23430 *751*
L.Ontario 19230 *237* / 7425 *778*
L.Michigan 58020 *281* / 22395 *922*
L.Erie 25680 *64* / 9915 *210*
L.de Nicaragua 8270 *70* / 3190 *230*
Great Bear Lake 31790 *319* / 12270 *1047*
L.Athabasca 8080 *91* / 3120 *299*
Great Slave Lake 28440 *140* / 10980 *459*
Nettilling Lake 5250 / 2030
L.Winnipeg 24510 *21* / 9460 *69*
Reindeer Lake 6390 / 2470

INLAND WATERS

water surface area □ = 1 000 sq km / 386 sq miles

deepest point 229 metres / 751 feet

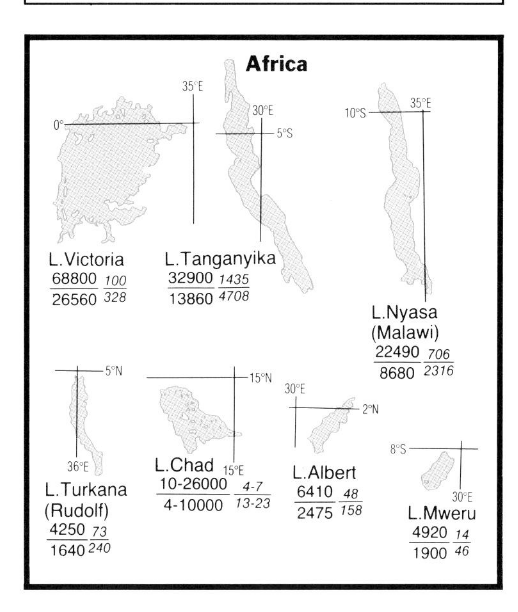

Africa

L.Victoria 68800 *100* / 26560 *328*
L.Tanganyika 32900 *1435* / 13860 *4708*
L.Nyasa (Malawi) 22490 *706* / 8680 *2316*
L.Turkana (Rudolf) 10-26000 *4-7* / 4-10000 *13-23*
L.Chad 4250 *73* / 1640 *240*
L.Albert 6410 *48* / 2475 *158*
L.Mweru 4920 *14* / 1900 *46*

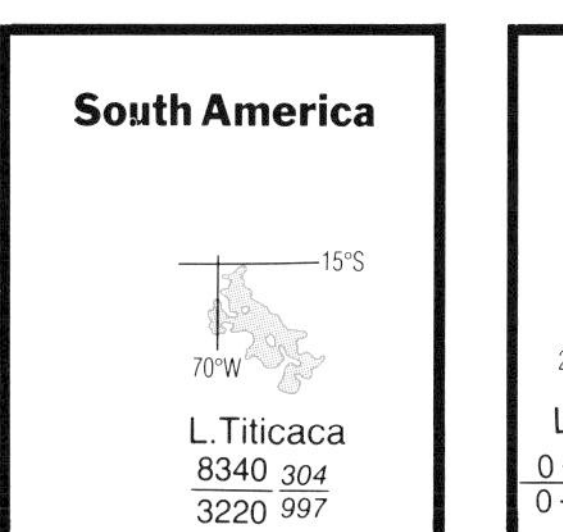

South America

L.Titicaca 8340 *304* / 3220 *997*

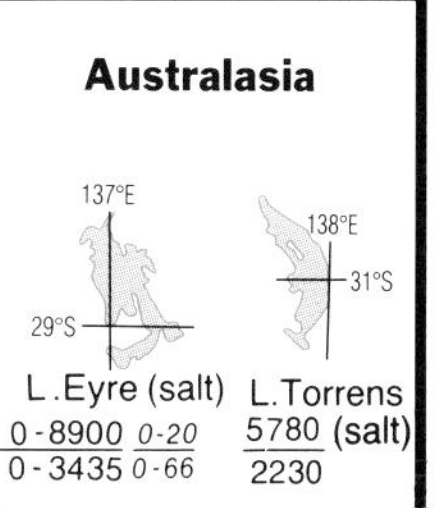

Australasia

L.Eyre (salt) 0-8900 *0-20* / 0-3435 *0-66*
L.Torrens 5780 (salt) / 2230

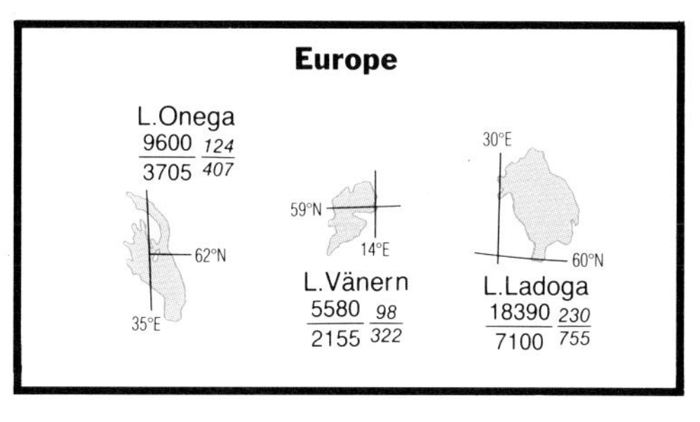

Europe

L.Onega 9600 *124* / 3705 *407*
L.Vänern 5580 *98* / 2155 *322*
L.Ladoga 18390 *230* / 7100 *755*

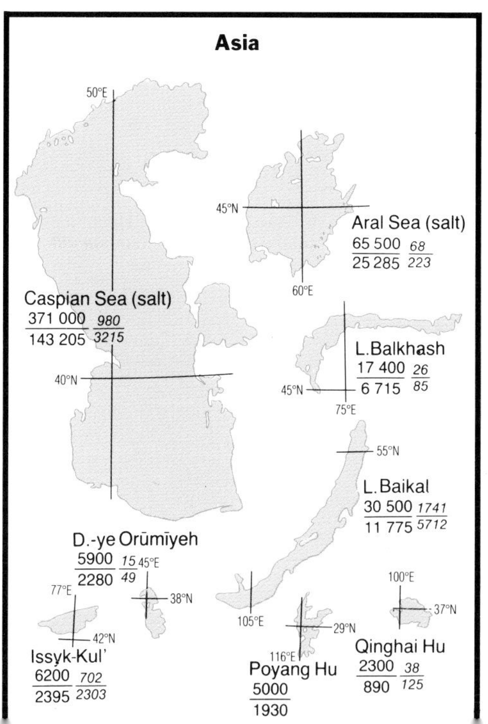

Asia

Aral Sea (salt) 65 500 *68* / 25 285 *223*
Caspian Sea (salt) 371 000 *980* / 143 205 *3215*
L.Balkhash 17 400 *26* / 6 715 *85*
L.Baikal 30 500 *1741* / 11 775 *5712*
D.-ye Orūmīyeh 5900 *15* / 2280 *49*
Issyk-Kul' 6200 *702* / 2395 *2303*
Poyang Hu 5000 / 1930
Qinghai Hu 2300 *38* / 890 *125*

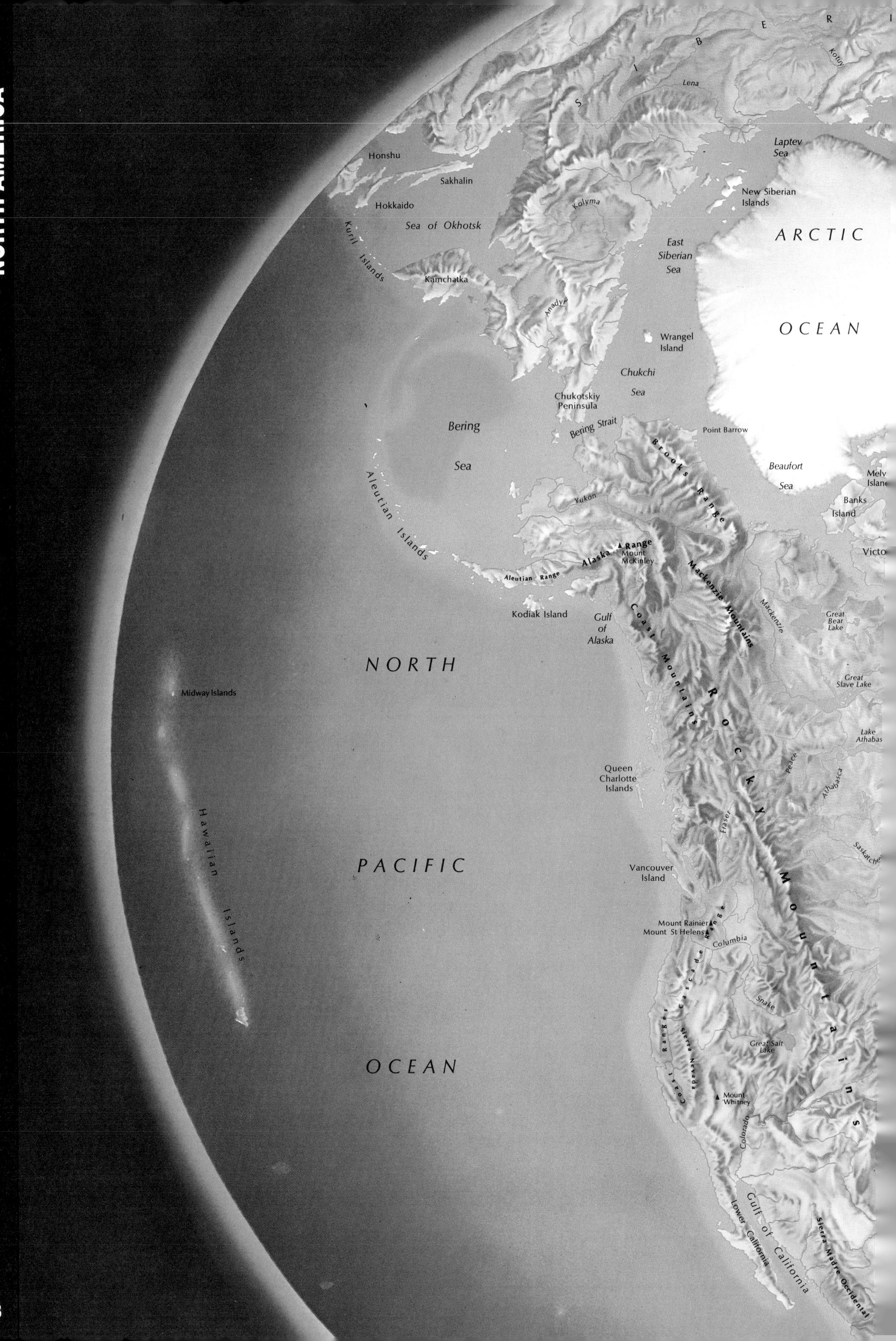

SIBERIA

Kotuy

Lena

Honshu

Sakhalin

Hokkaido

Kolyma

Laptev
Sea

New Siberian
Islands

Sea of Okhotsk

Kuril Islands

Kamchatka

ARCTIC

East
Siberian
Sea

OCEAN

Wrangel
Island

Chukchi
Sea

Anadyr

Chukotskiy
Peninsula

Bering

Point Barrow

Bering Strait

Brooks Range

Beaufort
Sea

Melv
Islan

Sea

Yukon

Banks
Island

Aleutian Islands

Alaska Range
Mount
McKinley

Victo

Mackenzie Mountains

Aleutian Range

Mackenzie

Kodiak Island

Gulf
of
Alaska

Coast Mountains

Great
Bear
Lake

NORTH

R
O
C
K
Y

Great
Slave Lake

Midway Islands

Lake
Athabas

Peace

Athabasca

Queen
Charlotte
Islands

Saskatche

PACIFIC

Hawaiian Islands

Fraser

M
o
u
n
t
a
i
n
s

Vancouver
Island

Mount Rainier
Mount St Helens

Cascade Range

Columbia

OCEAN

Snake

Coast Ranges

Cassiar

Sierra Nevada

Great Salt
Lake

Mount
Whitney

Colorado

Coast

Sierra Madre Occidental

Gulf of California

Lower California

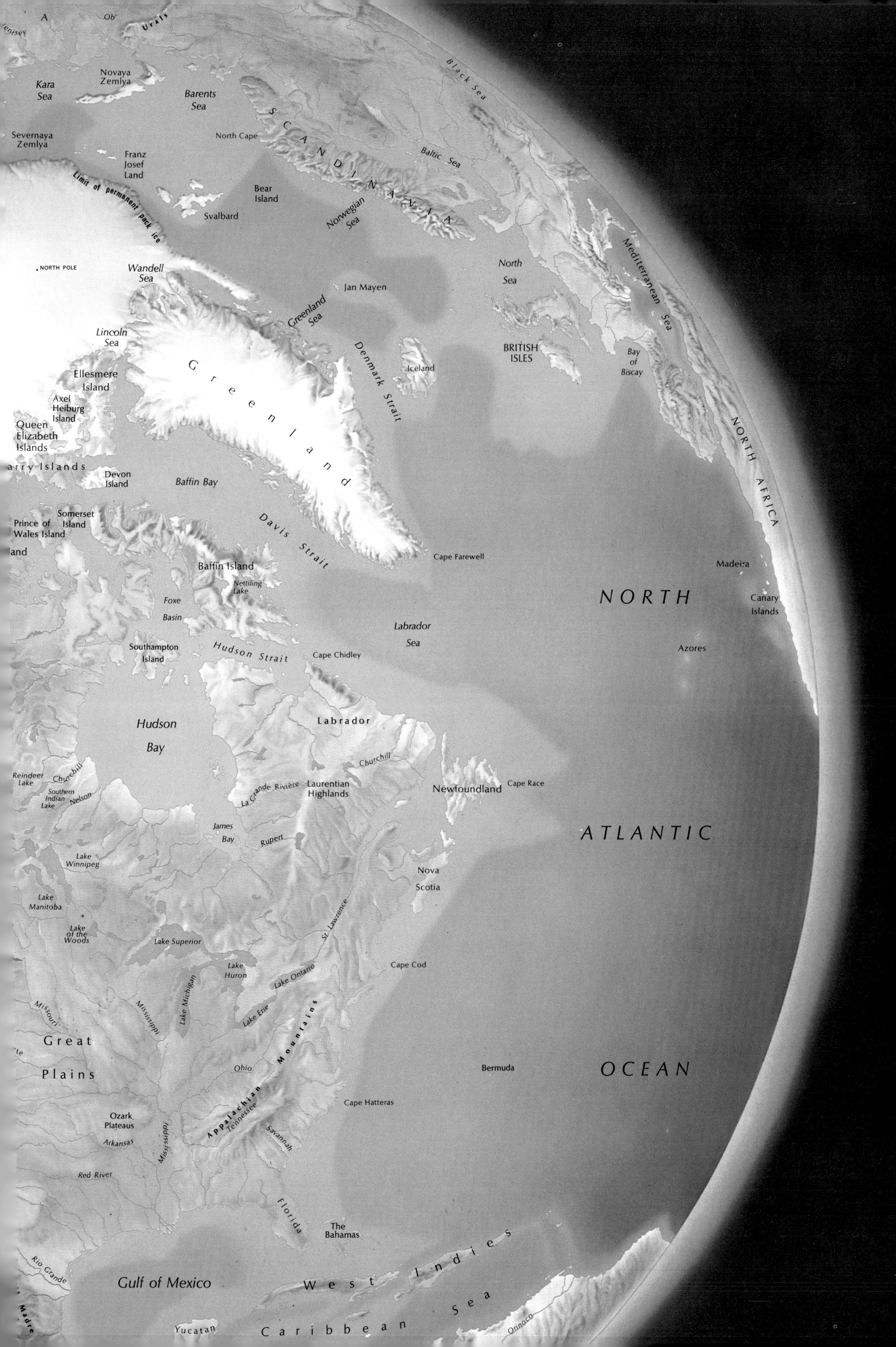

Ob'
Urals
Kara Sea
Novaya Zemlya
Barents Sea
Severnaya Zemlya
North Cape
SCANDINAVIA
Black Sea
Franz Josef Land
Baltic Sea
Limit of permanent pack ice
Bear Island
Svalbard
Norwegian Sea
NORTH POLE
Wandell Sea
Jan Mayen
North Sea
Mediterranean Sea
Greenland Sea
Lincoln Sea
Denmark Strait
Iceland
BRITISH ISLES
Bay of Biscay
Ellesmere Island
Greenland
Axel Heiburg Island
Queen Elizabeth Islands
NORTH AFRICA
Devon Island
Baffin Bay
Somerset Island
Prince of Wales Island
Davis Strait
Cape Farewell
Baffin Island
Nettiling Lake
Madeira
NORTH
Foxe Basin
Canary Islands
Labrador Sea
Southampton Island
Hudson Strait
Cape Chidley
Azores
Hudson Bay
Labrador
Churchill
Reindeer Lake
Southern Indian Lake
Nelson
La Grande Rivière
Laurentian Highlands
Newfoundland
Cape Race
ATLANTIC
James Bay
Rupert
Lake Winnipeg
Nova Scotia
Lake Manitoba
Lake of the Woods
Lake Superior
St Lawrence
Lake Huron
Lake Ontario
Cape Cod
Lake Michigan
Mississippi
Missouri
Lake Erie
Great Plains
Ohio
Mountains
Bermuda
OCEAN
Appalachian
Tennessee
Cape Hatteras
Ozark Plateaus
Arkansas
Savannah
Red River
Florida
The Bahamas
West Indies
Rio Grande
Gulf of Mexico
Caribbean Sea
Yucatan
Orinoco

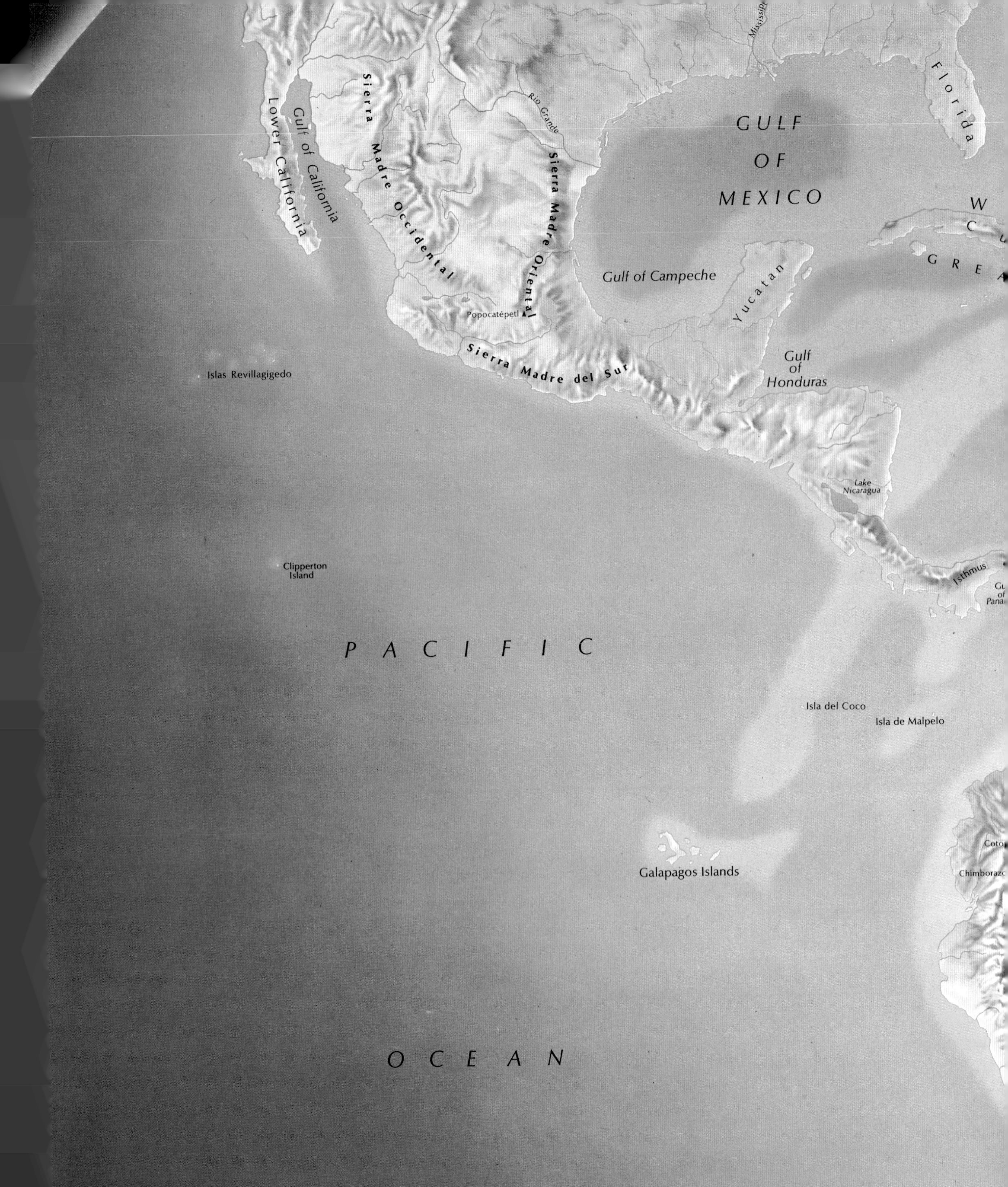

Sierra Madre Occidental

Lower California

Gulf of California

Sierra Madre Oriental

Rio Grande

Mississippi

Florida

GULF
OF
MEXICO

W
C

GREA

Gulf of Campeche

Yucatan

Popocatépetl ▲

Sierra Madre del Sur

Gulf
of
Honduras

Islas Revillagigedo

Lake
Nicaragua

Clipperton
Island

Isthmus

Gu
of
Pana

PACIFIC

Isla del Coco

Isla de Malpelo

Coto

Chimborazo

Galapagos Islands

OCEAN

Bermuda

B A H A M A S

Sargasso
Sea

St

a

b

W
E
S
T

Hispaniola

Puerto
Rico

I
N
D
I
E
S

amaica

GREATER ANTILLES

CARIBBEAN

SEA

LESSER ANTILLES

Gulf
of
Darien

Lake
Maracaibo

Trinidad

ama

Cauca

Occidental

Magdalena

Cordillera

Cordillera Oriental

L
L
A
N
O
S

Orinoco

Roraima ▲

Guiana Highlands

Branco

Mouths
of the
Amazon

Negro

Japurá

Amazon

Putumayo

Amazon

Marañón

Juruá

Purus

Madeira

Tapajós

Xingu

Tocantins

Parnaíba

Ucayali

ascarán

A
N
D
E
S

Madre de Dios

Lake
Titicaca

Ancohuma ▲

**Mato
Grosso**

Araguaia

Tocantins

São Francisco

Brazilian Highlands

Lake
Poopó

GRAN CHACO

Salar
de
Uyuni

Atacama Desert

Paraguay

Pilcomayo

Paraná

Paraná

Galapagos Islands

A

N

Lake
Poopó

Gran Chaco

Pilcomayo

Bermejo

Paraguay

Paraná

Uruguay

Salado

Paraná

Plate

San Félix   San Ambrosio

D

Aconcagua

Pampas

E

Colorado

Negro

Juan Fernández

S

Chubut

Chico

Patagonia

Deseado

Falkland
Islands

SOUTH

Sala y Gomez

Tierra del
Fuego

Easter Island

Cape Horn

Drake   Passage

PACIFIC

Elephant Island

South
Shetland
Islands

King
George I.

Ducie Island

Graham Land

ANTARCTIC PENINSULA

Palmer Land

Henderson Island

Pitcairn Island

Peter I Island

Bellingshausen
Sea

Ror

OCEAN

Ellsworth
Land

Rapa

Amundsen
Sea

Lesser
Antarctica

A N T

Marie   Byrd
Land

Rockefeller
Plateau

Ross
Ice
Shelf

Ross

Sea

Mount Erebus

Scott Island

T R

Oates
Land

Chatham
Islands

Antipodes

Balleny Islands

Bounty
Islands

New
Zealand

Campbell Island

INDI

St Helena

S O U T H

Tristan da Cunha

Gough Island

Cunene

South Georgia

Orange River

Kalahari
Desert

South
Sandwich
Islands

Cape
of
Good Hope

A T L A N T I C

South Orkney
Islands

Limpopo

Bouvet Island

Madagascar

Weddell

Sea

Lazarev
Sea

Prince Edward
Islands

Limit of permanent pack ice

O C E A N

e Shelf

Queen Maud Land

R C T I C A

Îles Crozet

Antarctica

Enderby Land

SOUTH POLE

Greater

Îles Kerguelen

Macdonald Islands
Heard Island

St Paul
Amsterdam Island

orge V
and

Wilkes Land

OCEAN

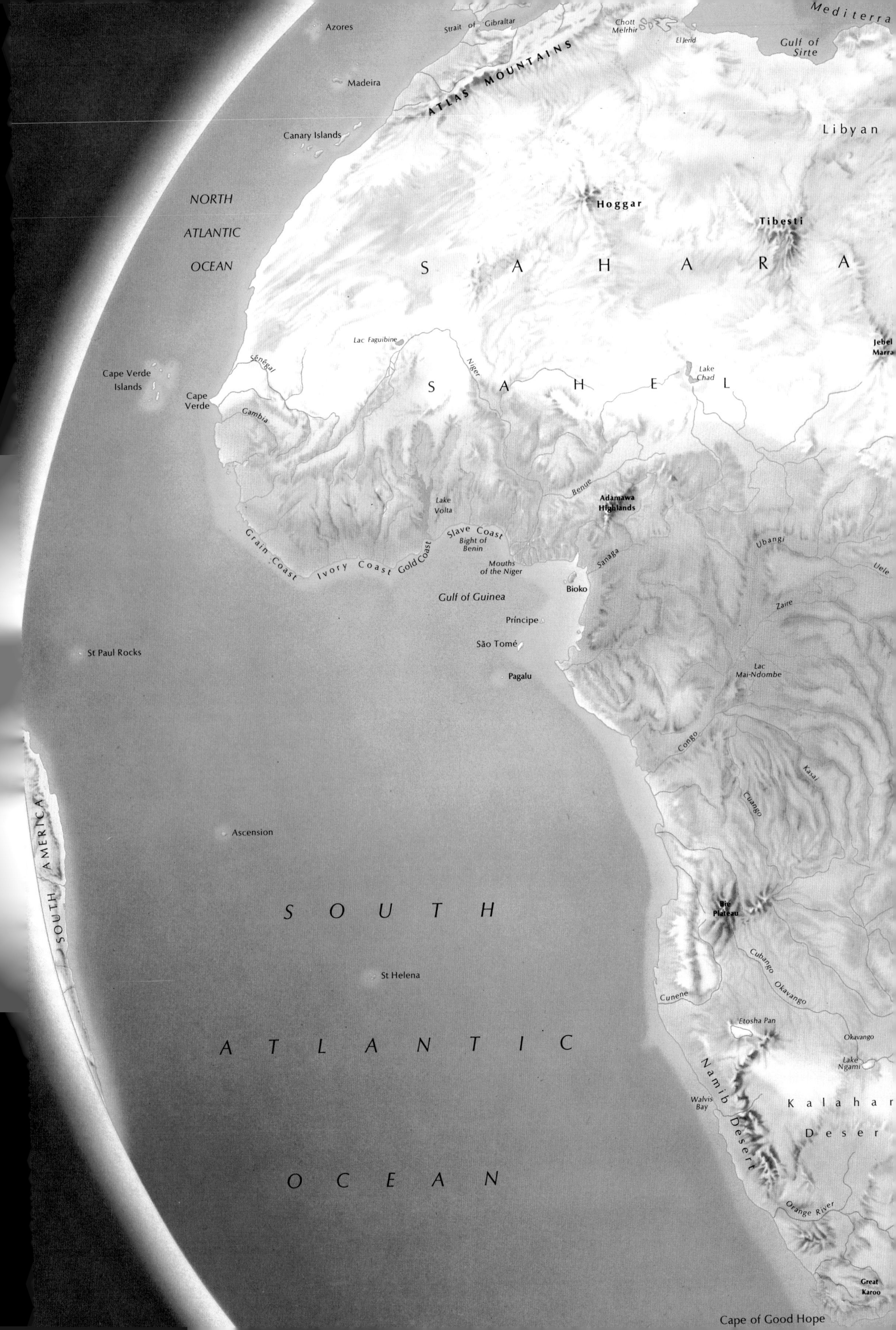

Mediterra

Gulf of
Sirte

Azores

Strait of Gibraltar

Chott
Melrhir

El Jerid

Madeira

ATLAS MOUNTAINS

Libyan

Canary Islands

NORTH

Hoggar

Tibesti

ATLANTIC

S   A   H   A   R   A

OCEAN

Jebel
Marra

Cape Verde
Islands

Lac Faguibine

Lake
Chad

Senegal

S

A   H   E   L

Niger

Cape
Verde

Gambia

Benue

Adamawa
Highlands

Ubangi

Uele

Lake
Volta

Slave Coast

Sanaga

Grain Coast

Bight of
Benin

Zaire

Ivory Coast Gold Coast

Mouths
of the Niger

Bioko

Lac
Mai-Ndombe

Gulf of Guinea

St Paul Rocks

Príncipe

São Tomé

Pagalu

Kasai

Congo

SOUTH AMERICA

Cuango

Ascension

SOUTH

Bie
Plateau

Cubango

Okavango

St Helena

Cunene

Okavango

Etosha Pan

Lake
Ngami

ATLANTIC

Walvis
Bay

Namib Desert

Kalahar

Deser

OCEAN

Orange River

Great
Karoo

Cape of Good Hope

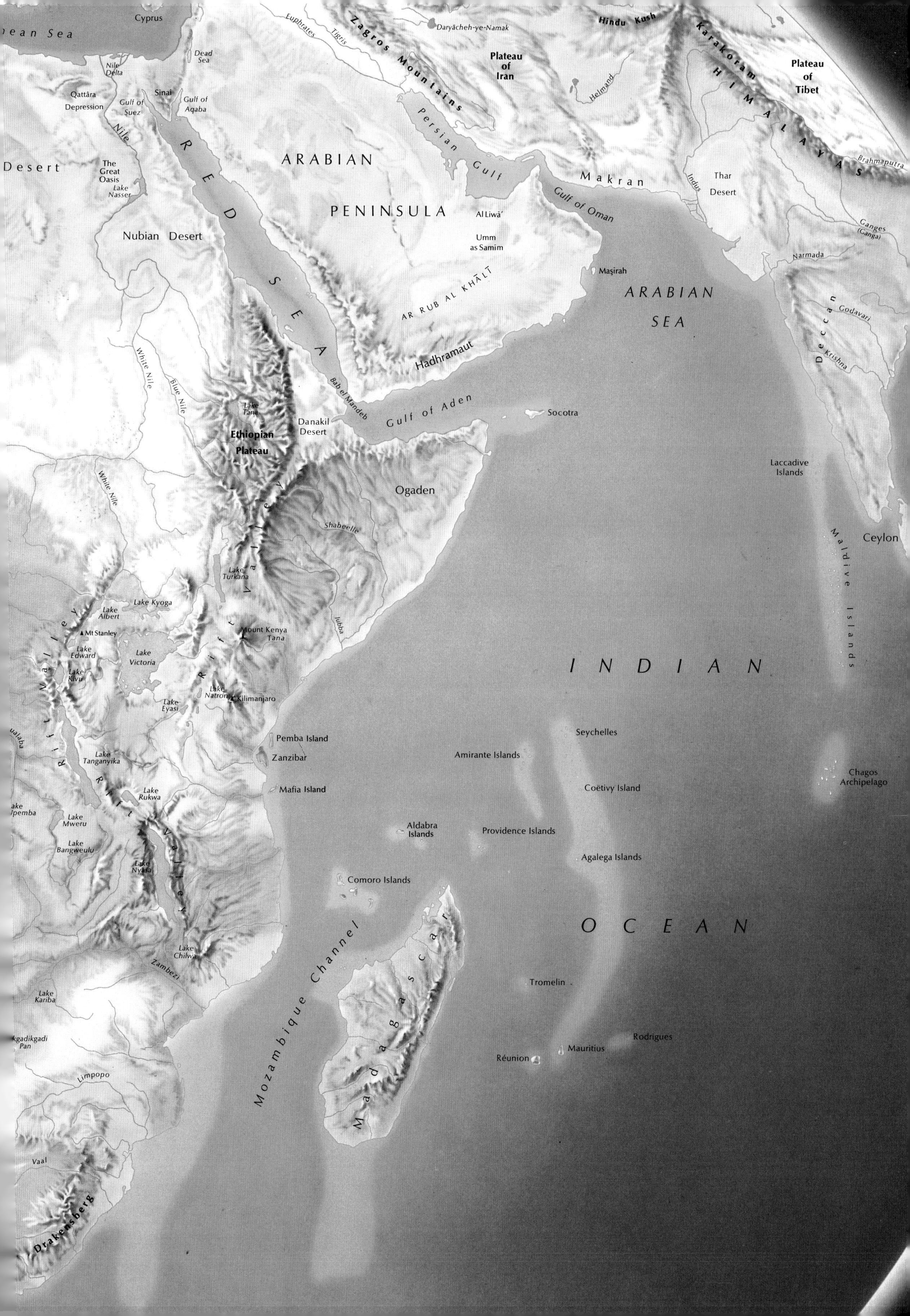

Cyprus
Dead Sea
Nile Delta
Qattâra Depression
Gulf of Suez
Sinai
Gulf of Aqaba
Nile
Desert
The Great Oasis
Lake Nasser
Nubian Desert
RED SEA
ARABIAN
PENINSULA
Euphrates
Tigris
Zagros Mountains
Daryācheh-ye-Namak
Plateau of Iran
Hindu Kush
Karakoram
HIMALAYAS
Plateau of Tibet
Helmand
Persian Gulf
Makran
Gulf of Oman
Indus
Thar Desert
Brahmaputra
Ganges (Ganga)
Narmada
Al Liwā'
Umm as Samīm
AR RUB AL KHĀLĪ
Maşirah
ARABIAN SEA
Godavari
Deccan
Krishna
Hadhramaut
Bab el Mandeb
Gulf of Aden
Socotra
White Nile
Blue Nile
Lake Tana
Ethiopian Plateau
Danakil Desert
Ogaden
Laccadive Islands
Shabeelle
Ceylon
Maldive Islands
Lake Turkana
Lake Kyoga
Lake Albert
Mt Stanley
Mount Kenya
Tana
Juba
Lake Edward
Lake Victoria
Lake Kivu
Rift Valley
INDIAN
Lake Natron
Kilimanjaro
Lake Eyasi
Seychelles
Pemba Island
Zanzibar
Amirante Islands
Chagos Archipelago
Lake Tanganyika
Coëtivy Island
Mafia Island
Lake Rukwa
Lake Mweru
Aldabra Islands
Providence Islands
Lake Bangweulu
Agalega Islands
Lake Nyasa
Comoro Islands
OCEAN
Lake Chilwa
Zambezi
Mozambique Channel
Madagascar
Tromelin
Lake Kariba
Rodrigues
Mauritius
Réunion
Limpopo
Vaal
Drakensberg

NORTH POLE

ARCTIC

Ellesmere Island

Greenland
Sea

Svalbard

Bear
Island

Hudson Bay

Baffin Island

Davis Strait

G r e e n l a n d

Greenland

LABRADOR

Denmark Strait

Cape Farewell

Iceland

Jan Mayen

Norwegian

Sea

Faeroe Islands

N O R T H

Shetland

Orkney

S C A N D I

Lake
Vänern

Lake
Vättern

Rockall

British
Isles

Grampians

North

Sea

B

A T L A N T I C

Irish Sea

Severn

Thames

Elbe

Oder

Rhine

N O R

R

English Channel

Seine

O C E A N

Loire

Bay
of
Biscay

Massif
Central

Rhône

Mt. Blanc

A L P S

Po

Adriatic

Apennines

D

Azores

Cantabrian Mts

Garonne

Pyrenees

Ebro

Corsica

Tagus

Balearic Islands

Sardinia

Guadalquivir

M E D I T E R

Strait of Gibraltar

Madeira

Sicily

Malta

A T L A S   M O U N T A I N S

Chott Melrhir

Canary Islands

El Jerid

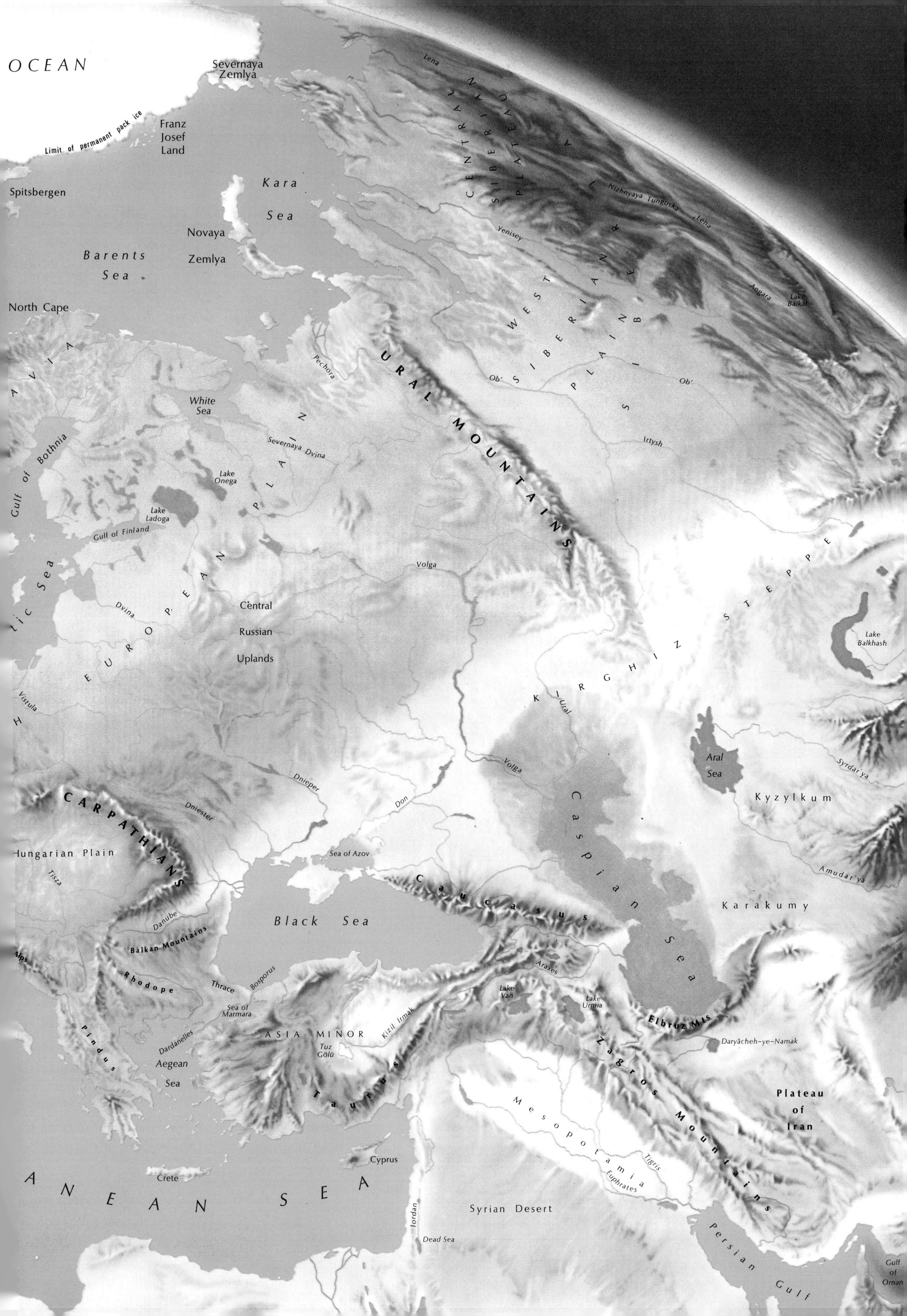

OCEAN

Severnaya
Zemlya

Limit of permanent pack ice

Franz
Josef
Land

Spitsbergen

*Kara
Sea*

Novaya
Zemlya

*Barents
Sea*

North Cape

Pechora

*White
Sea*

Severnaya Dvina

E U R O P E A N   P L A I N

Lake
Onega

Lake
Ladoga

Gulf of Finland

Gulf of Bothnia

Dvina

Baltic Sea

Vistula

Central
Russian
Uplands

Volga

URAL MOUNTAINS

WEST SIBERIAN PLAINS

CENTRAL SIBERIAN PLATEAU

Lena

Nizhnyaya Tunguska

Lena

Yenisey

Angara

Lake
Baikal

Ob'

Ob'

Irtysh

Lake
Balkhash

CARPATHIANS

Dnieper

Dniester

Don

Volga

Ural

K I R G H I Z   S T E P P E

Aral
Sea

K y z y l k u m

Syrdar'ya

Hungarian Plain

Tisza

Sea of Azov

C a u c a s u s

C a s p i a n   S e a

Amudar'ya

K a r a k u m y

Danube

Balkan Mountains

Rhodope

Black   Sea

Araxes

Lake
Van

Lake
Urmia

Elbruz Mts

Daryācheh-ye-Namak

Alps

Pindus

Thrace

Bosporus

Sea of
Marmara

Dardanelles

ASIA MINOR

Kizil Irmak

T a u r u s

Z a g r o s   M o u n t a i n s

**Plateau
of
Iran**

Aegean
Sea

Tuz
Gölü

M e s o p o t a m i a

Tigris

Euphrates

Crete

Cyprus

N E A N   S E A

Jordan

Dead Sea

Syrian Desert

*Persian
Gulf*

Gulf
of
Oman

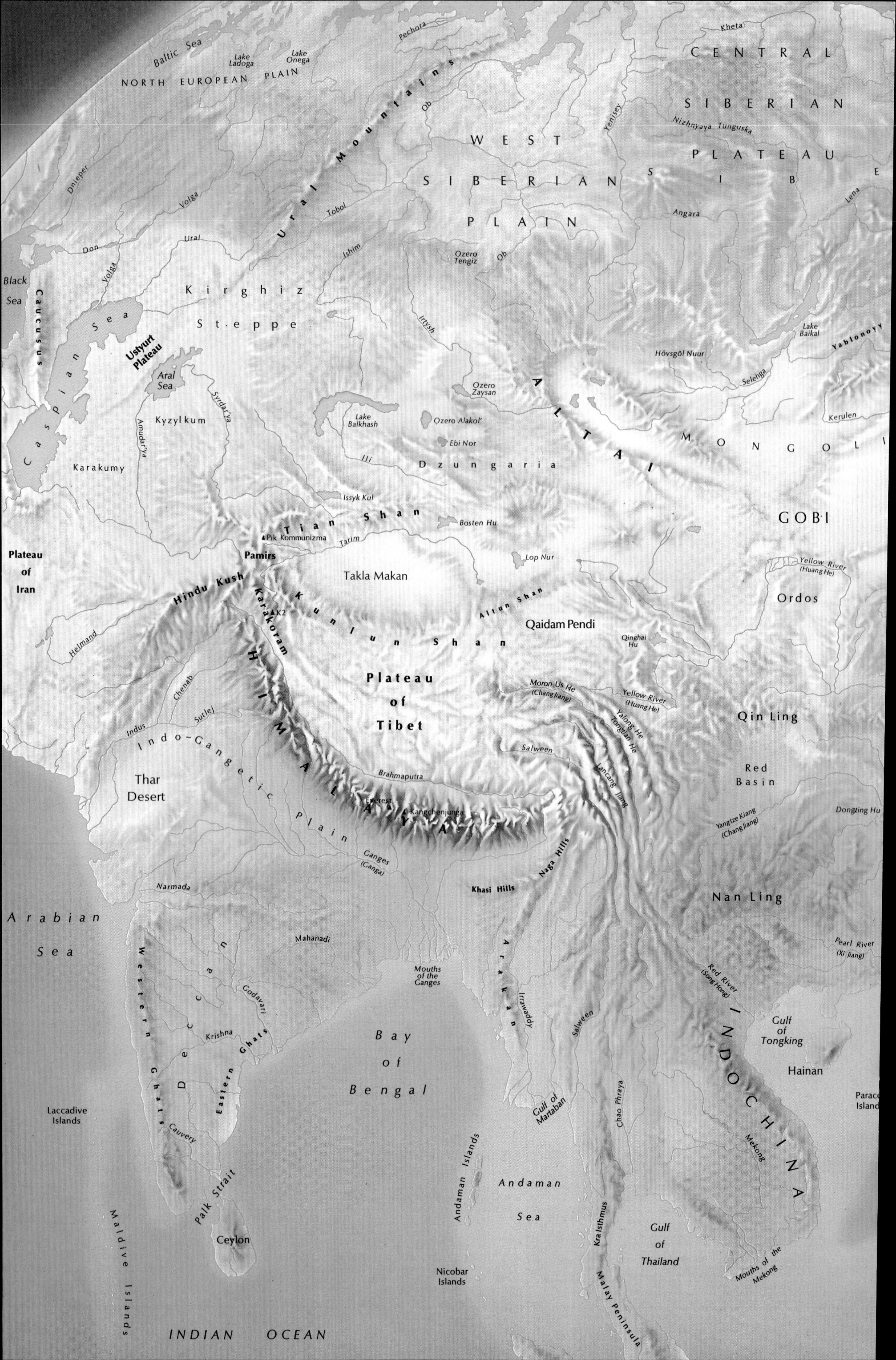

Baltic Sea

Lake Ladoga

Lake Onega

Pechora

Kheta

CENTRAL

NORTH EUROPEAN PLAIN

SIBERIAN

Nizhnyaya Tunguska

PLATEAU

Dnieper

Ural Mountains

Ob

WEST

SIBERIAN

S I B E

Volga

Tobol

SIBERIAN

PLAIN

Yenisey

Ural

Ishim

PLAIN

Lena

Don

Ob

Angara

Volga

Black Sea

Caucusus

K i r g h i z

Ozero Tengiz

Lake Baikal

Yablonoyy

Caspian Sea

S t e p p e

Irtysh

Hövsgöl Nuur

Selenga

Ustyurt Plateau

Ozero Zaysan

A L T A I

M O N G O L I

Kerulen

Aral Sea

Lake Balkhash

Ozero Alakol'

Kyzyl kum

Ebi Nor

Amudar'ya

Syrdar'ya

Ili

D z u n g a r i a

G O B I

Karakumy

Issyk Kul

Tian Shan

Bosten Hu

Plateau of Iran

Pik Kommunizma

Tarim

Lop Nur

Yellow River (Huang He)

Pamirs

Takla Makan

Altun Shan

Ordos

Hindu Kush

Karakoram

K2

Kunlun Shan

Qaidam Pendi

Qinghai Hu

Helmand

H I M A L A Y A

Plateau of Tibet

Qin Ling

Chenab

Moron Us He (Chang Jiang)

Yellow River (Huang He)

Indus

Sutlej

Yalong He

Tongtian He

Red Basin

Indo-Gangetic Plain

Brahmaputra

Salween

Lancang Jiang

Yangtze Kiang (Chang Jiang)

Thar Desert

Everest

Kangchenjunga

Dongting Hu

Narmada

Ganges (Ganga)

Naga Hills

Nan Ling

Khasi Hills

Arabian Sea

Mahanadi

Arakan

Pearl River (Xi Jiang)

Western Ghats

Deccan

Godavari

Red River (Song Hong)

Gulf of Tongking

Krishna

Eastern Ghats

B a y

Irrawady

Hainan

Laccadive Islands

Cauvery

o f

Mouths of the Ganges

Gulf of Martaban

Mekong

Paracel Islands

Palk Strait

B e n g a l

Salween

INDOCHINA

Maldive Islands

Andaman Islands

Andaman Sea

Chao Phraya

Gulf of Thailand

Ceylon

Kra Isthmus

Nicobar Islands

Malay Peninsula

Mouths of the Mekong

INDIAN OCEAN

Nunivak
Island

Bering

Sea

Aleutian Islands

Komandorskiye
Ostrova

Yana

Indigirka

Kolyma

Anadyr

Verkhoyanskiy Khrebet

Lena

ilyuУ

R

I

A

Aldan

Shilka

hrebet

Greater Khingan Range

Hulun
Nur

Manchuria

Songhua

Amur

Ussuri

Oz
Khanka

Kht. Dzhugdzhur

Sea
of
Okhotsk

Kamchatka

Sakhalin

Tatarskiy Proliv

Sikhote Alin

Hokkaido

Kuril Islands

N O R T H

Midway
Islands

Changbai Shan

Sea
of
Japan

H
o
n
s
h
u

Bo Hai

Korea

Yellow River
(Huang He)

Yellow
Sea

Korea Strait

Shikoku

Kyushu

P A C I F I C

Great Plain of China

Yangtze Kiang
(Chang Jiang)

Poyang Hu

East

China

Sea

Taiwan Strait

Bonin Islands

O C E A N

Ryukyu Islands

Volcano
Islands

Taiwan

M
a
r
i
a
n
a
s

Marshall Islands

South

China

Sea

P
H
I
L
I
P
P
I
N
E
S

Luzon

Guam

Kiribati

Mindoro

Samar

C
a
r
o
l
i
n
e
  I
s
l
a
n
d
s

Palawan

Panay

Negros

atly
lands

Sulu

Mindanao

Sea

Borneo

New Ireland

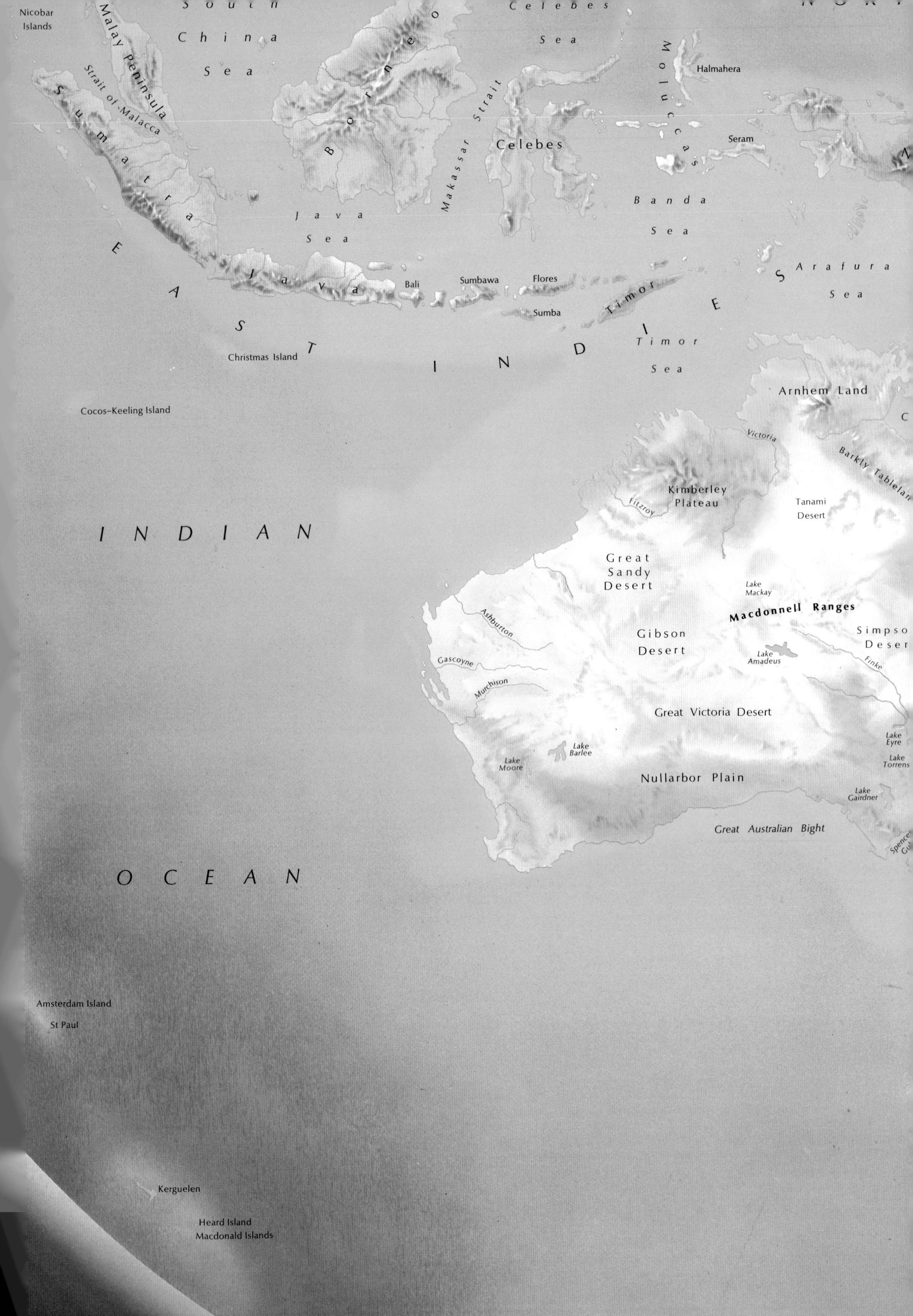

Nicobar Islands
South China Sea
Celebes Sea
Malay Peninsula
Strait of Malacca
Sumatra
Borneo
Makassar Strait
Celebes
Moluccas
Halmahera
Seram
Banda Sea
Java Sea
Java
Bali
Sumbawa
Flores
Sumba
Timor
Arafura Sea
Timor Sea
EAST INDIES
Christmas Island
Cocos-Keeling Island
Arnhem Land
Victoria
Barkly Tableland
Kimberley Plateau
Fitzroy
Tanami Desert
INDIAN
Great Sandy Desert
Lake Mackay
Macdonnell Ranges
Ashburton
Gibson Desert
Simpson Desert
Gascoyne
Lake Amadeus
Finke
Murchison
Great Victoria Desert
Lake Eyre
Lake Barlee
Lake Moore
Lake Torrens
Nullarbor Plain
Lake Gairdner
Great Australian Bight
Spencer Gulf
OCEAN
Amsterdam Island
St Paul
Kerguelen
Heard Island
Macdonald Islands
ANTARCTICA

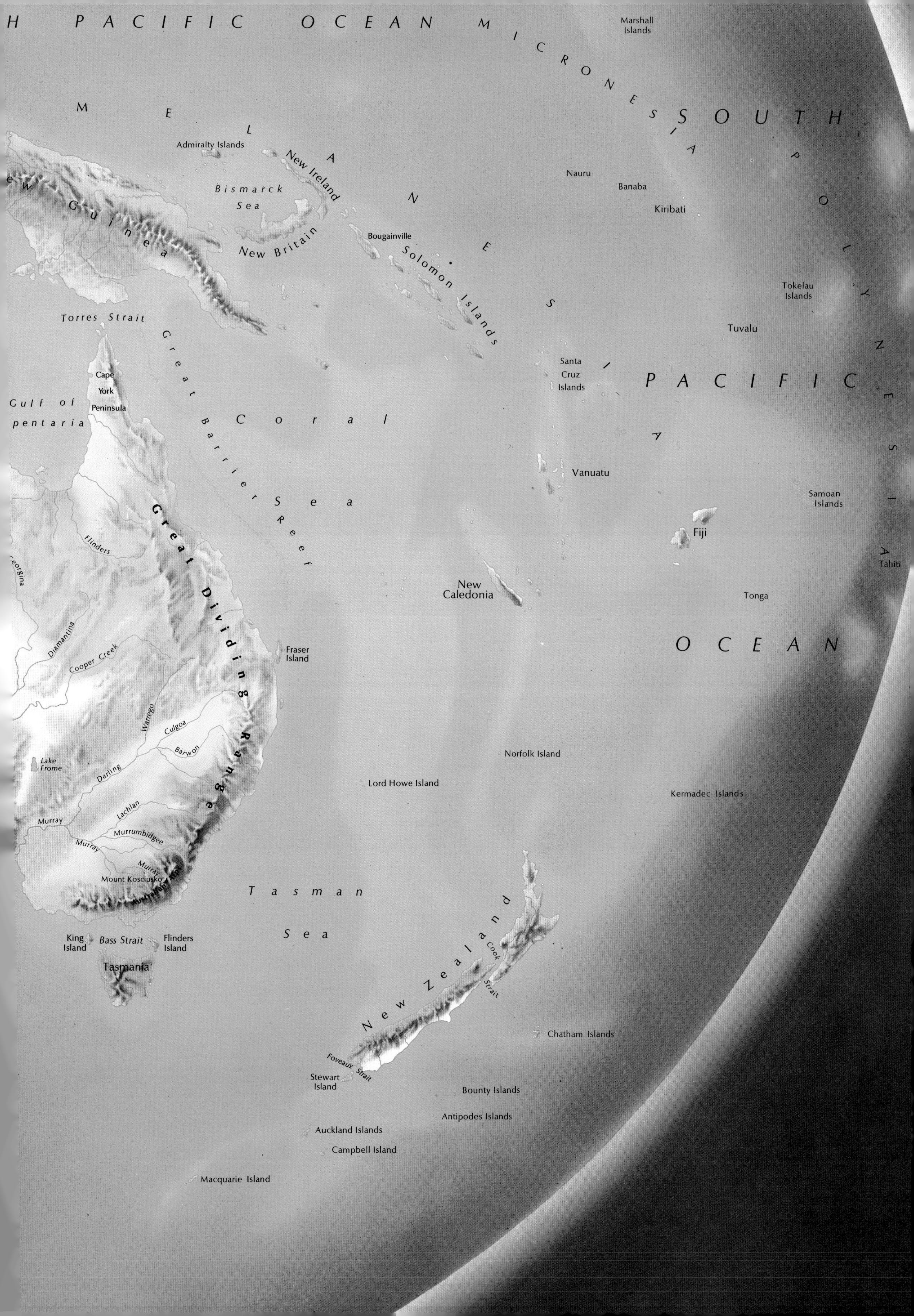

H PACIFIC OCEAN MICRONESIA SOUTH

Marshall Islands

MELANESIA POLYNESIA

Admiralty Islands

New Ireland

Bismarck Sea

New Britain

Bougainville

Solomon Islands

Nauru

Banaba

Kiribati

ew Guinea

Torres Strait

Gulf of pentaria

Cape York Peninsula

Great Barrier Reef

Coral Sea

Santa Cruz Islands

PACIFIC

Tokelau Islands

Tuvalu

Vanuatu

Samoan Islands

Fiji

Tahiti

Flinders

eorgina

Great Dividing Range

New Caledonia

Tonga

OCEAN

Diamantina

Cooper Creek

Fraser Island

Lake Frome

Warrego

Culgoa

Barwon

Darling

Lachlan

Murrumbidgee

Murray

Murray

Murray

Mount Kosciusko

Australian Alps

Norfolk Island

Lord Howe Island

Kermadec Islands

King Island

Bass Strait

Flinders Island

Tasmania

Tasman Sea

New Zealand

Cook Strait

Chatham Islands

Foveaux Strait

Stewart Island

Bounty Islands

Antipodes Islands

Auckland Islands

Campbell Island

Macquarie Island

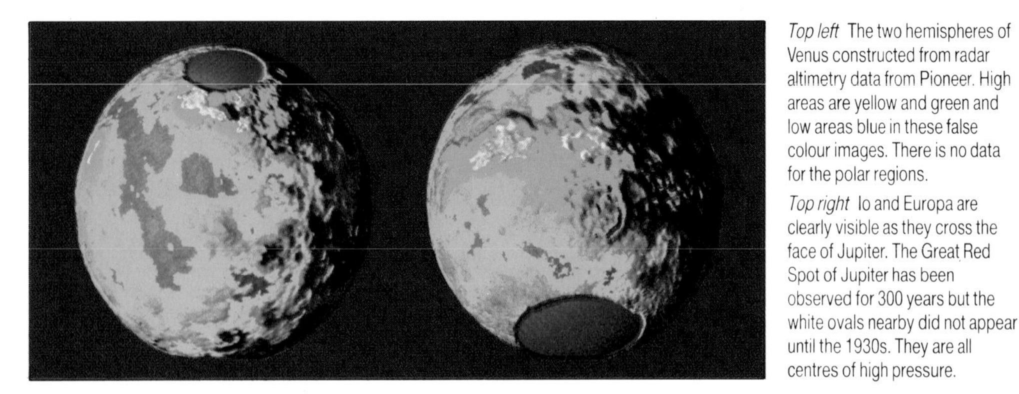

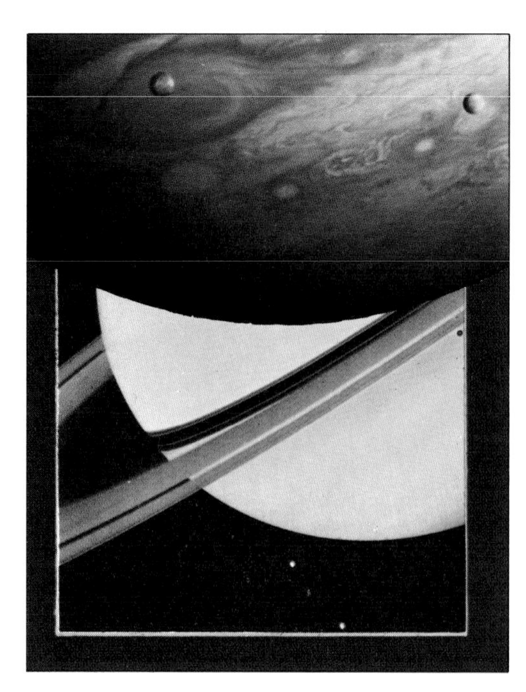

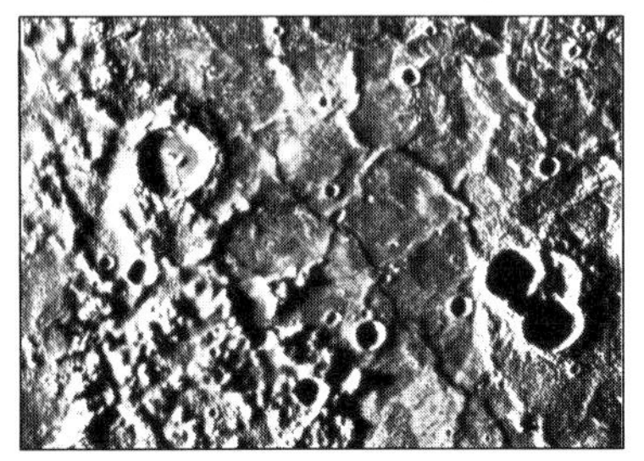

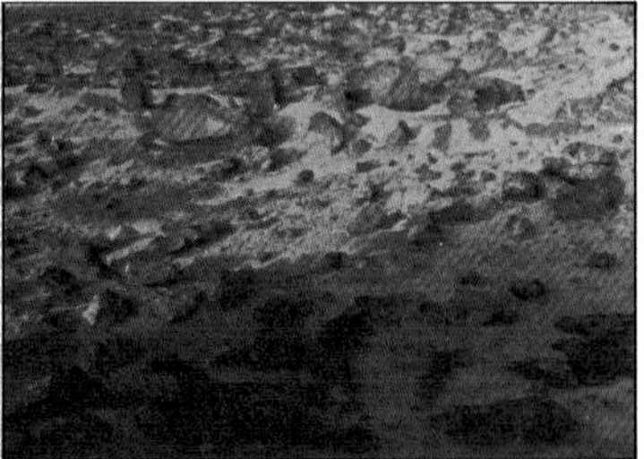

Top left The two hemispheres of Venus constructed from radar altimetry data from Pioneer. High areas are yellow and green and low areas blue in these false colour images. There is no data for the polar regions.

Top right Io and Europa are clearly visible as they cross the face of Jupiter. The Great Red Spot of Jupiter has been observed for 300 years but the white ovals nearby did not appear until the 1930s. They are all centres of high pressure.

Far left The Caloris basin of Mercury is the largest impact feature on the planet.
Right The rings of Saturn lie in the equatorial plane and consist of countless small ice-covered particles.
Left This Viking Lander 2 photograph shows a thin coating of ice that has accumulated at the base of rocks on the Martian soil.

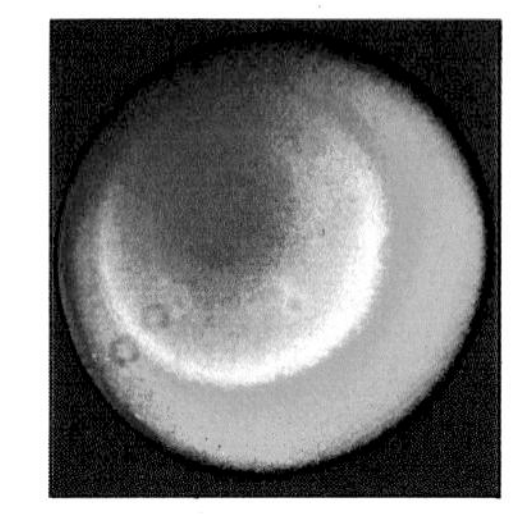

Left This photograph of Uranus in false colour was taken from 9.1 million km (5.7 million miles) by Voyager 2. The planet's atmosphere is deep, cold and remarkably clear, but the false colours enhance the polar region. Here, the suggestion is that a brownish haze of smog is concentrated over the pole.

Current theory suggests that the solar system condensed from a primitive solar nebula of gas and dust during an interval of a few tens of millions of years about 4600 million years ago. Gravity caused this nebula to contract, drawing most of its mass into the centre. Turbulence gave the original cloud a tendency to rotate faster and faster, forcing the remainder of the cloud into a disc shape.

The centre of the cloud heated up as it compressed, and so eventually became hot enough for the Sun to begin to shine, through nuclear energy released at its core. Meanwhile the surrounding disc of cloud cooled, allowing material to condense into solid form. Particles stuck together as they collided and progressively larger bodies were built up. These swept up most of the debris to form the planets, which now orbit the Sun.

EARTHLIKE PLANETS

Mercury is the nearest planet to the Sun, spinning three times for every two orbits around the Sun. It has an exceptionally large metallic core which may be responsible for Mercury's weak magnetic field. Mercury is an airless world subject to vast extremes of temperature, from −180°C (−292°F) at night to 430°C (806°F) near the middle of its long day. The Mariner 10 space probe, during the mid-1970s, revealed the surface to be dominated by heavily cratered areas.

Venus has a dense atmosphere of 96% carbon dioxide mixed with nitrogen, oxygen, sulphur dioxide and water vapour which hides the surface under permanent cloud and maintains a mean surface temperature of about 480°C (896°F). The planet's slow rotation means that weather systems are driven mostly by solar heat, rather than by spin. Westerly winds may blow up to 100 m/sec (328 ft/sec).

Mars has a thin atmosphere of about 96% carbon dioxide mixed with other minor gasses. The polar caps consist of semi-permanent water-ice and solid carbon dioxide. Day and night surface temperatures vary between about −120°C (−184°F) and −20°C (−4°F). Mars has two small satellites, Phobos and Deimos, each less than about 25km (15.5 miles) across, probably captured asteroids.

Mars also shows evidence of erosional processes. The effect of winds is seen in the form of the deposition of sand dunes. Dust storms frequently obscure the surface. The large channels, such as the 5000km (3107 miles) long Valles Marineris, may have been cut by flowing water. Water is abundant in the polar caps and may be widespread, held in as permafrost.

GAS GIANTS

Jupiter has at least 16 satellites and a debris ring system about 50,000km (31,070 miles) above the cloud tops. The outer atmosphere is all that can be directly observed of the planet itself. It is mostly hydrogen with lesser amounts of helium, ammonia, methane and water vapour. Jupiter's rapid rotation causes it to be flattened towards the poles. This rotation and heat flow from the interior cause complex weather patterns. Where cloud systems interact vast storms can occur in the form of vortices. Some last only a few days, but the most persistent of these, the Great Red Spot, has been present since it was first detected in the 17th century.

Saturn is the least dense of the planets. It has a stormy atmosphere situated above a 30,000km (18,640 miles) layer of liquid hydrogen and helium distorted by rotation.

The rings of Saturn are thought to be mostly made of icy debris, from 10m (33 ft) down to a few microns in size, derived from the break-up of a satellite. The rings are less than 1km thick.

Uranus, consisting mainly of hydrogen, was little known until Voyager 2 flew by it in 1986. The probe discovered ten new satellites and provided images of the planet's eleven icy rings of debris.

Neptune was visited by Voyager 2 in 1989. Six new satellites were discovered, one larger than Nereid, the smaller of the two known satellites. Triton, the largest satellite, was found to be smaller than previous estimates. The turbulent atmosphere is a mixture of hydrogen, helium and methane.

Pluto is usually the most distant planet from the Sun, but since 1983 the eccentricity of its orbit has brought it temporarily within the orbit of Neptune. The atmosphere is thought to be composed mostly of methane and smaller amounts of other gases.

	SUN	MERCURY	VENUS	EARTH	(MOON)	MARS	JUPITER	SATURN	URANUS	NEPTUNE	PLUTO
Mass (Earth=1)	333 400	0.055	0.815	1 (5.97 10²⁴kg)	0.012	0.107	317.8	95.2	14.5	17.2	0.003
Volume (Earth=1)	1 306 000	0.06	0.88	1	0.020	0.150	1 319	751	62	54	0.015?
Density (water=1)	1.41	5.43	5.24	5.52	3.34	3.94	1.33	0.70	1.30	1.76	1.1?
Equatorial diameter (km)	1 392 000	4 878	12 104	12 756	3 476	6 787	142 796	120 000	50 800	48 600	3 000?
Polar flattening	0	0	0	0.003	0	0.005	0.065	0.108	0.030	0.026	?
'Surface' gravity (Earth=1)	27.9	0.37	0.88	1	0.16	0.38	2.64	1.15	1.17	1.18	0.45?
Number of satellites greater than 100 km diameter	—	0	0	1	—	0	4	10	6	6	1
Total number of satellites	—	0	0	1	—	2	16	17	c.15	8	1
Period of rotation (in Earth days)	25.38	58.65	−243 (retrograde)	23hr 56m 4 secs	27.32	1.03	0.414	0.438	−0.72 (retrograde)	0.67	−6.39 (retrograde)
Length of year (in Earth days and years)	—	88 days	224.7 days	365.26 days	—	687 days	11.86 years	29.46 years	84.01 years	164.8 years	247.7 years
Distance from Sun (mean) Mkm	—	57.9	108.2	149.6	—	227.9	778.3	1 427	2 870	4 497	5 900

EARTH STRUCTURE

Internally, the Earth may be divided broadly into crust, mantle and core (*see right*).

The crust is a thin shell constituting only 0.2% of the mass of the Earth. The continental crust varies in thickness from 20 to 90km (12 to 56 miles) and is less dense than ocean crust. Two-thirds of the continents are overlain by sedimentary rocks of average thickness less than 2km (1.2 miles). Ocean crust is on average 7km (4.4 miles) thick. It is composed of igneous rocks, basalts and gabbros.

Crust and mantle are separated by the Mohorovičić Discontinuity (Moho). The mantle differs from the crust. It is largely igneous. The upper mantle extends to 350km (218 miles). The lower mantle has a more uniform composition. A sharp discontinuity defines the meeting of mantle and core. The inability of the outer core to transmit seismic waves suggests it is liquid. It is probably of metallic iron with other elements – sulphur, silicon, oxygen, potassium and hydrogen have all been suggested. The inner core is solid and probably of nickel-iron. Temperature at the core-mantle boundary is about 3700°C (5430°F) and 4000°–4500°C (7230°–8130°F) in the inner core.

THE ATMOSPHERE

The ancient atmosphere lacked free oxygen. Plant life added oxygen to the atmosphere and transferred carbon dioxide to the crustal rocks and the hydrosphere. The composition of air today at 79% nitrogen and 20% oxygen remains stable by the same mechanism.

Solar energy is distributed around the Earth by the atmosphere. Most of the weather and climate processes occur in the troposphere at the lowest level. The atmosphere also shields the Earth. Ozone exists to the extent of 2 parts per million and is at its maximum at 30km (19 miles). It is the only gas which absorbs ultra-violet radiation. Water-vapour and CO_2 keep out infra-red radiation.

Above 80km (50 miles) nitrogen and oxygen tend to separate into atoms which become ionized (an ion is an atom lacking one or more of its electrons). The ionosphere is a zone of ionized belts which reflect radio waves back to Earth. These electrification belts change their position dependent on light and darkness and external factors.

Beyond the ionosphere, the magnetosphere extends to outer space. Ionized particles form a plasma (a fourth state of matter, ie. other than solid, liquid, gas) held in by the Earth's magnetic field.

ORIGIN AND DEVELOPMENT OF LIFE

Primitive life-forms (blue-green algae) are found in rocks as old as 3500Ma (million years) and, although it cannot yet be proved, the origin of life on Earth probably dates back to about 4000Ma. It seems likely that the oxygen levels in the atmosphere increased only slowly at first, probably to about 1% of the present amount by 2000Ma. As the atmospheric oxygen built up so the protective ozone layer developed to allow organisms to live in shallower waters. More highly developed photosynthesising organisms led to the development of oxygen breathing animals. The first traces of multicellular life occur about 1000Ma; by 700Ma complex animals, such as jellyfish, worms and primitive molluscs, had developed.

Organisms developed hard parts that allowed their preservation as abundant fossils at about 570Ma. This coincided with a period of explosive evolution of marine life. Fishes appeared about 475Ma and by 400Ma land plants had developed. Between 340 and 305Ma dense vegetation covered the land, amphibians emerged from the sea, and by about 250Ma had given rise to reptiles and the first mammals. These expanded hugely about 65Ma.

EARTHQUAKES

Earthquakes are the manifestation of a slippage at a geological fault. The majority occur at tectonic plate boundaries. The interior of a plate tends to be stable and less subject to earthquakes. When plates slide past each other strain energy is suddenly released. Even though the amount of movement is very small the energy released is colossal. It

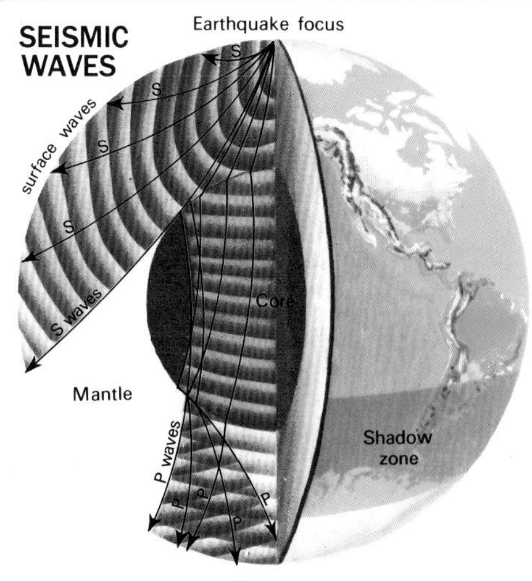

THE EARTH'S SHELLS

oceanic crust
Lithosphere
depth (km) 350
continental crust
Moho
upper mantle
transition zone
900
lower mantle
seismic discontinuities
2900
core-mantle discontinuity
outer core
4700
5150
transition zone
inner core
6370

SEISMIC WAVES

Earthquake focus
surface waves
S waves
S
Mantle
Core
P waves
Shadow zone

Above In an earthquake the shock generates vibrations, or seismic waves, which radiate in all directions from the focus. Surface waves travel close to the surface of the Earth. They cause most damage in the ground and most damage to structures.

Other waves known as body waves pass through the body of the Earth. Primary (P) waves are compressional. They are able to travel through solids and fluids and cause the particles of the Earth to vibrate in the direction of travel. Secondary (S) waves are transverse, or shear, waves. They can only pass through solids.

is transferred in shock waves.

Most earthquakes originate at not very great depths – 5km (3 miles) or so. Some, however, may be as deep as 700km (435 miles). The precise cause of these very deep earthquakes is not known. The point from which the earthquake is generated is the focus and the point on the surface immediately above the focus is the epicentre.

The Richter Scale is used to define the magnitude of earthquakes. In the Scale each unit is ten times the intensity of the next lower on the scale. The intensity is recorded by seismographs. There is no upper limit but the greatest magnitude yet recorded is 8.9.

VOLCANOES

Almost all the world's active volcanoes, numbering 500–600 are located at convergent plate boundaries. Those are the volcanoes which give spectacular demonstrations of volcanic activity. Yet far greater volcanic activity continues unnoticed and without cessation at mid-ocean ridges where magma from the upper mantle is quietly being extruded on to the ocean floor to create new crustal material.

Chemical composition of magmas and the amount of gas they contain determine the nature of a volcanic eruption. Gas-charged basalts produce cinder cones. Violent eruptions usually occur when large clouds of lava come into contact with water to produce fine-grained ash. When andesites are charged with gas they erupt with explosive violence.

Nuées ardentes (burning clouds) are extremely destructive. They are produced by magmas which erupt explosively sending molten lava fragments and gas at great speeds down the mountain sides.

In spite of the destructiveness of many volcanoes people still live in their vicinity because of the fertile volcanic soils. Geothermal energy in regions of volcanic activity is another source of attraction.

GRAVITY AND MAGNETISM

The Earth is spheroidal in form because it is a rotating body. Were it not so it would take the form of a sphere. The shape is determined by the mass of the Earth and its rate of rotation. Centrifugal force acting outwards reduces the pull of gravity acting inwards so that gravity at the equator is less than at the poles. Uneven distribution of matter within the Earth distorts the shape taken up by the mean sea-level surface (the geoid). Today the belief is that electric currents generated in the semi-molten outer core are responsible for the magnetic field. The Earth's magnetic poles have experienced a number of reversals, the north pole becoming the south and vice-versa.

ROCK AND HYDROLOGICAL CYCLES

Right In the most familiar cycle rain falls onto the land, drains to the sea, evaporates, condenses into cloud and is precipitated onto the land again. Water is also released and recirculated. In the rock cycle rocks are weathered and eroded, forming sediments which are compacted into rocks that are eventually exposed and then weathered again.

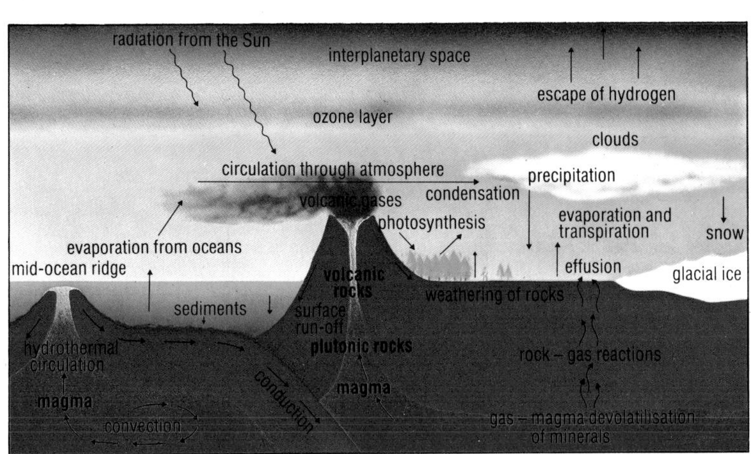

radiation from the Sun
interplanetary space
escape of hydrogen
ozone layer
clouds
circulation through atmosphere
precipitation
volcanic gases
condensation
evaporation and transpiration
snow
photosynthesis
evaporation from oceans
effusion
glacial ice
mid-ocean ridge
volcanic rocks
weathering of rocks
sediments
surface run-off
rock – gas reactions
hydrothermal circulation
plutonic rocks
magma
conduction
magma
convection
gas – magma devolatilisation of minerals

EARTHQUAKES AND VOLCANOES

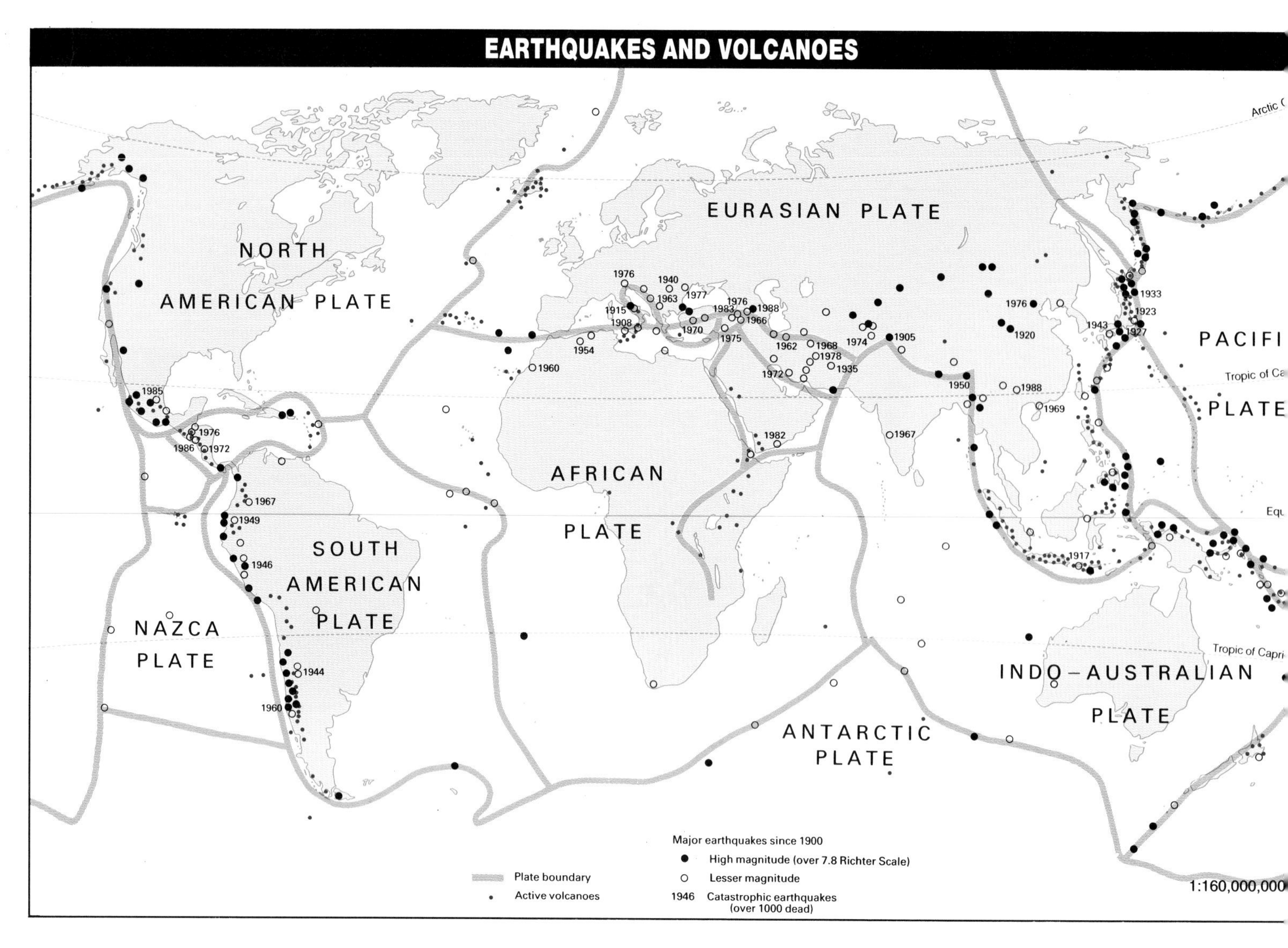

NORTH AMERICAN PLATE

EURASIAN PLATE

PACIFIC PLATE

AFRICAN PLATE

NAZCA PLATE

SOUTH AMERICAN PLATE

INDO–AUSTRALIAN PLATE

ANTARCTIC PLATE

Tropic of Cancer

Tropic of Capricorn

Equator

Arctic Circle

Major earthquakes since 1900
● High magnitude (over 7.8 Richter Scale)
○ Lesser magnitude
1946 Catastrophic earthquakes (over 1000 dead)

▨ Plate boundary
· Active volcanoes

1:160,000,000

ECONOMIC MINERALS

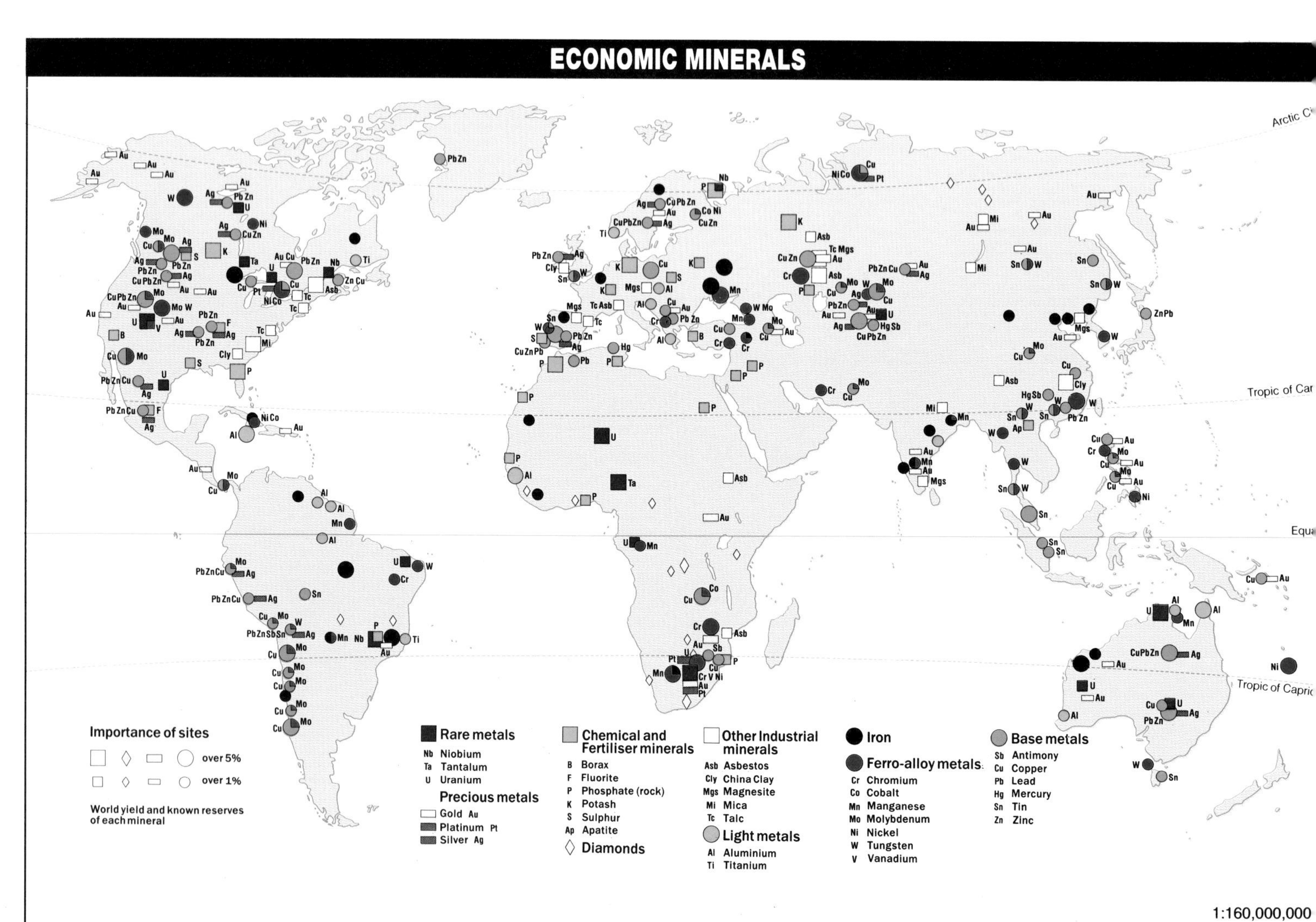

Importance of sites

□ ◇ ▭ ○ over 5%
□ ◇ ▭ ○ over 1%

World yield and known reserves of each mineral

■ **Rare metals**
Nb Niobium
Ta Tantalum
U Uranium

Precious metals
□ Gold Au
▨ Platinum Pt
■ Silver Ag

◇ **Diamonds**

▨ **Chemical and Fertiliser minerals**
B Borax
F Fluorite
P Phosphate (rock)
K Potash
S Sulphur
Ap Apatite

□ **Other Industrial minerals**
Asb Asbestos
Cly China Clay
Mgs Magnesite
Mi Mica
Tc Talc

● **Iron**

● **Ferro-alloy metals**
Cr Chromium
Co Cobalt
Mn Manganese
Mo Molybdenum
Ni Nickel
W Tungsten
V Vanadium

● **Light metals**
Al Aluminium
Ti Titanium

● **Base metals**
Sb Antimony
Cu Copper
Pb Lead
Hg Mercury
Sn Tin
Zn Zinc

1:160,000,000

64

TEMPERATURE: JANUARY

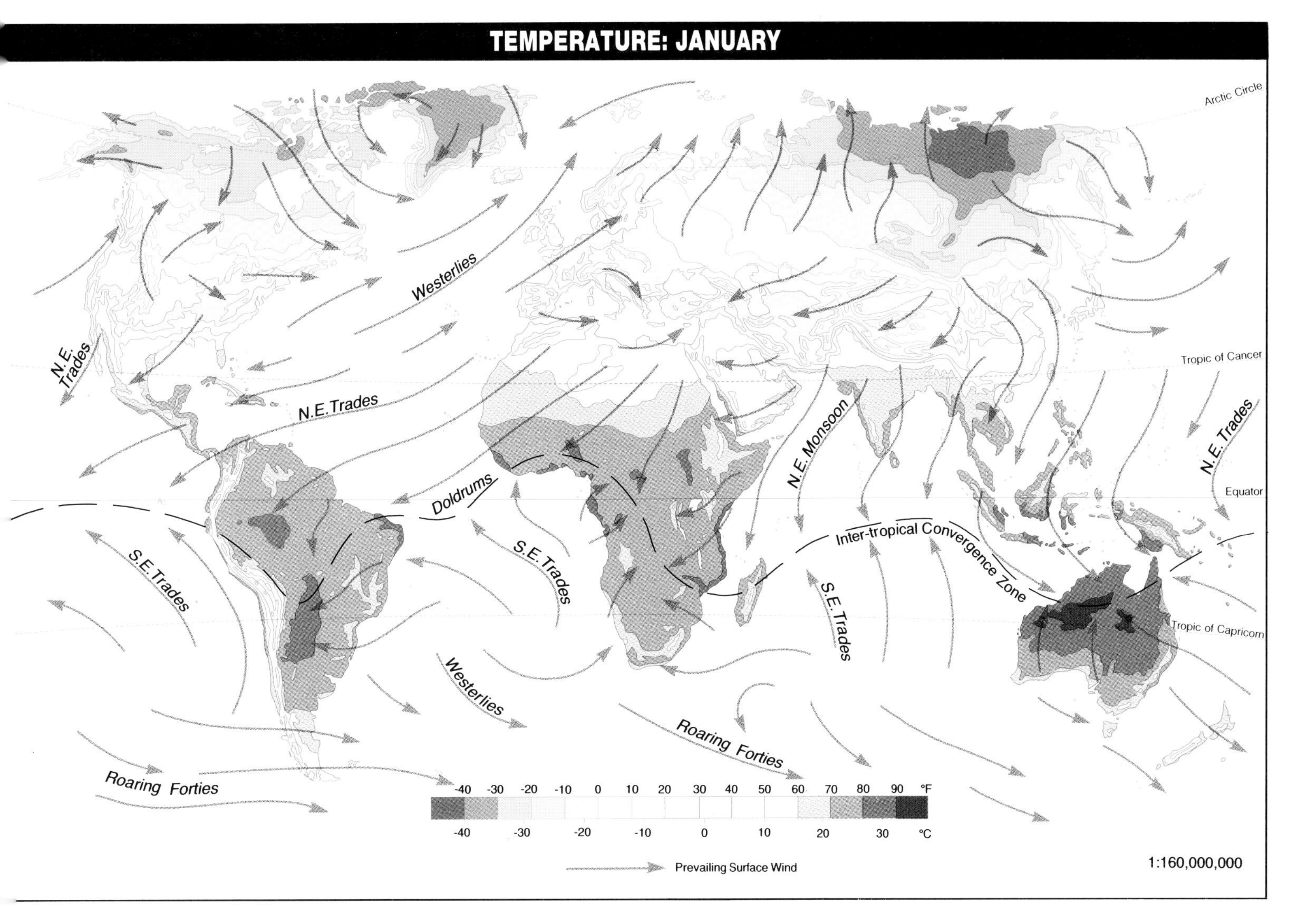

Arctic Circle
Westerlies
N.E. Trades
N.E. Trades
Tropic of Cancer
N.E. Monsoon
N.E. Trades
Equator
Doldrums
Inter-tropical Convergence Zone
S.E. Trades
S.E. Trades
S.E. Trades
Tropic of Capricorn
Westerlies
Roaring Forties
Roaring Forties
-40 -30 -20 -10 0 10 20 30 40 50 60 70 80 90 °F
-40 -30 -20 -10 0 10 20 30 °C
Prevailing Surface Wind
1:160,000,000

TEMPERATURE: JULY

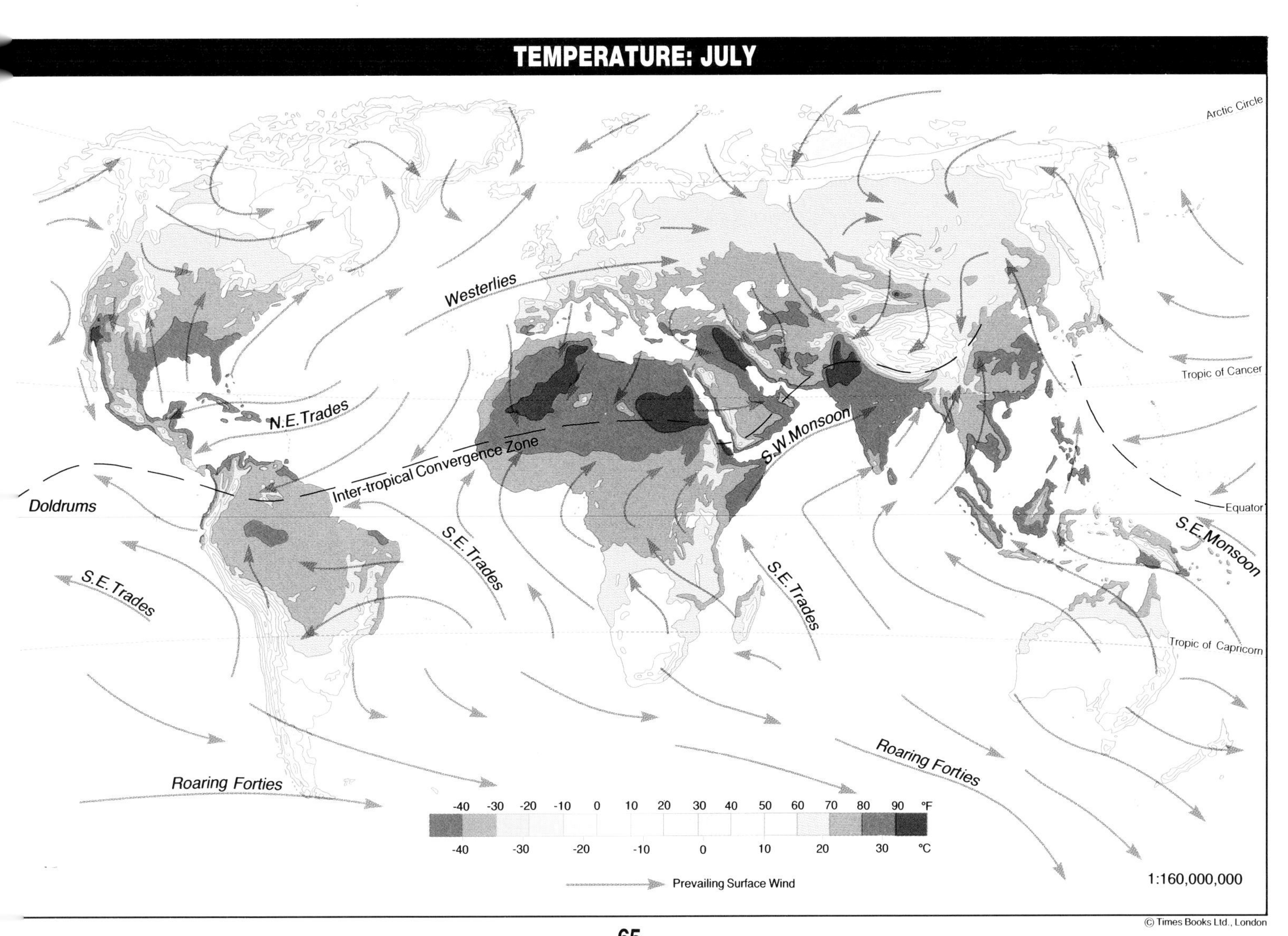

Arctic Circle
Westerlies
Tropic of Cancer
N.E. Trades
S.W. Monsoon
Inter-tropical Convergence Zone
Doldrums
Equator
S.E. Monsoon
S.E. Trades
S.E. Trades
S.E. Trades
Tropic of Capricorn
Roaring Forties
Roaring Forties
-40 -30 -20 -10 0 10 20 30 40 50 60 70 80 90 °F
-40 -30 -20 -10 0 10 20 30 °C
Prevailing Surface Wind
1:160,000,000

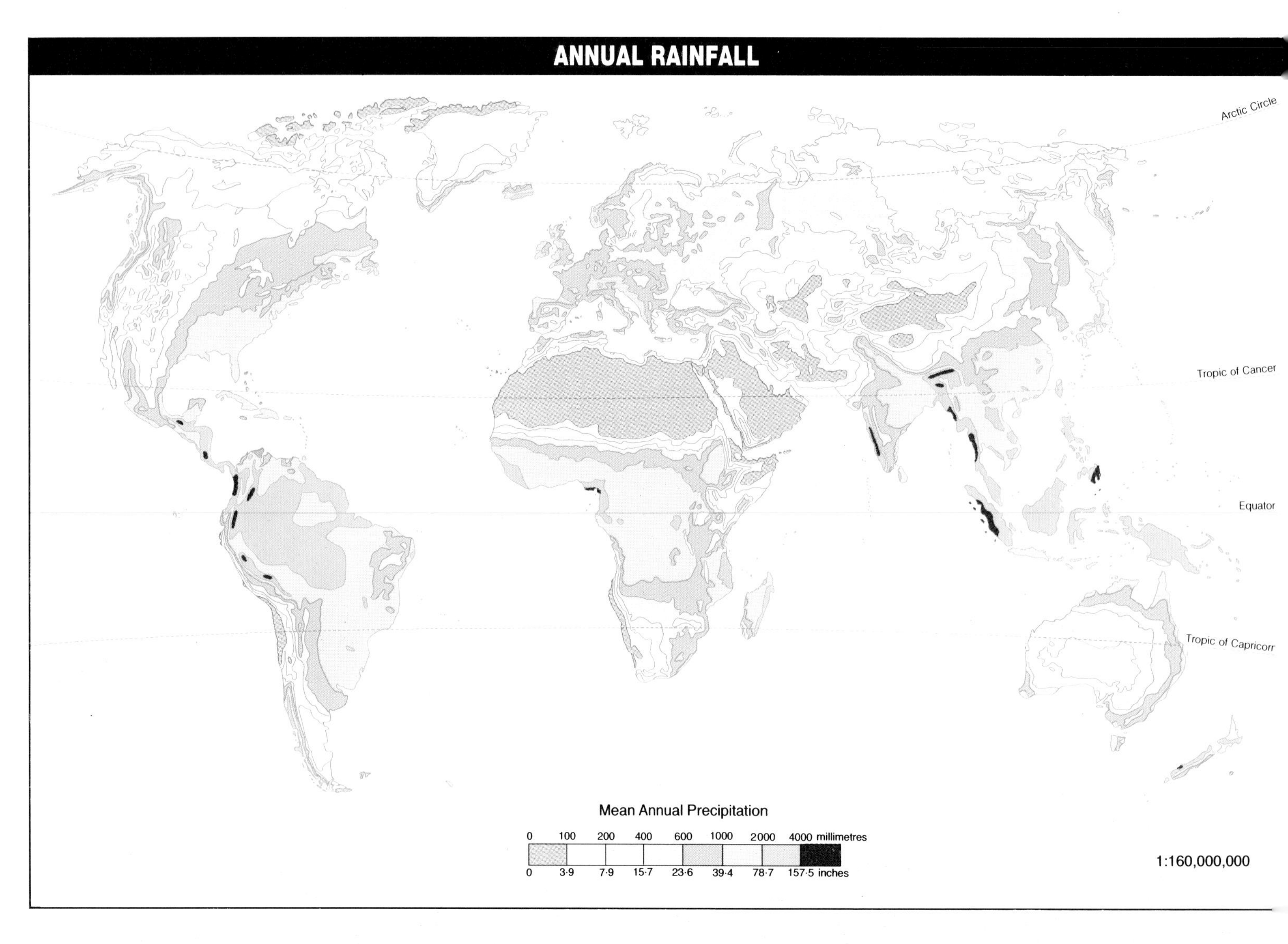

Mean Annual Precipitation

0	100	200	400	600	1000	2000	4000 millimetres
0	3·9	7·9	15·7	23·6	39·4	78·7	157·5 inches

1:160,000,000

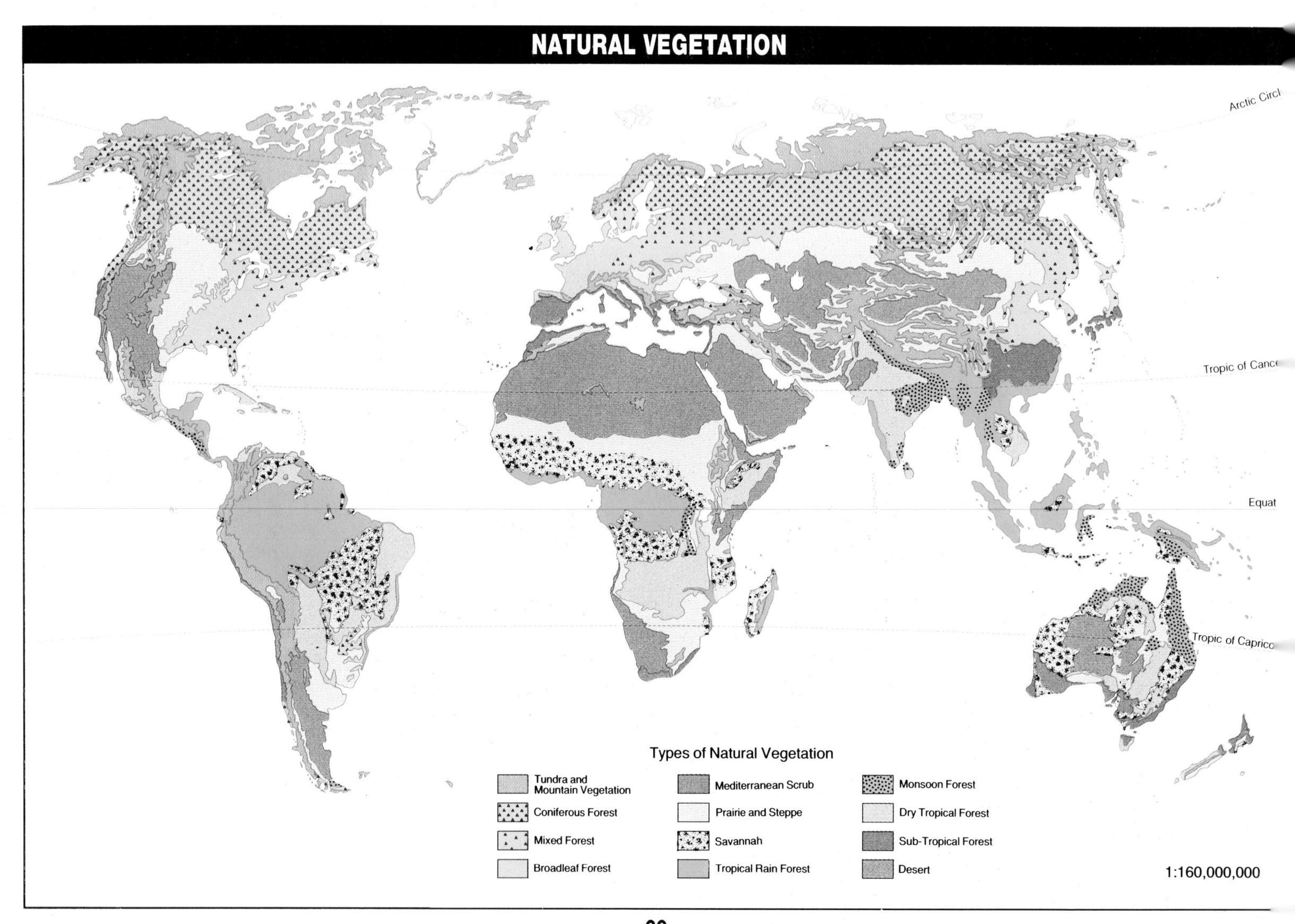

Types of Natural Vegetation

Tundra and Mountain Vegetation	Mediterranean Scrub	Monsoon Forest
Coniferous Forest	Prairie and Steppe	Dry Tropical Forest
Mixed Forest	Savannah	Sub-Tropical Forest
Broadleaf Forest	Tropical Rain Forest	Desert

1:160,000,000

POPULATION DENSITY

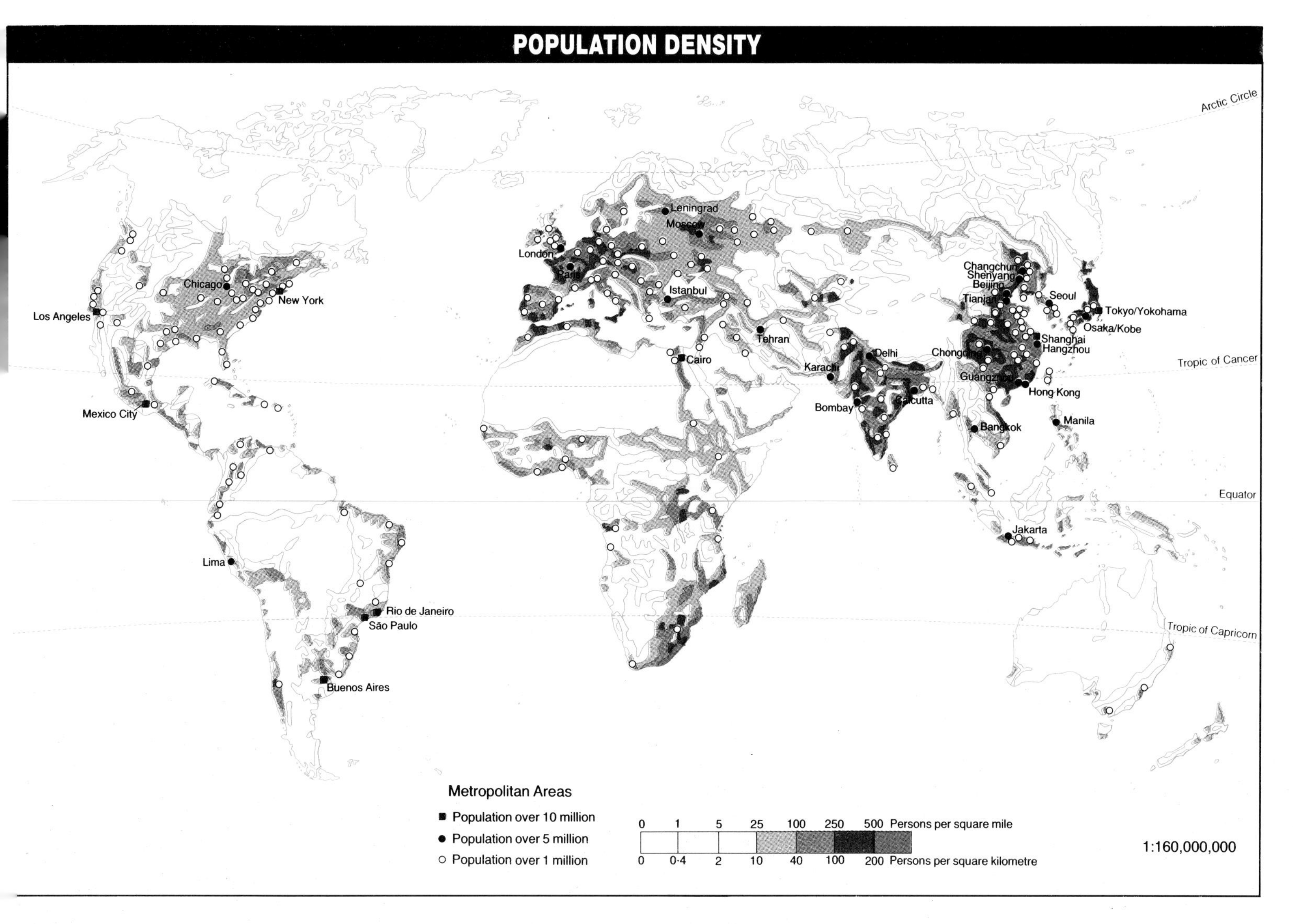

Metropolitan Areas

■ Population over 10 million
● Population over 5 million
○ Population over 1 million

0	1	5	25	100	250	500	Persons per square mile
0	0·4	2	10	40	100	200	Persons per square kilometre

1:160,000,000

POPULATION CHANGE

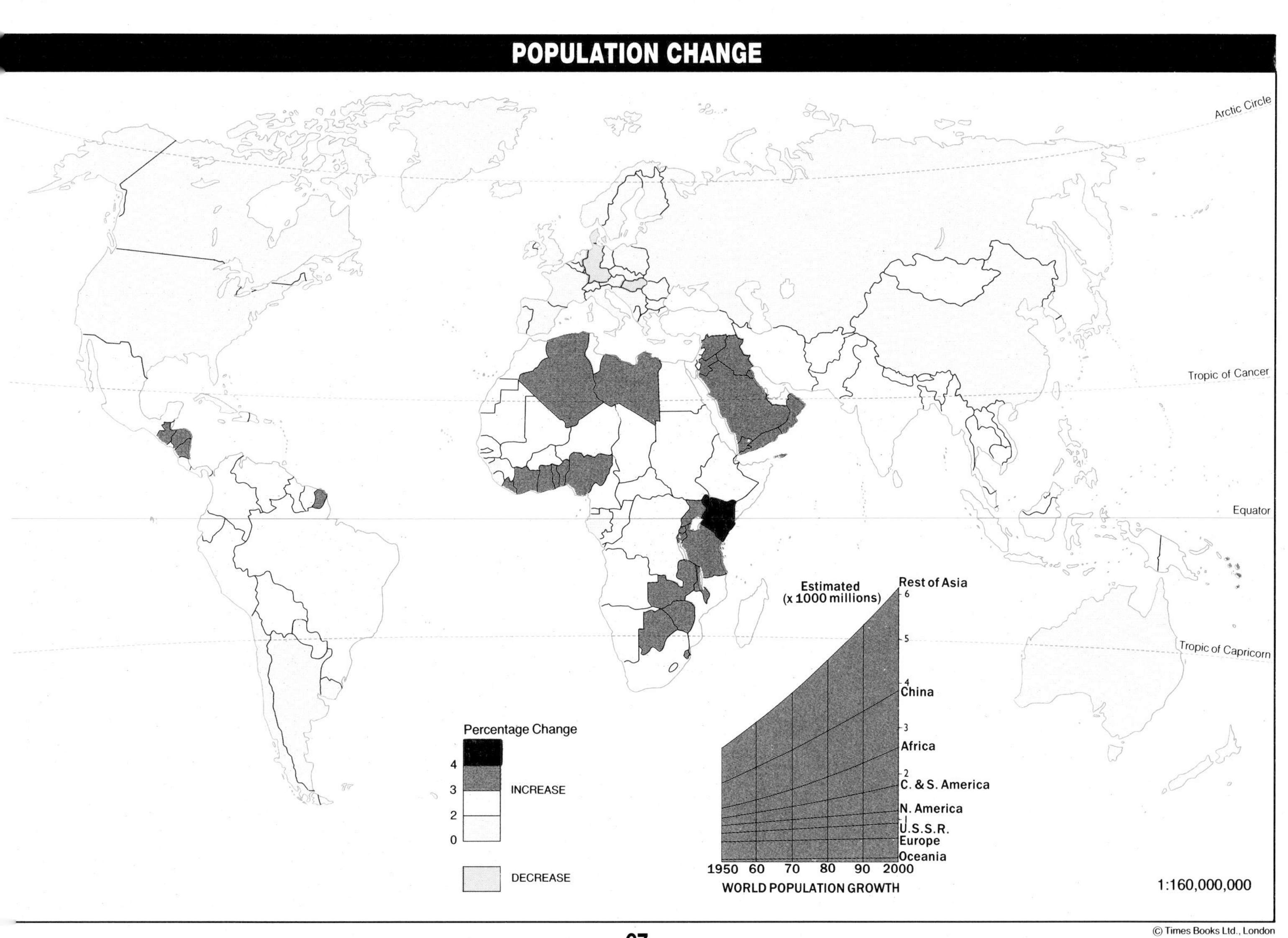

Percentage Change

4
3   INCREASE
2
0

DECREASE

Estimated (x 1000 millions)

Rest of Asia
China
Africa
C. & S. America
N. America
U.S.S.R.
Europe
Oceania

1950 60 70 80 90 2000
WORLD POPULATION GROWTH

1:160,000,000

67

TIME ZONES

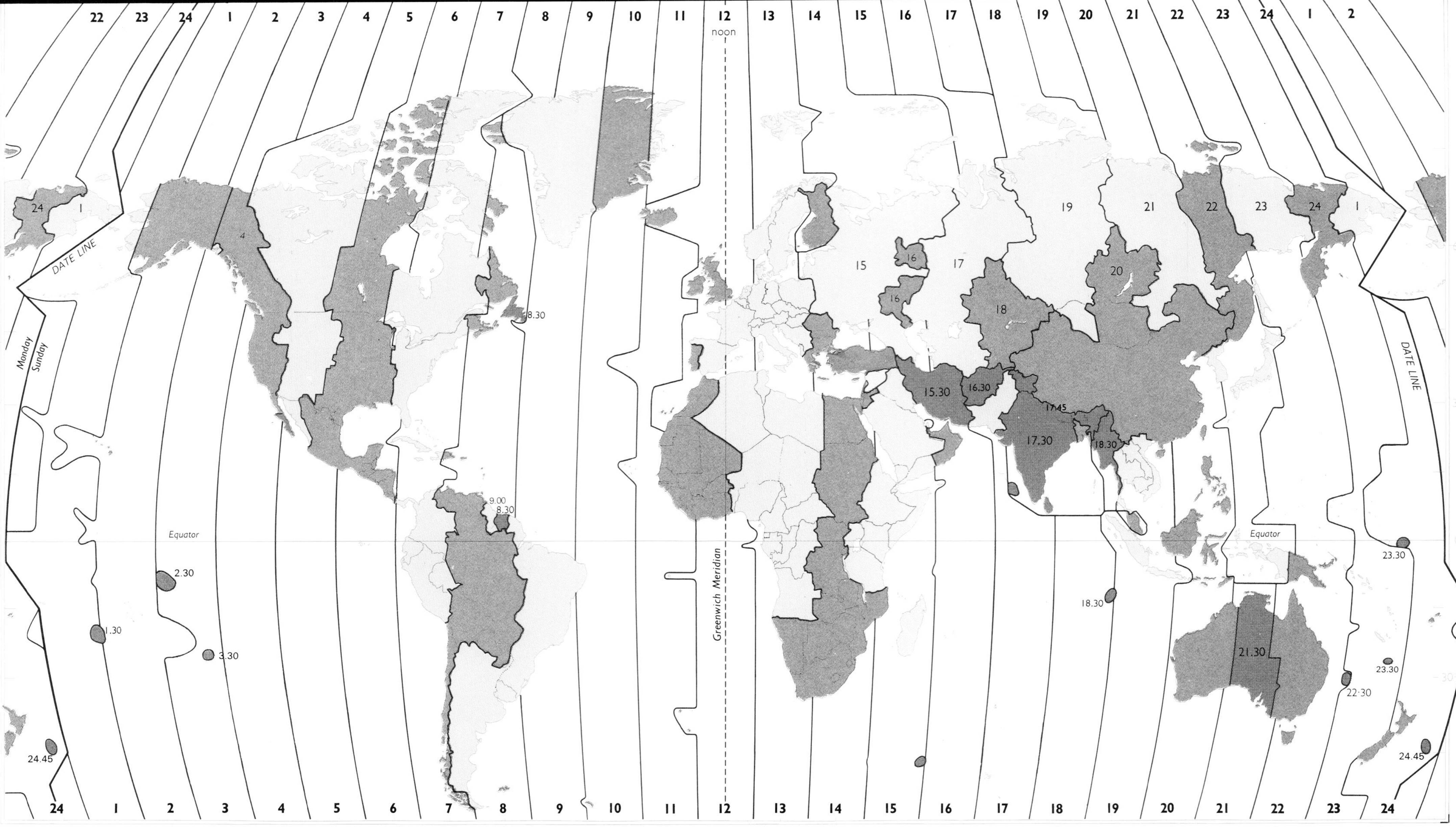

DATE LINE

noon

Greenwich Meridian

Equator

Monday
Sunday

DATE LINE

Equator

1:105,000,000

Zone times (given in bold figures at the top
and bottom of map) are the Standard Times
kept on land and sea compared with 12 hours
(noon) Greenwich Mean Time. Daylight
Saving Time (normally one hour in advance of
local Standard time), which is observed by
certain countries for part of the year, is not
shown on the map.

68

This page explains the main symbols, lettering style and height/depth colours used on the reference maps on pages 2 to 76. The scale of each map is indicated at the foot of each page. Abbreviations used on the maps appear at the beginning of the index.

BOUNDARIES

▬▬▬▬▬▬	International
▬▬ ▬▬ ▬▬ ▬▬	International under Dispute
▪ ▪ ▪ ▪ ▪ ▪ ▪	Cease Fire Line
▬▬▬▬▬▬	Autonomous or State
··············	Administrative
▬▬ ▬▬ ▬▬	Maritime (National)
▬ ▬ ▬ ▬ ▬	International Date Line

COMMUNICATIONS

══════	Motorway/Express Highway
▭▭▭▭▭▭	Under Construction
▬▬▬▬▬	Major Highway
▬▬▬▬▬	Other Roads
▬ ▬ ▬ ▬	Under Construction
▬ ▬ ▬ ▬ ▬	Track
	Road Tunnel
·········	Car Ferry
▬▬▬▬▬	Main Railway
▬▬▬▬▬	Other Railway
▬ ▬ ▬ ▬	Under Construction
	Rail Tunnel
▬ ▬ ▬ ▬ ▬	Rail Ferry
▬ ▬ ▬ ▬ ▬	Canal
⊕	International Airport
✈	Other Airport

LAKE FEATURES

	Freshwater
	Saltwater
	Seasonal
	Salt Pan

LANDSCAPE FEATURES

	Glacier, Ice Cap
	Marsh, Swamp
	Sand Desert, Dunes

OTHER FEATURES

	River
	Seasonal River
≍	Pass, Gorge
	Dam, Barrage
	Waterfall, Rapid
	Aqueduct
	Reef
▴4231	Summit, Peak
.217	Spot Height, Depth
⌣	Well
▵	Oil Field
▲	Gas Field
Gas/Oil	Oil/Natural Gas Pipeline
Gemsbok Nat. Pk	National Park
.·.UR	Historic Site

LETTERING STYLES

CANADA	Independent Nation
FLORIDA	State, Province or Autonomous Region
Gibraltar (U.K.)	Sovereignty of Dependent Territory
Lothian	Administrative Area
LANGUEDOC	Historic Region
Loire *Vosges*	Physical Feature or Physical Region

TOWNS AND CITIES

Square symbols denote capital cities

			Population
■	●	**New York**	over 5 000 000
■	●	**Montréal**	over 1 000 000
▫	○	Ottawa	over 500 000
▪	●	**Québec**	over 100 000
▫	○	St John's	over 50 000
▫	○	Yorkton	over 10 000
▫	○	Jasper	under 10 000

Built-up-area

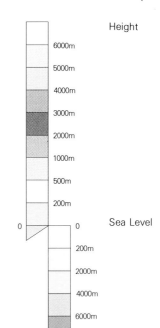

Height

| 6000m |
| 5000m |
| 4000m |
| 3000m |
| 2000m |
| 1000m |
| 500m |
| 200m |

0 — 0 — Sea Level

| 200m |
| 2000m |
| 4000m |
| 6000m |
| 8000m |

Depth

Map labels

ARCTIC OCEAN

Novo Sibirskiye Ostrova
Os. Vrangelya (Wrangel I.)
BEAUFORT SEA
Ellesmere Island
Nares Str.
Parry Is.
Melville I.
Banks I.
Victoria I.
Devon I.
Thule
BAFFIN BAY
GREENLAND
Scoresbysund
Denmark Strait
Godhavn
Godthåb
Julianehåb
ICELAND
Reykjavík

Barrow
USA
ALASKA
Arctic Circle
Inuvik
Gt. Bear L.
Mackenzie
Yukon
Fairbanks
UNITED

Anadyr
Bering Str.
Nome
St. Lawrence I.
Anchorage
Seward
Whitehorse
Gt. Slave L.
HUDSON BAY
Churchill
Baffin I.
Davis Str.

Magadan
BERING SEA
Juneau
CANADA
Goose Bay
Sept Iles
Newfoundland

Petropavlovsk-Kamchatskiy
Aleutian Islands
Edmonton
Saskatoon
Calgary
Regina
Winnipeg
Thunder Bay
L. Superior
Québec
Montréal
Ottawa
St John
St John's
Halifax

Victoria
Vancouver
Seattle
NORTH
Portland
Minneapolis
L. Michigan
L. Huron
Milwaukee
Detroit
Toronto
Buffalo
Cleveland
Boston
New York
Philadelphia

AMERICA
Salt Lake City
Denver
Chicago
Pittsbg.
Baltimore
Washington
Norfolk

San Francisco
UNITED STATES OF
Kansas City
St Louis
Cincinnati

Los Angeles
AMERICA
Oklahoma City
Memphis
Atlanta
NORTH ATLANTIC OCEAN
Azores (Port)
Lisbon

Phoenix
Dallas
Birmingham
Madeira (Port)
Casablanca

San Diego
El Paso
San Antonio
Jacksonville
Bermuda (UK)
Canary Is. (Sp)
La'youn

NORTH PACIFIC OCEAN
Houston
New Orleans
Tampa
Nouakchott
Dakar
Banjul
Bissau

Midway I. (USA)
Tropic of Cancer
Monterrey
MEXICO
GULF OF MEXICO
Miami
Havana
THE BAHAMAS
CAPE VERDE
Conakry
Freetown
Mon

Wake I. (USA)
Honolulu
Hawaiian Is. (USA)
Hawaii
Guadalajara
Tampico
Veracruz
CUBA
Hispaniola
HAITI
DOM. REP.
San Juan
P.R.
Leeward Is.

Marshall Is.
Mexico City
Acapulco
BELIZE
JAMAICA
Kingston
CARIBBEAN SEA
Windward Is.

International Date Line
Guatemala
GUA.
HOND.
Tegucigalpa
NIC.
Managua
Barranquilla
Panamá
TRIN. TOB.
Georgetown
Paramaribo
Cayenne

Clipperton (Fr.)
San Salvador
C.R.
San José
PANAMA
Maracaibo
Caracas
VENEZUELA
GUYANA
SUR.
FR. GUI.

KIRIBATI
Banaba
Equator
Galapagos Is. (Ec.)
Medellin
Bogotá
COLOMBIA
Orinoco
Belém

TUVALU
Phoenix Is.
Quito
ECUAD.
Guayaquil
Manaus
Amazon
Fortaleza
Fernando de Noronha (Braz.)

Marquesas (Fr.)
BRAZIL
Recife
Ascension (UK)

VANUATU
FIJI
Suva
Society Is. (Fr.)
Tuamotu (Fr.)
PERU
Callao
Lima
Cuzco
SOUTH AMERICA
Salvador

Ís. Wallis (Fr.)
W. SAMOA
Samoa (USA)
Tahiti
La Paz
BOLIVIA
Sucre
Brasília
Trindade (Braz.)

New Caledonia
Nouméa
TONGA
Cook Is.
Rarotonga
Pitcairn I. (UK)
Tropic of Capricorn
Sala y Gómez (Chile)
Arica
Antofagasta
São Paulo
Rio de Janeiro
Santos
SOUTH

SOUTH PACIFIC OCEAN
Easter I. (Chile)
PARAGUAY
Asunción
Pôrto Alegre

Norfolk I. (Aus)
AUSTRALASIA
Kermadec Is. (NZ)
Córdoba
S. Miguel de Tucumán
Paraná
Tristan da Cu (UK)

Auckland
Valparaíso
Rosario
URUG.
Montevideo

NEW ZEALAND
Wellington
Juan Fernández (Chile)
Santiago
Buenos Aires
ARGENTINA
Concepción
Bahía Blanca

Christchurch
Chatham Is. (NZ)
Pto. Montt

Invercargill
Dunedin
Stewart I. (NZ)
Bounty Is. (NZ)
Antipodes Is. (NZ)

Auckland Is. (NZ)
Campbell I.

Macquarie I. (Aus)

Falkland Is. (UK)
Stanley
Sth. Georgia (UK)
Punta Arenas
C. Horn

Population Key

Capitals | Cities & Towns
■ ● over 5 million
■ ● over 1 million
□ ○ under 1 million

Colours used to denote countries have no political significance

Index

For more information about each country refer to the States and Territories section (page number in bold type). For large scale map refer to map section (page number in italic).

AFRICA

Country		
Algeria	**4**	*48*
Angola	**4**	*51*
Benin	**7**	*48*
Botswana	**8**	*51*
Burkina	**9**	*48*
Burundi	**9**	*50*
Cameroon	**9**	*48–49*
Cape Verde	**10**	*48*
Central African Republic	**10**	*50*
Chad	**11**	*49*
Comoros	**12**	*51*
Congo	**13**	*50*
Djibouti	**14**	*50*
Egypt	**15**	*49*
Equatorial Guinea	**15**	*48*
Ethiopia	**15**	*48*
Gabon	**16**	*50*
Gambia	**16**	*48*
Ghana	**17**	*48*
Guinea	**18**	*48*
Guinea-Bissau	**18**	*48*
Ivory Coast	**21**	*48*
Kenya	**22**	*50*
Lesotho	**23**	*51*
Liberia	**23**	*48*
Libya	**23**	*49*
Madagascar	**24**	*51*
Malawi	**24**	*51*
Mali	**25**	*48*
Mauritania	**25**	*48*
Mauritius	**26**	*51*
Morocco	**26**	*48*
Mozambique	**27**	*51*
Namibia	**27**	*51*
Niger	**28**	*48*
Nigeria	**28**	*48*
Rwanda	**31**	*50*
São Tomé & Principe	**32**	*48*
Senegal	**32**	*48*
Seychelles	**32**	*51*
Sierra Leone	**32**	*48*
Somalia	**33**	*50*
South Africa	**33**	*51*
Sudan	**34**	*49*
Swaziland	**34**	*51*
Tanzania	**35**	*50–51*
Togo	**36**	*48*
Tunisia	**36**	*48*
Uganda	**37**	*50*
Zaire	**43**	*50–51*
Zambia	**43**	*51*
Zimbabwe	**43**	*51*

AMERICA, North & Central

Country		
Antigua & Barbuda	**5**	*69*
Bahamas	**6**	*69*
Barbados	**7**	*69*
Belize	**8**	*70*
Canada	**9**	*54–55*
Costa Rica	**13**	*70*
Cuba	**13**	*69*
Dominica	**14**	*69*
Dominican Republic	**14**	*69*
El Salvador	**15**	*70*
Grenada	**18**	*69*
Guatemala	**18**	*70*
Haiti	**18**	*69*
Honduras	**19**	*70*
Jamaica	**21**	*69*
Mexico	**26**	*69*
Nicaragua	**28**	*70*
Panama	**29**	*70*
St Kitts-Nevis	**31**	*69*
St Lucia	**31**	*69*
St Vincent	**31**	*69*
Trinidad & Tobago	**36**	*69*
USA	**39**	*56–57*

AMERICA, South

Country		
Argentina	**5**	*74*
Bolivia	**8**	*72–73*
Brazil	**8**	*72–73*
Chile	**11**	*74*
Colombia	**12**	*72*
Ecuador	**15**	*72*
Guyana	**18**	*73*
Paraguay	**29**	*74*

1:70 000 000
(45° N & S)

Peru **29** *72*	Japan **21** *28–29*	Taiwan **35** *31*	Vanuatu **42** *33*
Surinam **34** *73*	Jordan **21** *40*	Thailand **36** *30*	Western Samoa **42** *33*
Uruguay **41** *74*	North Korea **22** *28*	Turkey **36** *40*	
Venezuela **42** *72*	South Korea **22** *28*	USSR **37** *24–25*	**EUROPE**
	Kuwait **22** *41*	UAE **38** *41*	Albania **4** *17*
ASIA	Laos **23** *30*	Vietnam **42** *30*	Andorra **4** *15*
Afghanistan **4** *42*	Lebanon **23** *45*	Yemen **43** *50*	Austria **6** *18*
Bahrain **6** *41*	Malaysia **24** *30*	Yemen, South **43** *38*	Belgium **7** *13*
Bangladesh **6** *43*	Maldives **25** *44*		Bulgaria **8** *17*
Bhutan **7** *43*	Mongolia **26** *26*	**AUSTRALASIA**	Cyprus **13** *45*
Brunei **8** *27*	Nepal **27** *43*	Australia **5** *32–34*	Czechoslovakia **14** *18–19*
Burma **9** *30*	Oman **29** *38*	Fiji **16** *33*	Denmark **14** *11*
Cambodia **9** *30*	Pakistan **29** *42*	Kiribati **22** *33*	Finland **16** *12*
China **11** *31*	Philippines **30** *27*	Nauru **27** *33*	France **16** *14*
India **19** *42–44*	Qatar **30** *41*	New Zealand **28** *35*	East Germany **17** *18*
Indonesia **20** *27*	Saudi Arabia **32** *40–41*	Papua New Guinea **29** *32*	West Germany **17** *18*
Iran **20** *41*	Singapore **32** *30*	Solomon Islands **33** *33*	Greece **17** *17*
Iraq **20** *40–41*	Sri Lanka **34** *44*	Tonga **36** *33*	Hungary **19** *18–19*
Israel **20** *45*	Syria **35** *40*	Tuvalu **37** *33*	Iceland **19** *12*

Ireland **20** *9*
Italy **21** *16*
Liechtenstein **24** *16*
Luxembourg **24** *13*
Malta **25** *16*
Monaco **26** *14*
Netherlands **27** *13*
Norway **28** *12*
Poland **30** *18–19*
Portugal **30** *15*
Romania **30** *17*
San Marino **31** *16*
Spain **34** *15*
Sweden **35** *12*
Switzerland **35** *16*
UK **38** *6–9*
Vatican City **42**
Yugoslavia **43** *16–17*

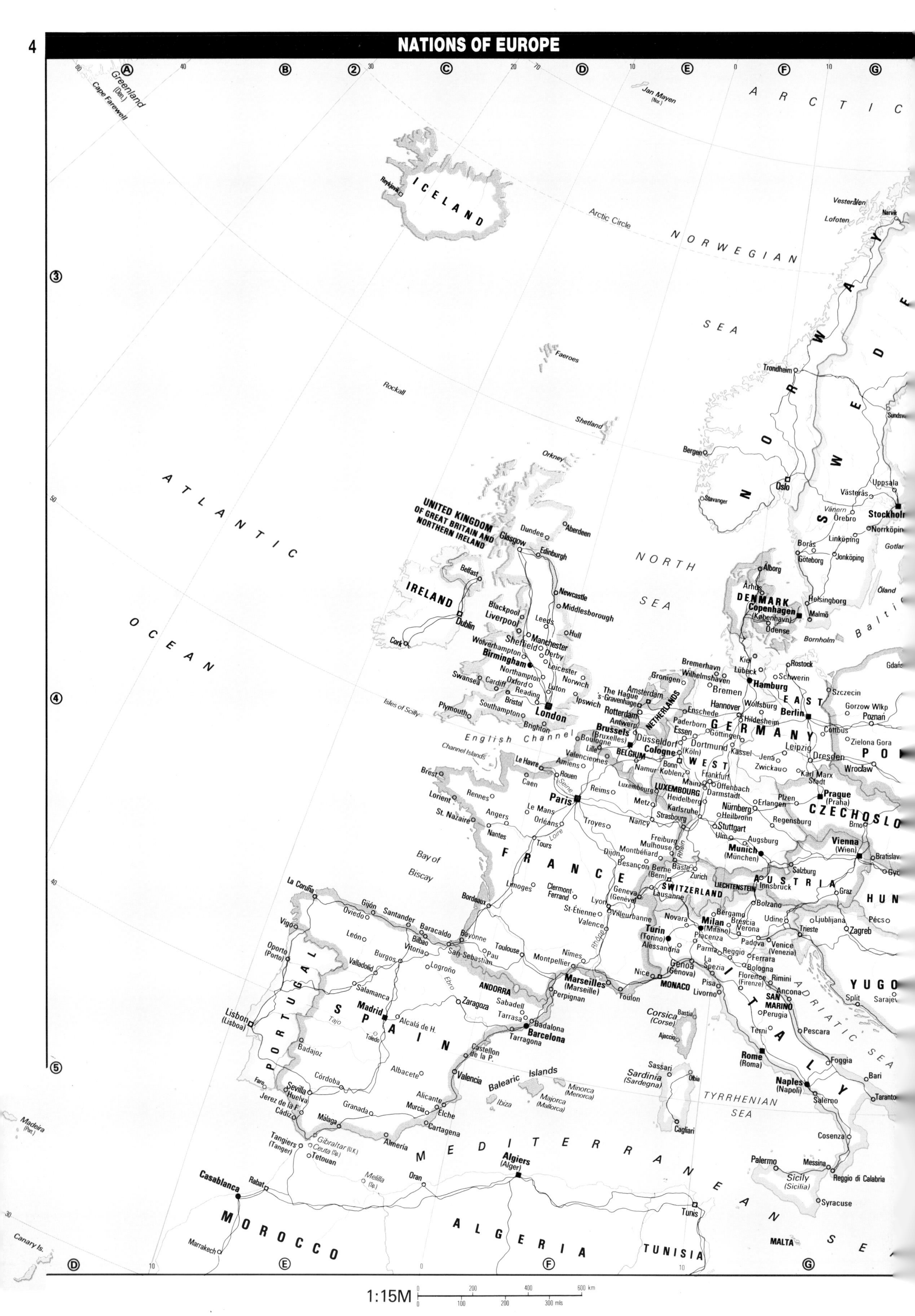

Greenland
Cape Farewell

ICELAND
Reykjavík

ARCTIC

Jan Mayen (Nor.)

NORWEGIAN SEA

Arctic Circle

Vesterålen
Lofoten
Narvik

N O R W A Y

Trondheim

Sundsvall

Faeroes

Rockall

Shetland

Orkney

Bergen
Stavanger
Oslo

S W E D E N

Uppsala
Västerås
Stockholm
Örebro
Norrköping
Borås
Linköping
Jönköping
Göteborg
Gotland
Öland

ATLANTIC OCEAN

UNITED KINGDOM
OF GREAT BRITAIN AND
NORTHERN IRELAND

Dundee
Aberdeen
Glasgow
Edinburgh
Newcastle
Belfast
Middlesborough

IRELAND

Blackpool
Liverpool
Leeds
Hull
Manchester
Dublin
Sheffield
Derby
Wolverhampton
Cork
Leicester
Birmingham
Norwich
Northampton
Swansea
Cardiff
Oxford
Ipswich
Bristol
Reading
Luton
London
Plymouth
Southampton
Brighton
Isles of Scilly

NORTH SEA

DENMARK
Ålborg
Århus
Copenhagen
(København)
Odense
Bornholm

Kiel
Lübeck
Schwerin
Rostock
Bremerhaven
Wilhelmshaven
Hamburg
Bremen
Hannover
Wolfsburg

Baltic

Helsingborg
Malmö

Gdańsk
Szczecin
Gorzow Wlkp
Poznań

EAST GERMANY
Berlin

P O

Channel Islands

English Channel

The Hague
's-Gravenhage
Amsterdam
Groningen
Enschede
NETHERLANDS
Rotterdam
Antwerp
Brussels
(Bruxelles)
BELGIUM
Düsseldorf
Lille
Boulogne
Valenciennes
Namur
Cologne
(Köln)
Bonn
Essen
Dortmund
Paderborn
Hildesheim
Göttingen
Kassel
WEST GERMANY
Frankfurt
Mainz
Offenbach
Darmstadt
Jena
Zwickau
Karl Marx
Stadt
Leipzig
Dresden
Erlangen
Plzeň
CZECHOSLO
Wrocław
Zielona Gora
Cottbus

Le Havre
Amiens
Rouen
Caen
Reims
Seine
Luxembourg
LUXEMBOURG
Metz
Heidelberg
Koblenz
Nürnberg
Heilbronn
Regensburg
Prague
(Praha)
Brno

Brest
Rennes
Lorient
St. Nazaire
Angers
Nantes

Paris
Le Mans
Orléans
Troyes
Loire
Tours
Nancy
Strasbourg
Karlsruhe
Stuttgart
Augsburg
Ulm
Munich
(München)
Salzburg
Vienna
(Wien)
Bratislav

Bay of
Biscay

F R A N C E

Limoges
Clermont-Ferrand
Dijon
Besançon
Mulhouse
Montbéliard
Freiburg
Berne
(Bern)
Basle
Zurich
Innsbruck
AUSTRIA
Graz
HUN

La Coruña
Vigo
Oviedo
Gijón
Santander
León
Baracaldo
Bilbao
Vitoria
Bayonne
San Sebastián
Pau
Toulouse
Burgos
Logroño
Ebro

Lyon
Villeurbanne
St-Étienne
Valence
Nîmes
Montpellier
Geneva
(Genève)
Lausanne
SWITZERLAND
LIECHTENSTEIN
Bolzano
Bergamo
Brescia
Novara
Verona
Udine
Trieste
Ljubljana
Zagreb
Pécs

PORTUGAL
Oporto
(Porto)
Valladolid
Salamanca
Lisbon
(Lisboa)
Tajo
Badajoz

Zaragoza
Sabadell
Tarrasa
ANDORRA
Perpignan
Marseilles
(Marseille)
Toulon
MONACO
Nice
Turin
(Torino)
Alessandria
Novara
Piacenza
Milan
(Milano)
Padova
Venice
(Venezia)
Ferrara
YUGO
Reggio
Parma
La
Spezia
Genoa
(Genova)
Bologna
Livorno
Florence
(Firenze)
Rimini
Ancona
Split
Sarajev
SAN
MARINO
Pisa
Perugia
Pescara
ADRIATIC SEA

Madrid
Alcalá de H.
Toledo
Badalona
Barcelona
Tarragona

S P A I N

Córdoba
Albacete
Castellón
de la P.
Valencia
Balearic Islands
Minorca
(Menorca)
Sardinia
(Sardegna)
Olbia
Corsica
(Corse)
Bastia
Ajaccio
Terni
Rome
(Roma)
Foggia
Bari
Sassari

Madeira
(Port.)

Faro
Sevilla
Huelva
Jerez de la F.
Cádiz
Granada
Málaga
Murcia
Elche
Alicante
Cartagena
Almería
Ibiza
Majorca
(Mallorca)
TYRRHENIAN SEA
Cagliari
Naples
(Napoli)
Salerno
Taranto
I T A L Y

Canary Is.

Tangiers
(Tanger)
Gibraltar (U.K.)
Ceuta (Sp.)
Tetouan
Melilla
(Sp.)
Oran
M E D I T E R R A N E A N
Algiers
(Alger)
Palermo
Cosenza
Messina
Sicily
(Sicilia)
Reggio di Calabria

Casablanca
Rabat
Marrakech

M O R O C C O

A L G E R I A

Tunis
Syracuse
MALTA
TUNISIA
S E A

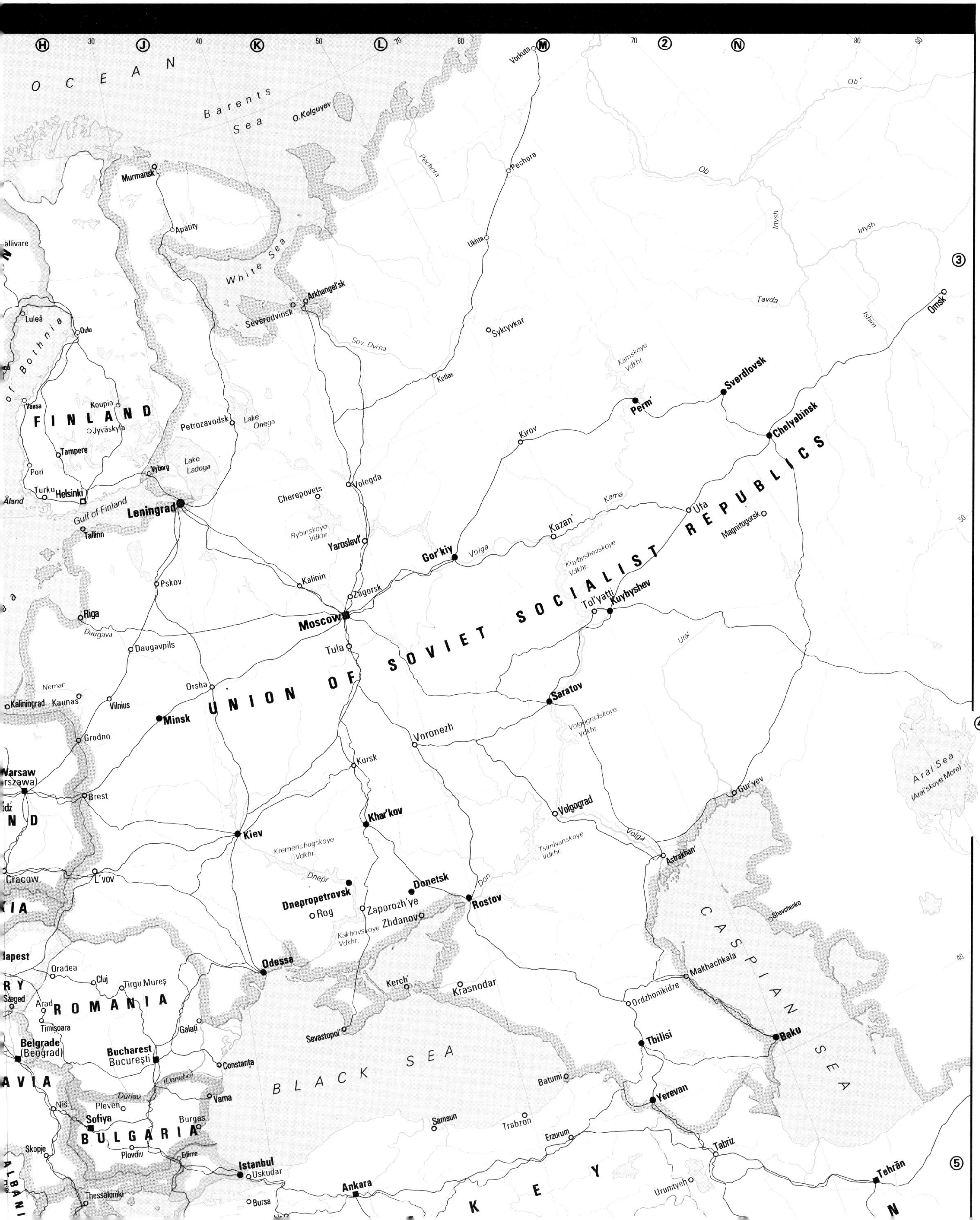

H 30 J 40 K 50 L 70 60 M 70 ② N 80 80

O C E A N

Barents Sea
O.Kolguyev

Ob'

Vorkuta

Murmansk

Apatity

Pechora

White Sea

Ukhta

Pechora

Ob

Irtysh

Irtysh

③

Severodvinsk

Arkhangel'sk

Syktyvkar

Kotlas

Tavda

Ishim

Omsk

Koupio

Jyväskyla

Petrozavodsk

Lake Onega

Kirov

Kamskoye Vdkhr.

Perm'

Sverdlovsk

Chelyabinsk

F I N L A N D

Luleå

Oulu

Tampere

Pori

Turku

Helsinki

Vyborg

Lake Ladoga

Vologda

Cherepovets

Kama

Kazan'

Ufa

Magnitogorsk

Leningrad

Gulf of Finland

Yaroslavl'

Volga

Gor'kiy

Kuybyshevskoye Vdkhr.

U N I O N   O F   S O V I E T   S O C I A L I S T   R E P U B L I C S

Åland

Tallinn

Rybinskoye Vdkhr.

Kalinin

Zagorsk

Tol'yatti

Kuybyshev

Riga

Psков

Moscow

Ural

Daugava

Daugavpils

Tula

Neman

Orsha

Kaliningrad

Kaunas

Vilnius

Saratov

Minsk

Voronezh

Volgogradskoye Vdkhr.

Grodno

Warsaw
(Warszawa)

Brest

Kursk

Aral Sea
(Aral'skoye More)

④

Łódź

ND

Khar'kov

Volgograd

Gur'yev

Cracow

L'vov

Kremenchugskoye Vdkhr.

Dnepr

Donetsk

Don

Astrakhan'

Tsimlyanskoye Vdkhr.

Volga

KIA

Dnepropetrovsk

Rog

Zaporozh'ye

Zhdanov

Rostov

Shevchenko

C A S P I A N

apest

Oradea

Cluj

Tirgu Mureş

Kakhovskoye Vdkhr.

Odessa

Makhachkala

RY

Szeged

Arad

R O M A N I A

Galaţi

Kerch'

Krasnodar

Ordzhonikidze

S E A

Timişoara

Belgrade
(Beograd)

Bucharest
Bucureşti

Constanţa

(Danube)

Sevastopol

Tbilisi

Baku

AVIA

Niš

Dunav

Pleven

B U L G A R I A

Varna

B L A C K   S E A

Batumi

Yerevan

Sofiya

Burgas

Skopje

Plovdiv

Edirne

Istanbul

Uskudar

Samsun

Trabzon

Erzurum

Tabriz

K E Y

⑤

ALBANI

Thessaloniki

Bursa

Ankara

Urumtyeh

Tehrān

N

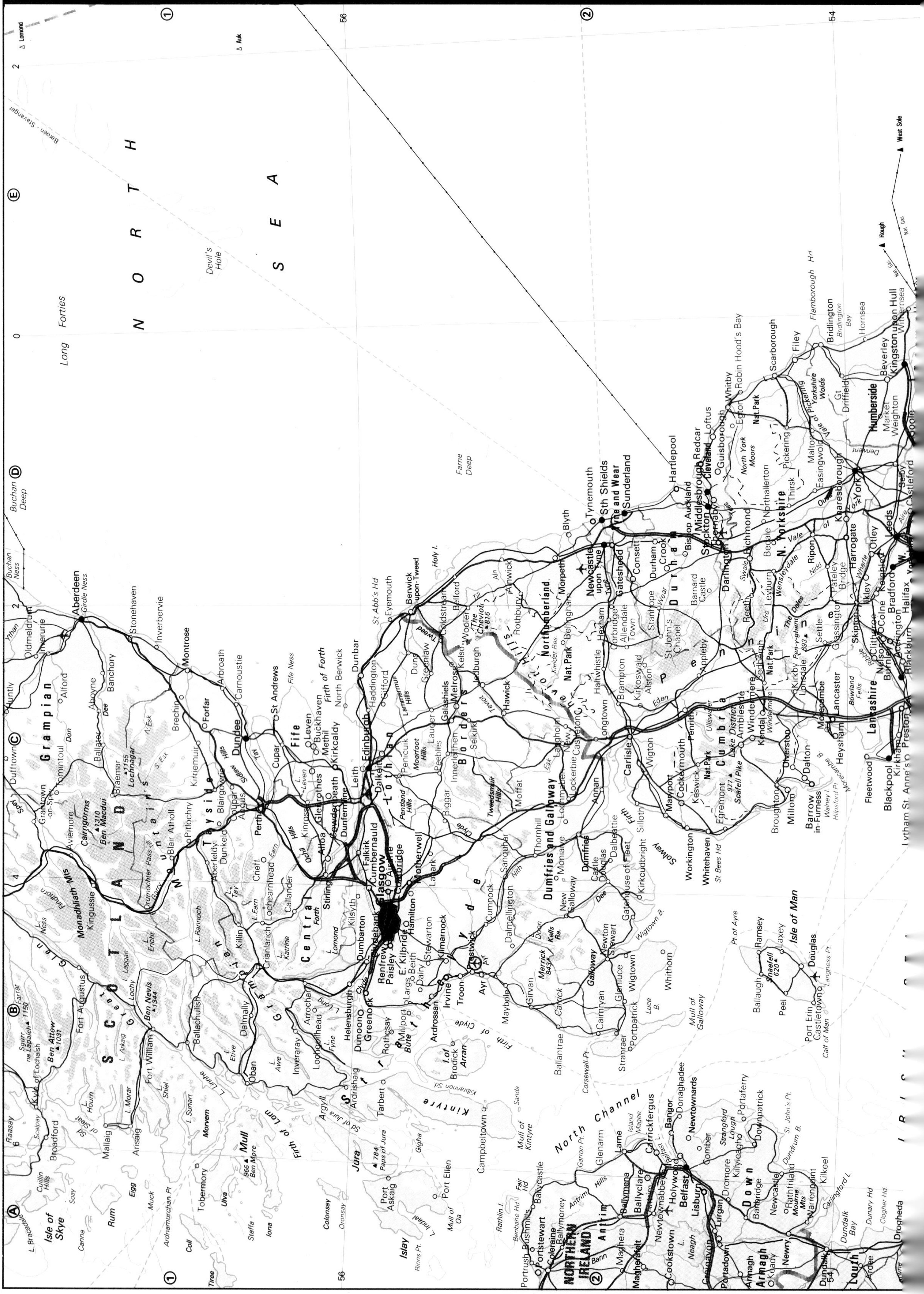

N O R T H   S E A

I R I S H   S E A

North Channel

Firth of Forth

Firth of Clyde

S C O T L A N D

Grampian

Highlands / Mountains

Tayside

Central

Strathclyde

Borders

Dumfries and Galloway

Cheviot Hills

Pennines

Northumberland Nat. Park

Lake District Nat. Park

Cumbria

Lancashire

N. Yorkshire

Humberside

Cleveland

Durham

The and Wear

Yorkshire Wolds

North York Moors

NORTHERN IRELAND

Antrim

Down

Isle of Man

Isle of Skye

Mull

Jura

Islay

Arran

Kintyre

Galloway

Long Forties

Devil's Hole

Farne Deep

Buchan Deep

Aberdeen · Girdle Ness

Dundee

Perth

Edinburgh

Glasgow

Paisley

Greenock

Ayr

Kilmarnock

Carlisle

Newcastle upon Tyne

Gateshead

Sunderland

Sth Shields

Tynemouth

Hartlepool

Middlesbrough

Stockton

Darlington

Durham

York

Leeds

Bradford

Harrogate

Kingston upon Hull

Scarborough

Whitby

Bridlington

Belfast

Bangor

Newtownards

Lisburn

Ballymena

Coleraine

Portrush

Larne

Ben Nevis ▲ 1344

Ben Macdui ▲ 1310

Lochnagar ▲ 1155

Cairngorms

Monadhliath Mts

Cuillin Hills

Fort William

Oban

Inveraray

Stirling

Falkirk

Dumbarton

Hamilton

Motherwell

Dumfries

Stranraer

Scafell Pike 977 ▲

1:2M

| 0 | 25 | 50 | 75 | 100 km |

| 0 | 25 | | 50 mls | |

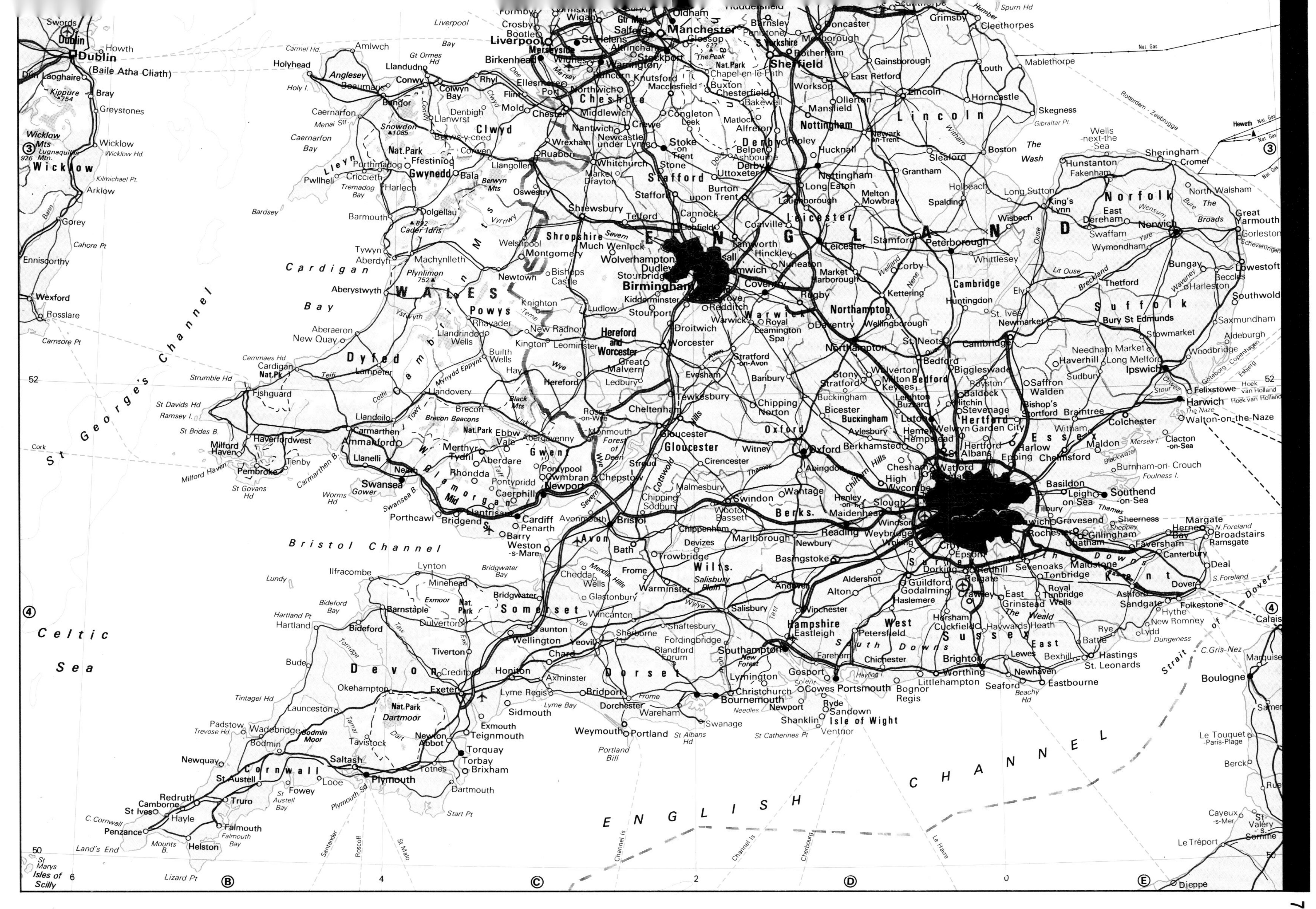
ENGLAND
WALES
Norfolk
Suffolk
Lincoln
Essex
Kent
Sussex
Dorset
Devon
Cornwall
Somerset
Wilts.
Berks.
Oxford
Gloucester
Hampshire
Cheshire
Stafford
Shropshire
Powys
Dyfed
Clwyd
Gwynedd
Wicklow
ENGLISH CHANNEL
Bristol Channel
Cardigan Bay
St George's Channel
Celtic Sea
Strait of Dover
The Wash
Isle of Wight
Isles of Scilly
Birmingham
Manchester
Liverpool
Sheffield
Nottingham
Leicester
Northampton
Cambridge
Ipswich
Norwich
Great Yarmouth
Lowestoft
Southend-on-Sea
Brighton
Southampton
Portsmouth
Bournemouth
Bristol
Cardiff
Swansea
Plymouth
Exeter
Dover
Calais
Boulogne
Dieppe
Dublin (Baile Atha Cliath)
Holyhead
Aberystwyth
Penzance
Land's End
Lizard Pt
Le Havre
Cherbourg
Channel Is
Roscoff
St Malo

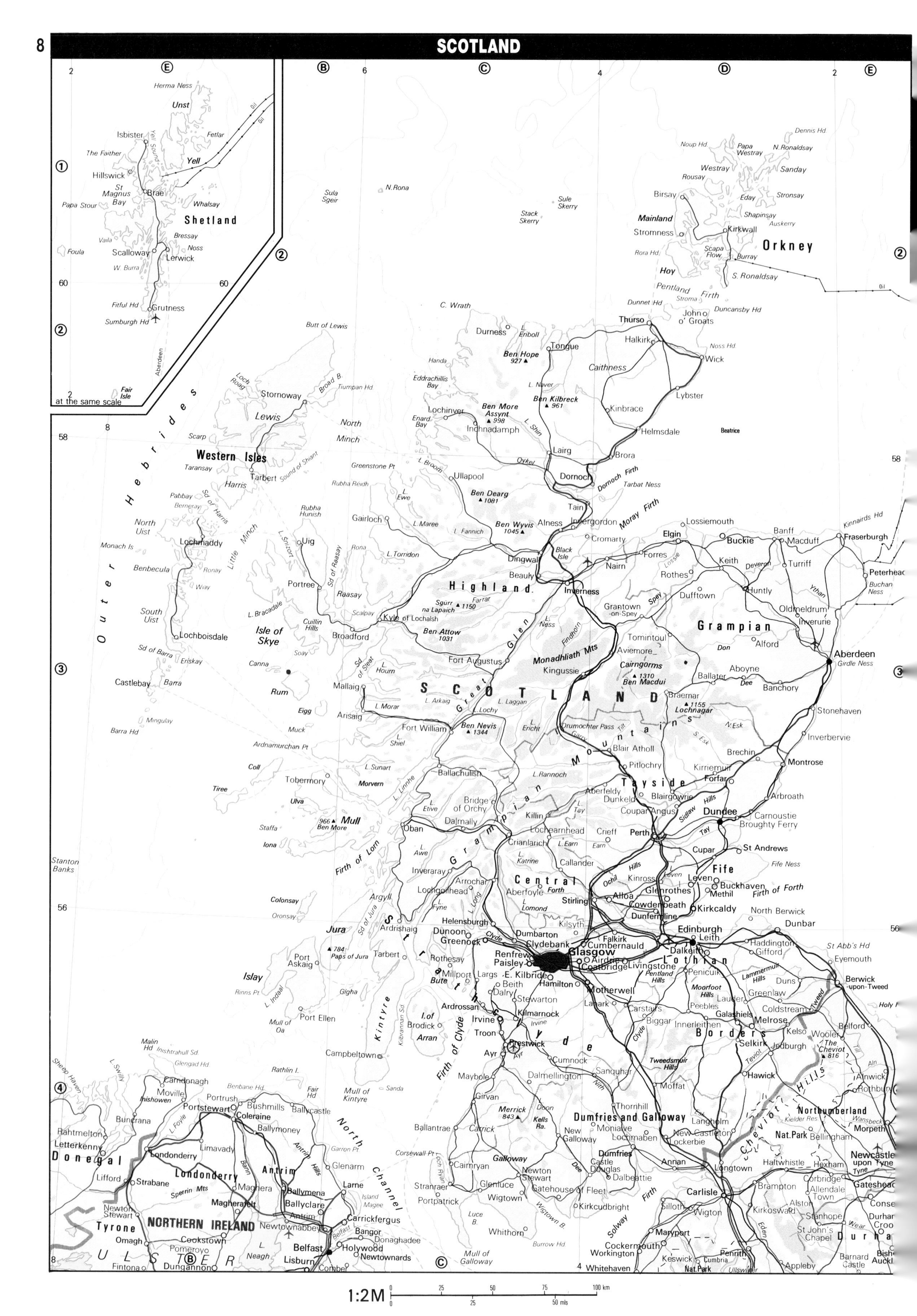

Herma Ness
Unst
Fetlar
Isbister
Yell Sound
Yell
The Faither
Hillswick
St Magnus Bay
Brae
Papa Stour
Whalsay
Shetland
Bressay
Vaila
Noss
Foula
Scalloway
Lerwick
W. Burra
Fitful Hd
Grutness
Sumburgh Hd
Aberdeen
Fair Isle
at the same scale
Oil
N. Rona
Sula Sgeir
Stack Skerry
Sule Skerry
Dennis Hd
Noup Hd
Papa Westray
N. Ronaldsay
Westray
Sanday
Rousay
Birsay
Eday
Stronsay
Mainland
Shapinsay
Auskerry
Stromness
Kirkwall
Orkney
Rora Hd
Scapa Flow
Burray
Hoy
S. Ronaldsay
Pentland Firth
Stroma
Dunnet Hd
Duncansby Hd
John o' Groats
C. Wrath
Butt of Lewis
Durness
L. Eriboll
Thurso
Halkirk
Tongue
Ben Hope 927
Noss Hd
Wick
Handa
Caithness
Eddrachillis Bay
L. Naver
Lybster
Loch Roag
Broad B.
Tiumpan Hd
Stornoway
Ben Kilbreck 961
Kinbrace
Lewis
Lochinver
Ben More Assynt 998
Enard Bay
North Minch
Inchnadamph
L. Shin
Helmsdale
Beatrice
Scarp
Lairg
Western Isles
Brora
Taransay
Greenstone Pt
L. Broom
Oykel
Tarbert
Sound of Shiant
Ullapool
Dornoch
Dornoch Firth
Harris
Rubha Reidh
Tarbat Ness
Pabbay
Sd of Harris
Berneray
L. Ewe
Ben Dearg 1081
Tain
Outer Hebrides
Rubha Hunish
Gairloch
L. Maree
Ben Wyvis 1045
Alness
Invergordon
Moray Firth
Lossiemouth
North Uist
L. Fannich
Cromarty
Elgin
Buckie
Banff
Macduff
Kinnairds Hd
Fraserburgh
Lochmaddy
Little Minch
L. Snizort
Uig
Sd of Raasay
Rona
L. Torridon
Dingwall
Black Isle
Forres
Monach Is
Nairn
Keith
Deveron
Turriff
Benbecula
Ronay
Beauly
Rothes
Peterhead
Wiay
Portree
Raasay
Highland
Inverness
Huntly
Buchan Ness
Ythan
Dufftown
South Uist
L. Bracadale
Sgùrr na Lapaich 1150
Farrar
Grantown -on-Spey
Spey
Oldmeldrum
Cuillin Hills
Scalpay
Kyle of Lochalsh
Inverurie
Lochboisdale
Isle of Skye
Broadford
Ben Attow 1031
L. Ness
Findhorn
Grampian
Tomintoul
Sd of Barra
Eriskay
Soay
Alford
Don
Aviemore
Aberdeen
Girdle Ness
Canna
Sd of Sleat
L. Hourn
Fort Augustus
Great Glen
Monadhliath Mts
Cairngorms
Kingussie
1310 Ben Macdui
Aboyne
Castlebay
Barra
Mallaig
Ballater
Dee
Banchory
Rum
L. Arkaig
S C O T L A N D
L. Laggan
Braemar
1155 Lochnagar
Eigg
L. Morar
Stonehaven
Arisaig
L. Lochy
Mingulay
Ben Nevis 1344
L. Ericht
Drumochter Pass
N. Esk
Barra Hd
Muck
Fort William
L. Shiel
Garry
Tilt
Mountains
S. Esk
Inverbervie
Ardnamurchan Pt
Blair Atholl
Brechin
Coll
L. Sunart
Pitlochry
Montrose
Kirriemuir
Tobermory
Morvern
Ballachulish
L. Linnhe
L. Rannoch
Tiree
Forfar
Tayside
Aberfeldy
Dunkeld
Sidlaw Hills
Arbroath
Ulva
Bridge of Orchy
Blairgowrie
L. Etive
Coupar Angus
Carnoustie
Mull
966 Ben More
Killin
L. Tay
Dundee
Broughty Ferry
Staffa
Dalmally
Grampian
Oban
Lochearnhead
Crieff
Perth
Tay
Iona
Crianlarich
L. Earn
Earn
St Andrews
L. Awe
L. Katrine
Cupar
Callander
Fife Ness
Stanton Banks
Firth of Lorn
Inveraray
Ochil Hills
Fife
Arrochar
Kinross
Leven
Central
Forth
Lochgoilhead
Aberfoyle
Glenrothes
Buckhaven
Methil
Firth of Forth
Argyll
Alloa
Colonsay
L. Fyne
L. Long
L. Lomond
Stirling
Cowdenbeath
Kirkcaldy
North Berwick
Oronsay
Dunfermline
Strathclyde
Helensburgh
Kilsyth
Dunbar
Jura
Sd of Jura
Ardrishaig
Dunoon
Dumbarton
Edinburgh
Leith
Greenock
Clyde
Clydebank
Falkirk
Cumbernauld
Haddington
St Abb's Hd
784 Paps of Jura
Tarbert
Renfrew
Glasgow
Dalkeith
Gifford
Port Askaig
Rothesay
Paisley
Airdrie
Lothian
Eyemouth
Islay
Millport
Largs
E. Kilbride
Coatbridge
Livingstone
Penicuik
Berwick -upon-Tweed
Bute
Beith
Hamilton
Pentland Hills
Lammermuir Hills
Duns
Rinns Pt
Gigha
Dalry
Motherwell
Moorfoot Hills
Greenlaw
L. Indaal
Stewarton
Lanark
Carstairs
Peebles
Lauder
Coldstream
Tweed
Holy I.
Ardrossan
Port Ellen
Kintyre
I. of Arran
Brodick
Irvine
Kilmarnock
Biggar
Galashiels
Mull of Oa
Kilbrannan Sd
Clyde
Innerleithen
Melrose
Belford
Troon
Borders
Kelso
Wooler
Malin Hd
Inishtrahull Sd
Prestwick
Selkirk
Jedburgh
The Cheviot 816
Campbeltown
Ayr
Firth of Clyde
Cumnock
Tweedsmuir Hills
Teviot
Till
Sheep Haven
Glengad Hd
Rathlin I.
Aln
Alnwick
Carndonagh
Maybole
Dalmellington
Sanquhar
Hawick
Moville
Benbane Hd
Fair Hd
Mull of Kintyre
Sanda
Nith
Moffat
Cheviot Hills
Rothbury
Inishowen
Portrush
Bushmills
Ballycastle
Girvan
Portstewart
Coleraine
Merrick 843
Doon
Thornhill
Buncrana
North Channel
Kells Ra.
Dumfries and Galloway
Northumberland
Kielder Res.
Ballymoney
Ballantrae
Carrick
Langholm
Wansbeck
Rathmelton
New Galloway
Moniaive
Lochmaben
New Castleton
Morpeth
Letterkenny
L. Foyle
Limavady
Antrim Hills
Garron Pt
Lockerbie
Nat. Park
Bellingham
Donegal
Londonderry
Corsewall Pt
Dumfries
Newcastle upon Tyne
Antrim
Glenarm
Loch Ryan
Galloway
Castle Douglas
Annan
Longtown
Haltwhistle
Hexham
Tyne
Lifford
Strabane
Londonderry
Bann
Cairnryan
Newton Stewart
Dee
Corbridge
Gateshead
Sperrin Mts
Maghera
Ballymena
Larne
Stranraer
Glenluce
Dalbeattie
Allendale Town
Island Magee
Gatehouse of Fleet
Carlisle
Brampton
Magherafelt
Ballyclare
Portpatrick
Wigtown
Firth
Newton Stewart
Antrim
Kirkcudbright
Silloth
Wigton
Alston
Consett
Carrickfergus
Kirkoswald
Tyrone
NORTHERN IRELAND
Newtownabbey
Luce B.
Wigtown B.
Solway
Eden
Stanhope
Durham
Belfast L.
Bangor
Whithorn
Wear
Omagh
Cookstown
Donaghadee
Maryport
St John's Chapel
Durham
Pomeroy
L. Neagh
Belfast
Holywood
Burrow Hd
Cockermouth
Workington
Penrith
ULSTER
Newtownards
Mull of Galloway
Cumbria
Barnard Castle
Fintona
Dungannon
Lisburn
Comber
Whitehaven
Keswick
Nat. Park
Ullswater
Appleby
1:2M
0 25 50 75 100 km
0 25 50 mls

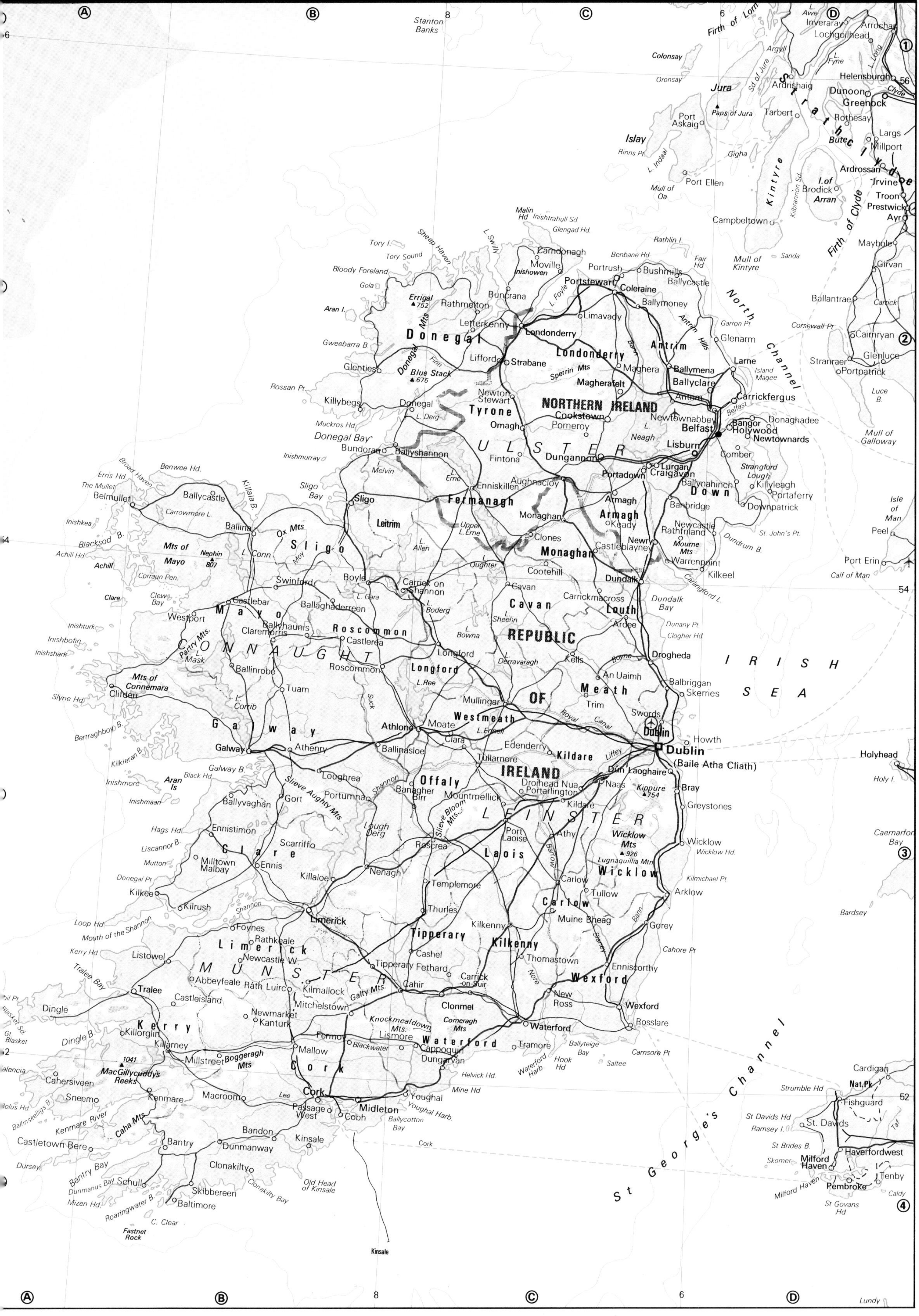

A   B   8   C   6   D

① Firth of Lorn
Colonsay
Oronsay   Argyll   L. Awe   Inveraray   Arrochar
Lochgoilhead   L. Long
Jura   Sd of Jura   L. Fyne   Helensburgh   56
Paps of Jura   Tarbert   Dunoon   Greenock
Port Askaig   Rothesay   Clyde
Islay   Gigha   Butec   Largs   Millport
Rinns Pt.   Mull of   Brodick   Ardrossan
Port Ellen   Oa   Arran   I. of   Irvine
Kintyre   Kilbrannon Sd.   Troon   ②
Campbeltown   Prestwick   Ayr
Mull of   Maybole
Kintyre   Sanda   Girvan

Malin   Inishtrahull Sd.   Ballantrae   Carrick
Hd.   Glengad Hd.   Corsewall Pt.   Cairnryan   ②
Tory I.   Carndonagh   Benbane Hd.   Fair   Stranraer   Glenluce
Tory Sound   Moville   Portrush   Bushmills   Hd.   Luce
Bloody Foreland   Inishowen   Portstewart   Ballycastle   Garron Pt.   Glenarm   B.
Gola   BunCrana   Coleraine   Antrim   Portpatrick   Isle
Errigal   Rathmelton   L. Foyle   Limavady   Ballymoney   Hills   Island   of
Aran I.   ▲752   Letterkenny   Londonderry   Maghera   Ballymena   Magee   Man
Gweebarra B.   Donegal   Londonderry   Magherafelt   Ballyclare   Larne   Peel
Rossan Pt.   Mts   Lifford   Strabane   Antrim   Carrickfergus   Mull of
Glenties   Blue Stack   Newton   Sperrin Mts   NORTHERN IRELAND   Belfast   Bangor   Galloway
Killybegs   ▲676   Stewart   Cookstown   Newtownabbey   Donaghadee
Donegal   Omagh   Pomeroy   Lisburn   Holywood   Port Erin
Muckros Hd.   Tyrone   ULSTER   L.   Newtownards   54
Donegal Bay   Dungannon   Neagh   Comber   Calf of Man
Inishmurray   Bundoran   Ballyshannon   Fintona   Portadown   Craigavon   Strangford
Sligo   L.   Enniskillen   Aughnacloy   Lurgan   Killyleagh   Lough
Bay   Melvin   Fermanagh   Monaghan   Armagh   Ballynahinch   Portaferry
Sligo   L. Erne   Keady   Banbridge   Downpatrick
Leitrim   Upper   Clones   Armagh   Newcastle   St. John's Pt.
L. Erne   Monaghan   Castleblayney   Rathfriland   Mourne
L.   Cootehill   Mts   Warrenpoint
Allen   Carrick on   Cavan   Dundalk   Kilkeel   Port Erin
Boyle   Shannon   Carrickmacross   Louth   Carlingford L.
Swinford   L. Gara   Cavan   Dundalk   Dundalk   Port Erin
Mts of   Nephin   Ballaghaderreen   L. Boderg   Bay
Mayo   807   L.   Clogher Hd.
Castlebar   Claremorris   L.   Sheelin   REPUBLIC   Dunany Pt.
Westport   Ballyhaunis   Bowna   Ardee   IRISH
Clew   Castlerea   Roscommon   Longford   OF   Drogheda
Bay   Ballinrobe   Roscommon   Derravaragh   Kells   SEA
Inishturk   Mask   Tuam   Longford   An Uaimh   Balbriggan
Inishbofin   Party Mts   L. Ree   Meath   Skerries
CONNAUGHT   L. Corrib   Westmeath   Trim   Swords
Mts of   Mullingar   Royal   Howth
Connemara   Galway   Athlone   Moate   L. Ennell   Canal   Dublin
Clifden   Athenry   Clara   Dublin
Galway   Ballinasloe   Edenderry   Kildare   (Baile Atha Cliath)   Holyhead
Shannon   Tullamore   Liffey   Dún Laoghaire   Holy I.
Bertraghboy B.   Loughrea   IRELAND   Naas   Kippure   Bray
Slyne Hd.   Slieve Aughty Mts   Offaly   Droihead Nua   ▲754   Greystones
Galway B.   Portumna   Banagher   Portarlington   Kildare
Inishmore   Gort   Birr   Mountmellick   Athy   Caernarfon
Aran Is   Ballyvaughan   Lough   LEINSTER   Wicklow   Bay
Inishmaan   Hags Hd.   Ennistimon   Derg   Port   Mts   ③
Liscannor B.   Scarriff   Laoise   Lugnaquillia Mtn   Wicklow
Clare   Slieve Bloom Mts   Laois   ▲926   Wicklow Hd.
Mutton   Milltown   Ennis   Roscrea   Carlow   WICKLOW   Kilmichael Pt.
Malbay   Killaloe   Nenagh   Barrow   Tullow   Arklow
Donegal Pt.   Kilkee   Templemore   Carlow   Bardsey
Loop Hd.   Kilrush   Shannon   Thurles   Muine Bheag   Gorey
Mouth of the Shannon   Foynes   Limerick   Kilkenny   Nore   Wexford
Kerry Hd.   Listowel   Rathkeale   Tipperary   Enniscorthy
Tralee Bay   Limerick   Newcastle W.   Cashel   Thomastown
Tralee   Abbeyfeale   Ráth Luirc   MUNSTER   Carrick   New
Dingle   Castleisland   Kilmallock   Tipperary   Fethard   on-Suir   Ross   Cahore Pt.
Kerry   Newmarket   Galty Mts   Clonmel   Wexford   Rosslare
MacGillycuddy's   Kanturk   Mitchelstown   Comeragh   Waterford
1041 ▲ Reeks   Killarney   Fermoy   Knockmealdown   Mts   Helvick Hd.
Cahersiveen   Millstreet   Boggeragh   Mts   Lismore   Waterford   Tramore   St George's Channel
Sneem   Macroom   Mts   Mallow   Cappoquin   Dungarvan   Waterford   Cardigan
Kenmare River   Lee   Cork   Youghal   Harb.   Hook   Nat. Pk.
Kenmare   CORK   Blackwater   Mine Hd.   Hd.   Fishguard   52
Caha Mts   Bandon   Midleton   Youghal Harb.   Strumble Hd.   St Davids Hd.
Castletown Bere   Dunmanway   Cobh   Ballycotton   Cork   St Davids
Bantry   Kinsale   Bay   Ramsey I.   Milford
Dursey   Bantry Bay   Clonakilty   Old Head   St Brides B.   Haverfordwest   Haven
Schull   of Kinsale   Skomer   Milford   Pembroke   Tenby
Mizen Hd.   Skibbereen   St Govans   Haven   Caldy
Roaringwater B.   Baltimore   Hd.   ④
C. Clear   Fastnet   Lundy
Rock   Kinsale

A   B   8   C   6   D

1:3M   0   25   50   75   100 km

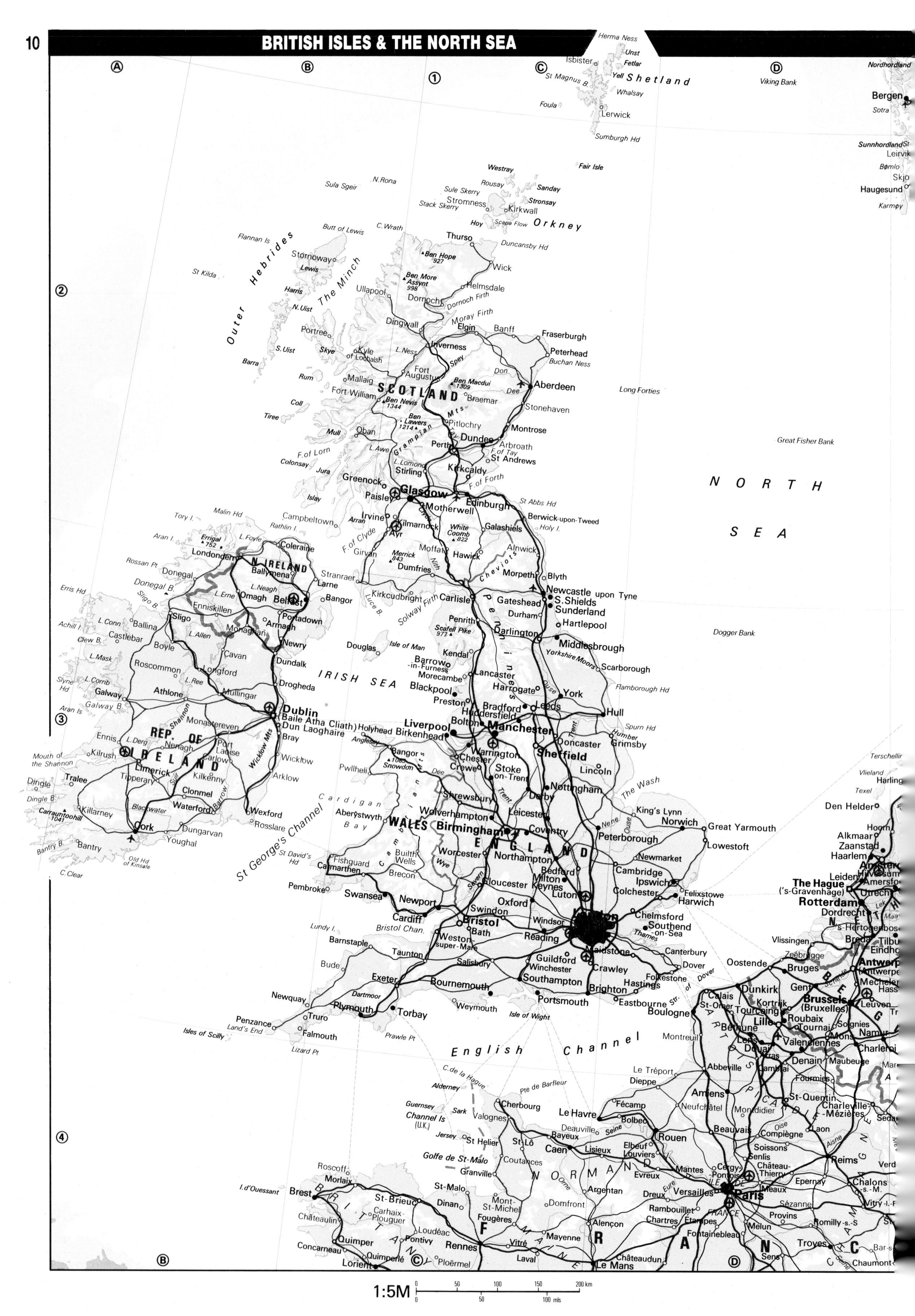
Herma Ness
Unst
Isbister
Fetlar
Yell
Shetland
St Magnus B.
Whalsay
Foula
Lerwick
Sumburgh Hd
Viking Bank
Nordhordland
Bergen
Sotra
Sunnhordland
Leirvik
Bømlo
Skjo
Haugesund
Karmøy
Fair Isle
Westray
Sanday
Rousay
Stronsay
Sule Skerry
Stromness
Stack Skerry
Kirkwall
Hoy
Scapa Flow
Orkney
Sula Sgeir
N.Rona
Butt of Lewis
C.Wrath
Thurso
Duncansby Hd
Flannan Is
Outer Hebrides
Stornoway
Lewis
Ben Hope
927
Wick
St Kilda
The Minch
Ben More Assynt
998
Helmsdale
Harris
Ullapool
Dornoch
Dornoch Firth
N.Uist
Dingwall
Moray Firth
Elgin
Banff
Fraserburgh
Portree
Peterhead
Buchan Ness
S.Uist
Skye
Kyle of Lochalsh
L.Ness
Inverness
Spey
Barra
Fort Augustus
Don
Aberdeen
Rum
Mallaig
Ben Macdui
1309
Dee
Long Forties
Fort William
SCOTLAND
Braemar
Ben Nevis
1344
Coll
Stonehaven
Tiree
Ben Lawers
1214
Grampian Mts
Pitlochry
Mull
Oban
Montrose
Tay
Perth
Dundee
Arbroath
Great Fisher Bank
F.of Lorn
L.Awe
F.of Tay
Colonsay
St Andrews
L.Lomond
Jura
Stirling
Kirkcaldy
F.of Forth
Greenock
NORTH SEA
Islay
Paisley
Glasgow
Edinburgh
St Abbs Hd
Motherwell
Malin Hd
Campbeltown
Irvine
Berwick-upon-Tweed
Tory I.
Rathlin I.
Arran
Kilmarnock
Galashiels
Holy I.
Clyde
White Coomb
822
Aran I.
Errigal
752
L.Foyle
Coleraine
Ayr
F.of Clyde
Tweed
Londonderry
Moffat
Hawick
Alnwick
Girvan
Merrick
843
Cheviots
Rossan Pt
N.IRELAND
Dumfries
Ballymena
Morpeth
Blyth
Donegal
Stranraer
Nith
Larne
Newcastle upon Tyne
Donegal B.
Erris Hd
L.Erne
L.Neagh
Kirkcudbright
Gateshead
S.Shields
Sligo B.
Omagh
Belfast
Bangor
Luce B.
Solway Firth
Carlisle
Sunderland
Enniskillen
Penrith
Durham
Achill I.
L.Conn
Ballina
Sligo
Portadown
Hartlepool
Armagh
Monaghan
Darlington
Dogger Bank
Clew B.
Castlebar
L.Allen
Newry
Douglas
Isle of Man
Scafell Pike
972
Middlesbrough
Boyle
Cavan
Pennines
Yorkshire Moors
L.Mask
Dundalk
Kendal
Barrow-in-Furness
Scarborough
Roscommon
Longford
Morecambe
Lancaster
Slyne Hd
L.Corrib
L.Ree
IRISH SEA
Drogheda
Harrogate
Blackpool
Flamborough Hd
Galway
Athlone
Mullingar
Preston
York
Galway B.
Ouse
Leeds
Bradford
Aran Is.
Dublin
Baile Atha Cliath
Huddersfield
Hull
Shannon
Monastereven
Liverpool
Bolton
Manchester
Spurn Hd
REP. OF IRELAND
Dun Laoghaire
Holyhead
Birkenhead
Humber
Ennis
L.Derg
Nenagh
Bray
Anglesey
Doncaster
Grimsby
Port Laoise
Warrington
Terschelling
Mouth of the Shannon
Kilrush
Wicklow Mts
Bangor
Sheffield
Carlow
Wicklow
Chester
Crewe
Snowdon
1085
Stoke-on-Trent
Lincoln
Vlieland
Limerick
Kilkenny
Pwllheli
Dee
Harlingen
Dingle
Tralee
Tipperary
Suir
Arklow
Trent
Nottingham
The Wash
Texel
Dingle B.
Clonmel
Barrow
Cardigan Bay
Cambrian Mts
Shrewsbury
Derby
Den Helder
Carrauntoohill
1041
Killarney
Blackwater
Waterford
Wexford
Aberystwyth
Wolverhampton
Leicester
King's Lynn
Norwich
Great Yarmouth
Rosslare
WALES
Birmingham
Coventry
Nene
Ouse
Hoorn
Cork
Dungarvan
St George's Channel
Peterborough
Alkmaar
Bantry
Youghal
ENGLAND
Lowestoft
Zaanstad
Bantry B.
St David's Hd
Worcester
Builth Wells
Northampton
Haarlem
Old Hd of Kinsale
Fishguard
Wye
Newmarket
Amsterdam
C.Clear
Carmarthen
Bedford
Cambridge
Leiden
Hilversum
Brecon
Milton Keynes
Ipswich
Amersfoort
Pembroke
Severn
Gloucester
Luton
Colchester
Felixstowe
The Hague ('s-Gravenhage)
Utrecht
Swansea
Newport
Oxford
Harwich
Rotterdam
Dordrecht
Cardiff
Swindon
Chelmsford
Lundy I.
Bristol
Windsor
London
Southend-on-Sea
's-Hertogenbosch
Bristol Chan.
Bath
Thames
Barnstaple
Weston-super-Mare
Reading
Breda
Tilburg
Vlissingen
Eindhoven
Taunton
Maidstone
Canterbury
Guildford
Zeebrugge
Antwerpen
Bude
Salisbury
Winchester
Crawley
Dover
Oostende
Bruges
Exeter
Folkestone
Str. of Dover
Southampton
Bournemouth
Hastings
Gent
Mechelen
Newquay
Dartmoor
Brighton
Dunkirk
Brussels (Bruxelles)
Leuven
Plymouth
Torbay
Weymouth
Portsmouth
Eastbourne
Calais
St-Omer
Kortrijk
Tourcoing
Truro
Isle of Wight
Boulogne
Roubaix
Penzance
Land's End
Lille
Tournai
Soignies
Isles of Scilly
Falmouth
Béthune
Mons
Namur
Prawle Pt
English Channel
Montreuil
Lens
Valenciennes
Charleroi
Lizard Pt
Douai
Arras
Cambrai
Denain
Maubeuge
Le Tréport
C.de la Hague
Dieppe
Abbeville
Alderney
Pte de Barfleur
Fourmies
Amiens
Guernsey
Sark
Cherbourg
Fécamp
St-Quentin
Channel Is (U.K.)
Valognes
Le Havre
Bolbec
Neufchâtel
Montdidier
Charleville-Mézières
Sedan
Jersey
Deauville
Seine
Oise
St Helier
St Lô
Bayeux
Rouen
Beauvais
Compiègne
Laon
Caen
Lisieux
Elbeuf
Louviers
Soissons
Aisne
Golfe de St-Malo
Coutances
Senlis
Reims
Roscoff
Granville
NORMANDIE
Mantes
Cergy-Pontoise
Château-Thierry
Verd
Morlaix
Orne
Evreux
Epernay
I.d'Ouessant
Brest
St-Malo
Argentan
Eure
Meaux
Châlons-s.-M.
St-Brieuc
Dinan
Mont-St-Michel
Domfront
Dreux
Versailles
Paris
Carhaix-Plouguer
Sézanne
Vitry-l.-F.
Châteaulin
Fougères
Rambouillet
Chartres
Etampes
ILE DE FRANCE
Provins
Loudéac
Mayenne
Alençon
Melun
Romilly-s.-S.
BRITTANY
Fontainebleau
Quimper
Pontivy
Rennes
Vitré
MAINE
Troyes
Concarneau
Quimperlé
Laval
Châteaudun
Bar-s.
Lorient
Ploërmel
Le Mans
Sens
Chaumont
FRANCE
CHAMPAGNE
PICARDIE
BELGIQUE
NEDERLAND
1:5M
0 50 100 150 200 km
0 50 100 mls

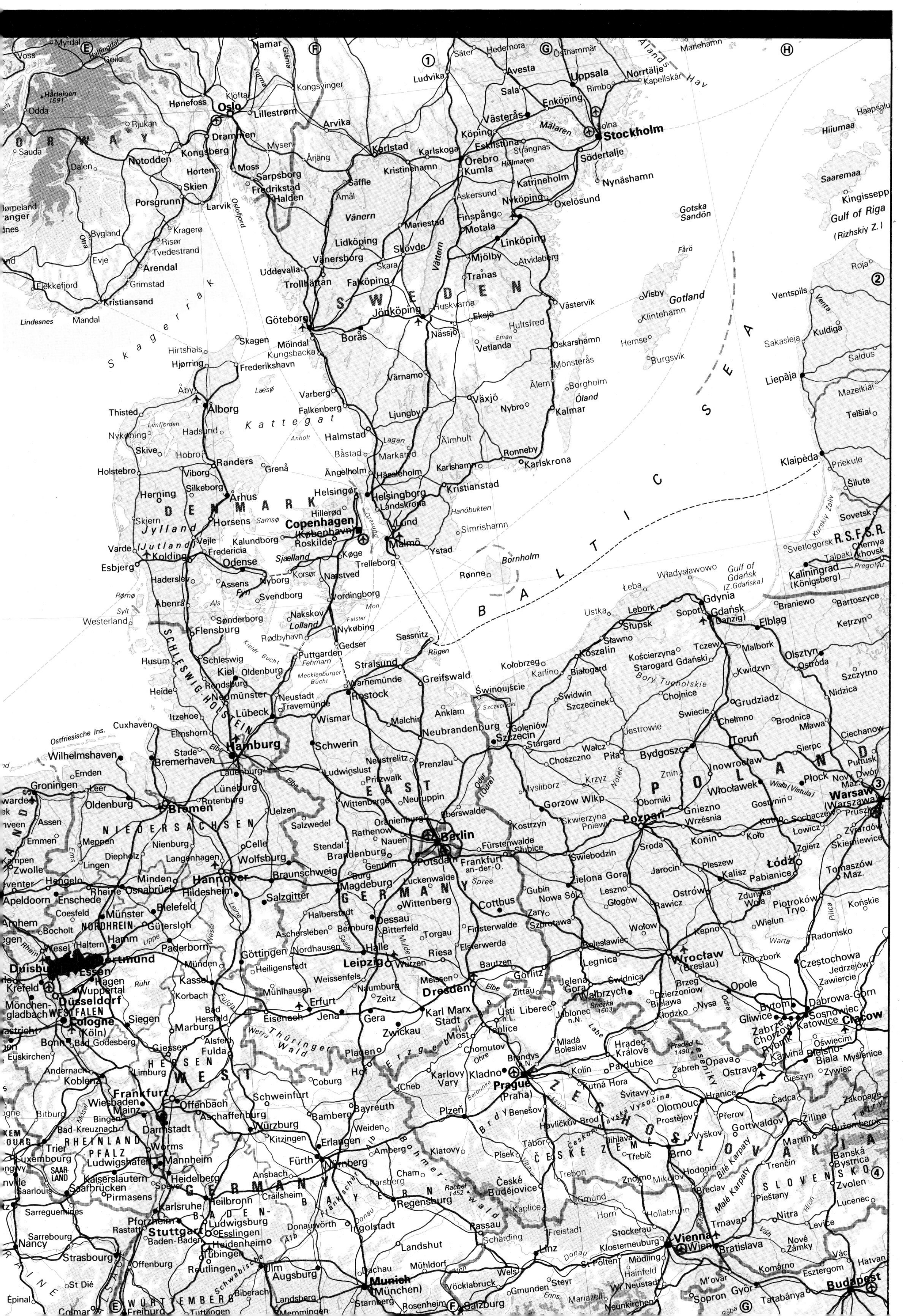
NORWAY
SWEDEN
DENMARK
EAST GERMANY
WEST GERMANY
POLAND
CZECHOSLOVAKIA
R.S.F.S.R.
Skagerrak
Kattegat
BALTIC SEA
Gulf of Riga
(Rizhskiy Z.)
Gulf of Gdańsk
(Z. Gdańska)
Ålands Hav
Oslo
Stockholm
Copenhagen
(København)
Berlin
Hamburg
Warsaw
(Warszawa)
Prague
(Praha)
Vienna
(Wien)
Budapest
Munich
(München)
Göteborg
Malmö
Gdańsk
(Danzig)
Gdynia
Szczecin
Poznań
Wrocław
(Breslau)
Łódź
Kraków
Kaliningrad
(Königsberg)
Klaipėda
Liepāja
Ventspils
Gotland
Öland
Bornholm
Hiiumaa
Saaremaa
Fårö
Gotska Sandön
Uppsala
Västerås
Örebro
Norrköping
Linköping
Jönköping
Växjö
Kalmar
Karlskrona
Kristianstad
Helsingborg
Lund
Ystad
Trelleborg
Halmstad
Borås
Trollhättan
Vänern
Vättern
Mälaren
Karlstad
Ålborg
Århus
Odense
Esbjerg
Randers
Kolding
Fredericia
Vejle
Horsens
Sjælland
Fyn
Lolland
Falster
Jylland
(Jutland)
Flensburg
Kiel
Lübeck
Rostock
Stralsund
Greifswald
Schwerin
Wismar
Neubrandenburg
Potsdam
Frankfurt an-der-O.
Magdeburg
Halle
Leipzig
Dresden
Karl Marx Stadt
Erfurt
Jena
Gera
Zwickau
Cottbus
Dessau
Bremen
Bremerhaven
Wilhelmshaven
Hannover
Braunschweig
Wolfsburg
Osnabrück
Münster
Bielefeld
Dortmund
Essen
Duisburg
Düsseldorf
Cologne
(Köln)
Bonn
Koblenz
Frankfurt
Wiesbaden
Mainz
Darmstadt
Mannheim
Heidelberg
Karlsruhe
Stuttgart
Nürnberg
Würzburg
Regensburg
Augsburg
Ulm
Salzburg
Linz
Brno
Bratislava
Ostrava
Olomouc
Plzeň
České Budějovice
Katowice
Częstochowa
Opole
Toruń
Bydgoszcz
Olsztyn
Elbląg
Koszalin
Słupsk
Kołobrzeg
Świnoujście
Zielona Gora
Gorzów Wlkp
NIEDERSACHSEN
SCHLESWIG-HOLSTEIN
NORDRHEIN-WESTFALEN
HESSEN
RHEINLAND-PFALZ
SAAR-LAND
BADEN-WÜRTTEMBERG
BAYERN
ČESKÉ ZEMĚ
SLOVENSKO
Thüringer Wald
Erzgebirge
Böhmer Wald
Elbe
Oder
(Odra)
Wisła (Vistula)
Donau

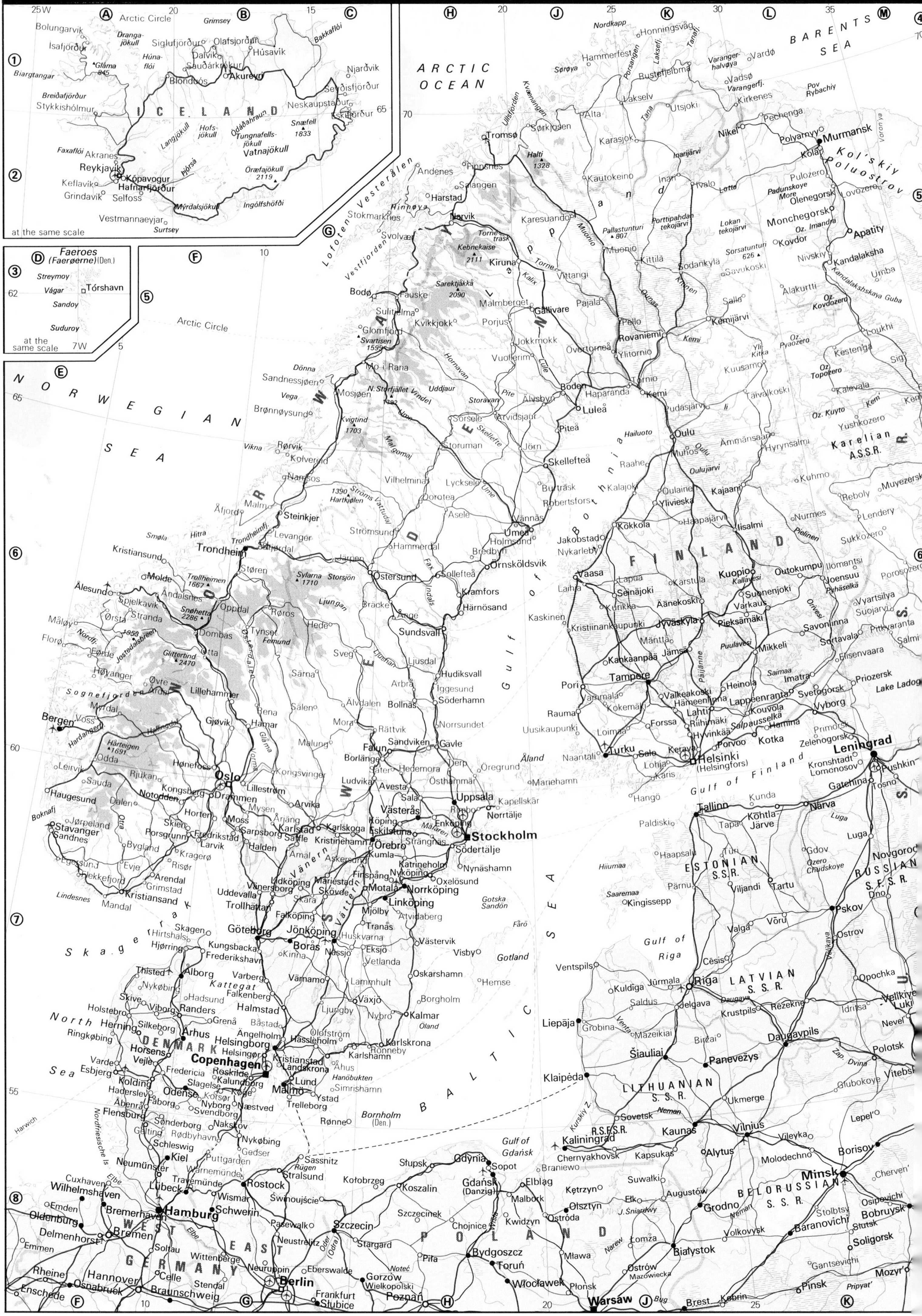

ICELAND inset

Bolungarvik, Isafjörður, Drangajökull, Grimsey, Siglufjörður, Ólafsfjörður, Bakkaflói, Húsavik, Dalvik, Sauðárkrókur, Akureyri, Njarðvik, Biargtangar, Glámа 845, Húnflói, Blönduós, Seyðisfjörður, Breiðafjörður, Stykkishólmur, Neskaupstaður, Langjökull, Hofsjökull, Öskjuvatn, Snæfell 1833, Faxaflói, Akranes, Tungnafellsjökull, Reykjavik, Kópavogur, Hafnarfjörður, Selfoss, Vatnajökull, Öræfajökull 2119, Keflavik, Grindavik, Þjórsá, Mýrdalsjökull, Ingólfshöfði, Vestmannaeyjar, Surtsey

at the same scale

FAEROES inset

Faeroes (Faerøerne)(Den.), Streymoy, Vágar, Tórshavn, Sandoy, Suðuroy
at the same scale 7W

ARCTIC OCEAN

NORWEGIAN SEA

Nordkapp, Honningsvåg, Hammerfest, Tromsø, Narvik, Bodø, Trondheim, Bergen, Oslo, Stavanger, Kristiansand, Göteborg, Malmö, Copenhagen, Hamburg, Bremen, Berlin

FINLAND: Helsinki, Turku, Tampere, Oulu, Vaasa, Kuopio, Rovaniemi

SWEDEN: Stockholm, Uppsala, Göteborg, Malmö, Luleå, Umeå, Sundsvall, Gävle, Örebro, Norrköping, Linköping, Jönköping

Leningrad, Tallinn, Riga, Vilnius, Kaliningrad, Minsk, Warsaw, Gdańsk, Szczecin, Murmansk

DENMARK, NORWAY, SWEDEN, FINLAND, POLAND, ESTONIAN S.S.R., LATVIAN S.S.R., LITHUANIAN S.S.R., BELORUSSIAN S.S.R., RUSSIAN S.F.S.R., KARELIAN A.S.S.R., WEST GERMANY, EAST GERMANY

BARENTS SEA, BALTIC SEA, Gulf of Bothnia, Gulf of Finland, Gulf of Riga, Gulf of Gdańsk, Skagerrak, Kattegat, North Sea, Lake Ladoga

1:7.5M

0 100 200 300 km
0 50 100 150 mls

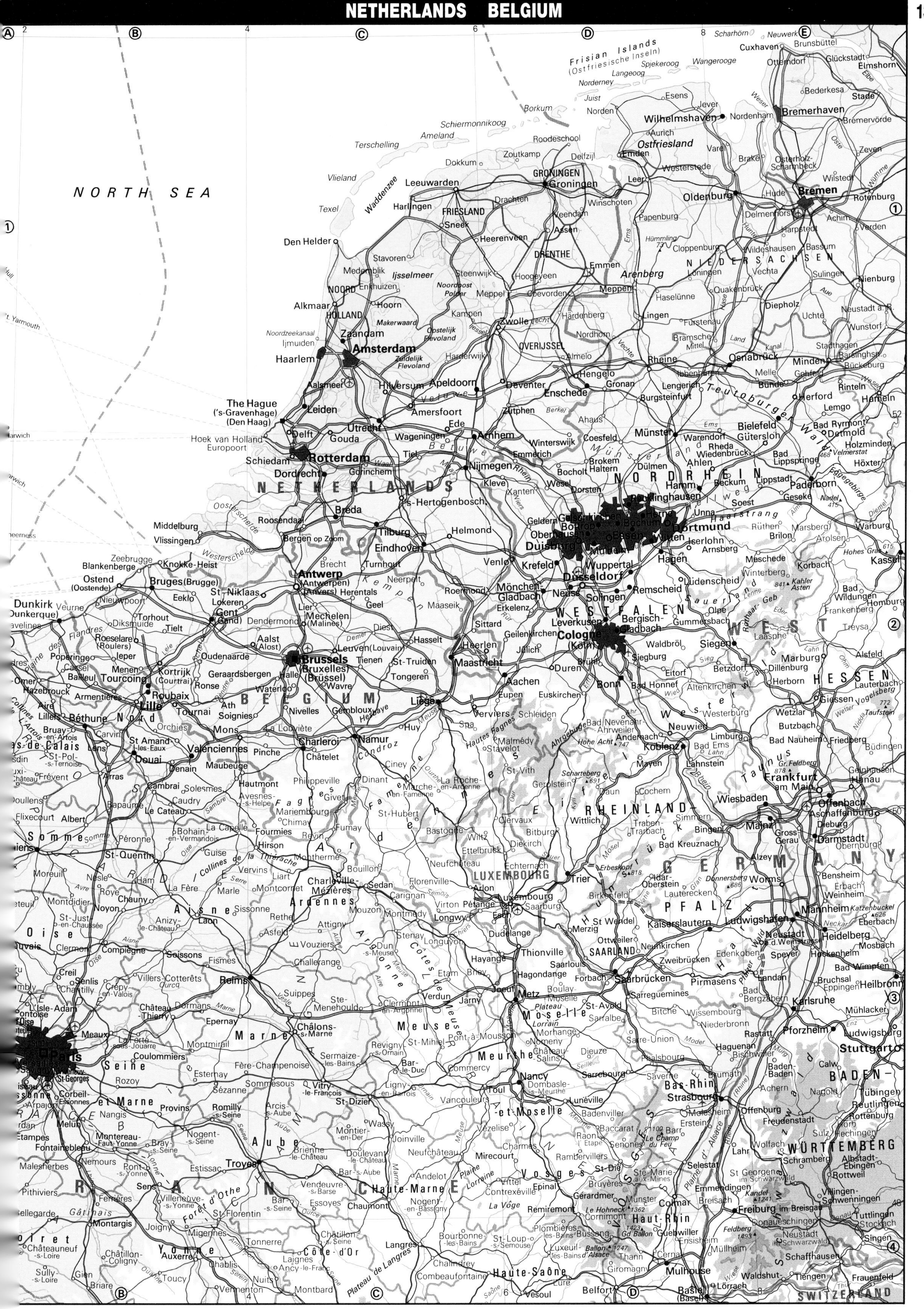
NORTH SEA
Frisian Islands
(Ostfriesische Inseln)
Borkum
Norderney
Juist
Langeoog
Spiekeroog
Wangerooge
Schiermonnikoog
Ameland
Terschelling
Vlieland
Texel
Waddenzee
Den Helder
Leeuwarden
Harlingen
FRIESLAND
Sneek
Heerenveen
Dokkum
Drachten
GRONINGEN
Groningen
Delfzijl
Zoutkamp
Roodeschool
Veendam
Assen
DRENTHE
Emmen
Hoogeveen
Coevorden
Meppel
Steenwijk
Noordoost Polder
IJsselmeer
Stavoren
Medemblik
Enkhuizen
Hoorn
NOORD HOLLAND
Alkmaar
Markerwaard
Zaandam
Amsterdam
Noordzeekanaal
IJmuiden
Haarlem
Oostelijk Flevoland
Zuidelijk Flevoland
Kampen
Zwolle
OVERIJSSEL
Harderwijk
Hilversum
Apeldoorn
Deventer
Aalsmeer
Leiden
The Hague
('s-Gravenhage)
(Den Haag)
Amersfoort
Veluwe
Utrecht
Delft
Gouda
Hoek van Holland
Europoort
Schiedam
Rotterdam
Dordrecht
Gorinchem
Ede
Arnhem
Wageningen
Tiel
Betuwe
Nijmegen
Zutphen
Almelo
Hengelo
Enschede
Gronan
Nordhorn
Hardenberg
NETHERLANDS
's-Hertogenbosch
Breda
Tilburg
Eindhoven
Helmond
Roosendaal
Bergen op Zoom
Oosterschelde
Westerschelde
Middelburg
Vlissingen
Zeebrugge
Blankenberge
Knokke-Heist
Ostend
(Oostende)
Bruges (Brugge)
Eeklo
St-Niklaas
Lokeren
Gent
(Gand)
Antwerp
(Antwerpen)
(Anvers)
Herentals
Turnhout
Geel
Kempen
Lier
Mechelen
(Malines)
Aalst
(Alost)
Dendermonde
Brussels
(Bruxelles)
(Brüssel)
Leuven (Louvain)
Tienen
Diest
Hasselt
St-Truiden
Tongeren
Maaseik
Roermond
Venlo
Sittard
Heerlen
Maastricht
Liège
Huy
Namur
Wavre
Waterloo
Nivelles
Gembloux
Charleroi
Châtelet
Mons
La Louvière
Soignies
Ath
Tournai
Kortrijk
(Courtrai)
Roeselare
(Roulers)
Ieper
Poperinge
Menen
Oudenaarde
Geraardsbergen
Ronse
Dunkirk
(Dunkerque)
Nieuwpoort
Diksmuide
Torhout
Tielt
Veurne
Flandres
BELGIUM
Verviers
Spa
Hautes Fagnes
Malmédy
Stavelot
St-Vith
Dinant
Ciney
Condroz
Famenne
Marche-en-Famenne
La Roche-en-Ardenne
Bastogne
St-Hubert
Philippeville
Givet
Chimay
Mariembourg
Fumay
Ardenne
Bouillon
Neufchâteau
Arlon
Virton
LUXEMBOURG
Luxembourg
Ettelbruck
Diekirch
Echternach
Wiltz
Clervaux
Esch
Dudelange
Longwy
Pétange
Lille
Roubaix
Tourcoing
Armentières
Hazebrouck
Béthune
Lens
Douai
Valenciennes
Arras
Cambrai
Maubeuge
Denain
St-Amand-les-Eaux
Orchies
Nord
Pas-de-Calais
St-Pol-s-Ternoise
Frévent
Doullens
Albert
Bapaume
Péronne
Le Cateau
Caudry
Solesmes
Avesnes-s-Helpe
Hautmont
Fourmies
Hirson
La Capelle
Bohain-en-Vermandois
St-Quentin
Guise
Vervins
Somme
Amiens
Montdidier
Roye
Nesle
Ham
Chauny
La Fère
Laon
Marle
Noyon
Oise
Compiègne
Soissons
Clermont
Creil
Senlis
Chantilly
Crépy-en-Valois
Villers-Cotterêts
Anizy-le-Château
Aisne
Sissonne
Rethel
Asfeld
Montcornet
Charleville-Mézières
Sedan
Carignan
Mouzon
Ardennes
Attigny
Vouziers
Argonne
Stenay
Montmédy
Reims
Fismes
Château-Thierry
Dormans
Epernay
Marne
Châlons-s-Marne
Suippes
Ste-Menehould
Verdun
Clermont-en-Argonne
Meuse
St-Mihiel
Pont-à-Mousson
Metz
Thionville
Hayange
Briey
Etain
Jarny
Hagondange
Boulay-Moselle
Moselle
Plateau Lorrain
Forbach
Saarbrücken
Sarreguemines
St-Avold
Morhange
Sarralbe
Bitche
Wissembourg
Niederbronn
Haguenau
Bischwiller
Sarre-Union
Dieuze
Château-Salins
Nomeny
Meurthe
Nancy
Lunéville
Dombasle-s-Meurthe
Toul
Commercy
Bar-le-Duc
Ligny-en-Barrois
Vitry-le-François
St-Dizier
Sermaize-les-Bains
Revigny-s-Ornain
Vaucouleurs
Sarrebourg
Phalsbourg
Saverne
Bas-Rhin
Strasbourg
Molsheim
Erstein
Baccarat
Raon-l'Etape
Senones
St-Dié
Rambervillers
Charmes
Mirecourt
Vézelise
Epinal
Vosges
Remiremont
Gérardmer
Le Hohneck
Munster
Colmar
Haut-Rhin
Guebwiller
Ensisheim
Mulhouse
Thann
Cernay
Belfort
Giromagny
Plombières-les-Bains
Luxeuil-les-Bains
Ballon d'Alsace
Gd Ballon
Sélestat
Ste-Marie-aux-Mines
Plaine d'Alsace
Neufchâteau
Contrexéville
Vittel
La Vôge
Bourbonne-les-Bains
St-Loup-s-Semouse
Haute-Saône
Vesoul
Lure
Langres
Plateau de Langres
Chalindrey
Combeaufontaine
Haute-Marne
Chaumont
Joinville
Montier-en-Der
Andelot
Nogent-en-Bassigny
Bar-s-Aube
Brienne-le-Château
Vendeuvre-s-Barse
Aube
Troyes
Bar-s-Seine
Essoyes
Châtillon-s-Seine
Côte-d'Or
Laignes
Ancy-le-Franc
Montbard
Tonnerre
Chablis
Nuits
Vermenton
Auxerre
Yonne
Joigny
Migennes
St-Florentin
Forêt d'Othe
Sens
Villeneuve-s-Yonne
Pont-s-Yonne
Montereau-Faut-Yonne
Bray-s-Seine
Nogent-s-Seine
Romilly-s-Seine
Estissac
Provins
Nangis
Sézanne
Esternay
Montmirail
Fère-Champenoise
Sommesous
Seine-et-Marne
Coulommiers
Meaux
La Ferté-sous-Jouarre
Paris
St-Denis
Pontoise
L'Isle-Adam
Corbeil-Essonnes
Melun
Fontainebleau
Nemours
Etampes
Malesherbes
Pithiviers
Gâtinais
Montargis
Châteauneuf-s-Loire
Châtillon-Coligny
Sully-s-Loire
Gien
Briare
Toucy
Loiret
Ferrières
Emden
Ostfriesland
Aurich
Norden
Esens
Jever
Wilhelmshaven
Nordenham
Varel
Brake
Westerstede
Leer
Oldenburg
Papenburg
Winschoten
Delmenhorst
Bremen
Bremerhaven
Cuxhaven
Brunsbüttel
Otterndorf
Glückstadt
Elmshorn
Bederkesa
Stade
Bremervörde
Zeven
Osterholz-Scharmbeck
Wilstedt
Rotenburg
Achim
Verden
Harpstedt
Wildeshausen
Bassum
Cloppenburg
Vechta
Löningen
NIEDERSACHSEN
Sulingen
Nienburg
Diepholz
Quakenbrück
Haselünne
Meppen
Arenberg
Lingen
Fürstenau
Bramsche
Uchte
Neustadt a. R.
Wunstorf
Stadthagen
Minden
Bückeburg
Rinteln
Hameln
Osnabrück
Rheine
Lengerich
Burgsteinfurt
Teutoburger Wald
Herford
Lemgo
Bad Rymont
Detmold
Bielefeld
Gütersloh
Münster
Warendorf
Rheda
Wiedenbrück
Ahlen
Coesfeld
Ahaus
Winterswijk
Emmerich
Kleve
Xanten
Wesel
Bocholt
Borken
Haltern
Dülmen
Dorsten
NORDRHEIN-WESTFALEN
Hamm
Beckum
Lippstadt
Paderborn
Bad Lippspringe
Höxter
Holzminden
Geseke
Soest
Unna
Recklinghausen
Gelsenkirchen
Herne
Bochum
Bottrop
Oberhausen
Essen
Dortmund
Witten
Duisburg
Mülheim
Krefeld
Geldern
Iserlohn
Hagen
Arnsberg
Brilon
Marsberg
Arolsen
Warburg
Kassel
Korbach
Meschede
Winterberg
Lüdenscheid
Sauerland
Wuppertal
Düsseldorf
Remscheid
Solingen
Neuss
Mönchen-Gladbach
Erkelenz
Geilenkirchen
Jülich
Leverkusen
Bergisch-Gladbach
Cologne
(Köln)
Gummersbach
Olpe
Waldbröl
Siegen
Siegburg
Düren
Aachen
Eupen
Bonn
Brühl
Euskirchen
Bad Honnef
Eitorf
Altenkirchen
Betzdorf
Westerwald
Bad Wildungen
Frankenberg
Treysa
Marburg
Alsfeld
Dillenburg
Herborn
HESSEN
Lauterbach
Giessen
Vogelsberg
Wetzlar
Butzbach
Bad Nauheim
Friedberg
Büdingen
Limburg
Bad Ems
Lahnstein
Koblenz
Neuwied
Andernach
Mayen
Bad Neuenahr-Ahrweiler
Ahrgebirge
Hohe Acht
Schleiden
Eifel
Gerolstein
Daun
Cochem
Wittlich
RHEINLAND-PFALZ
Traben-Trarbach
Bitburg
Trier
Hunsrück
Simmern
Bingen
Bad Kreuznach
Mainz
Wiesbaden
Frankfurt am Main
Offenbach
Hanau
Aschaffenburg
Dieburg
Darmstadt
Gross-Gerau
Taunus
Gr. Feldberg
Idar-Oberstein
Birkenfeld
Lauterecken
Donnersberg
Alzey
Worms
Bensheim
Erbach
Weinheim
Mannheim
Ludwigshafen
Kaiserslautern
Heidelberg
Eberbach
Mosbach
Neustadt a.d. Weinstrasse
Speyer
Hockenheim
Edenkoben
Haardt
Pfälzer Wald
Landau
Pirmasens
Zweibrücken
Neunkirchen
Ottweiler
St Wendel
Merzig
Saarlouis
SAARLAND
Bad Bergzabern
Bad Wimpfen
Bruchsal
Eppingen
Heilbronn
Karlsruhe
Mühlacker
Pforzheim
Ludwigsburg
Stuttgart
Calw
Rastatt
Baden-Baden
Achern
Nagold
BADEN-WÜRTTEMBERG
Tübingen
Reutlingen
Rottenburg
Horb
Sulz
Hechingen
Offenburg
Freudenstadt
Lahr
Wolfach
Schramberg
Albstadt-Ebingen
Rottweil
St Georgen im Schwarzwald
Villingen-Schwenningen
Tuttlingen
Stockach
Donaueschingen
Neustadt im Schwarzwald
Singen
Schwarzwald
Emmendingen
Kandel
Breisach
Freiburg im Breisgau
Feldberg
Müllheim
Schaffhausen
Waldshut-Tiengen
Lörrach
Basle
(Basel)
Frauenfeld
SWITZERLAND
GERMANY
FRANCE

1:2.5M
0 25 50 75 100 km
0 25 50 mls

EAST GERMANY

WEST GERMANY

HESSEN

WESTFALEN

RHEINLAND

PFALZ

SAAR LAND

BADEN

WÜRTEMBERG

BAYERN

AUSTRIA

SWITZERLAND

BELGIUM

LUXEMBOURG

LORRAINE

PICARDIE

NORMANDIE

BRETAGNE

POITOU

GASCOGNE

LANDES

ROUSSILLON

ANDORRA

NAVARRA

PAIS VASCOS

ASTURIAS

CORSICA (CORSE)

MONACO

LIECHTENSTEIN

F R A N C E

English Channel

BAY OF BISCAY (MAR CANTÁBRICO)

Ligurian Sea

Golfe du Lion

Cities and towns (selected, as legible):

London, Paris, Brussels, Antwerp, Cologne (Köln), Düsseldorf, Duisburg, Essen, Frankfurt, Wiesbaden, Mannheim, Stuttgart, Karlsruhe, München (Munich), Augsburg, Nürnberg, Strasbourg, Nancy, Metz, Luxembourg, Reims, Lille, Calais, Dunkerque, Amiens, Rouen, Le Havre, Caen, Cherbourg, Brest, Rennes, Nantes, Angers, Le Mans, Tours, Orléans, Bourges, Dijon, Besançon, Lyon, Saint-Étienne, Clermont-Ferrand, Limoges, Poitiers, Bordeaux, Toulouse, Montpellier, Nîmes, Avignon, Marseilles, Nice, Cannes, Grenoble, Chambéry, Annecy, Geneva (Genève), Lausanne, Berne (Bern), Zürich, Basle (Basel), Milan (Milano), Turin (Torino), Genoa (Genova), Bologna, Florence (Firenze), Pisa, Bastia, Perpignan, Carcassonne, Pau, Bayonne, Biarritz, San Sebastián, Bilbao, Santander, Gijón, Oviedo, León, Pamplona, Logroño, Vitoria

1:5M

0	50	100	150	200 km

0	50	100 mls

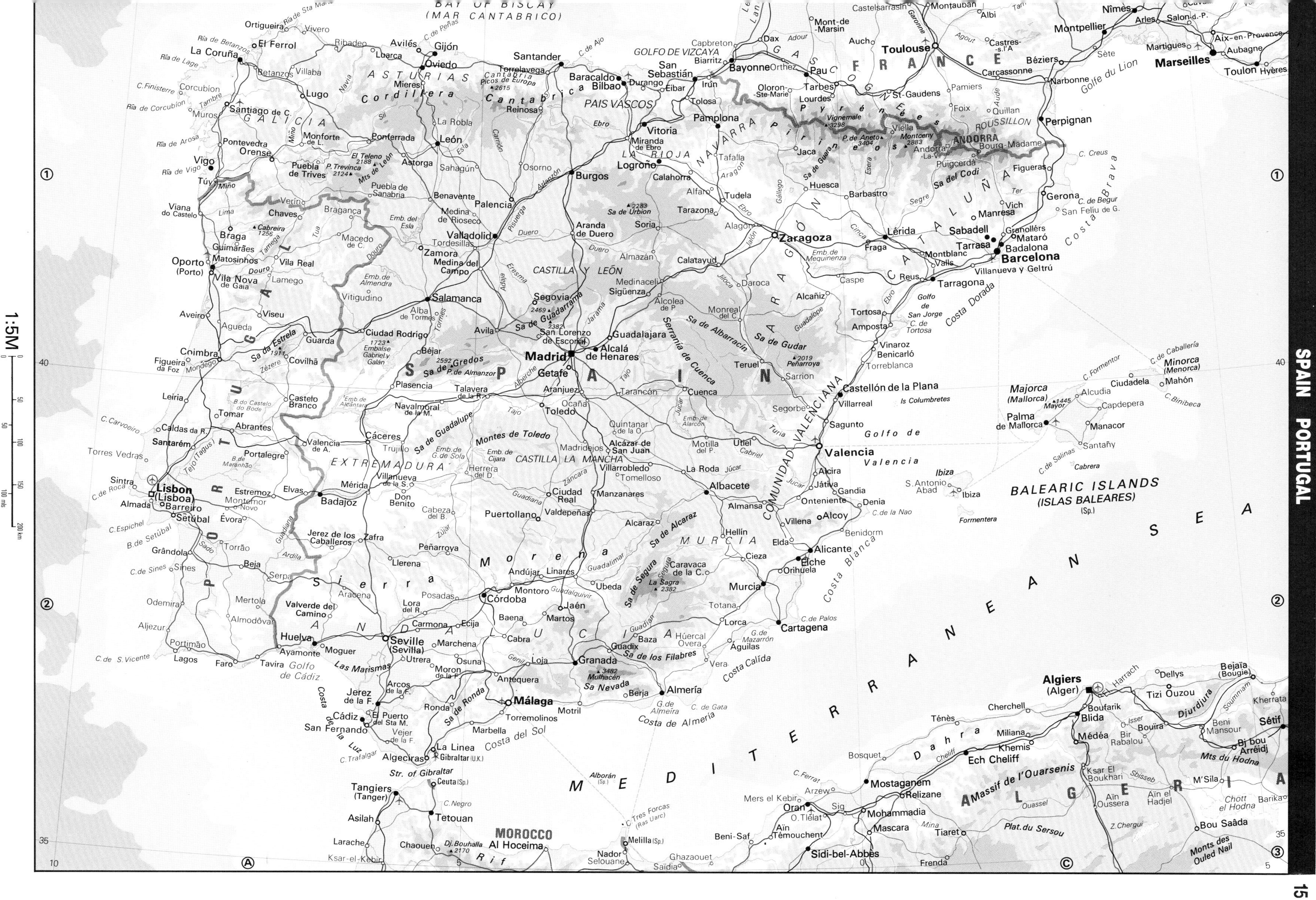
BAY OF BISCAY
(MAR CANTABRICO)
GOLFO DE VIZCAYA
Golfe du Lion
M E D I T E R R A N E A N   S E A
BALEARIC ISLANDS
(ISLAS BALEARES)
(Sp.)
Majorca
(Mallorca)
Minorca
(Menorca)
Ibiza
Formentera
Golfo de Valencia
Str. of Gibraltar
F R A N C E
ANDORRA
S P A I N
P O R T U G A L
A L G E R I A
MOROCCO
Madrid
Lisbon
(Lisboa)
Barcelona
Valencia
Seville
(Sevilla)
Zaragoza
Málaga
Bilbao
Oporto
(Porto)
Toulouse
Marseilles
Algiers
(Alger)
Oran
Tangiers
(Tanger)
Gibraltar (U.K.)
Ceuta (Sp.)
Melilla (Sp.)
Tetouan
Al Hoceima
Mostaganem
Sidi-bel-Abbès
Perpignan
Montpellier
Granada
Córdoba
Murcia
Alicante
Cartagena
Almería
Cádiz
Huelva
Badajoz
Salamanca
Valladolid
Burgos
León
Oviedo
Gijón
Santander
San Sebastián
Pamplona
Vitoria
Logroño
Lérida
Tarragona
Castellón de la Plana
Teruel
Cuenca
Toledo
Albacete
Jaén
Coimbra
Faro
Braga
Vigo
La Coruña
Santiago de C.
Lugo
Orense
Pyrénées
Cordillera Cantabrica
Sa de Guadarrama
Sa de Gredos
Sierra Morena
Sa Nevada
Serranía de Cuenca
Montes de Toledo
CASTILLA Y LEÓN
CASTILLA LA MANCHA
EXTREMADURA
ANDALUCIA
GALICIA
ASTURIAS
PAIS VASCOS
CATALUÑA
ARAGÓN
NAVARRA
COMUNIDAD VALENCIANA
MURCIA
Costa Brava
Costa Dorada
Costa Blanca
Costa del Sol
Costa de Almería
Tajo
Ebro
Duero
Guadiana
Guadalquivir
Júcar
Rif
1:5M
0 50 100 150 200 km
0 50 100 mls

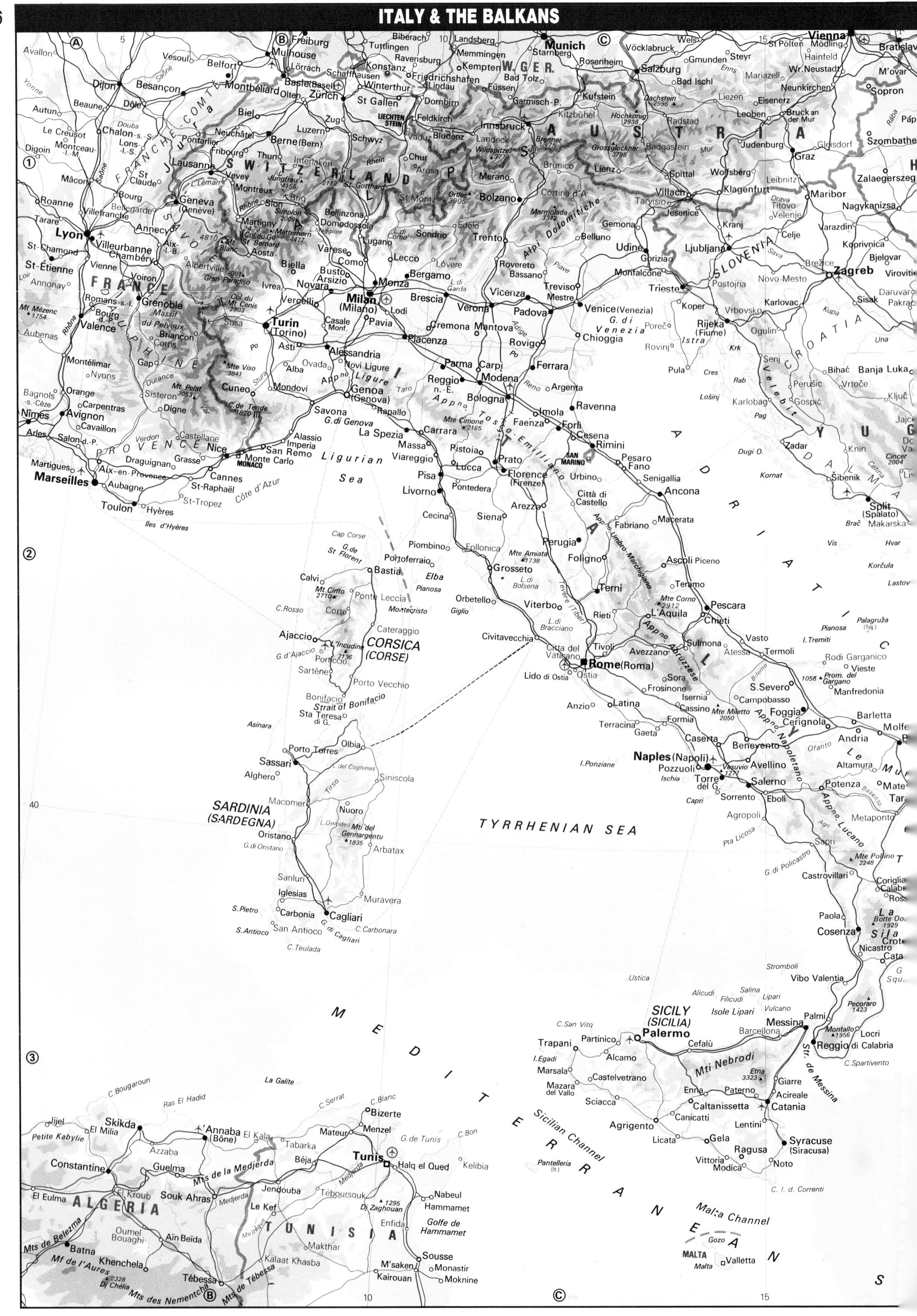
ITALY & THE BALKANS
FRANCE
SWITZERLAND
AUSTRIA
W. GER.
SLOVENIA
CROATIA
ITALY
ALGERIA
TUNISIA
CORSICA (CORSE)
SARDINIA (SARDEGNA)
SICILY (SICILIA)
MALTA
Ligurian Sea
TYRRHENIAN SEA
ADRIATIC
MEDITERRANEAN
Sicilian Channel
Malta Channel
Strait of Bonifacio
Str. de Messina
Munich
Vienna
Bratislava
Salzburg
Innsbruck
Graz
Klagenfurt
Zürich
Berne (Bern)
Lausanne
Geneva (Genève)
Basle (Basel)
Lyon
Grenoble
Marseilles
Toulon
Nice
Monte Carlo
MONACO
Turin (Torino)
Milan (Milano)
Genoa (Genova)
Venice (Venezia)
Trieste
Ljubljana
Zagreb
Rijeka (Fiume)
Bologna
Florence (Firenze)
Pisa
Livorno
Ancona
Perugia
Pescara
Rome (Roma)
Naples (Napoli)
Salerno
Foggia
Potenza
Cosenza
Reggio di Calabria
Messina
Palermo
Catania
Syracuse (Siracusa)
Trapani
Agrigento
Cagliari
Sassari
Olbia
Ajaccio
Bastia
Tunis
Bizerte
Sousse
Constantine
'Annaba (Bône)
Valletta
Mte Viso 3841
Gran Paradiso 4061
Mt Blanc 4810
Matterhorn 4477
Grossglockner 3798
Marmolada 3342
Mte Amiata 1738
Mte Corno 2912
Vesuvio 1277
Etna 3323
1:5M

0 50 100 150 200 km
0 50 100 mls

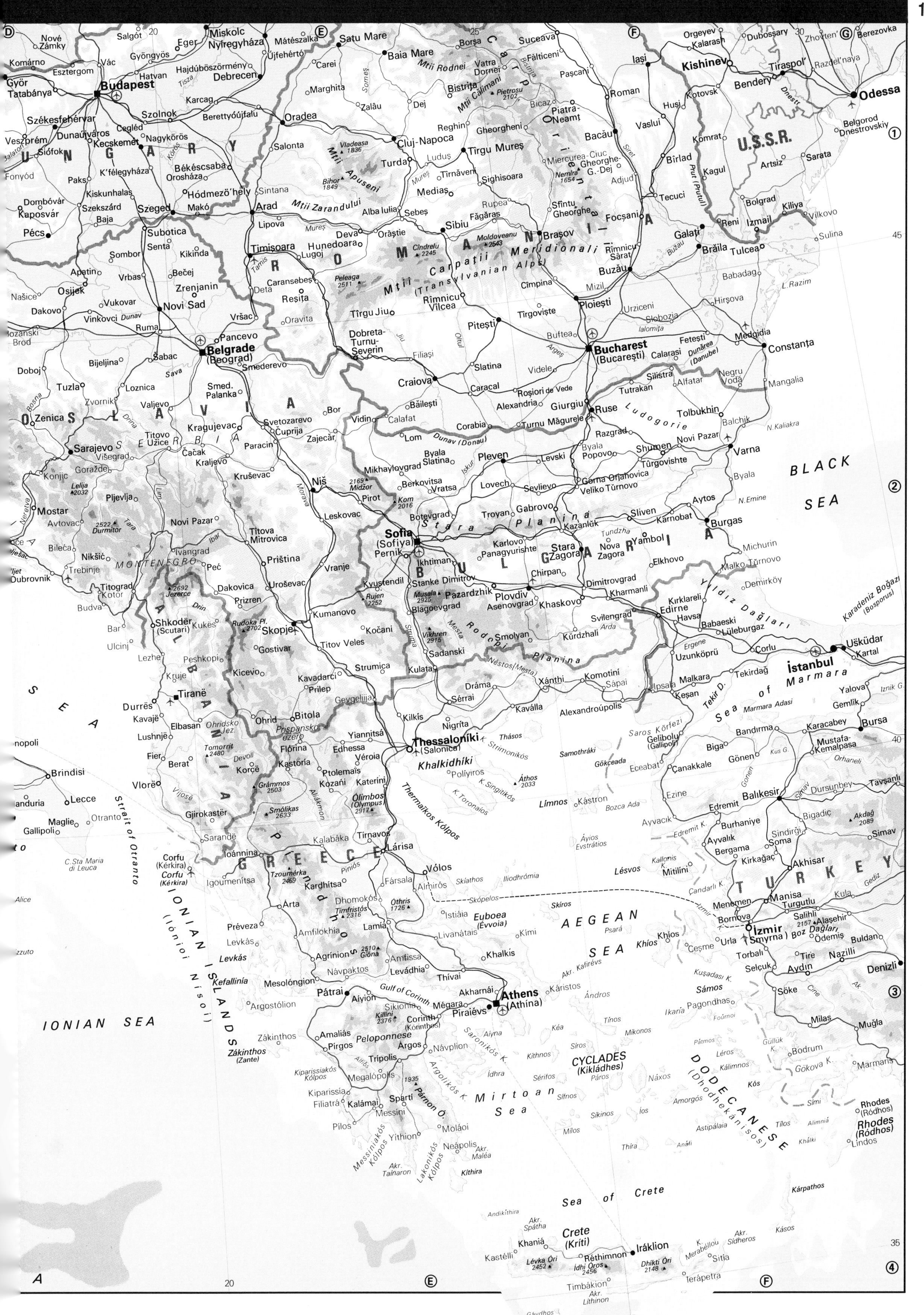

Nové Zámky
Komárno
Esztergom
Győr
Tatabánya
Salgótarján
Gyöngyös
Vác
Hatvan
Eger
Miskolc
Nyíregyháza
Mátészalka
Hajdúböszörmény
Debrecen
Budapest
Székesfehérvár
Dunaújváros
Veszprém
Siófok
Fonyód
Paks
Kiskunhalas
Dombóvár
Kaposvár
Szekszárd
Baja
Pécs
Cegléd
Kecskemét
Nagykőrös
Szolnok
Karcag
Berettyóújfalu
Kiskunfélegyháza
Békéscsaba
Orosháza
Hódmezővásárhely
Szeged
Makó
H U N G A R Y
Satu Mare
Újfehértó
Carei
Baia Mare
Mtii Rodnei
Borşa
Suceava
Fălticeni
Vatra Dornei
Bistriţa
Mtii Călimani
Pietrosu 2102
Marghita
Zalău
Dej
Oradea
Salonta
Cluj-Napoca
Reghin
Gheorgheni
Bicaz
Piatra-Neamţ
Roman
Paşcani
Iaşi
Bacău
Vladeasa 1836
Mtii Apuseni
Bihor 1849
Turda
Luduş
Tîrgu Mureş
Tîrnăveni
Sighisoara
Mediaş
Miercurea-Ciuc
Gheorghe-G.-Dej
Nemira 1654
Adjud
Vaslui
Bîrlad
Tecuci
Sintana
Arad
Mtii Zarandului
Alba Iulia
Sebeş
Rupea
Făgăraş
Sfîntu Gheorghe
Focşani
Lipova
Deva
Orăştie
Sibiu
Braşov
Moldoveanu 2543
Cindrelu 2245
Timişoara
Hunedoara
Lugoj
R O M A N I A
Carpaţii Meridionali
(Transylvanian Alps)
Carpaţi Orientali
Rîmnicu Sărat
Galaţi
Brăila
Buzău
Caransebeş
Reşiţa
Peleaga 2511
Rîmnicu Vîlcea
Cîmpina
Mizil
Ploieşti
Tîrgu Jiu
Tîrgovişte
Piteşti
Buftea
Bucharest (Bucureşti)
Urziceni
Slobozia
Fetesti
Hirşova
Medgidia
Constanţa
Babadag
Tulcea
Sulina
L. Razim
Dobreta-Turnu-Severin
Filiaşi
Slatina
Craiova
Caracal
Videle
Roşiori de Vede
Alexandria
Giurgiu
Călăraşi
Silistra
Tutrakan
Alfatar
Negru Vodă
Mangalia
Kishinev
Orgeyev
Kalarash
Dubossary
Zhovten'
Berezovka
Tiraspol'
Razdel'naya
Bendery
Odessa
Kotovsk
Belgorod Dnestrovskiy
Komrat
U.S.S.R.
Kagul
Artsiz
Sarata
Bolgrad
Izmail
Kiliya
Vilkovo
Reni
Prut (Prutul)
Siret
Apatin
Sombor
Vrbas
Subotica
Senta
Kikinda
Bečej
Zrenjanin
Novi Sad
Osijek
Našice
Vukovar
Dakovo
Vinkovci
Ruma
Vršac
Pančevo
Belgrade (Beograd)
Smederevo
Šabac
Bijeljina
Slavonski Brod
Doboj
Tuzla
Loznica
Zvornik
Valjevo
Smed. Palanka
Zenica
Sarajevo
Višegrad
Goražde
Konjic
Lelija 2032
Pljevlja
Mostar
Avtovac
Durmitor 2522
Bileća
Nikšić
Trebinje
Dubrovnik
Kotor
Budva
Bar
Ulcinj
Titograd
MONTENEGRO
Ivangrad
Peć
Novi Pazar
Titova Mitrovica
Priština
Dakovica
Prizren
Uroševac
Titovo Užice
Čačak
Kraljevo
Kragujevac
Kruševac
Paracin
Svetozarevo
Ćuprija
Zaječar
Bor
Vidin
Calafat
Lom
Niš
Pirot
Leskovac
Vranje
Midžor 2169
Kumanovo
Skopje
Tetovo
Gostivar
Kičevo
Titov Veles
Kočani
Štip
Strumica
Kavadarci
Prilep
Bitola
Ohrid
Ohridsko Jez.
Prespansko ezero
Gevgelija
Y U G O S L A V I A
S E R B I A
Shkodër (Scutari)
Kukës
Lezhë
Peshkopi
Krujë
Tiranë
Durrës
Kavajë
Elbasan
Lushnjë
Fier
Berat
Korçë
Vlorë
Tomorrit 2480
Gjirokastër
Sarandë
A L B A N I A
Jezerce 2692
Rudoka Pl. 2702
Drin
Băileşti
Corabia
Turnu Măgurele
Ruse
Ludogorie
Razgrad
Tolbukhin
Balchik
N. Kaliakra
Varna
Shumen
Novi Pazar
Tŭrgovishte
Byala
Popovo
Levski
Pleven
Mikhaylovgrad
Byala Slatina
Berkovitsa
Vratsa
Lovech
Sevlievo
Gorna Oryahovitsa
Veliko Tŭrnovo
Troyan
Gabrovo
Kom 2016
Botevgrad
Stara Planina
Kazanlŭk
Sliven
Karnobat
Aytos
Burgas
N. Emine
Sofia (Sofiya)
Pernik
Ikhtiman
Karlovo
Panagyurishte
Stara Zagora
Nova Zagora
Yambol
Elkhovo
Michurin
Malko Tŭrnovo
Kyustendil
Stanke Dimitrov
Rujen 2252
Musala 2925
Pazardzhik
Plovdiv
Asenovgrad
Chirpan
Dimitrovgrad
Khaskovo
Kharmanli
Svilengrad
Blagoevgrad
Vikhren 2915
Smolyan
Kŭrdzhali
Sadanski
Rodopi Planina
B U L G A R I A
Tundzha
Mesta
Struma
Arda
BLACK SEA
Kırklareli
Edirne
Havsa
Babaeski
Lüleburgaz
Demirköy
Yıldız Dağları
Karadeniz Boğazı (Bosporus)
Uzunköprü
Ergene
Çorlu
İstanbul
Üsküdar
Kartal
Malkara
Tekirdağ
Tekir D.
Keşan
İpsala
Sea of Marmara
Marmara Adası
Yalova
İznik G.
Gemlik
Karacabey
Bursa
Bandırma
Mustafa-Kemalpaşa
Orhaneli
Gelibolu (Gallipoli)
Saros Körfezi
Eceabat
Çanakkale
Biga
Gönen
Kus G.
Ezine
Balıkesir
Dursunbey
Tavşanlı
Edremit
Bigadiç
Akdağ 2089
Ayvacık
Edremit K.
Burhaniye
Ayvalık
Sındırgı
Simav
Soma
Bergama
Kırkağaç
Akhisar
Çandarlı K.
Menemen
Manisa
Turgutlu
Kula
Gediz
Bornova
Salihli
Alaşehir
Boz Dağları 2157
Ödemiş
İzmir (Smyrna)
Çeşme
Urla
Torbalı
Tire
Buldan
Nazilli
Selçuk
Aydın
Denizli
Kuşadası K.
Söke
Çine
Milas
Muğla
Bodrum
Gökova K.
Marmaris
T U R K E Y
Kavála
Dráma
Xánthi
Komotiní
Sápai
Néstos (Mesta)
Alexandroúpolis
Sérrai
Kilkís
Nigríta
Thessaloníki (Salonica)
K. Strimonikós
Thásos
Samothráki
Gökçeada
Límnos
Kástron
Bozca Ada
Khalkidhikí
Políyiros
K. Singitikós
Áthos 2033
K. Toronaíos
Thermaïkos Kólpos
Yiannitsá
Edhessa
Véroia
Flórina
Kastoría
Ptolemaïs
Kozaní
Kateríni
Grámmos 2503
Smólikas 2633
Óros Ólimbos (Olympus) 2917
Aliákmon
Tírnavos
Kalabáka
Lárisa
Ioánnina
Igoumenítsa
Corfu (Kérkira)
Tzouméka 2469
Kardhítsa
Piniós
Vólos
Fársala
Almirós
Skiathos
Iliodhrómia
Skópelos
Dhomokós
Óthris 1726
Tímfristós 2316
Lamía
Árta
Préveza
Amfilokhía
Levkás
Istiáia
Euboea (Évvoia)
Skíros
Límni
Livanátais
Kími
Khalkís
Agrínion
Gióna 2510
Amfissa
Levádhia
Thívai
Návpaktos
Mesolóngion
Kefallinía
Argostólion
Pátrai
Aiyion
Gulf of Corinth
Mégara
Akharnaí
Athens (Athína)
Piraiévs
Kíllini 2376
Corinth (Kórinthos)
Zákinthos (Zante)
Amaliás
Pírgos
Peloponnese
Árgos
Návplion
Trípolis
Megalópolis
Kiparissiakós Kólpos
Kiparissía
Filiatrá
Kalámai
Spartí
Messíni
Pílos
Yíthion
Molái
Neápolis
Akr. Maléa
Akr. Taínaron
Messiniakós Kólpos
Lakonikós Kólpos
Kíthira
Párnon Óros 1935
Argolikós K.
Saronikós K.
Aíyina
Kéa
Ándros
Tínos
Míkonos
Síros
Kíthnos
Sérifos
Sífnos
Mílos
Páros
Náxos
Íos
Amorgós
Thíra
Anáfi
Sikinos
CYCLADES (Kikládhes)
AEGEAN SEA
Psará
Khíos
Kalifrévs
Akr.
Áyios Evstrátios
Lésvos
Kallonís K.
Mitilíni
Ikaría
Pagondhas
Fournoi
Sámos
Pátmos
Léros
Kálimnos
Kós
Güllük K.
DODECANESE (Dhodhekánisos)
Astipálaia
Tílos
Símí
Alimniá
Khálki
Rhodes (Ródhos)
Líndos
Kárpathos
Kásos
Mirtoan Sea
Sea of Crete
Andikíthira
Akr. Spátha
Khaniá
Kastélli
Crete (Kríti)
Réthimnon
Iráklion
Lévka Óri 2452
Ídhi Óros 2456
Dhíkti Óri 2148
K. Merabéllou
Akr. Sídheros
Sitía
Ierápetra
Timbákion
Akr. Líthinon
Gávdhos
GREECE
Pindhos
IONIAN SEA
IONIAN ISLANDS (Iónioi Nísoi)
Strait of Otranto
Brindisi
Lecce
Nardò
Maglie
Otranto
Gallipoli
C. Sta Maria di Leuca
Alice
ADRIATIC SEA
Monopoli
20
25
30
35
40
45
A
D
E
F
G
1
2
3
4

NORTH SEA

Ⓐ Ⓑ Ⓒ Ⓓ
① ② ③ ④

SWEDEN
Göteborg · Jönköping · Huskvarna · Västervik · Hultsfred
Mölndal · Borås · Nässjö · Eksjö
Skagen · Varberg · Vetlanda
Hjørring · Falkenberg · Värnamo · Älem · Borgholm
Thisted · Åbya · Ljungby · Växjö · Öland · Kalmar
Ålborg · Læsø · Halmstad · Markaryd · Älmhult
Nykøbing · Hadsund · Båstad · Ängelholm · Hässleholm · Karlshamn
Skive · Hobro · Randers · Grenå · Helsingør · Helsingborg · Ronneby · Karlskrona
Holstebro · Viborg · Hillerød · Landskrona · Kristianstad
Herning · Silkeborg · Århus · Anholt · Simrishamn
DENMARK
Skjern · Horsens · Samsø · Copenhagen (København) · Lund · Hanöbukten
Jylland (Jutland) · Vejle · Kalundborg · Roskilde · Malmö · Ystad
Varde · Kolding · Fredericia · Sjælland · Køge · Trelleborg
Esbjerg · Haderslev · Odense · Nyborg · Korsør · Næstved · Rønne · Bornholm
Sylt · Åbenrå · Als · Svendborg · Vordingborg · BALT
Rømø · Sønderborg · Nakskov · Mon · B
Westerland · Flensburg · Lolland · Falster · Rødbyhavn · Nykøbing
Husum · Schleswig · Kieler Bucht · Puttgarden · Gedser · Sassnitz · Ustka
SCHLESWIG-HOLSTEIN · Kiel · Fehmarn · Mecklenburger Bucht · Rügen · Stralsund · Kołobrzeg · Karlino · Białogard
Heide · Rendsburg · Oldenburg · Warnemünde · Greifswald · Świnoujście · Swidwin · Szczecinek
Neumünster · Lübeck · Travemünde · Rostock · Z Szczeciński · Szczecin · Stargard
Itzehoe · Elmshorn · Wismar · Schwerin · Malchin · Anklam · Neubrandenburg · Goleniów · Wałcz
Cuxhaven · Stade · Hamburg · Lauenburg · Ludwigslust · Neustrelitz · Prenzlau · Myślibórz · Piła
Wilhelmshaven · Bremerhaven · Lüneburg · Pritzwalk · Oranienburg · Eberswalde · Gorzów Wlkp. · Noteć
Emden · Leer · Oldenburg · Rotenburg · Salzwedel · Uelzen · Wittenberge · Rathenow · Nauen · Berlin · Kostrzyn · Skwierzyna · Pniewy · Oborniki · POZNAŃ
NIEDERSACHSEN · Celle · Wolfsburg · Stendal · Brandenburg · Potsdam · Frankfurt an-der-Oder · Świebodzin · Sroda
Groningen · Assen · Meppen · Nienburg · Hannover · Braunschweig · Burg · Magdeburg · **GERMANY** · Fürstenwalde · Spree · Zielona Góra
Leeuwarden · Emmen · Lingen · Minden · Hildesheim · Salzgitter · Halberstadt · Bernburg · Wittenberg · Luckenwalde · Gubin · Nowa Sól
Den Helder · Zwolle · Rheine · Osnabrück · Bielefeld · Göttingen · Aschersleben · Dessau · Bitterfeld · Cottbus · Zary · Głogów
Hoorn · Deventer · Apeldoorn · Münster · Gütersloh · Paderborn · Nordhausen · Halle · Torgau · Finsterwalde · Sprotawa
Alkmaar · Amsterdam · Arnhem · Coesfeld · Hamm · Münden · Kassel · Heiligenstadt · Leipzig · Riesa · Elsterwerda · Wołów
Haarlem · Utrecht · Nijmegen · Bocholt · **NORDRHEIN** · Wesel · Haltern · Lippe · Korbach · Mühlhausen · Naumburg · Meissen · Bautzen · Bolesławiec
The Hague · Leiden · Hilversum · Wesel · Duisburg · Dortmund · Münden · Bad Hersfeld · Erfurt · Jena · Gera · Weissenfels · Zeitz · Dresden · Görlitz · Jelenia Góra · Legnica · **WROCŁAW** (Breslau)
Rotterdam · Dordrecht · Maas · Krefeld · Essen · Hagen · Wuppertal · Ruhr · Marburg · Alsfeld · Fulda · Eisenach · Zwickau · Karl Marx Stadt · Zittau · Liberec · Świdnica · Wałbrzych · Dzierżoniow
Vlissingen · Breda · Tilburg · Eindhoven · Venlo · Mönchengladbach · Düsseldorf · **WESTFALEN** · Siegen · Giessen · Limburg · **HESSEN** · Thüringer Wald · Plauen · Hof · Most · Teplice · Ústí · Jablonec · n.N. · Śnieżka · Kłodzko
Oostende · Bruges · Gent · Antwerp (Antwerpen) · Mechelen · Hasselt · Aachen · Cologne (Köln) · Bonn · Bad Godesberg · Koblenz · Frankfurt am Main · Erzgebirge · Cheb · Chomutov · Brandýs · Mladá · Hradeç Králové · Praděd
Brussels (Bruxelles/Brüssel) · Leuven · Maastricht · Euskirchen · Andernach · Wiesbaden · Mainz · Offenbach · Schweinfurt · Coburg · Karlovy Vary · Kladno · Kolín · Pardubice · 1490
Lille · Roubaix · Tournai · Solignies · Liège · St-Truiden · Bitburg · Mosel · Bad-Kreuznach · Darmstadt · Aschaffenburg · Würzburg · Bamberg · Bayreuth · Weiden · **PRAGUE** (Praha) · Kutná Hora · Zabreł
Béthune · Valenciennes · Mons · Charleroi · Namur · **RHEINLAND-PFALZ** · Trier · Worms · Mannheim · Kitzingen · Erlangen · Amberg · Plzeň · Beroun · Brdy · Benešov · Svitavy · Olomouc
Douai · Arras · Denain · Maubeuge · Ardennes · **LUXEMBOURG** · Luxembourg · Arlon · Longwy · SAARLAND · Ludwigshafen · Heidelberg · Ansbach · Nürnberg · Böhmer-wald · Klatovy · Písek · Tábor · **ČESKÉ ZEMĚ** · Uhlava · Prostějov
Cambrai · Fourmies · Charleville-Mézières · Sedan · Thionville · Saarlouis · Kaiserslautern · Saarbrücken · Speyer · Fürth · Alb · Parsberg · Regensburg · České Budějovice · Třebíč · Brno
St-Quentin · Oise · Laon · Aisne · Verdun · Metz · Pirmasens · Karlsruhe · Heilbronn · Crailsheim · Donau · Rachel · Passau · Trebon · Znojmo · Mikulov · Hodon · Brec
Compiègne · Château-Thierry · Reims · Meuse · Nancy · Sarrebourg · Pforzheim · **BADEN** · Ludwigsburg · **BAYERN** · Donauwörth · Schärding · Horn · Hollabrunn · Vyskov
Soissons · Marne · Épernay · Sarreguemines · Stuttgart · Baden-Baden · Heidenheim · Ingolstadt · Landshut · Freistadt · Stockerau · **VIENNA** (Wien)
Provins · Romilly-s-S · St-Dizier · Toul · Strasbourg · Offenburg · Tübingen · Reutlingen · Alb · Augsburg · Dachau · Mühldorf · Linz · Mödling · Bratislava
Troyes · Vitry-l.-F. · Bar-s-A. · Épinal · St-Dié · Colmar · **WÜRTTEMBERG** · Biberach · Ulm · Landsberg · Memmingen · Kempten · München/Munich · Starnberg · Rosenheim · Vöcklabruck · Wels · St Pölten · Wr. Neustadt · Sopron
Sens · Joigny · Chaumont · Langres · Freiburg · Schwarzwald · Ravensburg · Bad Tölz · Salzburg · Gmunden · Steyr · Mariazell · Neunkirchen
Auxerre · Avallon · Vesoul · Belfort · Mulhouse · Lörrach · Konstanz · Friedrichshafen · Lindau · Füssen · Garmisch-P. · Kufstein · Bad Ischl · Liezen · Eisenerz · M'óvár
Montbéliard · Basle (Basel) · Schaffhausen · Winterthur · St Gallen · Dornbirn · Kitzbühel · Hochkönig 2938 · Radstad · Leoben · Bruck an der Mur · Szombath
Dijon · Besançon · Doubs · Olten · Zürich · Zug · Feldkirch · Innsbruck · **AUSTRIA** · Dachstein 2996 · Badgastein · Judenburg · Graz
FRANCHE-COMTÉ · Biel · Luzern · Schwyz · **LIECHTENSTEIN** · Vaduz · Bludenz · Landeck · Brenner 1370 · Grossglockner 3798 · Villach · Klagenfurt · Gleisdorf · Zalaegerszeg
Beaune · Le Creusot · Chalon-s-S · Lons-le-S · Pontarlier · Neuchâtel · Berne (Bern) · Interlaken · Rhein · Chur · Arosa · Wildspitze 3777 · Lienz · Spittal · Wolfsberg · Leibnitz · Nagykanizsa
Digoin · Mâcon · Bourg · Geneva (Genève) · Lausanne · Vevey · Thun · **SWITZERLAND** · Jungfrau 4158 · St Moritz · Merano · Bolzano · Cortina d'A · Tarvisio · Maribor · Varazdin
Roanne · Villefranche · Annecy · L'Léman · Montreux · Brig · St Gotthard · Ortles 3899 · Marmolada 3342 · Gemona · Kranj · Celje · Koprivnica
Lyon · Aix · Chambéry · Martigny · Simplon 2009 · Bellinzona · Bolzano · **ALPI** · Dolomitiche · Udine · Gorizia · Ljubljana · Brežice · Bjelovar
St-Chamond · St-Étienne · Voiron · Mt Blanc 4810 · Gd St Bernard · Matterhorn 4477 · Lugano · di Como · Sondrio · Edolo · Trento · Belluno · Monfalcone · Postojna · Novo Mesto · Daruva
Annonay · Grenoble · Albertville · Gran Paradiso 4061 · Aosta · Varese · Lecco · L. di Garda · Rovereto · Bassano · Treviso · Trieste · Koper · Poreč · Rijeka (Fiume) · Istra · Sisak
Romans-s.-I · du Pelvoux 4103 · Ivrea · Biella · Busto Arsizio · Bergamo · Brescia · Verona · Vicenza · Mestre · Venice (Venezia) · Rovinj · Oglulin · Una
Valence · Col du Mt Cenis 2803 · Briançon · Vercelli · Novara · Monza · **MILAN** (Milano) · Lodi · Mantova · Padova · Venezia · Chioggia · **YUG**
Montélimar · Mte Viso 3841 · Gap · Susa · **TURIN** (Torino) · Casale Monf. · Pavia · Cremona · **ITALY** · Rovigo · G. di Venezia
Aubenas · Alessandria · Asti · Piacenza

1:5M
0 · 50 · 100 · 150 · 200 km
0 · 50 · 100 mls

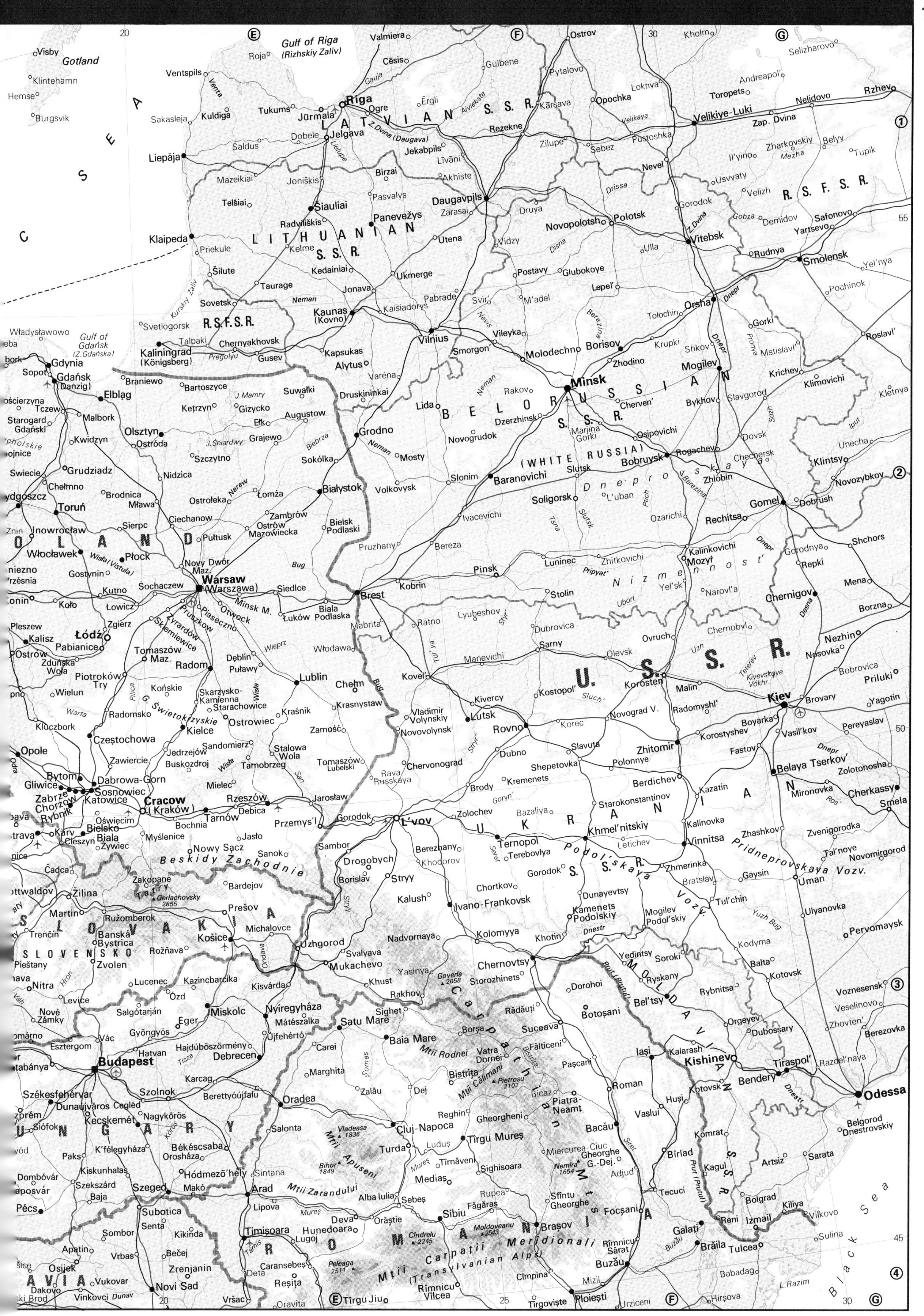
Gulf of Riga
(Rizhskiy Zaliv)
Visby
Gotland
Klintehamn
Hemse
Burgsvik
SEA
C
Ventspils
Venta
Roja
Valmiera
Cēsis
Gauja
Gulbene
Ostrov
Kholm
Selizharovo
Pytalovo
Andreapol'
Loknya
Toropets
Rzhev
Riga
Jūrmala
Tukums
Kuldīga
Sakasleja
Ogre
Ērgli
Aiviekste
LATVIAN S.S.R.
Kārsava
Opochka
Velikiye-Luki
Nelidovo
Zap. Dvina
Dobele
Jelgava
Z. Dvina (Daugava)
Rezekne
Velikaya
Pustoshka
Saldus
Lielupe
Jekabpils
Zilupe
Sebez
Liepāja
Līvāni
Il'yino
Zharkovskiy
Mezha
Belyy
Tupik
Mazeikiai
Joniškis
Birzai
Akhiste
Nevel
Usvyaty
Drissa
Telšiai
Šiauliai
Pasvalys
Daugavpils
Gorodok
Velizh
R. S. F. S. R.
Radviliškis
Panevežys
Zarasai
Druya
Novopolotsk
Polotsk
Z. Dvina
Gobza
Demidov
Safonovo
Yartsevo
Klaipeda
LITHUANIAN S.S.R.
Kelme
Utena
Vidzy
Disna
Ulla
Vitebsk
Rudnya
Smolensk
Yel'nya
Priekule
Šilute
Kedainiai
Ukmerge
Postavy
Glubokoye
Lepel'
Pochinok
Taurage
Jonava
Pabrade
Svir'
M'adel
Orsha
Dnepr
Sovetsk
Neman
Kaunas
(Kovno)
Kaisiadorys
Nevis
Berezina
Tolochin
Gorki
Roslavl'
Kurskiy Zaliv
R.S.F.S.R.
Svetlogorsk
Vilnius
Vileyka
Krupki
Pronya
Władysławowo
Gulf of Gdańsk
(Z. Gdańska)
Talpaki
Chernyakhovsk
Kaliningrad
(Königsberg)
Pregolya
Gusev
Kapsukas
Alytus
Smorgon'
Molodechno
Borisov
Shkov
Mstislavl'
Gdynia
Sopot
Gdańsk
(Danzig)
Braniewo
Varėna
Zhodino
Mogilev
Krichev
Klimovichi
Elbląg
Bartoszyce
Druskininkai
Minsk
Kletnya
Tczew
J. Mamry
Suwałki
Rakov
Neman
Starogard Gdański
Malbork
Kętrzyn
Gizycko
Lida
BELORUSSIAN S.S.R.
Cherven'
Bykhov
Slavgorod
Ełk
Augustow
Dzerzhinsk
Olsztyn
Ostróda
Kwidzyn
J. Śniardwy
Grajewo
Biebrza
Grodno
Marjina Gorki
Osipovichi
Iput
Unecha
Novogrudok
Dovsk
Grudziadz
Szczytno
Sokółka
Mosty
(WHITE RUSSIA)
Bobruysk
Rogachev
Chechersk
Klintsy
Swiecie
Nidzica
Slutsk
Dnepro
Chełmno
Narew
Białystok
Slonim
Baranovichi
Berezina
Zhlobin
Novozybkov
Bydgoszcz
Brodnica
Ostrołeka
Łomża
Volkovysk
Soligorsk
L'uban
Gomel
Dobrush
Toruń
Mława
Ptich
Ciechanow
Zambrów
Ivacevichi
Ozarichi
Rechitsa
Sierpc
Ostrów Mazowiecka
Bielsk Podlaski
Tsna
Inowrocław
Pułtusk
Dnepr
Shchors
POLAND
Włocławek
Płock
Wisła (Vistula)
Pruzhany
Bereza
Kalinkovichi
Gorodnya
Mozyr
Nowy Dwór Maz.
Zhitkovichi
Gostynin
Bug
Luninec
Repki
Pinsk
Pripyat'
Nizmennost'
Warsaw
(Warszawa)
Siedlce
Kobrin
Yel'sk
Mena
Kutno
Sochaczew
Brest
Stolin
Narovl'a
Chernigov
Konin
Koło
Łowicz
Minsk M.
Biała Podlaska
Ubort
Desna
Borzna
Zgierz
Otwock
Łuków
Mabrita
Ratno
Lyubeshov
Dubrovica
Chernobyl
Pleszew
Łódź
Żyrardów
Piaseczno
Styr'
Kalisz
Pabianice
Skierniewice
Pruszków
Ovruch
Nezhin
Ostrów
Tomaszów Maz.
Wieprz
Włodawa
Sarny
Uzh
Nosovka
Zduńska Wola
Dęblin
Puławy
Tur'ya
Manevichi
Olevsk
U. S. S. R.
Bobrovica
Piotrków Try
Radom
Teterev
Priluki
Wieluń
Końskie
Lublin
Chełm
Kovel'
Korosten'
Malin
Kiyevskoye Vdkhr.
Skarzysko-Kamienna
Starachowice
Krasnystaw
Kostopol'
Kivercy
Warta
Radomsko
G. Świetokrzyskie
Kraśnik
Vladimir Volynskiy
Lutsk
Sluch'
Radomyshl'
Kiev
Brovary
Yagotin
Ostrowiec
Kluczbork
Kielce
Zamość
Novovolynsk
Rovno
Korec
Novograd V.
Boyarka
Vasil'kov
Pereyaslav
Częstochowa
Sandomierz
Stalowa Wola
Slavuta
Zhitomir
Korostyshev
Opole
Zawiercie
Jędrzejów
Tomaszów Lubelski
Dubno
Fastov
Dnepr
Odra
Buskozdroj
Tarnobrzeg
Chervonograd
Shepetovka
Polonnye
Belaya Tserkov'
Zolotonosha
Bytom
Dabrowa-Gorn
San
Rava Russkaya
Kremenets
Berdichev
Gliwice
Sosnowiec
Mielec
Brody
Kazatin
Mironovka
Cherkassy
Zabrze
Chorzów
Katowice
Cracow
(Kraków)
Rzeszów
Jarosław
Goryn'
Starokonstantinov
Smela
Rybnik
Dębica
Zolochev
Bazaliya
UKRAINIAN
Ros'
Oświęcim
Bochnia
Tarnów
Przemyśl
Gorodok
L'vov
Khmel'nitskiy
Kalinovka
Zhashkov
Zvenigorodka
Bielsko Biała
Karv.
Cieszyn
Żywiec
Myślenice
Jasło
Berezhany
Ternopol
Letichev
Vinnitsa
Pridneprovskaya Vozv.
Nowy Sącz
Sanok
Sambor
Khodorov
Terebovlya
Podol'skaya
Tal'noye
Novomirgorod
Beskidy Zachodnie
Drogobych
Seret
Gorodok
S.S.R.
Zhmerinka
Čadca
Zakopane
Tatry
Gerlachovsky 2655
Bardejov
Borislav
Stryy
Bratslav
Gaysin
Uman
Žilina
Chortkov
Dunayevtsy
Vozv.
Martin
Prešov
Kalush
Ivano-Frankovsk
Kamenets Podolskiy
Tul'chin
Ružomberok
Mogilev Podol'skiy
Ulyanovka
Trenčín
Banská Bystrica
SLOVAKIA
Michalovce
Yuzh Bug
Košice
Uzhgorod
Nadvornaya
Kolomyya
Khotin
Dnestr
Pervomaysk
SLOVENSKO
Rožňava
Ondava
Svalyava
Kodyma
Piešťany
Zvolen
Mukachevo
Yedintsy
Soroki
Balta
Hron
Yasinya
Goverla 2058
Chernovtsy
Storozhinets
Kotovsk
Nitra
Lucenec
Kazincbarcika
Kisvárda
Khust
Ryskany
Voznesensk
Levice
Ózd
Rakhov
Dorohoi
MOLDAVIAN
Rybnitsa
Váh
Nové Zámky
Salgótarján
Miskolc
Nyíregyháza
Carpathian
Prut (Prutul)
Bel'tsy
Veselinovo
Sighet
Rădăuţi
Botoşani
Gyöngyös
Eger
Mátészalka
Satu Mare
Orgeyev
Zhovten'
Suceava
Dubossary
Vác
Hatvan
Újfehértó
Carei
Baia Mare
Borşa
Berezovka
Esztergom
Hajdúböszörmény
Vatra Dornei
Fălticeni
Budapest
Tisza
Debrecen
Mtii Rodnei
Iaşi
Kalarash
Kishinev
Tiraspol'
Razdel'naya
Somes
Bistriţa
Paşcani
Marghita
Mtii Călimani
Pietrosu 2102
Bendery
Karcag
Bicaz
Roman
Dnestr
Székesfehérvár
Szolnok
Berettyóújfalu
Oradea
Zalău
Dej
Kotovsk
Odessa
Dunaújváros
Cegléd
Nagykörös
Piatra-Neamţ
Huşi
Siófok
Kecskemét
HUNGARY
Körös
Reghin
Gheorgheni
Vaslui
Belgorod Dnestrovskiy
Salonta
Cluj-Napoca
Bacău
Viadeasa 1836
Komrat
Békéscsaba
Mtii Apuseni
Turda
Luduş
Tîrgu Mureş
Miercurea-Ciuc
Gheorghe G.-Dej
Siret
Paks
K'félegyháza
Orosháza
Mureş
Tîrnăveni
Nemira 1654
Bîrlad
Artsiz
Sarata
Kiskunhalas
Bihor 1849
Sighisoara
Adjud
Dombóvár
Szekszárd
Hódmezővásárhely
Sintana
Mediaş
Kagul
Kaposvár
Szeged
Makó
Arad
Mtii Zarandului
Alba Iulia
Sebeş
Rupea
Sfîntu Gheorghe
Tecuci
Bolgrad
Baja
Făgăraş
Focşani
Kiliya
Pécs
Subotica
Lipova
Mureş
Deva
Orăştie
Sibiu
Reni
Izmail
Vilkovo
Senta
Kikinda
Timişoara
Hunedoara
Cindrelu 2245
Moldoveanu 2543
Braşov
Galaţi
Black Sea
Sombor
ROMANIA
Lugoj
Mtii Carpaţii Meridionali
Brăila
Sulina
Apatin
Vrbas
Bečej
Tamiş
(Transylvanian Alps)
Rîmnicu Sărat
Tulcea
Osijek
Zrenjanin
Caransebeş
Peleaga 2511
Buzău
Babadag
Vukovar
Novi Sad
Reşiţa
Rîmnicu Vîlcea
Cîmpina
Mizil
L. Razim
Dakovo
Vinkovci
Dunav
Vršac
Tîrgu Jiu
Oravita
Tîrgovişte
Ploieşti
Urziceni
Hirşova
20
25
30
45
50
55
E
F
G
1
2
3
4

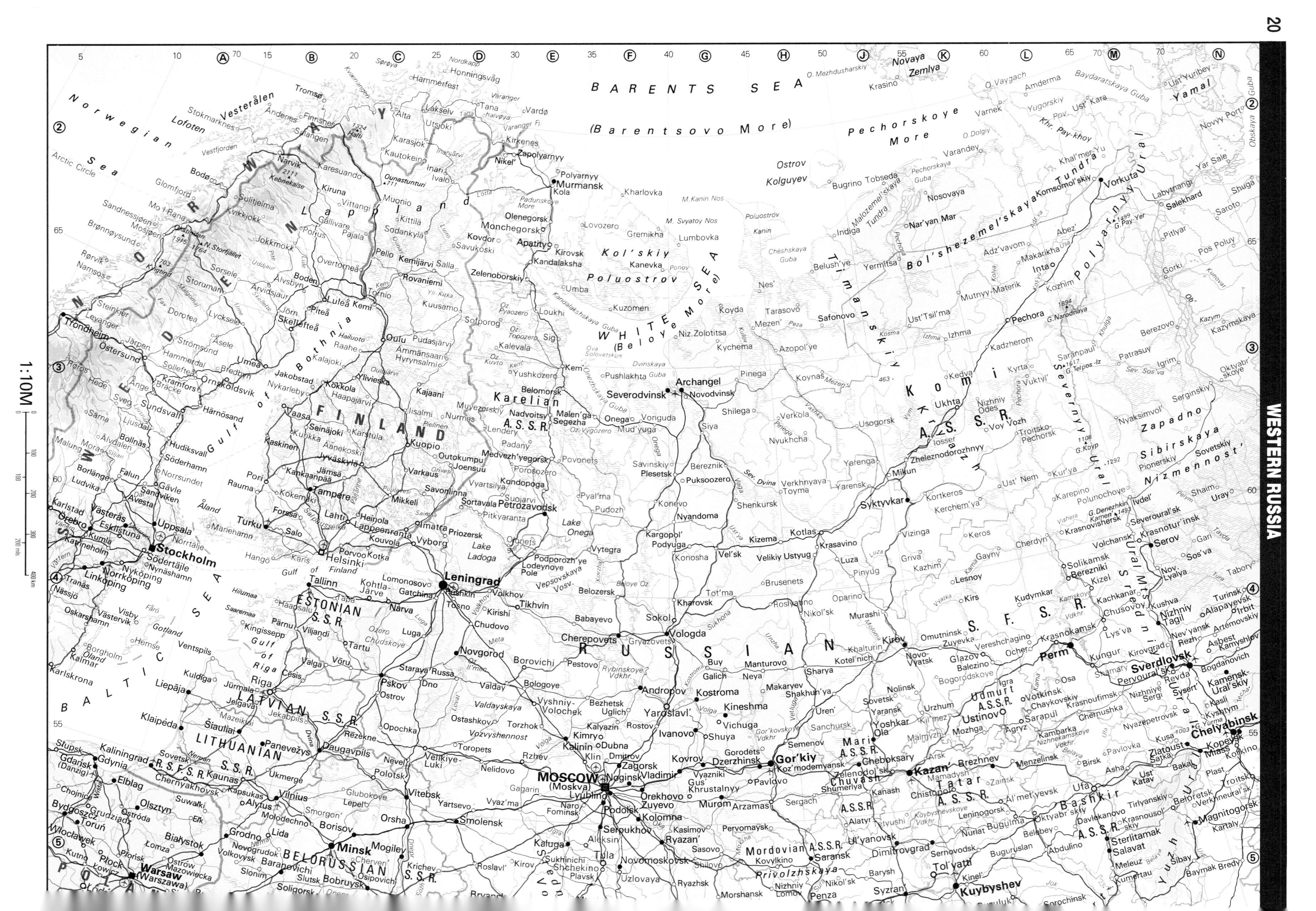

BARENTS SEA
(Barentsovo More)
Pechorskoye More
Norwegian Sea
WHITE SEA (Beloye More)
Gulf of Bothnia
Gulf of Finland
Gulf of Riga
BALTIC SEA
Arctic Circle
NORWAY
SWEDEN
FINLAND
Lapland
Kol'skiy Poluostrov
Karelian A.S.S.R.
ESTONIAN S.S.R.
LATVIAN S.S.R.
LITHUANIAN S.S.R.
BELORUSSIAN S.S.R.
R.S.F.S.R.
RUSSIAN S.F.S.R.
Komi A.S.S.R.
Udmurt A.S.S.R.
Tatar A.S.S.R.
Bashkir A.S.S.R.
Mari A.S.S.R.
Chuvash A.S.S.R.
Mordovian A.S.S.R.
Timanskiy Kryazh
Polyarnyy Ural
Severnyy Ural
Ural Mts
Zapadno Sibirskaya Nizmennost'
Bol'shezemel'skaya Tundra
Yamal
Novaya Zemlya
Ostrov Kolguyev
Lofoten
Vesterålen
Åland
Gotland
Öland
MOSCOW (Moskva)
Leningrad
Helsinki
Stockholm
Tallinn
Riga
Vilnius
Minsk
Warsaw (Warszawa)
Archangel
Murmansk
Gor'kiy
Kazan'
Kuybyshev
Perm
Sverdlovsk
Chelyabinsk
Lake Ladoga
Lake Onega
1:10M
0 100 200 300 400 km
0 100 200 mls

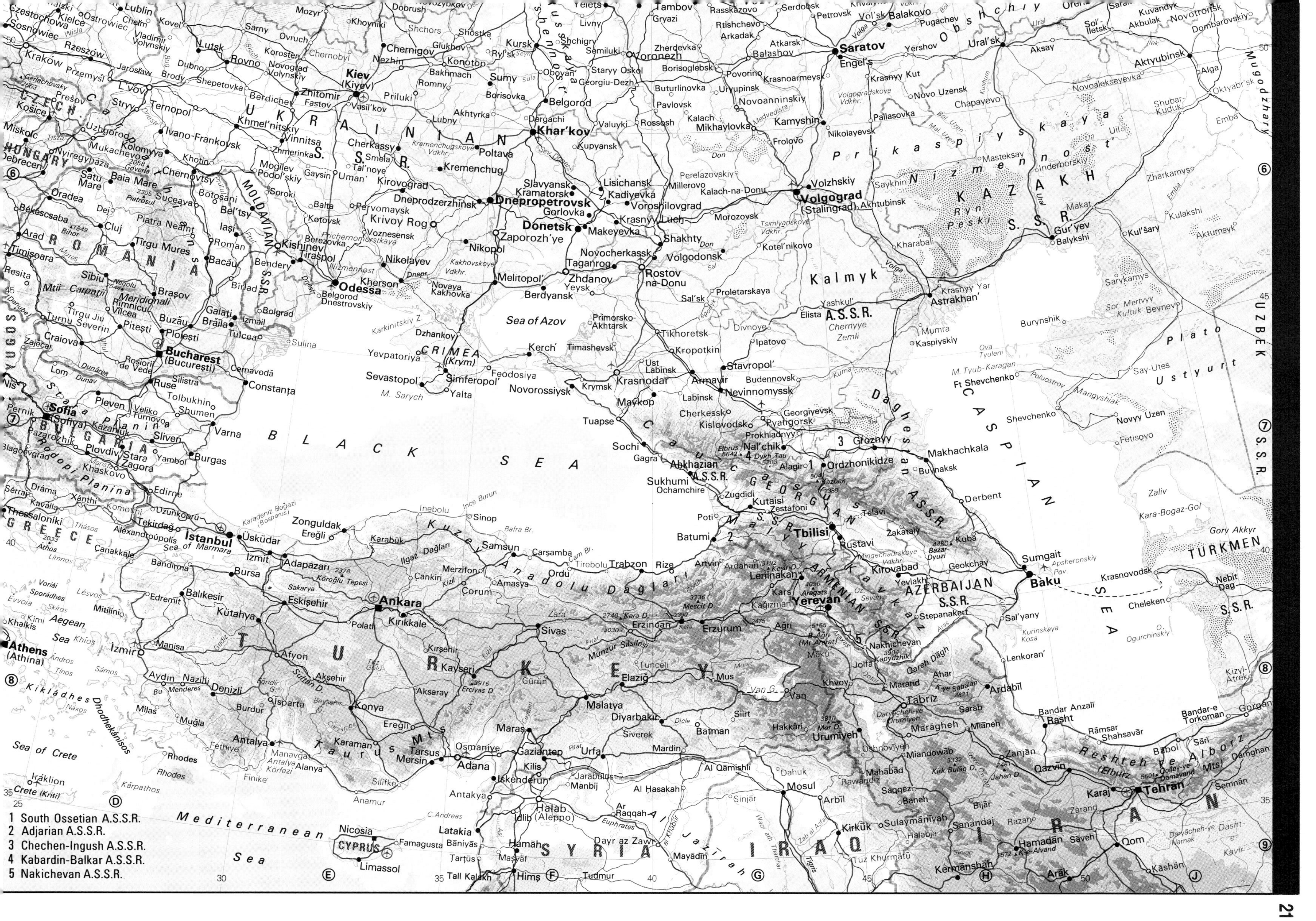

1 South Ossetian A.S.S.R.
2 Adjarian A.S.S.R.
3 Chechen-Ingush A.S.S.R.
4 Kabardin-Balkar A.S.S.R.
5 Nakichevan A.S.S.R.

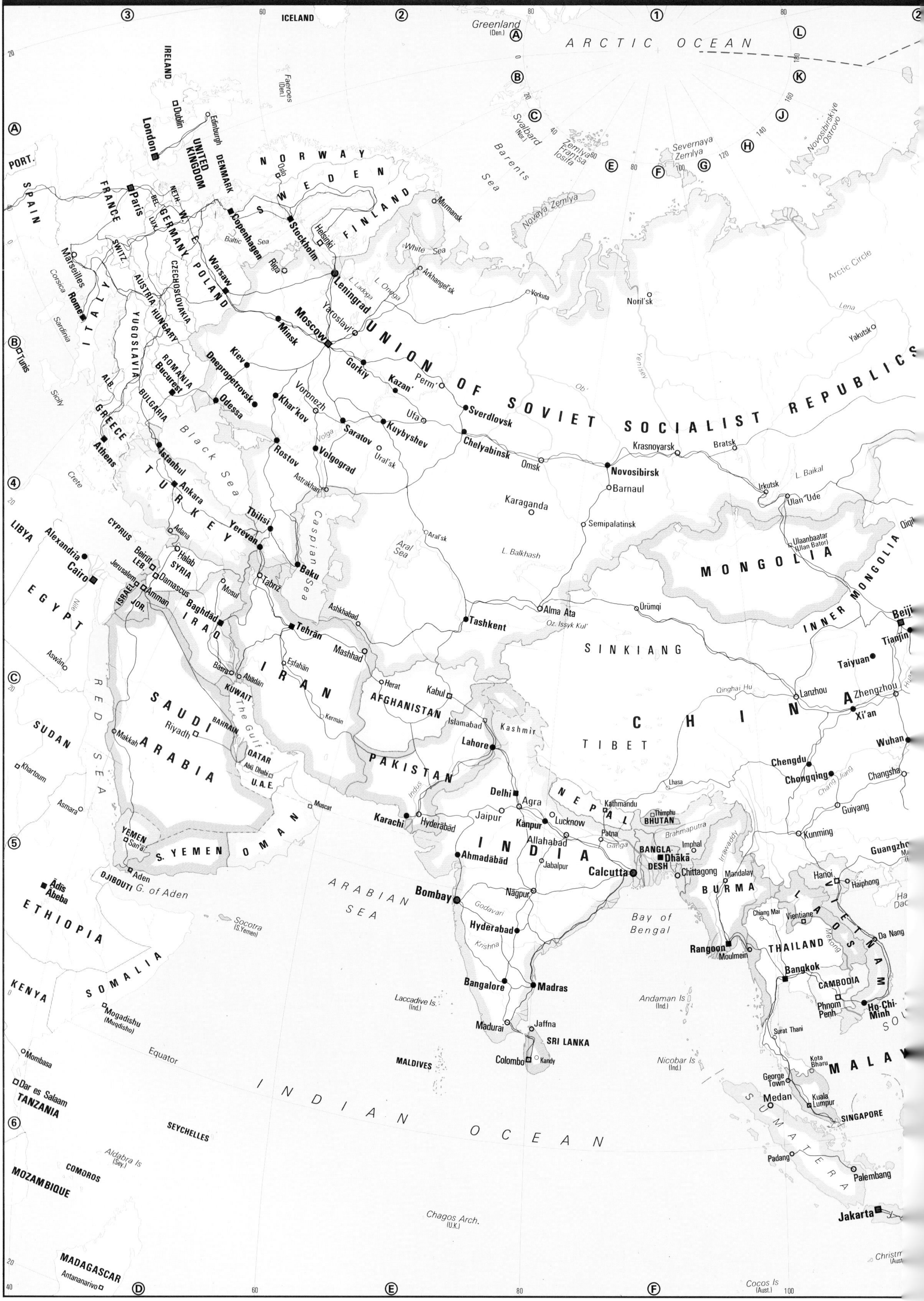

③   60   ICELAND   ②   80   ①   80   Ⓛ   ②

Ⓐ *Greenland* (Den.)   A R C T I C   O C E A N

IRELAND   Ⓑ

□ Dublin   Ⓒ *Svalbard* (Nor.)   *Zemlya Frantsa Iosifa*   Ⓚ

Edinburgh   Ⓔ   80   Ⓖ   120   Ⓗ   140   *Novosibirskiye Ostrova*

Ⓐ **London**   **UNITED**   Ⓕ   100   Ⓖ   *Severnaya Zemlya*   Ⓙ

KINGDOM   *Barents*   *Sea*

PORT.   Oslo   **NORWAY**   *Sea*

FRANCE   Paris ■   Murmansk   *Novaya Zemlya*

SPAIN   Marseilles   Copenhagen ■   Stockholm ■   Helsinki   Arkhangel'sk   *Lena*   Arctic Circle

Corsica   **GERMANY**   **POLAND**   Warsaw ■   Riga   L. Ladoga   L. Onega   Vorkuta   Noril'sk   Yakutsk

Ⓑ Rome ■   **ITALY**   CZECHOSLOVAKIA   **Leningrad** ■   Yaroslavl'   **U N I O N**   **O F**   **S O V I E T**   **S O C I A L I S T**   **R E P U B L I C S**

Tunis □   Sardinia   AUSTRIA   HUNGARY   **Moscow** ■   Minsk   Gorkiy

Sicily   YUGOSLAVIA   ROMANIA   Kiev   Kazan'   Perm'

BULGARIA   Bucurest   Dnepropetrovsk   Voronezh   Ufa   Sverdlovsk

GREECE   Istanbul   Odessa   Khar'kov   Saratov   Kuybyshev   Chelyabinsk   Krasnoyarsk   Bratsk

Ⓑ Athens   *Black*   *Sea*   Rostov   Volgograd   *Volga*   Omsk   **Novosibirsk**   Irkutsk

Crete   **T U R K E Y**   Ankara   Astrakhan'   Ural'sk   Barnaul   Ulan Ude

Ⓓ   CYPRUS   Yerevan   Tbilisi   *Caspian Sea*   Karaganda   L. Baikal

LIBYA   Alexandria □   Adana   Baku   *Aral Sea*   Aral'sk   Semipalatinsk   L. Balkhash   Ulaanbaatar (Ulan Bator)

Cairo ■   Beirut   Ḥalab   **SYRIA**   Tabriz   **M O N G O L I A**   Qiqi

EGYPT   Jerusalem   LEB.   Damascus   Mosul   Alma Ata   Ürümqi   **INNER MONGOLIA**

ISRAEL ■   Amman   Baghdād ■   Tehrān ■   Oz. Issyk Kul'   Beiji

Ⓒ   JOR.   **IRAQ**   Eşfahān   Mashhad   Tashkent   **S I N K I A N G**   Taiyuan   Tianjin

Aswān   SUDAN   Basra   Abadan   Ashkhabad   Herat   Kabul   Lanzhou   Zhengzhou   Xi'an   Wuhan

RED SEA   **SAUDI**   KUWAIT   **I R A N**   Kermān   **AFGHANISTAN**   Islamabad   *Kashmir*   **C H I N A**   Qinghai Hu   Chengdu   Chongqing   Changsha

Khartoum   **A R A B I A**   BAHRAIN   *The Gulf*   **T I B E T**   Lhasa   Guiyang

Riyadh   QATAR   Lahore   Delhi   Agra   Kathmandu   Kunming

Makkah   Abū Dhabi □   U.A.E.   **PAKISTAN**   Jaipur   Kanpur   Lucknow   **NEPAL**   Thimphu   **BHUTAN**   Guangzho

Asmara   Muscat   Karachi   Hyderābād   Allahabad   Patna   *Brahmaputra*   Imphal

Ⓒ   YEMEN   Şan'ā   **OMAN**   **I N D I A**   Ahmadābād   Jabalpur   **BANGLA-**   **DESH** ■ Dhāka   Chittagong   Mandalay

Ⓐdiş Abeba ■   DJIBOUTI   Aden   S. YEMEN   *G. of Aden*   Calcutta ■   **BURMA**

Socotra (S. Yemen)   *ARABIAN SEA*   Bombay ■   *Godavari*   Nāgpur   Hanoi   Haiphong

ETHIOPIA   Hyderabad   *Krishna*   *Bay of Bengal*   Rangoon ■   **THAILAND**   Chiang Mai   Vientiane   Da Nang

KENYA   SOMALIA   Bangalore   Madras   *Andaman Is* (Ind.)   Moulmein   Bangkok ■   **CAMBODIA**

Mogadishu (Muqdisho)   Madurai   Jaffna   **SRI LANKA**   Phnom Penh □   Ho-Chi-Minh ●

Mombasa   *Laccadive Is.* (Ind.)   Colombo □   Kandy   *Nicobar Is* (Ind.)   Kota Bharu   **M A L A W**

Ⓓ   *Equator*   MALDIVES   George Town

□ Dar es Salaam   *I N D I A N*   *O C E A N*   Medan   Kuala Lumpur

TANZANIA   SEYCHELLES   SINGAPORE

Ⓕ   COMOROS   *Chagos Arch.* (U.K.)   Padang   *S U M A T E R A*   Palembang

MOZAMBIQUE   Aldabra Is (Sey.)

MADAGASCAR   Antananarivo

Ⓓ   60   Ⓔ   80   Ⓕ   *Cocos Is* (Aust.)   100

1:40M   0   400   800   1200   1600 km   0   400   800 mls

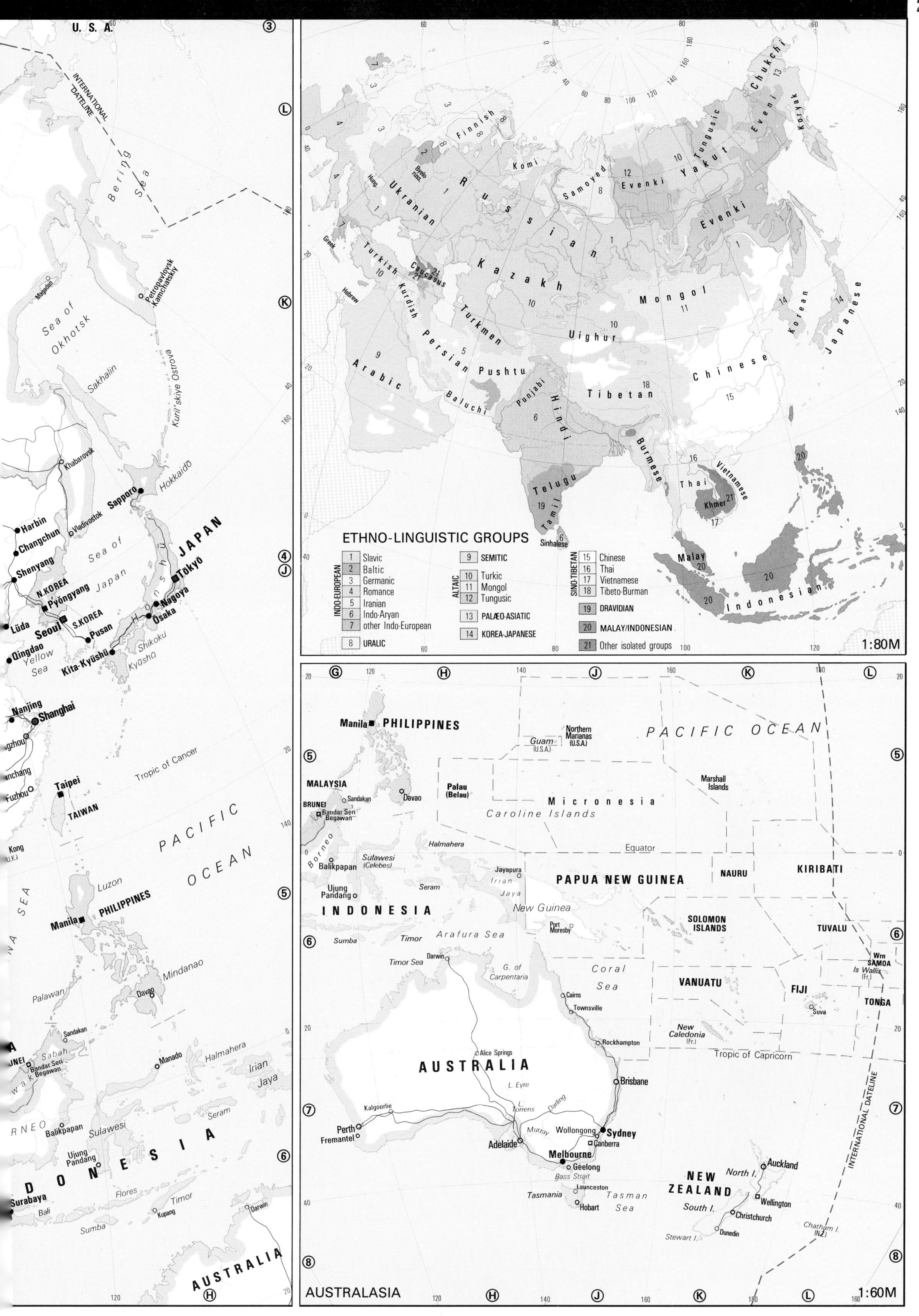

ETHNO-LINGUISTIC GROUPS

INDO-EUROPEAN
1 Slavic
2 Baltic
3 Germanic
4 Romance
5 Iranian
6 Indo-Aryan
7 other Indo-European

8 URALIC

ALTAIC
9 SEMITIC
10 Turkic
11 Mongol
12 Tungusic

13 PALÆO-ASIATIC

14 KOREA-JAPANESE

SINO-TIBETAN
15 Chinese
16 Thai
17 Vietnamese
18 Tibeto-Burman

19 DRAVIDIAN

20 MALAY/INDONESIAN

21 Other isolated groups

1:80M

AUSTRALASIA   1:60M

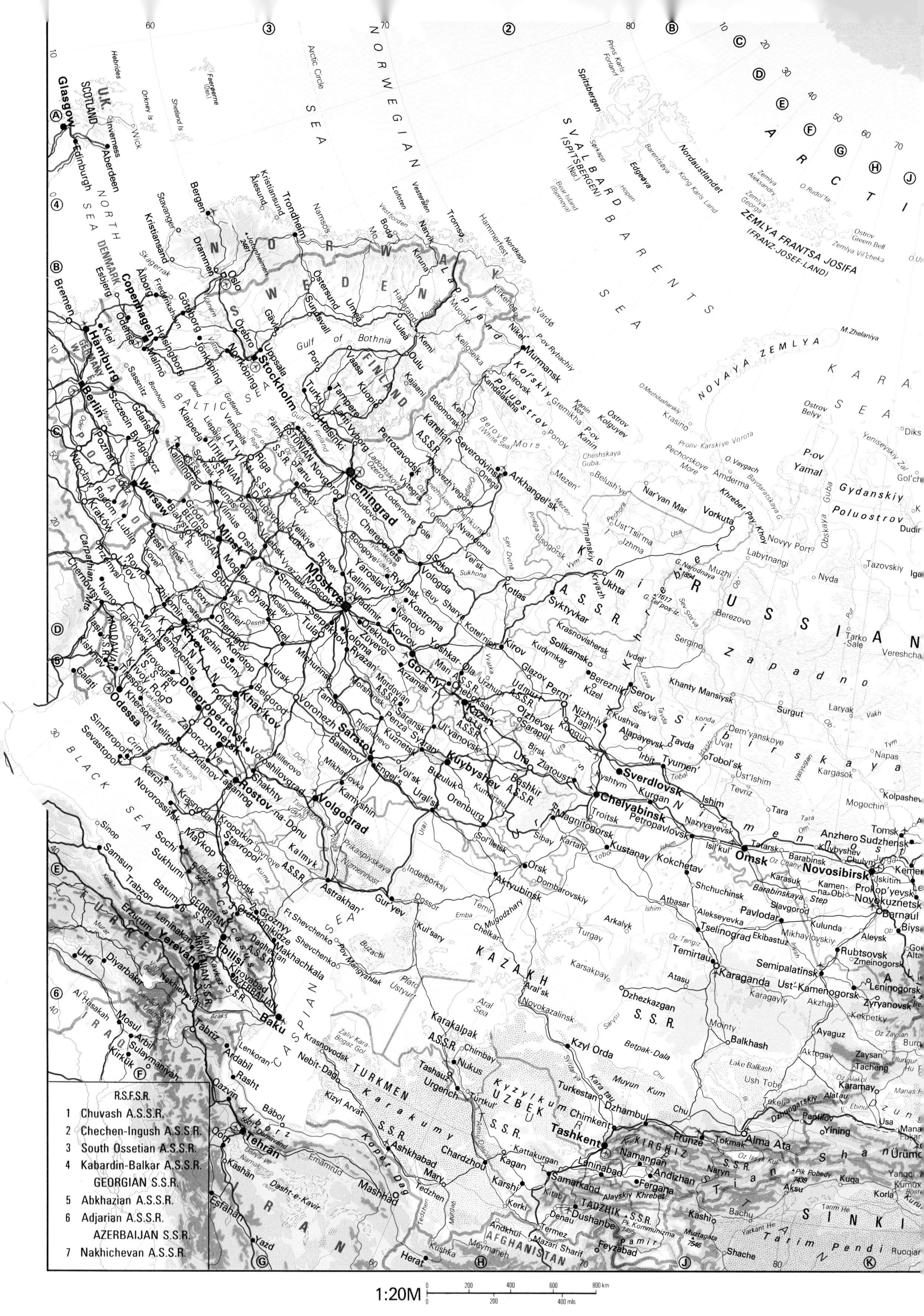

R.S.F.S.R.
1 Chuvash A.S.S.R.
2 Chechen-Ingush A.S.S.R.
3 South Ossetian A.S.S.R.
4 Kabardin-Balkar A.S.S.R.
GEORGIAN S.S.R.
5 Abkhazian A.S.S.R.
6 Adjarian A.S.S.R.
AZERBAIJAN S.S.R.
7 Nakhichevan A.S.S.R.

1:20M

| 0 | 200 | 400 | 600 | 800 km |

| 0 | 200 | 400 mls |

Grid references (top): ① ② ③ ④ ⑤ ⑥ S T U R Q P O N M L

Waters and seas

ARCTIC OCEAN
LAPTEV SEA
EAST SIBERIAN SEA
CHUKCHI SEA
BERING STRAIT (Bering Str.)
BERING SEA
SEA OF OKHOTSK
SEA OF JAPAN
YELLOW SEA
Bo Hai

Islands and land areas

SEVERNAYA ZEMLYA (NORTH LAND)
Ostrov Komsomolets
Ostrov Bol'shevik
Oktyabr'skoy Revolyutsii
Ostrov Shmidta
NOVOSIBIRSKYE OSTROVA (NEW SIBERIAN ISLANDS)
Ostrova De Longa
O. Bennetta
O. Novaya Sibir
O. Malyy Lyakhovskiy
O. Bol'shoy Lyakhovskiy
Ostrov Kotel'nyy
O. Bel'kovskiy
Ostrov Fadeyevskiy
Wrangel I.
O. Ayon
SAKHALIN
KAMCHATKA
Kuril Islands (Kuril'skiye Ostrova)
HOKKAIDO
HONSHU
SHIKOKU
KYUSHU
St. Lawrence I. (USA)
St. Matthew I. (USA)

Mountains and regions

Gory Byrranga
Poluostrov Taymyr
Gory Putorana
Sredne Sibirskoye Ploskogorye
SIBERIAN S.F.S.R.
VERKHOYANSKIY KHREBET
Khrebet Cherskogo
KOLYMSKOYE NAGORYE
KORYAKSKOYE NAGORYE
SREDINNYY KHREBET
Khrebet Orulgan
YAKUT A.S.S.R.
Aldanskoye Nagorye
STANOVOY KHREBET
Dzhugdzhur
SIKHOTE ALIN
BURYAT A.S.S.R.
Yablonovyy Khrebet
TUVA A.S.S.R.
Tannu Ola
MANCHURIA
MONGOLIA
INNER MONGOLIA
Ala Shan
Qilian Shan
Altun Shan
GREAT WALL
Ordos
NORTH KOREA
SOUTH KOREA
JAPAN

Cities and towns (selected)

Yakutsk
Magadan
Petropavlovsk-Kamchatskiy
Noril'sk
Khatanga
Tiksi
Nordvik
Verkhoyansk
Oymyakon
Aldan
Tommot
Lensk
Mirnyy
Suntar
Olekminsk
Bratsk
Ust'-Kut
Kirensk
Bodaybo
Irkutsk
Ulan Ude
Angarsk
Chita
Ulaanbaatar
Khabarovsk
Komsomol'sk-na-Amure
Nikolayevsk
Svobodnyy
Blagoveshchensk
Belogorsk
Birobidzhan
Yuzhno-Sakhalinsk
Korsakov
Vladivostok
Nakhodka
Ussuriysk
Harbin
Changchun
Shenyang
Jilin
Mudanjiang
Qiqihar
Hailar
Jinzhou
Beijing (Peking)
Tianjin (Tientsin)
Baotou
Datong
Hohhot
Yinchuan
Lanzhou
Taiyuan
Shijiazhuang
Jinan
Qingdao
Yantai
Xuzhou
Pyongyang
Seoul (Soul)
Inch'on
Taejon
Taegu
Pusan
Kwangju
Mokp'o
TOKYO
Yokohama
Osaka
Kyoto
Nagoya
Sapporo
Hakodate
Aomori
Sendai
Niigata
Fukuoka
Nagasaki
Kagoshima
Kumamoto
Kita Kyushu
Sasebo

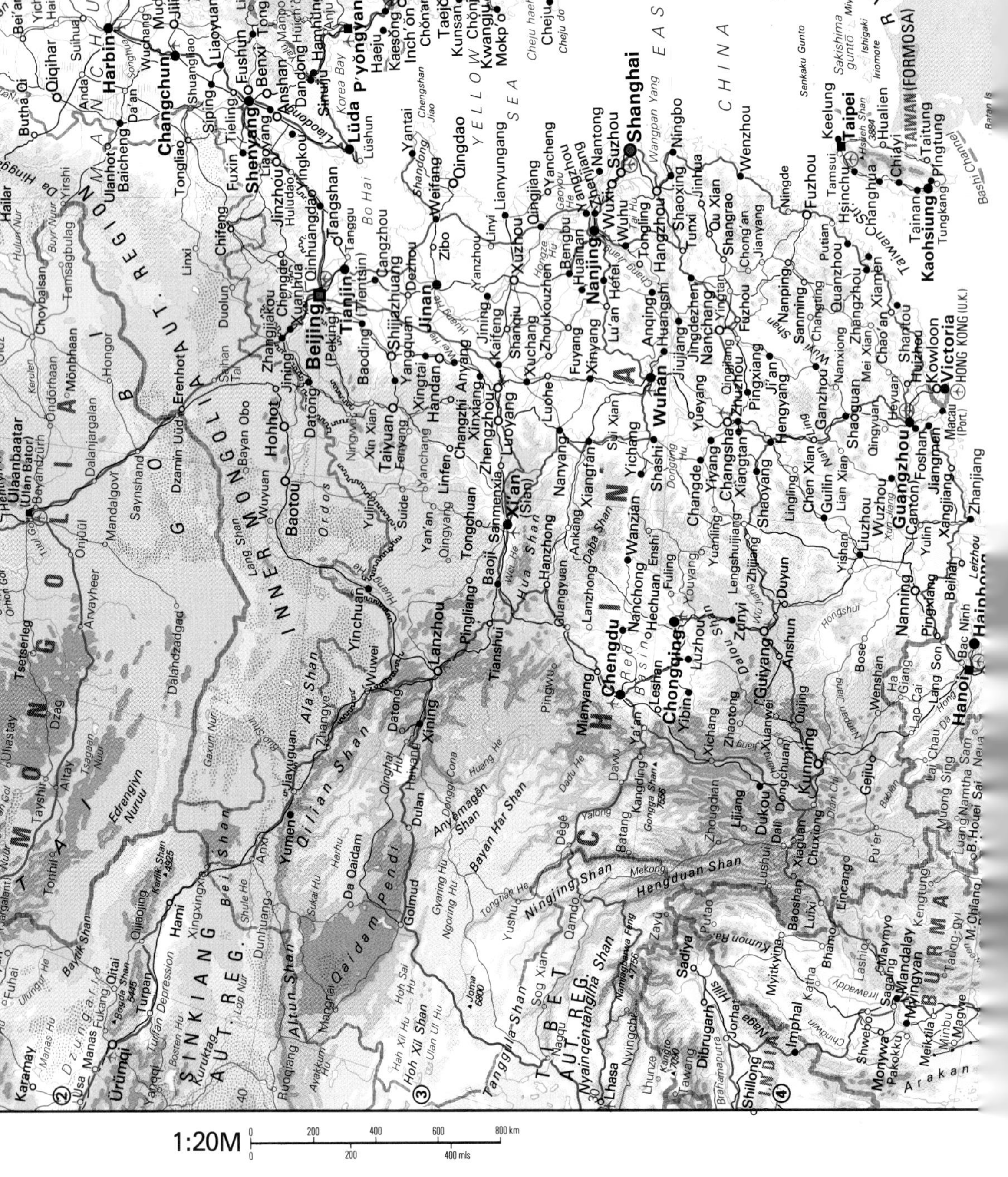

1:20M

200 400 600 800 km
200 400 mils

SEA OF OKHOTSK
SEA OF JAPAN
YELLOW SEA
EAST CHINA SEA
PACIFIC OCEAN
Kuril Islands
(Kuril'skiye Ostrova)
RYUKYU ISLANDS
KAMCHATKA
SAKHALIN
HOKKAIDŌ
HONSHU
SHIKOKU
KYŪSHŪ
NORTH KOREA
SOUTH KOREA
MONGOLIA
CHINA
INNER MONGOLIA AUT. REGION
SINKIANG AUT. REG.
TIBET AUT. REG.
U.S.S.R.
BURMA
INDIA
TAIWAN (FORMOSA)
Tropic of Cancer
Beijing
(Peking)
Shanghai
Tianjin
(Tientsin)
Tōkyō
Yokohama
Ōsaka
Kyōto
Nagoya
Kōbe
Sapporo
Seoul
P'yŏngyang
Pusan
Vladivostok
Khabarovsk
Harbin
Shenyang
Changchun
Irkutsk
Ulan Bator
Novosibirsk
Krasnoyarsk
Chita
Hohhot
Baotou
Lanzhou
Chengdu
Chongqing
Wuhan
Nanjing
Hangzhou
Guangzhou
(Canton)
Victoria
HONG KONG (U.K.)
Macau
(Port.)
Taipei
Kaohsiung
Hanoi
Kunming
Lhasa
Ürümqi
Xi'an
(Sian)
Mandalay
Qaidam Pendi
Hengduan Shan

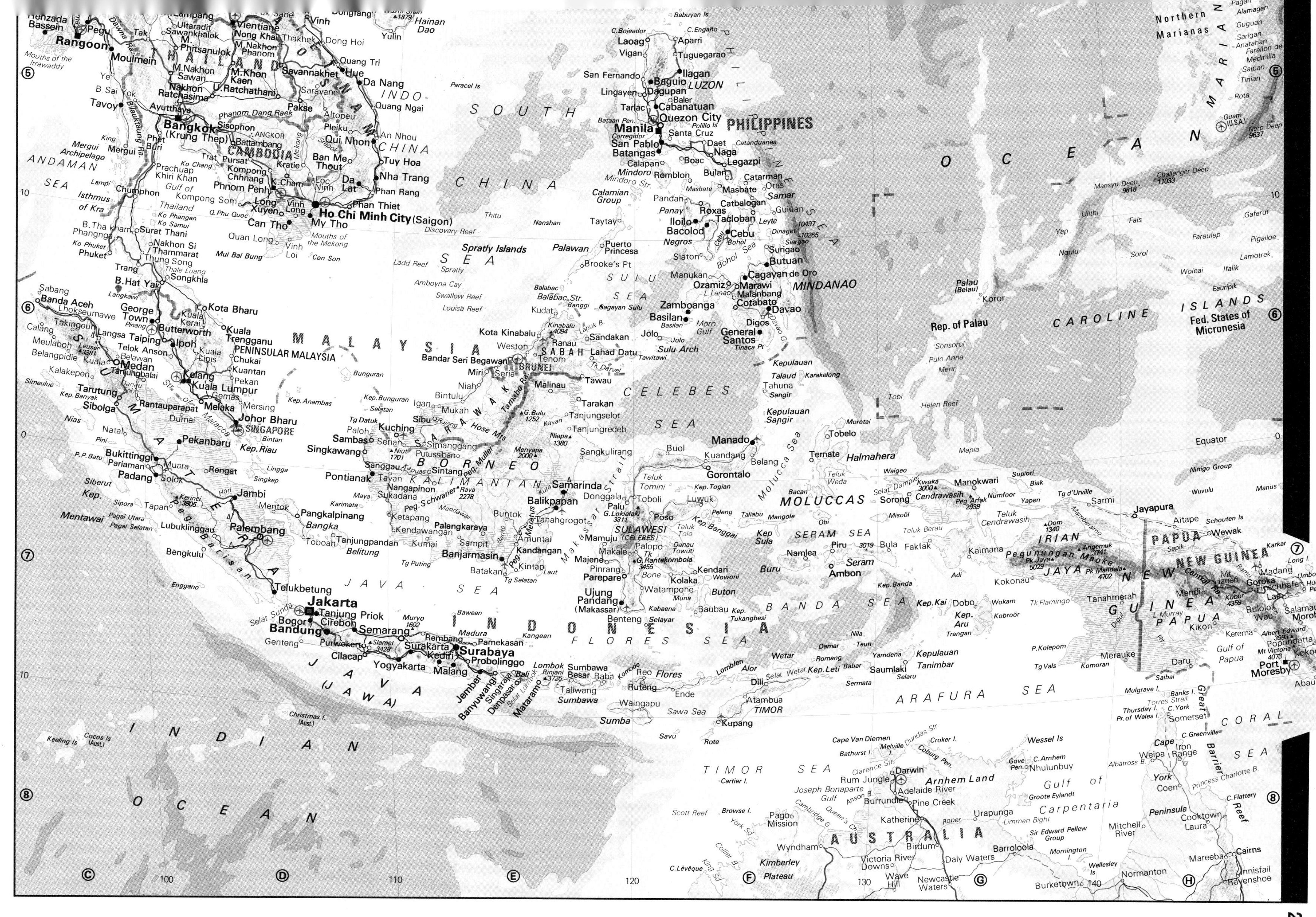

SOUTH CHINA SEA
PHILIPPINES
LUZON
MINDANAO
Manila
Quezon City
Cebu
Davao
Zamboanga
Iloilo
Bacolod
Cagayan de Oro
Legazpi
Baguio
SULU SEA
CELEBES SEA
Molucca Sea
BANDA SEA
SERAM SEA
FLORES SEA
JAVA SEA
TIMOR SEA
ARAFURA SEA
CORAL SEA
ANDAMAN SEA
Gulf of Thailand
Gulf of Carpentaria
Gulf of Papua
PHILIPPINE SEA
O C E A N
I N D I A N O C E A N
CAROLINE ISLANDS
Fed. States of Micronesia
Rep. of Palau
Koror
Northern Marianas
Guam (U.S.A.)
Challenger Deep 11033
Equator
M A L A Y S I A
PENINSULAR MALAYSIA
SABAH
SARAWAK
BRUNEI
B O R N E O
K A L I M A N T A N
SULAWESI (CELEBES)
MOLUCCAS
Halmahera
Seram
Buru
TIMOR
Flores
Sumba
Sumbawa
Lombok
Bali
Madura
J A V A (J A W A)
I N D O N E S I A
S U M A T E R A
IRIAN JAYA
PAPUA NEW GUINEA
NEW GUINEA
Jayapura
Port Moresby
Lae
Madang
Wewak
A U S T R A L I A
Arnhem Land
Cape York Peninsula
Darwin
Cairns
Kimberley Plateau
Great Barrier Reef
THAILAND
Bangkok (Krung Thep)
CAMBODIA
Phnom Penh
INDO-CHINA
Ho Chi Minh City (Saigon)
Da Nang
Hue
Vientiane
Rangoon
Moulmein
Hainan Dao
Kuala Lumpur
SINGAPORE
Johor Bharu
Kota Kinabalu
Bandar Seri Begawan
Kuching
Jakarta
Bandung
Semarang
Surabaya
Yogyakarta
Medan
Padang
Palembang
Pekanbaru
Pontianak
Banjarmasin
Balikpapan
Samarinda
Ujung Pandang (Makassar)
Manado
Ambon
Kupang
Dili
Sorong
Manokwari
Merauke
Spratly Islands
Palawan
Mindoro
Samar
Leyte
Negros
Panay
Christmas I. (Aust.)
Cocos Is (Aust.)

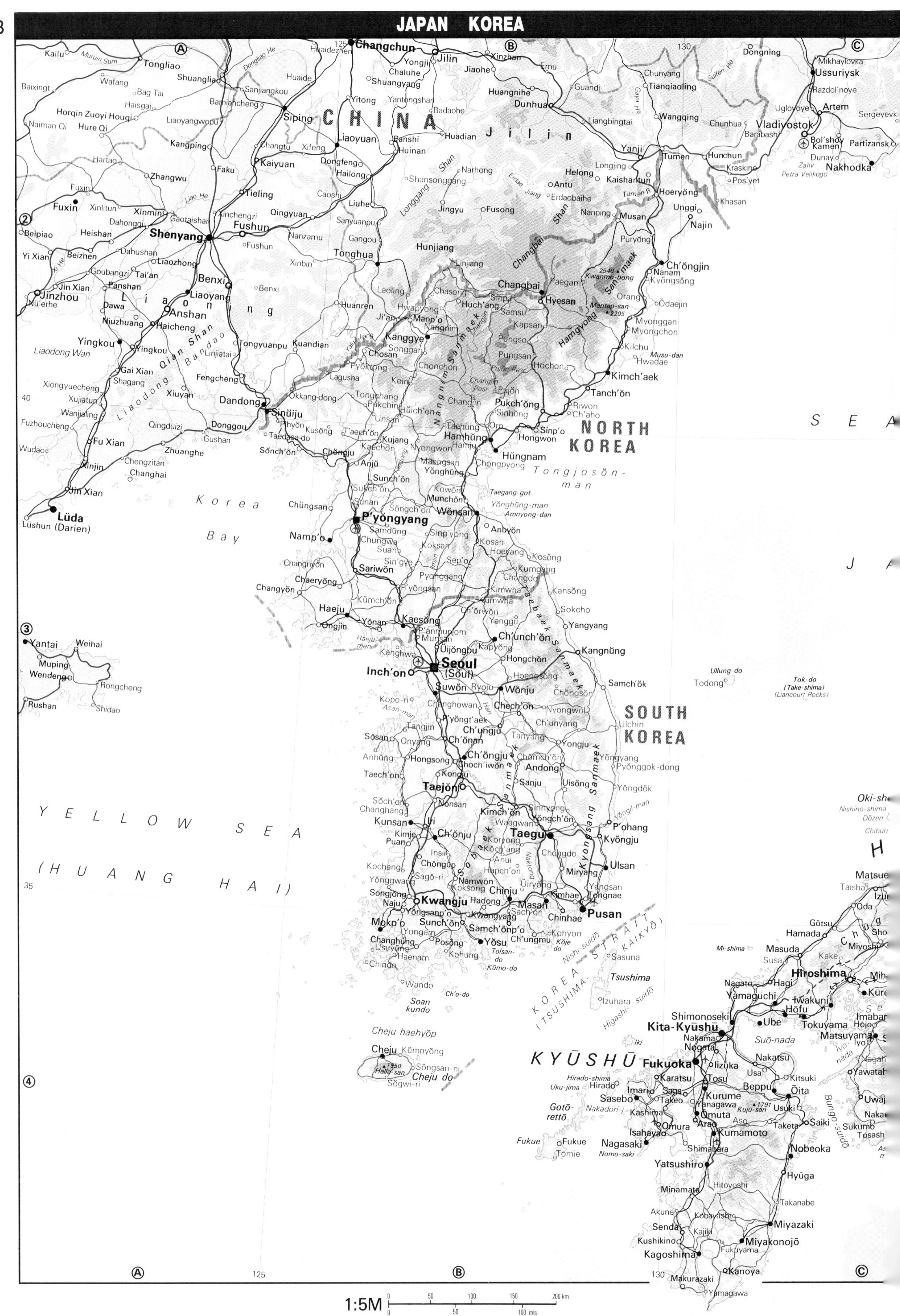

Kailu
Muruin Sum
Tongliao
Shuangliao
Dongliao He
Huaidezhen
Changchun
Jilin
Xinzhen
Emu
Chunyang
Dongning
Mikhaylovka
Ussuriysk

Baixingt
Wafang
Bag Tai
Haisgai
Sanjiangkou
Yongji
Chaluhe
Jiaohe
Huangnihe
Guandi
Tianqiaoling
Razdol'noye
Artem

Horqin Zuoyi Houqi
Hure Qi
Bamiancheng
Yitong
Yantongshan
Badaohe
Dunhua
Liangbingtai
Wangqing
Chunhua
Uglovoye
Sergeyevk

Naiman Qi
Hartao
Changtu
Xifeng
Dongfeng
Shan
Narhong
Shansonggang
Yanji
Tumen
Hunchun
Barabash
Dunay
Vladivostok

Fuxin
Xinlitun
Xinmin
Gaotaishan
Siping
Panshi
Huinan
Laoling
Huadian
Jingyu
Fusong
Changbai Shan
Longjing
Kaishantun
Helong
Antu
Erdaobaihe
Nanping
Unggi
Pos'yet
Khasan
Zaliv Petra Velikogo
Partizansk
Bol'shoy Kamen
Kraskino
Nakhodka

Belpiao
Heishan
Fuxin
Beizhen
Dahongqi
Liaoyuan
Tonghua
Hunjiang
Linjiang
Chasong
Simju
Paegam
Musan
Puryong
Najin
Shenyang
Fushun
Nanzamu
Xinbin
Laoling
Huch'ang
Hwapyong
Samsu
Kapsan
Myonggan
Myongchon
Ch'ongjin
Nanam
Kyongsong

②
Fuxin
Tieling
Qingyuan
Sanyuanpu
Gangou
Ji'an
Kanggye
Nangnim
Pungso
Orang
Ōdaejin

Fushun
Benxi
Huanren
Manp'o
Songgan
Kwanmo-bong
2540
San-maek
Mantap-san
2205

Benxi
Kuandian
Chonchon
Chosan
Pyŏktong
Chongsang
Hwadae
Kilchu

Goubangzi
Tai'an
Haicheng
Liaoyang
Fengcheng
Pukch'ong
Riwon
Ch'aho
Kimch'aek

Jinzhou
Jin Xian
Dahushan
Anshan
Qian Shan
Linjiatai
Tongyuanpu
Pukch'ong
Tanch'ŏn

Mu'erhe
Panshan
Niuzhuang
Yingkou
Bandao
Dandong
Sinŭiju
Ch'ongju
Chongju
Pyŏngsan
Changjin Resr
Pujŏn
Changjin
Taehung
Sinhŭng
Hamhung
Hŭich'ŏn
Hamgyong
Hongwon
Sinp'o

Liaodong Wan
Gai Xian
Shagang
Okkang-dong
Taedong-do
P'ihyon
Kusŏng
Unsan
Kujang
Tŏkch'ŏn
Maengsan
Yŏnghŭng
Kowŏn
Wŏnsan

Xiongyuecheng
Xujiatun
Wanjialing
Fuzhoucheng
Qingduizi
Gushan
Changhe
40
Sŏnch'ŏn
Anjŭ
Sunch'ŏn
Sunan
Chungsan
Songch'on
P'yŏngyang
Samdŭng
Suan
Sŏngch'on
Chongpyong
NORTH KOREA
Tongjosŏn-man
Yŏnghŭng-man
Amnyong-dan

Wudao
Jin Xian
Xinjin
Zhuanghe
Changhai
Chengzitan
K o r e a
B a y
Namp'o
Chungwa
Sin'gye
Sep'o
Kumgang
Kŭmhwa
Anbyŏn
Kosŏng
SEA

Lüda
Lüshun (Darien)
Changyŏn
Sariwŏn
Sin'gye
Pyonggang
Ch'ŏrwon
Kŭmhwa
Sokcho
Yangyang
J A

③
Yantai
Weihai
Muping
Wendeng
Rongcheng
Rushan
Shidao
Haeju
Ongjin
Changnyŏn
Chaeryŏng
Kŭmch'ŏn
Yŏnan
Kaesŏng
P'anmunjŏm
Munsan
Kanghwa
Uijŏngbu
Kapyŏng
Ch'unch'ŏn
Yangp'yŏng
Hongch'ŏn
Kangnŭng
Samch'ŏk
Ullŭng-do
Todong

Seoul (Sŏul)
Inch'on
Suwŏn
Ryoju
Wŏnju
Hoengsŏng
Chŏngsŏn
Tok-do (Take-shima) (Liancourt Rocks)

Kopo-ri
Changhowan
P'yŏngt'aek
Han
Chech'on
Nyongwol
Ch'unyang
Ulchin
SOUTH KOREA

Asan-man
Tangjin
Ansŏng
Onyang
Ch'ungju
Tanyang
Yongju
Yŏngyang
Pyŏnggok-dong

Sŏsan
Hongsong
Ch'ŏnan
Chŏch'iwŏn
Ch'ŏngju
Chŭmch'ŏn
Andong
Uisŏng
Yŏngdŏk

Anhŭng
Kongju
Sanju
Y E L L O W   S E A
Taech'on
Changhang
Nonsan
Sinnyong
Kimch'ŏn
Waegwan
Yŏngil-man

(H U A N G   H A I)
35
Kunsan
Ih
Ch'ŏnju
Koryong
Taegu
Kyŏngju
P'ohang

Kimje
Puan
Insil
Kŏch'ang
Anui
Hapch'on
Chongdo
Ulsan

Kochang
Chŏngŭp
Namwŏn
Koksong
Chinju
Miryang
Yangsan
Tongnae

Yŏnggwang
Sagŏ-ri
Hadong
Sach'on
Kimhae
Pusan

Songjong
Naju
Yŏngsanp'o
Kwangju
Kwangyang
Masan
Chinhae
Kohyon
Kŏje do
Nishino-shima
Dōzen
Chiburi
Oki-sh

Mokp'o
Sunch'ŏn
Samch'ŏnp'o
Ch'ungmu
Nishi-suidō
Tsushima
Matsue
Taisha
Izu

Changhŭng
Posŏng
Yŏsu
Kŭmo-do
Izuhara-suidō
K O R E A   S T R A I T
(TSUSHIMA-KAIKYŌ)
Sasuna
Gōtsu
Oda
Sho
Miyoshi

Usuyŏng
Haenam
Chindo
Yongam
Kohŭng
Tolsan-do
Higashi-suidō
Hamada
Masuda
Susa
Hagi
Hiroshima
Kure
Mih

Wando
Ch'o-do
Soan kundo
Tsushima
Mi-shima
Nagato
Yamaguchi
Iwakuni
Hōfu
Se

Cheju haehyŏp
Kŭmnyŏng
Sŏngsan-ni
Shimonoseki
Kita-Kyūshū
Nakama
Ube
Tokuyama
Hojo
Matsuyama
Iyo
Imabar
Nagah
nada

Cheju
1350
Halla-san
Sŏngwi-ri
Sŏgwi-ri
Cheju do
Iki
K Y Ū S H Ū
Fukuoka
Iizuka
Nakatsu
Usa
Kitsuki
Beppu
Bungo-suidō
Uwaj
Nakai

④
Fukue
Fukue
Tōmie
Nomo-saki
Gotō-rettō
Hirado-shima
Uku-jima
Hirado
Imari
Saga
Tosu
Kurume
Yanagawa
Ōita
Usuki
Saiki
Sukumo
Tosash

Nakadori-j.
Kashima
Takeo
Ōmura
Arao
Kuju-san
1791
Aso
Taketa
Nobeoka

Nagasaki
Isahaya
Shimabara
Ōmuta
Kumamoto
Yatsushiro
Hyūga

Minamata
Hitoyoshi
Takanabe

Akune
Kobayashi
Sendai
Kushikino
Kajiki
Miyazaki

Kushikino
Kagoshima
Fukuyama
Miyakonojō
Makurazaki
Kánoya
Yamagawa

CHINA
J i l i n
L i a o n i n g
Liao He
Liaodong Wan
Dawa
Liaozhong
Yingkou
Xinmin
H l

1:5M

0   50   100   150   200 km

0   50   100 mls

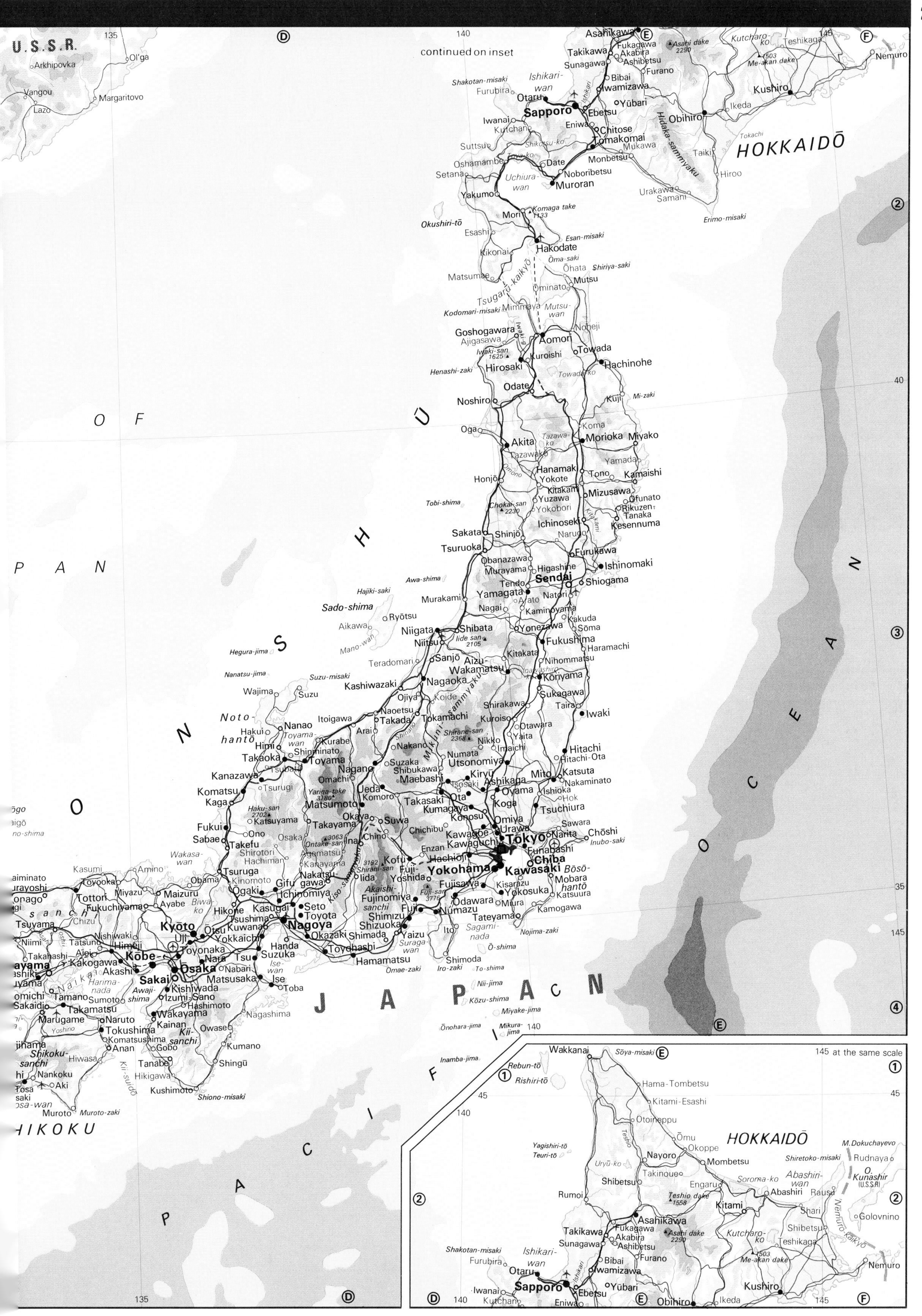

U.S.S.R.
135
Arkhipovka
Ol'ga
Vangou
Margaritovo
Lazo

continued on inset
140

Asahikawa
Takikawa Fukagawa
Sunagawa Akabira Ashibetsu
Ashai dake 2290
Kutcharo-ko Teshikaga
Nemuro

Shakotan-misaki
Furubira Ishikari-wan
Otaru Bibai Iwamizawa
Yūbari Furano
Obihiro
Hidaka-sammyaku
Kushiro
Ikeda

Iwanai Sapporo Ebetsu
Kutchan Eniwa Chitose
Suttsu Shikotsu-ko Tomakomai Mukawa
Oshamambe Date Monbetsu Taiki Hiro
Setana Uchiura-wan Noboribetsu Urakawa Samani
Yakumo Muroran

HOKKAIDŌ

Erimo-misaki

②

Okushiri-tō Mori Komaga take 1133
Esashi Esan-misaki

Kikonai Hakodate Ōma-saki Shiriya-saki
Matsumae Ōhata
Mutsu

Tsugaru-kaikyō Ōminato

OF JAPAN

Kodomari-misaki Mimmaya Mutsu-wan
Goshogawara Noheji
Ajigasawa Aomori
Iwaki-san 1625 Kuroishi Towada
Henashi-zaki Hirosaki Hachinohe
Odate Towada-ko

Noshiro Kuji Mi-zaki
Oga Koma
Akita Tazawa-ko Morioka Miyako
Tazawako Yamada
Honjō Omono Hanamaki Tōno Kamaishi
Yokote Kitakami
Yuzawa Mizusawa
Tobi-shima Chōkai-san 2230 Yokobori Ōfunato
Rikuzen-Tanaka Kesennuma
Sakata Shinjō Ichinoseki Naruko
Tsuruoka Furukawa
Obanazawa Murayama Higashine Ishinomaki
Tendo Shiogama
Awa-shima Yamagata Ayato Natori Sendai
Hajiki-saki Murakami Nagai Kaminoyama
Sado-shima Kakuda
Ryōtsu Yonezawa Sōma
Aikawa Shibata Fukushima
Niigata Niitsu Iide san 2105 Kitakata Haramachi
Mano-wan Sanjō Aizu Nihommatsu
Hegura-jima Teradomari Wakamatsu Kōriyama
Nanatsu-jima Nagaoka Sukagawa Taira
Wajima S Kashiwazaki Ojiya Shirakawa Iwaki
Suzu-misaki Koide Kuroiso
Suzu Naoetsu Tokamachi Otawara
Noto-hantō Nakano Nikko Yaita Hitachi
Nanao Takada Arai Numata Imaichi Hitachi-Ota
Hakui Itoigawa Shirane-san 2368
Himi Toyama-wan Kurabe Suzaka Shibukawa Utsunomiya Mito
Takaoka Shimminato Toyama Nagano Kiryū Ashikaga Katsuta
Kanazawa Tsubata Ueda Maebashi Oyama Nakaminato
Komatsu Tsurugi Omachi Komoro Takasaki Ishioka Tsuchiura
Kaga Yari-take 3180 Isezaki Koga
Fukui Katsuyama Matsumoto Takayama Konosu Omiya Sawara
Haku-san 2702 Okaya Chichibu Kawagoe Urawa Chōshi
Sabae Osaka Suwa Kawaguchi Tokyo Narita Inubo-saki
Takefu Shirotori Chino Enzan Kawasaki Funabashi
Tsuruga Hachiman Nakatsu Ina Kōfu Hachiōji Chiba Bōsō-hantō
Obama Ogaki Gifu Ichinomiya Agematsu Shirani-sen 3192 Fuji-Yoshida Yokohama Kawasaki Mobara
Kasumi Maizuru Kiso Fujinomiya Fujisawa Kisarazu
Tottori Miyazu Ayabe Kasugai Seto Akaishi-sanchi Fuji Odawara Yokosuka
Fukuchiyama Chizu Hikone Nagoya Shimizu Miura Kamogawa
Tsuyama Biwa-ko Kuwana Shizuoka Numazu Ito Sagami-nada
Niimi Tatsuno Nishiwaki Ōtsu Yokkaichi Okazaki Yaizu Tateyama
Himeji Uji Handa Hamamatsu Shimoda Nojima-zaki
Takahashi Aioi Kyōto Suzuka Toyohashi Ōmae-zaki Iro-zaki Ō-shima
Ayama Kakogawa Kōbe Nara Nabari Ise Toba To-shima
Okayama Akashi Sakai Osaka Matsusaka Ise-wan
Kurashiki Sumoto Izumi-Sano Kishiwada Nii-jima
Onomichi Harima-nada Awaji-shima Hashimoto Kōzu-shima Miyake-jima
Sakaide Tamano Takamatsu Naruto Wakayama Kainan Nagashima
Marugame Yoshino Tokushima Kumano Shingū JAPAN
Jihama Komatsushima Anan Kii-sanchi Ōnohara-jima Mikura-jima 140
Shikoku-sanchi Hiwasa Gobo
Tosa Nankoku Kainan Tanabe Hikigawa
Tosa-wan Muroto Muroto-zaki Kushimoto Shiono-misaki

HIKOKU

Naito Yamaguchi

Iga

PACIFIC OCEAN

40

③

145

35

④

Ⓔ

Inamba-jima
Sōya-misaki Ⓔ Wakkanai
145 at the same scale
① Rishiri-tō Rebun-tō Hama-Tombetsu
Kitami-Esashi ①
45 140 45

Yagishiri-tō Ōmu Okoppe
Teuri-tō Nayoro Mombetsu M.Dokuchayevo
Uryū-ko Rudnaya
② Okoppe Shiretoko-misaki Ⓞ. Kunashir
Rumoi Takinoue Engaru (U.S.S.R.)
Shibetsu Soroma-ko Abashiri-wan
HOKKAIDŌ Teshio dake 1558 Abashiri Rausu
Takikawa Fukagawa Kitami Shari Nemuro-kaikyō
Shakotan-misaki Akabira Asahikawa Asahi dake Shibetsu Golovnino
Furubira Sunagawa Ashibetsu 2290 1503
Ishikari-wan Bibai Me-akan dake Kutcharo-ko Teshikaga
② Iwamizawa Furano Nemuro ②
Otaru Yūbari Kushiro
Iwanai Sapporo Ebetsu
Kutchan Eniwa
Ⓓ 140 Ⓔ Obihiro Ⓕ Ikeda

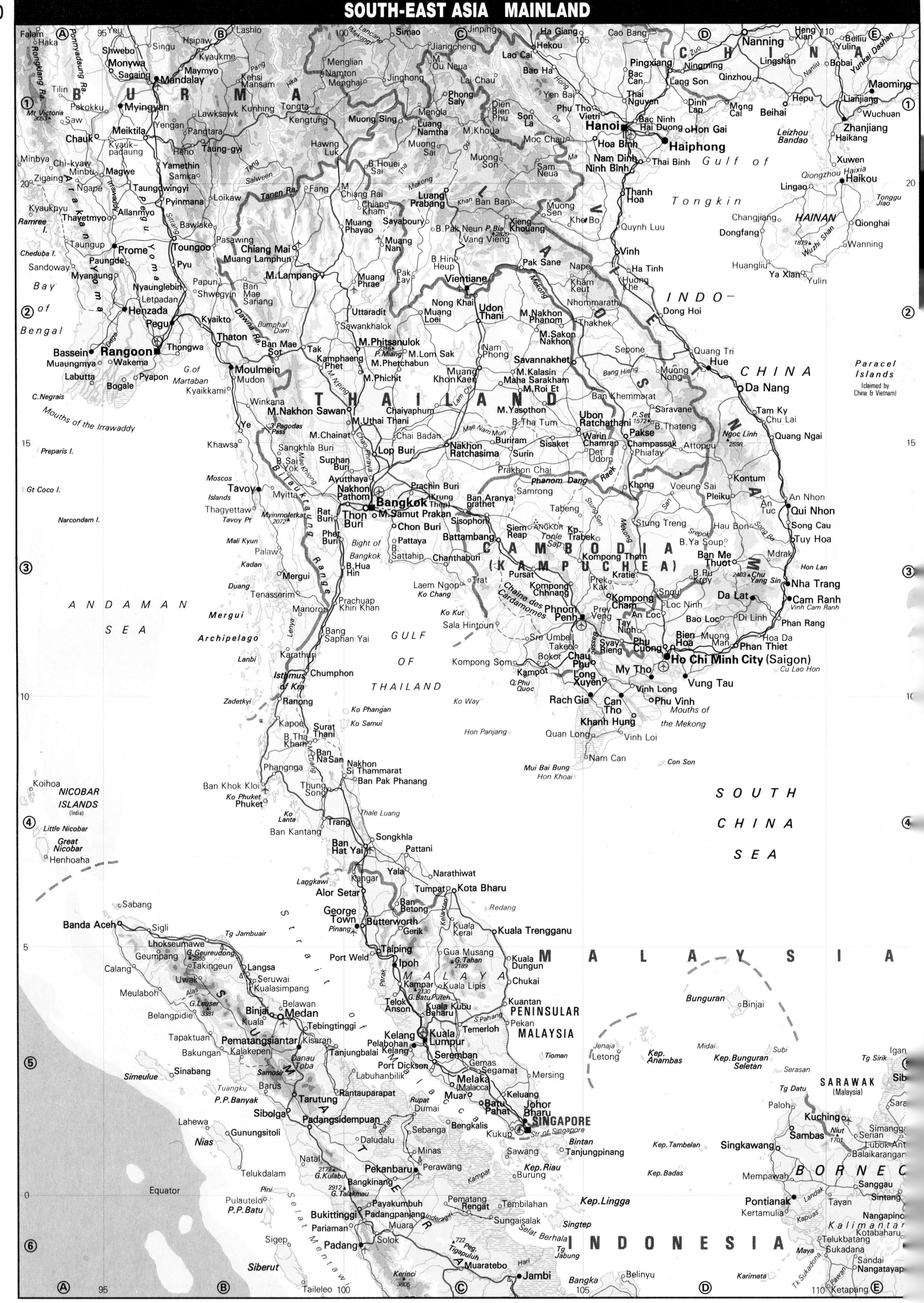
BURMA
Mandalay
Maymyo
Sagaing
Monywa
Shwebo
Myingyan
Meiktila
Chauk
Pakokku
Magwe
Minbu
Yamethin
Pyinmana
Taungdwingyi
Allanmyo
Prome
Thayetmyo
Toungoo
Pyu
Henzada
Pegu
Rangoon
Bassein
Thaton
Moulmein
Mudon
Kyaikkami
Ye
Tavoy
Mergui
Tenasserim
Lashio
Hsipaw
Kyaukme
Kengtung
Taung-gyi
Loikaw
Kalaw
Sandoway
Kyaukpyu
Ramree I.
Cheduba I.
Bay of Bengal
G. of Martaban
Mouths of the Irrawaddy
Preparis I.
Gt Coco I.
Narcondam I.
ANDAMAN SEA
Mergui Archipelago
Moscos Islands
THAILAND
Bangkok
Chiang Mai
Chiang Rai
M. Lampang
Nan
Phrae
Uttaradit
M. Phitsanulok
M. Nakhon Sawan
Lop Buri
Ayutthaya
Nakhon Pathom
Samut Prakan
Chon Buri
Pattaya
Nakhon Ratchasima
Udon Thani
Nong Khai
Ubon Ratchathani
Surin
Buriram
Khon Kaen
Chanthaburi
Trat
Prachuap Khiri Khan
Chumphon
Ranong
Surat Thani
Nakhon Si Thammarat
Phuket
Songkhla
Hat Yai
Pattani
Yala
Narathiwat
Bight of Bangkok
GULF OF THAILAND
Isthmus of Kra
Ko Phangan
Ko Samui
LAOS
Vientiane
Luang Prabang
Pak Sane
Savannakhet
Pakse
Attopeu
Saravane
Xieng Khouang
Phong Saly
Luang Namtha
Muong Sing
CAMBODIA (KAMPUCHEA)
Phnom Penh
Battambang
Siem Reap
Angkor
Tonle Sap
Kompong Thom
Kompong Cham
Kompong Chhnang
Pursat
Kratie
Kompong Som
Kampot
VIETNAM
Hanoi
Haiphong
Hon Gai
Nam Dinh
Ninh Binh
Thanh Hoa
Vinh
Ha Tinh
Dong Hoi
Quang Tri
Hue
Da Nang
Quang Ngai
Kontum
Pleiku
Qui Nhon
Tuy Hoa
Ban Me Thuot
Nha Trang
Cam Ranh
Da Lat
Phan Rang
Phan Thiet
Bien Hoa
Ho Chi Minh City (Saigon)
Vung Tau
My Tho
Can Tho
Vinh Long
Rach Gia
Long Xuyen
Chau Phu
Mouths of the Mekong
Con Son
Cao Bang
Lang Son
Lao Cai
Dien Bien Phu
CHINA
Nanning
Beihai
Zhanjiang
Maoming
Haikou
HAINAN
Gulf of Tongkin
Paracel Islands (claimed by China & Vietnam)
SOUTH CHINA SEA
MALAYSIA
Kota Bharu
Kuala Trengganu
Alor Setar
George Town
Butterworth
Taiping
Ipoh
Kuala Lumpur
Kelang
Seremban
Port Dickson
Melaka (Malacca)
Johor Bharu
SINGAPORE
Kuantan
PENINSULAR MALAYSIA
Tioman
Langkawi
Straits of Malacca
INDONESIA
Banda Aceh
Medan
Pematangsiantar
Tebingtinggi
Sibolga
Padangsidempuan
Pekanbaru
Padang
Bukittinggi
Jambi
Danau Toba
Simeulue
Nias
Siberut
Kep. Riau
Kep. Lingga
Bangka
Kep. Anambas
Bunguran
SARAWAK (Malaysia)
Kuching
Pontianak
Singkawang
BORNEO
Equator
NICOBAR ISLANDS (India)
Little Nicobar
Great Nicobar
1:10M
0 100 200 300 400 km
0 100 200 mls

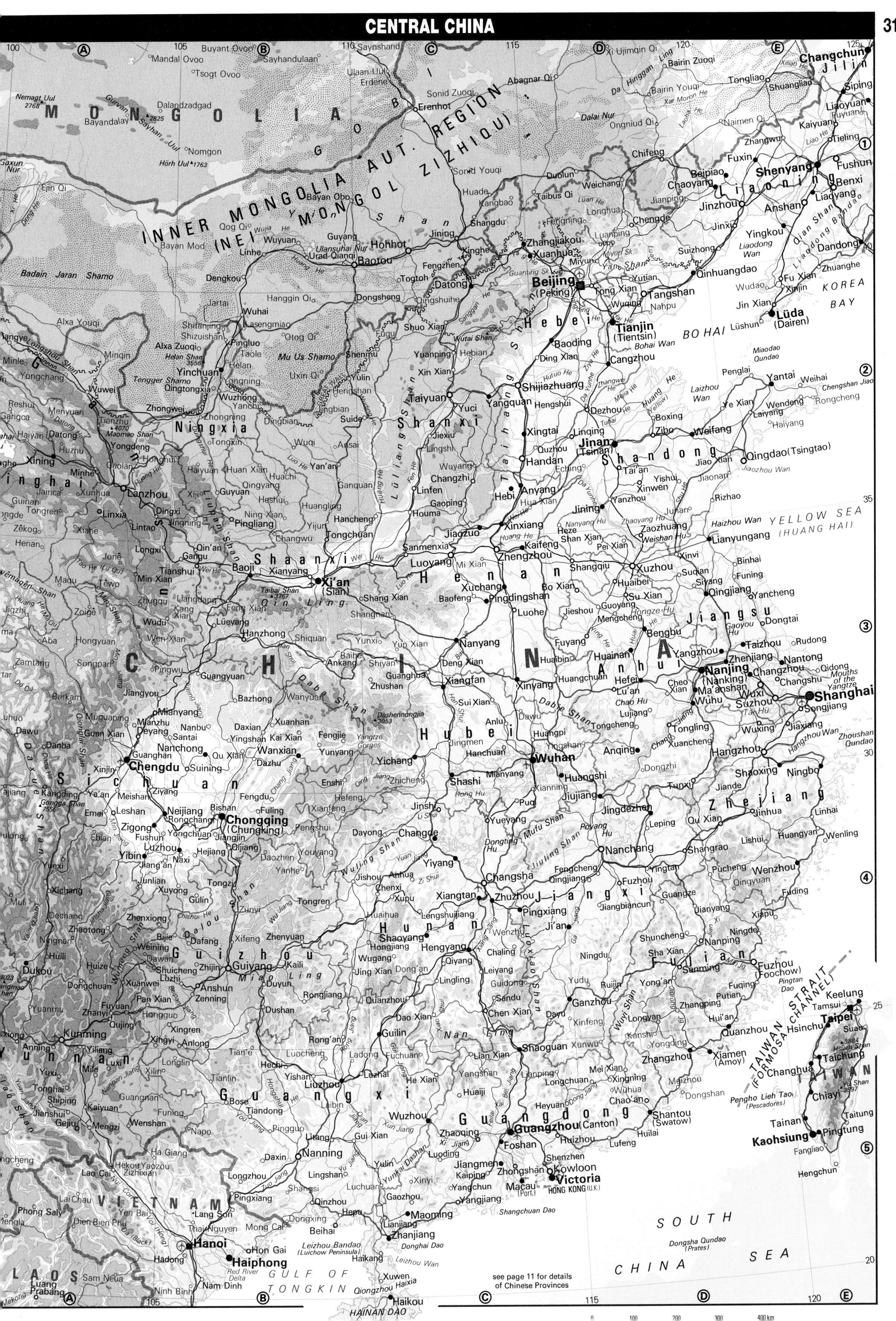
M O N G O L I A
G O B I
INNER MONGOLIA AUT. REGION
(NEI MONGOL ZIZHIQU)
Badain Jaran Shamo
Mu Us Shamo
Tengger Shamo
Ningxia
Shaanxi
Shanxi
Hebei
Henan
Shandong
Jiangsu
Anhui
Hubei
Hunan
Jiangxi
Zhejiang
Fujian
Guangdong
Guangxi
Guizhou
Sichuan
Yunnan
Liaoning
Jilin
Qinghai
C H I N A
VIETNAM
LAOS
TAIWAN
Beijing (Peking)
Tianjin (Tientsin)
Shanghai
Nanjing (Nanking)
Wuhan
Chongqing (Chungking)
Chengdu
Xi'an (Sian)
Lanzhou
Zhengzhou
Jinan (Tsinan)
Taiyuan
Shijiazhuang
Baotou
Hohhot
Yinchuan
Xining
Shenyang
Lüda (Dairen)
Changchun
Qingdao (Tsingtao)
Hangzhou
Nanchang
Changsha
Guiyang
Kunming
Nanning
Guangzhou (Canton)
Fuzhou (Foochow)
Xiamen (Amoy)
Shantou (Swatow)
Taipei
Kaohsiung
Taichung
Keelung
Hanoi
Haiphong
Victoria
Kowloon
HONG KONG (U.K.)
Macau (Port.)
Haikou
HAINAN DAO
BO HAI
Bohai Wan
KOREA BAY
YELLOW SEA (HUANG HAI)
SOUTH CHINA SEA
GULF OF TONGKIN
TAIWAN STRAIT (FORMOSA CHANNEL)
Leizhou Bandao (Luichow Peninsula)
Qin Ling
Taihang Shan
Daba Shan
Nan Ling
Wuyi Shan
Huang He
Chang Jiang
see page 11 for details of Chinese Provinces

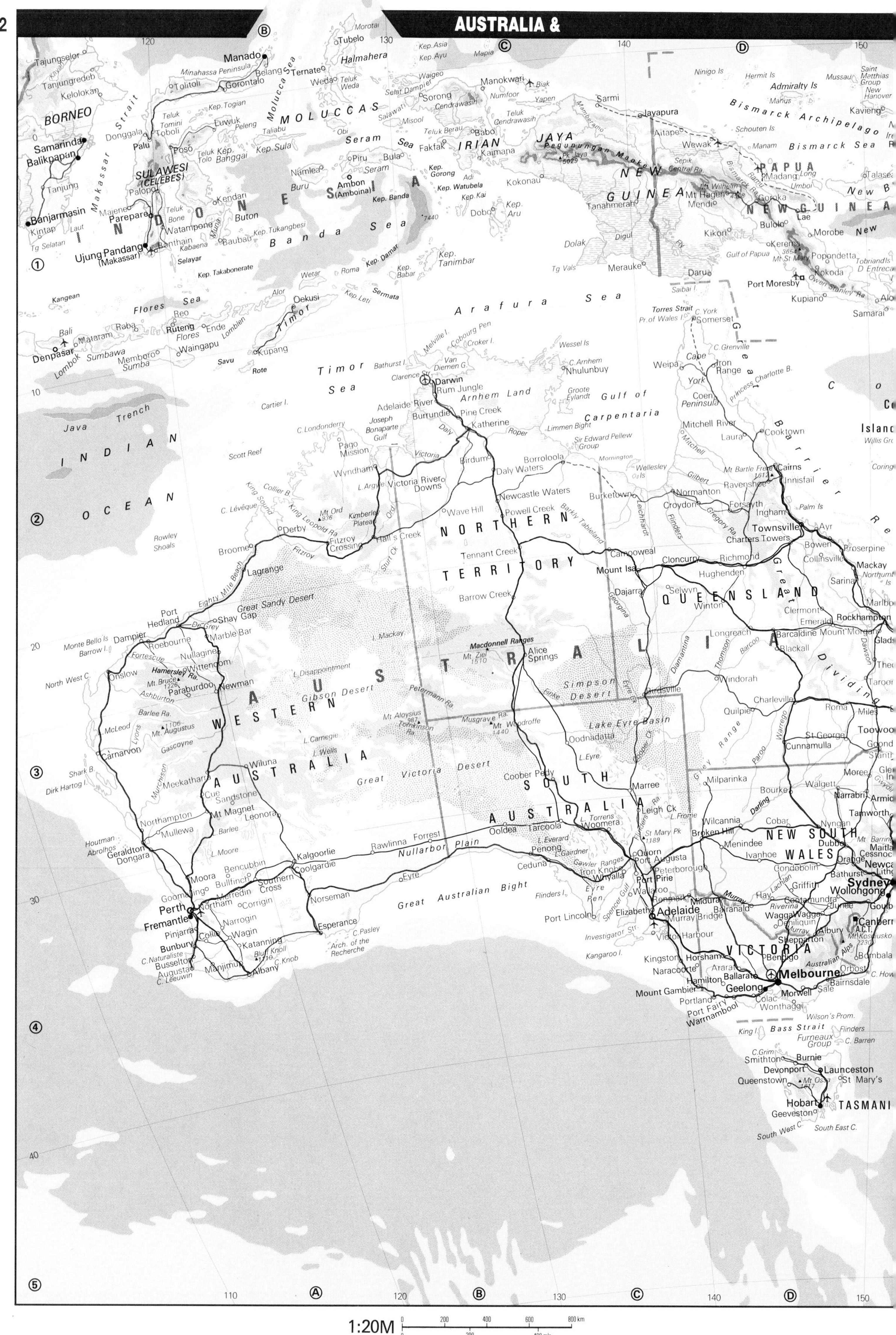
BORNEO
Samarinda
Balikpapan
Banjarmasin
Tanjung
Makassar Strait
Manado
Tolitoli
Gorontalo
Donggala
Palu
Poso
SULAWESI (CELEBES)
Palopo
Parepare
Watampone
Kendari
Buton
Ujung Pandang (Makassar)
Bonthain
Baubau
Ternate
Tubelo
Halmahera
Morotai
Molucca Sea
MOLUCCAS
Seram
Ambon (Amboina)
Namlea
Buru
Banda Sea
Kep. Banda
Kep. Tanimbar
Kep. Aru
Dobo
Fakfak
Manokwari
Biak
Sorong
Jayapura
Sarmi
IRIAN JAYA
Kaimana
Kokonau
Tanahmerah
Merauke
Dolak
NEW GUINEA
PAPUA NEW GUINEA
Aitape
Wewak
Madang
Mt Hagen
Mendi
Lae
Goroka
Bulolo
Kikori
Kerema
Popondetta
Kokoda
Port Moresby
Kupiano
Samarai
Daru
Bismarck Archipelago
Bismarck Sea
Admiralty Is
Kavieng
Arafura Sea
Timor Sea
Timor
Kupang
Flores
Flores Sea
Ende
Ruteng
Sumbawa
Sumba
Waingapu
Bali
Denpasar
Lombok
Mataram
Raba
INDONESIA
Torres Strait
C. York
Weipa
Cape York Peninsula
Coen
Cooktown
Cairns
Innisfail
Townsville
Ingham
Charters Towers
Bowen
Proserpine
Mackay
Rockhampton
Gulf of Carpentaria
Great Barrier Reef
Darwin
Rum Jungle
Katherine
Arnhem Land
Nhulunbuy
Borroloola
Daly Waters
Newcastle Waters
Tennant Creek
Barrow Creek
Alice Springs
Macdonnell Ranges
NORTHERN TERRITORY
Wyndham
Kununurra
Victoria River Downs
Derby
Broome
Fitzroy Crossing
Hall's Creek
Port Hedland
Dampier
Roebourne
Onslow
Carnarvon
Newman
Paraburdoo
Wittenoom
Meekatharra
Wiluna
Cue
Mt Magnet
Leonora
Geraldton
Dongara
Kalgoorlie
Coolgardie
Norseman
Esperance
Perth
Fremantle
Bunbury
Busselton
Albany
WESTERN AUSTRALIA
Great Sandy Desert
Gibson Desert
Great Victoria Desert
Nullarbor Plain
Great Australian Bight
Simpson Desert
Lake Eyre Basin
L. Eyre
Oodnadatta
Coober Pedy
Woomera
Tarcoola
Ooldea
Ceduna
Port Augusta
Port Pirie
Whyalla
Port Lincoln
Adelaide
Elizabeth
Murray Bridge
Kangaroo I.
SOUTH AUSTRALIA
Mount Isa
Cloncurry
Camooweal
Burketown
Normanton
Croydon
Richmond
Hughenden
Winton
Longreach
Barcaldine
Blackall
Emerald
Clermont
Windorah
Charleville
Quilpie
Roma
Cunnamulla
St George
Toowoomba
QUEENSLAND
Great Dividing Range
Bourke
Broken Hill
Wilcannia
Cobar
Menindee
Mildura
Balranald
Hay
Griffith
Wagga Wagga
Albury
Dubbo
Orange
Bathurst
Sydney
Wollongong
Canberra
A.C.T.
Tamworth
Moree
Narrabri
NEW SOUTH WALES
VICTORIA
Melbourne
Geelong
Ballarat
Bendigo
Horsham
Hamilton
Mount Gambier
Portland
Warrnambool
Sale
Bairnsdale
Bass Strait
Burnie
Devonport
Launceston
Queenstown
Hobart
TASMANIA
INDIAN OCEAN
Java Trench
1:20M
0 200 400 600 800 km
0 200 400 mls

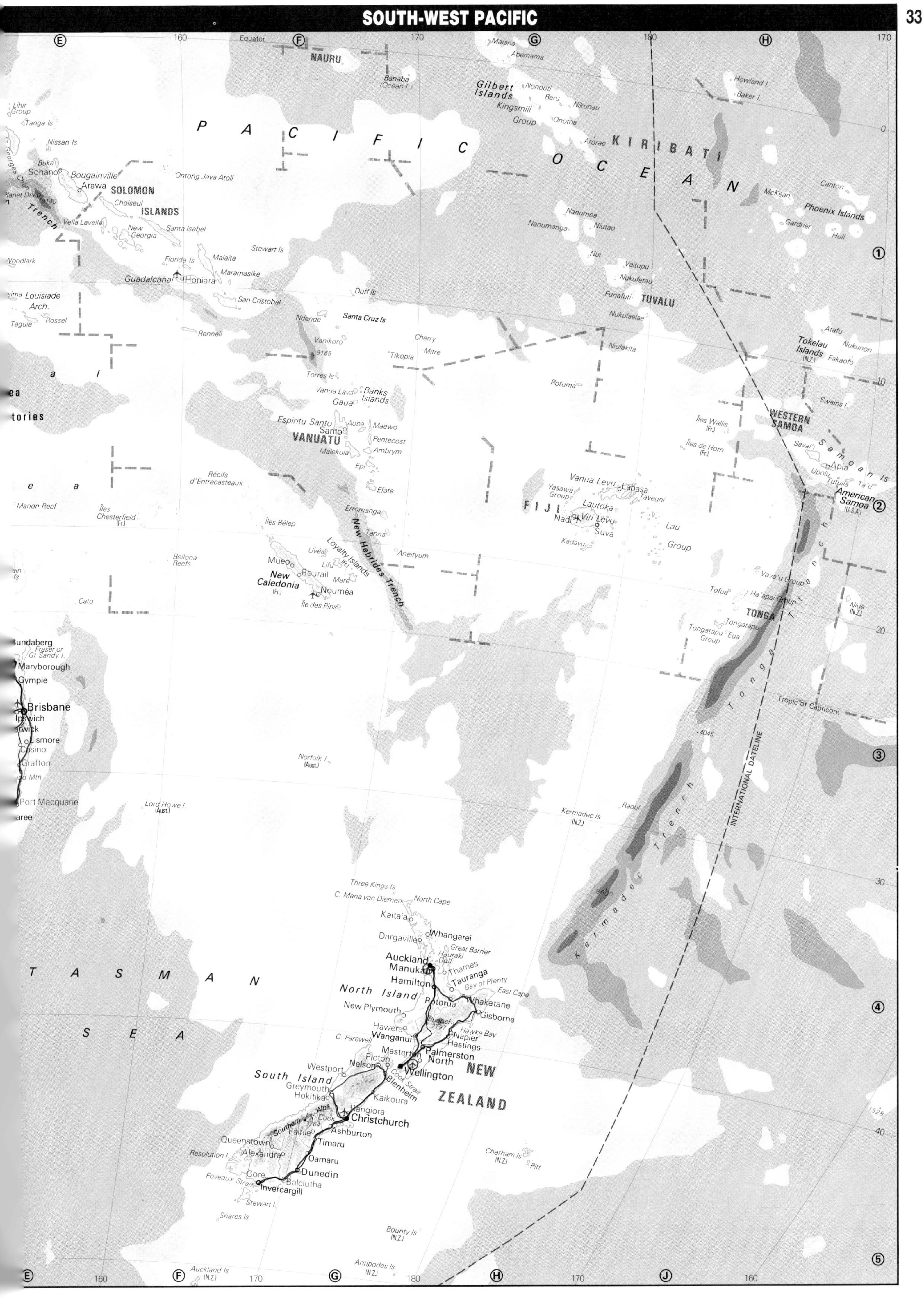

PACIFIC OCEAN

KIRIBATI

Maiana
Abemama
Nonouti
Beru Nikunau
Onotoa
Arorae

Howland I.
Baker I.

Canton
McKean
Phoenix Islands
Gardner
Hull

Lihir
Group
Tanga Is
Nissan Is

Buka
Sohano
Bougainville
Arawa
SOLOMON
Choiseul
Vella Lavella
New Georgia Santa Isabel
ISLANDS

St. George's Chan.
Planet Deep 9140
Trench

Woodlark

sima Louisiade
Arch.
Tagula Rossel

Florida Is
Guadalcanal Honiara
San Cristobal
Stewart Is
Malaita
Maramasike

Ontong Java Atoll

**Gilbert
Islands**
Kingsmill
Group

Nanumea
Nanumanga Niutao

Nui

Vaitupu
Nukufetau
Funafuti **TUVALU**

Nukulaelae

Duff Is

Ndende
Santa Cruz Is
Vanikoro
9165
Torres Is

Cherry
Tikopia Mitre

Rennell

Niulakita

Rotuma

Atafu
Nukunon
**Tokelau
Islands**
(N.Z.) Fakaofo

Swains I.

**WESTERN
SAMOA**

Vanua Lava
Gaua
**Banks
Islands**

Îles Wallis
(Fr.)

Îles de Horn
(Fr.)

Savai'i
Apia
Upolu
Tutuila Ta'u
**American
Samoa**
(U.S.A.)

Espiritu Santo
Santo
Aoba Maewo
VANUATU Pentecost
Malekula Ambrym
Epi

Récifs
d'Entrecasteaux

Îles Bélep

Marion Reef
Îles
Chesterfield
(Fr.)

tories

ea

a

Bellona
Reefs

Cato

Erromanga

New Hebrides Trench

Tanna

Efate

Aneityum

Loyalty Islands
Uvéa
Lifu
Maré

Mueo
Bourail
**New
Caledonia**
(Fr.) Nouméa

Île des Pins

Yasawa
Group
FIJI
Nadi Viti Levu
Suva

Vanua Levu Labasa
Lautoka Taveuni

Kadavu

Lau
Group

Vava'u Group

Tofua
Ha'apai Group
Tongatapu 'Eua
Tongatapu
Group Niue
(N.Z.)

Tonga

Tonga Trench

Kermadec Trench

Bundaberg
Fraser or
Gt Sandy I.
Maryborough
Gympie
Brisbane
Ipswich
rwick Lismore
Casino
Grafton
d Mtn
Port Macquarie
aree

Lord Howe I.
(Aust.)

Norfolk I.
(Aust.)

4045

Tropic of Capricorn

INTERNATIONAL DATELINE

Kermadec Is
(N.Z.)

Raoul

TASMAN

SEA

Three Kings Is
C. Maria van Diemen North Cape
Kaitaia
Dargaville Whangarei

Great Barrier
Auckland
Manukau Hauraki
Gulf Thames
North Island Hamilton Tauranga
Rotorua Bay of Plenty
New Plymouth East Cape
Hawera Ruapehu Whakatane
2797 Gisborne
Wanganui Napier
C. Farewell Masterton Hawke Bay
Picton Palmerston Hastings
Nelson North
Westport **Wellington** **NEW**
South Island Blenheim Cook Strait
Greymouth Kaikoura **ZEALAND**
Hokitika
Alps Rangiora
Cook **Christchurch**
Southern Fairlie
Queenstown Ashburton
Alexandra Timaru
Resolution I. Oamaru
Gore Dunedin
Foveaux Strait Balclutha
Invercargill
Stewart I.
Snares I.

Chatham Is
(N.Z.) Pitt

1528

Bounty Is
(N.Z.)

Antipodes Is
(N.Z.)

Auckland Is
(N.Z.)

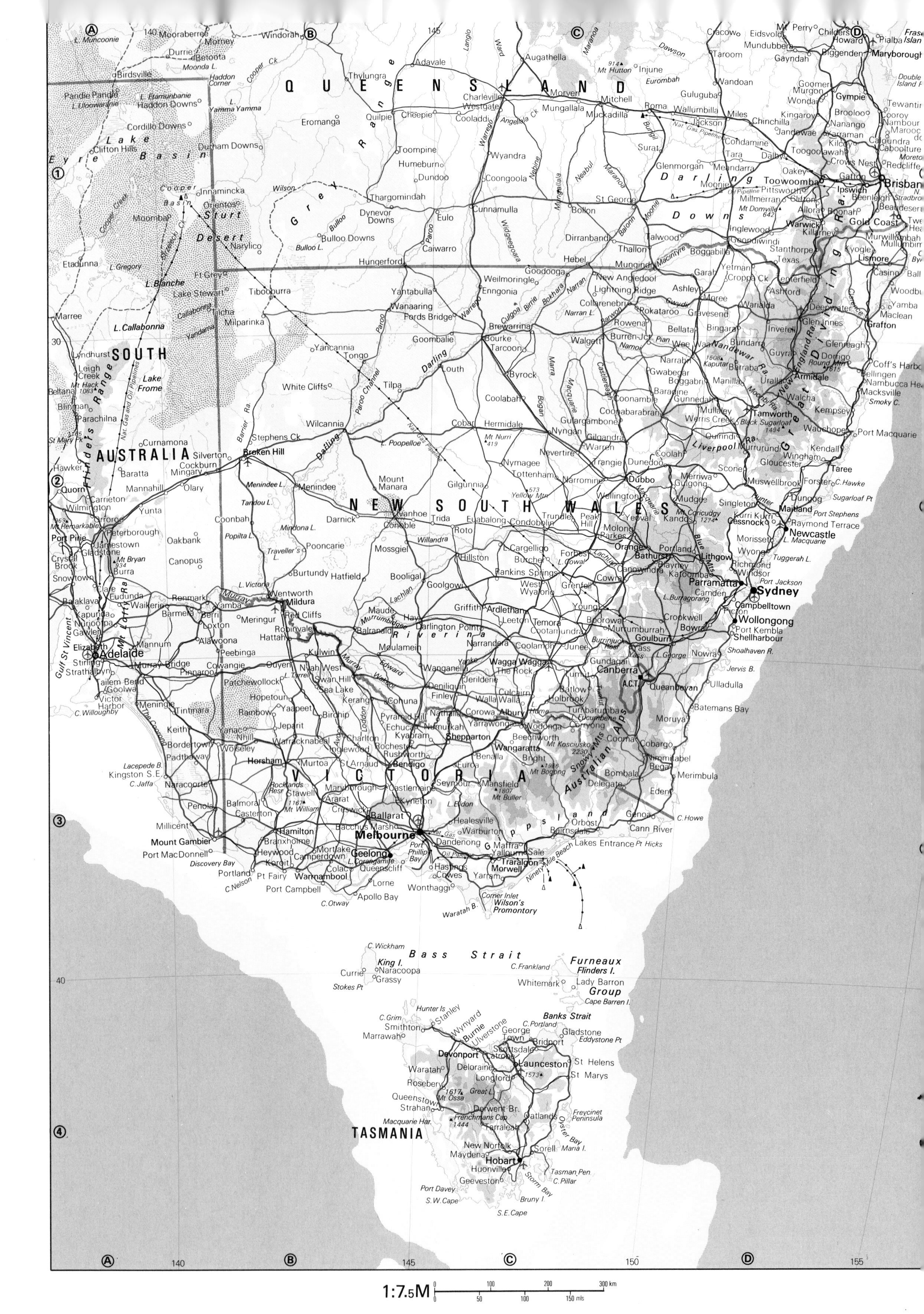

QUEENSLAND
NEW SOUTH WALES
VICTORIA
SOUTH AUSTRALIA
TASMANIA
A.C.T.
Brisbane
Sydney
Melbourne
Adelaide
Canberra
Hobart
Newcastle
Wollongong
Geelong
Ballarat
Bendigo
Launceston
Toowoomba
Ipswich
Gold Coast
Parramatta
Broken Hill
Mildura
Wagga Wagga
Albury
Dubbo
Tamworth
Armidale
Orange
Bathurst
Goulburn
Queanbeyan
Shepparton
Wangaratta
Horsham
Hamilton
Warrnambool
Mount Gambier
Port Pirie
Devonport
Burnie
Bass Strait
Great Dividing Ra.
Australian Alps
Snowy Mts
Mt Kosciusko 2230
Darling Downs
Grey Range
Sturt Desert
Lake Eyre Basin
Flinders Ranges
Riverina
Gippsland
Furneaux Group
Flinders I.
King I.
Port Phillip Bay
Wilson's Promontory
Murray
Darling
Lachlan
Murrumbidgee
1:7.5M

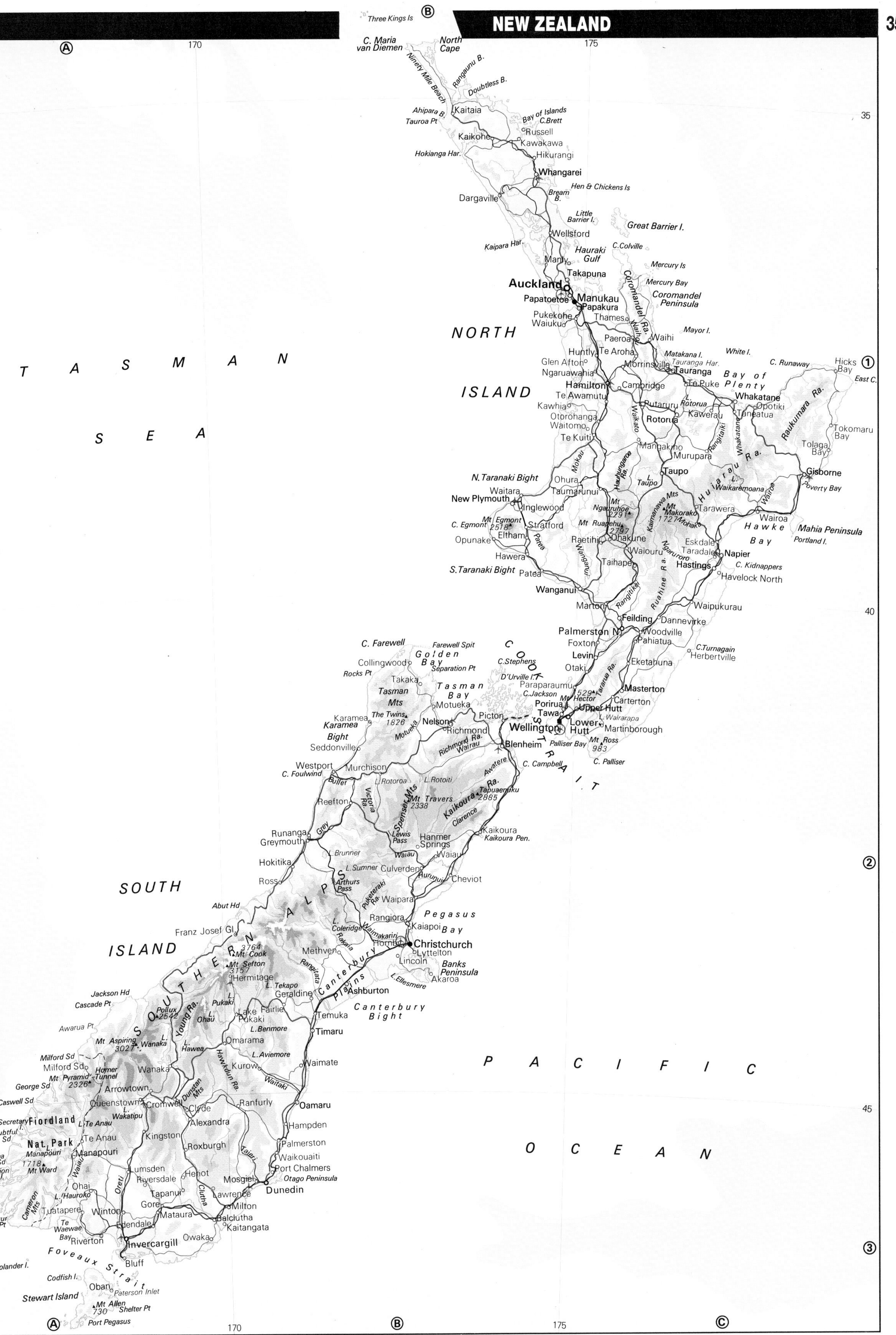

Three Kings Is

C. Maria
van Diemen
North
Cape
Rangaunu B.
Ninety Mile Beach
Doubtless B.
Ahipara B.
Tauroa Pt
Kaitaia
Bay of Islands
C. Brett
Russell
Kaikohe
Kawakawa
Hokianga Har.
Hikurangi
Whangarei
Hen & Chickens Is
Bream
B.
Dargaville
Little
Barrier I.
Great Barrier I.
Wellsford
Kaipara Har.
Manly
C. Colville
Hauraki
Gulf
Mercury Is
Takapuna
Mercury Bay
Auckland
Manukau
Coromandel
Peninsula
Papatoetoe
Papakura
Pukekohe
Thames
Waiuku
Paeroa
Waihi
Huntly
Te Aroha
Mayor I.
Glen Afton
Morrinsville
Matakana I.
White I.
Ngaruawahia
Cambridge
Tauranga Har.
C. Runaway
Hicks
Bay
Hamilton
Te Puke
Bay of
Plenty
East C.
Te Awamutu
Cambridge
Tauranga
Whakatane
Kawhia
Rotorua
Kawerau
Opotiki
Otorohanga
Taneatua
Waitomo
Rotorua
Te Kuiti
Murupara

NORTH

ISLAND

T A S M A N

S E A

Mangakino
Waikato
Raukumara Ra.
Tokomaru
Bay
N. Taranaki Bight
Ohura
L. Taupo
Taupo
Taumarunui
Waikaremoana
Tolaga
Bay
Waitara
New Plymouth
Mt
Ngauruhoe
2291
Mt
Makorako
1727
Gisborne
Poverty Bay
Inglewood
Mohaka
Mt
Egmont
2518
Stratford
Mt Ruapehu
2797
Wairoa
C. Egmont
Eltham
Ohakune
Tarawera
Hawke
Opunake
Raetihi
Waiouru
Eskdale
Bay
Hawera
Waipukurau
Taradale
Napier
Mahia Peninsula
S. Taranaki Bight
Patea
Taihape
Hastings
Havelock North
C. Kidnappers
Portland I.
Wanganui
Marton
Waipukurau
Feilding
Dannevirke
Palmerston N.
Woodville
C. Turnagain
Herbertville
Foxton
Pahiatua
Levin
Eketahuna
Otaki
Paraparaumu
Masterton
C. Stephens
Carterton
C. Jackson
Mt
Hector
1529
Martinborough
Porirua
Upper Hutt
Wairarapa
Tawa
Wellington
Lower
Hutt
Mt Ross
983

C. Farewell
Farewell Spit
Collingwood
Golden
Bay
Separation Pt
Rocks Pt
Takaka
Tasman
Bay
D'Urville I.
Palliser Bay
C. Palliser
Tasman
Mts
Motueka
The Twins
1826
Nelson
Picton
Karamea
Richmond
Blenheim
Karamea
Bight
Richmond Ra.
Wairau
Seddonville
Westport
Murchison
Awatere
C. Campbell
C. Foulwind
Buller
L. Rotoroa
Mt Travers
2338
Kaikoura Ra.
Tapuaenuku
2885
Reefton
Victoria
Ra.
Spenser Mts
Clarence
Runanga
Lewis
Pass
Hanmer
Springs
Kaikoura
Greymouth
Grey
Waiau
Kaikoura Pen.
Hokitika
L. Sumner
Culverden
Ross
Arthurs
Pass
Waiau
Hurunui
Cheviot
Abut Hd
L.
Coleridge
Waimakariri
Waipara
Pegasus
Bay
Franz Josef Gl
Rangiora
Mt Cook
3764
Kaiapoi
Mt Sefton
3157
Methven
Rakaia
Christchurch
Hermitage
Rangitata
Hornby
Lyttelton
L. Tekapo
Geraldine
Lincoln
Banks
Peninsula
Jackson Hd
Pollux
2542
Ohau
Lake Fairlie
Ashburton
Akaroa
Cascade Pt
Pukaki
L. Ellesmere
L. Pukaki
Temuka
Canterbury
Bight
Awarua Pt
Mt Aspiring
3027
Wanaka
L.
Benmore
Timaru
Milford Sd
Hawea
L. Aviemore
Milford Sd
Mt Pyramid
2326
Wanaka
Kurow
Waimate
George Sd
Homer
Tunnel
Omarama
Waitaki
Caswell Sd
Arrowtown
Cromwell
Ranfurly
Oamaru
Secretary
Queenstown
Clyde
Doubtful
Sd
L.
Wakatipu
Alexandra
Hampden
Te Anau
Kingston
Roxburgh
Palmerston
Fiordland
Te Anau
Nat. Park
Manapouri
Waikouaiti
Manapouri
Lumsden
Port Chalmers
Mt Ward
Riversdale
Heriot
Mosgiel
Otago Peninsula
Ohai
Tapanui
Lawrence
Dunedin
Mt Allen
730
Gore
Milton
Winton
Mataura
Balclutha
Riverton
Edendale
Kaitangata
Invercargill
Owaka
Bluff
Foveaux Strait
Solander I.
Codfish I.
Stewart Island
Oban
Paterson Inlet
Shelter Pt
Port Pegasus

SOUTH

ISLAND

SOUTHERN ALPS

P A C I F I C

O C E A N

0   50   100   150   200 km

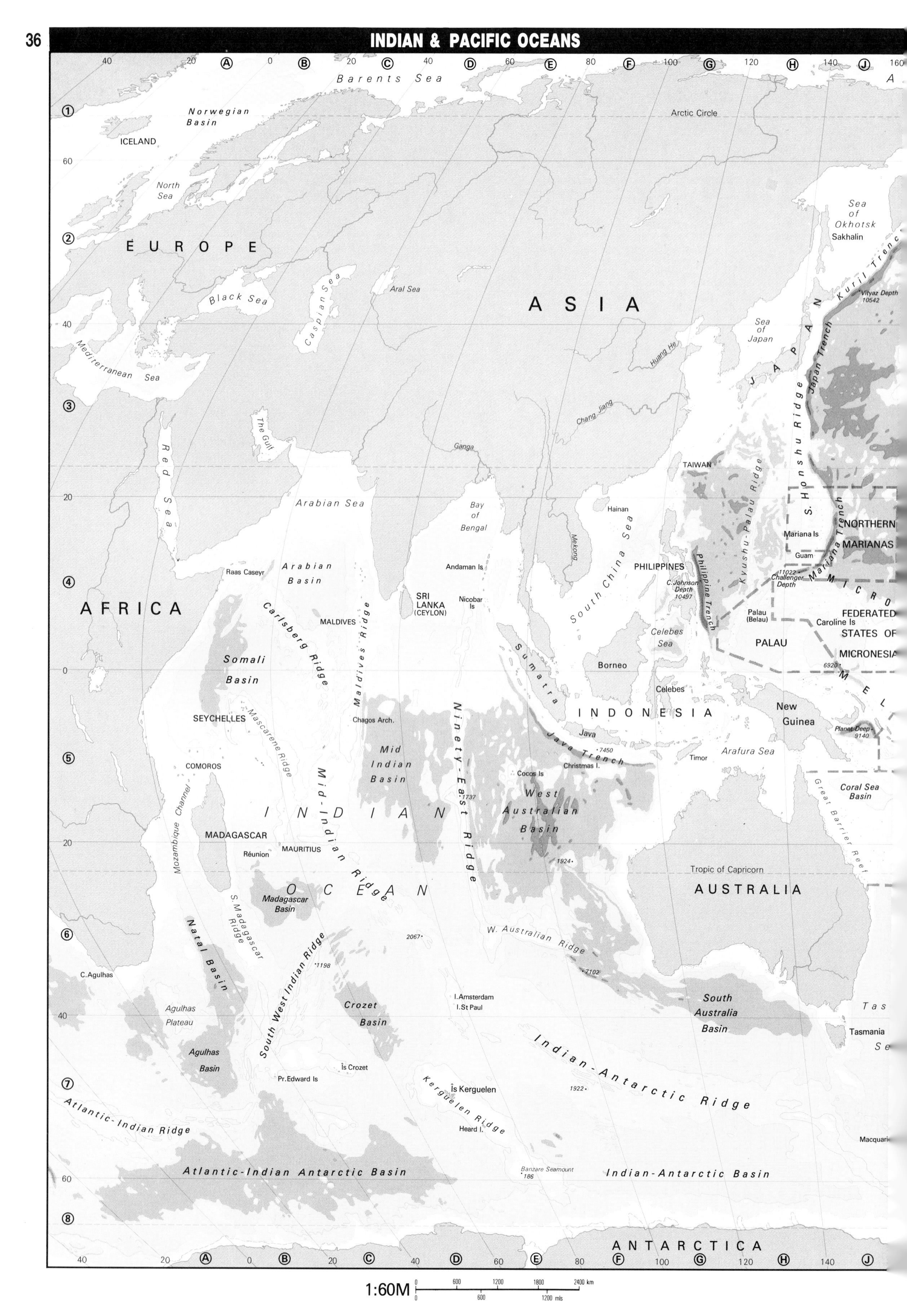

Barents Sea

Norwegian Basin

Arctic Circle

ICELAND

North Sea

EUROPE

Sea of Okhotsk

Sakhalin

ASIA

Black Sea

Caspian Sea

Aral Sea

Sea of Japan

Vityaz Depth 10542

Mediterranean Sea

The Gulf

Chang Jiang

JAPAN

Kuril Trench

S. Honshu Ridge

Japan Trench

Red Sea

Ganga

TAIWAN

Kyushu-Palau Ridge

Mariana Trench

Arabian Sea

Bay of Bengal

Hainan

NORTHERN MARIANAS

Mariana Is

MICRO

Arabian Basin

AFRICA

Raas Caseyr

Carlsberg Ridge

Maldives Ridge

SRI LANKA (CEYLON)

Andaman Is

Nicobar Is

South China Sea

PHILIPPINES

Philippine Trench

C. Johnson Depth 10497

Guam

11022 Challenger Depth

Palau (Belau)

Caroline Is

FEDERATED STATES OF MICRONESIA

MALDIVES

Somali Basin

SEYCHELLES

Mascarene Ridge

Chagos Arch.

Mid Indian Basin

Ninety-East Ridge

Sumatra

Celebes Sea

Borneo

Celebes

INDONESIA

PALAU

6920

MEL

New Guinea

Planet Deep 9140

COMOROS

MADAGASCAR

Réunion

MAURITIUS

S. Madagascar Ridge

Mid-Indian Ridge

INDIAN

Madagascar Basin

OCEAN

Java

Java Trench

7450

Christmas I.

West Australian Basin

Cocos Is

737

1924

Timor

Arafura Sea

Coral Sea Basin

Tropic of Capricorn

AUSTRALIA

Great Barrier Reef

Natal Basin

C.Agulhas

Agulhas Plateau

Agulhas Basin

South West Indian Ridge

Crozet Basin

Îs Crozet

Pr.Edward Is

1198

2067

W. Australian Ridge

I.Amsterdam I.St Paul

7102

Indian-Antarctic Ridge

South Australia Basin

Tasmania

Tas

Sea

Macquarie

Atlantic-Indian Ridge

Kerguelen Ridge

Îs Kerguelen

Heard I.

1922

Banzare Seamount 186

Indian-Antarctic Basin

Atlantic-Indian Antarctic Basin

ANTARCTICA

1:60M

0   600   1200   1800   2400 km
0   600   1200 mils

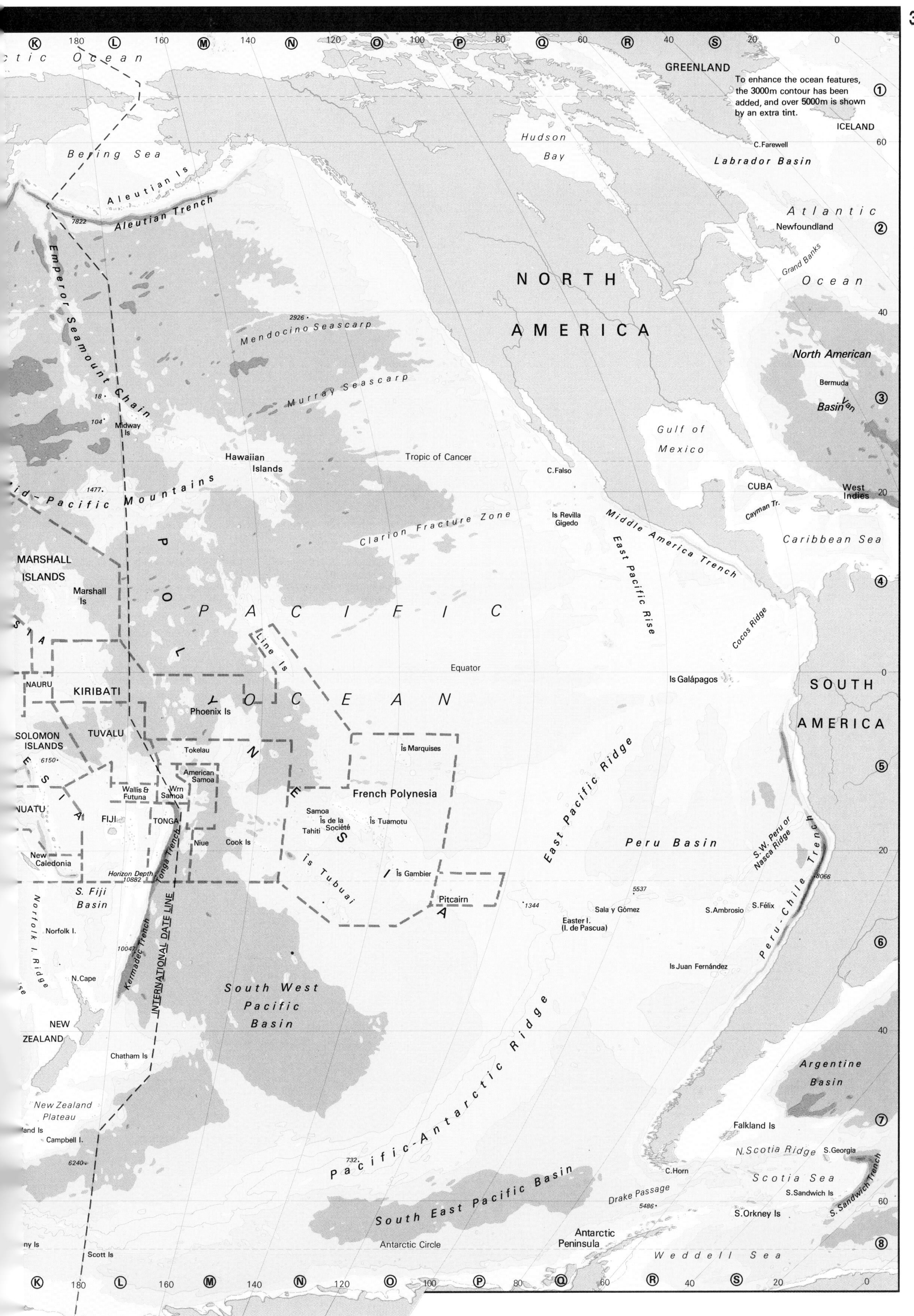

Ⓚ 180 Ⓛ 160 Ⓜ 140 Ⓝ 120 Ⓞ 100 Ⓟ 80 Ⓠ 60 Ⓡ 40 Ⓢ 20 0

ctic Ocean

GREENLAND

To enhance the ocean features,
the 3000m contour has been
added, and over 5000m is shown
by an extra tint.

ICELAND

Bering Sea

Hudson
Bay

C.Farewell

Labrador Basin

60 ①

60 ②

Atlantic

Newfoundland

Aleutian Is

Aleutian Trench

7822

Grand Banks

Ocean

NORTH

AMERICA

North American

Bermuda

Basin Van ③

Emperor Seamount Chain

2926

Mendocino Seascarp

40

Murray Seascarp

Gulf of
Mexico

C.Falso

18

104 Midway
Is

Hawaiian
Islands

Tropic of Cancer

CUBA

Cayman Tr.

West
Indies 20

id-Pacific Mountains

1477

Caribbean Sea ④

Clarion Fracture Zone

Is Revilla
Gigedo

Middle America Trench

East Pacific Rise

MARSHALL
ISLANDS

Marshall
Is

P

PACIFIC

Equator

Is Galápagos

0

SOUTH

AMERICA

Cocos Ridge

NAURU

KIRIBATI

O

L

Y

Line Is

Phoenix Is

TUVALU

N

Tokelau

Îs Marquises

French Polynesia

⑤

20

6150

Wallis &
Futuna

American
Samoa

E

Samoa
Îs de la
Société

Îs Tuamotu

East Pacific Ridge

Peru Basin

S.W. Peru or
Nasca Ridge

SOLOMON
ISLANDS

NUATU

FIJI

Wrn
Samoa

TONGA

S

Tahiti

5537

Peru-Chile Trench

New
Caledonia

Niue

Cook Is

Îs Tubuai

Îs Gambier

8066

Horizon Depth
10882

I

Pitcairn

A

Norfolk
I. Ridge

Norfolk I.

1344

Sala y Gómez

S.Ambrosio

S.Félix

40

⑥

Is Juan Fernández

N.Cape

Easter I.
(I. de Pascua)

10047

S. Fiji
Basin

Kermadec Trench

INTERNATIONAL DATE LINE

South West
Pacific
Basin

NEW

ZEALAND

Chatham Is

Argentine

Basin

*New Zealand
Plateau*

732

Pacific-Antarctic Ridge

Falkland Is

N.Scotia Ridge S.Georgia

⑦

land Is

Campbell I.

Scotia Sea

S.Sandwich Is

6240

Drake Passage

C.Horn

S.Sandwich Trench

60

ny Is

Scott Is

5486

S.Orkney Is

Antarctic
Peninsula

Antarctic Circle

Weddell Sea ⑧

Ⓚ 180 Ⓛ 160 Ⓜ 140 Ⓝ 120 Ⓞ 100 Ⓟ 80 Ⓠ 60 Ⓡ 40 Ⓢ 20 0

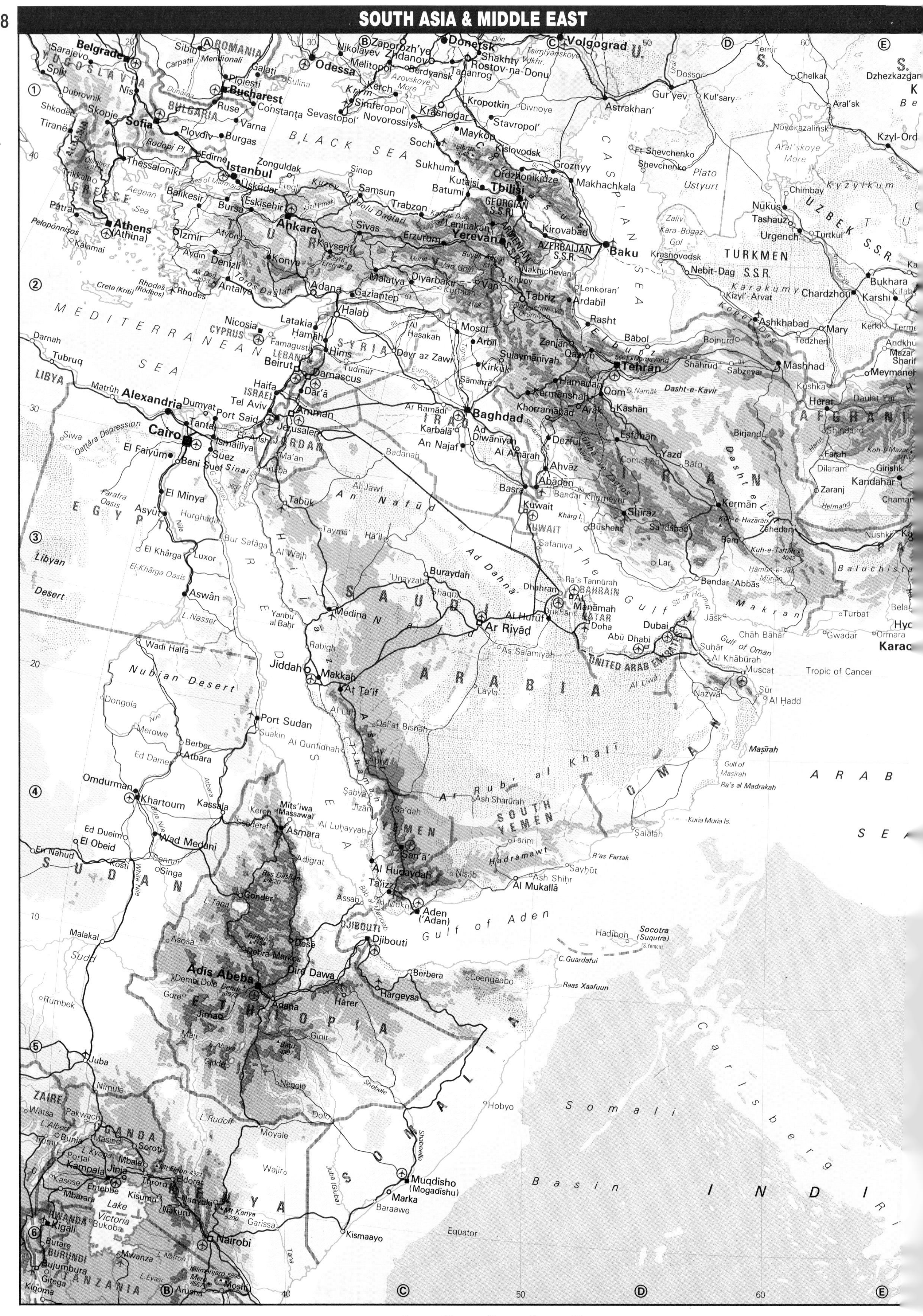
Belgrade
Sarajevo
Split
YUGOSLAVIA
Dubrovnik
Shkodër
Tiranë
ALBANIA
Skopje
Sofia
BULGARIA
Nis
Ruse
Varna
Plovdiv
Burgas
Bucharest
Ploiești
ROMANIA
Sibiu
Galați
Constanța
Sulina
Odessa
Nikolayev
Zaporozh'ye
Zhdanov
Melitopol'
Berdyansk
Donetsk
Shakhty
Rostov-na-Donu
Taganrog
Volgograd
Kerch
Simferopol'
Sevastopol'
Novorossiysk
Krasnodar
Kropotkin
Divnoye
Stavropol'
Maykop
Sochi
Kislovodsk
Sukhumi
Kutaisi
Tbilisi
Batumi
Groznyy
Ordzhonikidze
Makhachkala
Astrakhan'
Gur'yev
Dossor
Kul'sary
Temir
Chelkar
Dzhezkazgan
Aral'sk
Novokazalinsk
Kzyl-Ord
Ft Shevchenko
Shevchenko
Plato Ustyurt
Aral'skoye More
Kyzylkum
Chimbay
Nukus
Tashauz
Urgench
Turtkul'
UZBEK
S.S.R.
Zaliv Kara-Bogaz Gol
Krasnovodsk
Nebit-Dag
TURKMEN S.S.R.
Karakumy
Kizyl'-Arvat
Chardzhou
Bukhara
Karshi
Ashkhabad
Mary
Kerki
Tedzhen
BLACK SEA
CASPIAN SEA
Thessaloniki
GREECE
Edirne
Istanbul
Üsküdar
Zonguldak
Sinop
Samsun
Trabzon
Aegean Sea
Balikesir
Bursa
Eskişehir
Ankara
Sivas
Erzurum
Leninakan
Yerevan
GEORGIAN S.S.R.
ARMENIAN S.S.R.
AZERBAIJAN S.S.R.
Kirovabad
Baku
Pátrai
Pelopónnisos
Athens (Athina)
Kálamai
Izmir
Afyon
Aydin
Denizli
Konya
Kayseri
TURKEY
Malatya
Diyarbakir
Van
Nakhichevan
Khvoy
Lenkoran'
Tabriz
Ardabīl
Rasht
Crete (Kriti)
Rhodes
Antalya
Adana
Gaziantep
Halab
MEDITERRANEAN SEA
Nicosia
CYPRUS
Latakia
Hamāh
Hims
SYRIA
Al Hasakah
Mosul
Arbīl
Dayr az Zawr
Zanjān
Qazvīn
Bābol
Tehrān
Bojnurd
Shāhrud
Sabzevār
Mashhad
Darnah
Tubruq
LIBYA
Beirut
LEBANON
Damascus
Tudmur
Sulaymānīyah
Kirkūk
Sāmarrā'
Hamadān
Qom
Dasht-e-Kavir
Kushka
Herat
Haifa
ISRAEL
Tel Aviv
Dar'ā
Matrûh
Alexandria
Dumyat
Port Said
Tanta
Cairo
Ismailiya
Amman
Jerusalem
JORDAN
Ar Ramādī
Baghdad
IRAQ
Karbalā'
Ad Dīwānīyah
An Najaf
Kermānshāh
Khorramābād
Arāk
Kāshān
Esfahān
Yazd
Birjand
AFGHANISTAN
Shindand
Siwa
Qattâra Depression
El Faiyûm
Beni Suef
Suez
Sinai
Ma'an
Aqaba
Badanah
Al Amārah
Dezfūl
Ahvāz
Abādān
Basra
Kuwait
KUWAIT
Bandar Khomeyni
Kharg I.
Bushehr
Shīrāz
Kermān
Dasht-e-Lūt
IRAN
Bam
Zāhedān
Farah
Dilaram
Girishk
Kandahar
Zaranj
Chaman
Farafra Oasis
El Minya
Asyût
Hurghada
EGYPT
Tabūk
Al Jawf
An Nafūd
Tayma'
Hā'il
Al Wajh
Bur Safâga
El Khârga
Luxor
El-Khârga Oasis
Libyan Desert
Aswân
L. Nasser
Buraydah
'Unayzah
Shaqrā
Ad Dahnā
Safaniya
Ra's Tannūrah
Dhahran
BAHRAIN
Manāmah
QATAR
Doha
The Gulf
Str. of Hormuz
Lar
Bandar 'Abbās
Makran
Jāsk
Chāh Bahār
Gwadar
Ormara
Baluchistan
Turbat
Medina
SAUDI ARABIA
Ar Riyāḍ
Al Hufūf
Yanbu' al Baḥr
Rabigh
Jiddah
Makkah
At Tā'if
As Salamiyah
Layla'
Dubai
Abū Dhabi
UNITED ARAB EMIRATES
Al Liwā
Suhār
Al Khābūrah
Muscat
Gulf of Oman
Tropic of Cancer
Sūr
Al Hadd
Nazwa
Wadi Halfa
Nubian Desert
Dongola
Merowe
Port Sudan
Suakin
Al Qunfidhah
Qal'at Bishah
Berber
Atbara
Ed Damer
Rub' al Khālī
Maṣīrah
Gulf of Maṣīrah
Ra's al Madrakah
OMAN
ARABIAN SEA
Omdurman
Khartoum
Kassala
Keren
Mits'iwa (Massawa)
Asmara
Ṣabyā
Jīzān
Ash Sharūrah
SOUTH YEMEN
Ṣa'dah
YEMEN
Ṣan'ā'
Al Luḥayyah
Al Hudaydah
Ta'izz
Tarīm
Ḥadramawt
Kuria Muria Is.
Ṣalālah
R'as Fartak
Sayḥūt
Ash Shiḥr
Al Mukallā
Nişāb
Ed Dueim
El Obeid
En Nahud
Wad Medani
Sennar
Kosti
Singa
SUDAN
White Nile
Adigrat
L. Tana
Gonder
Assab
Bāb al Mandab
Aden ('Adan)
Gulf of Aden
DJIBOUTI
Djibouti
Hadiboh
Socotra (Suqutra)
C. Guardafui
Malakal
Sudd
Asosa
Dese
Debre Markos
Ādīs Ābeba
Dire Dawa
Berbera
Ceerigaabo
Raas Xaafuun
Dembi Dolo
Gore
Jimma
Adama
Harer
Hargeysa
ETHIOPIA
Rumbek
Gīnīr
Juba
Nimule
Negele
Shebele
Hobyo
Somali Basin
Carlsberg Ridge
ZAIRE
Watsa
Pakwach
L. Albert
L. Rudolf
Dolo
SOMALIA
UGANDA
Bunia
Masindi
Soroti
Moyale
Fort Portal
Kampala
Jinja
Mbale
Mt Elgon 4321
Wajir
Tororo
Eldoret
Entebbe
Kisumu
Kasese
Mbarara
Lake Victoria
Bukoba
Nanyuki
Nakuru
Mt Kenya 5200
KENYA
Garissa
Muqdisho (Mogadishu)
Marka
Baraawe
Kismaayo
Equator
INDIAN
RWANDA
Kigali
Butare
BURUNDI
Bujumbura
Gitega
Kigoma
Mwanza
L. Natron
L. Eyasi
Kilimanjaro 5895
Arusha
Moshi
TANZANIA
Nairobi
Tana
Juba (Giuba)
Shabeelle

1:20M
0 200 400 600 800 km
0 200 400 mls

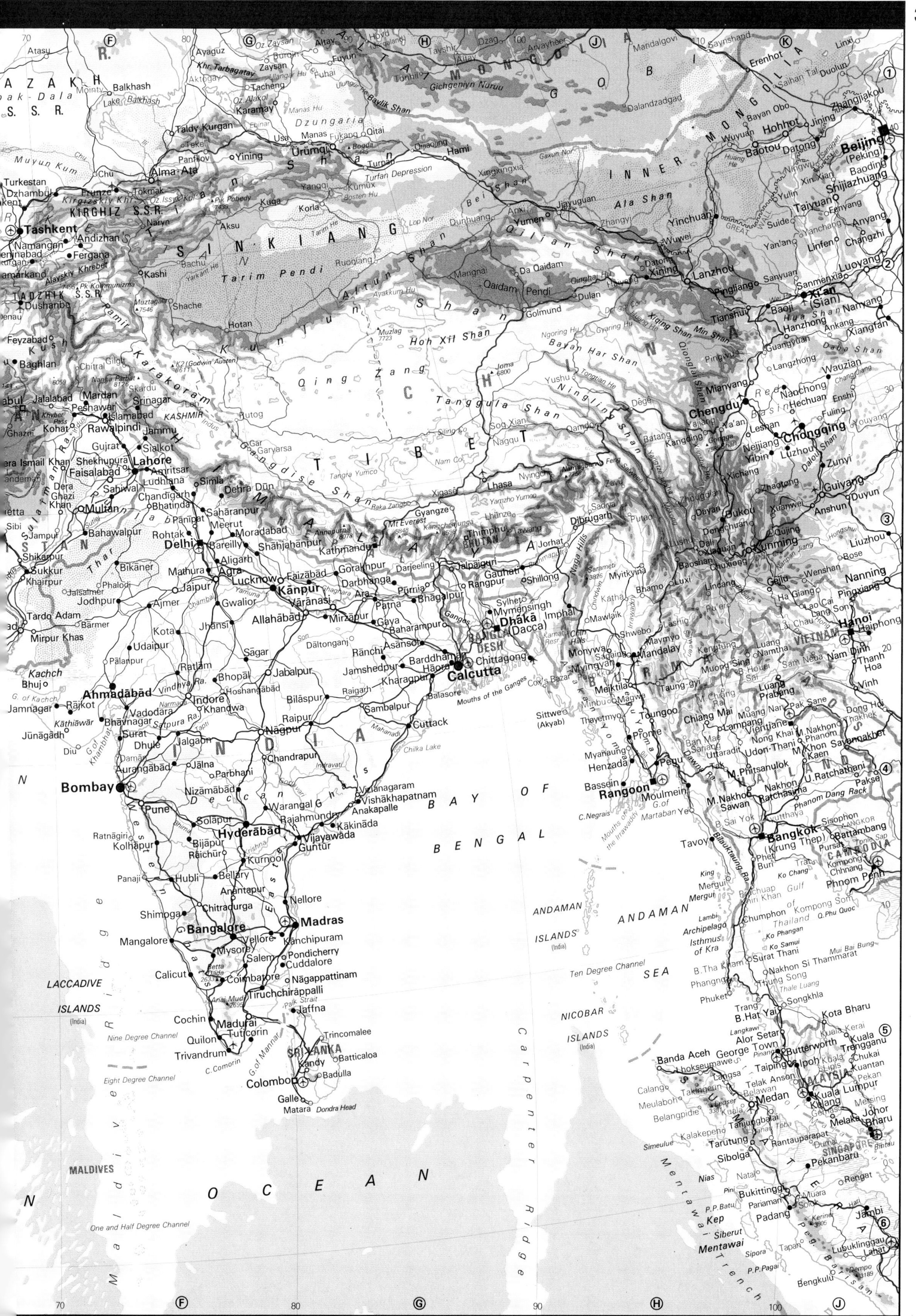

KAZAKH S.S.R.
Balkhash
Lake Balkhash
Ayaguz
Zaysan
Tacheng
Karamay
Altay
Fuyun
ALTAI
MONGOLIA
GOBI
Gichgeniyn Nuruu
Erenhot
Dzungaria
Taldy Kurgan
Yining
Ürümqi
Hami
Turfan Depression
Alma-Ata
Frunze
Tokmak
KIRGHIZ S.S.R.
Tashkent
Namangan
Andizhan
Fergana
Kashi
Aksu
Kuqa
Korla
SINKIANG
Tarim Pendi
TADZHIK S.S.R.
Dushanbe
Pamir
Shache
Hotan
Kun Lun Shan
Qaidam Pendi
Golmund
Dulan
Xining
Lanzhou
INNER MONGOLIA
Ala Shan
Baotou
Hohhot
Datong
Beijing
(Peking)
Shijiazhuang
Taiyuan
Yinchuan
Zhangjiakou
Jiuquan
Yumen
Qilian Shan
Luoyang
Xi'an
(Sian)
Tianshui
Baoji
Hanzhong
Xiangfan
Anyang
Changzhi
Linfen
Chengdu
Chongqing
Zunyi
Guiyang
Kunming
Nanning
Hanoi
Haiphong
VIETNAM
Hoh Xil Shan
Bayan Har Shan
Qing Zang
Tanggula Shan
TIBET
Lhasa
Gangdise Shan
Karakoram
KASHMIR
Srinagar
Peshawar
Islamabad
Rawalpindi
Jammu
Sialkot
Lahore
Amritsar
Faisalabad
Multan
Bahawalpur
Ludhiana
Simla
Chandigarh
Dehra Dūn
Meerut
Delhi
Moradabad
Bareilly
Aligarh
Agra
Mathura
Jaipur
Bikaner
Jodhpur
Ajmer
Gwalior
Lucknow
Kānpur
Allahābād
Vārānasi
Patna
Kathmandu
Thimphu
BHUTAN
HIMALAYA
Mt Everest
Darjeeling
Jalpaiguri
Gauhati
Shillong
Dibrugarh
Imphal
Dhākā
(Dacca)
BANGLADESH
Chittagong
Calcutta
Mouths of the Ganges
Jamshedpur
Rānchi
Kharagpur
Sukkur
Thar
Kota
Udaipur
Jhānsi
Sāgar
Jabalpur
Bhopāl
Indore
Ahmadābād
Rājkot
Jāmnagar
Bhāvnagar
Vadodara
Surat
Nāgpur
Raipur
Bilāspur
Cuttack
Sambalpur
INDIA
Jalgaon
Aurangābād
Bombay
Pune
Solapur
Hyderābād
Warangal
Vishākhapatnam
Vizianagaram
Rajahmundry
Kākināda
Vijayawāda
Guntūr
Kurnool
Bellary
Hubli
Panaji
Kolhāpur
Bijāpur
Deccan
Nellore
Madras
Bangalore
Mysore
Mangalore
Calicut
Salem
Pondicherry
Cuddalore
Coimbatore
Tiruchchirāppalli
Madurai
Tuticorin
Cochin
Quilon
Trivandrum
Jaffna
Trincomalee
SRI LANKA
Kandy
Batticaloa
Colombo
Galle
Matara
Dondra Head
LACCADIVE ISLANDS
(India)
Nine Degree Channel
Eight Degree Channel
One and Half Degree Channel
MALDIVES
Maldive Ridge
Carpenter Ridge
INDIAN OCEAN
BAY OF BENGAL
ANDAMAN ISLANDS
(India)
ANDAMAN SEA
Ten Degree Channel
NICOBAR ISLANDS
(India)
BURMA
Myitkyina
Bhamo
Mandalay
Monywa
Meiktila
Sittwe
(Akyab)
Prome
Toungoo
Henzada
Bassein
Rangoon
Pegu
Moulmein
G. of Martaban
Tavoy
Mergui
Chiang Mai
Lampang
Vientiane
LAOS
THAILAND
Udon Thani
Khon Kaen
Nakhon Ratchasima
Bangkok
(Krung Thep)
Phnom Penh
CAMBODIA
Battambang
Gulf of Thailand
Isthmus of Kra
Chumphon
Surat Thani
Nakhon Si Thammarat
Phuket
Songkhla
Kota Bharu
Alor Setar
George Town
Butterworth
Ipoh
Kuala Lumpur
MALAYSIA
Melaka
Johor Bharu
SINGAPORE
Banda Aceh
Medan
Sibolga
Pekanbaru
Padang
Bukittinggi
Jambi
Bengkulu
SUMATERA
Mentawai Trench
Simeulue
Nias
Siberut

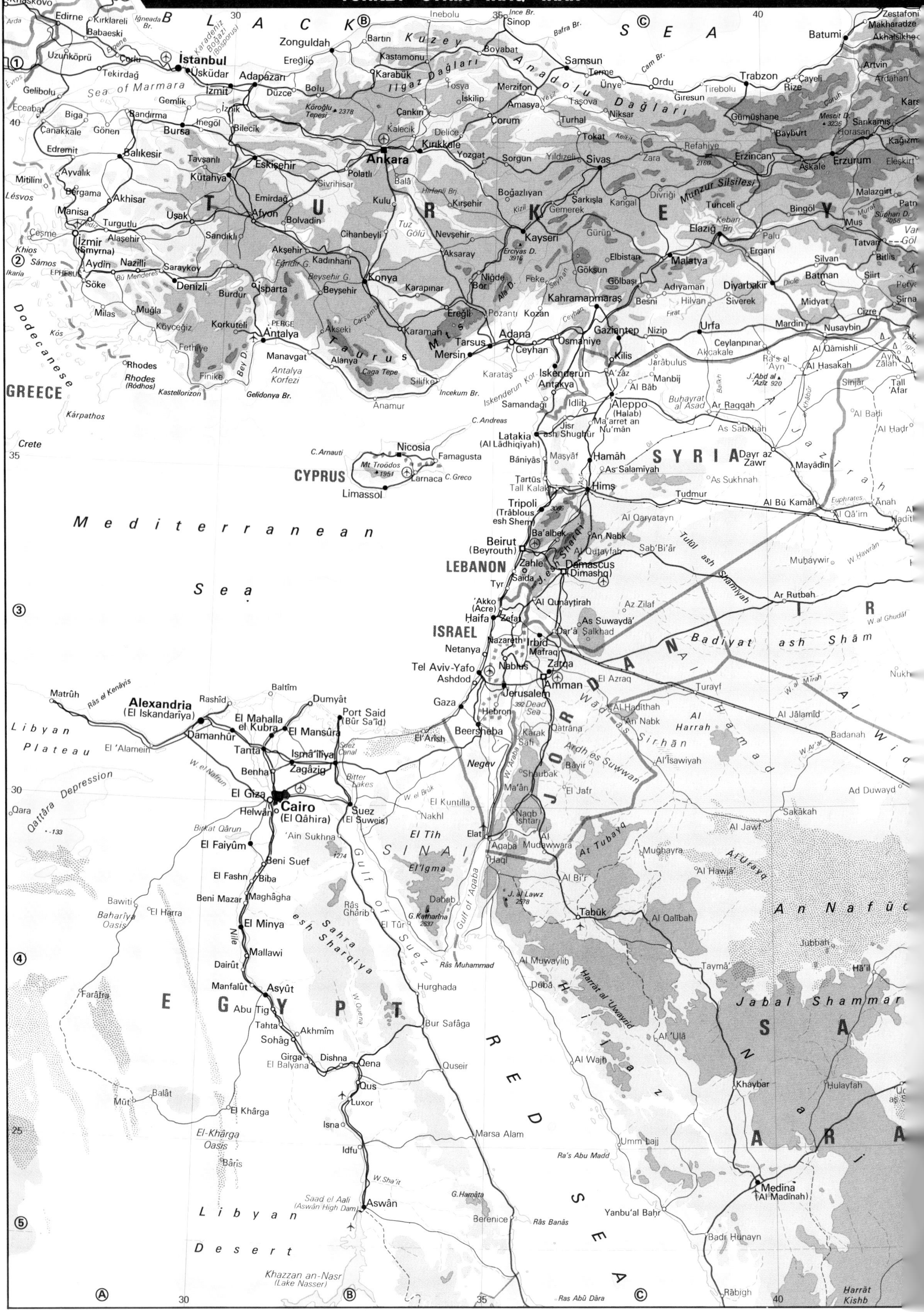
B L A C K S E A
Sea of Marmara
Mediterranean Sea
TURKEY
SYRIA
CYPRUS
LEBANON
ISRAEL
JORDAN
EGYPT
GREECE
RED SEA
SINAI
Gulf of Suez
Gulf of 'Aqaba
Libyan Plateau
Libyan Desert
Qattâra Depression
Badiyat ash Shām
An Nafūd
Jabal Shammar
Kuzey Anadolu Dağları
Ilgaz Dağları
Taurus Mts
Munzur Silsilesi
Istanbul
Üsküdar
Edirne
Kırklareli
Babaeski
Uzunköprü
Çorlu
Tekirdağ
Gelibolu
Çanakkale
Biga
Gönen
Bandırma
Bursa
İnegöl
Bilecik
İzmit
İznik
Adapazarı
Düzce
Bolu
Zonguldak
Ereğli
Bartın
Karabük
Kastamonu
Inebolu
Sinop
Boyabat
Samsun
Terme
Ünye
Ordu
Giresun
Tirebolu
Trabzon
Rize
Çayeli
Batumi
Artvin
Ardahan
Kars
Gümüşhane
Bayburt
Erzurum
Erzincan
Aşkale
Ankara
Kırıkkale
Çankırı
Çorum
Amasya
Tokat
Sivas
Yozgat
Kayseri
Malatya
Elazığ
Diyarbakır
Batman
Siirt
Bitlis
Tatvan
Muş
Bingöl
Tunceli
Balıkesir
Edremit
Ayvalık
Bergama
Manisa
İzmir (Smyrna)
Çeşme
Aydın
Nazilli
Söke
Milas
Muğla
Denizli
Uşak
Kütahya
Eskişehir
Afyon
Isparta
Burdur
Antalya
Konya
Karaman
Ereğli
Niğde
Adana
Tarsus
Mersin
Ceyhan
Osmaniye
Gaziantep
Kahramanmaraş
Urfa
Mardin
Nusaybin
Iskenderun
Antakya
Kilis
Aleppo (Halab)
Idlib
Latakia (Al Lādhiqīyah)
Bāniyās
Ţarţūs
Hamāh
Hims
Ar Raqqah
Dayr az Zawr
Al Hasakah
Al Qāmishli
Tudmur
Al Bū Kamāl
Damascus (Dimashq)
Beirut (Beyrouth)
Tripoli
Saida
Tyr
Zahle
Nicosia
Famagusta
Larnaca
Limassol
Haifa
Netanya
Tel Aviv-Yafo
Ashdod
Gaza
Jerusalem
Beersheba
Amman
Irbid
Zarqa
Elat
Aqaba
Ma'ān
Tabūk
Alexandria (El Iskandarîya)
Damanhûr
Tanta
Benha
El Mahalla el Kubra
El Mansûra
Dumyât
Port Said (Bûr Sa'îd)
Ismâ'îlîya
Zagâzig
Cairo (El Qâhira)
El Gîza
Helwân
Suez (El Suweis)
El Faiyûm
Beni Suef
El Minya
Mallawi
Asyût
Sohâg
Qena
Luxor
Isna
Idfu
Aswân
Hurghada
Bur Safâga
Quseir
Marsa Alam
Berenice
El Khârga
Bawiti
Farâfra
Matrûh
El 'Alamein
Medina (Al Madīnah)
Yanbu'al Bahr
Khaybar
Taymā'
Ha'il
Rābigh
30
35
40
25
A
B
C
1
2
3
4
5

1:7.5M 0 100 200 300 km 0 50 100 150 mls

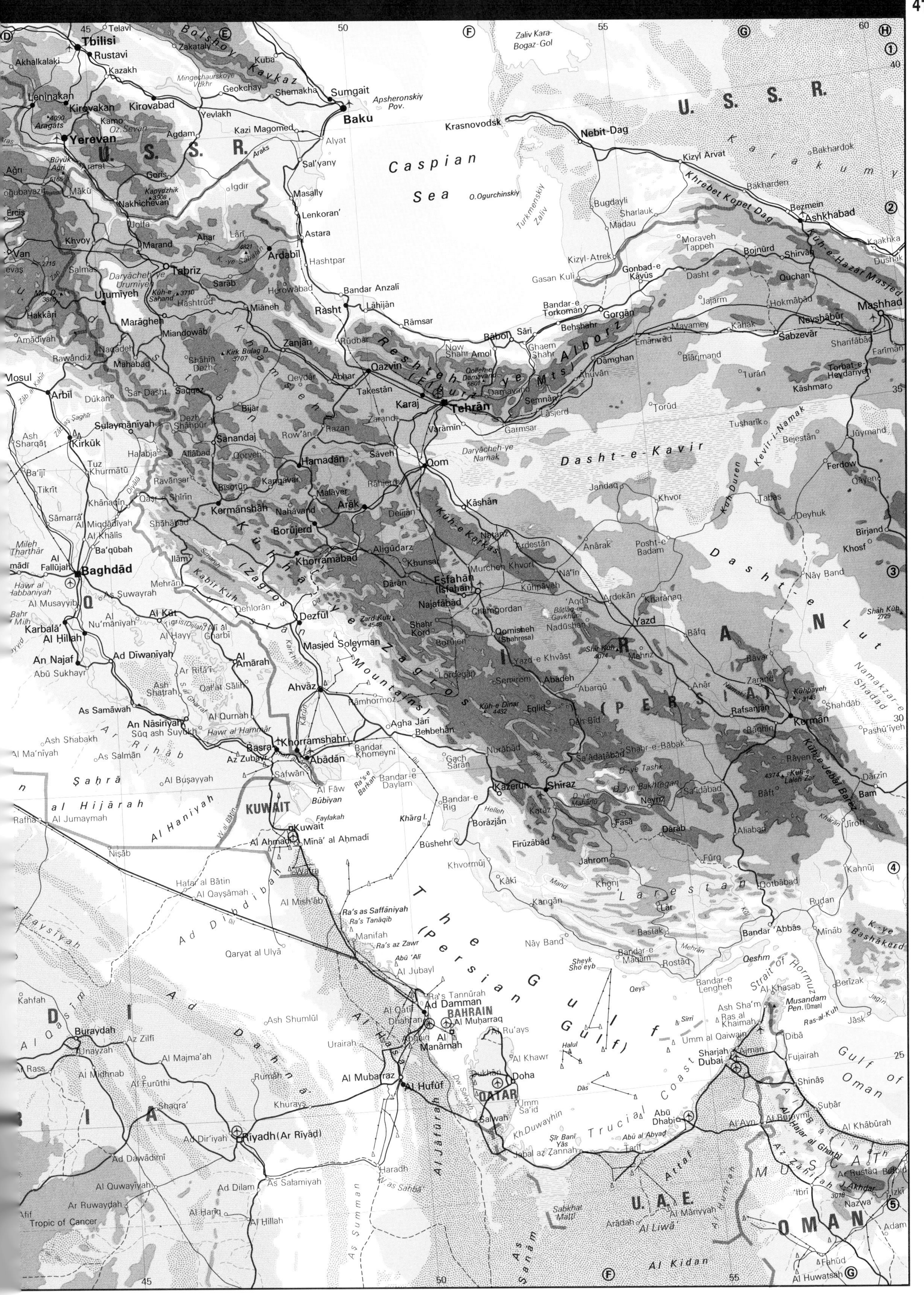

U. S. S. R.
Caspian Sea
Tbilisi
Baku
Yerevan
Tabriz
Tehrān
Baghdād
Kuwait
KUWAIT
BAHRAIN
QATAR
Doha
U. A. E.
OMAN
I R A N (P E R S I A)
Dasht-e-Kavir
Dasht-e Lut
The Gulf (Persian Gulf)
Gulf of Oman
Strait of Hormuz
Zagros Mountains
Reshteh-ye Alborz (Elburz)
Mashhad
Esfahān
Shīrāz
Kermān
Yazd
Basra
Riyadh (Ar Riyāḍ)
Tropic of Cancer

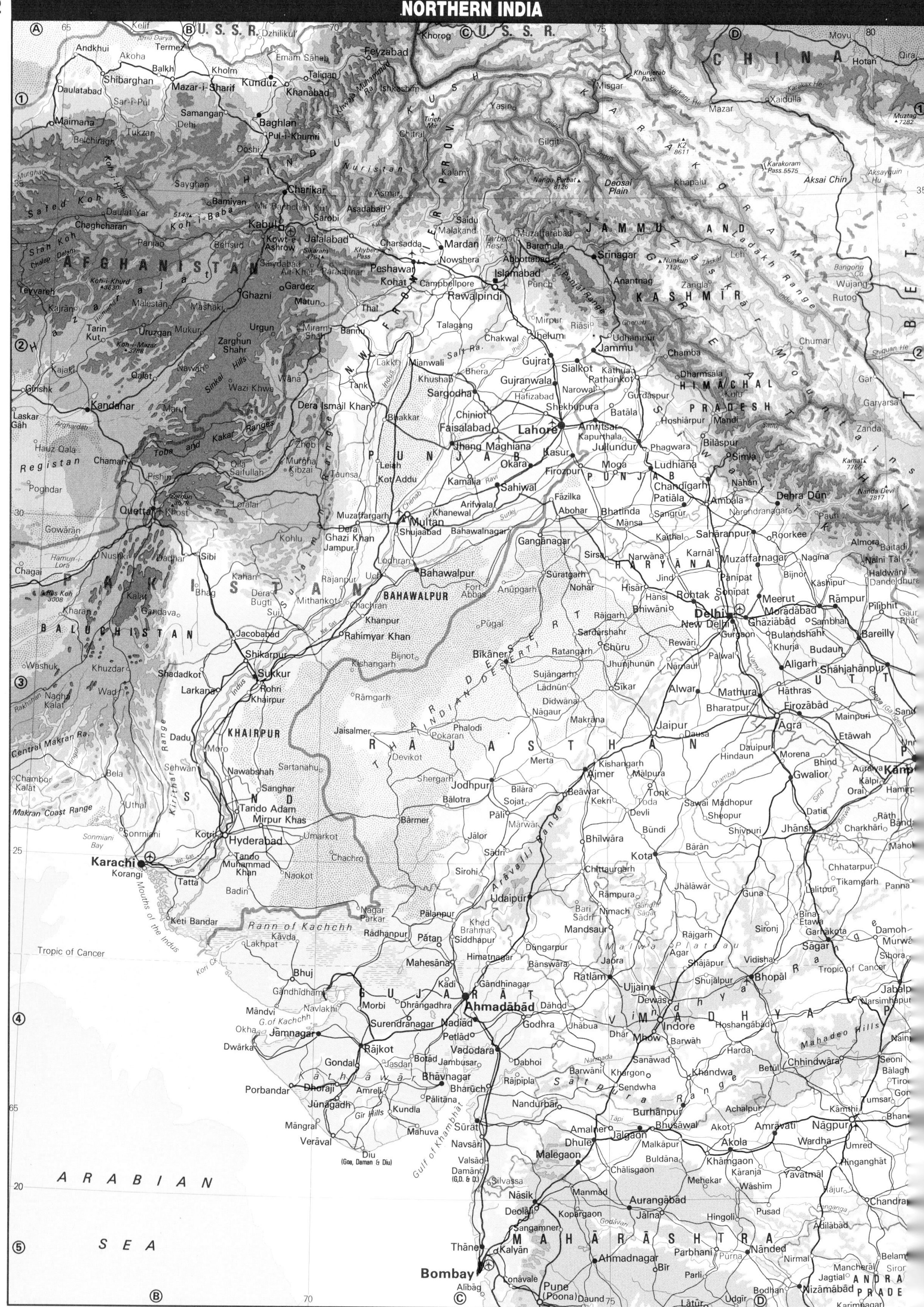
U. S. S. R.
CHINA
TIBET
AFGHANISTAN
PAKISTAN
BALUCHISTAN
JAMMU AND KASHMIR
HIMACHAL PRADESH
PUNJAB
HARYANA
RAJASTHAN
GUJARAT
MADHYA PRADESH
MAHARASHTRA
UTTAR PRADESH
THAR (INDIAN DESERT)
ARABIAN SEA
Tropic of Cancer
Rann of Kachchh
G. of Kachchh
Gulf of Khambhat
Mouths of the Indus
Karakoram Range
Ladakh Range
Zaskar Mountains
Pir Panjal Range
Salt Ra.
Sulaiman Range
Kirthar Range
Aravalli Range
Vindhya Range
Satpura Range
Mahadeo Hills
Malwa Plateau
Hindu Kush
Koh-i-Baba
Safed Koh
Toba and Kakar Ranges
Registan
Deosai Plain
Aksai Chin
K2 8611
Nanga Parbat 8126
Kabul
Kandahar
Mazar-i-Sharif
Peshawar
Islamabad
Rawalpindi
Lahore
Faisalabad
Multan
Quetta
Hyderabad
Karachi
Sukkur
Bahawalpur
Srinagar
Jammu
Simla
Chandigarh
Ludhiana
Amritsar
Delhi
New Delhi
Meerut
Agra
Jaipur
Ajmer
Jodhpur
Bikaner
Kota
Gwalior
Jhansi
Bhopal
Indore
Ujjain
Udaipur
Ahmadabad
Vadodara
Rajkot
Bhavnagar
Surat
Nasik
Aurangabad
Nagpur
Bombay
Pune (Poona)
Diu (Goa, Daman & Diu)
1:7.5M
0 100 200 300 km
0 50 100 150 mls

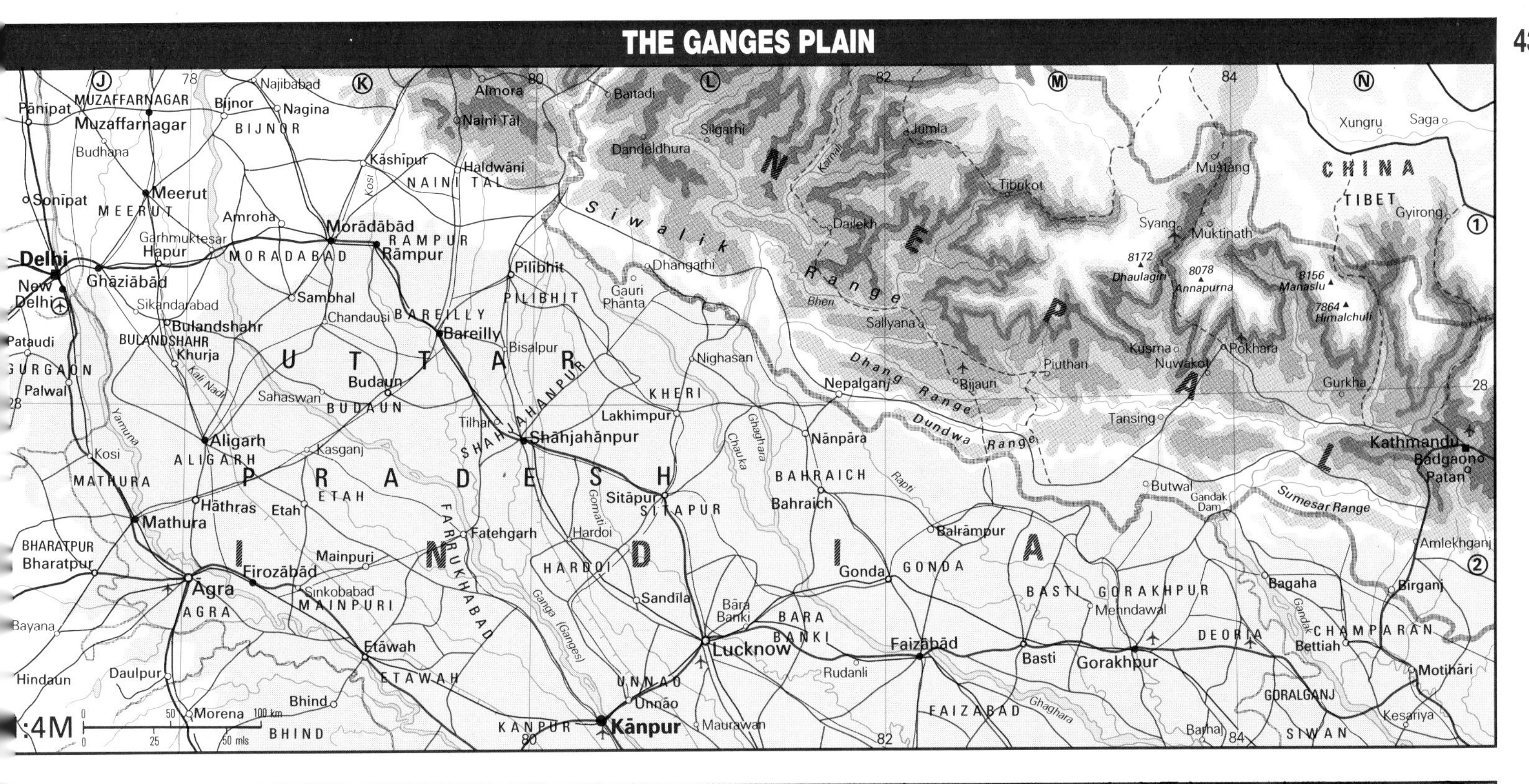
Delhi
New Delhi
Muzaffarnagar
Meerut
Ghāziābād
Morādābād
Rāmpur
Bareilly
Pilibhit
Shāhjahānpur
Aligarh
Mathura
Agra
Firozābād
Etāwah
Lucknow
Kānpur
Unnāo
Faizābād
Gorakhpur
Basti
Gonda
Bahraich
Sitāpur
Hardoi
Lakhimpur
Kathmandu
Patan
Pokhara
Butwal
Bettiah
Motihāri
Birganj
U T T A R P R A D E S H
I N D I A
N E P A L
CHINA
TIBET
Siwalik Range
Dhang Range
Dundwa Range
Sumesar Range
1:4M

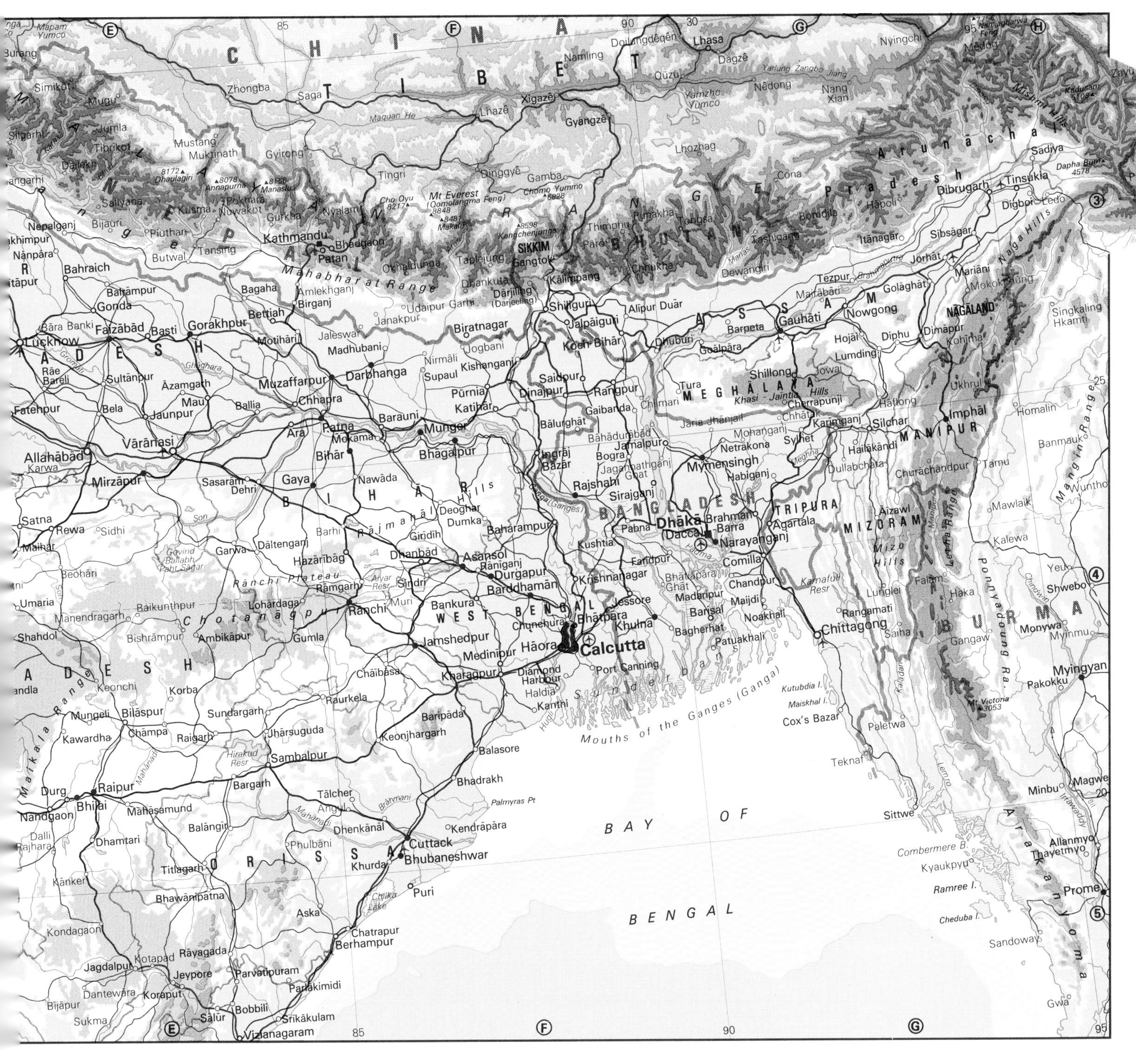
C H I N A
T I B E T
N E P A L
Lhasa
Xigazê
Gyangzê
Mt Everest
Kathmandu
Patan
SIKKIM
Gangtok
Dārjiling
B H U T A N
Thimphu
Arunāchal Pradesh
A S S A M
Gauhāti
Shillong
M E G H Ā L A Y A
NĀGĀLAND
Kohima
MANIPUR
Imphāl
TRIPURA
Agartala
MIZORAM
B A N G L A D E S H
Dhākā (Dacca)
Narayanganj
Chittagong
Cox's Bazar
Lucknow
Allahābād
Vārānasi
Patna
Gaya
Muzaffarpur
Darbhanga
Bhāgalpur
B I H Ā R
Dhanbād
Asansol
Ranchi
Jamshedpur
W E S T B E N G A L
Hāora
Calcutta
Khulna
Jessore
Kharagpur
Cuttack
Bhubaneshwar
Puri
O R I S S A
Sambalpur
Raipur
Bhilai
Durg
Berhampur
Vizianagaram
Srikākulam
Mouths of the Ganges (Ganga)
B A Y O F B E N G A L
B U R M A
Mahabharat Range
Rājmahāl Hills
Chota Nagpur
Ponnyadoung Ra.
Arakan Yoma
Prome
Sittwe
Myingyan
Magwe

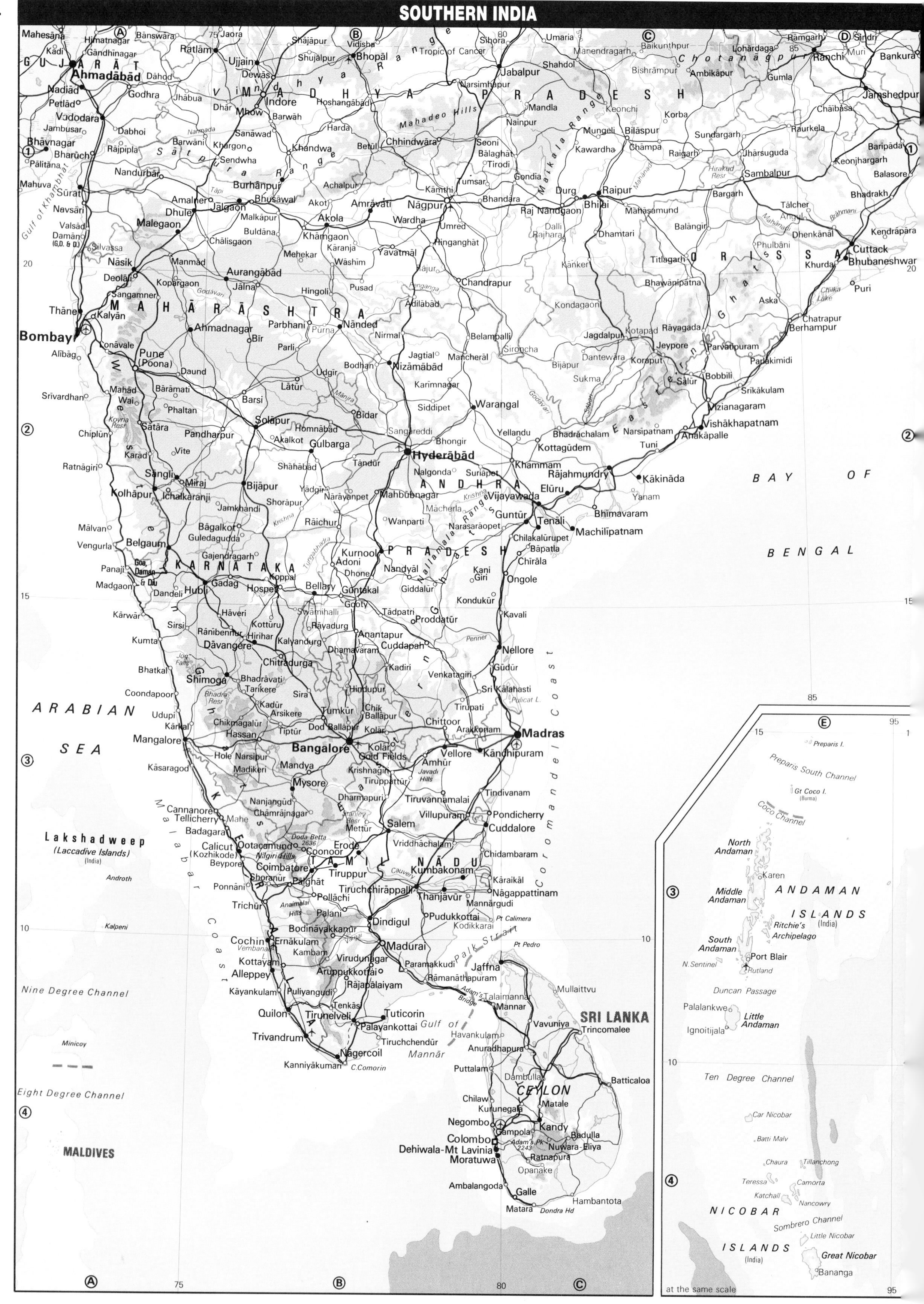
SOUTHERN INDIA
ARABIAN SEA
BAY OF BENGAL
SRI LANKA
CEYLON
MALDIVES
Lakshadweep
(Laccadive Islands)
(India)
ANDAMAN ISLANDS
(India)
NICOBAR ISLANDS
(India)
at the same scale
1:7.5M

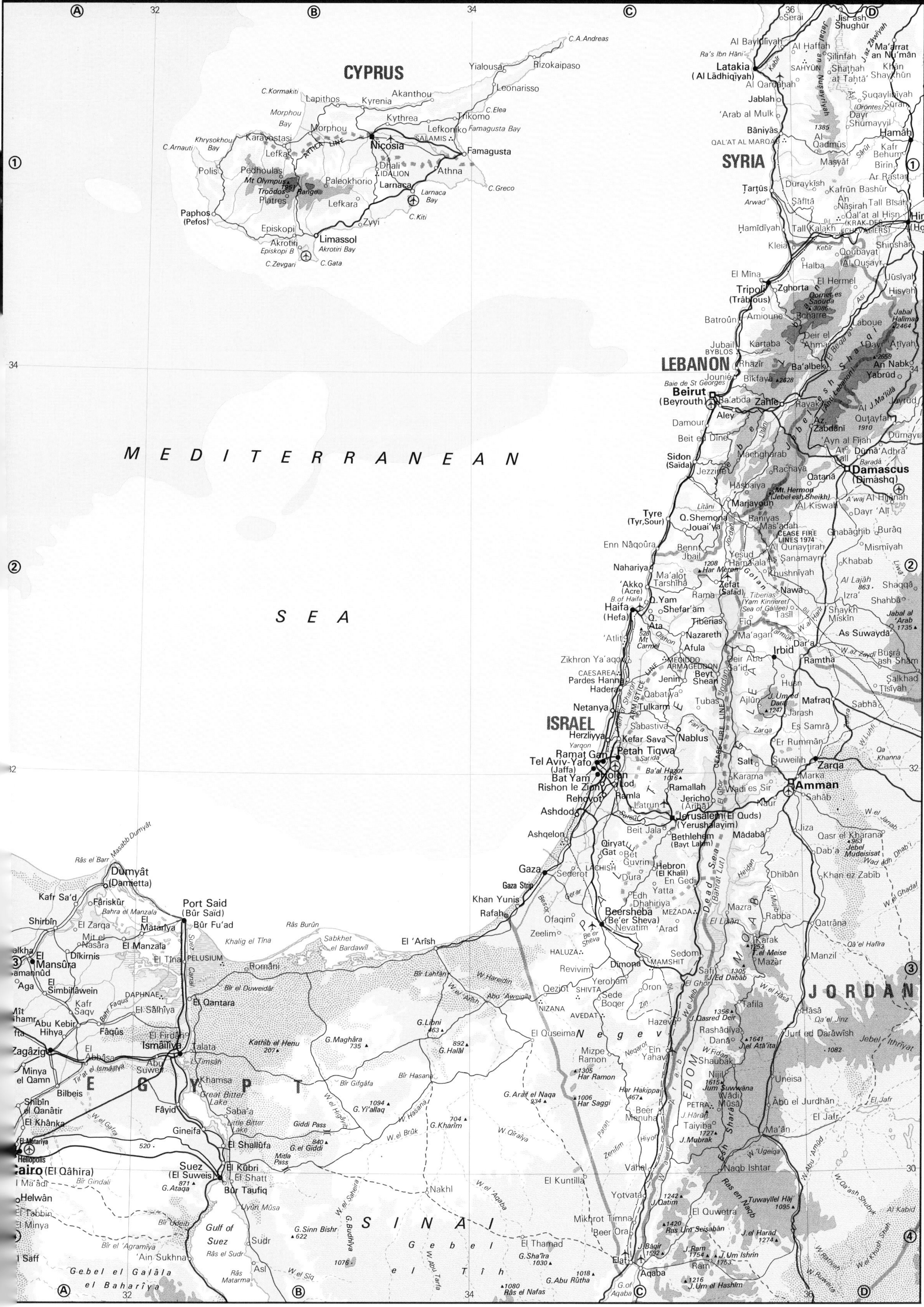

Ⓐ 32 Ⓑ 34 Ⓒ 36 Ⓓ

CYPRUS

C.A.Andreas
Rizokaipaso
C.Kormakiti Lapithos Akanthou Yialousa
Morphou Kyrenia Leonarisso
Bay Khrysokhou Karavostasi Kythrea Trikomo C.Elea
Bay Morphou Lefka Lefkoniko Famagusta Bay
C.Arnauti Nicosia SALAMIS
Polis Pedhoulas Dhali Famagusta
Mt Olympus IDALION Athna
Troödos Paleokhorio Larnaca C.Greco
Plátres Lefkara Larnaca Bay
Paphos Episkopi Zyyi C.Kiti
(Pefos) Limassol
Akrotiri Akrotiri Bay
Episkopi B
C.Zevgari C.Gata

Jisr ash Serai
Al Bayliiyah Al Haffah Silinfah
Ra's Ibn Hani SAHYUN Jaa Zawiyah Ma'arrat
Latakia an Nu'man
(Al Ladhiqiyah) Al Qardahah Shathah Khan
Jablah at Tahta Shaykhun
'Arab al Mulk (Orontes) Suqaylibiyah
Baniyas Suran
QAL'AT AL MARQAB 1385 Al Qadmus Dayr
Masyat Shumayyil **Hamah**
Tartus Durayksh Kafr Behum
Arwad Salta An Birin
Nasirah Bashur Ar Rastan
Hamidiyah Qal'at al Hisn
Tall Kalakh (KRAK DES **Hims**
Kleia (CHEVALIERS) **Homs**
Halba Qoubayat Shinshar
El Mina Al 'Qusayr
Tripoli El Hermel Yusiyah
(Trablous) Zghorta Hisyah
Batroun Amioune Qornet es
Saouda Jabal
Jubail Kartaba 3086▲ Halimat
BYBLOS Deir el Al Bedd 2464▲
Rhazir Ahmar 2659 Atiyah
LEBANON Ba'albek An Nabk
Jounié Bikfaya ▲2628 Yabrud
Baie de St Georges Rayak Jayrud
Beirut Ba'abda Zahle Qutayfah
(Beyrouth) Aley Zabdani Duma
Damour Beit el Dine Ayn al Fijah 1910
Beit ed Dine Az 'Adhra'
Sidon Machgharah Zabdani Barada Ma'lula
(Saida) Jezzine Rachaya **Damascus**
Qatana (Dimashq)
Hasbaiya Mt.Hermon Al Kiswah
(Jebel esh Sheikh) A'waj Al Hijanah
Litani Marjayoun Dayr 'Ali
Tyre Q.Shemona Mas'adah
(Tyr,Sour) Jouai'ya Baniyas Ghabaghib Buraq
Benn Hama ala CEASE FIRE Al Qunaytirah Sanamayn Mismiyah
Enn Naqoura Jbail LINES 1974 Khushniyah Al Lajah Khabab
Yesud Golan 863 Shaqqa
Nahariya 1208 Har Meron Nawa
Ma'alot Zefat Tiberias Shaykh Jabal al
'Akko Tarshiha (Safad) (Yam Kinneret) Miskin 'Arab 1735
(Acre) Rama Sea of Galilee) Izra' Shahba
B.of Haifa Q.Yam Fid Tasil Shuqqa
Haifa Shefar'am Nazareth Ma'agan
(Hefa) 'Atlit Ma'agan Nawa As Suwayda'
Mt Afula Dar'a
'Atlit Carmel Deir Abu Irbid Ramtha
528 Sa'id W.az Zaydi Busra
Zikhron Ya'aqov ARMAGEDDON Jenin Husn ash Sham
CAESAREA Beyt Ajlun Salkhad Tisiyah
Pardes Hanna Shean 1247 Jarash Es Samra
Hadera Qabatiya Er Rumman Sabha
Netanya Tubas Fari'a Zarqa Qa'
Tulkarm Zarqa Khanna
SHARON Sabastiya Salt Suweilih Zarqa
ISRAEL Nablus Karama **Amman** Marka
Herzliyya Kefar Sava Wadi es Sir Sahab
Ramat Gan Petah Tiqwa Ba'al Hazor Naur
Tel Aviv-Yafo Holon 1016▲ Jericho Jiza Qasr el Kharana
(Jaffa) Sarida Ramallah (Ariha) Dab'a Jebel
Bat Yam Lod Latrun Mudeisisat
Rishon le Zion Ramallah Madaba Wadi ddh Dhabi'
Rehovot Ramla **Jerusalem**(El Quds) Qasr el Kharana
Ashdod Latrun (Yerushalayim)
Ashqelon Beit Jala Bethlehem
Qiryat Bet (Bayt Lahm) Mazra
Gat Guvrin Hebron En Gedi
Gaza LACHISH (El Khalil) Rabba
Gaza Strip Sederot Dura Yatta Dhiban Khan ez Zabib
Khan Yunis Gerar Edh Mazra
Rafah Besor Dahiriya Qatrana
Ofaqim Gerar Beersheba MEZADA El Lisan Karak
Be'er (Be'er Sheva) Qa'el Hafira
Zeelim Sheva Arad El Meise
El 'Arish Sabkhet Nevatim Sedom
el Bardawil Safi Mazar Manzil
HALUZA Dimona MAMSHIT 1305
Romani W.el Ghadaf
Revivim W.el Hureidin Yeroham 1356▲ **JORDAN**
Qeziot SHIVTA Sede Oron El Ghor Jurf ed Darawish
NIZANA Boqer Tafila Qa'el Jinz
AVEDAT Hazeva 1641 Jebel
El Quseima Negev Rashadiya El Atá'ita Ithriyat
Dana 1082
Mizpe PETRA Abu el Jurdhan
G.Libni Ramon Ein El Jafr
863 Har Ramon Yahav Nijil
892▲ Negarot 1615▲ El Jafr
G.Halal Er Rafid Suwwana Wadi
J.Harun Musa Abu el Jurdhan
G.Arad el Naqa Har Hakippa Taiyiba
934 467▲ 1727 Ma'an
1006▲ Beer 1094 J.Mubrak
Har Saggi Menuha

M E D I T E R R A N E A N S E A

EGYPT

Masabb Dumyat
Ras el Barr
Dumyât Kafr Sa'd Fariskûr
(Damietta) Bahra el Manzala
Shirbîn El Zarqa Port Said Ras Burûn
El Matarîya (Bûr Saîd) Ras Burûn
El Manzala Bûr Fu'âd Khalig el Tîna
alkha El Mansûra Mit el Sabkhet
El Qantara El 'Arîsh el Bardawîl
amanhûd Dîkirnis PELUSIUM Sabkhet
Aga El Simbillâwein El Tîna Români
El Shâtt Bîr el Duweidâr
amr Kafr DAPHNAE El Qantara Bîr el Duweidâr
hamr Saqv El Sâlhîya
Abu Kebîr Fâqûs Bîr Lahfan
Hihya El Firdân Kathib el Henu Abu Aweigila
Zagâzig Ismaîlîya 207 W.el Arish
Minya El Abbâsa Talata Kathib el Henu NIZANA
el Qamn Timsâh G.Maghâra El Quseima
Bilbeis 735 892 El Quseima
Shibîn Khamsa G.Halâl
el Qanâtir Abu Bîr Hasani
El Khânka Suwer G.Yi'allaq 463
Minya Fâyid Bîr Gifgâfa 704 El Thamad
El Metariya Great Bitter G.Khârim W.el Hasana G.Arad el Naqa
Heliopolis Lake 1094 Beer Ora
airo (El Qâhira) Gineifa Saba'a Yi'allaq W.Qira'iya
I Ma'âdi 520 Saba'a W.el Brûk
Helwân 840 El Giddi Zenifim
Tabbin Suez El Giddi Vahel
Minya (El Suweis) Mitla El Kuntilla J.Qatim
I Saff Bîr Gindali El Kûbri Pass Naqb Ishtar
El Shattûfa Naqb Ishtar
Bûr Taufîq Nakhl Mikhrot Timna 1420 W.Qa'ash Shubk
871▲ El Shatt W.el 'Aqaba Ras Um Seisaban Al Kabid
G.Ataqa Bûr Taufîq 1242▲ El Quweira
Sudr J.Qatim Wâdi
'Ain Sukhna Ras el Sudr El Thamad 1754 Ram
Gebel el Galâla SINAI G.Buchiya J.Um Ishrin
el Baharîya Asl 1076 1753
G.Sinn Bishr Gebel 1752
Tir at el 622 el Tîh J.Bâqir 1216 J.Um al Hashim
'Agramîya Ras Elat 1532 1754
Matarma Wel Siq Aqaba
G.Sha'ira Ras Um Seisaban
1030 G.Abu Rûtha
1080 1018
Râs el Nafas G.of
Aqaba

1:2.5M

0 25 50 75 100 km
0 25 50 mls

Ⓐ 32 Ⓑ 34 Ⓒ 36 Ⓓ

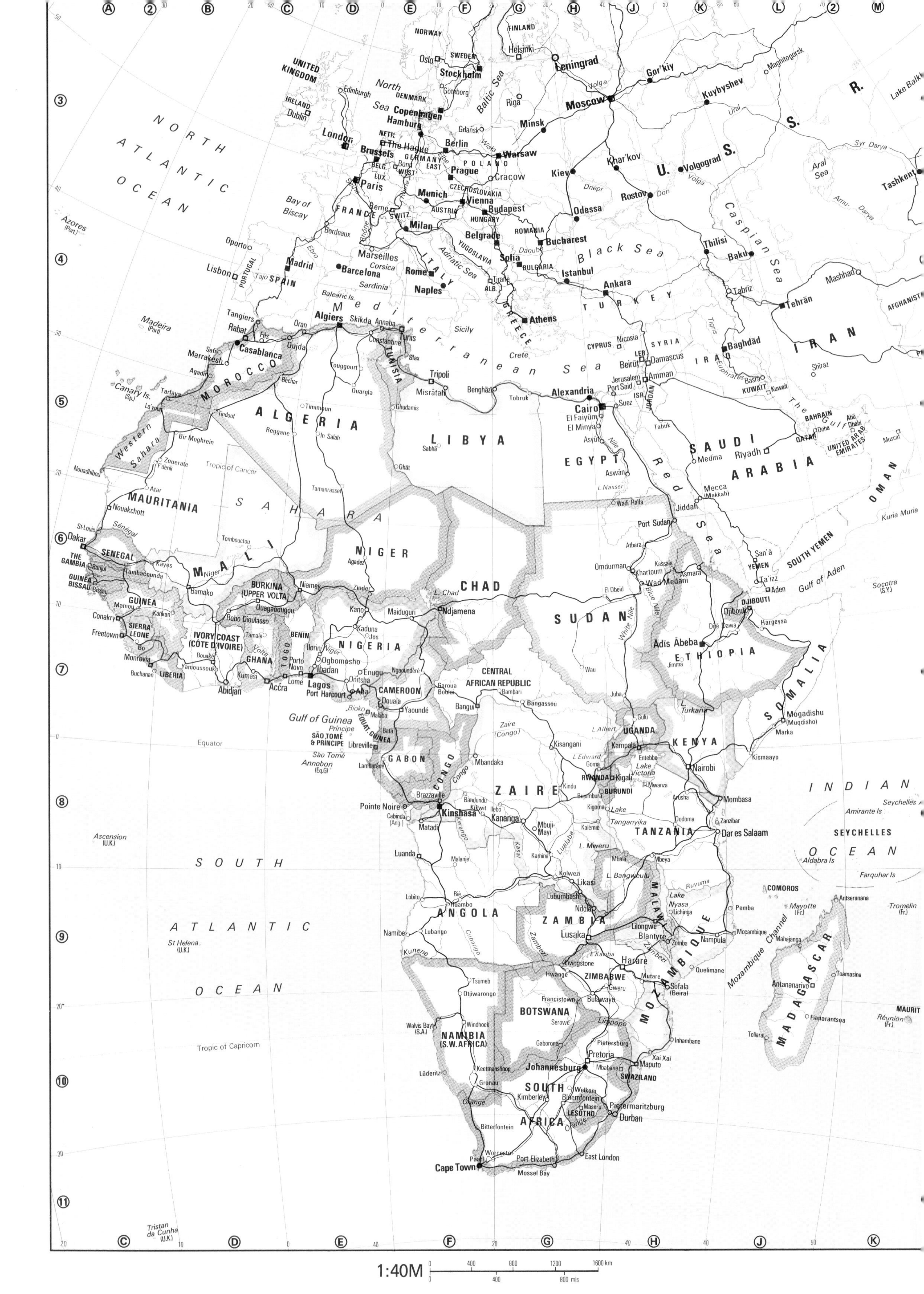
NORTH ATLANTIC OCEAN
SOUTH ATLANTIC OCEAN
INDIAN OCEAN
Mediterranean Sea
Black Sea
Caspian Sea
Red Sea
North Sea
Baltic Sea
Gulf of Guinea
Gulf of Aden
Mozambique Channel
Bay of Biscay
Adriatic Sea
The Gulf
Tropic of Cancer
Equator
Tropic of Capricorn
SAHARA
NORWAY
FINLAND
SWEDEN
UNITED KINGDOM
IRELAND
DENMARK
NETH.
BELG.
LUX.
GERMANY WEST
GERMANY EAST
POLAND
CZECHOSLOVAKIA
AUSTRIA
HUNGARY
SWITZ.
FRANCE
PORTUGAL
SPAIN
ITALY
YUGOSLAVIA
ROMANIA
BULGARIA
ALB.
GREECE
TURKEY
U. S. S. R.
CYPRUS
SYRIA
LEB.
ISR.
JORDAN
IRAQ
IRAN
KUWAIT
BAHRAIN
QATAR
UNITED ARAB EMIRATES
SAUDI ARABIA
OMAN
YEMEN
SOUTH YEMEN
AFGHANISTAN
MOROCCO
Western Sahara
ALGERIA
TUNISIA
LIBYA
EGYPT
MAURITANIA
MALI
NIGER
CHAD
SUDAN
SENEGAL
THE GAMBIA
GUINEA BISSAU
GUINEA
SIERRA LEONE
LIBERIA
IVORY COAST (CÔTE D'IVOIRE)
BURKINA (UPPER VOLTA)
GHANA
TOGO
BENIN
NIGERIA
CAMEROON
CENTRAL AFRICAN REPUBLIC
EQUAT. GUINEA
SÃO TOMÉ & PRINCIPE
GABON
CONGO
ZAIRE
UGANDA
KENYA
RWANDA
BURUNDI
TANZANIA
ETHIOPIA
DJIBOUTI
SOMALIA
ANGOLA
ZAMBIA
MALAWI
MOZAMBIQUE
ZIMBABWE
BOTSWANA
NAMIBIA (S.W. AFRICA)
SOUTH AFRICA
LESOTHO
SWAZILAND
MADAGASCAR
COMOROS
SEYCHELLES
Azores (Port.)
Madeira (Port.)
Canary Is. (Sp.)
Ascension (U.K.)
St Helena (U.K.)
Tristan da Cunha (U.K.)
Socotra (S.Y.)
Mayotte (Fr.)
Réunion (Fr.)
Tromelin (Fr.)
Aldabra Is
Amirante Is
Farquhar Is
Bioko
Principe
São Tomé
Annobon (Eq.G)
Corsica
Sardinia
Sicily
Crete
Balearic Is.
Oslo
Stockholm
Helsinki
Leningrad
Moscow
Gor'kiy
Kuybyshev
Magnitogorsk
Riga
Minsk
Edinburgh
Dublin
London
Copenhagen
Hamburg
Göteborg
Gdańsk
Berlin
Warsaw
The Hague
Brussels
Bonn
Paris
Prague
Cracow
Munich
Vienna
Budapest
Berne
Milan
Bordeaux
Marseilles
Oporto
Lisbon
Madrid
Barcelona
Rome
Naples
Belgrade
Sofia
Bucharest
Tirane
Athens
Istanbul
Ankara
Kiev
Odessa
Khar'kov
Volgograd
Rostov
Tbilisi
Baku
Tabriz
Tehrān
Mashhad
Tashkent
Nicosia
Beirut
Damascus
Baghdād
Shiraz
Basra
Kuwait
Jerusalem
Amman
Port Said
Suez
Alexandria
Cairo
El Faiyūm
El Minya
Asyūt
Aswān
Wadi Halfa
Tabuk
Medina
Riyadh
Doha
Abu Dhabi
Muscat
Mecca (Makkah)
Jiddah
Port Sudan
San'a
Ta'izz
Aden
Tangiers
Rabat
Fès
Casablanca
Safi
Marrakesh
Agadir
Oran
Algiers
Skikda
Annaba
Constantine
Tunis
Sfax
Oujda
Touggourt
Ouargla
Béchar
Tarfaya
La'youn
Tindouf
Timimoun
Reggane
In Salah
Ghudamis
Tripoli
Misrātah
Benghāzi
Tobruk
Sabha
Ghāt
Tamanrasset
Bir Moghrein
Zouerate
F'derik
Nouadhibou
Atar
Nouakchott
St-Louis
Dakar
Banjul
Tambacounda
Kayes
Bissau
Mamou
Conakry
Kankan
Freetown
Bo
Monrovia
Buchanan
Bamako
Tombouctou
Niamey
Agadez
Zinder
Ouagadougou
Bobo Dioulasso
Tamale
Bouaké
Yamoussoukro
Abidjan
Kumasi
Accra
Lomé
Porto Novo
Lagos
Ibadan
Ogbomosho
Ilorin
Kaduna
Jos
Kano
Maiduguri
Enugu
Onitsha
Aba
Port Harcourt
Ndjamena
L. Chad
Ngaoundéré
Garoua
Bouar
Douala
Yaoundé
Malabo
Bata
Libreville
Lambaréné
Bambari
Bangui
Bangassou
Khartoum
Omdurman
Atbara
Kassala
Wad Medani
Asmara
El Obeid
Wau
Juba
Djibouti
Dire Dawa
Hargeysa
Adis Abeba
Jimma
Mogadishu (Muqdisho)
Marka
Kismaayo
Gulu
L. Albert
L. Turkana
Kampala
Entebbe
Kisangani
L. Edward
Goma
Kigali
Lake Victoria
Bujumbura
Mwanza
Nairobi
Arusha
Mombasa
Kigoma
Lake Tanganyika
Dodoma
Zanzibar
Dar es Salaam
Mbandaka
Brazzaville
Kinshasa
Pointe Noire
Cabinda (Ang.)
Matadi
Bandundu
Kikwit
Ilebo
Kananga
Mbuji-Mayi
Kindu
Kalemie
Kamina
L. Mweru
Mbala
Mbeya
Kolwezi
Likasi
L. Bangweulu
Lubumbashi
Ndola
Luanda
Malanje
Lobito
Bié
Huambo
Namibe
Lubango
Lake Nyasa
Lichinga
Lilongwe
Blantyre
Zomba
Lusaka
L. Kariba
Livingstone
Hwange
Harare
Mutare
Nampula
Moçambique
Pemba
Quelimane
Sofala (Beira)
Tsumeb
Otjiwarongo
Windhoek
Walvis Bay (S.A.)
Francistown
Bulawayo
Gweru
Serowe
Gaborone
Pietersburg
Pretoria
Johannesburg
Mbabane
Maputo
Xai Xai
Inhambane
Keetmanshoop
Lüderitz
Grunau
Kimberley
Welkom
Bloemfontein
Maseru
Pietermaritzburg
Durban
Bitterfontein
Worcester
Paarl
Cape Town
Port Elizabeth
Mossel Bay
East London
Antseranana
Mahajanga
Antananarivo
Toamasina
Fianarantsoa
Toliara
Volga
Ural
Dnepr
Don
Danube
Elbe
Wisła
Rhine
Rhône
Ebro
Tajo
Tigris
Euphrates
Syr Darya
Amu Darya
Aral Sea
Lake Balkhash
Nile
White Nile
Blue Nile
Niger
Sénégal
Volta
Congo
Zaire (Congo)
Kasai
Kwango
Lualaba
Kunene
Cubango
Zambezi
Limpopo
Orange
Ruvuma
1:40M
0 400 800 1200 1600 km
0 400 800 mls

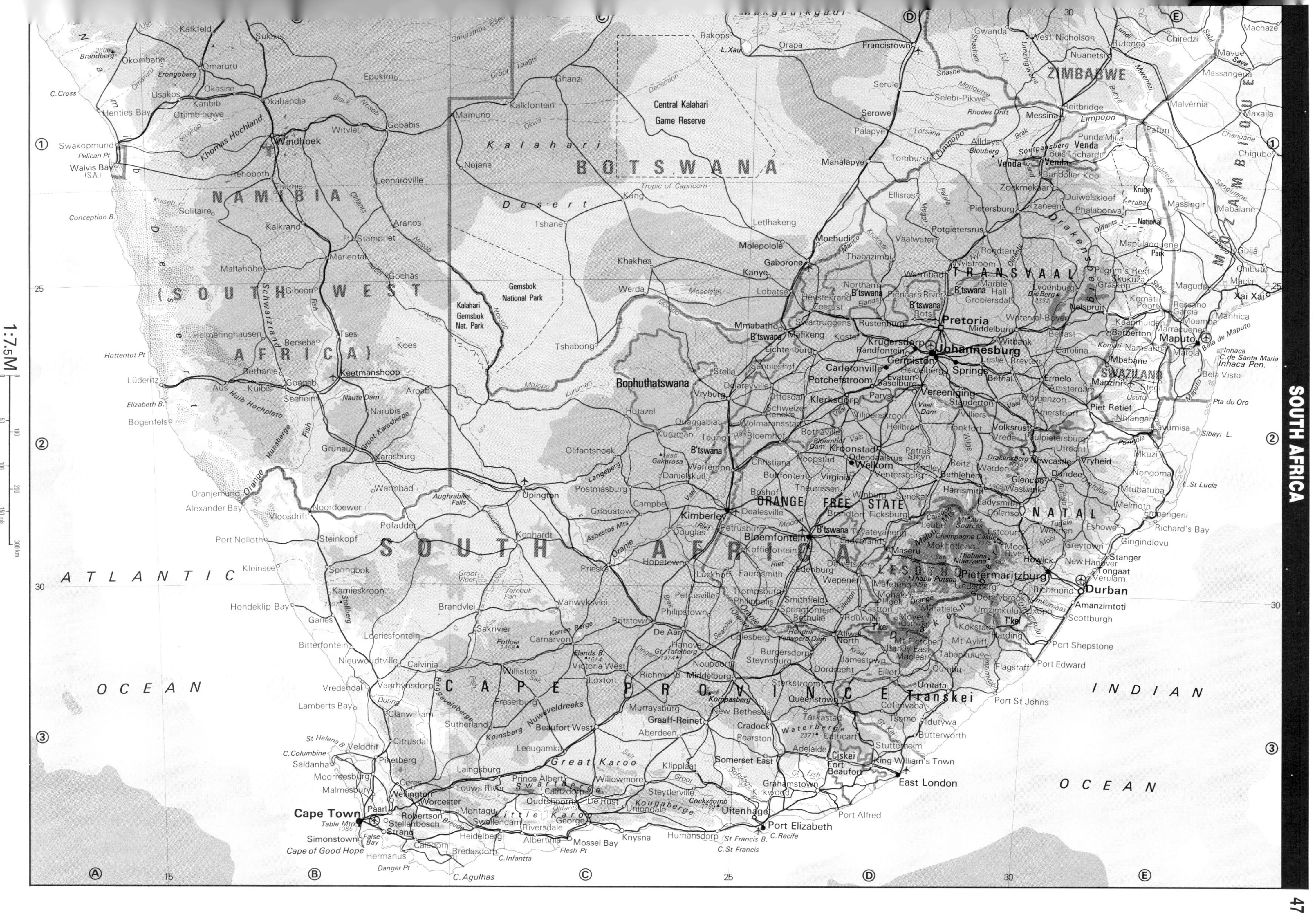
BOTSWANA
ZIMBABWE
MOZAMBIQUE
NAMIBIA
(SOUTH WEST AFRICA)
SOUTH AFRICA
TRANSVAAL
NATAL
ORANGE FREE STATE
CAPE PROVINCE
LESOTHO
SWAZILAND
Transkei
Ciskei
Bophuthatswana
INDIAN OCEAN
ATLANTIC OCEAN
Kalahari Desert
Central Kalahari Game Reserve
Gemsbok National Park
Kalahari Gemsbok Nat. Park
Great Karoo
Little Karoo
Drakensberg
Tropic of Capricorn
Pretoria
Johannesburg
Durban
Cape Town
Port Elizabeth
East London
Bloemfontein
Kimberley
Pietermaritzburg
Maputo
Windhoek
Gaborone
Maseru
Mbabane
Walvis Bay (S.A.)
Lüderitz
Upington
Orange
Vaal
Limpopo
Molopo
C. Agulhas
Cape of Good Hope
1:7.5M
0 100 200 300 km
0 50 100 150 mls

40N 30W

Flores
São Jorge   Angra Do
Faial   Heroismo
Pico   Terceira
Azores
(Açores)
(Portugal)   São Miguel
Ponta
Delgada   Formigas
Santa
Maria
at the same scale

Lisbon
(Lisboa)   Beja   Badajoz   Albacete   Ibiza   BALEARIC ISLANDS   Sardinia   Cagliari
(Islas Baleares)   (Sardegna)
PORTUGAL   Sierra   Ciudad   Murcia   Alicante
Morena   Real   M E D I T
Córdoba   Linares   Cartagena
Faro   Huelva   Seville   Granada   Algiers   Tizi   Bejaïa   Skikda   Annaba   Bizer
(Sevilla)   (Alger)   Ouzou   (Bougie)   (Philippeville)   (Bône)   Beja
C. de S.   Cádiz   Málaga   Almería   Cherchell   Ech   Constantine   Souk   El Kef
Vincente   Str. of   Gibraltar (U.K.)   Mostaganem   Cheliff   Blida   Ahras   Kairouan
Tangier   Ceuta (Sp)   Oran   Ignil-Izane   Sétif   Tébessa   El Jem
(Tanger)   Melilla   Mascara   Tiaret   Bou Saâda   M'sila   Aurès   Sfax
Larache   (SP.)   Sidi bel-Abbès   El Boukhari   Biskra   Batna   Kasserine
Ksar-El-Kebir   Taourit   Saïda   Djelfa   Chott   Gafsa
Kenitra   Taza   Oujda   Laghouat   Melrhir   Gabès
Rabat   Ain   Mecheria   El Oued   Touggourt   Medenine
Casablanca   Meknès   Fès   Beni   Ain   Ksar   Tozeur
(El-Dar-El-Beida)   Azrou   Mathar   Sefra   ech Chergui   **TUNISI**
El Jadida   Missour   Figuig   El Oued   Tataouine
Oued   Midelt   Bouârfa   Ghardaïa   Ouargla   Dehibat
Safi   Zem   M   Béchar   Atlas Saharien   Grand Erg   Ghadames
Beni Mellal   El Rachida   Abadla   Ft. Lallemand   Oriental
Essaouira   O   R   Ouarzazate   El Golea   El Gassi   Ghadamès
Marrakech   Jbel   Sarhro   Beni   Grand Erg Occidental   El Gassi
Toubkal   C   Zagora   Abbès   Hassi
4165   Tiznit   Tata   Hamada du Dra   Tabelbala   Timimoun   Inifel
Agadir   Anti Atlas   Jbel Ouarkziz   Tinfouchi   Ohanet
Ilhas Selvagens   Haut   Tan-Tan   Hamada Tounassine   Plateau du   Tin
(Port.)   Tarfaya   Hassi   A L G E R I A   Tademait   Fouye
Canary Islands   La'youn   Mdakane   Bordj   Hamada de Tinrhert
(Islas Canarias)   Saguia el Hamra   Adrar   Omar Driss   In Amenas
(Spain)   Lanzarote   Smara   Bj Flye   Reggane   Tassili   Sarda
Santa Cruz   De La Palma   Arrecife   El Farsia   Ste Marie   Aoulef   N'Ajjer   Ghat
La Palma   Fuerteventura   Tindouf   El Eglab   Plaine du   Arak   Adrar   Zaouatanlaz
Gomera   Tenerife   W   Bir Moghrein   Chegga   Chenachèn   Tidikelt   In Ecker   Idelès   Djanet
Hierro   Las   De Tenerife   S   Aioun Abd el Malek   In Salah   Hoggar   In Afaleleh
Palmas   Gran   Karet   El Mzereb   Erg   Abalessa   2918   In Ezzane
De Gran   Canaria   El Hank   Chech   (Ahaggar)   Silet   Tamanrasset
Canaria   B. de Rio de Oro   Erg Iguidi   El Mreiti   Erg   Tamanrasset   A
Dakhla   Guelta   Chech   El Haricha   Tanezrouft   Tahat   In Ebeggi
Zemmur   Ausert   Bir Zreigat   Troudenni   Bidon 5   2918
Nouadhibou   Azefal   Ouadâne   Oguilet   (Ruins)   Ténéré
Ras   Tichla   Ouarane   Khenachich   El Guettâra   du
Nouadhibou   Adrar   Zouerate   In Dagouber   Mt Gréboun   Tafassasset
I. Tidra   Chinguetti   T'dérik   El   Aguelhok   1944   Ifni
C. Mirik   Atar   Tourine   M A U R I T A N I A   Djouf   Tessalit   In Guezzam
Akjoujt   Araouane   Tin   Iférouane   Air
Nouakchott   El   Zaouaten   Talak   Timia
Tidjikja   El Merelé   Guir   Ardar   Agadez
Tichitt   Aklé   Azaouad   des   Kidal   Ingal   Erg du Ténéré
Boutilimit   Aouana   Dhar   Haggaguerete   Iforas   Anéfis   N I G E R
Rosso   Tamchaket   Oualata   Tassili du Hoggar   Zegueren   Tasker
St-Louis   Aleg   Hodh   Araouane   Timetrine   Abala
Dagana   Kiffa   Néma   Tombouctou   Monts   Ménaka   Tahoua
Louga   Matam   Mbout   Niger   Gourma   Gao   Tchin   Tillia   Tanout
Thiès   Kébémer   Timbédra   Goundam   Rharous   Ansongo   Tabaradene   Madaoua   Zinder   Gouré
Dakar   Touba   Karagoro   L. Faguibine   M A L I   Ingal   Keita   Dakoro
Rufisque   Diourbel   Linguère   Niafounké   Bourem   Mayahi   Maradi   Nguru   Gashua
SENEGAL   Bakel   Niono   L. Débo   Aderbissinat   Gumel
Kaolack   Kaffrine   Kidira   Nioro   Nara   Sokolo   Say   Dogondoutchi   Dosso   Sokoto   Daura   Hadejia
THE   Banjul   Tambacounda   Du Sahel   Diéma   Massina   Ségou   Birnin N'Konni   Goudoumaria   Zaria   Potis
GAMBIA   Bafoulabé   Kolokani   Mopti   Djibo   Niamey   Sokoto   Katsina   Kano   Hadejia
Diouloulou   Kayes   Bandiagara   Téra   Ouallam   Illéla   Tessaoua   Kari
Bignona   Kédougou   Kita   Dienné   Dori   Birnin-Kebbi   Kaura   Namoda   Yashi
Ziguinchor   Sédhiou   Bamako   San   Tougan   Ouahigouya   Gaya   Gusau   Funtua
Bissau   Bafatá   Kéniéba   Koulikoro   Nouna   BURKINA   Kantchari   Birnin-Kebbi   Kaduna   Bauchi
GUINEA   Bolama   Siguiri   Kangaba   Dédougou   Yako   Kaya   Dogondoutchi   Minna   Bida   Jos
BISSAU   Catió   Fouta   Labé   Dinguiraye   Koudougou   Ouagadougou   Nat   Say   Zungeru   Kano   Gombe
Arquipélago   C. Verga   Boké   Dabola   Bougouni   Sikasso   Fada N'Gourma   Jebba   Kainji   Minna
dos Bijagós   Fria   Dalaba   Kouroussa   Bobo   Boromo   Tenkodogo   Malanville   Resr   Zaria   Numa
GUINEA   Boffa   Kindia   Kankan   Dioulasso   Pama   Kandi   Nikki   Zungeru   Kaduna
Conakry   Mamou   Faranah   Maninian   Tingrela   Gaoua   Gambaga   Mango   Yelwa   Bembéréké   N I G E R I A
Forécariah   Kabala   Odienné   Diébougou   Tumu   Wa   Kandi   Nikki   Minna   Lafia
Kambia   SIERRA   Kissidougou   Korhogo   Boundiali   Wa   Bolgatanga   Djougou   Yashikera   Keffi   Shendam
Port Loko   LEONE   Beyla   Ferkéssédougou   White   Yendi   Kanté   Parakou   Bida   Shaki   Shendam
Freetown   Makeni   Niakaramandougou   Volta   Tamale   Bassila   Savé   Ilorin   Baro   Wokari
Moyamba   Mano   Voinjama   Séguéla   Black   Bole   Sokodé   Shaki   Ogbomosho   Okoja   Makurdi   Gashaka
Sherbro   Loma   Nzérékoré   Bouaké   Volta   Salaga   Kpélimé   Ibadan   Oshogbo   Katsina   Gombe
Bonthe   Mts   Macenta   Katiola   Bondoukou   Bassar   Atakpamé   Iwo   Ife   Okene   Ala   Mt
Robertsport   Danané   Bouaflé   Berekum   Wenchi   Jasikan   Apomey   Owo   Otukpo   Gotel
Bomi   Man   IVORY   Ganhoué   Sunyani   Pobé   Benin   Enugu   Mamfé   Mts
Hills   Duékoué   COAST   Abengourou   Mampong Volta   Kumasi   Abeokuta   City   Abakaliki   Bamenda
Monrovia   Guiglo   Daloa   GHANA   Bibiani   Pobé   Lagos   Sapele   CAMER
Buchanan   LIBERIA   Yamoussoukro   Kintampo   Dunkwa   Koforidua   Porto   Onitsha   Mamfé
Chiehn   (CÔTE D'IVOIRE)   Agboville   Enchi   Nsawam   Novo   Owerri   Aba   Bafoussam
River   Mt Niete   Soubré   Adzopé   Lomé   Keta   Warri   Calabar   Buea
Cess   Abidjan   Winneba   Cotonou   Forcados   Owerri   Aba   Nkongsamba
Greenville   Sassandra   Grand   Accra   Oba   Nsawam   Port   Bonny   Bali
San Pédro   Bassam   Cape Coast   Quidah   Harcourt   Cameroun   Yabassi
Harper   Tabou   C. Takoradi   Bight of Benin   Mouths   4095   Limbe   Douala
C. Palmas   Sekondi   Three Points   of the R. Niger   Malabo   Edea
Three Points   Bight of   Kribi
Biafra   EQUATORIAL   Bata   Ebebiyin
GUINEA   Nyong   Ebolowa
GULF OF GUINEA   S. TOME &   Río   Ambam
PRINCIPE   Cocobeach   Medouneu
São Tomé   Libreville   Pte   Evinayong
Azano   GABON   Ndjolé

Madeira
(Portugal)   Porto
Santo
Funchal   Deserta
Grande

25W
Sto Antão
S Luzia
S Vincente   Sal
S Nicolau
CAPE VERDE   Boa
Fogo   S Tiago   Vista
Brava   Praia   Maio
at the same scale   **15N**

1:15M
0   200   400   600 km
0   100   200   300 mls

Pagalu
(Equat. Guinea)

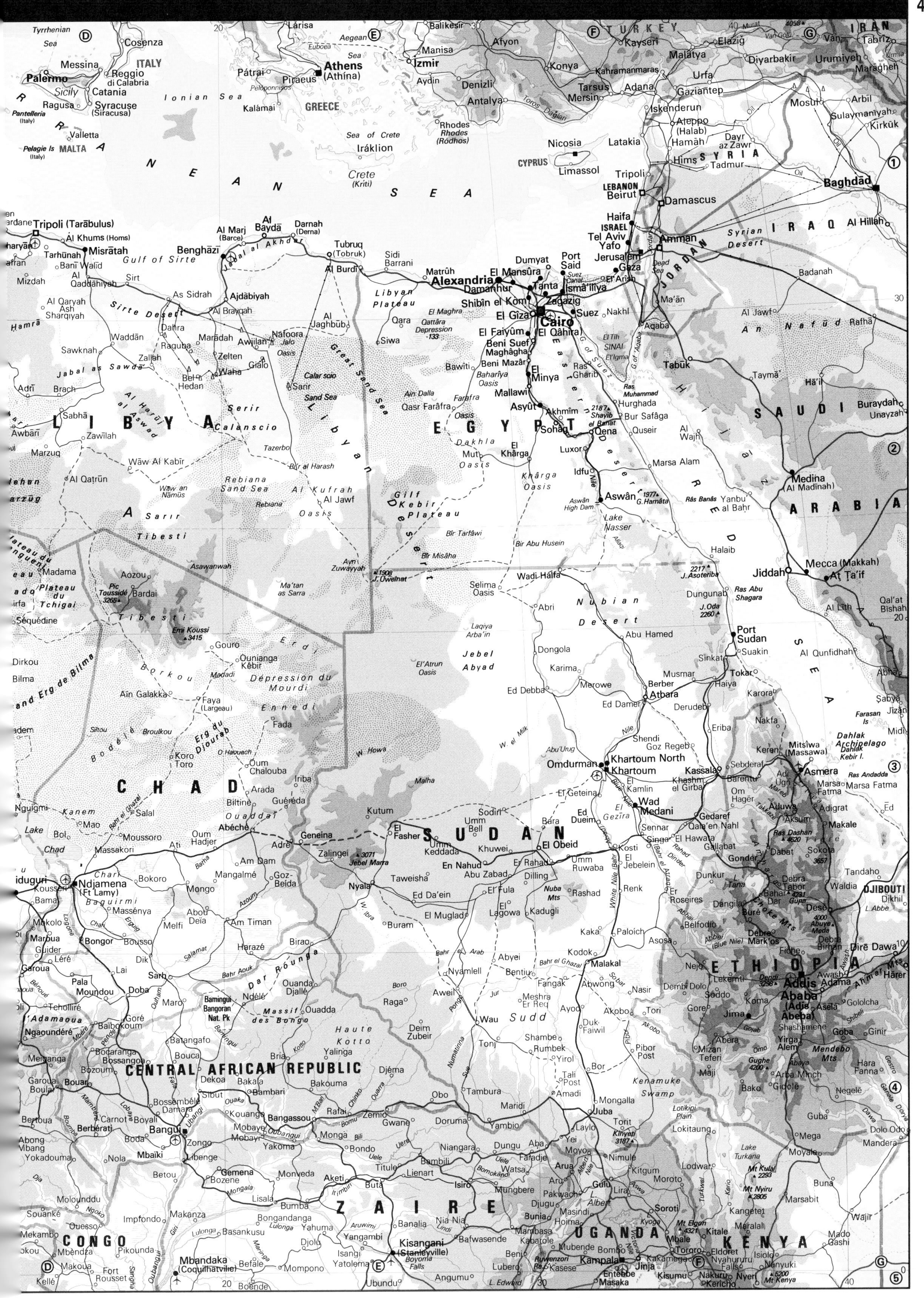

Tyrrhenian Sea
Cosenza
ITALY
Messina
Palermo
Reggio di Calabria
Sicily
Catania
Ragusa
Syracuse (Siracusa)
Pantelleria (Italy)
Valletta
Pelagie Is (Italy)
MALTA
Lárisa
Aegean Sea
Euboea
Athens (Athína)
Pátrai
Piraeus
Peloponnisos
Ionian Sea
Kalámai
GREECE
Balikesir
Manisa
Izmir
Aydin
Afyon
Denizli
Antalya
Konya
TURKEY
Kayseri
Malatya
Elazig
Diyarbakir
Kahramanmaras
Urfa
Gaziantep
Tarsus
Adana
Mersin
Iskenderun
Aleppo (Halab)
Hamah
Dayr az Zawr
Hims
SYRIA
Tadmur
Latakia
Tripoli
LEBANON
Beirut
Damascus
Nicosia
CYPRUS
Limassol
Rhodes
Rhodes (Ródhos)
Sea of Crete
Iráklion
Crete (Kríti)
MEDITERRANEAN SEA
IRAN
Van
Tabriz
Urumiyeh
Maragheh
Mosul
Arbil
Sulaymaniyah
Kirkuk
Baghdad
IRAQ
Al Hillah
Syrian Desert
Haifa
ISRAEL
Tel Aviv Yafo
Jerusalem
Amman
JORDAN
Dead Sea
Gaza
El Arish
Ma'an
Aqaba
Badanah
Al Jawf
An Nafud
Rafha
Tabuk
Tayma
Ha'il
SAUDI ARABIA
Buraydah
Unayzah
Medina (Al Madinah)
Yanbu al Bahr
Mecca (Makkah)
At Ta'if
Jiddah
Al Lith
Qal'at Bishah
Al Qunfidhah
Abha
Sabya
Jizan
Farasan Is
Midi
Al Wajh
HIJAZ
RED SEA
Tripoli (Tarabulus)
Al Khums (Homs)
Misratah
Tarhunah
Bani Walid
Al Qaddahiyah
Sirt
Mizdah
Gulf of Sirte
Benghazi
Al Marj (Barce)
Al Bayda
Darnah (Derna)
Jabal al Akhdar
Tubruq (Tobruk)
Al Burdi
Sidi Barrani
As Sidrah
Ajdabiyah
Al Brayqah
Al Qaryah Ash Sharqiyah
Sirte Desert
Hamra
Waddan
Dahra
Raguba
Maradah
Awjilah
Nafoora
Jalo Oasis
Zelten
Sawknah
Zallah
Jabal as Sawda
Wah
Gialo
Bel Hedan
Adri
Brach
Sabha
Awbari
LIBYA
Zawilah
Marzuq
Al Qatrun
Waw Al Kabir
Al Harui al Aswad
Serir Calanscio
Tazerbo
Bir al Harash
Rebiana Sand Sea
Rebiana
Al Kufrah Oasis
Al Jawf
Sarir Tibesti
Waw an Namus
Al Jaghbub
Calanscio
Sarir
Sand Sea
Great Sand Sea
Libyan Desert
Matrûh
Alexandria
Damanhur
El Mansura
Dumyat
Port Said
Suez Canal
Tanta
Isma'iliya
Zagazig
Shibin el Kom
El Giza
Cairo (El Qahira)
Suez
Nakhl
El Tih
SINAI
El 'Igma
G. of Suez
G. of 'Aqaba
Libyan Plateau
El Maghra
Qattara Depression -133
Qara
Siwa
El Faiyum
Beni Suef
Maghagha
Beni Mazar
Bawiti
Bahariya Oasis
El Minya
Ras Gharib
Mallawi
Ain Dalla
Qasr Farafra
Farafra Oasis
Asyut
Akhmim
Sohag
Qena
2187 Shayib el Banat
Ras Muhammad
Hurghada
Bur Safaga
Quseir
EGYPT
Dakhla Oasis
Mut
El Kharga
Kharga Oasis
Luxor
Idfu
Nile
Aswan
Aswan High Dam
1977 G. Hamata
Ras Banas
Marsa Alam
Eastern Desert
Gilf Kebir Plateau
Bir Tarfawi
Bir Misaha
Bir Abu Husein
Lake Nasser
Allaqi
Ayn Zuwayyah
1908 J. Uwelnat
Ma'tan as Sarra
Selima Oasis
Wadi Halfa
2217 J. Asoteriba
Halaib
Dungunab
Ras Abu Shagara
J. Oda 2260
Abri
Nubian Desert
Abu Hamed
Port Sudan
Suakin
Laqiya Arba'in
Jebel Abyad
Dongola
Karima
Merowe
El'Atrun Oasis
Sinkat
Tokar
Musmar
Berber
Atbara
Haiya
Ed Debba
Ed Damer
Derudeb
Karora
Nakfa
Eriba
Shendi
Goz Regeb
Keren
Mitsiwa (Massawa)
Dahlak Archipelago
Dahlak Kebir I.
Abu 'Urug
W. el Milk
W. Howa
Omdurman
Khartoum North
Khartoum
Kassala
Sebderat
Barentu
Asmera
Ras Andadda
Marsa Fatma
Adi Ugri
Om Hager
Adigrat
Aduwa
Aksum
Ed
El Geteina
Kamlin
Khashm el Girba
Wad Medani
Gezira
Blue Nile
Ed Dueim
Gedaref
Qala'en Nahl
Sennar
Singa
El Hawata
Gallabat
Makale
Ras Dashan 4620
Dabat
Sokota
3657
Gonder
Tana
Bahar Dar
Debra Tabor
4231 Guna
Dangila
Bure
Debre Mark'os
Blue Nile
Choke Mts
4000 Abuye Meda
Dese
Tandaho
Waldia
DJIBOUTI
Dikhil
L. Abbe
Debra Birhan
Dire Dawa
Harer
Ahmar Mts
Awash
Adama
Addis Ababa (Adis Abeba)
Dendi 3256
Asela
Gololcha
Shashamene
Goba
Ginir
Mendebo Mts
Yirga Alem
Hara Panna
Gestro
Arba Minch
Gidole
Guhe 4200
Neqele
Genale Dorya
Bako
Guba
Mega
Dolo Odo
Mandera
Moyale
ETHIOPIA
Ambo
Jima
Koma
Gore
Lekemti
Dembi Dolo
Nejo
Asosa
Fiche
Sodo
Gojeb
Omo
Abera
Mizan Teferi
Maji
Ahmara
Er Roseires
Belfodio
Dunkur
Kurmuk
Renk
Jebelein
Kosti
White Nile
Umm Ruwaba
El Obeid
SUDAN
Bara
Umm Bell
Sodiri
Kutum
Malha
El Fasher
Umm Keddada
Khuwei
En Nahud
Er Rahad
Abu Zabad
Dilling
Taweisha
El Fula
Nuba Mts
Rashad
Kadugli
El Lagowa
El Muglad
Ed Da'ein
Buram
Nyala
Jebel Marra 3071
Zalingei
Geneina
Adre
Kaka
Paloich
Kodok
Malakal
Sobat
Nasir
Abwong
Fangak
Bentiu
Bahr el Ghazal
Bahr el Arab
Abyei
Nyamlell
Aweil
Meshra Er Req
Raga
Wau
Sudd
Ayod
Akobo
Tori
Duk Faiwil
Pibor Post
Shambe
Rumbek
Yirol
Tonj
Deim Zubeir
Bor
Tali Post
Amadi
Tambura
Maridi
Kenamuke Swamp
Lotikipi Plain
Mongalla
Juba
Torit
Kinyeti 3187
Lokitaung
Lake Turkana
Mt Kulal 2293
Mt Nyiru 2805
Marsabit
Buna
Wajir
Lodwar
Moroto
Kitgum
Nimule
Yei
Moyo
Laylo
Gulu
Lira
Soroti
Kangetet
Maralal
Kitale
Mt Elgon 4321
Mbale
Tororo
Eldoret
Nyahururu Falls
Isiolo
Nanyuki
5200 Mt Kenya
Nakuru
Kericho
Nyeri
Kisumu
UGANDA
KENYA
Mado Gashi
Kampala
Entebbe
Jinja
Kakamega
Masaka
Ruwenzori
Kasese
Mubende
Bombo
Hoima
Masindi
L. Albert
Bunia
Djugu
Pakwach
Arua
Aru
Faradje
Watsa
Dungu
Aba
Yambio
Doruma
Niangara
Isiro
Bambili
Mungbere
Mambasa
Beni
Lubero
L. Edward
Kabatole
Bafwasende
Banalia
Nia Nia
Kisangani (Stanleyville)
Boyoma Falls
Angumu
Ubundu
Lienart
Buta
Titule
Bondo
Akeli
Bumba
Lisala
Monveda
Gemena
Bozene
Libenge
Zongo
Mobaye
Mobayi
Yakoma
Bangassou
Gwane
Zemio
Rafai
Obo
Djéma
Bakouma
Yalinga
Bria
Kotto
Haute Kotto
Ouadda
Massif des Bongo
Bamingui Bangoran Nat. Pk
Ndélé
Ouanda Djallé
Dar Rounga
Birao
CENTRAL AFRICAN REPUBLIC
Bouca
Batangafo
Kaga Bandoro
Dekoa
Bakala
Bambari
Sibut
Bossembélé
Damara
Bangui
Kouango
Boda
Mbaïki
Carnot
Boyali
Berbérati
Bouar
Bozoum
Bossangoa
Bodaranga
Meiganga
Garoua Boulai
Bertoua
Abong Mbang
Yokadouma
Nola
Ngaoundéré
Adamaoua
Tcholliré
Baibokoum
Goré
Maro
Doba
Moundou
Pala
Sarh
Lai
Kélo
Bongor
Bousso
Melfi
Am Timan
Abou Deïa
Mongo
Salamat
Harazé
Dik
Guider
Léré
Garoua
Bénoué
Marqua
Mokolo
Kousseri
Maiduguri
Ndjamena (Ft Lamy)
Chari
Baguirmi
Massénya
Bokoro
Bama
Mangalmé
Goz Beida
Am Dam
Oum Hadjer
Ati
Abéché
Ouaddai
Biltine
Guéréda
Iriba
Arada
Mao
Kanem
Bol
Lake Chad
Moussoro
Massakori
Bahr el Ghazal
Salal
Nguigmi
CHAD
Koro Toro
Oum Chalouba
O. Haouach
Erg du Djourab
Bodélé
Broulkou
Siltou
Fada
Ennedi
Faya (Largeau)
Aïn Galakka
Dépression du Mourdi
Ounianga Kébir
Madadi
Borkou
Gouro
Erdi
Emi Koussi 3415
Tibesti
Bardai
Pic Toussidé 3265
Aozou
Asawanwah
Madama
Plateau du Tchigai
Plateau du Manguéni
Séguédine
Dirkou
Bilma
Grand Erg de Bilma
Kousseri
Sangha
Ubangi
CONGO
Souanké
Moloundou
Ouesso
Mekambo
Mbendza
Makoua
Fort Rousset
Kellé
Impfondo
Makanza
Bongandanga
Lulonga
Basankusu
Yahuma
Djolu
Yangambi
Isangi
Yatolema
Mompono
Befale
Mbandaka (Coquilhatville)
Boende
ZAIRE

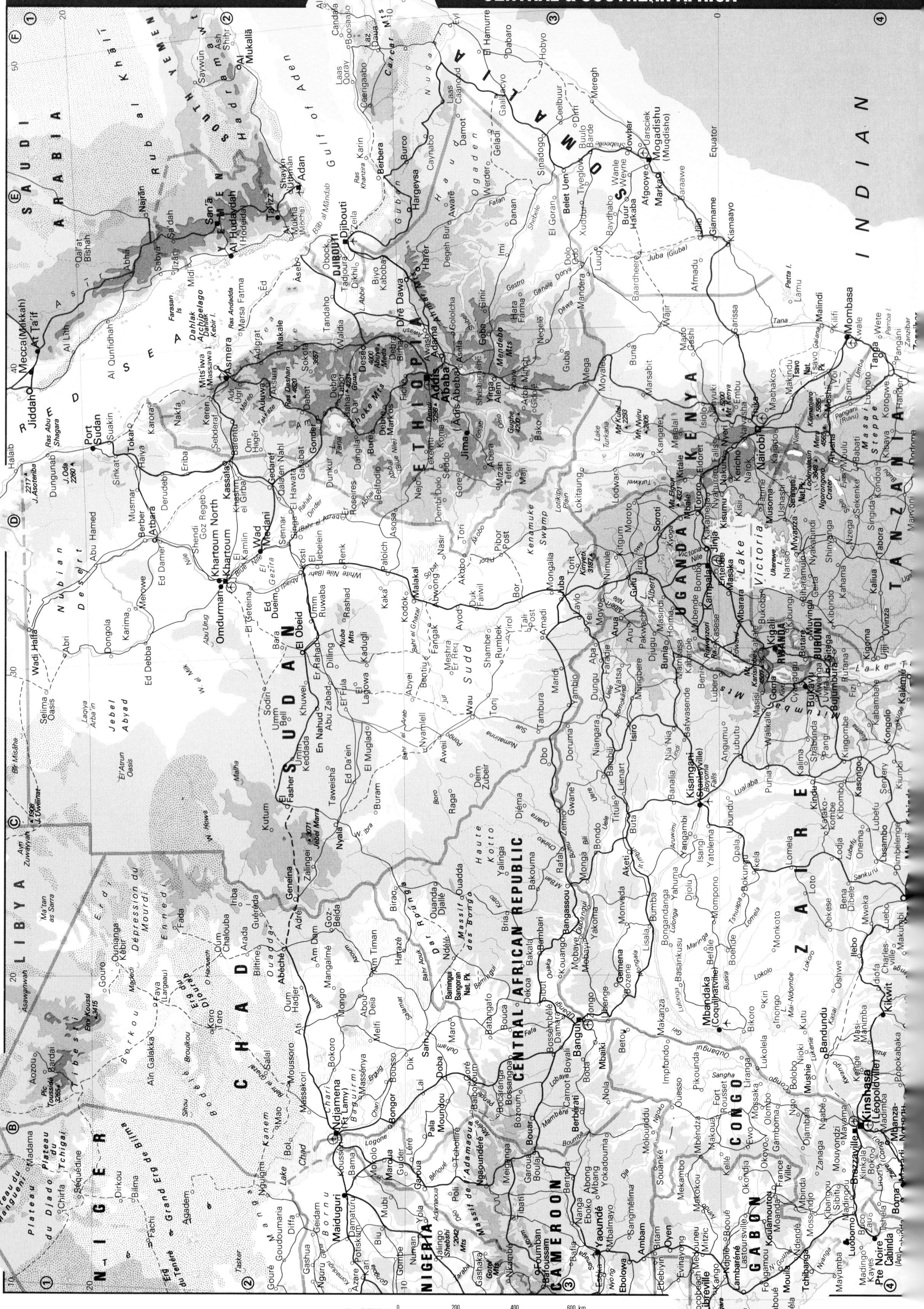

SAUDI ARABIA

YEMEN

SOUTH YEMEN

Mecca (Mekkah)
At Ta'if
Jiddah
Jiddah
San'a
Al Hudaydah
Ta'izz
Aden
Adan

Gulf of Aden

RED SEA

SUDAN

Khartoum
Omdurman
Khartoum North
Port Sudan
Atbara
El Obeid

ETHIOPIA

Asmera
Addis Ababa
Adama
Dire Dawa
Harer
Makale

DJIBOUTI

SOMALIA

Mogadishu (Muqdisho)
Berbera
Kismaayo

KENYA

Nairobi
Mombasa
Malindi

UGANDA

Kampala
Entebbe
Jinja

Lake Victoria

RWANDA
Kigali

BURUNDI
Bujumbura

TANZANIA

CHAD

N'djamena (Ft. Lamy)

NIGER

LIBYA

NIGERIA

Maiduguri

CAMEROON

Yaoundé

CENTRAL AFRICAN REPUBLIC

Bangui

GABON

Libreville
Port Gentil

CONGO

Brazzaville

ZAIRE

Kinshasa (Léopoldville)
Kisangani (Stanleyville)
Mbandaka (Coquilhatville)

INDIAN

Equator

1:15M

0 200 400 600 km
0 100 200 300 mls

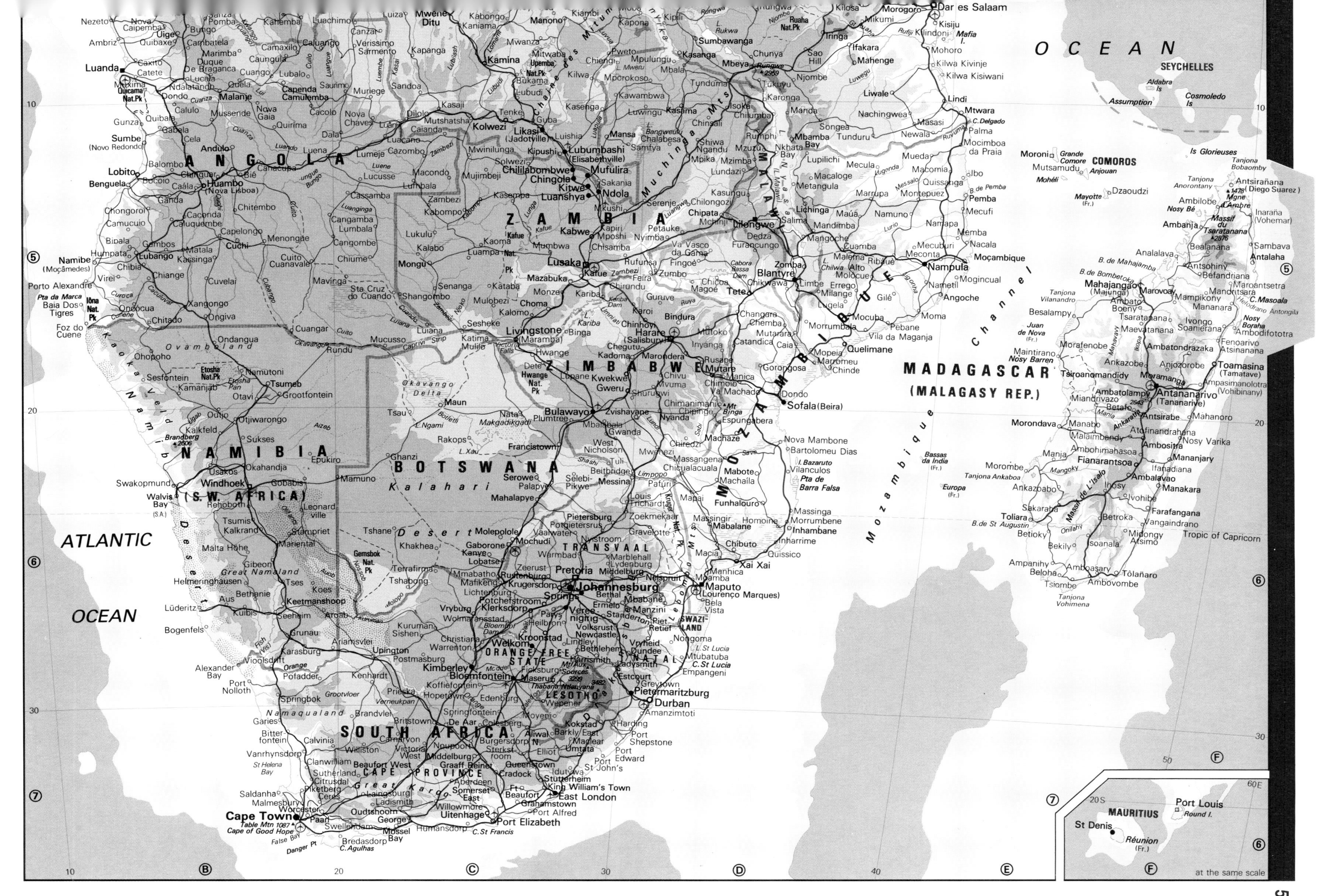

OCEAN
ATLANTIC
OCEAN
ANGOLA
ZAMBIA
MALAWI
ZIMBABWE
MOZAMBIQUE
BOTSWANA
Kalahari
Desert
NAMIBIA
(S.W. AFRICA)
Namib Desert
TRANSVAAL
ORANGE FREE STATE
NATAL
SWAZILAND
LESOTHO
SOUTH AFRICA
CAPE PROVINCE
MADAGASCAR
(MALAGASY REP.)
Mozambique Channel
COMOROS
SEYCHELLES
MAURITIUS
Tropic of Capricorn
Luanda
Lobito
Benguela
Huambo
(Nova Lisboa)
Lubumbashi
(Elisabethville)
Lusaka
Ndola
Kitwe
Lilongwe
Blantyre
Harare
(Salisbury)
Bulawayo
Livingstone
Windhoek
Walvis Bay
Gaborone
Pretoria
Johannesburg
Maputo
(Lourenço Marques)
Sofala (Beira)
Bloemfontein
Kimberley
Pietermaritzburg
Durban
East London
Port Elizabeth
Cape Town
Dar es Salaam
Nampula
Quelimane
Moroni
Mahajanga
Antananarivo
(Tananarive)
Toamasina
(Tamatave)
Fianarantsoa
Toliara
Port Louis
St Denis
Réunion (Fr.)
at the same scale

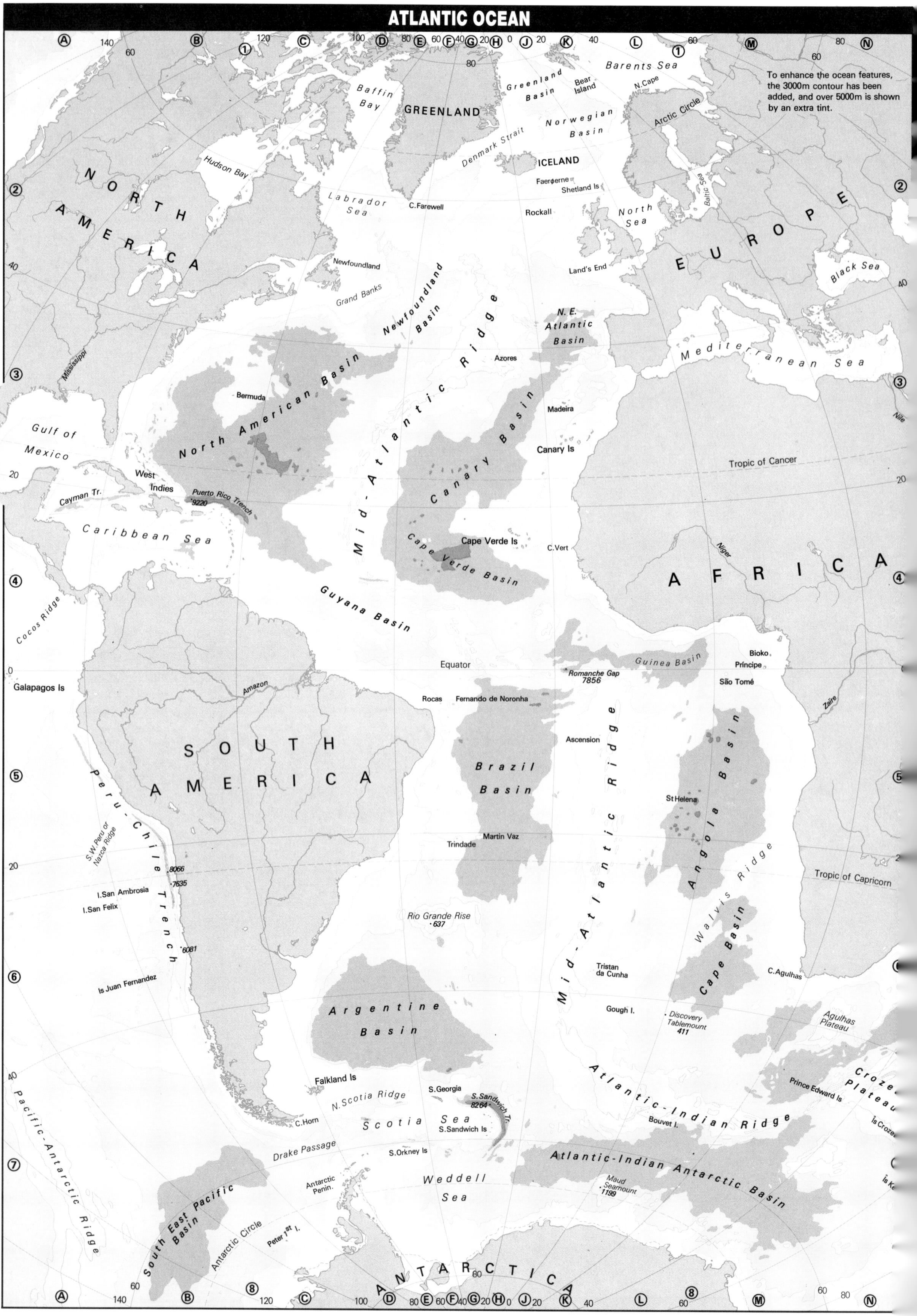

Ⓐ 140 Ⓑ 120 Ⓒ 100 Ⓓ 80 Ⓔ 60 Ⓕ 40 Ⓖ 20 Ⓗ 0 Ⓙ 20 Ⓚ 40 Ⓛ 60 Ⓜ 80 Ⓝ

To enhance the ocean features, the 3000m contour has been added, and over 5000m is shown by an extra tint.

Barents Sea

Baffin Bay

GREENLAND

Greenland Basin

Bear Island

N.Cape

Arctic Circle

① 80 ①

Denmark Strait

Norwegian Basin

ICELAND

Faerøerne

Shetland Is

North Sea

Ⓐ ② *Hudson Bay* ②

N O R T H

A M E R I C A

Labrador Sea

C.Farewell

Rockall

Land's End

E U R O P E

Baltic Sea

40 40

Black Sea

Newfoundland

Grand Banks

Newfoundland Basin

N.E. Atlantic Basin

Mediterranean Sea

Mississippi

③ Bermuda *North American Basin* Azores ③

Mid-Atlantic Ridge

Madeira

Gulf of Mexico

20 West Indies

Cayman Tr.

Canary Basin

Canary Is

20

Puerto Rico Trench 9220

Caribbean Sea

Cape Verde Is

Cape Verde Is

C.Vert

A F R I C A

Ⓐ ④ Cocos Ridge *Cape Verde Basin* ④

Niger

Guyana Basin

Bioko

Príncipe

Equator *Guinea Basin* São Tomé

0 Galapagos Is 0

Amazon

Rocas Fernando de Noronha

Zaire

Peru or Nazca Ridge

Ascension

S O U T H

A M E R I C A

Brazil Basin

Mid-Atlantic Ridge

⑤ St Helena *Angola Basin* ⑤

Peru-Chile Trench

Martin Vaz

Trindade

8066

7635

Walvis Ridge

20 I.San Ambrosia 20

I.San Felix *Rio Grande Rise* 637

Tristan da Cunha

Cape Basin

C.Agulhas

6081

Is Juan Fernandez

⑥ *Argentine* Gough I. ⑥

Basin

Discovery Tablemount 411

Agulhas Plateau

Falkland Is

S.Georgia

Crozet Plateau

40 N.Scotia Ridge S.Sandwich Tr. Prince Edward Is 40

C.Horn *Scotia* 8264 Is Crozet

Sea S.Sandwich Is

Bouvet I.

Drake Passage S.Orkney Is *Atlantic-Indian Ridge*

⑦ *Pacific-Antarctic Ridge* *Weddell* *Atlantic-Indian Antarctic Basin* ⑦

Antarctic *Sea*

Penin. Maud Seamount Is Ke

1159

South East Pacific Basin

Peter Ist I.

Antarctic Circle

A N T A R C T I C A

Ⓐ 140 Ⓑ 120 Ⓒ 100 Ⓓ 80 Ⓔ 60 Ⓕ 40 Ⓖ 20 Ⓗ 0 Ⓙ 20 Ⓚ 40 Ⓛ 60 Ⓜ 80 Ⓝ

⑧ 60 ⑧

1:60M 0 600 1200 1800 2400 km

0 600 1200 mls

Arctic Ocean

U.S.S.R.

Chukchi Sea

Bering Strait

Bering Sea

Beaufort Sea

GREENLAND
(Denmark)

Aleutian Islands

A l a s k a

Yukon

Prudhoe Bay

Inuvik

Queen Elizabeth Islands

Banks I.

Victoria I.

Ellesmere I.

Thule

Devon I.

Resolute

ICELAND

Reykjavik

Denmark Strait

Anchorage

Fairbanks

Dawson

Whitehorse

Alexander Arch.

Juneau

Great Bear L.

Mackenzie

Baffin Bay

Baffin I.

Q. Charlotte Is.

Prince Rupert

Prince George

Arctic Circle

Yellowknife

Great Slave L.

Hay River

Southampton I.

Hudson Strait

Labrador Sea

C A N A D A

Vancouver I.

Fraser

Dawson Creek

Peace

Uranium City

Athabasca

Athabasca

L. Athabasca

Churchill

Hudson Bay

Inukjuac

Schefferville

Churchill Falls

Goose Bay

Newfoundland

Victoria

Vancouver

Seattle

Columbia

Portland

Edmonton

Calgary

Saskatchewan

Saskatoon

Regina

Medicine Hat

Spokane

Great Falls

Butte

Snake

L. Winnipeg

Winnipeg

Kenora

James Bay

Moosonee

Chibougamau

Sept-Iles

Anticosti I.

St John's

Charlottetown

San Francisco

Sacramento

Reno

Salt Lake City

Colorado

Denver

Missouri

Fargo

Duluth

Thunder Bay

L. Superior

Sault Ste Marie

Sudbury

L. Huron

Québec

Moncton

St. John

Fredericton

Halifax

Minneapolis

St Paul

Omaha

Milwaukee

Chicago

L. Michigan

Detroit

Toronto

Ottawa

L. Ontario

L. Erie

Buffalo

Boston

U N I T E D   S T A T E S

Los Angeles

San Bernardino

San Diego

Tijuana

Phoenix

Tucson

Albuquerque

Pueblo

Arkansas

Kansas City

St Louis

Wichita

Indianapolis

Cleveland

Ohio

Cincinatti

Baltimore

Philadelphia

Washington

New York

Newport News

Norfolk

O F   A M E R I C A

Amarillo

Oklahoma City

Red

Nashville

Memphis

Mississippi

Birmingham

Atlanta

Charleston

Savannah

ATLANTIC OCEAN

Bermuda (U.K.)

Tropic of Cancer

Guadalupe (Mex.)

G. de California

Ciudad Juárez

El Paso

Fort Worth

Dallas

Jackson

Mobile

Tallahassee

Jacksonville

Hermosillo

Chihuahua

San Antonio

Austin

Baton Rouge

New Orleans

M E X I C O

Monterrey

Torreón

Corpus Christi

Houston

Tampa

Miami

THE BAHAMAS

Nassau

Sargasso Sea

Mazatlán

Durango

Gulf of Mexico

Habana

CUBA

Guantánamo

DOMINICAN REP.

Pto Rico (U.S.A.)

San Juan

ANTIGUA & BARBUDA

Revilla Gigedo Is. (Mex.)

Tampico

Rio Grande

Mérida

HAITI

Port-au-Prince

Santo Domingo

St Kitts - Nevis

Guadalajara

Mexico

Veracruz

JAMAICA

Kingston

DOMINICA

ST LUCIA

BARBADOS

ST VINCENT

Acapulco

BELIZE

Belmopan

CARIBBEAN SEA

GRENADA

TRINIDAD & TOBAGO

Netherlands Antilles

P A C I F I C

GUATEMALA

Guatemala

S.Salvador

EL SALVADOR

HONDURAS

Tegucigalpa

NICARAGUA

Managua

Sta Marta

Barranquilla

Maracaibo

Caracas

Cd Guayana

Clipperton (Fr.)

O C E A N

COSTA RICA

S.José

PANAMA

Panamá

Medellín

Orinoco

V E N E Z U E L A

I.del Coco (C.R)

Malpelo (Col.)

Bueraventura

Quito

Bogotá

C O L O M B I A

Cáli

Negro

Equator

Galapagos Is (Ecu.)

ECUADOR

PERU

B R A Z I L

1:35M

0   250   500   750   1000   1250 km

0   250   500   750mls

Names underlined indicate
Province/State capitals

1:15M

McClintock B.
C. Evans
Nyeboes Land
Kap asker
Seydisfjörður
Eskiföll

Axel Heiberg Island
Empire Land
Alert
Hazen Land
Grönnes
H'safjörður
Siglufjörður
Blönduós
Akureyri
Húsavík

United States Ra.
Washington Land
Daugaard Jensen Land
Hornafjördur
Vatneyri
Borgarnes
Langjökull
Þórshöfn

Eureka
Fosheim Pen.
Greely Fjord
Darling Pen.
Kane Basin
Inglefield Land
Humboldt Gletscher
ICELAND
Stykkishólmur
Reykjavík
Keflavík
Selfoss
Vík
Vestmannaeyjar

Graham I.
Otto Fj.
Roanes Pen.
Johan Pen.
Etah
Prudhoe Ld
Hayes Pen.
Haffners Bjerg ▲1433
Steenstrups Gletscher
H01 ▲3231

GriseFjord
Coburg I.
Glacier Str.
Mackinson Inlet
K. Parry
Thule
Dundas
Melville Bugt
K. York
Knud Rasmussens Land
Roland
Kap Gustav Holm

Jones Sound
Lady Ann Str.
C. Sherard
C. Liverpool
Nûgssuaq
Kraulshavn
Upernavik
Prøven
Svartenhuk Halvø
Kong Christian IX Land
Scoresby Sd
Gunbjörn Fjeld ▲3380
Mt Forel ▲3360
Ammassalik (Angmagssalik)
Dannebrog Ø

Devon Island ▲1887
Philpots Pen.
Lancaster Sound
Bylot I. ▲1889
Pond Inlet
C. Macculloch
Nûgssuaq
Umanak
Sarqaq
Uvkusigssat
Ubekendt Ejland
Disko
Rittenbenk
Pîkiutdleq

BAFFIN BAY
Arctic Bay
Brodeur Peninsula
Borden Peninsula
Eclipse Sound
Buchan Gulf
Scott Inlet
C. Christian
C. Raper
Qutdligssat
Diskofjord
Godhavn
Disko Bugt
Jakobshavn
Christianshåb
Egedesminde
Kangâtsiaq
Agto
Sukkertoppen ▲1737
Napassoq
Atangmik
Gyldenlöves Fjord
Skjoldungen
Tingmiarmiut

Brodeur Peninsula
Admiralty Inlet
Henry Kater Pen.
Horne Bay
Holsteinsborg
Itivdleq
Kangâmiut
Sukkertoppen
Gotthåb (Nuuk)
Færingehavn
Kap Cort Adelaer

Barnes Icecap
Clyde
Penny Highlands ▲2591
Cumberland Peninsula
Pangnirtung
C. Dyer
Kobberminebugt
Nunatakker
Fiskenæsset
Frederikshåb

Jens Munk I.
Koch I.
Bray I.
Rowley I.
Foley I.
Spencer I.
Prince Charles I.
Airforce I.
Cumberland Sound
C. Mercy
Cyrus Field B.
Loks Land
Narssaq
Kap Farvel
Cape Farewell (Kap Farvel)
Narssaq
Julianehåb (Qaqortoq)
Narssarssuaq
Prins Christian Sund

Igloolik
Hall Beach
Parry B.
C. Wilson
Nettilling Lake
Amadjuak Lake
Hall Peninsula
Lemieux Is
Meta Incognito Peninsula
Frobisher Bay
Lake Harbour
Edgell I.
Oagssimiut
Nanortalik

Melville Peninsula
Foxe Basin
C. Dominion
C. Dorchester
Nuvukjuak
Cape Dorset
Salisbury I.
Nottingham I.
Big I.
C. de la Nouvelle France
Frobisher Bay
Resolution I.
Button Is
C. Chidley

Repulse Bay
Committee
Simpson Pen.
Wales
Foxe Channel
Coral Harbour
Bell Pen.
Evans Str.
Southampton Island
Mansel I.
Ivujivik
Salluit
Kangiqsujuaq
Hopes Advance
Akpatok I.
N. Aulatsivik I.
Torngat Mts
Saglek B.
Hebron

Pelly Bay
Wager B.
Roes Welcome Sd
Fisher Str.
Coats I.
New Quebec Crater
Arnaud
Kangirsuk
Ungava Bay
Kangiqsualujjuaq
Nutak
S. Aulatsivik I.
Cod I.
Nain
Davis Inlet

Rae Isthmus
Chesterfield Inlet
Baker Foreland
C. Low
Nottingham I.
Kettlestone Bay
Smith I.
Povungnituk
Payne
R. aux Feuilles
Koksoak
Kuujjuaq
R. de la Baleine
George
Saglek
Hopedale
Makkovik
Whitegull L.
Davis Inlet

Rankin Inlet
Tavani
Maguse River
Eskimo Pt
Inukjuac
King George Is
Nastapoka Islands
L. Minto
Caniapiscau
L. Lower Seal
L. Upper Seal
L. Bienville
Schefferville
L. Caniapiscau
Rigolet
Hamilton Inlet
Cartwright
Domino
Port Hope Simpson
Battle Harbour

HUDSON BAY
Churchill
C. Churchill
C. Tatnam
Belcher Is
Poste-de-la-Baleine
C. Henrietta Maria
Long I.
Gde R.de-la Baleine
Kaniapiscow
Ashuanipi
Lac Joseph
Churchill Falls
Emeril
Wabush
Labrador City
Smallwood Resr
N.W. River
Goose Bay
Blanc Sablon
C. Bauld
St Anthony
Englee
Belle I.

York Factory
Hayes
Fort Severn
Severn
Winisk L.
Winisk
Nitchequon
Gde R. de la Baleine
Sakami
Gagnon
Natashquan R.
Harrington Har.
Daniel's Har.
Port au Choix
Port Saunders
St Barbe
White B.
Grey I.
Twillingate
Lewisporte
Botwood
NEWFOUNDLAND
Gander
Bonavista
St John's

Gods L.
Big Trout Lake
Attawapiskat
Fort George
James Bay
Akimiski I.
Eastmain
Charlton I.
Broadback
Rupert
Lac Mistassini
Lac Plétipi
Baie-du-Poste
Rés Manicouagan
Sept-Îles
Port Cartier
Anticosti Island
Gulf of Saint Lawrence
Gaspé
Gaspé Peninsula
Corner Brook
Stephenville
Channel Port aux Basques
C. Ray
Grand Bank
St Pierre
Placentia Bay
Carbonear
Avalon Pen.
Trepassey
C. Race

Cat Lake
Pikangikum L.
Pickle Lake
Fort Hope
Lansdowne House
Moosonee
Ft Rupert
Lac Evans
Chibougamau
Matagami
Rés Gouin
Senneterre
Dolbeau
Betsiamites
Baie-Comeau
Matane
Rimouski
Campbellton
Bathurst
Chatham
PRINCE EDWARD I.
Cape Breton I.
Glace Bay
Sydney
Magdalen Is
North
Port Hawkesbury

ONTARIO
Sioux Lookout
Savant Lake
Lac Seul
Auden
Nakina
Geraldton
Longlac
Hearst
Kapuskasing
Cochrane
Amos
Val-d'Or
Rouyn
Noranda
New Liskeard
La Sarre
Senneterre
Réservoir Cabonga
La Tuque
Québec
Lévis
Montmagny
Edmundston
Fredericton
Saint John
NEW BRUNSWICK
Amherst
Moncton
NOVA SCOTIA
Truro
New Glasgow
Charlottetown
Digby
Windsor

Dryden
Vermilion Bay
Ft Frances
Rainy L.
Atikokan
Thunder Bay
Isle Royale
N.P.I.
Marathon
Michipicoten
Wawa
Chapleau
Timmins
Kirkland Lake
Ville-Marie
Temiscaming
Mattawa
North Bay
Sudbury
Pembroke
Renfrew
Smiths Falls
Ottawa
Hull
Montréal
St Jérôme
Shawinigan
Trois Rivières
Joliette
Sorel
St Hyacinthe
Sherbrooke
Thetford Mines
Mont Laurier
Drummondville
MAINE
Bangor
Waterville
Augusta
Lewiston
Bath
Portland
Yarmouth
C. Sable
Liverpool
Bridgewater
Bay of Fundy
Halifax
Dartmouth
Sable I.
ATLANTIC OCEAN

LAKE SUPERIOR
Duluth
Superior
Apostle Is
Ironwood
Iron Mountain
Hancock
Marquette
Escanaba
Sault Ste Marie
Soo
Elliot Lake
Manitoulin I.
Sudbury
Nipissing
L. Nipissing
Tobermory
Owen Sd
Georgian Bay
Midland
Orillia
Peterborough
Cobourg
Belleville
Kingston
Watertown
Adirondack Mts
Lake Placid
Ogdensburg
Gloversville
Schenectady
Albany
Concord
Manchester
Lowell
Boston
Providence
New Bedford
Nantucket

Virginia
Hibbing
Bemidji
Grand Rapids
Rice Lake
St Cloud
Wausau
Rhinelander
WISCONSIN
Green Bay
Marinette
Menominee
Sheboygan
Manitowoc
MICHIGAN
Cadillac
Traverse City
Alpena
Saginaw
Bay City
Flint
Lansing
Grand Rapids
Kalamazoo
London
LAKE HURON
LAKE MICHIGAN
Toronto
L. Ontario
Hamilton
St Catharines
Buffalo
Rochester
Syracuse
Utica
Ithaca
Binghamton
Elmira
Scranton
NEW YORK
Hartford
CONN.
MASS.
Worcester
Springfield
Bridgeport
New Haven
Long Island
Newport

St Paul
Minneapolis
Faribault
Rochester
Austin
Mason City
La Crosse
Madison
Milwaukee
Racine
Kenosha
Chicago
Gary
Detroit
Windsor
L. Erie
Cleveland
Akron
VERMONT
NEW HAMPSHIRE
Burlington
Montpelier
Rutland

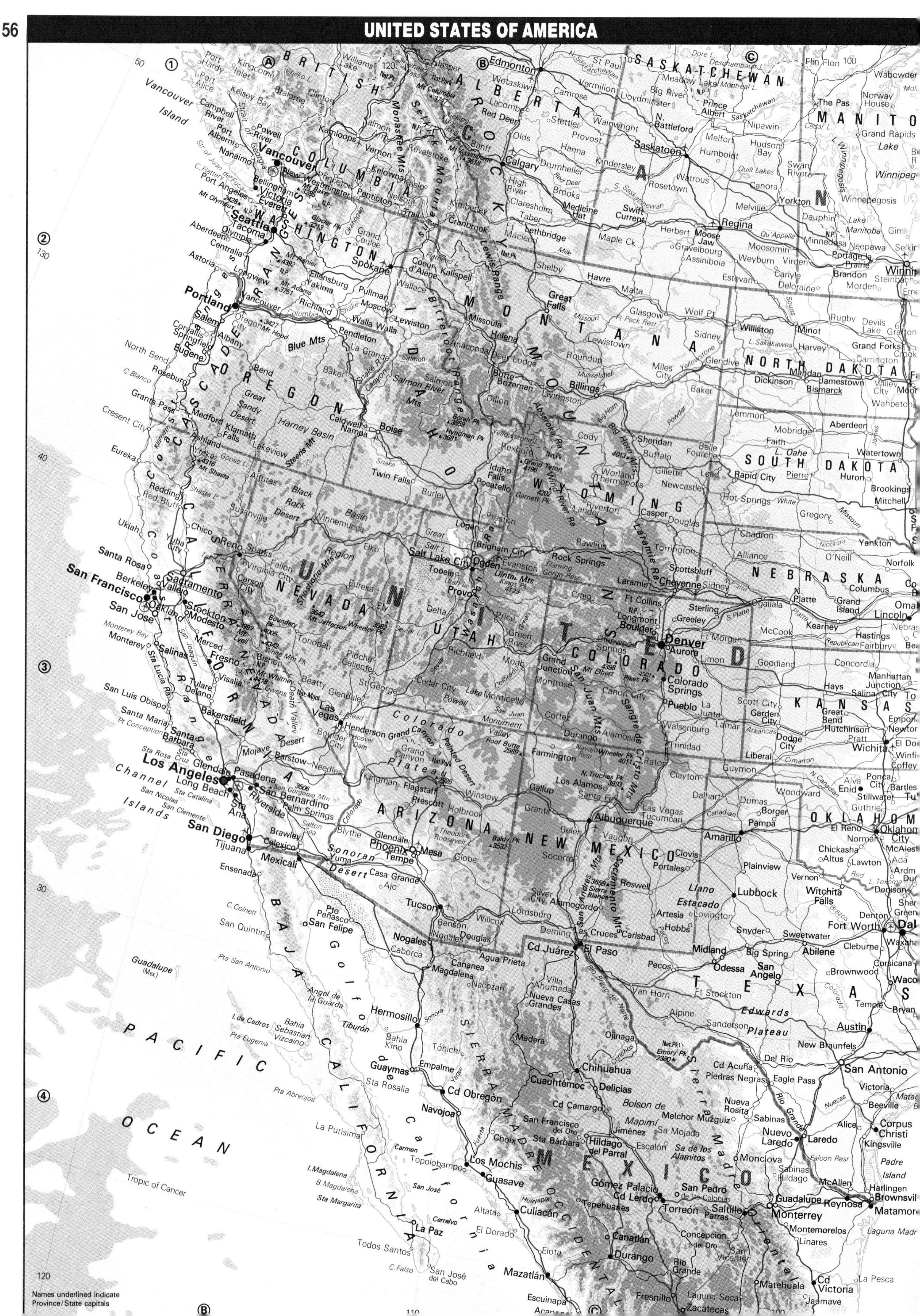

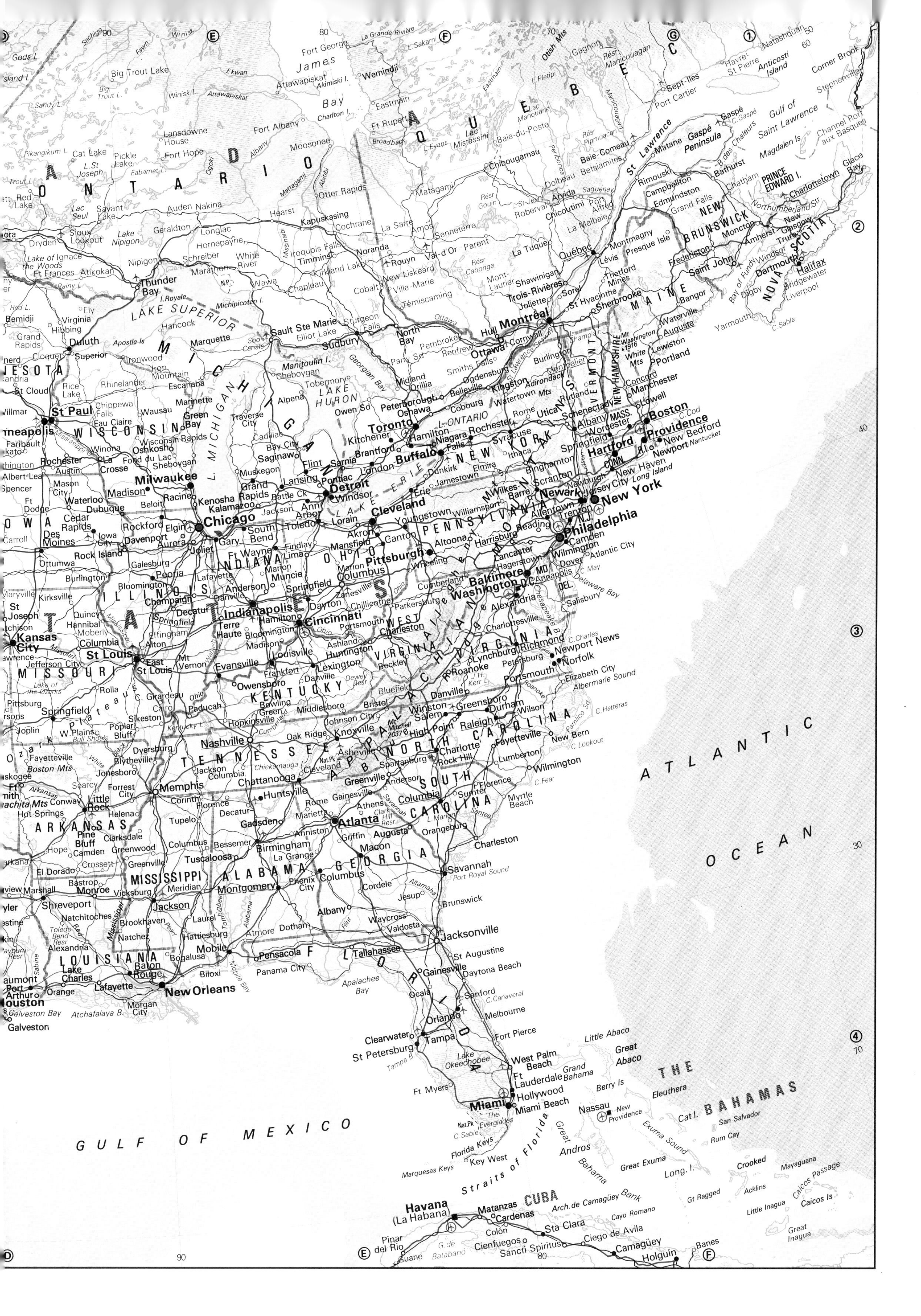

James Bay
Q U E B E C
O N T A R I O
LAKE SUPERIOR
LAKE HURON
L. ONTARIO
L. MICHIGAN
L A K E E R I E
Gulf of Saint Lawrence
St Lawrence
Gaspé Peninsula
Anticosti Island
PRINCE EDWARD I.
NEW BRUNSWICK
NOVA SCOTIA
MAINE
VERMONT
NEW HAMPSHIRE
MASS.
CONN.
R.I.
N.J.
MD
DEL.
D.C.
NEW YORK
PENNSYLVANIA
OHIO
INDIANA
ILLINOIS
WISCONSIN
MICHIGAN
IOWA
MISSOURI
KENTUCKY
TENNESSEE
WEST VIRGINIA
VIRGINIA
NORTH CAROLINA
SOUTH CAROLINA
GEORGIA
ALABAMA
MISSISSIPPI
ARKANSAS
LOUISIANA
FLORIDA
U N I T E D S T A T E S
APPALACHIAN MOUNTAINS
Blue Ridge
Ozark Plateau
Montréal
Québec
Ottawa
Toronto
Hamilton
Thunder Bay
Sudbury
Halifax
Saint John
Fredericton
Charlottetown
Boston
Providence
Hartford
New York
Philadelphia
Baltimore
Washington
Pittsburgh
Cleveland
Detroit
Buffalo
Chicago
Milwaukee
St Paul
Minneapolis
Indianapolis
Cincinnati
Columbus
Louisville
St Louis
Kansas City
Nashville
Memphis
Atlanta
Birmingham
Charlotte
Raleigh
Richmond
Norfolk
Columbia
Charleston
Savannah
Jacksonville
Tallahassee
Montgomery
Jackson
Little Rock
Baton Rouge
New Orleans
Mobile
Pensacola
Houston
Galveston
Orlando
Tampa
St Petersburg
Miami
Miami Beach
Key West
Florida Keys
A T L A N T I C O C E A N
G U L F O F M E X I C O
THE BAHAMAS
Great Abaco
Grand Bahama
Nassau
Andros
Eleuthera
Straits of Florida
CUBA
Havana (La Habana)
Matanzas
Cardenas
Sta Clara
Cienfuegos
Camagüey
Holguín
Banes
Pinar del Rio
Mt Mitchell 2037
Mt Washington 1916
C. Hatteras
C. Cod
C. Canaveral
C. Sable
Chesapeake Bay
Delaware Bay
Long Island
Albemarle Sound
Pamlico Sd
Okeechobee
The Everglades
90
80
70
60
50
40
30

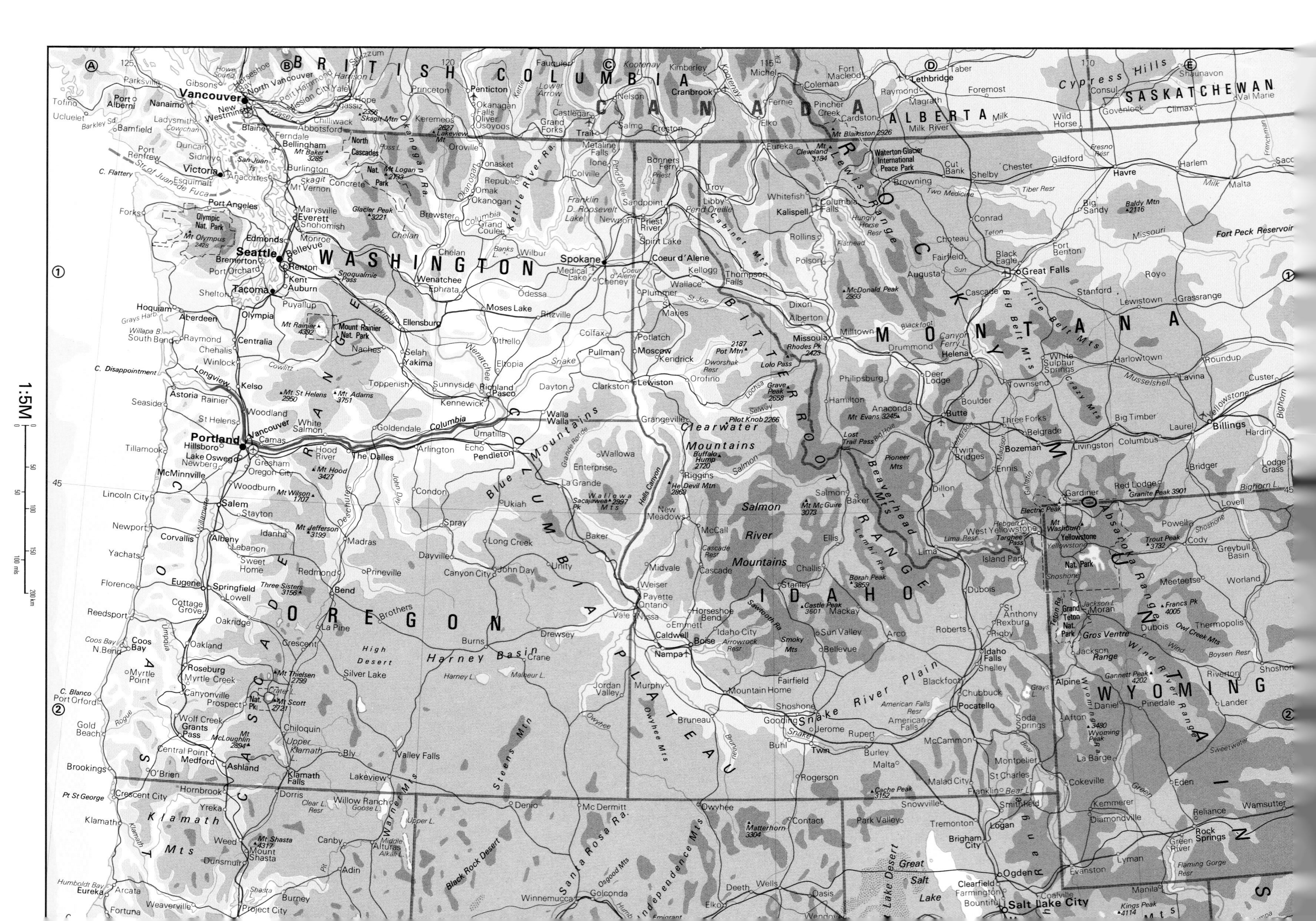

BRITISH COLUMBIA
CANADA
ALBERTA
SASKATCHEWAN
WASHINGTON
OREGON
IDAHO
MONTANA
WYOMING
ROCKY MOUNTAINS
COLUMBIA PLATEAU
CASCADE RANGE
COAST RANGES
BITTERROOT RANGE
Vancouver
Victoria
Seattle
Tacoma
Olympia
Spokane
Portland
Salem
Eugene
Boise
Helena
Great Falls
Billings
Butte
Missoula
Pocatello
Salt Lake City
Ogden
Great Salt Lake
Snake River Plain
Salmon River Mountains
Clearwater Mountains
Blue Mountains
Wind River Range
Absaroka Range
Yellowstone Nat. Park
Mount Rainier Nat. Park
Olympic Nat. Park
Klamath Mts
1:5M
0 50 100 150 200 km
0 50 100 mls

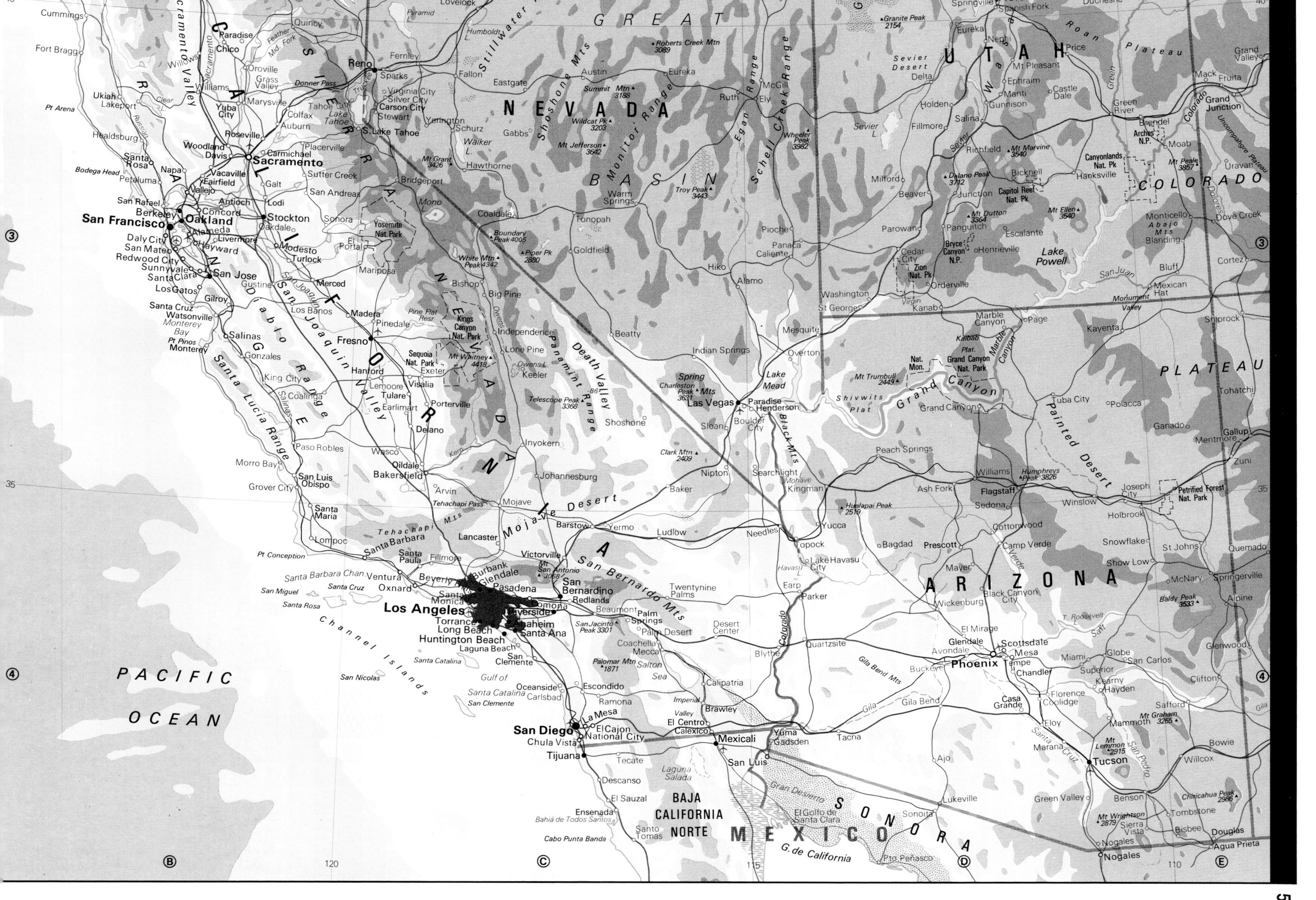

UTAH
NEVADA
CALIFORNIA
ARIZONA
COLORADO
MEXICO
BAJA CALIFORNIA NORTE
SONORA
GREAT BASIN
PLATEAU
SIERRA NEVADA
PACIFIC OCEAN
Mojave Desert
Painted Desert
Death Valley
San Joaquin Valley
Sacramento Valley
Diablo Range
Santa Lucia Range
Panamint Range
San Bernardino Mts
Shoshone Mts
Monitor Range
Schell Creek Range
Egan Range
Channel Islands
Lake Mead
Lake Powell
Grand Canyon
Salton Sea
G.de California
San Francisco
Oakland
San Jose
Sacramento
Stockton
Fresno
Bakersfield
Los Angeles
Long Beach
San Diego
Tijuana
Mexicali
Reno
Las Vegas
Phoenix
Tucson
Flagstaff
San Bernardino
Pasadena
Santa Barbara
Yuma
Nogales

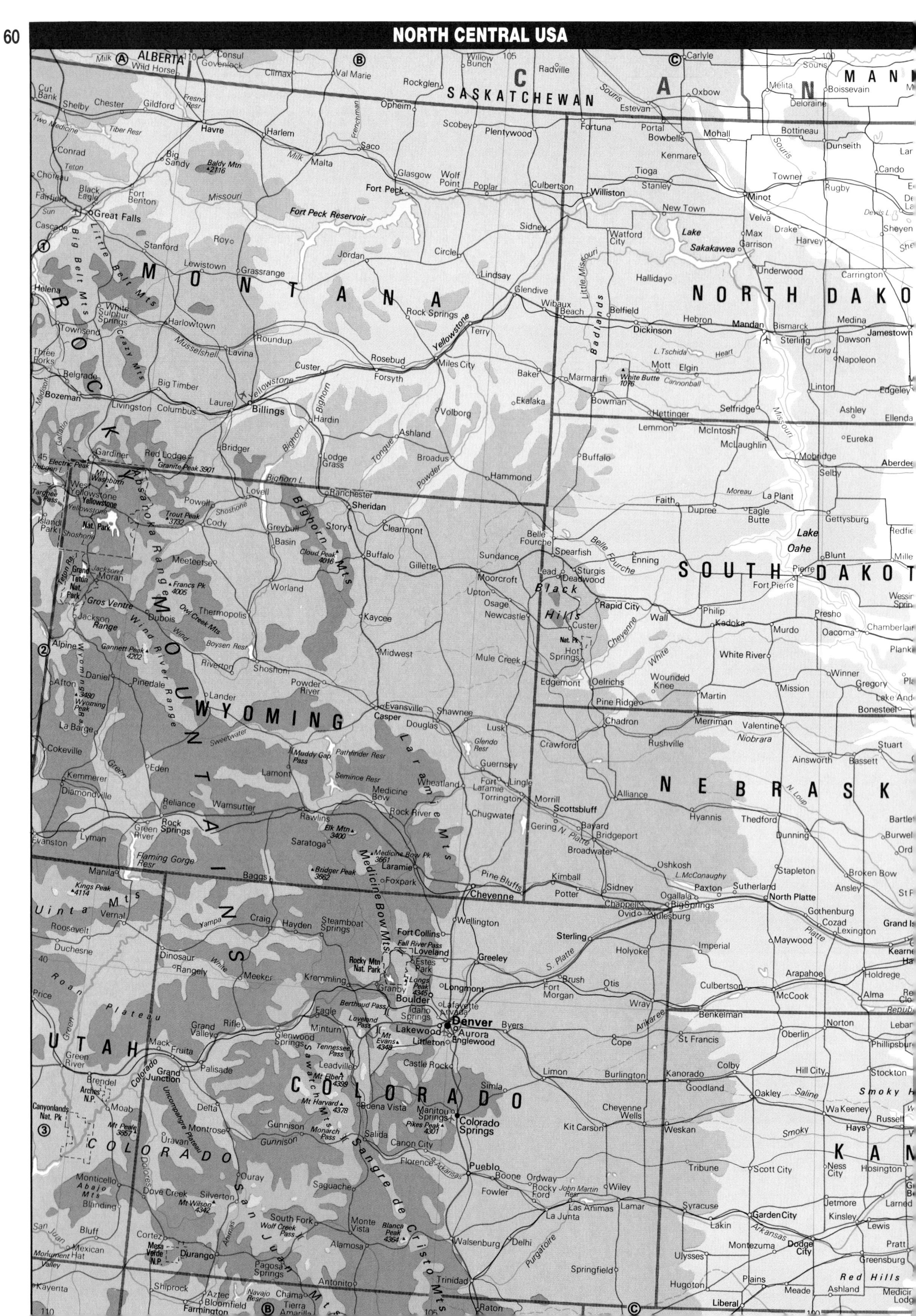
ALBERTA
SASKATCHEWAN
CANADA
MANITOBA
MONTANA
NORTH DAKOTA
SOUTH DAKOTA
NEBRASKA
WYOMING
COLORADO
UTAH
KANSAS
ROCKY MOUNTAINS
Milk
Consul
Govenlock
Wild Horse
Climax
Val Marie
Willow Bunch
Radville
Carlyle
Souris
Rockglen
Oxbow
Estevan
Melita
Boissevain
Deloraine
Cut Bank
Shelby
Chester
Gildford
Fresno Resr
Opheim
Scobey
Plentywood
Fortuna
Portal
Bowbells
Mohall
Bottineau
Dunseith
Two Medicine
Tiber Resr
Havre
Harlem
Frenchman
Saco
Kenmare
Cando
Conrad
Big Sandy
Baldy Mtn 2116
Milk
Malta
Tioga
Towner
Rugby
Teton
Choteau
Glasgow
Wolf Point
Stanley
Minot
Fairfield
Black Eagle
Fort Benton
Missouri
Fort Peck
Poplar
Culbertson
Williston
Sun
Great Falls
Fort Peck Reservoir
New Town
Velva
Devils L.
Cascade
Drake
Sheyenne
Max
Garrison
Lake Sakakawea
Harvey
Watford City
Sidney
Roy
Stanford
Jordan
Circle
Big Belt Mts
Little Belt Mts
Lewistown
Grassrange
Lindsay
Underwood
Carrington
Halliday
Helena
Glendive
Little Missouri
Badlands
White Sulphur Springs
Rock Springs
Wibaux
Beach
Belfield
Dickinson
Hebron
Mandan
Bismarck
Medina
Jamestown
Harlowtown
Yellowstone
Terry
Sterling
Dawson
Townsend
Crazy Mts
Musselshell
Roundup
L. Tschida
Heart
Long L.
Napoleon
Three Forks
Lavina
Rosebud
Miles City
Mott
Elgin
Belgrade
Custer
Forsyth
Baker
Marmarth
White Butte 1076
Cannonball
Linton
Edgeley
Madison
Big Timber
Bozeman
Laurel
Bighorn
Ekalaka
Bowman
Selfridge
Ashley
Livingston
Columbus
Billings
Hardin
Volborg
Hettinger
Ellendale
Gallatin
Lemmon
McIntosh
McLaughlin
Ashland
Missouri
Eureka
Gardiner
Red Lodge
Bridger
Tongue
Broadus
Lodge Grass
Buffalo
Mobridge
Aberdeen
Electric Peak
Granite Peak 3901
Powder
Hebgen L.
Mt Washburn
Selby
West Yellowstone
Yellowstone
Bighorn L.
Hammond
Targhee Pass
Lovell
Ranchester
Moreau
La Plant
Powell
Shoshone
Sheridan
Faith
Dupree
Eagle Butte
Gettysburg
Island Park
Trout Peak 3732
Cody
Nat. Park
Shoshone L.
Greybull
Story
Clearmont
Absaroka Range
Bighorn Mts
Basin
Cloud Peak 4016
Lake Oahe
Belle Fourche
Spearfish
Belle Fourche
Blunt
Teton Ra.
Grand Teton Nat. Park
Jackson L.
Moran
Meeteetse
Buffalo
Gillette
Sundance
Lead
Sturgis
Deadwood
Enning
Pierre
Fort Pierre
Francs Pk 4005
Worland
Moorcroft
Upton
Black Hills
Gros Ventre
Dubois
Thermopolis
Osage
Newcastle
Rapid City
Philip
Presho
Jackson
Range
Owl Creek Mts
Kaycee
Wall
Kadoka
Murdo
Oacoma
Chamberlain
Wind River Range
Wind
Boysen Resr
Custer
Cheyenne
Nat. Pk
Alpine
Gannett Peak 4202
Wyoming Range
Riverton
Midwest
Mule Creek
Hot Springs
White
White River
Daniel
Pinedale
Shoshoni
Edgemont
Oelrichs
Wounded Knee
Winner
Gregory
Afton
Wyoming Peak 3480
Lander
Powder River
Mission
Martin
Pine Ridge
Bonesteel
La Barge
Evansville
Shawnee
Casper
Douglas
Lusk
Chadron
Merriman
Valentine
Cokeville
Sweetwater
Muddy Gap Pass
Pathfinder Resr
Glendo Resr
Crawford
Rushville
Niobrara
Stuart
Green
Eden
Guernsey
Ainsworth
Bassett
Kemmerer
Lamont
Seminoe Resr
Laramie Mts
Fort Laramie
Lingle
Diamondville
Medicine Bow
Wheatland
Torrington
Morrill
Alliance
N. Loup
Reliance
Wamsutter
Rock River
Scottsbluff
Hyannis
Thedford
Green River
Rock Springs
Rawlins
Elk Mtn. 3400
Chugwater
Gering
N. Platte
Bayard
Bridgeport
Dunning
Evanston
Lyman
Saratoga
Broadwater
Burwell
Flaming Gorge Resr
Medicine Bow Pk 3661
Laramie
Oshkosh
Stapleton
Broken Bow
Manila
Bridger Peak 3662
L. McConaughy
Kings Peak 4114
Baggs
Foxpark
Pine Bluffs
Kimball
Potter
Sidney
Paxton
Sutherland
North Platte
Ansley
Uinta Mts
Vernal
Cheyenne
Chappell
Ogallala
Big Springs
Gothenburg
Medicine Bow Mts
Ovid
Julesburg
Cozad
Lexington
Roosevelt
Yampa
Craig
Hayden
Steamboat Springs
Fort Collins
Wellington
Grand Island
Duchesne
Fall River Pass
Loveland
Sterling
Holyoke
Imperial
Maywood
Platte
Kearney
Dinosaur
Rocky Mtn Nat. Park
Estes Park
Greeley
S. Platte
Rangely
White
Meeker
Kremmling
Longs Peak 4345
Longmont
Brush
Otis
Arapahoe
Holdrege
Roan
Granby
Boulder
Fort Morgan
Culbertson
McCook
Alma
Price
Plateau
Berthoud Pass
Lafayette
Arvada
Wray
Benkelman
Eagle
Idaho Springs
Denver
Byers
Norton
Green
Grand Valley
Rifle
Loveland Pass
Minturn
Lakewood
Aurora
Englewood
Littleton
Arikaree
St Francis
Oberlin
Phillipsburg
Glenwood Springs
Mt Evans 4348
Cope
UTAH
Mack
Fruita
Tennessee Pass
Green River
Colorado
Grand Junction
Palisade
Leadville
Castle Rock
Limon
Burlington
Kanorado
Colby
Hill City
Stockton
Brendel
Arches N.P.
Mt Elbert 4399
Goodland
Simla
Oakley
Saline
Smoky Hill
Uncompahgre Plateau
Delta
Mt Harvard 4378
Buena Vista
Manitou Springs
Colorado Springs
Cheyenne Wells
WaKeeney
Russell
Canyonlands Nat. Pk
Moab
Sawatch Mts
Pikes Peak 4301
Mt Peale 3857
Montrose
Gunnison
Monarch Pass
Kit Carson
Weskan
Smoky
Hays
Uravan
Gunnison
Salida
Canon City
Dolores
Florence
Arkansas
Pueblo
Tribune
Scott City
Ness City
Hoisington
Ouray
Sangre de Cristo Mts
Boone
Ordway
Monticello
Abajo Mts
Saguache
Fowler
Rocky Ford
John Martin Resr
Wiley
Jetmore
Larned
Dove Creek
Silverton
Mt Wilson 4342
Blanding
La Junta
Las Animas
Lamar
Syracuse
Garden City
Kinsley
South Fork
Wolf Creek Pass
Monte Vista
Blanca Peak 4364
Lakin
Arkansas
Lewis
San Juan
Bluff
Cortez
Animas
San Juan Mts
Alamosa
Walsenburg
Delhi
Purgatoire
Montezuma
Dodge City
Pratt
Mexican Hat
Monument Valley
Mesa Verde N.P.
Durango
Pagosa Springs
Springfield
Ulysses
Greensburg
Antonito
Trinidad
Plains
Red Hills
Kayenta
Shiprock
Aztec
Bloomfield
Farmington
Navajo Resr
Chama
Tierra Amarilla
Raton
Hugoton
Liberal
Meade
Ashland
Medicine Lodge
110
105
100
45
40
A
B
C
1
2
3

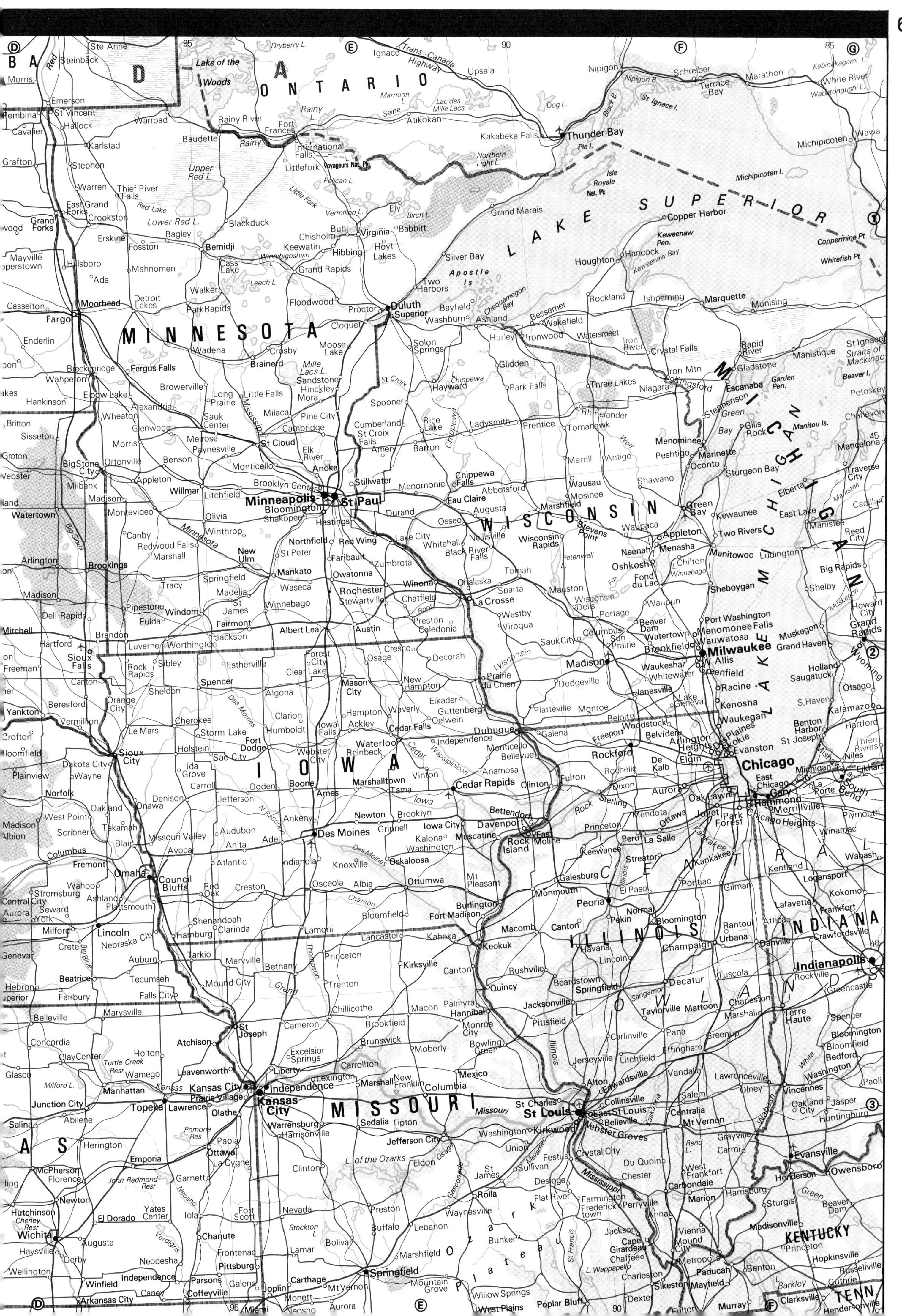
ONTARIO
Lake of the Woods
Trans-Canada Highway
Thunder Bay
LAKE SUPERIOR
Isle Royale Nat. Pk
Keweenaw Pen.
Apostle Is
MINNESOTA
WISCONSIN
MICHIGAN
LAKE MICHIGAN
IOWA
ILLINOIS
INDIANA
MISSOURI
KENTUCKY
TENN.
CENTRAL LOWLAND
Ozark Plateau
Winnipeg
Fargo
Moorhead
Grand Forks
Duluth
Superior
Minneapolis
St Paul
St Cloud
Rochester
Mankato
Sioux Falls
Sioux City
Omaha
Council Bluffs
Lincoln
Des Moines
Cedar Rapids
Davenport
Dubuque
Waterloo
Madison
Milwaukee
Green Bay
Appleton
Oshkosh
La Crosse
Eau Claire
Chicago
Rockford
Peoria
Springfield
Champaign
Indianapolis
St Louis
Kansas City
Independence
St Joseph
Topeka
Wichita
Springfield
Jefferson City
Columbia
Evansville
Grand Rapids
Muskegon
Kalamazoo
South Bend
Gary
Hammond
Marquette
Escanaba
Traverse City
Sault Ste Marie
Mississippi
Missouri
Des Moines
Illinois
Wabash
95
90
85
D
E
F
G
1
2
3

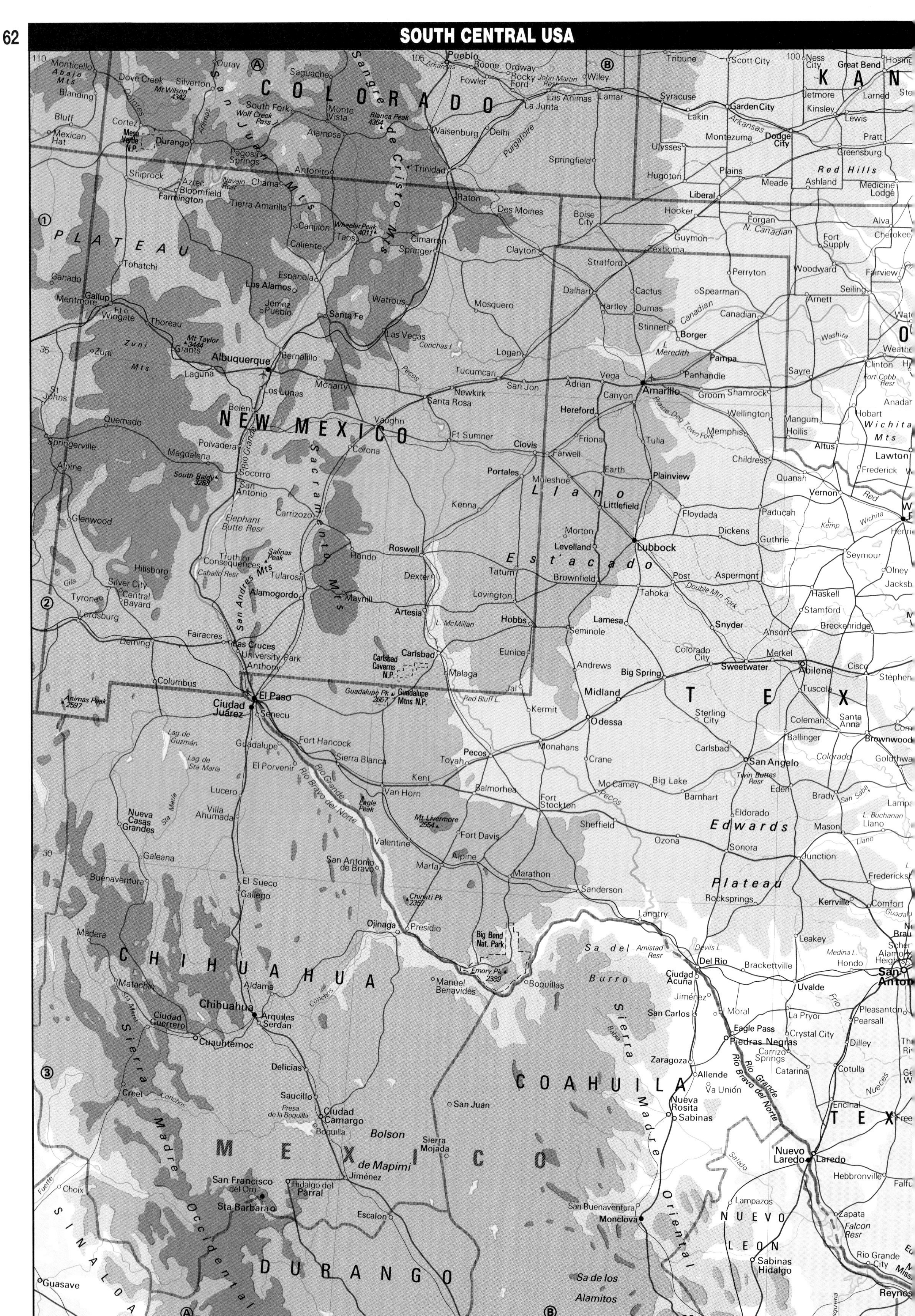
COLORADO
NEW MEXICO
CHIHUAHUA
COAHUILA
MEXICO
DURANGO
NUEVO LEON
SINALOA
PLATEAU
Llano Estacado
Edwards Plateau
Sangre de Cristo Mts
San Juan Mts
Sacramento Mts
San Andres Mts
Sierra Madre Occidental
Sierra Madre Oriental
Bolson de Mapimi
Pueblo
Albuquerque
Santa Fe
El Paso
Ciudad Juárez
Amarillo
Lubbock
Midland
Odessa
San Angelo
Abilene
Chihuahua
Laredo
Nuevo Laredo
Del Rio
Roswell
Las Cruces
Carlsbad
Alamogordo
Monclova
Rio Grande
Pecos

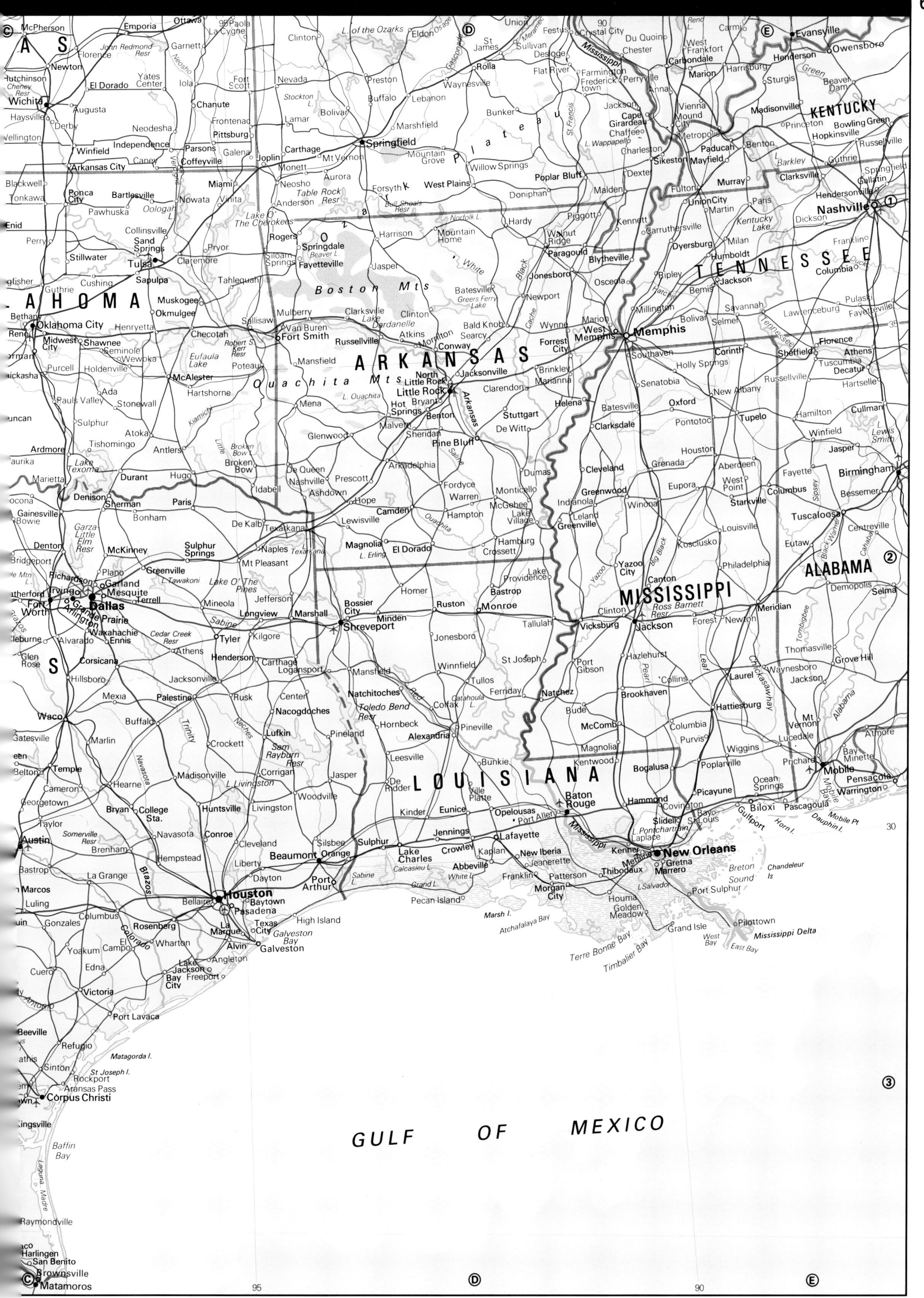
KENTUCKY
TENNESSEE
ARKANSAS
MISSISSIPPI
ALABAMA
LOUISIANA
AHOMA
Ozark Plateau
Boston Mts
Ouachita Mts
GULF OF MEXICO
Evansville
Owensboro
Nashville
Memphis
Springfield
Tulsa
Oklahoma City
Fort Smith
Little Rock
North Little Rock
Hot Springs
Pine Bluff
Texarkana
Shreveport
Dallas
Fort Worth
Waco
Austin
Houston
Galveston
Beaumont
Port Arthur
Lake Charles
Lafayette
Baton Rouge
New Orleans
Jackson
Vicksburg
Monroe
Alexandria
Natchez
Hattiesburg
Meridian
Tuscaloosa
Birmingham
Mobile
Pensacola
Biloxi
Gulfport
Corpus Christi
Brownsville
Matamoros
Wichita
Mississippi
Arkansas
Red
Brazos
Colorado
Trinity
Sabine
Mississippi Delta
Atchafalaya Bay
Terre Bonne Bay
Timbalier Bay
Breton Sound
Chandeleur Is
L. Pontchartrain
Galveston Bay
Matagorda I.
Baffin Bay
Laguna Madre
Toledo Bend Resr
Sam Rayburn Resr
Lake O' The Cherokees
Table Rock Resr
L. of the Ozarks
Kentucky Lake
95
90
30
35

LAKE SUPERIOR

LAKE MICHIGAN

LAKE HURON

LAKE ERIE

Georgian Bay

MINNESOTA

WISCONSIN

MICHIGAN

ONTARIO

CANADA

IOWA

ILLINOIS

INDIANA

OHIO

MISSOURI

KENTUCKY

TENNESSEE

WEST VIRGINIA

ARKANSAS

CUMBERLAND PLATEAU

Ozark Plateau

Allegheny

Clinch Mountains

Major cities: Thunder Bay, Duluth, Superior, St Paul, Milwaukee, Madison, Green Bay, Chicago, Detroit, Cleveland, Columbus, Cincinnati, Indianapolis, St Louis, Louisville, Nashville, Toledo, Sudbury, Sault Ste Marie, Sault, Ste Marie, London, Sarnia, Windsor, Akron, Canton, Youngstown, Dayton, Springfield, Lexington, Evansville, Peoria, Rockford, Cedar Rapids, Davenport, Rock Island, Dubuque, La Crosse, Rochester, Winona, Eau Claire, Wausau, Appleton, Oshkosh, Fond du Lac, Sheboygan, Manitowoc, Grand Rapids, Lansing, Flint, Saginaw, Bay City, Muskegon, Kalamazoo, Battle Creek, Ann Arbor, Gary, Hammond, South Bend, Fort Wayne, Lafayette, Terre Haute, Bloomington, Muncie, Anderson, Kokomo, Marion, Champaign, Urbana, Decatur, Springfield, Bloomington, Quincy, Galesburg

1:5M

0 50 100 150 200 km
0 50 100 mls

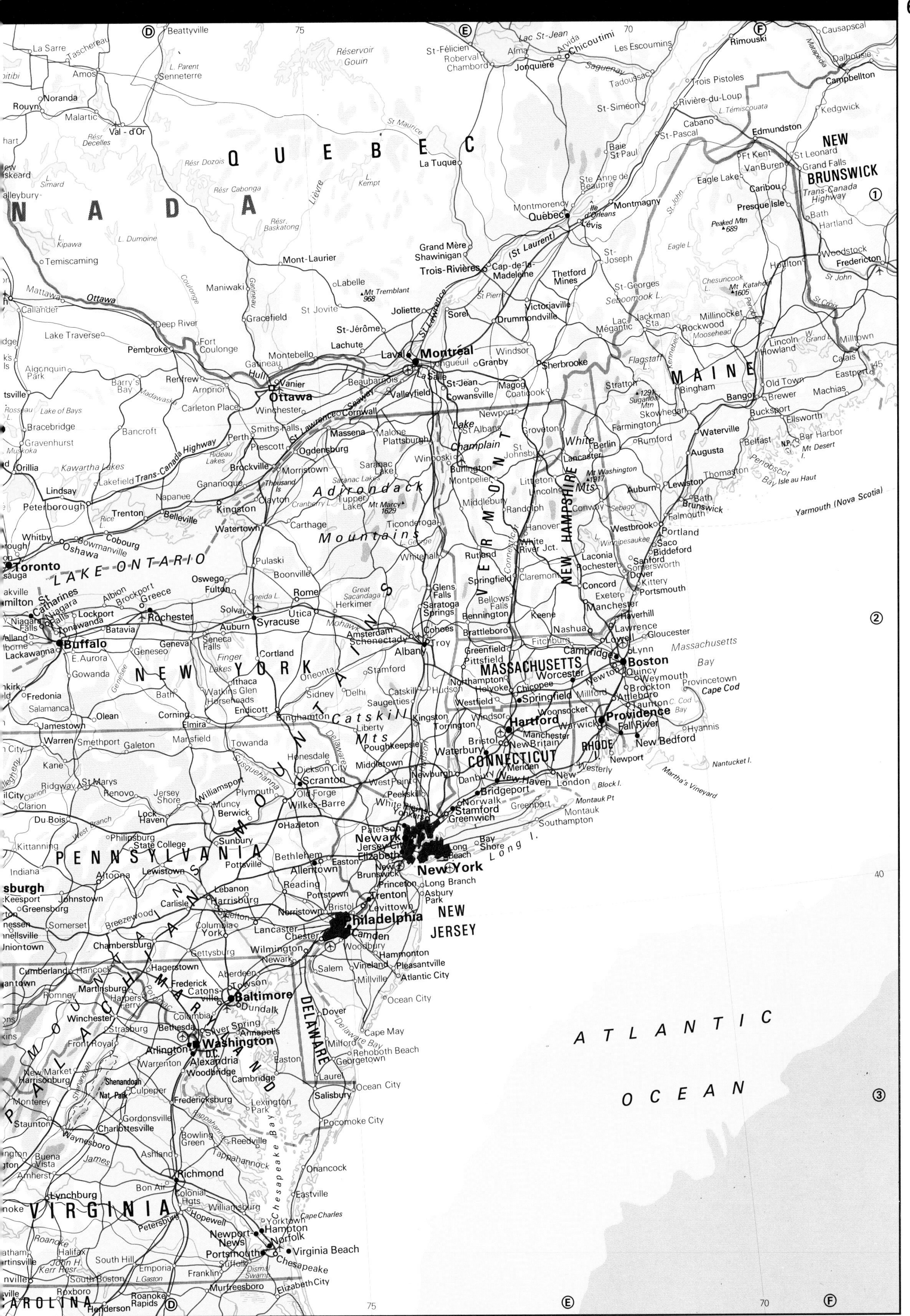
QUEBEC
CANADA
NEW BRUNSWICK
MAINE
VERMONT
NEW HAMPSHIRE
MASSACHUSETTS
CONNECTICUT
RHODE
NEW YORK
PENNSYLVANIA
NEW JERSEY
DELAWARE
MARYLAND
VIRGINIA
CAROLINA
APPALACHIAN MOUNTAINS
ATLANTIC
OCEAN
LAKE ONTARIO
Adirondack Mountains
Catskill Mts
White Mts
Lake Champlain
Long I.
Cape Cod
Massachusetts Bay
Chesapeake Bay
Delaware Bay
Trans-Canada Highway
St Lawrence Seaway
Beattyville
La Sarre
Amos
Noranda
Rouyn
Malartic
Val - d'Or
Senneterre
Réservoir Gouin
St-Félicien
Roberval
Chambord
Lac St-Jean
Alma
Jonquière
Chicoutimi
Arvida
Saguenay
Les Escoumins
Rimouski
Causapscal
Dalhousie
Campbellton
Tadoussac
Trois Pistoles
Rivière-du-Loup
St-Siméon
Cabano
Edmundston
St-Pascal
Baie St Paul
La Tuque
Ste Anne de Beaupré
Montmorency
Québec
Lévis
Montmagny
Ft Kent
VanBuren
St Leonard
Grand Falls
Eagle Lake
Caribou
Presque Isle
Bath
Hartland
Peaked Mtn 689
Woodstock
Fredericton
St John
Houlton
Grand Mère
Shawinigan
Trois-Rivières
Cap-de-la-Madeleine
Thetford Mines
St-Joseph
St-Georges
Mont-Laurier
Maniwaki
Labelle
Mt Tremblant 968
Mt Katahdin 1605
Millinocket
Rockwood
Moosehead L.
Ottawa
Mattawa
Callander
Deep River
Gracefield
St Jovite
Joliette
Sorel
Victoriaville
Drummondville
Jackman Sta.
Lac Mégantic
Lake Traverse
Pembroke
Fort Coulonge
Montebello
St-Jérôme
Lachute
Laval
Montréal
Longueuil
Granby
Windsor
Sherbrooke
Flagstaff L.
Lincoln
Howland
Milltown
Calais
Eastport
Algonquin Park
Barry's Bay
Renfrew
Arnprior
Gatineau
Hull
Vanier
Beauharnois
La Salle
St-Jean
Cowansville
Magog
Coaticook
Stratton
Sugarloaf Mtn 1291
Bingham
Bangor
Old Town
Brewer
Machias
Carleton Place
Winchester
Valleyfield
Cornwall
Newport
Skowhegan
Bucksport
Ellsworth
Bracebridge
Bancroft
Smiths Falls
Massena
Malone
Plattsburgh
St Albans
Groveton
Farmington
Waterville
Bar Harbor
Mt Desert I.
Gravenhurst
Perth
Prescott
Ogdensburg
Saranac Lake
Winooski
Burlington
Montpelier
St Johnsbury
Berlin
Lancaster
Rumford
Augusta
Belfast
Orillia
Brockville
Morristown
Mt Washington 1917
Littleton
Lincoln
Lewiston
Auburn
Thomaston
Lakefield
Gananoque
Lindsay
Napanee
Kingston
Clayton
Tupper Lake
Mt Marcy 1629
Middlebury
Randolph
Conway
Bath
Brunswick
Falmouth
Peterborough
Trenton
Belleville
Watertown
Carthage
Ticonderoga
Hanover
Westbrook
Portland
Yarmouth (Nova Scotia)
Whitby
Cobourg
Oshawa
Bowmanville
Toronto
Whitehall
Rutland
White River Jct.
Laconia
Rochester
Saco
Biddeford
Sanford
Somersworth
Dover
Kittery
Portsmouth
Pulaski
Boonville
Oswego
Fulton
Rome
Glens Falls
Springfield
Claremont
Concord
Exeter
Manchester
St Catharines
Niagara Falls
Lockport
Tonawanda
Albion
Brockport
Greece
Rochester
Solvay
Syracuse
Utica
Herkimer
Saratoga Springs
Bellows Falls
Bennington
Keene
Haverhill
Lawrence
Gloucester
Buffalo
Batavia
Auburn
Geneva
Seneca Falls
Amsterdam
Schenectady
Cohoes
Troy
Albany
Brattleboro
Nashua
Lowell
Lynn
Lackawanna
E. Aurora
Geneseo
Cortland
Greenfield
Pittsfield
Fitchburg
Cambridge
Boston
Gowanda
Ithaca
Oneonta
Stamford
Northampton
Holyoke
Chicopee
Worcester
Newton
Quincy
Weymouth
Brockton
Provincetown
Fredonia
Salamanca
Watkins Glen
Horseheads
Bath
Sidney
Delhi
Catskill
Saugerties
Hudson
Westfield
Springfield
Milford
Attleboro
Taunton
Olean
Corning
Elmira
Endicott
Binghamton
Kingston
Windsor
Hartford
Woonsocket
Providence
Jamestown
Liberty
Torrington
Manchester
Warwick
Fall River
New Bedford
Hyannis
Warren
Smethport
Galeton
Mansfield
Towanda
Poughkeepsie
Bristol
New Britain
Waterbury
Newport
Nantucket I.
Martha's Vineyard
Kane
Honesdale
Dickson City
Middletown
Meriden
Westerly
Scranton
West Point
Newburgh
Danbury
New Haven
New London
Block I.
Ridgway
St Marys
Renovo
Jersey Shore
Williamsport
Plymouth
Old Forge
Wilkes-Barre
Peekskill
White Plains
Bridgeport
Norwalk
Stamford
Greenwich
Greenport
Montauk Pt
Montauk
Southampton
Clarion
Du Bois
Lock Haven
Muncy
Berwick
Yonkers
Hazleton
Paterson
Newark
Jersey City
Elizabeth
Bay Shore
Long Beach
Philipsburg
State College
Sunbury
Kittanning
Indiana
Altoona
Lewistown
Pottsville
Bethlehem
Allentown
Easton
New Brunswick
New York
Reading
Princeton
Long Branch
Asbury Park
Johnstown
Lebanon
Harrisburg
Carlisle
Pottstown
Trenton
Bristol
Levittown
Greensburg
Somerset
Breezewood
Elizabethtown
Columbia
York
Norristown
Philadelphia
Lancaster
Chester
Camden
Woodbury
Chambersburg
Gettysburg
Wilmington
Newark
Hammonton
Pleasantville
Atlantic City
Cumberland
Hancock
Hagerstown
Aberdeen
Salem
Vineland
Millville
Martinsburg
Frederick
Catonsville
Towson
Baltimore
Dundalk
Romney
Harpers Ferry
Ocean City
Winchester
Columbia
Dover
Strasburg
Bethesda
Silver Spring
Annapolis
Cape May
Front Royal
Washington D.C.
Arlington
Alexandria
Milford
Rehoboth Beach
Georgetown
Warrenton
Woodbridge
Easton
New Market
Harrisonburg
Shenandoah Nat. Park
Culpeper
Cambridge
Laurel
Ocean City
Salisbury
Monterey
Fredericksburg
Lexington Park
Staunton
Gordonsville
Charlottesville
Waynesboro
Pocomoke City
Bowling Green
Reedville
Tappahannock
Buena Vista
Ashland
James
Amherst
Richmond
Onancock
Lynchburg
Bon Air
Colonial Hgts
Eastville
Williamsburg
Hopewell
Petersburg
Cape Charles
Yorktown
Hampton
Newport News
Norfolk
Portsmouth
Virginia Beach
Roanoke
Halifax
John H. Kerr Resr
South Hill
Suffolk
Chesapeake
Emporia
Franklin
Dismal Swamp
South Boston
L. Gaston
Roxboro
Roanoke Rapids
Murfreesboro
Elizabeth City
Henderson
75
70
45
40

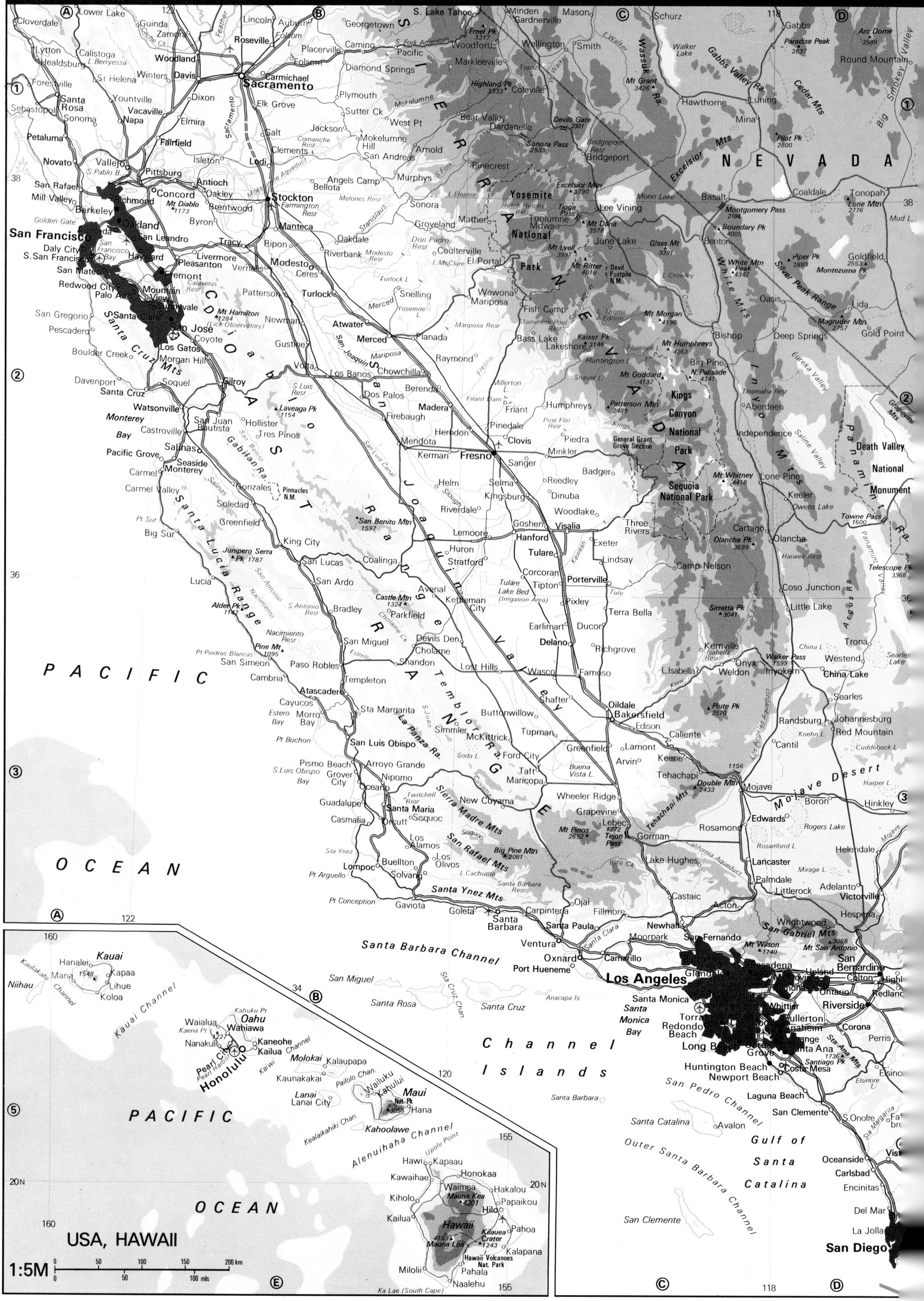

CALIFORNIA HAWAII

N E V A D A

Sacramento

Stockton

San Francisco

Oakland
Berkeley
Daly City
S. San Francisco
San Mateo
Redwood City
Palo Alto
Mountain View
Sunnyvale
Santa Clara
San Jose
Los Gatos

Santa Cruz
Monterey
Pacific Grove
Seaside
Carmel

Fresno
Clovis
Madera
Merced

S A N   J O A Q U I N   V A L L E Y

Visalia
Tulare
Hanford
Lemoore

Bakersfield
Oildale
Delano

S I E R R A   N E V A D A

Yosemite National Park

Sequoia National Park
Kings Canyon National Park
Mt Whitney 4418

Death Valley National Monument

Bishop
Big Pine
Lone Pine

Mojave Desert

Lancaster
Palmdale
Victorville

San Bernardino
Riverside
Los Angeles
Santa Monica
Long Beach
Anaheim
Santa Ana
Huntington Beach
Newport Beach

Oceanside
Carlsbad
Encinitas
Del Mar
La Jolla
San Diego

Santa Barbara
Ventura
Oxnard

Gulf of Santa Catalina

Santa Catalina

P A C I F I C

O C E A N

Channel Islands

Santa Barbara Channel

San Miguel
Santa Rosa
Santa Cruz
Anacapa
San Clemente

USA, HAWAII

P A C I F I C

O C E A N

Kauai
Hanalei
Kapaa
Lihue
Koloa

Niihau

Oahu
Waialua
Wahiawa
Kaneohe
Kailua
Nanakuli
Honolulu
Pearl City

Molokai
Kaunakakai

Lanai
Lanai City

Maui
Kahului
Wailuku
Hana
Haleakala Nat. Pk

Kahoolawe

Hawaii
Waimea
Mauna Kea 4201
Mauna Loa 4169
Hilo
Kailua
Kilauea Crater
Hawaii Volcanoes Nat. Park
Pahala
Naalehu
Ka Lae (South Cape)

1:5M   50 100 150 200 km
        50   100 mils

1:2.5M   25   50   75   100 km
          25   50 mils

KENTUCKY
VIRGINIA
TENNESSEE
NORTH CAROLINA
SOUTH CAROLINA
GEORGIA
ALABAMA
FLORIDA

CUMBERLAND PLATEAU
APPALACHIAN MTS
BLUE RIDGE
Great Smoky Mts
Clinch Mts
Mountains
Cumberland
Mt Rogers 1743
Mt Mitchell 2037
Great Smoky Mts Nat. Park
Mt Oglethorpe

Bowling Green
Corbin
Harlan
Big Stone Gap
Middlesboro
Albany
Russellville
Springfield
Gallatin
Hendersonville
Nashville
Lebanon
Cookeville
Livingston
Dale Hollow L.
Norris L.
Center Hill L.
Crossville
Oak Ridge
Harriman
Knoxville
Morristown
Greeneville
Kingsport
Bristol
Elizabethton
Johnson City
Abingdon
Boone
Murfreesboro
Franklin
McMinnville
Shelbyville
Manchester
Tullahoma
Dayton
Chickamauga Lake
Athens
Cleveland
Red Bank
Chattanooga
East Ridge
Bridgeport
Maryville
Gatlinburg
Hillsville
Galax
Martinsville
Chatham
Halifax
Kerr Resr
South Hill
Emporia
South Boston
L. Gaston
Danville
Roxboro
Portsmouth
Suffolk
Chesapeake
Franklin
Dismal Swamp
Murfreesboro
Ahoskie
Elizabeth City
Kitty Hawk
Albemarle Sd
Manteo
Roanoke Rapids
Henderson
Enfield
Mt Airy
Reidsville
Winston-Salem
Burlington
Durham
Chapel Hill
Cary
Raleigh
Rocky Mt
Tarboro
Wilson
Windsor
Williamston
Phelps Lake
Greenville
Washington
Englehard
High Point
Greensboro
Lexington
Thomasville
Statesville
Salisbury
Asheboro
Sanford
Smithfield
Goldsboro
La Grange
Kinston
New Bern
Pamlico
Pamlico Sound
Cape Hatteras
Hickory
Lenoir
Morganton
Asheville
Waynesville
Hendersonville
Brevard
Franklin
Murphy
L. Norman
Kannapolis
Concord
Gastonia
Shelby
Albemarle
Charlotte
Monroe
Pinehurst
Southern Pines
Fayetteville
Dunn
Neuse
Clinton
Havelock
Morehead City
Cape Lookout
Jacksonville
Elizabethtown
Burgaw
Onslow Bay
Cape Fear
Wilmington
Carolina Beach
Lumberton
Whiteville
Laurinburg
Rockingham
Landrum
Gaffney
Spartanburg
Rock Hill
Lancaster
Chester
Union
Greenville
Easley
Westminster
Toccoa
Hartwell Resr
Anderson
Laurens
Whitmire
Kershaw
Cheraw
Darlington
Florence
Marion
Pee Dee
Conway
Long Bay
Myrtle Beach
Newberry
Greenwood
Saluda
Abbeville
Elberton
Calhoun Falls
Johnston
Batesburg
Lake Murray
Camden
Columbia
Cayce
Sumter
Lake City
Broad
Clark Hill Resr
Aiken
Orangeburg
L. Marion
Manning
Santee
Moultrie
Georgetown
St Stephen
Bamberg
St George
Goose Creek
Cape Romain
Allendale
Varnville
Walterboro
Charleston
Estill
Ridgeland
Beaufort
St Helena Sound
Port Royal Sound
Blue Ridge
Dalton
Calhoun
Dahlonega
Gainesville
Sidney Lanier
Etowah
Buford
Allatoona L.
Cedartown
Marietta
Smyrna
Roswell
Decatur
Atlanta
Bremen
E. Point
College Park
Forest Park
Covington
Carrollton
Newnan
Griffin
Eatonton
Athens
Washington
Thomson
Augusta
N. Augusta
Edisto
Savannah
L. Sinclair
Milledgeville
Louisville
Waynesboro
Oconee
Ogeechee
Wrightsville
Barnesville
La Grange
Thomaston
Macon
Warner Robins
Perry
Dublin
Swainsboro
Statesboro
Eastman
Vidalia
Lyons
Pembroke
Savannah
Windsor Forest
St Catherines I.
McRae
Ocmulgee
Altamaha
Baxley
Ludowici
Jesup
Hazlehurst
Fitzgerald
Douglas
Darien
St Simons I.
Satilla
Waycross
Brunswick
St Andrew Sound
Alapaha
Homerville
Folkston
St Marys
Kingsland
Okefenokee Swamp
Fernandina Beach
Americus
Cordele
Dawson
Cuthbert
Walter F. George Resr
Flint
Ashburn
Albany
Tifton
Blakely
Camilla
Moultrie
Thomasville
Valdosta
Bainbridge
Ochlockonee
L. Seminole
Chattahoochee
Columbus
Phenix City
Opelika
Auburn
L. Martin
Lanett
Alexander City
Roanoke
Sylacauga
Talladega
Anniston
Center Point
Birmingham
Mountain Brook
Homewood
Bessemer
Clanton
Prattville
Montgomery
Selma
Fort Deposit
Union Springs
Eufaula
Troy
Ozark
Enterprise
Daleville
Dothan
Opp
Florala
Evergreen
Andalusia
Conecuh
Huntsville
Guntersville L.
Scottsboro
Tennessee
Trion
Ft Payne
Guntersville
Rome
Arab
Attalla
Gadsden
Weiss L.
Rainbow City
L. Lewis Smith
Chattahoochee
Talladega
De Funiak Springs
Marianna
Valparaiso
Fort Walton Beach
Tallahassee
Panama City
St Andrew Bay
Lynn Haven
Crawfordville
Carrabelle
Apalachicola
Apalachicola Bay
Port St Joe
C. San Blas
St George I.
Apalachee Bay
Perry
Greenville
Jasper
Live Oak
Lake City
Baldwin
Jacksonville
Jacksonville Beach
Orange Park
St Augustine
Palatka
High Springs
Gainesville
Suwannee
Chiefland
Williston
Bunnell
Ormond Beach
Daytona Beach
Ocala
George
St Johns
New Smyrna Beach
Waccasassa Bay
Wildwood
Leesburg
L. Apopka
Sanford
Winter Park
Titusville
Brooksville
Winter Garden
Pine Hills
Orlando
Cape Canaveral
Merritt Island
Cocoa
Hudson
Dade City
Disney World
Rockledge
Dunedin
Clearwater
Largo
Pinellas Park
St Petersburg
Lakeland
Plant City
Tampa
Tampa Bay
Ruskin
L. Kissimmee
Melbourne
Palm Bay
Lake Wales
Avon Park
Gifford
Vero Beach
Palmetto
Bradenton
Wauchula
Sebring
Peace
Istokpoga
Fort Pierce
Sarasota
Arcadia
Okeechobee
Lake Okeechobee
Stuart
Port Charlotte
Punta Gorda
Charlotte Harb.
Caloosahatchee
Pine I.
La Belle
Fort Myers
Pahokee
Belle Glade
South Bay
Riviera Beach
W. Palm Beach
Palm Beach
Lake Worth
Boynton Beach
Delray Beach
Boca Raton
Pompano Beach
Ft Lauderdale
Bonita Springs
Naples
The Everglades
Plantation
Hollywood
Carol City
N. Miami Beach
Hialeah
N. Miami
Miami
Miami Beach
Big Cypress Swamp
Marco
C. Romano
Ten Thousand Islands
South Miami
Coral Gables
Cutler Ridge
Biscayne Bay
Homestead
Florida City
National Park
Ponce de Leon Bay
Cape Sable
Florida Bay
Florida Keys
Key Largo
Islamorada
Big Pine Key
Marathon
Boca Chica Key
Key West
Marquesas Keys
Straits of Florida

ATLANTIC OCEAN
GULF OF MEXICO

THE BAHAMAS
Little Abaco
Cooper's Town
Little Bahama Bank
West End
Marsh Harbour
Grand Bahama
Freeport City
Lucaya
Great Abaco
Bimini Is.
Berry Is.
Nassau
Nicholl's Town
Adelaide
New Providence
Andros Town
Andros
Great Bahama Bank
Kemp's Bay

A B C
1 2 3 4
85 80 35 30 25

0 50 100 150 200 km

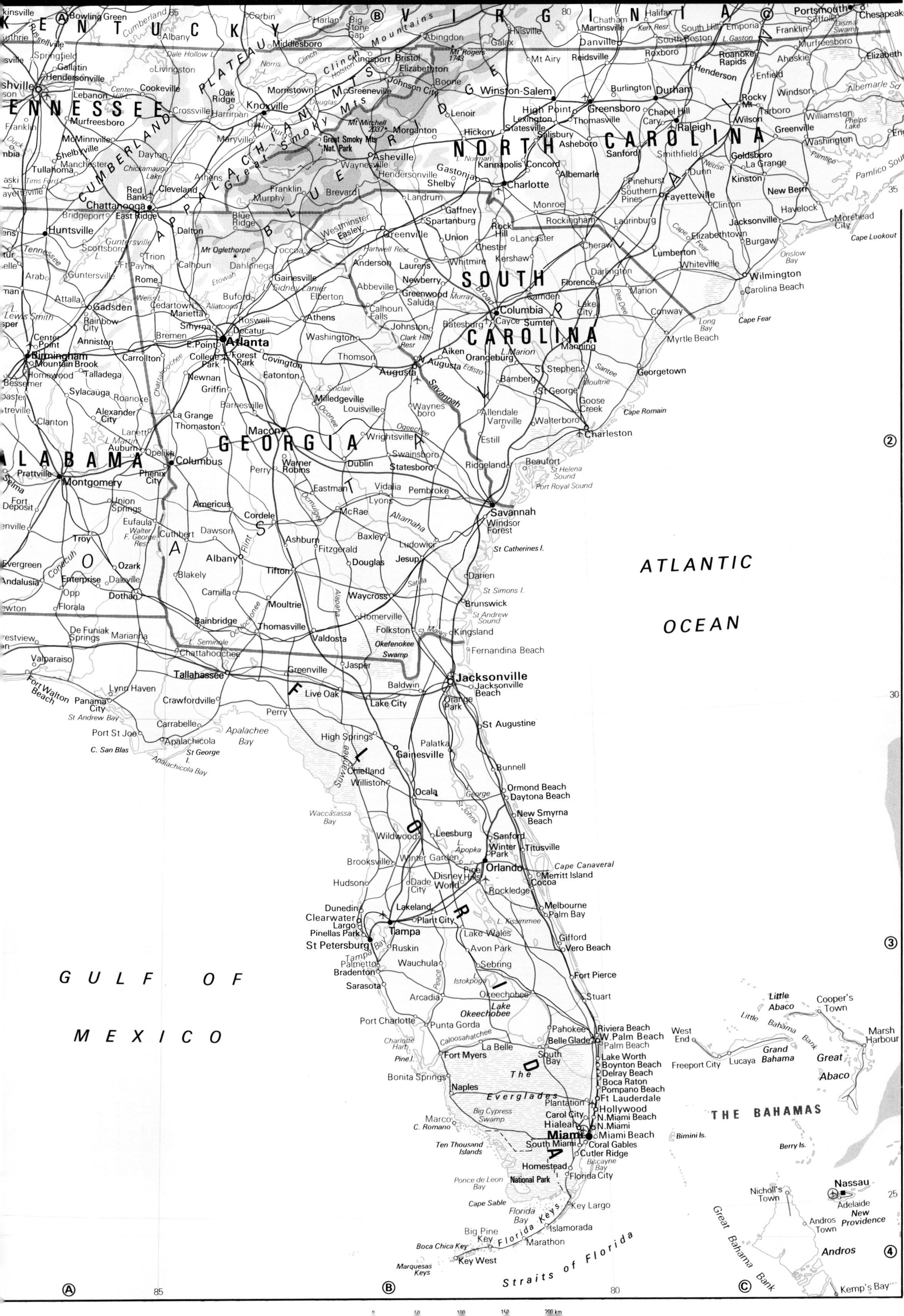

ATLANTIC OCEAN

NEW HAMPSHIRE
VERMONT
MASSACHUSETTS
CONNECTICUT
RHODE ISLAND
NEW YORK
PENNSYLVANIA
NEW JERSEY
DELAWARE
MARYLAND
VIRGINIA
WEST VIRGINIA

Boston
Providence
Hartford
Springfield
Worcester
Albany
Troy
Schenectady
Syracuse
Rochester
Buffalo
Scranton
Wilkes-Barre
New York
Newark
Jersey City
Paterson
Trenton
Philadelphia
Camden
Wilmington
Baltimore
Washington
Arlington
Harrisburg
Lancaster
York
Atlantic City
Cape May
Cape Cod
Nantucket Island
Martha's Vineyard
Long Island
Long Island Sound
New Bedford
Fall River
New Haven
Bridgeport
Stamford
Poughkeepsie
Lake Ontario

1:2.5M

0   25   50   75   100 km
0   25   50 mls

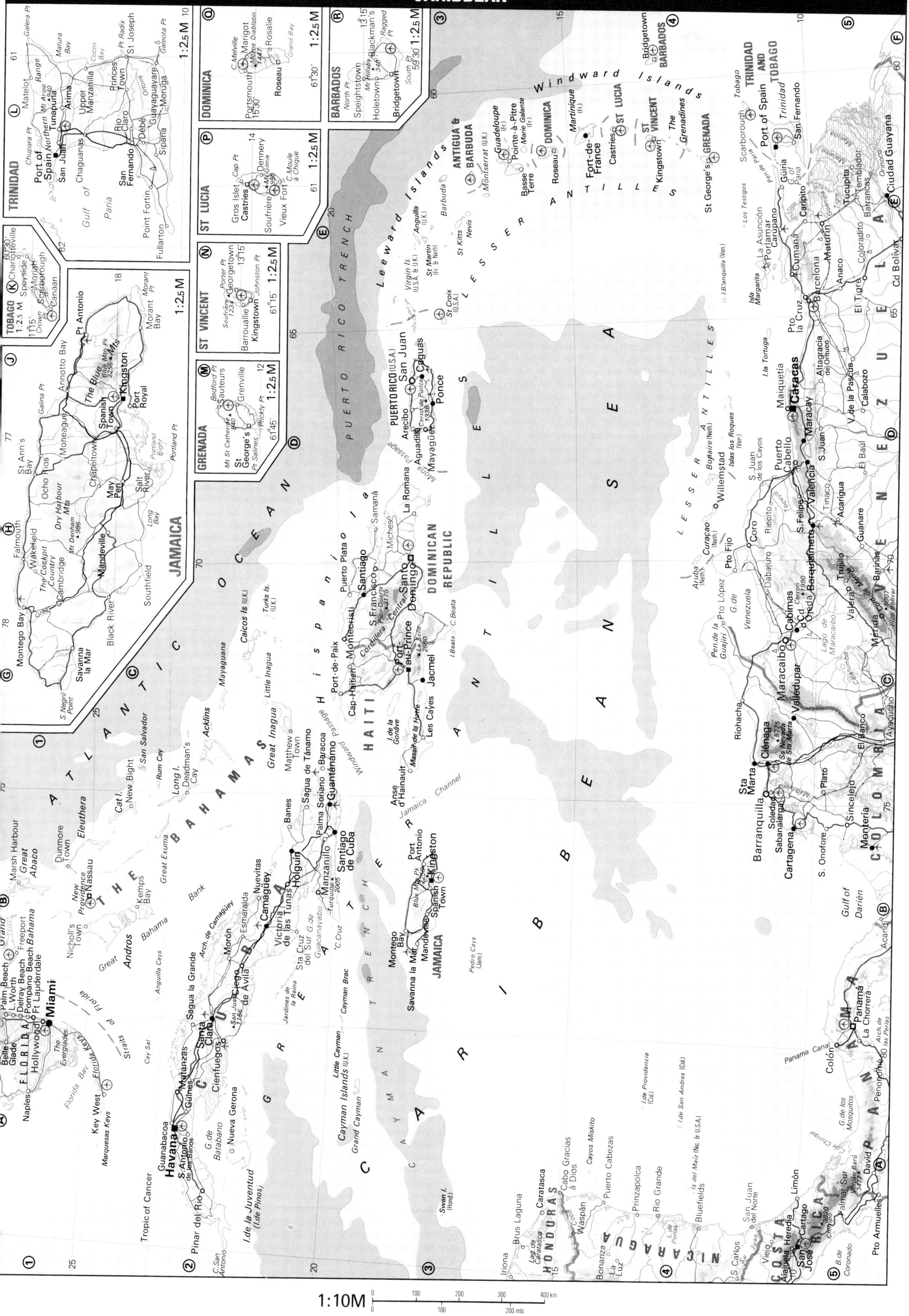

TRINIDAD

Matelot
Galera Pt
Mt Aripo Northern Range 940
Matura Bay
Princes Town
St Joseph
Arima
Upper Manzanilla
Pt Radix
Port of Spain
San Juan
Guayaguayare
Moruga
Rio Claro
Débe
Siparia
San Fernando
Gulf of Paria
Point Fortin
Fullarton

L

TOBAGO
1:2.5 M
Charlotteville
60°30'
Speyside
11°15'
Moriah
Scarborough
Crown Pt
Canaan
K

Q DOMINICA 1:2.5 M
C Melville
Portsmouth
Marigot
Morne Diablotin 1447
Rosalie
Roseau 1530'
61°30'
Grand Bay

R BARBADOS 1:2.5 M
13°15'
Blackman's
Ragged Pt
Speightstown
North Pt
BRIDGETOWN
Bathsheba
Mt Hillaby 340
Holetown
59°30'
Bridgetown

P ST LUCIA 1:2.5 M
Gros Islet
Cap Pt
Dennery
C Moule
à Chique
Castries
Soufrière 950
Vieux Fort
61

N ST VINCENT 1:2.5 M
Porter Pt
13°15'
Georgetown
Soufrière 1234
Barrouallie
Kingstown
61°15'

M GRENADA 1:2.5 M
Bedford Pt
Sauteurs
Grenville
Mt St Catherine 840
St George's
Prickly Pt
Pt Salines
61°45'
12

JAMAICA
Montego Bay
Falmouth
St Ann's Bay
Galina Pt
Annotto Bay
Pt Antonio
Wakefield
Ocho Rios
Port Maria
Moneague
The Blue Mtns 2256 Mts
Chapeltown
Dry Harbour Mts
Mt Denham 966
Spanish Town
KINGSTON
Port Royal
Cambridge
May Pen
Salt River
Portland Pt
Mandeville
The Cockpit Country
Black River
Southfield
Savanna la Mar
Long Bay
S Negril Point

ANTIGUA & BARBUDA (U.K.)
Montserrat (U.K.)
Guadeloupe (Fr.)
Pointe-à-Pitre
Basse Terre
Marie Galante
DOMINICA
Roseau
MARTINIQUE (Fr.)
Fort-de-France
ST LUCIA
Castries
ST VINCENT
Kingstown
The Grenadines
GRENADA
St George's
Windward Islands
Leeward Islands
LESSER ANTILLES

TRINIDAD AND TOBAGO
Tobago
Scarborough
Port of Spain
San Fernando
BARBADOS
Bridgetown

Barbuda
Anguilla (U.K.)
St Martin (Fr. & Neth.)
St Kitts
Nevis
St Barth (Fr.)
Virgin Is (U.S.A. & U.K.)
St Croix (U.S.A.)

PUERTO RICO (U.S.A.)
San Juan
Arecibo
Caguas
Aguadilla
Cerro de Punta 1338
Mayagüez
Ponce
Mona

DOMINICAN REPUBLIC
Santo Domingo
Santiago
Puerto Plata
S. Francisco
Miches
Samaná
La Romana
Pico Duarte 3175
Cordillera Central
C. Beata
I. Beata
I. de la Gonâve

HAITI
Port-au-Prince
Cap-Haïtien
Port-de-Paix
Jacmel
Les Cayes
La Selle 2680
Massif de la Hotte
Anse d'Hainault
Île de la Gonâve
Hispaniola
Windward passage

THE BAHAMAS
Marsh Harbour
Great Abaco
Dunmore Town
Eleuthera
Nicholl's Town
New Providence
NASSAU
Cat I.
New Bight
Kemps Bay
Andros
Great Exuma
San Salvador
Rum I.
Long I.
Deadman's Cay
Ackins
Crooked I.
Mayaguana
Little Inagua
Great Inagua
Matthew Town
Caicos Is (U.K.)
Turks Is. (U.K.)

Miami
Palm Beach
L. Worth
Delray Beach
Pompano Beach
Ft Lauderdale
Hollywood
FLORIDA
Naples
Key West
Marquesas Keys
Florida Keys
Florida Bay
The Everglades
Straits of Florida
Tropic of Cancer

CUBA
HAVANA
Matanzas
Guanabacoa
Güines
Cienfuegos
Santa Clara
Pinar del Río
Nueva Gerona
I. de la Juventud (I. de Pinos)
G. de Batabanó
Sagua la Grande
Morón
Ciego de Ávila
San Juan 1156
Victoria de las Tunas
Camagüey
Nuevitas
Holguín
Banes
Santiago de Cuba
Manzanillo
Sta Cruz del Sur
Bayamo
Guantánamo
Baracoa
Palma Soriano
C. Cruz
Esmeralda
Arch. de Camagüey
Jardines de la Reina
Cayman Islands (U.K.)
Grand Cayman
Little Cayman
Cayman Brac
Cayman Trench

HONDURAS
Cabo Gracias à Dios
Puerto Cabezas
Caratasca
Brus Laguna
Waspán

NICARAGUA
Bluefields
Rio Grande
Puerto Cabezas
Prinzapolca
Is del Maíz (Nic. & U.S.A.)
Cayos Miskito

COSTA RICA
Limón
San José
Cartago
Alajuela
Heredia
David
Cerro Chirripó 3837

PANAMA
PANAMÁ
Colón
La Chorrera
Penonomé
Panama Canal
Gulf of Darién
Arch. de las Perlas
G. de los Mosquitos

COLOMBIA
Barranquilla
Cartagena
Sta Marta
Ciénaga
Riohacha
Valledupar
Soledad
Sabanalarga
Sincelejo
Montería
Plato
El Banco
S. Onofre
Sierra Nevada de Sta Marta 5775
I. de San Andrés (Col.)
I. de Providencia (Col.)

VENEZUELA
CARACAS
Maracaibo
Maracay
Valencia
Barquisimeto
Barcelona
Cumaná
Coro
Puerto Cabello
Cabimas
Ciudad Guayana
Ciudad Bolívar
Mérida
Trujillo
Barinas
San Fernando
Maiquetía
Porlamar
La Asunción
Carúpano
Güiria
Maturín
El Tigre
Caripito
Anaco
Tucupita
Calabozo
El Baúl
Guanare
Acarigua
San Felipe
San Carlos
Tinaco
El Banco
Pico Bolívar 5007
Isla Margarita
I. la Tortuga
I. la Orchila
Los Roques (Ven.)
Islas los Roques (Ven.)
La Blanquilla (Ven.)
Los Testigos
Bonaire (Neth.)
Curaçao (Neth.)
Aruba (Neth.)
Willemstad
Pen. de Paria
G. de Paria
Orinoco
Lago de Maracaibo
Pen. de la Guajira

ATLANTIC OCEAN
CARIBBEAN SEA
PUERTO RICO TRENCH
CAYMAN TRENCH

TRINIDAD
1:2.5 M
DOMINICA 1:2.5 M
BARBADOS 1:2.5 M
ST LUCIA 1:2.5 M
ST VINCENT 1:2.5 M
GRENADA 1:2.5 M
TOBAGO 1:2.5 M

1:10M
0 100 200 300 400 km
0 100 200 mls

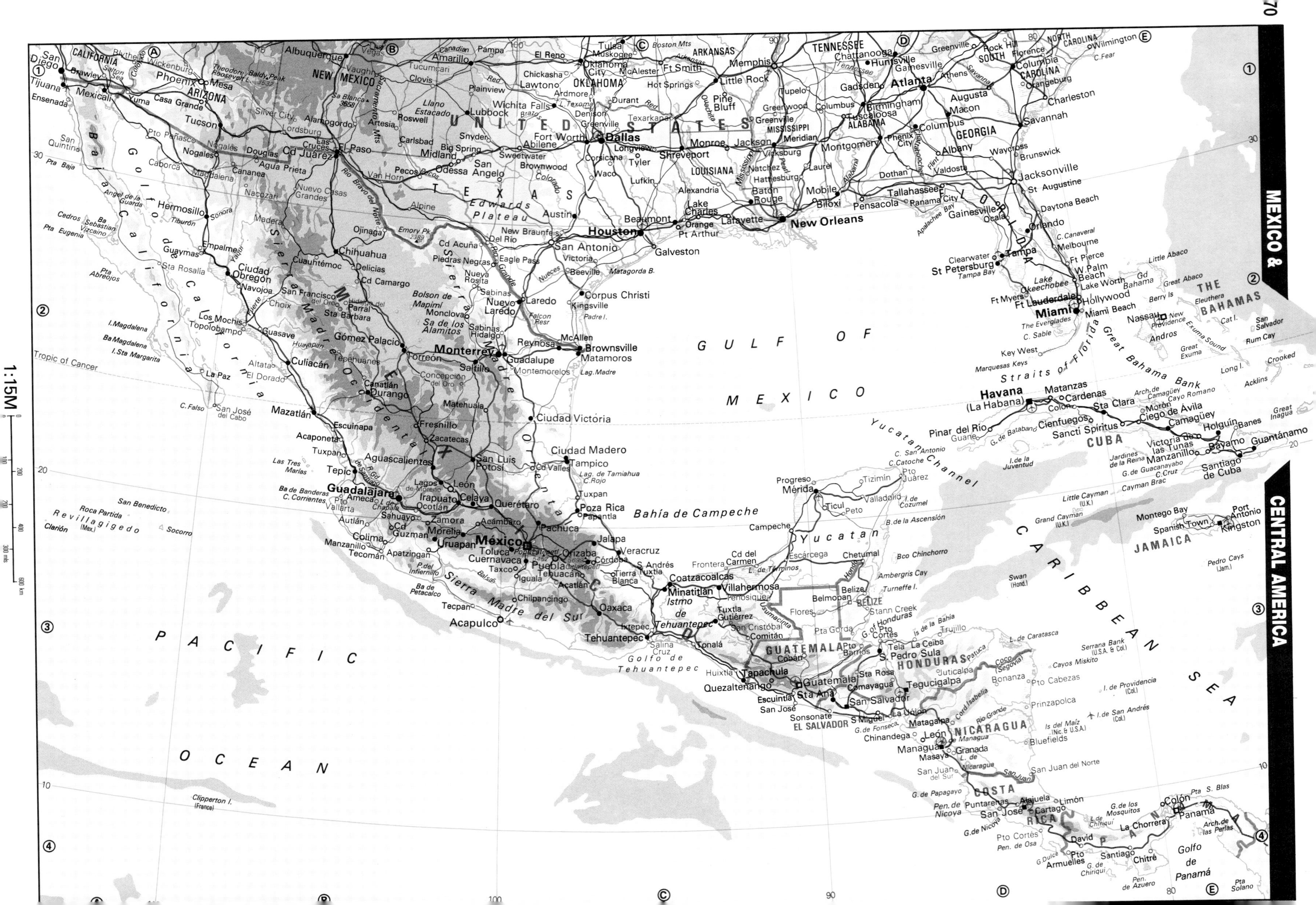
G U L F O F M E X I C O
C A R I B B E A N S E A
P A C I F I C O C E A N
Bahía de Campeche
Golfo de Tehuantepec
G o l f o d e C a l i f o r n i a
B a j a C a l i f o r n i a
Sierra Madre Occidental
Sierra Madre Oriental
Sierra Madre del Sur
Yucatan Channel
Straits of Florida
Great Bahama Bank
Tropic of Cancer
UNITED STATES
T E X A S
FLORIDA
GEORGIA
ALABAMA
MISSISSIPPI
LOUISIANA
ARKANSAS
OKLAHOMA
TENNESSEE
NEW MEXICO
ARIZONA
CALIFORNIA
SOUTH CAROLINA
NORTH CAROLINA
THE BAHAMAS
CUBA
JAMAICA
BELIZE
GUATEMALA
HONDURAS
EL SALVADOR
NICARAGUA
COSTA RICA
PANAMA
México
Guadalajara
Monterrey
Houston
Dallas
New Orleans
Atlanta
Miami
Havana (La Habana)
Kingston
Acapulco
Veracruz
Mérida
Belmopan
Guatemala
San Salvador
Tegucigalpa
Managua
San José
Panamá
Revillagigedo
Clipperton I. (France)
1:15M
0 200 400 600 km
0 100 200 300 mls

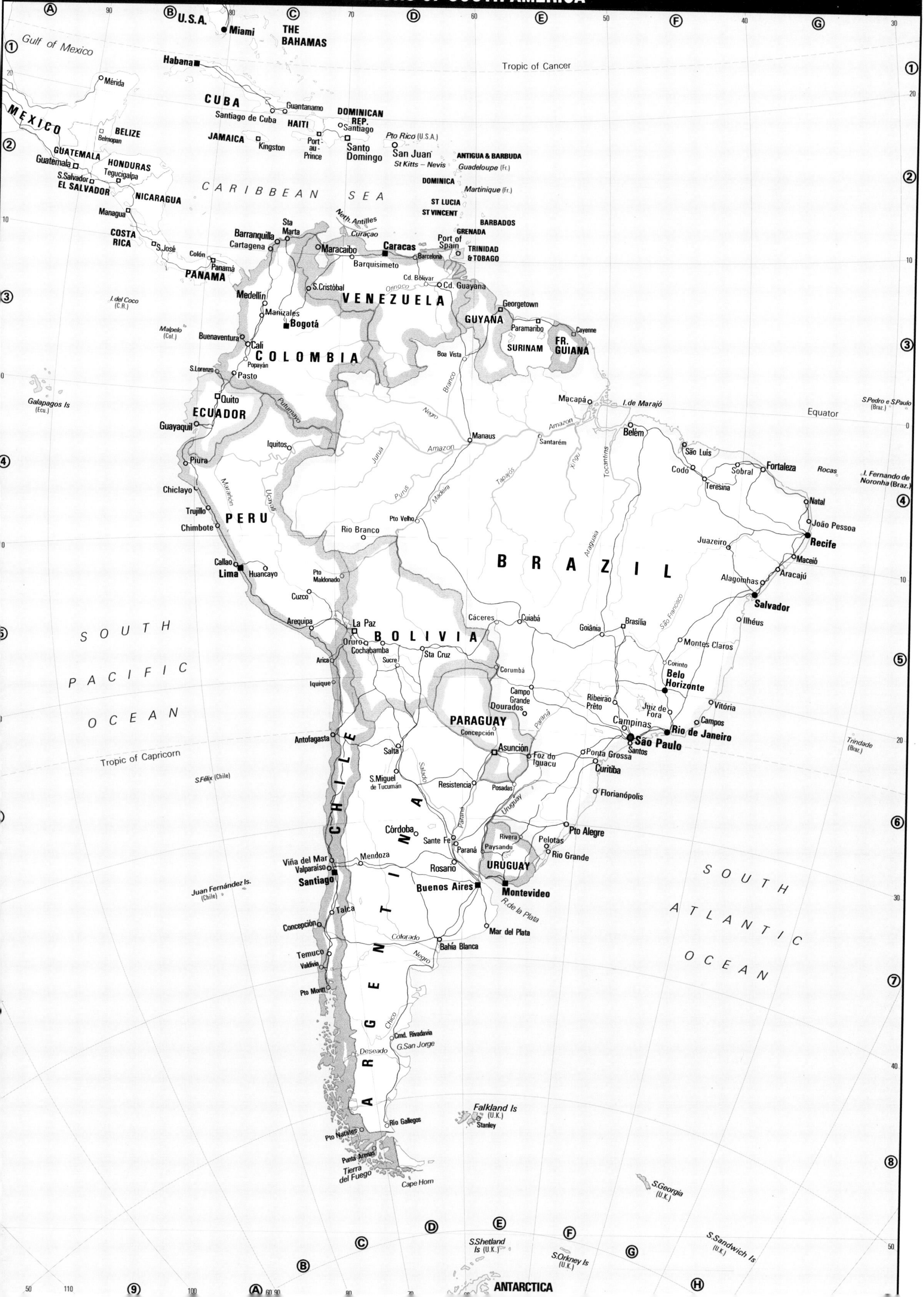

Gulf of Mexico

Tropic of Cancer

U.S.A.
Miami
THE BAHAMAS
Habana
Mérida

MEXICO

CUBA
Santiago de Cuba
Guantanamo
JAMAICA
Kingston
HAITI
Port-au-Prince
DOMINICAN REP.
Santiago
Santo Domingo
Pto Rico (U.S.A.)
San Juan
St Kitts – Nevis
ANTIGUA & BARBUDA
Guadeloupe (Fr.)
DOMINICA
Martinique (Fr.)
ST LUCIA
ST VINCENT
BARBADOS
GRENADA
Port of Spain
TRINIDAD & TOBAGO

BELIZE
Belmopan
GUATEMALA
Guatemala
HONDURAS
Tegucigalpa
S.Salvador
EL SALVADOR
NICARAGUA
Managua
COSTA RICA
S.José
Colón
Panamá
PANAMA

CARIBBEAN SEA

I.del Coco (C.R.)

Malpelo (Col.)

Barranquilla
Sta Marta
Cartagena
Neth. Antilles
Curaçao
Maracaibo
Caracas
Barcelona
Barquisimeto
Cd. Bolívar
Orinoco
Cd. Guayana

Medellín
Manizales
Bogotá
S.Cristóbal
VENEZUELA
GUYANA
Georgetown
Paramaribo
Cayenne
FR. GUIANA
SURINAM

Buenaventura
Cali
COLOMBIA
Popayán
Boa Vista
Branco

S.Lorenzo
Pasto
Quito
ECUADOR
Guayaquil
Putumayo

Macapá
I. de Marajó
Equator
S.Pedro e S.Paulo (Braz.)

Galapagos Is (Ecu.)

Iquitos
Marañón
Amazon
Manaus
Santarém
Amazon
Belém
São Luís
Fortaleza
Rocas
I. Fernando de Noronha (Braz.)

Piura
Negro
Juruá
Purús
Madeira
Tapajós
Xingú
Tocantins
Araguaia
Codó
Teresina
Sobral
Natal
João Pessoa
Recife

Chiclayo
Trujillo
PERU
Chimbote
Pto Velho
Rio Branco
BRAZIL
Juazeiro
Maceió
Aracajú

Callao
Lima
Huancayo
Pto Maldonado
Cuzco
Ucayali
Alagoinhas
Salvador
Ilhéus

Arequipa
La Paz
Cáceres
Cuiabá
Goiânia
Brasília
São Francisco
Montes Claros

SOUTH PACIFIC OCEAN

Oruro
Cochabamba
BOLIVIA
Sucre
Sta Cruz
Corumbá
Corinto
Belo Horizonte
Vitória

Arica
Iquique
Campo Grande
Dourados
Ribeirão Prêto
Juiz de Fora
Campos

Tropic of Capricorn
Antofagasta
PARAGUAY
Concepción
Paraná
Campinas
São Paulo
Santos
Rio de Janeiro
Trindade (Braz.)

S.Félix (Chile)
Salta
Salado
Asunción
Foz do Iguacu
Ponta Grossa
Curitiba

S.Miguel de Tucumán
Resistencia
Posadas
Florianópolis

CHILE
Córdoba
Santa Fe
Paraná
Uruguay
Rivera
Paysandu
Pto Alegre
Pelotas
Rio Grande

Juan Fernández Is. (Chile)
Viña del Mar
Valparaíso
Santiago
Mendoza
Rosario
ARGENTINA
URUGUAY
Montevideo

Talca
Buenos Aires
R.de la Plata

Concepción
Colorado
Negro
Bahía Blanca
Mar del Plata

SOUTH ATLANTIC OCEAN

Temuco
Valdivia
Pto Montt

Chico
Cmd. Rivadavia
Deseado
G.San Jorge

Falkland Is (U.K.)
Stanley

Rio Gallegos
Pto Natales
Punta Arenas
Tierra del Fuego
Cape Horn

S.Georgia (U.K.)

ANTARCTICA
S.Shetland Is (U.K.)
S.Orkney Is (U.K.)
S.Sandwich Is (U.K.)

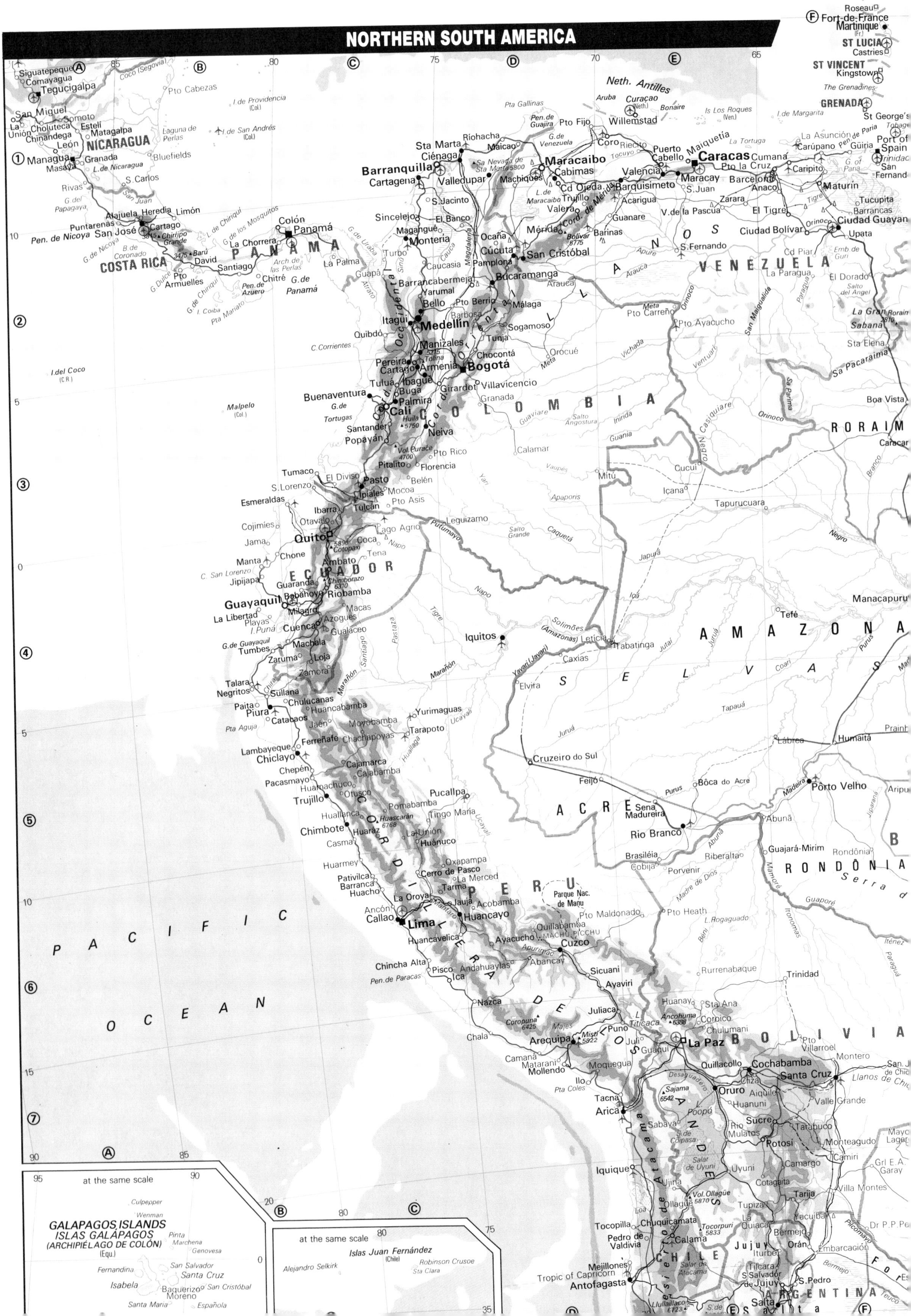

Roseau
(F) Fort-de-France
Martinique (Fr)
ST LUCIA
Castries
ST VINCENT
Kingstown
The Grenadines
GRENADA
St George's
Port of Spain
(Fr)
San Fernando
Trinidad
G. of Paria
Tobago

A 85 B 80 C 75 D 70 E 65

Siguatepeque
Comayagua
Tegucigalpa
Coco (Segovia)
Pto Cabezas
I. de Providencia (Col)
I. de San Andrés (Col)
San Miguel
La Unión
Choluteca
Chinandega Esteli
León Matagalpa
NICARAGUA
① Managua
Masaya Granada
L. de Nicaragua
Bluefields
Rivas S. Carlos
San Juan
B. de Papagaya
Alajuela Heredia Limón
Puntarenas San José Cartago
Pen. de Nicoya 3815 Chirripó Grande
G. de Nicoya 3475 Barú
B. de Coronado
COSTA RICA David
Pto Armuelles Chitré
G. Dulce G. de Chiriquí
Pen. de Azuero
I. Coiba Pta Mariato

Laguna de Perlas
G. de los Mosquitos
Colón
Panamá
PANAMA
La Chorrera
La Palma
Arch. de las Perlas
G. de Panamá

Pta Gallinas
Pen. de Guajira
Aruba (Neth) Curaçao (Neth)
Bonaire
Is Los Roques (Ven)
I. de Margarita
La Asunción
Carúpano Pen. de Paria Güiria

Riohacha
Maicao
G. de Venezuela
Pto Fijo Willemstad
Coro Riecito
Sta Marta Ciénaga
Sa Nevada de Sta Marta 5800
Barranquilla
Cartagena
Valledupar
Machiques
Maracaibo
Cabimas
Cd Ojeda
L. de Maracaibo
Trujillo
Valera Cord. de Mérida
Mérida
Bolívar 5775
Tucacoy Pto Cabello Maiquetia
Valencia Maracay
Barquisimeto S. Juan
Acarigua
Guanare
Barinas
Apure
CARACAS
Pto la Cruz
Barcelona Anaco
El Tigre
Zarara
V. de la Pasua
Cumana
Caripito
Maturín
Tucupita
Barrancas
Ciudad Guayan
Upata

S. Jacinto
El Banco
Magangué
Sincelejo
Montería
Turbo
Caucasia
Ocaña
Cúcuta
Pamplona
San Cristóbal
Bucaramanga
Arauca
Arauca
Cd Piar
Emb. de Guri
El Dorado
Salto del Angel
La Gran Sabana
Roraima 2810
Sta Elena
Sa Pacaraima

Quibdó
C. Corrientes
Barrancabermeja
Yarumal
Bello
Pto Berrio
Málaga
Sogamoso
Pto Carreño
Orocué
Vichada
Casiquiare
Boa Vista
RORAIM
Caracar

Itagüi MEDELLIN
Manizales
Pereira 5215 Tolima
Cartago Armenia
Tuluá Ibagué
Buenaventura S. de Buga
Palmira
Cali
Santander
Popayán
Huila 5750
Neiva
Pto Purace 4700
Pitalito
Florencia
Chocontá
BOGOTÁ
Villavicencio
Granada
Meta
Guaviare
Inírida
Salto Angostura
Guainía
Mitú
Cucui
Içana
Negro
Branco

COLOMBIA

Malpelo (Col.)
G. de Tortugas

Tumaco
El Diviso
S. Lorenzo
Pasto
Ipiales
Mocoa
Pto Rico
Calamar
Vaupés
Apaporis
Tapurucuara

Esmeraldas
Cojimíes
Jama
Otavalo Ibarra
Tulcán
Pto Asis
Putumayo
Leguizamo
Caquetá
Içá

Manta QUITO 5896 Coca
C. San Lorenzo Chone Cotopaxi Napo Tena
Jipijapa Ambato Japurá
Guaranda Chimborazo 5370 Riobamba
Guayaquil Milagro Macas
La Libertad Bababoyo
Playas Azogues
I. Puná Cuenca Gualáceo
G. de Guayaquil Machala Santiago
Tumbes Loja Pastaza
Zaruma Zamora Marañón

ECUADOR

Iquitos
(Amazonas) Leticia
Tabatinga
Caxias
Jutaí
Juruá
Tefé
AMAZONA

Talara
Negritos
Paita
Piura
Catacaos
Pta Aguja
Sullana
Chulucanas
Jaén
Huancabamba
Moyobamba
Yurimaguas
Tarapoto
Huallaga
Ucayali
Yavari (Javari)
Elvira
Yavari
SELVA
Juruá
Tapauá
Cruzeiro do Sul
Feijó
Purus
Bôca do Acre
Lábrea
Humaitá
Prainh

Lambayeque
Chiclayo
Chepén
Pacasmayo
Ferreñafe
Cajamarca
Cajabamba
Pucallpa
Purus
Sena Madureira
Abunã
ACRE
Rio Branco
Abuná
Guajará-Mirim
Madeira Pôrto Velho
Aripu
RONDÔNIA
Serra d

Trujillo
Huamachuco
Otusco
Pomabamba
Tingo María
Juruá
Cobija
Brasiléia
Riberalta
Porvenir
Rondônia

Chimbote
Casma
Huallanca Huascarán 6768
Huaraz
La Unión
Huánuco
Oxapampa
Madre de Dios
Pto de Dios
Pto Heath
L. Rogaguado
Guaporé
Itonomas
Iténez

Huarmey
Pativilca
Barranca
Huacho
Ancón
Callao
Cerro de Pasco
La Merced
Tarma
La Oroya
Jauja Acobamba
Huancayo
Parque Nac. de Manu
Pto Maldonado
Rurrenabaque
Beni
Trinidad

LIMA
Huancavelica
Ayacucho
Apurimac
MACHU PICCHU
Quillabamba
Cuzco
Sicuani
Ayaviri
Abancay
Andahuaylas
Huanay
Sta Ana
Ancohuma 6388
Corico
Chulumani

PERU

Chincha Alta
Pisco
Ica
Pen. de Paracas
Nazca
Chala
Coropuna 6425
Majes
Juliaca
L. Titicaca
Puno
Juli
Guaqui
La Paz
Montero
BOLIVIA
Pto Villarroel
Llanos de Chi

Arequipa Misti 5922
Camana
Matarani Mollendo
Moquegua
Ilo
Pta Coles
Tacna
Arica
Desaguadero
Sajama 6542
Oruro
Huanuni
Poopó
Quillacollo Cochabamba
Oploca
Aiquile
Santa Cruz
Sucre
Valle Grande
Montero
San J de Chic

PACIFIC OCEAN

Iquique
Sabaya
S. de Coipasa
Poopó
Tarabuco
Monteagudo
Camiri
Mayo
Lagar

Tocopilla
Chuquicamata
Pedro de Valdivia
Vol. Ollagüe 5870
Loa
Salar de Uyuni
Uyuni
Tupiza
Potosí
Camargo
Cotagaita
Tarija
Villa Montes
Dr P.P.Pe

Mejillones
S. Salvador
Antofagasta
Calama
S. Pedro
Pedro
Llullaillaco 6723
Salar de Atacama
Tilcara
S. Salvador de Jujuy
Jujuy
Orán
Embarcación
Tropic of Capricorn
CHILE
Desierto de Atacama
ANDES
Sajama
ARGENTINA
Salta

at the same scale

95 90
GALAPAGOS ISLANDS
ISLAS GALÁPAGOS
(ARCHIPIÉLAGO DE COLÓN) (Equ.)
Culpepper
Wenman
Pinta
Marchena
Genovesa
B 20 80 C
Fernandina
Santa Cruz
Isabela
Baquerizo Moreno
San Cristóbal
Española

at the same scale
80 75
Islas Juan Fernández (Chile)
Alejandro Selkirk
Robinson Crusoe
Sta Clara

I.del Coco (C.R.)

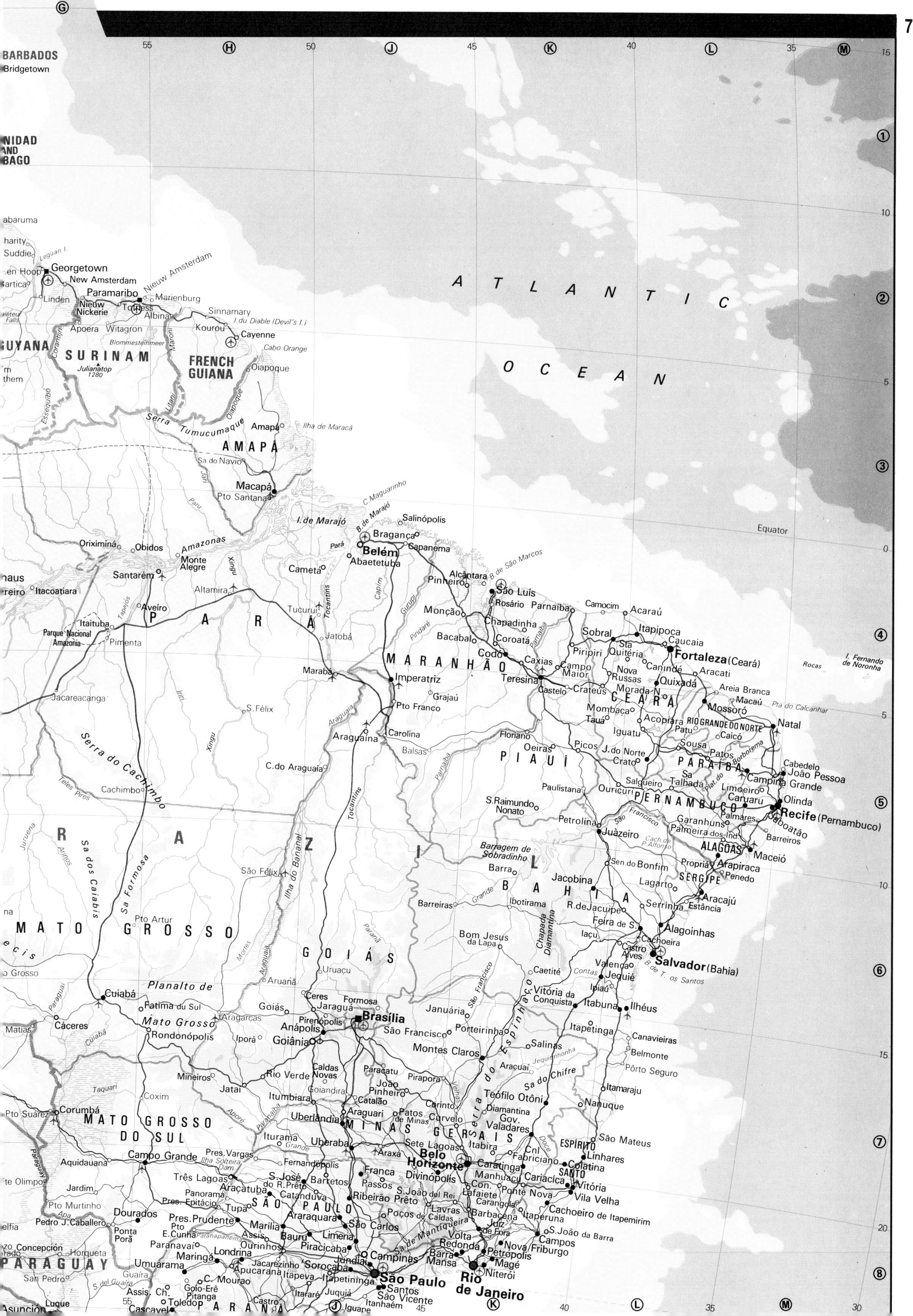
BARBADOS
Bridgetown
ATLANTIC OCEAN
Equator
Georgetown
New Amsterdam
Paramaribo
Nieuw Amsterdam
Marienburg
Linden
Nieuw Nickerie
Totness
Albina
Sinnamary
Kourou
Cayenne
I.du Diable (Devil's I.)
Apoera
Witagron
Blommestenmeer
Cabo Orange
SURINAM
FRENCH GUIANA
Julianatop 1280
Oiapoque
Serra Tumucumaque
Amapá
Ilha de Maracá
AMAPÁ
Sa do Navio
Macapá
Pto Santana
C. Maguarinho
B. de Marajó
I. de Marajó
Salinópolis
Bragança
Belém
Capanema
Abaetetuba
Pará
Oriximiná
Óbidos
Amazonas
Monte Alegre
Santarém
Cametá
Xingu
Itacoatiara
Altamira
Aveiro
Tucuruí
Tocantins
Capim
Gurupi
Alcântara
B. de São Marcos
Pinheiro
São Luís
Rosário
Parnaíba
Camocim
Acaraú
Itaituba
Tapajós
Parque Nacional Amazonia
Pimenta
PARÁ
Jatobá
Monção
Chapadinha
Bacabal
Coroatá
Pindaré
Sobral
Itapipoca
Caucaia
Fortaleza (Ceará)
Sta Quitéria
Canindé
Piripiri
Codó
Caxias
Campo Maior
Nova Russas
Quixadá
Aracati
Rocas
I. Fernando de Noronha
MARANHÃO
Teresina
Marabá
Imperatriz
Castelo
Crateús
Morada Nova
CEARÁ
Areia Branca
Macaú
Mossoró
Pta do Calcanhar
Jacareacanga
Grajaú
Pto Franco
S. Félix
Iriri
Mombaça
Tauá
Acopiara
Iguatu
Patu
RIO GRANDE DO NORTE
Caicó
Natal
Araguaia
Carolina
Araguaína
Floriano
Oeiras
Picos
J. do Norte
Crato
Sousa
Patos
Borborema
PARAÍBA
Cabedelo
João Pessoa
Campina Grande
Serra do Cachimbo
Balsas
C. do Araguaia
PIAUÍ
Sa Talhada
Plat. do
Salgueiro
Ouricuri
Paulistana
Limoeiro
Caruaru
Olinda
Recife (Pernambuco)
Teles Pires
Cachimbo
S. Raimundo Nonato
PERNAMBUCO
Garanhuns
Palmares
Jaboatão
Palmeira dos Índ.
Barreiros
Petrolina
Juàzeiro
Cach. de P. Afonso
ALAGOAS
Maceió
São Francisco
Barragem de Sobradinho
Sen. do Bonfim
Propriá
Arapiraca
Penedo
Juruena
Arinos
Sa dos Caiabis
Sa Formosa
BRAZIL
São Félix
Ilha do Bananal
Barra
Jacobina
SERGIPE
Lagarto
Aracajú
Estância
Serrinha
BAHIA
Barreiras
Grande
Ibotirama
R. de Jacuípe
Chapada Diamantina
Feira de S.
Alagoinhas
Pto Artur
MATO GROSSO
Paraná
Mortes
Bom Jesus da Lapa
Iaçu
Cachoeira
Castro Alves
Salvador (Bahia)
B. de T. os Santos
GOIÁS
Uruaçu
Caetité
Contas
Valença
Jequié
Ipiaú
Cuiabá
Planalto de Mato Grosso
Aruanã
Vitória da Conquista
Itabuna
Ilhéus
Cáceres
Fatima du Sul
Goiás
Ceres
Jaragua
Formosa
Brasília
Januária
Matias
Aragarças
Rondonópolis
Pirenópolis
Anápolis
Goiânia
Iporá
São Francisco
Porteirinha
Itapetinga
Canavieiras
Salinas
Belmonte
Montes Claros
Jequitinhonha
Pôrto Seguro
Serra do Espinhaço
Taquari
Mineiros
Jataí
Rio Verde
Caldas Novas
Paracatu
Pirapora
Araçuaí
Sa do Chifre
Itamaraju
Coxim
Itumbiara
Goiandira
João Pinheiro
Catalão
Teófilo Otôni
Nanuque
Corumbá
Pto Suárez
MATO GROSSO DO SUL
Aporé
Uberlândia
Araguari
Patos de Minas
Corinto
Curvelo
Diamantina
Gov. Valadares
MINAS GERAIS
São Mateus
Iturama
Uberaba
Araxá
Sete Lagoas
Itabira
ESPÍRITO SANTO
Linhares
Aquidauana
Campo Grande
Pres. Vargas
Ilha Solteira Dam
Fernandópolis
Belo Horizonte
Caratinga
Cnl Fabriciano
Colatina
Paraguay
Pte Olimpo
Três Lagoas
S. José do R. Prêto
Barretos
Franca
Passos
Divinópolis
Manhuaçu
Cariacica
Vitória
Vila Velha
Jardim
Panorama
Araçatuba
Catanduva
S. João del Rei
Con. Lafaiete
Ponte Nova
Carangola
Pto Murtinho
Pres. Epitácio
Tupã
SÃO PAULO
Ribeirão Prêto
Lavras
Barbacena
Itaperuna
Cachoeiro de Itapemirim
Pedro J. Caballero
Dourados
Pres. Prudente
Araraquara
Poços de Caldas
São Carlos
Serra da Mantiqueira
Juiz de Fora
S. João da Barra
Campos
Ponta Porã
Pto E. Cunha
Marília
Assis
Bauru
Limeira
Paranapanema
Concepción
Horqueta
Paranavaí
Ourinhos
Piracicaba
Volta Redonda
Nova Friburgo
Petrópolis
PARAGUAY
Umuarama
Maringá
Londrina
Jacarezinho
Apucarana
Sorocaba
Jundiaí
Campinas
Barra Mansa
Magé
Niterói
Rio de Janeiro
San Pedro
Guaíra
S. del Guaira
C. Mourão
Itapeva
Itapetininga
São Paulo
Assis. Ch.
Goio-Erê
Pitanga
Itararé
Juquiá
Santos
São Vicente
Itanhaém
Asunción
Luque
Toledo
Cascavel
Castro
PARANÁ
Iguape

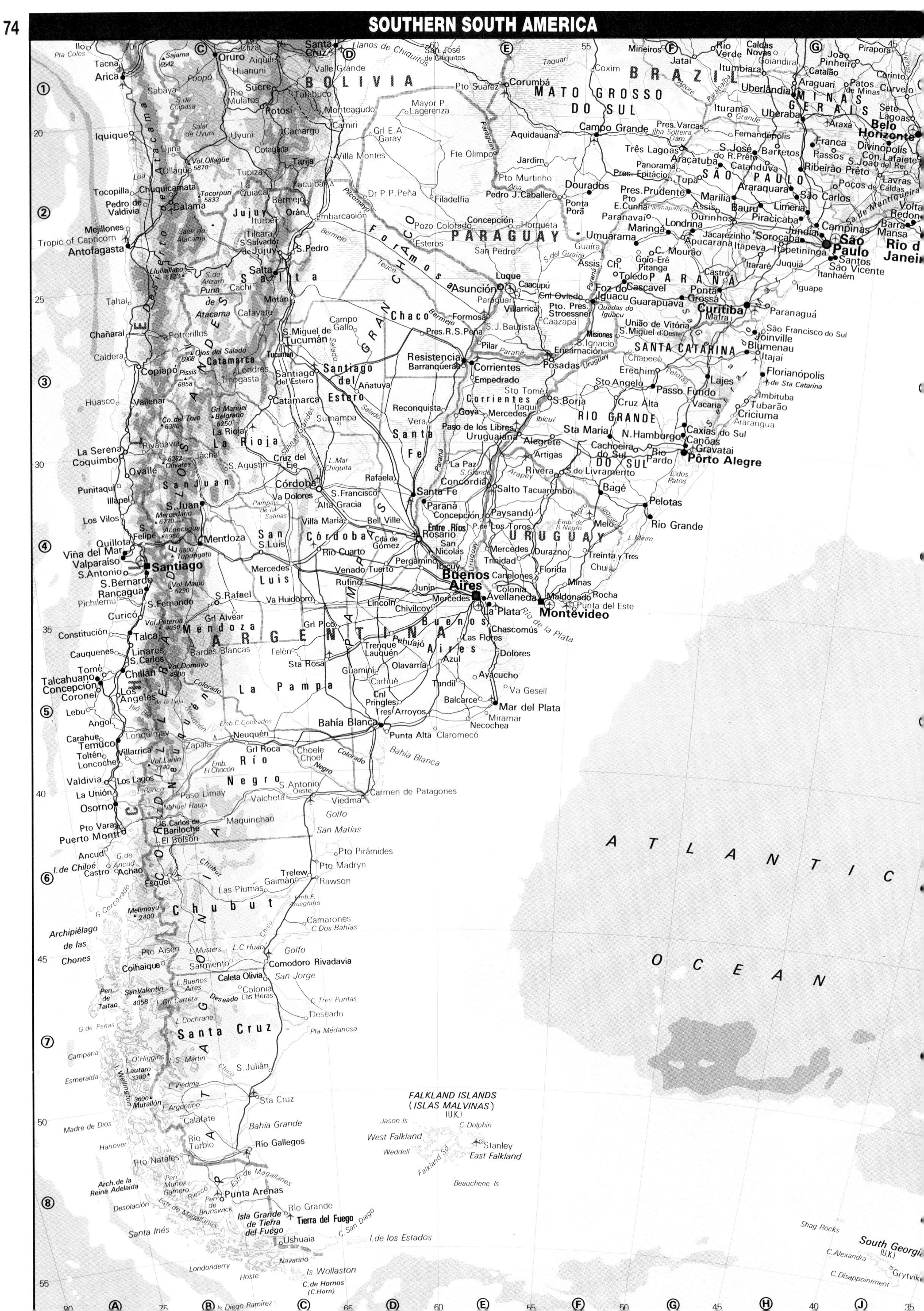
B O L I V I A
B R A Z I L
MATO GROSSO DO SUL
M I N A S G E R A I S
S Ã O P A U L O
P A R A N Á
SANTA CATARINA
RIO GRANDE DO SUL
P A R A G U A Y
U R U G U A Y
A R G E N T I N A
Tropic of Capricorn
Desierto de Atacama
Gran Chaco
Chaco
Formosa
Salta
Jujuy
Tucumán
Santiago del Estero
Catamarca
La Rioja
San Juan
San Luis
Córdoba
Santa Fe
Corrientes
Entre Ríos
Mendoza
La Pampa
Buenos Aires
Neuquén
Río Negro
Chubut
Santa Cruz
Tierra del Fuego
Cordillera de los Andes
Patagonia
Pampas
Arica
Iquique
Antofagasta
Copiapó
La Serena
Valparaíso
Santiago
Concepción
Temuco
Valdivia
Osorno
Puerto Montt
Punta Arenas
Ushuaia
Oruro
Sucre
Potosí
Tarija
Asunción
Resistencia
Rosario
Buenos Aires
La Plata
Montevideo
Mar del Plata
Bahía Blanca
Comodoro Rivadavia
Río Gallegos
Campo Grande
Curitiba
Florianópolis
Pôrto Alegre
São Paulo
Santos
Belo Horizonte
Rio de Janeiro
FALKLAND ISLANDS
(ISLAS MALVINAS)
(U.K.)
West Falkland
East Falkland
Stanley
I.de los Estados
Is Wollaston
C.de Hornos
(C.Horn)
Shag Rocks
South Georgia
(U.K.)
Grytviken
A T L A N T I C
O C E A N

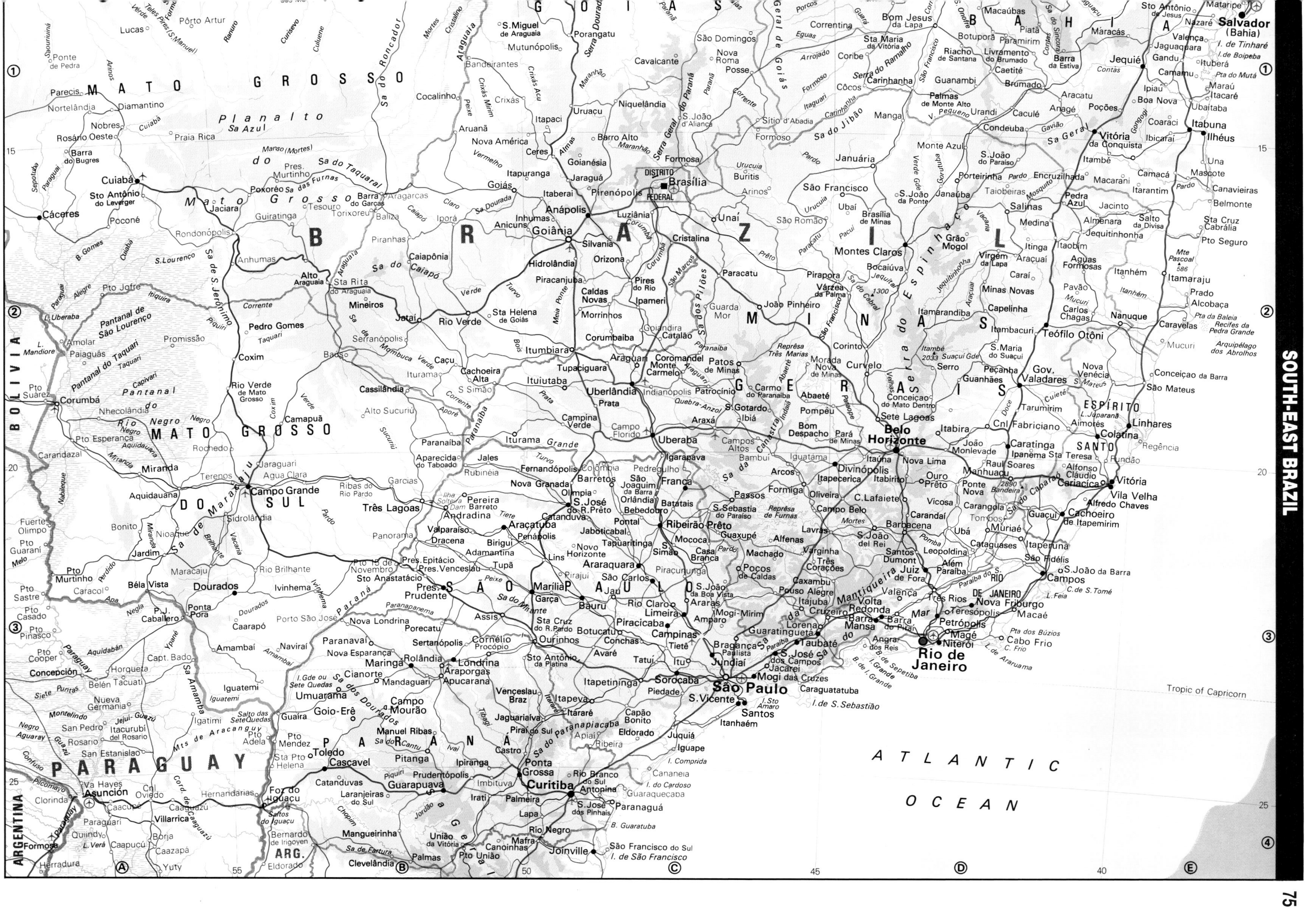
ATLANTIC
OCEAN
Tropic of Capricorn
BAHIA
MINAS GERAIS
ESPÍRITO SANTO
RIO DE JANEIRO
SÃO PAULO
PARANÁ
GOIÁS
MATO GROSSO
MATO GROSSO DO SUL
DISTRITO FEDERAL
BRAZIL
BOLIVIA
PARAGUAY
ARGENTINA
ARG.
Salvador (Bahia)
Ilhéus
Itabuna
Jequié
Vitória da Conquista
Teófilo Otôni
Gov. Valadares
Vitória
Vila Velha
Cachoeiro de Itapemirim
Campos
Rio de Janeiro
Niterói
Petrópolis
Belo Horizonte
Juiz de Fora
Montes Claros
Uberaba
Uberlândia
São Paulo
Santos
Campinas
Ribeirão Prêto
Curitiba
Joinville
Brasília
Goiânia
Anápolis
Campo Grande
Cuiabá
Corumbá
Asunción
Londrina
Maringá
Cascavel
Dourados
Três Lagoas
0
100
200
300 km

Portland
Seattle
Vancouver I.
Prince Rupert
Vancouver
Juneau
Vadzu
Anchorage
6194
Mt McKinley
Yukon
Teller
Bering Str.
Vankarem
Ayan
Blagoveshchensk
CHINA
Skovorodino
Chul'man
Amur
Chita
Ula Ud
Calgary
Edmonton
Dawson
Fairbanks
Alaska
(U.S.A.)
Kolyma
Pevek
Ambarchik
Ust'Nera
Aldan
Saskatoon
120
ROCKY MTS
Norman Wells
Inuvik
Prudhoe Bay
Barrow
Chukchi Sea
Wrangel I.
(O. Vrangel'ya)
70
Polyarn'yy
Indigirka
Verkhoyansk
Yakutsk
Kazach'ye
Chita
Flin Flon
Gt Bear L.
Yellowknife
Mackenzie
Gt Slave L.
East Siberian Sea
Kazach'ye
Zhigansk
Ust'Kut
Irkuts
L. Athabasca
CANADA
Coppermine
Banks I.
Victoria I.
McClure Str.
80
Novosibirskiye
Ostrova
Tiksi
Lena
U.
L. Winnipeg
4
90
Churchill
Queen
Elizabeth
Islands
N.Magnetic Pole
(1980)
Resolute
Laptev Sea
Nordvik
Tree Limit
S.
Krasnoyarsk
D
C
B
A
A
B
C
D
Hudson
Bay
Southampton I.
G.of Boothia
Ellesmere I.
North Pole
Eureka
Severnaya
Zemlya
Khatanga
Noril'sk
Turukhansk
Yenisey
Novosibirsk
Ba
S.
S.
Foxe Basin
Baffin I.
Resolute
Alert
Zemlya
Frantsa
Iosifa
Dikson
Dudinka
James B.
Fort George
Inukjuac
Tree Limit
Hudson Str.
Pond Inlet
Thule
Narres Str.
Lincoln Sea
Nord
Novaya Zemlya
Kara Sea
Nadym
Salekhard
Ob
Berezovo
Vorkuta
R.
Omsk
Tobol'sk
Tselino
3
Scheffervil
Hebron
Nain
Davis Str.
Godhavn
(Qeqertarsuaq)
Sondre Stromfjord
Greenland
(Den.)
Baffin
Bay
Upernavik
Svalbard
(Spitsbergen)
(Nor.)
Greenland
Sea
Barents
Sea
Uralskiy
Khrebet
Serov
Sverdlovsk
Perm'
Magnitogorsk
Labrador
Sea
Godthåb
(Nuuk)
G
Watkins Bjerge
3700
Scoresbysund
Bjørnøya
(Bear I.)
(Nor.)
Mezen'
Syktyvkar
Kotlas
Kirov
Ufa
Orsk
Gulf of
St Lawrence
60
Julianehåb
(Qaqortoq)
Ammassalik
(Angmagssalik)
K. Farvel
Denmark Strait
Jan Mayen (Nor.)
Norwegian
Nordkapp
Tromsø
Murmansk
Sev.Dvina
Arkhangel'sk
White Sea
Kazan'
Kuybyshev
Aktyubinsk
Newfoundland
Gander
2
ATLANTIC OCEAN
30
Reykjavik
ICELAND
1
Sea
Arctic Circle
0
NORWAY
Narvik
SWEDEN
Umeå
Oulu
FINLAND
12
30
Leningrad
Yaroslavl
Gor'kiy
11

2
30
1
0
12
30
11
ATLANTIC OCEAN
Antarctic Circle
60
Falkland Is
(U.K.)
Scotia
Sea
Orcadas
(Arg.)
S. Orkney
Is (U.K.)
Signy (U.K.)
Sanae
(S.A.)
Dakshin Gangotri (India)
Novolazarevskaya (U.S.S.R.)
Prinsesse
Astrid Kyst
Asuka (Japan)
Prinsesse
Ragnhild
Kyst
Syowa (Jap.)
Molodezhnaya
(U.S.S.R.)
INDIAN
Weddell
Sea
Georg Von Neumayer
(F.R.G.)
Dronning Maud Land
Enderby Land
ARGENTINA
S. Shetland
Is (U.K.)
King George I.
9
8
10
11
Graham
Land
Coats Land
Halley
(U.K.)
Mawson
(Aust.)
Heard I.
(Aust.)
Tierra del
Fuego
Palmer
Arch.
Antarctic
Peninsula
12
13
General Belgrano II
(Arg.)
Mac. Robertson Land
3355
Pr. Charles Mts
C. Darnley
Amery
Ice Shelf
CHILE
3
14
Palmer Land
Alexander I.
Ronne
Ice
Shelf
Berkner
I.
Lambert Gl.
Davis (Aust.)
15
Charcot I.
Pensacola
Mts
GREATER
American
Highland
Bellingshausen
Sea
Ellsworth
Land
Siple
(U.S.)
5140
Vinson Massif
F
Transantarctic
South Pole
Amundsen-Scott
(U.S.)
E
ANTARCTICA
F
G
H
PACIFIC
H
G
Peter I Øy
(Nor.)
Thurston I.
3022
Mt Seelig
LESSER
ANTARCTICA
E
Mts
Queen Mary
Land
Mirnyy (U.S.S.R.)
OCEAN
90
Walgreen Coast
Mt Sidley
4181
Marie
Byrd Land
Siple I.
Russkaya
(U.S.S.R.)
Mt Kirkpatrick
4528
Mt Markham
Ross Ice
Shelf
Roosevelt
I.
C. Colbeck
80
Vostok
(U.S.S.R.)
Victoria Land
Knox Coast
Casey
(Aust.)
C. Poinsett
Shackleton
Ice Shelf
Amundsen
Sea
4
120
Ross Sea
Scott
(N.Z.)
Mt Murdo
Wilkes Land
George V
Land
Terre
Adélie
Dumont d'Urville (Fr.)
C. Adare
Leningradskaya
(U.S.S.R.)
George V
Land
S.Magnetic Pole
(1980)
average minimum extent of sea ice
70
Oates Land
Balleny Is
5
150
6
180
7
150
8
Sturge I.
Scott I.

King George Island
62°S
60°S
1
2
58°30'W
3
4
5
6
7
0 10 20 30km

Antarctic Research Stations
1 Commandante Ferraz (Brazil)
2 Artowskiy (Poland)
3 Teniente Jubany (Argentina)
4 Artigas (Uruguay)
5 Bellinghausen (Ussr)
6 Teniente Rodolfo Marsh (Chile)
7 Great Wall (China)
8 Captain Arturo Prat (Chile)
9 Esperanza (Argentina)
10 General Bernardo O'Higgins (Chile)
11 Marambio (Argentina)
12 Palmer (USA)
13 Faraday (UK)
14 General San Martin (Argentina)
15 Rothera (UK)

1:40M
0 400 800 1200 1600 km
0 400 800 mls

International Boundary
State Boundary
Department Boundary
City Limits
Borough, District Boundary
Military Zones
Armistice, Ceasefire Line
Demilitarised Zone
Main Railways (Station)
Other Railways (Bridge)
Projected Railways
Underground Railway (Station)
Aerial Cableway, Funicular
Metro Stations (M)
Special Highway (Projected)
Main Road
Secondary Road
Other Road, Street
Track
Road Tunnel
Bridge, Flyover

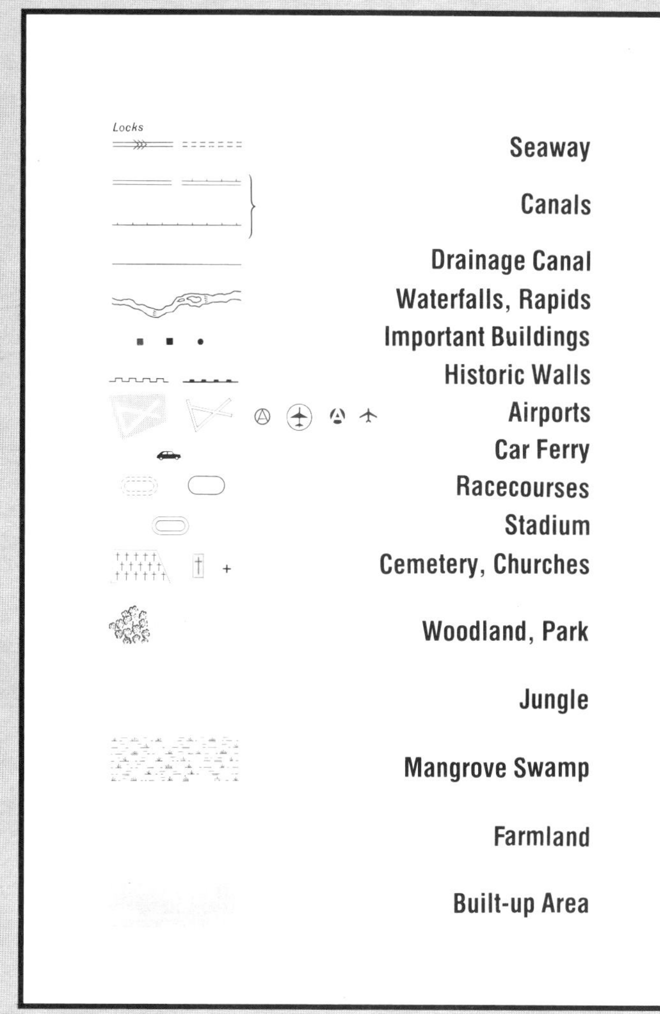
Locks
Seaway
Canals
Drainage Canal
Waterfalls, Rapids
Important Buildings
Historic Walls
Airports
Car Ferry
Racecourses
Stadium
Cemetery, Churches
Woodland, Park
Jungle
Mangrove Swamp
Farmland
Built-up Area

Amsterdam 81
Athens 83
Auckland 86
Bangkok 84
Barcelona 80
Beijing 84
Berlin 82
Bombay 87
Boston 89
Brussels 81
Buenos Aires 92
Cairo 88
Calcutta 87
Chicago 89
Copenhagen 83
Delhi 87
Geneva 82
Hamburg 82
Hong Kong 84
Istanbul 88
Jerusalem 88
London 78
Los Angeles 91
Madrid 80
Manhattan 90
Melbourne 86
Mexico City 92
Milan 82
Montreal 89
Moscow 83
Nairobi 88
New York 90
Osaka 85
Ottawa 89
Paris 79
Perth 86
Rio de Janeiro 92
Rome 80
San Francisco 91
Santiago 92
São Paulo 92
Seoul 85
Shanghai 84
Singapore 87
Stockholm 83
Sydney 86
Tokyo 85
Toronto 89
Vienna 81
Washington 91

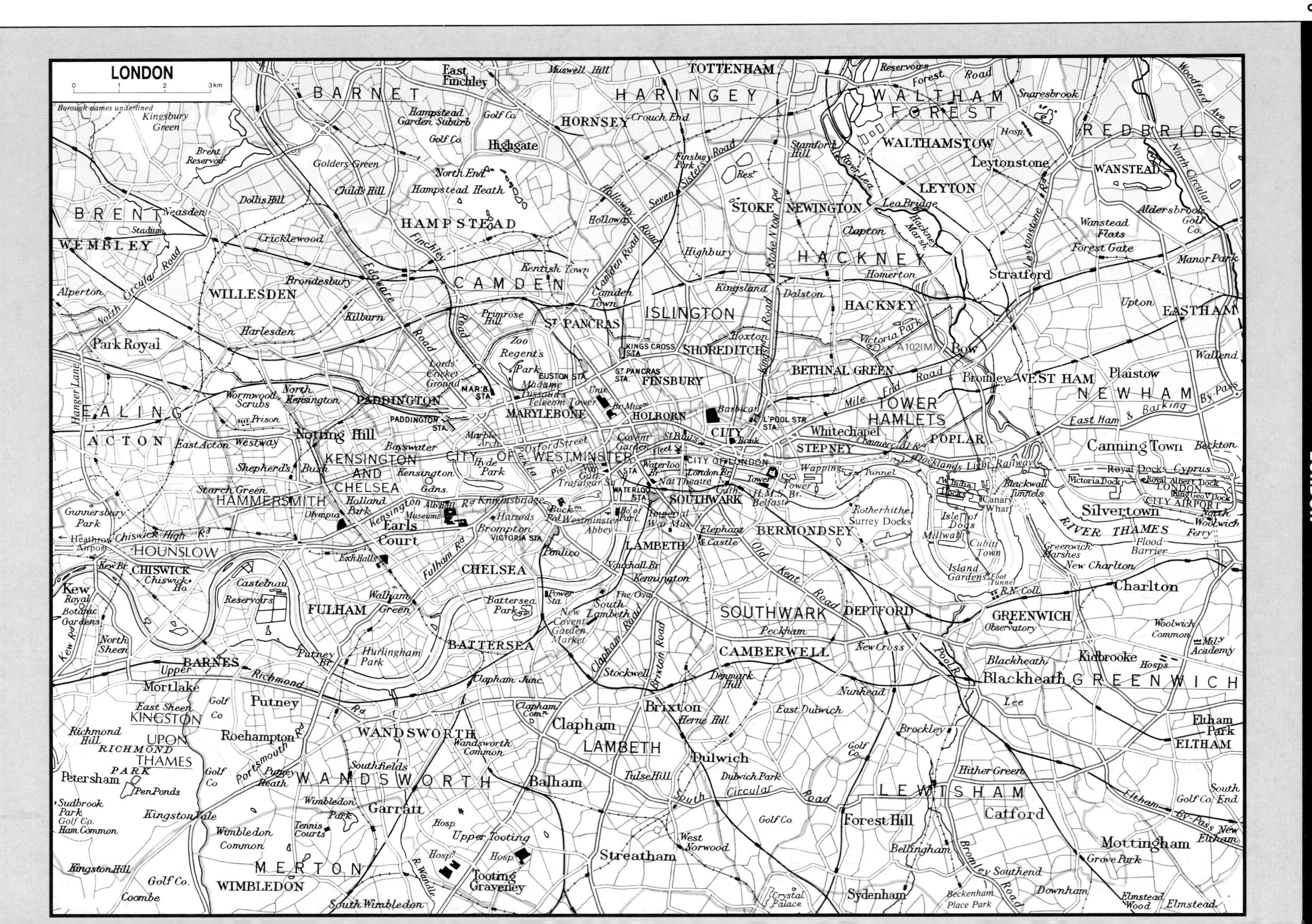
LONDON
0 1 2 3km
Borough names underlined
BARNET
East Finchley
Muswell Hill
TOTTENHAM
HARINGEY
Reservoirs
Forest Road
WALTHAM FOREST
Snaresbrook
Woodford Ave.
Kingsbury Green
Hampstead Garden Suburb
Golf Co.
HORNSEY
Crouch End
WALTHAMSTOW
Hosp.
REDBRIDGE
Brent Reservoir
Highgate
Finsbury Park
Seven Sisters Road
Stamford Hill
River Lea
Leytonstone
WANSTEAD
North Circular
Golders Green
North End
Res.
LEYTON
Childs Hill
Hampstead Heath
Holloway Road
STOKE NEWINGTON
Lea Bridge
Hackney Marsh
Aldersbrook
Dollis Hill
BRENT
Neasden
HAMPSTEAD
Holloway
Clapton
Wanstead Flats
Stadium
Cricklewood
Camden Road
Highbury
Stoke N'ton Rd
HACKNEY
Leytonstone Rd
Forest Gate
WEMBLEY
Finchley
Kentish Town
Homerton
Stratford
Manor Park
North Circular Road
Brondesbury
CAMDEN
Camden Town
Kingsland
Dalston
Alperton
WILLESDEN
ISLINGTON
HACKNEY
Upton
EASTHAM
Kilburn
Primrose Hill
ST PANCRAS
Victoria Park
Bow
Harlesden
Edgware Road
Zoo
Regent's Park
KINGS CROSS STA
SHOREDITCH
Hoxton
A102(M)
Wallend
Park Royal
Lords' Cricket Ground
EUSTON STA
ST PANCRAS STA.
FINSBURY
BETHNAL GREEN
Bromley
WEST HAM
Plaistow
Hanger Lane
Wormwood Scrubs
North Kensington
MAR'B. STA.
Madame Tussaud's
Telecom Tower
Univ.
Br. Mus.
Barbican
Mile End Road
TOWER HAMLETS
NEWHAM
By Pass
EALING
PADDINGTON
MARYLEBONE
HOLBORN
L'POOL STR STA.
Whitechapel
East Ham & Barking
Prison
PADDINGTON STA.
Marble Arch
Covent Garden
St. Pauls
CITY
Bank
Commercial Rd
POPLAR
ACTON
East Acton
Westway
Notting Hill
Bayswater
Oxford Street
Fleet St.
STEPNEY
Canning Town
Beckton
KENSINGTON AND CHELSEA
CITY OF WESTMINSTER
CITY OF LONDON
Docklands Light Railway
Shepherd's Bush
Kensington Gdns.
Hyde Park
Piccadilly
Nat. Gall.
Trafalgar Sq.
Waterloo Br.
London Br.
Tower
Wapping
Tunnel
Royal Docks
Cyprus
Starch Green
HAMMERSMITH
Holland Park
Albert Hall
Museums
Rd
Knightsbridge
Harrods
Buck'm Pal.
WATERLOO STA.
Nat. Theatre
Cath.
SOUTHWARK
H.M.S. Belfast
Tower Br.
West India Docks
Blackwall Tunnels
Victoria Dock
Royal Albert Dock
King Geo. V Dock
LONDON CITY AIRPORT
Gunnersbury Park
Olympia
Kensington
Earls Court
Brompton
VICTORIA STA.
Westminster Abbey
Ho. of Parl.
Imperial War Mus.
Elephant & Castle
Rotherhithe
Surrey Docks
Canary Wharf
Silvertown
North Woolwich
Heathrow Airport
Chiswick High Rd.
HOUNSLOW
Fulham Rd
Pimlico
LAMBETH
BERMONDSEY
Isle of Dogs
Millwall
RIVER THAMES
Woolwich Ferry
Kew Br.
CHISWICK
Chiswick Ho.
Exh. Halls
CHELSEA
Vauxhall Br.
Old Kent Road
Cubitt Town
Greenwich Marshes
Flood Barrier
Kennington
Island Gardens
Foot Tunnel
New Charlton
Kew
Royal Botanic Gardens
Castelnau Reservoirs
Walham Green
Power Sta.
The Oval
South Lambeth
R.N. Coll.
Charlton
FULHAM
Battersea Park
New Covent Garden Market
SOUTHWARK
DEPTFORD
GREENWICH
Observatory
Woolwich Common
Kew Rd
North Sheen
Clapham Road
Brixton Road
Peckham
Mil'y Academy
Putney Br.
Hurlingham Park
BATTERSEA
New Cross
Pool R.
CAMBERWELL
BARNES
Upper Richmond
Clapham Junc.
Stockwell
Denmark Hill
Blackheath
Kidbrooke
Hosps.
Mortlake
Blackheath
GREENWICH
East Sheen
Golf Co
Putney
Rd
Nunhead
Lee
KINGSTON UPON THAMES
Clapham Comn.
Clapham
Brixton
Herne Hill
East Dulwich
Richmond Hill
RICHMOND PARK
Roehampton
Portsmouth Rd
WANDSWORTH
Wandsworth Common
LAMBETH
Brockley
Eltham Park
ELTHAM
Southfields
Putney Heath
Dulwich
Petersham
Pen Ponds
WANDSWORTH
Balham
Tulse Hill
Dulwich Park
South Circular Road
Hither Green
LEWISHAM
South Golf Co. End
Sudbrook Park
Golf Co.
Ham Common
Kingston Vale
Wimbledon Park
Garratt
Forest Hill
Catford
Eltham By-Pass
New Eltham
Wimbledon Common
Tennis Courts
Upper Tooting
Hosp.
West Norwood
Bellingham
Mottingham
Kingston Hill
MERTON
R. Wandle
Tooting Graveney
Streatham
Bromley Road
Southend
Grove Park
Golf Co.
WIMBLEDON
Coombe
South Wimbledon
Crystal Palace
Sydenham
Beckenham Place Park
Downham
Elmstead Wood
Elmstead

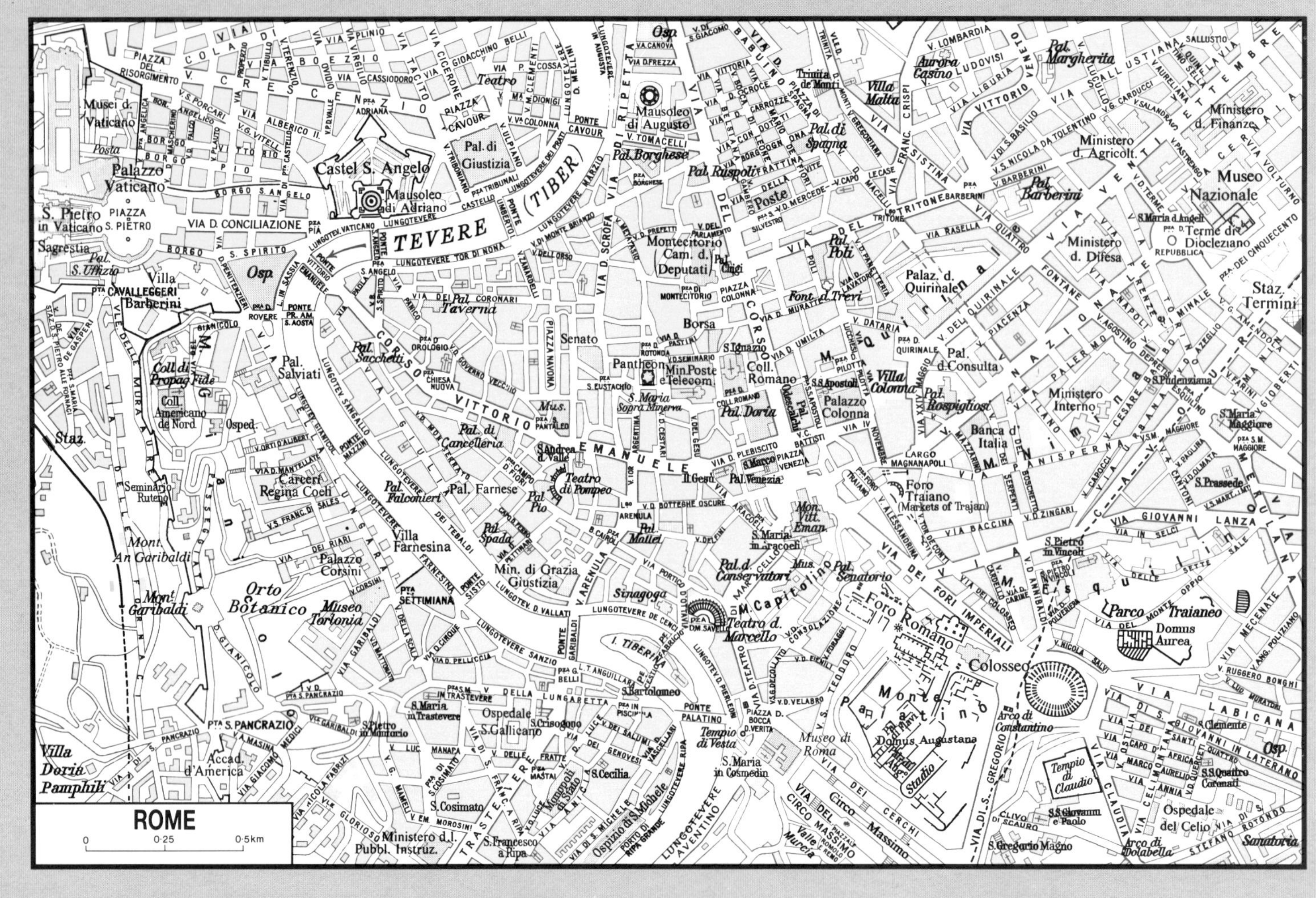

ROME

0   0.25   0.5km

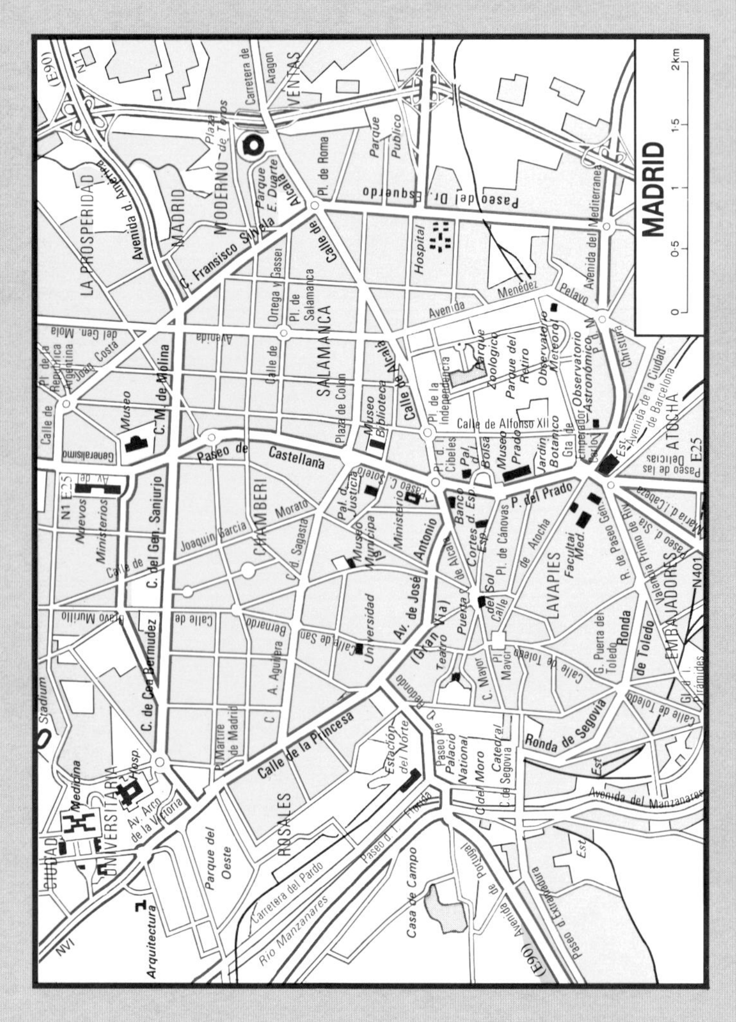

MADRID

2km
1.5
1
0.5
0

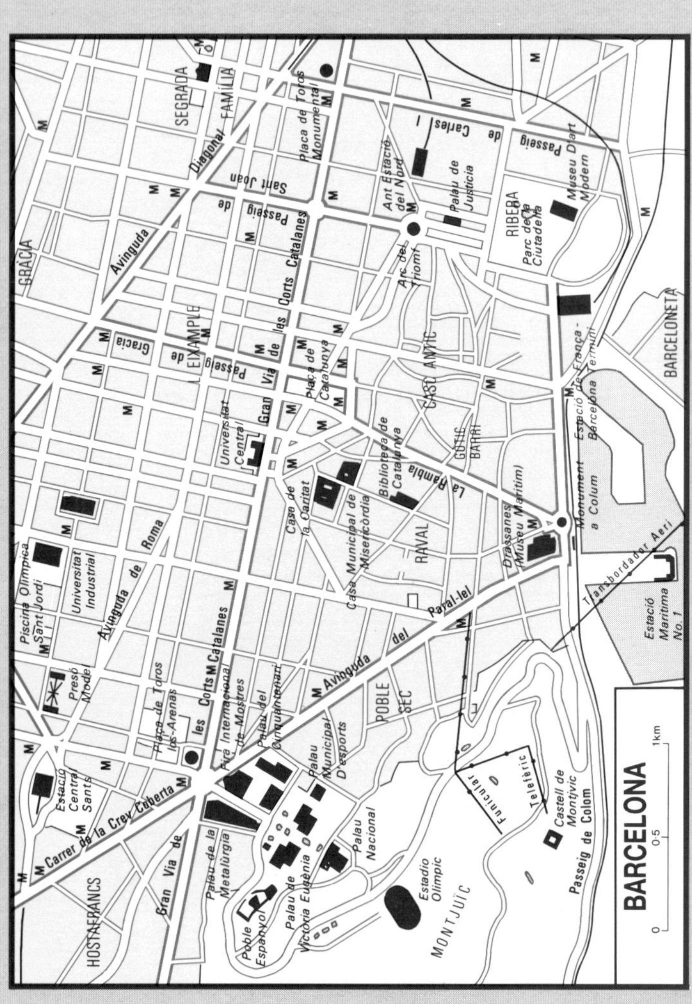

BARCELONA

1km
0.5
0

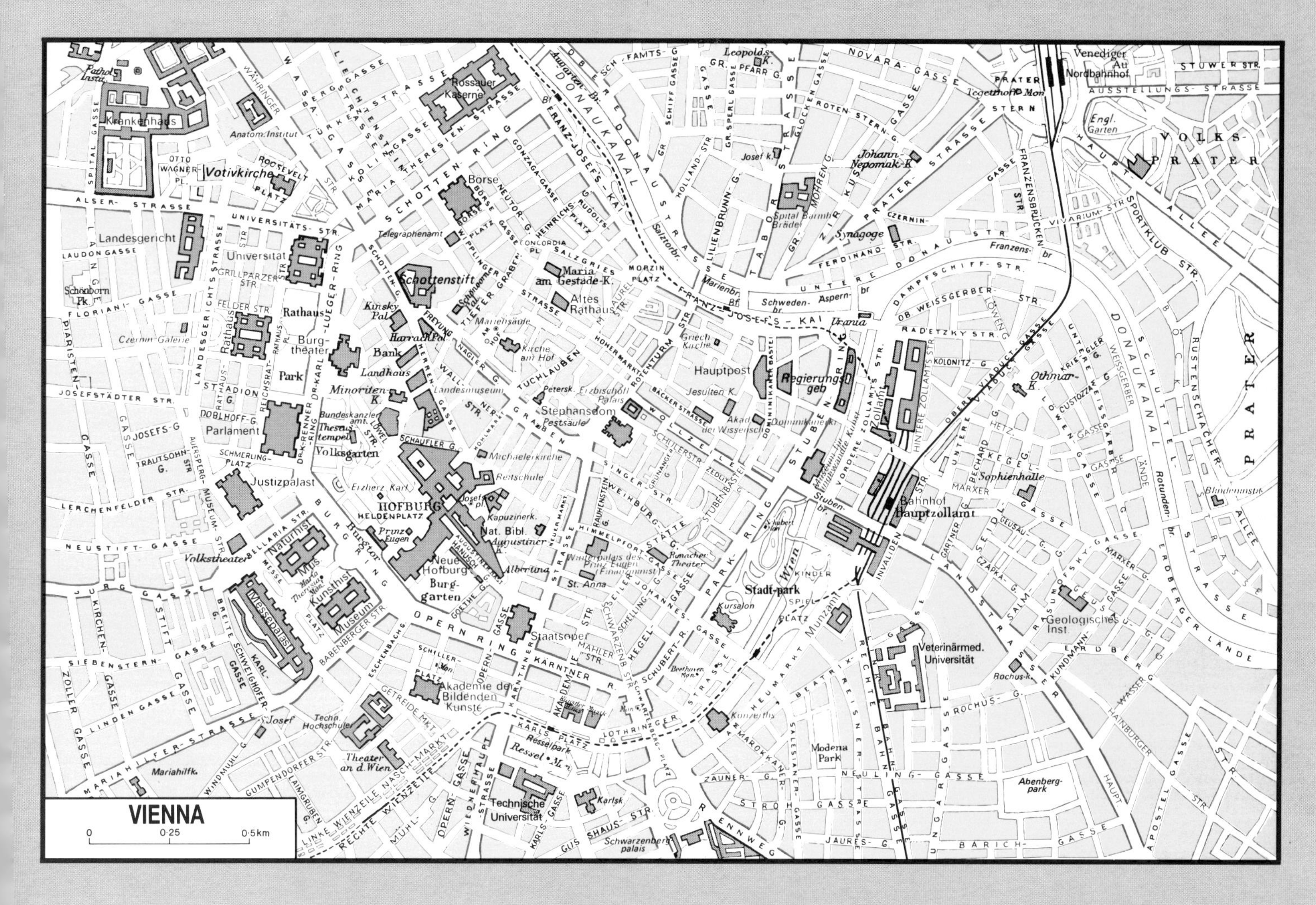
VIENNA
0 0·25 0·5km
Votivkirche
Rossauer Kaserne
Landesgericht
Universität
Rathaus
Parlament
Burg-theater
Volksgarten
Justizpalast
HOFBURG
HELDENPLATZ
Neue Hofburg
Burg-garten
Kunsthist. Museum
Naturhist. Mus.
Messepalast
Volkstheater
Staatsoper
Akademie der Bildenden Künste
Technische Universität
Karlsk.
Schwarzenberg palais
Stadt-park
Hauptpost
Regierungs-geb
Bahnhof Hauptzollamt
Stephansdom
Schottenstift
Börse
Maria am Gestade-K.
Altes Rathaus
Sophienhalle
Geologisches Inst
Veterinärmed. Universität
Modena Park
Abenberg-park
Nordbahnhof
Venediger Au
PRATER
VOLKS-PRATER
DONAUKANAL
FRANZ-JOSEFS-KAI
SCHOTTEN RING
OPERN RING
KÄRNTNER RING
PARK RING
STUBEN RING
LANDSTRASSE HAUPT
DONAU KANAL
Krankenhaus
Anatom. Institut
Telegraphenamt
Landhaus
Minoriten-K.
Bank
Kapuzinerk.
Nat. Bibl.
Albertina
St. Anna
Kursalon
Karlsplatz
Ressel park
Theater an d. Wien
Techn. Hochschule
Mariahilf.
Urania
Johann-Nepomuk-K.
Synagoge
Othmar-K.
Rochus-K.

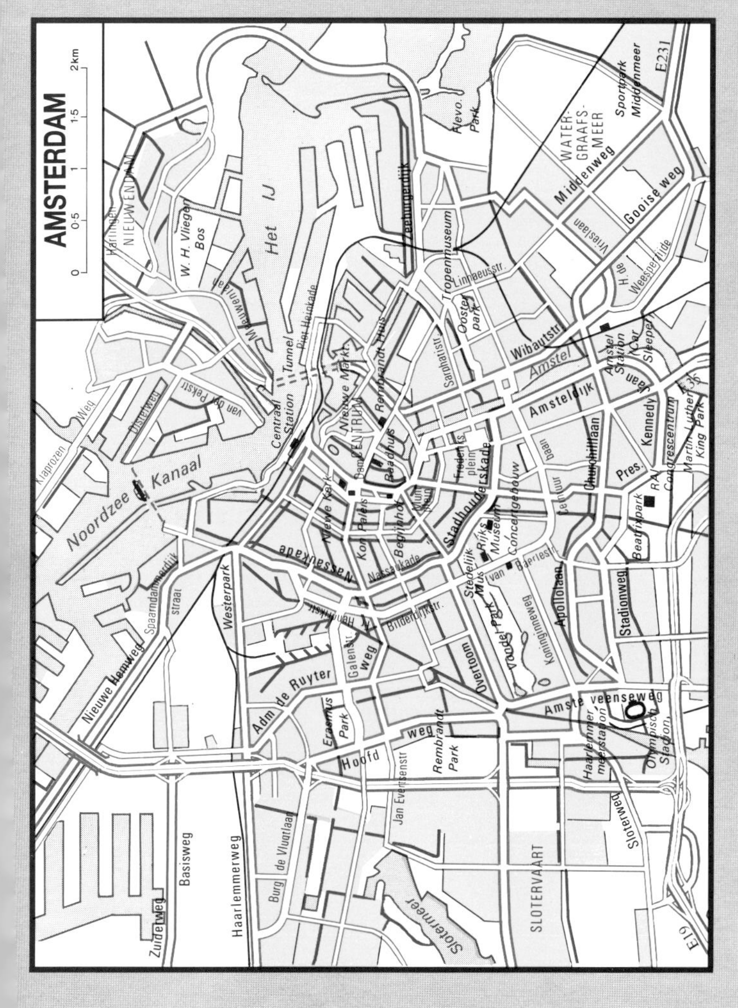
AMSTERDAM
0 0·5 1 1·5 2km
Het IJ
Noordzee Kanaal
W. H. Vliegen Bos
Central Station
CENTRUM
Amstel
Amstel Station
Oosterpark
Tropenmuseum
Vondel Park
Rijks Museum
Concertgebouw
Stadionweg
Olympisch Stadion
Rembrandt Park
Erasmus Park
Westerpark
Wibautstr.
Middenweg
Gooise weg
WATER-GRAAFS-MEER
Sportpark Middenmeer
Flevo Park
RAI
Congrescentrum
Haarlemmerweg
Basisweg
Sloterweg
SLOTERVAART
Nieuwe Hemweg
Zuiderweg
Adm. de Ruyter
Jan Evertsenstr
Apollolaan
Stadhouderskade
Nassaukade
Kennedy
Pres.
E231
E19

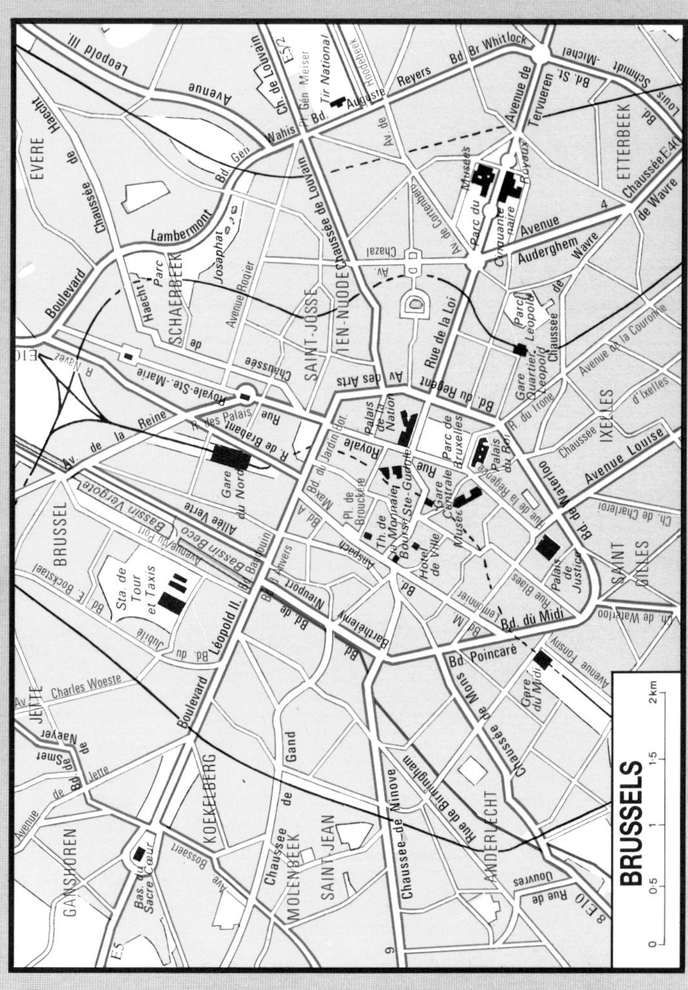
BRUSSELS
0 0·5 1 1·5 2km
EVERE
SCHAERBEEK
SAINT-JOSSE-TEN-NOODE
BRUSSEL
KOEKELBERG
MOLENBEEK SAINT-JEAN
ANDERLECHT
GANSHOREN
JETTE
IXELLES
SAINT GILLES
ETTERBEEK
Gare du Nord
Gare Centrale
Gare du Midi
Gare Quartier Léopold
Palais de Justice
Palais de la Nation
Parc de Bruxelles
Parc du Cinquantenaire
Parc Léopold
Musées
Hôtel de Ville
Bourse
Bas. du Sacré Cœur
Sta. de Tour et Taxis
Bassin Vergote
Bassin Béco
Chaussée de Louvain
Chaussée de Gand
Chaussée de Ninove
Chaussée de Mons
Chaussée de Wavre
Avenue Louise
Rue de la Loi
Bd. du Midi
Bd. Poincaré
Bd. Léopold II
Rue de Birmingham
Av. de Tervueren
Bd. Lambermont
Bd. Général Wahis
Bd. Auguste Reyers
Av. Charles Woeste
Rue de Mérode
Av. de Stalingrad
Av. du Roi
E10

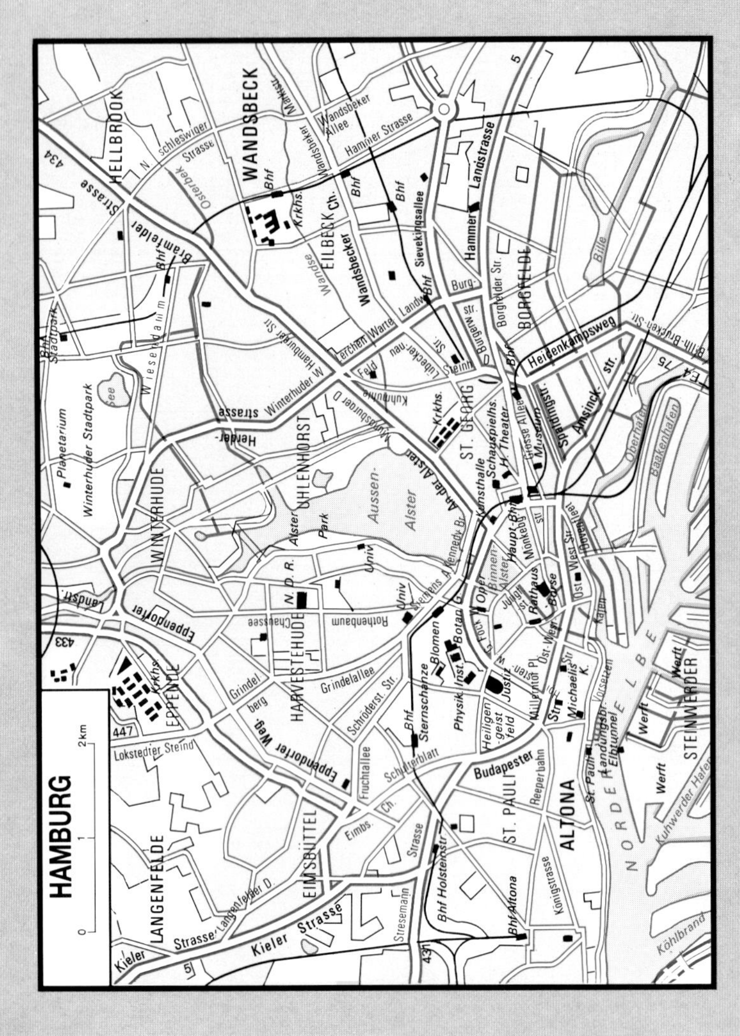
HAMBURG
0 1 2km
WANDSBECK
EILBECK
BARMBEK
ST. GEORG
ALTONA
ST. PAULI
EIMSBÜTTEL
HARVESTEHUDE
UHLENHORST
WINTERHUDE
EPPENDORF
LANGENFELDE
STEINWERDER
BORGFELDE
HELLBROOK
Aussen-Alster
Winterhuder Stadtpark
Planetarium
NORDERELBE

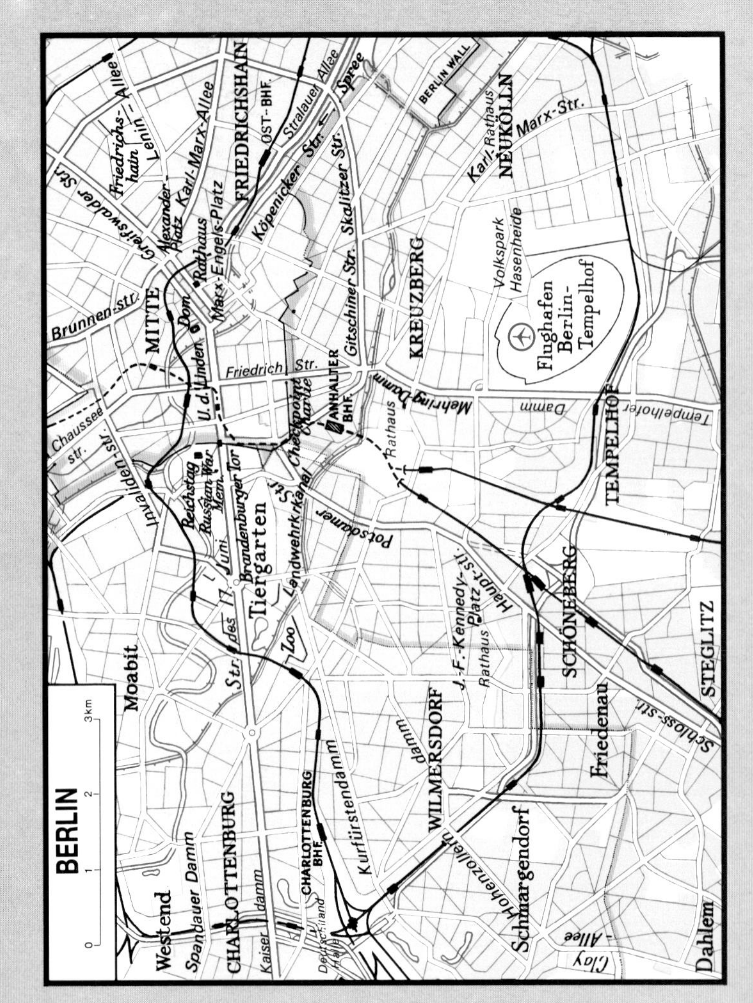
BERLIN
0 1 2 3km
MITTE
FRIEDRICHSHAIN
KREUZBERG
NEUKÖLLN
TEMPELHOF
SCHÖNEBERG
STEGLITZ
WILMERSDORF
CHARLOTTENBURG
Moabit
Tiergarten
Friedenau
Schmargendorf
Dahlem
Westend
Flughafen Berlin-Tempelhof
Volkspark Hasenheide
Kurfürstendamm
Spandauer Damm
BERLIN WALL

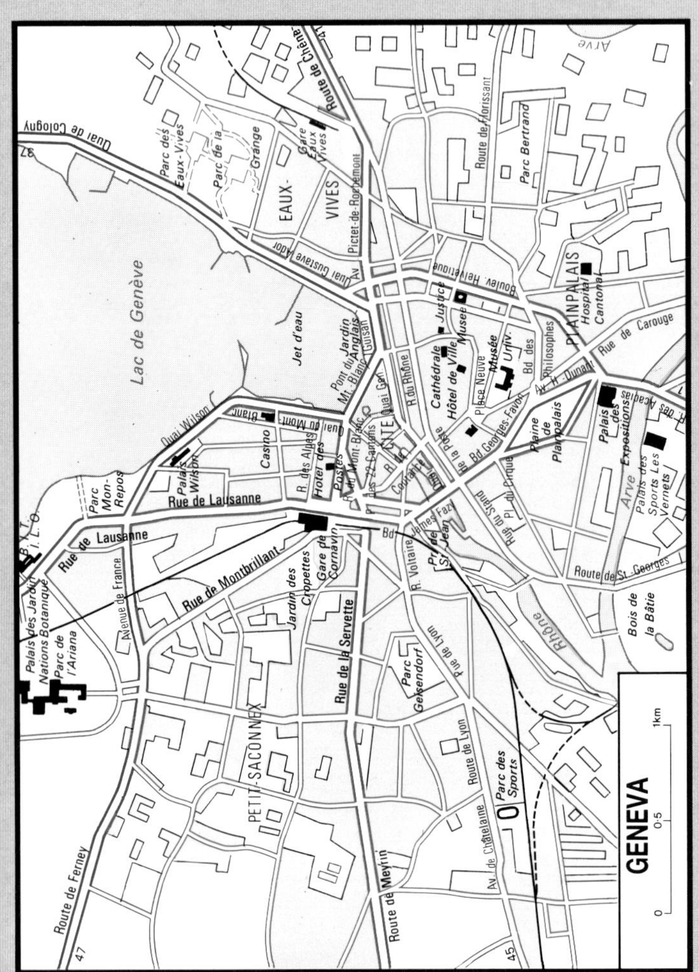
GENEVA
0 0.5 1km
Lac de Genève
EAUX-VIVES
PLAINPALAIS
PETIT-SACONNEX
Jet d'eau
Gare de Cornavin
Rue de Lausanne
Rue de Montbrillant
Parc des Eaux-Vives
Parc de la Grange
Palais des Nations
Jardin Botanique
Parc de l'Ariana
Cathédrale
Rhône
Arve
Route de Meyrin
Route de Ferney

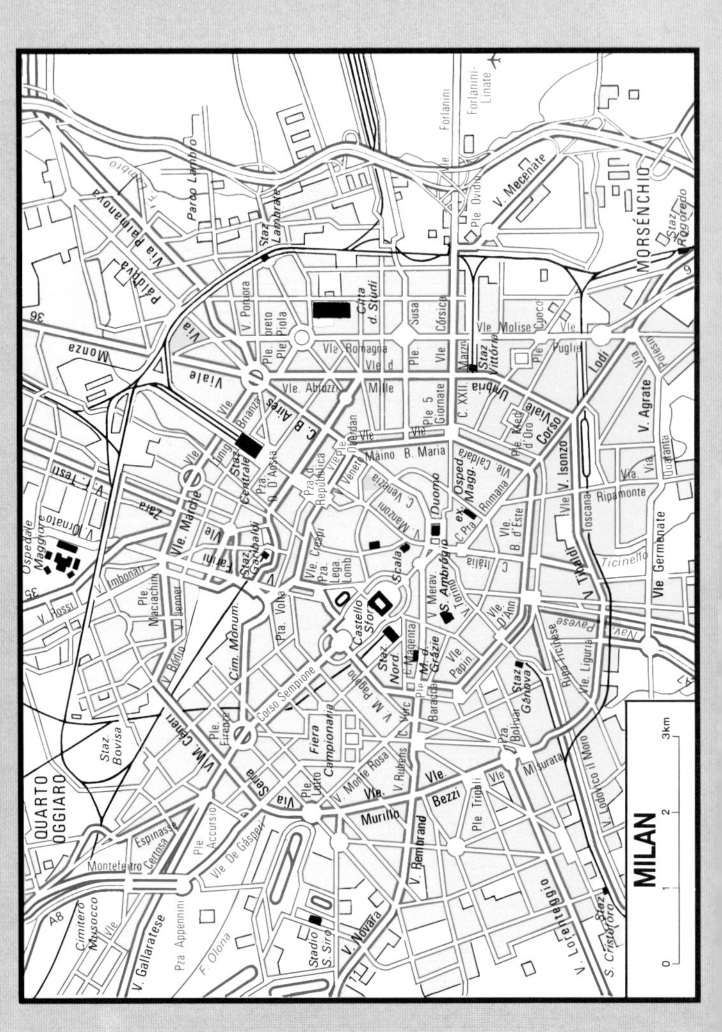
MILAN
0 1 2 3km
Duomo
Staz. Centrale
Castello Sforzesco
Scala
S. Ambrogio
Fiera Campionaria
Stadio S. Siro
QUARTO OGGIARO
MORSENCHIO
Parco Lambro
Città d. Studi

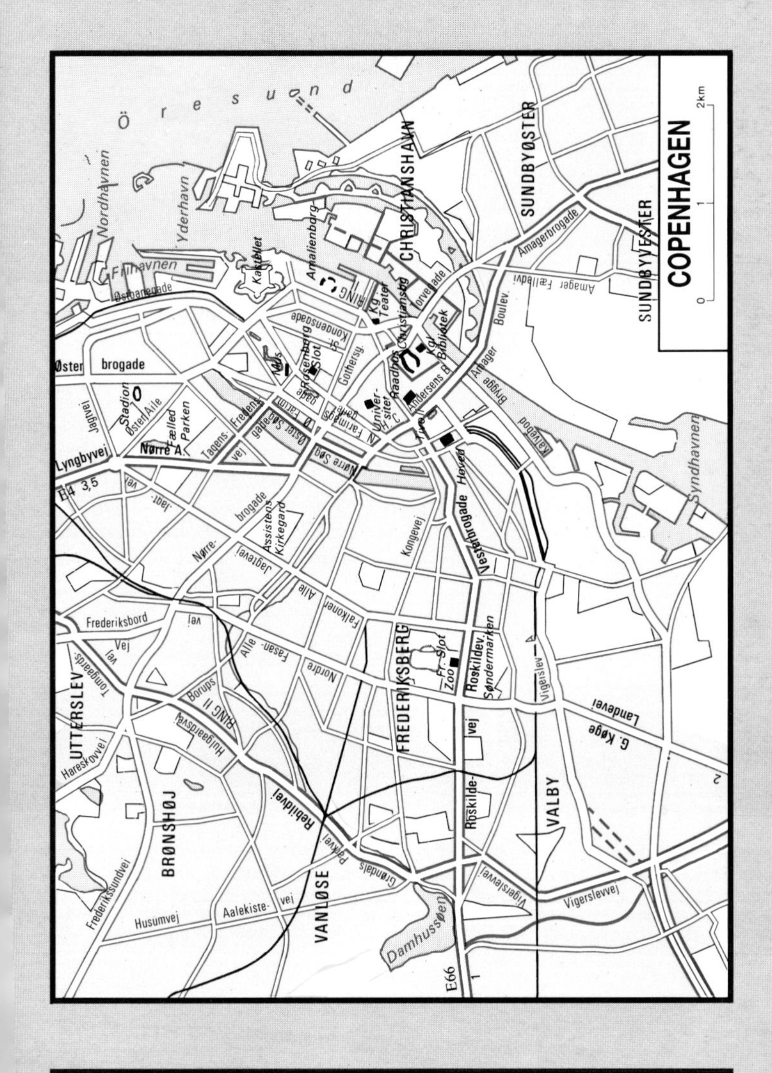

COPENHAGEN

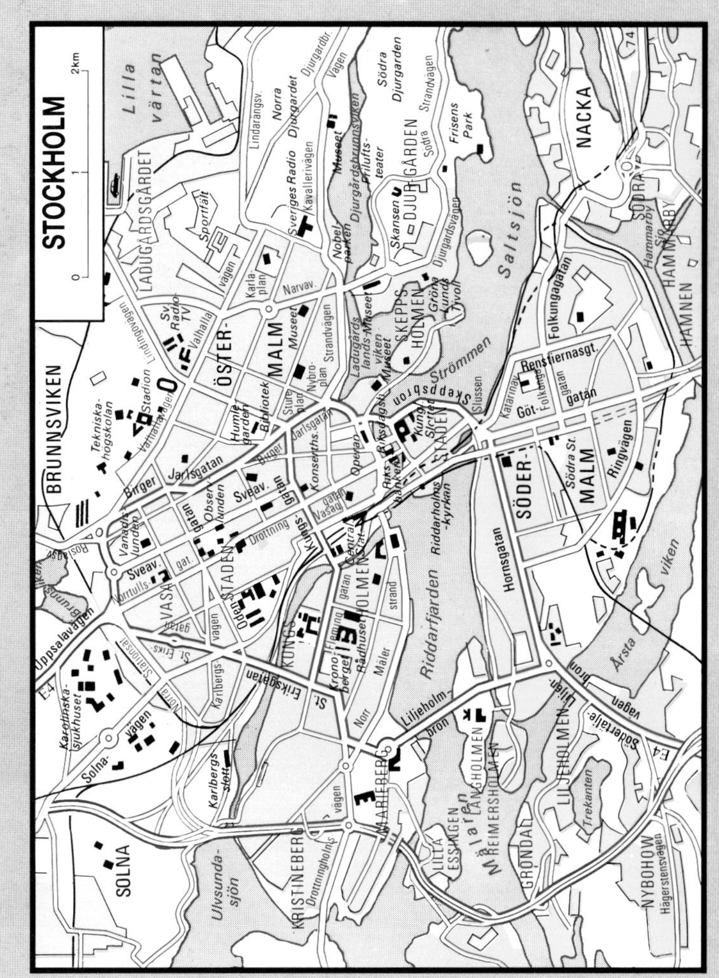

STOCKHOLM

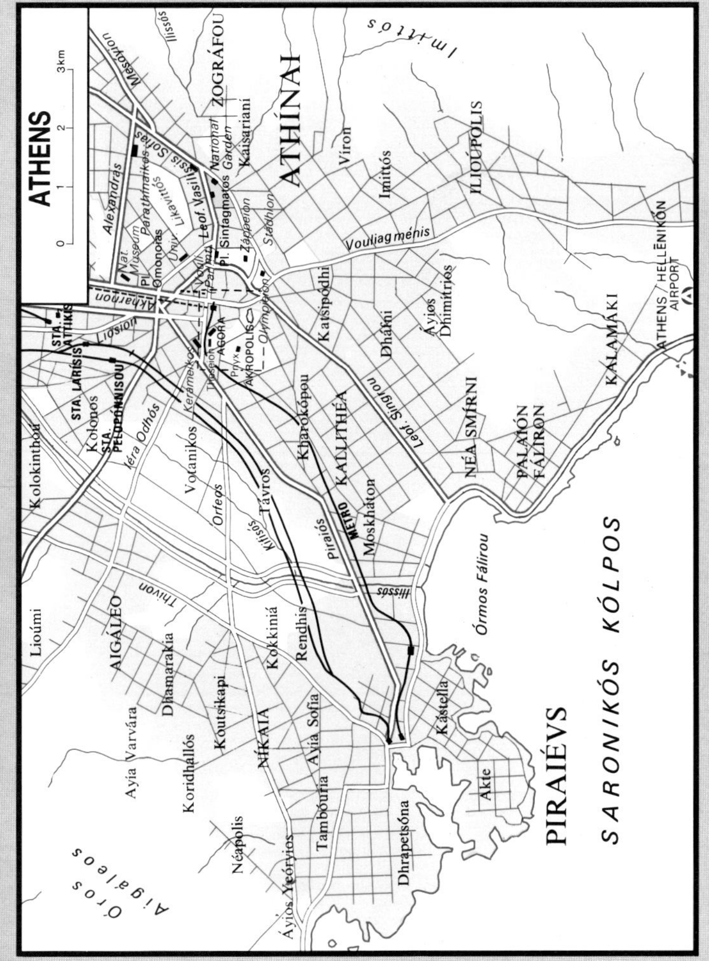

ATHENS

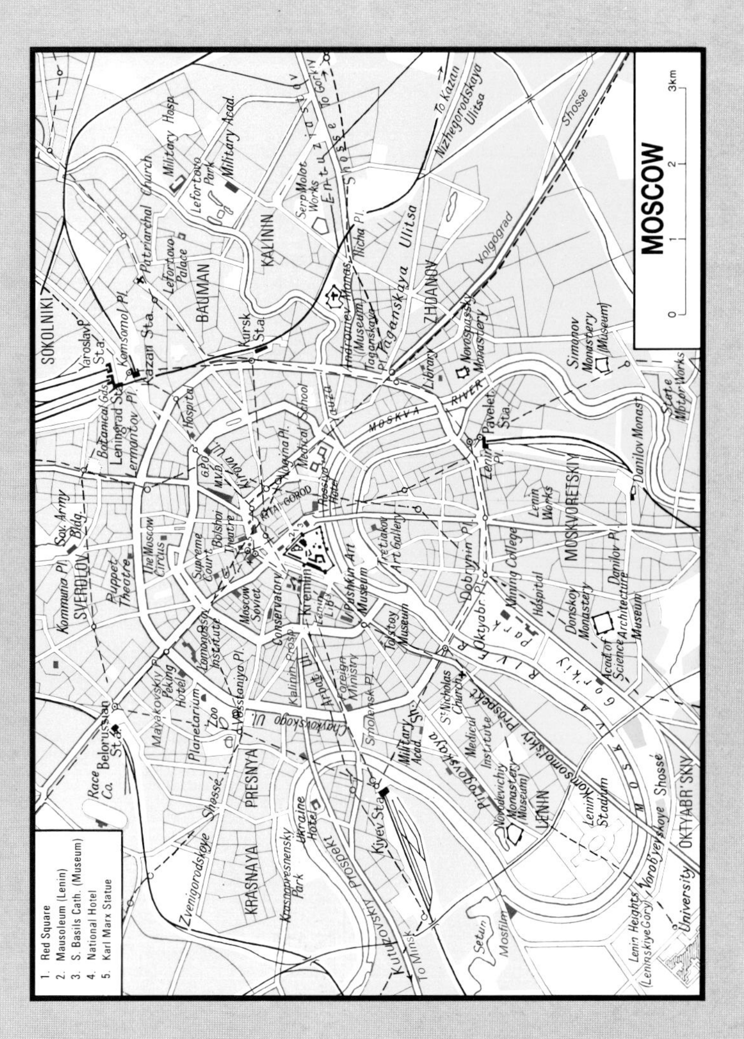

MOSCOW

1. Red Square
2. Mausoleum (Lenin)
3. S. Basil's Cath. (Museum)
4. National Hotel
5. Karl Marx Statue

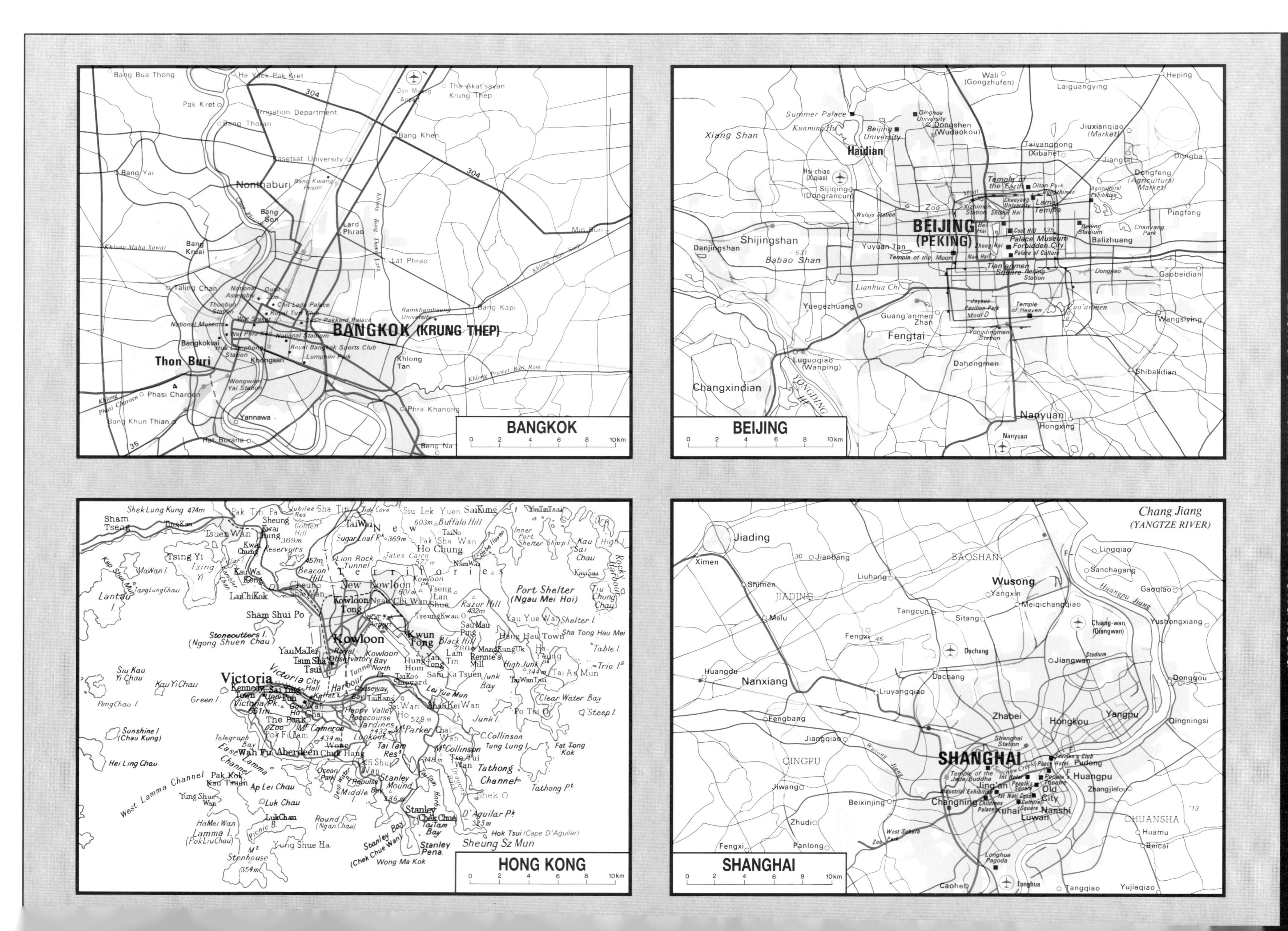
BANGKOK
BANGKOK (KRUNG THEP)
Thon Buri
Nonthaburi
BEIJING
BEIJING (PEKING)
Haidian
Fengtai
Shijingshan
Changxindian
HONG KONG
Kowloon
Victoria
Lantau
SHANGHAI
Chang Jiang
(YANGTZE RIVER)
Wusong
Jiading
Nanxiang
0 2 4 6 8 10km

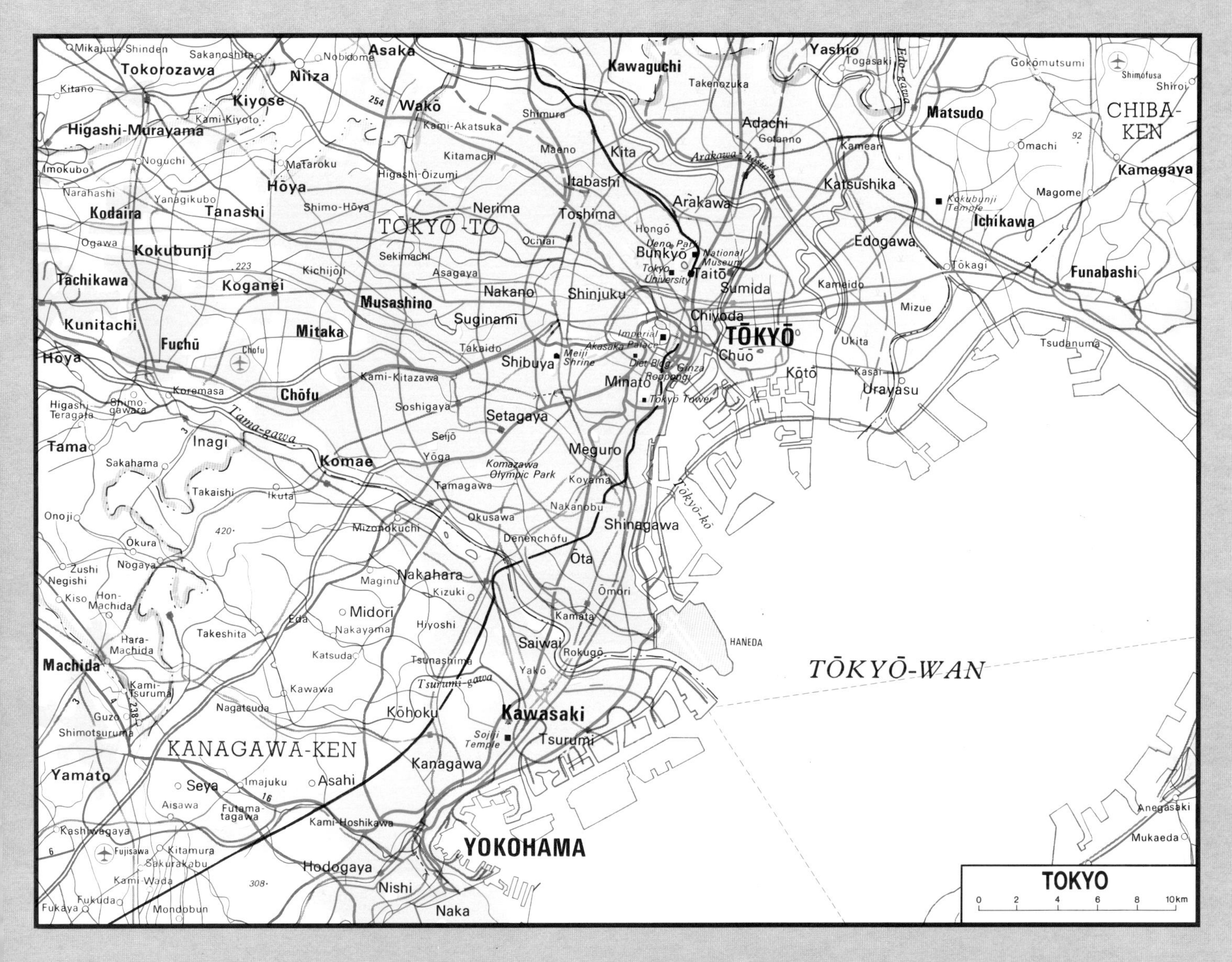
TOKYO
TŌKYŌ
TŌKYŌ-TO
TŌKYŌ-WAN
KANAGAWA-KEN
CHIBA-KEN
YOKOHAMA
Kawasaki
Kawaguchi
Tokorozawa
Niiza
Asaka
Kiyose
Wakō
Higashi-Murayama
Hōya
Kodaira
Tanashi
Kokubunji
Koganei
Tachikawa
Musashino
Mitaka
Kunitachi
Fuchū
Chōfu
Komae
Inagi
Tama
Machida
Yamato
Matsudo
Ichikawa
Funabashi
Urayasu
Adachi
Katsushika
Edogawa
Arakawa
Itabashi
Nerima
Toshima
Kita
Bunkyō
Taitō
Sumida
Shinjuku
Nakano
Suginami
Chiyoda
Chūō
Minato
Kōtō
Shibuya
Setagaya
Meguro
Shinagawa
Ota
Nakahara
Saiwai
Kanagawa
Tsurumi
Hodogaya
Nishi
Naka
Kamagaya
Tsudanuma
Tama-gawa
Tsurumi-gawa
Arakawa-hōsuiro
Edo-gawa
Tōkyō-kō
HANEDA
Imperial Palace
Meiji Shrine
Tokyo Tower
Komazawa Olympic Park
Sojiji Temple
Kokubunji Temple
Tokyo University
National Museum
0 2 4 6 8 10km

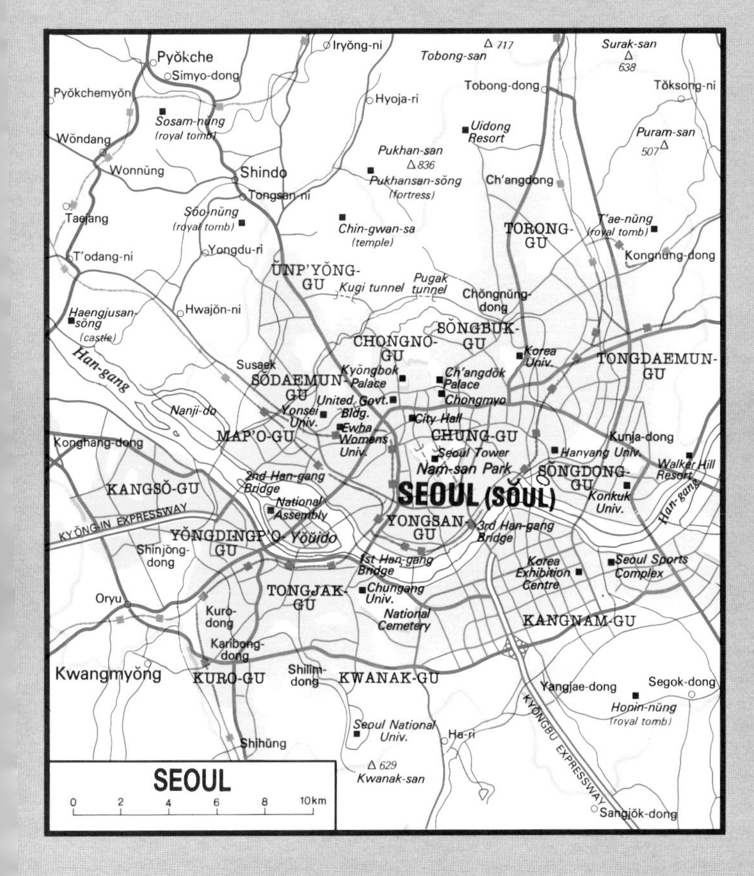
SEOUL
SEOUL (SŎUL)
Han-gang
KANGSŎ-GU
YŎNGDŬNGP'O-GU
TONGJAK-GU
KURO-GU
KWANAK-GU
KANGNAM-GU
YONGSAN-GU
MAP'O-GU
SŎDAEMUN-GU
CHONGNO-GU
SŎNGBUK-GU
TONGDAEMUN-GU
TORONG-GU
ŬNP'YŎNG-GU
CHUNG-GU
SŎNGDONG-GU
Kwangmyŏng
Yŏido
Nam-san Park
City Hall
Seoul Tower
Korea Univ.
Yonsei Univ.
Ewha Womens Univ.
National Assembly
Seoul National Univ.
Seoul Sports Complex
Korea Exhibition Centre
National Cemetery
Walker Hill Resort
Bukhansan
Tobong-san
Kwanak-san
KYŎNGBU EXPRESSWAY
KYŎNGIN EXPRESSWAY
0 2 4 6 8 10km

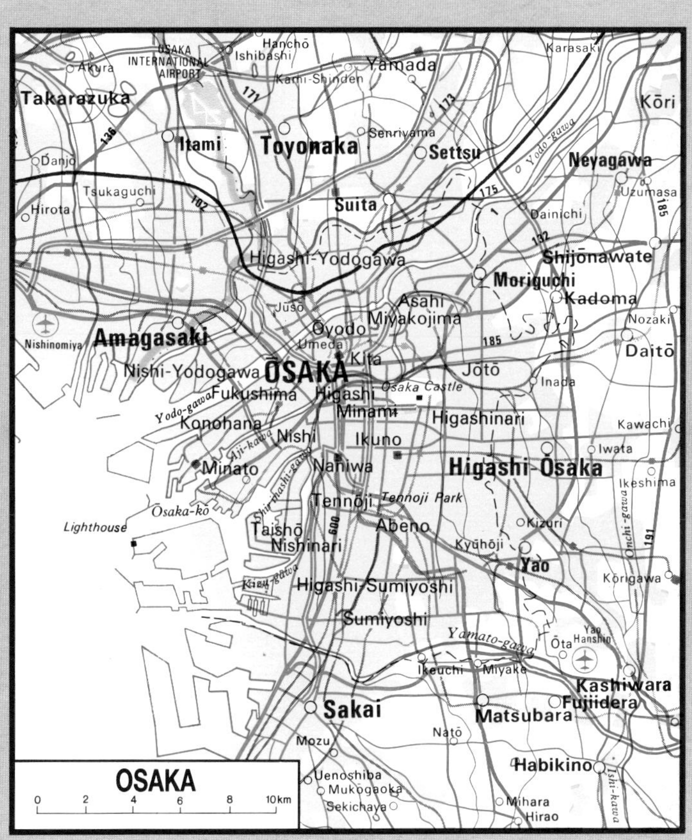
OSAKA
ŌSAKA
OSAKA INTERNATIONAL AIRPORT
Takarazuka
Itami
Toyonaka
Suita
Settsu
Neyagawa
Kōri
Moriguchi
Kadoma
Daitō
Amagasaki
Higashi-Yodogawa
Yodogawa
Nishi-Yodogawa
Kita
Miyakojima
Asahi
Jōtō
Fukushima
Konohana
Nishi
Minami
Higashi
Higashinari
Ikuno
Naniwa
Minato
Tennōji
Abeno
Taishō
Nishinari
Higashi-Osaka
Higashi-Sumiyoshi
Sumiyoshi
Yao
Sakai
Matsubara
Fujiidera
Kashiwara
Habikino
Osaka Castle
Tennoji Park
Yodo-gawa
Yamato-gawa
Ōsaka-kō
Lighthouse
0 2 4 6 8 10km

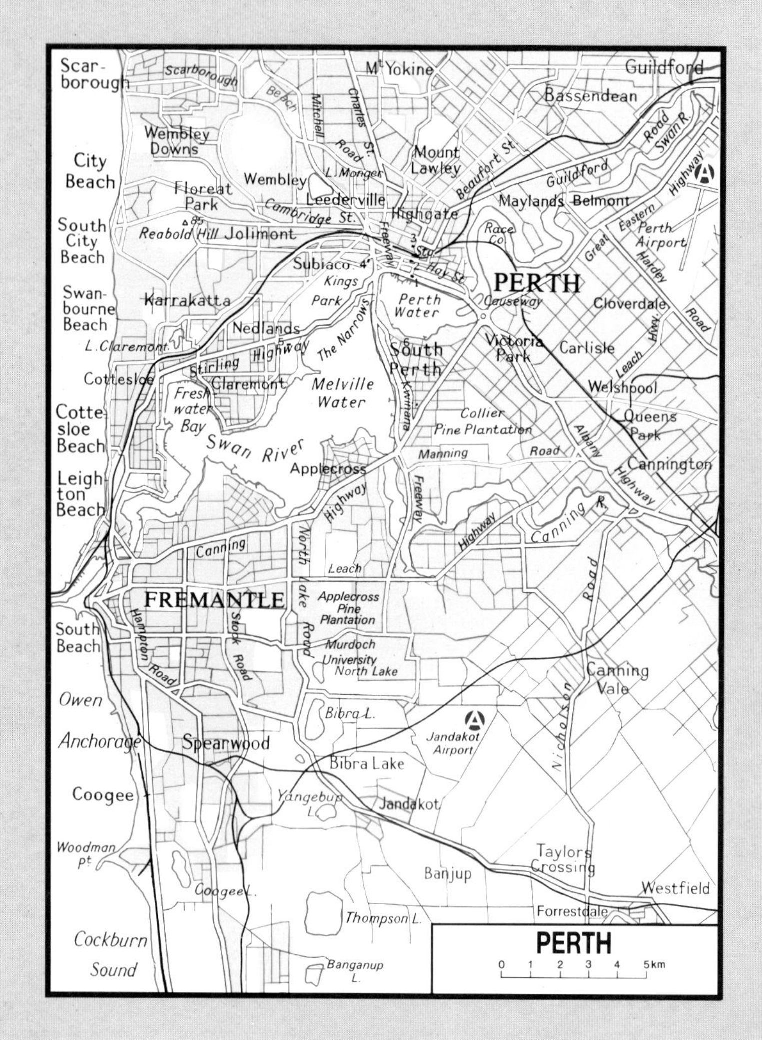

PERTH
0 1 2 3 4 5km

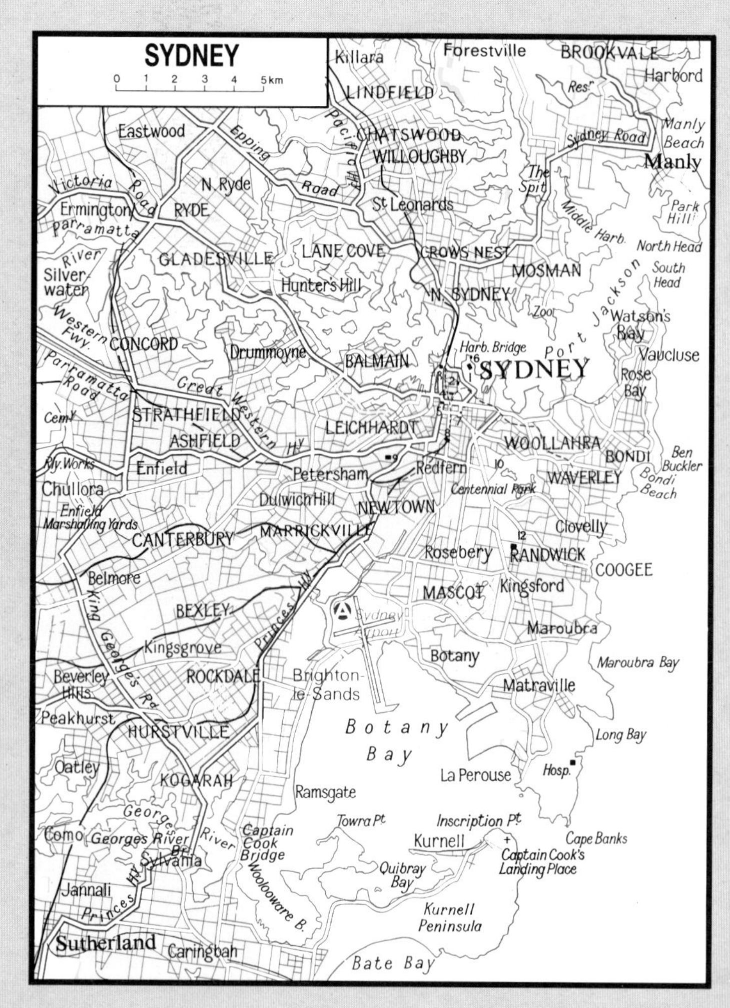

SYDNEY
0 1 2 3 4 5km

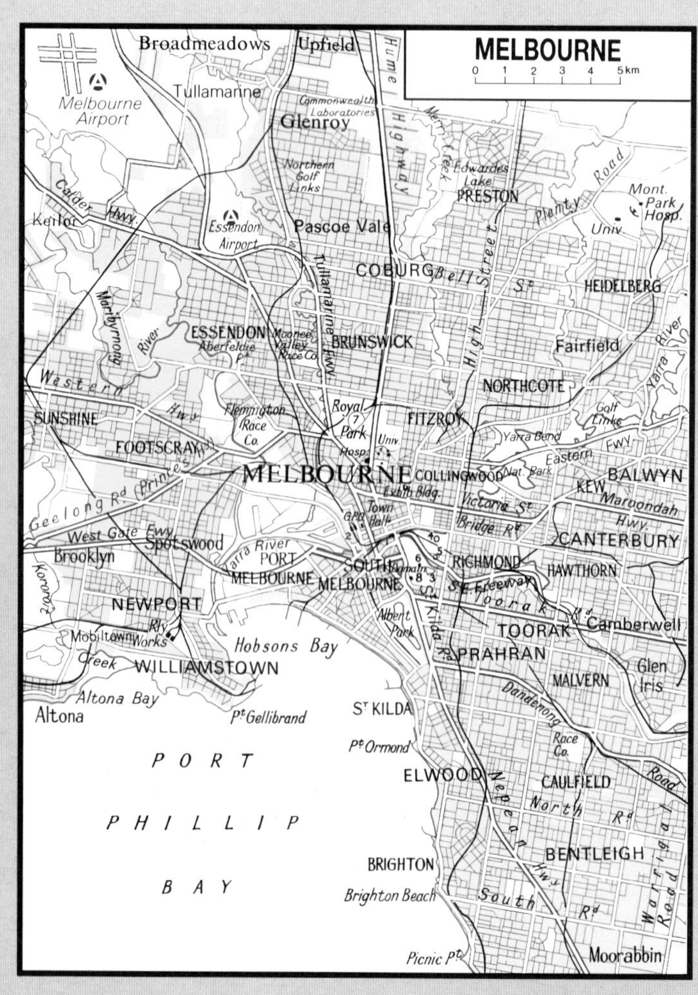

MELBOURNE
0 1 2 3 4 5km

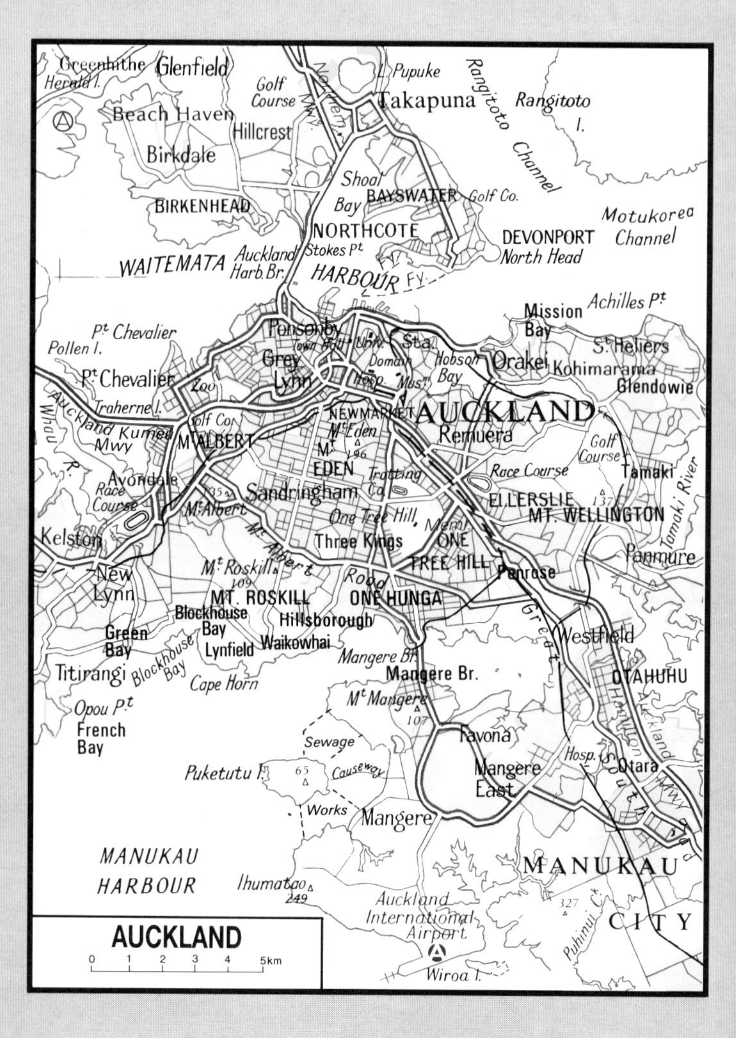

AUCKLAND
0 1 2 3 4 5km

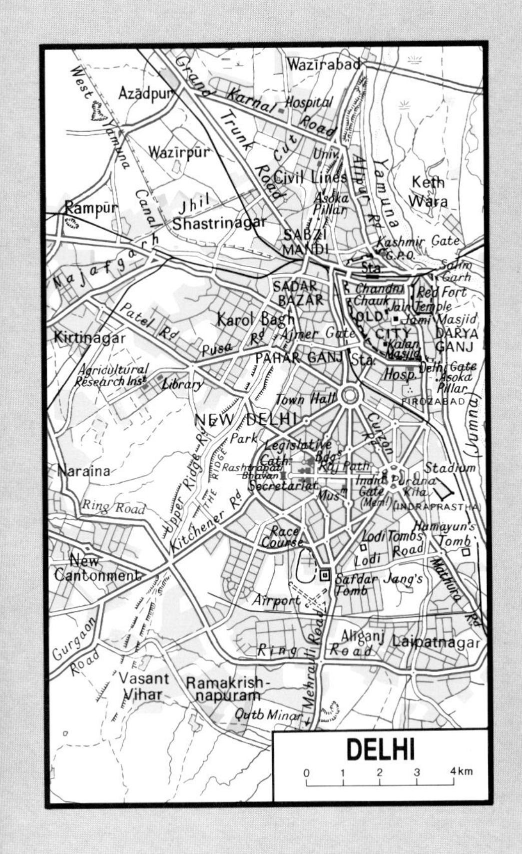

DELHI

0 1 2 3 4km

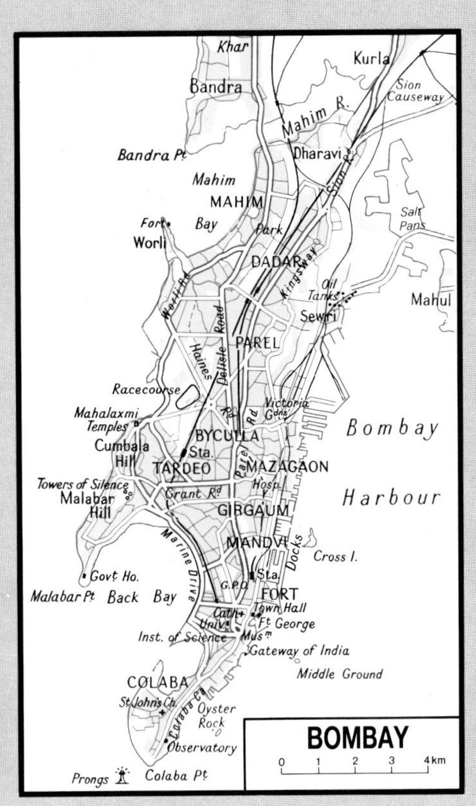

BOMBAY

0 1 2 3 4km

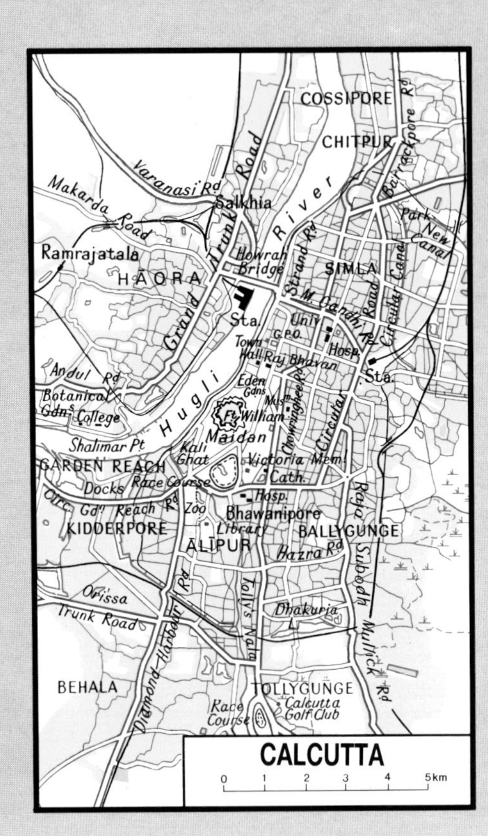

CALCUTTA

0 1 2 3 4 5km

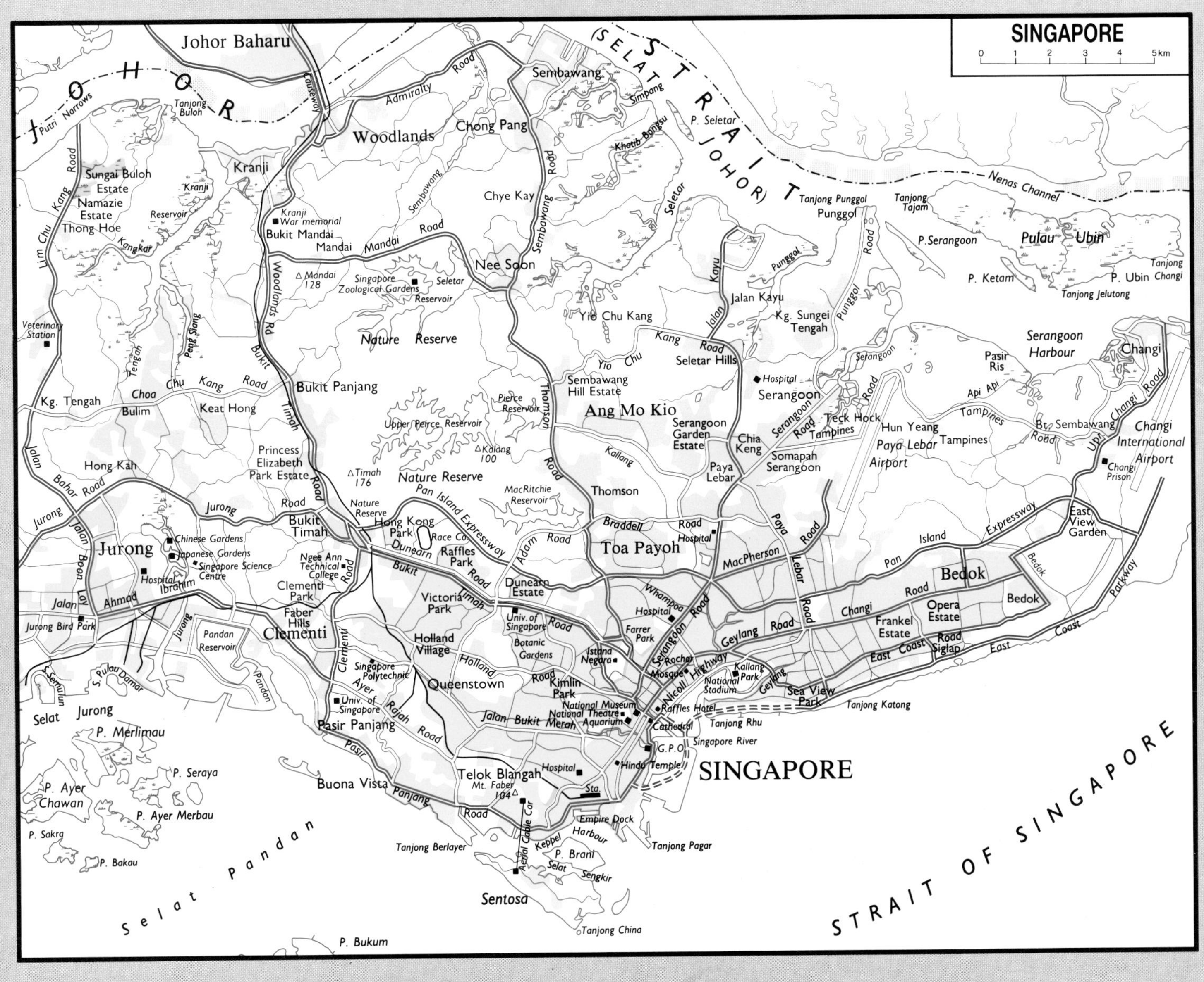

SINGAPORE

0 1 2 3 4 5km

SINGAPORE

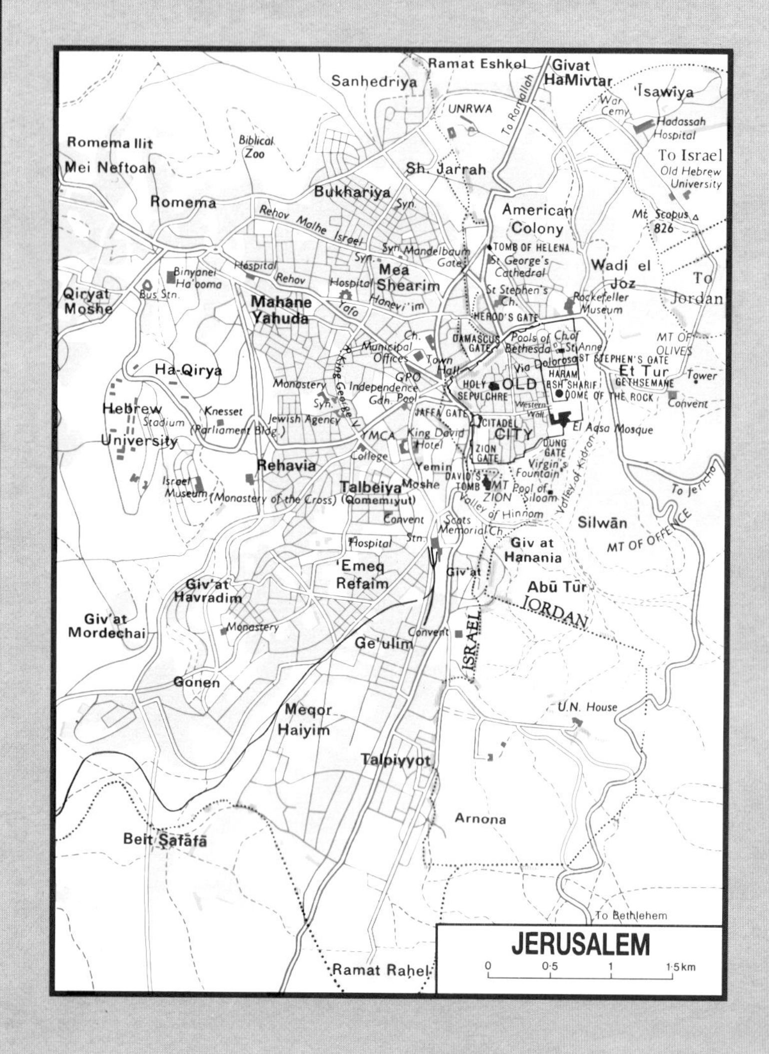

JERUSALEM

0   0·5   1   1·5km

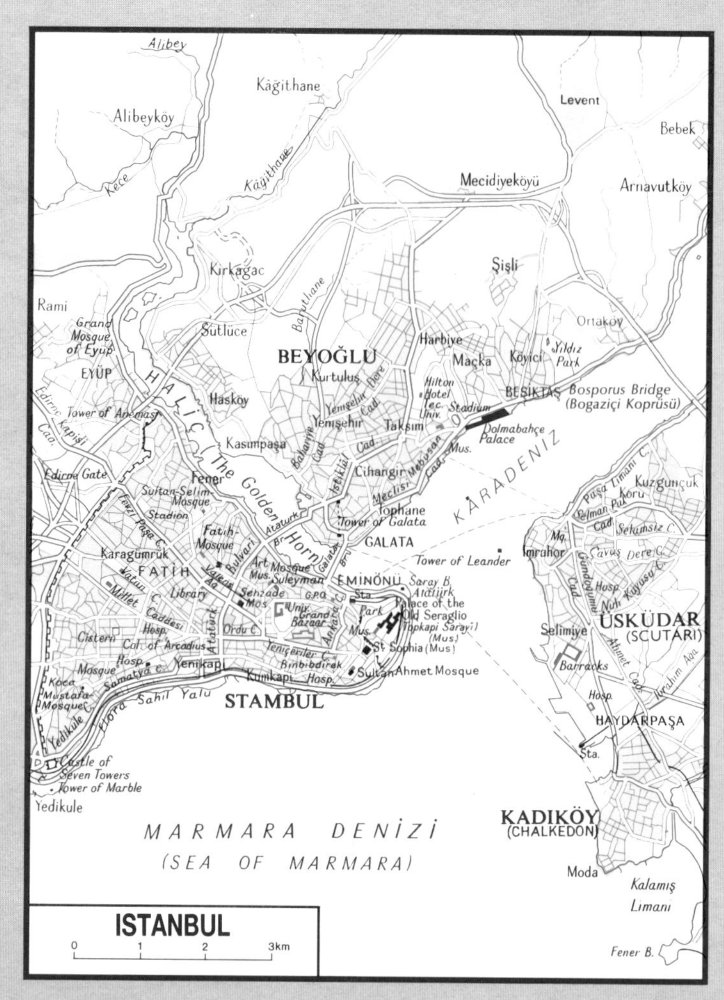

ISTANBUL

0   1   2   3km

Fener B.

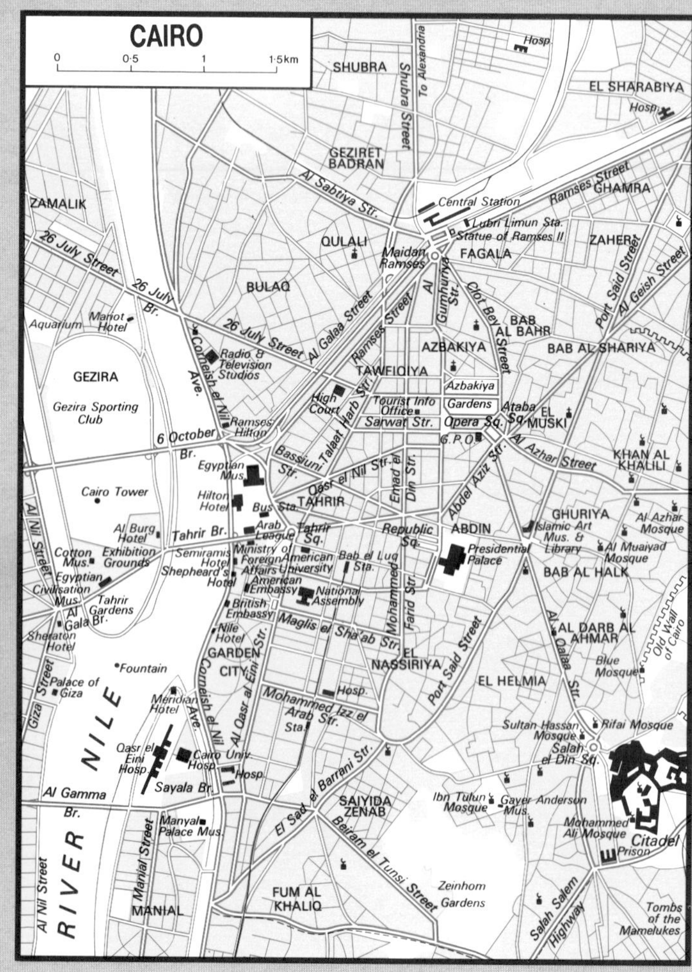

CAIRO

0   0·5   1   1·5km

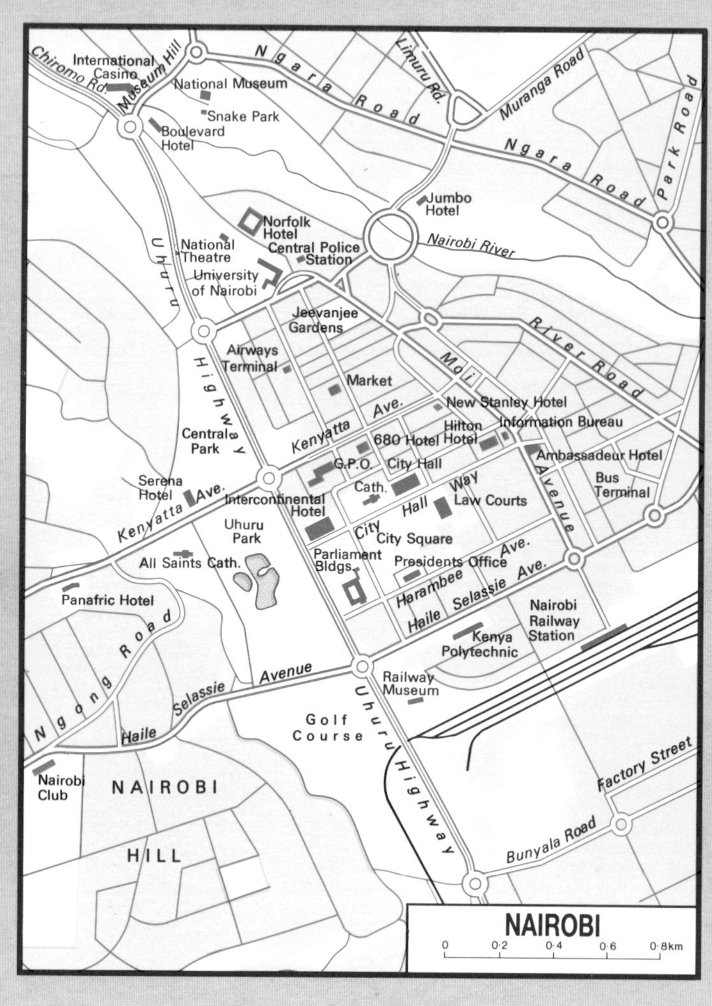

NAIROBI

0   0·2   0·4   0·6   0·8km

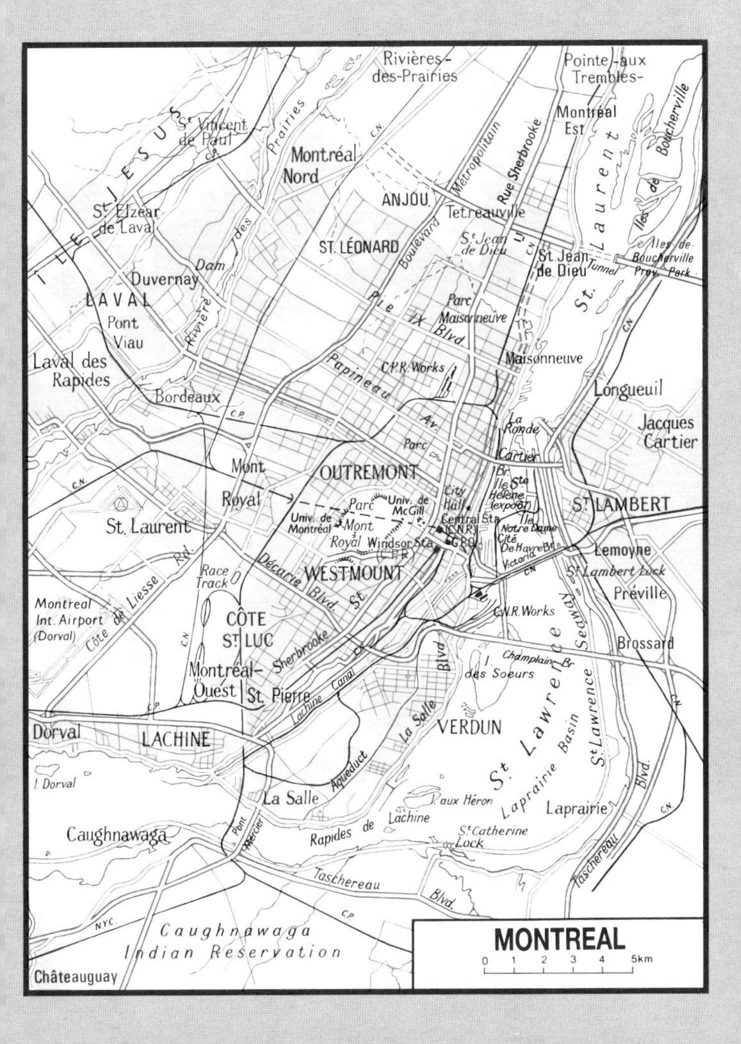
MONTREAL
0 1 2 3 4 5km
Rivières-des-Prairies
Pointe-aux-Trembles
Montréal Est
Montréal Nord
ANJOU
Tetreauville
ST. LÉONARD
St. Jean de Dieu
Boucherville
St. Elzear de Laval
Duvernay
LAVAL
Pont Viau
Laval des Rapides
Bordeaux
Maisonneuve
Longueuil
Jacques Cartier
Mont Royal
OUTREMONT
St. Laurent
ST. LAMBERT
Lemoyne
WESTMOUNT
Préville
CÔTE ST. LUC
Brossard
Montreal Int. Airport (Dorval)
Montréal-Ouest
St. Pierre
Dorval
LACHINE
VERDUN
La Salle
Lapraírie
Caughnawaga
Caughnawaga Indian Reservation
Châteauguay
St. Lawrence
Lachine Canal
Papineau
Sherbrooke
Tunnel

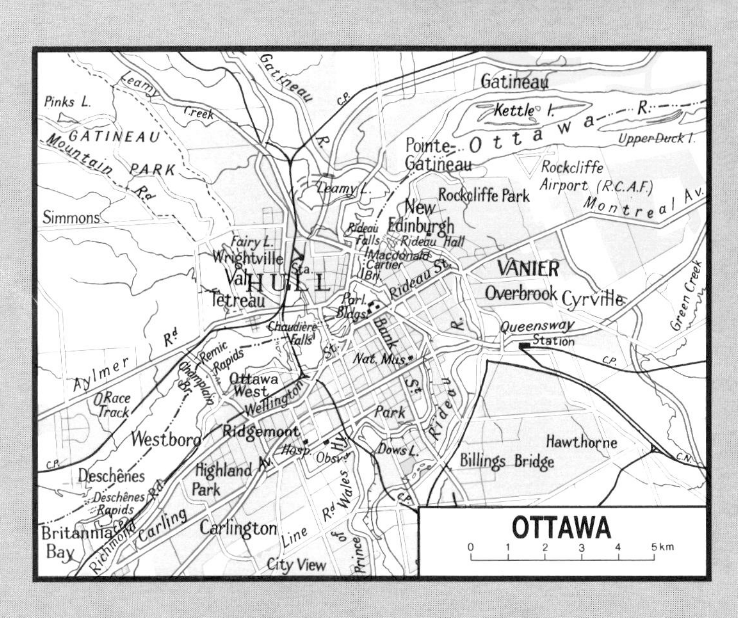
OTTAWA
0 1 2 3 4 5km
Gatineau
Kettle I.
Ottawa R.
Pinks L.
GATINEAU PARK
Mountain Rd
Leamy L.
Pointe-Gatineau
Rockcliffe Airport (R.C.A.F.)
Rockcliffe Park
Montreal Av.
New Edinburgh
Simmons
Rideau Hall
Fairy L.
Wrightville
Val Tetreau
HULL
VANIER
Overbrook
Cyrville
Green Creek
Queensway Station
Aylmer Rd
Chaudière Falls
Remic Rapids
Nat. Mus.
Race Track
Ottawa West
Wellington
Park
Westboro
Ridgemont
Dows L.
Hawthorne
Billings Bridge
Deschênes
Highland Park
Deschênes Rapids
Britannia Bay
Carling Av.
Carlington
City View
Richmond Rd.
Prince of Wales Dr.
Bank St.
Rideau R.

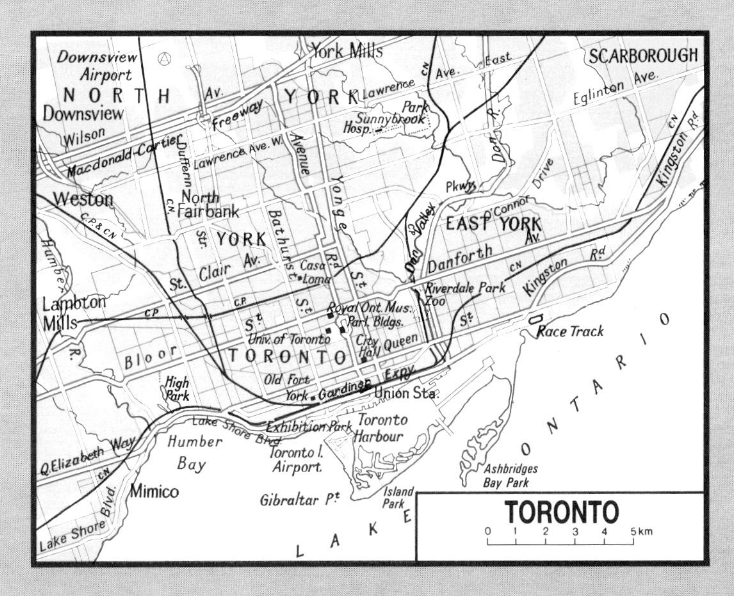
TORONTO
0 1 2 3 4 5km
Downsview Airport
York Mills
SCARBOROUGH
NORTH YORK
Lawrence Ave.
Eglinton Ave.
Downsview
Sunnybrook Park
Wilson
Macdonald-Cartier Freeway
Lawrence Ave. W.
Weston
North Fairbank
YORK
EAST YORK
O'Connor Drive
Danforth Av.
St. Clair Av.
Casa Loma
Kingston Rd
Lambton Mills
Royal Ont. Mus.
Parl. Bldgs.
Riverdale Park
Zoo
Race Track
Bloor St.
Univ. of Toronto
TORONTO
City Hall
Queen
High Park
Old Fort York
Gardiner Expy.
Union Sta.
Exhibition Park
Toronto Harbour
Humber Bay
Lake Shore Blvd.
Toronto I. Airport
Q. Elizabeth Way
Mimico
Gibraltar Pt.
Island Park
Ashbridges Bay Park
LAKE ONTARIO
Yonge St.
Bathurst St.
Humber R.
Don R.

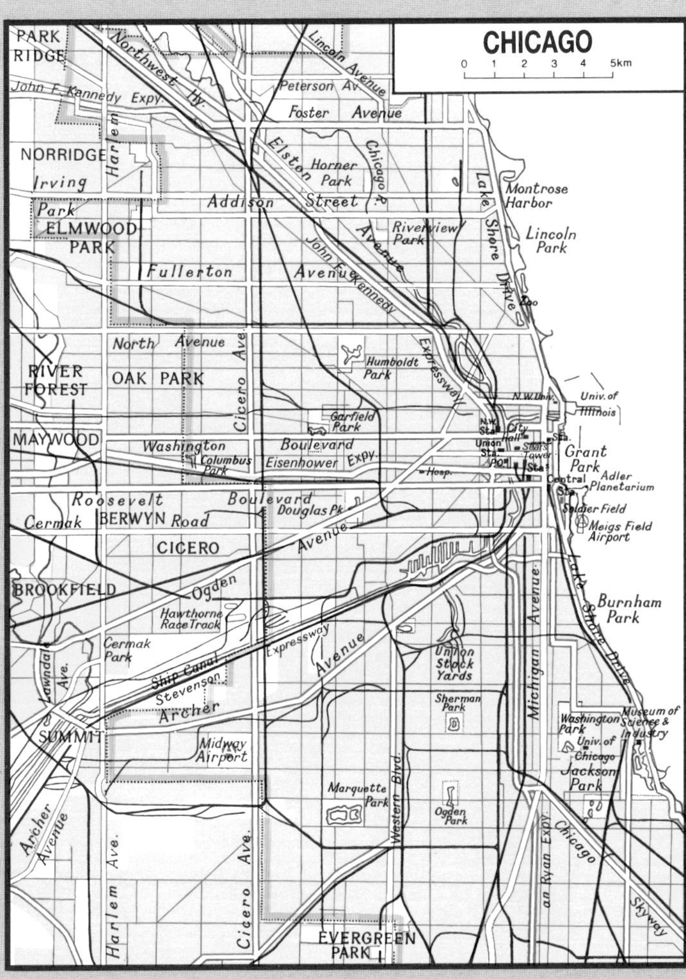
CHICAGO
0 1 2 3 4 5km
PARK RIDGE
Northwest Hy.
Lincoln Avenue
John F. Kennedy Expy.
Peterson Av.
Foster Avenue
NORRIDGE
Irving Park
Horner Park
Elston Avenue
Montrose Harbor
Addison Street
Riverview Park
Lincoln Park
ELMWOOD PARK
Fullerton Avenue
Kennedy Expressway
Lake Shore Drive
North Avenue
Humboldt Park
RIVER FOREST
OAK PARK
Univ. of Illinois
Garfield Park
MAYWOOD
Washington Boulevard
Columbus Park
Eisenhower Expy.
Grant Park
Adler Planetarium
Roosevelt Road
Cermak
BERWYN
Douglas Pk.
Soldier Field
Meigs Field Airport
CICERO
BROOKFIELD
Ogden Avenue
Hawthorne Race Track
Burnham Park
Cermak Park
Union Stock Yards
Ship Canal
Stevenson Expressway
Archer Avenue
Sherman Park
SUMMIT
Midway Airport
Washington Park
Museum of Science & Industry
Univ. of Chicago
Jackson Park
Marquette Park
Ogden Park
Harlem Ave.
Cicero Ave.
Western Blvd.
Michigan Avenue
Dan Ryan Expy.
Chicago Skyway
EVERGREEN PARK

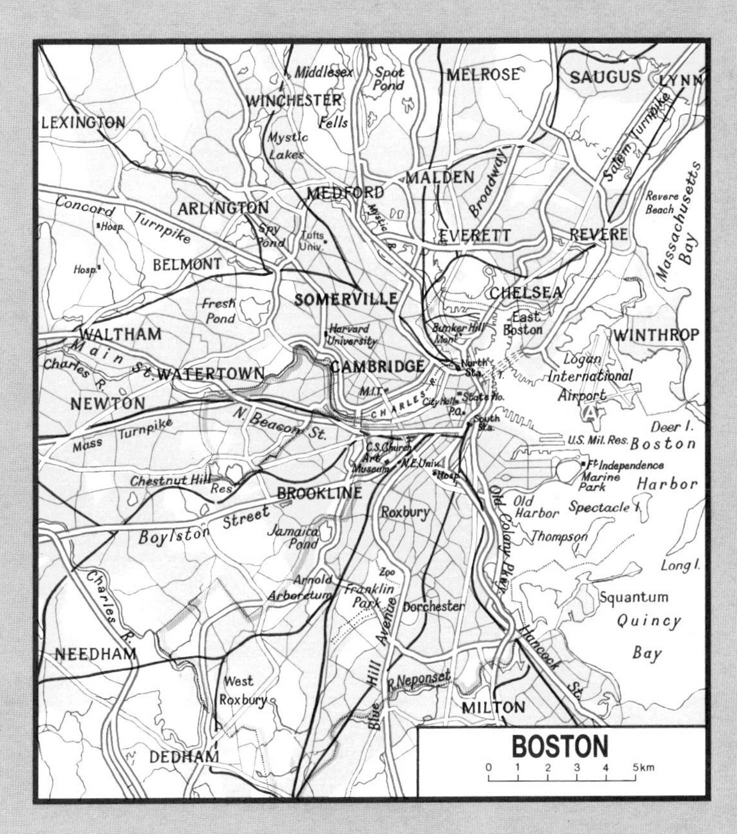
BOSTON
0 1 2 3 4 5km
Middlesex Fells
Spot Pond
MELROSE
SAUGUS
LYNN
WINCHESTER
LEXINGTON
Mystic Lakes
Salem Turnpike
MEDFORD
MALDEN
Broadway
Concord Turnpike
ARLINGTON
Revere Beach
Spy Pond
Tufts Univ.
EVERETT
REVERE
Massachusetts Bay
BELMONT
CHELSEA
Fresh Pond
SOMERVILLE
East Boston
WALTHAM
Harvard University
Bunker Hill Mont.
WINTHROP
Main St.
WATERTOWN
CAMBRIDGE
Logan International Airport
Charles R.
M.I.T.
NEWTON
Mass Turnpike
N. Beacon St.
Deer I.
Boston Harbor
Chestnut Hill Res.
BROOKLINE
Ft. Independence Marine Park
Roxbury
Old Harbor
Spectacle I.
Boylston Street
Jamaica Pond
Thompson
Long I.
Arnold Arboretum
Franklin Park
Dorchester
Old Colony Pkwy.
Squantum
Quincy Bay
NEEDHAM
West Roxbury
Blue Hill Avenue
R. Neponset
Hancock St.
MILTON
DEDHAM

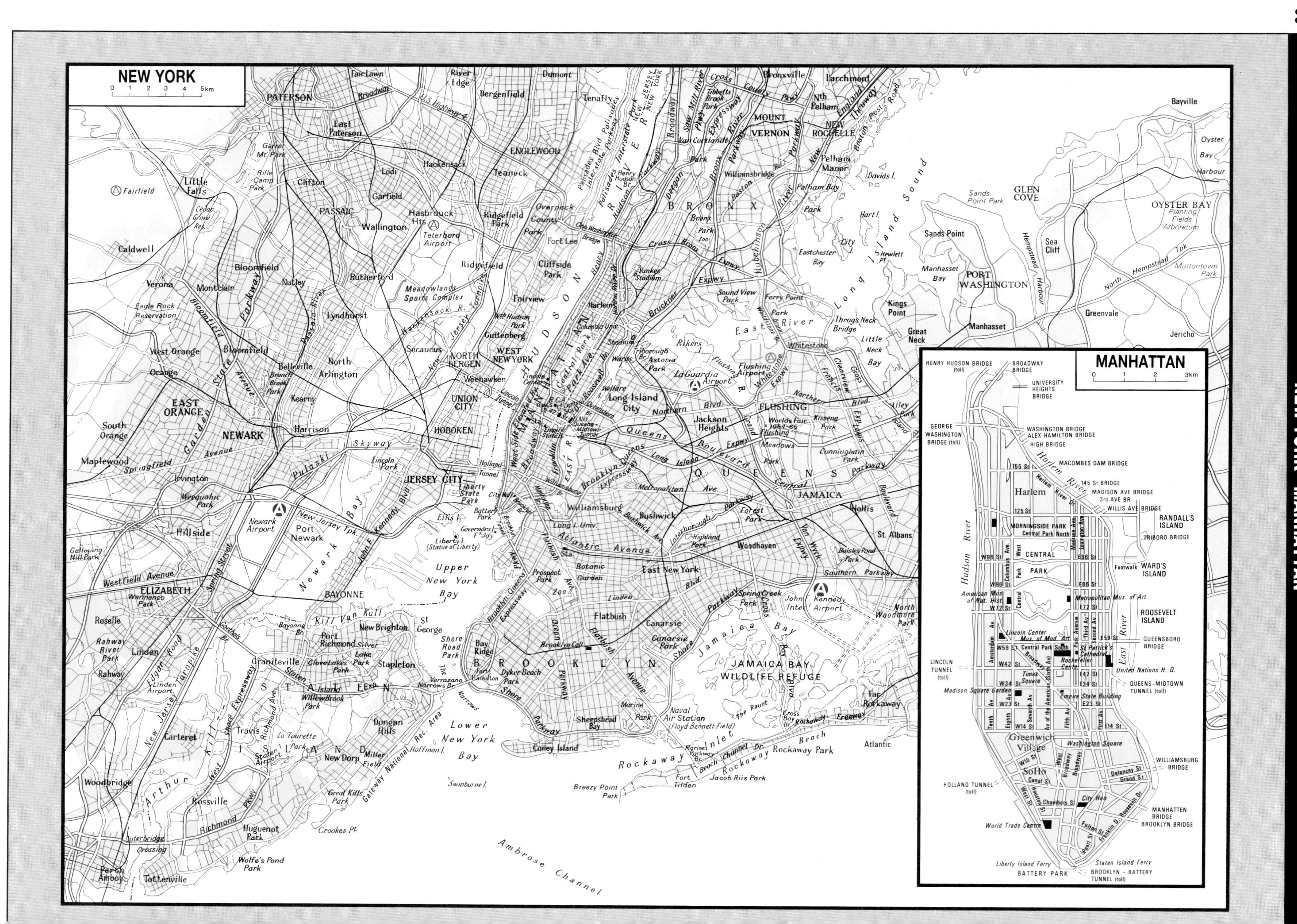
NEW YORK
0 1 2 3 4 5km
MANHATTAN
0 1 2 3km
PATERSON
PASSAIC
NEWARK
EAST ORANGE
ELIZABETH
BAYONNE
JERSEY CITY
HOBOKEN
UNION CITY
WEST NEW YORK
NORTH BERGEN
ENGLEWOOD
MOUNT VERNON
NEW ROCHELLE
GLEN COVE
PORT WASHINGTON
OYSTER BAY
JAMAICA
FLUSHING
JAMAICA BAY WILDLIFE REFUGE
Newark Airport
Upper New York Bay
Lower New York Bay
Ambrose Channel
Long Island Sound
Hudson River
East River
Harlem River
CENTRAL PARK
Greenwich Village
SoHo
BATTERY PARK

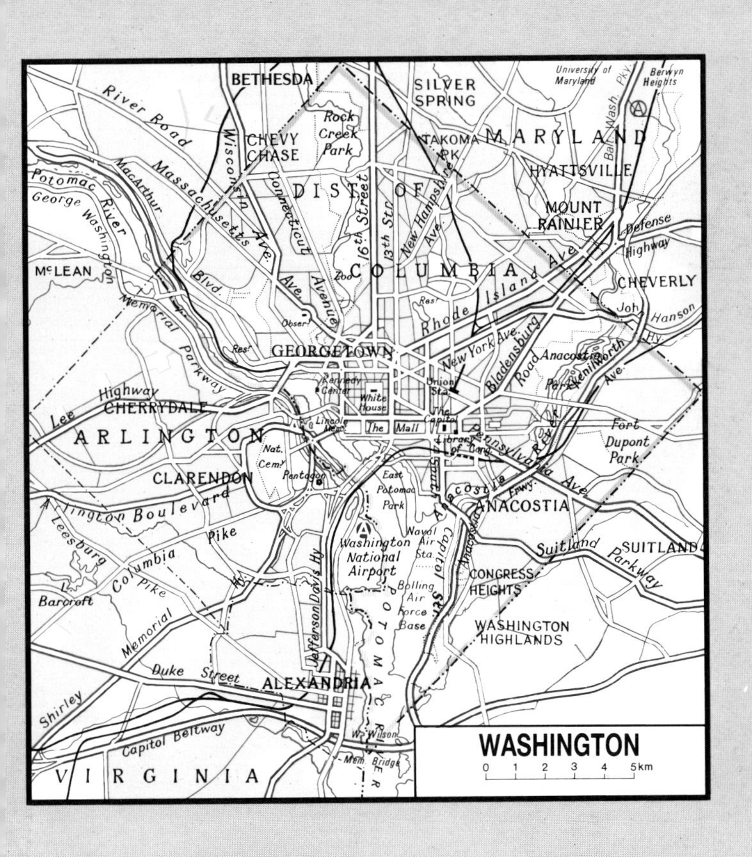

WASHINGTON

River Road
BETHESDA
SILVER SPRING
Rock Creek Park
CHEVY CHASE
University of Maryland
TAKOMA PK.
Defense Highway
Berwyn Heights
MARYLAND
HYATTSVILLE
MOUNT RAINIER
DISTRICT OF COLUMBIA
CHEVERLY
McLEAN
Potomac River
George Washington Memorial Parkway
Wisconsin Ave.
Massachusetts Ave.
16th Street
New Hampshire Ave.
Rhode Island Ave.
New York Ave.
Bladensburg
Anacostia
Baltimore Wash. Pkwy.
GEORGETOWN
White House
The Mall
Capitol
Pennsylvania Ave.
Joh. Hanson Hy.
Fort Dupont Park
CHERRYDALE
ARLINGTON
CLARENDON
Arlington Boulevard
Nat. Cem.
Pentagon
Washington National Airport
East Potomac Park
ANACOSTIA
Suitland Parkway
CONGRESS HEIGHTS
SUITLAND
Lee Highway
Leesburg Pike
Columbia Pike
Barcroft
Memorial
Shirley
Duke Street
ALEXANDRIA
Bolling Air Force Base
WASHINGTON HIGHLANDS
Jefferson Davis Hy.
Capital Beltway
VIRGINIA
W. Wilson Mem. Bridge

WASHINGTON
0 1 2 3 4 5km

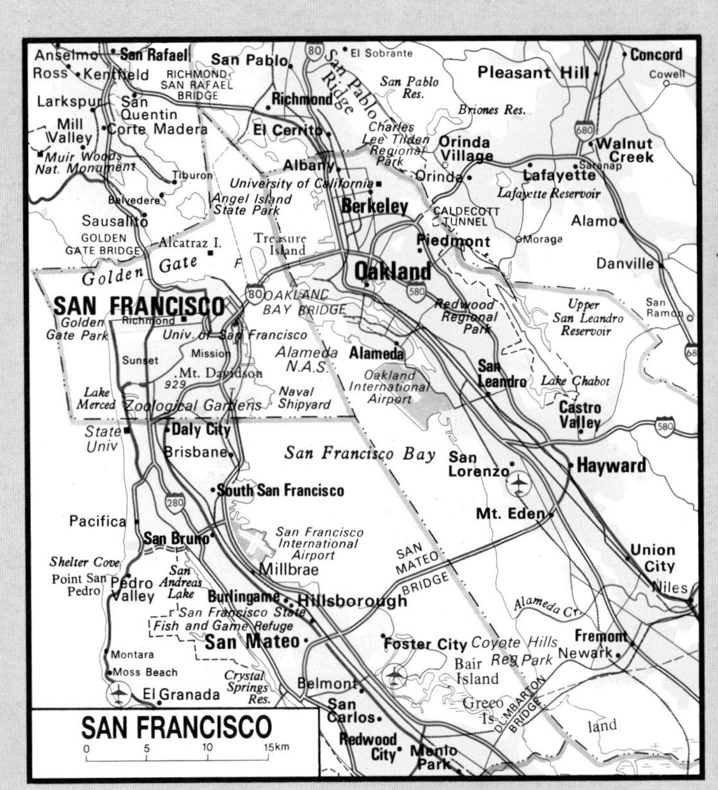

SAN FRANCISCO

Anselmo
San Rafael
San Pablo
El Sobrante
Concord
Pleasant Hill
Cowell
Ross
Kentfield
RICHMOND SAN RAFAEL BRIDGE
Richmond
San Pablo Res.
Larkspur
San Corte Madera
El Cerrito
Briones Res.
Mill Valley
Charles Lee Tilden Regional Park
Orinda Village
Walnut Creek
Muir Woods Nat. Monument
Tiburon
Albany
Orinda
Lafayette
Alamo
Sausalito
Belvedere
University of California
Angel Island State Park
Berkeley
Lafayette Reservoir
Danville
GOLDEN GATE BRIDGE
Alcatraz I.
Treasure Island
Piedmont
CALDECOTT TUNNEL
Moraga
San Ramon
Golden Gate
Oakland
SAN FRANCISCO
Golden Gate Park
Univ. of San Francisco
OAKLAND BAY BRIDGE
Redwood Regional Park
Upper San Leandro Reservoir
Richmond
Mission
Alameda
San Leandro
Sunset
Mt. Davidson 929
Alameda N.A.S.
Lake Merced
Zoological Gardens
Naval Shipyard
Oakland International Airport
Castro Valley
State Univ
Daly City
Brisbane
San Francisco Bay
San Lorenzo
Lake Chabot
Hayward
Pacifica
South San Francisco
Mt. Eden
San Bruno
San Francisco International Airport
SAN MATEO BRIDGE
Union City
Shelter Cove
Pedro Valley
San Andreas Lake
Millbrae
Niles
Point San Pedro
San Francisco State Fish and Game Refuge
Burlingame
Hillsborough
Coyote Hills Reg. Park
Fremont
Newark
Montara
San Mateo
Foster City
Bair Island
Moss Beach
Belmont
Greco Is.
DUMBARTON BRIDGE
El Granada
Crystal Springs Res.
San Carlos
land
Redwood City
Menlo Park

SAN FRANCISCO
0 5 10 15km

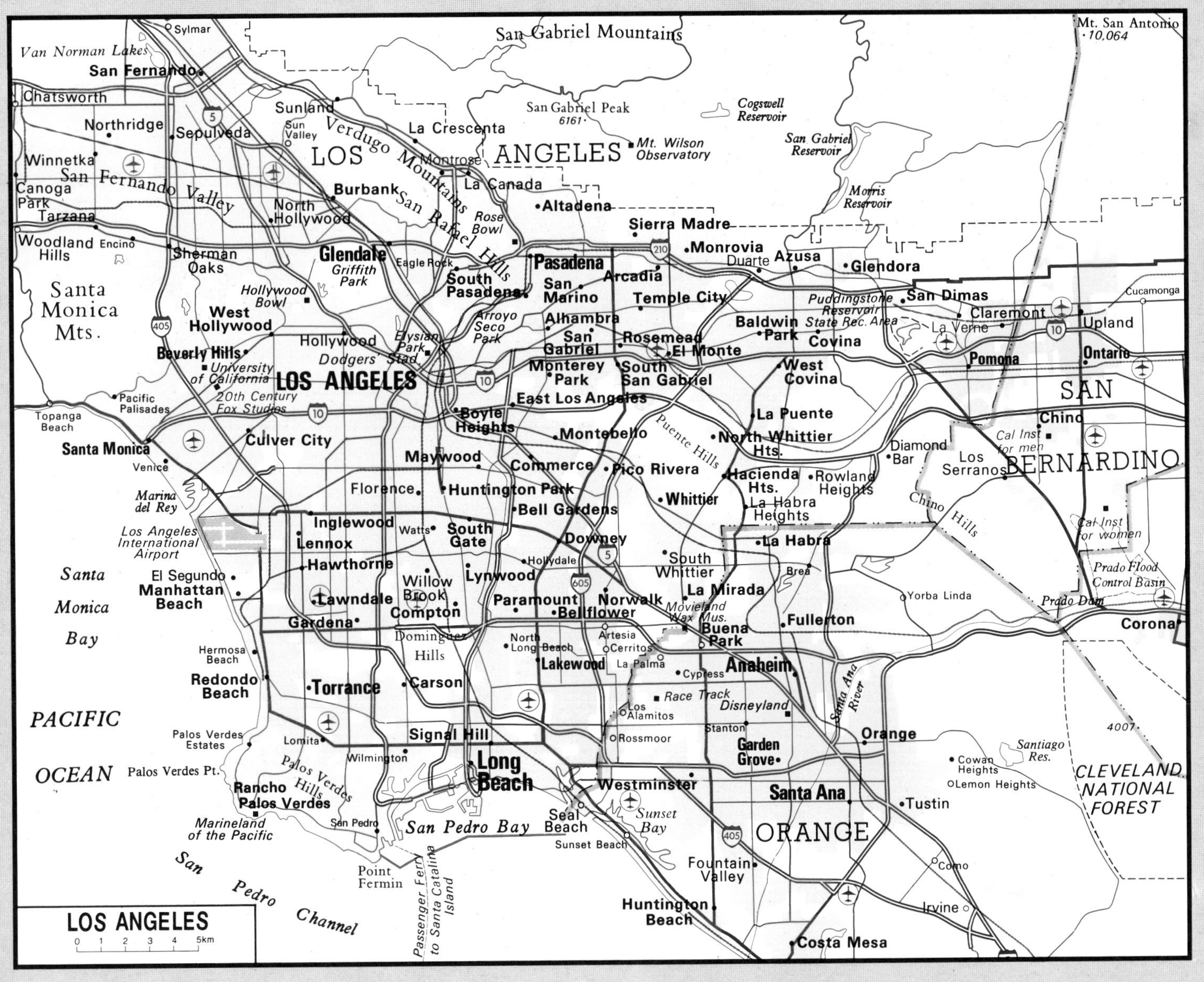

LOS ANGELES

San Gabriel Mountains
Mt. San Antonio 10,064
Van Norman Lakes
Sylmar
San Fernando
Chatsworth
Cogswell Reservoir
San Gabriel Peak 6161
San Gabriel Reservoir
Sunland
Verdugo Mountains
La Crescenta
Northridge
Sepulveda
Sun Valley
Montrose
Mt. Wilson Observatory
Winnetka
San Fernando Valley
LOS ANGELES
Morris Reservoir
Canoga Park
Tarzana
Burbank
San Rafael Hills
La Canada
Altadena
Sierra Madre
Woodland Hills
Encino
North Hollywood
Rose Bowl
Monrovia
Duarte
Azusa
Glendora
Santa Monica Mts.
Sherman Oaks
Glendale
Griffith Park
Eagle Rock
South Pasadena
Pasadena
Arcadia
Temple City
Puddingstone Reservoir
San Dimas
Cucamonga
Hollywood Bowl
San Marino
Claremont
West Hollywood
Hollywood
Alhambra
San Gabriel
Rosemead
Covina
La Verne
Beverly Hills
University of California
20th Century Fox Studios
Elysian Park
Dodgers Stad.
El Monte
Baldwin Park
West Covina
Pomona
Ontario
Topanga Beach
Pacific Palisades
LOS ANGELES
Boyle Heights
Monterey Park
South San Gabriel
La Puente
SAN BERNARDINO
Santa Monica
Venice
Culver City
Montebello
North Whittier Hts.
Diamond Bar
Los Serranos
Chino
Marina del Rey
Maywood
Commerce
Pico Rivera
Hacienda Hts.
Rowland Heights
Cal Inst for men
Florence
Huntington Park
Whittier
La Habra Heights
Chino Hills
Los Angeles International Airport
Inglewood
Bell Gardens
Santa Monica Bay
Lennox
Watts
South Gate
Downey
South Whittier
La Habra
Brea
Cal Inst for women
Hawthorne
Hollydale
Prado Flood Control Basin
El Segundo
Manhattan Beach
Lawndale
Willow Brook
Lynwood
Norwalk
La Mirada
Movieland Wax Mus.
Prado Dam
Gardena
Compton
Paramount
Bellflower
Buena Park
Fullerton
Yorba Linda
Corona
Hermosa Beach
Dominguez Hills
North Long Beach
Artesia
Cerritos
La Palma
Redondo Beach
Torrance
Carson
Lakewood
Anaheim
Palos Verdes Estates
Lomita
Wilmington
Signal Hill
Los Alamitos
Race Track
Disneyland
Santa Ana River
Orange
Santa Monica
Palos Verdes Hills
Rancho Palos Verdes
Long Beach
Westminster
Garden Grove
Santa Ana
Tustin
Cowan Heights
Santiago Res.
Lemon Heights
CLEVELAND NATIONAL FOREST
PACIFIC OCEAN
Palos Verdes Pt.
San Pedro
San Pedro Bay
Seal Beach
Sunset Bay
Fountain Valley
Marineland of the Pacific
Point Fermin
Sunset Beach
ORANGE
Como
Passenger Ferry to Santa Catalina Island
Rossmoor
Stanton
Huntington Beach
Costa Mesa
Irvine
San Pedro Channel

LOS ANGELES
0 1 2 3 4 5km

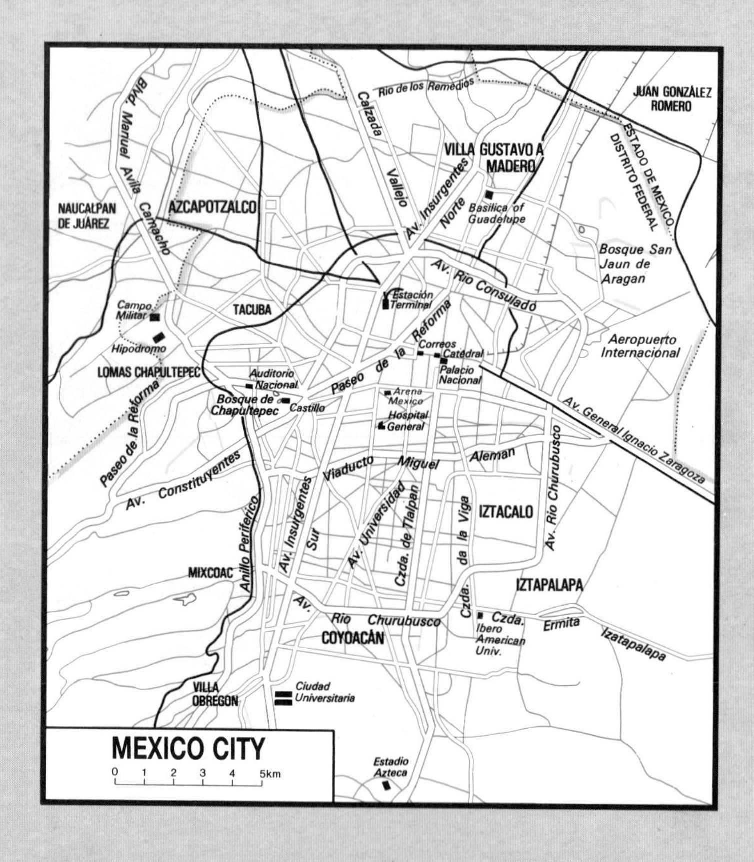

MEXICO CITY

0 1 2 3 4 5km

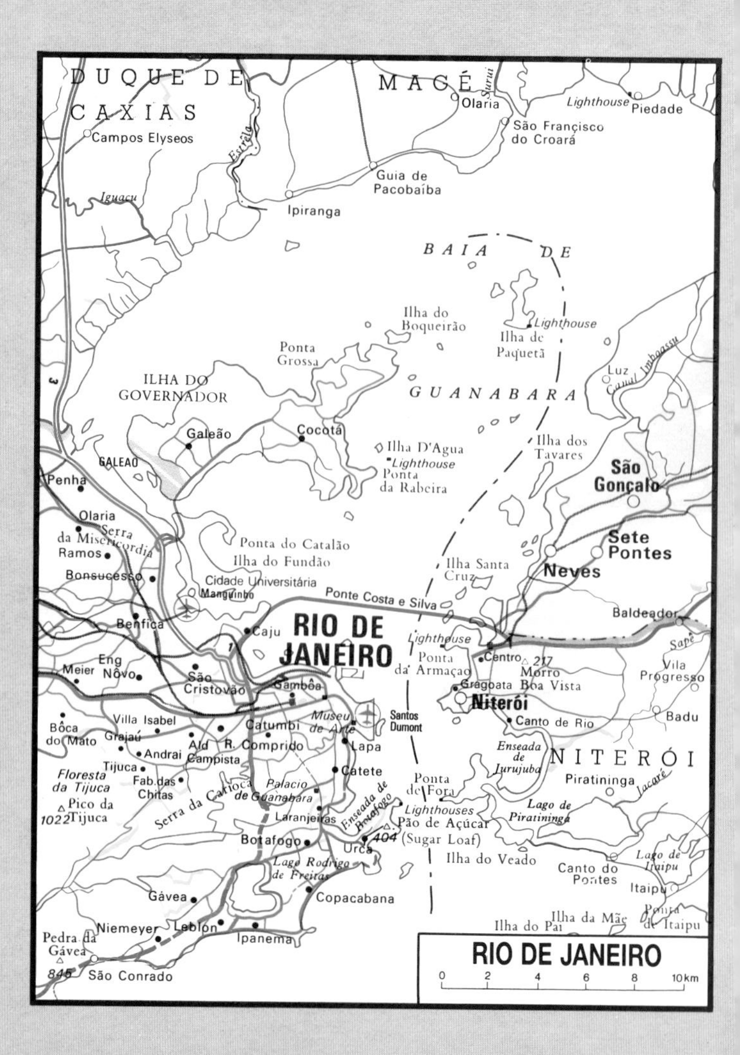

SAO PAULO

0 1 2 3 4 5km

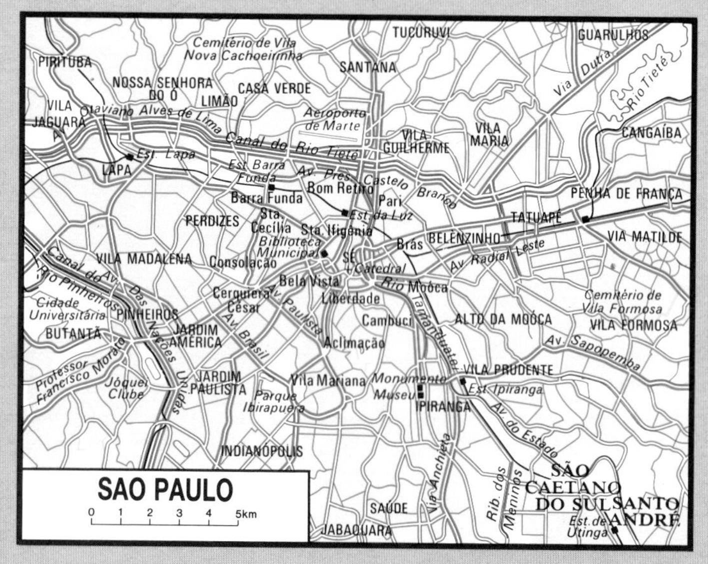

SANTIAGO

0 1 2 3 4 5km

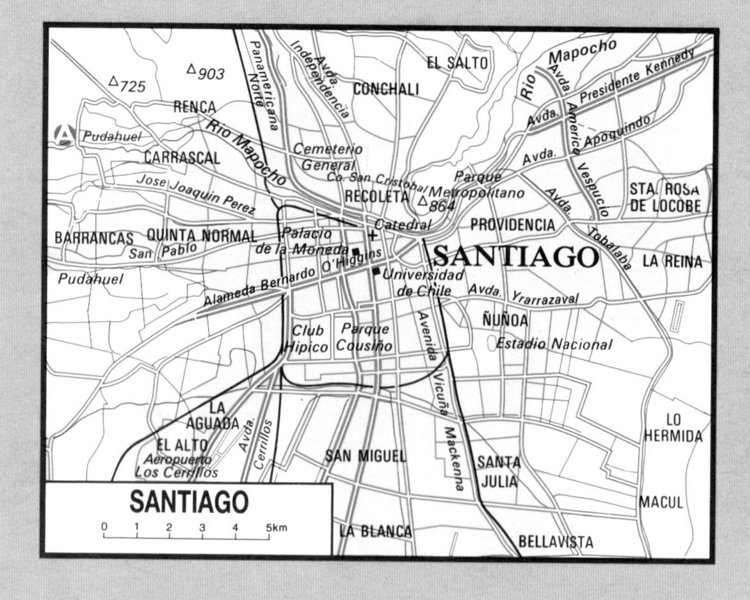

RIO DE JANEIRO

0 2 4 6 8 10km

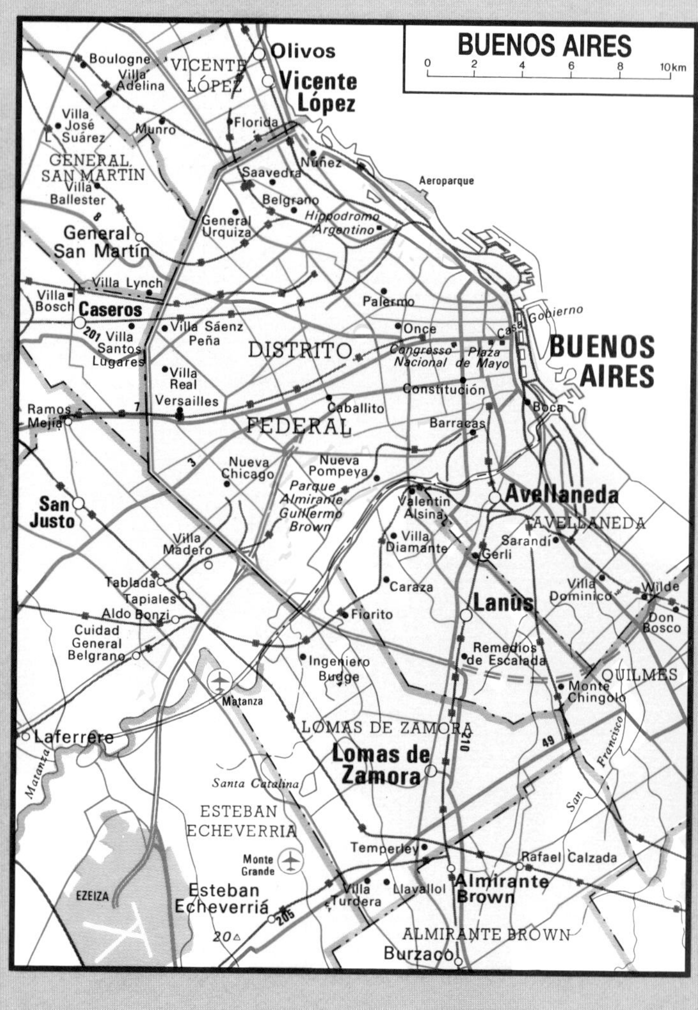

BUENOS AIRES

0 2 4 6 8 10km

The roman alphabet is used world-wide. Yet the sounds of Latin from which it was inherited were far too few to allow the alphabet to be applied unaltered to the languages of the world. As a result numerous modifications have been made by adding supplementary letters, by changing the original letters or by adding accents or other diacritical signs.

This brief guide is intended to give no more than an indication of the English language equivalents of the more important letters or combinations of letters in the various alphabets used in the Atlas. An English word is added in brackets to illustrate the sound intended.

FRENCH
There are four nasal vowels:
am an aen em en aon   ā
aim ain en eim ein im in   ē
om on   ō
um un   eũ
ā ē ō eũ are like a in hart; e in met; o in corn; oo in book pronounced nasally.
au, eau = o (no); é = ay (lay); è, ê, = e (met); oi oî = wa (wand)
c + a = k; c + e or i = ç = s (sit)
ch = sh (fresh); g + a, o or u = g (got)
g + e or i = j = zh⁺; gn = ni (onion)
gu = g (got); gü = gw (iguana)
ll = l or y; qu = k; th = t
u = between e in few and oo in too

SPANISH
c + a, o or u = k; c + e or i = th (thin) or s (sit)
ch = ch (cheese); g + a, o or u = g (got)
g + e or i = kh*; gu + a, o or u = gw (iguana)
gu + e or i = g (got); j = kh*; ñ = ny (canyon);
ll = y (yes)
qu + a, o or u = kw (quick); qu + e or i = k (kite)
y = y (yes); z = th (thin) or z depending on dialect

ITALIAN
c + a, o or u = k; c + e or i = ch (cheese)
ch = k
g + a, o or u = g (got); g + e or i = j (jet)
gh = g (got); gli = lli (million)
qu = kw (quick); z = ts or dz

ROMANIAN
ă = a in relative
â = i in ravine
c + a, o or u = k
c + e or i = ch (cheese); ch = k
g + a, o or u = g (got); g + e or i = j (jet)
ş = sh (fresh); ţ = ts (sits)

PORTUGUESE
ã, ãe = French ē
õa, õe = French ō
c + a, o or u = k; c + e or i = s
ç = s; ch = sh (fresh)
ih = lli (million)
x = sh (fresh); z = z but = zh when final

GERMAN
ä = e (met); au = ow (down)
äu = oy (boy); c = ts (sits)
ch = kh*; ei, ey = eye (= y in why)
eu = oy (boy); g = g (got)
ie = ie (retrieve); j = y (yes)
ö = oo (book); s = z but s when final
sch = sh (fresh); sp, st = shp, sht
ü = French u; v = f; w = v; z = ts (sits)

DUTCH
aa ee are long vowels
c + e or i or z = s, otherwise k
ij = eye (= y in why)

SCANDINAVIAN
å = aw (law); ä = e (met)
ø = oo (book); øj = oy (boy)
j = y (yes)

ICELANDIC
ð = dh = th (then)
hv = kw; ll = tl; p = th

FINNISH
ay = eye (= y in why)
j = y; y = French u; w = v

HUNGARIAN
a = aw (law); cs = ch (cheese); ccs = chch;
gy = d + y (dew)
j = y; ny = ny (canyon)
s = sh (fresh); ss = shsh
sz = s (sit); ty = t + y (yes)
zs = zh⁺
ai = e (met); av = au or av
dh = th (then); th = th (thin)
kh = kh*; oi = i (ravine)
ou = oo (too)

TURKISH
c = j (jet); ç = ch (cheese)
ö = oo (book); ş = sh
ü = French u
ı and i = i (ravine)

RUSSIAN
ay = a + y (yes)
e = e or ye
ë = yaw; ëy = yoy
ch = ch (cheese); sh = sh (fresh)
sh ch = sh ch (fresh cheese)
ts = ts (sits)
ya = ya (yam); z = z (zoo)
zh = zh (measure)
' = sound of y (yes)
" = silent

OTHER SLAVONIC

§S-C	Pol	Cz	
c	c	c	= ts (sits)
	ć		= ts + y (yes)
č	cz	č	= ch (cheese)
ć			= t + y (yes)
đ		ď	= d + y (yes)
		ě	= e (mother)
h	ch	ch	= kh*
j	j	j	= y (yes)
	ł		= w (wood)
nj	ń	ň	= ny (canyon)
		ř	= rzh*
š	sz	š	= sh (fresh)
		ť	= t + y (yes)
ž	ż, rz, ź	ž	= zh*

ARABIC
long vowels have a macron (bar), ā
dh = th (then)
h = h (hat); j = (jet)
gh = French r, pronounce as g (got)
kh = kh* q = g (got)
' and ' are best treated as glottal stops
ḍ ḥ ṣ ṭ ẓ = d, h, s, t, z
Note: 1. in Egypt and Sudan g = g (got)
      2. in NW Africa Dj = j (jet)
          ou = w (wadi)

FARSI (IRAN)
Can be read as Arabic above. Stress is on the last syllable.

SOMALI
long vowels are aa, ee, ii, oo, uu
c is silent = glottal stop
dh = th (then)
g = g (got); q = k (kite)
sh = sh (fresh); w = w (wadi)
x = kh*

MALAY – INDONESIAN
As English except
c = ch (cheese)

CHINESE (PINYIN)
q = ch (church); c = ts (sits)
x = hs = h + s

zh = s in measure;
kh = ch in Scottish loch
     = German ch in achtung

§S-C = Serbo-Croat
Pol = Polish
Cz = Czech

A

ABLATION   The loss of water from ice and snow surfaces, by melting and run-off, calving of icebergs, evaporation and snow-blowing.

ABRASION   The wearing down or away of rocks by friction.

ABSOLUTE HUMIDITY   The amount of water vapour in a specified amount of air, frequently expressed as grams of water vapour per kilogram of dry air containing the vapour.

ABYSSAL   Usually applied to the very deep parts of the oceans, over 3km below the surface.

ACCRETION   The growth of objects by collection of additional material, usually of smaller size. Ice particles in the atmosphere can grow by this process.

ACID PRECIPITATION   Rain and snow with a pH of less than 5.6.

ADVECTION   Movement of a property in air and water by their motion. Usually applied to horizontal rather than vertical motion.

AEOLIAN   Related to winds. Thus aeolian geomorphology is concerned with the processes whereby wind removes, distributes and deposits materials of the earth's surface.

AGGLOMERATE   A rock made of small pieces of lava that have been fused by heat.

AGGRADATION   The building up of a land surface by deposition of material by wind, water or ice.

AGGREGATE   A loose collection of rock fragments.

ALLUVIAL PLAIN   A plain, usually at low altitude, made of alluvium.

ANTICYCLONE   An extensive region of relatively high atmospheric pressure, usually a few thousand kilometres across, in which the low level winds spiral outwards, clockwise in the northern hemisphere and anticlockwise in the southern hemisphere.

ARCHIPELAGO   A sea or lake containing numerous islands, such as the area between Sumatra and the Philippines.

ARTESIAN WELL   A well which taps water held under pressure in rocks below the surface. The pressure results in a well water level higher than the highest part of the water-bearing rocks.

ATOLL   A coral reef surrounding a lagoon found in the tropical oceans.

AURORA BOREALIS (Northern Lights)   Flashing lights in the atmosphere some 400km above polar regions caused by solar particles being trapped in the earth's magnetic field.

AVALANCHE   The sudden and rapid movement of ice, snow, earth and rock down a slope.

AZIMUTH   Horizontal angle between two directions.

B

BADLANDS   Highly dissected landscapes, usually associated with poorly consolidated materials and sparse vegetation cover.

BAR   A usually sandy feature, lying parallel to the coast and frequently underwater.

BARCHAN   A crescentic sand dune whose horns point in the direction of dune movement.

BAROGRAPH   An instrument for recording atmospheric pressure. The output is a graph of pressure changes through time.

BAROMETER   An instrument for measuring atmospheric pressure. The reading is either by measuring the height of a column of mercury or by the compression or expansion of a series of vacuum chambers.

BARRIER REEF   A coral reef characterized by the presence of a lagoon or body of water between it and the associated coastline.

BASALT   A fine-grained and dark coloured igneous rock.

BASE LEVEL   The lower limit to the operation of erosional processes generating on land – usually defined with reference to the role of running water. Sea level is the most general form of base level.

BASIN   An area of land encompassing the water flow into any specific river channel – hence usually known as a drainage basin.

BATHOLITH   A large mass of intrusive igneous rock.

BATHYMETRY   Measurement of water depth.

BAUXITE   The main ore of aluminium.

BEACH   A coastal accumulation of various types of sediment, usually sands and pebbles.

BEAUFORT SCALE   A scale of wind speed devised by Admiral Sir Francis Beaufort based on effects of winds on ships. Later modified to include land-based phenomena.

BENCH MARK   A reference point used in the measurement of land height in topographic surveying.

BENTHIC   Relating to plants, animals and other organisms that inhabit the floors of lakes, seas and oceans.

BERGSCHRUND   The crevasse existing at the head of a glacier because of the movement of glacier ice away from the rock wall.

BIGHT   A bend in a coast forming an open bay, or the bay itself.

BIOMASS   The mass of biological material present per plant or animal, per community or per unit area.

BIOME   A mixed community of plants and animals occupying a large area of continental size.

BIOSPHERE   The zone at the interface of the earth's surface, ocean and atmosphere where life is found.

BIOTA   The entire collection of species or organisms, plants and animals found in a given region.

BISE   A cold, dry northerly to north-easterly wind occurring in the mountains of Central Europe in winter.

BLACK EARTH   A black soil rich in humus, found extensively in temperate grasslands such as the Russian Steppes.

BLOW HOLE   Vertical shaft leading from a sea cave to the surface. Air and water are frequently forced through it by advancing seas.

BORE   A large solitary wave which moves up funnel-shaped rivers and estuaries.

BOREAL   A descriptive term, usually of climate and forest, to characterize conditions in middle to high latitudes.

BOURNE   A river channel on chalk terrain that flows after heavy rain.

BUTTE   A small, flat-topped and often steep-sided hill standing isolated on a flat plain. *(see picture below)*

C

CALDERA   A depression, usually several kilometres across.

CALVING   The breaking away of a mass of ice from a floating glacier or ice shelf to form an iceberg.

CANYON   A steep sided valley, usually found in semi-arid and arid areas.

CAPE   An area of land jutting out into water, frequently as a peninsula or promontory.

CARDINAL POINTS   The four principal compass points, north, east, south and west.

CATARACT   A large waterfall over a precipice.

CHINOOK   A warm, dry wind that blows down the eastern slopes of the Rocky Mountains of North America.

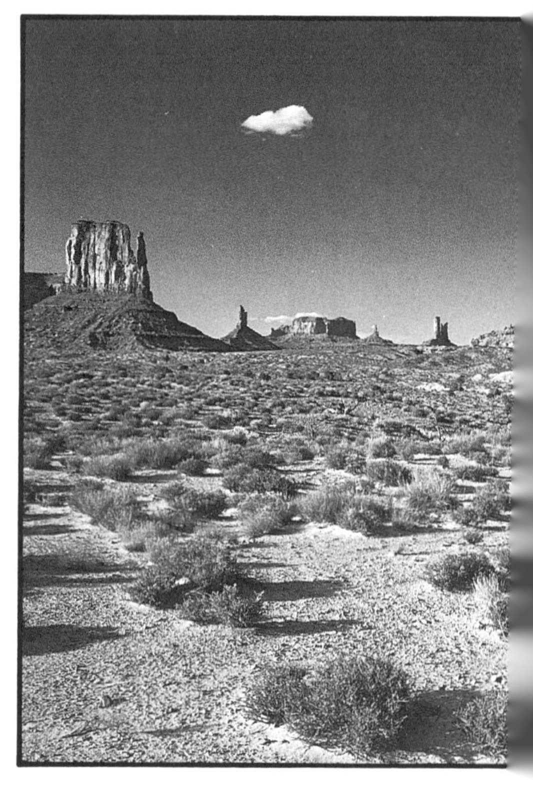

Above Butte, Monument Valley, Arizona USA. This type of flat-topped, steep sided hill is characteristic of the arid plateau region of the western United States.

CIRQUE OR CORRIE   A hollow, open downstream but bounded upstream by a curved, steep headwall, with a gently sloping floor. Found in areas that have been glaciated.

CLIMATE   The long-term atmospheric characteristics of a specified area.

CLOUD   A collection of a vast number of small water droplets or ice crystals or both in the atmosphere.

COL   A pass or saddle between two mountain peaks.

COLD FRONT   A zone of strong horizontal temperature gradient in the atmosphere moving such that, for the surface observer, cold air replaces warm.

CONDENSATION   The process of formation of liquid water from water vapour.

CONFLUENCE   The 'coming together' of material

flows, most usually used in fluids such as the atmosphere and oceans.

CONGLOMERATE   A rock which comprises or contains rounded pebbles more than about 2mm in diameter.

CONTINENTAL DRIFT   The movement of continents relative to each other. (See *Plate Tectonics*)

CONTINENTAL SHELF   A portion of the continental crust below sea level that slopes gently seaward forming an extension of the adjacent coastal plain separated from the deep ocean by the steeply sloping continental slope.

CONTINENTAL SLOPE   Lies on the seaward edge of the continental shelf and slopes steeply to the ocean floor.

CONTOUR   A line on a map that joins points of equal height or equal depth.

CONVECTION CURRENT   A current resulting from convection which is a mode of mass transport within a fluid (especially heat) resulting in movement and mixing of properties of that fluid.

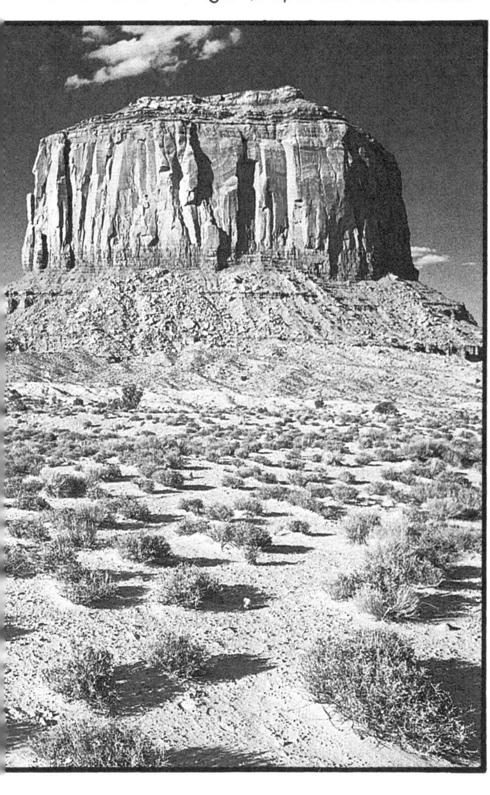

CONVERGENCE   The opposite of divergence which is the outflowing mass of fluid. Hence convergence is the inflowing of such mass.

CORAL REEF   Large structures fringing islands and coastlines consisting mostly of corals and algae.

CORDILLERA   A system of mountain ranges consisting of a number of more or less parallel chains of mountain peaks – such as in the Rocky Mountains.

CRATER   A depression at the top of a volcano where a vent carrying lava and gasses reaches the surface.

CRATON   A continental area that has experienced little internal deformation in the last 600 million years.

CREVASSE   A deep fissure in the surface of a body of ice.

CYCLONE   A region of relatively low atmospheric pressure about 2000 km across around which air rotates anticlockwise in the northern hemisphere and clockwise in the southern.

D

DATUM LEVEL   Something (such as a fixed point or assumed value) used as a basis for calculating or measuring. Frequently a height of ground relative to which other heights are assessed.

DECLINATION   Angular distance north or south from the equator measured along a line of longitude.

DECIDUOUS FOREST   Forest in which the trees shed their leaves at a particular time, season or growth stage. The most common manifestation is the shedding in winter.

DEFLATION   The process whereby the wind removes fine materials from the surface of a beach or desert.

DEGRADATION   The lowering and often flattening of a land surface by erosion.

DELTA   Accumulations of sediment deposited at the mouths of rivers. The Nile and Mississippi deltas are two famous examples.

DENUDATION   The laying bare of underlying rocks or strata by the removal of overlying material.

DEPOSITION   The laying down of material, which, in geomorphological terms, was previously carried by wind, liquid water or ice.

DEPRESSION   See *cyclone*

DESALINIZATION   To take out the salt content of a material. Usually applied to the extraction of salt from sea water to give fresh water.

DESERT   An area in which vegetation cover is sparse or absent and precipitation is low in amount. Deserts can be hot or cold.

DISCHARGE   The volume of flow of fluid in a given time period.

DISSECTED PLATEAU   A relatively flat, high level area of land which has been cut by streams.

DIURNAL   Occurring everyday or having a daily cycle.

DIVERGENCE   A spreading of material. Frequently found in high pressure areas (anticyclones) in the atmosphere where air spirals outwards from the centre.

DOLDRUMS   A zone of light, variable winds and low atmospheric pressure near or slightly north of the equator.

DRAINAGE   The flow of material (usually a fluid) over the earth's surface due to the force of gravity. Most familiarly seen as rivers.

DRIFT ICE   Ice bodies drifting in ocean currents.

DROUGHT   Dryness caused by lack of precipitation, most easily seen in the hot, dry desert areas of the world.

DROWNED VALLEY   A valley which has been filled with water due to a rise of sea level relative to the level with which the river mouth was previously in accord.

DRUMLIN   A depositional landform, usually made of glacially-derived material, which has been streamlined by the passage of overlying ice.

DRY VALLEY   A valley which is seldom, if ever, occupied by a stream channel.

DUNE   An accumulation of sand deposited and shaped by wind.

DUST   Solid particles carried in suspension by the atmosphere.

DYKE   A sheet-like intrusion of igneous rock, usually oriented vertically, which cuts across the structural planes of the host rocks.

E

EARTH PILLAR   A pinnacle of soil or other unconsolidated material that is protected from erosion by the presence of a stone at the top.

EARTHQUAKE   A series of shocks and tremors resulting from the sudden release of pressure along active faults and in areas of volcanic activity.

EBB TIDE   Tide receding to or at its lowest point.

ECLIPSE, LUNAR   The total or partial obscuring of the Moon by the Earth lying on a line between the Moon and the Sun.

ECLIPSE, SOLAR   The total or partial obscuring of the Sun by the Moon lying on a line between the Sun and the Earth.

ECOLOGY   A branch of science that studies the relations of plants and animals with each other and with their non-living environment.

ECOSYSTEM   An entity within which ecological relations operate.

EPICENTRE   The point on the earth's surface which lies directly above the focus of an earthquake.

EQUINOX   The time of year when the sun is directly overhead at noon at the equator.

ERG   A sand desert.

EROSION   The group of processes whereby debris is loosened or dissolved and removed from any part of the earth's surface.

ERRATIC   A rock that has been carried to its present location by a glacier.

ESCARPMENT   A linear land form with one steep side (scarp slope) and one less steep side (dip slope).

ESKER   A sinuous ridge of coarse gravel which has been deposited by a meltwater stream normally flowing underneath a glacier.

ESTUARY   The sections of a river which flow into the sea and are influenced by tidal currents.

EVAPORATION   The diffusion of water vapour into the atmosphere from freely exposed water surfaces.

EXFOLIATION   The weathering of a rock by the peeling off of surface layers.

F

FATHOM   A unit of length equal to six feet, most usually used in measuring depth of water.

FAULT   A crack or fissure in rock, resulting from tectonic movement.

FAUNA   Animals or animal life of an area.

FEN   A low lying area partially covered by water which is characterized by accumulations of peat.

FJORD   A glacially eroded valley whose floor is occupied by the sea.

FIRTH   A sea inlet, particularly in Scotland.

FLORA   Plants or plant life in an area.

FLUVIOGLACIAL   The activity of rivers which are fed by water melted from glaciers.

FOG   An accumulation of water droplets or ice crystals in the atmosphere such that visibility is reduced to 1km or less.

FÖHN WIND   A strong, gusty, warm, down-slope wind which occurs on the lee side of a mountain range.

FOLD   A bend in rock strata resulting from movement of the crustal rocks.

FOOD CHAIN   The transfer of food from one type of organism to another in a sequence.

FORD   A shallow part of a river that allows easy crossing.

FRACTURE   The splitting of material into parts: usually concerned with geological materials.

FRAZIL ICE   Fine spikes of ice in suspension in water, usually associated with the freezing of sea water.

FRONT   A transition zone between air of different density, temperature and humidity.

FROST   A situation resulting from air temperatures falling to 0°C – either in the air (air frost) or at the ground (ground frost).

FUMAROLE   A small, volcanic vent through which hot gasses are emitted.

G

GABBRO   A basic igneous rock, usually coarse grained and dark grey to black in colour.

GEEST   Ancient alluvial sediments which still cover the land surfaces on which they were originally deposited.

GEODESY   The determination of the size and shape of the earth by survey and calculation.

GEOID   The shape of the earth at mean sea level.

GEOLOGY   Science that deals with the nature and origin of the earth's rocks and sediments.

GEOMORPHOLOGY   Science that deals with the nature and origin of landforms of the earth's surface.

GEOSYNCLINE   A very large depression, tens or hundreds of kilometres across and up to ten kilometres deep, the floor of which is built up by sedimentation.

GEYSER   A spring of geothermally heated water that erupts intermittently due to pressures beneath the surface. Old Faithful in Yellowstone National Park, USA, is the most famous example.

GLACIATION   The incursion of ice into (or over) a landscape resulting in a whole suite of glacial processes operating thereupon.

GLACIER   A large body of ice, in a valley or covering a much larger area. The largest are found in polar regions.

GLEN   Valley. Term especially used in Scotland.

GNEISS   A coarse-grained igneous rock that has been metamorphosed.

GONDWANALAND   A large continent which it is thought was split very early in geological time to form parts of Africa, Australia, Antarctica, South America and India.

GORGE   A deep and narrow section of a river valley, usually with very steep sides.

GRAVEL   Loose, rounded fragments of rock.

GREAT CIRCLE   A circle formed on the surface of the earth by the intersection of a plane through the centre of the earth with the surface. Lines of longitude and the Equator are great circles.

GROUND FROST   See *frost*

GROUND WATER   All water (gaseous, liquid or solid) lying below the earth's surface and not chemically combined with the minerals present.

GROYNE   A man-made barrier running across a beach and into the sea; constructed to reduce erosion of the beach by longshore currents.

GULF   A part of the sea that is partly or almost completely enclosed by land.

GULLY   A linear depression worn in the earth by running water after rains.

GUYOT   A flat-topped mountain on the sea floor which does not reach the sea surface.

GYRE   Large circulations of water in the world's oceans, involving the major currents.

H

HAFF   A coastal lagoon separated from the open seas by a sand spit.

HAIL   Solid precipitation which falls as ice particles from cumulonimbus clouds. Contrasts markedly with snow.

HEMISPHERE   Half of the earth, usually thought of in terms of its surface. The most familiar are the northern and southern hemispheres, bounded by the Equator.

HORIZON   Apparent junction of earth and sky.

HORSE LATITUDE   The latitude belts over the oceans at latitudes of 30–35° where winds are predominantly calm or light and weather is often hot and dry.

HOT SPOT   A small area of the earth's crust where an unusually high heat flow is associated with volcanic activity.

HOT SPRING   An emission of hot water at the land surface.

HURRICANE   A severe cyclone occurring in the tropics, characterized by high wind speeds and heavy precipitation.

HYDROLOGICAL CYCLE   The continuous movement of all forms of water (vapour, liquid and solid) on, in and above the earth.

HYDROSPHERE   The earth's water – saline, fresh, gaseous, liquid and solid.

HYGROMETER   A device for measuring the relative humidity of the atmosphere.

HYPSOGRAPHIC CURVE   A generalized profile of the earth and ocean floors which represents the proportions of the area of the surface at various altitudes above or below a datum.

I

ICEBERG   A large floating mass of ice detached from a glacier, usually tens of metres deep and can be several kilometres across.

ICE-CAP   A dome-shaped glacier with a generally outward flow of ice.

ICE FLOE   A piece of floating ice which is not attached to the land and is usually 2–3 metres thick.

ICE SHELF   A floating sheet of ice attached to an embayment in the coast.

IGNEOUS ROCK   Rock formed when molten material solidifies, either within the earth's crust or at the surface.

INSELBERG   A large, residual hill which overlooks a surrounding eroded plain.

INSOLATION   The amount of solar radiation received over a specified area and a specified time.

INTERNATIONAL DATE LINE   An arbitary line, roughly along the 180° longitude line, east and west of which the date differs by one day.

INVERSION (temperature)
An increase of temperature with height.

IRRIGATION   The supply of water to land by artificial means. Usually to improve agricultural productivity.

ISLAND ARC   A chain of islands with an arcuate plan form. The islands are usually volcanic in origin.

ISOBAR   A line drawn on diagrams joining equal values of atmospheric pressure. A particular kind of isopleth.

ISOPLETH   A line drawn on diagrams joining equal values of the plotted element.

ISOSTASY   The condition of balance between the rigid crustal elements of the earth's surface and the underlying, denser and more mobile material.

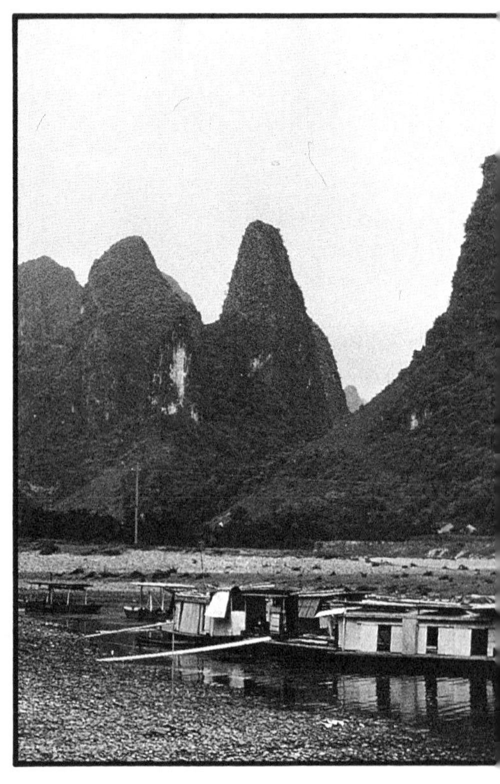

Above Limestone towers in the world's most spectacular karst region – Li River near Guilin, Guangxi Province, China. The towers are the result of erosional processes.

ISTHMUS   A narrow strip of land which connects two islands or two large land masses.

J

JOINT   A fracture or crack in a rock.

JUNGLE   An area of land overgrown with dense vegetation, usually in the tropics.

K

KAME   An irregular mound of stratified sediment deposited by, in association with stagnant ice.

KARST   Limestone areas which have distinctive landforms such as caves, sinks and frequently a lack of surface water. *(see picture above)*

KELP   A mass of large brown seaweeds.

KETTLE HOLE   An enclosed depression resulting from the melting of buried ice.

KNOT A measure of speed – one nautical mile per hour (1.15 mi hr^{-1}; 0.85 km hr^{-1}).

KOPJE A small hill or rock outcrop; term used particularly in South Africa.

KRILL Small marine animals, resembling shrimps.

L

LACCOLITH A mass of intrusive rock, usually with a horizontal base and causing the doming of overlying strata.

LAGOON A shallow pool separated from a larger body of water by a bar or reef.

LANDSAT An unmanned satellite that carries sensors to record the resources of the earth.

LANDSLIDE The movement downward under the influence of gravity of a mass of rock debris.

LATERITE A red clay formed by the weathering of rock that consists especially of compounds of iron and aluminium.

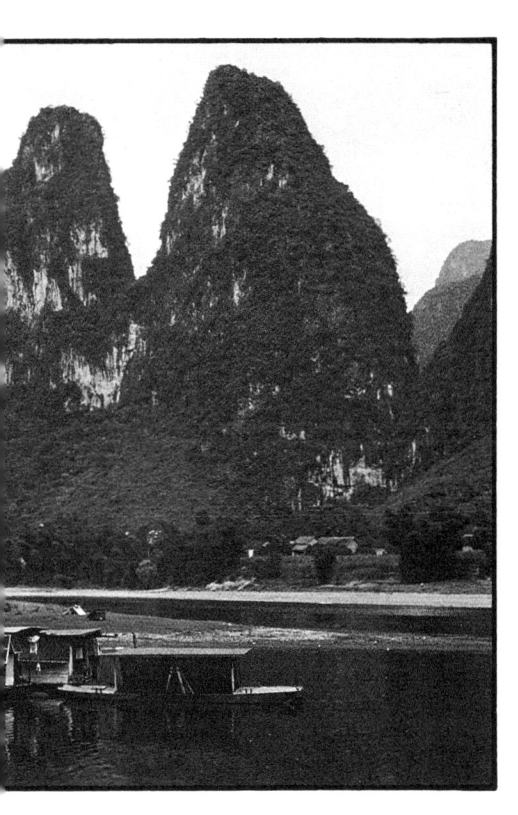

LAURASIA The northern part of Pangaea, a super-continent thought to have been broken up by continental drift.

LAVA Molten rock material that emerges from volcanoes and volcanic fissures.

LEACHING The downward movement of water through soil resulting in the removal of water-soluble materials from upper layers and their accumulation in lower layers.

LEEWARD To the lee (downwind, downstream) of an obstacle lying in a flow.

LEVEE A broad, long ridge running parallel and adjacent to a river on its flood-plain.

LIGNITE A brownish black coal in which the texture of the original wood is distinct.

LITHOSPHERE The earth's crust and a portion of the upper mantle that together comprise a layer of strength relative to the more easily deformable layer below.

LITTORAL A coastal region.

LLANOS An open grassy plain in S. America.

LOAM A crumbly soil consisting of a mixture of clay, silt and sand.

LOCH A lake or narrow sea inlet in Scotland.

LOESS Unconsolidated and frequently unstratified material deposited after transport by wind.

LONGSHORE CURRENT A current that runs along a coast. It may result in longshore drift, the transport of beach material along the coast.

LOW See *cyclone*

LUNAR MONTH The period of time between two successive new moons, being about 29½ days.

M

MAGMA Fused, molten rock material beneath the earth's crust from which igneous rocks are formed.

MAGNETIC ANOMALIES Areas with local surface variations in the earth's magnetic field relative to large-scale values.

MAGNETIC FIELD The field of force exerted by the earth by virtue of its being like a giant magnet. Its most familiar manifestation is in the behaviour of a compass.

MAGNETIC REVERSAL The reversal of the earth's magnetic field, such that a north-seeking compass points toward the South Pole. Such reversals have occurred in geological time.

MANTLE The zone within the earth's interior extending from 25 to 70km below the surface to a depth of 2900km.

MAP PROJECTION A mathematical device for representing a portion of all of the earth's curved surface on a flat surface.

MAP SCALE A measure of the ratio of distances represented on a map to their true value.

MAQUIS Scrub vegetation of evergreen shrubs characteristic of the western Mediterranean.

MARL A fine grained mixture of clay and silt with a high proportion of calcium carbonate.

MASSIF A large mountainous area, often quite distinct, containing several individual substantial mountains.

MEANDER A sinuously winding portion of a river channel; also applied to similar forms within larger flows, such as the atmosphere and oceans.

MEAN SEA LEVEL The level of the sea determined from a mean of the tidal ranges over periods of several months to several years.

METAMORPHIC ROCKS Rocks in which their composition, structure and texture have been significantly altered by the action of heat and pressure greater than that produced normally by burial.

METEOROLOGY The study of the workings of the atmosphere.

MILLIBAR A unit of pressure, most widely used in meteorology. The average pressure exerted by the atmosphere on the surface of the earth is just over 1013 millibars.

MISTRAL A cold, dry, north or northwest wind affecting the Rhone Valley.

MONSOON A wind regime with marked seasonal reversal in direction, most famously found in the Indian sub-continent.

MORAINE A landform resulting from the deposition of till by glaciers, taking on several

distinctive forms depending upon the location and mode of deposition.

N

NADIR A point that is vertically below the observer.

NASA National Aeronautics and Space Administration (USA).

NEAP TIDE A tide of minimum height occurring at the first and third quarter of the moon.

NÉVÉ Snow that is being compacted into ice, as found in the birth place of glaciers.

NUNATAK A mountain completely surrounded by an ice cap or ice sheet.

O

OASIS An area within a desert region where there is sufficient water to sustain animal and plant life throughout the year.

OCEAN BASIN A large depression in the ocean floor analogous to basins on land.

OCEANIC CRUST The portion of the earth's surface crust comprising largely sima (silica-magnesia rich rocks) about 5km thick. Underlies most of the world's oceans.

OCEAN RIDGE A ridge in the ocean floor, sometimes 150 to 1500 km wide and hundreds of metres high.

OCCLUSION The coming together of warm and cold fronts in cyclones in the latest stages of its evolution.

OROGENESIS The formation of mountains, such as the Andes and Rocky Mountains. The mechanism is still uncertain but is probably related to plate tectonics.

OUTWASH PLAIN Stratified material deposited by glacio-fluvial waters beyond the ice margin.

OXBOW LAKE A lake, usually curved in plan, occupying an abandoned section of meandering river.

P

PACK ICE Ice formed on sea surface when water temperatures fall to about −2°C and floating free under the influence of currents and wind.

PAMPAS An extensive, generally grass-covered plain of temperate South America east of the Andes.

PANGAEA The name given to a postulated continental landmass which split up to produce most of the present northern hemisphere continents.

PASS A narrow passage over relatively low ground in a mountain range.

PEDIMENT A smooth, erosional land surface typically sloping from the foot of a high-land area to a local base level.

PELAGIC The part of an aquatic system that excludes its margins and substrate; it is essentially the main part of the water body.

PENEPLAIN The supposed end land form resulting from erosional processes wearing down an initially uplifted block.

PENUMBRA A region of partial darkness in a shadow surrounding the region of total darkness (umbra), such as seen in an eclipse.

PERIHELION   The point in its orbit about the sun that a planet is closest to the sun.

PIEDMONT GLACIER   A glacier which spreads out into a lobe as it flows onto a lowland.

PILLOW LAVA   Lava that has solidified, probably under water, in rounded masses.

PLACER DEPOSIT   A sediment, such as in the bed of a stream, which contains particles of valuable minerals.

PLAIN   Extensive area of level or rolling treeless country.

PLANKTON   Small freshwater and marine organisms that tend to move with water currents and comprise the food of larger and higher order organisms.

PLATE TECTONICS   A theory which holds that the earth's surface is divided into several major rigid plates which are in motion with respect to each other and the underlying mantle. Continental drift results from plate motion and earthquakes, volcanoes and mountain-building tend to occur at the plate boundaries.

PLUTONIC ROCK   Rock material that has formed at depth where cooling and crystallization have occurred slowly.

POLAR WANDERING   The movements of the North and South Poles throughout geological time relative to the positions of the continents.

POLDER   A low lying area of land that has been reclaimed from the sea or a lake by artificial means and is kept free of water by pumping.

PRECIPITATION   The deposition of water from the atmosphere in liquid and solid form. Rain, snow, hail and dew are the most familiar forms.

PRAIRIE   An extensive area of level or rolling, almost treeless grassland in North America.

PRESSURE GRADIENT   The change per unit distance of pressure, perhaps most frequently met in atmospheric studies. The cause of winds.

Q

QUARTZ   A crystalline mineral consisting of silicon dioxide that is a major constituent of many rocks.

QUICKSAND   Water-saturated sand that is semi-liquid and cannot bear the weight of heavy objects.

R

RADAR   A device that transmits radio waves and locates objects in the vicinity by analysis of the waves reflected back from them (radio detection and ranging).

RADIATION   The transmission of energy in the form of electromagnetic waves and requiring no intervening medium.

RAIN SHADOW   An area experiencing relatively low rainfall because of its position on the leeward side of a hill.

RAISED BEACH   An emerged shoreline represented by stranded marine deposits and wave cut platforms, usually backed by former cliffs.

RANGE   An open region over which livestock may roam and feed, particularly in North America.

RAVINE   A narrow, steep sided valley usually formed by running water.

REEF   A rocky construction found at or near sea-level; coral reefs are perhaps the most familiar type.

RELATIVE HUMIDITY   The amount of water vapour in an air sample relative to the amount the sample could hold if it were saturated at the same temperature; expressed as a percentage.

REMOTE SENSING   The observation and measurement of an object without touching it.

RHUMB LINE   An imaginary line on the surface of the earth which makes equal oblique angles with all lines of longitude so that it forms a spiral coiling round the poles but never reaching them. This would be the course sailed by a ship following a single compass direction.

RIA   An inlet of the sea formed by the flooding of river valleys by rising sea or sinking land. Contrast to fjords which are drowned glacial valleys.

RIFT VALLEY   A valley formed when the area between two parallel faults sinks.

RIVER TERRACE   A step like land form in the flood plain of rivers due to the river incising further into the plain and leaving remnants of its former flood plain at levels higher than the present level of the river channel.

ROARING FORTIES   The area between 40° and 50°S, so called because of the high speeds of the winds occurring there. Sometimes applied to the winds themselves.

RUN-OFF   The section of the hydrological cycle connecting precipitation to channel flow.

S

SALINITY   The presence of salts in the waters and soils of arid, semi-arid and coastal areas.

SALT-MARSH   Vegetated mud-flats found commonly on many low-lying coasts in a wide range of temperate environments.

SANDBANK   A large deposit of sand, usually in a river or coastal waters.

SANDSTORM   A wind storm driving clouds of sand, most usually in hot, dry deserts.

SAVANNAH   A grassland region of the tropics and sub-tropics.

SCHIST   Medium to coarse-grained crystalline metamorphic rock.

SEA-FLOOR SPREADING   The phenomenon when tectonic plates move apart.

SEAMOUNT   A mountain or other area of high relief on the sea-floor which does not reach the surface.

SEASAT   A satellite especially designed to sense remotely wind and sea conditions on the oceans.

SEDIMENTARY ROCK   Rock composed of the fragments of older rocks which have been eroded and the debris deposited by wind and water, often as distinct strata.

SEISMIC WAVE   Wave resulting from the movements of materials in earthquakes.

SEISMOLOGY   Science that deals with earthquakes and other vibrations of the earth.

SHALE   A compacted sedimentary rock, usually with fine-grained particles.

SHALLOW-FOCUS EARTHQUAKE   An earthquake with a focus (or centre) at a shallow level relative to the earth's surface.

SIAL   The part of the earth's crust with a composition dominated by minerals rich in silicon and aluminium.

SIDEREAL DAY   A period of complete rotation of the earth on its axis, about 23 hours 56 minutes.

SILL   A tabular sheet of igneous rock injected along the bedding planes of sedimentary and volcanic formations.

SILT   An unconsolidated material of small particles ranging in size from about 2 to 60 micrometres.

SIMA   The part of the earth's crust with a composition dominated by minerals rich in silicon and magnesium.

SOIL CREEP   The slow movement downslope of soil, usually resulting in thinning of soils on the upper reaches and accumulations on the lower.

SOLIFLUCTION   The slow movement downslope of water saturated, seasonally thawed materials.

SOLSTICE   The days of maximum declination of the sun measured relative to the equator. When

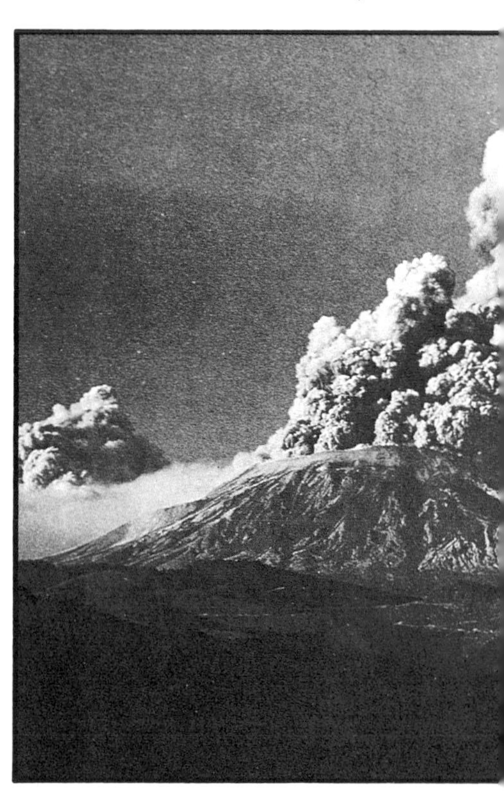

Above On May 18 1980, Mt St Helens demonstrated a plinian eruption (a kind first described by Pliny the Elder). The apparent smoke cloud is pulverised ash.

the midday sun is overhead at 23½°N it gives the longest day in the northern hemisphere and the shortest day in the southern. The reverse applies when the sun is overhead at 23½°S.

SPIT   Usually linear deposits of beach material attached at one end to land and free at the other.

SPRING TIDE   A tide of greater than average range occurring at or around the times of the new and full moon.

SQUALL   A sudden, violent wind, often associated with rain or hail; frequently occurs under cumulonimbus clouds.

STALACTITE   A deposit of calcium carbonate, rather like an icicle, hanging from the roof of a cave.

STALAGMITE   A deposit of calcium carbonate growing up from the floor of a cave due to the constant drip of water from the roof.

STANDARD TIME The officially established time, with reference to Greenwich Mean Time, of a region or country.

STEPPE Mid-latitude grasslands with few trees, most typically found in USSR.

STORM SURGE Changes in sea level caused by extreme weather events, notably the winds in storms.

STRAIT A narrow passage joining two large bodies of water.

STRIAE Scratches of a rock surface due to the passage over it of another rock of equal or greater hardness.

SUBDUCTION ZONE An area where the rocks comprising the sea floor are forced beneath continental rocks at a plate margin to be reincorporated in the magma beneath the earth's crust.

SUBSEQUENT RIVER A stream which follows a course determined by the structure of the local bedrock.

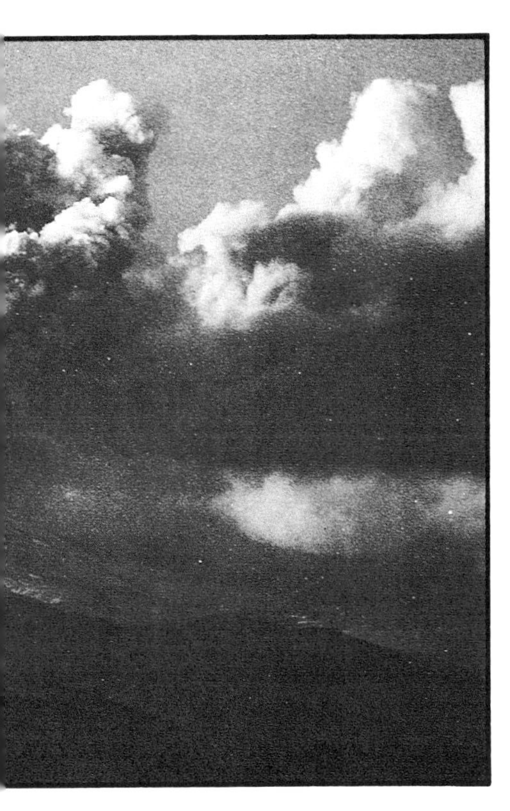

SUBSIDENCE Usually applied to the sinking of air in the atmosphere or the downward movement of the earth's surface.

SUBSOIL The layer of weathered material that underlies the surface soil.

SUDD Floating vegetable matter that forms obstructive masses in the upper White Nile.

SUNSPOT Relatively dark regions on the disk of the sun with surface temperature of about 4500K compared to the more normal 6000K of the rest of the surface.

SURGE A sudden excess over the normal value, usually of a flow of material (soil, ice, water).

SWELL A long, perturbation (usually wavelike) of a water surface that continues beyond its cause (eg a strong wind).

TAIGA The most northerly coniferous forest of cold temperature regions found in Canada, Alaska and Eurasia.

TECTONIC Concerned with the broad structures of the earth's rocks and the processes of faulting, folding and warping that form them.

TETHYS OCEAN An ocean formed in the Palaeozoic Era which extended from what is now the Mediterranean Sea eastwards as far as South-east Asia.

THERMOCLINE A layer of water or a lake or sea that separates an upper, warmer, oxygen-rich zone from a lower, colder, oxygen-poor zone and in which temperature decreases by 1°C for every metre of increased depth.

THRUST FAULT A low-angle reverse fault.

THUNDERSTORM A cloud in which thunder and lightning occur, usually associated with heavy precipitation and strong winds.

TIDAL BORE A large solitary wave that moves up funnel-shaped rivers and estuaries with the rising tide, especially spring tides.

TIDAL CURRENT The periodic horizontal motions of the sea, generated by the gravitational attraction of the moon and sun, typically of $1ms^{-1}$ on continental shelves.

TIDE The regular movements of the seas due to the gravitational attraction of the moon and sun, most easily observed as changes in coastal sea levels.

TOPOGRAPHY The configuration of a land surface, including its relief and the position of its natural and man-made features.

TOR An exposure of bedrock usually as blocks and boulders, forming an abrupt, steep sided culmination of a more gentle rise to the summits of hills. Famous tors exist on Dartmoor.

TORNADO A violent, localized rotating storm with winds of $100ms^{-1}$ circulating round a funnel cloud some 100m in diameter. Frequent in mid-western USA.

TRADE WIND Winds with an easterly component which blow from the subtropic high pressure areas around 30° toward the equator.

TROPICAL CYCLONE See *hurricane*

TROPOSPHERE The portion of the earth's atmosphere between the earth's surface and a height about 15–20km. This layer contains virtually all the world's weather. Mean temperatures decrease and mean wind speeds increase with height in the troposphere.

TSUNAMI Sea-surface waves caused by submarine earthquakes and volcanic activity. Popularly called tidal waves.

TURBULENCE Chaotic and apparently random fluctuations in fluid flow, familiarly seen in the behaviour of smoke, either from a cigarette, a chimney or a volcano.

TUNDRA Extensive, level, treeless and marshy regions lying polewards of the taiga.

TYPHOON A term used in the Far East to describe tropical cyclones or hurricanes.

UMBRA A region of total shadow, especially in an eclipse.

UPWELLING The upward movement of deeper water towards the sea surface.

V

VARVE A sediment bed deposited in a body of water within the course of one year.

VOE An inlet or narrow bay of the Orkney or Shetland Islands.

VOLCANIC ASH Ash emitted from a volcano.

VOLCANO An opening through which magma, molten rock ash or volatiles erupts onto the earth's surface. Also used to describe the landform produced by the erupted material. *(see picture below left)*

W

WADI An ephemeral river channel in deserts.

WARM FRONT An atmospheric front whereby, as it passes over an individual on the ground, warm air replaces cold.

WATERFALL A vertical or very steep descent of water in a stream.

WATERSHED A boundary dividing and separating the areas drained by different rivers.

WATERSPOUT A funnel-shaped, rotating cloud that forms occasionally over water when the atmosphere is very unstable. Akin to tornadoes which occur over land.

WATER TABLE The level below which the ground is wholly and permanently saturated with water.

WAVE HEIGHT The vertical extent of a wave.

WAVE LENGTH The horizontal extent of a wave, most easily seen as the distance along the direction of wave movement between crests or troughs.

WAVE PERIOD The time taken for a complete cycle of the oscillation occurring within a wave.

WAVE VELOCITY The velocity of a wave form, best seen by concentrating on one part of the wave such as its crest or trough.

WEATHERING The alteration by physical, chemical and biological processes of rocks and sediments in the top metres of the earth's crust. So called because this material is exposed to the effects of atmospheric and atmospherically related conditions.

WEATHER ROUTEING Choosing a route for a ship or aeroplane to minimise the deleterious effects of weather.

WESTERLIES Winds with a westerly component occurring between latitudes of about 35° and 60°. The whole regime forms a 'vortex' around each of the poles and forms a major element in world climate.

WHIRLWIND A general term to describe rotating winds of scales up to that of a tornado, usually a result of intense convection over small areas.

WILLY-WILLY Australasian term for a tropical cyclone or hurricane.

WINDSHEAR The variation of speed or direction or both of wind over a distance.

Y

YARDANG A desert landform, usually but not always, of unconsolidated material, shaped by and lying roughly along the direction of the wind.

Z

ZENITH A point that is vertically above the observer: the opposite of nadir.

ZOOPLANKTON One of the three kinds of plankton, including mature representatives of many animal groups such as Protozoa and Crustacea.

A

ABBREVIATIONS	FULL FORM	ENGLISH FORM
a.d.	an der	on the
Appno	Appennino	mountain range
Aqued.	Aqueduct	aqueduct
Arch.	Archipelago	
	Archipiélago	archipelago
A.S.S.R.	Autonomous Soviet Socialist Republic	Autonomous Soviet Socialist Republic

B

ABBREVIATIONS	FULL FORM	ENGLISH FORM
B.	1. Bahía, Baía, Baie, Bay, Bucht, Bukhta, Bugt	bay
	2. Ban	village
	3. Barrage,	dam
	4. Bir, Bîr, Bi'r	well
Bj	Bordj	fort
Bol.	Bol'sh, -oy	big
Br.	1. Branch	branch
	2. Bridge, Brücke	bridge
	3. Burun	cape
Brj	Baraj, -i	dam
Bu.	Büyük	big

C

ABBREVIATIONS	FULL FORM	ENGLISH FORM
C.	Cabo, Cap, Cape	cape
Can.	Canal	canal
Cat.	Cataract, Catarata	cataract
Cd	Ciudad	town
Ch.	Chott	salt lake
Chan.	Channel	channel
Ck	Creek	creek
Cnia	Colonia	colony
Cnl	Coronel	colonel
Co., Cord.	Cordillera	mountain chain
Cuch.	Cuchillas	hills, ridge

D

ABBREVIATIONS	FULL FORM	ENGLISH FORM
D.	1. Dağ, Dagh, Dağı, Dağları	mountain, range
	2. dake	mountain
	3. Daryâcheh	lake
Dj.	Djebel	mountain
Dr.	Doctor	Doctor

E

ABBREVIATIONS	FULL FORM	ENGLISH FORM
E.	East	east
Eil.	Eiland(en)	island(s)
Emb.	Embalse	reservoir
Escarp.	Escarpment	escarpment
Estr.	Estrecho	strait

F

ABBREVIATIONS	FULL FORM	ENGLISH FORM
F.	Firth	estuary
Fj.	2. Fjord, Fjörður	fjord
Ft	Fort	fort

G

ABBREVIATIONS	FULL FORM	ENGLISH FORM
G.	1. Gebel	mountain
	2. Ghedir	well
	3. Göl, Gölü	lake
	4. Golfe, Golfo, Gulf	Gulf
	5. Gora, -gory	mountain, range
	6. Guba	gulf, bay
	7. Gunung	mountain
Gd, Gde	Grand, Grande	grand
Gdor	Gobernador	governor
Geb.	Gebirge	mountain range
Gez.	Gezira	island
Ghub.	Ghubbat	bay
Gl.	Glacier	glacier
Gr.	Grosser	greater
Grl	General	general
Gt, Gtr	Great, Groot, -e, Greater	greater

H

ABBREVIATIONS	FULL FORM	ENGLISH FORM
H.	1. Hawr	lake
	2. Hoch	high
	3. Hora, Hory	mountain(s)
Har.	Harbour, Harbor	harbour
Hd	Head	head
Hg.	Hegy	mountain
Hgts	Heights	heights
Hwy	Highway	highway

I

ABBREVIATIONS	FULL FORM	ENGLISH FORM
I.	Ile, Ilha, Insel, Isla, Island, Isle Isola,	island
	Isole	islands
In.	1. Inner	inner
	2. Inlet	inlet
Is	Iles, Ilhas, Islands, Isles, Islas	islands
Isth.	Isthmus	isthmus

J

ABBREVIATIONS	FULL FORM	ENGLISH FORM
J.	1. Jabal, Jebel, Jibâl	mountain, mountains
	2. Järvi, Jaure, Jezero	lake
	3. Jazira	island
	4. Jökull	glacier
	5. Juan	John
Jct.	Junction	junction

K

ABBREVIATIONS	FULL FORM	ENGLISH FORM
K.	1. Kaap, Kap, Kapp	cape
	2. kaikyō	channel, strait
	3. Kato	lower
	4. Karang	reef
	5. ko	lake
	6. Kûh(hā)	mountain(s)
	7. Kólpos	gulf
	8. Kopf	peak, hill
	9. Kuala	estuary
Kep.	Kepulauan	islands
Kg	Kampong	village
Kh.	Khawr	wadi, river
Khr.	Khrebet	mountain range
Kör.	Körfez, -i	gulf, bay
Kp.	Kompong	settlement on river

L

ABBREVIATIONS	FULL FORM	ENGLISH FORM
L.	1. Lac, Lago, Lagoa, Lake, Liman, Limni, Loch, Lough	lake
	2. Lam	river
Lag.	Lagoon, Laguna, Lagune, Lagoa	lagoon
Ld.	Land	land
Lit.	Little	little

M

ABBREVIATIONS	FULL FORM	ENGLISH FORM
M.	1. Meer	sea, lake
	2. Mys	cape
m	metre, -s	metre(s)
Mal.	Malyy	small
Mf	Massif	mountain group
Mgna	Montagna	mountain
Mgne	Montagne(s)	mountain(s)
Mon.	Monasterio, Monastery	monastery
Mt	Mont, Mount	mountain
Mte	Monte	mountain
Mti	Monti, Munţii	mountains, range
Mtn	Mountain	mountain
Mts	Monts, Mountains, Montañas, Montes	mountains

N

ABBREVIATIONS	FULL FORM	ENGLISH FORM
N.	1. Nam	south
	2. Neu-, Ny-	new
	3. Noord, Nord, Norte, North, Norra, Nørre	north
	4. Nos	cape
Nat.	National	national
Nat. Pk	National Park	national park
Ndr	Nieder	lower
N.E.	North East	north east
Nizh.	Nizhne-, Nizhniy, Nizhniye, Nizhnyaya	lower
Nizm.	Nizmennost'	lowland
N.M.	National Monument	national monument
N.O.	NoordOost, Nord-Ost	north east
Nov.	Novaya, Novyy	new
N.P.	National Park	national park
N.W.	North West	north west

O

ABBREVIATIONS	FULL FORM	ENGLISH FORM
O.	1. Old	old
	2. Oost, Ost	east
	3. Ostrov	island
O	1. Öst(er)	east
	2. -øy	island
Or.	Oros(Ori)	mountain(s)
Orm.	Ormos	bay
Ova	Ostrova	islands
Oz.	Ozero, Ozera	lake(s)

P

ABBREVIATIONS	FULL FORM	ENGLISH FORM
P.	1. Pass, Passo	pass
	2. Pic, Pico, Pizzo	peak
	3. Pulau	island
Pass.	Passage	passage
Peg.	Pegunungan	mountains
Pen.	Peninsula, Penisola	peninsula
Per.	Pereval	pass
Pk	1. Park	park
	2. Peak, Pik	peak
Pl.	Planina	mountain range
Pla.	Playa	beach
Plat.	Plateau, Planalto	plateau
Plosk.	Ploskogor'ye	plateau
Pov	Poluostrov	peninsula
Pr.	1. Prince	prince
	2. Proliv	strait
Pres.	Presidente	president
Promy	Promontory	promontory
Pt	1. Petit, -e	small
	2. Point	point
	3. Pont	bridge
Pta	1. Ponta, Punta	point
	2. Puerta	pass
Pte	1. Pointe	point
	2. Ponte, Puente	bridge
Pto	1. Ponto	point
	2. Porto, Puerto	port
Pzo	Pizzo	peak

Q

ABBREVIATIONS	FULL FORM	ENGLISH FORM
Q.	1. Qal'at	fortress
	2. Qarat	mountain

R

ABBREVIATIONS	FULL FORM	ENGLISH FORM
R.	1. Reka, Rio, Río, River, Rivière, Rûd, Rzeka	river
Ra.	Range	range
Rap.	Rapids	rapids
Rca	Rocca	rock, mountain
Rd	Road	road
Res.	Reserve, Reservation	reserve, reservation
Resr	Reservoir	reservoir
Rge	Ridge	ridge
Rly	Railway	railway
R.S.F.S.R.	Russian Soviet Federated Socialist Republic	Russian Soviet Federated Social Republic
Rte	Route	route

S

ABBREVIATIONS	FULL FORM	ENGLISH FORM
S.	1. Salar, Salina	salt marsh
	2. San, São	saint
	3. See	sea, lake
	4. seto	strait
	5. sjø	lake
	6. Sør, South, Sud	south
	7. Sungai	river
s.	sur	on
Sa	Serra, Sierra	mountain range
Sab.	Sabkhat	salt flats
Sd	Sound, Sund	sound
S.E.	South East	south east
Seb.	Sebjet, Sebkhat, Sebkra	salt marsh, lagoon
Sev.	Severo-, Severnaya, -nyy	north
Sh.	1. Sha'ib	watercourse
	2. Shaṭṭ	river-mouth
	3. shima	island
Sp.	Spitze	peak
S.S.R.	Soviet Socialist Republic	Soviet Socialist Republic
St	Saint	saint
Sta	Santa	saint
Ste	Sainte	saint
Sten.	Stenon	pass, strait
Sto	Santo	saint
Str.	Strait	strait
S.W.	South West	south west

T

ABBREVIATIONS	FULL FORM	ENGLISH FORM
T.	1. Tal	valley
	2. Tall, Tell	hill, mountain
	3. Tepe, Tepesi	peak, hill
Talsp.	Talsperre	dam
Tg	Tanjung	cape
Tk	Teluk	bay
Tr.	Trench, Trough	trench, trough
Tun.	Tunnel	tunnel

U

ABBREVIATIONS	FULL FORM	ENGLISH FORM
U.	Uad	wadi
Ug	Ujung	cape
Unt.	Unter	lower

V

ABBREVIATIONS	FULL FORM	ENGLISH FORM
V.	1. Val, Valle	valley
	2. Väster, Vest, Vester	west
	3. Vatn	lake
	4. Ville	town
Va	Villa	town
Vdkhr.	Vodokhranilishche	reservoir
Verkh.	Verkhnyaya	upper
Vol.	Volcán, Volcano, Vulkan	volcano
Vost.	Vostochnyy	eastern
Vozv.	Vozvyshennost'	upland

W

ABBREVIATIONS	FULL FORM	ENGLISH FORM
W.	1. Wadi	wadi
	2. Wald	forest
	3. Wan	gulf, bay
	4. Water	water
	5. Well	well
	6. West	west

Y

ABBREVIATIONS	FULL FORM	ENGLISH FORM
Yuzh.	Yuzhno-, Yuzhnyy	south

Z

ABBREVIATIONS	FULL FORM	ENGLISH FORM
Z	1. Zahrez	intermittent lake
	2. Zaliv	gulf, bay
	3. Zatoka	
Zap.	Zapad-naya, Zapadno-, Zapadnyy	western
Zem.	Zemlya	country, land

Introduction to the index

In the index, the first number refers to the page, and the following letter and number to the section of the map in which the index entry can be found. For example, Paris 14C2 means that Paris can be found on page 14 where column C and row 2 meet.

Abbreviations used in the index

Afghan	Afghanistan	Hung	Hungary	Port	Portugal	Arch	Archipelago
Alb	Albania	Indon	Indonesia	Rom	Romania	B	Bay
Alg	Algeria	Irish Rep	Ireland	S Arabia	Saudi Arabia	C	Cape
Ant	Antarctica	N Ire	Ireland, Northern	Scot	Scotland	Chan	Channel
Arg	Argentina	Leb	Lebanon	Sen	Senegal	Gl	Glacier
Aust	Australia	Lib	Liberia	S Africa	South Africa	I(s)	Island(s)
Bang	Bangladesh	Liech	Liechtenstein	S Yemen	South Yemen	Lg	Lagoon
Belg	Belgium	Lux	Luxembourg	Switz	Switzerland	L	Lake
Bol	Bolivia	Madag	Madagascar	Tanz	Tanzania	Mt(s)	Mountain(s)
Bulg	Bulgaria	Malay	Malaysia	Thai	Thailand	O	Ocean
Cam	Cameroon	Maur	Mauritania	Turk	Turkey	P	Pass
Camb	Cambodia	Mor	Morocco	USSR	Union of Soviet Socialist	Pass	Passage
Can	Canada	Mozam	Mozambique		Republics	Pen	Peninsula
CAR	Central African Republic	Neth	Netherlands	UAE	United Arab Emirates	Plat	Plateau
Czech	Czechoslovakia	NZ	New Zealand	UK	United Kingdom	Pt	Point
Den	Denmark	Nic	Nicaragua	USA	United States of America	Res	Reservoir
Dom Rep	Dominican Republic	Nig	Nigeria	Urug	Uruguay	R	River
E Germ	East Germany	Nor	Norway	Ven	Venezuela	S	Sea
El Sal	El Salvador	Pak	Pakistan	Viet	Vietnam	Sd	Sound
Eng	England	PNG	Papua New Guinea	W Germ	West Germany	Str	Strait
Eq Guinea	Equatorial Guinea	Par	Paraguay	Yugos	Yugoslavia	V	Valley
Eth	Ethiopia	Phil	Philippines	Zim	Zimbabwe		
Fin	Finland	Pol	Poland				

A

Aachen W Germ	18B2	Aberdeen Scot	8D3	Abu Suweir Egypt	45B3
Aalsmeer Neth	13C1	Aberdeen, S Dakota		Abu Tarfa, Wadi Egypt	45B4
Aalst Belg	13C2	USA	56D2	Abut Head, C NZ	35B2
Äänekoski Fin	12K6	Aberdeen, Washington		Abu Tig Egypt	40B4
Aba China	31A3	USA	56A2	Abu'Urug, Well Sudan	50D2
Aba Nigeria	48C4	Aberdeen L Can	54J3	Abuye Meda, Mt Eth	50D2
Aba Zaïre	50D3	Aberdyfi Wales	7B3	Abu Zabad Sudan	50C2
Abādān Iran	41E3	Aberfeldy Scot	8D3	Abwong Sudan	50D3
Abādeh Iran	41F3	Aberfoyle Scot	8C3	Åby Den	18B1
Abadla Alg	48B1	Abergavenny Wales	7C4	Abyei Sudan	50C3
Abaeté Brazil	75C2	Aberystwyth Wales	7B3	Acadia Nat Pk USA	65F2
Abaeté, R Brazil	75C2	Abez' USSR	20L2	Acámbaro Mexico	70B2
Abaetetuba Brazil	73J4	Abhā S Arabia	50E2	Acandí Colombia	69B5
Abagnar Qi China	31D1	Abhar Iran	41E2	Acaponeta Mexico	70B2
Abajo Mts USA	59E3	Abidjan Ivory Coast	48B4	Acapulco Mexico	70B3
Abakaliki Nigeria	48C4	Abilene, Kansas USA	61D3	Acaraú Brazil	73L4
Abakan USSR	25L4	Abilene, Texas USA	62C2	Acarigua Ven	72E2
Abala Niger	48C3	Abingdon Eng	7D4	Acatlán Mexico	70C3
Abalessa Alg	48C2	Abingdon USA	64C3	Accra Ghana	48B4
Abancay Peru	72D6	Abitibi, R Can	55K4	Accrington Eng	6C3
Abarqū Iran	41F3	Abitibi,L Can	55L5	Achalpur India	42D4
Abashiri Japan	29E2	Abkhazian ASSR,		Achao Chile	74B6
Abashiri-wan, B Japan	29E2	Republic USSR	21G7	Achern W Germ	13E3
Abau PNG	27H7	Abohar India	42C2	Achill Hd, Pt Irish Rep	9A3
Abaya, L Eth	50D3	Abomey Benin	48C4	Achill I Irish Rep	10A3
Abbai, R Eth/Sudan	50D2	Abong Mbang Cam	50B3	Achim W Germ	13E1
Abbe, L Eth/Djibouti	50E2	Abou Deïa Chad	50B2	Achinsk USSR	25L4
Abbeville France	14C1	Aboyne Scot	8D3	Acireale, Sicily	16D3
Abbeville, Louisiana USA	63D3	Abqaiq S Arabia	41E4	Ackley USA	61E2
Abbeville, S Carolina		Abrantes Port	15A2	Acklins, I The Bahamas	69C2
USA	67B2	Abreojos, Punta, Pt		Acobamba Peru	72D6
Abbotsford Can	58B1	Mexico	70A2	Aconcagua, Mt Chile	74B4
Abbotsford USA	64A2	Abri Sudan	50D1	Acopiara Brazil	73L5
Abbottabad Pak	42C2	Abrolhos, Is Aust	32A3	Açores, Is = Azores	
'Abd al 'Aziz, Jebel, Mt		Abrolhos, Arquipélago		Acre = 'Akko	
Syria	40D2	dos Brazil	75E2	Acre, State Brazil	72D5
Abdulino USSR	20J5	Absaroka Range, Mts		Acton USA	66C3
Abéché Chad	50C2	USA	56B2	Ada USA	63C2
Abengourou Ivory Coast	48B4	Abū al Abyaḍ, I UAE	41F5	Adaja, R Spain	15B1
Åbenrå Den	18B1	Abū 'Ali, I S Arabia	41E4	Adam Oman	41G5
Abeokuta Nigeria	48C4	Abu 'Amūd, Wadi		Adama Eth	50D3
Abera Eth	50D3	Jordan	45D3	Adamantina Brazil	75B3
Aberaeron Wales	7B3	Abu 'Aweigîla, Well		Adamaoua, Region	
Aberdare Wales	7C4	Egypt	45C3	Cam/Nig	50B3
Aberdeen, California		Abū Dhabi UAE	41F5	Adamaoua, Massif de l',	
USA	66C2	Abū el Jurdhān Jordan	45C3	Mts Cam	50B3
Aberdeen, Maryland		Abu Hamed Sudan	50D2	Adams USA	68D1
USA	65D3	Abu Kebir Hihya Egypt	45A3	Adam's Bridge India/Sri	
Aberdeen, Mississippi		Abunã Brazil	72E5	Lanka	44B4
USA	63E2	Abunã, R Bol/Brazil	72E6	Adams,Mt USA	56A2
Aberdeen S Africa	47C3	Abu Rûtha, Gebel, Mt		Adam's Peak, Mt Sri	
		Egypt	45C4	Lanka	44C4
		Abū Sukhayr Iraq	41D3	'Adan = Aden	

Adana Turk	21F8	Adzopé Ivory Coast	48B4
Adapazari Turk	21E7	Adz'va, R USSR	20K2
Adare,C Ant	76F7	Adz'vavom USSR	20K2
Adavale Aust	34B1	Aegean Sea Greece	17E3
Ad Dahnā', Region S		Afghanistan, Republic	
Arabia	41E4	Asia	38E2
Ad Damman S Arabia	41F4	Afgooye Somalia	50E3
Ad Dawādimi S Arabia	41D5	'Afif S Arabia	41D5
Ad Dibdibah, Region S		Afikpo Nigeria	48C4
Arabia	41E4	Åfjord Nor	12G6
Ad Dilam S Arabia	41E5	Aflou Alg	48C1
Ad Dir'iyah S Arabia	41E5	Afmadu Somalia	50E3
Addis Ababa Eth	50D3	Afollé, Region Maur	48A3
Ad Dīwaniyah Iraq	41D3	Afton, New York USA	68C1
Ad Duwayd S Arabia	40D3	Afton, Wyoming USA	58D2
Adel USA	61E2	Afula Israel	45C2
Adelaide Aust	32C4	Afyon Turk	21E8
Adelaide Bahamas	67C4	Aga Egypt	45A3
Adelaide, Base Ant	76G3	Agadem Niger	50B2
Adelaide Pen Can	54J3	Agadez Niger	48C3
Adelaide River Aust	27G8	Agadir Mor	48B1
Adelanto USA	66D3	Agar India	42D4
Aden S Yemen	38C4	Agartala India	43G4
Aden,G of Somalia/S.		Agassiz Can	58B1
Yemen	38C4	Agboville Ivory Coast	48B4
Aderbissinat Niger	48C3	Agdam USSR	40E1
Adhrā' Syria	45D2	Agematsu Japan	29C3
Adi, I Indon	27G7	Agen France	14C3
Adige, R Italy	16C1	Agha Jāri Iran	41E3
Adigrat Eth	50D2	Agnibilékrou Ivory Coast	48B4
Adilābād India	42D5	Agout, R France	14C3
Adin USA	58B2	Agra India	42D3
Adirondack Mts USA	65E2	Aǧri Turk	41D2
Adi Ugri Eth	50D2	Agri, R Italy	16D2
Adıyaman Turk	40C2	Agrigento, Sicily	16C3
Adjud Rom	17F1	Agrihan, I Marianas	26H5
Admiralty I USA	54E4	Agrínion Greece	17E3
Admiralty Inlet, B Can	55K2	Agropoli Italy	16C2
Admiralty Is PNG	32D1	Agryz USSR	20J4
Adoni India	44B2	Agto Greenland	55N3
Adour, R France	14B3	Agua Clara Brazil	75B3
Adra Spain	15B2	Aguadilla Puerto Rico	69D3
Adrar Alg	48B2	Agua Prieta Mexico	70B1
Adrar, Mts Alg	48C2	Aguaray Guazú Par	75A3
Adrar, Region Maur	48A2	Aguascalientes Mexico	70B2
Adrar Soutouf, Region		Aguas Formosas Brazil	75D2
Mor	48A2	Agueda Port	15A1
Adré Chad	50C2	Aguelhok Mali	48C3
Adri Libya	49D2	Agüenit, Well Mor	48A2
Adrian, Michigan USA	64C2	Águilas Spain	15B2
Adrian, Texas USA	62B1	Aguja, Puerta Peru	72B5
Adriatic S Italy/Yugos	16C2	Agulhas Basin Indian O	36C7
Aduwa Eth	50D2	Agulhas,C S Africa	51C7
Adycha, R USSR	25P3		

Agulhas Plat

Amasya

Agulhas Plat *Indian O* 36C6
Ahaggar = Hoggar
Ahar *Iran* 21H8
Ahaus *W Germ* 13D1
Ahipara B *NZ* 35B1
Ahlen *W Germ* 13D2
Ahmadābād *India* 42C4
Ahmadnagar *India* 44A2
Ahmar Mts *Eth* 50E3
Ahoskie *USA* 67C1
Ahr, R *W Germ* 13D2
Ahrgebirge, Mts *W Germ* 13D2
Åhus *Sweden* 12G7
Ahuvān *Iran* 41F2
Ahvāz *Iran* 41E3
Aiajuela *Costa Rica* 69A4
Aigoual, Mount *France* 14C3
Aikawa *Japan* 29C3
Aiken *USA* 67B2
Ailao Shan, Upland *China* 31A5
Aimorés *Brazil* 75D2
Aïn Beïda *Algeria* 16B3
Ain Beni Mathar *Mor* 48B1
Ain Dalla, Well *Egypt* 49E2
Aïn el Hadjel *Alg* 15C2
Aïn Galakka *Chad* 50B2
Aïn Oussera *Alg* 15C2
Aïn Sefra *Alg* 48B1
'Ain Sukhna *Egypt* 40B4
Ainsworth *USA* 60D2
Aïn Témouchent *Alg* 15B2
Aioi *Japan* 29B4
Aïoun Abd el Malek, Well *Maur* 48B2
Aïoun El Atrouss *Maur* 48B3
Aiquile *Bol* 72E7
Aïr, Desert Region *Niger* 48C3
Airdrie *Scot* 8D4
Aire *France* 13B2
Aire, R *Eng* 6D3
Aire, R *France* 13C3
Airforce I *Can* 55L3
Aishihik *Can* 54E3
Aisne, Department *France* 13B3
Aisne, R *France* 14C2
Aitape *PNG* 32D1
Aitape *PNG* 27H7
Aiviekste, R *USSR* 19F1
Aix-en-Provence *France* 14D3
Aix-les-Bains *France* 14D2
Aiyar Res *India* 43F4
Aíyion *Greece* 17E3
Aíyna, I *Greece* 17E3
Aizawl *India* 43G4
Aizeb, R *Namibia* 51B6
Aizu-Wakamatsu *Japan* 29D3
Ajaccio, Corsica 16B2
Ajaccio, G d', Corsica 16B2
Ajdabiyah *Libya* 49E1
Ajigasawa *Japan* 29E2
Ajlun *Jordan* 45C2
Ajman *UAE* 41G4
Ajmer *India* 42C3
Ajo *USA* 59D4
Ajo, Cabo de, C *Spain* 15B1
Ak, R *Turk* 17F3
Akabira *Japan* 29D2
Akaishi-sanchi, Mts *Japan* 29C3
Akalkot *India* 44B2
Akanthou *Cyprus* 45B1
Akaroa *NZ* 35B2
Akashi *Japan* 29B4
Akbulak *USSR* 21K5
Akçakale *Turk* 40C2
Akchar, Watercourse *Maur* 48A2
Aketi *Zaïre* 50C3
Akhalkalaki *USSR* 41D1
Akhalsikhe *USSR* 40D1
Akharnái *Greece* 17E3
Akhdar, Jabal al, Mts *Libya* 49E1
Akhdar, Jebel, Mt *Oman* 41G5
Akhisar *Turk* 40A2
Akhiste *USSR* 19F1
Akhmîm *Egypt* 49F2
Akhtubinsk *USSR* 21H6
Akhtyrka *USSR* 21E5
Aki *Japan* 29B4
Akimiski I *Can* 55K4
Akita *Japan* 29E3
Akjoujt *Maur* 48A3
'Akko *Israel* 45C2
Aklavik *Can* 54E3
Aklé Aouana, Desert Region *Maur* 48B3
Akobo *Eth* 50D3
Akobo, R *Sudan/Eth* 50D3
Akoha *Afghan* 42B1
Akola *India* 42D4
Akot *India* 42D4
Akpatok I *Can* 55M3
Ákra Kafirévs, C *Greece* 17E3
Ákra Líthinon, C *Greece* 17E4
Ákra Maléa, C *Greece* 17E3
Akranes *Iceland* 12A2
Ákra Sídheros, C *Greece* 17F3
Ákra Spátha, C *Greece* 17E3
Ákra Taínaron, C *Greece* 17E3
Akron *USA* 57E2
Akrotiri *Cyprus* 45B1
Akrotiri B *Cyprus* 45B1
Aksai Chin, Mts *China* 42D1
Aksaray *Turk* 21E8
Aksay *USSR* 21J5
Aksayquin Hu, L *China* 42D1
Akşehir *Turk* 40B2
Akseki *Turk* 40B2
Aksenovo Zilovskoye *USSR* 25N4
Aksha *USSR* 26E1
Aksu *China* 39G1
Aksu *China* 24J5
Aksum *Eth* 50D2
Aktogay *USSR* 24J5
Aktumsyk *USSR* 21K6
Aktyubinsk *USSR* 24G4
Akureyri *Iceland* 12B1
Akyab = Sittwe
Akzhal *USSR* 24K5
Alabama, R *USA* 63E2
Alabama, State *USA* 57E3
Alabaster *USA* 67A2
Ala Dağları, Mts *Turk* 40C2
Alagir *USSR* 21G7
Alagoas, State *Brazil* 73L5
Alagoinhas *Brazil* 73L6
Alagón *Spain* 15B1
Al Ahmadi *Kuwait* 41E4
Alajuela *Costa Rica* 70D3
Alakanuk *USA* 54B3
Alakol, Ozero, L *USSR* 24K5
Alakurtti *USSR* 12L5
Alamagan, I *Pacific O* 27H5
Al Amarah *Iraq* 41E3
Alameda *USA* 59B3
Alamo *USA* 59C3
Alamogordo *USA* 62A2
Alamo Heights *USA* 62C3
Alamosa *USA* 62A1
Åland, I *Fin* 12H6
Alanya *Turk* 21E8
Alapaha, R *USA* 67B2
Alapayevsk *USSR* 24H4
Alarcón, Embalse de, Res *Spain* 15B2
Alaşehir *Turk* 40A2
Ala Shan, Mts *China* 26D3
Alaska, State *USA* 54C3
Alaska,G of *USA* 54D4
Alaska Range, Mts *USA* 54C3
Alassio *Italy* 16B2
Alatyr' *USSR* 20H5
Alawoona *Aust* 34B2
Al'Ayn *UAE* 41G5
Alayskiy Khrebet, Mts *USSR* 39F2
Alazeya, R *USSR* 25R3
Alba *Italy* 14D3
Al Bāb *Syria* 40C2
Albacete *Spain* 15B2
Alba de Tormes *Spain* 15A1
Al Badi *Iraq* 40D2
Alba Iulia *Rom* 17E1
Albania, Republic *Europe* 17D2
Albany *Aust* 32A4
Albany, Georgia *USA* 67B2
Albany, Kentucky *USA* 64B3
Albany, New York *USA* 65E2
Albany, Oregon *USA* 56A2
Albany, R *Can* 55K4
Albarracin, Sierra de, Mts *Spain* 15B1
Al Batinah, Region *Oman* 41G5
Albatross B *Aust* 27H8
Al Bayda *Libya* 49E1
Al Baylūliyah *Syria* 45C1
Albemarle *USA* 67B1
Albemarle Sd *USA* 67C1
Alberche, R *Spain* 15B1
Albert *France* 13B2
Alberta, Province *Can* 54G4
Albert Edward, Mt *PNG* 27H7
Albertinia *S Africa* 47C3
Albert,L *Uganda/Zaïre* 50D3
Albert Lea *USA* 57D2
Albert Nile, R *Uganda* 50D3
Alberton *USA* 58D1
Albertville *France* 14D2
Albi *France* 14C3
Albia *USA* 61E2
Albina *Surinam* 73H2
Albion, Michigan *USA* 64C2
Albion, Nebraska *USA* 61D2
Albion, New York *USA* 65D2
Al Bi'r *S Arabia* 40C4
Alborán, I *Spain* 15B2
Ålborg *Den* 12G7
Al Brayqah *Libya* 49D1
Albstadt-Ebingen *W Germ* 13E3
Al Bū Kamāl *Syria* 40D3
Albuquerque *USA* 56C3
Al Buraymi *Oman* 41G5
Al Burdi *Libya* 49E1
Albury *Aust* 32D4
Al Buşayyah *Iraq* 41E3
Alcalá de Henares *Spain* 15B1
Alcamo, Sicily 16C3
Alcañiz *Spain* 15B1
Alcântara *Brazil* 73K4
Alcántara, Embalse de, Res *Spain* 15A2
Alcaraz *Spain* 15B2
Alcaraz, Sierra de, Mts *Spain* 15B2
Alcázar de San Juan *Spain* 15B2
Alcira *Spain* 15B2
Alcobaça *Brazil* 75E2
Alcolea de Pinar *Spain* 15B1
Alcoy *Spain* 15B2
Alcudia *Spain* 15C2
Aldabra Is *Indian O* 46J8
Aldama *Mexico* 62A3
Aldan *USSR* 25O4
Aldan, R *USSR* 25P4
Aldanskoye Nagor'ye, Upland *USSR* 25O4
Aldeburgh *Eng* 7E3
Alderney, I *Channel Is* 14B2
Aldershot *Eng* 7D4
Aleg *Maur* 48A3
Alegre, R *Brazil* 75A2
Alegrete *Brazil* 74E3
Aleksandrovsk Sakhalinskiy *USSR* 25Q4
Alekseyevka *USSR* 24J4
Aleksin *USSR* 20F5
Älem *Sweden* 18D1
Além Paraíba *Brazil* 75D3
Alençon *France* 14C2
Alenuihaha Chan *Hawaiian Is* 66E5
Aleppo *Syria* 21F8
Alert *Can* 55M1
Alès *France* 14C3
Alessandria *Italy* 16B2
Ålesund *Nor* 24B3
Aleutian Ra, Mts *USA* 54C4
Aleutian Trench *Pacific O* 37L2
Alexander Arch *USA* 54E4
Alexander Bay *S Africa* 47B2
Alexander City *USA* 67A2
Alexander I *Ant* 76G3
Alexandra *NZ* 35A3
Alexandra,C *South Georgia* 74J8
Alexandra Fjord *Can* 55L2
Alexandria *Egypt* 49E1
Alexandria, Louisiana *USA* 57D3
Alexandria, Minnesota *USA* 57D2
Alexandria, Virginia *USA* 57F3
Alexandroúpolis *Greece* 17F2
Aley *Leb* 45C2
Aleysk *USSR* 24K4
Al Fallujah *Iraq* 41D3
Alfaro *Spain* 15B1
Alfatar *Bulg* 17F2
Al Faw *Iraq* 41E4
Alfensas *Brazil* 75C3
Alfiós, R *Greece* 17E3
Alfonso Cláudio *Brazil* 75D3
Alford *Scot* 8D3
Alfredo Chaves *Brazil* 75D3
Alfreton *Eng* 7D3
Al Furuthi *S Arabia* 41E4
Alga *USSR* 21K6
Algeciras *Spain* 15A2
Alger = Algiers
Algeria, Republic *Africa* 48B2
Alghero, Sardinia 16B2
Algiers *Alg* 15C2
Algona *USA* 61E2
Algonquin Park *Can* 65D1
Al Ḥadd *Oman* 38D3
Al Hadithah *Iraq* 40D3
Al Hadithah *S Arabia* 40C3
Al Ḥaḍr *Iraq* 40D2
Al Haffah *Syria* 45D1
Al Ḥajar al Gharbī, Mts *Oman* 41G5
Al Hamad, Desert Region *Jordan/S Arabia* 40C3
Al Haniyah, Desert Region *Iraq* 41E4
Al Ḥariq *S Arabia* 41E5
Al Harrah, Desert Region *S Arabia* 40C3
Al Haruj al Aswad, Upland *Libya* 49D2
Al Hasa, Region *S Arabia* 41E4
Al Ḥasakah *Syria* 40D2
Al Hawjā' *S Arabia* 40C4
Al Hayy *Iraq* 41E3
Al Hijānah *Syria* 45D2
Al Ḥillah *Iraq* 41D3
Al Ḥillah *S Arabia* 41E5
Al Hoceima *Mor* 15B2
Al Ḥudaydah *Yemen* 50E2
Al Hufūf *S Arabia* 41E4
Al Humrah, Region *UAE* 41F5
Al Huwatsah *Oman* 41G5
Aliabad *Iran* 41E2
Aliabad *Iran* 41G4
Aliákmon, R *Greece* 17E2
Ali al Gharbi *Iraq* 41E3
Alibāg *India* 44A2
Alicante *Spain* 15B2
Alice *USA* 56D4
Alice, Punta, Pt *Italy* 16D3
Alice Springs *Aust* 32C3
Alicudi, I *Italy* 16C3
Aligarh *India* 42D3
Aligudarz *Iran* 41E3
Ali-Khel *Afghan* 42B2
Alimniá, I *Greece* 17F3
Alipur Duār *India* 43F3
Aliquippa *USA* 64C2
Al' Isawiyah *S Arabia* 40C3
Aliwal North *S Africa* 47D3
Al Jaghbūb *Libya* 49E2
Al Jalamid *S Arabia* 40D3
Al Jawf *Libya* 49E2
Al Jawf *S Arabia* 40C4
Al Jazirah *Syria/Iraq* 21G8
Al Jazirah, Desert Region *Syria/Iraq* 40D2
Aljezur *Port* 15A2
Al Jubayl *S Arabia* 41E4
Al Jumaymah *S Arabia* 41D4
Al Kabid, Desert *Jordan* 45D4
Al Kahfah *S Arabia* 41D4
Al Kāmil *Oman* 41E4
Al Khābūr, R *Syria* 40D2
Al Khābūrah *Oman* 41G5
Al Khālis *Iraq* 41D3
Al Khaşab *Oman* 41G4
Al Khawr *Qatar* 41F4
Al Khums *Libya* 49D1
Al Kidan, Region *S Arabia* 41F5
Al Kiswah *Syria* 45D2
Alkmaar *Neth* 18A2
Al Kufrah Oasis *Libya* 49E2
Al Kut *Iraq* 41E3
Allahabad *India* 43E3
Al Lajah, Mt *Syria* 45D2
Allakaket *USA* 54C3
Allanmyo *Burma* 30B2
Allatoona L *USA* 67B2
Alldays *S Africa* 47D1
Allegheny, R *USA* 65D2
Allegheny Mts *USA* 57F3
Allendale *USA* 67B2
Allendale Town *Eng* 6C2
Allen, Lough, L *Irish Rep* 10B3
Allen,Mt *NZ* 35A3
Allentown *USA* 65D2
Alleppey *India* 44B4
Aller, R *France* 14C2
Alliance *USA* 60C2
Al Līth *S Arabia* 50E1
Al Liwā', Region *UAE* 41F5
Alloa *Scot* 8D3
Allora *Aust* 34D1
Alma *Can* 65E1
Alma, Michigan *USA* 64C2
Alma, Nebraska *USA* 60D2
Alma Ata *USSR* 39F1
Almada *Port* 15A2
Al Madinah = Medina
Al Majma'ah *S Arabia* 41E4
Al Manāmah *Bahrain* 41F4
Al Ma'niyah *Iraq* 41D3
Almanor,L *USA* 59B2
Almansa *Spain* 15B2
Al Mariyyah *UAE* 41F5
Al Marj *Libya* 49E1
Almas, R *Brazil* 75C2
Almazán *Spain* 15B1
Alme, R *W Germ* 13E2
Almelo *Neth* 13D1
Almenara *Brazil* 75D2
Almendra, Embalse de, Res *Spain* 15A1
Almería *Spain* 15B2
Almería, Golfo de *Spain* 15B2
Al'met'yevsk *USSR* 20J5
Älmhult *Sweden* 18C1
Al Midhnab *S Arabia* 41D4
Al Miqdadiyah *Iraq* 41E3
Almirós *Greece* 17E3
Al Mish'ab *S Arabia* 41E4
Almodôvar *Port* 15A2
Almora *India* 42D3
Al Mubarraz *S Arabia* 41E4
Al Mudawwara *Jordan* 40C4
Al Muḩarraq *Bahrain* 41F4
Al Mukallā *S Yemen* 38C4
Al Mukhā *Yemen* 50E2
Al Musayyib *Iraq* 41D3
Al Muwayliḩ *S Arabia* 40C4
Alness *Scot* 8C3
Aln, R *Eng* 6D2
Al Nu'maniyah *Iraq* 41E3
Alnwick *Eng* 6D2
Alor, I *Indon* 27F7
Alor Setar *Malay* 30C4
Alost = Aalst
Alotau *PNG* 32E2
Aloysius,Mt *Aust* 32B3
Alpena *USA* 64C1
Alpi Dolomitiche, Mts *Italy* 16C1
Alpine, Arizona *USA* 59E4
Alpine, Texas *USA* 62B2
Alpine, Wyoming *USA* 58D2
Alps, Mts *Europe* 16B1
Al Qaddāhiyah *Libya* 49D1
Al Qadmus *Syria* 45D1
Al Qā'im *Iraq* 40D3
Al Qalībah *S Arabia* 40C4
Al Qamishlī *Syria* 40D2
Al Qardāḩah *Syria* 45D1
Al Qaryah Ash Sharqiyah *Libya* 49D1
Al Qaryatayn *Syria* 40C3
Al Qasim, Region *S Arabia* 41D4
Al Qatif *S Arabia* 41E4
Al Qatrun *Libya* 49D2
Al Qayşamah *S Arabia* 41E4
Al Qunayţirah *Syria* 40C3
Al Qunfidhah *S Arabia* 50E2
Al Qurnah *Iraq* 41E3
Al Quşayr *Syria* 45D1
Al Quţayfah *Syria* 45D2
Al Quwayiyah *S Arabia* 41E5
Als, I *Den* 18B1
Alsace, Region *France* 14D2
Alsace, Plaine d' *France* 13D3
Alsfeld *W Germ* 18B2
Alston *Eng* 6C2
Alta *Nor* 12J5
Alta Gracia *Arg* 74D4
Altagracia de Orituco *Ven* 69D5
Altai, Mts *Mongolia* 26B2
Altamaha, R *USA* 67B2
Altamira *Brazil* 73H4
Altamura *Italy* 16D2
Altanbulag *Mongolia* 26D1
Altata *Mexico* 70B2
Altay *China* 24K5
Altay *Mongolia* 25L5
Altay, Mts *USSR* 24K5
Altenkirchen *W Germ* 13D2
Alto Araguaia *Brazil* 75B2
Alto Molócue *Mozam* 51D5
Alton *Eng* 7D4
Alton *USA* 64A3
Altoona *USA* 65D2
Alto Sucuriú *Brazil* 75B2
Altrincham *Eng* 7C3
Altun Shan, Mts *China* 39G2
Alturas *USA* 58B2
Altus *USA* 62C2
Al'Ula *S Arabia* 40C4
Alula *Somalia* 50E2
Al Urayq, Desert Region *S Arabia* 40C4
Alva *USA* 62C1
Alvarado *USA* 63C2
Älvdalen *Sweden* 12G6
Alvin *USA* 63C3
Älvsbyn *Sweden* 12J5
Al Wajh *S Arabia* 40C4
Alwar *India* 42D3
Al Widyan, Desert Region *Iraq/S Arabia* 40D3
Alxa Youqi *China* 31A2
Alxa Zuoqi *China* 31B2
Alyat *USSR* 41E2
Alytus *USSR* 12J8
Alzey *W Germ* 13E3
Amadi *Sudan* 50D3
Amadiyah *Iraq* 41D2
Amadjuak L *Can* 55L3
Åmål *Sweden* 12G7
Amalat, R *USSR* 25N4
Amaliás *Greece* 17E3
Amalner *India* 42C4
Amambaí *Brazil* 75A3
Amambaí, R *Brazil* 75B3
Amamba, Serra, Mts *Par/Brazil* 75A3
Amami, I *Japan* 26F4
Amami gunto, Arch *Japan* 26F4
Amapá *Brazil* 73H3
Amapá, State *Brazil* 73H3
Amarillo *USA* 62B1
Amasya *Turk* 21F7

Batabanó, G de **Bhiwāni**

Batabanó, G de *Cuba* 70D2
Batakan *Indon* 27E7
Batāla *India* 42D2
Batang *China* 26C3
Batangafo *CAR* 50B3
Batangas *Phil* 27F5
Batan Is *Phil* 26F4
Batatais *Brazil* 75C3
Batavia *USA* 65D2
Batemans Bay *Aust* 34D3
Batesburg *USA* 67B2
Batesville, Arkansas *USA* 63D1
Batesville, Mississippi *USA* 63E2
Bath *Can* 65F1
Bath *Eng* 7C4
Bath, Maine *USA* 65F2
Bath, New York *USA* 65D2
Batha, R *Chad* 50B2
Bathawana Mt *Can* 64C1
Bathurst *Aust* 32D4
Bathurst *Can* 55M5
Bathurst,C *Can* 54F2
Bathurst I *Aust* 32C2
Bathurst I *Can* 54H2
Bathurst Inlet, B *Can* 54H3
Batié *Burkina* 48B4
Bāţin, Wadi al, Watercourse *Iraq* 41E4
Bāţlāq-e-Gavkhūni, Salt Flat *Iran* 41F3
Batlow *Aust* 34C3
Batman *Turk* 40D2
Batna *Algeria* 16B3
Baton Rouge *USA* 57D3
Batroûn *Leb* 45C1
Battambang *Camb* 30C3
Batticaloa *Sri Lanka* 44C4
Batti Malv, I, Nicobar Is *Indian O* 44E4
Battle *Eng* 7E4
Battle Creek *USA* 57E2
Battle Harbour *Can* 55N4
Battle Mountain *USA* 58C2
Batumi *USSR* 21G7
Batu Pahat *Malay* 30C5
Bat Yam *Israel* 45C2
Baubau *Indon* 32B1
Bauchi *Nigeria* 48C3
Baudette *USA* 61E1
Bauld,C *Can* 55N4
Baunt *USSR* 25N4
Bauru *Brazil* 73J8
Baús *Brazil* 75B2
Bautzen *E Germ* 18C2
Bawean, I *Indon* 27E7
Bawîti *Egypt* 49E2
Bawku *Ghana* 48B3
Bawlake *Burma* 30B2
Bawlen *Aust* 34A2
Baxley *USA* 67B2
Bayamo *Cuba* 70E2
Bayana *India* 43J2
Bayandalay *Mongolia* 31A1
Bayandzürh *Mongolia* 25M5
Bayan Har Shan, Mts *China* 26C3
Bayan Mod *China* 31A1
Bayan Obo *China* 31B1
Bayard, Nebraska *USA* 60C2
Bayard, New Mexico *USA* 62A2
Bayburt *Turk* 40D1
Bay City, Michigan *USA* 57E2
Bay City, Texas *USA* 63C3
Baydaratskaya Guba, B *USSR* 24H3
Baydhabo *Somalia* 50E3
Bayern, State *W Germ* 18C3
Bayeux *France* 14B2
Bayfield *USA* 64A1
Bayir *Jordan* 40C3
Baykal, Ozero, L = Baikal, L
Baykalskiy Khrebet, Mts *USSR* 26D1
Baykit *USSR* 25L3
Baylik Shan, Mts *China/Mongolia* 25L5
Baymak *USSR* 20K5
Bay Minette *USA* 63E2
Bayonne *France* 14B3
Bayreuth *W Germ* 18C3
Bay St Louis *USA* 63E2
Bay Shore *USA* 65E2
Bays,L of *Can* 65D1
Baytik Shan, Mts *China* 26B2
Bayt Lahm = Bethlehem
Baytown *USA* 63D3
Baza *Spain* 15B2
Bazaliya *USSR* 19F3
Bazar-Dyuzi, Mt *USSR* 21H7
Bazaruto, Ilha *Mozam* 51D6
Bazas *France* 14B3
Bazhong *China* 31B3
Bcharre *Leb* 45D1
Beach *USA* 60C1
Beach Haven *USA* 68C3
Beachy Head *Eng* 7E4
Beacon *USA* 68D2
Bealanana *Madag* 51E5
Bear, R *USA* 58D2
Beardstown *USA* 64A2
Bear I *Barents S* 24C2
Bear L *USA* 58D2
Bear Valley *USA* 66B1
Beata, Cabo, C *Dom Rep* 69C3
Beata, Isla *Dom Rep* 69C3
Beatrice *USA* 56D2
Beatrice, Oilfield *N Sea* 8D2
Beatton River *Can* 54F4
Beatty *USA* 56B3
Beattyville *Can* 65D1
Beauchene Is *Falkland Is* 74E8
Beaudesert *Aust* 34D1
Beaufort *USA* 67B2
Beaufort S *Can/USA* 54D2
Beaufort West *S Africa* 47C3
Beauharnois *Can* 65E1
Beauly *Scot* 8C3
Beaumaris *Wales* 7B3
Beaumont, California *USA* 59C4
Beaumont, Texas *USA* 57D3
Beaune *France* 14C2
Beauvais *France* 14C2
Beaver *USA* 54D3
Beaver, Utah *USA* 59D3
Beaver, R *Can* 54G4
Beaver Creek *Can* 54D3
Beaver Dam, Kentucky *USA* 64B3
Beaver Dam, Wisconsin *USA* 64B2
Beaverhead Mts *USA* 58D1
Beaver I *USA* 64B1
Beaver L *USA* 63D1
Beāwar *India* 42C3
Bebedouro *Brazil* 75C3
Beccles *Eng* 7E3
Bečej *Yugos* 17E1
Béchar *Alg* 48B1
Beckley *USA* 57E3
Beckum *W Germ* 13E2
Bedale *Eng* 6D2
Bederkesa *W Germ* 13E1
Bedford *Eng* 7D3
Bedford, Indiana *USA* 64B3
Bedford, Pennsylvania *USA* 68A3
Bedford, County *Eng* 7D3
Bedford Pt *Grenada* 69M2
Beech Creek *USA* 68B2
Beechey Pt *USA* 54D2
Beechworth *Aust* 34C3
Beenleigh *Aust* 34D1
Beer Menuha *Israel* 45C3
Beer Ora *Israel* 45C4
Beersheba *Israel* 40B3
Be'er Sheva = Beersheba
Be'er Sheva, R *Israel* 45C3
Beeville *USA* 56D4
Befale *Zaïre* 50C3
Befandriana *Madag* 51E5
Bega *Aust* 34C3
Begicheva, Ostrov, I = Bol'shoy Begichev, Ostrov
Begur, C de *Spain* 15C1
Behbehan *Iran* 41F3
Behshahr *Iran* 41F2
Behsud *Afghan* 42B2
Bei'an *China* 26F2
Beihai *China* 31B5
Beijing *China* 31D2
Beiliu *China* 30E1
Beipan Jiang, R *China* 31B4
Beipiao *China* 31E1
Beira = Sofala
Beirut *Leb* 40C3
Bei Shan, Mts *China* 26C2
Beitbridge *Zim* 47E1
Beit ed Dine *Leb* 45C2
Beith *Scot* 8C4
Beit Jala *Israel* 45C3
Beizhen *China* 28A2
Beja *Port* 15A2
Béja *Tunisia* 16B3
Bejaïa *Alg* 15C2
Béjar *Spain* 15A1
Bejestān *Iran* 41G3
Békéscsaba *Hung* 19E3
Bekily *Madag* 51E6
Bela *India* 43E3
Bela *Pak* 42B3
Bel Air *USA* 68B3
Belampalli *India* 44B2
Belang *Indon* 27F6
Belangpidie *Indon* 27C6
Belau = Palau
Béla Vista *Brazil/Par* 75A3
Bela Vista *Mozam* 47E2
Belawan *Indon* 27C6
Belaya, R *USSR* 20K4
Belaya Tserkov' *USSR* 19G3
Belcher Chan *Can* 55J2
Belcher Is *Can* 55L4
Belchiragh *Afghan* 42B1
Belebey *USSR* 20J5
Belém *Brazil* 73J4
Belén *Colombia* 72C3
Belén *Par* 75A3
Belen *USA* 56C3
Bélep., Iles *New Caledonia* 33F2
Belet Uen *Somalia* 50E3
Belezma, Mts de *Algeria* 16B3
Belfast *N Ire* 9C2
Belfast *S Africa* 47E2
Belfast Lough, Estuary *N Ire* 9C2
Belfield *USA* 60C1
Belfodio *Eth* 50D2
Belford *Eng* 6D2
Belfort *France* 14D2
Belgaum *India* 44A2
Belgium, Kingdom *N W Europe* 18A2
Belgorod *USSR* 21F5
Belgorod Dnestrovskiy *USSR* 21E6
Belgrade *USA* 58D1
Belgrade *Yugos* 17E2
Bel Hedan *Libya* 49D2
Belitung, I *Indon* 27D7
Belize *Belize* 70D3
Belize, Republic *Cent America* 70D3
Bel'kovskiy, Ostrov, I *USSR* 25P2
Bellac *France* 14C2
Bella Coola *Can* 54F4
Bellaire *USA* 63C3
Bellary *India* 44B2
Bellata *Aust* 34C1
Bellefonte *USA* 68B2
Belle Fourche *USA* 56C2
Belle Fourche, R *USA* 60C2
Bellegarde *France* 14D2
Belle Glade *USA* 67B3
Belle I *Can* 55N4
Belle-Ile, I *France* 14B2
Belle Isle,Str of *Can* 55N4
Belleville *Can* 55L5
Belleville, Illinois *USA* 64B3
Belleville, Kansas *USA* 61D3
Bellevue, Idaho *USA* 58D2
Bellevue, Iowa *USA* 64A2
Bellevue, Washington *USA* 58B1
Bellingen *Aust* 34D2
Bellingham *Eng* 6C2
Bellingham *USA* 56A2
Bellingshausen, Base *Ant* 76G2
Bellingshausen S *Ant* 76G3
Bellinzona *Switz* 16B1
Bello *Colombia* 72C2
Bellona Reefs *Nouvelle Calédonie* 33E3
Bellota *USA* 66B1
Bellows Falls *USA* 65E2
Bell Pen *Can* 55K3
Belluno *Italy* 16C1
Bell Ville *Arg* 74D4
Belmont *USA* 68B1
Belmonte *Brazil* 73L7
Belmopan *Belize* 70D3
Belogorsk *USSR* 26F1
Beloha *Madag* 51E6
Belo Horizonte *Brazil* 73K7
Beloit, Kansas *USA* 61D3
Beloit, Wisconsin *USA* 57E2
Belomorsk *USSR* 24E3
Beloretsk *USSR* 20K5
Belorussian SSR, Republic *USSR* 20D5
Belo-Tsiribihina *Madag* 51E5
Beloye More, S = White Sea
Beloye Ozero, L *USSR* 20F3
Belozersk *USSR* 20F3
Belper *Eng* 7D3
Belpre *USA* 64C3
Beltana *Aust* 34A2
Belton *USA* 63C2
Bel'tsy *USSR* 19F3
Belukha, Mt *USSR* 24K5
Belush'ye *USSR* 20H2
Belvidere, Illinois *USA* 64B2
Belvidere, New Jersey *USA* 68C2
Belyy, Ostrov, I *USSR* 24J2
Bembe *Angola* 51B4
Bembéréké *Benin* 48C3
Bemidji *USA* 57D2
Bemis *USA* 63E1
Bena Dibele *Zaïre* 50C4
Benalla *Aust* 34C3
Ben Attow, Mt *Scot* 8C3
Benavente *Spain* 15A1
Benbane Hd, Pt *N Ire* 9C2
Benbecula, I *Scot* 8B3
Bencubbin *Aust* 32A4
Bend *USA* 56A2
Ben Dearg, Mt *Scot* 8C3
Bender Beyla *Somalia* 50E3
Bendery *USSR* 19F3
Bendigo *Aust* 32D4
Benešov *Czech* 18C3
Benevento *Italy* 16C2
Bengal,B of *Asia* 39G4
Ben Gardane *Tunisia* 49D1
Bengbu *China* 31D3
Benghazi *Libya* 49E1
Bengkulu *Indon* 27D7
Benguela *Angola* 51B5
Benha *Egypt* 40B3
Ben Hope, Mt *Scot* 8C2
Beni *Zaïre* 50C3
Béni, R *Bol* 72E6
Beni Abbès *Alg* 48B1
Benicarló *Spain* 15C1
Benidorm *Spain* 15B2
Beni Mansour *Alg* 15C2
Beni Mazâr *Egypt* 49F2
Beni Mellal *Mor* 48B1
Benin, Republic *Africa* 48C4
Benin City *Nigeria* 48C4
Beni-Saf *Alg* 15B2
Beni Suef *Egypt* 49F2
Benkelman *USA* 60C3
Ben Kilbreck, Mt *Scot* 8C2
Ben Lawers, Mt *Scot* 10C2
Ben Macdui, Mt *Scot* 8D3
Ben More *Scot* 8B3
Ben More Assynt, Mt *Scot* 8C2
Benmore,L *NZ* 35B2
Bennetta, Ostrov, I *USSR* 25R2
Ben Nevis, Mt *Scot* 8C3
Bennington *USA* 65E2
Bennt Jbail *Leb* 45C2
Bénoué, R *Cam* 50B3
Bensheim *W Germ* 13E3
Benson, Arizona *USA* 56B3
Benson, Minnesota *USA* 61D1
Benteng *Indon* 27F7
Bentiu *Sudan* 50C3
Bento Gomes, R *Brazil* 75A2
Benton, Arkansas *USA* 63D2
Benton, California *USA* 66C2
Benton, Kentucky *USA* 64B3
Benton Harbor *USA* 64B2
Benue, R *Nigeria* 48C4
Ben Wyvis, Mt *Scot* 8C3
Benxi *China* 31E1
Beograd = Belgrade
Beohari *India* 43E4
Beppu *Japan* 28C4
Berat *Alb* 17D2
Berau, Teluk, B *Indon* 27G7
Berber *Sudan* 50D2
Berbera *Somalia* 50E2
Berbérati *CAR* 50B3
Berdichev *USSR* 21D6
Berdyansk *USSR* 21F6
Berea *USA* 64C3
Berekum *Ghana* 48B4
Berenda *USA* 66B2
Berenice *Egypt* 40C5
Berens, R *Can* 54J4
Berens River *Can* 54J4
Beresford *USA* 61D2
Berettyóújfalu *Hung* 19E3
Bereza *USSR* 19F2
Berezhany *USSR* 19E3
Berezina, R *USSR* 19F2
Bereznik *USSR* 20G3
Berezniki *USSR* 24G4
Berezovka *USSR* 21E6
Berezovo *USSR* 24H3
Bergama *Turk* 40A2
Bergamo *Italy* 16B1
Bergen *Nor* 12F6
Bergen *USA* 68B1
Bergen op Zoom *Neth* 13C2
Bergerac *France* 14C3
Bergisch-Gladbach *W Germ* 13D2
Berhampur *India* 44C2
Beringa, Ostrov, I *USSR* 25S4
Beringovskiy *USSR* 25U3
Bering S *USA/USSR* 37K2
Bering Str *USA/USSR* 76C6
Berizak *Iran* 41G4
Berja *Spain* 15B2
Berkel, R *Neth/W Germ* 13D1
Berkeley *USA* 56A3
Berkeley Spring *USA* 68A3
Berkhamsted *Eng* 7D4
Berkner I *Ant* 76F2
Berkovitsa *Bulg* 17E2
Berkshire, County *Eng* 7D4
Berkshire Hills *USA* 68D1
Berlin *E Germ* 18C2
Berlin, New Hampshire *USA* 65E2
Bermejo *Bol* 72F8
Bermejo, R *Arg* 74E3
Bermuda, I *Atlantic O* 53M5
Bern = Berne
Bernalillo *USA* 62A1
Bernardo de Irigoyen *Arg* 75B4
Bernardsville *USA* 68C2
Bernburg *E Germ* 18C2
Berne *Switz* 16B1
Berneray, I *Scot* 8B3
Bernier B *Can* 55K2
Berounka, R *Czech* 18C3
Berri *Aust* 34B2
Berriane *Alg* 48C1
Berry, Region *France* 14C2
Berryessa,L *USA* 66A1
Berry Is *The Bahamas* 57F4
Berryville *USA* 68B3
Berseba *Namibia* 47B2
Berthoud P *USA* 60B3
Bertoua *Cam* 50B3
Beru, I *Kiribati* 33G1
Berwick *USA* 65D2
Berwick-upon-Tweed *Eng* 6C2
Berwyn Mts *Wales* 7C3
Besalampy *Madag* 51E5
Besançon *France* 14D2
Beskidy Zachodnie, Mts *Pol* 19E3
Besni *Turk* 40C2
Besor, R *Israel* 45C3
Bessemer, Alabama *USA* 67A2
Bessemer, Michigan *USA* 64B1
Betafo *Madag* 51E5
Betanzos *Spain* 15A1
Bet Guvrin *Israel* 45C3
Bethal *S Africa* 47D2
Bethanie *Namibia* 47B2
Bethany, Missouri *USA* 61E2
Bethany, Oklahoma *USA* 63C1
Bethel, Alaska *USA* 54B3
Bethel, Connecticut *USA* 68D2
Bethel Park *USA* 64C2
Bethesda *USA* 65D3
Bethlehem *Israel* 45C3
Bethlehem *S Africa* 47D2
Bethlehem *USA* 65D2
Bethulie *S Africa* 47D3
Béthune *France* 14C1
Betioky *Madag* 51E6
Betoota *Aust* 34B1
Betou *Congo* 50B3
Betpak Dala, Steppe *USSR* 39E1
Betroka *Madag* 51E6
Betsiamites *Can* 55M5
Bettendorf *USA* 64A2
Bettiah *India* 43E3
Betul *India* 42D4
Betuwe, Region *Neth* 13C2
Betwa, R *India* 42D3
Betws-y-coed *Wales* 7C3
Betzdorf *W Germ* 13D2
Beverley *Eng* 7D3
Beverly *USA* 68E1
Beverly Hills *USA* 66C3
Bexhill *Eng* 7E4
Bey Dağları *Turk* 40B2
Beyla *Guinea* 48B4
Beypore *India* 44B3
Beyrouth = Beirut
Beyşehir *Turk* 40B2
Beyşehir Gölü, L *Turk* 21E8
Beyt Shean *Israel* 45C2
Bezhetsk *USSR* 20F4
Béziers *France* 14C3
Bezmein *USSR* 41G2
Beznosova *USSR* 26D1
Bhadgaon *Nepal* 43F3
Bhadrachalam *India* 44C2
Bhadrakh *India* 43F4
Bhadra Res *India* 44B3
Bhadravati *India* 44B3
Bhag *Pak* 42B3
Bhagalpur *India* 43F3
Bhakkar *Pak* 42C2
Bhandara *India* 42D4
Bharatpur *India* 42D3
Bharuch *India* 42C4
Bhatiapara Ghat *Bang* 43F4
Bhatinda *India* 42C2
Bhatkal *India* 44A3
Bhatpara *India* 43F4
Bhavnagar *India* 42C4
Bhawanipatna *India* 43E5
Bhera *Pak* 42C2
Bheri, R *Nepal* 43E3
Bhilai *India* 43E4
Bhilwara *India* 42C3
Bhimavaram *India* 44C2
Bhind *India* 42D3
Bhiwani *India* 42D3

Bhongir Boro

Bhongir *India* 44B2
Bhopāl *India* 42D4
Bhubaneshwar *India* 43F4
Bhuj *India* 42B4
Bhusāwal *India* 42D4
Bhutan, Kingdom *Asia* 22F4
Biak, I *Indon* 27G7
Biala Podlaska *Pol* 19E2
Bialogard *Pol* 18D2
Bialystok *Pol* 19E2
Biargtangar, C *Iceland* 12A1
Biārjmand *Iran* 41G2
Biarritz *France* 14B3
Biba *Egypt* 40B4
Bibai *Japan* 29E2
Bibala *Angola* 51B5
Biberach *W Germ* 18B3
Bibiani *Ghana* 48B4
Bicaz *Rom* 17F1
Bicester *Eng* 7D4
Bicknell *USA* 59D3
Bida *Nigeria* 48C4
Bidar *India* 44B2
Bidbid *Oman* 41G5
Biddeford *USA* 65E2
Bideford *Eng* 7C6
Bideford B *Eng* 7B4
Bidon 5 *Alg* 48C2
Bié *Angola* 51B5
Biebrza, R *Pol* 19E2
Biel *Switz* 16B1
Bielawa *Pol* 18D2
Bielefeld *W Germ* 18B2
Biella *Italy* 16B1
Bielsk Podlaski *Pol* 19E2
Bien Hoa *Viet* 30D3
Bienville, Lac *Can* 55L4
Biferno, R *Italy* 16C2
Biga *Turk* 40A1
Bigadiç *Turk* 17F3
Big Belt Mts *USA* 58D1
Big Bend Nat Pk *USA* 62B3
Big Black, R *USA* 63E2
Big Blue, R *USA* 61D2
Big Cypress Swamp *USA* 67B3
Big Delta *USA* 54D3
Biggar *Scot* 8D4
Biggar Kindersley *Can* 54H4
Biggenden *Aust* 34D1
Biggleswade *Eng* 7D3
Big Hole, R *USA* 58D1
Bighorn, R *USA* 60B1
Bighorn L *USA* 60B1
Bighorn Mts *USA* 60B2
Bight of Benin, B *W Africa* 48C4
Bight of Biafra, B *Cam* 48C4
Big I *Can* 55L3
Big Lake *USA* 62B2
Bignona *Sen* 48A3
Big Pine *USA* 59C3
Big Pine Key *USA* 67B4
Big Pine Mt *USA* 66C3
Big Rapids *USA* 64B2
Big River *Can* 54H4
Big Sandy *USA* 58D1
Big Sioux, R *USA* 61D2
Big Smokey V *USA* 66D1
Big Spring *USA* 56C3
Big Springs *USA* 60C2
Big Stone City *USA* 61D1
Big Stone Gap *USA* 64C3
Big Sur *USA* 66B2
Big Timber *USA* 58E1
Big Trout L *Can* 55J4
Big Trout Lake *Can* 55K4
Bihać *Yugos* 16D2
Bihār *India* 43F3
Bihār, State *India* 43F4
Biharamulo *Tanz* 50D4
Bihor, Mt *Rom* 21C6
Bijagós, Arquipélago dos Is *Guinea-Bissau* 48A3
Bijāpur *India* 44B2
Bijāpur *India* 44C2
Bijār *Iran* 41E2
Bijauri *Nepal* 43E3
Bijeljina *Yugos* 17D2
Bijie *China* 31B4
Bijnor *India* 42D3
Bijnot *Pak* 42C3
Bikāner *India* 42C3
Bikfaya *Leb* 45C2
Bikin *USSR* 26G2
Bikoro *Zaïre* 50B4
Bilāra *India* 42C3
Bilaspur *India* 42D2
Bilauktaung Range, Mts *Thai/Burma* 30B3
Bilbao *Spain* 15B1
Bilbeis *Egypt* 45A3
Bilé, R *Czech* 18D3
Bileća *Yugos* 17D2
Bilecik *Turk* 40B1
Bili, R *Zaïre* 50C3
Bilibino *USSR* 25S3
Billings *USA* 56C2
Bilma *Niger* 50B2
Biloxi *USA* 57E3
Biltine *Chad* 50C2
Bimini Is *Bahamas* 67C3
Bina-Etawa *India* 42D4
Bindura *Zim* 51D5
Binga *Zim* 51C5
Binga, Mt *Zim/Mozam* 51D5
Bingara *Aust* 34D1
Bingen *W Germ* 18B3
Bingham *USA* 65F1
Binghamton *USA* 57F2
Bingöl *Turk* 40D2
Binhai *China* 31D3
Binibeca, Cabo, C *Spain* 15C2
Bintan, I *Indon* 27D6
Bintulu *Malay* 27E6
Bió Bió, R *Chile* 74B5
Bioko, I *Eq Guinea* 48C4
Bir *India* 44B2
Bîr Abu Husein, Well *Egypt* 49E2
Bi'r al Harash, Well *Libya* 49E2
Birao *CAR* 50C2
Biratnagar *Nepal* 43F3
Birchip *Aust* 34B3
Birch L *USA* 61E1
Birch Mts *Can* 54G4
Bird *Can* 55J4
Birdsville *Aust* 32C3
Birdum *Aust* 32C2
Bîr el 'Agramîya, Well *Egypt* 45A4
Bîr el Duweidâr, Well *Egypt* 45B3
Birganj *Nepal* 43E3
Bîr Gifgâfa, Well *Egypt* 45B3
Bîr Gindali, Well *Egypt* 45A4
Bîr Hasana, Well *Egypt* 45B3
Birigui *Brazil* 75B3
Birın *Syria* 45D1
Birjand *Iran* 41G3
Birkat Qârun, L *Egypt* 40B4
Birkenfeld *W Germ* 13D3
Birkenhead *Eng* 7C3
Bîrlad *Rom* 21D6
Bîr Lahfân, Well *Egypt* 45B3
Birmingham *Eng* 7C3
Birmingham *USA* 57E3
Bîr Misâha, Well *Egypt* 49E2
Bir Moghrein *Maur* 48A2
Birnin-Kebbi *Nigeria* 48C3
Birobidzhan *USSR* 26G2
Birr *Irish Rep* 9C3
Bir Rabalou *Alg* 15C2
Birrie, R *Aust* 34C1
Birsay *Scot* 8D2
Birsk *USSR* 20K4
Bîr Tarfâwi, Well *Egypt* 49E2
Bîr Udelb, Well *Egypt* 45B4
Biryusa, R *USSR* 25L4
Birzăi *USSR* 12J7
Bir Zreigat, Well *Maur* 48B2
Bisalpur *India* 43K1
Bisbee *USA* 59E4
Biscay,B of *France/Spain* 14A2
Biscayne B *USA* 67B3
Bischwiller *France* 13D3
Biscotasi L *Can* 64C1
Bishan *China* 31B4
Bishop *USA* 56B3
Bishop Auckland *Eng* 6D2
Bishops Castle *Eng* 7C3
Bishop's Stortford *Eng* 7E4
Bishrāmpur *India* 43E4
Biskra *Alg* 48C1
Bismarck *USA* 56C2
Bismarck Arch *PNG* 32D1
Bismarck Range, Mts *PNG* 32D1
Bismarck S *PNG* 32D1
Bisotūn *Iran* 41E3
Bissau *Guinea-Bissau* 48A3
Bissett *Can* 57D1
Bistcho L *Can* 54G4
Bistrita, R *Rom* 17F1
Bitam *Gabon* 50B3
Bitburg *W Germ* 18B3
Bitche *France* 13D3
Bitlis *Turk* 40D2
Bitola *Yugos* 17E2
Bitterfeld *E Germ* 18C2
Bitterfontein *S Africa* 47B3
Bitter Lakes *Egypt* 40B3
Bitteroot Range, Mts *USA* 56B2
Biu *Nigeria* 48D3
Biwa-ko, L *Japan* 29D3
Biyo Kaboba *Eth* 50E2
Biysk *USSR* 24K4
Bizerte *Tunisia* 16B3
Bjelovar *Yugos* 16D1
Bj Flye Ste Marie *Alg* 48B2
Bjørnøya, I = Bear I
Black, R *USA* 63D1
Blackall *Aust* 32D3
Black B *Can* 64B1
Blackburn *Eng* 6C3
Blackburn,Mt *USA* 54D3
Black Canyon City *USA* 59D4
Blackduck *USA* 61E1
Black Eagle *USA* 58D1
Blackfoot *USA* 58D2
Blackfoot, R *USA* 58D1
Black Hd, Pt *Irish Rep* 9B3
Black Hills *USA* 54H5
Black Isle, Pen *Scot* 8C3
Blackman's *Barbados* 69Q2
Black Mts *USA* 59D3
Black Mts *Wales* 7C4
Black Nosob, R *Namibia* 47B1
Blackpool *Eng* 6C3
Black River *Jamaica* 69H1
Black River Falls *USA* 64A2
Black Rock Desert *USA* 56B2
Black S *USSR/Europe* 24E5
Blacksburg *USA* 64C3
Black Sugarloaf, Mt *Aust* 34D2
Black Volta, R *W Africa* 48B4
Black Warrior, R *USA* 63E2
Blackwater, R *Eng* 7E4
Blackwater, R *Irish Rep* 10B3
Blackwell *USA* 63C1
Blagoevgrad *Bulg* 17E2
Blagoveshchensk *USSR* 25O4
Blaikiston,Mt *Can* 58D1
Blaine *USA* 58B1
Blair *USA* 61D2
Blair Atholl *Scot* 8D3
Blairgowrie *Scot* 8D3
Blakely *USA* 67C2
Blanca, Bahía, B *Arg* 74D5
Blanca Peak, Mt *USA* 62A1
Blanc, C *Tunisia* 16B3
Blanche, L *Aust* 34A1
Blanc, Mont, Mt *France/Italy* 16B1
Blanco,C *USA* 56A2
Blanc Sablon *Can* 55N4
Blandford Forum *Eng* 7C4
Blanding *USA* 59E3
Blankenberge *Belg* 13B2
Blanquilla, Isla *Ven* 69E4
Blantyre *Malawi* 51D5
Blasket Sd *Irish Rep* 9A3
Blaye *France* 14B2
Blayney *Aust* 34C2
Blenheim *NZ* 33G5
Blida *Alg* 15C2
Blind River *Can* 64C1
Blinman *Aust* 34A2
Block I *USA* 65E2
Block Island Sd *USA* 68E2
Bloemfontin *S Africa* 47D2
Bloemhof *S Africa* 47D2
Bloemhof Dam, Res *S Africa* 47D2
Blommesteinmeer, L *Surinam* 73G3
Blönduós *Iceland* 12A1
Bloomfield, Indiana *USA* 64B3
Bloomfield, Iowa *USA* 61E2
Bloomfield, Nebraska *USA* 61D2
Bloomfield, New Mexico *USA* 62A1
Bloomington, Illinois *USA* 64B2
Bloomington, Indiana *USA* 64B3
Bloomington, Minnesota *USA* 61E2
Bloomsburg *USA* 68B2
Blossburg *USA* 68B2
Blosseville Kyst, Mts *Greenland* 55Q3
Blouberg, Mt *S Africa* 47D1
Bludenz *Austria* 18B3
Bluefield *USA* 57E3
Bluefields *Nic* 72B1
Blue Hill *USA* 60D2
Blue Knob, Mt *USA* 68A2
Blue Mountain Peak, Mt *Jamaica* 69J1
Blue Mt *USA* 68B2
Blue Mts *Aust* 34D2
Blue Mts *USA* 56A2
Blue Mts, The *Jamaica* 69J1
Blue Nile = Abbai
Blue Nile *Ethiopia* = Bahr el Azraq
Blue Nile, R *Sudan* 50D2
Bluenose L *Can* 54G3
Blue Ridge *USA* 67C2
Blue Ridge Mts *USA* 57E3
Blue Stack, Mt *Irish Rep* 9C2
Bluff *NZ* 35A3
Bluff *USA* 59E3
Bluff Knoll, Mt *Aust* 32A4
Blumenau *Brazil* 74G3
Blunt *USA* 60D2
Bly *USA* 58B2
Blyth *Eng* 6D2
Blythe *USA* 56B3
Blytheville *USA* 57E3
Bo *Sierra Leone* 48A4
Boac *Phil* 27F5
Boa Nova *Brazil* 75D1
Boardman *USA* 64C2
Boa Vista *Brazil* 71D3
Boa Vista, I *Cape Verde* 48A4
Bobai *China* 30E1
Bobbili *India* 44C2
Bobo Dioulasso *Burkina* 48B3
Bobrovica *USSR* 19G2
Bobruysk *USSR* 20D5
Boca Chica Key, I *USA* 67B4
Bôca do Acre *Brazil* 72E5
Bocaiúva *Brazil* 75D2
Bocaranga *CAR* 50B3
Boca Raton *USA* 67B3
Bochnia *Pol* 19E3
Bocholt *W Germ* 18B2
Bochum *W Germ* 13D2
Bocoio *Angola* 51B5
Boda *CAR* 50B3
Bodaybo *USSR* 25N4
Bodega Head, Pt *USA* 59B3
Bodélé, Desert Region *Chad* 50B2
Boden *Sweden* 12J5
Boderg, L *Irish Rep* 9C3
Bodhan *India* 44B2
Bodināyakkanūr *India* 44B3
Bodmin *Eng* 7B4
Bodmin Moor, Upland *Eng* 7B4
Bodø *Nor* 12G5
Bodrum *Turk* 17F3
Boende *Zaïre* 50C4
Boffa *Guinea* 48A3
Bogale *Burma* 30B2
Bogalusa *USA* 63E2
Bogan, R *Aust* 34C2
Bogande *Burkina* 48B3
Boğazlıyan *Turk* 40C2
Bogdanovich *USSR* 20L4
Bogda Shan, Mt *China* 26B2
Bogenfels *Namibia* 47B2
Boggabilla *Aust* 34D1
Boggabri *Aust* 34C2
Bognor Regis *Eng* 7D4
Bogong, Mt *Aust* 34C3
Bogor *Indon* 27D7
Bogorodskoye *USSR* 25Q4
Bogotá *Colombia* 72D3
Bogotol *USSR* 25K4
Bogra *Bang* 43F4
Bo Hai, B *China* 31D2
Bohain-en-Vermandois *France* 13B3
Bohai Wan, B *China* 31D2
Bohmer-wald, Upland *W Germ* 18C3
Bohol, I *Phil* 27F6
Bohol S *Phil* 27F6
Boipeba, Ilha de *Brazil* 75E1
Bois, R *Brazil* 75B2
Bois Blanc I *USA* 64C1
Boise *USA* 56B2
Boise City *USA* 62B1
Bois, Lac des *Can* 54F3
Boissevain *Can* 60C1
Bojador,C *Mor* 48A2
Bojeador, C *Phil* 27F5
Bojnurd *Iran* 41G2
Boké *Guinea* 48A3
Bokhara, R *Aust* 34C1
Boknafjord, Inlet *Nor* 12F7
Boko *Congo* 50B4
Bokor *Camb* 30C3
Bokoro *Chad* 50B2
Bokungu *Zaïre* 50C4
Bol *Chad* 50B2
Bolama *Guinea-Bissau* 48A3
Bolbec *France* 14C2
Bole *Ghana* 48B4
Bolesławiec *Pol* 18D2
Bolgatanga *Ghana* 48B3
Bolgrad *USSR* 21D6
Bolivar, Missouri *USA* 63D1
Bolivar, Tennessee *USA* 63E1
Bolívar, Mt *Ven* 72D2
Bolivia, Republic *S America* 72E7
Bollnäs *Sweden* 12H6
Bollon *Aust* 34C1
Bolobo *Zaïre* 50B4
Bologna *Italy* 16C2
Bologoye *USSR* 20E4
Bolon' *USSR* 26G1
Bolon', Oz, L *USSR* 26G2
Bolsena, L di *Italy* 16C2
Bol'shevik, Ostrov, I *USSR* 25M2
Bol'shezemel'skaya Tundra, Plain *USSR* 20J2
Bol'shoy Anyuy, R *USSR* 25S3
Bol'shoy Begichev, Ostrov, I *USSR* 25N2
Bol'shoy Irgiz, R *USSR* 21H5
Bol'shoy Kamen *USSR* 28C2
Bol'shoy Kavkaz, Mts = Caucasus
Bol'shoy Lyakhovskiy, Ostrov, I *USSR* 25Q2
Bol'shoy Uzen, R *USSR* 21H6
Bolson de Mapimí, Desert *Mexico* 56C4
Bolton *Eng* 7C3
Bolu *Turk* 40B1
Bolungarvik *Iceland* 12A1
Bolus Hd, Pt *Irish Rep* 9A4
Bolvadin *Turk* 40B2
Bolzano *Italy* 16C1
Boma *Zaïre* 50B4
Bombala *Aust* 32D4
Bombay *India* 44A2
Bombetoka, Baie de, B *Madag* 51E5
Bombo *Uganda* 50D3
Bom Despacho *Brazil* 75C2
Bomdila *India* 43G3
Bomi Hills *Lib* 48A4
Bom Jesus da Lapa *Brazil* 73K6
Bomnak *USSR* 25O4
Bomokandi, R *Zaïre* 50C3
Bomu, R *CAR/Zaïre* 50C3
Bon Air *USA* 65D3
Bonaire, I *Caribbean S* 69D4
Bonanza *Nic* 70D3
Bonavista *Can* 55N5
Bon, C *Tunisia* 16C3
Bondo *Zaïre* 50C3
Bondoukou *Ivory Coast* 48B4
Bône = 'Annaba
Bonesteel *USA* 60D2
Bonfim *Guyana* 73G3
Bongandanga *Zaïre* 50C3
Bongo, Massif des, Upland *CAR* 50C3
Bongor *Chad* 50B2
Bonham *USA* 63C2
Bonifacio, Corsica 16B2
Bonifacio,Str of, Chan, Corsica/Sardinia 16B2
Bonin Is = Ogasawara Gunto
Bonita Springs *USA* 67B3
Bonito *Brazil* 75A3
Bonn *W Germ* 18B2
Bonners Ferry *USA* 58C1
Bonny *Nigeria* 48C4
Bonthain *Indon* 32A1
Bonthe *Sierra Leone* 48A4
Booaaso *Somalia* 50E2
Booligal *Aust* 34B2
Boonah *Aust* 34D1
Boone, Colorado *USA* 62B1
Boone, Iowa *USA* 61E2
Boone, North Carolina *USA* 67B1
Boonville *USA* 65D2
Boorowa *Aust* 34C2
Boothia,G of *Can* 55J2
Boothia Pen *Can* 55J2
Bootle *Eng* 7C3
Booué *Gabon* 50B4
Bophuthatswana, Self governing homeland *S Africa* 47C2
Boquillas *Mexico* 62B3
Bor *Sudan* 50D3
Bor *Turk* 40B2
Bor *Yugos* 17E2
Borah Peak, Mt *USA* 56B2
Borås *Sweden* 12G7
Borazjan *Iran* 41F4
Bordeaux *France* 14B3
Borden I *Can* 54G2
Borden Pen *Can* 55K2
Bordentown *USA* 68C2
Borders, Region *Scot* 8D4
Bordertown *Aust* 34B3
Bordj bou Arréidj *Alg* 15C2
Bordj Omar Driss *Alg* 48C2
Borgå = Porvoo
Borgarnes *Iceland* 55Q3
Borger *USA* 56C3
Borgholm *Sweden* 12H7
Borislav *USSR* 19E3
Borisoglebsk *USSR* 21G5
Borisov *USSR* 20D5
Borisovka *USSR* 21F5
Borja *Par* 75A4
Borkou, Desert Region *Chad* 50B2
Borkum, I *W Germ* 13D1
Borlänge *Sweden* 12H6
Borneo, I *Indon/Malaysia* 27E6
Bornholm, I *Den* 12H7
Bornova *Turk* 17F3
Bornu, Region *Nigeria* 48D3
Boro, R *Sudan* 50C3

Borogontsy **Buriram**

Borogontsy *USSR* **25P3**
Boromo *Burkina* **48B3**
Boron *USA* **66D3**
Borovichi *USSR* **20E4**
Borroloola *Aust* **32C2**
Borsa *Rom* **17E1**
Borūjen *Iran* **41F3**
Borūjerd *Iran* **41E3**
Bory Tucholskie, Region *Pol* **18D2**
Borzna *USSR* **19G2**
Borzya *USSR* **25N4**
Bose *China* **31B5**
Boshof *S Africa* **47D2**
Bosna, R *Yugos* **17D2**
Bōsō-hantō, B *Japan* **29D3**
Bosporus = Karadeniz Boğazi
Bosquet *Alg* **15C2**
Bossangoa *CAR* **50B3**
Bossèmbélé *CAR* **50B3**
Bossier City *USA* **63D2**
Bosten Hu, L *China* **24K5**
Boston *Eng* **7D3**
Boston *USA* **57F2**
Boston Mts *USA* **57D3**
Botād *India* **42C4**
Botevgrad *Bulg* **17E2**
Bothaville *S Africa* **47D2**
Bothnia,G of *Fin/ Sweden* **20B3**
Botletli, R *Botswana* **51C6**
Botoşani *Rom* **21D6**
Botswana, Republic *Africa* **51C6**
Botte Donato, Mt *Italy* **16D3**
Bottineau *USA* **60C1**
Bottrop *W Germ* **13D2**
Botucatu *Brazil* **75C3**
Botuporã *Brazil* **75D1**
Botwood *Can* **55N5**
Bouaké *Ivory Coast* **46D7**
Bouar *CAR* **50B3**
Bouârfa *Mor* **48B1**
Bouca *CAR* **50B3**
Boufarik *Alg* **15C2**
Bougainville, I *PNG* **33E1**
Bougaroun, C *Algeria* **16B3**
Bougie = Bejaïa
Bougouni *Mali* **48B3**
Bouhalla, Djebel, Mt *Mor* **15A2**
Bouillon *France* **13C3**
Bouïra *Alg* **15C2**
Bou Izakarn *Mor* **48B2**
Boulay-Moselle *France* **13D3**
Boulder, Colorado *USA* **56C2**
Boulder, Montana *USA* **58D1**
Boulder City *USA* **56B3**
Boulder Creek *USA* **66A2**
Boulogne *France* **14C1**
Boumba, R *CAR/Cam* **50B3**
Bouna *Ivory Coast* **48B4**
Boundary Peak, Mt *USA* **56B3**
Boundiali *Ivory Coast* **48B4**
Bountiful *USA* **58D2**
Bounty Is *NZ* **33G5**
Bourail *New Caledonia* **33F3**
Bourbonne-les-Bains *France* **13C4**
Bourem *Mali* **48B3**
Bourg *France* **14D2**
Bourg de Péage *France* **14D2**
Bourges *France* **14C2**
Bourg-Madame *France* **14C3**
Bourgogne, Region *France* **14C2**
Bourke *Aust* **34C2**
Bournemouth *Eng* **7D4**
Bou Saâda *Alg* **15C2**
Bousso *Chad* **50B2**
Boutilimit *Maur* **48A3**
Bouvet I *Atlantic O* **52J7**
Bowbells *USA* **60C1**
Bowen *Aust* **32D2**
Bowie, Arizona *USA* **59E4**
Bowie, Texas *USA* **63C2**
Bowland Fells *Eng* **6C3**
Bowling Green, Kentucky *USA* **57E3**
Bowling Green, Missouri *USA* **63D1**
Bowling Green, Ohio *USA* **64C2**
Bowling Green, Virginia *USA* **65D3**
Bowman *USA* **60C1**
Bowmanville *Can* **65D2**
Bowna, L *Irish Rep* **9C3**
Bowral *Aust* **34D2**
Bo Xian *China* **31D3**
Boxing *China* **31D2**
Boyabat *Turk* **40B1**
Boyali *CAR* **50B3**
Boyarka *USSR* **19G2**
Boyd *Can* **54J4**
Boyertown *USA* **68C2**
Boyle *Irish Rep* **10B3**
Boyne, R *Irish Rep* **9C3**
Boynton Beach *USA* **67B3**
Boyoma Falls *Zaïre* **50C3**
Boysen Res *USA* **58E2**
Bozanski Brod *Yugos* **17D1**
Bozca Ada, I *Turk* **17F3**
Boz Dağlari, Mts *Turk* **17F3**
Bozeman *USA* **56B2**
Bozen = Bolzano
Bozene *Zaïre* **50B3**
Bozoum *CAR* **50B3**
Brač, I *Yugos* **16D2**
Bracadale, Loch, Inlet *Scot* **8B3**
Bracciano, L di *Italy* **16C2**
Bracebridge *Can* **65D1**
Brach *Libya* **49D2**
Bräcke *Sweden* **12H6**
Brackettville *USA* **62B3**
Bradenton *USA* **67B3**
Bradford *Eng* **6D3**
Bradford *USA* **68A2**
Bradley *USA* **66B3**
Brady *USA* **62C2**
Brae *Scot* **8E1**
Braemar *Scot* **8D3**
Braga *Port* **15A1**
Bragança *Brazil* **73J4**
Bragança *Port* **15A1**
Bragança Paulista *Brazil* **75C3**
Brahman-Baria *Bang* **43G4**
Brāhmani, R *India* **43F4**
Brahmaputra, R *India/ Bang* **43G3**
Brăila *Rom* **21D6**
Brainerd *USA* **57D2**
Braintree *Eng* **7E4**
Brak, R *S Africa* **47C3**
Brake *W Germ* **13E1**
Brakna, Region *Maur* **48A3**
Bralorne *Can* **54F4**
Brampton *Can* **65D2**
Brampton *Eng* **6C2**
Bramsche *W Germ* **13D1**
Branco, R *Brazil* **72F3**
Brandberg, Mt *Namibia* **51B6**
Brandenburg *E Germ* **18C2**
Brandfort *S Africa* **47D2**
Brandon *Can* **56D2**
Brandon *USA* **61D2**
Brandvlei *S Africa* **47C3**
Brandýs-nad-Laben *Czech* **18C2**
Braniewo *Pol* **19D2**
Brantford *Can* **57E2**
Branxholme *Aust* **34B3**
Bras d'Or Lakes *Can* **55M5**
Brasiléia *Brazil* **72E6**
Brasília *Brazil* **73J7**
Brasília de Minas *Brazil* **75D2**
Braşov *Rom* **17F1**
Bratislava *Czech* **18D3**
Bratsk *USSR* **25M4**
Bratslav *USSR* **19F3**
Brattleboro *USA* **65E2**
Braunschweig *W Germ* **18C2**
Brava, I *Cape Verde* **48A4**
Brawley *USA* **56B3**
Bray *Irish Rep* **9C3**
Bray I *Can* **55L3**
Bray-sur-Seine *France* **13B3**
Brazil, Republic *S America* **71E5**
Brazil Basin *Atlantic O* **52G5**
Brazos, R *USA* **56D3**
Brazzaville *Congo* **50B4**
Brdy, Upland *Czech* **18C3**
Breaksea Sd *NZ* **35A3**
Bream B *NZ* **35B1**
Brechin *Scot* **8D3**
Brecht *Belg* **13C2**
Breckenridge, Minnesota *USA* **61D1**
Breckenridge, Texas *USA* **62C2**
Breckland *Eng* **7E3**
Breclav *Czech* **18D3**
Brecon *Wales* **7C4**
Brecon Beacons, Mts *Wales* **7C4**
Brecon Beacons Nat Pk *Wales* **7B3**
Breda *Neth* **18A2**
Bredasdorp *S Africa* **47C3**
Bredbyn *Sweden* **12H6**
Bredy *USSR* **20K5**
Breede, R *S Africa* **47B3**
Breezewood *USA* **65D2**
Breiðafjörður, B *Iceland* **12A1**
Breisach *W Germ* **13D3**
Bremen *USA* **67A2**
Bremen *W Germ* **18B2**
Bremerhaven *W Germ* **18B2**
Bremerton *USA* **58B1**
Bremervörde *W Germ* **13E1**
Brendel *USA* **59E3**
Brenham *USA* **63C2**
Brenner, P *Austria/Italy* **18C3**
Brenner, Pass *Austria* **14E2**
Brentwood *USA* **66B2**
Brescia *Italy* **16C1**
Breslau = Wrocław
Bressay, I *Scot* **8E1**
Bressuire *France* **14B2**
Brest *France* **14B2**
Brest *USSR* **19E2**
Bretagne, Region *France* **14B2**
Breteuil *France* **13B3**
Breton Sd *USA* **63E3**
Breton Woods *USA* **68C2**
Brett,C *NZ* **35B1**
Brevard *USA* **67B1**
Brewarrina *Aust* **34C1**
Brewer *USA* **65F2**
Brewster, New York *USA* **68D2**
Brewster, Washington *USA* **58C1**
Brewton *USA* **67A2**
Breyten *S Africa* **47D2**
Brezhnev *USSR* **20J4**
Brežice *Yugos* **16D1**
Bria *CAR* **50C3**
Briançon *France* **14D3**
Briare *France* **14C2**
Bridgend *Wales* **7C4**
Bridge of Orchy *Scot* **8C3**
Bridgeport, Alabama *USA* **67A2**
Bridgeport, California *USA* **59C3**
Bridgeport, Connecticut *USA* **65E2**
Bridgeport, Nebraska *USA* **60C2**
Bridgeport, Texas *USA* **63C2**
Bridgeport Res *USA* **66C1**
Bridger *USA* **58E1**
Bridger Peak *USA* **60B2**
Bridgeton *USA* **68C3**
Bridgetown *Barbados* **69R3**
Bridgewater *Can* **55M5**
Bridgewater *USA* **68E2**
Bridgwater *Eng* **7C4**
Bridgwater B *Eng* **7C4**
Bridlington *Eng* **6D2**
Bridlington Bay *Eng* **6E3**
Bridport *Aust* **34C4**
Bridport *Eng* **7C4**
Brienne-le-Château *France* **13C3**
Briey *France* **13C3**
Brig *Switz* **16B1**
Brigham City *USA* **56B2**
Bright *Aust* **34C3**
Brighton *Eng* **7D4**
Brilhante, R *Brazil* **75A3**
Brilon *W Germ* **13E2**
Brindisi *Italy* **17D2**
Brinkley *USA* **63D2**
Brisbane *Aust* **33E3**
Bristol, Connecticut *USA* **65E2**
Bristol *Eng* **7C4**
Bristol, Pennsylvania *USA* **65E2**
Bristol, Rhode Island *USA* **68E2**
Bristol, Tennessee *USA* **57E3**
Bristol *USA* **64C3**
Bristol Chan *Eng/Wales* **7B4**
British Columbia, Province *Can* **54F4**
British Empire Range, Mts *Can* **55K1**
British Mts *Can* **54E3**
Brits *S Africa* **47D2**
Britstown *S Africa* **47C3**
Britton *USA* **61D1**
Brive *France* **14C2**
Brixham *Eng* **7C4**
Brno *Czech* **18D3**
Broad, R *USA* **67B2**
Broadalbin *USA* **68C1**
Broadback, R *Can* **55L4**
Broad Bay, Inlet *Scot* **8B2**
Broadford *Scot* **8C3**
Broad Haven, B *Irish Rep* **9B2**
Broadstairs *Eng* **7E4**
Broadus *USA* **60B1**
Broadwater *USA* **60C2**
Brochet *Can* **54H4**
Brock I *Can* **54G2**
Brockport *USA* **65D2**
Brockton *USA* **68E1**
Brockville *Can* **65D2**
Brockway *USA* **68A2**
Brodeur Pen *Can* **55K2**
Brodick *Scot* **8C4**
Brodnica *Pol* **19D2**
Brody *USSR* **21D5**
Brokem Haltern *W Germ* **13D2**
Broken Bow, Nebraska *USA* **60D2**
Broken Bow, Oklahoma *USA* **63D2**
Broken Bow L *USA* **63D2**
Broken Hill *Aust* **32D4**
Bromsgrove *Eng* **7C3**
Brønnøysund *Nor* **12G5**
Bronx, Borough, New York *USA* **68D2**
Brooke's Pt *Phil* **27E6**
Brookfield, Missouri *USA* **61E3**
Brookfield, Wisconsin *USA* **64B2**
Brookhaven *USA* **57D3**
Brookings, Oregon *USA* **58B2**
Brookings, South Dakota *USA* **56D2**
Brookline *USA* **68E1**
Brooklyn *USA* **61E2**
Brooklyn, Borough, New York *USA* **68D2**
Brooklyn Center *USA* **61E1**
Brooks *Can* **54G4**
Brooks Range, Mts *USA* **54C3**
Brooksville *USA* **67B3**
Brooloo *Aust* **34D1**
Broome *Aust* **32B2**
Broom, Loch, Estuary *Scot* **8C3**
Brora *Scot* **8D2**
Brothers *USA* **58B2**
Broughton *Eng* **6C2**
Broughty Ferry *Scot* **8D3**
Broulkou, Well *Chad* **50B2**
Brovary *USSR* **19G2**
Browerville *USA* **61E1**
Brownfield *USA* **62B2**
Brownsville *USA* **56D4**
Brownwood *USA* **56D3**
Browse I *Aust* **27F8**
Bruay-en-Artois *France* **13B2**
Bruce,Mt *Aust* **32A3**
Bruce Pen *Can* **64C1**
Bruchsal *W Germ* **13E3**
Bruck an der Mur *Austria* **18D3**
Brugge = Bruges
Bruges *Belg* **13B2**
Brühl *W Germ* **13D2**
Brûk, Wadi el *Egypt* **45B3**
Brumado *Brazil* **75D1**
Brumath *France* **13D3**
Bruneau *USA* **58C2**
Bruneau, R *USA* **58C2**
Brunei, State *Borneo* **27E6**
Brunico *Italy* **16C1**
Brunner,L *NZ* **35B2**
Brunsbüttel *W Germ* **13E1**
Brunswick, Georgia *USA* **57E3**
Brunswick, Maine *USA* **65F2**
Brunswick, Mississippi *USA* **61E3**
Brunswick,Pen de *Chile* **74B8**
Bruny I *Aust* **34C4**
Brusenets *USSR* **20G3**
Brush *USA* **60C2**
Brus Laguna *Honduras* **69A3**
Brüssel = Brussels
Brussels *Belg* **18A2**
Bruxelles = Brussels
Bruyères *France* **13D3**
Bryan *USA* **56D3**
Bryan,Mt *Aust* **34A2**
Bryansk *USSR* **20E5**
Bryant *USA* **63D2**
Bryce Canyon Nat Pk *USA* **59D3**
Brzeg *Pol* **18D2**
Būbiyan, I *Kuwait* **41E4**
Bubu, R *Tanz* **50D4**
Bubye, R *Zim* **47E1**
Bucaramanga *Colombia* **72D2**
Buchan, Oilfield *N Sea* **8E3**
Buchanan *Lib* **48A4**
Buchanan,L *USA* **62C2**
Buchan Deep *N Sea* **8E3**
Buchan G *Can* **55L2**
Buchan Ness, Pen *Scot* **10C2**
Buchans *Can* **55N5**
Bucharest *Rom* **17F2**
Buchon,Pt *USA* **66B3**
Bückeburg *W Germ* **13E1**
Buckeye *USA* **59D4**
Buckhaven *Scot* **8D3**
Buckie *Scot* **8D3**
Buckingham *Eng* **7D3**
Bucksport *USA* **65F2**
Buco Zau *Congo* **50B4**
Bucureşti = Bucharest
Budapest *Hung* **19D3**
Budaun *India* **42D3**
Bude *Eng* **7B4**
Bude *USA* **63D2**
Budennovsk *USSR* **21G7**
Budhana *India* **43J1**
Budhīya, Gebel *Egypt* **45B4**
Büdingen *W Germ* **13E2**
Budva *Yugos* **17D2**
Buéa *Cam* **48C4**
Buellton *USA* **66B3**
Buenaventura *Colombia* **72C3**
Buenaventura *Mexico* **62A3**
Buena Vista, Colorado *USA* **60B3**
Buena Vista, Virginia *USA* **65D3**
Buena Vista L *USA* **66C3**
Buenos Aires *Arg* **74E4**
Buenos Aires, State *Arg* **74E5**
Buenos Aires, Lago *Arg* **74B7**
Buffalo, Mississipi *USA* **63D1**
Buffalo, New York *USA* **57F2**
Buffalo, S Dakota *USA* **60C1**
Buffalo, Texas *USA* **63C2**
Buffalo, Wyoming *USA* **56C2**
Buffalo, R *S Africa* **47E2**
Buffalo Hump, Mt *USA* **58C1**
Buffalo L *Can* **54G3**
Buffalo Narrows *Can* **54H4**
Buford *USA* **67B2**
Buftea *Rom* **17F2**
Bug, R *Pol/USSR* **19E2**
Buga *Colombia* **72C3**
Bugdayli *USSR* **41F2**
Bugrino *USSR* **20H2**
Bugulma *USSR* **20J5**
Buguruslan *USSR* **20J5**
Buḩayrat al Asad, Res *Syria* **40C2**
Buhl, Idaho *USA* **58D2**
Buhl, Minnesota *USA* **61E1**
Builth Wells *Wales* **7C3**
Bujumbura *Burundi* **50C4**
Buka, I *PNG* **33E1**
Bukama *Zaïre* **51C4**
Bukavu *Zaïre* **50C4**
Bukhara *USSR* **38E2**
Bukittinggi *Indon* **27D7**
Bukoba *Tanz* **50D4**
Bula *Indon* **27G7**
Bulan *Phil* **27F5**
Bulandshahr *India* **42D3**
Bulawayo *Zim* **51C6**
Buldan *Turk* **17F3**
Buldāna *India* **42D4**
Bulgan *Mongolia* **26D2**
Bulgaria, Republic *Europe* **17E2**
Buller, R *NZ* **35B2**
Buller,Mt *Aust* **34C3**
Bullfinch *Aust* **32A4**
Bulloo, R *Aust* **34B1**
Bulloo Downs *Aust* **34B1**
Bulloo L *Aust* **34B1**
Bull Shoals Res *USA* **63D1**
Bulolo *PNG* **32D1**
Bultfontein *S Africa* **47D2**
Bulu, Gunung, Mt *Indon* **27E6**
Bumba *Zaïre* **50C3**
Bu Menderes, R *Turk* **21D8**
Bumphal Dam *Thai* **30B2**
Buna *Kenya* **50D3**
Bunbury *Aust* **32A4**
Buncrana *Irish Rep* **9C2**
Bundaberg *Aust* **33E3**
Bundarra *Aust* **34D2**
Bünde *W Germ* **13E1**
Bundi *India* **42D3**
Bungay *Eng* **7E3**
Bungil, R *Aust* **34C1**
Bungo *Angola* **51B4**
Bungo-suidō, Str *Japan* **28B4**
Bunguran, I *Indon* **27D6**
Bunguran, Kepulauan, I *Indon* **27D6**
Bunia *Zaïre* **50D3**
Bunker *USA* **63D1**
Bunkie *USA* **63D2**
Bunnell *USA* **67B3**
Buntok *Indon* **27E7**
Buol *Indon* **27F6**
Buram *Sudan* **50C2**
Burang *China* **43E2**
Burāq *Syria* **45D2**
Buraydah *S Arabia* **41D4**
Burbank *USA* **59C4**
Burcher *Aust* **34C2**
Burco *Somalia* **50E3**
Burdur *Turk* **21E8**
Burē *Eth* **50D2**
Bure, R *Eng* **7E3**
Bureinskiy Khrebet, Mts *USSR* **26G1**
Bureya *USSR* **26F2**
Būr Fu'ad *Egypt* **45B3**
Burg *E Germ* **18C2**
Burgas *Bulg* **17F2**
Burgaw *USA* **67C2**
Burgersdorp *S Africa* **47D3**
Burgos *Spain* **15B1**
Burgsteinfurt *W Germ* **13D1**
Burgsvik *Sweden* **19D1**
Burhaniye *Turk* **17F3**
Burhānpur *India* **42D4**
Buriram *Thai* **30C2**

Buritis *Brazil* 75C2
Burketown *Aust* 32C2
Burkina, Republic *W Africa* 48B3
Burks Falls *Can* 65D1
Burley *USA* 56B2
Burlington, Colorado *USA* 60C3
Burlington, Iowa *USA* 57D2
Burlington, New Jersey *USA* 68C2
Burlington, North Carolina *USA* 67C1
Burlington, Vermont *USA* 57F2
Burlington, Washington *USA* 58B1
Burma, Republic *Asia* 39H3
Burnet *USA* 62C2
Burney *USA* 58B2
Burnham *USA* 68B2
Burnham-on-Crouch *Eng* 7E4
Burnie *Aust* 32D5
Burnley *Eng* 6C3
Burns *USA* 58C2
Burns Lake *Can* 54F4
Burqin *China* 24K5
Burra *Aust* 34A2
Burragorang,L *Aust* 34D2
Burray, I *Scot* 8D2
Burren Junction *Aust* 34C2
Burrinjuck Res *Aust* 34C2
Burro, Serranías del, Mts *Mexico* 62B3
Burrow Head, Pt *Scot* 8C4
Burrundie *Aust* 27G8
Bursa *Turk* 21D7
Bur Safâga *Egypt* 40B4
Bûr Saïd = Port Said
Bûr Taufiq *Egypt* 45B4
Burton *USA* 64C2
Burton upon Trent *Eng* 7D3
Burtrask *Sweden* 12J6
Burtundy *Aust* 34B2
Buru, I *Indon* 27F7
Burundi, Republic *Africa* 50C4
Burwell *USA* 60D2
Bury *Eng* 7C3
Buryat ASSR, Republic *USSR* 25N4
Burynshik *USSR* 21J6
Bury St Edmunds *Eng* 7E3
Bushan *China* 28A3
Büshehr *Iran* 41F4
Bushmills *N Ire* 9C2
Busira, R *Zaïre* 50B4
Buskozdroj *Pol* 19E2
Buşrá ash Shām *Syria* 45D2
Bussang *France* 13D4
Busselton *Aust* 32A4
Busto Arsizio *Italy* 16B1
Buta *Zaïre* 50C3
Butare *Rwanda* 50C4
Bute, I *Scot* 8C4
Butha Qi *China* 26F2
Butler *USA* 65D2
Buton, I *Indon* 32B1
Butta *Togo* 48C4
Butte *USA* 56B2
Butterworth *Malay* 30C4
Butterworth *S Africa* 47D3
Butt of Lewis, C *Scot* 10B2
Button Is *Can* 55M3
Buttonwillow *USA* 66C3
Butuan *Phil* 27F6
Buturlinovka *USSR* 21G5
Butwal *Nepal* 43E3
Butzbach *W Germ* 13E2
Buulo Barde *Somalia* 50E3
Buur Hakaba *Somalia* 50E3
Buxton *Eng* 7D3
Buy *USSR* 20G4
Buyant Ovoo *Mongolia* 31B1
Buynaksk *USSR* 21H7
Buyr Nuur, L *Mongolia* 25N5
Büyük Ağrı Dağı, Mt *Turk* 21G8
Büyük Menderes, R *Turk* 40A2
Buzău *Rom* 17F1
Buzău, R *Rom* 17F1
Búzios, Ponta dos, Pt *Brazil* 75D3
Buzuluk *USSR* 20J5
Buzzards B *USA* 68E2
Byala *Bulg* 17F2
Byala Slatina *Bulg* 17E2
Byam Martin, Chan *Can* 54H2
Byam Martin I *Can* 54H2
Byblos, Hist site *Lebanon* 45C1
Bydgoszcz *Pol* 19D2
Byers *USA* 60C3
Bygland *Nor* 12F7
Bykhov *USSR* 19G2
Bylot I *Can* 55L2
Byrock *Aust* 34C2
Byron *USA* 66B2
Byron, C *Aust* 34D1
Bytantay, R *USSR* 25P3
Bytom *Pol* 19D2

C

Caacupú *Par* 74E3
Caaguazú *Par* 75A4
Caála *Angola* 51B5
Caapucú *Par* 75A4
Caarapó *Brazil* 75B3
Caazapá *Par* 74E3
Caballería, Cabo de, C *Spain* 15C1
Caballo Res *USA* 62A2
Cabanatuan *Phil* 27F5
Cabano *Can* 65F1
Cabedelo *Brazil* 73M5
Cabeza del Buey *Spain* 15A2
Cabimas *Ven* 72D1
Cabinda *Angola* 50B4
Cabinda, Province *Angola* 50B4
Cabinet Mts *USA* 58C1
Cabo Frio *Brazil* 75D3
Cabonga,Réservoire *Can* 55L5
Caboolture *Aust* 34D1
Cabora Bassa Dam *Mozam* 51D5
Caborca *Mexico* 70A1
Cabot Str *Can* 55M5
Cabra *Spain* 15B2
Cabral, Serra do, Mts *Brazil* 75D2
Cabreira, Mt *Port* 15A1
Cabrera, I *Spain* 15C2
Cabriel, R *Spain* 15B2
Čačak *Yugos* 17E2
Cacapon, R *USA* 68A3
Cáceres *Brazil* 73G7
Cáceres *Spain* 15A2
Cache, R *USA* 63D1
Cache Creek, R *USA* 66A1
Cache Peak, Mt *USA* 58D2
Cachi *Arg* 74C3
Cachimbo *Brazil* 73G5
Cachimbo, Serra do, Mts *Brazil* 73G5
Cachoeira *Brazil* 73L6
Cachoeira Alta *Brazil* 75B2
Cachoeira de Paulo Afonso, Waterfall *Brazil* 73L5
Cachoeira do Sul *Brazil* 74F4
Cachoeiro de Itapemirim *Brazil* 73K8
Cachuma,L *USA* 66C3
Cacolo *Angola* 51B5
Caconda *Angola* 51B5
Cactus *USA* 62B1
Caçu *Brazil* 75B2
Caculé *Brazil* 75D1
Caculuvar, R *Angola* 51B5
Čadca *Czech* 19D3
Cader Idris, Mt *Wales* 7C3
Cadillac *USA* 57E2
Cádiz *Spain* 15A2
Cádiz, Golfo de, G *Spain* 15A2
Caen *France* 14B2
Caernarfon *Wales* 7B3
Caernarfon B *Wales* 7B3
Caerphilly *Wales* 7C4
Caesarea, Hist Site *Israel* 45C2
Caetité *Brazil* 75D1
Cafayate *Arg* 74C3
Caga Tepe, Mt *Turk* 40B2
Cagayan de Oro *Phil* 27F6
Cagayan Sulu, I *Phil* 27E6
Cagliari, Sardinia 16B3
Cagliari, G di, Sardinia 16B3
Caguas *Puerto Rico* 69D3
Cahaba, R *USA* 67A2
Cahir *Irish Rep* 9C3
Cahore Pt *Irish Rep* 9C3
Cahors *France* 14C3
Caia *Mozam* 51D5
Caiabis, Serra dos, Mts *Brazil* 73G6
Caianda *Angola* 51C5
Caiapó, R *Brazil* 75B2
Caiapônia *Brazil* 75B2
Caiapó, Serra do, Mts *Brazil* 75B2
Caicó *Brazil* 73L5
Caicos Is *Caribbean S* 69C2
Caicos Pass *The Bahamas* 57F4
Cairngorms, Mts *Scot* 8D3
Cairnryan *Scot* 8C4
Cairns *Aust* 32D2
Cairo *Egypt* 40B3
Cairo *USA* 57E3
Caithness *Scot* 8D2
Caiwarro *Aust* 34B1
Cajabamba *Peru* 72C5
Cajamarca *Peru* 72C5
Calabar *Nigeria* 48C4
Calabozo *Ven* 69D5
Calafat *Rom* 17E2
Calafate *Arg* 74B8
Calahorra *Spain* 15B1
Calais *France* 14C1
Calais *USA* 65F1
Calama *Chile* 74C2
Calamar *Colombia* 72D3
Calamian Group, Is *Phil* 27E5
Calang *Indon* 27C6
Calanscio Sand Sea *Libya* 49E2
Calapan *Phil* 27F5
Calarasi *Rom* 17F2
Calatayud *Spain* 15B1
Calaveras Res *USA* 66B2
Calcasieu L *USA* 63D3
Calcutta *India* 43F4
Caldas da Rainha *Port* 15A2
Caldas Novas *Brazil* 73J7
Caldera *Chile* 74B3
Caldwell *USA* 56B2
Caledon *S Africa* 47B3
Caledon, R *S Africa* 47D3
Caledonia, Minnesota *USA* 64A2
Caledonia, New York *USA* 68B1
Caleta Olivia *Arg* 74C7
Calexico *USA* 56B3
Calgary *Can* 54G4
Calhoun *USA* 67B2
Calhoun Falls *USA* 67B2
Cali *Colombia* 72C3
Calicut *India* 44B3
Caliente, California *USA* 66C3
Caliente, Nevada *USA* 56B3
Caliente, New Mexico *USA* 62A1
California, State *USA* 56A3
California Aqueduct *USA* 66C3
California, G de *Mexico* 70A1
Calimera,Pt *India* 44B3
Calipatria *USA* 59C4
Calitzdorp *S Africa* 47C3
Callabonna, R *Aust* 34B1
Callabonna,L *Aust* 34A1
Callander *Can* 65D1
Callander *Scot* 8C3
Callao *Peru* 72C6
Callicoon *USA* 68C2
Caloosahatchee, R *USA* 67B3
Caloundra *Aust* 34D1
Caltanissetta, Sicily 16C3
Caluango *Angola* 51B4
Calulo *Angola* 51B5
Caluquembe *Angola* 51B5
Calvi, Corsica 16B2
Calvinia *S Africa* 47B3
Calw *W Germ* 13E3
Camacari *Brazil* 75E1
Camagüey *Cuba* 70E2
Camagüey,Arch de, Is *Cuba* 70E2
Camamu *Brazil* 75E1
Camaná *Peru* 72D7
Camapuã *Brazil* 75B2
Camargo *Bol* 72E8
Camarillo *USA* 66C3
Camarones *Arg* 74C6
Camas *USA* 58B1
Camaxilo *Angola* 51B4
Cambatela *Angola* 51B4
Cambodia, Republic *S E Asia* 30C3
Camborne *Eng* 7B4
Cambrai *France* 14C1
Cambria *USA* 66B3
Cambrian Mts *Wales* 7C3
Cambridge *Can* 64C2
Cambridge *Eng* 7E3
Cambridge *Jamaica* 69H1
Cambridge, Maryland *USA* 65D3
Cambridge, Massachussets *USA* 65E2
Cambridge, Minnesota *USA* 61E1
Cambridge *NZ* 35C1
Cambridge, Ohio *USA* 64C2
Cambridge, County *Eng* 7D3
Cambridge Bay *Can* 54H3
Cambridge G *Aust* 27F8
Cam Burun, Pt *Turk* 21F7
Camden, Arkansas *USA* 57D3
Camden *Aust* 34D2
Camden, New Jersey *USA* 65E3
Camden, New York *USA* 68C1
Camden, South Carolina *USA* 67B2
Cameron, Missouri *USA* 61E3
Cameron, Texas *USA* 63C2
Cameron I *Can* 54H2
Cameron Mts *NZ* 35A3
Cameroon, Federal Republic *Africa* 50B3
Cameroun, Mt *Cam* 48C4
Cametá *Brazil* 73J4
Camilla *USA* 67B2
Camino *USA* 66B1
Camiri *Bol* 72F8
Camocim *Brazil* 73K4
Camooweal *Aust* 32C2
Camorta, I, Nicobar Is *Indian O* 44E4
Campana, I *Chile* 74A7
Campbell *S Africa* 47C2
Campbell,C *NZ* 35B2
Campbell I *NZ* 37K7
Campbell,Mt *Can* 54E3
Campbellpore *Pak* 42C2
Campbell River *Can* 54F5
Campbellsville *USA* 64B3
Campbellton *Can* 55M5
Campbelltown *Aust* 34D2
Campbeltown *Scot* 8C4
Campeche *Mexico* 70C3
Campeche, B de *Mexico* 70C2
Camperdown *Aust* 34B3
Campina Grande *Brazil* 73L5
Campinas *Brazil* 73J8
Campina Verde *Brazil* 75C2
Camp Nelson *USA* 66C2
Campo *Cam* 48C4
Campobasso *Italy* 16C2
Campo Belo *Brazil* 75C3
Campo Florido *Brazil* 75C2
Campo Gallo *Arg* 74D3
Campo Grande *Brazil* 74F2
Campo Maior *Brazil* 73K4
Campo Mourão *Brazil* 74F2
Campos *Brazil* 75D3
Campos Altos *Brazil* 75C2
Camp Verde *USA* 59D4
Cam Ranh *Viet* 30D3
Camrose *Can* 54G4
Camucuio *Angola* 51B5
Canaan *Tobago* 69K1
Canaan *USA* 68D1
Canacupa *Angola* 51B5
Canada, Dominion *N America* 53F3
Cañada de Gómez *Arg* 74D4
Canadensis *USA* 68C2
Canadian *USA* 62B1
Canadian, R *USA* 56C3
Çanakkale *Turk* 21D7
Canandaigua *USA* 68B1
Canandaigua L *USA* 68B1
Cananea *Mexico* 70A1
Cananeia *Brazil* 75C4
Canarias, Islas = Canary Is
Canary Basin *Atlantic O* 52G3
Canary Is *Atlantic O* 48A2
Canastra, Serra da, Mts *Brazil* 75C3
Canatlán *Mexico* 70B2
Canaveral,C *USA* 57E4
Canavieiras *Brazil* 73L7
Canberra *Aust* 32D4
Canby, California *USA* 58B2
Canby, Minnesota *USA* 61D2
Candala *Somalia* 50E2
Çandarlı Körfezi, B *Turk* 17F3
Candlewood,L *USA* 68D2
Cando *USA* 60D1
Candor *USA* 68B1
Canelones *Urug* 74E4
Caney *USA* 63C1
Cangamba *Angola* 51C5
Cangombe *Angola* 51C5
Cangzhou *China* 31D2
Caniapiscau, R *Can* 55M4
Caniapiscau,L *Can* 55M4
Canicatti, Sicily 16C3
Canindé *Brazil* 73L4
Canisteo *USA* 68B1
Canisteo, R *USA* 68B1
Canjilon *USA* 62A1
Çankırı *Turk* 40B1
Canna, I *Scot* 8B3
Cannanore *India* 44B3
Cannes *France* 14D3
Cannock *Eng* 7C3
Cannonball, R *USA* 60C1
Cann River *Aust* 34C3
Canõas *Brazil* 74F3
Canoinhas *Brazil* 75B4
Canon City *USA* 60B3
Canopus *Aust* 34B2
Canora *Can* 54H4
Canowindra *Aust* 34C2
Cantabria, Region *Spain* 15B1
Cantabrica, Cord, Mts *Spain* 14A3
Canterbury *Eng* 7E4
Canterbury Bight, B *NZ* 35B2
Canterbury Plains *NZ* 35B2
Can Tho *Viet* 30D4
Cantil *USA* 66D3
Canton = Guangzhou
Canton, Mississippi *USA* 63E2
Canton, Missouri *USA* 64A2
Canton, Ohio *USA* 57E2
Canton, Pensylvania *USA* 68B2
Canton, S Dakota *USA* 61D2
Canton, I *Phoenix Is* 33H1
Cantu, Serra do, Mts *Brazil* 75B3
Canyon *USA* 62B2
Canyon City *USA* 58C2
Canyon Ferry L *USA* 58D1
Canyonlands Nat Pk *USA* 59E3
Canyonville *USA* 58B2
Canzar *Angola* 51C4
Cao Bang *Viet* 30D1
Caoshi *China* 28B2
Capanema *Brazil* 73J4
Capão Bonito *Brazil* 75C3
Caparaó, Serra do, Mts *Brazil* 75D3
Capbreton *France* 14B3
Cap Corse, C, Corsica 16B2
Cap de la Hague, C *France* 14B2
Cap-de-la-Madeleine *Can* 65E1
Capdepera *Spain* 15C2
Cape, Cabo etc : *see also individual cape name*
Cape Barren I *Aust* 34C4
Cape Basin *Atlantic O* 52J6
Cape Breton I *Can* 55N5
Cape Coast *Ghana* 48B4
Cape Cod B *USA* 65E2
Cape Fear, R *USA* 67C2
Cape Girardeau *USA* 63E1
Cape Horn *Chile* 74C8
Cape Johnson Depth *Pacific O* 36H4
Capelinha *Brazil* 75D2
Cape Lisburne *USA* 54B3
Capelongo *Angola* 51B5
Cape May *USA* 65E3
Cape Mendocino *USA* 54F5
Capenda Camulemba *Angola* 51B4
Cape Parry *Can* 54F2
Cape Province *S Africa* 47C3
Cape Town *S Africa* 47B3
Cape Verde, Is *Atlantic O* 52G4
Cape Verde Basin *Atlantic O* 52G4
Cape York Pen *Aust* 32D2
Cap-Haïtien *Haiti* 69C3
Capim, R *Brazil* 73J4
Capitán Bado *Par* 75A3
Capitol Reef Nat Pk *USA* 59E3
Capivari, R *Brazil* 75A2
Cappoquin *Irish Rep* 9C3
Cap Pt *St Lucia* 69P2
Capri, I *Italy* 16C2
Caprivi Strip, Region *Namibia* 51C5
Caquetá, R *Colombia* 72D4
Caracal *Rom* 17E2
Caracaraí *Brazil* 72F3
Caracas *Ven* 72E1
Caracol *Brazil* 75A3
Caraguatatuba *Brazil* 75C3
Carahue *Chile* 74B5
Caraí *Brazil* 75D2
Carandaí *Brazil* 75D3
Carandazal *Brazil* 75A2
Carangola *Brazil* 73K8
Caransebeş *Rom* 17E1
Caratasca *Honduras* 69A3
Caratasca, L de, Lg *Honduras* 70D3
Caratinga *Brazil* 75D2
Caravaca de la Cruz *Spain* 15B2
Caravelas *Brazil* 75E2
Carbonara, C, Sardinia 16B3
Carbondale, Illinois *USA* 64B3
Carbondale, Pennsylvania *USA* 68C2
Carbonear *Can* 55N5
Carbonia, Sardinia 16B3
Carcajou *Can* 54G4
Carcar Mts *Somalia* 50E2
Carcassonne *France* 14C3
Carcross *Can* 54E3
Cardamomes, Chaîne des, Mts *Camb* 30C3
Cardenas *Cuba* 70D2
Cardiff *Wales* 7C4
Cardigan *Wales* 7B3
Cardigan B *Wales* 7B3
Cardoso, Ilha do *Brazil* 75C4
Carei *Rom* 17E1
Careiro *Brazil* 73G4
Carey *USA* 64C2
Carhaix-Plouguer *France* 14B2
Carhué *Arg* 74D5
Cariacíca *Brazil* 73K8

Caribbean S *Cent America* 71C2
Caribou *Can* 54J4
Caribou *USA* 65F1
Caribou Mts, Alberta *Can* 54G4
Caribou Mts, British Columbia *Can* 54F4
Carignan *France* 13C3
Carinhanha *Brazil* 75D1
Carinhanha, R *Brazil* 75D1
Caripito *Ven* 72F1
Carleton Place *Can* 65D1
Carletonville *S Africa* 47D2
Carlin *USA* 58C2
Carlingford, L *N Ire* 9C2
Carlinville *USA* 64B3
Carlisle *Eng* 6C2
Carlisle *USA* 65D2
Carlos Chagas *Brazil* 75D2
Carlow *Irish Rep* 9C3
Carlow, County *Irish Rep* 9C3
Carlsbad, California *USA* 59C4
Carlsbad, New Mexico *USA* 56C3
Carlsbad Caverns Nat Pk *USA* 62B2
Carlsberg Ridge *Indian O* 36E4
Carlyle *Can* 54H5
Carmacks *Can* 54E3
Carmarthen *Wales* 7B4
Carmarthen B *Wales* 7B4
Carmel, California *USA* 66B2
Carmel, New York *USA* 68D2
Carmel Hd, Pt *Wales* 7B3
Carmel,Mt *Israel* 45C2
Carmel Valley *USA* 66B2
Carmen, I *Mexico* 56B4
Carmen de Patagones *Arg* 74D6
Carmi *USA* 64B3
Carmichael *USA* 59B3
Carmo do Paranaiba *Brazil* 75C2
Carmona *Spain* 15A2
Carnacá *Brazil* 75E2
Carnarvon *Aust* 32A3
Carnarvon *S Africa* 47C3
Carndonagh *Irish Rep* 9C2
Carnegie,L *Aust* 32B3
Car Nicobar, I, Nicobar Is *Indian O* 44E4
Carnot *CAR* 50B3
Carnoustie *Scot* 8D3
Carnsore Pt *Irish Rep* 9C3
Carol City *USA* 67B3
Carolina *Brazil* 73J5
Carolina *S Africa* 47E2
Carolina Beach *USA* 67C2
Caroline Is *Pacific O* 36J4
Carpathian Mts *Rom* 19F3
Carpathians, Mts *E Europe* 21C6
Carpentaria,G of *Aust* 32C2
Carpenter Ridge *Indian O* 39H5
Carpentras *France* 14D3
Carpi *Italy* 16C2
Carpinteria *USA* 66C3
Carrabelle *USA* 67B3
Carrara *Italy* 16C2
Carrauntoohill, Mt *Irish Rep* 10B3
Carrick *Scot* 8C4
Carrickfergus *N Ire* 9D2
Carrickmacross *Irish Rep* 9C3
Carrick-on-Suir *Irish Rep* 9C3
Carrieton *Aust* 34A2
Carrington *USA* 54J5
Carrión, R *Spain* 15B1
Carrizo Springs *USA* 62C3
Carrizozo *USA* 62A2
Carroll *USA* 57D2
Carrollton, Georgia *USA* 67A2
Carrollton, Kentucky *USA* 64B3
Carrollton, Missouri *USA* 61E3
Carrowmore,L *Irish Rep* 9B2
Carruthersville *USA* 63E1
Carşamba *Turk* 21F7
Carşamba, R *Turk* 21E8
Carson City *USA* 56B3
Carsonville *USA* 64C2
Carstairs *Scot* 8D4
Cartagena *Colombia* 69B4
Cartagena *Spain* 15B2
Cartago *Colombia* 72C3
Cartago *Costa Rica* 70D4
Cartago *USA* 66C2
Carterton *NZ* 35C2
Carthage, Missouri *USA* 63D1
Carthage, New York *USA* 65D2
Carthage, Texas *USA* 63D2
Cartier I *Timor S* 32B2
Cartwright *Can* 55N4
Caruaru *Brazil* 73L5
Carúpano *Ven* 72F1
Carvin *France* 13B2
Carvoeiro, Cabo, C *Port* 15A2
Cary *USA* 67C1
Casablanca *Mor* 48B1
Casa Branca *Brazil* 75C3
Casa Grande *USA* 56B3
Casale Monferrato *Italy* 16B1
Cascade *USA* 58D1
Cascade Pt *NZ* 35A2
Cascade Ranges, Mts *USA* 56A2
Cascade Res *USA* 58C2
Cascavel *Brazil* 74F2
Caserta *Italy* 16C2
Casey, Base *Ant* 76G9
Cashel *Irish Rep* 9C3
Casino *Aust* 33E3
Casma *Peru* 72C5
Casmalia *USA* 66B3
Caspe *Spain* 15C1
Casper *USA* 56C2
Caspian S *USSR* 24G5
Cass *USA* 65D3
Cassamba *Angola* 51C5
Cassel *France* 13B2
Casselton *USA* 61D1
Cassiar Mts *Can* 54E3
Cassilândia *Brazil* 75B2
Cassino *Italy* 16C2
Cass Lake *USA* 61E1
Castaic *USA* 66C3
Castellane *France* 14D3
Castello, Città di *Italy* 16C2
Castellón de la Plana *Spain* 15C1
Castelo *Brazil* 73K5
Castelo Branco *Port* 15A2
Castelsarrasin *France* 14C3
Castelvetrano, Sicily 16C3
Casterton *Aust* 34B3
Castilla la Mancha, Region *Spain* 15B2
Castilla y León, Region *Spain* 15B1
Castlebar *Irish Rep* 10B3
Castlebay *Scot* 8B3
Castleblayney *Irish Rep* 9C2
Castle Dale *USA* 59D3
Castle Douglas *Scot* 8D4
Castleford *Eng* 6D3
Castlegar *Can* 58C1
Castlemaine *Aust* 34B3
Castle Mt *USA* 66B3
Castle Peak, Mt *USA* 58D2
Castlereagh, R *Aust* 34C2
Castle Rock *USA* 60C3
Castletown *Eng* 6B2
Castletown Bere *Irish Rep* 9B4
Castres-sur-l'Agout *France* 14C3
Castries *St Lucia* 69P2
Castro *Arg* 74B6
Castro *Brazil* 74F2
Castro Alves *Brazil* 73L6
Castrovillari *Italy* 16D3
Castroville *USA* 66B2
Caswell Sd *NZ* 35A2
Cat, I *The Bahamas* 70E2
Catacaos *Peru* 72B5
Cataguases *Brazil* 75D3
Catahoula L *USA* 63D2
Catalão *Brazil* 75C2
Cataluña, Region *Spain* 15C1
Catamarca *Arg* 74C3
Catamarca, State *Arg* 74C3
Catandica *Mozam* 51D5
Catanduanes, I *Phil* 27F5
Catanduva *Brazil* 74G2
Catanduvas *Brazil* 75B4
Catania, Sicily 16D3
Catanzaro *Italy* 16D3
Catarina *USA* 62C3
Catarman *Phil* 27F5
Catatumbo, R *Ven* 69C5
Catawissa *USA* 68B2
Catbalogan *Phil* 27F5
Cateraggio, Corsica 16B2
Catete *Angola* 51B4
Cathcart *S Africa* 47D3
Catio *Guinea-Bissau* 48A3
Cat Lake *Can* 55J4
Cato, I *Aust* 33E3
Catoche,C *Mexico* 70D2
Catoctin Mt *USA* 68B3
Catonsville *USA* 65D3
Catskill *USA* 65E2
Catskill Mts *USA* 65E2
Cauca, R *Colombia* 72D2
Caucaia *Brazil* 73L4
Caucasia *Colombia* 72C2
Caucasus, Mts *USSR* 21G7
Caudry *France* 13B2
Caungula *Angola* 51B4
Cauquenes *Chile* 74B5
Causapscal *Can* 65F1
Cauvery, R *India* 44B3
Cavaillon *France* 14D3
Cavalcante *Brazil* 75C1
Cavalier *USA* 61D1
Cavally, R *Lib* 48B4
Cavan *Irish Rep* 9C3
Cavan, County *Irish Rep* 9C3
Caxias *Brazil* 72D4
Caxias do Sul *Brazil* 74F3
Caxito *Angola* 51B4
Cayce *USA* 67B2
Çayeli *Turk* 40D1
Cayenne *French Guiana* 73H3
Cayman Brac, I, Cayman Is *Caribbean S* 70E3
Cayman Is *Caribbean S* 69A3
Cayman Trench *Caribbean S* 69A3
Caynabo *Somalia* 50E3
Cayo Romano, I *Cuba* 70E2
Cayos Miskito, Is *Nic* 70D3
Cay Sal, I *Caribbean S* 69A2
Cayucos *USA* 66B3
Cayuga L *USA* 68B1
Cazenovia *USA* 68C1
Cazombo *Angola* 51C5
Ceará = Fortaleza
Ceará, State *Brazil* 73K5
Cebu *Phil* 27F5
Cebu, I *Phil* 27F5
Cecilton *USA* 68C3
Cecina *Italy* 16C2
Cedar, R *USA* 61E2
Cedar City *USA* 56B3
Cedar Creek Res *USA* 63C2
Cedar Falls *USA* 61E2
Cedar L *Can* 54J4
Cedar Mts *USA* 66D1
Cedar Rapids *USA* 57D2
Cedartown *USA* 67A2
Cedros, I *Mexico* 70A2
Cedros, Isla de *Mexico* 56B4
Ceduna *Aust* 32C4
Ceelbuur *Somalia* 50E3
Ceerigaabo *Somalia* 50E2
Cefalù, Sicily 16C3
Cegléd *Hung* 19D3
Cela *Angola* 51B5
Celaya *Mexico* 70B2
Celebes = Sulawesi
Celebes S *S E Asia* 27F6
Celina *USA* 64C2
Celje *Yugos* 16D1
Celle *W Germ* 18C2
Celtic S *British Is* 7A4
Cemmaes Hd, Pt *Wales* 7B3
Cendrawasih, Pen *Indon* 27G7
Center *USA* 63D2
Center Hill L *USA* 67A1
Center Moriches *USA* 68D2
Center Point *USA* 67A2
Central *USA* 62A2
Central, Region *Scot* 8C3
Central African Republic *Africa* 50B3
Central City, Nebraska *USA* 61D2
Central City, Pennsylvania *USA* 68A2
Central Falls *USA* 68E2
Centralia, Illinois *USA* 64B3
Centralia, Washington *USA* 56A2
Central Kalahari Game Res *Botswana* 47C1
Central Makran Ra, Mts *Pak* 42A3
Central Point *USA* 58B2
Central Range, Mts *PNG* 27H7
Central Square *USA* 68B1
Centreville, Alabama *USA* 67A2
Centreville, Maryland *USA* 68B3
Ceram = Seram
Ceram Sea = Seram Sea
Ceres *Brazil* 73J7
Ceres *S Africa* 47B3
Ceres *USA* 66B2
Cergy-Pontoise *France* 14C2
Cerignola *Italy* 16D2
Cernavodă *Rom* 21D7
Cernay *France* 13D4
Cerralvo, I *Mexico* 56C4
Cerro de Pasco *Peru* 72C6
Cerro de Punta, Mt *Puerto Rico* 69D3
Cerron, Mt *Ven* 69C4
Cerros Colorados, Embalse, Res *Arg* 74C5
Cesena *Italy* 16C2
Cesis *USSR* 20C4
České Budějovice *Czech* 18C3
České Zemé, Region *Czech* 18C3
Českomoravská Vysočina Region *Czech* 18D3
Çeşme *Turk* 17F3
Cessnock *Aust* 32E4
Cetina, R *Yugos* 16D2
Ceuta *N W Africa* 15A2
Ceyhan *Turk* 40C2
Ceyhan, R *Turk* 40C2
Ceylanpinar *Turk* 40C2
Ceylon, I *Indian Oc* 44C4
Ceylon, Republic = Sri Lanka
Chaa-Khol *USSR* 25L4
Châteaudun *France* 14C2
Chablis *France* 13B4
Chachapoyas *Peru* 72C5
Chachran *Pak* 42C3
Chachro *Pak* 42C3
Chaco, State *Arg* 74D3
Chad, Republic *Africa* 50B2
Chad, L *C Africa* 50B2
Chadron *USA* 56C2
Chaeryŏng *N Korea* 28B3
Chaffee *USA* 63E1
Chagai *Pak* 42A3
Chagda *USSR* 25P4
Chaghcharan *Afghan* 42B2
Chagos Arch *Indian O* 36E5
Chaguanas *Trinidad* 69L1
Chāh Bahār *Iran* 38E3
Ch'aho *N Korea* 28A2
Chai Badan *Thai* 30C2
Chaibasa *India* 43F4
Chaiyaphum *Thai* 30C2
Chakwal *Pak* 42C2
Chala *Peru* 72D7
Chalabesa *Zambia* 51D5
Chalap Dalam, Mts *Afghan* 42A2
Chaleurs, B des *Can* 57G2
Chalindrey *France* 13C4
Chaling *China* 31C4
Chalisgaon *India* 42D4
Challenger Deep *Pacific O* 27H5
Challerange *France* 13C3
Challis *USA* 58D2
Châlons-sur-Marne *France* 13C3
Chalon sur Saône *France* 14C2
Chaluhe *China* 28B2
Cham *W Germ* 18C3
Chama *USA* 62A1
Chaman *Pak* 42B2
Chamba *India* 42D2
Chambal, R *India* 42D3
Chamberlain *USA* 60D2
Chambersburg *USA* 65D3
Chambéry *France* 14D2
Chambly *France* 13B3
Chambord *Can* 65E1
Chambor Kalat *Pak* 42A3
Chamgordan *Iran* 41F3
Champa *India* 43E4
Champagne, Region *France* 14C2
Champagne Castle, Mt *Lesotho* 47D2
Champaign *USA* 57E2
Champaran, District *India* 43N2
Champassak *Laos* 30D3
Champlain,L *USA* 57F2
Chāmrajnagar *India* 44B3
Chañaral *Chile* 74B3
Chandalar *USA* 54D3
Chandalar, R *USA* 54D3
Chandeleur Is *USA* 63E3
Chandigarh *India* 42D2
Chandler *USA* 59D4
Chandpur *Bang* 43G4
Chandrapur *India* 42D5
Changane, R *Mozam* 47E1
Changara *Mozam* 51D5
Changbai *China* 28B2
Changbai Shan, Mts *China* 28B2
Changchun *China* 28B2
Changde *China* 31C4
Changdo *N Korea* 28A3
Changhai *China* 28A3
Changhang *S Korea* 28A3
Changhowan *S Korea* 28A3
Changhua *Taiwan* 26E4
Changhŭng *S Korea* 28A4
Changjiang *China* 30D2
Chang Jiang, R *China* 31D3
Changjin *N Korea* 28B2
Changjin, R *N Korea* 28A2
Changjin Res *N Korea* 28A2
Changnyŏn *N Korea* 28B3
Changsha *China* 31C4
Changshu *China* 31E3
Changwu *China* 31B2
Changyŏn *N Korea* 28A3
Changzhi *China* 31C2
Changzhou *China* 31E3
Channel Is *British Isles* 14B2
Channel Is *USA* 56B3
Channel Port-aux-Basques *Can* 55N5
Chanthaburi *Thai* 30C3
Chantilly *France* 13B3
Chantrey Inlet, B *Can* 55J3
Chanute *USA* 63C1
Chany, Ozero, L *USSR* 24J4
Chao'an *China* 31D5
Chao Hu, L *China* 31D3
Chao Phraya, R *Thai* 30C3
Chaouen *Mor* 15A2
Chaoyang *China* 31E1
Chapada Diamantina, Mts *Brazil* 73K6
Chapadinha *Brazil* 73K4
Chapala, L de *Mexico* 70B2
Chapayevo *USSR* 21J5
Chapecó *Brazil* 74F3
Chapel-en-le-Frith *Eng* 7D3
Chapel Hill *USA* 67C1
Chapeltown *Jamaica* 69H1
Chapleau *Can* 55K5
Chaplino, Mys, C *USSR* 25U3
Chaplygin *USSR* 20G5
Chappell *USA* 60C2
Charcot I *Ant* 76G3
Chard *Eng* 7C4
Chardzhou *USSR* 38E2
Charente, R *France* 14C2
Chari, R *Chad* 50B2
Chari Baguirmi, Region *Chad* 50B2
Charikar *Afghan* 42B1
Chariton, R *USA* 61E2
Charity *Guyana* 73G2
Charkhari *India* 42D3
Charleroi *Belg* 13C2
Charles,C *USA* 57F3
Charleston, Illinois *USA* 64B3
Charleston, Missouri *USA* 63E1
Charleston, S Carolina *USA* 57F3
Charleston, W Virginia *USA* 57E3
Charleston Peak, Mt *USA* 59C3
Charles Town *USA* 68B3
Charlestown *USA* 68D1
Charlesville *Zaïre* 50C4
Charleville *Aust* 32D3
Charleville-Mézières *France* 14C2
Charlevoix *USA* 64B1
Charlotte, Michigan *USA* 64C2
Charlotte, N Carolina *USA* 57E3
Charlotte Harbor, B *USA* 67B3
Charlottesville *USA* 57F3
Charlottetown *Can* 55M5
Charlotteville *Tobago* 69K1
Charlton *Aust* 34B3
Charlton I *Can* 57F1
Charmes *France* 13D3
Charsadda *Pak* 42C2
Charters Towers *Aust* 32D3
Chartres *France* 14C2
Chascomús *Arg* 74E5
Chasong *N Korea* 28A2
Châteaubriant *France* 14B2
Châteaulin *France* 14B2
Châteauneuf-sur-Loire *France* 13B4
Châteauroux *France* 14C2
Château-Salins *France* 13D3
Château-Thierry *France* 14C2
Châtelet *Belg* 13C2
Châtellerault *France* 14C2
Chatfield *USA* 61E2
Chatham *Eng* 7F6
Chatham, Massachusetts *USA* 68E2
Chatham, New Brunswick *Can* 55M5
Chatham, New York *USA* 68D1
Chatham, Ontario *Can* 64C2
Chatham, Virginia *USA* 65D3
Chatham Is *NZ* 33H5
Chatham Str *USA* 54E4
Châtillon *France* 14C2
Châtillon-Coligny *France* 13B4
Châtillon-sur-Seine *France* 13C4
Chatrapur *India* 43E5
Chatsworth *USA* 68C3
Chattahoochee *USA* 67B2
Chattahoochee, R *USA* 67A2
Chattanooga *USA* 57E3
Chauk *Burma* 30A1
Chauka, R *India* 43L2
Chaumont *France* 14D2
Chauny *France* 13B3
Chau Phu *Viet* 30D3

Chaura **Clyde**

Chaura, I, Nicobar Is *Indian O* 44E4
Chaves *Port* 15A1
Chaykovskiy *USSR* 20J4
Cheb *Czech* 18C2
Cheboksary *USSR* 24F4
Cheboygan *USA* 57E2
Chechersk *USSR* 19G2
Chech'on *S Korea* 28B3
Checotah *USA* 63C1
Cheddar *Eng* 7C4
Cheduba I *Burma* 30A2
Cheepie *Aust* 34B1
Chegga *Maur* 48B2
Chegutu *Zim* 51D5
Chehalis *USA* 58B1
Cheju *S Korea* 28B4
Cheju Do, I *S Korea* 28B4
Cheju Haehyŏp, Str *S Korea* 28B4
Chekunda *USSR* 25P4
Chelan,L *USA* 58B1
Cheleken *USSR* 21J8
Chélia, Dj, Mt *Algeria* 16B3
Cheliff, R *Alg* 15C2
Chelkar *USSR* 38D1
Chełm *Pol* 19E2
Chełmno *Pol* 19D2
Chelmsford *Eng* 7E4
Cheltenham *Eng* 7C4
Chelyabinsk *USSR* 24H4
Chelyushin, Mys, C *USSR* 25M2
Chemba *Mozam* 51D5
Chemung, R *USA* 68B1
Chenab, R *India/Pak* 42D2
Chenachen *Alg* 48B2
Chenango, R *USA* 68C1
Cheney *USA* 58C1
Cheney Res *USA* 63C1
Chengde *China* 31D1
Chengdu *China* 31A3
Chengshan Jiao, Pt *China* 31E2
Chengzitan *China* 28A3
Chenxi *China* 31C4
Chen Xian *China* 31C4
Cheo Xian *China* 31D3
Chepén *Peru* 72C5
Chepstow *Wales* 7C4
Chequamegon B *USA* 64A1
Cher, R *France* 14C2
Cheraw *USA* 67C2
Cherbourg *France* 14B2
Cherchell *Alg* 15C2
Cherdyn *USSR* 20K3
Cheremkhovo *USSR* 25M4
Cherepovets *USSR* 20F4
Cherkassy *USSR* 21E6
Cherkessk *USSR* 21G7
Chernigov *USSR* 21E5
Chernobyl *USSR* 19G2
Chernovtsy *USSR* 21D6
Chernushka *USSR* 20K4
Chernyakhovsk *USSR* 20C5
Chernyye Zemli, Region *USSR* 21H6
Cherokee, Iowa *USA* 61D2
Cherokee, Oklahoma *USA* 62C1
Cherokees,L o'the *USA* 63D1
Cherrapunji *India* 43G3
Cherry, I *Solomon Is* 33F2
Cherskiy *USSR* 25S3
Cherskogo, Khrebet, Mts *USSR* 25Q3
Cherven' *USSR* 20D5
Chervonograd *USSR* 19E2
Chesapeake *USA* 65D3
Chesapeake B *USA* 65D3
Chesham *Eng* 7D4
Cheshire *USA* 68D1
Cheshire, County *Eng* 7C3
Chëshskaya Guba, B *USSR* 20H2
Chester, California *USA* 59B2
Chester *Eng* 7C3
Chester, Illinois *USA* 64B3
Chester, Massachusets *USA* 68D1
Chester, Montana *USA* 58D1
Chester, Pennsylvania *USA* 65D3
Chester, S Carolina *USA* 67B2
Chester, Vermont *USA* 68D1
Chester, R *USA* 68B3
Chesterfield *Eng* 7D3
Chesterfield, Îles *Nouvelle Calédonie* 33E2
Chesterfield Inlet *Can* 55J3
Chestertown *USA* 68B3
Chesuncook L *USA* 65F1
Chetumal *Mexico* 70D3
Cheviot *NZ* 35B2
Cheviots, Hills *Eng/Scot* 10C2
Cheyenne *USA* 60C2
Cheyenne, R *USA* 60C2
Cheyenne Wells *USA* 60C3
Chhapra *India* 43E3
Chhātak *Bang* 43G3
Chhatarpur *India* 42D4
Chhindwāra *India* 42D4
Chhukha *Bhutan* 43F3
Chiange *Angola* 51B5
Chiang Kham *Thai* 30C2
Chiang Mai *Thai* 30B2
Chiayi *Taiwan* 31E5
Chiba *Japan* 29E3
Chibia *Angola* 51B5
Chibougamau *Can* 55L4
Chiburi-jima, I *Japan* 28B3
Chibuto *Mozam* 47E1
Chicago *USA* 57E2
Chicago Heights *USA* 64B2
Chichagof I *USA* 54E4
Chichester *Eng* 7D4
Chichibu *Japan* 29C3
Chichi-jima, I *Japan* 26H4
Chickamauga L *USA* 57E3
Chickasawhay, R *USA* 63E2
Chickasha *USA* 56D3
Chicken *USA* 54D3
Chiclayo *Peru* 72B5
Chico *USA* 56A3
Chico, R *Arg* 74C6
Chicoa *Mozam* 51D5
Chicopee *USA* 65E2
Chicoutimi *Can* 55L5
Chicualacuala *Mozam* 51D6
Chidambaram *India* 44B3
Chidley,C *Can* 55M3
Chiefland *USA* 67B3
Chiehn *Lib* 48B4
Chiengi *Zambia* 51C4
Chiers, R *France* 13C3
Chieti *Italy* 16C2
Chifeng *China* 31D1
Chifre, Serra do, Mts *Brazil* 73K7
Chigmit Mts *USA* 54C2
Chigubo *Mozam* 47E1
Chihuahua *Mexico* 70B2
Chihuahua, State *Mexico* 62A3
Chik Ballāpur *India* 44B3
Chikmagalūr *India* 44B3
Chikwawa *Malawi* 51D5
Chi-kyaw *Burma* 30A1
Chilakalūrupet *India* 44C2
Chilaw *Sri Lanka* 44B4
Childers *Aust* 34D1
Childress *USA* 62B2
Chile, Republic 71C6
Chililabombwe *Zambia* 51C5
Chilka L *India* 43F5
Chilko L *Can* 54F4
Chillán *Chile* 74B5
Chillicothe, Missouri *USA* 61E3
Chillicothe, Ohio *USA* 64C3
Chilmari *India* 43G3
Chiloé, Isla de *Chile* 74B6
Chilongozi *Zambia* 51D5
Chiloquin *USA* 58B2
Chilpancingo *Mexico* 70C3
Chiltern Hills, Upland *Eng* 7D4
Chilton *USA* 64B2
Chilumba *Malawi* 51D5
Chi-lung = Keelung
Chilwa, L *Malawi* 51D5
Chimanimani *Zim* 51D5
Chimay *Belg* 13C2
Chimbay *USSR* 24G5
Chimborazo, Mt *Ecuador* 72C4
Chimbote *Peru* 72C5
Chimkent *USSR* 24H5
Chimoio *Mozam* 51D5
China, Republic *Asia* 22F4
China Lake *USA* 66D3
Chinandega *Nic* 70D3
Chinati Peak, Mt *USA* 62B3
Chincha Alta *Peru* 72C6
Chinchilla *Aust* 34D1
Chinde *Mozam* 51D5
Chindo *S Korea* 28A4
Chindwin, R *Burma* 43G4
Chingola *Zambia* 51C5
Chinguar *Angola* 51B5
Chinguetti *Maur* 48A2
Chinhae *S Korea* 28B3
Chinhoyi *Zim* 51D5
Chiniot *Pak* 42C2
Chinju *S Korea* 28B3
Chinko, R *CAR* 50C3
Chino *Japan* 29C3
Chinsali *Zambia* 51D5
Chioggia *Italy* 16C1
Chipata *Zambia* 51D5
Chipinge *Zim* 51D6
Chiplūn *India* 44A2
Chippenham *Eng* 7C4
Chippewa, R *USA* 64A1
Chippewa Falls *USA* 57D2
Chippewa,L *USA* 64A1
Chipping Norton *Eng* 7D4
Chipping Sodbury *Eng* 7C4
Chira, R *Peru* 72B4
Chīrāla *India* 44C2
Chiredzi *Zim* 51D6
Chirfa *Niger* 50B1
Chiricahua Peak, Mt *USA* 59E4
Chiriquí, G de *Panama* 70D4
Chiriquí, Lago de *Panama* 72B2
Chirpan *Bulg* 17F2
Chirripó Grande, Mt *Costa Rica* 72B2
Chirundu *Zim* 51C5
Chisamba *Zambia* 51C5
Chisholm *USA* 61E1
Chishui He, R *China* 31B4
Chisimaio = Kismaayo
Chistopol *USSR* 20H4
Chita *USSR* 26E1
Chitado *Angola* 51B5
Chitembo *Angola* 51B5
Chitose *Japan* 29D2
Chitradurga *India* 44B3
Chitral *Pak* 42C1
Chitré *Panama* 72B2
Chittagong *Bang* 43G4
Chittaurgarh *India* 42C4
Chittoor *India* 44B3
Chiume *Angola* 51C5
Chivilcoy *Arg* 74D4
Chivu *Zim* 51D5
Chizu *Japan* 29B3
Choch'iwŏn *S Korea* 28A3
Chocontá *Colombia* 72D2
Ch'o-do, I *S Korea* 28A4
Choele Choel *Arg* 74C5
Choiseul, I *Solomon Is* 33E1
Choix *Mexico* 70B2
Chojnice *Pol* 19D2
Chokai-san, Mt *Japan* 29D3
Choke Mts *Eth* 50D2
Chokurdakh *USSR* 25Q2
Cholame *USA* 66B3
Cholame Creek, R *USA* 66B3
Cholet *France* 14B2
Choluteca *Honduras* 72A1
Choma *Zambia* 51C5
Chŏmch'ŏn *S Korea* 28A3
Chomo Yummo, Mt *China/India* 43F3
Chomutov *Czech* 18C2
Chona, R *USSR* 25M3
Ch'ŏnan *S Korea* 28B3
Chon Buri *Thai* 30C3
Chonchon *N Korea* 28A2
Chone *Ecuador* 72C4
Chones, Archipiélago de las *Chile* 74B6
Chongdo *S Korea* 28A3
Ch'ŏngjin *N Korea* 28B2
Chŏngju *N Korea* 28B3
Ch'ŏngju *S Korea* 28B3
Chongoroi *Angola* 51B5
Chongpyong *N Korea* 28A3
Chongqing *China* 31B4
Chŏngsŏn *S Korea* 28A3
Chŏngŭp *S Korea* 28B3
Ch'ŏnju *S Korea* 28B3
Cho Oyu, Mt *China/Nepal* 43F3
Chopim, R *Brazil* 75B4
Chorley *Eng* 6C3
Chortkov *USSR* 19F3
Ch'ŏrwŏn *S Korea* 28B3
Chorzow *Pol* 19D2
Chosan *N Korea* 28A2
Chōshi *Japan* 29E3
Choszczno *Pol* 18D2
Chotanāgpur, Region *India* 43E4
Choteau *USA* 58D1
Chott ech Chergui, L *Alg* 48C1
Chott El Hodna, L *Alg* 15C2
Chott Melrhir, L *Alg* 48C1
Chowchilla *USA* 66B2
Choybalsan *Mongolia* 25N5
Christchurch *Eng* 7D4
Christchurch *NZ* 33G5
Christiana *S Africa* 47D2
Christian,C *Can* 55M2
Christianshab *Greenland* 55N3
Christmas I *Indian O* 36G5
Chu *USSR* 24J5
Chu, R *USSR* 24J5
Chubbuck *USA* 58D2
Chubut, R *Arg* 74C6
Chubut, State *Arg* 74C6
Chudovo *USSR* 20E4
Chudskoye Ozero, L *USSR* 24D4
Chugach Mts *USA* 54D3
Chūgoku-sanchi, Mts *Japan* 28B3
Chugwater *USA* 60C2
Chui *Urug* 74F4
Chukai *Malay* 30C5
Chukchagirskoye, Oz, L *USSR* 26G1
Chukotskiy Khrebet, Mts *USSR* 25T3
Chukotskiy Poluostrov, Pen *USSR* 25U3
Chu Lai *Viet* 30D2
Chula Vista *USA* 59C4
Chulman *USSR* 26F1
Chulucanas *Peru* 72B5
Chulumani *Bol* 72E7
Chulym *USSR* 24K4
Chulym, R *USSR* 25K4
Chuma, R *USSR* 25L4
Chumar *India* 42D2
Chumikan *USSR* 25P4
Chumphon *Thai* 30B3
Ch'unch'ŏn *S Korea* 28B3
Chunchura *India* 43F4
Ch'ungju *S Korea* 28B3
Chungking = Chongqing
Ch'ungmu *S Korea* 28A4
Chŭngsan *N Korea* 28B3
Chungwa *N Korea* 28A3
Chunhua *China* 28C2
Chunya *Tanz* 51D4
Chunya, R *USSR* 25M3
Chunyang *China* 28B2
Ch'unyang *S Korea* 28A3
Chupara Pt *Trinidad* 69L1
Chuquicamata *Chile* 74C2
Chur *Switz* 16B1
Churāchāndpur *India* 43G4
Churapcha *USSR* 25P3
Churchill *Can* 55J4
Churchill, R, Labrador *Can* 55M4
Churchill, R, Manitoba *Can* 55J4
Churchill,C *Can* 55J4
Churchill Falls *Can* 55M4
Churchill L *Can* 54H4
Chūru *India* 42C3
Chusovoy *USSR* 20K4
Chuvash ASSR *USSR* 20H4
Chuxiong *China* 26D4
Chu Yang Sin, Mt *Viet* 30D3
Cianorte *Brazil* 75B3
Ciechanow *Pol* 19E2
Ciego de Ávila *Cuba* 70E2
Ciénaga *Colombia* 72D1
Cienfuegos *Cuba* 70D2
Cieszyn *Pol* 19D3
Cieza *Spain* 15B2
Cihanbeyli *Turk* 40B2
Cijara, Embalse de, Res *Spain* 15B2
Cilacap *Indon* 27D7
Cimarron *USA* 62B1
Cimarron, R *USA* 62C1
Cimone, Monte, Mt *Italy* 16C2
Cîmpina *Rom* 17F1
Cinca, R *Spain* 15C1
Cincer, Mt *Yugos* 16D2
Cincinatti *USA* 57E3
Cindrelu, Mt *Rom* 17E1
Cine, R *Turk* 17F3
Ciney *Belg* 13C2
Cinto, Monte, Mt, *Corsica* 16B2
Circle, Alaska *USA* 54D3
Circle, Montana *USA* 60B1
Circleville *USA* 64C3
Cirebon *Indon* 27D7
Cirencester *Eng* 7D4
Cisco *USA* 62C2
Citlaltepetl, Vol *Mexico* 70C3
Citrusdal *S Africa* 47B3
Ciudad Acuña *Mexico* 70B2
Ciudad Bolívar *Ven* 72F2
Ciudad Camargo *Mexico* 70B2
Ciudad del Carmen *Mexico* 70C3
Ciudadela *Spain* 15C2
Ciudad Guayana *Ven* 72F2
Ciudad Guzman *Mexico* 70B3
Ciudad Juárez *Mexico* 70B1
Ciudad Lerdo *Mexico* 56C4
Ciudad Madero *Mexico* 70C2
Ciudad Obregon *Mexico* 70B2
Ciudad Ojeda *Ven* 69C4
Ciudad Piar *Ven* 72F2
Ciudad Real *Spain* 15B2
Ciudad Rodrigo *Spain* 15A1
Ciudad Valles *Mexico* 70C2
Ciudad Victoria *Mexico* 70C2
Civitavecchia *Italy* 16C2
Cizre *Turk* 40D2
Clacton-on-Sea *Eng* 7E4
Claire,L *Can* 54G4
Clairton *USA* 65D2
Clanton *USA* 67A2
Clanwilliam *S Africa* 47B3
Clara *Irish Rep* 9C3
Clare *USA* 64C2
Claremont *USA* 65E2
Claremore *USA* 63C1
Clarence, R *Aust* 34D1
Clarence, R *NZ* 35B2
Clarence Str *Aust* 32C2
Clarendon *USA* 63D2
Clarenville *Can* 55N5
Claresholm *Can* 54G4
Clarinda *USA* 61D2
Clarion, Iowa *USA* 61E2
Clarion, Pennsylvania *USA* 65D2
Clarión, I *Mexico* 70A3
Clarion, R *USA* 65D2
Clarion Fracture Zone *Pacific O* 37M4
Clark Hill Res *USA* 57E3
Clark Mt *USA* 59C3
Clark,Pt *Can* 64C2
Clarksburg *USA* 64C3
Clarksdale *USA* 57D3
Clarkston *USA* 58C1
Clarksville, Arkansas *USA* 63D1
Clarksville, Tennessee *USA* 67A1
Claro, R *Brazil* 75B2
Claromecó *Arg* 74E5
Clay Center *USA* 61D3
Claymore, Oilfield *N Sea* 8E2
Clayton, New Mexico *USA* 56C3
Clayton, New York *USA* 65D2
Clear, C *Irish Rep* 10B3
Clearfield, Pennsylvania *USA* 68A2
Clearfield, Utah *USA* 58D2
Clear L *USA* 59B3
Clear Lake *USA* 61E2
Clear Lake Res *USA* 58B2
Clearmont *USA* 60B2
Clearwater *USA* 57E4
Clearwater Mts *USA* 58C1
Cleburne *USA* 56D3
Cleethorpes *Eng* 7D3
Clements *USA* 66B1
Clermont *Aust* 32D3
Clermont *France* 13B3
Clermont-en-Argonne *France* 13C3
Clermont-Ferrand *France* 14C2
Clervaux *Lux* 13D2
Cleveland, Mississippi *USA* 63D2
Cleveland, Ohio *USA* 57E2
Cleveland, Tennessee *USA* 67B1
Cleveland, Texas *USA* 63C2
Cleveland, County *Eng* 6D2
Clevelândia *Brazil* 75B4
Cleveland,Mt *USA* 58D1
Clew B *Irish Rep* 10B3
Clifton, Arizona *USA* 59E4
Clifton *Aust* 34D1
Clifton, New Jersey *USA* 68C2
Clifton Hills *Aust* 34A1
Clinch, R *USA* 67B1
Clinch Mts *USA* 67B1
Clinton, Arkansas *USA* 63D1
Clinton *Can* 54F4
Clinton, Connecticut *USA* 68D2
Clinton, Iowa *USA* 64A2
Clinton, Massachusetts *USA* 68E1
Clinton, Mississippi *USA* 63D2
Clinton, Missouri *USA* 63D1
Clinton, N Carolina *USA* 67C2
Clinton, New Jersey *USA* 68C2
Clinton, Oklahoma *USA* 62C1
Clinton-Colden L *Can* 54H3
Clipperton I *Pacific O* 70B3
Clitheroe *Eng* 6C3
Cliza *Bol* 72E7
Clogher Hd, Pt *Irish Rep* 9C3
Clonakilty B *Irish Rep* 9B4
Cloncurry *Aust* 32D3
Clones *Irish Rep* 9C3
Clonmel *Irish Rep* 9C3
Cloppenburg *W Germ* 13E1
Cloquet *USA* 57D2
Clorinda *Arg* 75A4
Cloud Peak, Mt *USA* 60B2
Cloverdale *USA* 66A1
Clovis, California *USA* 66C2
Clovis, New Mexico *USA* 56C3
Cluj *Rom* 21C6
Cluj-Napoca *Rom* 17E1
Clutha, R *NZ* 35A3
Clwyd, County *Wales* 7C3
Clwyd, R *Wales* 7C3
Clyde *Can* 55M2

Clyde Cranston

Clyde NZ 35A3
Clyde USA 68B1
Clyde, R Scot 8C4
Clydebank Scot 8C4
Coachella USA 59C4
Coahuila, State Mexico 62B3
Coaldale USA 59C3
Coalinga USA 59B3
Coalville Eng 7D3
Coalville USA 58D2
Coaraci Brazil 75E1
Coari, R Brazil 72F5
Coastal Plain USA 67A2
Coast Mts Can 54E4
Coast Ranges, Mts USA 56A2
Coatbridge Scot 8C4
Coatesville USA 68C3
Coaticook Can 65E1
Coats I Can 55K3
Coats Land, Region Ant 76F1
Coatzacoalcas Mexico 70C3
Cobalt Can 55L5
Cobán Guatemala 70C3
Cobar Aust 32D4
Cobargo Aust 34C3
Cobija Bol 72E6
Cobleskill USA 68C1
Cobourg Can 55L5
Cobourg Pen Aust 32C2
Coburg W Germ 18C2
Coca Ecuador 72C4
Cocalinho Brazil 75B1
Cochabamba Bol 72E7
Cochem W Germ 13D2
Cochin India 44B4
Cochrane, Ontario Can 55K5
Cochrane, Lago Arg/Chile 74B7
Cockburn Aust 34B2
Cockermouth Eng 6C2
Cockeysville USA 68B3
Cockpit Country,The Jamaica 69H1
Cockscomb, Mt S Africa 47C3
Coco, R Honduras/Nic 70D3
Cocoa USA 67B3
Cocobeach Eq Guinea 48C4
Coco Channel Andaman Is/Burma 44E3
Coco, Isla del Costa Rica 53K8
Côcos Brazil 75D1
Cocos B Trinidad 69L1
Cocos Is Indian O 36F5
Cocos Ridge Pacific O 37P4
Cod,C USA 57F2
Codfish I NZ 35A3
Cod I Can 55M4
Codi, Sierra del, Mts Spain 15C1
Codó Brazil 73K4
Cody USA 56C2
Coen Aust 27H8
Coesfeld W Germ 18B2
Coeur d'Alene USA 56B2
Coeur d'Alene L USA 58C1
Coevorden Neth 13D1
Coffeyville USA 56D3
Coff's Harbour Aust 34D2
Cofimvaba S Africa 47D3
Coghinas, Lago del, Sardinia 16B2
Cognac France 14B2
Cohocton USA 68B1
Cohocton, R USA 68B1
Cohoes USA 65E2
Cohuna Aust 34B3
Coiba, Isla Panama 72B2
Coihaique Chile 74B7
Coimbatore India 44B3
Coimbra Port 15A1
Cojimies Ecuador 72B3
Cokeville USA 58D2
Colac Aust 32D4
Colatina Brazil 73K7
Colbeck,C Ant 76F6
Colby USA 14B2
Colchester Eng 7E4
Colchester USA 68D2
Coldstream Scot 8D4
Coldwater USA 64C2
Coleman Can 58D1
Coleman, Michigan USA 64C2
Coleman, Texas USA 62C2
Colenso S Africa 47D2
Coleraine N Ire 9C2
Coleridge,L NZ 35B2
Colesberg S Africa 47D3
Coles, Puerta Peru 72D7
Coleville USA 66C1
Colfax, California USA 59B3
Colfax, Louisiana USA 63D2
Colfax, Washington USA 58C1
Colhué Huapí, Lago Arg 74C7
Colima Mexico 70B3
Coll, I Scot 8B3
Collarenebri Aust 34C1
College Park, Georgia USA 67B2
College Park, Washington DC USA 68B3
College Station USA 63C2
Collie Aust 32A4
Collier B Aust 32B2
Collines de l'Artois, Hills France 13A2
Collines de la Thiérache, Hills France 13B3
Collingwood Can 64C2
Collingwood NZ 35B2
Collins, Mississippi USA 63E2
Collins, New York USA 68A1
Collinson Pen Can 54H2
Collinsville Aust 32D3
Collinsville, Illinois USA 64B3
Collinsville, Oklahoma USA 63C1
Colmar France 14D2
Colne Eng 6C3
Colnett, Cabo, C Mexico 56B3
Cologne W Germ 18B2
Colômbia Brazil 75C3
Colombia USA 65D3
Colombia, Republic S America 72D3
Colombo Sri Lanka 44B4
Colón Arg 74E4
Colon Cuba 70D2
Colón Panama 72C2
Colón, Arch. de = Galapagos Is
Colonia Urug 74E4
Colonia Las Heras Arg 74C7
Colonial Heights USA 65D3
Colonsay, I Scot 8B3
Coloradito Ven 69E5
Colorado, R, Buenos Aires Arg 74D5
Colorado, R, Texas USA 56D3
Colorado, R USA/Mexico 56B3
Colorado, State USA 56C3
Colorado City USA 62B2
Colorado Plat USA 56B3
Colorado Springs USA 56C3
Columbia, Maryland USA 68B3
Columbia, Mississippi USA 63E2
Columbia, Missouri USA 57D3
Columbia, Pennsylvania USA 65D2
Columbia, S Carolina USA 57E3
Columbia, Tennessee USA 57E3
Columbia, R USA 56A2
Columbia Falls USA 58D1
Columbia,Mt Can 54G4
Columbia Plat USA 58C1
Columbine,C S Africa 47B3
Columbretes, Islas Spain 15C2
Columbus, Georgia USA 57E3
Columbus, Indiana USA 64B3
Columbus, Mississippi USA 57E3
Columbus, Montana USA 58E1
Columbus, Nebraska USA 56D2
Columbus, New Mexico USA 62A2
Columbus, Ohio USA 57E2
Columbus, Texas USA 63C3
Columbus, Wisconsin USA 64B2
Colville USA 58C1
Colville, R USA 54C3
Colville,C NZ 35C1
Colville L Can 54F3
Colwyn Bay Wales 7C3
Comanche USA 62C2
Comanche Res USA 66B1
Comandante Ferraz, Base Ant 76G2
Comayagua Honduras 70D3
Combeaufontaine France 13C4
Comber N Ire 9D2
Combermere B Burma 43G5
Comeragh Mts Irish Rep 9C3
Comfort USA 62C2
Comilla Bang 43G4
Comitán Mexico 70C3
Commercy France 13C3
Committee B Can 55K3
Como Italy 16B1
Comodoro Rivadavia Arg 74C7
Como, L di Italy 16B1
Comorin,C India 44B4
Comoros, Is, Republic Indian O 51E5
Compiègne France 14C2
Comprida, Ilha Brazil 75C3
Comunidad Valenciana, Region Spain 15B2
Cona China 43G3
Conakry Guinea 48A4
Concarneau France 14B2
Conceiçao da Barra Brazil 75E2
Conceição do Araguaia Brazil 73J5
Conceiçao do Mato Dentro Brazil 75D2
Concepción Arg 74E4
Concepción Brazil/Par 75A3
Concepción Chile 74B5
Concepción Par 74E2
Concepción del Oro Mexico 70B2
Conception B Namibia 47A1
Conception,Pt USA 56A3
Conchas Brazil 75C3
Conchas L USA 62B1
Conchos, R Mexico 56C4
Concord, California USA 59B3
Concord, New Hampshire USA 57F2
Concord, North Carolina USA 67B1
Concordia Arg 74E4
Concordia USA 56D3
Concrete USA 58B1
Condamine Aust 34D1
Condeuba Brazil 75D1
Condobolin Aust 32D4
Condon USA 58B1
Condroz, Mts Belg 13C2
Conecuh, R USA 67A2
Conesus L USA 68B1
Confuso, R Par 75A3
Congleton Eng 7C3
Congo, R W Africa 46F8
Congo, Republic Africa 46F8
Congo,R = Zaire
Coniston Can 64C1
Conneaut USA 64C2
Connecticut, R USA 65E2
Connecticut, State USA 57F2
Connellsville USA 65D2
Connersville USA 64B3
Conn, Lough, L Irish Rep 10B3
Conoble Aust 34B2
Conrad USA 58D1
Conroe USA 63C2
Conselheiro Lafaiete Brazil 75D3
Consett Eng 6D2
Con Son, Is Viet 30D4
Constanţa Rom 21D7
Constantine Algeria 16B3
Constitución Chile 74B5
Contact USA 58D2
Contas, R Brazil 73K6
Contrexéville France 13C3
Contwoyto L Can 54H3
Conway, Arkansas USA 57D3
Conway, New Hampshire USA 65E2
Conway, South Carolina USA 67C2
Conwy Wales 7C3
Conwy, R Wales 7C3
Coober Pedy Aust 32C3
Cookeville USA 67A1
Cook Inlet, B USA 54C3
Cook Is Pacific O 37L5
Cook,Mt NZ 35B2
Cookstown N Ire 9C2
Cook Str NZ 33G5
Cooktown Aust 32D2
Coolabah Aust 34C2
Cooladdi Aust 34C1
Coolah Aust 34C2
Coolamon Aust 34C2
Coolgardie Aust 32B4
Coolidge USA 59D4
Cooma Aust 34C3
Coonabarabran Aust 34C2
Coonambie Aust 34C2
Coonbah Aust 34B2
Coondapoor India 44A3
Coongoola Aust 34C1
Coonoor India 44B3
Cooper Basin Aust 34B1
Cooper Creek, R Aust 34B1
Cooper's Town Bahamas 67C3
Cooperstown, New York USA 68C1
Cooperstown, North Dakota USA 61D1
Coorong,The Aust 34A3
Cooroy Aust 34D1
Coos B USA 58B2
Coos Bay USA 58B2
Cootamundra Aust 32D4
Cootehill Irish Rep 9C2
Cope USA 60C3
Copenhagen Den 18C1
Copiapó Chile 74B3
Copper Center USA 54D3
Copper Cliff Can 64C1
Copper Harbor USA 64B1
Coppermine Can 54G3
Coppermine, R Can 54G3
Coppermine Pt Can 64C1
Coquilhatville = Mbandaka
Coquimbo Chile 74B3
Corabia Rom 17E2
Coral Gables USA 67B3
Coral Harbour Can 55K3
Coral S Aust/PNG 32E2
Coral Sea Basin Pacific O 36J5
Coral Sea Island Territories Aust 32E2
Corangamite,L Aust 34B3
Corantijn, R Guyana/Surinam 73G3
Corbeil-Essonnes France 13B3
Corbin USA 64C3
Corbridge Eng 6D2
Corby Eng 7D3
Corcoran USA 66C2
Corcovado, Golfo, G Chile 74B6
Corcubíon Spain 15A1
Cordele USA 57E3
Cordillera Cantabrica, Mts Spain 15A1
Cordillera Central, Mts Dom Rep/Haiti 69C3
Cordillera de Caaguazú Par 75A4
Cordillera Isabelia, Mts Nic 70D3
Cordillera Occidental, Mts Colombia 72C2
Cordillera Oriental, Mts Colombia 72C3
Cordillo Downs Aust 34B1
Córdoba Arg 74D4
Córdoba Mexico 70C3
Córdoba Spain 15B2
Córdoba, State Arg 74D4
Cordova USA 54D3
Corfu Greece 17D3
Corfu, I Greece 17D3
Coribe Brazil 75D1
Coricudgy,Mt Aust 34D2
Corigliano Calabro Italy 16D3
Coringa Is Aust 32E2
Corinth Greece 17E3
Corinth, Mississippi USA 57E3
Corinth, New York USA 68D1
Corinth, Gulf of Greece 17E3
Corinto Brazil 73K7
Cork Irish Rep 10B3
Çorlu Turk 40A1
Cornel Fabriciano Brazil 73K7
Cornélio Procópio Brazil 75B3
Corner Brook Can 55N5
Corner Inlet, B Aust 34C3
Cornimont France 13D4
Corning USA 65D2
Corno, Monte, Mt Italy 16C2
Cornwall Can 55L5
Cornwall, County Eng 7B4
Cornwall,C Eng 7B4
Cornwall I Can 54H2
Cornwallis I Can 55J2
Coro Ven 72E1
Coroatá Brazil 73K4
Coroico Bol 72E7
Coromandel Brazil 75C2
Coromandel Coast India 44C3
Coromandel Pen NZ 35C1
Coromandel Range, Mts NZ 35C1
Corona, California USA 66D4
Corona, New Mexico USA 62A2
Coronado, B. de Costa Rica 72B2
Coronation G Can 54G3
Coronel Chile 74B5
Coronel Fabriciano Brazil 75D2
Coronel Oviedo Par 74E3
Coronel Pringles Arg 74D5
Coropuna, Mt Peru 72D7
Corowa Aust 34C3
Corps France 14D3
Corpus Christi USA 56D4
Corpus Christi,L USA 63C3
Corraun Pen Irish Rep 9B3
Corregidor, I Phil 27F5
Corrente, R, Bahia Brazil 75D1
Corrente, R, Goias Brazil 75C1
Corrente, R, Mato Grosso Brazil 75B2
Correntina Brazil 75D1
Corrib, Lough, L Irish Rep 10B3
Corrientes Arg 74E3
Corrientes, State Arg 74E3
Corrientes, Cabo, C Colombia 72C2
Corrientes, Cabo, C Mexico 70B2
Corrigan USA 63D2
Corrigin Aust 32A4
Corryong Aust 34C3
Corse = Corsica
Corsewall Pt Scot 8C4
Corsica, I Medit S 16B2
Corsicana USA 56D3
Cort Adelaer, Kap, C Greenland 55O3
Corte, Corsica 16B2
Cortez USA 56C3
Cortina d'Ampezzo Italy 16C1
Cortland USA 65D2
Çoruh, R Turk 21G7
Çorum Turk 21F7
Corumbá Brazil 73G7
Corumbá, R Brazil 75C2
Corumbaiba Brazil 75C2
Corvallis USA 58B2
Corvo, I Azores 48A1
Corwen Wales 7C3
Cosenza Italy 16D3
Cosmoledo Is Seychelles 51E5
Coso Junction USA 66D2
Costa Blanca, Region Spain 15B2
Costa Brava, Region Spain 15C1
Costa Calída, Region Spain 15B2
Costa de Almería, Region Spain 15B2
Costa de la Luz, Region Spain 15A2
Costa del Sol, Region Spain 15B2
Costa Dorada, Region Spain 15C1
Costa Mesa USA 66D4
Costa Rica, Republic Cent America 70D3
Cotabato Phil 27F6
Cotagaita Bol 72E8
Côte d'Azur, Region France 14D3
Côte D'Ivoire = Ivory Coast
Côte-d'Or, Department France 13C4
Côtes de Meuse, Mts France 13C3
Cothi, R Wales 7B4
Cotonou Benin 48C4
Cotopaxi, Mt Ecuador 72C4
Cotswold Hills, Upland Eng 7C4
Cottage Grove USA 58B2
Cottbus E Germ 18C2
Cottonwood USA 59D4
Cotulla USA 62C3
Coudersport USA 68A2
Coulommiers France 13B3
Coulonge, R Can 65D1
Coulterville USA 66B2
Council USA 54B3
Council Bluffs USA 56D2
Coupar Angus Scot 8D3
Courtrai = Kortrijk
Coutances France 14B2
Coventry Eng 7D3
Covilhã Port 15A1
Covington, Georgia USA 67B2
Covington, Kentucky USA 64C3
Covington, Louisiana USA 63D2
Covington, Virginia USA 65D3
Cowal,L Aust 34C2
Cowangie Aust 34B3
Cowansville Can 65E1
Cowdenbeath Scot 8D3
Cowes Aust 34C3
Cowes Eng 7D4
Cowichan L Can 58B1
Cowlitz, R USA 58B1
Cowra Aust 34C2
Coxim Brazil 73H7
Coxim, R Brazil 75B2
Coxsackie USA 68D1
Cox's Bazar Bang 43G4
Coyote USA 66B2
Cozad USA 60D2
Cozumel, Isla de Mexico 70D2
Cracow Aust 34D1
Cracow Pol 19D2
Cradock S Africa 47D3
Craig USA 56C2
Craigavon N Ire 9C2
Crailsheim W Germ 18C3
Craiova Rom 17E2
Cranberry L USA 65E2
Cranbrook Can 54G5
Crane, Oregon USA 58C2
Crane, Texas USA 62B2
Cranston USA 68E2

De Long Mts Dubā

De Long Mts *USA* 54B3
Deloraine *Aust* 34C4
Deloraine *Can* 54H5
Delray Beach *USA* 67B3
Del Rio *USA* 56C4
Delta *USA* 56B3
Delta Res *USA* 68C1
Dembi Dolo *Eth* 50D3
Demer, R *Belg* 13C2
Demidov *USSR* 19G1
Deming *USA* 62A2
Demirköy *Turk* 17F2
Demopolis *USA* 63E2
Dem'yanskoye *USSR* 24H4
Denain *France* 14C1
Denau *USSR* 39E2
Denbigh *Wales* 7C3
Dendermond *Belg* 13C2
Dendi, Mt *Eth* 50D3
Dèndre, R *Belg* 13B2
Dengkou *China* 31B1
Deng Xian *China* 31C3
Den Haag = The Hague
Denham,Mt *Jamaica* 69H1
Den Helder *Neth* 18A2
Denia *Spain* 15C2
Deniliquin *Aust* 32D4
Denio *USA* 58C2
Denison, Iowa *USA* 61D2
Denison, Texas *USA* 56D3
Denizli *Turk* 21D8
Denmark, Kingdom *Europe* 12F7
Denmark Str *Greenland/Iceland* 76C1
Dennery *St Lucia* 69P2
Dennis Head, Pt *Scot* 8D2
Denpasar *Indon* 27E7
Denton, Maryland *USA* 68C3
Denton, Texas *USA* 56D3
D'Entrecasteaux Is *PNG* 32E1
Denver *USA* 56C3
Déo, R *Cam* 50B3
Déo, R *Cam/Nigeria* 48D4
Deoghar *India* 43F4
Deolāli *India* 42C5
Deoria, District *India* 43M2
Deosai Plain *India* 42D1
Depew *USA* 68A1
Deposit *USA* 68C1
Deputatskiy *USSR* 25Q3
De Queen *USA* 63D2
Dera Bugti *Pak* 42B3
Dera Ghazi Khan *Pak* 42C3
Dera Ismail Khan *Pak* 42C2
Derbent *USSR* 21H7
Derby *Aust* 32B2
Derby, Connecticut *USA* 68D2
Derby *Eng* 7D3
Derby, Kansas *USA* 63C1
Derby, County *Eng* 7D3
Dergachi *USSR* 21F5
Derg, Lough, L *Irish Rep* 10B3
De Ridder *USA* 63D2
Derna = Darnah
Derravaragh, L *Irish Rep* 9C3
Derry *USA* 68E1
Derudeb *Sudan* 50D2
De Rust *S Africa* 47C3
De Ruyter *USA* 68C1
Derwent, R *Eng* 6D3
Derwent Bridge *Aust* 34C4
Desaguadero, R *Bol* 72E7
Descanso *Mexico* 59C4
Deschutes, R *USA* 58B2
Desē *Eth* 50D2
Deseado *Arg* 74C7
Deseado, R *Arg* 74C7
Deserta Grande, I *Madeira* 48A1
Desert Center *USA* 59C4
Desert Peak, Mt *USA* 59D2
Desloge *USA* 63D1
Des Moines, Iowa *USA* 57D2
Des Moines, New Mexico *USA* 62B1
Des Moines, R *USA* 61E2
Desna, R *USSR* 21E5
Desolación, I *Chile* 74B8
Des Plaines *USA* 64B2
Dessau *E Germ* 18C2
Destruction Bay *Can* 54E3
Deta *Rom* 17E1
Dete *Zim* 51C5
Detmold *W Germ* 13E2
Detroit *USA* 57E2
Detroit Lakes *USA* 61D1
Det Udom *Thai* 30D3
Deva *Rom* 17E1
Deventer *Neth* 18B2
Deveron, R *Scot* 8D3
Devikot *India* 42C3
Devil Postpile Nat Mon *USA* 66C2
Devils Den *USA* 66C3
Devils Gate, P *USA* 66C1
Devil's Hole, Region *N Sea* 6E1
Devil's Island = Diable, Isla du
Devils L, N Dakota *USA* 60D1
Devils L, Texas *USA* 62B3
Devils Lake *USA* 56D2
Devizes *Eng* 7D4
Devli *India* 42D3
Devoll, R *Alb* 17E2
Devon, County *Eng* 7B4
Devon I *Can* 55J2
Devonport *Aust* 32D5
Dewangiri *Bhutan* 43G3
Dewās *India* 42D4
Dewetsdorp *S Africa* 47D2
Dewey Res *USA* 57E3
De Witt *USA* 63D2
Dewsbury *Eng* 6D3
Dexter, Missouri *USA* 63E1
Dexter, New Mexico *USA* 62B2
Deyang *China* 31A3
Deyhuk *Iran* 41G3
Dezfūl *Iran* 41E3
Dezhou *China* 31D2
Dezh Shāhpūr *Iran* 41E2
Dhab'i, Wadi edh *Jordan* 45D3
Dhahran *S Arabia* 41F4
Dhākā *Bang* 43G4
Dhali *Cyprus* 45B1
Dhamavaram *India* 44B3
Dhamtari *India* 43E4
Dhanbād *India* 43F4
Dhangarhi *Nepal* 43E3
Dhang Range, Mts *Nepal* 43M1
Dhankuta *Nepal* 43F3
Dhār *India* 42D4
Dharmapuri *India* 44B3
Dharmsāla *India* 42D2
Dhar Oualata, Desert Region *Maur* 48B3
Dhaulagiri, Mt *Nepal* 43E3
Dhenkānāl *India* 43F4
Dhībān *Jordan* 45C3
Dhíkti Óri, Mt *Greece* 17F3
Dhodhekánisos = Dodecanese
Dhomokós *Greece* 17E3
Dhone *India* 44B2
Dhoraji *India* 42C4
Dhrāngadhra *India* 42C4
Dhuburi *India* 43F3
Dhule *India* 42C4
Diable, Isle du *French Guiana* 73H2
Diablo,Mt *USA* 66B2
Diablo Range, Mts *USA* 59B3
Diamantina *Brazil* 73K7
Diamantina, R *Aust* 32D3
Diamantino *Brazil* 75A1
Diamond Harbour *India* 43F4
Diamond Springs *USA* 66B1
Diamondville *USA* 58D2
Dibā *UAE* 41G4
Dibaya *Zaïre* 51C4
Dibrugarh *India* 43G3
Dickens *USA* 62B2
Dickinson *USA* 56C2
Dickson *USA* 67A1
Dickson City *USA* 65D2
Dicle, R *Turk* 21G8
Didwāna *India* 42C3
Die Berg, Mt *S Africa* 47E2
Diébougou *Burkina* 48B3
Dieburg *W Germ* 13E3
Diego Ramírez, Islas *Chile* 74C9
Diégo Suarez = Antsirañana
Diekirch *Lux* 13D3
Diéma *Mali* 48B3
Dien Bien Phu *Viet* 30C1
Diepholz *W Germ* 18B2
Dieppe *France* 14C2
Diest *Belg* 13C2
Dieuze *France* 13D3
Diffa *Niger* 48D3
Digboi *India* 43H3
Digby *Can* 55M5
Digne *France* 14D3
Digoin *France* 14C2
Digos *Phil* 27F6
Digul, R *Indon* 32C1
Dihang, R *India/China* 43G3
Dijlah = Tigris
Dijon *France* 14C2
Dik *Chad* 50B3
Dikhil *Djibouti* 50E2
Dīkirnis *Egypt* 45A3
Diksmuide *Belg* 13B2
Dikson *USSR* 24K2
Dilaram *Afghan* 38E2
Dili *Indon* 27F7
Di Linh *Viet* 30D3
Dillenburg *W Germ* 13E2
Dilley *USA* 62C3
Dilling *Sudan* 50C2
Dillingham *USA* 54C4
Dillon *USA* 56B2
Dillsburg *USA* 68B2
Dilolo *Zaïre* 51C5
Dimāpur *India* 43G3
Dimashq = Damascus
Dimbelenge *Zaïre* 50C4
Dimbokro *Ivory Coast* 48B4
Dimitrovgrad *Bulg* 17F2
Dimitrovgrad *USSR* 20H5
Dimona *Israel* 45C3
Dinaget, I *Phil* 27F5
Dinajpur *India* 43F3
Dinan *France* 14B2
Dinant *Belg* 13C2
Dinar *Turk* 40B2
Dinder, R *Sudan* 50D2
Dindigul *India* 44B3
Dingbian *China* 31B2
Dinggyê *China* 43F3
Dingle *Irish Rep* 10A3
Dingle B *Irish Rep* 10A3
Dinguiraye *Guinea* 48A3
Dingwall *Scot* 8C3
Dingxi *China* 31A2
Ding Xian *China* 31D2
Dinh Lap *Viet* 30D1
Dinosaur *USA* 60B2
Dinuba *USA* 66C2
Diouloulou *Sen* 48A3
Diphu *India* 43G3
Dire Dawa *Eth* 50E3
Dirk Hartog, I *Aust* 32A3
Dirkou *Niger* 50B2
Dirranbandi *Aust* 34C1
Dirri *Somalia* 50E3
Disappointment,C *South Georgia* 74J8
Disappointment,C *USA* 58B1
Disappointment,L *Aust* 32B3
Discovery B *Aust* 34B3
Discovery Reef *S China Sea* 27E5
Discovery Tablemount *Atlantic O* 52J7
Dishna *Egypt* 40B4
Disko *Greenland* 55N3
Disko Bugt, B *Greenland* 55N3
Diskofjord *Greenland* 55N3
Dismal Swamp *USA* 65D3
Disna, R *USSR* 19F1
Disney World *USA* 67B3
Distrito Federal *Brazil* 75C2
Diu *India* 42C4
Divinópolis *Brazil* 73K8
Divnoye *USSR* 21G6
Divriği *Turk* 40C2
Dixon, California *USA* 66B1
Dixon, Illinois *USA* 64B2
Dixon, Montana *USA* 58D1
Dixon Entrance, Sd *Can/USA* 54E4
Diyālā, R *Iraq* 41E3
Diyarbakir *Turk* 21G8
Diz, R *Iran* 41E3
Dja, R *Cam* 50B3
Djado,Plat du *Niger* 50B1
Djambala *Congo* 50B4
Djanet *Alg* 48C2
Djedi, Watercourse *Alg* 48C1
Djelfa *Alg* 48C1
Djéma *CAR* 50C3
Djenné *Mali* 48B3
Djibo *Burkina* 48B3
Djibouti *Djibouti* 50E2
Djibouti, Republic *E Africa* 50E2
Djolu *Zaïre* 50C3
Djougou *Benin* 48C4
Djourab, Erg du, Desert Region *Chad* 50B2
Djugu *Zaïre* 50D3
Djúpivogur *Iceland* 12C2
Djurdjura, Mts *Alg* 15C2
Dmitriya Lapteva, Proliv, Str *USSR* 25P2
Dmitrov *USSR* 20F4
Dnepr, R *USSR* 21E6
Dneprodzerzhinsk *USSR* 21E6
Dnepropetrovsk *USSR* 21F6
Dneprovskaya Nizmennost', Region *USSR* 20D5
Dnestr, R *USSR* 21C6
Dno *USSR* 20E4
Doba *Chad* 50B3
Dobele *USSR* 19E1
Dobo *Indon* 32C1
Doboj *Yugos* 17D2
Dobrush *USSR* 21E5
Doce, R *Brazil* 73K7
Doctor P P Peña *Par* 74D2
Dod *India* 44B3
Doda Betta, Mt *India* 44B3
Dodecanese, Is. *Greece* 17F3
Dodge City *USA* 56C3
Dodgeville *USA* 64A2
Dodoma *Tanz* 50D4
Dog L *Can* 64B1
Dog L *Can* 64C1
Dōgo, I *Japan* 29B3
Dogondoutchi *Niger* 48C3
Doğubayazit *Turk* 41D2
Doha *Qatar* 41F4
Doilungdêqên *China* 43G3
Dokkum *Neth* 13D1
Dokuchayevo, Mys, C *USSR* 29F2
Dolak, I *Indon* 32C1
Doland *USA* 61D2
Dolbeau *Can* 55L5
Dôle *France* 14D2
Dolgellau *Wales* 7C3
Dolgeville *USA* 68C1
Dolgiy, Ostrov, I *USSR* 20K2
Dolo Odo *Eth* 50E3
Dolores *Arg* 74E5
Dolores, R *USA* 60B3
Dolphin and Union Str *Can* 54G3
Dolphin,C *Falkland Is* 74E8
Dom, Mt *Indon* 27G7
Dombarovskiy *USSR* 24G4
Dombås *Nor* 12F6
Dombasle-sur-Meurthe *France* 13D3
Dombóvár *Hung* 17D1
Domfront *France* 14B2
Dominica, I *Caribbean S* 69E3
Dominican Republic *Caribbean S* 69C3
Dominion,C *Can* 55L3
Domino *Can* 55N4
Domna *USSR* 26E1
Domodossola *Italy* 16B1
Domuyo, Vol *Arg* 74B5
Domville,Mt *Aust* 34D1
Don, R *Scot* 8D3
Don, R *USSR* 21G6
Donaghadee *N Ire* 9C2
Donau, R *Austria/W Germ* 18C3
Donaueschingen *W Germ* 13E4
Donauwörth *W Germ* 18C3
Don Benito *Spain* 15A2
Doncaster *Eng* 7D3
Dondo *Angola* 51B4
Dondo *Mozam* 51D5
Dondra Head, C *Sri Lanka* 44C4
Donegal *Irish Rep* 10B3
Donegal, County *Irish Rep* 9C2
Donegal B *Irish Rep* 10B3
Donegal Mts *Irish Rep* 9C2
Donegal Pt *Irish Rep* 9B3
Donetsk *USSR* 21F6
Dong'an *China* 31C4
Dongara *Aust* 32A3
Dongchuan *China* 31A4
Dongfang *China* 30D2
Dongfeng *China* 28B2
Donggala *Indon* 32A1
Donggi Cona, L *China* 26C3
Donggou *China* 28A3
Donghai Dao, I *China* 31C5
Dong He, R *China* 31A1
Dong Hoi *Viet* 30D2
Dong Jiang, R *China* 31C5
Dongliao He, R *China* 28A2
Dongning *China* 28C2
Dongola *Sudan* 50D2
Dongshan *China* 31D5
Dongsha Qundao, I *China* 26E4
Dongsheng *China* 31C2
Dongtai *China* 31E3
Dongting Hu, L *China* 31C4
Dongxing *China* 31B5
Dongzhi *China* 31D3
Doniphan *USA* 63D1
Donji Vakuf *Yugos* 16D2
Dönna, I *Nor* 12G5
Donner P *USA* 59B3
Donnersberg, Mt *W Germ* 13D3
Donnybrook *S Africa* 47D2
Don Pedro Res *USA* 66B2
Doon, Loch, L *Scot* 8C4
Do Qu, R *China* 31A3
Dorbirn *Austria* 14D2
Dorchester *Eng* 7C4
Dorchester,C *Can* 55L3
Dordogne, R *France* 14C2
Dordrecht *Neth* 18A2
Dordrecht *S Africa* 47D3
Dorest Peak, Mt *USA* 68D1
Dori *Burkina* 48B3
Doring, R *S Africa* 47B3
Dorking *Eng* 7D4
Dormans *France* 13B3
Dornbirn *Austria* 18B3
Dornoch *Scot* 8C3
Dornoch Firth, Estuary *Scot* 8D3
Dorotea *Sweden* 12H6
Dorrigo *Aust* 34D2
Dorris *USA* 58B2
Dorset, County *Eng* 7C4
Dorset, Cape *Can* 55L3
Dorsten *W Germ* 13D2
Dortmund *W Germ* 18B2
Doruma *Zaïre* 50C3
Dosatuy *USSR* 25N4
Doshi *Afghan* 42B1
Dos Palos *USA* 66B2
Dosso *Niger* 48C3
Dossor *USSR* 24G5
Dothan *USA* 57E3
Douai *France* 14C1
Douala *Cam* 50A3
Double Island Pt *Aust* 34D1
Double Mountain Fork, R *USA* 62B2
Double Mt *USA* 66C3
Doubs, R *France* 14D2
Doubtful Sd *NZ* 35A3
Douentza *Mali* 48B3
Douglas, Arizona *USA* 56C3
Douglas, Georgia *USA* 67B2
Douglas, I of Man *British Is* 6B2
Douglas *S Africa* 47C2
Douglas, Wyoming *USA* 56C2
Douglas L *USA* 67B1
Doulevant-le-Château *France* 13C2
Doullens *France* 13B2
Dourada, Serra, Mts *Brazil* 75B2
Dourada, Serra, Mts *Brazil* 75C1
Dourados *Brazil* 73H8
Dourados, R *Brazil* 75B3
Dourados, Serra dos, Mts *Brazil* 75B3
Dourdan *France* 13B3
Douro, R *Port* 15A1
Dove, R *Eng* 7D3
Dove Creek *USA* 62A1
Dover, Delaware *USA* 65D3
Dover *Eng* 7E4
Dover, New Hampshire *USA* 65E2
Dover, New Jersey *USA* 68C2
Dover, Ohio *USA* 64C2
Dover,Str of *Eng/France* 7E4
Dovsk *USSR* 19G2
Down, County *N Ire* 9C2
Downingtown *USA* 68C3
Downpatrick *N Ire* 9D2
Downsville *USA* 68C1
Doylestown *USA* 68C2
Dozen, I *Japan* 28B3
Dozois, Réservoir *Can* 65D1
Dr'aa, Watercourse *Mor* 48A2
Dracena *Brazil* 75B3
Drachten *Neth* 13D1
Dracut *USA* 68E1
Draguignan *France* 14D3
Drake *USA* 60C1
Drakensberg, Mt *S Africa* 47D2
Drake Passage *Atlantic O/Pacific O* 52E7
Dráma *Greece* 17E2
Drammen *Nor* 12G7
Drangajökull, Ice cap *Iceland* 12A1
Drava, R *Yugos* 16D1
Drenthe, Province *Neth* 13D1
Dresden *E Germ* 18C2
Dreux *France* 14C2
Drewsey *USA* 58C2
Driftwood *USA* 68A2
Drin, R *Alb* 17E2
Drina, R *Yugos* 17D2
Drissa, R *USSR* 19F1
Drogheda *Irish Rep* 9C3
Drogobych *USSR* 19E3
Droihead Nua *Irish Rep* 9C3
Droitwich *Eng* 7C3
Dromore *N Ire* 9C2
Dronning Maud Land, Region *Ant* 76F12
Drumheller *Can* 54G4
Drummond *USA* 58D1
Drummond I *USA* 64C1
Drummondville *Can* 65E1
Drumochter Pass *Scot* 8C3
Druskininkai *USSR* 19E2
Druzhina *USSR* 25Q3
Dryberry L *Can* 61E1
Dryden *Can* 55J5
Dryden *USA* 68B1
Dry Harbour Mts *Jamaica* 69H1
Duang, I *Burma* 30B3
Duba *S Arabia* 40C4

Dubai **Elmira**

Dubai *UAE* 41G4
Dubawnt, R *Can* 54H3
Dubawnt L *Can* 54H3
Dubbo *Aust* 32D4
Dublin *Irish Rep* 9C3
Dublin *USA* 67B2
Dublin, County *Irish Rep* 9C3
Dubna *USSR* 20F4
Dubno *USSR* 21D5
Dubois, Idaho *USA* 58D2
Du Bois *USA* 65D2
Dubois, Wyoming *USA* 58E2
Dubossary *USSR* 19F3
Dubrovica *USSR* 19F2
Dubrovnik *Yugos* 17D2
Dubuque *USA* 57D2
Duchesne *USA* 59D2
Duck, R *USA* 67A1
Ducor *USA* 66C3
Dudelange *Lux* 13D3
Dudinka *USSR* 24K3
Dudley *Eng* 7C3
Dudypta, R *USSR* 25L2
Duekoué *Ivory Coast* 48B4
Duero, R *Spain* 15B1
Duff Is *Solomon Is* 33F1
Dufftown *Scot* 8D3
Dugi Otok, I *Yugos* 16C2
Duisburg *W Germ* 18B2
Duiwelskloof *S Africa* 47E1
Dūkan *Iraq* 41E3
Duk Faiwil *Sudan* 50D3
Dukhān *Qatar* 41F4
Dukou *China* 31A4
Dulan *China* 26C3
Dulce, Golfo *Costa Rica* 70D4
Dullabchara *India* 43G4
Dülmen *W Germ* 13D2
Duluth *USA* 57D2
Dulverton *Eng* 7C4
Dūmā *Syria* 45D2
Dumai *Indon* 27D6
Dumas *USA* 56C3
Ḑumayr *Syria* 45D2
Dumbarton *Scot* 8C4
Dumer Rbia *Mor* 48B1
Dumfries *Scot* 8D4
Dumfries and Galloway, Region *Scot* 8C4
Dumka *India* 43F4
Dumoine,L *Can* 65D1
Dumont d'Urville, Base *Ant* 76G8
Dumyat *Egypt* 49F1
Dunărea, R *Rom* 17F2
Dunany Pt *Irish Rep* 9C3
Dunav, R *Bulg* 17E2
Dunav, R *Yugos* 17D1
Dunay *USSR* 28C2
Dunayevtsy *USSR* 19F3
Dunbar *Scot* 8D4
Duncan *USA* 63C2
Duncannon *USA* 68B2
Duncan Pass, Chan *Andaman Is* 44E3
Duncansby Head, Pt *Scot* 8D2
Dundalk *Irish Rep* 9C2
Dundalk *USA* 68B3
Dundalk B *Irish Rep* 9C3
Dundas *Greenland* 55M2
Dundas Pen *Can* 54G2
Dundas Str *Aust* 27G8
Dundee *S Africa* 47E2
Dundee *Scot* 8D3
Dundee *USA* 68B1
Dundoo *Aust* 34B1
Dundrum B *N Ire* 9D2
Dundwa Range, Mts *Nepal* 43M2
Dunedin *NZ* 33G5
Dunedin *USA* 67B3
Dunedoo *Aust* 34C2
Dunfermline *Scot* 8D3
Dungannon *N Ire* 9C2
Dūngarpur *India* 42C4
Dungarvan *Irish Rep* 9C3
Dungeness, Pen *Eng* 7E4
Dungog *Aust* 34D2
Dungu *Zaïre* 50C3
Dungunab *Sudan* 50D1
Dunhua *China* 28B2
Dunhuang *China* 26C2
Dunkeld *Scot* 8D3
Dunkerque = Dunkirk
Dunkirk *France* 13B2
Dunkirk *USA* 57F2
Dunkur *Eth* 50D2
Dunkwa *Ghana* 48B4
Dun Laoghaire *Irish Rep* 10B3
Dunmanus *Irish Rep* 9B4
Dunmore *USA* 68C2
Dunmore Town *The Bahamas* 69B1
Dunn *USA* 67C1
Dunnet Head, Pt *Scot* 8D2
Dunning *USA* 60C2
Dunoon *Scot* 8C4
Duns *Scot* 8D4
Dunseith *USA* 60C1
Dunsmuir *USA* 58B2
Dunstan Mts *NZ* 35A2
Dun-sur-Meuse *France* 13C3
Duolun *China* 31D1
Dupree *USA* 60C1
Duque de Braganca *Angola* 51B4
Du Quoin *USA* 64B3
Dura *Israel* 45C3
Durance, R *France* 14D3
Durand *USA* 64A2
Durango *Mexico* 70B2
Durango *Spain* 15B1
Durango *USA* 56C3
Durant *USA* 56D3
Duraykish *Syria* 45D1
Durazno *Urug* 74E4
Durban *S Africa* 47E2
Duren *W Germ* 13D2
Durg *India* 43E4
Durgapur *India* 43F4
Durham *Eng* 6D2
Durham, N Carolina *USA* 57F3
Durham, New Hampshire *USA* 68E1
Durham, County *Eng* 6D2
Durham Downs *Aust* 34B1
Durmitor, Mt *Yugos* 17D2
Durness *Scot* 8C2
Durrës *Alb* 17D2
Durrie *Aust* 34B1
Dursunbey *Turk* 17F3
D'Urville I *NZ* 35B2
Dushak *USSR* 41H2
Dushan *China* 31B4
Dushanbe *USSR* 39E2
Dushore *USA* 68B2
Dusky Sd *NZ* 35A3
Düsseldorf *W Germ* 18B2
Dutton,Mt *USA* 59D3
Duyun *China* 31B4
Düzce *Turk* 40B1
Dvina, R *USSR* 20D4
Dvinskaya Guba, B *USSR* 20F2
Dwārka *India* 42B4
Dworshak Res *USA* 58C1
Dyer,C *Can* 55M3
Dyersburg *USA* 57E3
Dyfed, County *Wales* 7B3
Dykh Tau, Mt *USSR* 21G7
Dynevor Downs *Aust* 34B1
Dzag *Mongolia* 26C2
Dzamïn Üüd *Mongolia* 26E2
Dzamin Üüd *Mongolia* 25M5
Dzaoudzi, Mayotte *Indian O* 51E5
Dzavhan Gol, R *Mongolia* 26C2
Dzerzhinsk *USSR* 20G4
Dzhalinda *USSR* 25O4
Dzhambul *USSR* 24J5
Dzhankoy *USSR* 21E6
Dzhezkazgan *USSR* 38E1
Dzhilikul' *USSR* 42B1
Dzhugdzhur, Khrebet, Mts *USSR* 25P4
Dzhungarskiy Alatau, Mts *USSR* 24J5
Dzierzoniow *Pol* 18D2
Dzungaria Basin *China* 39G1

E

Eabamet L *Can* 55K4
Eagle, Colorado *USA* 60B3
Eagle Butte *USA* 60C1
Eagle L, California *USA* 58B2
Eagle L, Maine *USA* 65F1
Eagle Lake *USA* 65F1
Eagle Mountain L *USA* 63C2
Eagle Pass *USA* 56C4
Eagle Peak, Mt *USA* 62A2
Eagle Plain *Can* 54E3
Earlimart *USA* 59C3
Earn, R *Scot* 8D3
Earn, Loch, L *Scot* 8C3
Earp *USA* 59D4
Earth *USA* 62B2
Easingwold *Eng* 6D2
Easley *USA* 67B2
East Aurora *USA* 65D2
East B *USA* 63E2
Eastbourne *Eng* 7E4
East Branch Delaware, R *USA* 68C1
East C *NZ* 33G4
East Chicago *USA* 64B2
East China Sea *China/Japan* 26F3
East Dereham *Eng* 7E3
Easter I *Pacific O* 37O6
Eastern Ghats, Mts *India* 43E5
East Falkland, Is *Falkland Is* 74E8
Eastgate *USA* 59C3
East Germany, Republic *Europe* 18C2
East Grand Forks *USA* 61D1
East Grinstead *Eng* 7D4
Easthampton *USA* 68D1
East Hampton *USA* 68D2
East Kilbride *Scot* 8C4
East Lake *USA* 64B2
Eastleigh *Eng* 7D4
East Liverpool *USA* 64C2
East London *S Africa* 47D3
Eastmain *Can* 55L4
Eastmain, R *Can* 55L4
Eastman *USA* 67B2
East Moline *USA* 64A2
Easton, Maryland *USA* 65D3
Easton, Pennsylvania *USA* 65D2
East Orange *USA* 68C2
East Pacific Ridge *Pacific O* 37O5
East Pacific Rise *Pacific O* 37O4
East Point *USA* 67B2
Eastport *USA* 65F2
East Retford *Eng* 7D3
East Ridge *USA* 67A1
East St Louis *USA* 57D3
East Siberian S *USSR* 25R2
East Sussex, County *Eng* 7E4
Eastville *USA* 65D3
East Walker, R *USA* 66C1
Eatonton *USA* 67B2
Eau Claire *USA* 61E2
Eauripik, I *Pacific O* 27H6
Ebbw Vale *Wales* 7C4
Ebebiyin *Eq Guinea* 50B3
Ebensburg *USA* 68A2
Eberbach *W Germ* 13E3
Eberswalde *E Germ* 18C2
Ebetsu *Japan* 29D2
Ebian *China* 31A4
Ebinur, L *China* 24K5
Eboli *Italy* 16D2
Ebolowa *Cam* 50B3
Ebro, R *Spain* 15B1
Eceabat *Turk* 40A1
Ech Cheliff *Alg* 15C2
Eching *China* 31D2
Echo *USA* 58C1
Echo Bay *Can* 54G3
Echternach *Lux* 13D3
Echuca *Aust* 34B3
Ecija *Spain* 15A2
Eclipse Sd *Can* 55K2
Ecuador, Republic *S America* 72C4
Ed *Eth* 50E2
Eday, I *Scot* 8D2
Ed Da'ein *Sudan* 50C2
Ed Damer *Sudan* 50D2
Ed Debba *Sudan* 50D2
Eddrachillis B *Scot* 8C2
Ed Dueim *Sudan* 50D2
Eddystone Pt *Aust* 34C4
Ede *Neth* 13C1
Edea *Cam* 50A3
Eden *Aust* 34C3
Eden, Texas *USA* 62C2
Eden, Wyoming *USA* 58E2
Eden, R *Eng* 6C2
Edenburg *S Africa* 47D2
Edendale *NZ* 35A3
Edenderry *Irish Rep* 9C3
Edenkoben *W Germ* 13D3
Eder, R *W Germ* 13E2
Edgeley *USA* 60D1
Edgell I *Can* 55M3
Edgemont *USA* 60C2
Edgeøya, I *Svalbard* 24D2
Edgewood *USA* 68B3
Edh Dhahiriya *Israel* 45C3
Edhessa *Greece* 17E2
Edinburg *USA* 62C3
Edinburgh *Scot* 8D3
Edirne *Turk* 21D7
Edison *USA* 66C3
Edisto, R *USA* 67B2
Edmonds *USA* 58B1
Edmonton *Can* 54G4
Edmore *USA* 60D1
Edmundston *Can* 55M5
Edna *USA* 63C3
Edolo *Italy* 16C1
Edom, Region *Jordan* 45C3
Edremit *Turk* 21D8
Edremit Körfezi, B *Turk* 17F3
Edrengiyn Nuruu, Mts *Mongolia* 26C2
Edson *Can* 54G4
Edward, R *Aust* 34B3
Edward,L *Uganda/Zaïre* 50C4
Edwards *USA* 66D3
Edwards Plat *USA* 56C3
Edwardsville *USA* 64B3
Eeklo *Belg* 13B2
Efate, I *Vanuatu* 33F2
Effingham *USA* 57E3
Egadi,I, *Sicily* 16C3
Egan Range, Mts *USA* 59D3
Egedesminde *Greenland* 55N3
Egegik *USA* 54C4
Eger *Hung* 19E3
Egersund *Nor* 12F7
Eggegebirge, Mts *W Germ* 13E2
Egg Harbor City *USA* 68C3
Eglinton I *Can* 54G2
Egmont,C *NZ* 35B1
Egmont,Mt *NZ* 35B1
Egremont *Eng* 6C2
Eğridir Gölü, L *Turk* 40B2
Egton *Eng* 6D2
Eguas, R *Brazil* 75C1
Egvekinot *USSR* 25T3
Egypt, Republic *Africa* 49E2
Eibar *Spain* 15B1
Eidsvold *Aust* 34D1
Eifel, Region *W Germ* 13D2
Eigg, I *Scot* 8B3
Eight Degree Chan *Indian O* 39F5
Eighty Mile Beach *Aust* 32B2
Eildon,L *Aust* 34C3
Eindhoven *Neth* 18B2
Ein Yahav *Israel* 45C3
Eisenach *E Germ* 18C2
Eisenerz *Austria* 18C3
Eitorf *W Germ* 13D2
Ejin qi *China* 31A1
Ekalaka *USA* 60C1
Eketahuna *NZ* 35C2
Ekibastuz *USSR* 24J4
Ekimchan *USSR* 25P4
Eksjö *Sweden* 12H7
Ekwan, R *Can* 57E1
El Abbâsa *Egypt* 45A3
El'Alamein *Egypt* 40A3
Elands, R *S Africa* 47D2
Elands Berg, Mt *S Africa* 47C3
El'Arîsh *Egypt* 40B3
Elat *Israel* 40B4
El' Atrun Oasis *Sudan* 50C2
Elazığ *Turk* 21F8
El Azraq *Jordan* 40C3
Elba, I *Italy* 16C2
El Balyana *Egypt* 49F2
El Banco *Colombia* 72D2
Elbasan *Alb* 17E2
El Baúl *Ven* 69D5
Elbe, R *E Germ/W Germ* 18C2
El Beqa'a, R *Leb* 45D1
Elberta *USA* 64B2
Elbert,Mt *USA* 56C3
Elberton *USA* 67B2
Elbeuf *France* 14C2
Elbistan *Turk* 40C2
Elbląg *Pol* 19D2
El Bolsón *Arg* 74B6
Elbow Lake *USA* 61D1
Elbrus, Mt *USSR* 21G7
Elburz Mts = Reshteh-ye Alborz
El Cajon *USA* 59C4
El Campo *USA* 63C3
El Centro *USA* 59C4
Elche *Spain* 15B2
El Chocón, Embalse, Res *Arg* 74C5
Elda *Spain* 15B2
El-Dar-El-Beida = Casablanca
El'dikan *USSR* 25P3
El Diviso *Colombia* 72C3
El Djouf, Desert Region *Maur* 48B2
Eldon *USA* 63D1
Eldorado *Arg* 75B4
El Dorado, Arkansas *USA* 57D3
Eldorado *Brazil* 75C3
El Dorado, Kansas *USA* 56D3
El Dorado *Mexico* 70B2
Eldorado, Texas *USA* 62B2
El Dorado *Ven* 72F2
Eldoret *Kenya* 50D3
Eldred *USA* 68A2
Elea, C *Cyprus* 45C1
Eleanor,L *USA* 66C1
Electric Peak, Mt *USA* 58D2
El Eglab, Region *Alg* 48B2
Elephant Butte Res *USA* 62A2
Eleşkirt *Turk* 40D2
El Eulma *Algeria* 16B3
Eleuthera, I *The Bahamas* 57F4
El Faiyûm *Egypt* 40B4
El Farsia, Well *Mor* 48B2
El Fasher *Sudan* 50C2
El Fashn *Egypt* 40B4
El Ferrol *Spain* 15A1
El Firdân *Egypt* 45B3
El Fula *Sudan* 50C2
El Gassi *Alg* 48C1
El Geteina *Sudan* 50D2
El Gezira, Region *Sudan* 50D2
El Ghor, V *Israel/Jordan* 45C3
Elgin, Illinois *USA* 57E2
Elgin, N Dakota *USA* 60C1
Elgin *Scot* 8D3
El Gîza *Egypt* 40B3
El Golea *Alg* 48C1
El Golfo de Santa Clara *Mexico* 59D4
Elgon,Mt *Uganda/Kenya* 50D3
El Goran *Eth* 50E3
El Guettara, Well *Mali* 48B2
El Hamurre *Somalia* 50E3
El Hank, Region *Maur* 48B2
El Haricha, Desert Region *Mali* 48B2
El Harra *Egypt* 40A4
El Harrach *Alg* 15C2
El Hawata *Sudan* 50D2
El'Igma, Desert Region *Egypt* 40B4
Elisabethville = Lubumbashi
Elisenvaara *USSR* 12K6
El Iskandarîya = Alexandria
Elista *USSR* 21G6
Elizabeth *Aust* 32C4
Elizabeth *USA* 65E2
Elizabeth B *Namibia* 47B2
Elizabeth City *USA* 57F3
Elizabeth Is *USA* 68E2
Elizabethton, Tennessee *USA* 67B1
Elizabethtown, Kentucky *USA* 64B3
Elizabethtown, N Carolina *USA* 67C2
Elizabethtown, Pennsylvania *USA* 68B2
El Jadida *Mor* 48B1
El Jafr *Jordan* 40C3
El Jafr, L *Jordan* 45D3
El Jebelein *Sudan* 50D2
El Jem *Tunisia* 48D1
Elk *Pol* 19E2
Elk, R, Maryland/Penn *USA* 68C3
Elk, R, W Virginia *USA* 64C3
Elkader *USA* 61E2
El Kala *Algeria* 16B3
El Kamlin *Sudan* 50D2
El Kef *Tunisia* 48C1
Elk Grove *USA* 66B1
El Khalil = Hebron
El Khânka *Egypt* 45A3
El Khârga *Egypt* 40B4
El-Khârga Oasis *Egypt* 40B4
Elkhart *USA* 64B2
El Khenachich, Desert Region *Mali* 48B2
Elkhorn, R *USA* 61D2
Elkhovo *Bulg* 17F2
Elkins *USA* 65D3
Elkland *USA* 68B2
Elk Mt *USA* 60B2
Elko *Can* 58C1
Elko *USA* 56B2
El Kroub *Algeria* 16B3
Elkton *USA* 68C3
El Kûbri *Egypt* 45B3
El Kuntilla *Egypt* 40B3
El Lagowa *Sudan* 50C2
Ellef Ringnes I *Can* 54H2
Ellendale *USA* 60D1
Ellen,Mt *USA* 59D3
Ellensburg *USA* 56A2
Ellenville *USA* 68C2
Ellesmere I *Can* 55K2
Ellesmere,L *NZ* 35B2
Ellesmere Port *Eng* 7C3
Ellicott City *USA* 68B3
Elliot *S Africa* 47D3
Elliot Lake *Can* 55K5
Ellis *USA* 58D2
El Lisān, Pen *Jordan* 45C3
Ellisras *S Africa* 47D1
Ellsworth *USA* 65F2
Ellsworth Land, Region *Ant* 76F3
El Ma'âdi *Egypt* 45A4
El Maghra, L *Egypt* 49E1
El Mahalla el Kubra *Egypt* 40B3
El Mansûra *Egypt* 40B3
El Manzala *Egypt* 45A3
El Matarîya *Egypt* 45A3
El Matarîya *Egypt* 45B3
Elmer *USA* 68C3
El Merejé, Desert Region *Maur/Mali* 48B3
El Milia *Algeria* 16B3
El Mina *Leb* 45C1
El Minya *Egypt* 40B4
Elmira, California *USA* 66B1

Elmira

Fatehpur

Elmira, New York *USA* 57F2
El Mirage *USA* 59D4
El Moral *Mexico* 62B3
El Mreiti, Well *Maur* 48B2
Elmshorn *W Germ* 18B2
El Muglad *Sudan* 50C2
El Mzereb, Well *Mali* 48B2
El Obeid *Sudan* 50D2
El Oued *Alg* 48C1
Eloy *USA* 59D4
El Paso *USA* 56C3
El Portal *USA* 59B3
El Porvenir *Mexico* 62A2
El Puerto del Sta Maria *Spain* 15A2
El Qâhira = Cairo
El Qantara *Egypt* 45B3
El Quds = Jerusalem
El Quseima *Egypt* 45C3
El Quwetra *Jordan* 45C4
El Reno *USA* 56D3
Elsa *Can* 54E3
El Saff *Egypt* 45A4
El Sâlhîya *Egypt* 45B3
El Salvador, Republic *Cent America* 70D3
El Sauzal *Mexico* 59C4
El Shallûfa *Egypt* 45B3
El Shatt *Egypt* 45B4
El Simbillâwein *Egypt* 45A3
Elsinore L *USA* 66D4
Elsterwerde *E Germ* 18C2
El Sueco *Mexico* 62A3
El Suweis = Suez
El Tabbin *Egypt* 45A4
El Teleno, Mt *Spain* 15A1
Eltham *NZ* 35B1
El Thamad *Egypt* 45C4
El Tigre *Ven* 72F2
El Tîh, Desert Region *Egypt* 40B4
El Tîna *Egypt* 45B3
Eltopia *USA* 58C1
El Tûr *Egypt* 40B4
Elûru *India* 44C2
Elvas *Port* 15A2
Elvira *Brazil* 72D5
Elvira,C *Can* 54H2
Elwood *USA* 64B2
Ely *Eng* 7E3
Ely, Minnesota *USA* 57D2
Ely, Nevada *USA* 56B3
Elyria *USA* 64C2
El Zarqa *Egypt* 45A3
Emâmrûd *Iran* 41G2
Emâm Sâheb *Afghan* 42B1
Eman, R *Sweden* 18D1
Emba *USSR* 21K6
Emba, R *USSR* 21K6
Embalse de Ricobayo, Res = Embalse del Esla
Embarcación *Arg* 74D2
Embarras Portage *Can* 54G4
Embu *Kenya* 50D4
Emden *W Germ* 18B2
Emei *China* 31A4
Emerald *Aust* 32D3
Emeril *Can* 55M4
Emerson *Can* 54J5
Emigrant P *USA* 58C2
Emi Koussi, Mt *Chad* 50B1
Emirdağ *Turk* 40B2
Emmaus *USA* 68C2
Emmen *Neth* 18B2
Emmendingen *W Germ* 13D3
Emmerich *W Germ* 13D2
Emmett *USA* 58C2
Emmitsburg *USA* 68B3
Emory Peak, Mt *USA* 56C4
Empalme *Mexico* 70A2
Empangeni *S Africa* 47E2
Empedrado *Arg* 74E3
Emperor Seamount Chain *Pacific O* 37K2
Emporia, Kansas *USA* 63C1
Emporia, Virginia *USA* 65D3
Emporium *USA* 68A2
Ems, R *W Germ* 18B2
Emu *China* 28B2
Enard B *Scot* 8C2
Encarnación *Par* 74E3
Enchi *Ghana* 48B4
Encinal *USA* 62C3
Encinitas *USA* 66D4
Encruzilhada *Brazil* 75D2
Ende *Indon* 32B1
Enderby Land, Region *Ant* 76G11
Enderlin *USA* 61D1
Endicott *USA* 65D2
Endicott Mts *USA* 54C3
Enfida *Tunisia* 16C3
Enfield *USA* 67C1
Engaño, C *Phil* 27F5
Engaru *Japan* 29D2
En Gedi *Israel* 45C3
Engel's *USSR* 21H5
Enggano, I *Indon* 27D7
England *UK* 10C3
Englee *Can* 55N4
Englehard *USA* 67C1
Englehart *Can* 65D1
Englewood *USA* 60C3
English Channel *Eng/ France* 10C3
Enid *USA* 63C1
Eniwa *Japan* 29D2
Enji, Well *Maur* 48B3
Enkhuizen *Neth* 13C1
Enköping *Sweden* 12H7
Enna, Sicily 16C3
En Nahud *Sudan* 50C2
Ennedi, Desert Region *Chad* 50C2
Ennell, L *Irish Rep* 9C3
Enngonia *Aust* 34C1
Enning *USA* 60C2
Ennis *Irish Rep* 10B3
Ennis, Montana *USA* 58D1
Ennis, Texas *USA* 63C2
Enniscorthy *Irish Rep* 9C3
Enniskillen *N Ire* 9C2
Enn Nâqoûra *Leb* 45C2
Enns, R *Austria* 18C3
Enschede *Neth* 12F8
Ensenada *Mexico* 70A1
Enshi *China* 31B3
Ensisheim *France* 13D4
Entebbe *Uganda* 50D4
Enterprise, Alabama *USA* 67A2
Enterprise, Oregon *USA* 58C1
Entre Ríos, State *Arg* 74E4
Enugu *Nigeria* 48C4
Enz, R *w Germ* 13E3
Enzan *Japan* 29C3
Epernay *France* 14C2
Ephesus *Turk* 40A2
Ephraim *USA* 59D3
Ephrata, Pennsylvania *USA* 68B2
Ephrata, Washington *USA* 58C1
Epi, I *Vanuatu* 33F2
Épinal *France* 14D2
Episkopi *Cyprus* 45B1
Episkopi B *Cyprus* 45B1
Epping *Eng* 7E4
Eppingen *W Germ* 13E3
Epsom *Eng* 7D4
Epukiro *Namibia* 47B1
Eqlid *Iran* 41F3
Equator 46D7
Equatorial Guinea, Republic *W Africa* 48C4
Equinox Mt *USA* 68D1
Equinunk *USA* 68C2
Erbach *W Germ* 13E3
Erbeskopf, Mt *W Germ* 13D3
Erciş *Turk* 41D2
Erciyas Dağları, Mt *Turk* 21F8
Erdaobaihe *China* 28B2
Erdao Jiang, R *China* 28B2
Erdene *Mongolia* 31C1
Erdenet *Mongolia* 26D2
Erdi, Desert Region *Chad* 50C2
Erechim *Brazil* 74F3
Ereğli *Turk* 40B1
Ereğli *Turk* 40B2
Erenhot *China* 26E2
Eresma, R *Spain* 15B1
Erft, R *W Germ* 13D2
Erfurt *E Germ* 18C2
Ergani *Turk* 40C2
Erg Chech, Desert Region *Alg/Mali* 48B2
Erg du Ténéré, Desert Region *Niger* 48D3
Ergene, R *Turk* 40A1
Erg Iguidi, Region *Alg/ Mauritania* 48B2
Ergli *USSR* 19F1
Erguig, R *Chad* 50B2
Ergun', R *USSR/China* 25N4
Ergun Zuoqi *China* 25O4
Eriba *Sudan* 50D2
Eriboll, Loch, Inlet *Scot* 8C2
Ericht, Loch, L *Scot* 8C3
Erie *USA* 57F2
Erie,L *Can/USA* 57E2
Erimo-misaki, C *Japan* 29D2
Eriskay, I *Scot* 8B3
Eritrea, Region *Eth* 50D2
Erkelenz *W Germ* 13D2
Erlangen *W Germ* 18C3
Erling,L *USA* 63D2
Ermelo *S Africa* 47D2
Ernâkulam *India* 44B4
Erne, L *N Ire* 9C2
Erode *India* 44B3
Eromanga *Aust* 34B1
Erongoberg, Mt *Namibia* 47B1
Er Rachida *Mor* 48B1
Er Rahad *Sudan* 50D2
Errego *Mozam* 51D5
Errigal, Mt *Irish Rep* 10B2
Erris Head, Pt *Irish Rep* 10A3
Erromanga, I *Vanuatu* 33F2
Er Roseires *Sudan* 50D2
Er Rummân *Jordan* 45C2
Erskine *USA* 61D1
Erstein *France* 13D3
Erzgebirge, Upland *E Germ* 18C2
Erzincan *Turk* 21F8
Erzurum *Turk* 21G8
Esan-misaki, C *Japan* 29D2
Esashi *Japan* 29D2
Esbjerg *Den* 18B1
Escalante *USA* 59D3
Escalón *Mexico* 56C4
Escanaba *USA* 57E2
Escárcega *Mexico* 70C3
Esch *Lux* 13C3
Escondido *USA* 59C4
Escuinapa *Mexico* 70B2
Escuintla *Guatemala* 70C3
Eséka *Cam* 50B3
Esens *W Germ* 13D1
Esera, R *Spain* 15C1
Eşfahān *Iran* 41F3
Eshowe *S Africa* 47E2
Esh Sharā, Upland *Jordan* 45C3
Esk, R *Scot* 8D4
Eskdale *NZ* 35C1
Eskifjörður *Iceland* 12C1
Eskilstuna *Sweden* 12H7
Eskimo Lakes *Can* 54E3
Eskimo Point *Can* 55J3
Eskişehir *Turk* 21E8
Esla, R *Spain* 15A1
Esla, Embalse del, Res *Spain* 15A1
Esmeralda *Cuba* 69B2
Esmeralda, I *Chile* 74A7
Esmeraldas *Ecuador* 72C3
Espalion *France* 14C3
Espanola *Can* 64C1
Espanola *USA* 62A1
Esperance *Aust* 32B4
Esperanza, Base *Ant* 76G2
Espichel, Cabo, C *Port* 15A2
Espinhaço, Serra do, Mts *Brazil* 75D2
Espírito Santo, State *Brazil* 75D2
Espiritu Santo, I *Vanuatu* 33F2
Espungabera *Mozam* 51D6
Esquel *Arg* 74B6
Esquimalt *Can* 58B1
Es Samrā *Jordan* 45D2
Essaouira *Mor* 48B1
Essen *W Germ* 18B2
Essequibo, R *Guyana* 73G3
Essex, County *Eng* 7E4
Essexville *USA* 64C2
Esslingen *W Germ* 18B3
Essonne, Department *France* 13B3
Essoyes *France* 13C3
Estados, Isla de los *Arg* 74D8
Estância *Brazil* 73L6
Estcourt *S Africa* 47D2
Esteí *Nic* 72A1
Esternay *France* 13B3
Estero B *USA* 66B3
Esteros *Par* 74D2
Estes Park *USA* 60B2
Estevan *Can* 54H5
Estherville *USA* 61E2
Estill *USA* 67B2
Estissac *France* 13B3
Estonian SSR, Republic *USSR* 20C4
Estrella, R *USA* 66B3
Estremoz *Port* 15A2
Esztergom *Hung* 19D3
Etadunna *Aust* 34A1
Etah *Can* 55L2
Etah *India* 43K2
Etam *France* 13C3
Étampes *France* 14C2
Etamunbanie,L *Aust* 34A1
Etāwah *India* 42D3
Ethiopia, Republic *Africa* 50D3
Etive, Loch, Inlet *Scot* 8C3
Etna, Vol, Sicily 16C3
Etosha Nat Pk *Namibia* 51B5
Etosha Pan, Salt L *Namibia* 51B5
Etowah, R *USA* 67B2
Ettelbruck *Lux* 13C3
Eua, I *Tonga* 33H3
Euabalong *Aust* 34C2
Euboea, I *Greece* 17E3
Euclid *USA* 64C2
Eucumbene,L *Aust* 34C3
Eudunda *Aust* 34A2
Eufala L *USA* 63C1
Eufaula *USA* 67A2
Eugene *USA* 56A2
Eugenia, Punta, Pt *Mexico* 70A2
Eulo *Aust* 34C1
Eunice, Louisiana *USA* 63D2
Eunice, New Mexico *USA* 62B2
Eupen *W Germ* 13D2
Euphrates, R *Iraq/Syria* 40D3
Eupora *USA* 63E2
Eure, R *France* 14C2
Eureka, California *USA* 58B2
Eureka *Can* 55K1
Eureka, Montana *USA* 58C1
Eureka, Nevada *USA* 56B3
Eureka, S Dakota *USA* 60D1
Eureka, Utah *USA* 59D3
Eureka Sd *Can* 55K2
Eureka V *USA* 66D2
Euroa *Aust* 34C3
Eurombah, R *Aust* 34C1
Europa, I *Mozam Chan* 51E6
Europoort *Neth* 13C2
Euskirchen *W Germ* 18B2
Eutaw *USA* 63E2
Evans,C *Can* 55K1
Evans,L *Can* 55L4
Evans,Mt, Colorado *USA* 60B3
Evans,Mt, Montana *USA* 58D1
Evans Str *Can* 55K3
Evanston, Illinois *USA* 64B2
Evanston, Wyoming *USA* 56B2
Evansville, Indiana *USA* 57E3
Evansville, Wyoming *USA* 60B2
Evaton *S Africa* 47D2
Everard,L *Aust* 32C4
Everest,Mt *China/Nepal* 39G3
Everett, Pennsylvania *USA* 68A2
Everett, Washington *USA* 56A2
Everett,Mt *USA* 68D1
Everglades,The, Swamp *USA* 57E4
Evergreen *USA* 67A2
Evesham *Eng* 7D3
Evinayong *Eq Guinea* 50B3
Evje *Nor* 12F7
Évora *Port* 15A2
Evoron, Oz, L *USSR* 26G1
Evreux *France* 14C2
Évvoia = Euboea
Ewe, Loch, Inlet *Scot* 8C3
Ewo *Congo* 50B4
Excelsior Mt *USA* 66C1
Excelsior Mts *USA* 66C1
Excelsior Springs *USA* 61E3
Exe, R *Eng* 7C4
Exeter, California *USA* 59C3
Exeter *Eng* 7C4
Exeter, New Hampshire *USA* 65E2
Exmoor *Eng* 7C4
Exmouth *Eng* 7C4
Extremadura, Region *Spain* 15A2
Exuma Sd *The Bahamas* 70E2
Eyasi, L *Tanz* 50D4
Eyemouth *Scot* 8D4
Eyl *Somalia* 50E3
Eyre *Aust* 32B4
Eyre Creek, R *Aust* 32C3
Eyre,L *Aust* 32C3
Eyre Pen *Aust* 32C4
Ezine *Turk* 17F3

F

Faber L *Can* 54G3
Fåborg *Den* 12F7
Fabriano *Italy* 16C2
Fachi *Niger* 50B2
Fada *Chad* 50C2
Fada N'Gourma *Burkina* 48C3
Faddeyevskiy, Ostrov, I *USSR* 25Q2
Faenza *Italy* 16C2
Færingehavn *Greenland* 55N3
Faerøerne = Faeroes
Faeroes, Is *N Atlantic Oc* 12D3
Fafa, R *CAR* 50B3
Fafan, R *Eth* 50E3
Făgăras *Rom* 17E1
Fagnes, Region *Belg* 13C2
Faguibine,L *Mali* 48B3
Fahūd *Oman* 41G5
Faial, I *Azores* 48A1
Fairacres *USA* 62A2
Fairbanks *USA* 54D3
Fairbault *USA* 55J5
Fairborn *USA* 64C3
Fairbury *USA* 56D2
Fairfax *USA* 68B3
Fairfield, California *USA* 59B3
Fairfield, Connecticut *USA* 68D2
Fairfield, Idaho *USA* 58D2
Fairfield, Montana *USA* 58D1
Fairfield, Ohio *USA* 64C3
Fair Head, Pt *N Ire* 9C2
Fair Isle, I *Scot* 10C2
Fairlie *NZ* 35B2
Fairmont, Minnesota *USA* 61E2
Fairmont, W Virginia *USA* 64C3
Fairport *USA* 68B1
Fairview *USA* 62C1
Fairweather,Mt *USA* 54E4
Fais, I *Pacific O* 27H6
Faisalabad *Pak* 42C2
Faith *USA* 60C1
Faither,The, Pen *Scot* 8E1
Fakaofo, I *Tokelau Is* 33H1
Fakenham *Eng* 7E3
Fakfak *Indon* 32C1
Faku *China* 28A2
Falam *Burma* 43G4
Falcon Res *Mexico/USA* 70C2
Falémé, R *Mali/Sen/ Guinea* 48A3
Falfurrias *USA* 62C3
Falkenberg *Sweden* 12G7
Falkirk *Scot* 8D4
Falkland Is, Dependency *S Atlantic* 74D8
Falkland Sd *Falkland Is* 74E8
Falköping *Sweden* 12G7
Fallbrook *USA* 66D4
Fallon *USA* 56B3
Fall River *USA* 65E2
Fall River P *USA* 60B2
Falls City *USA* 61D2
Falmouth *Eng* 7B4
Falmouth *Jamaica* 69H1
Falmouth, Maine *USA* 65E2
Falmouth, Massachusetts *USA* 68E2
Falmouth Bay *Eng* 7B4
False B *S Africa* 47B3
Falso,C *Mexico* 70A2
Falster, I *Den* 18C2
Fălticeni *Rom* 17F1
Falun *Sweden* 12H6
Famagusta *Cyprus* 40B2
Famagusta B *Cyprus* 45B1
Famenne, Region *Belg* 13C2
Famoso *USA* 66C3
Fang *Thai* 30B2
Fangak *Sudan* 50D3
Fangliao *Taiwan* 31E5
Fannich, L *Scot* 8C3
Fano *Italy* 16C2
Fâqûs *Egypt* 45A3
Faraday, Base *Ant* 76G3
Faradje *Zaïre* 50C3
Farafangana *Madag* 51E6
Farafra Oasis *Egypt* 49E2
Farah *Afghan* 38E2
Farallon de Medinilla, I *Pacific O* 27H5
Farallon de Pajaros, I *Marianas* 26H4
Faranah *Guinea* 48A3
Farasan Is *S Arabia* 50E2
Faraulep, I *Pacific O* 27H6
Fareham *Eng* 7D4
Farewell,C *Greenland* 55O4
Farewell,C *NZ* 33G5
Farewell Spit, Pt *NZ* 35B2
Fargo *USA* 56D2
Fari'a, R *Israel* 45C2
Faribault *USA* 57D2
Faridpur *Bang* 43F4
Farimān *Iran* 41G2
Fâriskûr *Egypt* 45A3
Farmington, Maine *USA* 65E2
Farmington, Missouri *USA* 63D1
Farmington, New Hampshire *USA* 68E1
Farmington, New Mexico *USA* 56C3
Farmington, Utah *USA* 58D2
Farmington Res *USA* 66B2
Farne Deep *N Sea* 6D2
Faro *Port* 15A2
Fårö, I *Sweden* 12H7
Farquhar Is *Indian O* 46K9
Farrar, R *Scot* 8C3
Farrell *USA* 64C2
Farrukhabad, District *India* 43K2
Fársala *Greece* 17E3
Fartura, Serra de, Mts *Brazil* 75B4
Farwell *USA* 62B2
Fasā *Iran* 41F4
Fastov *USSR* 21D5
Fatehgarh *India* 43K2
Fatehpur *India* 43E3

Fatima du Sul Fulton

Fatima du Sul *Brazil* 73H7
Fauquier *Can* 58C1
Fauresmith *S Africa* 47D2
Fauske *Nor* 12H5
Faversham *Eng* 7E4
Fawn, R *Can* 55K4
Fax, R *Sweden* 12H6
Faxaflói, B *Iceland* 12A2
Faya *Chad* 50B2
Fayette *USA* 63E2
Fayetteville, Arkansas *USA* 57D3
Fayetteville, N Carolina *USA* 57F3
Fayetteville, Tennessee *USA* 67A1
Fâyid *Egypt* 45B3
Faylakah, I *Kuwait* 41E4
Fäzilka *India* 42C2
Fdérik *Maur* 48A2
Fear,C *USA* 57F3
Feather, R *USA* 66B1
Feather Middle Fork, R *USA* 59B3
Fécamp *France* 14C2
Fehmarn, I *W Germ* 18C2
Feia, Lagoa *Brazil* 75D3
Feijó *Brazil* 72D5
Feilai Xai Bei Jiang, R *China* 31C5
Feilding *NZ* 35C2
Feira *Zambia* 51D5
Feira de Santan *Brazil* 73L6
Feke *Turk* 40C2
Feldberg, Mt *W Germ* 13D4
Feldkirch *Austria* 18B3
Felixstowe *Eng* 10D3
Femund, L *Nor* 12G6
Fengcheng *China* 28A2
Fengdu *China* 31B4
Fengjie *China* 31B3
Fengning *China* 31D1
Feng Xian *China* 31B3
Fengzhen *China* 31C1
Fen He, R *China* 31C2
Fenoarivo Atsinanana *Madag* 51E5
Feodosiya *USSR* 21F7
Ferdow *Iran* 41G3
Fère-Champenoise *France* 13B3
Fergana *USSR* 39F1
Fergus Falls *USA* 61D1
Ferkessedougou *Ivory Coast* 48B4
Fermanagh, County *N Ire* 9C2
Fernandina Beach *USA* 67B2
Fernando de Noronha, Isla *Brazil* 73M4
Fernandópolis *Brazil* 75B3
Fernando Poo, I = Bioko
Ferndale *USA* 58B1
Fernie *Can* 58C1
Fernley *USA* 59C3
Ferrara *Italy* 16C2
Ferrat, Cap, C *Alg* 15B2
Ferreñafe *Peru* 72C5
Ferriday *USA* 63D2
Ferrières *France* 13B3
Fès *Mor* 48B1
Festus *USA* 63D1
Feteşti *Rom* 17F2
Fethard *Irish Rep* 9C3
Fethiye *Turk* 40A2
Fetisovo *USSR* 21J7
Fetlar, I *Scot* 8E1
Feuilles, Rivière aux, R *Can* 55L4
Feyzabad *Afghan* 24J6
Ffestiniog *Wales* 7C3
Fianarantsoa *Madag* 51E6
Fiche *Eth* 50D3
Ficksburg *S Africa* 47D2
Fidan, Wadi *Jordan* 45C3
Fier *Alb* 17D2
Fife, Region *Scot* 8D3
Fife Ness, Pen *Scot* 8D3
Figeac *France* 14C3
Figueira da Foz *Port* 15A1
Figueras *Spain* 15C1
Figuig *Mor* 48B1
Fiji, Is *Pacific O* 33G2
Filabres, Sierra de los, Mts *Spain* 15B2
Filadelfia *Par* 73G8
Filey *Eng* 6D2
Filiaşi *Rom* 17E2
Filiatrá *Greece* 17E3
Filicudi, I *Italy* 16C3
Fillmore, California *USA* 59C4
Fillmore, Utah *USA* 59D3
Findhorn, R *Scot* 8C3
Findlay *USA* 57E2
Finger Lakes *USA* 65D2
Fingoè *Mozam* 51D5
Finike *Turk* 21E8
Finisterre, Cabo, C *Spain* 15A1
Finke, R *Aust* 32C3
Finland, Republic *N Europe* 20C3
Finland,G of *N Europe* 12J7
Finlay, R *Can* 54F4
Finlay Forks *Can* 54F4
Finley *Aust* 34C3
Finn, R *Irish Rep* 9C2
Finnsnes *Nor* 12H5
Finschhafen *PNG* 27H7
Finspång *Sweden* 12H7
Finsterwalde *E Germ* 18C2
Fintona *N Ire* 9C2
Fiordland Nat Pk *NZ* 35A3
Fiq *Syria* 45C2
Firat, R *Turk* 21F8
Firebaugh *USA* 66B2
Firenze = Florence
Firozābād *India* 42D3
Firozpur *India* 42C2
Firth of Clyde, Estuary *Scot* 8C4
Firth of Forth, Estuary *Scot* 8D3
Firth of Lorn, Estuary *Scot* 8B3
Firth of Tay, Estuary *Scot* 10C2
Firūzābād *Iran* 41F4
Fish, R *Namibia* 47B2
Fish, R *S Africa* 47C3
Fish Camp *USA* 66C2
Fishers I *USA* 68D2
Fisher Str *Can* 55K3
Fishguard *Wales* 7B4
Fiskenæsset *Greenland* 55N3
Fismes *France* 13B3
Fitchburg *USA* 65E2
Fitful Head, Pt *Scot* 8E2
Fitzgerald *USA* 67B2
Fitzroy, R *Aust* 32B2
Fitzroy Crossing *Aust* 32B2
Fitzwilliam I *Can* 64C1
Fiume = Rijeka
Fizi *Zaïre* 50C4
Flagstaff *S Africa* 47D3
Flagstaff *USA* 56B3
Flagstaff L *USA* 65E1
Flamborough Head, C *Eng* 6D2
Flaming Gorge Res *USA* 56C2
Flamingo, Teluk, B *Indon* 27G7
Flandres, Plaine des *Belg/France* 13B2
Flannan Isles *Scot* 8B2
Flathead L *USA* 56B2
Flat River *USA* 63D1
Flattery,C *Aust* 27H8
Flattery,C *USA* 56A2
Fleetwood *Eng* 6C3
Flekkefjord *Nor* 12F7
Fleming Deep *Pacific O* 26H4
Flemington *USA* 68C2
Flensburg *W Germ* 18B2
Flinders, I *Aust* 32C4
Flinders, I *Aust* 32D5
Flinders, R *Aust* 32D2
Flinders Range, Mts *Aust* 32C4
Flin Flon *Can* 54H4
Flint *USA* 57E2
Flint *Wales* 7C3
Flint, R *USA* 57E3
Flixecourt *France* 13B2
Floodwood *USA* 64A1
Florala *USA* 67A2
Florence, Alabama *USA* 57E3
Florence, Arizona *USA* 59D4
Florence, Colorado *USA* 60B3
Florence *Italy* 16C2
Florence, Kansas *USA* 63C1
Florence, Oregon *USA* 58B2
Florence, S Carolina *USA* 57F3
Florence L *USA* 66C2
Florencia *Colombia* 72C3
Florentine Ameghino, Embalse, Res *Arg* 74C6
Florenville *Belg* 13C3
Flores *Guatemala* 70D3
Flores, I *Azores* 48A1
Flores, I *Indon* 32B1
Flores S *Indon* 27E7
Floriano *Brazil* 73K5
Florianópolis *Brazil* 74G3
Florida *Urug* 74E4
Florida, State *USA* 70D2
Florida B *USA* 67B3
Florida City *USA* 67B3
Florida Is *Solomon Is* 33E1
Florida Keys, Is *USA* 57E4
Florida,Strs of *USA* 57E4
Flórina *Greece* 17E2
Florø *Nor* 12F6
Floydada *USA* 62B2
Fly, R *PNG* 32D1
Focşani *Rom* 17F1
Foggia *Italy* 16D2
Fogo, I *Cape Verde* 48A4
Foix *France* 14C3
Foleyet *Can* 64C1
Foley I *Can* 55L3
Foligno *Italy* 16C2
Folkestone *Eng* 7E4
Folkston *USA* 67B2
Follonica *Italy* 16C2
Folsom *USA* 66B1
Fonda *USA* 68C1
Fond-du-Lac *Can* 54H4
Fond du Lac *USA* 57E2
Fonseca, G de *Honduras* 70D3
Fontainbleau *France* 14C2
Fontenay-le-Comte *France* 14B2
Fonyód *Hung* 17D1
Foochow = Fuzhou
Foraker, Mt *USA* 54C3
Forbach *France* 13D3
Forbes *Aust* 34C2
Forcados *Nigeria* 48C4
Ford City *USA* 66C3
Førde *Nor* 12F6
Fordingbridge *Eng* 7D4
Fords Bridge *Aust* 34C1
Fordyce *USA* 63D2
Forécariah *Guinea* 48A4
Forel,Mt *Greenland* 55P3
Foremost *Can* 58D1
Forest *Can* 64C2
Forest *USA* 63E2
Forest City, Iowa *USA* 61E2
Forest City, Pennsylvania *USA* 68C2
Forest of Dean *Eng* 7C4
Forest Park *USA* 67B2
Forestville *USA* 66A1
Forêt d'Othe *France* 13B3
Forfar *Scot* 8D3
Forgan *USA* 62B1
Forks *USA* 58B1
Forlì *Italy* 16C2
Formby *Eng* 7C3
Formentera, I *Spain* 15C2
Formentor, Cabo, C *Spain* 15C1
Formia *Italy* 16C2
Formigas, I *Azores* 48A1
Formosa = Taiwan
Formosa *Arg* 74E3
Formosa *Brazil* 73J7
Formosa, State *Arg* 74D2
Formosa Channel = Taiwan Str
Formosa, Serra, Mts *Brazil* 73G6
Formoso *Brazil* 75C1
Formoso, R *Brazil* 75C1
Forres *Scot* 8D3
Forrest *Aust* 32B4
Forrest City *USA* 57D3
Forsayth *Aust* 32D2
Forssa *Fin* 12J6
Forster *Aust* 34D2
Forsyth, Missouri *USA* 63D1
Forsyth, Montana *USA* 60B1
Fort Abbas *Pak* 42C3
Fort Albany *Can* 55K4
Fortaleza *Brazil* 73L4
Fort Augustus *Scot* 8C3
Fort Beaufort *S Africa* 47D3
Fort Benton *USA* 58D1
Fort Bragg *USA* 59B3
Fort Cobb Res *USA* 62C1
Fort Collins *USA* 56C2
Fort Coulonge *Can* 65D1
Fort Davis *USA* 62B2
Fort-de-France *Martinique* 69E4
Fort Deposit *USA* 67A2
Fortescue, R *Aust* 32A3
Fort Frances *Can* 55J5
Fort Frances *Can* 57D2
Fort Franklin *Can* 54F3
Fort George *Can* 55L4
Fort Good Hope *Can* 54F3
Fort Grey *Aust* 34B1
Forth, R *Scot* 8C3
Fort Hancock *USA* 62A2
Fort Hope *Can* 55K4
Forties, Oilfield *N Sea* 8F3
Fort Kent *USA* 65F1
Fort Lallemand *Alg* 48C1
Fort Lamy = Ndjamena
Fort Laramie *USA* 60C2
Fort Lauderdale *USA* 57E4
Fort Liard *Can* 54F3
Fort Mackay *Can* 54G4
Fort Macleod *Can* 54G5
Fort McMurray *Can* 54G4
Fort McPherson *Can* 54E3
Fort Madison *USA* 64A2
Fort Morgan *USA* 56C2
Fort Myers *USA* 57E4
Fort Nelson *Can* 54F4
Fort Norman *Can* 54F3
Fort Payne *USA* 67A2
Fort Peck *USA* 60B1
Fort Peck Res *USA* 56C2
Fort Pierce *USA* 57E4
Fort Pierre *USA* 60C2
Fort Plain *USA* 68C1
Fort Providence *Can* 54G3
Fort Resolution *Can* 54G3
Fort Rousset *Congo* 50B4
Fort Rupert *Can* 55L4
Fort St James *Can* 54F4
Fort St John *Can* 54F4
Fort Scott *USA* 63D1
Fort Selkirk *Can* 54E3
Fort Severn *Can* 55K4
Fort Shevchenko *USSR* 21J7
Fort Simpson *Can* 54F3
Fort Smith *Can* 54G3
Fort Smith *USA* 57D3
Fort Smith, Region *Can* 54F3
Fort Stockton *USA* 56C3
Fort Sumner *USA* 62B2
Fort Supply *USA* 62C1
Fortuna, California *USA* 58B2
Fortuna, N Dakota *USA* 60C1
Fort Vermilion *Can* 54G4
Fort Walton Beach *USA* 67A2
Fort Wayne *USA* 57E2
Fort William *Scot* 8C3
Fort Wingate *USA* 62A1
Fort Worth *USA* 56D3
Fort Yukon *USA* 54D3
Foshan *China* 31C5
Fosheim Pen *Can* 55K2
Fosston *USA* 61D1
Fougamou *Gabon* 50B4
Fougères *France* 14B2
Foula, I *Scot* 8D1
Foulness I *Eng* 7E4
Foulwind,C *NZ* 35B2
Foumban *Cam* 50B3
Foum el Alba, Region *Mali* 48B2
Fourmies *France* 14C1
Foúrnoi, I *Greece* 17F3
Fouta Djallon, Mts *Guinea* 48A3
Foveaux Str *NZ* 33F5
Fowey *Eng* 7B4
Fowler *USA* 62B1
Fox, R *USA* 64B2
Foxe Basin, G *Can* 55K3
Foxe Chan *Can* 55K3
Foxe Pen *Can* 55L3
Foxpark *USA* 60B2
Foxton *NZ* 35C2
Foyle, Lough, Estuary *Irish Rep/N Ire* 10B2
Foz do Cuene *Angola* 51B5
Foz do Iguaçu *Brazil* 74F3
Frackville *USA* 68B2
Fraga *Spain* 15C1
Framingham *USA* 68E1
Franca *Brazil* 73J8
France, Republic *Europe* 14C2
France Ville *Gabon* 50B4
Franche Comté, Region *France* 14D2
Francistown *Botswana* 47D1
Francs Peak, Mt *USA* 58E2
Frankenberg *W Germ* 13E2
Frankfort, Indiana *USA* 64B2
Frankfort, Kentucky *USA* 57E3
Frankfort, New York *USA* 68C1
Frankfort *S Africa* 47D2
Frankfurt am Main *W Germ* 18B2
Frankfurt an-der-Oder *E Germ* 18C2
Fränkischer Alb, Upland *W Germ* 18C3
Franklin, Idaho *USA* 58D2
Franklin, Indiana *USA* 64B3
Franklin, Louisiana *USA* 63D3
Franklin, Massachusetts *USA* 68E1
Franklin, N Carolina *USA* 67B1
Franklin, New Hampshire *USA* 68E1
Franklin, New Jersey *USA* 68C2
Franklin, Pennsylvania *USA* 65D2
Franklin, Tennessee *USA* 67A1
Franklin, Virginia *USA* 65D3
Franklin B *Can* 54F2
Franklin D Roosevelt, L *USA* 58C1
Franklin Mts *Can* 54F3
Franklin Str *Can* 54J2
Franklinville *USA* 68A1
Franz Josef Glacier *NZ* 35B2
Franz-Josef-Land = Zemlya Frantsa Josifa
Fraser, R *Can* 54F5
Fraserburg *S Africa* 47C3
Fraserburgh *Scot* 8D3
Fraser I *Aust* 34D1
Frederica *USA* 68C3
Fredericia *Den* 18B1
Frederick, Maryland *USA* 65D3
Frederick, Oklahoma *USA* 62C2
Fredericksburg, Texas *USA* 62C2
Fredericksburg, Virginia *USA* 65D3
Fredericktown *USA* 64A3
Fredericton *Can* 55M5
Frederikshåp *Greenland* 55N3
Frederikshavn *Den* 12G7
Fredonia *USA* 65D2
Fredrikstad *Nor* 12G7
Freehold *USA* 68C2
Freel Peak, Mt *USA* 66C1
Freeman *USA* 61D2
Freeport, Illinois *USA* 64B2
Freeport, Texas *USA* 63C3
Freeport *The Bahamas* 69B1
Freer *USA* 62C3
Freetown *Sierra Leone* 48A4
Freiburg *W Germ* 18B3
Freiburg im Breisgau *W Germ* 13D3
Freistadt *Austria* 18C3
Fremantle *Aust* 32A4
Fremont, California *USA* 66B2
Fremont, Nebraska *USA* 61D2
Fremont, Ohio *USA* 64C2
French Guiana, Dependency *S America* 73H3
Frenchman, R *USA* 60B1
Frenchmans Cap, Mt *Aust* 34C4
French Polynesia, Is *Pacific O* 37M5
Frenda *Alg* 15C2
Fresnillo *Mexico* 70B2
Fresno *USA* 56B3
Fresno, R *USA* 66C2
Fresno Res *USA* 58D1
Freudenstadt *W Germ* 13E3
Frévent *France* 13B2
Freycinet Pen *Aust* 34C4
Fria *Guinea* 48A3
Friant *USA* 66C2
Friant Dam *USA* 66C2
Fribourg *Switz* 16B1
Friedberg *W Germ* 13E2
Friedrichshafen *W Germ* 18B3
Friesland, Province *Neth* 13C1
Frio, R *USA* 62C3
Frio, Cabo, C *Brazil* 75D3
Friona *USA* 62B2
Frobisher B *Can* 55M3
Frobisher Bay *Can* 55M3
Frobisher L *Can* 54H4
Frolovo *USSR* 21G6
Frome *Eng* 7C4
Frome, R *Eng* 7C4
Frome,L *Aust* 32C4
Frontenac *USA* 63D1
Frontera *Mexico* 70C3
Front Royal *USA* 65D3
Frosinone *Italy* 16C2
Fruita *USA* 60B3
Frunze *USSR* 39F1
Fuchuan *China* 31C5
Fuding *China* 31E4
Fuerte, R *Mexico* 70B2
Fuerte Olimpo *Brazil* 75A3
Fuerte Olimpo *Par* 74E2
Fuerteventura, I *Canary Is* 48A2
Fugu *China* 31C2
Fuhai *China* 26B2
Fujairah *UAE* 41G4
Fuji *Japan* 29C3
Fujian, Province *China* 31D4
Fujin *China* 26G2
Fujinomiya *Japan* 29C3
Fuji-san, Mt *Japan* 29D3
Fujisawa *Japan* 29C3
Fuji-Yoshida *Japan* 29C3
Fukagawa *Japan* 29D2
Fukang *China* 24K5
Fukuchiyama *Japan* 29D3
Fukue *Japan* 28A4
Fukue, I *Japan* 28A4
Fukui *Japan* 29D3
Fukuoka *Japan* 28C4
Fukushima *Japan* 29E3
Fukuyama *Japan* 29C4
Fulda *USA* 61D2
Fulda *W Germ* 18B2
Fulda, R *W Germ* 18B2
Fuling *China* 31B4
Fullarton *Trinidad* 69L1
Fullerton *USA* 66D4
Fulton, Illinois *USA* 64A2

Glomfjord Groom

Glomfjord *Nor* 12G5
Glorieuses, Isles *Madag* 51E5
Glossop *Eng* 7C3
Gloucester *Aust* 34D2
Gloucester *Eng* 7C4
Gloucester *USA* 68E1
Gloucester, County *Eng* 7C4
Gloversville *USA* 68C1
Glubokoye *USSR* 19F1
Glückstadt *W Germ* 13E1
Glukhov *USSR* 21E5
Gmünd *Austria* 18D3
Gmunden *Austria* 18C3
Gniezno *Pol* 19D2
Goa, Daman and Diu, Union Territory *India* 44A2
Goageb *Namibia* 47B2
Goälpāra *India* 43G3
Goba *Eth* 50D3
Gobabis *Namibia* 47B1
Gobi, Desert *China/Mongolia* 31B1
Gobo *Japan* 29C4
Gobza, R *USSR* 19G1
Gochas *Namibia* 47B1
Godalming *Eng* 7D4
Godāvari, R *India* 44C2
Goddard,Mt *USA* 66C2
Goderich *Can* 64C2
Godhavn *Greenland* 55N3
Godhra *India* 42C4
Gods L *Can* 57D1
Godthåb *Greenland* 55N3
Godwin Austen, Mt = K2
Goffstown *USA* 68E1
Gogama *Can* 64C1
Gohfeld *W Germ* 13E1
Goiandira *Brazil* 75C2
Goianésia *Brazil* 75C2
Goiânia *Brazil* 71F5
Goiás *Brazil* 75B2
Goiás, State *Brazil* 73J6
Goio-Erê *Brazil* 75B3
Gojab, R *Eth* 50D3
Gökçeada, I *Turk* 17F2
Gökova Körfezi, B *Turk* 17F3
Goksu, R *Turk* 21F8
Göksun *Turk* 40C2
Golāghāt *India* 43G3
Gola, I *Irish Rep* 9B2
Gölbaşı *Turk* 40C2
Gol'chikha *USSR* 24K2
Golconda *USA* 58C2
Gold *USA* 68B2
Gold Beach *USA* 58B2
Gold Coast *Aust* 34D1
Golden B *NZ* 35B2
Goldendale *USA* 58B1
Golden Gate, Chan *USA* 66A2
Golden Meadow *USA* 63D3
Goldfield *USA* 59C3
Gold Point *USA* 66D2
Goldsboro *USA* 67C1
Goldthwaite *USA* 62C2
Goleniów *Pol* 18C2
Goleta *USA* 66C3
Golmud *China* 26C3
Gololcha *Eth* 50E3
Golovnino *USSR* 29F2
Goma *Zaïre* 50C4
Gomati *India* 43L2
Gombe *Nigeria* 48D3
Gomel *USSR* 19G2
Gomera, I *Canary Is* 48A2
Gómez Palacio *Mexico* 70B2
Gonam, R *USSR* 25O4
Gonâve, Isla de la *Cuba* 69C3
Gonbad-e Kāvūs *Iran* 41G2
Gonda *India* 43E3
Gondal *India* 42C4
Gonder *Eth* 50D2
Gondia *India* 43E4
Gönen *Turk* 40A1
Gonen, R *Turk* 17F3
Gongga Shan, Mt *China* 31A4
Gonghe *China* 31A2
Gongogi, R *Brazil* 75D1
Gongola, R *Nigeria* 48D3
Gonzales, California *USA* 66B2
Gonzales, Texas *USA* 63C3
Good Hope,C of *S Africa* 47B3
Gooding *USA* 58D2
Goodland *USA* 60C3
Goodooga, R *Aust* 34C1
Goole *Eng* 7D3
Goolgowi *Aust* 34C2
Goolwa *Aust* 34A3
Goomalling *Aust* 32A4
Goombalie *Aust* 34C2
Goomeri *Aust* 34D1
Goondiwindi *Aust* 34D1
Goose Bay *Can* 55N4
Goose Creek *USA* 67C2
Goose L *USA* 58B2
Gooty *India* 44B2
Goraka *PNG* 32D1
Gorakhpur *India* 43E3
Gora Koyp, Mt *USSR* 20K3
Gora Munku Sardyk, Mt *USSR/Mongolia* 25L4
Gora Narodnaya, Mt *USSR* 20K3
Gora Pay-Yer, Mt *USSR* 20L2
Gora Telpos-Iz, Mt 20K3
Goražde *Yugos* 17D2
Gordon *USA* 54D2
Gordonsville *USA* 65D3
Goré *Chad* 50B3
Gore *Eth* 50D3
Gore *NZ* 35A3
Gore Topko, Mt *USSR* 25P4
Gorey *Irish Rep* 9C3
Gorgān *Iran* 41F2
Gorinchem *Neth* 13C2
Goris *USSR* 41E2
Gorizia *Italy* 16C1
Gorki, Belorusskaya S.S.R. *USSR* 19G2
Gorki, Rossiyskaya S.F.S. R. *USSR* 20M2
Gor'kiy *USSR* 24F4
Gor'kovskoye Vodokhranilishche, Res *USSR* 20G4
Gorleston *Eng* 7E3
Görlitz *E Germ* 18C2
Gorlovka *USSR* 21F6
Gorman *USA* 66C3
Gorna Orjahovica *Bulg* 17F2
Gorno-Altaysk *USSR* 26B1
Gornozavodsk *USSR* 26H2
Goro Denezhkin Kamen', Mt *USSR* 20K3
Gorodets *USSR* 20G4
Gorodnya *USSR* 19G2
Gorodok, Belorusskaya S.S.R. *USSR* 19G1
Gorodok, Ukrainskaya S. S.R. *USSR* 19E3
Gorodok, Ukrainskaya S. S.R. *USSR* 19F3
Goroka *PNG* 27H7
Gorongosa *Mozam* 51D5
Gorontalo *Indon* 27F6
Goro Yurma, Mt *USSR* 20L4
Gorutuba, R *Brazil* 75D2
Goryachinsk *USSR* 25M4
Gory Akkyr, Upland *USSR* 21J7
Gory Byrranga, Mts *USSR* 25L2
Goryn', R *USSR* 19F3
Gory Putorana, Mts *USSR* 25L3
Góry Świetokrzyskie, Upland *Pol* 19E2
Gory Tel'pos-iz, Mt *USSR* 24G3
Gorzów Wielkopolski *Pol* 12H8
Goshen *USA* 66C2
Goshogawara *Japan* 29E2
Gospić *Yugos* 16D2
Gosport *Eng* 7D4
Gostivar *Yugos* 17E2
Gostynin *Pol* 19D2
Göteborg *Sweden* 12G7
Gotel Mts *Nig* 50B3
Gothenburg *USA* 60C2
Gotland, I *Sweden* 12H7
Gotō-rettō, Is *Japan* 28B4
Gotska Sandön, I *Sweden* 12H7
Gōtsu *Japan* 28C4
Göttingen *W Germ* 18B2
Gottwaldov *Czech* 19D3
Goubangzi *China* 28A2
Gouda *Neth* 13C2
Goudoumaria *Niger* 50B2
Gough I *Atlantic O* 52H7
Gouin, Réservoire *Can* 55L5
Goulburn *Aust* 34C2
Goumbou *Mali* 48B3
Goundam *Mali* 48B3
Gouré *Niger* 50B2
Gourma Rharous *Mali* 48B3
Gouro *Chad* 50B2
Govenlock *Can* 58E1
Gove Pen *Aust* 27G8
Goverla, Mt *USSR* 21C6
Governador Valadares *Brazil* 75D2
Govind Ballabh Paht Sāgar, L *India* 43E4
Gowārān *Afghan* 42B3
Gower *Wales* 7B4
Goya *Arg* 74E3
Goz-Beïda *Chad* 50C2
Gozo, I *Malta* 16C3
Goz Regeb *Sudan* 50D2
Graaff-Reinet *S Africa* 47C3
Gracefield *Can* 65D1
Gracias à Dios, Cabo *Honduras* 69A4
Grafton *Aust* 33E3
Grafton, N Dakota *USA* 61D1
Grafton, W Virginia *USA* 64C3
Graham I *Can* 54E4
Graham,Mt *USA* 59E4
Grahamstown *S Africa* 47D3
Grajaú *Brazil* 73J5
Grajewo *Pol* 19E2
Grámmos, Mt *Alb/Greece* 17E2
Grampian, Mts *Scot* 8C3
Grampian, Region *Scot* 8D3
Granada *Colombia* 72D3
Granada *Nic* 72A1
Granada *Spain* 15B2
Granby *Can* 65E1
Granby *USA* 60B2
Gran Canaria, I *Canary Is* 48A2
Gran Chaco, Region *Arg* 74D3
Grand, R, Michigan *USA* 64B2
Grand, R, Missouri *USA* 61E2
Grand B *Dominica* 69Q2
Grand Bahama, I *The Bahamas* 57F4
Grand Ballon, Mt *France* 13D4
Grand Bank *Can* 55N5
Grand Banks *Atlantic O* 52F2
Grand Bassam *Ivory Coast* 48B4
Grand Canyon *USA* 59D3
Grand Canyon Nat Pk *USA* 59D3
Grand Cayman, I, Cayman Is *Caribbean S* 69A3
Grand Coulee *USA* 58C1
Grande, R, Bahia *Brazil* 73K6
Grande, R, Minas Gerais/São Paulo *Brazil* 75C2
Grande, Bahía, B *Arg* 74C8
Grande Comore, I *Comoros* 51E5
Grande, Ilha *Brazil* 75D3
Grande Prairie *USA* 63C2
Grand Erg de Bilma, Desert Region *Niger* 50B2
Grand Erg Occidental, Desert *Alg* 48C1
Grand Erg Oriental, Desert *Alg* 48C2
Grande Rivière de la Baleine, R *Can* 55L4
Grande Ronde, R *USA* 58C1
Gran Desierto *USA* 59D4
Grand Falls, New Brunswick *Can* 55M5
Grand Falls, Newfoundland *Can* 55N5
Grand Forks *Can* 58C1
Grand Forks *USA* 61D1
Grand Gorge *USA* 68C1
Grand Haven *USA* 64B2
Grand Island *USA* 60D2
Grand Isle *USA* 63E2
Grand Junction *USA* 60B3
Grand L *USA* 63D3
Grand Marais *USA* 64A1
Grand Mère *Can* 65E1
Grândola *Port* 15A2
Grand Prairie *Can* 54G4
Grand Rapids *Can* 54J4
Grand Rapids, Michigan *USA* 64B2
Grand Rapids, Minnesota *USA* 64A1
Grand St Bernard, Col du, P *Italy/Switz* 16B1
Grand Teton, Mt *USA* 56B2
Grand Teton Nat Pk *USA* 58D2
Grand Valley *USA* 60B3
Grangeville *USA* 58C1
Granite Peak, Mt, Montana *USA* 58E1
Granite Peak, Mt, Utah *USA* 59D2
Granollérs *Spain* 15C1
Gran Paradiso, Mt *Italy* 16B1
Grantham *Eng* 7D3
Grant,Mt *USA* 66C1
Grantown-on-Spey *Scot* 8D3
Grants *USA* 62A1
Grants Pass *USA* 58B2
Granville *France* 14B2
Granville *USA* 68D1
Granville L *Can* 54H4
Grão Mogol *Brazil* 75D2
Grapevine *USA* 66C3
Grapevine Mts *USA* 66D2
Graskop *S Africa* 47E1
Gras, Lac de *Can* 54G3
Grasse *France* 14D3
Grassington *Eng* 6D2
Grassrange *USA* 58E1
Grass Valley *USA* 59B3
Gravatai *Brazil* 74F4
Gravelbourg *Can* 54H5
Gravelines *France* 13B2
Gravelotte *S Africa* 51D6
Gravenhurst *Can* 65D2
Grave Peak, Mt *USA* 58D1
Gravesend *Aust* 34D1
Gravesend *Eng* 7E4
Grays Harbour, B *USA* 58B1
Grays L *USA* 58D2
Grayson *USA* 64C3
Grayville *USA* 64B3
Graz *Austria* 18D3
Great, R *Jamaica* 69H1
Great Abaco, I *The Bahamas* 57F4
Great Australian Bight, G *Aust* 32B4
Great B, New Hampshire *USA* 68E1
Great B, New Jersey *USA* 68C3
Great Bahama Bank *The Bahamas* 70E2
Great Barrier I *NZ* 35C1
Great Barrier Reef, Is *Aust* 32D2
Great Barrington *USA* 68D1
Great Basin *USA* 59C2
Great Bear L *Can* 54F3
Great Bend *USA* 62C1
Great Bitter L *Egypt* 45B3
Great Cacapon *USA* 68A3
Great Coco I *Burma* 44E3
Great Dividing Range, Mts *Aust* 32D3
Great Driffield *Eng* 6D2
Great Egg Harbor, B *USA* 68C3
Greater Antarctica, Region *Ant* 76F10
Greater Antilles, Is *Caribbean S* 69B2
Greater London, Metropolitan County *Eng* 7D4
Greater Manchester, Metropolitan County *Eng* 7C3
Great Exuma, I *The Bahamas* 70E2
Great Falls *USA* 58D1
Great Fish, R *S Africa* 47D3
Great Glen, V *Scot* 8C3
Great Himalayan Range, Mts *Asia* 43F3
Great Inagua, I *The Bahamas* 57F4
Great Karoo, Mts *S Africa* 47C3
Great Kei, R *S Africa* 47D3
Great L *Aust* 34C4
Great Malvern *Eng* 7C3
Great Namaland, Region *Namibia* 51B6
Great Nicobar, I *Indian O* 44E4
Great Ormes Head, C *Wales* 7C3
Great Pt *USA* 68E2
Great Ragged, I *The Bahamas* 57F4
Great Ruaha, R *Tanz* 51D4
Great Sacandaga L *USA* 65E2
Great Salt L *USA* 58D2
Great Salt Lake Desert *USA* 58D2
Great Sand Sea *Libya/Egypt* 49E2
Great Sandy Desert *Aust* 32B3
Great Sandy Desert *USA* 56A2
Great Sandy I = Fraser I
Great Slave L *Can* 54G3
Great Smoky Mts *USA* 67B1
Great Smoky Mts Nat Pk *USA* 67B1
Great South B *USA* 68D2
Great Tafelberg, Mt *S Africa* 47C3
Great Victoria Desert *Aust* 32B3
Great Wall *China* 31B2
Great Yarmouth *Eng* 7E3
Gréboun, Mont *Niger* 48C2
Greco, C *Cyprus* 45C1
Gredos, Sierra de, Mts *Spain* 15A1
Greece *USA* 65D2
Greece, Republic *Europe* 17E3
Greeley *USA* 60C2
Greely Fjord *Can* 55K1
Greem Bell, Ostrov, I *USSR* 24H1
Green, R, Kentucky *USA* 64B3
Green, R, Utah *USA* 59D3
Green B *USA* 64B1
Green Bay *USA* 64B2
Greencastle, Indiana *USA* 64B3
Greencastle, Pennsylvania *USA* 68B3
Greene *USA* 68C1
Greeneville *USA* 67B1
Greenfield, California *USA* 66B2
Greenfield, California *USA* 66C3
Greenfield, Massachusetts *USA* 68D1
Greenfield, Wisconsin *USA* 64B2
Greenland, Dependency *N Atlantic O* 55O2
Greenland, I *Atlantic O* 52F1
Greenland Basin *Greenland S* 52H1
Greenland Sea *Greenland* 76B1
Greenlaw *Scot* 8D4
Greenock *Scot* 8C4
Greenport *USA* 68D2
Green River, Utah *USA* 59D3
Green River, Wyoming *USA* 58E2
Greensboro, Maryland *USA* 68C3
Greensboro, N Carolina *USA* 67C1
Greensburg, Kansas *USA* 62C1
Greensburg, Kentucky *USA* 64B3
Greensburg, Pennsylvania *USA* 65D2
Greenstone Pt *Scot* 8C3
Greenup *USA* 64B3
Green Valley *USA* 59D4
Greenville, Alabama *USA* 67A2
Greenville *Lib* 48B4
Greenville, Mississippi *USA* 63D2
Greenville, N Carolina *USA* 67C1
Greenville, N Hampshire *USA* 68E1
Greenville, Ohio *USA* 64C2
Greenville, S Carolina *USA* 67B2
Greenville, Texas *USA* 63C2
Greenville, Florida *USA* 67B2
Greenville,C *Aust* 27H8
Greenwich *Eng* 7E4
Greenwich *USA* 68D2
Greenwood, Delaware *USA* 68C3
Greenwood, Mississippi *USA* 63D2
Greenwood, S Carolina *USA* 67B2
Greers Ferry L *USA* 63D1
Gregory *USA* 60D2
Gregory,L *Aust* 34A1
Gregory Range, Mts *Aust* 32D2
Greifswald *E Germ* 18C2
Gremikha *USSR* 20F2
Grenå *Den* 12G7
Grenada *USA* 63E2
Grenada, I *Caribbean S* 69E4
Grenadines,The, Is *Caribbean S* 69E4
Grenfell *Aust* 34C2
Grenoble *France* 14D2
Grenville *Grenada* 69M2
Grenville,C *Aust* 32D2
Gresham *USA* 58B1
Gretna *USA* 63D3
Grey, R *NZ* 35B2
Greybull *USA* 58E2
Grey Is *Can* 55N4
Greylock,Mt *USA* 68D1
Greymouth *NZ* 35B2
Grey Range, Mts *Aust* 32D3
Greystones *Irish Rep* 9C3
Greytown *S Africa* 47E2
Griffin *USA* 67B2
Griffith *Aust* 34C2
Grim,C *Aust* 32D5
Grimsby *Can* 65D2
Grimsby *Eng* 7D3
Grimsey, I *Iceland* 12B1
Grimstad *Nor* 12F7
Grinnell *USA* 61E2
Grinnell Pen *Can* 55J2
Grise Fjord *Can* 55K2
Griva *USSR* 20J3
Grobina *USSR* 12J7
Groblersdal *S Africa* 47D2
Grodno *USSR* 19E2
Gromati, R *India* 43E3
Gronan *W Germ* 13D1
Groningen *Neth* 18B2
Groningen, Province *Neth* 13D1
Groom *USA* 62B1

Harrisburg **Hønefoss**

Harrisburg, Pennsylvania *USA* 68B2
Harrismith *S Africa* 47D2
Harrison *USA* 63D1
Harrisonburg *USA* 65D3
Harrison,C *Can* 55N4
Harrisonville *USA* 61E3
Harris,Sound of, Chan *Scot* 8B3
Harrisville *USA* 64C2
Harrogate *Eng* 6D2
Har Saggi, Mt *Israel* 45C3
Ḩarsīr, Wadi al *Syria* 45D2
Harstad *Nor* 12H5
Hartao *China* 28A2
Hartbees, R *S Africa* 47C2
Hårteigen, Mt *Nor* 12F6
Hartford, Connecticut *USA* 68D2
Hartford, Michigan *USA* 64B2
Hartford, S Dakota *USA* 61D2
Hartkjølen, Mt *Nor* 12G6
Hartland *Can* 65F1
Hartland *Eng* 7B4
Hartland Pt *Eng* 7B4
Hartlepool *Eng* 6D2
Hartley *USA* 62B1
Hartselle *USA* 67A2
Hartshorne *USA* 63C2
Hartwell Res *USA* 67B2
Hartz, R *S Africa* 47C2
Hārūn, Jebel, Mt *Jordan* 45C3
Har Us Nuur, L *Mongolia* 25L5
Harut, R *Afghan* 38E2
Harvard,Mt *USA* 60B3
Harvey *USA* 60C1
Harwich *Eng* 7E4
Haryāna, State *India* 42D3
Hāsā *Jordan* 45C3
Hasana, Wadi *Egypt* 45B3
Hāsā, Wadi el *Jordan* 45C3
Hāsbaiya *Leb* 45C2
Hase, R *W Germ* 13E1
Haselünne *W Germ* 13D1
Hashimoto *Japan* 29C4
Hashtpar *Iran* 41E2
Hashtrūd *Iran* 41E2
Haskell *USA* 62C2
Haslemere *Eng* 7D4
Hassan *India* 44B3
Hasselt *Belg* 18B2
Hassi Inifel *Alg* 48C2
Hassi Mdakane, Well *Alg* 48B2
Hassi Messaoud *Alg* 48C1
Hässleholm *Sweden* 12G7
Hastings *Aust* 34C3
Hastings *Eng* 7E4
Hastings, Minnesota *USA* 61E2
Hastings, Nebraska *USA* 56D2
Hastings *NZ* 35C1
Hatchie, R *USA* 63E1
Hatfield *Aust* 34B2
Hāthras *India* 42D3
Ha Tinh *Viet* 30D2
Hattah *Aust* 34B2
Hatteras,C *USA* 57F3
Hattiesburg *USA* 63E2
Hatvan *Hung* 19D3
Hau Bon *Viet* 30D3
Haud, Region *Eth* 50E3
Haugesund *Nor* 12F7
Hauhungaroa Range, Mts *NZ* 35C1
Hauraki G *NZ* 35B1
Hauroko,L *NZ* 35A3
Haut Atlas, Mts *Mor* 48B1
Haute Kotto, Region *CAR* 50C3
Haute-Marne, Department *France* 13C3
Haute-Saône, Department *France* 13D4
Hautes Fagnes, Mts *Belg/W Germ* 13C2
Haut, Isle au *USA* 65F2
Hautmont *France* 13C2
Haut-Rhin, Department *France* 13D4
Hauz Qala *Afghan* 42A2
Havana *Cuba* 70D2
Havana *USA* 64A2
Havankulam *Sri Lanka* 44B4
Havasu L *USA* 59D4
Havelock *USA* 67C2
Havelock North *NZ* 35C1
Haverhill *Eng* 7E3
Haverhill *USA* 68E1
Hāveri *India* 44B3
Haverstraw *USA* 68D2
Havlíčkův Brod *Czech* 18D3
Havre *USA* 58E1
Havre de Grace *USA* 68B3
Havre-St-Pierre *Can* 55M4
Havsa *Turk* 17F2
Hawaii, Is, State *Pacific O* 66E5
Hawaii Volcanoes Nat Pk *Hawaiian Is* 66E5
Hawea,L *NZ* 35A2
Hawera *NZ* 35B1
Hawi *Hawaiian Is* 66E5
Hawick *Scot* 8D4
Hawkdun Range, Mts *NZ* 35A2
Hawke B *NZ* 35C1
Hawke,C *Aust* 34D2
Hawker *Aust* 34A2
Hawley *USA* 68C2
Hawng Luk *Burma* 30B1
Hawr al Habbaniyah, L *Iraq* 41D3
Hawr al Hammár, L *Iraq* 41E3
Ḩawrān, Wadi, R *Iraq* 40D3
Hawthorne *USA* 66C1
Hay *Aust* 34B2
Hay *Eng* 7C3
Hay, R *Can* 54G3
Hayange *France* 13C3
Haycock *USA* 54B3
Hayden, Arizona *USA* 59D4
Hayden, Colorado *USA* 60B2
Hayes, R *Can* 55J4
Hayes Halvø, Region *Greenland* 55M2
Hayes, Mt *USA* 54D3
Hayle *Eng* 7B4
Hayling, I *Eng* 7D4
Haymarket *USA* 68B3
Hay River *Can* 54G3
Hays *USA* 60D3
Haysville *USA* 63C1
Hayward, California *USA* 66A2
Hayward, Wisconsin *USA* 64A1
Haywards Heath *Eng* 7D4
Hazarajat, Region *Afghan* 42A2
Hazard *USA* 64C3
Hazāribāg *India* 43F4
Hazebrouck *France* 13B2
Hazelhurst *USA* 63D2
Hazelton *Can* 54F4
Hazen B *USA* 54B3
Hazen L *Can* 55L1
Hazen Str *Can* 54G2
Hazeva *Israel* 45C3
Hazleton *USA* 68C2
Healdsburg *USA* 66A1
Healesville *Aust* 34C3
Heard I *Indian O* 36E7
Hearne *USA* 63C2
Hearst *Can* 57E2
Heart, R *USA* 60C1
Hebbronville *USA* 62C3
Hebei, Province *China* 31D2
Hebel *Aust* 34C1
Heber City *USA* 58D2
Hebgen L *USA* 58D2
Hebi *China* 31C2
Hebian *China* 31C2
Hebron *Can* 55M4
Hebron *Israel* 45C3
Hebron, N. Dakota *USA* 60C1
Hebron, Nebraska *USA* 61D2
Hecate Str *Can* 54E4
Hechi *China* 31B5
Hechingen *W Germ* 13E3
Hecla and Griper B *Can* 54G2
Hector,Mt *NZ* 35C2
Hede *Sweden* 12G6
Hedemora *Sweden* 12H6
He Devil Mt *USA* 58C1
Heerenveen *Neth* 18B2
Heerlen *Neth* 13C2
Hefa = Haifa
Hefei *China* 31D3
Hefeng *China* 31B4
Hegang *China* 26G2
Hegura-jima, I *Japan* 29C3
Heho *Burma* 30B1
Heiburg I *Can* 55J2
Heidan, R *Jordan* 45C3
Heide *W Germ* 18B2
Heidelberg, Cape Province *S Africa* 47C3
Heidelberg, Transvaal *S Africa* 47D2
Heidelberg *W Germ* 18B3
Heidenheim *W Germ* 18C3
Heihe *China* 25O4
Heilbron *S Africa* 47D2
Heilbronn *W Germ* 18B3
Heiligenstadt *E Germ* 18C2
Heinola *Fin* 12K6
Heishan *China* 28A2
Hejiang *China* 31B4
Hekla, Mt *Iceland* 55R3
Hekou *Viet* 30C1
Hekou Yaozou Zizhixian *China* 31A5
Helan *China* 31B2
Helan Shan, Mt *China* 31B2
Helena, Arkansas *USA* 63D2
Helena, Montana *USA* 58D1
Helendale *USA* 66D3
Helen Reef *Pacific O* 27G6
Helensburgh *Scot* 8C3
Heliopolis *Egypt* 45A3
Helleh, R *Iran* 41F4
Hellín *Spain* 15B2
Hells Canyon, R *USA* 58C1
Hellweg, Region *W Germ* 13D2
Helm *USA* 66B2
Helmand, R *Iran/Afghan* 38E2
Helmeringhausen *Namibia* 47B2
Helmond *Neth* 13C2
Helmsdale *Scot* 8D2
Helodrano Antongila, B *Madag* 51F5
Helong *China* 28B2
Helsingborg *Sweden* 12G7
Helsingfors = Helsinki
Helsingør *Den* 18C1
Helsinki *Fin* 12J6
Helston *Eng* 7B4
Helvick Hd, Pt *Irish Rep* 9C3
Helwân *Egypt* 40B4
Hemel Hempstead *Eng* 7D4
Hempstead *USA* 63C2
Hemse *Sweden* 12H7
Henan *China* 31A3
Henan, Province *China* 31C3
Hen and Chickens Is *NZ* 35B1
Henashi-zaki, C *Japan* 29C2
Henderson, Kentucky *USA* 64B3
Henderson, N. Carolina *USA* 67C1
Henderson, Nevada *USA* 59D3
Henderson, Texas *USA* 63D2
Hendersonville, N. Carolina *USA* 67B1
Hendersonville, Tennessee *USA* 67A1
Hendrik Verwoerd Dam *S Africa* 47D3
Hengchun *Taiwan* 31E5
Hengduan Shan, Mts *China* 26C4
Hengelo *Neth* 18B2
Hengshan *China* 31B2
Hengshui *China* 31D2
Heng Xian *China* 30D1
Hengyang *China* 31C4
Henhoaha, Nicobar Is 30A4
Henley-on-Thames *Eng* 7D4
Henlopen,C *USA* 68C3
Henniker *USA* 68E1
Henrietta *USA* 62C2
Henrietta Maria,C *Can* 55K4
Henrieville *USA* 59D3
Henryetta *USA* 63C1
Henry Kater Pen *Can* 55M3
Henties Bay *Namibia* 47A1
Hentiyn Nuruu, Mts *Mongolia* 26D2
Henzada *Burma* 30B2
Hepu *China* 31B5
Herat *Afghan* 38E2
Herbert *Can* 54H4
Herbertville *NZ* 35C2
Herborn *W Germ* 13E2
Heredia *Costa Rica* 69A4
Hereford *Eng* 7C3
Hereford *USA* 62B2
Hereford & Worcester, County *Eng* 7C3
Herentals *Belg* 13C2
Herford *W Germ* 13E1
Herington *USA* 61D3
Heriot *NZ* 35A3
Herkimer *USA* 68C1
Herma Ness, Pen *Scot* 8E1
Hermanus *S Africa* 47B3
Hermidale *Aust* 34C2
Hermitage *NZ* 35B2
Hermit Is *PNG* 32D1
Hermon, Mt *Leb/Syria* 45C2
Hermosillo *Mexico* 70A2
Hernandarias *Par* 75B4
Herndon *USA* 68B2
Herne *W Germ* 13D2
Herne Bay *Eng* 7E4
Herning *Den* 18B1
Herowābad *Iran* 41E2
Herradura *Arg* 75A4
Herrera del Duque *Spain* 15B2
Hershey *USA* 68B2
Hertford *Eng* 7D4
Hertford, County *Eng* 7D4
Herzliyya *Israel* 45C2
Hesbaye, Region *Belg* 13C2
Hesdin *France* 13A2
Heshui *China* 31B2
Hesperia *USA* 66D3
Hessen, State *W Germ* 18B2
Hetch Hetchy Res *USA* 66C2
Hettinger *USA* 60C1
Heuts Plateaux *Mor/Alg* 48B1
Hewett, Oilfield *N Sea* 7E3
Hexham *Eng* 6C2
He Xian *China* 31C5
Heysham *Eng* 6C2
Heystekrand *S Africa* 47D2
Heyuan *China* 31C5
Heywood *Aust* 34B3
Heze *China* 31D2
Hialeah *USA* 67B3
Hibbing *USA* 61E1
Hickory *USA* 67B1
Hicks Bay *NZ* 35C1
Hicks,Pt *Aust* 34C3
Hico *USA* 63C2
Hidaka-sammyaku, Mts *Japan* 29D2
Hidalgo del Parral *Mexico* 70B2
Hidrolândia *Brazil* 75C2
Hierro, I *Canary Is* 48A2
Higashine *Japan* 29D3
Higashi-suidō, Str *Japan* 28B4
Higāyib, Wadi el *Egypt* 45B3
High Desert *USA* 58B2
High Island *USA* 63D3
Highland *USA* 66D3
Highland, Region *Scot* 8C3
Highlander, Oilfield *N Sea* 8E2
Highland Peak, Mt *USA* 66C1
Highlands Falls *USA* 68C2
High Point *USA* 67B1
High Prairie *Can* 54G4
High River *Can* 54G4
High Springs *USA* 67B3
Hightstown *USA* 68C2
High Wycombe *Eng* 7D4
Hiiumaa, I *USSR* 12J7
Hijaz, Region *S Arabia* 40C4
Hikigawa *Japan* 29C4
Hiko *USA* 59C3
Hikone *Japan* 29C3
Hikurangi *NZ* 35B1
Hildago del Parral *Mexico* 56C4
Hildesheim *W Germ* 18B2
Hillaby,Mt *Barbados* 69R2
Hill City *USA* 60D3
Hillerød *Den* 18C1
Hillsboro, N. Dakota *USA* 61D1
Hillsboro, New Hampshire *USA* 68E1
Hillsboro, New Mexico *USA* 62A2
Hillsboro, Ohio *USA* 64C3
Hillsboro, Oregon *USA* 58B1
Hillsboro, Texas *USA* 63C2
Hillston *Aust* 34C2
Hillsville *USA* 64C3
Hillswick *Scot* 8E1
Hilo *Hawaiian Is* 66E5
Hilpsford, Pt *Eng* 6C2
Hilton *USA* 68B1
Hilvan *Turk* 40C2
Hilversum *Neth* 18B2
Himāchal Pradesh, State *India* 42D2
Himalaya = Great Himalayan Range
Himalaya, Mts *Asia* 39G3
Himalchuli, Mt *Nepal* 43N1
Himatnagar *India* 42C4
Himeji *Japan* 29C4
Himi *Japan* 29D3
Ḩimş *Syria* 45D1
Hinckley *Eng* 7D3
Hinckley, Minnesota *USA* 61E1
Hinckley Res *USA* 68C1
Hindaun *India* 42D3
Hindu Kush, Mts *Afghan* 42B1
Hindupur *India* 44B3
Hines Creek *Can* 54G4
Hinganghāt *India* 42D4
Hingol, R *Pak* 42B3
Hingoli *India* 42D5
Hinkley *USA* 66D3
Hinnøya, I *Nor* 12H5
Hinsdale *USA* 68D1
Hinton *USA* 62C1
Hirado *Japan* 28A4
Hirado-shima, I *Japan* 28A4
Hirakud Res *India* 43E4
Hirfanli Baraji, Res *Turk* 40B2
Hirihar *India* 44B3
Hiroo *Japan* 29D2
Hirosaki *Japan* 29E2
Hiroshima *Japan* 28C4
Hirson *France* 13C3
Hirşova *Rom* 17F2
Hirtshals *Den* 18B1
Hisār *India* 42D3
Hispaniola, I *Caribbean S* 69C3
Ḩisyah *Syria* 45D1
Hīt *Iraq* 40D3
Hitachi *Japan* 29E3
Hitachi-Ota *Japan* 29D3
Hitchin *Eng* 7D4
Hitoyoshi *Japan* 28C4
Hitra, I *Nor* 12F6
Hiuchi-nada, B *Japan* 29B4
Hiwasa *Japan* 29B4
Hiyon, R *Israel* 45C3
Hjørring *Den* 18B1
Hka, R *Burma* 30B1
Ho *Ghana* 48C4
Hoa Binh *Viet* 30D1
Hoa Da *Viet* 30D3
Hobart *Aust* 34C4
Hobart *USA* 62C2
Hobbs *USA* 62B2
Hobro *Den* 18B1
Hobyo *Somalia* 50E3
Ho Chi Minh City *Viet* 30D3
Hochkonig, Mt *Austria* 18C3
Hochon *N Korea* 28A2
Hockenheim *W Germ* 13E3
Hodeida = Al Ḩudaydah
Hódmezö'hely *Hung* 17E1
Hodna, Monts du *Alg* 15C2
Hodonin *Czech* 18D3
Hoek van Holland *Neth* 13C2
Hoengsŏng *S Korea* 28A3
Hoeryŏng *N Korea* 28B2
Hoeyang *N Korea* 28A3
Hof *W Germ* 18C2
Höfn *Iceland* 55R3
Hofsjökull, Mts *Iceland* 12B2
Hōfu *Japan* 28C4
Hoggar, Upland *Alg* 48C2
Hohe Acht, Mt *W Germ* 13D2
Hohes Gras, Mts *W Germ* 13E2
Hohhot *China* 31C1
Hoh Sai Hu, L *China* 26C3
Hoh Xil Shan, Mts *China* 39G2
Hoima *Uganda* 50D3
Hojāi *India* 43G3
Hojo *Japan* 28B4
Hokianga Harbour, B *NZ* 35B1
Hokitika *NZ* 35B2
Hokkaidō, I *Japan* 26H2
Hokmābād *Iran* 41G2
Hokota *Japan* 29D3
Holbeach *Eng* 7E3
Holbrook *Aust* 34C3
Holbrook *USA* 59D4
Holden *USA* 59D3
Holdenville *USA* 63C1
Holdrege *USA* 60D2
Hole Narsipur *India* 44B3
Holetown *Barbados* 69Q2
Holguín *Cuba* 69B2
Hollabrunn *Austria* 18D3
Holland *USA* 64B2
Hollidaysburg *USA* 68A2
Hollis *USA* 62C2
Hollister *USA* 66B2
Holly Springs *USA* 63E2
Hollywood, California *USA* 66C3
Hollywood, Florida *USA* 67B3
Holman Island *Can* 54G2
Holmsund *Sweden* 12J6
Holon *Israel* 45C2
Holstebro *Den* 18B1
Holstein *USA* 61D2
Holsteinborg *Greenland* 55N3
Holston, R *USA* 67B1
Holt *USA* 64C2
Holton *USA* 61D3
Holy Cross *USA* 54C3
Holyhead *Wales* 7B3
Holy I *Eng* 6D3
Holy I *Wales* 7B3
Holyoke, Colorado *USA* 60C2
Holyoke, Massachusetts *USA* 68D1
Holywood *N Ire* 9D2
Holzminden *W Germ* 13E2
Homalin *Burma* 43G4
Homburg *W Germ* 13E2
Home B *Can* 55M3
Homer, Louisiana *USA* 63D2
Homer *USA* 54C4
Homer Tunnel *NZ* 35A2
Homerville *USA* 67B2
Homestead *USA* 67B3
Homewood *USA* 67A2
Homnābād *India* 44B2
Homoine *Mozam* 51D6
Homs = Al Khums
Homs = Himş
Homs *Syria* 29J5
Hondeklip B *S Africa* 47B3
Hondo, New Mexico *USA* 62A2
Hondo, Texas *USA* 62C3
Hondo, R *Mexico* 70D3
Honduras, Republic *Cent America* 70D3
Honduras,G of *Honduras* 70D3
Hønefoss *Nor* 12G6

Honesdale
Ingersoll

Honesdale USA 68C2
Honey L USA 59B2
Hong, R = Nui Con Voi
Hong, R Viet 30C1
Hon Gai Viet 30D1
Hongchŏn S Korea 28A3
Hongguo China 31A4
Hong Hu, L China 31C4
Honghui China 31B2
Hongjiang China 31C4
Hong Kong, Colony S E Asia 31C5
Hongor Mongolia 26E2
Hongshui He, R China 31B5
Hongsong S Korea 28A3
Hongwon N Korea 28A3
Hongyuan China 31A3
Hongze Hu, L China 31D3
Honiara Solomon Is 33E1
Honiton Eng 7C4
Honjō Japan 29D3
Hon Khoai, I Camb 30C4
Hon Lan, I Viet 30D3
Honnigsvåg Nor 12K4
Honningsvåg Nor 20D1
Honokaa Hawaiian Is 66E5
Honolulu Hawaiian Is 66E5
Hon Panjang, I Viet 30C4
Honshū, I Japan 26G3
Hood,Mt USA 58B1
Hood River USA 58B1
Hoogeveen Neth 13D1
Hooker USA 62B1
Hook Head, C Irish Rep 9C3
Hoonah USA 54E4
Hooper Bay USA 54B3
Hoopstad S Africa 47D2
Hoorn Neth 18A2
Hoosick Falls USA 68D1
Hoover Dam USA 56B3
Hope, Arkansas USA 63D2
Hopedale Can 55M4
Hopen, I Svalbard 24D2
Hopes Advance,C Can 55M3
Hopetoun Aust 34B3
Hopetown S Africa 47C2
Hopewell, Pennsylvania USA 68A2
Hopewell, Virginia USA 65D3
Hopkinsville USA 64B3
Hoquiam USA 58B1
Horasan Turk 40D2
Horb W Germ 13E3
Hordiyo Somalia 50E2
Hörh Uul, Mt Mongolia 31B1
Horizon Depth Pacific O 37L6
Hormuz,Str of Oman/Iran 41G4
Horn Austria 18D3
Horn, C Iceland 55Q3
Hornavan, L Sweden 12H5
Hornbeck USA 63D2
Hornbrook USA 58B2
Hornby NZ 35B2
Horncastle Eng 7D3
Hornell USA 68B1
Hornepayne Can 55K5
Horn I USA 63E2
Horn, Îles de Pacific O 33H2
Horn Mts Can 54F3
Hornos, Cabo de, C Chile 74C9
Hornsea Eng 6D3
Horqin Zuoyi Houqi China 28A2
Horqueta Par 74E2
Horseheads USA 68B1
Horsens Den 18C1
Horseshoe Bay Can 58B1
Horseshoe Bend USA 58C2
Horsham Aust 34B3
Horsham Eng 7D4
Horten Nor 12G7
Horton, R Can 54F3
Hose Mts Borneo 27E6
Hoshangabad India 42D4
Hoshiārpur India 42D2
Hosington USA 62C1
Hospet India 44B2
Hoste, I Chile 74C9
Hotan China 39F2
Hotazel S Africa 47C2
Hot Springs, Arkansas USA 63D2
Hot Springs, S. Dakota USA 60C2
Hottah L Can 54G3
Hotte, Massif de la, Mts Haiti 69C3
Hottentot Pt Namibia 47A2
Houghton USA 64B1
Houlton USA 65F1
Houma China 31C2
Houma USA 63D3
Hourn, Loch, Inlet Scot 8C3
Housatonic, R USA 68D2
Houston, Mississippi USA 63E2
Houston, Texas USA 63C3
Houtman, Is Aust 32A3
Houtzdale USA 68A2
Hovd Mongolia 26C2
Hövsgol Nuur, L Mongolia 26D1
Howard Aust 34D1
Howard City USA 64B2
Howa, Wadi, Watercourse Sudan/Chad 50C2
Howe,C Aust 34C3
Howe Sd Can 58B1
Howick S Africa 47E2
Howland USA 65F1
Howth Irish Rep 9C3
Höxter W Germ 13E2
Hoy, I Scot 8D2
Høyanger Nor 12F6
Hoyt Lakes USA 61E1
Hradec-Králové Czech 18D2
Hranice Czech 19D3
Hron, R Czech 19D3
Hsinchu Taiwan 31E5
Hsipaw Burma 30B1
Hsüeh Shan, Mt Taiwan 31E5
Huab, R Namibia 47A1
Huachi China 31B2
Huacho Peru 72C6
Huade China 31C1
Huadian China 28B2
Huaibei China 31D3
Huaibin China 31D3
Huaide China 28A2
Huaidezhen China 28A2
Huai He, R China 31D3
Huaihua China 31C4
Huaiji China 31C5
Huainan China 31D3
Hualapai Peak, Mt USA 59D3
Hualien Taiwan 26F4
Huallaga, R Peru 72C5
Huallanca Peru 72C5
Huamachuco Peru 72C5
Huambo Angola 51B5
Huanay Bol 72E7
Huancabamba Peru 72C5
Huancavelica Peru 72C6
Huancayo Peru 72C6
Huangchuan China 31D3
Huang Hai = Yellow S
Huang He, R China 31D2
Huangling China 31B2
Huangliu China 30D2
Huangnihe China 28B2
Huangpi China 31C3
Huangshi China 31D3
Huangyan China 31E4
Huanren China 28B2
Huanuco Peru 72C5
Huanuni Bol 74C1
Huan Xian China 31B2
Huaráz Peru 72C5
Huarmey Peru 72C6
Huascarán, Mt Peru 72C5
Huasco Chile 74B3
Hua Xian China 31C2
Huayapan, R Mexico 70B2
Hubei, Province China 31C3
Hubli India 44B2
Huch'ang N Korea 28B2
Hucknell Torkard Eng 7D3
Huddersfield Eng 7D3
Hude W Germ 13E1
Hudiksvall Sweden 12H6
Hudson, Florida USA 67B3
Hudson, Michigan USA 64C2
Hudson, New York USA 68D1
Hudson, R USA 68D1
Hudson B Can 55K4
Hudson Bay Can 54H4
Hudson Falls USA 68D1
Hudson Str Can 55L3
Hue Viet 30D2
Huelva Spain 15A2
Húercal Overa Spain 15B2
Huesca Spain 15B1
Hughenden Aust 32D3
Hughes USA 54C3
Hugli, R India 43F4
Hugo USA 63C2
Hugoton USA 62B1
Hui'an China 31D4
Huiarau Range, Mts NZ 35C1
Huib Hochplato, Plat Namibia 47B2
Hüich'on N Korea 28B2
Huila, Mt Colombia 72C3
Huilai China 31D5
Huili China 31A4
Huinan China 28B2
Huixtla Mexico 70C3
Huize China 31A4
Huizhou China 31C5
Ḩulayfah S Arabia 40D4
Hulin China 26G2
Hull Can 65D1
Hull Eng 6D3
Hull, I Phoenix Is 33H1
Hultsfred Sweden 18D1
Hulun Nur, L China 25N5
Humaitá Brazil 72F5
Humansdorp S Africa 47C3
Humber, R Eng 7D3
Humberside, County Eng 6D3
Humboldt Can 54H4
Humboldt, Iowa USA 61E2
Humboldt, Tennessee USA 63E1
Humboldt, R USA 58C2
Humboldt B USA 58B2
Humboldt Gletscher, Gl Greenland 55M2
Humboldt L USA 59C3
Humeburn Aust 34C1
Hume,L Aust 34C3
Hümmling, Hill W Germ 13D1
Humpata Angola 51B5
Humphreys USA 66C2
Humphreys,Mt, California USA 66C2
Humphreys Peak, Mt, Arizona USA 59D3
Húnaflóri, B Iceland 12A1
Hunan, Province China 31C4
Hunchun China 28C2
Hunedoara Rom 17E1
Hungary, Republic Europe 19D3
Hungerford Aust 34B1
Hüngnam N Korea 28B3
Hungry Horse Res USA 58D1
Hunjiang China 28B2
Hunsberge, Mts Namibia 47B2
Hunsrück, Mts W Germ 13D3
Hunstanton Eng 7E3
Hunte, R W Germ 13E1
Hunter, R Aust 34D2
Hunter Is Aust 34C4
Huntingburg USA 64B3
Huntingdon Eng 7D3
Huntingdon, Indiana USA 64B2
Huntingdon, Pennsylvania USA 68A2
Huntington USA 64C3
Huntington Beach USA 66C4
Huntington L USA 66C2
Huntly NZ 35C1
Huntly Scot 8D3
Hunt, Mt Can 54F3
Huntsville, Alabama USA 67A2
Huntsville Can 65D1
Huntsville, Texas USA 63C2
Huong Khe Viet 30D2
Huon Peninsula PNG 27H7
Huonville Aust 34C4
Hurd,C Can 64C1
Hure Qi China 28A2
Hurghada Egypt 40B4
Hurley USA 64A1
Huron, California USA 66B2
Huron, S. Dakota USA 61D2
Huron,L Can/USA 64C1
Hurunui, R NZ 35B2
Hurup, Ostrov, I USSR 25Q5
Húsavik Iceland 12B1
Huşi Rom 17F1
Huskvarna Sweden 12G7
Husn Jordan 45C2
Husum W Germ 18B2
Hutchinson USA 56D3
Hutton,Mt Aust 34C1
Hutuo He, R China 31D2
Huy Belg 13C2
Huzhu China 31A2
Hvar, I Yugos 16D2
Hwadae N Korea 28A2
Hwange Zim 51C5
Hwange Nat Pk Zim 51C5
Hwapyong N Korea 28A2
Hyannis, Massachusetts USA 68E2
Hyannis, Nebraska USA 60C2
Hyargas Nuur, L Mongolia 26C2
Hydaburg USA 54E4
Hyde Park USA 68D2
Hyderābād India 44B2
Hyderabad Pak 42B3
Hyères France 14D3
Hyères, Iles d', Is France 14D3
Hyesan N Korea 28B2
Hyndman USA 68A3
Hyndman Peak, Mt USA 56B2
Hyrynsalmi Fin 20D3
Hythe Eng 7E4
Hyvinkää Fin 12J6

I

Iaçu Brazil 73K6
Ialomiţa, R Rom 17F2
Iaşi Rom 17F1
Ibadan Nigeria 48C4
Ibagué Colombia 72C3
Ibar, R Yugos 17E2
Ibarra Ecuador 72C3
Ibbenbüren W Germ 13D1
Ibiá Brazil 75C2
Ibicaraí Brazil 75E1
Ibicuí, R Brazil 74E3
Ibicuy Arg 74E4
Ibiza Spain 15C2
Ibiza, I Spain 15C2
Ibo Mozam 51E5
Ibotirama Brazil 73K6
Ibra, Wadi, Watercourse Sudan 50C2
'Ibri Oman 41G5
Ica Peru 72C6
Içá, R Brazil 72E4
Içana Brazil 72E3
Iceland, Republic N Atlantic O 12A1
Icha USSR 25R4
Ichalkaranji India 44A2
Ichinomiya Japan 29C3
Ichinosek Japan 29E3
Icy C USA 54B2
Idabell USA 63D2
Ida Grove USA 61D2
Idaho, State USA 58D2
Idaho City USA 58C2
Idaho Falls USA 58D2
Idaho Springs USA 60B3
Idalion, Hist Site Cyprus 45B1
Idanha USA 58B2
Idar Oberstein W Germ 13D3
Idehan Marzug, Desert Libya 49D2
Idehan Ubari, Desert Libya 49D2
Idelès Alg 48C2
Ideriym Gol, R Mongolia 26C2
Idfu Egypt 40B5
Ídhi Óros, Mt Greece 17E3
Ídhra, I Greece 17E3
Idiofa Zaïre 50B4
Idlib Syria 40C2
Idritsa USSR 12K7
Idutywa S Africa 47D3
Ieper Belg 13B2
Ierápetra Greece 17F3
Ifakara Tanz 51D4
Ifalik, I Pacific O 27H6
Ifanadiana Madag 51E6
Ife Nigeria 48C4
Iférouane Niger 48C3
Igan Malay 27E6
Igarapava Brazil 75C3
Igarka USSR 24K3
Igatimi Par 75A3
Igdir Iran 41E2
Iggesund Sweden 12H6
Iglesias, Sardinia 16B3
Igloolik Can 55K3
Ignace Can 57D2
Iğneada Burun, Pt Turk 40A1
Ignil-Izane Alg 48C1
Ignoitijala Andaman Is 44E3
Igoumenítsa Greece 17E3
Igra USSR 20J4
Igrim USSR 20L3
Iguaçu, Quedas do, Falls Arg/Brazil 74F3
Iguala Mexico 70C3
Iguape Brazil 74G2
Iguatama Brazil 75C3
Iguatemi Brazil 75B3
Iguatemi, R Brazil 75A3
Iguatu Brazil 73L5
Iguéla Gabon 50A4
Ihosy Madag 51E6
Iida Japan 29D3
Iide-san, Mt Japan 29C3
Iisalmi Fin 12K6
Iizuka Japan 28B4
Ijebu Nigeria 48C4
Ijmuiden Neth 13C1
Ijssel, R Neth 13C1
Ijsselmeer, S Neth 18B2
Ikaria, I Greece 17F3
Ikeda Japan 29E2
Ikela Zaïre 50C4
Ikhtiman Bulg 17E2
Iki, I Japan 28A4
Ikopa, R Madag 51E5
Ilagan Phil 27F5
Ilam Iran 41E3
Ilanskiy USSR 26C1
Ilebo Zaïre 50C4
Île de France, Region France 14C2
Ile d'Orleans Can 65E1
Ilek, R USSR 21K5
Ilfracombe Eng 7B4
Ilgaz Dağları, Mts Turk 40B1
Ilha do Bananal, Region Brazil 73H6
Ilha Grande, B de Brazil 75D3
Ilha Grande ou Sete Quedas, I Brazil 75B3
Ilha Solteira Dam Brazil 75B3
Ilhéus Brazil 73L6
Iliamna L USA 54C4
Ilim, R USSR 26D1
Il'inskiy USSR 26H2
Iliodhrómia, I Greece 17E3
Ilion USA 68C1
Ilkley Eng 6D3
Illapel Chile 74B4
Illéla Niger 48C3
Illinois, R USA 64A3
Illinois, State USA 64B2
Illizi Alg 48C2
Il'men, Ozero, L USSR 20E4
Ilo Peru 72D7
Iloilo Phil 27F5
Ilomantsi Fin 12L6
Ilorin Nigeria 48C4
Il'yino USSR 19G1
Imabari Japan 28B4
Imaichi Japan 29C3
Imari Japan 28A4
Imatra Fin 20D3
Imbituba Brazil 74G3
Imbituva Brazil 75B4
Imi Eth 50E3
Imjin, R N Korea 28A3
Imlay USA 58C2
Imola Italy 16C2
Imperatriz Brazil 73J5
Imperia Italy 16B2
Imperial USA 60C2
Imperial V USA 59C4
Impfondo Congo 50B3
Imphal India 43G4
Ina Japan 29C3
In Afaleleh, Well Alg 48C2
Inamba-jima, I Japan 29C4
In Amenas Alg 48C2
Inaraña Madag 51F5
Inari Fin 12K5
Inarijärvi, L Fin 12K5
Inawashiro-ko, L Japan 29D3
In Belbel Alg 48C2
Ince Burun, Pt Turk 21F7
Incekum Burun, Pt Turk 40B2
Inchnadamph Scot 8C2
Inch'on S Korea 28B3
Indaal, Loch, Inlet Scot 8B4
In Dagouber, Well Mali 48B2
Indaiá, R Brazil 75C2
Indals, R Sweden 12H6
Independence, California USA 66C2
Independence, Iowa USA 61E2
Independence, Kansas USA 63C1
Independence, Missouri USA 61E3
Independence Mts USA 58C2
Inderborskiy USSR 21J6
India, Federal Republic Asia 39F3
Indiana USA 65D2
Indiana, State USA 64B2
Indian-Antarctic Basin Indian O 36F7
Indian-Antarctic Ridge Indian O 36F7
Indianapolis USA 64B3
Indian Desert = Thar Desert
Indian Harbour Can 55N4
Indian O 36E5
Indianola, Iowa USA 61E2
Indianola, Mississippi USA 63D2
Indianópolis Brazil 75C2
Indian Springs USA 59C3
Indiga USSR 20H2
Indigirka, R USSR 25Q3
Indo-China, Region S E Asia 30D2
Indonesia, Republic S E Asia 27F7
Indore India 42D4
Indre, R France 14C2
Indus, R Pak 42B3
Indus, Mouths of the Pak 42B4
In Ebeggi, Well Alg 48C2
Inebolu Turk 21E7
In Ecker Alg 48C2
Inegöl Turk 40A1
In Ezzane Alg 48D2
Infantta, C S Africa 47C3
Infiernillo, Pico del, Mt Mexico 70B3
Ingal Niger 48C3
Ingersoll Can 64C2

Jiande
Karak

Jiande China 31D4
Jiang'an China 31B4
Jiangbiancun China 31D4
Jiangcheng China 31A5
Jiangmen China 31C5
Jiangsu, Province China 31D3
Jiangxi, Province China 31C4
Jiangyou China 31A3
Jianping China 31D1
Jianshui China 31A5
Jian Xi, R China 31D4
Jianyang China 31D4
Jiaohe China 28B2
Jiaonan China 31E2
Jiao Xian China 31E2
Jiaozhou Wan, B China 31E2
Jiaozuo China 31C2
Jiaxiang China 31E3
Jiayuguan China 26C3
Jibão, Serra do, Mts Brazil 75C2
Jiddah S Arabia 50D1
Jieshou China 31D3
Jiexiu China 31C2
Jigzhi China 31A3
Jihlava Czech 18D3
Jijel Algeria 16B3
Jilib Somalia 50E3
Jilin China 28B2
Jilin, Province China 28B2
Jiloca, R Spain 15B1
Jima Eth 50D3
Jiménez, Coahuila Mexico 62B3
Jinan China 31D2
Jind India 42D3
Jingbian China 31B2
Jingdezhen China 31D4
Jinghong China 30C1
Jingmen China 31C3
Jingning China 31B2
Jing Xian China 31B4
Jingyu China 28B2
Jinhua China 31D4
Jining Nei Mongol China 31C1
Jining, Shandong China 31D2
Jinja Uganda 50D3
Jinping China 30C1
Jinsha Jiang, R China 31A4
Jinshi China 31C4
Jinxi China 31E1
Jin Xian China 31E2
Jinzhou China 31E1
Jiparaná, R Brazil 72F5
Jipijapa Ecuador 72B4
Jiroft Iran 41G4
Jishou China 31B4
Jisr ash Shughūr Syria 40C2
Jiu, R Rom 17E2
Jiujiang China 31D4
Jiuling Shan, Hills China 31C4
Jiulong China 31A4
Jiulong Jiang, R China 31D4
Jixi China 26G2
Jiza Jordan 45C3
Jīzān S Arabia 50E2
Joal Sen 48A3
João Monlevade Brazil 75D2
João Pessoa Brazil 73M5
João Pinheiro Brazil 73J7
Jodhpur India 42C3
Joensuu Fin 12K6
Joeuf France 13C3
Jogbani India 43F3
Jog Falls India 44A3
Johannesburg S Africa 47D2
Johannesburg USA 59C3
Johan Pen Can 55L2
John Day USA 58C2
John Day, R USA 58B1
John H Kerr L USA 57F3
John H. Kerr Res USA 65D3
John Martin Res USA 62B1
John o'Groats Scot 8D2
John Redmond Res USA 63C1
Johnsonburg USA 68A2
Johnson City, New York USA 68C1
Johnson City, Tennessee USA 67B1
Johnston USA 67B2
Johnston Pt St Vincent 69N2
Johnstown, New York USA 68C1
Johnstown, Pennsylvania USA 65D2
Johor Bharu Malay 30C5
Joigny France 14C2
Joinville Brazil 74G3
Joinville France 13C3
Jok, R USSR 20J5
Jokkmokk Sweden 12H5
Jolfa Iran 21H8
Joliet USA 57E2
Joliette Can 55L5
Jolo Phil 27F6
Jolo, I Phil 27F6
Joma, Mt China 39H2
Jonava USSR 19E1
Jonê China 31A3
Jonesboro, Arkansas USA 57D3
Jonesboro, Louisiana USA 63D2
Jones Sd Can 55K2
Joniškis USSR 19E1
Jönköping Sweden 12G7
Jonquière Can 65E1
Joplin USA 57D3
Jordan, Montana USA 60B1
Jordan, New York USA 68B1
Jordan, Kingdom S W Asia 40C3
Jordan, R Israel 45C2
Jordan Valley USA 58C2
Jordão, R Brazil 75B4
Jorhāt India 43G3
Jörn Sweden 20C2
Jørpeland Nor 12F7
Jos Nigeria 48C3
Joseph Bonaparte G Aust 32B2
Joseph City USA 59D3
Joseph, Lac Can 55M4
Jotunheimen, Mt Nor 24B3
Jouai'ya Leb 45C2
Jounié Leb 45C2
Jowai India 43G3
Jowhar Somalia 50E3
Juan de Fuca,Str of Can/USA 54F5
Juan de Nova, I Mozam Chan 51E5
Juan Fernández, Islas Pacific O 72Q
Juàzeiro Brazil 73K5
Juàzeiro do Norte Brazil 73L5
Juba Sudan 50D3
Juba, R Somalia 50E3
Jubail Leb 45C1
Jubany, Base Ant 76G2
Jubbah S Arabia 40D4
Júcar, R Spain 15B2
Judenburg Austria 18C3
Juist, I W Germ 13D1
Juiz de Fora Brazil 73K8
Jujuy, State Arg 74C2
Julesburg USA 60C2
Juli Peru 72E7
Juliaca Peru 72D7
Julianatop, Mt Surinam 73G3
Julianehåb Greenland 55O3
Jülich W Germ 13D2
Jullundur India 42D2
Jumla Nepal 43E3
Jum Suwwāna, Mt Jordan 45C3
Jūnāgadh India 42C4
Junan China 31D2
Junction, Texas USA 62C2
Junction, Utah USA 59D3
Junction City USA 56D3
Jundiaí Brazil 74G2
Juneau USA 54E4
Junee Aust 32D4
June Lake USA 66C2
Jungfrau, Mt Switz 16B1
Juniata, R USA 68B2
Junín Arg 74D4
Junipero Serra Peak, Mt USA 66B2
Junlian China 31A4
Juparanã, Lagoa Brazil 75D2
Juquiá Brazil 74G2
Jur, R Sudan 50C3
Jura, I Scot 8C4
Jura, Mts France 14D2
Jura,Sound of, Chan Scot 8C3
Jurf ed Darāwish Jordan 45C3
Jurga USSR 24K4
Jūrmala USSR 20C4
Juruá, R Brazil 72E4
Juruena, R Brazil 73G6
Jūsiyah Syria 45D1
Jutaí, R Brazil 72E4
Juticalpa Honduras 70D3
Jutland, Pen = Jylland
Juventud, Isla de la Cuba 69A2
Jūymand Iran 41G3
Jylland, Pen Den 18B1
Jyväskyla Fin 12K6

K

K2, Mt China/India 39F2
Kaakhka USSR 41G2
Kaapmuiden S Africa 47E2
Kabaena Indon 27F7
Kabaena, I Indon 32B1
Kabala Sierra Leone 48A4
Kabale Uganda 50D4
Kabalo Zaïre 50C4
Kabambare Zaïre 50C4
Kabarole Uganda 50D3
Kabinakagami L Can 64C1
Kabinda Zaïre 50C4
Kabir, R Syria 45C1
Kabir Kuh, Mts Iran 41E3
Kabompo Zambia 51C5
Kabompo, R Zambia 51C5
Kabongo Zaïre 51C4
Kabul Afghan 42B2
Kachchh,G of India 42B4
Kachkanar USSR 20K4
Kachug USSR 25M4
Kadan, I Burma 30B3
Kadi India 42C4
Kadınhanı Turk 40B2
Kadiri India 44B3
Kadiyevka USSR 21F6
Kadoka USA 60C2
Kadoma Zim 51C5
Kadugli Sudan 50C2
Kaduna Nigeria 48C3
Kaduna, R Nigeria 48C3
Kadūr India 44B3
Kadusam, Mt China 43H3
Kadzherom USSR 20K3
Kaechon N Korea 28A3
Kaédi Maur 48A3
Kaena Pt Hawaiian Is 66E5
Kaesŏng N Korea 28B3
Kafanchan Nigeria 48C4
Kaffrine Sen 48A3
Kafr Behum Syria 45D1
Kafr Sa'd Egypt 45A3
Kafr Saqv Egypt 45A3
Kafrūn Bashūr Syria 45D1
Kafue Zambia 51C5
Kafue, R Zambia 51C5
Kafue Nat Pk Zambia 51C5
Kaga Japan 29D3
Kagan USSR 24H6
Kağizman Turk 21G7
Kagul USSR 19F3
Kāhak Iran 41G2
Kahama Tanz 50D4
Kahan Pak 42B3
Kahemba Zaïre 51B4
Kahler Asten, Mt W Germ 13E2
Kahnūj Iran 41G4
Kahoka USA 64A2
Kahoolawe, I Hawaiian Is 66E5
Kahramanmaraş Turk 40C2
Kahuku Pt Hawaiian Is 66E5
Kahului Hawaiian Is 66E5
Kaiapoi NZ 35B2
Kaibab Plat USA 59D3
Kaieteur Falls Guyana 73G2
Kaifeng China 31C3
Kai, Kepulauan, Arch Indon 27G7
Kaikohe NZ 35B1
Kaikoura NZ 33G5
Kaikoura Pen NZ 35B2
Kaikoura Range, Mts NZ 35B2
Kaili China 31B4
Kailu China 28A2
Kailua Hawaii 66E5
Kailua, Oahu Hawaiian Is 66E5
Kaimana Indon 27G7
Kaimenawa Mts NZ 35C1
Kainan Japan 29C4
Kainji Res Nigeria 48C3
Kaipara Harbour, B NZ 35B1
Kaiping China 31C5
Kairouan Tunisia 16C3
Kaiser Peak, Mt USA 66C2
Kaiserslautern W Germ 14D2
Kaishantun China 28B2
Kaisiadorys USSR 19E2
Kaitaia NZ 35B1
Kaitangata NZ 35A3
Kaithal India 42D3
Kaiwi Chan Hawaiian Is 66E5
Kai Xian China 31B3
Kaiyuan, Liaoning China 28A2
Kaiyuan, Yunnan China 31A5
Kajaani Fin 12K6
Kajaki Afghan 42B2
Kajiado Kenya 50D4
Kajrān Afghan 42B2
Kaka Sudan 50D2
Kakabeka Falls Can 64B1
Kakamega Kenya 50D3
Kake Japan 28B4
Kakhovskoye Vodokhranilishche, Res USSR 24E5
Kāki Iran 41F4
Kākināda India 44C2
Kakogawa Japan 29B4
Kaktovik USA 54D2
Kakuda Japan 29D3
Kalaat Khasba Tunisia 16B3
Kalabáka Greece 17E3
Kalabo Zambia 51C5
Kalach USSR 21G5
Kalach-na-Donu USSR 21G6
Kaladan, R Burma/India 43G4
Ka Lae, C Hawaiian Is 66E5
Kalahari Desert Botswana 51C6
Kalahari Gemsbok Nat Pk S Africa 47C2
Kalajoki Fin 20C3
Kalakan USSR 25N4
Kalakepen Indon 27C6
Kalam Pak 42C1
Kalámai Greece 17E3
Kalamazoo USA 57E2
Kalapana Hawaiian Is 66E5
Kalarash USSR 19F3
Kalat Pak 42B3
Kalaupapa Hawaiian Is 66E5
Kalecik Turk 40B1
Kalémié Zaïre 50C4
Kalevala USSR 20E2
Kalewa Burma 43G4
Kalgoorlie Aust 32B4
Kali, R India/Nepal 43E3
Kalima Zaïre 50C4
Kalimantan, Terr Indon 27E7
Kálimnos, I Greece 17F3
Kālimpang India 43F3
Kali Nadi, R India 43K1
Kalinigrad USSR 12J8
Kalinin USSR 20F4
Kaliningrad USSR 20B5
Kalinkovichi USSR 21D5
Kalinovka USSR 19F3
Kalispell USA 56B2
Kalisz Pol 19D2
Kaliua Tanz 50D4
Kalix, R Sweden 12J5
Kalkfeld Namibia 51B6
Kalkfontein Botswana 47C1
Kallavesi, L Fin 12K6
Kallonis Kólpos, B Greece 17F3
Kalmar Sweden 12H7
Kalmyk ASSR, Republic USSR 21H6
Kalomo Zambia 51C5
Kalona USA 64A2
Kalpeni, I India 44A3
Kālpi India 42D3
Kaluga USSR 20F5
Kalundborg Den 12G7
Kalush USSR 19E3
Kalyān India 44A2
Kalyandurg India 44B3
Kalyazin USSR 20F4
Kama, R USSR 20J3
Kamaishi Japan 29E3
Kamalia Pak 42C2
Kamanjab Namibia 51B5
Kamara China 25O4
Kamat, Mt India/China 42D2
Kambam India 44B4
Kambarka USSR 20J4
Kambia Sierra Leone 48A4
Kamchatka, Pen USSR 25S4
Kamenets Podolskiy USSR 19F3
Kamenka USSR 20G5
Kamen-na-Obi USSR 24K4
Kamenskoya USSR 25S3
Kamensk-Ural'skiy USSR 20L4
Kamieskroon S Africa 47B3
Kamilukuak L Can 54H3
Kamina Zaïre 51C4
Kaminak L Can 55J3
Kaminoyama Japan 29D3
Kamloops Can 54F4
Kamo USSR 41E1
Kamogawa Japan 29D3
Kampala Uganda 50D3
Kampar Malay 30C5
Kampen Neth 18B2
Kamphaeng Phet Thai 30B2
Kampot Camb 30C3
Kampuchea = Cambodia
Kamskoye Vodokhranilishche, Res USSR 20K4
Kāmthi India 42D4
Kamyshin USSR 21H5
Kamyshlov USSR 20L4
Kanaaupscow, R Can 55L4
Kanab USA 59D3
Kananga Zaïre 50C4
Kanash USSR 20H4
Kanayama Japan 29C3
Kanazawa Japan 29D3
Kānchipuram India 44B3
Kandagan Indon 27E7
Kandahar Afghan 42B2
Kandalaksha USSR 24E3
Kandalakshskaya Guba, B USSR 12L5
Kandel, Mt W Germ 13D3
Kandi Benin 48C3
Kandos Aust 34C2
Kandy Sri Lanka 44C4
Kane USA 65D2
Kane Basin, B Can 55L1
Kanem, Desert Region Chad 50B2
Kaneohe Hawaiian Is 66E5
Kanevka USSR 20F2
Kang Botswana 47C1
Kangaba Mali 48B3
Kangal Turk 40C2
Kangâmiut Greenland 55N3
Kangān Iran 41F4
Kangar Malay 30C4
Kangaroo I Aust 32C4
Kangatsiaq Greenland 55N3
Kangavar Iran 41E3
Kangbao China 31C1
Kangchenjunga, Mt Nepal/China 39G3
Kangding China 31A4
Kangean, Is Indon 32A1
Kangerdlugssuaq, B Greenland 55P3
Kangerdlugssuatsaiq, B Greenland 55P3
Kangetet Kenya 50D3
Kanggye N Korea 28B2
Kanghwa S Korea 28B3
Kangiqsualujjuaq Can 55M4
Kangiqsujuak Can 55L3
Kangirsuk Can 55L3
Kangnŭng S Korea 28B3
Kango Gabon 50B3
Kangping China 28A2
Kangto, Mt China/India 26C4
Kang Xian China 31B3
Kaniama Zaïre 51C4
Kani Giri India 44B2
Kanin Nos, Pt USSR 24F3
Kanin, Poluostrov, Pen USSR 20G2
Kankaanpää Fin 12J6
Kankakee USA 64B2
Kankakee, R USA 64B2
Kankan Guinea 48B3
Kānker India 43E4
Kannapolis USA 67B1
Kanniyākumari India 44B4
Kano Nigeria 48C3
Kanorado USA 60C3
Kānpur India 43E3
Kansas, R USA 61D3
Kansas, State USA 56D3
Kansas City USA 57D3
Kanshi China 31D5
Kansk USSR 26C1
Kansŏng S Korea 28A3
Kantchari Burkina 48C3
Kanté Togo 48C4
Kanthi India 43F4
Kantishna USA 54C3
Kanturk Irish Rep 9B3
Kanye Botswana 47D1
Kaohsiung Taiwan 26E4
Kaoka Veld, Plain Namibia 51B5
Kaolack Sen 48A3
Kaoma Zambia 51C5
Kapaa Hawaiian Is 66E5
Kapaau Hawaiian Is 66E5
Kapanga Zaïre 51C4
Kapellskär Sweden 12H7
Kap Farvel = Farewell, C
Kapiri Zambia 51C5
Kaplan USA 63D2
Kaplice Czech 18C3
Kapoe Thai 30B4
Kapona Zaïre 51C4
Kaposvár Hung 17D1
Kapsan N Korea 28A2
Kapsukas USSR 20C5
Kapuas, R Indon 27E6
Kapunda Aust 34A2
Kapurthala India 42D2
Kapuskasing Can 55K5
Kapuskasing, R Can 64C1
Kaputar, Mt Aust 34D2
Kapydzhik, Mt USSR 21H8
Kapyŏng S Korea 28A3
Kara, R Turk 21G8
Karabük Turk 40B1
Karacabey Turk 17F2
Karachi Pak 42B4
Karād India 44A2
Kara Dağları, Mt Turk 21F7
Karadeniz Boğazi, Str Turk 21D7
Karaftit USSR 26E1
Karaganda USSR 24J5
Karagayly USSR 24J5
Karaginskiy, Ostrov, I USSR 25S4
Kāraikāl India 44B3
Karaj Iran 41F2
Karak Jordan 40C3

Karakalpak ASSR, Republic *USSR* 24G5
Karakax He, R *China* 42D1
Karakelong, I *Indon* 27F6
Karakoram, Mts *India* 42D1
Karakoram P *India/China* 42D1
Karakoro, Watercourse *Maur/Mali* 48A3
Karakumy, Desert *USSR* 24G6
Karama *Jordan* 45C3
Karaman *Turk* 21E8
Karamay *China* 24K5
Karamea *NZ* 35B2
Karamea Bight, B *NZ* 35B2
Kāranja *India* 42D4
Karanlik, R *Turk* 21E8
Karapınar *Turk* 40B2
Kara S *USSR* 24J2
Karasburg *Namibia* 47B2
Karasjok *Nor* 12K5
Karasuk *USSR* 24J4
Karataş *Turk* 40C2
Kara Tau, Mts *USSR* 24H5
Karathuri *Burma* 30B3
Karatsu *Japan* 28B4
Karaul *USSR* 24K2
Karavostasi *Cyprus* 45B1
Karāz *Iran* 41F4
Karbalā' *Iraq* 41D3
Karcag *Hung* 19E3
Kardhítsa *Greece* 17E3
Karelian ASSR, Republic *USSR* 20E3
Karen *Andaman Is* 44E3
Karepino *USSR* 20K3
Karesvando *Sweden* 12J5
Karet, Desert Region *Maur* 48B2
Kargasok *USSR* 24K4
Kargopol' *USSR* 20F3
Kari *Nigeria* 48D3
Kariba *Zim* 51C5
Kariba Dam *Zambia/Zim* 51C5
Kariba, L *Zambia/Zim* 51C5
Karibib *Namibia* 47B1
Karima *Sudan* 50D2
Karimata, I *Indon* 27D7
Karimganj *India* 43G4
Karimnagar *India* 44B2
Karin *Somalia* 50E2
Karis *Fin* 12J6
Karisimbe, Mt *Zaïre* 50C4
Káristos *Greece* 17E3
Kārkal *India* 44A3
Karkar, I *PNG* 27H7
Karkheh, R *Iran* 41E3
Karkinitskiy Zaliv, B *USSR* 21E6
Karlik Shan, Mt *China* 25L5
Karlino *Pol* 18D2
Karl Marx Stadt *E Germ* 18C2
Karlobag *Yugos* 16D2
Karlovac *Yugos* 16D1
Karlovo *Bulg* 17E2
Karlovy Vary *Czech* 18C2
Karlshamn *Sweden* 12G7
Karlskoga *Sweden* 12G7
Karlskrona *Sweden* 12H7
Karlsruhe *W Germ* 18B3
Karlstad *Sweden* 12G7
Karlstad *USA* 61D1
Karluk *USA* 54C4
Karnafuli Res *Bang* 43G4
Karnāl *India* 42D3
Karnātaka, State *India* 44A2
Karnobat *Bulg* 17F2
Karoi *Zim* 51C5
Karonga *Malawi* 51D4
Karora *Sudan* 50D2
Kárpathos, I *Greece* 17F3
Karrats Fjord *Greenland* 55N2
Karree Berge, Mts *S Africa* 47C3
Kars *Turk* 21G7
Karsakpay *USSR* 24H5
Kārsava *USSR* 19F1
Karshi *USSR* 38E2
Karskiye Vorota, Proliv, Str *USSR* 24G2
Karstula *Fin* 12J6
Kartaba *Leb* 45C1
Kartal *Turk* 17F2
Kartaly *USSR* 20L5
Karthaus *USA* 68A2
Kārūn, R *Iran* 41E3
Karwa *India* 43E3
Kārwār *India* 44A3
Karymskoye *USSR* 26E1
Kasai, R *Zaïre* 50B4
Kasaji *Zaïre* 51C5
Kasama *Zambia* 51D5
Kasanga *Tanz* 51D4
Kāsaragod *India* 44A3
Kasba L *Can* 54H3
Kasempa *Zambia* 51C5
Kasenga *Zaïre* 51C5
Kasese *Uganda* 50D3
Kasganj *India* 43K2
Kāshān *Iran* 41F3
Kashi *China* 39F2
Kashima *Japan* 28B4
Kāshipur *India* 42D3
Kashiwazaki *Japan* 29D3
Kāshmar *Iran* 41G2
Kashmir, State *India* 22E4
Kasimov *USSR* 20G5
Kaskaskia, R *USA* 64B3
Kaskinen *Fin* 12J6
Kasli *USSR* 20L4
Kaslo *Can* 54G5
Kasongo *Zaïre* 50C4
Kasongo-Lunda *Zaïre* 51B4
Kásos, I *Greece* 17F3
Kaspiyskiy *USSR* 21H6
Kassala *Sudan* 50D2
Kassel *W Germ* 18B2
Kasserine *Tunisia* 48C1
Kassinga *Angola* 51B5
Kastamonu *Turk* 40B1
Kastélli *Greece* 17E3
Kastellorizon, I *Greece* 40A2
Kastoría *Greece* 17E2
Kástron *Greece* 17F3
Kasugai *Japan* 29D3
Kasumi *Japan* 29B3
Kasungu *Malawi* 51D5
Kasur *Pak* 42C2
Kataba *Zambia* 51C5
Katahdin,Mt *USA* 65F1
Katako-kombe *Zaïre* 50C4
Katalla *USA* 54D3
Katangli *USSR* 25Q4
Katanning *Aust* 32A4
Katchall, I, Nicobar Is *Indian O* 44E4
Kateríni *Greece* 17E2
Kates Needle, Mt *Can/USA* 54E4
Katharîna, Gebel, Mt *Egypt* 40B4
Katherine *Aust* 32C2
Kāthiāwār, Pen *India* 42C4
Kathib el Henu, hill *Egypt* 45B3
Kathmandu *Nepal* 43F3
Kathua *India* 42D2
Katihār *India* 43F3
Katima Mulilo *Namibia* 51C5
Katiola *Ivory Coast* 48B4
Katmai,Mt *USA* 54C4
Katni *India* 43E4
Katoomba *Aust* 34D2
Katowice *Pol* 19D2
Katrineholm *Sweden* 12H7
Katrine, Loch, L *Scot* 8C3
Katsina *Nigeria* 48C3
Katsina, R *Cam/Nigeria* 48C4
Katsina Ala *Nigeria* 48C4
Katsuta *Japan* 29D3
Katsuura *Japan* 29D3
Katsuyama *Japan* 29C3
Kattakurgan *USSR* 24H5
Kattegat, Str *Den/Sweden* 12G7
Katzenbuckel, Mt *W Germ* 13E3
Kauai, I *Hawaiian Is* 66E5
Kauai Chan *Hawaiian Is* 66E5
Kaulakahi Chan *Hawaiian Is* 66E5
Kaunakakai *Hawaiian Is* 66E5
Kaunas *USSR* 20C5
Kaura Namoda *Nigeria* 48C3
Kautokeino *Nor* 12J5
Kavadarci *Yugos* 17E2
Kavajë *Alb* 17D2
Kavali *India* 44B3
Kavālla *Greece* 17E2
Kavda *India* 42B4
Kavieng *PNG* 32E1
Kawagoe *Japan* 29C3
Kawaguchi *Japan* 29C3
Kawaihae *Hawaiian Is* 66E5
Kawakawa *NZ* 35B1
Kawambwa *Zambia* 51C4
Kawardha *India* 43E4
Kawartha Lakes *Can* 65D2
Kawasaki *Japan* 29D3
Kaweah, R *USA* 66C2
Kawerau *NZ* 35C1
Kawhia *NZ* 35B1
Kaya *Burkina* 48B3
Kayan, R *Indon* 27E6
Kāyankulam *India* 44B4
Kaycee *USA* 60B2
Kayenta *USA* 59D3
Kayes *Mali* 48A3
Kayseri *Turk* 21F8
Kazach'ye *USSR* 25P2
Kazakh *USSR* 41E1
Kazakh SSR, Republic *USSR* 24G5
Kazan' *USSR* 20H4
Kazanlük *Bulg* 17F2
Kazan Retto, Is *Japan* 26H4
Kazatin *USSR* 19F3
Kazbek, Mt *USSR* 21G7
Kāzerūn *Iran* 41F4
Kazhim *USSR* 20J3
Kazi Magomed *USSR* 41E1
Kazincbarcika *Hung* 19E3
Kazym, R *USSR* 20M3
Kazymskaya *USSR* 20M3
Kéa, I *Greece* 17E3
Keady *N Ire* 9C2
Kealaikahiki Chan *Hawaiian Is* 66E5
Kearney *USA* 56D2
Kearny *USA* 59D4
Keban Baraji, Res *Turk* 40C2
Kébémer *Sen* 48A3
Kebili *Tunisia* 48C1
Kebir, R *Leb/Syria* 45D1
Kebnekaise, Mt *Sweden* 12H5
Kecskemét *Hung* 19D3
Kedainiai *USSR* 19E1
Kedgwick *Can* 65F1
Kediri *Indon* 27E7
Kédougou *Sen* 48A3
Kedva *USSR* 20J3
Keele Pk, Mt *Can* 54E3
Keeler *USA* 59C3
Keeling Is *Indian O* 27C8
Keelung *Taiwan* 26F4
Keene, California *USA* 66C3
Keene, New Hampshire *USA* 65E2
Keetmanshoop *Namibia* 47B2
Keewanee *USA* 64B2
Keewatin *USA* 64A1
Keewatin, Region *Can* 55J3
Kefallinía, I *Greece* 17E3
Kefar Sava *Israel* 45C2
Keffi *Nigeria* 48C4
Keflavík *Iceland* 55Q3
Keg River *Can* 54G4
Kehsi Mansam *Burma* 30B1
Keita *Niger* 48C3
Keith *Aust* 34B3
Keith *Scot* 8D3
Keith Arm, B *Can* 54F3
Keithley *Eng* 6C3
Kekertuk *Can* 55M3
Kekri *India* 42D3
Kelang *Malay* 30C5
Kelantan, R *Malay* 30C4
Kelibia *Tunisia* 16C3
Kelif *USSR* 42B1
Kelkit, R *Turk* 40C1
Kellé *Congo* 50B4
Kellett,C *Can* 54F2
Kellogg *USA* 58C1
Kelloselka *Fin* 24D3
Kells *Irish Rep* 33B9
Kells Range, Hills *Scot* 8C4
Kelme *USSR* 19E1
Kelowna *Can* 54G5
Kelsey Bay *Can* 54F4
Kelso *Scot* 8D4
Kelso *USA* 58B1
Kem' *USSR* 24E3
Kem', R *USSR* 20E3
Ke Macina *Mali* 48B3
Kemerovo *USSR* 24K4
Kemi *Fin* 12J5
Kemi, R *Fin* 12K5
Kemijärvi *Fin* 12K5
Kemmerer *USA* 58D2
Kempen, Region *Belg* 13C2
Kemp,L *USA* 62C2
Kemps Bay *The Bahamas* 69B2
Kempsey *Aust* 34D2
Kempten *W Germ* 18C3
Kempt,L *Can* 65E1
Kenai *USA* 54C3
Kenai Pen *USA* 54C3
Kenamuke Swamp *Sudan* 50D3
Kendal *Eng* 6C2
Kendall *Aust* 34D2
Kendari *Indon* 32B1
Kendawangan *Indon* 27E7
Kendrāpara *India* 43F4
Kendrick *USA* 58C1
Kenedy *USA* 63C3
Kenema *Sierra Leone* 48A4
Kenge *Zaïre* 50B4
Kengtung *Burma* 30B1
Kenhardt *S Africa* 47C2
Kéniéba *Mali* 48A3
Kenitra *Mor* 48B1
Kenmare *USA* 60C1
Kenna *USA* 62B2
Kennebec, R *USA* 65F1
Kennebunk *USA* 68E1
Kenner *USA* 63D3
Kennett *USA* 63E1
Kennett Square *USA* 68C3
Kennewick *USA* 58C1
Kenny Dam *Can* 54F4
Kenora *Can* 55J5
Kenosha *USA* 57E2
Kent, Texas *USA* 62B2
Kent, Washington *USA* 58B1
Kent, County *Eng* 7E4
Kentland *USA* 64B2
Kenton *USA* 64C2
Kent Pen *Can* 54H3
Kentucky, R *USA* 64C3
Kentucky, State *USA* 57E3
Kentucky L *USA* 57E3
Kentwood, Louisiana *USA* 63D2
Kentwood, Michigan *USA* 64B2
Kenya, Republic *Africa* 50D3
Kenya,Mt *Kenya* 50D4
Keokuk *USA* 64A2
Keonchi *India* 43E4
Keonjhargarh *India* 43F4
Kepno *Pol* 19D2
Kerala, State *India* 44B3
Kerang *Aust* 34B3
Kerava *Fin* 12K6
Kerch' *USSR* 21F6
Kerchem'ya *USSR* 20J3
Kerema *PNG* 32D1
Keremeos *Can* 58C1
Keren *Eth* 50D2
Kerguelen, Is *Indian O* 36E7
Kerguelen Ridge *Indian O* 36E7
Kericho *Kenya* 50D4
Kerinci, Mt *Indon* 27D7
Kerio, R *Kenya* 50D3
Kerkenna, Îles *Tunisia* 48D1
Kerki *USSR* 38E2
Kérkira = Corfu
Kermadec Is *Pacific O* 33H3
Kermadec Trench *Pacific O* 33H4
Kermān *Iran* 41G3
Kerman *USA* 66B2
Kermānshāh *Iran* 41E3
Kermit *USA* 62B2
Kern, R *USA* 59C3
Kernville *USA* 66C3
Keros *USSR* 20J3
Kerrville *USA* 62C2
Kerry Hd *Irish Rep* 9B3
Kershaw *USA* 67B2
Kerulen, R *Mongolia* 25N5
Kerzaz *Alg* 48B2
Keşan *Turk* 17F2
Kesariya *India* 43N2
Kesennuma *Japan* 29E3
Kesir Dağları, Mt *Turk* 21G7
Kestenga *USSR* 12L5
Keswick *Eng* 6C2
Keta *Ghana* 48C4
Ketapang *Indon* 27E7
Ketchikan *USA* 54E4
Keti Bandar *Pak* 42B4
Kętrzyn *Pol* 19E2
Kettering *Eng* 7D3
Kettering *USA* 64C3
Kettle, R *Can* 58C1
Kettleman City *USA* 66C2
Kettle River Range, Mts *USA* 58C1
Kettlestone B *Can* 55L3
Keuka L *USA* 68B1
Kevir-i-Namak, Salt Flat *Iran* 41G3
Kewaunee *USA* 64B2
Keweenaw B *USA* 64B1
Keweenaw Pen *USA* 64B1
Key Harbour *Can* 64C1
Key Largo *USA* 67B3
Key West *USA* 57E4
Kezhma *USSR* 25M4
Khabab *Syria* 45D2
Khabarovsk *USSR* 26G2
Khabūr, al, R *Syria* 21G8
Khairpur *Pak* 42B3
Khairpur, Division *Pak* 42B3
Khakhea *Botswana* 47C1
Khalig el Tîna, B *Egypt* 45B3
Khalij Maşirah, G *Oman* 38D4
Khálki, I *Greece* 17F3
Khalkidhíki, Pen *Greece* 17E2
Khalkís *Greece* 17E3
Khal'mer-Yu *USSR* 20L2
Khalturin *USSR* 20H4
Khambhat,G of *India* 42C4
Khamgaon *India* 42D4
Kham Keut *Laos* 30C2
Khammam *India* 44C2
Khamsa *Egypt* 45B3
Khamseh, Mts *Iran* 41E2
Khan, R *Laos* 30C2
Khanabad *Afghan* 42B1
Khānaqin *Iraq* 41E3
Khandwa *India* 42D4
Khanewal *Pak* 42C2
Khan ez Zabib *Jordan* 45D3
Khanh Hung *Viet* 30D4
Khaniá *Greece* 17E3
Khanka, Oz, L *USSR* 26G2
Khanpur *Pak* 42C3
Khan Shaykhun *Syria* 45D1
Khanty-Mansiysk *USSR* 24H3
Khan Yunis *Israel* 45C3
Khapalu *India* 42D1
Khapcheranga *USSR* 26E2
Kharabali *USSR* 21H6
Kharagpur *India* 43F4
Kharan *Pak* 42B3
Kharan, R *Iran* 41G4
Kharanaq *Iran* 41F3
Kharg, I *Iran* 41F4
Khârga Oasis *Egypt* 49F2
Khargon *India* 42D4
Kharîm, Gebel, Mt *Egypt* 45B3
Khar'kov *USSR* 21F6
Kharlovka *USSR* 20F2
Kharmanli *Bulg* 17F2
Kharovsk *USSR* 20G4
Khartoum *Sudan* 50D2
Khartoum North *Sudan* 50D2
Khasan *USSR* 28C2
Khashm el Girba *Sudan* 50D2
Khasi-Jaintia Hills *India* 43G3
Khaskovo *Bulg* 17F2
Khatanga *USSR* 25M2
Khatangskiy Zaliv, Estuary *USSR* 25N2
Khatyrka *USSR* 25T3
Khawsa *Burma* 30B3
Khaybar *S Arabia* 40C4
Khazzan an-Nasr, L *Egypt* 40B5
Khe Bo *Viet* 30C2
Khed Brahma *India* 42C4
Khemis *Alg* 15C2
Khenchela *Algeria* 16B3
Kheri, District *India* 43L1
Kherrata *Alg* 15D2
Kherson *USSR* 21E6
Khilok *USSR* 25N4
Khíos *Greece* 17F3
Khíos, I *Greece* 17F3
Khmel'nitskiy *USSR* 21D6
Khodorov *USSR* 19E3
Kholm *Afghan* 42B1
Kholm *USSR* 19G1
Khomas Hochland, Mts *Namibia* 47B1
Khong *Laos* 30D3
Khonj *Iran* 41F4
Khor *USSR* 26G2
Khor Duwayhin, B *UAE* 41F5
Khorog *USSR* 42C1
Khorramabad *Iran* 41E3
Khorramshahr *Iran* 41E3
Khosf *Iran* 41G3
Khost *Pak* 42B2
Khotin *USSR* 21D6
Khoyniki *USSR* 21E5
Khrebet Kopet Dag, Mts *USSR/Iran* 41G2
Khrebet Pay-khoy, Mts *USSR* 20L2
Khrysokhou B *Cyprus* 45B1
Khulga, R *USSR* 20L3
Khulna *Bang* 43F4
Khunjerab P *China/India* 42D1
Khunsar *Iran* 41F3
Khurays *S Arabia* 41E4
Khurda *India* 43F4
Khurja *India* 42D3
Khushab *Pak* 42C2
Khushnıyah *Syria* 45C2
Khush Shah, Wadi el *Jordan* 45D4
Khust *USSR* 19E3
Khuwei *Sudan* 50C2
Khuzdar *Pak* 42B3
Khvalynsk *USSR* 21H5
Khvor *Iran* 41G3
Khvormūj *Iran* 41F4
Khvoy *Iran* 21G8
Khwaja Muhammad Ra, Mts *Afghan* 42C1
Khyber P *Afghan/Pak* 42C2
Kiambi *Zaïre* 51C4
Kiamichi, R *USA* 63C2
Kibangou *Congo* 50B4
Kibaya *Tanz* 50D4
Kibombo *Zaïre* 50C4
Kibondo *Tanz* 50D4
Kibungu *Rwanda* 50D4
Kicevo *Yugos* 17E2
Kicking Horse P *Can* 54G4
Kidal *Mali* 48C3
Kidderminster *Eng* 7C3
Kidira *Sen* 48A3
Kidnappers,C *NZ* 35C1
Kiel *W Germ* 18C2
Kielce *Pol* 19E2
Kielder Res *Eng* 6C2
Kieler Bucht, B *W Germ* 18C2
Kiev *USSR* 21E5
Kifab *USSR* 38E2
Kiffa *Maur* 48A3

Kowloon La'nga Co

Kowloon *Hong Kong* 31C5
Kowŏn *N Korea* 28A3
Kowt-e-Ashrow *Afghan* 42B2
Köyceğiz *Turk* 40A2
Koyda *USSR* 20G2
Koyna Res *India* 44A2
Koynas *USSR* 20H3
Koyukuk *USA* 54C3
Kozan *Turk* 40C2
Kozańi *Greece* 17E2
Kozhikode = Calicut
Kozhim *USSR* 20K2
Koz'modemyansk *USSR* 20H4
Kozu-shima, I *Japan* 29C4
Kpalimé *Togo* 48C4
Kraai, R *S Africa* 47D3
Kragerø *Nor* 12F7
Kragujevac *Yugos* 17E2
Kra,Isthmus of *Burma/Malay* 30B3
Krak des Chevaliers, Hist Site *Syria* 45D1
Kraków = Cracow
Kraljevo *Yugos* 17E2
Kramatorsk *USSR* 21F6
Kramfors *Sweden* 12H6
Kranj *Yugos* 16C1
Krasavino *USSR* 20H3
Krasino *USSR* 24G2
Kraskino *USSR* 28C2
Kraśnik *Pol* 19E2
Krasnoarmeysk *USSR* 21H5
Krasnodar *USSR* 21F7
Krasnokamsk *USSR* 20K4
Krasnotur'insk *USSR* 20L4
Krasnoufimsk *USSR* 20K4
Krasnousol'skiy *USSR* 20K5
Krasnovishersk *USSR* 20K3
Krasnovodsk *USSR* 21J7
Krasnoyarsk *USSR* 25L4
Krasnystaw *Pol* 19E2
Krasnyy Kut *USSR* 21H5
Krasnyy Luch *USSR* 21F6
Krasnyy Yar *USSR* 21H6
Kratie *Camb* 30D3
Kraulshavn *Greenland* 55N2
Krefeld *W Germ* 18B2
Kremenchug *USSR* 21E6
Kremenchugskoye Vodokhranilische, Res *USSR* 21E6
Kremenets *USSR* 19F2
Kremming *USA* 60B2
Kribi *Cam* 48C4
Krichev *USSR* 20E5
Krishna, R *India* 44B2
Krishnagiri *India* 44B3
Krishnanagar *India* 43F4
Kristiansand *Nor* 12F7
Kristianstad *Sweden* 12G7
Kristiansund *Nor* 24B3
Kristiinankaupunki *Fin* 12J6
Kristinehamn *Sweden* 12G7
Kríti = Crete
Krivoy Rog *USSR* 21E6
Krk, I *Yugos* 16C1
Krokodil, R *S Africa* 47D1
Kronotskaya Sopka, Mt *USSR* 25S4
Kronotskiy, Mys, C *USSR* 25S4
Kronprins Frederik Bjerge, Mts *Greenland* 55P3
Kronshtadt *USSR* 12K7
Kroonstad *S Africa* 47D2
Kropotkin *USSR* 21G6
Kruger Nat Pk *S Africa* 47E1
Krugersdorp *S Africa* 47D2
Kruje *Alb* 17D2
Krung Thep = Bangkok
Krupki *USSR* 19F2
Kruševac *Yugos* 17E2
Krustpils *USSR* 12K7
Krym = Crimea
Krym, Pen *USSR* 24E5
Krymsk *USSR* 21F7
Krzyz *Pol* 18D2
Ksar El Boukhari *Alg* 15C2
Ksar-el-Kebir *Mor* 15A2
Ksour, Mts des *Alg* 48C1
Kuala *Indon* 27C6
Kuala Dungun *Malay* 30C5
Kuala Kerai *Malay* 30C4
Kuala Kubu Baharu *Malay* 30C5
Kuala Lipis *Malay* 30C5
Kuala Lumpur *Malay* 30C5
Kuala Trengganu *Malay* 30C4
Kuandang *Indon* 27F6
Kuandian *China* 28A2
Kuantan *Malay* 30C5
Kuba *USSR* 21H7
Kubor, Mt *PNG* 27H7
Kuching *Malay* 27E6
Kudat *Malay* 27E6
Kudymkar *USSR* 20J4
Kufstein *Austria* 18C3
Kuh Duren, Upland *Iran* 41G3
Kuh-e Dinar, Mt *Iran* 41F3
Kuh-e-Hazār Masjed, Mts *Iran* 41G2
Kuh-e Jebal Barez, Mts *Iran* 41G4
Kuh-e Karkas, Mts *Iran* 41F3
Kuh-e Laleh Zar, Mt *Iran* 41G4
Kuh-e Sahand, Mt *Iran* 41E2
Kuh-e-Taftān, Mt *Iran* 38E3
Kuhhaye Alvand, Mts *Iran* 21H9
Kuhhaye Sabalan, Mts *Iran* 21H8
Kuhhā-ye Zagros, Mts *Iran* 41E3
Kuhmo *Fin* 12K6
Kuhpāyeh *Iran* 41F3
Kuhpāyeh, Mt *Iran* 41G3
Kuh-ye Bashakerd, Mts *Iran* 41G4
Kuh-ye Sabalan, Mt *Iran* 41E2
Kuibis *Namibia* 47B2
Kuiseb, R *Namibia* 47B1
Kujang *N Korea* 28A3
Kuji *Japan* 29E2
Kuju-san, Mt *Japan* 28B4
Kukës *Alb* 17E2
Kukup *Malay* 30C5
Kul, R *Iran* 41G4
Kula *Turk* 17F3
Kulakshi *USSR* 21K6
Kulal,Mt *Kenya* 50D3
Kulata *Bulg* 17E2
Kuldiga *USSR* 20C4
Kulov, R *USSR* 20G2
Kul'sary *USSR* 21J6
Kulu *India* 42D2
Kulu *Turk* 40B2
Kulunda *USSR* 24J4
Kulwin *Aust* 34B2
Kuma, R *USSR* 21H7
Kumagaya *Japan* 29C3
Kumai *Indon* 27E7
Kumak *USSR* 21L5
Kumamoto *Japan* 28C4
Kumano *Japan* 29C4
Kumanovo *Yugos* 17E2
Kumasi *Ghana* 48B4
Kumba *Cam* 48C4
Kumbakonam *India* 44B3
Kümch'ŏn *N Korea* 28A3
Kumertau *USSR* 20K5
Kumgang *N Korea* 28A3
Kumla *Sweden* 12H7
Kümnyŏng *S Korea* 28A4
Kümo-do, I *S Korea* 28A4
Kumta *India* 44A3
Kumüx *China* 39G1
Kumwha *S Korea* 28B3
Kunar, R *Afghan* 42C2
Kunashir, Ostrov, I *USSR* 29F2
Kunda *USSR* 12K7
Kundla *India* 42C4
Kunduz *Afghan* 42B1
Kunene, R = Cunene R
Kungsbacka *Sweden* 12G7
Kungur *USSR* 20K4
Kunhing *Burma* 30B1
Kunlun Shan, Mts *China* 39G2
Kunming *China* 31A4
Kunovat, R *USSR* 20M3
Kunsan *S Korea* 28B3
Kuopio *Fin* 12K6
Kupa, R *Yugos* 16D1
Kupang *Indon* 32B2
Kupiano *PNG* 32D2
Kupreanof I *USA* 54E4
Kupyansk *USSR* 21F6
Kuqa *China* 39G1
Kura, R *USSR* 21H8
Kurabe *Japan* 29C3
Kurashiki *Japan* 29C4
Kurayoshi *Japan* 29B3
Kurdistan, Region *Iran* 41E2
Kürdzhali *Bulg* 17F2
Kure *Japan* 28C4
Kureyka, R *USSR* 25L3
Kurgan *USSR* 24H4
Kurikka *Fin* 12J6
Kuril Is *USSR* 25Q5
Kuril'skiye Ostrova, Is = Kuril Is
Kuril Trench *Pacific O* 36J2
Kurinskaya Kosa, Sand Spit *USSR* 21H8
Kurnool *India* 44B2
Kuroishi *Japan* 29D2
Kuroiso *Japan* 29D3
Kurow *NZ* 35B2
Kurri Kurri *Aust* 34D2
Kursk *USSR* 21F5
Kurskiy Zaliv, Lg *USSR* 19E1
Kuruktag, R *China* 26B2
Kuruman *S Africa* 47C2
Kuruman, R *S Africa* 47C2
Kurume *Japan* 28C4
Kurunegala *Sri Lanka* 44C3
Kurunktag, R *China* 24K5
Kur'ya *USSR* 20K3
Kusa *USSR* 20K4
Kuşadasi Körfezi, B *Turk* 17F3
Kus Golü, L *Turk* 17F2
Kushimoto *Japan* 29D4
Kushiro *Japan* 29E2
Kushka *USSR* 38E2
Kushtia *Bang* 43F4
Kushum, R *USSR* 21J5
Kushva *USSR* 24H4
Kuskokwim, R *USA* 54B3
Kuskokwim Mts *USA* 54C3
Kusma *Nepal* 43E3
Kusŏng *N Korea* 28B3
Kustanay *USSR* 24H4
Kuta, R *Indon* 27E7
Kütahya *Turk* 21D8
Kutaisi *USSR* 21G7
Kutchan *Japan* 29D2
Kutcharo-ko, L *Japan* 29E2
Kutná Hora *Czech* 18D3
Kutno *Pol* 19D2
Kutu *Zaïre* 50B4
Kutubdia I *Bang* 43G4
Kutum *Sudan* 50C2
Kuujjuaq *Can* 55M4
Kuusamo *Fin* 12K5
Kuvandyk *USSR* 21K5
Kuvbyshev *USSR* 29L3
Kuwait *Kuwait* 41E4
Kuwait, Sheikhdom *S W Asia* 38C3
Kuwana *Japan* 29C3
Kuybyshev *USSR* 24G4
Kuybyshev *USSR* 24J4
Kuybyshevskoye Vodokhranilishche, Res *USSR* 20H5
Kuyto, Ozero, L *USSR* 20E2
Kuytun *USSR* 25M4
Kuzey Anadolu Dağları, Mts *Turk* 21F7
Kuzomen *USSR* 20F2
Kvænangen, Sd *Nor* 20C2
Kvigtind, Mt *Nor* 12G5
Kvikkjokk *Sweden* 20B2
Kwale *Kenya* 50D4
Kwangju *S Korea* 28B3
Kwango, R *Zaïre* 50B4
Kwangyang *S Korea* 28A3
Kwanmo-bong, Mt *N Korea* 28A2
Kwekwe *Zim* 51C5
Kwidzyn *Pol* 19D2
Kwigillingok *USA* 54B4
Kwoka, Mt *Indon* 27G7
Kyabram *Aust* 34C3
Kyaikkami *Burma* 30B2
Kyaikto *Burma* 30B2
Kyakhta *USSR* 26D1
Kyaukme *Burma* 30B1
Kyauk-padaung *Burma* 30B1
Kyaukpyu *Burma* 30A2
Kychema *USSR* 20G2
Kyle of Lochalsh *Scot* 10B2
Kyll, R *W Germ* 13D2
Kyneton *Aust* 34B3
Kyoga, L *Uganda* 50D3
Kyogle *Aust* 34D1
Kyŏngju *S Korea* 28B3
Kyongsang Sanmaek, Mts *S Korea* 28A3
Kyŏngsŏng *N Korea* 28A2
Kyoto *Japan* 29D3
Kyrenia *Cyprus* 45B1
Kyrta *USSR* 20K3
Kyshtym *USSR* 24H4
Kythrea *Cyprus* 45B1
Kyūshū, I *Japan* 28B4
Kyushu-Palau Ridge *Pacific O* 36H4
Kyustendil *Bulg* 17E2
Kyusyur *USSR* 25O2
Kyzyl *USSR* 26C1
Kyzylkum, Desert *USSR* 24H5
Kzyl Orda *USSR* 24H5

L

Laas Caanood *Somalia* 50E3
Laasphe *W Germ* 13E2
Laas Qoray *Somalia* 50E2
La Asunción *Ven* 72F1
La Barge *USA* 58D2
Labé *Guinea* 48A3
Labe, R *Czech* 18D2
Labelle *Can* 65E1
La Belle *USA* 67B3
Labinsk *USSR* 21G7
Laboué *Leb* 45D1
Labrador, Region *Can* 55M4
Labrador City *Can* 55M4
Labrador S *Can/Greenland* 55N4
Lábrea *Brazil* 72F5
Labuk B *Malay* 27E6
Labutta *Burma* 30A2
Labytnangi *USSR* 20M2
La Capelle *France* 13B2
Laccadive Is = Lakshadweep
Laccadive Is *India* 39F4
La Ceiba *Honduras* 70D3
Lacepede B *Aust* 34A3
La Châtre *France* 14C2
Lachish, Hist Site *Israel* 45C3
Lachlan, R *Aust* 32D4
La Chorrera *Panama* 72C2
Lachute *Can* 65E1
Lackawanna *USA* 65D2
Lac la Biche *Can* 54G4
Lac L'eau Claire *Can* 55L4
Lac Mégantic *Can* 65E1
Lacombe *Can* 54G4
Laconia *USA* 65E2
La Coruña *Spain* 15A1
La Crosse *USA* 57D2
La Cruces *USA* 56C3
La Cygne *USA* 63D1
Ladakh Range, Mts *India* 42D2
Ladd Reef *S China Sea* 27E6
Ladnun *India* 42C3
Ladoga, L *USSR* 20E3
Ladong *China* 31B5
Ladozhskoye Oz, L = Ladoga, L
Lady Ann Str *Can* 55K2
Lady Barron *Aust* 34C4
Ladybrand *S Africa* 47D2
Ladysmith *S Africa* 47D2
Ladysmith *USA* 64A1
Lae *PNG* 32D1
Laem Ngop *Thai* 30C3
Laesø, I *Den* 18C1
Lafayette, Colorado *USA* 60B3
Lafayette, Indiana *USA* 57E2
Lafayette, Louisiana *USA* 57D3
La Fère *France* 13B3
La-Ferté-sous-Jouarre *France* 13B3
Lafia *Nigeria* 48C4
Lafiagi *Nigeria* 48C4
La Flèche *France* 14B2
La Galite, I *Tunisia* 16B3
Lagan, R *Sweden* 18C1
Lagarto *Brazil* 73L6
Laggan, L *Scot* 8C3
Laghouat *Alg* 48C1
Lago Agrio *Ecuador* 72C4
Lagos *Nigeria* 48C4
Lagos *Port* 15A2
Lagos de Moreno *Mexico* 70B2
La Grande *USA* 56B2
La Grande Rivière, R *Can* 55L4
Lagrange *Aust* 32B2
La Grange, Georgia *USA* 57E3
La Grange, Kentucky *USA* 64B3
La Grange, N Carolina *USA* 67C1
La Grange, Texas *USA* 63C3
La Gran Sabana, Mts *Ven* 72F2
Laguna *USA* 62A2
Laguna Beach *USA* 59C4
Laguna Seca *Mexico* 56C4
Lagusha *N Korea* 28B2
Lahad Datu *Malay* 27E6
Lahijan *Iran* 41F2
Lahn, R *W Germ* 13D2
Lahnstein *W Germ* 13D2
Lahore *Pak* 42C2
Lahr *W Germ* 13D3
Lahti *Fin* 12K6
Lai *Chad* 50B3
Laibin *China* 31B5
Lai Chau *Viet* 30C1
Laignes *France* 13C4
Laihia *Fin* 12J6
Laingsburg *S Africa* 47C3
Lairg *Scot* 8C2
Laiyang *China* 31E2
Laizhou Wan, B *China* 31D2
Laja, Lago de la *Chile* 74B5
Lajes *Brazil* 74F3
La Jolla *USA* 66D4
La Junta *USA* 56C3
Lake Andes *USA* 60D2
Lake Cargelligo *Aust* 34C2
Lake Charles *USA* 57D3
Lake City, Florida *USA* 67B2
Lake City, Minnesota *USA* 61E2
Lake City, S Carolina *USA* 67C2
Lake District, Region *Eng* 6C2
Lake Elsinore *USA* 66D4
Lake Eyre Basin *Aust* 32C3
Lakefield *Can* 65D2
Lake Geneva *USA* 64B2
Lake George *USA* 68D1
Lake Harbour *Can* 55M3
Lake Havasu City *USA* 59D4
Lake Hughes *USA* 66C3
Lakehurst *USA* 68C2
Lake Isabella *USA* 66C3
Lake Jackson *USA* 63C3
Lakeland *USA* 67B3
Lake of the Woods *Can* 55J5
Lake Oswego *USA* 58B1
Lakeport *USA* 59B3
Lake Providence *USA* 63D2
Lake Pukaki *NZ* 35B2
Lakes Entrance *Aust* 34C3
Lakeshore *USA* 66C2
Lake Stewart *Aust* 34B1
Lake Traverse *Can* 65D1
Lakeview *USA* 56A2
Lakeview Mt *Can* 58B1
Lake Village *USA* 63D2
Lake Wales *USA* 67B3
Lakewood, California *USA* 66C4
Lakewood, Colorado *USA* 60B3
Lakewood, New Jersey *USA* 68C2
Lakewood, Ohio *USA* 64C2
Lake Worth *USA* 67B3
Lakhimpur *India* 43E3
Lakhpat *India* 42B4
Lakin *USA* 62B1
Lakki *Pak* 42C2
Lakonikós Kólpos, G *Greece* 17E3
Lakota *Ivory Coast* 48B4
Laksefjord, Inlet *Nor* 12K4
Lakselv *Nor* 12K4
Lakshadweep, Is, Union Territory *India* 44A3
La Libertad *Ecuador* 72B4
La Linea *Spain* 15A2
Lalitpur *India* 42D4
La Loche *Can* 54H4
La Louvière *Belg* 13C2
La Luz *Nic* 69A4
La Malbaie *Can* 55L5
Lamar, Colorado *USA* 56C3
Lamar, Missouri *USA* 63D1
La Marque *USA* 63C3
Lambaréné *Gabon* 50B4
Lambayeque *Peru* 72B5
Lambert Glacier *Ant* 76F10
Lamberts Bay *S Africa* 47B3
Lambertville *USA* 68C2
Lambton,C *Can* 54F2
Lam Chi, R *Thai* 30C2
Lamego *Port* 15A1
La Merced *Peru* 72C6
Lamesa *USA* 62B2
La Mesa *USA* 59C4
Lamía *Greece* 17E3
Lammermuir Hills *Scot* 8D4
Lammhult *Sweden* 12G7
Lamoni *USA* 61E2
Lamont, California *USA* 66C3
Lamont, Wyoming *USA* 60B2
Lamotrek, I *Pacific O* 27H6
Lamotte-Beuvron *France* 13B4
La Moure *USA* 60D1
Lampasas *USA* 62C2
Lampeter *Wales* 7B3
Lamu *Kenya* 50E4
Lanai, I *Hawaiian Is* 66E5
Lanai City *Hawaiian Is* 66E5
Lanao, L *Phil* 27F6
Lanark *Scot* 8D4
Lanbi, I *Burma* 30B3
Lancang, R *China* 30C1
Lancashire, County *Eng* 6C3
Lancaster, California *USA* 59C4
Lancaster *Eng* 6C2
Lancaster, Missouri *USA* 61E2
Lancaster, New Hampshire *USA* 65E2
Lancaster, New York *USA* 68A1
Lancaster, Ohio *USA* 64C3
Lancaster, Pennsylvania *USA* 57F3
Lancaster, S Carolina *USA* 67B2
Lancaster Sd *Can* 55K2
Landan *W Germ* 13E3
Landeck *Austria* 18C3
Lander *USA* 56C2
Landes, Les, Region *France* 14B3
Landrum *USA* 67B1
Landsberg *W Germ* 18C3
Lands End, C *Can* 54F2
Land's End, Pt *Eng* 7B4
Landshut *W Germ* 18C3
Làndskrona *Sweden* 12G7
Lanett *USA* 67A2
La'nga Co, L *China* 43E2

Langdon Linhai

Langdon *USA* 60D1
Langeberg, Mts *S Africa* 47C2
Langenhagen *W Germ* 18B2
Langeoog, I *W Germ* 13D1
Langholm *Scot* 8D4
Langjökull, Mts *Iceland* 12A2
Langkawi, I *Malay* 30B4
Langlo, R *Aust* 34C1
Langness, Pt *Eng* 6B2
Langon *France* 14B3
Langres *France* 14D2
Langres, Plateau de *France* 13C4
Langsa *Indon* 27C6
Lang Shan, Mts *China* 26D2
Lang Son *Viet* 30D1
Langtry *USA* 62B3
Languedoc, Region *France* 14C3
Lanin, Vol *Arg* 74B5
Lansdale *USA* 68C2
Lansdowne House *Can* 55K4
Lansford *USA* 68C2
Lansing *USA* 57E2
Lanzarote, I *Canary Is* 48A2
Lanzhou *China* 31A2
Laoag *Phil* 27F5
Lao Cai *Viet* 30C1
Laoha He, R *China* 31D1
Laois, County *Irish Rep* 9C3
Laoling *China* 28A2
Laon *France* 13B3
La Oroya *Peru* 72C6
Laos, Republic *S E Asia* 30C2
Lapa *Brazil* 75C4
Lapalisse *France* 14C2
La Palma *Panama* 72C2
La Palma, I *Canary Is* 48A2
La Pampa, State *Arg* 74C5
La Panza Range, Mts *USA* 66B3
La Paragua *Ven* 72F2
La Paz *Arg* 74E4
La Paz *Bol* 72E7
La Paz *Mexico* 70A2
La Perouse Str *Japan/USSR* 26H2
La Pine *USA* 58B2
Lapithos *Cyprus* 45B1
Laplace *USA* 63D2
La Plant *USA* 60C1
La Plata *Arg* 74E4
La Porte *USA* 64B2
Laporte *USA* 68B2
Lappeenranta *Fin* 12K6
Lappland, Region *Fin/Sweden* 12H5
La Pryor *USA* 62C3
Laptev S *USSR* 25O2
Lapua *Fin* 12J6
La Purísima *Mexico* 56B4
Laqiya Arba'in, Well *Sudan* 50C1
La Quiaca *Arg* 74C2
L'Aquila *Italy* 16C2
Lar *Iran* 41F4
Larache *Mor* 15A2
Laramie *USA* 56C2
Laramie Mts *USA* 60B2
Laramie Range, Mts *USA* 56C2
Laranjeiras do Sul *Brazil* 75B4
Laredo *USA* 56D4
Larestan, Region *Iran* 41F4
Largeau = Faya
Largo *USA* 67B3
Largs *Scot* 8C4
Lari *Iran* 41E2
La Rioja *Arg* 74C3
La Rioja, Region *Spain* 15B1
La Rioja, State *Arg* 74C3
Lárisa *Greece* 17E3
Larkana *Pak* 42B3
Larnaca *Cyprus* 40B3
Larnaca B *Cyprus* 45B1
Larne *N Ire* 9C2
Larned *USA* 62C1
La Robla *Spain* 15A1
La Roche-en-Ardenne *Belg* 13C2
La Rochelle *France* 14B2
La Roche-sur-Yon *France* 14B2
La Roda *Spain* 15B2
La Romana *Dom Rep* 69D3
La Ronge *Can* 54H4
Larvik *Nor* 12F7
Lar'yak *USSR* 24J3
La Sagra, Mt *Spain* 15B2
La Salle *Can* 65E1
La Salle *USA* 64B2
Las Animas *USA* 62B1
La Sarre *Can* 55L5
Las Cruces *USA* 62A2
La Selle, Mt *Haiti* 69C3
Lasengmiao *China* 31B2
La Serena *Chile* 74B3
Las Flores *Arg* 74E5
Lashio *Burma* 30B1
La Sila, Mts *Italy* 16D3
Lasjerd *Iran* 41F2
Laskar Gāh *Afghan* 42A2
Las Marismas, Marshland *Spain* 15A2
Las Palmas de Gran Canaria *Canary Is* 48A2
La Spezia *Italy* 16B2
Las Plumas *Arg* 74C6
Lassen Peak, Mt *USA* 58B2
Lassen Volcanic Nat Pk *USA* 58B2
Lastoursville *Gabon* 50B4
Lastovo, I *Yugos* 16D2
Las Tres Marias, Is *Mexico* 70B2
Las Vegas *USA* 56B3
Latakia *Syria* 40C2
Latina *Italy* 16C2
La Tortuga, I *Ven* 72E1
Latrobe *Aust* 34C4
Latrun *Israel* 45C3
La Tuque *Can* 55L5
Lātūr *India* 44B2
Latvian SSR, Republic *USSR* 20C4
Lauder *Scot* 8D4
Lauenburg *W Germ* 18B2
Lau Group, Is *Fiji* 33H2
Launceston *Aust* 32D5
Launceston *Eng* 7B4
La Unión *Chile* 74B6
La Unión *El Salvador* 70D3
La Unión *Peru* 72C5
Laura *Aust* 32D2
Laurel, Delaware *USA* 65D3
Laurel, Maryland *USA* 68B3
Laurel, Mississippi *USA* 57E3
Laurel, Montana *USA* 58E1
Laurens *USA* 67B2
Laurinburg *USA* 67C2
Lausanne *Switz* 16B1
Laut, I *Indon* 27E7
Lautaro *Chile* 74B7
Lauterbach *W Germ* 13E2
Lauterecken *W Germ* 13D3
Laval *Can* 65E1
Laval *France* 14B2
Laveaga Peak, Mt *USA* 66B2
Lavina *USA* 58E1
La Vôge, Region *France* 13C3
Lavras *Brazil* 73K8
Lavrentiya *USSR* 54A3
Lavumisa *Swaziland* 47E2
Lawksawk *Burma* 30B1
Lawrence, Kansas *USA* 61D3
Lawrence, Massachusetts *USA* 65E2
Lawrence *NZ* 35A3
Lawrenceburg *USA* 63E1
Lawrenceville, Illinois *USA* 64B3
Lawrenceville, Pennsylvania *USA* 68B2
Lawton *USA* 56D3
Lawz, Jebel al, Mt *S Arabia* 40C4
Laxey *Eng* 6B2
Layla' *S Arabia* 38C3
Laylo *Sudan* 50D3
La'youn *Mor* 48A2
Laz Daua *Somalia* 50E2
Lazo *USSR* 29C2
Lead *USA* 56C2
Leadville *USA* 60B3
Leaf, R *USA* 63E2
Leakey *USA* 62C3
Leamington Spa, Royal *Eng* 7D5
Leavenworth *USA* 61E3
Łeba *Pol* 19D2
Lebanon, Kansas *USA* 60D3
Lebanon, Missouri *USA* 63D1
Lebanon, Oregon *USA* 58B2
Lebanon, Pennsylvania *USA* 65D2
Lebanon, Tennessee *USA* 64B3
Lebanon, Republic *S W Asia* 40C3
Lebec *USA* 66C3
Lebombo Mts *Mozam/S Africa/Swaziland* 51D6
Lębork *Pol* 19D2
Lebu *Chile* 74B5
Le Cateau *France* 13B2
Lecce *Italy* 17D2
Lecco *Italy* 16B1
Le Champ du Feu, Mt *France* 13D3
Le Creusot *France* 14C2
Ledbury *Eng* 7C3
Ledo *India* 43H3
Lee *USA* 68D1
Leech L *USA* 61E1
Leeds *Eng* 10C3
Leek *Eng* 7C3
Leer *W Germ* 18B2
Leesburg, Florida *USA* 67B3
Leesburg, Virginia *USA* 68B3
Leesville *USA* 63D2
Leeton *Aust* 34C2
Leeugamka *S Africa* 47C3
Leeuwarden *Neth* 18B2
Leeuwin,C *Aust* 32A4
Lee Vining *USA* 66C2
Leeward Is *Caribbean S* 69E3
Lefka *Cyprus* 45B1
Lefkara *Cyprus* 45B1
Lefkoniko *Cyprus* 45B1
Legazpi *Phil* 27F5
Legnica *Pol* 18D2
Leguan Island *Guyana* 73G2
Leguizamo *Peru* 72D4
Leh *India* 42D2
Le Havre *France* 14C2
Lehi *USA* 59D2
Lehigh, R *USA* 68C2
Lehighton *USA* 68C2
Le Hohneck, Mt *France* 13D3
Leiah *Pak* 42C2
Leibnitz *Austria* 18D3
Leicester *Eng* 7D3
Leicester, County *Eng* 7D3
Leichhardt, R *Aust* 32C2
Leiden *Neth* 18A2
Leie, R *Belg* 13B2
Leigh Creek *Aust* 32C4
Leigh on Sea *Eng* 7E4
Leighton Buzzard *Eng* 7D4
Leine, R *W Germ* 18B2
Leinster, Region *Irish Rep* 9C3
Leipzig *E Germ* 18C2
Leiria *Port* 15A2
Leirvik *Nor* 12F7
Leith *Scot* 8D4
Leiyang *China* 31C4
Leizhou Bandao, Pen *China* 31B5
Leizhou Wan, B *China* 31C5
Lek, R *Neth* 18A2
Le Kef *Tunisia* 16B3
Lekemti *Eth* 50D3
Leland *USA* 63D2
Lelija, Mt *Yugos* 17D2
Léman, Lac *France/Switz* 16B1
Le Mans *France* 14C2
Le Mars *USA* 61D2
Lemgo *W Germ* 13E1
Lemhi Range, Mts *USA* 58D2
Lemieux Is *Can* 55M3
Lemmon *USA* 56C2
Lemmon,Mt *USA* 59D4
Lemoore *USA* 59C3
Lempdes *France* 14C2
Lemro, R *Burma* 43G4
Le Murge, Region *Italy* 16D2
Lena, R *USSR* 25O3
Lendery *USSR* 20E3
Lengerich *W Germ* 13D1
Lengshuijiang *China* 31C4
Leninabad *USSR* 39E1
Leninakan *USSR* 24F5
Leningrad *USSR* 20E4
Leningradskaya, Base *Ant* 76F7
Leninogorsk, Tatar ASSR *USSR* 20J5
Leninogorsk *USSR* 26B1
Leninsk-Kuznetskiy *USSR* 24K4
Leninskoye *USSR* 26G2
Lenkoran' *USSR* 21H8
Lenne, R *W Germ* 13E2
Lenoir *USA* 67B1
Lenox *USA* 68D1
Lens *France* 13B2
Lensk *USSR* 25N3
Lentini, Sicily 16C3
Lenya, R *Burma* 30B3
Leoben *Austria* 16C1
Leominster *Eng* 7C3
Leominster *USA* 68E1
León *Mexico* 70B2
León *Nic* 72A1
León *Spain* 15A1
Leonardville *Namibia* 47B1
Leonarisso *Cyprus* 45C1
Leonora *Aust* 32B3
Leopoldina *Brazil* 75D3
Léopoldville = Kinshasa
Lepel *USSR* 20D5
Leping *China* 31D4
Le Puy *France* 14C2
Léré *Chad* 50B3
Leribe *Lesotho* 47D2
Lérida *Spain* 15C1
Léros, I *Greece* 17F3
Le Roy *USA* 68B1
Lerwick *Scot* 10C1
Les Cayes *Haiti* 69C3
Les Escoumins *Can* 65F1
Leshan *China* 31A4
Leskovac *Yugos* 17E2
Leslie *S Africa* 47D2
Lesnoy *USSR* 20J4
Lesosibirsk *USSR* 25L4
Lesotho, Kingdom *S Africa* 47D2
Lesozavodsk *USSR* 26G2
Les Sables-d'Olonne *France* 14B2
Lesser Antarctica, Region *Ant* 76E4
Lesser Antilles, Is *Caribbean S* 69E3
Lésvos, I *Greece* 17F3
Leszno *Pol* 18D2
Letaba, R *S Africa* 47E1
Letha Range, Mts *Burma* 43G4
Lethbridge *Can* 54G5
Lethem *Guyana* 73G3
Letichev *USSR* 19F3
Leticia *Colombia* 72E4
Leti, Kepulauan, I *Indon* 32B1
Letlhakeng *Botswana* 47D1
Le Touquet-Paris-Plage *France* 7E4
Letpadan *Burma* 30B2
Le Tréport *France* 14C1
Letterkenny *Irish Rep* 9C2
Leuser, Mt *Indon* 27C6
Leuven *Belg* 18A2
Levádhia *Greece* 17E3
Levanger *Nor* 12G6
Levelland *USA* 62B2
Leven *Scot* 8D3
Leven, Loch, L *Scot* 8D3
Lévêque,C *Aust* 27F8
Leverkusen *W Germ* 13D2
Levice *Czech* 19D3
Levin *NZ* 35C2
Lévis *Can* 55L5
Levittown *USA* 65E2
Lévka Óri, Mt *Greece* 17E3
Levkás *Greece* 17E3
Levkás, I *Greece* 17E3
Lévque,C *Aust* 32B2
Levski *Bulg* 17F2
Lewes *Eng* 7E4
Lewis *USA* 62C1
Lewis, I *Scot* 10B2
Lewisburg *USA* 68B2
Lewis P *NZ* 35B2
Lewis Range, Mts *USA* 56B2
Lewis Smith,L *USA* 67A2
Lewiston, Idaho *USA* 56B2
Lewiston, Maine *USA* 57F2
Lewistown, Montana *USA* 56C2
Lewistown, Pennsylvania *USA* 65D2
Lewisville *USA* 63D2
Lexington, Kentucky *USA* 57E3
Lexington, Missouri *USA* 61E3
Lexington, N Carolina *USA* 67B1
Lexington, Nebraska *USA* 60D2
Lexington, Virginia *USA* 65D3
Lexington Park *USA* 65D3
Leyburn *Eng* 6D2
Leyte, I *Phil* 27F5
Lezhe *Alb* 17D2
Lhasa *China* 39H3
Lhazê *China* 43F3
Lhokseumawe *Indon* 27C6
Lhozhag *China* 43G3
Lhunze *China* 26C4
Liancourt Rocks = Tok-do
Liangbingtai *China* 28B2
Liangdang *China* 31B3
Lianjiang *China* 31C5
Lianping *China* 31C5
Lian Xian *China* 31C5
Lianyungang *China* 31D3
Liaodong Bandao, Pen *China* 31E1
Liaodong Wan, B *China* 31E1
Liao He, R *China* 31E1
Liaoning, Province *China* 31E1
Liaoyang *China* 31E1
Liaoyangwopu *China* 28A2
Liaoyuan *China* 31E1
Liaozhong *China* 28A2
Liard, R *Can* 54F3
Liard River *Can* 54F4
Liart *France* 13C3
Liban, Jebel, Mts *Leb* 45C2
Libby *USA* 58C1
Libenge *Zaïre* 50B3
Liberal *USA* 56C3
Liberec *Czech* 18C2
Liberia, Republic *Africa* 48A4
Liberty, Missouri *USA* 61E3
Liberty, New York *USA* 65E2
Liberty, Pennsylvania *USA* 68B2
Liberty, Texas *USA* 63D2
Libni, Gebel, Mt *Egypt* 45B3
Libourne *France* 14B3
Libreville *Eq Guinea* 48C4
Libya, Republic *Africa* 49D2
Libyan Desert *Libya/Egypt/Sudan* 49E2
Libyan Plat *Egypt* 49E1
Licata, Sicily 16C3
Lichfield *Eng* 7D3
Lichinga *Mozam* 51D5
Lichtenburg *S Africa* 47D2
Licking, R *USA* 64C3
Lick Observatory *USA* 66B2
Licosa, Punta, Pt *Italy* 16C2
Lida *USA* 66D2
Lida *USSR* 20D5
LidKöping *Sweden* 12G7
Lido di Ostia *Italy* 16C2
Liechtenstein, Principality *Europe* 16B1
Liège *Belg* 18B2
Lielupe, R *USSR* 19E1
Lienart *Zaïre* 50C3
Lienz *Austria* 18C3
Liepaja *USSR* 12J7
Lier *Belg* 13C2
Lièvre, R *Can* 65E1
Liezen *Austria* 18C3
Liffey, R *Irish Rep* 9C3
Lifford *Irish Rep* 9C2
Lifu, I *Nouvelle Calédonie* 33F3
Lightning Ridge *Aust* 34C1
Ligny-en-Barrois *France* 13C3
Ligonha, R *Mozam* 51D5
Ligurian S *Italy* 16B2
Lihir Group, Is *PNG* 33E1
Lihue *Hawaiian Is* 66E5
Likasi *Zaïre* 51C5
Lille *France* 14C1
Lillehammer *Nor* 12G6
Lillers *France* 13B2
Lillestrøm *Nor* 12G7
Lilongwe *Malawi* 51D5
Lim, R *Yugos* 17D2
Lima *Peru* 72C6
Lima *USA* 57E2
Lima, R *Port* 15A1
Lima Res *USA* 58D2
Limassol *Cyprus* 40B3
Limavady *N Ire* 9C2
Limbe *Cam* 48C4
Limbe *Malawi* 51D5
Limburg *W Germ* 18B2
Limeira *Brazil* 73J8
Limerick *Irish Rep* 10B3
Limfjorden, L *Den* 18B1
Limmen Bight, B *Aust* 32C2
Límnos, I *Greece* 17F3
Limoeiro *Brazil* 73L5
Limoges *France* 14C2
Limón *Costa Rica* 70D4
Limon *USA* 56C3
Limousin, Region *France* 14C2
Limousin, Plateaux de *France* 14C2
Limpopo, R *Mozam* 47E1
Linares *Chile* 74B5
Linares *Mexico* 56D4
Linares *Spain* 15B2
Lincang *China* 26C4
Lincoln *Arg* 74D4
Lincoln *Eng* 7D3
Lincoln, Illinois *USA* 64B2
Lincoln, Maine *USA* 65F1
Lincoln, Nebraska *USA* 56D2
Lincoln, New Hampshire *USA* 65E2
Lincoln *NZ* 35B2
Lincoln, County *Eng* 7D3
Lincoln City *USA* 58B2
Lincoln Park *USA* 64C2
Lincoln Sea *Greenland* 76A2
L'Incudine, Mt, Corsica 16B2
Lindau *W Germ* 18B3
Linden *Guyana* 73G2
Lindesnes, C *Nor* 12F7
Lindi *Tanz* 51D4
Lindi, R *Zaïre* 50C3
Lindley *S Africa* 47D2
Líndos *Greece* 17F3
Lindsay, California *USA* 66C2
Lindsay *Can* 65D2
Lindsay, Montana *USA* 60B1
Line Is *Pacific O* 37M4
Linfen *China* 31C2
Lingao *China* 30D2
Lingayen *Phil* 27F5
Lingen *W Germ* 18B2
Lingga, I *Indon* 27D7
Lingle *USA* 60C2
Lingling *China* 31C4
Lingshan *China* 31B5
Lingshi *China* 31C2
Linguère *Sen* 48A3
Linhai, Zhejiang *China* 31E4

Mazara del Vallo Minnesota

Mazara del Vallo, Sicily 16C3
Mazar-i-Sharif *Afghan* 42B1
Mazarrón, Golfo de, G *Spain* 15B2
Mazatlán *Mexico* 70B2
Mazeikiai *USSR* 20C4
Mazra *Jordan* 45C3
Mbabane *Swaziland* 51D6
Mbaïki *CAR* 50B3
Mbala *Zambia* 51D4
Mbalabala *Zim* 51C6
Mbale *Uganda* 50D3
Mbalmayo *Cam* 50B3
Mbam, R *Cam* 50B3
Mbamba Bay *Tanz* 51D5
Mbandaka *Zaïre* 50B3
Mbanza Congo *Angola* 50B4
Mbanza-Ngungu *Zaïre* 50B4
Mbarara *Uganda* 50D4
M'Bari, R *CAR* 50C3
Mbèndza *Congo* 50B3
Mbére, R *Cam/CAR/Chad* 50B3
Mbeya *Tanz* 51D4
Mbinda *Congo* 50B4
Mbout *Maur* 48A3
Mbuji-Mayi *Zaïre* 50C4
Mbulu *Tanz* 50D4
Mcherrah, Region *Alg* 48B2
Mchinji *Malawi* 51D5
Mdrak *Viet* 30D3
Meade *USA* 62B1
Mead,L *USA* 56B3
Meadow Lake *Can* 54H4
Meadville *USA* 64C2
Me-akan dake, Mt *Japan* 29D2
Mealy Mts *Can* 55N4
Meandarra *Aust* 34C1
Meander River *Can* 54G4
Meath *Irish Rep* 9C3
Meaux *France* 14C2
Mecca *S Arabia* 50E1
Mecca *USA* 59C4
Mechanicville *USA* 68D1
Mechelen *Belg* 18A2
Mecheria *Alg* 48B1
Mecklenburger Bucht, B *E Germ* 18C2
Meconta *Mozam* 51D5
Mecuburi *Mozam* 51D5
Mecufi *Mozam* 51E5
Mecula *Mozam* 51D5
Medan *Indon* 27C6
Médanosa, Puerta, Pt *Arg* 74C7
Médéa *Alg* 15C2
Medellín *Colombia* 72C2
Medemblik *Neth* 13C1
Medenine *Tunisia* 48D1
Medford *USA* 56A2
Medgidia *Rom* 17F2
Mediaş *Rom* 17E1
Medical Lake *USA* 58C1
Medicine Bow *USA* 60B2
Medicine Bow Mts *USA* 60B2
Medicine Bow Peak, Mt *USA* 60B2
Medicine Hat *Can* 54G5
Medicine Lodge *USA* 62C1
Medina *Brazil* 75D2
Medina, N Dakota *USA* 60D1
Medina, New York *USA* 68A1
Medina *S Arabia* 40C5
Medinaceli *Spain* 15B1
Medina del Campo *Spain* 15A1
Medina de Rioseco *Spain* 15A1
Medina L *USA* 62C3
Medinipur *India* 43F4
Mediterranean S *Europe* 46E4
Medjerda, R *Tunisia/Alg* 16B3
Medjerda, Mts de la *Tunisia/Alg* 16B3
Mednogorsk *USSR* 21K5
Mednyy, Ostrov, I *USSR* 25S4
Mêdog *China* 43H3
Medouneu *Gabon* 50B3
Medvedista, R *USSR* 21G5
Medvezh'i Ova, Is *USSR* 25S2
Medvezh'yegorsk *USSR* 24E3
Meekatharra *Aust* 32A3
Meeker *USA* 60B2
Meerut *India* 42D3
Meeteetse *USA* 58E2
Mega *Eth* 50D3
Megalópolis *Greece* 17E3
Mégara *Greece* 17E3
Meghālaya, State *India* 43G3
Meghna, R *Bang* 43G4
Megiddo, Hist Site *Israel* 45C2
Mehekar *India* 42D4
Mehndawal *India* 43M2
Mehrān, R *Iran* 41F4
Mehriz *Iran* 41F3
Meia Ponte, R *Brazil* 75C2
Meiganga *Cam* 50B3
Meiktila *Burma* 30B1
Meishan *China* 31A4
Meissen *E Germ* 18C2
Mei Xian *China* 31D5
Meizhou *China* 31D5
Mejillones *Chile* 72D8
Mekambo *Gabon* 50B3
Meknès *Mor* 48B1
Mekong, R *Camb* 30D3
Mekong, Mouths of the *Viet* 30D4
Mekrou, R *Benin* 48C3
Melaka *Malay* 30C5
Melanesia, Region *Pacific O* 36J5
Melbourne *Aust* 32D4
Melbourne *USA* 57E4
Melchor Muźguiz *Mexico* 56C4
Meleuz *USSR* 20K5
Melfi *Chad* 50B2
Melfort *Can* 54H4
Melilla *N W Africa* 15B2
Melimoyu, Mt *Chile* 74B6
Melita *Can* 60C1
Melitopol' *USSR* 21F6
Melle *W Germ* 13E1
Mellégue, R *Tunisia/Alg* 16B3
Melmoth *S Africa* 47E2
Melo *Urug* 74F4
Melo, R *Brazil* 75A3
Melones Res *USA* 66B2
Melrose *Scot* 8D4
Melrose *USA* 61E1
Melton Mowbray *Eng* 7D3
Melun *France* 14C2
Melville *Can* 54H4
Melville Bugt, B *Greenland* 55M2
Melville,C *Dominica* 69Q2
Melville Hills *Can* 54F3
Melville I *Aust* 32C2
Melville I *Can* 54G2
Melville,L *Can* 55N4
Melville Pen *Can* 55K3
Memba *Mozam* 51E5
Memboro *Indon* 32A1
Memmingen *W Germ* 18C3
Memphis, Tennessee *USA* 57E3
Memphis, Texas *USA* 62B2
Mena *USA* 63D2
Mena *USSR* 19G2
Menai Str *Wales* 7B3
Ménaka *Mali* 48C3
Menasha *USA* 64B2
Mendawai, R *Indon* 27E7
Mende *France* 14C3
Mendebo Mts *Eth* 50D3
Mendi *PNG* 32D1
Mendip Hills, Upland *Eng* 7C4
Mendocino,C *USA* 58B2
Mendocino Seascarp *Pacific O* 37M3
Mendota, California *USA* 66B2
Mendota, Illinois *USA* 64B2
Mendoza *Arg* 74C4
Mendoza, State *Arg* 74C5
Menemen *Turk* 17F3
Menen *Belg* 13B2
Mengcheng *China* 31D3
Menghai *China* 30B1
Mengla *China* 31A5
Menglian *China* 30B1
Mengzi *China* 31A5
Menindee *Aust* 32D4
Menindee L *Aust* 34B2
Meningie *Aust* 34A3
Menominee *USA* 64B1
Menomonee Falls *USA* 64B2
Menomonie *USA* 64A2
Menongue *Angola* 51B5
Menorca, I = Minorca
Mentawi, Kepulauan, Is *Indon* 27C7
Mentmore *USA* 62A1
Mentok *Indon* 27D7
Mentor *USA* 64C2
Menyapa, Mt *Indon* 27E6
Menyuan *China* 31A2
Menzel *Tunisia* 16B3
Menzelinsk *USSR* 20J4
Meppel *Neth* 13D1
Meppen *W Germ* 18B2
Mequinenza, Embalse de Res *Spain* 15B1
Meramec, R *USA* 63D1
Merano *Italy* 16C1
Meratus, Pegunungan, Mts *Indon* 27E7
Merauke *Indon* 32D1
Merced *USA* 56A3
Merced, R *USA* 66B2
Mercedario, Mt *Arg* 74B4
Mercedes, Buenos Aires *Arg* 74E4
Mercedes, Corrientes *Arg* 74E3
Mercedes, San Luis *Arg* 74C4
Mercedes *Urug* 74E4
Mercury B *NZ* 35C1
Mercury Is *NZ* 35C1
Mercy B *Can* 54F2
Mercy,C *Can* 55M3
Meredith,L *USA* 62B1
Meregh *Somalia* 50E3
Mergui *Burma* 30B3
Mergui Arch *Burma* 30B3
Mérida *Mexico* 70D2
Mérida *Spain* 15A2
Mérida *Ven* 72D2
Mérida, Cordillera de *Ven* 72D2
Meridian *USA* 57E3
Merimbula *Aust* 34C3
Meringur *Aust* 34B2
Merir, I *Pacific O* 27G6
Merkel *USA* 62B2
Merowe *Sudan* 50D2
Merredin *Aust* 32A4
Merrick, Mt *Scot* 8C4
Merrill *USA* 64B1
Merrillville *USA* 64B2
Merrimack, R *USA* 68E1
Merriman *USA* 60C2
Merritt Island *USA* 67B3
Merriwa *Aust* 34D2
Mersea, I *Eng* 7E4
Mers el Kebir *Alg* 15B2
Mersey, R *Eng* 7C3
Merseyside, Metropolitan County *Eng* 7C3
Mersin *Turk* 21E8
Mersing *Malay* 30C5
Merta *India* 42C3
Merthyr Tydfil *Wales* 7C4
Mertola *Port* 15A2
Méru *France* 13B3
Meru, Mt *Tanz* 50D4
Merzifon *Turk* 21F7
Merzig *W Germ* 13D3
Mesa *USA* 56B3
Mesa Verde Nat Pk *USA* 62A1
Meschede *W Germ* 13E2
Mescit Dağ, Mt *Turk* 40D1
Meshra Er Req *Sudan* 50C3
Mesolóngion *Greece* 17E3
Mesquite, Nevada *USA* 59D3
Mesquite, Texas *USA* 63C2
Messalo, R *Mozam* 51D5
Messina *S Africa* 47D1
Messina, Sicily 16D3
Messina, Stretto de, Str *Italy/Sicily* 16D3
Messíni *Greece* 17E3
Messiniakós Kólpos, G *Greece* 17E3
Mesta, R = Néstos
Mesta, R *Bulg* 17E2
Mestre *Italy* 16C1
Meta, R *Colombia/Ven* 72D3
Meta, R *USSR* 20E4
Meta Incognito Pen *Can* 55M3
Metairie *USA* 63D3
Metaline Falls *USA* 58C1
Metán *Arg* 74D3
Metangula *Mozam* 51D5
Metaponto *Italy* 16D2
Methil *Scot* 8D3
Methuen *USA* 68E1
Methven *NZ* 35B2
Metlakatla *USA* 54E4
Metropolis *USA* 64B3
Mettur *India* 44B3
Metz *France* 14D2
Meulaboh *Indon* 27C6
Meurthe, R *France* 13D3
Meurthe-et-Moselle, Department *France* 13D3
Meuse, Department *France* 13C3
Meuse, R *Belg* 13C2
Meuse, R *France* 14D2
Mexborough *Eng* 7D3
Mexia *USA* 63C2
Mexicali *Mexico* 70A1
Mexican Hat *USA* 59E3
México *Mexico* 70C3
Mexico *USA* 61E3
Mexico, Federal Republic *Cent America* 70B2
Mexico,G of *Cent America* 70C2
Meymaneh *Afghan* 24H6
Mezada, Hist Site *Israel* 45C3
Mezen' *USSR* 24F3
Mezen', R *USSR* 20H3
Mézenc, Mount *France* 14C3
Mezha, R *USSR* 19G1
Mezhdusharskiy, Ostrov, I *USSR* 24G2
Mhow *India* 42D4
Miami, Arizona *USA* 59D4
Miami, Florida *USA* 57E4
Miami, Oklahoma *USA* 63D1
Miami Beach *USA* 57E4
Miandowab *Iran* 21H8
Miandrivazo *Madag* 51E5
Mianeh *Iran* 21H8
Mianwali *Pak* 42C2
Mianyang *China* 31A3
Mianyang *China* 31C3
Mianzhu *China* 31A3
Miaodao Qundao, Arch *China* 31E2
Miao Ling, Upland *China* 31B4
Miass *USSR* 20L5
Michalovce *Czech* 19E3
Michel *Can* 58D1
Miches *Dom Rep* 69D3
Michigan, State *USA* 57E2
Michigan City *USA* 64B2
Michigan,L *USA* 57E2
Michipicoten *Can* 64C1
Michipicoten I *Can* 55K5
Michurin *Bulg* 17F2
Michurinsk *USSR* 21G5
Micronesia, Is *Pacific O* 27H6
Micronesia, Region *Pacific O* 36J4
Mid Atlantic Ridge *Atlantic O* 52F4
Middelburg, Cape Province *S Africa* 47C3
Middelburg *Neth* 13B2
Middelburg, Transvaal *S Africa* 47D2
Middle Alkali L *USA* 58B2
Middle America Trench *Pacific O* 37O4
Middle Andaman, I *Indian O* 44E3
Middleboro *USA* 68E2
Middleburg, Pennsylvania *USA* 68B2
Middleburg, Virginia *USA* 68B3
Middleburgh *USA* 68C1
Middlebury *USA* 65E2
Middlesboro *USA* 57E3
Middlesbrough *Eng* 6D2
Middletown, Connecticut *USA* 68D2
Middletown, Delaware *USA* 68C3
Middletown, New York *USA* 65E2
Middletown, Ohio *USA* 64C3
Middletown, Pennsylvania *USA* 68B2
Middleville *USA* 68C1
Middlewich *Eng* 7C3
Midelt *Mor* 48B1
Mid Glamorgan, County *Wales* 7C4
Midi *Yemen* 50E2
Mid Indian Basin *Indian O* 36E5
Mid Indian Ridge *Indian O* 36E5
Midland *Can* 55L5
Midland, Michigan *USA* 64C2
Midland, Texas *USA* 56C3
Midleton *Irish Rep* 9B4
Midongy Atsimo *Madag* 51E6
Mid Pacific Mts *Pacific O* 37K4
Midvale *USA* 58C2
Midway Is *Pacific O* 37L3
Midwest *USA* 60B2
Midwest City *USA* 63C1
Midyat *Turk* 40D2
Midžor, Mt *Yugos* 17E2
Mielec *Pol* 19E2
Miercurea-Ciuc *Rom* 17F1
Mieres *Spain* 15A1
Mifflintown *USA* 68B2
Migennes *France* 13B4
Mihara *Japan* 28B4
Mikhaylovgrad *Bulg* 17E2
Mikhaylovka *USSR* 21G5
Mikhaylovka *USSR* 28C2
Mikhaylovskiy *USSR* 24J4
Mikhrot Timna *Israel* 45C4
Mikkeli *Fin* 12K6
Míkonos, I *Greece* 17F3
Mikulov *Czech* 18D3
Mikumi *Tanz* 51D4
Mikun *USSR* 20J3
Mikuni-sammyaku, Mts *Japan* 29D3
Mikura-jima, I *Japan* 29C4
Milaca *USA* 61E1
Milagro *Ecuador* 72C4
Milan *Italy* 16B1
Milan *USA* 63E1
Milange *Mozam* 51D5
Milano = Milan
Milas *Turk* 21D8
Milbank *USA* 61D1
Mildura *Aust* 32D4
Mile *China* 31A5
Mileh Tharthar, L *Iraq* 41D3
Miles *Aust* 32E3
Miles City *USA* 56C2
Miletto, Monte, Mt *Italy* 16C2
Milford, Connecticut *USA* 68D2
Milford, Delaware *USA* 65D3
Milford, Nebraska *USA* 61D2
Milford, New Hampshire *USA* 68E1
Milford, Pennsylvania *USA* 68C2
Milford, Utah *USA* 59D3
Milford Haven *Wales* 7B4
Milford Haven, Sd *Wales* 7B4
Milford L *USA* 61D3
Milford Sd *NZ* 35A2
Miliana *Alg* 15C2
Milk, R *Can/USA* 54G4
Milk, R *USA* 60B1
Mil'kovo *USSR* 25R4
Milk, Wadi el, Watercourse *Sudan* 50C2
Millau *France* 14C3
Millbrook *USA* 68D2
Milledgeville *USA* 67B2
Mille Lacs L *USA* 61E1
Mille Lacs, Lac des *Can* 61E1
Miller *USA* 60D2
Millerovo *USSR* 21G6
Millersburg *USA* 68B2
Millers Falls *USA* 68D1
Millerton *USA* 68D2
Millerton L *USA* 66C2
Millford, Massachusetts *USA* 65E2
Millicent *Aust* 34B3
Millington *USA* 63E1
Millinocket *USA* 65F1
Millmerran *Aust* 34D1
Millom *Eng* 6C2
Millport *Scot* 8C4
Millstreet *Irish Rep* 9B3
Milltown *Can* 65F1
Milltown *USA* 58D1
Mill Valley *USA* 66A2
Millville *USA* 65E3
Milne Land, I *Greenland* 55Q2
Milolii *Hawaiian Is* 66E5
Mílos, I *Greece* 17E3
Milparinka *Aust* 32D3
Milroy *USA* 68B2
Milton, Florida *USA* 67A2
Milton *NZ* 35A3
Milton, Pennsylvania *USA* 68B2
Milton Keynes *Eng* 7D3
Milwaukee *USA* 57E2
Mimmaya *Japan* 29D2
Mina *USA* 66C1
Mina, R *Alg* 15C2
Mina' al Aḩmadi *Kuwait* 41E4
Minab *Iran* 41G4
Minas *Urug* 74E4
Minas Gerais, State *Brazil* 73J7
Minas Novas *Brazil* 75D2
Minatitlán *Mexico* 70C3
Minbu *Burma* 30A1
Minbya *Burma* 30A1
Minch,Little, Sd *Scot* 8B3
Minch,North, Sd *Scot* 8B2
Minch,The, Sd *Scot* 10B2
Mindanao, I *Phil* 27F6
Minden, Louisiana *USA* 63D2
Minden, Nevada *USA* 66C1
Minden *W Germ* 18B2
Mindona L *Aust* 34B2
Mindoro, I *Phil* 27F5
Mindoro Str *Phil* 27F5
Minehead *Eng* 7C4
Mineiros *Brazil* 73H7
Mineola *USA* 63C2
Mineral Wells *USA* 62C2
Minersville *USA* 68B2
Mingary *Aust* 34B2
Mingechaurskoye Vodokhranilische, Res *USSR* 21H7
Mingulay, I *Scot* 8B3
Minhe *China* 31A2
Minicoy, I *India* 44A4
Min Jiang, R, Fujian *China* 31D4
Min Jiang, R, Sichuan *China* 31A4
Minkler *USA* 66C2
Minlaton *Aust* 34A2
Minle *China* 31A2
Minna *Nigeria* 48C4
Minneapolis *USA* 57D2
Minnedosa *Can* 54J4
Minnesota, R *USA* 61D2

Minnesota **Mosquito**

Minnesota, State *USA* 57D2
Miño, R *Spain* 15A1
Minorca, I *Spain* 15C1
Minot *USA* 56C2
Minqin *China* 31A2
Min Shan, Upland *China* 31A3
Minsk *USSR* 20D5
Minsk Mazowiecki *Pol* 19E2
Minto Inlet, B *Can* 54G2
Minto,L *Can* 55L4
Minturn *USA* 60B3
Minusinsk *USSR* 26C1
Min Xian *China* 31A3
Minya el Qamn *Egypt* 45A3
Miquelon *Can* 55N5
Mirage L *USA* 66D3
Mirah, Wadi al, Watercourse *Iraq/S Arabia* 40D3
Miraj *India* 44A2
Miramar *Arg* 74E5
Miram Shah *Pak* 42B2
Miranda *Brazil* 75A3
Miranda, R *Brazil* 75A2
Miranda de Ebro *Spain* 15B1
Mirante, Serra do, Mts *Brazil* 75B3
Mir Bachchen Küt *Afghan* 42B2
Mirecourt *France* 13C3
Miri *Malay* 27E6
Mirik,C *Maur* 48A3
Mirim, Lagoa, L *Brazil/Urug* 74F4
Mirnoye *USSR* 25K3
Mirnyy *USSR* 25N3
Mirnyy, Base *Ant* 76G9
Mironovka *USSR* 19G3
Mirpur *Pak* 42C2
Mirpur Khas *Pak* 42B3
Mirtoan S *Greece* 17E3
Miryang *S Korea* 28B3
Mirzāpur *India* 43E3
Misgar *Pak* 42C1
Mishawaka *USA* 64B2
Mi-shima, I *Japan* 28B4
Mishmi Hills *India* 43H3
Misima, I *PNG* 33E2
Misiones, State *Arg* 74F3
Miskolc *Hung* 19E3
Mismiyah *Syria* 45D2
Misoöl, I *Indon* 27G7
Misrātah *Libya* 49D1
Missinaibi, R *Can* 55K5
Missinaibi L *Can* 64C1
Mission, S Dakota *USA* 60C2
Mission, Texas *USA* 62C3
Mission City *Can* 58B1
Mississauga *Can* 65D2
Mississippi, R *USA* 57D3
Mississippi, State *USA* 57D3
Mississippi Delta *USA* 63E3
Missoula *USA* 56B2
Missour *Mor* 48B1
Missouri, R *USA* 57D2
Missouri, State *USA* 57D3
Missouri Valley *USA* 61D2
Mistassini,L *Can* 57F1
Misti, Mt *Peru* 72D7
Mitchell *Aust* 34C1
Mitchell *USA* 56D2
Mitchell, R *Aust* 32D2
Mitchell,Mt *USA* 57E3
Mitchell River *Aust* 27H8
Mît el Nasâra *Egypt* 45A3
Mît Ghamr *Egypt* 45A3
Mithankot *Pak* 42C3
Mitilíni *Greece* 17F3
Mitla Pass *Egypt* 45B3
Mito *Japan* 29E3
Mitre, I *Solomon Is* 33G2
Mits'iwa *Eth* 50D2
Mittel Land Kanal *W Germ* 13D1
Mitú *Colombia* 72D3
Mitumba, Chaine des, Mts *Zaïre* 51C4
Mitumbar Mts *Zaïre* 50C4
Mitwaba *Zaïre* 51C4
Mitzic *Gabon* 50B3
Miura *Japan* 29C3
Mi Xian *China* 31C3
Miyake, I *Japan* 26G3
Miyake-jima, I *Japan* 29C4
Miyako *Japan* 29E3
Miyako, I, Ryukyu Is *Japan* 26F4
Miyazu *Japan* 29C3
Miyoshi *Japan* 28C4
Miyun *China* 31D1
Miyun Shuiku, Res *China* 31D1
Mi-zaki, Pt *Japan* 29D2
Mizan Teferi *Eth* 50D3
Mizdah *Libya* 49D1
Mizil *Rom* 17F1
Mizo Hills *India* 43G4
Mizoram, Union Territory *India* 43G4
Mizpe Ramon *Israel* 45C3
Mizusawa *Japan* 29E3
Mjölby *Sweden* 12H7
Mkushi *Zambia* 51C5
Mkuzi *S Africa* 47E2
Mladá Boleslav *Czech* 18C2
Mlawa *Pol* 19E2
Mljet, I *Yugos* 17D2
Mmabatho *S Africa* 47D2
Moa, R *Sierra Leone* 48A4
Moab *USA* 56C3
Moab, Region *Jordan* 45C3
Moamba *Mozam* 47E2
Moanda *Congo* 50B4
Moanda *Gabon* 50B4
Moate *Irish Rep* 9C3
Moba *Zaïre* 51C4
Mobara *Japan* 29D3
Mobaye *CAR* 50C3
Mobayi *Zaïre* 50C3
Moberly *USA* 57D3
Mobile *USA* 57E3
Mobile B *USA* 57E3
Mobile Pt *USA* 63E2
Mobridge *USA* 56C2
Moçambique *Mozam* 51E5
Moçâmedes = Namibe
Moc Chau *Viet* 30C1
Mocha = Al Mukha
Mochudi *Botswana* 47D1
Mocimboa da Praia *Mozam* 51E5
Mocoa *Colombia* 72C3
Mococa *Brazil* 75C3
Mocuba *Mozam* 51D5
Modder, R *S Africa* 47D2
Modena *Italy* 16C2
Moder, R *France* 13D3
Modesto *USA* 56A3
Modesto Res *USA* 66B2
Modica, Sicily 16C3
Mödling *Austria* 18D3
Moffat *Scot* 8D4
Moga *India* 42D2
Mogadishu *Somalia* 50E3
Mogi das Cruzes *Brazil* 75C3
Mogilev *USSR* 19G2
Mogilev Podol'skiy *USSR* 21D6
Mogi-Mirim *Brazil* 75C3
Mogincual *Mozam* 51E5
Mogocha *USSR* 26E1
Mogochin *USSR* 24K4
Mogol, R *S Africa* 47D1
Moguer *Spain* 15A2
Mohaka, R *NZ* 35C1
Mohale's Hoek *Lesotho* 47D3
Mohall *USA* 60C1
Mohammadia *Alg* 15C2
Mohanganj *Bang* 43G4
Mohave,L *USA* 59D3
Mohawk *USA* 68C1
Mohawk, R *USA* 65E2
Mohéli, I *Comoros* 51E5
Mohoro *Tanz* 51D4
Mointy *USSR* 24J5
Mo i Rana *Nor* 12G5
Moissac *France* 14C3
Mojave *USA* 59C3
Mojave, R *USA* 66D3
Mojave Desert *USA* 56B3
Mokama *India* 43F3
Mokau, R *NZ* 35B1
Mokelumne, R *USA* 66B1
Mokelumne Aqueduct *USA* 66B1
Mokelumne Hill *USA* 66B1
Mokhotlong *Lesotho* 47D2
Moknine *Tunisia* 16C3
Mokokchung *India* 43G3
Mokolo *Cam* 50B2
Mokp'o *S Korea* 28B4
Moksha, R *USSR* 20G5
Moláoi *Greece* 17E3
Mold *Wales* 7C3
Moldavian SSR, Republic *USSR* 21D6
Molde *Nor* 12F6
Moldoveanu, Mt *Rom* 17E1
Molepolole *Botswana* 47D1
Molesheim *France* 13D3
Molfetta *Italy* 16D2
Mollendo *Peru* 72D7
Molodechno *USSR* 20D5
Molodezhnaya, Base *Ant* 76G11
Molokai, I *Hawaiian Is* 66E5
Moloma, R *USSR* 20H4
Molong *Aust* 34C2
Molopo, R *Botswana/S Africa* 47C2
Molounddu *Cam* 50B3
Molson L *Can* 56D1
Molucca S *Indon* 32B1
Moluccas, Is *Indon* 27F7
Moma *Mozam* 51D5
Mombaça *Brazil* 73K5
Mombasa *Kenya* 50D4
Mombetsu *Japan* 29D2
Mombuca, Serra da, Mts *Brazil* 75B2
Mompono *Zaïre* 50C3
Mon, I *Den* 18C2
Monach Is *Scot* 8B3
Monaco, Principality *Europe* 14D3
Monadhliath Mts *Scot* 8C3
Monaghan *Irish Rep* 9C2
Monaghan, County *Irish Rep* 9C2
Monahans *USA* 62B2
Mona Pass *Caribbean S* 69D3
Monarch P *USA* 60B3
Monashee Mts *Can* 54G4
Monastereven *Irish Rep* 10B3
Monastir *Tunisia* 16C3
Monbetsu *Japan* 29D2
Monção *Brazil* 73J4
Monchegorsk *USSR* 12L5
Mönchen-gladbach *W Germ* 18B2
Monclova *Mexico* 70B2
Moncton *Can* 55M5
Mondego, R *Port* 15A1
Mondovi *Italy* 16B2
Moneague *Jamaica* 69H1
Monessen *USA* 65D2
Monett *USA* 63D1
Monfalcone *Italy* 16C1
Monforte de Lemos *Spain* 15A1
Monga *Zaïre* 50C3
Mongala, R *Zaïre* 50C3
Mongalla *Sudan* 50D3
Mong Cai *Viet* 30D1
Mongo *Chad* 50B2
Mongolia, Republic *Asia* 26C2
Mongu *Zambia* 51C5
Mönhhaan *Mongolia* 25N5
Moniaive *Scot* 8D4
Monitor Range, Mts *USA* 59C3
Monkoto *Zaïre* 50C4
Monmouth *USA* 64A2
Monmouth *Wales* 7C4
Mono, R *Togo/Benin* 48C4
Mono L *USA* 59C3
Monopoli *Italy* 17D2
Monreal del Campo *Spain* 15B1
Monroe, Louisiana *USA* 63D2
Monroe, Michigan *USA* 64C2
Monroe, N Carolina *USA* 67B2
Monroe, Washington *USA* 58B1
Monroe, Wisconsin *USA* 64B2
Monroe City *USA* 61E3
Monrovia *Lib* 48A4
Monrovia *USA* 66D3
Mons *Belg* 18A2
Monson *USA* 68D1
Mont, Monte : *see also individual mt. name*
Montagu *S Africa* 47C3
Montague I *USA* 54D4
Montaigu *France* 14B2
Montallo, Mt *Italy* 16D3
Montana, State *USA* 56B2
Montañas de León, Mts *Spain* 15A1
Montargis *France* 14C2
Montauban *France* 14C3
Montauk *USA* 65E2
Montauk Pt *USA* 65E2
Montbard *France* 13C4
Montbéliard *France* 14D2
Mont Blanc *France/Italy* 16B1
Montblanc *Spain* 15C1
Montceau-les-Mines *France* 14C2
Mont Cenis, Col du, P *France/Italy* 16B1
Montceny, Mt *Spain* 15C1
Montcornet *France* 13C3
Mont-de-Marsin *France* 14B3
Montdidier *France* 14C2
Monteagudo *Bol* 72F7
Monte Alegre *Brazil* 73H4
Monte Azul *Brazil* 75D2
Montebello *Can* 65D1
Monte Bello Is *Aust* 32A3
Monte Carlo *Monaco* 14D3
Monte Carmelo *Brazil* 75C2
Montecristi *Dom Rep* 69C3
Montecristo, I *Italy* 16C2
Montego Bay *Jamaica* 69H1
Montélimar *France* 14C3
Montelindo, R *Par* 75A3
Montemorelos *Mexico* 70C2
Montemor-o-Novo *Port* 15A2
Montenegro, Region *Yugos* 17D2
Montepuez *Mozam* 51D5
Montereau-Faut-Yonne *France* 13B3
Monterey, California *USA* 56A3
Monterey, Virginia *USA* 65D3
Monterey B *USA* 56A3
Montería *Colombia* 72C2
Montero *Bol* 72F7
Monterrey *Mexico* 70B2
Montes Claros *Brazil* 73K7
Montes de Toledo, Mts *Spain* 15B2
Montevideo *Urug* 74E4
Montevideo *USA* 61D2
Monte Vista *USA* 62A1
Montezuma *USA* 62B1
Montezuma Peak, Mt *USA* 66D2
Montgomery, Alabama *USA* 57E3
Montgomery, Pennsylvania *USA* 68B2
Montgomery *Wales* 7C3
Montgomery P *USA* 66C2
Monthermé *France* 13C3
Monticello, Arkansas *USA* 63D2
Monticello, Iowa *USA* 64A2
Monticello, Minnesota *USA* 61E1
Monticello, New York *USA* 68C2
Monticello, Utah *USA* 56C3
Montier-en-Der *France* 13C3
Mont-Laurier *Can* 55L5
Montluçon *France* 14C2
Montmagny *Can* 55L5
Montmédy *France* 13C3
Montmirail *France* 13B3
Montmorency *Can* 65E1
Montoro *Spain* 15B2
Montoursville *USA* 68B2
Montpelier, Idaho *USA* 58D2
Montpelier, Ohio *USA* 64C2
Montpelier, Vermont *USA* 57F2
Montpellier *France* 14C3
Montréal *Can* 55L5
Montreuil *France* 14C1
Montreux *Switz* 16B1
Montrose, Colorado *USA* 56C3
Montrose, Pennsylvania *USA* 68C2
Montrose *Scot* 10C2
Montrose, Oilfield *N Sea* 8F3
Mont-St-Michel *France* 14B2
Montserrat, I *Caribbean S* 69E3
Monument V *USA* 56B3
Monveda *Zaïre* 50C3
Monywa *Burma* 30B1
Monza *Italy* 16B1
Monze *Zambia* 51C5
Mooi, R *S Africa* 47E2
Mooi River *S Africa* 47D2
Moomba *Aust* 34B1
Moonbi Range, Mts *Aust* 34D2
Moonda L *Aust* 34B1
Moonie *Aust* 34D1
Moonie, R *Aust* 34C1
Moonta *Aust* 34A2
Moora *Aust* 32A4
Mooraberree *Aust* 34B1
Moorcroft *USA* 60C2
Moore,L *Aust* 32A3
Moorfoot Hills *Scot* 8D4
Moorhead *USA* 56D2
Moorpark *USA* 66C3
Moorreesburg *S Africa* 47B3
Moose, R *Can* 55K4
Moosehead L *USA* 65F1
Moose Jaw *Can* 54H4
Moose Lake *USA* 61E1
Moosomin *Can* 54H4
Moosonee *Can* 55K4
Moosup *USA* 68E2
Mopeia *Mozam* 51D5
Mopti *Mali* 48B3
Moquegua *Peru* 72D7
Mora *Sweden* 12G6
Mora *USA* 61E1
Moradabad *India* 42D3
Morada Nova *Brazil* 73L5
Morada Nova de Minas *Brazil* 75C2
Morafenobe *Madag* 51E5
Moramanga *Madag* 51E5
Moran *USA* 58D2
Morant Bay *Jamaica* 69J2
Morant Pt *Jamaica* 69J2
Morar, Loch, L *Scot* 8C3
Moratuwa *Sri Lanka* 44B4
Morava, R *Austria/Czech* 18D3
Morava, R *Yugos* 17E2
Moraveh Tappeh *Iran* 41G2
Moray Firth, Estuary *Scot* 10C2
Morbi *India* 42C4
Mor Dağ, Mt *Turk* 41D2
Morden *Can* 54J5
Mordovian ASSR, Republic *USSR* 20G5
Moreau, R *USA* 60C1
Morecambe *Eng* 7C2
Morecambe B *Eng* 7C2
Moree *Aust* 32D3
Morehead *USA* 64C3
Morehead City *USA* 67C2
Morelia *Mexico* 70B3
Morena *India* 42D3
Morena, Sierra, Mts *Spain* 15A2
Moresby I *Can* 54E4
Moreton I *Aust* 34D1
Moreuil *France* 13B3
Morgan City *USA* 63D3
Morgan Hill *USA* 66B2
Morgan,Mt *USA* 66C2
Morganton *USA* 67B1
Morgantown *USA* 65D3
Morgenzon *S Africa* 47D2
Morhange *France* 13D3
Mori *Japan* 29E2
Moriah *Tobago* 69K1
Moriarty *USA* 62A2
Morioka *Japan* 29E3
Morisset *Aust* 34D2
Morkoka, R *USSR* 25N3
Morlaix *France* 14B2
Morne Diablotin, Mt *Dominica* 69Q2
Morney *Aust* 34B1
Mornington, I *Aust* 32C2
Moro *Pak* 42B3
Morobe *PNG* 32D1
Morocco, Kingdom *Africa* 48B1
Moro G *Phil* 27F6
Morogoro *Tanz* 51D4
Morombe *Madag* 51E6
Morón *Cuba* 69B2
Morondava *Madag* 51E6
Moron de la Frontera *Spain* 15A2
Moroni *Comoros* 51E5
Morotai, I *Indon* 27F6
Moroto *Uganda* 50D3
Morozovsk *USSR* 21G6
Morpeth *Eng* 6D2
Morphou *Cyprus* 45B1
Morphou B *Cyprus* 45B1
Morrill *USA* 60C2
Morrilton *USA* 63D1
Morrinhos *Brazil* 75C2
Morrinsville *NZ* 35C1
Morris *Can* 61D1
Morris *USA* 61D1
Morristown, New Jersey *USA* 68C2
Morristown, New York *USA* 65D2
Morristown, Tennessee *USA* 67B1
Morrisville, New York *USA* 68C1
Morrisville, Pennsylvania *USA* 68C2
Morro Bay *USA* 66B3
Morrumbala *Mozam* 51D5
Morrumbene *Mozam* 51D6
Morshansk *USSR* 20G5
Mortes, R = Manso
Mortes, R, Mato Grosso *Brazil* 73H6
Mortes, R, Minas Gerais *Brazil* 75D3
Mortlake *Aust* 34B3
Morton *USA* 62B2
Moruga *Trinidad* 69L1
Moruya *Aust* 34D3
Morven *Aust* 34C1
Morvern, Pen *Scot* 8C3
Morwell *Aust* 34C3
Mosbach *W Germ* 13E3
Moscos Is *Burma* 30B3
Moscow, Idaho *USA* 58C1
Moscow, Pennsylvania *USA* 68C2
Moscow *USSR* 24E4
Mosel, R *W Germ* 18B2
Moselebe, R *Botswana* 47C2
Moselle, Department *France* 13D3
Moselle, R *France* 13D3
Moses Lake *USA* 58C1
Mosgiel *NZ* 35B3
Moshi *Tanz* 50D4
Mosinee *USA* 64B2
Mosjøen *Nor* 12G5
Moskal'vo *USSR* 25Q4
Moskva = Moscow
Mosquero *USA* 62B1
Mosquito, R *Brazil* 75D2

Mosquitos, Golfo de los Panama 72B2
Moss Nor 12G7
Mossaka Congo 50B4
Mossâmedes = Namibe
Mossel Bay S Africa 47C3
Mossendjo Congo 50B4
Mossgiel Aust 34B2
Mossoró Brazil 73L5
Most Czech 18C2
Mostaganem Alg 15C2
Mostar Yugos 17D2
Mosty USSR 19E2
Mosul Iraq 41D2
Motala Sweden 12H7
Motherwell Scot 8D4
Motihári India 43E3
Motilla del Palancar Spain 15B2
Motloutse, R Botswana 47D1
Motril Spain 15B2
Mott USA 60C1
Motueka NZ 35B2
Motueka, R NZ 35B2
Mouila Gabon 50B4
Moulamein Aust 34B2
Mould Bay Can 54G2
Moule à Chique, Cap St Lucia 69P2
Moulins France 14C2
Moulmein Burma 30B2
Moulouya, R Mor 48B1
Moultrie USA 67B2
Moultrie,L USA 67C2
Mound City, Illinois USA 64B3
Mound City, Missouri USA 61D2
Moundou Chad 50B3
Moundsville USA 64C3
Mountain Brook USA 67A2
Mountain Grove USA 63D1
Mountain Home, Arkansas USA 63D1
Mountain Home, Idaho USA 58C2
Mountain View USA 66A2
Mountain Village USA 54B3
Mount Airy, Maryland USA 68B3
Mount Airy, N Carolina USA 67B1
Mount Ayliff S Africa 47D3
Mount Carmel USA 68B2
Mount Desert I USA 65F2
Mount Fletcher S Africa 47D3
Mount Gambier Aust 34B3
Mount Hagen PNG 32D1
Mount Holly USA 68C3
Mount Holly Springs USA 68B2
Mount Isa Aust 32C3
Mount Jackson USA 68A3
Mount Jewett USA 68A2
Mount Lofty Range, Mts Aust 34A2
Mount Magnet Aust 32A3
Mount Manara Aust 34B2
Mountmellick Irish Rep 9C3
Mount Morgan Aust 32E3
Mount Morris USA 68B1
Mount Perry Aust 34D1
Mount Pleasant, Texas USA 63D2
Mount Pleasant, Utah USA 59D3
Mount Pocono USA 68C2
Mount Rainier Nat Pk USA 58B1
Mounts B Eng 7B4
Mount Shasta USA 58B2
Mount Union USA 68B2
Mount Vernon, Alabama USA 63E2
Mount Vernon, Illinois USA 64B3
Mount Vernon, Missouri USA 63D1
Mount Vernon, Washington USA 58B1
Mourdi, Dépression du, Desert Region Chad 50C2
Mourne Mts N Ire 9C2
Moussoro Chad 50B2
Mouydir, Mts du Alg 48C2
Mouzon France 13C3
M'óvár Hung 18D3
Moville Irish Rep 9C2
Moy, R Irish Rep 9B2
Moyale Kenya 50D3
Moyamba Sierra Leone 48A4
Moyen Atlas, Mts Mor 48B1
Moyeni Lesotho 47D3
Moyero, R USSR 25M3
Moyo Uganda 50D3
Moyobamba Peru 72C5
Moyu China 42D1

Mozambique, Republic Africa 51D6
Mozambique Chan Madag/Mozam 51D6
Mozhga USSR 20J4
Mozyr' USSR 21D5
Mpanda Tanz 50D4
Mpika Zambia 51D5
Mporokoso Zambia 51D4
Mposhi Zambia 51C5
Mpraeso Ghana 48B4
Mpulungu Zambia 51D4
Mpwapwa Tanz 50D4
M'saken Tunisia 16C3
M'Sila Alg 15C2
Mstislavl' USSR 19G2
Mtsensk USSR 20F5
Mtubatuba S Africa 47E2
Mtwara Tanz 51E5
Muang Chainat Thai 30C2
Muang Chiang Rai Thai 30C2
Muang Kalasin Thai 30C2
Muang Khon Kaen Thai 30C2
Muang Lampang Thai 30B2
Muang Lamphun Thai 30B2
Muang Loei Thai 30C2
Muang Lom Sak Thai 30C2
Muang Nakhon Phanom Thai 30C2
Muang Nakhon Sawan Thai 30B2
Muang Nan Thai 30C2
Muang Phayao Thai 30C2
Muang Phetchabun Thai 30C2
Muang Phichit Thai 30C2
Muang Phitsanulok Thai 30C2
Muang Phrae Thai 30C2
Muang Roi Et Thai 30C2
Muang Sakon Nakhon Thai 30C2
Muang Samut Prakan Thai 30C3
Muang Uthai Thani Thai 30C2
Muang Yasothon Thai 30C2
Muar Malay 30C5
Muara Indon 27D7
Muaungmya Burma 30A2
Mubende Uganda 50D3
Mubi Nigeria 49D3
Mubrak, Jebel, Mt Jordan 45C3
Muchinga Mts Zambia 51D5
Much Wenlock Eng 7C3
Muck, I Scot 8B3
Muckadilla Aust 34C1
Muckros Hd, Pt Irish Rep 9B2
Mucuri Brazil 75E2
Mucuri, R Brazil 75D2
Mucusso Angola 51C5
Mudanjiang China 26F2
Muddy Gap P USA 60B2
Mudeisisat, Jebel, Mt Jordan 45D3
Mudgee Aust 34C2
Mud L USA 66D2
Mudon Burma 30B2
Mud'yuga USSR 20F3
Mueda Mozam 51D5
Mueo New Caledonia 33F3
Mufulira Zambia 51C5
Mufu Shan, Hills China 31C4
Mughayra S Arabia 40C4
Mugla Turk 40A2
Mugodzhary, Mts USSR 21K6
Mugu Nepal 43E3
Muguaping China 31A3
Muhaywir Iraq 40D3
Mühlacker W Germ 13E3
Mühldorf W Germ 18C3
Mühlhausen E Germ 18C2
Muhos Fin 12K6
Mui Bai Bung, C Camb 30C4
Muine Bheag Irish Rep 9C3
Mujib, Wadi Jordan 45C3
Mujimbeji Zambia 51C5
Mukachevo USSR 19E3
Mukah Malay 27E6
Mukawa Japan 29D2
Muko-jima, I Japan 26H4
Muktinath Nepal 43E3
Mukur Afghan 42B2
Mulberry USA 63D1
Mulde, R E Germ 18C2
Mule Creek USA 60C2
Muleshoe USA 62B2
Mulgrave I Aust 27H8
Mulhacén, Mt Spain 15B2
Mülheim W Germ 13D2
Mulhouse France 13D4
Muli China 31A4
Mull, I Scot 8C3
Mullaittvu Sri Lanka 44C4
Mullaley Aust 34C2
Muller, Pegunungan, Mts Indon 27E6
Mullet, The Pt Irish Rep 9A2
Mullewa Aust 32A3

Müllheim W Germ 13D4
Mullica, R USA 68C3
Mullingar Irish Rep 9C3
Mull of Kintyre, Pt Scot 8C4
Mull of Oa, C Scot 8B4
Mullumbimby Aust 34D1
Mulobezi Zambia 51C5
Multan Pak 42C2
Mumbwa Zambia 51C5
Mumra USSR 21H6
Muna Indon 27F7
München = Munich
Munchŏn N Korea 28A3
Muncie USA 64B2
Muncoonie,L Aust 34A1
Muncy USA 68B2
Münden W Germ 18B2
Mundubbera Aust 34D1
Mungallala Aust 34C1
Mungallala, R Aust 34C1
Mungbere Zaïre 50C3
Mungeli India 43E4
Munger India 43F3
Mungindi Aust 34C1
Munich W Germ 18C3
Munising USA 64B1
Muñoz Gamero,Pen Chile 74B8
Munsan S Korea 28A3
Munster France 13D3
Münster W Germ 18B2
Münsterland, Region W Germ 13D2
Munţii Apuseni, Mts Rom 17E1
Munţii Călimani, Mts Rom 17E1
Munţii Carpaţii Meridionali, Mts Rom 17E1
Munţii Rodnei, Mts Rom 17E1
Munţii Zarandului, Mts Rom 17E1
Munzur Silsilesi, Mts Turk 40C2
Muong Khoua Laos 30C1
Muong Man Viet 30D3
Muong Nong Laos 30D2
Muong Ou Neua Laos 30C1
Muong Sai Laos 30C1
Muong Sen Viet 30C2
Muong Sing Laos 30C1
Muong Son Laos 30C1
Muonio Fin 12J5
Muonio, R Fin/Sweden 12J5
Muping China 28A3
Muqdisho Somalia 50E3
Mur, R Austria 16C1
Murakami Japan 29D3
Murallón, Mt Arg/Chile 74B7
Murashi USSR 20H4
Murat, R Turk 40D2
Muravera, Sardinia 16B3
Murayama Japan 29D3
Murcheh Khvort Iran 41F3
Murchison NZ 35B2
Murchison, R Aust 32A3
Murcia Spain 15B2
Murcia, Region Spain 15B2
Murdo USA 60C2
Mureş, R Rom 17E1
Murfreesboro, N Carolina USA 67C1
Murfreesboro, Tennessee USA 67A1
Murg, R W Germ 13E3
Murgab, R USSR 24H6
Murghab, R Afghan 42A1
Murgha Kibzai Pak 42B2
Murgon Aust 34D1
Muri India 43F4
Muriaé Brazil 75D3
Muriege Angola 51C4
Murmansk USSR 20E2
Murom USSR 20G4
Muroran Japan 29E2
Muros Spain 15A1
Muroto Japan 29C4
Muroto-zaki, C Japan 29B4
Murphy, Idaho USA 58C2
Murphy, N Carolina USA 67B1
Murphys USA 66B1
Murray, Kentucky USA 64B3
Murray, Utah USA 58B2
Murray, R Aust 34B2
Murray Bridge Aust 34A3
Murray,L PNG 27H7
Murray,L USA 67B2
Murraysburg S Africa 47C3
Murray Seacarp Pacific O 37M3
Murrumbidgee, R Aust 34B2
Murrumburrah Aust 34C2
Murrurundi Aust 34D2
Murtoa Aust 34B3
Muruin Sum, R China 28A2
Murupara NZ 35C1
Murwāra India 43E4

Murwillumbah Aust 34D1
Muryo, Mt Indon 27E7
Muş Turk 40D2
Musala, Mt Bulg 17E2
Musan N Korea 28B2
Musandam Pen Oman 41G4
Muscat Oman 38D3
Muscatine USA 61E2
Musgrave Range, Mts Aust 32C3
Mushie Zaïre 50B4
Muskeget Chan USA 68E2
Muskegon USA 64B2
Muskegon, R USA 64B2
Muskogee USA 63C1
Muskoka,L Can 65D2
Musmar Sudan 50D2
Musoma Tanz 50D4
Mussau, I PNG 32D1
Musselshell, R USA 58E1
Mussende Angola 51B5
Mussidan France 14C3
Mustafa-Kemalpasa Turk 17F2
Mustang Nepal 43E3
Musters, Lago Arg 74C7
Musu-dan, C N Korea 28A2
Muswellbrook Aust 34D2
Mut Egypt 49E2
Mutá, Ponta do, Pt Brazil 75E1
Mutarara Mozam 51D5
Mutare Zim 51D5
Mutnyy Materik USSR 20K2
Mutoko Zim 51D5
Mutsamudu Comoros 51E5
Mutshatsha Zaïre 51C5
Mutsu Japan 29E2
Mutsu-wan, B Japan 29E2
Mutunópolis Brazil 75C1
Mu Us Shamo, Desert China 31B2
Muxima Angola 51B4
Muya USSR 25N4
Muyezerskiy USSR 20E3
Muyinga Burundi 50D4
Muyumba Zaïre 51C4
Muyun Kum, Desert USSR 39E1
Muzaffarābad Pak 42C2
Muzaffargarh Pak 42C2
Muzaffarnagar India 42D3
Muzaffarpur India 43F3
Muzhi USSR 24H3
Muzlag, Mt China 39G2
Muztagala, Mt China 39F2
Mvuma Zim 51D5
Mwanza Tanz 50D4
Mwanza Zaïre 51C4
Mweka Zaïre 50C4
Mwene Ditu Zaïre 51C4
Mwenezi Zim 51D6
Mwenezi, R Zim 47E1
Mwenga Zaïre 50C4
Mweru, L Zambia/Zaïre 51C4
Mwinilunga Zambia 51C5
Myanaung Burma 30B2
Myingyan Burma 30B1
Myinmoletkat, Mt Burma 30B3
Myitta Burma 30B3
Mymensingh Bang 43G4
Mynydd Eppynt Wales 7C3
Myojin, I Japan 26G3
Myongchon N Korea 28A2
Myonggan N Korea 28A2
Myrdal Nor 12F6
Myrdalsjökull, Mts Iceland 12B2
Myrtle Beach USA 67C2
Myrtle Creek USA 58B2
Mysen Nor 12G7
Mys Kanin Nos, C USSR 20G2
Myślenice Pol 19D3
Mysliborz Pol 18C2
Mysore India 44B3
Mys Sarych, C USSR 21E7
Mys Shmidta USSR 25T3
Mys Svyatoy Nos, C USSR 20F2
Mystic USA 68E2
Mys Tyub-Karagan, Pt USSR 21J7
Mys Zhelaniya, C USSR 24H2
My Tho Viet 30D3
Mytle Point USA 58B2
Mzimba Malawi 51D5
Mzuzú Malawi 51D5

N

Naalehu Hawaiian Is 66E5
Naantali Fin 12J6
Naas Irish Rep 9C3
Nabari Japan 29C4
Nabeul Tunisia 16C3
Nabileque, R Brazil 75A3
Nablus Israel 45C2
Nacala Mozam 51E5
Naches USA 58B1

Nachingwea Tanz 51D5
Nacimiento, R USA 66B3
Nacimiento Res USA 66B3
Nacogdoches USA 63D2
Nacozari Mexico 70B1
Nadel, Mt W Germ 13E2
Nadiād India 42C4
Nador Mor 15B2
Nadūshan Iran 41F3
Nadvoitsy USSR 20E3
Nadvornaya USSR 19E3
Naestved Den 18C1
Nafoora Libya 49E2
Naga Phil 27F5
Nagahama Japan 28B4
Naga Hills India 43H3
Nagai Japan 29C3
Nägäland, State India 43G3
Nagano Japan 29D3
Nagaoka Japan 29D3
Nägappattinam India 44B3
Nagar Parkar Pak 42C4
Nagasaki Japan 28B4
Nagashima Japan 29C4
Nagato Japan 28B4
Nägaur India 42C3
Nägercoil India 44B4
Nagha Kalat Pak 42B3
Nagina India 42D3
Nagold W Germ 13E3
Nagoya Japan 29D3
Nägpur India 42D4
Nagqu China 39H2
Nagykanizsa Hung 18D3
Nagykörös Hung 19D3
Naha, Okinawa Japan 26F4
Nähan India 42D2
Nahanni Butte Can 54F3
Nahariya Israel 45C2
Nahävand Iran 41E3
Nahe, R W Germ 13D3
Nahpu China 31D2
Nahuel Haupí, Lago Arg 74B6
Naimen Qi China 31E1
Nain Can 55M4
Nä'in Iran 41F3
Naini Tal India 42D3
Nainpur India 43E4
Nairn Scot 8D3
Nairobi Kenya 50D4
Najafābād Iran 41F3
Najd, Region S Arabia 40C4
Najin N Korea 28C2
Najrän S Arabia 50E2
Naju S Korea 28A3
Nakadori-jima Japan 28A4
Nakama Japan 28B4
Nakaminato Japan 29E3
Nakamura Japan 28B4
Nakano Japan 29C3
Nakano-shima, I Japan 29B3
Nakatsu Japan 28C4
Nakatsu-gawa Japan 29C3
Nakfa Eth 50D2
Nakhichevan USSR 21H8
Nakhl Egypt 45B4
Nakhodka USSR 28C2
Nakhon Pathom Thai 30C3
Nakhon Ratchasima Thai 30C3
Nakhon Si Thammarat Thai 30C4
Nakina, Ontario Can 55K4
Naknek USA 54C4
Nakskov Den 12G8
Naktong, R S Korea 28A3
Nakuru Kenya 50D4
Nal'chik USSR 21G7
Nalgonda India 44B2
Nallamala Range, Mts India 44B2
Nälüt Libya 49D1
Namaacha Mozam 47E2
Namak, L Iran 24G6
Namakzar-e Shadad, Salt Flat Iran 41G3
Namangan USSR 24J5
Namapa Mozam 51D5
Namaqualand, Region S Africa 51B7
Nambour Aust 34D1
Nambucca Heads Aust 34D2
Nam Can Viet 30D4
Nam Co, L China 39H2
Nam Dinh Viet 30D1
Nametil Mozam 51D5
Namib Desert Namibia 47A1
Namibe Angola 51B5
Namibia, UN Trust Territory Africa 51B6
Namlea Indon 27F7
Namling China 43F3
Namoi, R Aust 34C2
Nampa USA 58C2
Nampala Mali 48B3
Nam Phong Thai 30C2
Namp'o N Korea 28B3
Nampula Mozam 51D5

Pathfinder Res *USA*	60B2	Peixe, R, São Paulo *Brazil*	75B3	Perryville, Missouri *USA*	63E1
Patiala *India*	42D2	Pei Xian *China*	31D3	Persia = Iran	
Pativilca *Peru*	72C6	Pekan *Malay*	30C5	Persian Gulf = The Gulf	
Pátmos, I *Greece*	17F3	Pekanbaru *Indon*	27D6	Perth *Aust*	32A4
Patna *India*	43F3	Pekin *USA*	64B2	Perth *Can*	65D2
Patnos *Turk*	40D2	Peking = Beijing		Perth *Scot*	8D3
Patomskoye Nagor'ye, Upland *USSR*	25N4	Pelabohan Kelang *Malay*	30C5	Perth Amboy *USA*	68C2
Patos *Brazil*	73L5	Pelat, Mont *France*	14D3	Peru *USA*	64B2
Patos de Minas *Brazil*	75C2	Peleaga, Mt *Rom*	17E1	Peru, Republic *S America*	72D6
Patos, Lagoa dos, Lg *Brazil*	74F4	Peleduy *USSR*	25N4	Peru Basin *Pacific O*	37P5
Pátrai *Greece*	17E3	Pelee I *Can*	64C2	Peru-Chile Trench *Pacific O*	52E6
Patrasuy *USSR*	20L3	Peleng, I *Indon*	32B1	Perugia *Italy*	16C2
Patrocínio *Brazil*	75C2	Pelican L *USA*	61E1	Perušic *Yugos*	16D2
Patta I *Kenya*	50E4	Pelican Pt *S Africa*	47A1	Pervari *Turk*	40D2
Pattani *Thai*	30C4	Pello *Fin*	12J5	Pervomaysk, RSFSR *USSR*	20G5
Pattaya *Thai*	30C3	Pelly Bay *Can*	55J3	Pervomaysk, Ukraine SSR *USSR*	21E6
Patterson, California *USA*	66B2	Pelly Mts *Can*	54E3	Pervoural'sk *USSR*	20K4
Patterson, Louisiana *USA*	63D3	Pelotas *Brazil*	74F4	Pesaro *Italy*	16C2
Patterson Mt *USA*	66C2	Pelotas, R *Brazil*	74F3	Pescadero *USA*	66A2
Patton *USA*	68A2	Pelusium, Hist Site *Egypt*	45B3	Pescadores = Pengho Lieh Tao	
Patu *Brazil*	73L5	Pelvoux, Massif du, Mts *France*	14D2	Pescara *Italy*	16C2
Patuakhali *Bang*	43G4	Pelym, R *USSR*	20L3	Peshawar *Pak*	42C2
Patuca, R *Honduras*	70D3	Pemba *Mozam*	51E5	Peshkopi *Alb*	17E2
Pau *France*	14B3	Pemba, Baiá de, B *Mozam*	51E5	Peshtigo *USA*	64B1
Paulatuk *Can*	54F3	Pemba I *Tanz*	50D4	Pestovo *USSR*	20F4
Paulistana *Brazil*	73K5	Pembina *USA*	61D1	Petacalco, B de *Mexico*	70B3
Paulpietersburg *S Africa*	47E2	Pembroke *Can*	65D1	Petah Tiqwa *Israel*	45C2
Pauls Valley *USA*	63C2	Pembroke *USA*	67B2	Petaluma *USA*	59B3
Paungde *Burma*	30B2	Pembroke *Wales*	7B4	Pétange *Lux*	13C3
Pauri *India*	42D2	Penacook *USA*	68E1	Petauke *Zambia*	51D5
Pavão *Brazil*	75D2	Penápolis *Brazil*	75B3	Petenwell L *USA*	64B2
Pavia *Italy*	16B1	Peñarroya *Spain*	15A2	Peterborough *Aust*	34A2
Pavlodar *USSR*	24J4	Peñarroya, Mt *Spain*	15B1	Peterborough *Can*	65D2
Pavlovich *USSR*	25O4	Penarth *Wales*	7C4	Peterborough *Eng*	7D3
Pavlovka *USSR*	20K4	Peñas, Cabo de, C *Spain*	15A1	Peterborough *USA*	68E1
Pavlovo *USSR*	20G4	Penas, Golfo de, G *Chile*	74B7	Peterhead *Scot*	8E3
Pavlovsk *USSR*	21G5	Peña Trevinca, Mt *Spain*	15A1	Petermann Gletscher, Gl *Greenland*	55M1
Pawhuska *USA*	63C1	Pende, R *Chad/CAR*	50B3	Petermann Range, Mts *Aust*	32B3
Paw Paw *USA*	68A3	Pendleton *USA*	58C1	Peteroa, Vol *Arg/Chile*	74B5
Pawtucket *USA*	68E2	Pend Oreille, R *USA*	58C1	Peter 1 Øy, I *Ant*	76G4
Paxton *USA*	60C2	Penedo *Brazil*	73L6	Petersburg *USA*	54E4
Payette *USA*	58C2	Penganga, R *India*	42D5	Petersburg, Virginia *USA*	65D3
Payne,L *Can*	55L4	Pengho Lieh Tao, Is *Taiwan*	31D5	Petersfield *Eng*	7D4
Paynesville *USA*	61E1	Penglai *China*	31E2	Petite Kabylie, Hills *Algeria*	16B3
Paysandú *Urug*	74E4	Pengshui *China*	31B4	Petit Mècatina, Rivière du, R *Can*	55M4
Pazardzhik *Bulg*	17E2	Penicuik *Scot*	8D4	Petlad *India*	42C4
Peace, R *Can*	54G4	Peninsular Malaysia *Malay*	30C5	Peto *Mexico*	70D2
Peace, R *USA*	67B3	Penistone *Eng*	7D3	Petoskey *USA*	64C1
Peach Springs *USA*	59D3	Penner, R *India*	44B3	Petra, Hist Site *Jordan*	45C3
Peak District Nat Pk *Eng*	7D3	Pennine Chain, Mts *Eng*	6C2	Petra, Ostrova, Is *USSR*	25N2
Peaked Mt *USA*	65F1	Penns Grove *USA*	68C3	Petra Velikogo, Zaliv, B *USSR*	28C2
Peak Hill *Aust*	34C2	Pennsylvania, State *USA*	57F2	Petrified Forest Nat Pk *USA*	59E3
Peak,The, Mt *Eng*	7D3	Penn Yan *USA*	68B1	Petrolina *Brazil*	73K5
Peale,Mt *USA*	59E3	Penny Highlands, Mts *Can*	55M3	Petropavlovsk *USSR*	24H4
Pearl, R *USA*	63D2	Penobscot, R *USA*	65F1	Petropavlovsk-Kamchatskiy *USSR*	26J1
Pearl City *Hawaiian Is*	66E5	Penobscot B *USA*	65F2	Petrópolis *Brazil*	75D3
Pearl Harbor *Hawaiian Is*	66E5	Penola *Aust*	34B3	Petrovsk *USSR*	21H5
Pearsall *USA*	62C3	Penong *Aust*	32C4	Petrovsk Zabakal'skiy *USSR*	25M4
Pearston *S Africa*	47D3	Penonomé *Panama*	69A5	Petrovsk Zabaykal'skiy *USSR*	26D1
Peary Chan *Can*	54H2	Penrith *Eng*	6C2	Petrozavodsk *USSR*	20E3
Pebane *Mozam*	51D5	Pensacola *USA*	63E2	Petrusburg *S Africa*	47D2
Peć *Yugos*	17E2	Pensacola Mts *Ant*	76E2	Petrus Steyn *S Africa*	47D2
Peçanha *Brazil*	75D2	Pentecost, I *Vanuatu*	33F2	Petrusville *S Africa*	47C3
Pecan Island *USA*	63D3	Penticton *Can*	54G5	Pevek *USSR*	25T3
Pechenga *USSR*	12L5	Pentland Firth, Chan *Scot*	8D2	Peza, R *USSR*	20H2
Pechora *USSR*	20K2	Pentland Hills *Scot*	8D4	Pfälzer Wald, Region *W Germ*	13E2
Pechora, R *USSR*	20J2	Pen-y-ghent, Mt *Eng*	6C2	Pforzheim *W Germ*	18B3
Pechorskaya Guba, G *USSR*	20J2	Penza *USSR*	20H5	Phagwara *India*	42D2
Pechorskoye More, S *USSR*	20J2	Penzance *Eng*	7B4	Phalaborwa *S Africa*	47E1
Pecoraro, Mt *Italy*	16D3	Penzhina, R *USSR*	25S3	Phalodi *India*	42C3
Pecos *USA*	62B2	Penzhinskaya Guba, B *USSR*	25S3	Phalsbourg *France*	13D3
Pecos, R *USA*	62B2	Peoria *USA*	64B2	Phaltan *India*	44A2
Pécs *Hung*	19D3	Perak, R *Malay*	30C5	Phangnga *Thai*	30B4
Pedhoulas *Cyprus*	45B1	Perdido, R *Brazil*	75A3	Phanom Dang, Mts *Camb/Thai*	30C3
Pedra Azul *Brazil*	75D2	Pereira *Colombia*	72C3	Phan Rang *Viet*	30D3
Pedregulho *Brazil*	75C3	Pereira Barreto *Brazil*	75B3	Phan Thiet *Viet*	30D3
Pedro Cays, Is *Caribbean S*	69B3	Perelazovskiy *USSR*	21G6	Pharr *USA*	62C3
Pedro de Valdivia *Chile*	74C2	Pereyaslav *USSR*	19G2	Phelps L *USA*	67C1
Pedro Gomes *Brazil*	75B2	Pergamino *Arg*	74D4	Phenix City *USA*	67A2
Pedro Juan Caballero *Par*	75A3	Perge *Turk*	40B2	Phet Buri *Thai*	30B3
Pedro,Pt *Sri Lanka*	44C4	Peribonca, R *Can*	55L4	Phiafay *Laos*	30D3
Peebinga *Aust*	34B2	Périgueux *France*	14C2	Philadelphia, Mississippi *USA*	63E2
Peebles *Scot*	8D4	Perlas, Archipiélago de las *Panama*	72C2	Philadelphia, Pennsylvania *USA*	68C2
Pee Dee, R *USA*	67C2	Perlas, Laguna de *Nic*	69A4	Philip *USA*	60C2
Peekskill *USA*	68D2	Perm' *USSR*	20K4	Philippeville = Skikda	
Peel, I of Man *British Is*	6B2	Pernambuco = Recife		Philippeville *Belg*	13C2
Peel, R *Can*	54E3	Pernambuco, State *Brazil*	73L5	Philippine S *Pacific O*	27F5
Peel Sd *Can*	54J2	Pernik *Bulg*	17E2	Philippines, Republic *S E Asia*	27F5
Pefos = Paphos		Péronne *France*	13B3	Philippine Trench *Pacific O*	36H4
Peg Arfak, Mt *Indon*	27G7	Perpignan *France*	14C3	Philippolis *S Africa*	47D3
Pegasus B *NZ*	35B2	Perris *USA*	66D4	Philipsburg, Montana *USA*	58D1
Pegu *Burma*	30B2	Perry, Florida *USA*	67B2	Philipsburg, Pennsylvania *USA*	65D2
Pegunungan Maoke, Mts *Indon*	32C1	Perry, Georgia *USA*	67B2	Philip Smith Mts *USA*	54D3
Pegu Yoma, Mts *Burma*	30B2	Perry, New York *USA*	68A1	Philipstown *S Africa*	47C3
Pehuajó *Arg*	74D5	Perry, Oklahoma *USA*	63C1	Phillips B *Can*	55K1
Peixe, R, Mato Grosso *Brazil*	75B1	Perry River *Can*	54H3	Phillipsburg, Kansas *USA*	60D3
		Perrysburg *USA*	64C2	Phillipsburg, New Jersey *USA*	68C2
		Perryton *USA*	62B1	Philpots Pen *Can*	55K2
				Phnom Penh *Camb*	30C3
				Phoenix, Arizona *USA*	59D4
				Phoenix, New York *USA*	68B1
				Phoenix Is *Pacific O*	33H1
				Phoenixville *USA*	68C2
				Phong Saly *Laos*	30C1
				Phu Bia, Mt *Laos*	30C2
				Phu Cuong *Viet*	30D3
				Phuket *Thai*	30B4
				Phulbani *India*	43E4
				Phu Miang, Mt *Thai*	30C2
				Phu Set, Mt *Laos*	30D2
				Phu Tho *Viet*	30D1
				Phu Vinh *Viet*	30D4
				Piacenza *Italy*	16B1
				Pialba *Aust*	34D1
				Pian, R *Aust*	34C2
				Pianosa, I *Italy*	16C2
				Pianosa, I *Italy*	16D2
				Piaseczno *Pol*	19E2
				Piatã *Brazil*	75D1
				Piatra-Neamţ *Rom*	17F1
				Piauí, State *Brazil*	73K5
				Piave, R *Italy*	16C1
				Pibor, R *Sudan*	50D3
				Pibor Post *Sudan*	50D3
				Picardie, Region *France*	13B3
				Picayune *USA*	63E2
				Pichilemu *Chile*	74B4
				Pickering *Eng*	6D2
				Pickle Lake *Can*	55J4
				Pico, I *Azores*	48A1
				Pico Bolívar, Mt *Ven*	69C5
				Pico de Almanzor, Mt *Spain*	15A1
				Pico de Aneto, Mt *Spain*	15C1
				Pico Duarte, Mt *Dom Rep*	69C3
				Picos *Brazil*	73K5
				Picos de Europa, Mt *Spain*	15B1
				Picton *Aust*	34D2
				Picton *NZ*	35B2
				Piedade *Brazil*	75C3
				Piedra *USA*	66C2
				Piedras Blancas,Pt *USA*	66B3
				Piedras Negras *Mexico*	70B2
				Pie I *Can*	64B1
				Pieksämäki *Fin*	12K6
				Pielinen, L *Fin*	12K6
				Pienaar's River *S Africa*	47D2
				Pierre *USA*	60C2
				Pieštany *Czech*	19D3
				Pietermaritzburg *S Africa*	47E2
				Pietersburg *S Africa*	47D1
				Piet Retief *S Africa*	47E2
				Pietrosul, Mt *Rom*	17F1
				Pigailoe, I *Pacific O*	27H6
				Piggott *USA*	63D1
				Pihyŏn *N Korea*	28A3
				Pikangikum L *Can*	55J4
				Pikes Peak *USA*	60B3
				Piketberg *S Africa*	47B3
				Pikeville *USA*	64C3
				Pikiutaleq *Greenland*	55O3
				Pik Kommunizma, Mt *USSR*	39F2
				Pikounda *Congo*	50B3
				Pik Pobedy, Mt *China/USSR*	39G1
				Piła *Pol*	18D2
				Pilar *Par*	74E3
				Pilcomayo, R *Arg/Par/Bol*	74D2
				Pilgrim's Rest *S Africa*	47E1
				Pilibhit *India*	42D3
				Pilica, R *Pol*	19D2
				Pillar,C *Aust*	34C4
				Pilões, Serra dos, Mts *Brazil*	75C2
				Pilos *Greece*	17E3
				Pilot Knob, Mt *USA*	58C1
				Pilot Peak, Mt *USA*	66D1
				Pilottown *USA*	63E3
				Pimenta *Brazil*	73G4
				Pinang, I *Malay*	30C4
				Pinar del Rio *Cuba*	69A2
				Pinche *Belg*	13C2
				Pindaré, R *Brazil*	73J4
				Pindhos, Mts *Greece*	17E3
				Pine Bluff *USA*	63D2
				Pine Bluffs *USA*	60C2

Pine City *USA*	61E1
Pine Creek *Aust*	32C2
Pine Creek, R *USA*	68B2
Pinecrest *USA*	66C1
Pinedale, California *USA*	66C2
Pinedale, Wyoming *USA*	58E2
Pine Flat Res *USA*	66C2
Pinega *USSR*	20G3
Pinega, R *USSR*	20H3
Pine Grove *USA*	68B2
Pine Hills *USA*	67B3
Pinehurst *USA*	67C1
Pine I *USA*	67B3
Pineland *USA*	63D2
Pinellas Park *USA*	67B3
Pine Mt *USA*	66B3
Pine Point *Can*	54G3
Pine Ridge *USA*	60C2
Pines,L. o'the *USA*	63D2
Pineville *USA*	63D2
Pingdingshan *China*	31C3
Pingguo *China*	31B5
Pingliang *China*	31B2
Pingluo *China*	31B2
Pingtan Dao, I *China*	31D4
Pingtung *Taiwan*	31E5
Pingwu *China*	31A3
Pingxiang, Guangxi *China*	31B5
Pingxiang, Jiangxi *China*	31C4
Pinheiro *Brazil*	73J4
Pini, I *Indon*	27C6
Piniós, R *Greece*	17E3
Pinjarra *Aust*	32A4
Pinnacles Nat. Mon. *USA*	66B2
Pinnaroo *Aust*	34B3
Pinos,I de = Juventud, Isla de la	
Pinos,Mt *USA*	66C3
Pinos,Pt *USA*	59B3
Pinrang *Indon*	27E7
Pins, Île des *New Caledonia*	33F3
Pinsk *USSR*	21D5
Pinyug *USSR*	20H3
Pioche *USA*	59D3
Piombino *Italy*	16C2
Pioneer Mts *USA*	58D1
Pioner, Ostrov, I *USSR*	25K2
Pionerskiy *USSR*	20L3
Piotrków Trybunalski *Pol*	19D2
Piper, Oilfield *N Sea*	8F2
Piper Peak, Mt *USA*	66D2
Pipestone *USA*	61D2
Pipmuacan, Rés *Can*	57F2
Pipmudcan, Res *Can*	55M4
Piqua *USA*	64C2
Piquiri, R *Brazil*	75B4
Piracanjuba *Brazil*	75C2
Piracicaba *Brazil*	75C3
Piraçununga *Brazil*	75C3
Piraí do Sul *Brazil*	75C3
Piraiévs *Greece*	17E3
Pirajuí *Brazil*	75C3
Piranhas *Brazil*	75B2
Pirapora *Brazil*	75D2
Pirenópolis *Brazil*	75C2
Pires do Rio *Brazil*	75C2
Pírgos *Greece*	17E3
Pirineos, Mts *Spain/France*	14B3
Piripiri *Brazil*	73K4
Pirmasens *W Germ*	13D3
Pirot *Yugos*	17E2
Pir Panjal Range, Mts *Pak*	42C2
Piru *Indon*	27F7
Piru Creek, R *USA*	66C3
Pisa *Italy*	16C2
Pisco *Peru*	72C6
Piseco *USA*	68C1
Písek *Czech*	18C3
Pishin *Pak*	42B2
Pismo Beach *USA*	66B3
Pissis, Mt *Arg*	74C3
Pistoia *Italy*	16C2
Pisuerga, R *Spain*	15B1
Pit, R *USA*	58B2
Pitalito *Colombia*	72C3
Pitanga *Brazil*	74F2
Pitcairn, I *Pacific O*	37N6
Pite, R *Sweden*	12H5
Piteå *Sweden*	12J5
Pitești *Rom*	17E2
Pit Gorodok *USSR*	25L4
Pithiviers *France*	13B3
Pitkyaranta *USSR*	20E3
Pitlochry *Scot*	8D3
Pitlyar *USSR*	20M2
Pitt, I *NZ*	33H5
Pitt I *Can*	54F4
Pittsburg, California *USA*	66B1
Pittsburg, Kansas *USA*	63D1
Pittsburgh *USA*	65D2
Pittsfield, Illinois *USA*	64A3

Pittsfield Princeton

Pittsfield, Massachusetts USA 68D1
Pittston USA 68C2
Pittsworth Aust 34D1
Piura Peru 72B5
Piute Peak, Mt USA 66C3
Piuthan Nepal 43E3
Pixley USA 66C3
Pjórsá, R Iceland 12B2
Placentia B Can 55N5
Placerville USA 66B1
Plaine Lorraine, Region France 13C3
Plains USA 62B1
Plainview, Nebraska USA 61D2
Plainview, Texas USA 62B2
Planada USA 66B2
Planalto de Mato Grosso Plat Brazil 73H7
Planalto do Borborema, Plat Brazil 73L5
Planet Deep PNG 33E1
Plankinton USA 60D2
Plano USA 63C2
Plantation USA 67B3
Plant City USA 67B3
Plasencia Spain 15A1
Plast USSR 20L5
Plastun USSR 26G2
Plata, Río de la Arg/Urug 74E5
Plateau Lorrain France 13D2
Plato Colombia 69C5
Platres Cyprus 45B1
Platte USA 60D2
Platte, R USA 60C2
Platteville USA 64A2
Plattsburgh USA 65E2
Plattsmouth USA 61D2
Plauen E Germ 18C2
Plavsk USSR 20F5
Playas Ecuador 72B4
Pleasanton, California USA 66B2
Pleasanton, Texas USA 62C3
Pleasantville USA 68C3
Pleasure Ridge Park USA 64B3
Pleiku Viet 30D3
Plenty,B of NZ 35C1
Plentywood USA 60C1
Plesetsk USSR 20F3
Pleszew Pol 19D2
Pletipi,L Can 55L4
Pleven Bulg 17E2
Plevlja Yugos 17D2
Ploče Yugos 17D2
Płock Pol 19D2
Ploërmel France 14B2
Ploieşti Rom 17F2
Plombières-les-Bains France 13D4
Płońsk Pol 20C5
Plovdiv Bulg 17E2
Plummer USA 58C1
Plumtree Zim 51C6
Plymouth, California USA 66B1
Plymouth Eng 7B4
Plymouth, Indiana USA 64B2
Plymouth, Massachusetts USA 68E2
Plymouth, Pennsylvania USA 68C2
Plymouth B USA 68E2
Plymouth Sd Eng 7B4
Plynlimon, Mt Wales 7C3
Plzeň Czech 18C3
Pniewy Pol 18D2
Po Burkina 48B3
Po, R Italy 16C2
Pobé Benin 48C4
Pobedino USSR 26H2
Pocatello USA 54G5
Pochinok USSR 19G2
Poções Brazil 75D1
Pocomoke City USA 65D3
Poconé Brazil 75A2
Poços de Caldas Brazil 75C3
Podkamennaya Tunguska, R USSR 25L3
Podol'sk USSR 20F4
Podol'skaya Vozvyshennost', Upland USSR 19F3
Podporozh'ye USSR 20E3
Podyuga USSR 20G3
Pofadder S Africa 47B2
Poghdar Afghan 42A2
P'ohang S Korea 28B3
Poinsett,C Ant 76G9
Point Aust 34C2
Pointe-à-Pitre Guadeloupe 69E3
Pointe Noire Congo 50B4
Point Fairy Aust 34B3
Point Fortin Trinidad 69L1
Point Hope USA 54B3
Point L Can 54G3
Point Lay USA 54B3
Point Pleasant, New Jersey USA 68C2
Point Pleasant, W Virginia USA 64C3
Poitiers France 14C2
Poitou, Region France 14B2
Poix France 13A3
Pokaran India 42C3
Pokataroo Aust 34C1
Pokhara Nepal 43E3
Pokrovsk USSR 25O3
Polacca USA 59D3
Poland USA 68C1
Poland, Republic Europe 19D2
Polatlı Turk 40B2
Poli Cam 49D4
Policastro, G di Italy 16D3
Polillo Is Phil 27F5
Poliny Osipenko USSR 25P4
Polis Cyprus 45B1
Políyiros Greece 17E2
Pollachi India 44B3
Pollino, Monte, Mt Italy 16D3
Polonnye USSR 19F2
Polotsk USSR 19F1
Polson USA 58D1
Poltava USSR 21E6
Pölten Austria 16D1
Polunochoye USSR 20K3
Poluostrov Mangyshiak, Pen USSR 21J7
Poluostrov Rybachiy, Pen USSR 12L5
Polvadera USA 62A2
Polyarnyy, Murmansk USSR 20E2
Polyarnyy, Yakutskaya USSR 25Q2
Polyarnyy Ural, Mts USSR 20L2
Polynesia, Region Pacific O 37L4
Pomabamba Peru 72C5
Pomba, R Brazil 75D3
Pomeroy N Ire 9C2
Pomona USA 66D3
Pomona Res USA 61D3
Pompano Beach USA 67B3
Pompton Lakes USA 68C2
Ponca City USA 63C1
Ponce Puerto Rico 69D3
Ponce de Leon B USA 67B3
Pondicherry India 44B3
Pond Inlet Can 55L2
Ponferrada Spain 15A1
Pongara, Pte Eq Guinea 48C4
Pongo, R Sudan 50C3
Pongola, R S Africa 47E2
Ponnāni India 44B3
Ponnyadoung Range, Mts Burma 43G4
Ponoy USSR 24F3
Ponoy, R USSR 20G2
Pons France 14B2
Ponta Delgada Azores 48A1
Ponta Grossa Brazil 75B4
Pontal Brazil 75C3
Pont-à-Mousson France 13C3
Ponta Pora Brazil 75A3
Pontarlier France 14D2
Pontchartrain,L USA 63D2
Ponte de Pedra Brazil 75A1
Pontedera Italy 16C2
Pontefract Eng 7D3
Ponte Leccia, Corsica 16B2
Pontevedra Spain 15A1
Pontiac, Illinois USA 64B2
Pontiac, Michigan USA 64C2
Pontianak Indon 27D7
Pontivy France 14B2
Pontoise France 13B3
Pontotoc USA 63E2
Pont-sur-Yonne France 13B3
Pontypool Wales 7C4
Pontypridd Wales 7C4
Ponziane, I Italy 16C2
Poole Eng 7D4
Poona = Pune
Pooncarie Aust 34B2
Poopelloe,L Aust 34B2
Poopó, Lago Bol 72E7
Poorman USA 54C3
Popayán Colombia 72C3
Poperinge Belg 13B2
Popilta L Aust 34B2
Poplar USA 60B1
Poplar Bluff USA 63D1
Poplarville USA 63E2
Popocatepetl, Vol Mexico 70C3
Popokabaka Zaïre 50B4
Popondetta PNG 27H7
Popovo Bulg 17F2
Porangatu Brazil 75C1
Porbandar India 42B4
Porcos, R Brazil 75C1
Porcupine, R USA/Can 54D3
Poreč Yugos 16C1
Porecatu Brazil 75B3
Pori Fin 12J6
Porirua NZ 35B2
Porjus Sweden 12H5
Porlamar Venezuela 69E4
Poronaysk USSR 26H2
Porosozero USSR 20E3
Porsangen, Inlet Nor 12K4
Porsgrunn Nor 12F7
Portadown N Ire 9C2
Portaferry N Ire 9D2
Portage USA 64B2
Portal USA 60C1
Port Alberni Can 54F5
Portalegre Port 15A2
Portales USA 62B2
Port Alfred S Africa 47D3
Port Alice Can 54F4
Port Allegany USA 68A2
Port Allen USA 63D2
Port Angeles USA 58B1
Port Antonio Jamaica 69B3
Portarlington Irish Rep 9C3
Port Arthur USA 63D3
Port Askaig Scot 8B4
Port Augusta Aust 32C4
Port-au-Prince Haiti 69C3
Port Austin USA 64C2
Port Blair Andaman Is 44E3
Port Campbell Aust 34B3
Port Canning India 43F4
Port Cartier Can 55M5
Port Chalmers NZ 35B3
Port Charlotte USA 67B3
Port Chester USA 68D2
Port Clinton USA 64C2
Port Colborne Can 65D2
Port Davey, B Aust 34C4
Port-de-Paix Haiti 69C3
Port Dickson Malay 30C5
Port Edward S Africa 47E3
Porteirinha Brazil 75D2
Port Elgin Can 64C2
Port Elizabeth S Africa 47D3
Port Ellen Scot 8B4
Port Erin, I of Man British Is 6B2
Porter Pt St Vincent 69N2
Porterville USA 66C2
Port Fairy Aust 32D4
Port Gentil Gabon 50A4
Port Gibson USA 63D2
Port Hammond Can 58B1
Port Harcourt Nigeria 48C4
Port Hardy Can 54F4
Port Hawkesbury Can 55M5
Porthcawl Wales 7C4
Port Hedland Aust 32A3
Porthmadog Wales 7B3
Port Hope Simpson Can 55N4
Port Hueneme USA 66C3
Port Huron USA 64C2
Portimão Port 15A2
Port Jackson, B Aust 34D2
Port Jefferson USA 68D2
Port Jervis USA 68C2
Port Kembla Aust 34D2
Portland Eng 7C4
Portland, Indiana USA 64C2
Portland, Maine USA 65E2
Portland, New South Wales Aust 34C2
Portland, Oregon USA 58B1
Portland, Victoria Aust 34B3
Portland Bight, B Jamaica 69H2
Portland Bill, Pt Eng 7C4
Portland,C Aust 34C4
Portland I NZ 35C1
Portland Pt Jamaica 69H2
Port Laoise Irish Rep 9C3
Port Lavaca USA 63C3
Port Lincoln Aust 32C4
Port Loko Sierra Leone 48A4
Port Louis Mauritius 51F6
Port MacDonnell Aust 34B3
Port Macquarie Aust 34D2
Port Matilda USA 68A2
Port Moresby PNG 32D1
Port Nolloth S Africa 47B2
Port Norris USA 68C3
Porto = Oporto
Pôrto Alegre Brazil 74F4
Porto Alexandre Angola 51B5
Porto Armuelles Panama 69A5
Porto Artur Brazil 75A1
Pôrto 15 de Novembro Brazil 75B3
Pôrto dos Meinacos Brazil 75B1
Pôrto E Cunha Brazil 74F2
Pôrto Esperança Brazil 75A2
Portoferraio Italy 16C2
Port of Spain Trinidad 69L1
Pôrto Jofre Brazil 75A2
Pôrto Mendez Brazil 75B3
Pôrto Murtinho Brazil 75A3
Porto Novo Benin 48C4
Port Orchard USA 58B1
Port Orford USA 58B2
Pôrto Santa Helena Brazil 75B3
Porto Santo, I Madeira 48A1
Pôrto São José Brazil 75B3
Pôrto Seguro Brazil 73L7
Porto Torres, Sardinia 16B2
Pôrto União Brazil 75B4
Porto Vecchio, Corsica 16B2
Pôrto Velho Brazil 72F5
Portpatrick Scot 8C4
Port Pegasus, B NZ 35A3
Port Phillip B Aust 34B3
Port Pirie Aust 34A2
Portree Scot 8B3
Port Renfrew Can 58B1
Port Royal Jamaica 69J2
Port Royal Sd USA 67B2
Portrush N Ire 9C2
Port Said Egypt 45B3
Port St Joe USA 67A3
Port St Johns S Africa 47D3
Port Saunders Can 55N4
Port Shepstone S Africa 47E3
Portsmouth Dominica 69Q2
Portsmouth Eng 7D4
Portsmouth, New Hampshire USA 68E1
Portsmouth, Ohio USA 64C3
Portsmouth, Virginia USA 65D3
Port Stephens, B Aust 34D2
Portstewart N Ire 9C2
Port Sudan Sudan 50D2
Port Sulphur USA 63E3
Porttipahdan Tekojärvi, Res Fin 12K5
Portugal, Republic Europe 15A2
Portumna Irish Rep 9B3
Portville USA 68A1
Port Washington USA 64B2
Port Weld Malay 30C5
Porvenir Bol 72E6
Porvoo Fin 12K6
Posadas Arg 74E3
Posadas Spain 15A2
Posht-e Badam Iran 41G3
Poso Indon 27F7
Posŏng S Korea 28A4
Pos Poluy USSR 20M2
Posse Brazil 75C1
Post USA 62B2
Postavy USSR 19F1
Poste-de-la-Baleine Can 55L4
Postmasburg S Africa 47C2
Postojna Yugos 16C1
Pos'yet USSR 28C2
Potchefstroom S Africa 47D2
Poteau USA 63D1
Potenza Italy 16D2
Potgietersrus S Africa 47D1
Poth USA 62C3
Poti USSR 21G7
Potiskum Nigeria 48D3
Potlatch USA 58C1
Potloer, Mt S Africa 47C3
Pot Mt USA 58C1
Potomac, R USA 65D3
Potosí Bol 72E7
Potrerillos Chile 74C3
Potsdam E Germ 18C2
Potter USA 60C2
Pottstown USA 68C2
Pottsville USA 68B2
Poughkeepsie USA 68D2
Pouso Alegre Brazil 75C3
Poverty B NZ 35C1
Povonets USSR 20F3
Povorino USSR 21G5
Povungnituk Can 55L4
Powder, R USA 60B1
Powder River USA 60B2
Powell USA 58E2
Powell Creek Aust 32C2
Powell,L USA 59D3
Powell River Can 54F5
Powys, County Wales 7C3
Poxoréo Brazil 75B2
Poyang Hu, L China 31D4
Pozantı Turk 40C2
Poza Rica Mexico 70C2
Poznań Pol 18D2
Pozo Colorado Par 74E2
Pozzuoli Italy 16C2
Pra, R Ghana 48B4
Prachin Buri Thai 30C3
Prachuap Khiri Khan Thai 30B3
Praděd, Mt Czech 18D2
Pradelles France 14C3
Prado Brazil 75E2
Prague Czech 18C2
Praha = Prague
Praia Cape Verde 48A4
Praia Rica Brazil 75A1
Prainha Brazil 72F5
Prairie Dog Town Fork, R USA 62B2
Prairie du Chien USA 64A2
Prairie Village USA 61E3
Prakhon Chai Thai 30C3
Prata Brazil 75C2
Prata, R Brazil 75C2
Prates, I = Dongsha Qundao
Prato Italy 16C2
Prattsville USA 68C1
Prattville USA 67A2
Prawle Pt Eng 14B1
Predivinsk USSR 25L4
Predporozhnyy USSR 25Q3
Pregolyu, R USSR 19E2
Prek Kak Camb 30D3
Prentice USA 64A1
Prenzlau E Germ 18C2
Preparis I Burma 44E3
Přerov Czech 18D3
Prescott, Arizona USA 59D4
Prescott, Arkansas USA 63D2
Prescott Can 65D2
Presho USA 60C2
Presidencia Roque Sáenz Peña Arg 74D3
Presidente Epitácio Brazil 75B3
Presidente Murtinho Brazil 75B2
Presidente Prudente Brazil 75B3
Presidenté Vargas Brazil 73H8
Presidente Venceslau Brazil 75B3
Presidio USA 62B3
Prešov Czech 19E3
Presque Isle USA 65F1
Preston Eng 6C3
Preston, Idaho USA 56B2
Preston, Minnesota USA 61E2
Preston, Missouri USA 63D1
Prestwick Scot 8C4
Prêto Brazil 73J8
Prêto, R Brazil 75C2
Pretoria S Africa 47D2
Préveza Greece 17E3
Prey Veng Camb 30D3
Price USA 59D3
Prichard USA 63E2
Prichernomorskaya Nizmennost', Lowland USSR 21E6
Prickly Pt Grenada 69M2
Pridneprovskaya Vozvyshennost', Upland USSR 19F3
Priekule USSR 19E1
Prieska S Africa 47C2
Priest L USA 58C1
Priest River USA 58C1
Prikaspiyskaya Nizmennost', Region USSR 21H6
Prilep Yugos 17E2
Priluki USSR 21E5
Primavera, Base Ant 76G3
Primorsk USSR 12K6
Primorsko-Akhtarsk USSR 21F6
Prince Albert Can 54H4
Prince Albert S Africa 47C3
Prince Albert,C Can 54F2
Prince Albert Pen Can 54G2
Prince Albert Sd Can 54G2
Prince Charles I Can 55L3
Prince Charles Mts Ant 76F10
Prince Edward I Can 55M5
Prince Edward Is Indian O 36C7
Prince George Can 54F4
Prince Gustaf Adolf, S Can 54H2
Prince of Wales I Aust 27H8
Prince of Wales I Can 54H2
Prince of Wales I USA 54E4
Prince of Wales Str Can 54G2
Prince Patrick I Can 54F2
Prince Regent Inlet, Str Can 55J2
Prince Rupert Can 54E4
Princess Charlotte B Aust 32D2
Princes Town Trinidad 69L1
Princeton Can 54F5
Princeton, Illinois USA 64B2
Princeton, Kentucky USA 64B3
Princeton, Missouri USA 61E2
Princeton, New Jersey USA 68C2

Rock Rapids St-Hubert

Rock Rapids *USA* 61D2
Rock River *USA* 60B2
Rock Springs, Montana *USA* 60B1
Rocksprings, Texas *USA* 62B2
Rock Springs, Wyoming *USA* 58E2
Rocks Pt *NZ* 35B2
Rock,The *Aust* 34C3
Rockville, Connecticut *USA* 68D2
Rockville, Indiana *USA* 64B3
Rockville, Maryland *USA* 68B3
Rockwood *USA* 65F1
Rocky Ford *USA* 62B1
Rocky Island L *Can* 64C1
Rocky Mount *USA* 67C1
Rocky Mountain Nat Pk *USA* 60B2
Rocky Mts *Can/USA* 56B1
Rødbyhavn *Den* 18C2
Rodez *France* 14C3
Ródhos = Rhodes
Rodi Garganico *Italy* 16D2
Rodopi Planina, Mts *Bulg* 17E2
Roebourne *Aust* 32A3
Roedtan *S Africa* 47D1
Roer, R *Neth* 13D2
Roermond *Neth* 13C2
Roeselare *Belg* 13B2
Roes Welcome Sd *Can* 55K3
Rog *USSR* 26G2
Rogachev *USSR* 19F2
Rogaguado, Lago *Bol* 72E6
Rogers *USA* 63D1
Rogers City *USA* 64C1
Rogers L *USA* 66D3
Rogers,Mt *USA* 64C3
Rogerson *USA* 58D2
Roggeveldberge, Mts *S Africa* 47B3
Rogue, R *USA* 58B2
Rohri *Pak* 42B3
Rohtak *India* 42D3
Roja *USSR* 19E1
Rojo, Cabo, C *Mexico* 70C2
Rolândia *Brazil* 75B3
Rolla *USA* 63D1
Rollins *USA* 58D1
Roma = Rome
Roma *Aust* 34C1
Romain,C *USA* 67C2
Roman *Rom* 17F1
Romanche Gap *Atlantic O* 52H5
Romang, I *Indon* 27F7
Romania, Republic *E Europe* 21C6
Romano,C *USA* 67B3
Romans-sur-Isère *France* 14D2
Romblon *Phil* 27F5
Rome, Georgia *USA* 67A2
Rome *Italy* 16C2
Rome, New York *USA* 68C1
Rome *USA* 65D2
Romilly-sur-Seine *France* 14C2
Romney *USA* 65D3
Romny *USSR* 21E5
Rømø, I *Den* 18B1
Romoratin *France* 14C2
Rona, I *Scot* 8C3
Ronay, I *Scot* 8B3
Roncador, Serra do, Mts *Brazil* 75B1
Ronda *Spain* 15A2
Ronda, Sierra de, Mts *Spain* 15A2
Rondônia *Brazil* 72F6
Rondônia, State *Brazil* 72F6
Rondonópolis *Brazil* 75B2
Rong'an *China* 31B4
Rongchang *China* 31B4
Rongcheng *China* 31E2
Ronge, Lac la *Can* 54H4
Rongjiang *China* 31B4
Rong Jiang, R *China* 31B4
Rongklang Range, Mts *Burma* 30A1
Rønne *Den* 12G7
Ronneby *Sweden* 12H7
Ronne Ice Shelf *Ant* 76F2
Ronse *Belg* 13B2
Roodeschool *Neth* 13D1
Roof Butte, Mt *USA* 56C3
Roorkee *India* 42D3
Roosendaal *Neth* 13C2
Roosevelt *USA* 59D2
Roosevelt I *Ant* 76E6
Root, R *USA* 61E2
Roper, R *Aust* 32C2
Rora Head, Pt *Scot* 8D2
Roraima, Mt *Ven/Brazil/ Guyana* 72F2
Roraima, State *Brazil* 72F3
Røros *Nor* 20A3
Rørvik *Nor* 12G6
Ros' R *USSR* 19G3
Rosalie *Dominica* 69Q2
Rosamond *USA* 66C3
Rosamond L *USA* 66C3
Rosario *Arg* 74D4
Rosário *Brazil* 73K4
Rosario *Par* 75A3
Rosário Oeste *Brazil* 75A1
Roscoe *USA* 68C2
Roscoff *France* 14B2
Roscommon *Irish Rep* 10B3
Roscrea *Irish Rep* 9C3
Roseau *Dominica* 69Q2
Rosebery *Aust* 34C4
Rosebud *USA* 60B1
Roseburg *USA* 58B2
Rosenberg *USA* 63C3
Rosenheim *W Germ* 18C3
Rosetown *Can* 54H4
Roseville *USA* 66B1
Roskilde *Den* 12G7
Roslavl' *USSR* 20E5
Roslyatino *USSR* 20G4
Roşorii de Vede *Rom* 17E2
Ross *NZ* 35B2
Rossano *Italy* 16D3
Rossan Pt *Irish Rep* 10B3
Ross Barnett Res *USA* 63E2
Rosseau L *Can* 65D1
Rossel, I *PNG* 33E2
Ross Ice Shelf *Ant* 76E6
Ross L *USA* 58B1
Rosslare *Irish Rep* 9C3
Ross,Mt *NZ* 35C2
Rosso *Maur* 48A3
Rosso, C, Corsica 16B2
Ross-on-Wye *Eng* 7C4
Rossosh *USSR* 21F5
Ross River *Can* 54E3
Ross S *Ant* 76F6
Rostāq *Iran* 41F4
Rostock *E Germ* 18C2
Rostov *USSR* 20F4
Rostov-na-Donu *USSR* 21F6
Roswell, Georgia *USA* 67B2
Roswell, New Mexico *USA* 62B2
Rota, I *Pacific O* 27H5
Rote, I *Indon* 27F8
Rotenburg, Niedersachsen *W Germ* 18B2
Rothaar-Geb, Region *W Germ* 13E2
Rothbury *Eng* 6D2
Rothera, Base *Ant* 76G3
Rotherham *Eng* 7D3
Rothesay *Scot* 8C4
Rothes-on-Spey *Scot* 8D3
Roto *Aust* 34C2
Rotoiti,L *NZ* 35B2
Rotoroa,L *NZ* 35B2
Rotorua *NZ* 35C1
Rotorua,L *NZ* 35C1
Rottenburg *W Germ* 13E3
Rotterdam *Neth* 18A2
Rottweil *W Germ* 13E3
Rotuma, I *Fiji* 33G2
Roubaix *France* 13B2
Rouen *France* 14C2
Rough, Oilfield *N Sea* 6E3
Roulers = Roeselare
Round I *Mauritius* 51F6
Round Mountain *USA* 66D1
Round Mt *Aust* 34D2
Roundup *USA* 58E1
Rousay, I *Scot* 8D2
Roussillon, Region *France* 14C3
Rouxville *S Africa* 47D3
Rouyn *Can* 65D1
Rovaniemi *Fin* 12K5
Rovereto *Italy* 16C1
Rovigo *Italy* 16C1
Rovinj *Yugos* 16C1
Rovno *USSR* 21D5
Row'ān *Iran* 41E2
Rowena *Aust* 34C1
Rowley I *Can* 55L3
Rowley Shoals *Aust* 32A2
Roxas *Phil* 27F5
Roxboro *USA* 67C1
Roxburgh *NZ* 35A3
Roy *USA* 58E1
Royal Canal *Irish Rep* 9C3
Royale, Isle *USA* 64B1
Royal Leamington Spa *Eng* 7D3
Royal Oak *USA* 64C2
Royal Tunbridge Wells *Eng* 7E4
Royan *France* 14B2
Roye *France* 13B3
Royston *Eng* 7D3
Rožňava *Czech* 19E3
Rozoy *France* 13B3
Rtishchevo *USSR* 21G5
Ruabon *Wales* 7C3
Ruaha Nat Pk *Tanz* 51D4
Ruahine Range, Mts *NZ* 35C1
Ruapehu,Mt *NZ* 35C1
Rub' al Khālī, Desert *S Arabia* 38C4
Rubha Hunish, C *Scot* 8B3
Rubha Réidh, Pt *Scot* 8C3
Rubinéia *Brazil* 75B3
Rubtsovsk *USSR* 24K4
Ruby *USA* 54C3
Ruby Mts *USA* 59C2
Rudan *Iran* 41G4
Rudanli *India* 43L2
Rūdbār *Iran* 41E2
Rudnaya *USSR* 29F2
Rudnaya Pristan' *USSR* 26G2
Rudnya *USSR* 19G2
Rudoka Planina, Mt *Yugos* 17E2
Rudol'fa, Ostrov, I *USSR* 24G1
Rudong *China* 31E3
Rudyard *USA* 64C1
Ruffec *France* 14C2
Rufiji, R *Tanz* 51D4
Rufino *Arg* 74D4
Rufisque *Sen* 48A3
Rufunsa *Zambia* 51C5
Rugby *Eng* 7D3
Rugby *USA* 60C1
Rügen, I *E Germ* 12G8
Ruhr, R *W Germ* 13D2
Ruijin *China* 31D4
Rujen, Mt *Bulg/Yugos* 17E2
Rukwa, L *Tanz* 51D4
Rum, I *Scot* 8B3
Ruma *Yugos* 17D1
Rumāh *S Arabia* 41E4
Rumbek *Sudan* 50C3
Rum Cay, I *The Bahamas* 69C2
Rumford *USA* 65E2
Rum Jungle *Aust* 32C2
Rumoi *Japan* 29D2
Rumphi *Malawi* 51D5
Runanga *NZ* 35B2
Runaway,C *NZ* 35C1
Runcorn *Eng* 7C3
Rundu *Namibia* 51B5
Rungwa *Tanz* 51D4
Rungwa, R *Tanz* 51D4
Rungwe, Mt *Tanz* 51D4
Ruoqiang *China* 39G2
Ruo Shui, R *China* 26D2
Rupea *Rom* 17F1
Rupert *USA* 58D2
Rupert, R *Can* 55L4
Rur, R *W Germ* 13D2
Rurrenabaque *Bol* 72E6
Rusape *Zim* 51D5
Ruse *Bulg* 17F2
Rushville, Illinois *USA* 64A2
Rushville, Nebraska *USA* 60C2
Rushworth *Aust* 34B3
Rusk *USA* 63C2
Ruskin *USA* 67B3
Russell *NZ* 35B1
Russell *USA* 60D3
Russellville, Alabama *USA* 63E2
Russellville, Arkansas *USA* 63D1
Russellville, Kentucky *USA* 64B3
Russian, R *USA* 59B3
Russian S.F.S.R., Republic *USSR* 20E4
Russkaya, Base *Ant* 76F5
Russkiy, Ostrov, I *USSR* 25L2
Rustavi *USSR* 41E1
Rustenburg *S Africa* 47D2
Ruston *USA* 63D2
Rutana *Burundi* 50C4
Ruteng *Indon* 27F7
Rutenga *Zim* 47E1
Ruth *USA* 59C3
Rüthen *W Germ* 13E2
Rutland *USA* 65E2
Rutland, I *Andaman Is* 44E3
Rutog *China* 42D2
Ruvu = Pangani
Ruvuma, R *Tanz/Mozam* 51E5
Ruweila, Wadi *Jordan* 45D4
Ruwenzori Range, Mts *Uganda/Zaïre* 50D3
Ruya, R *Zim* 51D5
Ružomberok *Czech* 19D3
Rwanda, Republic *Africa* 50C4
Ryan, L *Scot* 8C4
Ryazan' *USSR* 20F5
Ryazhsk *USSR* 20G5
Rybinskoye Vodokhranilishche, Res *USSR* 20F4
Rybnitsa *USSR* 19F3
Ryde *Eng* 7D4
Rye *Eng* 7E4
Rye Patch Res *USA* 58C2
Ryl'sk *USSR* 21E5
Ryn Peski, Desert *USSR* 21H6
Ryoju *S Korea* 28A3
Ryōtsu *Japan* 29D3
Ryskany *USSR* 19F3
Ryūkyū Is *Japan* 26F4
Rzeszów *Pol* 19E2
Rzhev *USSR* 20E4

S

Sa'ādatābād *Iran* 41F3
Saad el Aali, Dam *Egypt* 40B5
Saale, R *E Germ* 18C2
Saar, R *W Germ* 13D3
Saarbrücken *W Germ* 13D3
Saarburg *W Germ* 13D3
Saaremaa, I *USSR* 12J7
Saarland, State *W Germ* 13D3
Saarlouis *W Germ* 13D3
Saba'a *Egypt* 45B3
Šabac *Yugos* 17D2
Sabadell *Spain* 15C1
Sabae *Japan* 29C3
Sabah, State *Malay* 27E6
Sabanalarga *Colomt a* 69C4
Sabang *Indon* 27C6
Sabari, R *India* 44C2
Sabastiya *Israel* 45C2
Sabaya *Bol* 72E7
Sab'Bi'ār *Syria* 40C3
Sabhā *Jordan* 45D2
Sabhā *Libya* 49D2
Sabi, R *Zim* 51D6
Sabie, R *S Africa* 47E2
Sabinas *Mexico* 70B2
Sabinas Hidalgo *Mexico* 70B2
Sabine, R *USA* 63C2
Sabine L *USA* 63D3
Sabkhat Maṭṭī, Salt Marsh *UAE* 41F5
Sabkhet el Bardawîl, Lg *Egypt* 45B3
Sable,C *Can* 55M5
Sable,C *USA* 67B3
Sable I *Can* 55M5
Şabyā *S Arabia* 50E2
Sabzevār *Iran* 41G2
Sacajawea Peak *USA* 58C1
Sacandaga Res *USA* 68C1
Sac City *USA* 61E2
Sachigo, R *Can* 57D1
Sach'on *S Korea* 28A3
Sachs Harbour *Can* 54F2
Saco, Maine *USA* 65E2
Saco, Montana *USA* 60B1
Sacramento *USA* 66B1
Sacramento, R *USA* 66B1
Sacramento, V *USA* 59B2
Sacramento Mts *USA* 62A2
Şa'dah *Yemen* 50E2
Sadanski *Bulg* 17E2
Sadiya *India* 43H3
Sado, R *Port* 15A2
Sado-shima, I *Japan* 29D3
Sādri *India* 42C3
Safad = Zefat
Safed Koh, Mts *Afghan* 42A2
Säffle *Sweden* 12G7
Safford *USA* 59E4
Saffron Walden *Eng* 7E3
Safi *Jordan* 40C3
Safi *Mor* 48B1
Şāfītā *Syria* 45D1
Safonovo *USSR* 19G1
Safwān *Iraq* 41E3
Saga *China* 43F3
Saga *Japan* 28B4
Sagaing *Burma* 30B1
Sagami-nada, B *Japan* 29C4
Sāgar *India* 42D4
Sag Harbor *USA* 68D2
Saginaw *USA* 64C2
Saginaw B *USA* 64C2
Saglek B *Can* 55M4
Sagŏ-ri *S Korea* 28A3
Saguache *USA* 62A1
Sagua de Tánamo *Cuba* 69B2
Sagua la Grande *Cuba* 69B2
Saguenay, R *Can* 57F2
Saguia el Hamra, Watercourse *Mor* 48A2
Sagunto *Spain* 15B2
Sahāb *Jordan* 45D3
Sahagún *Spain* 15A1
Sahara, Desert *N Africa* 48C2
Sahāranpur *India* 42D3
Sahaswan *India* 43K1
Saheira, Wadi el *Egypt* 45B4
Sahiwal *Pak* 42C2
Şaḩrā al Hijārah, Desert Region *Iraq* 41D3
Sahra esh Sharqiya, Desert Region *Egypt* 40B4
Sahuayo *Mexico* 70B2
Sahyūn, Hist Site *Syria* 45D1
Saibai I *Aust* 32D1
Saïda = Sidon
Sa'īdābad *Iran* 41G4
Saïdia *Mor* 15B2
Saidpur *Bang* 43F3
Saidu *Pak* 42C2
Saigō *Japan* 29B3
Saigon = Ho Chi Minh City
Saiha *India* 43G4
Saihan Tal *China* 26E2
Saijo *Japan* 29B4
Saiki *Japan* 28C4
Saimaa, L *Fin* 12K6
St Abb's Head, Pt *Scot* 8D4
St Albans *Eng* 7D4
St Albans, Vermont *USA* 65E2
St Albans, West Virginia *USA* 64C3
St Albans Head, C *Eng* 7C4
St Amand-les-Eaux *France* 13B2
St Amand-Mont Rond *France* 14C2
St Andrew B *USA* 67A3
St Andrews *Scot* 8D3
St Andrew Sd *USA* 67B2
Ste Anne *Can* 61D1
Ste Anne de Beaupré *Can* 65E1
St Ann's Bay *Jamaica* 69H1
St Anthony *Can* 55N4
St Anthony *USA* 58D2
St Arnaud *Aust* 34B3
St Augustin, Baie de, B *Madag* 51E6
St Augustine *USA* 67B3
St Austell *Eng* 7B4
St Austell Bay *Eng* 7B4
St-Avold *France* 13D3
St Bees Head, Pt *Eng* 6C2
St Brides B *Wales* 7B4
St-Brieuc *France* 14B2
St Catharines *Can* 65D2
St Catherine,Mt *Grenada* 69M2
St Catherines I *USA* 67B2
St Catherines Pt *Eng* 7D4
St-Chamond *France* 14C2
St Charles, Idaho *USA* 58D2
St Charles, Missouri *USA* 61E3
St Clair *USA* 64C2
St Clair,L *Can/USA* 64C2
St Clair Shores *USA* 64C2
St Claude *France* 14D2
St Cloud *USA* 61E1
St Croix, I *Caribbean S* 69E3
St Croix, R *Can/USA* 65F1
St Croix, R *USA* 64A1
St Croix Falls *USA* 64A1
St Davids Head, Pt *Wales* 7B4
St Denis *France* 13B3
St Denis *Réunion* 51F6
St-Dié *France* 13D3
St-Dizier *France* 13C3
St Elias, Mt *USA* 54D3
St Elias Mts *Can* 54E3
Saintes *France* 14B2
St-Étienne *France* 14C2
St-Félicien *Can* 65E1
St Florent, G de, Corsica 16B2
St Florent, Golfo de *Corse* 14D3
St-Florentin *France* 13B3
St Francis *USA* 60C3
St Francis, R *USA* 63D1
St Francis B *S Africa* 47C3
St Francis,C *S Africa* 47C3
St Gallen *Switz* 16B1
St-Gaudens *France* 14C3
St George *Aust* 34C1
St George, South Carolina *USA* 67B2
St George, Utah *USA* 59D3
St George I, Florida *USA* 67B3
St Georgen im Schwarzwald *W Germ* 13E3
St George,Pt *USA* 58B2
St-Georges *Can* 65E1
St George's *Grenada* 69M2
St George's Chan *Irish Rep/Wales* 7A4
St George's Chan *PNG* 33E1
St Gotthard, Pass *Switz* 16B1
St Govans Head, Pt *Wales* 7B4
St Helena *USA* 66A1
St Helena, I *Atlantic O* 52H5
St Helena B *S Africa* 47B3
St Helena Sd *USA* 67B2
St Helens *Aust* 34C4
St Helens *Eng* 7C3
St Helens *USA* 58B1
St Helens,Mt *USA* 58B1
St Helier, Jersey *Channel Is.* 14B2
St-Hubert *Belg* 13C2

St-Hyacinthe *Can*	55L5	Saipan, I *Pacific O*	27H5	Salon-de-Provence		San Antonio de Bravo		Sangrür *India*	42D2
St Ignace *USA*	64C1	Saiydabad *Afghan*	42B2	*France*	14D3	*Mexico*	62B2	Sangutane, R *Mozam*	47E1
St Ignace I *Can*	64B1	Sajama, Mt *Bol*	72E7	Salonica = Thessaloníki		San Antonio de los		San Ignacio *Arg*	74E3
St Ives, Cambs *Eng*	7D3	Sak, R *S Africa*	47C3	Salonta *Rom*	17E1	Banos *Cuba*	69A2	San Jacinto *Colombia*	72D2
St Ives, Cornwall *Eng*	7B4	Sakai *Japan*	29D4	Salpausselkä, Region *Fin*	12K6	San Antonio,Mt *USA*	66D3	San Jacinto Peak, Mt	
St James, Minnesota		Sakaidi *Japan*	29B4	Sal'sk *USSR*	21G6	San Antonio Oeste *Arg*	74D6	*USA*	59C4
USA	61E2	Sakaiminato *Japan*	28B3	Salt *Jordan*	45C2	San Antonio Res *USA*	66B3	Sanjiangkou *China*	28A2
St James, Missouri *USA*	63D1	Sakäkah *S Arabia*	40D4	Salt, R *S Africa*	47C3	San Ardo *USA*	66B2	Sanjö *Japan*	29D3
St James, C *Can*	54E4	Sakakawea,L *USA*	60C1	Salt, R *USA*	59D4	Sanäwad *India*	42D4	San João del Rei *Brazil*	74H2
St-Jean *Can*	65E1	Sakami,L *Can*	57F1	Salta *Arg*	74C2	San Benedicto, I *Mexico*	70A3	San Joaquin, R *USA*	66B2
St Jean-d'Angely *France*	14B2	Sakania *Zaïre*	51C5	Salta, State *Arg*	74C2	San Benito *USA*	63C3	San Joaquin Valley *USA*	66B2
St-Jean,L *Can*	65E1	Sakaraha *Madag*	51E6	Saltash *Eng*	7B4	San Benito, R *USA*	66B2	San Jon *USA*	62B1
St-Jérôme *Can*	65E1	Sakarya, R *Turk*	21E7	Saltillo *Mexico*	70B2	San Benito Mt *USA*	66B2	San Jorge, Golfo, G *Arg*	74C7
St Joe, R *USA*	58C1	Sakasleja *USSR*	19E1	Salt Lake City *USA*	58D2	San Bernardino *USA*	66D3	San Jorge, Golfo de, G	
Saint John *Can*	55M5	Sakata *Japan*	29D3	Salto Angostura,		San Bernardo *Chile*	74B4	*Spain*	15C1
St John, R *USA/Can*	65F1	Sakété *Benin*	48C4	Waterfall *Colombia*	72D3	San Bernardo Mts *USA*	59C4	San José *Costa Rica*	72B2
St Johns, Arizona *USA*	59E4	Sakhalin, I *USSR*	26H1	Salto da Divisa *Brazil*	75E2	San Blas,C *USA*	67A3	San José *Guatemala*	70C3
St John's *Can*	55N5	Sakishima guntö, Is		Salto das Sete Quedas		San Blas, Puerta, Pt		San Jose *USA*	66B2
St Johns, Michigan *USA*	64C2	*Japan*	26F4	*Brazil*	75B3	*Panama*	70E4	San José, I *Mexico*	56B4
St Johns, R *USA*	67B3	Sakrivier *S Africa*	47C3	Salto del Angel,		San Borja *Brazil*	74E3	San José de Chiquitos	
St Johnsbury *USA*	65E2	Sal, I *Cape Verde*	48A4	Waterfall *Ven*	72F2	San Carlos *Chile*	74B5	*Bol*	72F7
St John's Chapel *Eng*	6C2	Sal, R *USSR*	21G6	Salto del Guaíra,		San Carlos *Nic*	72B1	San José del Cabo	
St John's Pt *N Ire*	9D2	Sala *Sweden*	12H7	Waterfall *Brazil*	74E2	San Carlos *USA*	59D4	*Mexico*	56C4
St Johnsville *USA*	68C1	Salada, Laguna, L		Salto Grande, Waterfall		San Carlos de Bariloche		San José do Rio Prêto	
St-Joseph *Can*	65E1	*Mexico*	59C4	*Colombia*	72D4	*Arg*	74B6	*Brazil*	74G2
St Joseph, Louisiana		Salado, R, Sante Fe *Arg*	74D3	Salton S *USA*	59C4	Sanchursk *USSR*	20H4	San Joseé del Cabo	
USA	63D2	Salaga *Ghana*	48B4	Saltos do Iguaçu,		San Clemente *USA*	66D4	*Mexico*	70B2
St Joseph, Michigan		Sala Hintoun *Camb*	30C3	Waterfall *Arg*	75B4	San Clemente I *USA*	59C4	Sanju *S Korea*	28A3
USA	64B2	Salal *Chad*	50B2	Salto Tacuarembó *Urug*	74E4	San Cristóbal *Mexico*	70C3	San Juan *Arg*	74C4
St Joseph, Missouri *USA*	61E3	Şalälah *Oman*	38D4	Salt Range, Mts *Pak*	42C2	San Cristóbal·*Ven*	72D2	San Juan *Puerto Rico*	69D3
St Joseph *Trinidad*	69L1	Salamanca *Spain*	15A1	Salt River *Jamaica*	69H2	San Cristobal, I *Solomon*		San Juan *Trinidad*	69L1
St Joseph, R *USA*	64C2	Salamanca *USA*	68A1	Saluda *USA*	67B2	*Is*	33F2	San Juan *Ven*	72E2
St Joseph I *Can*	64C1	Salamat, R *Chad*	50B3	Sälür *India*	44C2	Sancti Spíritus *Cuba*	70E2	San Juan, Mt *Cuba*	69B2
St Joseph I *USA*	63C3	Salamaua *PNG*	27H7	Salvador *Brazil*	73L6	Sancy, Puy de, Mt		San Juan, R, California	
St Joseph,L *Can*	55J4	Salamis, Hist Site *Cyprus*	45B1	Salvador,L *USA*	63D3	*France*	14C2	*USA*	66B3
St-Junien *France*	14C2	Salangen *Nor*	12H5	Salwah *Qatar*	41F5	Sand, R *S Africa*	47D1	San Juan, R *Costa Rica/*	
St-Just-en-Chaussée		Salar de Arizaro, Salt		Salween, R *Burma*	30B1	Sanda, I *Scot*	8C4	*Nic*	70D3
France	13B3	Pan *Arg*	74C2	Sal'yany *USSR*	21H8	Sandakan *Malay*	27E6	San Juan, R, Utah *USA*	59D3
St Kilda, I *Scot*	8A3	Salar de Atacama, Salt		Salyersville *USA*	64C3	Sanday, I *Scot*	8D2	San Juan, State *Arg*	74C4
St Kitts, I *Caribbean S*	69E3	Pan *Chile*	74C2	Salzburg *Austria*	18C3	Sanderson *USA*	62B2	San Juan Bautista *Par*	74E4
St Lawrence, R *Can*	55M5	Salar de Coipasa, Salt		Salzgitter *W Germ*	18C2	Sandgate *Eng*	7E4	San Juan Bautista *USA*	66B2
Saint Lawrence,G of *Can*	55M5	Pan *Bol*	72E7	Salzwedel *E Germ*	18C2	San Diego *USA*	59C4	San Juan del Norte *Nic*	70D3
St Lawrence I *USA*	54B3	Salar de Uyuni, Salt Pan		Samagaltay *USSR*	26C1	San Diego, Cabo *Arg*	74C8	San Juan de los Cayos	
St Lawrence Seaway		*Bol*	72E8	Samaná *Dom Rep*	69D3	Sandikli *Turk*	40B2	*Ven*	69D4
Can/USA	65D2	Salavat *USSR*	20K5	Samandaği *Turk*	40C2	Sandila *India*	43E3	San Juan del Sur *Nic*	70D3
St Leonard *Can*	65F1	Salawati, I *Indon*	32C1	Samangan *Afghan*	42B1	Sandnes *Nor*	12F7	San Juan Is *USA*	58B1
St Leonards *Eng*	7E4	Sala y Gómez, I *Pacific*		Samani *Japan*	29D2	Sandnessjøen *Nor*	12G5	San Juan Mts *USA*	62A1
St-Lô *France*	14B2	*O*	37O6	Samannüd *Egypt*	45A3	Sandoa *Zaïre*	51C4	San Julián *Arg*	74C7
St-Louis *Sen*	48A3	Salbris *France*	14C2	Samar, I *Phil*	27F5	Sandomierz *Pol*	19E2	Sankuru, R *Zaïre*	50C4
St Louis *USA*	64A3	Saldanha *S Africa*	47B3	Samarai *PNG*	32E2	Sandoway *Burma*	43G5	San Leandro *USA*	66A2
St-Loup-sur-Semouse		Saldus *USSR*	19E1	Samarinda *Indon*	27E7	Sandown *Eng*	7D4	San Lorenzo *Ecuador*	72C3
France	13D4	Sale *Aust*	34C3	Samarkand *USSR*	39E2	Sandoy, I *Faeroes*	12D3	San Lorenzo, Cabo, C	
St Lucia, I *Caribbean S*	69E4	Salekhard *USSR*	20M2	Sämarr' *Iraq*	41D3	Sandpoint *USA*	58C1	*Ecuador*	72B4
St Lucia,L *S Africa*	47E2	Salem, Illinois *USA*	64B3	Sambalpur *India*	43E4	Sand Springs *USA*	63C1	San Lorenzo de Escorial	
St Magnus B *Scot*	8E1	Salem *India*	44B3	Sambas *Indon*	27D6	Sandstone *Aust*	32A3	*Spain*	15B1
St-Malo *France*	14B2	Salem, Massachusetts		Sambava *Madag*	51F5	Sandstone *USA*	61E1	San Lucas *USA*	66B2
St-Malo, Golfe de, B		*USA*	68E1	Sambhal *India*	42D3	Sandu *China*	31C4	San Luis *Arg*	74C4
France	14B2	Salem, New Jersey *USA*	68C3	Sambor *USSR*	19E3	Sandusky *USA*	64C2	San Luis *USA*	59D4
Ste-Marie-aux-Mines		Salem, New York *USA*	68D1	Sambre, R *France*	13B2	Sandviken *Sweden*	12H6	San Luis, State *Arg*	74C4
France	13D3	Salem, Oregon *USA*	58B2	Samch'ŏk *S Korea*	28B3	Sandwich *USA*	68E2	Šan Luis Canal *USA*	66B2
St Maries *USA*	58C1	Salem, Virginia *USA*	64C3	Samch'ŏnp'o *S Korea*	28A4	Sandy L *Can*	55J4	San Luis Obispo *USA*	66B3
St Martin, I *Caribbean S*	69E3	Sälen *Sweden*	12G6	Samdüng *N Korea*	28A3	San Estanislao *Par*	75A3	San Luis Obispo B *USA*	66B3
St Mary,Mt *PNG*	32D1	Salerno *Italy*	16C2	Same *Tanz*	50D4	San Felipe, Baja Cal		San Luis Potosí *Mexico*	70B2
St Mary Peak, Mt *Aust*	34A2	Salford *Eng*	7C3	Samfya *Zambia*	51C5	*Mexico*	56B3	San Luis Res *USA*	66B2
St Marys *Aust*	34C4	Salgót *Hung*	17D1	Samka *Burma*	30B1	San Felipe *Chile*	74B4	Sanluri, *Sardinia*	16B3
St Marys *USA*	65D2	Salgótarján *Hung*	19D3	Sam Neua *Laos*	30C1	San Felipe *Ven*	69D4	San Maigualida, Mts *Ven*	72E2
St Marys, I *Eng*	7A5	Salgueiro *Brazil*	73L5	Samoan Is *Pacific O*	33H2	San Felíu de Guixols		San Marcos *USA*	63C3
St Marys, R *USA*	67B2	Salida *USA*	60B3	Sámos, I *Greece*	17F3	*Spain*	15C1	San Martin, Base *Ant*	76G3
Saint Mathias Group, Is		Salihli *Turk*	17F3	Samothráki, I *Greece*	17F2	San Felix, Isla *Pacific O*	52D6	San Martin, Lago *Arg/*	
PNG	32E1	Salima *Malawi*	51D5	Sampit *Indon*	27E7	San Fernando *Chile*	74B4	*Chile*	74B7
St Maurice, R *Can*	65E1	Salina, Kansas *USA*	61D3	Sam Rayburn Res *USA*	63D2	San Fernando *Phil*	27F5	San Mateo *USA*	66A2
Ste-Menehould *France*	13C3	Salina, Utah *USA*	59D3	Samrong *Camb*	30C3	San Fernando *Spain*	15A2	San Matías *Bolivia*	73G7
St Michael *USA*	54B3	Salina, I *Italy*	16C3	Samsø, I *Den*	18C1	San Fernando *Trinidad*	69L2	San Matías, Golfo, G	
St Michaels *USA*	68B3	Salina Cruz *Mexico*	70C3	Samsu *N Korea*	28A2	San Fernando *USA*	66C3	*Arg*	74D6
St-Mihiel *France*	13C3	Salinas *Brazil*	75D2	Samsun *Turk*	40C1	San Fernando *Ven*	72E2	Sanmenxia *China*	31C3
St Moritz *Switz*	16B1	Salinas *USA*	66B2	San *Mali*	48B3	Sanford, Florida *USA*	67B3	San Miguel *El Salvador*	70D3
St-Nazaire *France*	14B2	Salinas, R *USA*	66B2	San, R *Camb*	30D3	Sanford, Maine *USA*	65E2	San Miguel *USA*	66B3
St Neots *Eng*	7D3	Salinas, Cabo de, C		San, R *Pol*	19E2	Sanford, N Carolina *USA*	67C1	San Miguel, I *USA*	66B3
St-Niklaas *Belg*	13C2	*Spain*	15C2	San'ä *Yemen*	50E2	Sanford *USA*	57E4	San Miguel de Tucumán	
St-Omer *France*	13B2	Salinas Grandes, Salt		Sanaga, R *Cam*	50B3	Sanford, Mt *USA*	54D3	*Arg*	74C3
St-Pascal *Can*	65F1	Pans *Arg*	74D3	San Agustín *Arg*	74C4	San Francisco *Arg*	74D4	San Miguel d'Oeste	
St Paul *Can*	54G4	Salinas Peak, Mt *USA*	62A2	San Ambrosia, Isla		San Francisco *Dom Rep*	69C3	*Brazil*	74F3
St Paul, Minnesota *USA*	61E2	Saline, R, Arkansas *USA*	63D2	*Pacific O*	52D6	San Francisco *USA*	66A2	Sanming *China*	31D4
St Paul, Nebraska *USA*	60D2	Saline, R, Kansas *USA*	60C3	Sanandaj *Iran*	41E2	San Francisco B *USA*	66A2	San Nicolas *Arg*	74D4
St Paul, I *Indian O*	36E6	Salines,Pt *Grenada*	69M2	San Andreas *USA*	66B1	San Francisco del Oro		San Nicolas, I *USA*	56B3
St Paul, R *Lib*	48A4	Saline V *USA*	66D2	San Andres, Isla de		*Mexico*	70B2	Sannieshof *S Africa*	47D2
St Peter *USA*	61E2	Salinópolis *Brazil*	73J4	*Caribbean S*	69A4	San Gabriel Mts *USA*	66D3	Sanniquellie *Lib*	48B4
St Petersburg *USA*	67B3	Salisbury = Harare		San Andres Mts *USA*	62A2	Sangamner *India*	42C5	Sanok *Pol*	19E3
St Pierre *USA*	55N5	Salisbury *Eng*	7D4	San Andrés Tuxtla		Sangamon, R *USA*	64B3	San Onofore *Colombia*	69B5
St Pierre,L *Can*	65E1	Salisbury, Maryland *USA*	65D3	*Mexico*	70C3	Sangar *USSR*	25O3	San Onofre *USA*	66D4
St-Pol-sur-Ternoise		Salisbury, North Carolina		San Angelo *USA*	62B2	Sangäreddi *India*	44B2	San Pablo *Phil*	27F5
France	13B2	*USA*	67B1	San Antioco, Sardinia	16B3	Sanger *USA*	66C2	San Pablo B *USA*	66A1
St Pölten *Austria*	18D3	Salisbury I *Can*	55L3	San Antioco, I, Sardinia	16B3	Sanggan He, R *China*	31C2	San Pédro *Ivory Coast*	48B4
St-Quentin *France*	13B3	Salisbury Plain *Eng*	7D4	Sant Antonia, Pt *Mexico*	56B4	Sanggau *Indon*	27E6	San Pedro, Jujuy *Arg*	74D2
St Raphaël *France*	14D3	Şalkhad *Syria*	45D2	San Antonio *Chile*	74B4	Sangha, R *Congo*	50B3	San Pedro *Par*	74E2
St-Siméon *Can*	65F1	Salla•*Fin*	12K5	San Antonio, New		Sanghar *Pak*	42B3	San Pedro, R *USA*	59D4
St Simons I *USA*	67B2	Sallisaw *USA*	63D1	Mexico *USA*	62A2	Sangir, I *Indon*	27F6	San Pedro Chan *USA*	66C4
St Stephen *USA*	67B2	Salluit *Can*	55L3	San Antonio, Texas *USA*	62C3	Sangir, Kepulauan, Is		San Pedro de los	
St Thomas *Can*	64C2	Sallyana *Nepal*	43E3	San Antonio, R,		*Indon*	27F6	Colonias *Mexico*	56C4
St Tropez *France*	14D3	Salmas *Iran*	41D2	California *USA*	66B2	Sangkhla Buri *Thai*	30B3	San Pedro Sula	
St Truiden *Belg*	13C2	Salmi *USSR*	12L6	San Antonio, R, Texas		Sangkulirang *Indon*	27E6	*Honduras*	70D3
St Vincent *USA*	61D1	Salmo *Can*	58C1	*USA*	63C3	Sängli *India*	44A2	San Pietro, I *Sardinia*	16B3
St Vincent, I *Caribbean*		Salmon *USA*	58D1	San Antonio Abad *Spain*	15C2	Sangmélima *Cam*	50B3	Sanquar *Scot*	8D4
S	69E4	Salmon, R *USA*	58C1	San Antonio,C *Cuba*	70D2	San Gorgonio Mt *USA*	56B3	San Quintin *Mexico*	70A1
St Vincent,G *Aust*	34A2	Salmon Arm *Can*	54G4	San Antonio, Cabo, C		Sangre de Cristo Mts		San Rafael *Arg*	74C4
St-Vith *W Germ*	13D2	Salmon River Mts *USA*	58C1	*Cuba*	69A2	*USA*	62A1	San Rafael *USA*	66A2
St Wendel *W Germ*	13D3	Salo *Fin*	12J6			San Gregorio *USA*	66A2	San Rafael Mts *USA*	66C3

San Remo Selvas

San Remo *Italy* 16B2
San Saba, R *USA* 62C2
San Salvador *El Salvador* 71B2
San Salvador, I *The Bahamas* 69C2
San Salvador de Jujuy *Arg* 74C2
San Sebastián *Spain* 15B1
San Severo *Italy* 16D2
San Simeon *USA* 66B3
Santa Ana *Bol* 72E7
Santa Ana *Guatemala* 70C3
Santa Ana *USA* 66D4
Santa Ana Mts *USA* 66D4
Santa Anna *USA* 62C2
Santa Barbara *Mexico* 70B2
Santa Barbara *USA* 66C3
Santa Barbara, I *USA* 66C4
Santa Barbara Chan *USA* 66B3
Santa Barbara Res *USA* 66C3
Santa Catalina, I *USA* 66C4
Santa Catalina,G of *USA* 66C4
Santa Catarina, State *Brazil* 74F3
Santa Catarina, Isla de *Brazil* 74G3
Santa Clara *Cuba* 69B2
Santa Clara *USA* 66B2
Santa Clara, R *USA* 66C3
Santa Cruz *Arg* 74C8
Santa Cruz *Bol* 72F7
Santa Cruz *Phil* 27F5
Santa Cruz *USA* 66A2
Santa Cruz, I *USA* 66C4
Santa Cruz, R *USA* 59D4
Santa Cruz, State *Arg* 74B7
Santa Cruz Cabrália *Brazil* 75E2
Santa Cruz Chan *USA* 66C3
Santa Cruz de la Palma *Canary Is* 48A2
Santa Cruz del Sur *Cuba* 69B2
Santa Cruz de Tenerife *Canary Is* 48A2
Santa Cruz do Cuando *Angola* 51C5
Santa Cruz do Rio Pardo *Brazil* 75C3
Santa Cruz Is *Solomon Is* 33F2
Santa Cruz Mts *USA* 66A2
Santa Elena *Ven* 72F3
Santa Fe *Arg* 74D4
Santa Fe *USA* 62A1
Santa Fe, State *Arg* 74D3
Santa Helena de Goiás *Brazil* 75B2
Santai *China* 31B3
Santa Inés, I *Chile* 74B8
Santa Isabel, I *Solomon Is* 33E1
Santa Lucia Range, Mts *USA* 66B2
Santa Luzia, I *Cape Verde* 48A4
Santa Margarita *USA* 66B3
Santa Margarita, R *USA* 66D4
Santa Margarita, Isla *Mexico* 70A2
Santa Maria *Brazil* 74F3
Santa Maria *USA* 66B3
Santa Maria, I *Azores* 48A1
Santa María, R, Chihuahua *Mexico* 62A2
Santa Maria, Cabo de, C *Mozam* 47E2
Santa Maria da Vitória *Brazil* 75D1
Santa Maria di Leuca, Capo, C *Italy* 17D3
Santa María Laguna de, L *Mexico* 62A2
Santa Marta *Colombia* 69C4
Santa Marta, Sierra Nevada de, Mts *Colombia* 72D1
Santa Monica *USA* 66C3
Santa Monica B *USA* 66C4
Santana *Brazil* 75D1
Santana do Livramento *Brazil* 74E4
Santander *Colombia* 72C3
Santander *Spain* 15B1
Santañy *Spain* 15C2
Santa Paula *USA* 66C3
Santa Quitéria *Brazil* 73K4
Santarém *Brazil* 73H4
Santarém *Port* 15A2
Santa Rita do Araguaia *Brazil* 75B2
Santa Rosa *Arg* 74D5
Santa Rosa, California *USA* 66A1
Santa Rosa *Honduras* 70D3
Santa Rosa, New Mexico *USA* 62B2
Santa Rosa, I *USA* 66B3
Santa Rosalía *Mexico* 70A2
Santa Rosa Range, Mts *USA* 58C2
Santa Talhada *Brazil* 73L5
Santa Teresa *Brazil* 75D2
Santa Teresa di Gallura, Sardinia 16B2
Santa Ynez, R *USA* 66B3
Santa Ynez Mts *USA* 66B3
Santee, R *USA* 67C2
Santiago *Chile* 74B4
Santiago *Dom Rep* 69C3
Santiago *Panama* 72B2
Santiago, R *Peru* 72C4
Santiago de Compostela *Spain* 15A1
Santiago de Cuba *Cuba* 69B2
Santiago del Estero *Arg* 74D3
Santiago del Estero, State *Arg* 74D3
Santiago Peak, Mt *USA* 66D4
Santo *Vanuatu* 33F2
Santo Amaro, Ilha *Brazil* 75C3
Santo Anastatácio *Brazil* 75B3
Santo Angelo *Brazil* 74F3
Santo Antão, I *Cape Verde* 48A4
Santo Antônio da Platina *Brazil* 75B3
Santo Antônio de Jesus *Brazil* 75E1
Santo Antônio do Leverger *Brazil* 75A2
Santo Domingo *Dom Rep* 69D3
Santos *Brazil* 75C3
Santos Dumont *Brazil* 75D3
Santo Tomas *Mexico* 59C4
Santo Tomé *Arg* 74E3
San Valentin, Mt *Chile* 74B7
San Vito, C, Sicily 16C3
Sanyuanpu *China* 28B2
Sanza Pomba *Angola* 51B4
São Carlos *Brazil* 75C3
São Domingos *Brazil* 75C1
São Félix, Mato Grosso *Brazil* 73H5
São Fidélis *Brazil* 75D3
São Francisco *Brazil* 75D2
São Francisco, R *Brazil* 73L5
São Francisco do Sul *Brazil* 74G3
São Francisco, Ilha de *Brazil* 75C4
São Gotardo *Brazil* 75C2
Sao Hill *Tanz* 51D4
São Jerônimo, Serra de, Mts *Brazil* 75A2
São João da Barra *Brazil* 75D3
São João da Boa Vista *Brazil* 75C3
São João d'Aliança *Brazil* 75C1
São João da Ponte *Brazil* 75D2
São João del Rei *Brazil* 75D3
São João do Paraíso *Brazil* 75D2
São Joaquim da Barra *Brazil* 75C3
São Jorge, I *Azores* 48A1
São José do Rio Prêto *Brazil* 75C3
São José dos Campos *Brazil* 75C3
São José dos Pinhais *Brazil* 75C4
São Lourenço, R *Brazil* 75A2
São Luís *Brazil* 73K4
São Marcos, R *Brazil* 75C2
São Marcos, Baia de, B *Brazil* 73K4
São Maria do Suaçui *Brazil* 75D2
São Mateus *Brazil* 75E2
São Mateus, R *Brazil* 75D2
São Miguel, I *Azores* 48A1
São Miguel de Araguaia *Brazil* 75B1
Saône, R *France* 14C2
São Nicolau, I *Cape Verde* 48A4
São Onofre, R *Brazil* 75D1
São Paulo *Brazil* 75C3
São Paulo, State *Brazil* 75B3
São Pedro e São Paulo, Is *Atlantic O* 71H3
São Raimundo Nonato *Brazil* 73K5
São Romão *Brazil* 75C2
São Sebastia do Paraíso *Brazil* 75C3
São Sebastião, Ilha de *Brazil* 75C3
São Simão, Goias *Brazil* 75B2
São Simão, São Paulo *Brazil* 75C3
São Tiago, I *Cape Verde* 48A4
São Tomé, I *W Africa* 48C4
São Tomé and Principe, Republic *W Africa* 48C4
São Tomé, Cabo de, C *Brazil* 75D3
Saoura, Watercourse *Alg* 48B2
Saouriuiná, R *Brazil* 75A1
São Vicente *Brazil* 75C3
São Vicente, Cabo de, C *Port* 15A2
São Vincente, I *Cape Verde* 48A4
Sápai *Greece* 17F2
Sapele *Nigeria* 48C4
Sapporo *Japan* 29E2
Sapri *Italy* 16D2
Sapulpa *USA* 63C1
Saqqez *Iran* 41E2
Sarab *Iran* 21H8
Sarajevo *Yugos* 17D2
Saraktash *USSR* 21K5
Sarala *USSR* 25K4
Saranac Lake *USA* 65E2
Sarandë *Alb* 17E3
Saranpaul' *USSR* 20L3
Saransk *USSR* 20H5
Sarapul *USSR* 20J4
Sarasota *USA* 67B3
Sarata *USSR* 17F1
Saratoga *USA* 60B2
Saratoga Springs *USA* 68D1
Saratov *USSR* 21H5
Saratovskoye Vodokhranilishche, Res *USSR* 21H5
Saravane *Laos* 30D2
Sarawak, State *Malay* 27E6
Saraykoy *Turk* 40A2
Sardalas *Libya* 49D2
Sar Dasht *Iran* 41E2
Sardegna = Sardinia
Sardinia, I *Medit S* 16B2
Sarektjåkkå, Mt *Sweden* 12H5
Sargodha *Pak* 42C2
Sarh *Chad* 50B3
Sarhro, Jbel, Mt *Mor* 48B1
Sari *Iran* 41F2
Sarida, R *Israel* 45C2
Sarigan, I *Pacific O* 27H5
Sarıkamış *Turk* 40D1
Sarina *Aust* 32D3
Sar-i-Pul *Afghan* 42B1
Sarir *Libya* 49E2
Sarir Tibesti, Desert *Libya* 49D2
Sariwŏn *N Korea* 28B3
Sark, I *Channel Is* 14B2
Şarkışla *Turk* 40C2
Sarmi *Indon* 27G7
Sarmiento *Arg* 74C7
Särna *Sweden* 12G6
Sarnia *Can* 64C2
Sarny *USSR* 19F2
Sarobi *Afghan* 42B2
Saronikós Kólpos, G *Greece* 17E3
Saros Körfezi, B *Turk* 17F2
Saroto *USSR* 20M2
Sarpsborg *Nor* 12G7
Sarqaq *Greenland* 55N2
Sarralbe *France* 13D3
Sarrebourg *France* 13D3
Sarreguemines *France* 13D3
Sarre-Union *France* 13D3
Sarrion *Spain* 15B1
Sartanahu *Pak* 42B3
Sartène, Corsica 16B2
Sarthe, R *France* 14B2
Sarüt, R *Syria* 45D1
Sarykamys *USSR* 21J6
Sarysu, R *USSR* 24H5
Sasarām *India* 43E4
Sasebo *Japan* 28B4
Saskatchewan, Province *Can* 54H4
Saskatchewan, R *Can* 54H4
Saskatoon *Can* 54H4
Saskylakh *USSR* 25N2
Sasolburg *S Africa* 47D2
Sasovo *USSR* 20G5
Sassandra *Ivory Coast* 48B4
Sassandra, R *Ivory Coast* 48B4
Sassari, Sardinia 16B2
Sassnitz *E Germ* 18C2
Sasuna *Japan* 28A4
Satara *India* 44A2
Satellite B *Can* 54G2
Säter *Sweden* 12H6
Satilla, R *USA* 67B2
Satka *USSR* 20K4
Satluj, R *India* 42D2
Satna *India* 43E4
Satpura Range, Mts *India* 42C4
Satu Mare *Rom* 21C6
Sauðárkrókur *Iceland* 12B1
Sauda *Nor* 12F7
Saudi Arabia, Kingdom *Arabian Pen* 38C3
Sauer, R *W Germ/Lux* 13D3
Sauerland, Region *W Germ* 13D2
Saugatuck *USA* 64B2
Saugerties *USA* 68D1
Sauk Center *USA* 61E1
Sauk City *USA* 64B2
Sault Ste Marie *Can* 64C1
Sault Ste Marie *USA* 64C1
Saumlaki *Indon* 27G7
Saumur *France* 14B2
Saurimo *Angola* 51C4
Sauteurs *Grenada* 69M2
Sava, R *Yugos* 17D2
Savai'i, I *Western Samoa* 33H2
Savalou *Benin* 48C4
Savannah, Georgia *USA* 67B2
Savannah, Tennessee *USA* 63E1
Savannah, R *USA* 67B2
Savannakhet *Laos* 30C2
Savanna la Mar *Jamaica* 69G1
Savant Lake *Can* 55J4
Savé *Benin* 48C4
Save, R *Mozam* 51D6
Saveh *Iran* 41F3
Saverne *France* 13D3
Savigny *France* 13B3
Savinskiy *USSR* 20F3
Savoie, Region *France* 14D2
Savona *Italy* 16B2
Savonlinna *Fin* 12K6
Savoonga *USA* 54A3
Savu, I *Indon* 32B2
Savukoski *Fin* 12K5
Savu S *Indon* 27F7
Saw *Burma* 30A1
Sawai Madhopur *India* 42D3
Sawankhalok *Thai* 30C2
Sawara *Japan* 29D3
Sawatch Mts *USA* 60B3
Sawda', Jabal as, Mts *Libya* 49D2
Sawknah *Libya* 49D2
Sawtooth Range, Mts *USA* 58C2
Sawu, I *Indon* 27F8
Saxmundham *Eng* 7E3
Saxton *USA* 68A2
Say *Niger* 48C3
Sayghan *Afghan* 42B1
Sayhandulaan *Mongolia* 31B1
Sayḥut *S Yemen* 38D4
Saykhin *USSR* 21H6
Saynshand *Mongolia* 26D2
Sayre, Oklahoma *USA* 62C1
Sayre, Pennsylvania *USA* 68B2
Say-Utes *USSR* 21J7
Sayville *USA* 68D2
Sázava, R *Czech* 18C3
Sbisseb, R *Alg* 15C2
Scafell Pike, Mt *Eng* 6C2
Scalloway *Scot* 8E1
Scalpay, I *Scot* 8C3
Scapa Flow, Sd *Scot* 8D2
Scarborough *Can* 65D2
Scarborough *Eng* 6D2
Scarborough *Tobago* 69K1
Scarp, I *Scot* 8B2
Schaffhausen *Switz* 16B1
Schärding *Austria* 18C3
Scharhörn, I *W Germ* 13E1
Scharteberg, Mt *W Germ* 13D2
Schefferville *Can* 55M4
Schelde, R *Belg* 13B2
Schell Creek Range, Mts *USA* 59D3
Schenectady *USA* 68D1
Schertz *USA* 62C3
Schiedam *Neth* 13C2
Schiermonnikoog, I *Neth* 13D1
Schleiden *W Germ* 13D2
Schleswig *W Germ* 18B2
Schleswig Holstein, State *W Germ* 18B2
Schoharie *USA* 68C1
Schouten Is *PNG* 32D1
Schramberg *W Germ* 13E3
Schreiber *Can* 55K5
Schull *Irish Rep* 9B4
Schurz *USA* 59C3
Schuykill Haven *USA* 68B2
Schuylkill, R *USA* 68C2
Schwabische Alb, Upland *W Germ* 18B3
Schwaner, Pegunungan, Mts *Indon* 27E7
Schwarzrand, Mts *Namibia* 47B2
Schwarzwald, Mts *W Germ* 13E3
Schweinfurt *W Germ* 18C2
Schweizer Reneke *S Africa* 47D2
Schwerin *E Germ* 18C2
Schwyz *Switz* 16B1
Sciacca *Italy* 16C3
Scilly, Isles of *Eng* 7A5
Scioto, R *USA* 64C3
Scobey *USA* 60B1
Scone *Aust* 34D2
Scoresby Sd *Greenland* 55Q2
Scotia Sea *Atlantic O* 52F7
Scotland *U K* 8C3
Scott, Base *Ant* 76F7
Scottburgh *S Africa* 47E3
Scott City *USA* 62B1
Scott I *Ant* 76G6
Scott Inlet, B *Can* 55L2
Scott,Mt *USA* 58B2
Scott Reef *Timor S* 32B2
Scottsbluff *USA* 60C2
Scottsboro *USA* 67A2
Scottsdale *Aust* 34C4
Scottsdale *USA* 59D4
Scranton *USA* 68C2
Scribner *USA* 61D2
Scunthorpe *Eng* 7D3
Scutari = Shkodër
Seacow, R *S Africa* 47C3
Seaford *Eng* 7E4
Seal, R *Can* 54J4
Sea Lake *Aust* 34B3
Searchlight *USA* 59D3
Searcy *USA* 63D1
Searles *USA* 66D3
Seaside, California *USA* 66B2
Seaside, Oregon *USA* 58B1
Seaside Park *USA* 68C3
Seattle *USA* 58B1
Sebago L *USA* 65E2
Sebastian Vizcaino, B *Mexico* 70A2
Sebastopol *USA* 66A1
Sebderaf *Eth* 50D2
Sebez *USSR* 19F1
Seboomook L *USA* 65F1
Sebring *USA* 67B3
Secretary I *NZ* 35A3
Sedalia *USA* 61E3
Sedan *France* 13C3
Sedbergh *Eng* 6C2
Seddonville *NZ* 35B2
Sede Boqer *Israel* 45C3
Sederot *Israel* 45C3
Sédhiou *Sen* 48A3
Sedom *Israel* 45C3
Sedona *USA* 59D4
Seeheim *Namibia* 47B2
Seelig,Mt *Ant* 76E4
Sefton,Mt *NZ* 35B2
Segamat *Malay* 30C5
Segezha *USSR* 20E3
Segorbe *Spain* 15B2
Ségou *Mali* 48B3
Segovia = Coco
Segovia *Spain* 15B1
Segre, R *Spain* 15C1
Séguéla *Ivory Coast* 48B4
Seguin *USA* 63C3
Segura, R *Spain* 15B2
Segura, Sierra de, Mts *Spain* 15B2
Sehwan *Pak* 42B3
Seiling *USA* 62C1
Seille, R *France* 13D3
Seinäjoki *Fin* 12J6
Seine, R *Can* 61E1
Seine, R *France* 13C4
Seine-et-Marne, Department *France* 13B3
Sekenke *Tanz* 50D4
Sekondi *Ghana* 48B4
Selah *USA* 58B1
Selaru, I *Indon* 27G7
Selatan, I *Indon* 27D6
Selat Dampier, Str *Indon* 27G7
Selat Lombok, Chan *Indon* 27E7
Selat Sunda, Str *Indon* 27D7
Selat Wetar, Chan *Indon* 27F7
Selawik *USA* 54C3
Selayar, I *Indon* 32B1
Selby *Eng* 6D3
Selby *USA* 60C1
Selçuk *Turk* 17F3
Selebi Pikwe *Botswana* 47D1
Selennyakh, R *USSR* 25Q3
Selestat *France* 13D3
Selfoss *Iceland* 55Q3
Selfridge *USA* 60C1
Selima Oasis *Sudan* 50C1
Selizharovo *USSR* 19G1
Selkirk *Can* 54J4
Selkirk *Scot* 8D4
Selkirk Mts *Can/USA* 54G4
Selma, Alabama *USA* 67A2
Selma, California *USA* 66C2
Selmer *USA* 63E1
Selouane *Mor* 15B2
Selvas, Region *Brazil* 72D5

South Shields *Eng* 6D2
South Taranaki Bight, B *NZ* 35B1
South Uist, I *Scot* 8B3
South West Africa = Namibia
South West C *Aust* 32D5
South West Indian Ridge *Indian O* 36D6
South West Pacific Basin *Pacific O* 37M6
South West Peru Ridge *Pacific O* 52D5
Southwold *Eng* 7E3
South Yemen, Republic *Arabian Pen* 38C4
South Yorkshire, County *Eng* 7D3
Soutpansberg, Mts *S Africa* 47D1
Sovetsk, RSFSR *USSR* 19E1
Sovetsk, RSFSR *USSR* 20H4
Sovetskaya Gavan' *USSR* 26G2
Sovetskiy *USSR* 20L3
Sōya-misaki, C *Japan* 29D1
Soyo Congo *Angola* 51B4
Sozh, R *USSR* 19G2
Spa *Belg* 13C2
Spain, Kingdom *S.W. Europe* 15
Spalato = Split
Spalding *Eng* 7D3
Spanish, R *Can* 64C1
Spanish Fork *USA* 59D2
Spanish Town *Jamaica* 69J1
Sparks *USA* 59C3
Sparta *USA* 64A2
Spartanburg *USA* 67B2
Spartí *Greece* 17E3
Spartivento, C *Italy* 16D3
Spassk *USSR* 26G2
Spearfish *USA* 60C2
Spearman *USA* 62B1
Speightstown *Barbados* 69R2
Spenard *USA* 54D3
Spence Bay *Can* 55J3
Spencer, Indiana *USA* 64B3
Spencer, Iowa *USA* 61D2
Spencer G *Aust* 32C4
Spencer I *Can* 55L3
Spenser Mts *NZ* 35B2
Sperrin Mts *N Ire* 9C2
Spey, R *Scot* 8D3
Speyer *W Germ* 18B3
Speyside *Tobago* 69K1
Spirit Lake *USA* 58C1
Spirit River *Can* 54G4
Spitsbergen, I *Svalbard* 24C2
Spitsbergen, Is = Svalbard
Spittal *Austria* 18C3
Spjekeroog, I *W Germ* 13D1
Spjelkavik *Nor* 12F6
Split *Yugos* 16D2
Spokane *USA* 58C1
Spooner *USA* 64A1
Sporádhes, Is = Dodecanese
Spratly, I *S China Sea* 27E6
Spratly Is *S China Sea* 27E6
Spray *USA* 58C2
Spree, R *E Germ* 18C2
Springbok *S Africa* 47B2
Springdale *USA* 63D1
Springer *USA* 62B1
Springerville *USA* 59E4
Springfield, Colorado *USA* 62B1
Springfield, Illinois *USA* 64B3
Springfield, Massachusetts *USA* 68D1
Springfield, Minnesota *USA* 61E2
Springfield, Missouri *USA* 63D1
Springfield, Ohio *USA* 64C3
Springfield, Oregon *USA* 58B2
Springfield, Tennessee *USA* 67A1
Springfield, Vermont *USA* 65E2
Springfontein *S Africa* 47D3
Spring Mts *USA* 59C3
Springs *S Africa* 47D2
Springville, New York *USA* 68A1
Springville, Utah *USA* 59D2
Springwater *USA* 68B1
Spruce Mt *USA* 58D2
Spurn Head, C *Eng* 7E3
Spuzzum *Can* 58B1
Squillace, G di *Italy* 16D3
Sredinnyy Khrebet, Mts *USSR* 25S4
Srednekolymsk *USSR* 25R3

Sredne-Russkaya Vozvyshennost', Upland *USSR* 20F5
Sredne Sibirskoye Ploskogorye, *USSR* 25M3
Sredniy Ural, Mts *USSR* 20K4
Srepok, R *Camb* 30D3
Sretensk *USSR* 26E1
Sre Umbell *Camb* 30C3
Srikakulam *India* 44C2
Sri Kalahasti *India* 44B3
Sri Lanka, Republic *S Asia* 39G5
Srinagar *Pak* 42C2
Srivardhan *India* 44A2
Sroda *Pol* 18D2
Stack Skerry, I *Scot* 8C2
Stade *W Germ* 13E1
Stadthagen *W Germ* 13E1
Staffa, I *Scot* 8B3
Stafford *Eng* 7C3
Stafford, County *Eng* 7C3
Stafford Springs *USA* 68D2
Stalingrad = Volgograd
Stallberg, Mt *S Africa* 47B3
Stallworthy,C *Can* 55J1
Stalowa Wola *Pol* 19E2
Stamford, Connecticut *USA* 68D2
Stamford *Eng* 7D3
Stamford, New York *USA* 68C1
Stamford, Texas *USA* 62C2
Stampriet *Namibia* 47B1
Standerton *S Africa* 47D2
Standish *USA* 64C2
Stanford *USA* 58D1
Stanger *S Africa* 47E2
Stanhope *Eng* 6C2
Stanislaus, R *USA* 66B2
Stanke Dimitrov *Bulg* 17E2
Stanley *Aust* 34C4
Stanley *Falkland Is* 74E8
Stanley, Idaho *USA* 58D2
Stanley, N Dakota *USA* 60C1
Stanley Res *India* 44B3
Stanleyville = Kisangani
Stann Creek *Belize* 70D3
Stanovoy Khrebet, Mts *USSR* 26F1
Stanthorpe *Aust* 34D1
Stanton Banks, Sand-bank *Scot* 8A3
Stapleton *USA* 60C2
Starachowice *Pol* 19E2
Stara Planiná, Mts *Bulg* 17E2
Staraya Russa *USSR* 20E4
Stara Zagora *Bulg* 17F2
Stargard *Pol* 18D2
Starkville *USA* 63E2
Starnberg *W Germ* 18C3
Starogard Gdański *Pol* 19D2
Starokonstantinov *USSR* 19F3
Start Pt *Eng* 7C4
Staryy Oskol *USSR* 21F5
State College *USA* 68B2
Staten I *USA* 68C2
Statesboro *USA* 67B2
Statesville *USA* 67B1
Staunton *USA* 65D3
Stavanger *Nor* 12F7
Stavelot *Belg* 13C2
Stavoren *Neth* 13C1
Stavropol' *USSR* 21G6
Stawell *Aust* 34B3
Stayton *USA* 58B2
Steamboat Springs *USA* 60B2
Steelton *USA* 68B2
Steens Mt *USA* 58C2
Steenstrups Gletscher, Gl *Greenland* 55N2
Steenwijk *Neth* 13D1
Stefansson I *Can* 54H2
Stegi *Swaziland* 47E2
Steinback *Can* 61D1
Steinkjer *Nor* 12G6
Steinkjer *Nor* 20A3
Steinkopf *S Africa* 47B2
Stella *S Africa* 47C2
Stellenbosch *S Africa* 47B3
Stenay *France* 13C3
Stendal *E Germ* 18C2
Stepanakert *USSR* 21H8
Stephen *USA* 61D1
Stephens,C *NZ* 35B2
Stephens Creek *Aust* 34B2
Stephenson *USA* 64B1
Stephenville *Can* 55N5
Stephenville *USA* 62C2
Sterkstroom *S Africa* 47D3
Sterling, Colorado *USA* 60C2
Sterling, Illinois *USA* 64B2
Sterling, Kansas *USA* 62C1
Sterling, N Dakota *USA* 60C1
Sterling City *USA* 62B2
Sterling Heights *USA* 64C2

Sterlitamak *USSR* 20K5
Stettler *Can* 54G4
Steubenville *USA* 64C2
Stevenage *Eng* 7D4
Stevens Point *USA* 64B2
Stevens Village *USA* 54D3
Stewart *Can* 54F4
Stewart *USA* 59C3
Stewart, R *Can* 54E3
Stewart I *NZ* 35A3
Stewart Is *Solomon Is* 33F1
Stewarton *Scot* 8C4
Stewart River *Can* 54E3
Stewartstown *USA* 68B3
Stewartville *USA* 61E2
Steynsburg *S Africa* 47D3
Steyr *Austria* 18C3
Steytlerville *S Africa* 47C3
Stikine, R *Can* 54F4
Stillwater, Minnesota *USA* 61E1
Stillwater, Oklahoma *USA* 63C1
Stillwater Range, Mts *USA* 59C3
Stinnett *USA* 62B1
Stirling *Aust* 34A2
Stirling *Scot* 8D3
Stjørdal *Nor* 12G6
Stockach *W Germ* 13E4
Stockbridge *USA* 68D1
Stockerau *Austria* 18D3
Stockholm *Sweden* 12H7
Stockport *Eng* 7C3
Stockton, California *USA* 66B2
Stockton *Eng* 6D2
Stockton, Kansas *USA* 60D3
Stockton L *USA* 63D1
Stoke-on-Trent *Eng* 7C3
Stokmarknes *Nor* 12G5
Stolbovoy, Ostrov, I *USSR* 25P2
Stolbtsy *USSR* 12K8
Stolin *USSR* 19F2
Stone *Eng* 7C3
Stone Harbor *USA* 68C3
Stonehaven *Scot* 8D3
Stonewall *USA* 63C2
Stony Stratford *Eng* 7D3
Storavan, L *Sweden* 12H5
Støren *Nor* 12G6
Storm B *Aust* 34C4
Storm Lake *USA* 61D2
Stornoway *Scot* 8B2
Storozhinets *USSR* 19F3
Storrs *USA* 68D2
Storsjön, L *Sweden* 12G6
Storuman *Sweden* 12H5
Story *USA* 60B2
Stoughton *USA* 68E1
Stour, R *Eng* 7E4
Stourbridge *Eng* 7C3
Stourport *Eng* 7C3
Stowmarket *Eng* 7E3
Strabane *N Ire* 9C2
Strahan *Aust* 34C4
Stralsund *E Germ* 18C2
Strand *S Africa* 47B3
Stranda *Nor* 12F6
Strangford Lough, L *Irish Rep* 9D2
Strängnäs *Sweden* 12H7
Stranraer *Scot* 8C4
Strasbourg *France* 14D2
Strasburg *USA* 65D3
Stratford, California *USA* 66C2
Stratford *Can* 64C2
Stratford, Connecticut *USA* 68D2
Stratford *NZ* 35B1
Stratford, Texas *USA* 62B1
Stratford-on-Avon *Eng* 7D3
Strathalbyn *Aust* 34A3
Strathclyde, Region *Scot* 8C4
Stratton *USA* 65E1
Streator *USA* 64B2
Stroma, I *Scot* 8D2
Stromboli, I *Italy* 16D3
Stromness *Scot* 8D2
Stromsburg *USA* 61D2
Stromsund *Sweden* 12H6
Ströms Vattudal, L *Sweden* 12G6
Stronsay, I *Scot* 8D2
Stroud *Eng* 7C4
Stroudsburg *USA* 68C2
Struma, R *Bulg* 17E2
Strumble Head, Pt *Wales* 7B3
Strumica *Yugos* 17E2
Stryy *USSR* 19E3
Stryy, R *USSR* 19E3
Strzelecki Creek, R *Aust* 34B1
Stuart, Florida *USA* 67B3
Stuart, Nebraska *USA* 60D2
Stuart L *Can* 54F4
Stubice *Pol* 12G8
Stung Sen, R *Camb* 30D3

Stung Treng *Camb* 30D3
Stura, R *Italy* 16B2
Sturge I *Ant* 76G7
Sturgeon Bay *USA* 64B2
Sturgeon Falls *Can* 65D1
Sturgis, Kentucky *USA* 64B3
Sturgis, Michigan *USA* 64B2
Sturgis, S Dakota *USA* 60C2
Sturt Creek, R *Aust* 32B2
Sturt Desert *Aust* 34B1
Stutterheim *S Africa* 47D3
Stuttgart *USA* 63D2
Stuttgart *W Germ* 18B3
Stykkishólmur *Iceland* 12A1
Styr', R *USSR* 19F2
Suaçui Grande, R *Brazil* 75D2
Suakin *Sudan* 50D2
Suan *N Korea* 28A3
Suao *Taiwan* 31E5
Subotica *Yugos* 17D1
Suceava *Rom* 21D6
Sucre *Bol* 72E7
Sucuriú, R *Brazil* 75B2
Sudan, Republic *Africa* 50C2
Sudbury *Can* 64C1
Sudbury *Eng* 7E3
Sudd, Swamp *Sudan* 50C3
Suddie *Guyana* 73G2
Sudr *Egypt* 45B4
Sue, R *Sudan* 50C3
Suez *Egypt* 40B4
Suez Canal *Egypt* 40B3
Suez,G of *Egypt* 40B4
Suffern *USA* 68C2
Suffolk, County *Eng* 7E3
Sugarloaf Mt *USA* 65E2
Sugarloaf Pt *Aust* 34D2
Sugoy, R *USSR* 25R3
Suḥar *Oman* 41G5
Sühbaatar *Mongolia* 26D1
Sui *Pak* 42B3
Suide *China* 31C2
Suifen He, R *China* 28C2
Suihua *China* 26F2
Suining *China* 31B3
Suippes *France* 13C3
Suir, R *Irish Rep* 10B3
Sui Xian *China* 31C3
Suizhong *China* 31E1
Sujangarh *India* 42C3
Sukadana *Indon* 27D7
Sukagawa *Japan* 29E3
Sukai Mu, L *China* 26C3
Sukch'ŏn *N Korea* 28B3
Sukhinichi *USSR* 20F5
Sukhona, R *USSR* 20G4
Sukhumi *USSR* 21G7
Sukkertoppen *Greenland* 55N3
Sukkertoppen Isflade, Ice field *Greenland* 55N3
Sukkozero *USSR* 12L6
Sukkur *Pak* 42B3
Sukma *India* 44C2
Sukses *Namibia* 51B6
Sukumo *Japan* 28B4
Sula, R *USSR* 21F5
Sulaiman Range, Mts *Pak* 42B3
Sula, Kepulauan, I *Indon* 32B1
Sula Sgeir, I *Scot* 8B2
Sulawesi, Is *Indon* 27E7
Sulaymaniyah *Iraq* 41E2
Sule Skerry, I *Scot* 8C2
Sulina *Rom* 17F1
Sulingen *W Germ* 13E1
Sulitjelma *Nor* 12H5
Sullana *Peru* 72B4
Sullivan *USA* 63D1
Sully-sur-Loire *France* 13B4
Sulmona *Italy* 16C2
Sulphur, Louisiana *USA* 63D2
Sulphur, Oklahoma *USA* 63C2
Sulphur Springs *USA* 63C2
Sultan Daǧlari, Mts *Turk* 21E8
Sultanpur *India* 43E3
Sulu Arch, Is *Phil* 27F6
Sulu S *Phil* 27E6
Sulz *W Germ* 13E3
Sumampa *Arg* 74D3
Sumatera, I *Indon* 27C6
Sumba, I *Indon* 27E8
Sumbawa, I *Indon* 27E7
Sumbawa Besar *Indon* 27E7
Sumbawanga *Tanz* 51D4
Sumbe *Angola* 51B5
Sumburgh Head, Pt *Scot* 8E2
Sumesar Ra, Mts *Nepal* 43N2
Sumgait *USSR* 21H7
Sumisu, I *Japan* 26H3
Summit Lake *Can* 54F4
Summit Mt *USA* 59C3
Sumner,L *NZ* 35B2
Sumoto *Japan* 29B4
Sumter *USA* 67B2
Sumy *USSR* 21E5
Sun, R *USA* 58D1

Sunagawa *Japan* 29D2
Sunan *N Korea* 28A3
Sunart, Loch, Inlet *Scot* 8C3
Sunbury *USA* 68B2
Sunch'ŏn *N Korea* 28B3
Sunch'ŏn *S Korea* 28B4
Sundance *USA* 60C2
Sundargarh *India* 43E4
Sunderbans, Swamp *India/Bang* 43F4
Sunderland *Eng* 6D2
Sundridge *Can* 65D1
Sundsvall *Sweden* 12H6
Sunnyside *USA* 58C1
Sunnyvale *USA* 59B3
Sun Prairie *USA* 64B2
Suntar *USSR* 25N3
Sun Valley *USA* 58D2
Sunyani *Ghana* 48B4
Suojarvi *USSR* 20E3
Suo-nada, B *Japan* 28B4
Suonenjoki *Fin* 12K6
Supaul *India* 43F3
Superior, Arizona *USA* 59D4
Superior, Nebraska *USA* 61D2
Superior, Wisconsin *USA* 64A1
Superior,L *Can/USA* 64B1
Suphan Buri *Thai* 30C3
Süphan Daǧ, Mt *Turk* 40D2
Supiori, I *Indon* 27G7
Suq ash Suyukh *Iraq* 41E3
Suqian *China* 31D3
Suqutra = Socotra
Sur *Oman* 38D3
Sura, R *USSR* 20H5
Surabaya *Indon* 27E7
Suraga-wan, B *Japan* 29C4
Surakarta *Indon* 27E7
Şuran *Syria* 45D1
Surat *Aust* 34C1
Surat *India* 42C4
Suratgarh *India* 42C3
Surat Thani *Thai* 30B4
Surendranagar *India* 42C4
Surf City *USA* 68C3
Surgut *USSR* 24J3
Suriapet *India* 44B2
Surigao *Phil* 27F6
Surin *Thai* 30C3
Surinam, Republic *S America* 73G3
Sur,Pt *USA* 66B2
Surrey, County *Eng* 7D4
Surtsey, I *Iceland* 12A2
Susa *Italy* 16B1
Susa *Japan* 28B4
Susaki *Japan* 29B4
Susanville *USA* 59B2
Susquehanna *USA* 68C2
Susquehanna, R *USA* 68B3
Sussex *USA* 68C2
Sussex West *Eng* 7D4
Sutherland *S Africa* 47C3
Sutherland *USA* 60C2
Sutlej, R *Pak* 42C2
Sutter Creek *USA* 59B3
Sutton *USA* 64C3
Suttsu *Japan* 29D2
Suwa *Japan* 29D3
Suwalki *Pol* 19E2
Suwannee, R *USA* 67B3
Suweilih *Jordan* 45C2
Suwŏn *S Korea* 28B3
Su Xian *China* 31D3
Suzaka *Japan* 29C3
Suzhou *China* 31E3
Suzu *Japan* 29D3
Suzuka *Japan* 29C4
Suzu-misaki, C *Japan* 29C3
Svalbard, Is *Barents S* 24C2
Svalyava *USSR* 19E3
Svartenhuk Halvø, Region *Greenland* 55N2
Svartisen, Mt *Nor* 12G5
Svay Rieng *Camb* 30D3
Sveg *Sweden* 12G6
Svendborg *Den* 12G7
Sverdlovsk *USSR* 24H4
Sverdrup Chan *Can* 55J1
Sverdrup Is *Can* 54H2
Svetlaya *USSR* 26G2
Svetlogorsk *USSR* 19E2
Svetogorsk *USSR* 12K6
Svetozarevo *Yugos* 17E2
Svilengrad *Bulg* 17F2
Svir' *USSR* 19F2
Svir', R *USSR* 20E3
Svitavy *Czech* 18D3
Svobodnyy *USSR* 26F1
Svolvær *Nor* 12G5
Swaffam *Eng* 7E3
Swain Reefs *Aust* 33E3
Swainsboro *USA* 67B2
Swains I *American Samoa* 33H2

Tongatapu, I *Tonga* 33H3
Tongatapu Group, Is *Tonga* 33H3
Tonga Trench *Pacific O* 33H3
Tongchang *N Korea* 28A2
Tongcheng *China* 31D3
Tongchuan *China* 31B2
Tongde *China* 31A2
Tongeren *Belg* 13C2
Tonggu Jiao, I *China* 30E2
Tonghai *China* 31A5
Tonghua *China* 28B2
Tongjosŏn-Man, S *N Korea* 28B3
Tongkin,G of *China/Viet* 30D1
Tongliao *China* 31E1
Tongling *China* 31D3
Tongnae *S Korea* 28A3
Tongo *Aust* 34B2
Tongren, Guizhou *China* 31B4
Tongren, Qinghai *China* 31A2
Tongsa *Bhutan* 43G3
Tongta *Burma* 30B1
Tongtian He, R *China* 26C3
Tongue *Scot* 8C2
Tongue, R *USA* 60B1
Tong Xian *China* 31D2
Tongxin *China* 31B2
Tongyuanpu *China* 28A2
Tongzi *China* 31B4
Tonhil *Mongolia* 25L5
Tónichi *Mexico* 56C4
Tonj *Sudan* 50C3
Tonk *India* 42D3
Tonkawa *USA* 63C1
Tonle Sap, L *Camb* 30C3
Tonnerre *France* 13C4
Tono *Japan* 29D3
Tonopah *USA* 59C3
Tooele *USA* 58D2
Toogoolawah *Aust* 34D1
Toompine *Aust* 34B1
Toowoomba *Aust* 34D1
Topaz L *USA* 66C1
Topeka *USA* 61D3
Topock *USA* 59D4
Topolobampo *Mexico* 56C4
Topozero, L *USSR* 20E2
Toppenish *USA* 58B1
Topsfield *USA* 68E1
Torbalı *Turk* 17F3
Torbat-e-Heydarīyeh *Iran* 41G2
Torbay *Eng* 7C4
Tordesillas *Spain* 15A1
Torgau *E Germ* 18C2
Torhout *Belg* 13B2
Tori *Eth* 50D3
Tori, I *Japan* 26H3
Torino = Turin
Torit *Sudan* 50D3
Torixoreu *Brazil* 75B2
Tormes, R *Spain* 15A1
Torne, R *Sweden* 12J5
Torneträsk, L *Sweden* 12H5
Torngat, Mts *Can* 55M4
Tornio *Fin* 12J5
Toro, Cerro del, Mt *Arg/Chile* 74C3
Toronto *Can* 65D2
Toropets *USSR* 20E4
Tororo *Uganda* 50D3
Toros, Dağları = Taurus Mts
Torquay *Eng* 7C4
Torrance *USA* 66C4
Torrão *Port* 15A2
Torreblanca *Spain* 15C1
Torre del Greco *Italy* 16C2
Torrelavega *Spain* 15B1
Torremolinos *Spain* 15B2
Torrens, L *Aust* 32C4
Torreón *Mexico* 70B2
Torres Is *Vanuatu* 33F2
Torres Str *Aust* 32D2
Torres Vedras *Port* 15A2
Torridge, R *Eng* 7B4
Torridon, Loch, Inlet *Scot* 8C3
Torrington, Connecticut *USA* 68D2
Torrington, Wyoming *USA* 60C2
Tórshavn *Faeroes* 12D3
Tortosa *Spain* 15C1
Tortosa, Cabo de, C *Spain* 15C1
Tortugas, Golfo de *Colombia* 72C3
Torūd *Iran* 41G2
Toruń *Pol* 19D2
Tory I *Irish Rep* 10B2
Tory Sol *Irish Rep* 9B2
Torzhok *USSR* 20E4
Tosa *Japan* 29B4
Tosashimizu *Japan* 28C4
Tosa-Wan, B *Japan* 29C4
To-shima, I *Japan* 29C4
Tosno *USSR* 12L7
Tosno *USSR* 20E4
Tosu *Japan* 28B4
Tosya *Turk* 40B1
Totana *Spain* 15B2
Tot'ma *USSR* 20G3
Totnes *Eng* 7C4
Totness *Surinam* 73G2
Tottenham *Aust* 34C2
Tottori *Japan* 29C3
Touba *Ivory Coast* 48B4
Touba *Sen* 48A3
Toubkal, Mt *Mor* 48B1
Toucy *France* 13B4
Tougan *Burkina* 48B3
Touggourt *Alg* 48C1
Tougué *Guinea* 48A3
Toul *France* 13C3
Toulon *France* 14D3
Toulouse *France* 14C3
Toumodi *Ivory Coast* 48B4
Toungoo *Burma* 30B2
Tourcoing *France* 13B2
Tourine *Maur* 48A2
Tournai *Belg* 13B2
Tours *France* 14C2
Touws River *S Africa* 47C3
Towada *Japan* 29E2
Towada-ko, L *Japan* 29E2
Towanda *USA* 68B2
Towne P *USA* 66D2
Towner *USA* 60C1
Townsend *USA* 58D1
Townsville *Aust* 32D2
Towson *USA* 68B3
Towy, R *Wales* 7C4
Toyah *USA* 62B2
Toya-ko, L *Japan* 29D2
Toyama *Japan* 29D3
Toyama-wan, B *Japan* 29C3
Toyohashi *Japan* 29C4
Toyonaka *Japan* 29C4
Toyooka *Japan* 29B3
Toyota *Japan* 29D3
Tozeur *Tunisia* 48C1
Traben-Trarbach *W Germ* 13D3
Trâblous = Tripoli, L
Trabzon *Turk* 40C1
Tracy, Minnesota *USA* 61D2
Tracy *USA* 66B2
Trafalgar, Cabo, C *Spain* 15A2
Trail *Can* 54G5
Tralee *Irish Rep* 10B3
Tramore *Irish Rep* 9C3
Tranås *Sweden* 12G7
Trang *Thai* 30B4
Trangan, I *Indon* 27G7
Trangie *Aust* 34C2
Transantarctic Mts *Ant* 76E3
Transkei, Self-governing homeland *S Africa* 47D3
Transvaal, Province *S Africa* 47D1
Transylvanian Alps, Mts = Munţii Carpaţii Meridionali
Trapani *Italy* 16C3
Traralgon *Aust* 34C3
Trarza, Region *Maur* 48A3
Trat *Thai* 30C3
Traveller's L *Aust* 34B2
Travemünde *W Germ* 18C2
Traverse City *USA* 64B2
Travers,Mt *NZ* 35B2
Travis,L *USA* 62C2
Třebíč *Czech* 18D3
Trebinje *Yugos* 17D2
Trebon *Czech* 18C3
Treinta y Tres *Urug* 74F4
Trelew *Arg* 74C6
Trelleborg *Sweden* 12G7
Tremadog B *Wales* 7B3
Tremblant,Mt *Can* 65E1
Tremiti, Is *Italy* 16D2
Tremont *USA* 68B2
Tremonton *USA* 58D2
Trenčín *Czech* 19D3
Trenque Lauquén *Arg* 74D5
Trent, R *Eng* 7D3
Trento *Italy* 16C1
Trenton *Can* 65D2
Trenton, Missouri *USA* 61E2
Trenton, New Jersey *USA* 68C2
Trepassey *Can* 55N5
Tres Arroyos *Arg* 74D5
Três Corações *Brazil* 75C3
Tres Forcas, Cabo, C *Mor* 15B2
Três Lagoas *Brazil* 74F2
Tres Pinos *USA* 66B2
Tres Puntas, Cabo *Arg* 74C7
Três Rios *Brazil* 75D3
Treviso *Italy* 16C1
Trevose Hd, Pt *Eng* 7B4
Treysa *W Germ* 13E2
Tribune *USA* 62B1
Trichur *India* 44B3
Trida *Aust* 34C2
Trier *W Germ* 13D3
Trieste *Italy* 16C1
Trikomo *Cyprus* 45B1
Trim *Irish Rep* 9C3
Trincomalee *Sri Lanka* 44C4
Trindade, I *Atlantic O* 52G6
Trinidad *Bol* 72F6
Trinidad *Urug* 74E4
Trinidad *USA* 62B1
Trinidad, I *Caribbean S* 69E4
Trinidad & Tobago, Is Republic *Caribbean S* 69E4
Trinity *USA* 63C2
Trinity, R *USA* 56D3
Trinity B *Can* 55N5
Trion *USA* 67A2
Tripoli *Leb* 45C1
Tripoli *Libya* 49D1
Trípolis *Greece* 17E3
Tripura, State *India* 43G4
Tristan da Cunha, Is *Atlantic O* 52H6
Trivandrum *India* 44B4
Trnava *Czech* 19D3
Trobriand Is *PNG* 32E1
Trois Pistoles *Can* 65F1
Trois-Riviéres *Can* 65E1
Troitsk *USSR* 24H4
Troitsko Pechorsk *USSR* 20K3
Trollhättan *Sweden* 12G7
Trollheimen, Mt *Nor* 12F6
Tromelin, I *Indian O* 46K9
Trompsburg *S Africa* 47D3
Tromsø *Nor* 12H5
Trona *USA* 66D3
Trondheim *Nor* 12G6
Trondheimfjord, Inlet *Nor* 12G6
Troödos Range, Mts *Cyprus* 45B1
Troon *Scot* 8C4
Tropic of Cancer 52J3
Tropic of Capricorn 52K6
Troudenni *Mali* 48B2
Trout L, Ontario *Can* 55J4
Trout Peak, Mt *USA* 58E2
Trout Run *USA* 68B2
Trowbridge *Eng* 7C4
Troy, Alabama *USA* 67A2
Troy, Montana *USA* 58C1
Troy, New York *USA* 68D1
Troy, Ohio *USA* 64C2
Troy, Pennsylvania *USA* 68B2
Troyan *Bulg* 17E2
Troyes *France* 13C3
Troy Peak, Mt *USA* 59C3
Trucial Coast, Region *UAE* 41F5
Truckee, R *USA* 59B3
Trujillo *Honduras* 70D3
Trujillo *Peru* 72C5
Trujillo *Spain* 15A2
Trujillo *Ven* 72D2
Trumbull,Mt *USA* 59D3
Trundle *Aust* 34C2
Truro *Can* 55M5
Truro *Eng* 7B4
Truth or Consequences *USA* 62A2
Tsagaan Nuur, L *Mongolia* 26C2
Tsagan-Tologoy *USSR* 26C1
Tsaratanana *Madag* 51E5
Tsau *Botswana* 51C6
Tsavo *Kenya* 50D4
Tsavo Nat Pk *Kenya* 50D4
Tschida,L *USA* 60C1
Tselinograd *USSR* 24J4
Tses *Namibia* 47B2
Tsetserleg *Mongolia* 26C2
Tsetserleg *Mongolia* 26D2
Tsévié *Togo* 48C4
Tshabong *Botswana* 47C2
Tshane *Botswana* 47C1
Tshela *Zaïre* 50B4
Tshibala *Zaïre* 51C4
Tshikapa *Zaïre* 50C4
Tshuapa, R *Zaïre* 50C4
Tsimlyanskoye Vodokhranilishche, Res *USSR* 21G6
Tsinan = Jinan
Tsingtao = Qingdao
Tsiombe *Madag* 51E6
Tsiroanomandidy *Madag* 51E5
Tsna, R *USSR* 19F2
Tsogt Ovoo *Mongolia* 31B1
Tsomo *S Africa* 47D3
Tsu *Japan* 29C4
Tsubata *Japan* 29C3
Tsuchiura *Japan* 29E3
Tsugarū-kaikyō, Str *Japan* 29E2
Tsumeb *Namibia* 51B5
Tsumis *Namibia* 51B6
Tsuruga *Japan* 29D3
Tsurugi *Japan* 29C3
Tsuruoka *Japan* 29D3
Tsushima *Japan* 29C3
Tsushima, Is *Japan* 28B4
Tsushima-Kaikyō = Korea Str
Tsuyama *Japan* 29C3
Tua, R *Port* 15A1
Tuamotu, Îles *Pacific O* 37M5
Tuapse *USSR* 21F7
Tuatapere *NZ* 35A3
Tuba City *USA* 59D3
Tubai, Îles *Pacific O* 37M6
Tubarão *Brazil* 74G3
Tubas *Israel* 45C2
Tübingen *W Germ* 18B3
Tubruq *Libya* 49E1
Tuckerton *USA* 68C3
Tucson *USA* 59D4
Tucumán, State *Arg* 74C3
Tucumcari *USA* 62B1
Tucupita *Ven* 72F2
Tudela *Spain* 15B1
Tudmur *Syria* 40C3
Tugela, R *S Africa* 47E2
Tuggerah L *Aust* 34D2
Tuguegarao *Phil* 27F5
Tugur *USSR* 25P4
Tuhai He, R *China* 31D2
Tukangbesi, Kepulauan, Is *Indon* 32B1
Tukangbesi, Kepulauan, Is *Indon* 27F7
Tuktoyaktuk *Can* 54E3
Tukums *USSR* 19E1
Tukuringra, Khrebet, Mts *USSR* 25O4
Tukuyu *Tanz* 51D4
Tukzar *Afghan* 42B1
Tula *USSR* 20F5
Tulare *USA* 66C2
Tulare Lake Bed *USA* 66C2
Tularosa *USA* 62A2
Tulcán *Ecuador* 72C3
Tulcea *Rom* 21D6
Tul'chin *USSR* 19F3
Tule, R *USA* 66C2
Tuli *Zim* 51C6
Tuli, R *Zim* 47D1
Tulia *USA* 62B2
Tulkarm *Israel* 45C2
Tullahoma *USA* 67A1
Tullamore *Irish Rep* 9C3
Tulle *France* 14C2
Tullos *USA* 63D2
Tullow *Irish Rep* 9C3
Tully *USA* 68B1
Tulsa *USA* 63C1
Tuluá *Colombia* 72C3
Tulul ash Shamīyah, Desert Region *Iran/Syria* 40C3
Tulun *USSR* 25M4
Tumaco *Colombia* 72C3
Tumany *USSR* 25R3
Tumbarumba *Aust* 34C3
Tumbes *Ecuador* 72B4
Tumen *China* 28B2
Tumen R *China/N Korea* 28B2
Tumkūr *India* 44B3
Tumpat *Malay* 30C4
Tumsar *India* 42D4
Tumu *Ghana* 48B3
Tumucumaque, Serra, Mts *Brazil* 73H3
Tumut *Aust* 34C3
Tumut, R *Aust* 34C3
Tunapuna *Trinidad* 69L1
Tunbridge Wells, Royal *Eng* 7E4
Tunceli *Turk* 40C2
Tunduma *Zambia* 51D4
Tunduru *Tanz* 51D5
Tundzha, R *Bulg* 17F2
Tungabhadra, R *India* 44B2
Tungkang *Taiwan* 26E4
Tungnafellsjökull, Mts *Iceland* 12B2
Tunguska, R *USSR* 25M3
Tuni *India* 44C2
Tunis *Tunisia* 16C3
Tunis, G de *Tunisia* 16C3
Tunisia, Republic *N Africa* 48C1
Tunja *Colombia* 72D2
Tunkhannock *USA* 68C2
Tunxi *China* 31D4
Tuolumne Meadows *USA* 66C2
Tupă *Brazil* 75B3
Tupaciguara *Brazil* 75C2
Tupelo *USA* 63E2
Tupik *USSR* 19G1
Tupiza *Bol* 72E8
Tupman *USA* 66C3
Tupper Lake *USA* 65E2
Tupungato, Mt *Arg* 74C4
Tura *India* 43G3
Tura *USSR* 25L3
Tura, R *USSR* 20L4
Turan *Iran* 41G2
Turan *USSR* 25L4
Turayf *S Arabia* 40C3
Turbat *Pak* 38E3
Turbo *Colombia* 72C2
Turda *Rom* 17E1
Turfan Depression *China* 24K5
Turgay *USSR* 24H5
Turgen Uul, Mt *Mongolia* 25L5
Turgutlu *Turk* 40A2
Turhal *Turk* 40C1
Türi *USSR* 12K7
Turia, R *Spain* 15B2
Turin *Italy* 16B1
Turinsk *USSR* 20L4
Turiy *USSR* 26G2
Turkana, L *Eth/Kenya* 50D3
Turkestan, Region *C Asia* 38E1
Turkey, Republic *W Asia* 40C2
Turkmenskiy Zaliv, B *USSR* 41F2
Turkmen SSR, Republic *USSR* 38D1
Turks Is *Caribbean S* 69C2
Turku *Fin* 12J6
Turkwel, R *Kenya* 50D3
Turlock *USA* 66B2
Turlock L *USA* 66B2
Turnagain,C *NZ* 35C2
Turneffe I *Belize* 70D3
Turners Falls *USA* 68D1
Turnhout *Belg* 13C2
Turnu Măgurele *Rom* 17E2
Turnu-Severin *Rom* 17E2
Turpan *China* 25K5
Turquino, Mt *Cuba* 69B2
Turriff *Scot* 8D3
Turtkul' *USSR* 38E1
Turtle Creek Res *USA* 61D3
Turukhansk *USSR* 25K3
Turuntayevo *USSR* 26D1
Turvo, R, Goias *Brazil* 75B2
Turvo, R, São Paulo *Brazil* 75C3
Tur'ya, R *USSR* 19E2
Tuscaloosa *USA* 63E2
Tuscarora Mt *USA* 68B2
Tuscola, Illinois *USA* 64B3
Tuscola, Texas *USA* 62C2
Tuscumbia *USA* 63E2
Tusharık *Iran* 41G3
Tussey Mt *USA* 68A2
Tuticorin *India* 44B4
Tutrakan *Bulg* 17F2
Tuttlingen *W Germ* 18B3
Tutuila, I *American Samoa* 33H2
Tuul Gol, R *Mongolia* 26D2
Tuva ASSR, Republic *USSR* 25L4
Tuvalu, Is *Pacific O* 33G1
Tuwayılel Haj, Mt *Jordan* 45C4
Tuxpan *Mexico* 70B2
Tuxpan *Mexico* 70C2
Tuxtla Gutiérrez *Mexico* 70C3
Túy *Spain* 15A1
Tuy Hoa *Viet* 30D3
Tuz Gölü, Salt L *Turk* 40B2
Tuz Khurmatu *Iraq* 41D3
Tuzla *Yugos* 17D2
Tweed, R *Eng/Scot* 8D4
Tweed Heads *Aust* 34D1
Tweedsmuir Hills *Scot* 8D4
Twentynine Palms *USA* 59C4
Twillingate *Can* 55N5
Twin Bridges *USA* 58D1
Twin Buttes Res *USA* 62B2
Twin Falls *USA* 58D2
Twins,The, Mt *NZ* 35B2
Twitchell Res *USA* 66B3
Two Harbors *USA* 64A1
Two Medicine, R *USA* 58D1
Two Rivers *USA* 64B2
Tygda *USSR* 25O4
Tyler *USA* 63C2
Tymovskoye *USSR* 26H1
Tynda *USSR* 26F1
Tyne, R *Eng* 6D2
Tyne and Wear, Metropolitan County *Eng* 6D2
Tynemouth *Eng* 6D2
Tynset *Nor* 12G6
Tyr = Tyre
Tyre *Leb* 45C2
Tyrone, New Mexico *USA* 62A2
Tyrone, Pennsylvania *USA* 68A2

Tyrone Vembanad L

Tyrone, County N Ire 9C2
Tyrrell,L Aust 34B3
Tyrrhenian S Italy 16C2
Tyuleni, Ova, Is USSR 21J7
Tyumen' USSR 24H4
Tyung, R USSR 25O3
Tywyn Wales 7B3
Tzaneen S Africa 47E1
Tzoumérka, Mt Greece 17E3

U

Uarsciek Somalia 50E3
Ubá Brazil 75D3
Ubaí Brazil 75D2
Ubaitaba Brazil 75E1
Ubangi, R CAR/Congo/Zaïre 50B3
Ubayyid, Wadi al, Watercourse Iraq 40D3
Ube Japan 28B4
Ubeda Spain 15B2
Ubekendt Ejland, I Greenland 55N2
Uberaba Brazil 75C2
Uberaba, Lagoa Brazil 75A2
Uberlândia Brazil 75C2
Ubon Ratchathani Thai 30D2
Ubort, R USSR 19F2
Ubundu Zaïre 50C4
Ucayali, R Peru 72D5
Uch Pak 42C3
Uchar, R USSR 25P4
Uchiura-wan, B Japan 29E2
Uchte W Germ 13E1
Ucluelet Can 58A1
Uda, R USSR 26C1
Udaipur India 42C4
Udaipur Garhi Nepal 43F3
Uddevalla Sweden 12G7
Uddjaur, L Sweden 12H5
Udgir India 44B2
Udhampur India 42D2
Udine Italy 16C1
Udmurt ASSR, Republic USSR 20J4
Udon Thani Thai 30C2
Udskaya Guba, B USSR 25P4
Udupi India 44A3
Udzha USSR 25N2
Ueda Japan 29C3
Uele, R Zaïre 50C3
Uelen USSR 25U3
Uelzen W Germ 18C2
Uere, R Zaïre 50C3
Ufa USSR 20K5
Ufa, R USSR 20K4
Ugab, R Namibia 51B6
Ugaila, R Tanz 50D4
Uganda, Republic Africa 50D3
'Ugeiqa, Wadi Jordan 45C3
Uglegorsk USSR 26H2
Uglich USSR 20F4
Uglovoye USSR 28C2
Ugra, R USSR 20F5
Uig Scot 8B3
Uige Angola 51B4
Üijŏngbu S Korea 28A3
Uil USSR 21J6
Uinta Mts USA 58D2
Üiryŏng S Korea 28A3
Uisŏng S Korea 28A3
Uitenhage S Africa 47D3
Újfehértó Hung 19E3
Uji Japan 29C4
Ujiji Tanz 50C4
Ujina Chile 74C2
Ujjain India 42D4
Ujung Pandang Indon 32A1
Ukerewe I Tanz 50D4
Ukhrul India 43G3
Ukhta USSR 20J3
Ukiah, California USA 59B3
Ukiah, Oregon USA 58C1
Ukiah USA 56A3
Ukmerge USSR 19E1
Ukrainian SSR, Republic USSR 21D6
Uku-jima, I Japan 28A4
Ulaanbaatar Mongolia 26D2
Ulaangom Mongolia 26C2
Ulaan Uul Mongolia 31C1
Ulan Bator = Ulaanbaatar
Ulangar Hu, L China 39G1
Ulanhot China 26F2
Ulan Ude USSR 26D1
Ulan Ul Hu, L China 26C3
Ul'beya, R USSR 25Q3
Ulchin S Korea 28B3
Ulcinj Yugos 17D2
Uldz Mongolia 26E2
Uliastay Mongolia 26C2
Ulithi, I Pacific O 27G5
Ulla USSR 19F1
Ulladulla Aust 34D3
Ullapool Scot 8C3
Ullsfjorden, Inlet Nor 12H5
Ullswater, L Eng 6C2
Ullung-do, I Japan 28C3
Ulm W Germ 18C3
Uloowaranie,L Aust 34A1
Ulsan S Korea 28B3
Ulster, Region N Ire 9C2
Ulungur He, R China 24K5
Ulungur Hu, L China 24K5
Ulva, I Scot 8B3
Ulverston Eng 6C2
Ulverstone Aust 34C4
Ulya, R USSR 25Q4
Ulyanovka USSR 19G3
Ul'yanovsk USSR 20H5
Ulysses USA 62B1
Uman' USSR 21E6
Umanak Greenland 55N2
Umaria India 43E4
Umarkot Pak 42B3
Umatilla USA 58C1
Umba USSR 20E2
Umba, R Tanz/Kenya 50D4
Umboi I PNG 32D1
Ume, R Sweden 12H6
Umea Sweden 12J6
Um ed Daraj, Jebel, Mt Jordan 45C2
Um el Hashim, Jebel, Mt Jordan 45C4
Umfolozi, R S Africa 47E2
Umiat USA 54C3
Um Ishrin, Jebel, Mt Jordan 45C4
Umkomaas, R S Africa 47E3
Umm al Qaiwain UAE 41G4
Umm Bell Sudan 50C2
Umm Keddada Sudan 50C2
Umm Lajj S Arabia 40C4
Umm Ruwaba Sudan 50D2
Umm Sa'id Qatar 41F5
Umniaiti, R Zim 51C5
Umpqua, R USA 58B2
Umred India 42D4
Umtali = Mutare
Umtata S Africa 47D3
Umuarama Brazil 75B3
Umzimkulu S Africa 47D3
Umzimkulu, R S Africa 47E3
Umzimvubu, R S Africa 47D3
Umzingwane, R Zim 47D1
Una Brazil 75E2
Una, R Yugos 16D1
Unadilla USA 68C1
Unadilla, R USA 68C1
Unaí Brazil 75C2
Unalakleet USA 54B3
Unayzah S Arabia 41D4
Uncasville USA 68D2
Uncompahgre Plat USA 60B3
Underberg S Africa 47D2
Underwood USA 60C1
Unecha USSR 20E5
Uneisa Jordan 45C3
Ungava B Can 55M4
Unggi N Korea 28C2
União de Vitória Brazil 74F3
Union, Missouri USA 63D1
Union, S Carolina USA 67B2
Union City, Pennsylvania USA 65D2
Union City, Tennessee USA 63E1
Uniondale S Africa 47C3
Union of Soviet Socialist Reps Asia 22D3
Union Springs USA 67A2
Uniontown USA 65D3
United Arab Emirates Arabian Pen 41F5
United Kingdom of Gt Britain & N Ireland N W Europe 4E3
United States of America 53H4
United States Range, Mts Can 55K1
Unity USA 58C2
University Park USA 62A2
Unna W Germ 13D2
Unnao India 43E3
Unsan N Korea 28A2
Unst, I Scot 8E1
Ünye Turk 40C1
Unzha, R USSR 20G4
Upata Ven 72F2
Upemba Nat Pk Zaïre 51C4
Upernavik Greenland 55N2
Upington S Africa 47C2
Upland USA 66D3
Upolu, I Western Samoa 33H2
Upper Hutt NZ 35C2
Upper Klamath L USA 58B2
Upper L USA 58B2
Upper Lough Erne, L N Ire 9C2
Upper Manzanilla Trinidad 69L1
Upper Red L USA 61E1
Upper Seal,L Can 55L4
Upperville USA 68B3
Uppsala Sweden 12H7
Upsala Can 61E1
Upton USA 60C2
'Uqlat as Suqur S Arabia 40D4
Uraba, Golfo de Colombia 72C2
Urad Qianqi China 31B1
Urairah S Arabia 41E4
Urakawa Japan 29D2
Ural, R USSR 21J5
Uralla Aust 34D2
Ural Mts USSR 20M4
Ural'sk USSR 21J5
Ural'skiy Khrebet, Mts USSR 24G4
Urandi Brazil 75D1
Uranium City Can 54H4
Urapunga Aust 27G8
Uravan USA 60B3
Urawa Japan 29C3
Uray USSR 20L3
Urbana, Illinois USA 64B2
Urbana, Ohio USA 64C2
Urbino Italy 16C2
Urbion, Sierra de, Mt Spain 15B1
Ure, R Eng 6C2
Uren' USSR 20H4
Urfa Turk 40C2
Urgench USSR 38E1
Urgun Afghan 42B2
Urla Turk 17F3
Uroševac Yugos 17E2
Uruaçu Brazil 75C1
Uruapan Mexico 70B3
Urucuia, R Brazil 75C2
Uruguaiana Brazil 74E3
Uruguay, R Urug/Arg 74E4
Uruguay, Republic S America 74E4
Urumiyeh Iran 41E2
Ürümqi China 39G1
Urup, I, Kuril Is USSR 26J2
Uruzgan Afghan 42B2
Uryu-ko, L Japan 29D2
Uryupinsk USSR 21G5
Urzhum USSR 20J4
Urziceni Rom 17F2
Usa China 39G1
Usa Japan 28B4
Usa, R USSR 20L2
Uşak Turk 40A2
Usakos Namibia 47B1
Ushakova, Ostrov, I USSR 24J1
Ushashi Tanz 50D4
Ush Tobe USSR 24J5
Ushuaia Arg 74C8
Ushumun USSR 25O4
Usk, R Wales 7C4
Üsküdar Turk 40A1
Usogorsk USSR 20H3
Usol'ye Sibirskoye USSR 25M4
Ussuri, R China/USSR 26G2
Ussuriysk USSR 28C2
Ust'-Belaya USSR 25T3
Ust'Bol'sheretsk USSR 25R4
Ustica, I, Sicily 16C3
Ústí-nad-Laben Czech 18C2
Ust'Ishim USSR 24J4
Ustka Pol 18D2
Ust'Kamchatsk USSR 25S4
Ust'-Kamenogorsk USSR 24K5
Ust' Kara USSR 20L2
Ust Karabula USSR 25L4
Ust' Katav USSR 20K5
Ust'-Kut USSR 25M4
Ust Labinsk USSR 21F6
Ust'Maya USSR 25P3
Ust' Nem USSR 20K3
Ust'Nera USSR 25Q3
Ust'Nyukzha USSR 25N4
Ust'Ordynskiy USSR 25M4
Ust' Tsil'ma USSR 20J2
Ust-'Umal'tu USSR 25P4
Ust'ya, R USSR 20G3
Ust' Yuribey USSR 20M2
Ustyurt, Plato, Plat USSR 24G5
Usuki Japan 28B4
Usumacinta, R Guatemala/Mexico 70C3
Usutu, R Swaziland 47E2
Usuyŏng S Korea 28A4
Usvyaty USSR 19G1
Utah, State USA 56B3
Utah L USA 59D2
Utena USSR 19F1
Uthal Pak 42B3
Utica USA 68C1
Utiel Spain 15B2
Utrecht Neth 18B2
Utrecht S Africa 47E2
Utrera Spain 15A2
Utsjoki Fin 12K5
Utsonomiya Japan 29D3
Uttaradit Thai 30C2
Uttar Pradesh, State India 43E3
Uttoxeter Eng 7D3
Uusikaupunki Fin 12J6
Uvalde USA 62C3
Uvat USSR 24H4
Uvéa, I New Caledonia 33F3
Uvinza Tanz 50D4
Uvira Zaïre 50C4
Uvkusigssat Greenland 55N2
Uvs Nuur, L Mongolia 26C1
Uwajima Japan 28C4
Uweinat, Jebel, Mt Sudan 50C1
Uxin Qi China 31B2
Uyandina, R USSR 25Q3
Uyar USSR 25L4
Uyuni Bol 72E8
Uyûn Mûsa, Well Egypt 45B4
Uzbek SSR, Republic USSR 38E1
Uzerche France 14C2
Uzh, R USSR 19F2
Uzhgorod USSR 19E3
Uzlovaya USSR 20F5
Uzunköprü Turk 40A1

V

Vaal, R S Africa 47C2
Vaal Dam, Res S Africa 47D2
Vaalwater S Africa 47D1
Vaasa Fin 12J6
Vác Hung 19D3
Vacaria Brazil 74F3
Vacaria, R, Mato Grosso do Brazil 75B3
Vacaria, R, Minas Gerais Brazil 75D2
Vacaville USA 59B3
Vadodara India 42C4
Vadsø Nor 12K4
Vaduz Liech 16B1
Vaga, R USSR 20G3
Váh, R Czech 19D3
Vahel Israel 45C3
Vaigai, R India 44B3
Vaila, I Scot 8E1
Vaitupu, I Tuvalu 33G1
Valcheta Arg 74C6
Valday USSR 20E4
Valdayskaya Vozvyshennost', Upland USSR 20E4
Val de la Pascua Ven 72E2
Valdepeñas Spain 15B2
Valdez USA 54D3
Valdivia Chile 74B5
Val d'Oise, Department France 13B3
Val-d'Or Can 65D1
Valdosta USA 67B2
Vale USA 58C2
Valença, Bahia Brazil 75E1
Valença, Rio de Janeiro Brazil 75D3
Valence France 14C3
Valencia Spain 15B2
Valencia Ven 72E1
Valencia, Region = Comunidad Valenciana
Valencia de Alcantara Spain 15A2
Valencia, Golfo de, G Spain 15C2
Valenciennes France 13B2
Valentine, Nebraska USA 60C2
Valentine, Texas USA 62B2
Vale of Pickering Eng 6D2
Vale of York Eng 6D2
Valera Ven 72D2
Valga USSR 12K7
Valjevo Yugos 17D2
Valkeakoski Fin 12J6
Valladolid Mexico 70D2
Valladolid Spain 15B1
Valle de la Pascua Ven 69D5
Valledupar Colombia 72D1
Valle Grande Bol 72F7
Vallejo USA 66A1
Vallenar Chile 74B3
Valle Pequeno Brazil 75D1
Valley City USA 61D1
Valley Falls USA 58B2
Valleyfield Can 65E1
Valls Spain 15C1
Valmiera USSR 19F1
Valognes France 14B2
Valparaíso Brazil 75B3
Valparaíso Chile 74B4
Valparaiso USA 67A2
Vals, R S Africa 47D2
Valsad India 42C4
Valuyki USSR 21F5
Valverde del Camino Spain 15A2
Vammala Fin 12J6
Van Turk 41D2
Vanavara USSR 25M3
Van Buren, Arkansas USA 63D1
Van Buren, Maine USA 65F1
Vancouleurs France 13C3
Vancouver Can 54F5
Vancouver USA 58B1
Vancouver I Can 54F5
Vandalia, Illinois USA 64B3
Vandalia, Ohio USA 64C3
Vanderhoof Can 54F4
Van Diemen,C Aust 27G8
Van Diemen G Aust 32C2
Vänern, L Sweden 12G7
Vänersborg Sweden 12G7
Van Etten USA 68B1
Vangaindrano Madag 51E6
Van Gölü, Salt L Turk 40D2
Vangou USSR 29C2
Vang Vieng Laos 30C2
Van Horn USA 62B2
Vanier Can 65D1
Vanikoro, I Solomon Is 33F2
Vanino USSR 26G2
Vankarem USSR 25U3
Vännäs Sweden 12H6
Vannes France 14B2
Vanrhynsdorp S Africa 47B3
Vansittart I Can 55K3
Vanua Lava, I Vanuatu 33F2
Vanua Levu, I Fiji 33G2
Vanuatu, Is, Republic Pacific O 37K5
Van Wert USA 64C2
Vanwyksvlei S Africa 47C3
Var, R France 14D3
Varamin Iran 41F2
Varanasi India 43E3
Varandey USSR 20K2
Varangerfjord, Inlet Nor 12K4
Varangerhalvøya, Pen Nor 12L4
Varazdin Yugos 16D1
Varberg Sweden 12G7
Varde Den 12F7
Vardø Nor 12L4
Varel W Germ 13E1
Varėna USSR 19E2
Varese Italy 16B1
Varginha Brazil 75C3
Varkaus Fin 12K6
Varna Bulg 17F2
Värnamo Sweden 12G7
Varnek USSR 20K2
Varnville USA 67B2
Várzea da Palma Brazil 75D2
Vashka, R USSR 20H3
Vasil'kov USSR 21E5
Vassar USA 64C2
Västerås Sweden 12H7
Västervik Sweden 12H7
Vasto Italy 16C2
Vaticano, Citta del Italy 16C2
Vatnajökull, Mts Iceland 12B2
Vatra Dornei Rom 17F1
Vättern, L Sweden 12G7
Vaughn USA 62A2
Vaupés, R Colombia 72D3
Vava'u Group, Is Tonga 33H2
Vavuniya Sri Lanka 44C4
Växjö Sweden 12G7
Vaygach, Ostrov, I USSR 24G2
Vecht, R Neth/W Germ 13D1
Vechta W Germ 13E1
Veendam Neth 13D1
Vega USA 62B1
Vega, I Nor 12G5
Vejer de la Frontera Spain 15A2
Vejle Den 12F7
Velddrif S Africa 47B3
Velebit, Mts Yugos 16D2
Velenje Yugos 16D1
Velhas, R Brazil 75D2
Velikaya, R, Rossiyskaya USSR 25T3
Velikaya, R, RSFSR USSR 19F1
Velikaya, R USSR 12K7
Velikiye Luki USSR 20E4
Velikiy Ustyug USSR 20H3
Veliko Tŭrnovo Bulg 17F2
Vélingara Sen 48A3
Velizh USSR 19G1
Vella Lavella, I Solomon Is 33E1
Vellore India 44B3
Velmerstat, Mt W Germ 13E2
Vel'sk USSR 20G3
Veluwe, Region Neth 13C1
Velva USA 60C1
Vembanad L India 44B4

ACKNOWLEDGEMENTS

PICTURE CREDITS
The sources for the photographs and illustrations appearing in the atlas are listed below.

page
48–61   Physical maps by Duncan Mackay, copyright © Times Books Ltd., London

62   *Venus* US Geological Survey, Flagstaff, Arizona
Mercury NSSDC/ NASA
Mars NSSDC/NASA
Jupiter NSSDC/NASA
Saturn NASA
Uranus Jet Propulsion Laboratory/NASA

63   *Rock and Hydrological Cycles* Encyclopaedia Universalis Editeur, Paris

90   *Manhattan* Adapted from map by Nicholson Publications Ltd.

94–99   Robert Harding Picture Library Ltd.

BIBLIOGRAPHY
G.L. Fitzpatrick and M.J. Modlin: *Direct Line Distances. International Edition* Metuchen N.J. and London, 1986

The Europa Year Book 1987 London, 1987

Ed. J. Paxton: *The Statesman's Year-book 1987–88*. London, 1987